THE CAMBRIDGE HISTORY OF
LATIN AMERICA

VOLUME II

Colonial Latin America

THE CAMBRIDGE HISTORY OF LATIN AMERICA

VOLUME II

Colonial Latin America

---

edited by
LESLIE BETHELL

Reader in Hispanic American and
Brazilian History at University College London

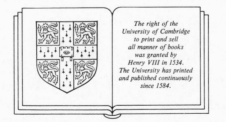

The right of the
University of Cambridge
to print and sell
all manner of books
was granted by
Henry VIII in 1534.
The University has printed
and published continuously
since 1584.

CAMBRIDGE UNIVERSITY PRESS

Cambridge

London   New York   New Rochelle
Melbourne   Sydney

Published by the Press Syndicate of the University of Cambridge
The Pitt Building, Trumpington Street, Cambridge CB2 IRP
32 East 57th Street, New York, NY 10022, USA
10 Stamford Road, Oakleigh, Melbourne 3166, Australia

First published 1984
Reprinted 1985

Printed in Great Britain by the University Press, Cambridge

Library of Congress catalogue card number: 83–19036

British Library Cataloguing in Publication Data

The Cambridge history of Latin America.
Vol. 2: Colonial Latin America
1. Latin America – History
I. Bethell, Leslie
980   F1410

ISBN 0 521 24516 8

UP

CONTENTS

PART FOUR. INTELLECTUAL AND CULTURAL LIFE

MAPS

FIGURES

NOTE ON CURRENCY AND MEASUREMENT

Various units of value and measurement are referred to in the text of the following chapters. It is not possible to give exact equivalents in modern terms, particularly as there were many local variations. The following explanations may prove helpful.

Peso	The silver peso of Mexico in the late eighteenth century was equal to the American dollar or 4*s*. 8*d*.
Real	The peso was divided into eight silver reales or twenty copper reales (*reales de vellón*).
Maravedí	The value of the maravedí varied widely and was often no more than an imaginary division of bigger coins, since for long periods there were no maravedí coins at all. The last ones to circulate, probably in the late seventeenth and early eighteenth centuries, were copper coins, often debased. One such coin was worth 1/34 part of a real de vellón.
Réis (sing. *real*)	Smallest Portuguese monetary unit; existed only as money of account.
Milréis	1,000 réis, usually written 1$000; worth 12*s*. in the middle of the seventeenth century.
Cruzado	The Portuguese cruzado was equal to 400 réis (480 réis in the first half of the eighteenth century); originally of gold, later silver.
Conto	A conto equalled 1,000$000 réis (1,000 milréis).
Fanega	A dry measure for cacao, wheat, maize, etc. Usually equal to 1.5 English bushels, but there were local variations, e.g. in Mexico, where the fanega of maize could be either 1.5 or 2.5 bushels (or 55 or 90.8 litres).
Quintal	Usually translated as 'hundredweight' and composed of 4 Spanish *arrobas* or 100 *libras*.
Arroba	The Spanish arroba weighed about 11.5 kg (25 lb). The Portuguese arroba weighed 14.5 kg (32 lb).

GENERAL PREFACE

In the English-speaking and English-reading world the multi-volume
Cambridge Histories planned and edited by historians of established
reputation, with individual chapters written by leading specialists in
their fields, have since the beginning of the century set the highest
standards of collaborative international scholarship. *The Cambridge
Modern History*, planned by Lord Acton, appeared in sixteen volumes
between 1902 and 1912. It was followed by *The Cambridge Ancient
History*, *The Cambridge Medieval History* and others. The *Modern History*
has now been replaced by *The New Cambridge Modern History* in fourteen
volumes, and *The Cambridge Economic History of Europe* has recently been
completed. Cambridge Histories of Islam, of Iran and of Africa are
published or near completion; in progress are Histories of China and
of Judaism, while Japan is soon to join the list.

In the early 1970s Cambridge University Press decided the time was
ripe to embark on a Cambridge History of Latin America. Since the
Second World War and particularly since 1960 research and writing on
Latin American history had been developing, and have continued to
develop, at an unprecedented rate – in the United States (by American
historians in particular, but also by British, European and Latin
American historians resident in the United States), in Europe (especially
in Britain and France) and increasingly in Latin America itself (where
a new generation of young professional historians, many of them
trained in the United States, Britain or Europe, had begun to emerge).
Perspectives had changed as political, economic and social realities in
Latin America – and Latin America's role in the world – had changed.
Methodological innovations and new conceptual models drawn from
the social sciences (economics, political science, historical demography,
sociology, anthropology) as well as from other fields of historical

research were increasingly being adopted by historians of Latin America. The Latin American Studies monograph series and the *Journal of Latin American Studies* had already been established by the Press and were beginning to publish the results of this new historical thinking and research.

In 1974 Dr Leslie Bethell, Reader in Hispanic American and Brazilian History at University College London, accepted an invitation to edit the Cambridge History of Latin America. For the first time a single editor was given responsibility for the planning, co-ordination and editing of an entire History. Contributors were drawn from the United States and Canada, Britain and Europe, and Latin America.

The Cambridge History of Latin America is the first large-scale, authoritative survey of Latin America's unique historical experience during almost five centuries from the first contacts between the native American Indians and Europeans (and the beginnings of the African slave trade) in the late fifteenth and early sixteenth centuries to the present day. (The Press has under consideration a separate Cambridge History of the native peoples of America – North, Middle and South – before the arrival of the Europeans.) Latin America is taken to comprise the predominantly Spanish- and Portuguese-speaking areas of continental America south of the United States – Mexico, Central America and South America – together with the Spanish-speaking Caribbean – Cuba, Puerto Rico, the Dominican Republic – and, by convention, Haiti. (The vast territories in North America lost to the United States by treaty and by war, first by Spain, then by Mexico, during the first half of the nineteenth century are for the most part excluded. Neither the British, French and Dutch Caribbean islands nor the Guianas are included even though Jamaica and Trinidad, for example, have early Hispanic antecedents and are now members of the Organisation of American States.) The aim is to produce a high-level synthesis of existing knowledge which will provide historians of Latin America with a solid base for future research, which students of Latin American history will find useful and which will be of interest to historians of other areas of the world. It is also hoped that the *History* will contribute more generally to a deeper understanding of Latin America through its history in the United States and in Europe and, not least, to a greater awareness of its own history in Latin America.

For the first time the volumes of a Cambridge History will be published in chronological order: Volumes I and II (Colonial Latin

America – with an introductory section on the native American peoples and civilizations on the eve of the European invasion) in 1984; Volume III (Latin America, Independence and Post-Independence, *c.* 1790–1870/80) in 1985; Volumes IV and V (Latin America, 1870/80–1930) in 1986; and Volumes VI–VIII (Latin America, 1930 to the present) as soon as possible thereafter. Each volume or set of volumes examines a period in the economic, social, political, intellectual and cultural history of Latin America. While recognizing the decisive impact on Latin America of external forces, of developments within what is now called the capitalist world system, and the fundamental importance of its economic, political and cultural ties first with Spain and Portugal, then with Britain, France and, to a lesser extent, Western Europe as a whole, and finally with the United States, the emphasis of the *History* will be upon the evolution of internal structures. Furthermore, the emphasis is clearly on the period since the establishment of all the independent Latin American states except Cuba at the beginning of the nineteenth century, which, compared with the colonial and independence periods, has been relatively neglected by historians of Latin America. The period of Spanish and Portuguese colonial rule from the sixteenth to the eighteenth centuries is the subject of two of the eight volumes. Six are devoted to the nineteenth and twentieth centuries and will consist of a mixture of general, comparative chapters built around major themes in Latin American history and chapters on the individual histories of the twenty independent Latin American countries (plus Puerto Rico), and especially the three major countries – Brazil, Mexico and Argentina. In view of its size, population and distinctive history, Brazil, which has often been neglected in general histories of Latin America, written for the most part by Spanish Americans or Spanish American specialists, will here receive the attention it deserves. The editor of the *History* is himself, above all, a specialist on Brazil.

An important feature of the *History* will be the bibliographical essays which accompany each chapter. These will give special emphasis to books and articles published during the past 15–20 years, that is to say, since the publication of Howard F. Cline (ed.), *Latin American History: essays in its study and teaching, 1898–1965* (2 vols., published for the Conference on Latin American History by the University of Texas Press, Austin, Texas, 1967), and Charles C. Griffin (ed.), *Latin America: a guide to the historical literature* (published for the Conference on Latin American History by the University of Texas Press, Austin, Texas, 1971); the latter was prepared during 1966–9 and included few works published after 1966.

PREFACE TO VOLUMES I AND II

The first two volumes of *The Cambridge History of Latin America*, which are closely integrated, are devoted to the three centuries of Spanish and Portuguese colonial rule from the first contacts between the native American Indians and Europeans at the end of the fifteenth and beginning of the sixteenth centuries to the revolutions and wars of independence at the beginning of the nineteenth century.

Man first entered the continent through the Bering Strait, perhaps as long ago as 35,000 B.C. There is some evidence of the possible presence of man in what is today Mexico as early as 20,000 B.C., but the oldest certain human finds – for example, at Tepexpan, north-east of Mexico City, and Lagôa Santa in Minas Gerais, Brazil – have been dated no earlier than 9,000–8,000 B.C. Agriculture in Mesoamerica dates from around 5,000 B.C., and the production of pottery from around 2,300 B.C. The earliest evidence of societies with political and religious structures can be found, in Mexico, at the Olmec sites, notably La Venta, and, in the Andes, at Chavin, both dating from before 1,000 B.C. By A.D 1500 there were states with highly structured economies and societies and highly developed cultures and religions, like the Aztec empire in Mexico and the Inca empire in the Central Andes, as well as more or less stable chiefdoms of varying degrees of complexity throughout, for example, the Caribbean and circum-Caribbean and, still, hundreds of nomadic or semi-nomadic tribes in North America, southern South America and Brazil. Research on pre-Columbian America has advanced rapidly during the past twenty or thirty years, especially in Mesoamerica, but also most recently in the Andes – and elsewhere. Important contributions to knowledge have been made by archaeologists, but also by linguists and palaeographers, geographers and botanists, even by mathematicians and astronomers and, above all, by anthropologists, ethnologists and ethnohistorians. The invaluable *Handbook of Latin American Studies* (1936–   ) has since 1960 included a section on publications in the important new field of ethnohistory. The *Handbook of South American Indians*, ed. Julian H. Steward (6 vols., Washington, D.C., 1946–50) and the *Handbook of Middle American Indians*, ed. Robert Wauchope (16 vols., Austin, Texas, 1964–76), remain indispensable, although the former in particular is now seriously out of date. No attempt has been made in *The Cambridge History of Latin America* to present a full-scale account of the evolution of the various indigenous American societies – in isolation from the rest of the world – during the two or three thousand years before the arrival of the Europeans. This belongs to another Cambridge *History*. However, the five chapters which form the first section of the first of these two volumes on colonial Latin America survey the native American peoples and civilizations on the eve of the European invasion.

The expansion of Europe in the fifteenth and sixteenth centuries and in particular Europe's 'discovery' of America, although not entirely neglected, have been largely excluded from this history of colonial Latin America. They are subjects which belong more properly to the history of Europe. There is in any case a vast literature on European expansion: for example, John H. Parry's classic *The age of reconnaissance: discovery, exploration and settlement 1450–1650* (London, 1963); V. Magalhães Godinho, notably *Os descobrimentos e a economia mundial* (2 vols., Lisbon, 1965); Samuel Eliot Morison, *The European discovery of America*, vol. II, *The southern voyages 1492–1616* (New York, 1974); and, most recently, G. V. Scammell, *The world encompassed: the first European maritime empires c. 800–1650* (London, 1981), which examines Norse, Hanse, Venetian and Genoese maritime explorations before turning to the Portuguese and Spanish and finally the Dutch, English and French. The first three chapters of the second section of Volume I of this history of Latin America examine the European invasion, subjugation and settlement of parts of the New World during the period from 1492 to 1570/80. The viewpoint is not, however, exclusively European. Equally important is the 'vision of the vanquished'. And post-conquest relations between the Spanish and Portuguese and the native Americans are given particular attention. The remaining five chapters of this section, the central core of the volume, examine the political and economic structures of the Spanish and Portuguese empires in America from the middle of the sixteenth to the end of the eighteenth centuries – to a large extent from a metropolitan perspective. There is some discussion of imperial rivalries, and the integration of Spanish America and Brazil into the new world economic system is also explored. The volume concludes with two chapters on the Catholic Church in colonial Latin America, but the reader is also referred to the *Historia General de la Iglesia en America Latina* which is being published in eleven volumes by CEHILA (Comisión de Estudios de Historia de la Iglesia en Latinoamérica) under the general direction of Enrique Dussel.

The second of these two volumes on colonial Latin America opens with two chapters on population trends and is then largely devoted to aspects of the internal economic and social history of colonial Spanish America (nine chapters) and colonial Brazil (four chapters) which have attracted most research interest during the past twenty years: for example, urban development; mining; land tenure and exploitation; labour systems, including African slavery; local economies and inter-colonial trade; social organisation and social change; Indians under colonial rule. Spanish America and Brazil have been for the most part treated separately. They have, on the whole, two different histories, two different historiographies. There are in any case few historians competent and willing to write comparatively about Spanish America and Brazil in the colonial period. The volume concludes with four chapters which survey the intellectual and cultural life – literature and ideas, architecture and art, music – of colonial Latin America.

A Cambridge *History*, as John F. Fairbank, one of the general editors of *The Cambridge History of China*, has written, is meant to be indebted to every single contributor to its field. More particularly in the case of these two volumes on colonial Latin America many of the historians who have themselves contributed chapters – nine American, eight continental European (two resident in the United States, one in Brazil), seven British (four resident in the United States) and seven Latin American (one resident in the United States, one in France) – also read and commented on the chapters of their colleagues. I am especially grateful in this respect to Dauril Alden, J. H. Elliott, Charles Gibson, Murdo J. Macleod, Richard M. Morse and Stuart B. Schwartz. In addition, Woodrow Borah, J. S. Cummins, Valerie Frazer, Olivia Harris and Enrique Tandeter provided critical assessments of several chapters. Most important was the advice and encouragement generously offered throughout the planning and editing of these volumes by my colleague John Lynch.

Patricia Williams at Cambridge University Press was largely responsible for initiating this project and continued to support it even after she left the Press. A number of editors at the Press have been involved in this *History*. I am particularly grateful to Elizabeth Wetton. The subeditors of the volumes were Cynthia Postan and Mandy Macdonald, after preliminary advice from Clare Davies-Jones. Nazneen Razwi at University College London offered invaluable secretarial assistance. The indexes were prepared by Alison Rowlatt.

Part One

POPULATION

1

THE POPULATION OF COLONIAL SPANISH AMERICA*

The New World was abundantly peopled when it was first invaded by the Spaniards. Population distribution was, however, uneven, with the heaviest concentrations of people in Mesoamerica and the central Andes, where native American societies had reached the highest levels of economic, social, political and cultural organization. According to circumstances, this distribution of population either helped or hindered the Spanish conquest of America, as it likewise affected Spanish colonization. The presence of a large native American population determined the shape both of the conquest itself and of the colonial structures. They, in their turn, were to influence the process of demographic change. This interaction between population and colonization is the central theme of this chapter, in which the three centuries of Spanish domination have been divided into two. The first part of the chapter deals with the initial sudden and violent clash between invaders and invaded, which was followed by a serious decline in the native American population. The intensity of the demographic catastrophe, and the reasons for it, are discussed. Consideration is also given to the impact of European and African immigration to the New World in the sixteenth and the first half of the seventeenth centuries. The second part examines the way the Indian population slowly recovered, from midway through the colonial period, and the white and mestizo population expanded rapidly, especially in the eighteenth century. The chapter concludes by examining the population of Spanish America, region by region, at the end of the colonial period.

* Translated from the original Spanish by Dr Richard Boulind; translation revised by the editor.

THE NATIVE AMERICANS: DEMOGRAPHIC COLLAPSE

Argument about the size of the native American population on the eve
of the European invasion has gone on for decades and shows no signs
of abating. Important in itself, it has a wider significance because of
the implications for any interpretation of the Spanish conquest and
colonization of America, its characteristics and effects. The higher the
population on the eve of the invasion, the more steeply it must have
fallen during the first century of Spanish colonialism. Nowadays
historians, anthropologists, archaeologists and ecologists seem to be
agreed that the pre-Columbian population was higher than their
colleagues of a generation ago used to believe, and certainly that it was
higher than at any time during the colonial period, although for Central
Mexico at least there is a tendency in the most recent studies to cut back
somewhat the highest figures so far proposed. Even so, no one suggests
a return to the old low figures.[1]

Of the 25 million estimated by S. F. Cook and W. Borah to have been
the population of central Mexico, the area lying between the Isthmus
of Tehuantepec and the frontier with the Chichimecas, in 1519, only
17 million native Americans survived four years after the European
invasion; in 1548, according to the same authors, only six million;
twenty years later, three million; about 1580, two million; and in the
early seventeenth century, around 1630, according to their most recent
estimates the Indians of central Mexico scarcely reached 750,000, that
is, only 3 per cent of the population before the conquest. The decrease
did not occur at the same rate everywhere: the low-lying lands along
the Gulf and the Pacific coasts witnessed the virtual disappearance of
the indigenous population earlier, and more suddenly; the highlands
retained their Indian population longer, and in a higher proportion.
Cook and Borah have also reconstructed the demographic history of
north-west Mexico and Yucatán, observing that population decline in
these areas was comparable with that experienced in central Mexico.
Even if the estimated pre-Hispanic native American population of
central Mexico is reduced by half, as William T. Sanders has suggested
it should be, the effect of the conquest still has to be considered
catastrophic. The decline would be from 12 million to 750,000; a fall

---

[1] See the Note on the native American population on the eve of the European invasions, *CHLA*
I, 145–6, and, for the most important contributions to the literature on the demographic collapse
which followed the conquest, see *CHLA* II, Bibliographical Essay 1.

of 90 per cent. For every sixteen Indians living there when Cortés landed there would scarcely be one a century later. (The Berkeley school's calculations suggest a collapse in the proportion of 33:1.)

The highest figures proposed for the pre-conquest population of the Antilles and Circum-Caribbean are by no means generally accepted, but there is no disagreement over the fact of the rapid destruction of the Indians in the region, only over its scale. Whether the island of Hispaniola (the most systematically studied) had a population of eight million or 100,000 in 1492, certainly there were only a few hundred survivors in 1570. Central America also experienced a major demographic disaster. Here however it seems that it stopped just in time for the native population to avoid the near extinction it had suffered in the Antilles. Ironically, economic stagnation came to this region so early that it relieved the pressure on the Indian population and thus saved many lives.[2]

The demographic history of Andean South America is better documented than that of the Antilles or the Isthmus. Native American society was more complex. It had already conducted its own censuses, and it was therefore easier for the Spanish to assess the population. Moreover, the dryness of the climate has helped to preserve the source materials for the colonial population. Even so, information on Andean demography is not as abundant as it is for Mexico.

In what is now Colombia, the native population shrank by more or less a quarter of its former size in the first three decades after the conquest. Tunja's population diminished from 232,407 in 1537 to 168,444 in 1564, according to the successive tribute counts analysed first by Juan Friede and later by G. Colmenares. In 1636, after a century of Spanish occupation, only 44,691 remained – less than a fifth of the original number.[3] Other highland areas in the eastern region of the country, like Santa Fe, Vélez, and Pamplona, lost comparable proportions.[4]

The Incas used to take a comprehensive census of those of their subjects who were liable for the payment of tribute. Knots tied

[2] See Murdo J. MacLeod, *Spanish Central America. A socioeconomic history 1520–1720* (Berkeley and Los Angeles, 1973), parts 1 and 2 *passim*.

[3] Germán Colmenares, *La provincia de Tunja en el Nuevo Reino de Granada: ensayo de historia social (1539–1800)* (Bogotá, 1970).

[4] Darío Fajardo, *El régimen de la encomienda en la provincia de Vélez (población indígena y economía)* (Bogotá, 1969); Germán Colmenares, *Encomienda y población en la provincia de Pamplona (1549–1650)* (Bogotá, 1969).

according to set conventions along cords that made up the *quipu* denoted individual figures. Plenty of *quipus* are preserved in museums, but knowledge of what they used to signify has been lost, in the same way that finding a single punched computer card nowadays would tell us nothing if the code book were lost. Luckily, Spanish treasury officials undertaking visitations sometimes asked the caciques to read off the *quipus* in the presence of a notary public. In these cases, the information was transferred to paper and so preserved. Because of this, for instance, we know how many Aymara and Uro tributaries the Inca had in Chucuito, district by district. Before the northern campaigns of Huascar, Chucuito contained 20,280 tribute-paying males between 30 and 60 years of age, equivalent to some 170,000 people in all. In his 1567 visitation, Díaz de San Miguel found a population of 63,012 there, showing that in 40 years it had fallen to only just over a third of its former size.[5] The visitation of Chucuito was one of several ordered by the marqués de Cañete as viceroy. Some of those ordered by Cañete's predecessor have survived. In the case of Peru, historical sources have by no means been exhausted. However, for the purpose of estimating the original native American population of Peru and tracing its development in the early colonial period the documentary base is still slender. N. David Cook in his most recent work has estimated that the population of what is today Peru stood at nine million at the time of the conquest, which suggests a relatively dense occupation of the land (although less dense than central Mexico), and fell to 1.3 million by 1570. From 1570 the margin of uncertainty that affects our demographic information is reduced. After the resettlement of the Indians, Viceroy Toledo counted them, in order to determine how much tribute each community should pay. As the native population fell, it was necessary to adjust the payments accordingly. From time to time, in a particular area, a fresh count was undertaken, and bore witness to the local decline in population. However, no second general census was undertaken until 1683. As far as Peru is concerned, Cook has reconstructed the general evolution of the population from 1570 to 1620 on the basis of these re-counts: he concludes that the Indian population of the highland region fell from 1.045 million to 585,000 and the coastal population collapsed from 250,000 to 87,000.

Those Indians who were *originarios*, that is who belonged to the

[5] Waldemar Espinoza Soriano (ed.), *Vista hecha a la provincia de Chucuito por García Diez de San Miguel en el año 1567* (Lima, 1964).

communities founded by Viceroy Toledo, were liable to pay tribute, whereas *forasteros*, that is, migrants and their descendants, were exempt. The 1683 general census was the first to differentiate between them, and the distinction it draws can be used to trace movements of population and to gauge internal migration. By the late seventeenth century, *originarios* were only a bare majority in the male population. No less than 45 per cent of male Indians were recorded as *forasteros*. In part, they compensated for the loss of tribute-paying Indians, though initially they represented a loss to their communities of origin. For this reason, censuses that enumerate tribute-paying Indians alone do not serve as measures for the development of the population in general. In the section of present-day Bolivia that has been studied, tribute-paying Indians decreased by 57 per cent. But if migrant Indians are taken into account, it turns out that the adult male population declined by only 22 per cent, and the population as a whole, that is, with women, children, and old people included, by 42 per cent. The presence of migrants, however, did not wholly compensate for demographic setbacks. Because they were migrants, they distorted the demographic structure as to sex and age. However, reproduction was not as rapid as it normally would have been in a stable community.

The population decline took longer in Peru than it did in Mexico. It did not end till after the great epidemic of 1719. Thus Peru reached its minimum population for the colonial period in the first decades of the eighteenth century, compared with the late sixteenth century in the case of Central America and the middle of the seventeenth in the highlands of New Spain and in New Granada. From the Amazon basin, from the *pampas* of southern South America, from the valleys of Chile as well, scattered but unquestionable evidence survives of a decline in population during the first century or so of Spanish colonial rule. It was not uniform all over Spanish America either in intensity or in duration, but there is no doubt that every region was affected.

In its extent this phenomenon is without parallel in the modern history of the world's population. Europeans colonized other continents – Africa and Asia – in the nineteenth century, but contact with the inhabitants there never brought any decrease in the indigenous population nearly so disastrous as it had in America. Only in the European occupation of the islands of the Pacific do we find analogies. What then caused this demographic disaster?

A privileged witness of events in the New World was the Dominican friar Bartolomé de Las Casas, writer of the impassioned indictment *Breve relación de la destrucción de las Indias*,[6] later translated into several other languages. It is in this book that we find the view – one which has prevailed down the centuries – that the population collapse can be explained by the violence that the conquerors inflicted on the native population. This allegation subsumes in one argument several sets of facts, ranging from purely warlike interventions and their usual corollary – the confiscation of food, plunder, rape, etc. – to others that were much more of an economic nature – the public or private exaction of tribute, enslavement, and the cruel overworking of the labour force in agricultural or mining enterprises.

Although no doubt all of them were destructive, the wars of conquest were not equally long, however, nor did they affect every section of the population and every area to the same extent. Moreover, it was the men who suffered the greatest losses in the wars, but their numbers had the least influence on the rate of reproduction of the population. War, then, caused short-term havoc, limited in extent and of short duration. War alone could not have set off so long and so deep a population decline as was seen in the American continent in the sixteenth century. If it had been the only cause, the native population would have recovered after quite a short time, as has happened in the case of modern populations that have been much worse hit by warfare. The specific effects of war need to be demonstrated in detail. If we study the age-pyramids for representative communities we can identify the victims of military conquest by age and by sex. By the same token, we can distinguish short-term effects from those of more extended significance.

Among the slaughters of warfare one has to include as well those that resulted from conflict among the American natives. Through the early colonial period, rebellious or nomadic Indians waged war on the settlements of those who had already been subdued or settled. Of these attacks there are plenty of examples, all equally deadly, from Guatemala, from the Mexican north-west, from New Granada, and from other frontier areas of the continent.

The oppressions visited by the conquerors upon those Indians who showed reluctance to hand over foodstuffs produced another batch of victims at the outset of colonization. This direct assault, however, was less serious than the harm caused by the confiscation of food reserves. The precarious nutritional balance that existed in what was a strictly

[6] *Obras escogidas de Fray Bartolomé de Las Casas* (Madrid, 1958), v, 134–81.

subsistence economy broke down under these exactions. Hunger took over. It impaired the physiques of the native Americans and left them a prey to various ills which eventually cost a greater or smaller number of individuals their lives.

Mobilization of the Indians to carry weapons or baggage, or as auxiliaries in the fighting, cost them more in labouring capacity than in reproductive potential. Labour was harder to replace. In an agrarian economy, a smaller workforce meant less production for community use. On the other hand, the shortage of husbands could always be compensated for by polygamy, as long as the shortage was not excessive. Colonial censuses exist for Peru in which, for every married Indian male, there are numerous 'widows' and 'spinsters', and the population of infants bears no relation to the number of recorded married couples. The terms 'widow' and 'spinster' in the censuses actually concealed relationships which did not conform with the monogamous ideal of the Iberian family.

An extreme case of the requisitioning of labour is to be seen in Nicaragua. There the Indians were constrained to carry timber from the forest to the coast for the building of the fleet which was to carry the conquering expedition to Peru. Later on, other Nicaraguan Indians were coerced into slavery, and carried off to South America. It has been estimated that as many as 448,000 slaves could have been taken to Peru in the 1,280 ships which sailed from Nicaraguan ports between 1527 and 1536.[7] Because of this massive forced migration the population of the Isthmus fell not just temporarily, but over the long term. Enslavement of Indians was not peculiar to Nicaragua. It happened in Yucatán and in Honduras, too, in order to supply Cuba with labour.

Labour was also requisitioned locally to furnish services to individuals and to the colonial authorities. The overall effect of such onslaughts was equally disastrous. Fr. Toribio de Motolinía called the rebuilding of Tenochtitlán 'the seventh plague', in view of the lives it cost. The grandiose construction programmes on which the religious orders embarked in Mexico between 1530 and 1570 took a heavy toll in human life, so much so that the authorities had to restrain the friars' enthusiasm for building.

It is frequently claimed that work in the mines caused the deaths of

[7] David R. Radell, 'The Indian slave trade and population of Nicaragua during the sixteenth century', in W. M. Denevan (ed.), *The native population of the Americas in 1492* (Madison, 1976), 67–76.

multitudes of Indians. It has been successfully demonstrated from census records, for example, how mining depopulated the area of Muzo (in present-day Colombia) in the middle of the seventeenth century.[8] However, it has also been pointed out that at the time when the mines went into large-scale operation and needed labour in abundance, the population had already shrunk by over a half. Large-scale mining aggravated population decline; it did not cause it.

The conquerors abused the native Americans time and again, without considering the consequences of what they were doing. The Indian population seemed so abundant that it looked as though the labour force would never be exhausted. However, faced with loss of life on such a scale, some officials were quick to raise their voices in alarm, and the crown responded. Laws were enacted which, for example, forbade native forced labour in the mines. Some abuses were mitigated, but the native population did not cease to diminish. By then, however, the cause was not so much the ill-treatment they were undergoing as the socio-economic regime to which they were subjected.

The conquest brought about a change of diet as well as a change in the methods of food production. The Spaniards brought to the Indies Mediterranean eating habits based on wheat, wine, olive oil, the meat of sheep and cattle, and sweeteners such as honey and sugar. Livestock and sugar-cane found in America optimal conditions in which to flourish; wheat was less favoured. In the hotter areas, the Antilles for example, the sugar plantations occupied the land that had been left vacant by the disappearance of the Indians. In densely peopled areas like those in New Spain, herds of cattle established themselves on land that had previously been inhabited. Both the livestock in these herds and the animals that ran wild (which were equally abundant) continually invaded the areas cultivated by the Indians of the neighbouring villages, destroying their crops and driving them off the land. The vacuum caused thereby tempted the landowners into expanding their estates and creating new ones. European agriculture and stock raising thus spread at the expense of the native Americans: the more European crops and livestock there were, the fewer Indians. Only in one case did the new livestock really bring the Indians any benefit. Both in the north of Mexico and in the pampas of the Río de la Plata, horses and cattle reproduced at a remarkable rate. The Indian hunters turned themselves

---

[8] Juan Friede, 'Demographic changes in the mining community of Muzo after the plague of 1629', *Hispanic American Historical Review* [*HAHR*], 47 (1967), 338–43.

into nomadic horsemen, became better fed, and enjoyed a mobility which made them feared.

The introduction of wheat caused fresh distortion, by obliging the Indians to change the crops they grew. Their best land had to be used to grow this cereal in order to pay the tribute and to supply the cities with food. Forced by this imposition, lacking experience in wheat cultivation, and disliking it as a food, the Indians grew it with great reluctance, and when they did, they derived lower yields from it than from their traditional grains, like maize. Consequently, the conquerors chose to take over the arable lands themselves – at the expense of native property rights, of course.

The initial depopulation made it easier to take land over in order to produce staples for colonial society, or for export to the mother country. The cacao and indigo of Guatemala furnish examples of these new cash crops. The deficiency in the native subsistence economy that this inflicted deepened the demographic decline still further. War and violence caused the initial contraction; social and economic change precipitated collapse.

Physical causes were reinforced by psychological factors. 'The surrender that those who have been conquered have to make to the victor of self-esteem, wealth, prosperity, and comfort inevitably has repercussions on the raising of children, whom they can no longer afford to support', the viceroy of Peru, the Marqués de Castelfuerte, wrote many years after the conquest, with reference to the depopulation of the province of Santa.[9] Pauperization, combined with the loss of their own culture, thus constricted the Indians' capacity to reproduce themselves. The population decline was thus due not only to the rise in mortality caused by violence and malnutrition, but also to a fall in the fertility rate resulting not so much from biological factors, though they probably also existed, as from individual decisions.

The size of the native American family began to fall early on. The *repartimiento* of Indians on the royal estates in Santo Domingo in 1514 shows less than one child per family, except in the households of polygamous caciques. Las Casas had noted, however, that at the time the Spaniards arrived, the Indians usually had from three to five children per family. In Huánuco, in the central Andes, it has been calculated that the average family shrank from about six members in Inca days to 2.5

[9] *Memorias de los virreyes que han gobernado el Perú durante el tiempo del coloniaje español*, III (Lima, 1859), 132.

in 1562.[10] The decrease stemmed in part from the breakup of marriages, but pre-eminently from the lower rate of child-bearing. In early seventeenth-century New Granada, half of the Indian families were childless. In the half that did have children, two was the most usual number, and a couple with as many as four was exceptional. The native family shrank apace. Abortion and infanticide were frequent, as Fr. Pedro de Córdoba attests. 'The women', he wrote from Santo Domingo,

worn out with labouring, have given up conceiving and bearing children, so that they will not expose themselves to the work piled upon work that is the lot of expectant or newly delivered mothers; their fear of the fatigue of child-bearing is so great that many of them, on finding themselves pregnant, have taken drugs so they will lose their babies, and have aborted them. And others, who have already given birth, kill their children with their own hands.[11]

Their despair did not merely limit the Indians' desire to have children. In extreme cases it provoked them into attempts on their own lives. Suicide because of ill-treatment, or in order to escape paying tribute, was relatively common. One witch-doctor even managed to induce a whole crowd of Indians to commit mass suicide.

Self-inflicted death or constricting one's own fertility were acts conditioned by the social context, but were nonetheless determined by human free will. On the other hand, epidemics provided a totally involuntary cause of population decline. These diseases, above all smallpox, malaria, measles, typhus, and influenza, which already regularly afflicted Europe, were transferred to the New World at an early date. They arrived with the conquerors, and found hosts who had no immunity against them. In contrast, the three Old World continents shared the same spectrum of diseases. Black Africa and the Far East had been exchanging disease-bearing agents with Europe for centuries along the trade routes which traversed the Sahara and the deserts of central Asia.

On the other hand America, and also Australasia, had stayed on the sidelines in this lethal interchange. The native Americans were isolated, living in relatively healthy conditions. When the Europeans invaded, carrying their endemic diseases with them, the native populations were

---

[10] Elda R. González and Rolando Mellafe, 'La función de la familia en la historia social hispanoamericana colonial', *Anuario del Instituto de Investigaciones Históricas*, 8 (Rosario, 1965), 57–71.

[11] *Colección de documentos inéditos relativos al descubrimiento, conquista y organización de las antiguas posesiones españolas*, XI (Madrid, 1869), 219.

protected by none of the appropriate immunities. The effects of these plagues on them were ferocious. Slightly later, Africa started sending its tropical infections direct to the coastal lands of America. Yellow fever came over in slave ships. By contrast, America had no disease to contribute to the world, save – some believe – syphilis, and even this is now generally doubted. The Indians were the more vulnerable because of the malnutrition caused by the change in their diet and because of the abuses of exploitation, so that the plague germs assailed them with virulence. The result was devastating. When the epidemic, or rather the complex of epidemics, passed on, there were many villages where only one in ten of the Indian population survived. As early as May 1519 the royal officials in Hispaniola reported that smallpox had decimated the island's natives. Cortés' men then took it with them to the mainland. The epidemic disrupted Aztec resistance and killed Montezuma's successor. From Mexico it spread to Central America, and thence passed on to the southern continent, which it invaded more than five years earlier than Spanish soldiers. When the Inca Huayna Capac died in 1524, it was smallpox that killed him – smallpox which Europeans had originally brought to America, and which thus caused the war for the succession to the throne which was going on when Pizarro arrived in Peru. It was smallpox that opened the American continents to Spanish domination. Without its aid, the conquerors could not have subjugated the mass of native Americans. A considerable part of the Indian population disappeared in the first epidemic.

Malaria established itself quickly in the tropical coastlands. Its onslaught possibly accounts for the fact that the depopulation of the *tierra caliente* was faster than that of the temperate highlands. In 1529 a new disease, measles, broke out in the Caribbean area, sweeping away a large part of what remained there of the native population. Mexico was hit by it in 1531, and from there it leapt to Central America. *Matlazahuatl*, as the Aztecs called typhus, laid New Spain low in 1545. A year later it struck New Granada and Peru. An epidemic of influenza, of a type that was very severe even in Europe, crossed the Atlantic around 1558, and proved to be particularly lethal for the native Americans, who, unlike the Europeans, were suffering from it for the first time. The American continent also underwent attacks of *cocoliztli*, a malignant form of fever. The epidemic caused by this disease in 1576 was one of the deadliest, so deadly, indeed, that it seriously affected production throughout New Spain and in Central America. The epidemic of 1588 spread from a different centre of infection: it broke out first in Cartagena, in a newly arrived cargo of slaves. From there it spread rapidly to Bogotá, and then passed on to Quito, Lima, Cuzco, Upper Peru, and Chile. Later on, it spread northwards to New Spain.

The chronological sequence shows epidemics recurring at about ten-year intervals throughout the sixteenth century. No generation ever had time to recover from one of these diseases before another, still more devastating, was upon it, carrying off more of the population. From one crisis to another, the active elements in the population diminished. All age groups suffered, but particularly the younger ones, and their removal impaired the population's ability to reproduce itself. The epidemics not only brought sudden death to tens of thousands of Indians; they gnawed away at future population growth.

In contrast a large number of the epidemics that broke out in the seventeenth century were of local origin and were geographically confined. Mexico and Central America registered epidemics of typhus, plague, or smallpox in 1607–8, 1631, 1686, and 1693–4. At the other end of the continent, Buenos Aires suffered consecutive onslaughts in 1642–3, 1652–3, 1670, 1675, 1694, 1700–5, 1717–20, 1734, and 1742. The sequences could be multiplied. There is no shortage of registers of the deaths. The dates of epidemics overlap, but that does not mean that the causes of them were the same. What the epidemics lost in continental range they gained in increasing frequency. Among the diseases that became endemic, yellow fever stands out. America's coastal lowlands offered the mosquito that carried it conditions for reproduction that resembled those in its African homeland. The coasts of Cuba, Veracruz and Yucatán were devastated by yellow fever in the middle of the seventeenth century. And Europeans in the urban centres figured heavily among the victims of the 'black vomit', as it was called.

In general, however, for a variety of reasons Europeans proved less vulnerable to the diseases than the Indians – perhaps because they had arrived from overseas already largely immune to them, perhaps because they had inherited mechanisms of defence against disease from their ancestors, certainly because they lived in healthier, more hygienic conditions.

IMMIGRATION AND SETTLEMENT

The voyages of exploration and the early conquests brought to America a handful of sailors, soldiers, officials, and clerics. Few of them proposed, when they first embarked, to settle in the New World. Dead or alive, however, many of them did stay there for ever. These men made up the first wave of a great procession which over the centuries was to bring millions of Europeans to America, north and south.

Although in the beginning the flow was spontaneous, it was soon regulated. The crown of Castile forbade certain categories of people from entering the Indies, so as to maintain the ideological purity of the newly conquered lands. Thus passage was barred to Moors, to Jews, to gypsies and to anyone who had ever been condemned by the Inquisition. The law restricted the passage of foreigners, and initially even of natives of the kingdoms of Aragon, to the New World. The principle was that emigration to America was to be confined to those who belonged to the crown of Castile.

Legally, passage to the Indies required official permission. From the original licences that are preserved in great numbers in the Archive of the Indies in Seville, the number of immigrants to America can be estimated and their main characteristics roughly delineated. So far as the *Catálogo de pasajeros a Indias* has been published it relates solely to the period from 1509 to 1559.[12] In its three volumes are 15,000 names – quite insufficient as a total for the emigration of the period. Some of the bundles of documents are now missing; more significantly, it was very common for people to embark without papers, and for seamen to desert their ships on reaching port in America. P. Boyd-Bowman therefore has had recourse to other techniques to complete the listings. To those included in the *Catálogo*, he has added all the names of Spaniards residing in the New World that he could extract from printed documentation, either public or private, up to the end of the sixteenth century. Although his *Indice geobiográfico* is also incomplete, it does include 45,000 names. According to him the total number of emigrants from Spain to America reaches about 200,000 for the whole of the sixteenth century; that is, an average of two thousand a year.

This last figure has been increased by M. Mörner, who has noted the growing capacity of the ships that crossed the Atlantic and therefore the likely average number of passengers they carried per voyage. The

[12] *Catálogo de pasajeros a Indias durante los siglos XVI, XVII y XVIII* (3 vols., Seville, 1940–6).

average figure of fifteen passengers during the years from 1506 to 1540 is said to have risen to twenty during the next two decades and 30 during the years between 1562 and 1625, reaching 40 during the years from 1626 to 1650. Multiplying these averages by the number of ships sailing, as recorded in the registers edited by Huguette and Pierre Chaunu,[13] he arrives at totals for each period and annual averages for the number of migrants. Mörner then concludes that the number of Spaniards who emigrated to the Indies was, over the whole of the sixteenth century, about 243,000; a further 195,000 went during the first half of the seventeenth century. The average number of people leaving Spain for America annually, therefore, was 2,600 during the sixteenth century and 3,900 during the first half of the seventeenth century. The calculations of Boyd-Bowman and Mörner are therefore quite close, and on another count the totals are fairly modest, even bearing in mind the limited population of Spain at the time, and are not at all comparable with the mass European migrations of the nineteenth and twentieth centuries.[14]

Although they cannot in themselves indicate the full extent of European migration in the sixteenth century, the *Catálogo* and the *Indice* do nonetheless offer representative samples of what the emigrant population was like. Naturally, the male sex predominated. The *Catálogo* shows that only 10 per cent of embarkation licences were issued to women. In this respect Boyd-Bowman distinguishes emigration by period. In the first stage, the proportion of women was very low, but in the middle of the sixteenth century it increased dramatically, and by the 1560s it came to exceed one quarter of the total. As for the proportions within the Spanish population in the early colonial period, however, one gets the impression from the little research done so far that the imbalance between the sexes was less than that indicated by the ships' registers. The higher mortality rate in the Indies for men, plus their wider geographical dispersion, perhaps explain the discrepancy. Nevertheless, in the period we are considering there were always fewer Spanish women than Spanish men in America.

In the interests of consolidating its hegemony there, the crown wanted to see a more stable and balanced Spanish population developing in America. It encouraged women to emigrate, and even whole families.

[13] Huguette and Pierre Chaunu, *Séville et l'Atlantique (1504–1650)*, 8 vols. (Paris, 1955–9).
[14] For the contributions of P. Boyd-Bowman and Magnus Mörner on Spanish migration to America during the colonial period, see *CHLA* II, Bibliographical Essay 1.

Both royal officials and encomenderos were encouraged to marry while in Spain, or to send for their wives and relatives to come over to join them in the New World. The high proportion of young men, most of them single, who were continually crossing the ocean frustrated this policy objective, for it meant that the chronic deficiency of Spanish women in America was never made up. For the same reason, more or less permanent relationships of Spanish men with native American women took root. The result was the formation in the population of a stratum of mestizos, not always differentiated as such. In fact, especially at the beginning, many mestizos were absorbed into the social stratum occupied by their fathers, enjoying their privileges and passing for Europeans.

The *Catálogo* and the *Indice*, as well as local census-rolls, are equally informative about where the Spanish migrants came from. The port of embarkation was Seville. Not surprisingly, therefore, Andalusia – and principally western Andalusia – consequently contributed more than a third of all emigrants, and Estremadura almost a sixth. The central zone of the peninsula, the two Castiles, and León contributed another third, the majority from Toledo, Valladolid, and Salamanca. Among the lands of the periphery, the Basque country, especially the province of Vizcaya, supplied quite a number of emigrants. The Basques drew attention to themselves, moreover, not so much through numbers as through the group cohesiveness they displayed once in the New World. In early seventeenth-century Potosí they were the predominant group, entering into open confrontation with the Andalusians, for instance in the so-called Vicuña War. As the sources testify, Catalans, Valencians and Aragonese, and also Galicians and Asturians, crossed the ocean in the sixteenth century, though their numbers were low. In spite of the prohibitions against them, more than a thousand foreigners also went openly to the Spanish Indies during the first century of colonization.

Among the emigrants were many hidalgos, some of whom possibly first rose to that rank in America. Besides merchants and officials, such members of the lower classes as peasants and artisans flocked across the ocean in great numbers. What is also noticeable is that far more emigrants came from cities and towns than from rural areas. The emigrants were quite often to return to the peninsula – with fortunes, with titles, with scars – but the majority of them put down roots in the New World. Three-quarters of a century after the first voyages of discovery there were about 150,000 people of Spanish ancestry in the

Indies, although, of course, not all of them had been born in Europe.
In his *Geografía y descripción universal de las Indias* (1574)[15] the cosmographer and chronicler Juan López de Velasco mentions some 225
Spanish cities and towns, whose inhabitants included 25,000 *vecinos*, or
full citizens. The total number of Spaniards in these American urban
centres can be estimated by counting six individual persons for each
extended family represented by one of these full citizens (i.e. 150,000).
It could well be that this multiplier should be larger, if we take probable
errors and omissions into account. By itself, the exact figure is of little
importance: what matters is the order of magnitude within which we
are to locate it. There were tens of thousands of Spaniards living in
America at a relatively early date, although they were very much a
minority compared with the millions of Indians who survived in the
Spanish dominions, even after the demographic catastrophe.

Half a century later, the itinerant Carmelite Antonio Vázquez de
Espinosa repeated, to some extent, the work of López de Velasco. In
his *Compendio y descripción de las Indias occidentales* (*c.* 1628)[16] he provides
a minimum figure of 75,000 *vecinos* (giving a Spanish population of
450,000). If we suppose that his errors and omissions are in the same
proportion as his predecessor's, the number of Spanish colonists in the
New World must have trebled between 1570 and 1620. Approximately
half of this increase resulted from immigration, according to the
statistics provided by Mörner. The rest of it came from natural growth
of the Spanish stock already in America. If this is so, in these 50 years
the Spaniards doubled their number by natural reproduction – a high
rate of fecundity by comparison with the standard rates for the time
in Europe.

Growth did not occur at the same rate in all areas. In some, the
increase was considerable; others stagnated, or even lost inhabitants.
From a comparison of López de Velasco and Vázquez de Espinosa it
is clear that the areas of most rapid growth for the white population
were the Audiencia of Charcas, owing to the mining boom there, and
the Audiencia of Quito, thanks to the rise of its coastal plantations and
of stock rearing in its hills. The number of Spaniards in Mexico also
grew, though not perhaps so rapidly. The Audiencias of Lima and

[15] Juan López de Velasco, *Geografía y descripción universal de las Indias* [1574] (Madrid, 1894; 2nd
edn, Madrid, 1971).
[16] Antonio Vázquez de Espinosa, *Compendio y descripción de las Indias* [*c.* 1628] (Washington, D.C.,
1948; 2nd edn, Madrid, 1969).

Bogotá occupy a central position in a table of white population growth-rates in the late sixteenth and early seventeenth centuries. Below them come the Audiencias of Guadalajara and Santo Domingo. The growth in the latter was entirely attributable to the increasing weight of Caracas and the area around it, as by this time the Caribbean islands were well into a period of decline. The Audiencias of Panama and of Guatemala seem to have been stagnating; Chile was actually losing population, owing to the bloody affrays between the Spaniards and the Araucanians that had been going on for more than four decades.

Europeans were not the only new settlers in the American continent. From the outset Africans, in the role of auxiliaries, formed part of the expeditionary forces, and soon their numbers increased. Their transfer to the New World was, however, involuntary, and it had an economic purpose. With the disappearance of the Indians in the Antilles and the beginnings of plantation agriculture, Las Casas proposed that African slaves be brought in to replace them as labourers. Africans had shown themselves well able to adapt to Caribbean conditions, and in the end they took the place of native Americans in the islands and the *tierra caliente* of the mainland. Africans were less needed in the mining areas of the sierras, although some were imported there, too, to carry out specialized tasks. Blacks were brought in all over the continent – including on the great stock-rearing haciendas – as they were inherently much more mobile than Indians. A large number of them went into domestic service and thereby raised their masters' social status. African slaves constituted a capital asset, and importation of them was regulated by commercial law. Just as in other mercantile activities, the state undertook a regulatory function in the slave trade.

The *conquistadores* and officials of the Spanish crown received the first licences to import slaves into America, as a reward for the services they had rendered or as compensation for personal expenditure incurred in the discovery or the conquest. Hernán Cortés and Pizarro both received such recognition. Soon the grants of licences to import slaves became far more widely available. It was no longer adequate to purchase slaves in Seville; instead, they had to be fetched from Africa and transported to ports authorized specially for the purpose in the New World – the ports of the Antilles, Veracruz, Nombre de Dios, and Cartagena.

Hard-pressed towards the end of the sixteenth century by its financial obligations, the crown of Castile instituted a monopoly from which it was to derive lucrative revenues. Each licence or contract (*asiento*) stipulated how long the privilege of importation was to last and the number of slaves to be transported under it. With some fluctuations this monopoly endured until after the beginning of the eighteenth century. The first companies to benefit from it were Portuguese. At the time subjects of the Spanish king, the Portuguese had substantial capital available and the benefit of long experience in the slave trade. From the factories they had set up in the Cape Verde islands and São Tomé they re-exported blacks captured along the coasts of Africa. The stay in the Portuguese factory that the captives necessarily underwent makes it difficult to identify their ethnic background and territorial origins. Nor did the slavers have any very precise knowledge of African geography or African societies. Broadly speaking, it appears that the Africans transported to the New World during the sixteenth century came from Senegambia, Guinea, or the mouth of the Congo river: that is to say, they were mostly either Mandingos, Minas, or Congos, if we follow the nomenclature used in the Indies. From the second quarter of the seventeenth century onwards, Angola took the lead, and came almost to monopolize the supply. Angolans appeared in Brazil first, because of the geographical proximity. From there, some were taken covertly to the Río de la Plata, and even to Peru.

The African slave trade reached a peak in the final quinquennium of the sixteenth century, when the crown of Castile granted licences for 26,100 slaves to be imported into its dominions. The commerce remained at this near-peak level for a quarter of a century, till the world economic crisis of the 1620s precipitated a decline. From 1641 to 1650 the trade was even officially suspended. At its peak, however, 3,500 *piezas de Indias* (pieces) entered Spanish America each year. Each *pieza* was equivalent to one slave of full strength to work, but women, children, and some of the men constituted only fractions of such a unit, calculated according to age and physical condition. If we total the licences and contracts recorded by Pierre and Huguette Chaunu[17] we find that the number of *piezas* whose exportation to the colonies was authorized by the Castilian crown between 1571 and 1640 was 170,000. Out of this total, 100,000 crossed in the first four decades of the seventeenth century. On the one hand, however, the heavy mortality the slaves suffered on the high seas reduced the proportion of them that was finally landed, while on the other, the legal restrictions were quite

[17] Chaunu, *Séville et l'Atlantique*.

often evaded, and there was no lack of smuggling of slaves. For his part, Philip Curtin estimates that Spanish America imported about 75,000 slaves during the sixteenth century and about 125,000 between 1600 and 1650: in all, about 200,000 in a century and a half.[18] This was less than half the number of Spaniards immigrating into America in the same period. However, we must bear in mind that for the migration of Spaniards to America the totals are gross, for that of Africans, net: the slaves were there to stay.

The level of reproduction among slaves was low. Apart from the harshness of their living and working conditions, which tended to cause them to deteriorate physically and die early, the distribution of the sexes was not in a natural ratio. Royal orders laid upon shippers the obligation to make the cargo of each slave ship at least one-third female; but even if this requirement had been enforced, it would still have left women far in the minority. The African contributed to the mingling of races in America. Unions of black men and Indian women produced the *zambo*, and those of white men and black women, the mulatto.

The conquest of the Philippines opened up a third channel by which immigrants reached America, as involuntarily as those from Africa. From the time of Legazpi's voyage in 1566 – and especially after the union of Spain and Portugal in 1580 – there arrived at Acapulco, from the west, several thousand Filipino slaves, plus some from China, Japan and even the East Indies. Most of them stayed in Mexico. The Lima census of 1613, however, records the presence there of 114 Asians: 38 Chinese or Filipinos, 20 Japanese, and 56 from 'Portuguese India' – a term which included Malays and Cambodians. For the most part they were artisans and domestic servants. This flow, never very large, stopped when Philip II prohibited the trade in Asians in 1597.

The advanced civilizations of Mesoamerica and the Andes had built metropolises, such as Tenochtitlán and Cuzco, equivalent in size and function to the great cities of the same period in Europe and Asia. Below them were spread a closely woven network of smaller cities and towns. In the area of the great empires, the Spaniards occupied these centres of native power and culture, supplanted the governing groups in them, and at once busied themselves reorganizing them. In general, they preferred to conquer the most populous, most urbanized areas. Some

[18] Philip Curtin, *The Atlantic slave trade: a census* (Madison, 1969).

native cities disappeared altogether; sometimes the Spaniards founded new ones. All in all, however, the original urban network survived. Where the Spaniards found a dispersed population – whether of hunters or of less intensive cultivators – they founded centres of their own to fulfil administrative or economic needs or to meet the requirements of the imperial system of communications. Zacatecas, Santiago de Chile, and Buenos Aires were all founded for such purposes.

By contrast with other colonial systems, that of Spain was, above all, an urban one. A high proportion of the immigrants, as we have seen, came from cities. Even for the rural migrants their journey to the Indies actually meant a drift to the city, its amenities, and its social distinctions. It was also essential for them, once settled in America, to be in groups. Scattered across so extensive a continent, the thousands of settlers arriving in the Indies would otherwise have been so diluted as to fall easy prey to the Indians. Congregated together, they were able to preserve their identity, their language, and their way of life. Even when their business kept them in the country for part of the year, they used to keep houses in the nearest town or city.

By law, Spaniards and Indians lived in different places. The Spaniards were forbidden to move into Indian townships and vice versa, except for those Indians needed to service the cities. Even the latter – artisans, for example – lived in parishes set apart. The multitude of workers and pedlars who came into the city daily lived outside its limits in satellite townships. Native Americans thus ceased to dominate the urban centres, but they did not become more dispersed. State and church were agreed: it suited them both for the Indians to be kept congregated together. Government and evangelization would thereby be facilitated, not to mention the fact that resettlement left large tracts of land unoccupied and free for the crown to use for rewarding the colonists. The policy of congregating the Indians together dates back to the Laws of Burgos of 1512, before the Spanish invasion of the mainland. It took a long time to complete the process, despite the Spanish monarchs' persistence. In Guatemala the friars managed to regroup the Indians speedily and successfully. By about 1550 most of them were living in newly founded townships. In central Mexico, the elder Velasco carried out an intensive campaign of resettlement during his term as viceroy from 1550 to 1564. It was left to Viceroy Montesclaros, between 1603 and 1605, to complete the work. It has been estimated that the second programme affected a quarter of a million people, a considerable

proportion of the remaining dispersed Indian population, though even
then not the whole of it.[19] The new townships housed an average of
400 to 500 tributaries: that is, 2,000 to 2,500 inhabitants. We have
already referred to the comprehensive resettlement accomplished in
1573 by Viceroy Toledo in Peru, which was on a bigger scale and more
systematic. Yucatán went the same way at this time. In New Granada
in 1602, Luis Henríquez as Visitor tried to concentrate the Indians; but
he was resisted by the encomenderos who would be affected by the
resettlement, as well as by the Indians themselves, and his purpose was
frustrated.

The Spaniards for the most part lived in the major cities, the Indians
in the smaller towns. In spite of the law, however, segregation into two
'republics' was never rigorously enforced. There was never any lack
of Indians in the cities, which indeed needed them if they were to
function efficiently. On the other hand, the Spaniards intruded little by
little into the wealthier Indian towns. And the townships they set up
on their own estates had a bottom stratum of Indian or mestizo peons.

DEMOGRAPHIC RECOVERY

Throughout the seventeenth and eighteenth centuries mortality rates
remained high. In particular, a very high proportion of the youngest
died. 'The tithe of children' was what it was called – more because there
was never a year in which it did not have to be paid, than because it
robbed the population of only a tenth. Over twice this rate of mortality
was considered normal, though there were variations, of course,
according to social stratum and ethnic category. In León – a town in
the Mexican Bajío – in the late eighteenth century, 19 per cent of Spanish
deaths were those of young children; among the people of mixed race
the figure was 36 per cent, and among the Indians 51 per cent. These
figures cover a broader category than that usually described as 'infant
mortality'.

Quite apart from the steady drain on life through the deaths of
individuals, every so often an exceptional death toll would ravage the
population. The parish registers of several predominantly Indian settlements in the Puebla–Tlaxcala region of central Mexico demonstrate
how these reverses occurred again and again. The parish registers of

[19] Howard F. Cline, 'Civil congregations of the Indians in New Spain, 1598–1606', *HAHR*, 29
(1949), 349–69.

Acatzingo, Zacatelco, and Cholula have been analysed.[20] Month after
month, in times of crisis, the numbers of baptisms and burials diverge.
With both physical and mental depression widespread, the sudden rise
in deaths brought in its wake an immediate decrease in births, or in
conceptions – whichever way one cares to put it – as well as in marriages
between couples of child-bearing age. Short crises with these effects
followed upon one another's heels throughout the second half of the
seventeenth century and the whole of the eighteenth. The reverses were
quite evenly spaced. In Zacatelco they were recorded in 1692, 1727,
1737, 1762, 1779, 1784, 1797, 1804–5, and 1813, not to mention some
less significant setbacks. The heaviest death tolls occurred in the first
three: in 1737, deaths quintupled from one year to the next; in 1692
and 1727 the crises took even more lives, but did not affect the number
of conceptions so acutely, so their consequences were less profoundly
disturbing. They were by no means moderate, however, either in their
geographical extent or in terms of individual damage. In 1813 burials
tripled once again in Zacatelco, while births shrank to barely half the
usual number.[21] The setbacks of 1692 and 1727 arose from epidemics
of measles, those of 1737, 1762, and 1779 from typhus (*matlazahuatl*),
that of 1797 from smallpox, and that of 1813 from influenza. The
diagnosis is not absolutely certain, but there is a growing consensus in
the aetiology of these Mexican epidemics. Those dating from 1761 in
Mexico City have been the subject of a detailed study.[22] More evidence
about the way each outbreak occurred, the surrounding circumstances,
and the effects of the epidemics survives from the better-documented
urban areas than from rural centres.

Hunger, so often an affliction during the period, was a very important
cause of excessive mortality. In the Bajío the peaks of mortality have
been related to periods of high food prices, and therefore to shortages
of maize.[23] Crises of subsistence used to precede or follow the attacks

[20] Thomas Calvo, *Acatzingo. Demografía de una parroquia mexicana* (Mexico, 1973); Claude Morin,
Santa Inés Zacatelco (1646–1812). Contribución a la demografía del México colonial (Mexico, 1973);
Elsa Malvido, 'Factores de despoblación y reposición de la población de Cholula (1641–1810)',
Historia Mexicana [HM], 89 (1973), 52–110.

[21] Thousands of miles south of Zacatelco, in the Andean valley of the river Colca, the parish of
Yanque manifests a whole litany of parallel tribulations: 1689, 1694, 1700, 1713, 1720–1, 1731,
1742, 1756, 1769, 1780, 1785, 1788, and 1790–1. The two series do not, however, coincide.
In Yanque, as for the rest of Peru, 1720 was a particularly fateful date; not so in Mexico. See
N. D. Cook, *The people of the Colca valley. A population study* (Boulder, 1982), 76.

[22] Donald B. Cooper, *Epidemic disease in Mexico City, 1761–1813. An administrative, social and medical
study* (Austin, 1965).

[23] D. A. Brading, *Haciendas and ranchos in the Mexican Bajío, León 1700–1860* (Cambridge, 1978),
174–204.

of infection. Bodies weakened by hunger were an easy prey to the viruses; on the other hand, by reducing the labour force, an epidemic would disrupt agriculture and therefore the food supply. Hunger also drove the Indians to flight. During the great famines of 1627–31 and 1648–56 tens of thousands of Mayas fled inland in search of food. Years later they had to be returned to their own villages by force.

Besides sicknesses and hunger there were natural disasters such as the earthquakes that levelled cities from time to time, causing high death tolls, especially in areas along the Pacific coast, where the youngest geological folds are to be found. According to the records we have, earthquakes occurred more often in the seventeenth and eighteenth centuries than they have done at any other time. For example, of the population of the *corregimientos* of Riobamba and Ambato in the Audiencia of Quito, 9 per cent and 14 per cent respectively died in the earthquake of 1797.[24]

The reduction in mortality rates that began to manifest itself – hesitantly and inconsistently – at the end of the eighteenth century is not easy to explain. Improvements in hygiene did not produce it, even though by that time a considerable effort was being made to improve public health. At best, its results were no more than partial. The most famous initiative in this field was the introduction of vaccination against smallpox in 1780. In 1797–8 a more energetic attempt followed this first step. Five years later, the authorities undertook an ambitious campaign across almost the whole continent. Heading it was the physician Francisco Javier de Balmis, who sailed from Corunna in 1803 with a medical team. He took with him as well dozens of children inoculated with the virus. The pustules that came up on their arms contained cultures which, staying active for many months and over great distances, secreted the vaccine that was to be applied to children and adults in the Indies.

The inoculation campaign began in the Canary Islands, continued in Puerto Rico, and from there went on to the northern coast of South America. In Barranquilla the expedition divided. One half, with José Salvany at its head, went inland towards Panama, and then southward. Salvany visited Bogotá, Quito, Cuenca, Piura, and Trujillo, and went on as far as Lima. Here there was another split: the main group travelled up to Arequipa and then penetrated via Puno into the altiplano, to

---

[24] Rosemary D. F. Bromley, 'Urban–rural demographic contrasts in Highland Ecuador: town recession in a period of catastrophe, 1778–1841', *Journal of Historical Geography*, 5 (1979), 292–3.

descend from there to the port of Buenos Aires, reaching it five years after they had left Spain. The other section travelled through the interior of Peru and then went on to Chile. Meanwhile, the team led by Balmis himself visited Cuba and Yucatán. In Mérida a third group split off, taking upon itself the task of bringing vaccination to the captaincy general of Guatemala. Balmis travelled to Veracruz, where he entered New Spain. There, Mexico City and Puebla were his chief fields of operation. He then went on through Zacatecas and Durango in the north, and sailed from Acapulco for Manila. His philanthropic work there completed, he finally returned to Cadiz, having travelled around the world distributing his health-giving inoculations.

Even though Balmis' medical team covered the whole of Spanish America, it was hard to reach all the inhabitants. Children were given priority. Some 100,000 were inoculated in Mexico between July 1804 and January 1806, but these could not have been more than a fifth of the number needing vaccination. The big cities and the ports were the places that benefited most from the campaign – and within them, naturally, the higher ranks in society. Although the vaccination was free, taking it to the peasants and other sections of the lower classes turned out to be difficult, for the vaccine was met with suspicion. More than the lives that the inoculation probably saved, the greatest legacy of Balmis' voyage may well have been the spreading of knowledge among the public and the medical profession.[25]

Death still reigned, but life was beginning to lift its head. As each crisis passed, marriages and conceptions multiplied, as though the people were trying to make up for lost time, or to fill the gap that disease had produced. Generally speaking, good years came to exceed bad, and in the good years births outnumbered deaths. In spite of the continuing high mortality rate in the infant and other age groups, the population grew. In Zacatelco, for example, the birth-rate exceeded 50 births per thousand inhabitants, while the death-rate worked out at around 40. The progressive increase in population, therefore, was over 1 per cent annually. From the scattered data available it is possible to suggest a number of reasons for this. Here and there, indications exist that Indian women were marrying younger, thus increasing the span during whch

[25] G. Díaz de Yraola, 'La vuelta al mundo de la expedición de la vacuna', *Anuario de Estudios Americanos*, 4 (1947), 105–62. See also M. M. Smith, 'The "Real expedición marítima de la vacuna" in New Spain and Guatemala', *Transactions of the American Philosophical Society*, 64 (1974), 1–74.

they were most likely to conceive. In eighteenth-century Oaxaca, girls married, on average, at the early age of fifteen or sixteen. This was only a few months earlier than the Indian women of León. Likewise, a smaller proportion of women remained single. Families also started to have more children, so that each generation easily maintained or even increased its numbers. Available evidence shows that fertility rates varied according to social and ethnic group. In general, women of European ancestry had more children than Indian women, and Indians more than those of African origin. The urban centres, where the Europeans were concentrated, also manifested a higher average number of children per family. In the Indies, the exact reverse occurred of what happens in contemporary industrial societies: the lower social strata did not have more children than the higher strata in colonial Spanish America. The great landowners around Buenos Aires, for example, had twice as many children living as did their day-labourers and their domestic servants. And creole women in the towns did not necessarily have a higher marriage rate, or marry any earlier.

Matrimony is a poor index of fecundity during the colonial period. A very considerable share of the procreation that went on occurred outside marriage. The registers of the parish of San Sebastián in the city of Lima reveal 40 per cent of infant baptisms as being of illegitimate children in the late sixteenth century; in the seventeenth century the percentage varied between 25 and 40.[26] In the port of Valparaíso, the illegitimacy rate hovered around the same figure of 40 per cent throughout the eighteenth century.[27] In the mining area of Charcas, in northern Mexico, it amounted to 29 per cent between 1690 and 1729.[28] In rural districts, where the people were less mobile and in any case preponderantly Indian, it came as low as 6 per cent, for example in the town of Acatzingo, already mentioned. Babies either had parents both of whose identities were known, or their father was unnamed, or they had been abandoned by their mothers, who thus remained anonymous. The two former categories were, of course, the more usual.

Both white and Indian couples gave birth to fewer illegitimate children than mixed couples. In Pelarco, a country parish in Chile, 63

[26] Claude Mazet, 'Population et société à Lima aux xvie et xviie siècles', *Cahiers des Amériques Latines*, 13–14 (1976), 53–100.
[27] René Salinas Meza, 'Carácteres generales de la evolución demográfica de un centro urbano chileno: Valparaíso, 1685–1830', *Historia*, 10 (1971), 177–204.
[28] Marcello Carmagnani, 'Demografía y sociedad. La estructura social de los centros mineros del norte de México, 1600–1720', *HM*, 21 (1972), 419–59.

per cent of the children recorded as mestizos at baptism between 1786 and 1796 were illegitimate: only 37 per cent had been conceived within regular marriages. Among the mulattos, 48 per cent were illegitimate. This fell to 39 per cent among the Indians, and as low as 20 per cent among the whites.[29] Although illegitimacy was no monopoly of those of mixed race, it nonetheless included a significant proportion of the offspring of the growing number of interracial unions. In spite of the barriers set up by law and by prejudice, these unions were increasingly common in the eighteenth century. The mestizo sector of the population grew the most rapidly – at the expense of the other ethnic groups. And it enjoyed a fertility rate second only to that of the whites, higher than that of the blacks, the mulattos, or the Indians.

It was no longer true, as it had been in the sixteenth and early seventeenth centuries, that demographic tendencies within the Indian world largely determined the size of the population of Spanish America. It was nevertheless a fact of no little significance that in the key areas of predominantly Indian settlement – central Mexico (from the middle of the seventeenth century) and the central Andes (from the early decades of the eighteenth century) – the Indian population began to recover from the lowest point of its decline, although as a general rule the process was slow and frequently interrupted by major epidemics. The returns from the tax of half a real that each Indian paid annually for cathedral building gave José Miranda an opportunity to calculate how the tributary population developed in three dioceses of New Spain. Between the middle and the end of the seventeenth century it increased by 32 per cent in the diocese of Mexico, by 53 per cent in that of Michoacán, and by 19 per cent in that of Puebla.[30] Charles Gibson's researches into the Aztecs of the Valley of Mexico, and those of Cook and Borah into the Mixteca Alta, show still higher proportions, in a period that admittedly was longer, for their work extends into the middle of the eighteenth century.[31] As for encomienda Indians in Yucatán, they almost tripled their numbers between 1688 and 1785.[32] Their rate of increase was a really notable one, of the order of 1.1 per

[29] H. Aranguiz Donoso, 'Notas para el estudio de una parroquia rural del siglo XVIII: Pelarco, 1786–1796', *Anales de la Facultad de Filosofía y Ciencias de la Educación* (1969), 37–42.

[30] José Miranda, 'La población indígena de México en el siglo XVII', *HM*, 12 (1963), 182–9.

[31] Charles Gibson, *The Aztecs under Spanish Rule. A history of the Indians of the Valley of Mexico, 1519–1810* (Stanford, 1964); Sherburne F. Cook and Woodrow Borah, *The population of the Mixteca Alta, 1520–1960* (Berkeley, 1968).

[32] Sherburne F. Cook and Woodrow Borah, *Essay in population history: Mexico and the Caribbean*, vol. II (Berkeley, 1974).

cent compounded annually. It has been estimated that the Indian population of Mexico increased by 44 per cent during the second half of the eighteenth century, the growth being greater on the periphery than in the central zone.[33] The further the eighteenth century advanced, the more demographic growth increased. Not everywhere, however: in fact, in the country parishes around Puebla already mentioned, the growth rate slowed down at the end of the century. Evidence that is partial, and sometimes contradictory, suggests that overall there was also a moderate demographic revival in the central Andes.

The slow progress in the rural world of the Indians contrasts with the more dramatic signs of population growth on the coasts, especially in recently settled regions along the Atlantic coast, as a result of internal population pressures and expanding European demand for agricultural products. Gauchos peopled the pampas of the Río de la Plata, while the ports experienced notable economic and demographic expansion. Ranchers and their livestock multiplied on the plains of the Orinoco. The northern coast of South America also prospered and, along with it, the islands of the Caribbean – Cuba, Hispaniola, and Puerto Rico. The northern frontier of New Spain was being pushed far back to the north, opening up space for colonization.

Population pressure arose also in some areas that were marginal to European demands, or at best linked to them only indirectly. In the isolated west of New Granada, the excess population of the north of Antioquia overflowed into the valleys to the south. J. J. Parsons has described how the colonists occupied the wastelands on the temperate slopes and brought them under cultivation.[34] In 1764 spontaneous settlement reached Caldas. In 1789, however, a royal cedula instructed officials to found agricultural colonies and to settle immigrants there. Early marriage and larger families produced a growth in population that the countryside around Antioquia was unable to support. Further south, settlement in the coastlands of Guayaquil grew notably compared to that of the sierra of Quito, largely in response to the growing demand of Lima and Mexico for Ecuadorean tobacco and cacao.[35] Chile provides a third example of rapid development. Its population expanded to meet the needs of nearby Lima rather than those of distant Europe.

[33] Delfina E. López Sarrelangue, 'Población indígena de Nueva España en el siglo XVIII', *HM*, 12 (1963), 516–30.
[34] James J. Parsons, *Antioqueño colonization in Western Colombia* (2nd edn, Berkeley, 1968).
[35] Michael T. Hamerly, *Historia social y económica de la antigua provincia de Guayaquil, 1763–1842* (Guayaquil, 1973).

The population of the diocese of Santiago is estimated to have doubled in the half-century following 1760.[36]

In this period of demographic expansion, sizeable human populations were displaced, over both short and long distances. The Indians congregated in villages during the late sixteenth century chose to spread out again. Their dispersal in Yucatán has been attributed to an ancient Indian preference in favour of scattered settlement.[37] In the sierra of Peru, the villages established in the time of Viceroy Toledo were abandoned for more practical reasons. In effect, by putting themselves far beyond the reach of the tax-collectors and the overseers of the *mita*, the Indians managed to evade the legal burdens they were supposed to bear. As has been stated above, they then appeared in 'foreign' terrain as 'strangers' who for that reason were exempt. According to the summary counts made by the tax official Orellana in 1754 and incorporated into the report by the Conde de Superunda on his period of office as viceroy, 57 per cent of the Indians in the diocese of Chuquisaca and La Paz were immigrants, or the offspring of immigrants, in the middle of the eighteenth century. In Cuzco the figure was 37 per cent, in Trujillo 30 per cent, in Lima 23 per cent, and in Arequipa and Huamanga, 18 per cent.[38] Indians arriving from outside flocked to the most fertile valleys, but also established themselves in the altiplano, where resources were scanty. Rather than positive ambition, it was dissatisfaction with the conditions of life in their existing communities that incited people to move. Migrant Indians settled as peons on Spanish-owned haciendas, but they also started to disperse across the countryside again. In the eighteenth century, the crown stopped insisting on the Indians' resettlement in towns, except on the frontiers, where a whole-hearted missionary offensive backed by the state succeeded in setting up missions and reservations in lands whose own inhabitants were unsubdued, from California to Patagonia. In an extension of its policy, the crown favoured lands being divided among the Indians to be held in individual ownership – a step which naturally tended to bring about a dispersion of the population. After the Jesuits were expelled, the strict order they had imposed on their missions disintegrated when they came into the care either of the civil authority

[36] Marcello Carmagnani, 'Colonial Latin American demography: growth of Chilean Population, 1700–1830', *Journal of Social History*, 1 (1967), 179–91.

[37] Nancy M. Farriss, 'Nucleation versus dispersal: the dynamics of population movement in colonial Yucatán,' *HAHR*, 58 (1978), 187–216.

[38] Nicolás Sánchez-Albornoz, *Indios y tributos en el Alto Perú* (Lima, 1978), 52.

or of other religious orders. The breakup was especially violent in Paraguay, where the natives either returned to the forest or migrated downstream to earn their living on the great coastal estates of the Río de la Plata. In 1772, five years after the expulsion of the Jesuits, *visitador* Larrázabal found there were still 80,352 Indians living in 30 former mission villages, but in 1797 only 54,388 remained. The rest had not died: rather, the deterioration of their villages had caused them to move.[39] In Mexico, on the other hand, there seem to have been more positive motivations behind internal migration. In the early days the Bajío had been a raiding ground for the nomadic Chichimeca, but it now turned out to have fertile soil, and it was occupied by settled Indians moving in from various parts of central Mexico. The prosperity of its agriculture caused the number of its inhabitants to multiply four and a half times during the second half of the seventeenth century and five times during the eighteenth century. The rise of cattle-rearing attracted migrants to the *provincias internas* in the north of New Spain, some of which were areas located beyond the frontiers of present-day Mexico.

IMMIGRATION IN THE EIGHTEENTH CENTURY

Migration from Europe remained a significant source of population growth in the late colonial period. Fifty-three thousand Spaniards are estimated to have migrated to America during the eighteenth century. An average of only 500 a year looks small, and certainly the number was lower than it had been in the sixteenth or seventeenth centuries. Many of the new arrivals occupied high positions in the civil, military and ecclesiastical bureaucracies, as well as in commerce. Some, however, came as settlers. The crown encouraged migration to the Indies, partly to provide an outlet for the surplus population of some regions of Spain. Many people from the Canaries crossed the Atlantic, initially to the Caribbean islands and then to the northern coasts of South America. Galicians, Asturians, and Castilians from the Cantabrian mountains flocked to the new agricultural colonies. In their geographical origins, the majority of these emigrants differed from those of the sixteenth century. They came from the north of Spain rather than the south, and now included large numbers of Catalans. The manufactures and primary products of Catalonia found excellent markets overseas. Any list of

[39] The Larrázabal census, Archivo General de la Nación, Buenos Aires, 9, 18.8.5, 18.8.6, and 18.8.7.

merchants reveals the presence of many people with Catalan surnames in all the great ports of Spanish America. The Spanish crown was also concerned to occupy the vast areas of land to which it had legal title but no effective possession, in an era of increasing conflict with other European powers. The abortive colonies that were set up in 1779 and 1786 in inhospitable areas of Patagonia were an attempt to realize this objective. In Cuba in the time of the intendant Ramírez, the Junta de Población Blanca (Board for White Settlement) deliberately fostered Spanish immigration to counterbalance the island's massive importation of African slaves.

The strongest migratory current of this period, however, remained the involuntary one – from Africa. After the 1640–51 ban on importing slaves into the Spanish dominions had been lifted, the crown hesitated between various different commercial formulas, all of them intended to combine the necessary influx of labour with a solid financial return. From being directly organized by the crown, the trade became based on a series of short-term agreements with different contractors. Then, profiting from the rapprochement between Spain and France that followed the change of dynasty in Madrid, in 1701 the Royal French Gulf of Guinea Company secured for itself the right of importing slaves into Spanish America. In 1713 the Treaty of Utrecht transferred this monopoly to England. The British government granted its rights to the South Sea Company, which supplied the Spanish Indies with slaves until 1750, except for brief interruptions caused by the wars at sea. The South Sea Company secured the right to maintain slave factories in Campeche, Veracruz, Havana, Cartagena, Portobelo, Panama, Caracas, and Buenos Aires. The factories turned into points for the penetration of Spanish America by English contraband goods, a business which was often more profitable than the trade in slaves.

The inability of the contractors, whether French or English, to dispose of the quotas of slaves agreed upon proves that the Spanish government had initially overestimated the demand for them. As the eighteenth century progressed, however, this demand intensified, but the English found they had to confront an active trade conducted by the French and the Dutch, smuggling in slaves from their Caribbean possessions. Philip Curtin estimates that between 1651 and 1760 about 344,000 Africans entered the Spanish dominions – an average of rather more than 3,000 a year. Of this number, 144,000 *piezas de Indias* were imported by the South Sea Company.

The sharp increase in the slave trade during the second half of the eighteenth century was due to the expanding cultivation of tropical crops, above all sugar, in the Caribbean. Between 1761 and 1810 about 300,000 Africans were imported into Spanish America, a rate of somewhat over 6,000 a year. Cuba and to a lesser extent Puerto Rico took almost the whole supply. African immigration totally transformed the ethnic makeup of the islands. According to la Torre's census, 44 per cent of the population of Cuba in 1774 was coloured and slaves constituted 37 per cent of the total. In 1817, 57 per cent of the population was coloured and slaves constituted 49 per cent.[40] By now blacks were in a majority. In contrast to Cuba (and even more sharply to Haiti, the western part of Hispaniola) only 3 per cent of the 100,000 or so inhabitants of Santo Domingo at the beginning of the nineteenth century were slaves, though there was also a small percentage of free blacks and mulattos. The African element was, however, important along the northern coast of South America, not so much in Barcelona and Cumaná in the east of Venezuela – where there were more Indians – as in the central valleys and coasts, above all in the Gulf of Maracaibo. The Atlantic coastlands of New Granada, centring on Cartagena, likewise had a high proportion of Africans in their population.

Towards the end of the colonial period, the population of Spanish America thus consisted of an elaborate mosaic of peoples. The Indians, the main stem of the population structure, made up about 45 per cent of it. They had in part reversed their long demographic decline, but had by no means recovered the numbers they had had at the time of the European invasion. From some areas they had disappeared completely or survived only as faint traces in the blood of the mestizos or *zambos*. In others, they constituted only a fraction of the population, often not the biggest fraction, but a dwindling minority well advanced on the road to complete assimilation. Where they still predominated, clinging tenaciously to their lands and languages – in the mountains and valleys of central Mexico, between the Isthmus of Tehuantepec and Costa Rica, in the south of New Granada (particularly in Quito), and throughout the Peruvian Andes and the Bolivian altiplano – their

[40] Ramiro Guerra y Sánchez, *Historia de la nación cubana* (Havana, 1952), I, 162.

growth was generally slow. The progeny of the *conquistadores* and of the Spanish migrants who followed them remained in a minority. Despite the rapid growth the white population had experienced, it did not amount to even a fifth of the population. Mestizos of one sort or another, and of one colour or another, constituted not much less than a third. Blacks were only 4 per cent. In the predominantly Indian areas the Hispanic community, consisting of Spaniards and creoles – white or mestizo, as the categories are not always separated in the censuses – was largely confined to the big cities or towns and the great estates. They themselves predominated in the sparsely inhabited Río de la Plata, and likewise in central Chile, in the southern coastal region and the centre of Peru, in the western valley of New Granada, and in the Venezuelan Andes. Outside South America, great concentrations of mestizos or whites were to be found in Costa Rica, in the north of New Spain, where native Americans had never been numerous, and also in parts of Santo Domingo, Cuba, and Puerto Rico.

Around 1800 Spanish America had about thirteen and a half million inhabitants, according to the added, adjusted and rounded figures of the censuses of the period. This is an approximate figure, and one which is probably on the low side. In fact, no allowance has been made for under-registration due to census errors or to wilful omissions for various reasons – fiscal, military, and other. Nor does it take account of Indians still unsubdued and not effectively incorporated into colonial society, but occupying territory under Spanish jurisdiction. (Spain itself at the time had a population of about ten and a half million.) New Spain, including the remote *provincias internas* and the two Californias, had the largest population. The six million there constituted 44 per cent of the total population of Spanish America; and of these, about nine-tenths were concentrated in the centre and the south of the viceroyalty. In some areas the population density was relatively high: Guanajuato, for example, registered 36 inhabitants per square kilometre. The Antilles and the captaincy general of Venezuela each totalled about 800,000 inhabitants, together accounting for 12 per cent of the population of Spanish America; the majority lived in Cuba and the region around Caracas. With 1,110,000 inhabitants, Central America – from Chiapas to Panama – had 8 per cent; and there Guatemala had the highest population density. The Andes, stretching from the coastlands of New Granada to the vast Peruvian altiplano, had a population of three and a half million, approximately 26 per cent of the total population of

Spanish America: 1,100,000 New Granadans (excluding Panamanians), 500,000 *quiteños* – counting inhabitants of both the coastal and the mountain regions – 1,300,000 Peruvians, and 600,000 inhabitants of Upper Peru. Mostly mountainous, the Andean region had population densities that tended to relate to altitude, with most people living in the valleys and along the coast. The temperate southern zone of Chile and the Río de la Plata – including the Banda Oriental (now Uruguay) and Paraguay with its decaying missions – in which the central valley of Chile was most densely populated, contained 1,300,000 inhabitants on one side of the Andes or the other: that is, a little over 10 per cent of the total population of Spanish America.

2

THE POPULATION OF COLONIAL BRAZIL*

The study and reconstruction of the Brazilian population during the colonial era, not only its size over three centuries but also its regional components and its rhythm and patterns of growth, is a task which is only now beginning to interest Brazilian scholars. Historical demography has begun to be accepted as a new research discipline with a rigorous, scientific methodology.[1] Without data, however, there is no demography, and in the case of Brazil there is practically no statistical information for the first 250 years of its existence. What useful information there is for the study of population is incomplete, indirect, and only in exceptional cases serialized. Therefore, no really elaborate demographic analysis can be carried out on the basis of this type of information. This is what is called the *pre-statistical phase* in Brazilian population studies.[2] During this period, no direct head-count was carried out, either on a general or regional, or even a sectoral basis. Moreover, church records (baptismal, marriage, and death registers), even when kept regularly, can hardly be said to have accounted for the whole population. What is worse, however, is that even these have rarely survived intact for posterity.

For the second half of the eighteenth century, the situation with regard to sources of information on the population of Brazil begins to improve. As a result of the mercantilist policies of the marquis of Pombal, the first direct censuses began to be carried out of the inhabitants of the colonial towns and cities, together with their

---

* Translated from the original Portuguese by Dr David Brookshaw.
[1] See, for example, the introduction to the development of historical demography in M. L. Marcílio (ed.), *Demografia histórica* (São Paulo, 1977; French edn, Paris, 1979).
[2] See M. L. Marcílio and L. Lisanti, 'Problèmes de l'histoire quantitative du Brésil: métrologie et démographie', in Centre National de la Recherche Scientifique, *L'histoire quantitative du Brésil de 1800 à 1930* (Paris, 1973), 29–58.

surrounding area, the municipalities. These censuses occasionally present lists of names, but usually exhibit general population characteristics with numerous and variable cross-references based on sex, age, marital status, colour, profession, social status, etc. Moreover, they become increasingly comprehensive and exact in their coverage of the population and scientific in their organization of data and elaboration of statistical tables.

Unfortunately, not all the captaincies of Brazil carried out an annual census of their inhabitants as the new laws of Portugal decreed from 1765. Worse still, many of the nominative lists and the general tables of inhabitants have been lost. The colonial census data which remain are scattered in national, regional, local, or Portuguese archives, or else lodged in church or private collections. The task of location, access, and organization is consequently all the more difficult.

For its part, the church also began to pay more careful attention to its records from the end of the eighteenth century. By this time, the number of dioceses and parishes had increased considerably. The guidelines laid down in the First Constitutions of the Archbishopric of Bahia (1707), which were drawn up on the occasion of the first Brazilian Synod, greatly contributed to the better organization and maintenance of parish records. In addition, more careful attention was given to the keeping of parish registers, which were organized more efficiently and more systematically from the latter decades of the eighteenth century. From this period onwards, the researcher has at his disposal more continuous and homogeneous series of documents, and more wide-ranging baptismal, marriage and death records for both the free and slave populations. As a result, from the 1760s we enter what is called the *proto-statistical phase* in Brazilian population studies. (The *statistical phase* itself begins with the first national census in Brazil in 1872, and the formation of the Civil Register of births, marriages, and deaths in 1890.)

THE DECLINE OF THE INDIAN POPULATION

How large was the native American population of Brazil at the time of its first contact with white Europeans in 1500? It is difficult, indeed impossible, to say with any precision, and any attempt at an estimate is bound to be subject to error.

The necessary information on which to base any calculation is limited almost exclusively to one or two scattered and fragmented reports by missionaries and colonial officials, and even these are only relevant to the latter decades of the sixteenth century. No head-count of the indigenous population was carried out either locally or regionally. Nor were any lists even drawn up of tributary or mission Indians. Furthermore, as we are concerned with a population which had scarcely embarked on its neolithic revolution, the archaeological remains are equally fragmentary. For this reason, not even modern archaeological techniques can help us to obtain a more exact idea of Brazilian palaeodemography.

Until recently, it was believed that the indigenous population of Brazil did not exceed one million at the time of the discoveries.[3] Today a much higher figure is accepted. The most comprehensive calculations are those of John Hemming, who gives us a total of 2,431,000 Indians in Brazil in 1500.[4] Far more is known about the steady and systematic process of destruction to which the indigenous population was subjected.

The entire Brazilian littoral was inhabited at the time of the discoveries by a number of scattered tribes, most of whom belonged to the Tupi–Guaraní family. 'All the peoples of this coast', Father Anchieta tells us, 'those who also extend some 200 leagues inland, speak the same language'.[5] The Tupi were, at the time, in the first stages of an agricultural revolution, with their plantations of manioc, corn, beans, peanuts, etc. They did not rear animals, but lived by hunting, fishing, gathering, and the crops they harvested. They were, however, semi-nomadic and their technology was little more advanced than that of the other tribes in the interior, who were of many and varied linguistic groups or, as Anchieta put it, 'barbarians speaking a variety of different languages'.

The coastal Indians experienced the first ravages of decimation upon their initial contact with the European colonizer. The shock of contact produced a real holocaust, virtually wiping out whole tribes. One of the main factors was the wars of extermination and enslavement waged

---

[3] Á. Rosenblat, *La población indígena de América desde 1492 hasta la actualidad* (Buenos Aires, 1945), 92.

[4] John Hemming, *Red Gold. The conquest of the Brazilian Indians* (London, 1978), appendix, 487–501. Compare the estimates of 2.5–3 million in J. H. Steward and L. C. Faron, *Native peoples of South America* (New York, 1959), 52. For even higher figures for the Amazon basin and greater Amazonia (five million and 6.8 million respectively), see William M. Denevan, 'The aboriginal population of Amazonia', in Denevan (ed.), *The native population of the Americas in 1492* (Madison, 1976), 205–34.

[5] Fr. José de Anchieta, *Informações do Brasil e de suas Capitanias (1584)* (São Paulo, 1964), 12.

by the colonizers against the Indians. Typical of these was the joint operation which lasted from 1564 to 1568 against the Tupinambá of the coastal areas around Rio de Janeiro and Bahia. Aided by information supplied by the Jesuits Nóbrega and Anchieta, and with the participation of Indians who had been pacified or were enemies of the Tupinambá, a formidable military campaign was organized which all but wiped them out. Some Indians who managed to escape took refuge in the area of Cabo Frio, from where they continued to harass the white colonizers. In 1574, however, after a series of brutal and violent campaigns, they were almost totally annihilated, and some 3,000 survivors were herded into two villages where they were submitted to a process of deculturalization by the Jesuits. A handful of other survivors managed to escape into the interior, to the area of the São Francisco river, or to the south, where they continued to resist the whites.

Similarly, on the Bahian littoral, the warlike Tupinambá sought to remain masters of their own vast territory, which stretched from the estuary of the São Francisco river in the north to Ilhéus in the south. However, the third governor-general of Brazil, Mem de Sá (1557–72), mounted a series of campaigns aimed at exterminating or enslaving the rebellious Indians. In the area of Salvador, the capital of the colony, he destroyed more than 300 Tupinambá villages. Some of the Indians were enslaved, the great majority were put to the sword, and the rest managed to flee to the interior. The campaign of violence and destruction continued, with the remaining villages put under constant attack. In 1596, a fresh campaign against the Tupinambá who still held out in the coastal area, and in which Jesuits and colonists collaborated, practically liquidated them through slaughter, enslavement, and confinement to missionary villages.

The same process was repeated further north, in the coastal area of Pernambuco. Here, the destruction or enslavement of the hostile Caeté Indians was vital to the growth and success of the sugar-cane plantations. Military expeditions were organized with the help of pacified or enemy tribes, and virtually wiped out the Caeté. Other tribes survived only because of their immediate surrender to the colonizers, as was the case of the Potiguar in the coastal region of Pernambuco and Paraíba, and of the Tabajara, Kiriri, Pau-caram and others in the north-eastern interior.

Apart from war, the importation of new diseases, many of an epidemic type, was a significant factor in the rapid decline of the Indian population. Hitherto isolated in their own world, the Indians suffered great losses through contact with smallpox, measles, syphilis, tuberculosis, tetanus, fevers of all types, leprosy, and pulmonary and intestinal infections which the Europeans brought with them.[6] It has been estimated, for example, that in the great smallpox epidemic of 1562–65, some 30,000 Indians perished in the Bahia *aldeias* alone.[7] The epidemic swept through the entire coastal belt and into the interior, where it even affected the Indians in Paraguay. This first epidemic, so catastrophic in its proportions, produced an imbalance between the number of surviving Indians and their rudimentary means of subsistence and social organization, resulting in a terrible famine in 1564 which further weakened the native population.

Apart from sporadic regional epidemics, there is evidence of a second great outbreak in 1597, which attacked the Indians throughout the coastal belt, but particularly in the north-eastern captaincies, where it even delayed the colonization of Rio Grande do Norte by whites. It has been estimated that, as early as 1570, the Brazilian Indian population had already fallen to 800,000; in other words, to just over a third of its original total.

During the seventeenth century, the process of demographic decline among the native population began to slow down as the Indians who had survived the shock of conquest and the violence and epidemics brought in its wake began to acquire greater resistance and ability to adapt to their new situation. Part of the population was either integrated into the colonial system through widespread race mixture, or placed under its yoke through forms of slavery or by being confined to missionary villages. However, the vast majority gradually pulled out of the areas appropriated for colonization, and retreated into the interior, where, generally speaking, they continued to resist as best they could.

Meanwhile, during the course of the seventeenth century, the need for labour on the coastal plantations caused colonists to mount a whole series of military expeditions into the interior for the purpose of

[6] For further information on the devastating effects of epidemics and disease transmitted by Europeans on the indigenous population see C. A. Moreira, 'O processo de interação ecológica e biótica entre os primeiros núcleos coloniais e os Tupinambá do Rio, Bahia e São Vicente, analisando com base da documentação fornecido por Anchieta, Nóbrega, Lery, Gabriel Soares de Souza e Hans Staden' (Museo do Indio, Rio de Janeiro, 1956, mimeo). Also Darcy Ribeiro, 'Convívio e contaminação', *Sociología* 18/1 (Mar. 1956), 3–50.

[7] Hemming, *Red Gold*, 144.

obtaining Indian slaves. These expeditions were organized in the most peripheral areas of the colony. The *bandeiras* set out from São Paulo in the south, while the *resgates* explored the river systems of the Amazon in search of Indians. The *bandeirantes*, generally of mixed European and Indian descent, systematically exterminated whole tribes throughout a vast territory and over a period of more than a century. Their expeditions practically cleared of Indians the area between the São Francisco river and the Paraguay–Paraná valley in the west, and in the far south they even reached the tribes and missions of the Río de la Plata. Mexia de Ovando was to claim, no doubt with considerable exaggeration, that in 1639 alone Paulista expeditionaries captured more than 200,000 Indians from the Jesuit missions of the Paraguay–Paraná river area, and that these were sold to the sugar producers of Rio de Janeiro, Espírito Santo, Bahia, and Pernambuco. Funes, less prone to fantasy, reports that between 1628 and 1630, the *bandeirantes* sold some 60,000 Indians in Rio de Janeiro, obtained largely as a result of slave raids on the Jesuit missions in Paraguay.[8]

To the north, in the state of Maranhão, the so-called *resgate* slave-hunting expeditions against the Indians of the interior, along with the impact of epidemics, the process of detribalization, and the campaigns of pacification waged against the coastal Indians, all had a severe effect on the Indian population. A letter from the bishop of Lisbon to the king of Portugal in 1617 states that

in the whole district [of the city of Maranhão], there is not a single Indian village left. Within a hundred leagues of Pará there is not a single Indian who is not at peace or has not been domesticated by the Portuguese, whom he fears even more than a slave fears his master. In the district of Ceará, there used to be 60 villages within a radius of 60 leagues. Today, not one remains, for they have all disappeared as a result of the activities of the slave hunters...In Pará, and along the banks of its great rivers, there were so many Indians and so many villages as to cause visitors to marvel. Now, few are those which have remained unscathed. The rest have perished as a result of the injustices to which the slave hunters subjected them...[9]

Equally severe accusations were reiterated on numerous occasions by the Jesuit António Vieira. In 1652, for example, he wrote that 'the entire region of Maranhão has been worn down, depopulated, and reduced to one or two scanty villages, and vast numbers of people have been

<hr />

[8] Mexía de Ovando, 'Libro o memorial práctico del Nuevo Mundo' [1639], in Rosenblat, *La población indígena*, 163–4.

[9] Arquivo Histórico Ultramarino (Lisbon) [AHU], Maranhão, caixa 2, MSS.

wiped out, or rather, we have wiped them out within a space of 30 years'.[10] Vieira himself calculated that in the first 40 years of the seventeenth century, more than two million Indians were killed and more than 500 villages destroyed along the coastal belt of Maranhão and its hinterland.[11] While the numbers were undoubtedly exaggerated, the vast scale of the destruction of the Indian population was not.

During the period of the Dutch occupation of the sugar captaincies, the new colonizer was seen by the Indian as a genuine 'liberator'. The Dutch immediately prohibited the enslavement of Indians and rules and regulations were drawn up in order to improve labour conditions. When the Dutch conquered the north-eastern provinces, they were shocked by the conditions in which the Indians lived, and by the fall in the population. According to Dutch reports, within a stretch of 800 miles along the Brazilian coast between Ceará and the São Francisco river, the native population had fallen within a century from many hundreds of thousands to less than 9,000.[12] With the departure of the Dutch in 1654, the Portuguese immediately resumed their slave-hunting campaigns, and once more pursued their policy of enslavement and destruction of the Indians.

Strong contributing factors to the demographic decline must have been the periodic local epidemics, especially of measles and smallpox, the most lasting of which was the plague of 1685–92 which swept through the coastal area from Pernambuco to Paranaguá. At this incipient stage of research in the field, we cannot know in terms of actual numbers the losses suffered by Brazilian Indians as a result of epidemics during the colonial period. All we can do at present is to point out their incidence, geographical extent, and chronology.[13]

During the last hundred years of the colonial period, the remaining Indians continued to be expelled from their lands, enslaved, decimated in wars or as a result of infectious diseases, or assimilated into the colonial system through race mixture or mission life. At the end of the seventeenth century Amazonia had been divided up amongst the missionary orders – Jesuits, Mercedarians, Capuchins, Carmelites and, in 1700, Franciscans. The Jesuits, in particular, pursued a policy of

[10] António Vieira, 'Informação sobre as coisas do Maranhão', in *Obras várias* (Lisbon, 1856), 213.
[11] Vieira, *Sermão e carta* (Porto, 1941), 101 and 118.
[12] Hemming, *Red Gold*, 286.
[13] A chronological study of epidemics affecting São Paulo during the seventeenth century was carried out by S. Buarque de Holanda, 'Movimentos da população em São Paulo no Século XVII', in *Revista do Instituto de Estudos Brasileiros*, 1 (1966), 51–111.

detribalization by confining the Indians in ever greater numbers to isolated villages (*aldeias*) where in the final analysis they were 'deculturated', homogenized, deprived of their cultural identity.[14] It must be said, however, that the Jesuits did at least manage to protect the natives from the far more brutal and devastating actions of the Portuguese colonists.

With the expulsion of the Jesuits from Brazil in 1759, which coincided with the launching of Pombal's new policies designed to stimulate population growth through race mixture, the indigenous population entered a new period of decline and absorption. The colonists were encouraged to spare no effort in implementing the crown's policy of detribalizing the Indians and integrating them into colonial life. Mixed marriage between Europeans and Indians was legalized. The Jesuit villages were all but abolished. In the region of the Seven Missions, east of the Uruguay river (in what is now Rio Grande do Sul), the large Indian population concentrated there 'virtually vanished overnight. The great majority of the Indians cast off the aspects of civilization they had acquired and returned to the bush. In 1801, the population of the area had fallen to less than 20,000, and by 1814, it had declined to such an extent that its numbers barely exceeded 8,000.'[15]

Epidemics of catastrophic proportions also continued to wreak havoc among the defenceless Indians. According to Hoornaert, at least ten great epidemics of smallpox and measles swept through the state of Maranhão between 1724 and 1776, one of the most serious of these being the one which assailed the city of Pará in 1724, causing more than 15,000 deaths.[16] Shortly before, a particularly severe epidemic of smallpox had devastated the coastal belt of São Paulo, reaching the inland settlements in 1702. The disease had been brought in by the slave ships from Africa. Buarque de Holanda refers to outbreaks of smallpox in São Paulo in 1720, 1724, 1726, 1730, 1737, 1744, 1746, and 1749.[17] An epidemic of measles in 1749–50 devastated the tribes of Amazonia, killing an estimated 30,000 Indians.[18]

[14] C. A. Moreira, 'Indios de Amazônia. O século do extermínio, 1750–1850' (Museo do Indio, Rio de Janeiro, mimeo, n.d.).

[15] Nicolau Dreys, *Noticia descritiva da Provincia do Rio Grande de São Pedro do Sul (1839)* (Porto Alegre, 1961), 155–6.

[16] E. Hoornaert (ed.), *História da Igreja no Brasil* (2nd edn, Petrópolis, 1979), 405.

[17] Buarque de Holanda, 'Movimentos', 77.

[18] P. M. Ashburn, *The ranks of death. A medical history of the conquest of America* (New York, 1947), 91.

When the general census was taken in 1798, only 252,000 'pacified' Indians were counted in the whole of Brazil, a figure which amounted to a mere 7.8 per cent of the total population. When all Indians, including those as yet unsubjugated, were taken into account in 1819, the native population was estimated at some 800,000 souls, a third of what it had been in 1500 and 18.2 per cent of the total population of Brazil.[19]

THE GROWTH OF THE WHITE COLONIZING POPULATION

Throughout the colonial period, the number of Europeans entering Brazil was relatively small. White immigrants tended to fall into one of the following categories: Portuguese settlers (the overwhelming majority); 'New Christians' (i.e. Jews) of various nationalities who were fleeing from persecution in the Old World; French, Spanish, Dutch, Italian and English incursionists; survivors of failed attempts at conquest and settlement on the part of the French, in Guanabara and northern Brazil; and the Dutch, in the coastal area between the Amazon and Bahia.

In the sixteenth century, what European immigration there was was limited to three main zones of settlement and bases for penetration: the coast of Pernambuco, Bahia and the Recôncavo, its surrounding area, and the coast of São Vicente. In these three areas of initial settlement, the cane plantation and the sugar mill were instrumental in attracting European colonization. The pattern of settlement was therefore influenced to a considerable degree by a colonial economy which was essentially agricultural in character. Consequently it was centred on the landed estate rather than on the urban conglomerations.

It is generally believed that at the time when the first governor-general arrived in Brazil in 1549, there were no more than three or four thousand European settlers in the whole of the colony. According to two contemporary estimates the number of inhabitants of European origin had increased to 20,000 by 1570 (over 60 per cent of the total in Bahia and Pernambuco) and approximately 30,000 by 1580 (over 80 per cent in Bahia and Pernambuco).[20] If these figures are valid, the number of whites in Brazil would have doubled in barely 50 years.

If one accepts the above figures, then whites in about 1600 would

---

[19] For further discussion of Indians in colonial Brazil, see Hemming, *CHLA* II, ch. 13.
[20] See Johnson, *CHLA* I, ch. 8, table I.

have represented about one-third of an estimated total population in the settled areas of Brazil of 100,000 (that is, excluding unsubjugated Indians).[21] In 1587, the capital city, Salvador da Bahia, including its surrounding area, would have boasted a population of some 2,000 European settlers, alongside 4,000 blacks and 6,000 Indians. The urban area itself would have contained less than 10 per cent of this total, the remainder being scattered throughout the sugar estates and small farms of the region. We know that the so-called New Christians formed a significant proportion of the white inhabitants. New Christians numbered some 5,000 at least in Pernambuco, where there were already two synagogues in the sixteenth century.[22]

During the period of Spanish domination (1580–1640), European emigration to Brazil was freer and was open to individuals of all nationalities provided that they were Catholics. Given this situation, many Spaniards entered the colony, preferring to settle in southern peripheral areas such as Santa Catarina, Paraná, and São Paulo. The number of New Christians (not only of Portuguese origin) also grew, thus swelling the white sector of the population. In the city of Salvador alone, the number of identifiable New Christians would seem to have represented between 10 and 20 per cent of the white population during the period 1635–45.[23] They were to be found as merchants, tradesmen, plantation owners, administrators and artisans. In the later years of Spanish domination, Europeans of non-Iberian origin arrived, mainly Dutch and English, and some of them stayed on in Brazil even after the expulsion of the Dutch from the coastal belt of Pernambuco in 1654. With the restoration of Portuguese independence in 1640, European emigration to Brazil was once again restricted to native Portuguese.

From the beginning of the seventeenth century, the crown pursued a policy of encouraging settlement along the northern coastal belt, in order to protect the area from incursion by other European nations. Two hundred Azorean families, for example, totalling about a thousand people, were settled on the coast of Maranhão in 1617. At the same time, other families from the Portuguese islands were settled in Pará and at other points along the northern coast.

[21] See M. L. Marcílio, 'Évolution historique de la population brasilienne jusqu'en 1872', in CICRED, *La population du Brésil* (Paris, 1974), 10. The best estimates for the total population of Brazil in 1550, 1600, and 1660, drawn from a variety of sources, are still to be found in Félix Contreiras Rodrigues, *Traços de economia social e política do Brasil colonial* (Rio de Janeiro, 1935).

[22] Castro Barreto, *Povoamento e população* (Rio de Janeiro, 1951), 55.

[23] A. Novinsky, *Cristãos novos na Bahia* (São Paulo, 1972), 67. See also Schwartz, *CHLA* II, ch. 12.

White immigration during the sixteenth and seventeenth centuries was on the whole both spontaneous and selective. From the beginning there was a preponderance of white adult males, and this fact encouraged a continuous process of miscegenation with Indians and Africans. The first white women arrived together with their families in 1537, in order to assist in the colonization of São Vicente. Nonetheless, few Portuguese migrated to Brazil in family groups. In 1551 the queen, at the request of missionaries, sent out a number of Portuguese orphan girls to Bahia. More accompanied Mem de Sá, the third governor-general. The exception to the rule was the organized migration of whole families from the Azores and Madeira as part of crown policy to protect strategically important and peripheral areas. Consequently, it was only in such areas that there emerged a pattern of settlement, land use, productive activity, and social organization which differed from the rest of Brazil. There, family enterprises, based on smallholdings and involved in food production either for subsistence or internal consumer demands, were favoured over slave labour and plantation agriculture for the export market. By the end of the seventeenth century whites (100,000) constituted a third of the total assimilated population of the settled areas of Brazil, estimated at 300,000.[24]

With the discovery of gold in central southern Brazil at the end of the seventeenth century, along the banks of the tributaries of the São Francisco river in Minas Gerais, there occurred the first mass migration in Brazilian demographic history. From then on the coastal area, and in particular the north-eastern littoral, where the mass of the white population was concentrated along with its slaves and Indian serfs, was no longer the only region capable of attracting settlers. A year after the first discovery of alluvial gold in Minas Gerais, the region suffered the first great increase in the general death rate as a result of the famine of 1697/8. Another severe famine followed in 1700/1, causing a further steep increase in the death rate. Nevertheless, within a few years the gold rush had totally transformed the geographical distribution of the colonial population, as well as its general size.

Apart from internal migration from various parts of Brazil to the gold-mining area, large numbers of Peninsular Portuguese emigrated to Minas Gerais. In 1700 Portugal had a population of about two million people. During the eighteenth century approximately 400,000 left for Brazil, despite efforts by the crown to place severe restrictions on

[24] M. L. Marcílio, 'Évolution historique', 10.

emigration.[25] The Portuguese came from all areas of the mother country, but especially from the Minho, the most densely populated province, and from all social classes and occupations, from the peasantry to the gentry, including artisans, tradesmen, priests, and many with no fixed occupation.

Such was the fascination which rumours of quick wealth induced during this period that within the first quarter of the eighteenth century the central southern region, including hitherto practically uninhabited lands, came to contain half the total colonial population. Trails to the interior were made and a huge subsidiary area opened up, particularly in the captaincy of São Paulo, which was turned into a producer of food supplies for the large population centres developing on the periphery of the gold- and diamond-mining regions of Minas Gerais, Goiás and Mato Grosso. Settlement here took on new characteristics: it was intensive, essentially urban, and was concentrated along the rivers and gold-yielding streams. Moreover, as gold was generally found in more inaccessible areas where the quality of the soil did not favour any type of agriculture, the arrival of vast numbers of settlers stimulated the development of an agricultural and pastoral economy by necessity some considerable distance from the mining areas themselves. The area of food production stretched from southern Minas and the Paraíba valley through to the southern part of the captaincy of São Paulo and beyond to the plains of Viamão in Rio Grande do Sul, where ranches supplied the mining areas with cattle for food and mules for transport.

During the 1760s and '70s, gold production entered a period of decline as alluvial deposits were worked out. As a result, there began a slow process of demographic decline and resettlement in new areas of economic attraction. This period coincided with the rise to power in Portugal of the marquis of Pombal, who embarked on a series of policies aimed at stimulating trade with Brazil and enlarging its population. Such policies had a double purpose: to increase the number of inhabitants in order to increase production, and to redeploy part of the population to frontier regions of strategic importance or areas of dispute between Portugal and other colonial nations.

During his regime, Pombal favoured and even encouraged Portu-

---

[25] Celso Furtado, in his *Formação Económica do Brasil* (11th edn, São Paulo, 1971), put immigration from Portugal in the eighteenth century at not less than 300,000 and perhaps as high as half a million.

guese emigration to Brazil, particularly from the impoverished and overpopulated Atlantic islands. These currents of migration were channelled directly to vulnerable coastal areas or to disputed frontier regions. Between 1748 and 1752, the Crown facilitated the settlement in Brazil of new immigrant families from the Azores and Madeira. During this period, 1,057 couples from the Azores were settled on the island of Santa Catarina, totalling, together with their offspring, 5,960 people. Some 4,000 couples were settled in Rio Grande do Sul. Another 21 families established themselves in Rio de Janeiro, and at the same time, ships carrying 400 to 500 islanders from the Azores arrived in Pará and Maranhão. It is not an easy task to produce evidence as to their exact numbers. As they were all peasant farmers, they founded small nuclei of population around land distributed in family plots, and involved in the production of food crops for subsistence and for the internal market. Because of family stability, the absence of slave labour, and an economy based essentially on the family unit, the birth-rate among these groups of islanders remained one of the highest in the entire Brazilian population. On the island of Santa Catarina, for example, the population in 1820 reached a density of 25 inhabitants per square kilometre.

Substantial European immigration in the eighteenth century, coupled with natural growth among the inhabitants of European origin, caused the white population to increase tenfold during the course of the century. The estimates made for 1798 reveal a white population of 1,010,000, or 31 per cent of the whole population, excluding non-pacified Indians.[26] European immigration was given further impetus by the transfer of the Portuguese court to the colony in 1808. According to official estimates, the white population totalled 1,302,000 in 1817/18,

---

[26] By royal order in 1797 all the Brazilian captaincies were thenceforth obliged to prepare annual censuses, by *município*, to be organized by local and regional *capitães-mores* and parish priests. See M. L. Marcílio, 'Les origines des recensements du Brésil', in S. Pascu (ed.), *Populatie sí Societete* (Cluj-Napoca, Rumania, 1980), 25–34. Not all did so in 1798, and these regional censuses are today dispersed in a number of archives (e.g. the Arquivo Histórico Ultramarino (Lisbon), the Arquivo Nacional do Rio de Janeiro, the Biblioteca Nacional do Rio de Janeiro, and Brazilian state archives). Moreover, censuses for the same captaincy found in two different archives can show different population totals. The estimates for 1798 accepted by most historians can be found in Contreiras Rodrigues, *Traços*. See, most recently, T. W. Merrick and D. H. Graham, *Population and economic development in Brazil: 1800 to the present* (Baltimore, 1979), 29. [Editor's note: for different, and lower, estimates of the total Brazilian population *c.* 1776 and *c.* 1800, and its racial composition, see the estimates by Alden, *CHLA* II, ch. 15, tables 1, 2 and 4.]

Table 1 *Gross birth and death rates and natural growth among the female
free population of the captaincy of São Paulo*

Year	Births per 1,000	Deaths per 1,000	% growth
1798	53.7	42.0	1.2
1808	54.7	42.2	1.2
1818	54.3	42.2	1.2
1828	56.7	42.7	1.4

Source: M. L. Marcílio, 'Crescimento demográfico e evolução agrária paulista, 1700–1836' (São Paulo, 1974 (mimeo)), 151. Model of the West family, A. J. Coale and D. Demeny, *Regional model life tables and stable populations* (Princeton, 1966), applied to the census registers of the captaincy of São Paulo.

and in 1822, the year in which Brazil achieved its political independence, whites constituted some 35 per cent of the total number of inhabitants.[27]

The growth and structure of the free population in general (including Indians, blacks, and mestizos as well as whites) during the colonial period, are only now becoming better known. The known birth and death rates are exceedingly high, whether in areas of subsistence agriculture, the plantation export economy, pastoral activity, or in the urban environment. Nevertheless, it would seem that in areas of mixed agriculture, based on free family labour, as was the case, for example, in the vast captaincy of São Paulo during the eighteenth century and the beginning of the nineteenth, fertility rates were considerably higher than in areas given over to one-crop export agriculture, operated by slave labour. In the same areas of subsistence agriculture, the death rate, though high, was not so high as elsewhere, thanks to the absence of periods of crisis such as epidemics and famine. For this reason, one can note that, over a long period of time, there was a more marked and more sustained growth rate among the free population in food- and cattle-producing areas, than in other areas of the territory (see table 1).

However, the areas given over to export agriculture or to mineral extraction attracted migrants, especially adult men and youths, from

[27] For 1817/18, see Antonio Rodrigues Velloso de Oliveira, *Memória* presented to Council of State on 28 July 1819, in *Revista do Instituto Histórico, Geográphico e Ethnográphico do Brasil*, 29/1 (1866). For 1822, see Anon., 'Memória estatística do Império do Brazil', *Revista do Instituto Histórico e Geográfico do Brasil* [RIHGB], 58 (1895), 91–9. See also Joaquim Norberto de Souza e Silva, 'População geral do Império', in *Relatório do Ministério do Império, 1870* (Rio de Janeiro, 1872), annex, for sources and estimates of Brazilian population at various dates beginning 1776.

Table 2 *Proportion of illegitimate children and foundlings in the free population of São Paulo (per 100 births)*

Period	Illegitimate	Foundlings	Total
1741–55	10.24	14.85	25.09
1756–70	18.28	14.72	33.00
1771–85	20.97	21.42	42.39
1786–1800	21.08	10.74	31.82
1801–15	26.26	15.64	41.90
1816–30	30.15	18.83	48.98
Total	22.02	16.17	38.19

Source: M. L. Marcílio, *La ville de São Paulo. Peuplement et population, 1750–1850* (Rouen, 1968), 183–4.

both within and outside the colony, to the detriment of less attractive areas of subsistence and pastoral agriculture or natural extraction. These areas either shed any surplus population, or reduced this surplus until it included only the poorest, most marginalized elements. There was as a result an imbalance in the sexes: a surplus of males in those areas directly linked to the world economy, and a surplus of females in areas of secondary economic activity. In both cases, the situation favoured miscegenation between the free white population and the dispossessed racial sectors consisting mainly of mulattos, Indians, and blacks.

At the same time it was not a situation favourable to the development of stable and legally constituted families, contributing rather to the rate of illegitimacy, which was considerable in the free population of the mixed agricultural areas (see table 2), but particularly intense in the areas of plantation agriculture and slave labour.

In turn, the death rate in food-producing agricultural areas was substantially lower in the long term than in mining areas, or in areas of export-based plantation agriculture. A better, more balanced diet, allied to the lower density of the population, which was more widely dispersed in areas of subsistence and pastoral agriculture, created natural protective barriers against the spread of epidemics and such catastrophes as famine. This sector of the population, with its relatively stable death rate, increased more rapidly than the white population of the plantation areas.

For their part, the white inhabitants of the plantation areas were more vulnerable to epidemics, infectious illnesses and parasitic ailments, because of the relative density of the population and the poorer quality of the diet, which was both unbalanced and deficient. A graph of the death rate would show considerable irregularity, with frequent peaks corresponding to epidemics and famine. The general imbalance and deficiency in dietary habits contributed to the increase in the rates of morbidity and mortality, which in turn shortened life expectancy. In the sugar-producing captaincy of Paraíba do Norte, recorded death rates among the free population for the year 1798 were classified by cause of death, and it was found that 67.1 per cent came under the category of death from infectious and parasitic diseases.[28]

It seems clear that the natural growth of the population was slightly lower among whites inside compared with whites outside the plantation system.

THE AFRICAN SLAVE TRADE

The third element in the population of colonial Brazil was black African, the result of the forced migration of Africans to be used as slave labour in all productive activities. The introduction of African slaves into Brazil was officially authorized, it would seem, in 1549, although Africans had been present since 1535, working on the sugar-cane plantations of São Vicente, and by 1570 there were already several thousand employed on sugar *engenhos*. Although the volume of slave traffic across the Atlantic has been the subject of much research and investigation, it is not possible to establish with any accuracy the total number of slaves imported from Africa over the centuries and the fluctuations in the trade. The case of Brazil is all the more frustrating because so much of the evidence, especially with regard to slave numbers, was burnt as a result of a decree-law at the end of the nineteenth century.

The economic historian Roberto Simonsen derived his figures from contemporary sources of information regarding the number of sugar mills and the amount of sugar produced. Co-ordinating this information with the estimated amount of manpower needed, he calculated that a probable total of 350,000 slaves would have been imported in the seventeenth century.[29] Another leading scholar, Mauricio Goulart, suggested that during the sixteenth century, the number of blacks

---

[28] See 'Mapa da população de toda a Capitania da Paraíba do Norte, 1798', MS in AHU, Paraíba, sheaf 19, doc. 38.
[29] R. Simonsen, *História econômica do Brasil* (3rd edn, São Paulo, 1957), 133.

entering the colony would not have exceeded 30,000; Indians were still being used in large numbers for labour on the plantations of Pernambuco and Bahia. In the following century, however, he suggests that between 1600 and 1630 an annual average of 2,500 blacks – a total, therefore, of 75,000 – would have entered Pernambuco and the neighbouring captaincies of Itamaracá, Paraíba, and Rio Grande do Norte, where there were 166 sugar mills in 1629. In the captaincy of Bahia, where there were only 50 mills at that time, he estimates that average yearly imports of slaves would not have exceeded 2,000. For the whole of Brazil, Goulart calculates that 200,000 blacks would have been imported between 1600 and 1650, averaging 4,000 per annum. With regard to the second half of the century, the same author suggests an annual figure of 6,000–7,000 slaves entering Brazil, making a total of 300,000–350,000. For the whole century, therefore, Goulart arrives at a total estimate of 500,000–550,000 imported blacks.[30]

The recent authoritative work of Philip Curtin produced figures close to those of Goulart. During the seventeenth century, the slave trade would have introduced 560,000 blacks into Brazil (average 5,600 per annum), a figure which corresponds to 41.8 per cent of the total number of Africans imported into the Americas during this period. According to his calculations, this total could be broken down to the following figures over the century: 100,000 between 1601 and 1625, 100,000 between 1626 and 1650, 185,000 between 1651 and 1675, and 175,000 between 1676 and the end of the century.[31]

For the eighteenth century, and focusing on the Minas Gerais region alone, Goulart calculated that between 1735 and 1760 some 160,000 slaves would have entered the captaincy, making an annual average of around 6,500. After this, annual imports would have fallen from 4,000 between 1760 and 1780 to 2,000 up to 1820. Therefore, a further 160,000 slaves would have entered the captaincy during those 60 years, making a grand total of 470,000 slaves for the mining area alone.[32] Simonsen's figure for the number of slaves imported into the mining areas during the eighteenth century was 600,000.[33] A rare document on the importation of slaves during the period, which exhibits annual totals and values of imports, tells us only that 233,023 slaves and 'young infants' were shipped from Benguela to Brazil between 1762 and 1799. If one ignores

[30] M. Goulart, *A escravidão africana no Brasil* (3rd edn, São Paulo, 1975), 98.
[31] Philip D. Curtin, *The Atlantic slave trade: a census* (Madison, 1969), 119.
[32] Goulart, *A escravidão*, 170.   [33] Simonsen, *História econômica*, 135.

the considerable losses on the high seas, the annual average comes out at 6,000.[34]

For Curtin, between 1701 and 1801, nearly two million Africans would have entered Brazil, or to be precise 1,891,400, a figure which represents 31.3 per cent of all slaves imported into the Americas during the same period. Breaking this figure down chronologically, Curtin estimates that 292,700 slaves would have entered the colony between 1701 and 1720 (a little under 15,000 per annum on average), 312,400 between 1721 and 1740 (a little over 15,000 per annum), 354,500 between 1741 and 1760 (almost 18,000 per annum), 325,900 between 1761 and 1780 (16,000 per annum), and 605,000 during the last 30 years from 1781 to 1810 (20,000 per annum).[35]

With regard to the total number of Africans entering Brazil during the first three centuries of colonization, the estimates of Goulart, Simonsen and Curtin bear a striking resemblance. Goulart's estimate comes to between 2,200,000 and 2,250,000. Curtin's figure is 2,501,400. Simonsen's total, which includes imports up to the end of the slave trade in 1850–1, comes out at 3,300,000.

There are only a few estimates of the slave population during the first centuries of the colonial period, and even these can only be regarded as tentative. It has been suggested that in 1600, the total number of black slaves would have amounted to 15,000, corresponding to 15 per cent of the total population, excluding tribal Indians. The slave population in 1680 has been estimated at 150,000. The first reliable figures, however, appear towards the end of the eighteenth century. According to the estimates for 1798, there were 1,361,000 black slaves in Brazil, constituting 42 per cent of the total population. On the other hand, according to the figures for 1819, slave numbers amounted to no more than 31 per cent of the population, their total being estimated at 1,107,389.[36]

We do know, however, that reproduction among black slaves in Brazil was, generally speaking, fairly low, the lowest of all sectors of society at all times. This can undoubtedly be attributed to the relatively low price of imported slaves, to the facilities made available by the

---

[34] 'Mappas dos escravos exportados desta Capitania de Benguella para o Brasil, desde o anno de 1762 até 1799'. Biblioteca Nacional do Rio de Janeiro, cod. 1, 31, 30, 96.

[35] Curtin, *The Atlantic slave trade*, 216. [Editor's note: for a different, and lower, estimate see also Alden, *CHLA* 11, ch. 15, table 5.]

[36] See table 5 below. [Editor's note: for a different estimate see Alden, *CHLA* 11, ch. 15, table 4.]

Table 3 *Proportion of married and widowed population in Paraíba by ethnic group and age category, 1798*

Age	Whites			Free blacks			Black slaves			Free mulattos			Mulatto slaves		
	Total	m/w*	%	Total	m/w	%	Total	m/w	%	Total	m/w	%	Total	m/w	%
10–20	2,130	382	17.9	426	81	19.0	1,182	86	7.3	2,143	307	14.3	258	37	14.3
20–30	2,100	983	46.8	504	184	36.5	1,522	326	21.4	2,507	1,220	48.7	352	126	35.8
30–40	4,700	3,337	71.0	1,463	763	52.1	2,982	853	28.6	5,198	3,406	65.5	731	363	49.6
Total	8,930	4,702	52.6	2,393	1,028	42.9	5,686	1,265	22.2	9,848	4,933	50.1	1,341	526	39.2

* Married/widowed.

Source: AHU, Paraíba, mapa de população, sheaf 20, doc. 38.

crown in support of the slave trade, and to the harsh conditions of life among the slave population, the absence of family stability, and the inadequacy of sanitary conditions.

In effect, the slaveowner had a vested interest in impeding the development of family stability and reproduction among slaves. Lawfully constituted families could create legal and particularly moral obstacles when consideration was being given to selling one of the members of a family. The cost and risk attached to rearing slaves until they reached a productive age were greater than the market price of an adult slave.

As a consequence, the incidence of slave marriage was almost nil, especially in the plantation and mining areas. In Vila Rica, for example, of the 2,783 slaves living there in 1804, only ten women and twelve men were registered as married.[37]

Table 3, showing the proportional distribution of the population of the captaincy of Paraíba in 1798 according to civil status, colour and social class, illustrates this tendency. We can see that only 22 per cent of black slaves at any time were legally married. The proportion was greater among assimilated mulatto slaves, with 39 per cent married or widowed.

There were always far more male than female slaves, especially in those areas directly dependent on the world economy. This was due to the selective importation of adult males, and further hindered marriages among slaves because of the constant lack of women. In the city of Vila Rica, Minas Gerais, even in the period of its decline (1804), there were 138 male slaves for every 100 females. The same bias towards males existed in the captaincy of Paraíba in 1798. Even in the marginal areas given over to subsistence agriculture, the imbalance between the sexes was considerable. For the captaincy of São Paulo, the following ratios of males among the slave population were calculated: 117 in 1798, 122 in 1808, 144 in 1818 and 154 in 1828.[38] The slave population was thus inevitably a producer of large numbers of illegitimate offspring. Equally, the rate of miscegenation with other ethnic groups was considerable, resulting in numerous ethnic variants which were to form the basis of a new Brazilian phenotype.

Finally, if one adds to these demographic characteristics of the black Brazilian slave population the very high death rate, especially among

---

[37] Iraci del Nero Costa, *Vila Rica: população (1719–1826)* (São Paulo, 1979), 245.
[38] Marcílio, 'Crescimento demográfico', 144.

infants, one can understand why the growth of the black population was so much slower than that of all other sectors of Brazil's colonial population. Everything would lead one to conclude that, generally speaking, the natural growth rate of the Brazilian slave population must have been constantly nil or even negative. Only the continual arrival of large numbers of new slaves maintained and indeed increased the total slave population.

RACE MIXTURE

The Brazilian population therefore grew out of three formative elements: indigenous Indian, European, and African. These, either in their 'pure' form, or mixed to a greater or lesser extent among themselves, began the process of moulding a new Brazilian ethnicity. It is true that the crown did not facilitate mixed marriages by law until relatively late in the colonial period. Indeed, it was only as a result of Pombal's policies that legislation favourable to mixed marriages was drawn up (decree of 4 April 1755). Even then only marriages between whites and Indians were permitted; Africans were excluded. On the other hand, in practice both the crown and the church tolerated interracial marriages from the very beginning of colonization.

Not that the process of race mixture in colonial Brazil was predominantly the product of legally constituted families. Race mixture, in all its permutations, was the result first and foremost of stable unions among consenting partners, which was the standard family institution among the poorest social strata, that is, among the non-white ethnic groups. Secondly, race mixture resulted from temporary extramarital unions, especially between the dominant ethnic group, the white colonizer, and the colonized strata – the Indians, slaves, and mestizos. The vast numbers of illegitimate children born in all regions of Brazil bear witness to this situation. In the tiny township of São Paulo during the last decades of the eighteenth century and the first decade of the nineteenth, over 40 per cent of births in the free population alone were illegitimate (see table 2 above). In Vila Rica de Ouro Preto, 52.2 per cent of free births in 1804 were illegitimate. Considering the total population, both free and slave, the proportion of illegitimates is quite astounding: in Vila Rica between 1719 and 1723, for example, 89.5 per cent of child baptisms were of bastards.[39]

It is difficult to estimate to what extent the process of miscegenation

[39] Costa, *Vila Rica.*

developed in Brazil. Difficulties begin with the very definition of the mestizo, and are compounded by the mestizo's own prejudiced attitude on the one hand, and on the other by social values which associate wealth and power with 'whiteness' and view poverty as proportional to darkness of skin. Skin colour therefore ceases to be a phenotypic and genetic characteristic and becomes a social determinant. As Darcy Ribeiro puts it,

any quantitative analysis of the racial composition of the Brazilian population, either in the past or the present, is fraught with difficulties, as one is obliged to work with figures which are more or less arbitrary. Even official data, when available, are not reliable, not only because of the lack of any uniform definitions of racial groups on the part of the census authorities, but because of the interference of prejudiced attitudes among the very population in which the census is being carried out.[40]

The mixed population was classified in colonial census registers as either 'mulatto' or 'brown'. Mestizos of Indian–white or Indian–black descent were sometimes included in the 'white' category, sometimes in the 'mulatto', and occasionally even in the 'black'. Consequently it is easy to understand why the proportion of mestizos is so low in almost all population surveys.[41]

On a regional level, according to the census of 1798 Paraíba counted 37 per cent of mestizos (*pardos*) among its inhabitants. Paraíba was a captaincy with plantations on the coastal belt and cattle-breeding lands in the interior, which pointed to the likelihood of intense race mixture, white–black on the coast, and Indian–white and Indian–black in the interior.[42] The white colonizer normally arrived without any family, preferring to use and exploit servile Indian or African women. Because of the gradual decline and assimilation of the indigenous population, the predominant form of race mixture was increasingly between white men and black women and their products. Only in the regions which were economically isolated from the colonial system did the *caboclo*, the product of the white man and the Indian woman, predominate.

To summarize the basic characteristics of the demography of colonial Brazil:

1. The population was largely agrarian in character throughout the

[40] D. Ribeiro, *As Américas e a civilização* (Petrópolis, 1977), 100.
[41] [Editor's note: see Alden, *CHLA* II, ch. 15, table 4.]
[42] Data from AHU, Paraíba, mapa de 1798.

whole colonial period. The very settlement of Brazil – its dispersal along the coastal belt and concentration at particular points along this belt – was determined essentially by agrarian priorities. Only mining managed to push significant numbers of settlers into the interior during the eighteenth century and increase the population significantly.

For the most part colonial cities and towns were offshoots of the landed estates, and the few urban conglomerations of any size owed their importance to the fact that they served as entrepots for the export of primary products and the import of goods, not least African slaves. At the end of the sixteenth century, there were only three cities – Salvador (the largest, with a population under 15,000), Rio de Janeiro, and Filipeia (present-day João Pessoa) – all of them ports, and fourteen towns. In the seventeenth century, the number of cities grew to seven (all ports), and there were 51 towns of modest size. During the eighteenth century there were ten cities, while the number of small towns increased to 118. However, at the end of the eighteenth century the largest city, Salvador, had only 50,000 inhabitants, followed by Rio de Janeiro with 45,000 (soon to overtake Salvador, however, as it doubled its population 1808–22), Recife, São Luís, and São Paulo with 20,000–25,000 each. Moreover it should be noted that these figures refer to the population of the municipal districts as a whole, which means that a large proportion of people lived in rural areas. By 1822, when Brazil become independent, two new cities and 44 new towns had been added.[43]

2. The colonization of Brazil during the period was always clearly dispersed and the distribution of the population extremely irregular and unequal. Furthermore, the actual dispersal of these inhabitants over the territory obeyed the periodic changes in the priorities of the colonial economy, which in turn were dependent on the fluctuations and requirements of the world economy.

As long as Brazilian sugar remained the principal export commodity, from the late sixteenth to the end of the seventeenth centuries, the cane plantations and sugar mills which were concentrated around Recife, Salvador, and to a lesser extent Rio de Janeiro accounted for the majority of the colonial population. Approximately 70 per cent of Brazilians during this period were distributed throughout the main sugar-growing areas, demarcated in the south by the area around Bahia

[43] See data contained in A. Azevedo, *Vilas e cidades do Brasil colonial* (São Paulo, 1956).

(the Recôncavo), and in the north by the valley of the Parnaíba river and including the hinterland, which was turned over to cattle raising and served as a complementary area to that of the sugar-cane plantations.

In the eighteenth century, the discovery of alluvial gold stimulated profound changes in the distribution of the population of Brazil. Considerable migration occurred within the colony, particularly from the sugar-growing areas of the north-east to the newly created gold-mining captaincies, and more especially the central eastern region of Minas Gerais. Gold, however, was also a determining factor in the arrival of continual levies of immigrants from Portugal and increasing numbers of slaves from Africa. Mining in turn caused the pattern of colonization to undergo profound changes, for it stimulated the formation or further development of extensive complementary areas which became suppliers of food and pack animals to the mining centres. These complementary areas included the captaincy of São Paulo, the extreme south of Brazil, the upper reaches of the São Francisco river, and finally the valley of the Paraíba river and southern Minas, both of which attracted large numbers of settlers. The city of Rio de Janeiro became the main port for the export of gold in the eighteenth century and for the importation of slaves and European goods. The southern captaincies – Rio de Janeiro (sugar, rice, and from 1790s coffee), São Paulo (sugar), Rio Grande do Sul (wheat and hides) – participated prominently in the agricultural renaissance of the late colonial period. There was a further shift in the colonial population, and the central southern region accounted for some 50 per cent of all Brazilians at the end of the eighteenth century. The captaincies of Minas Gerais, Bahia, Pernambuco, and Rio de Janeiro contained the largest regional concentrations of population.[44]

3. Certain specific and quite distinct demographic patterns may be distinguished in the development of the different components of colonial Brazil's population. Among the colonial elite, which was largely of European origin and by definition 'white', one finds:
(a) legally constituted families and corresponding family stability, although alongside a pattern of extra-marital sexual relations between the master and his slave women and servants, which

[44] See Marcílio, 'Évolution historique', and Alden, *CHLA* II, ch. 15, tables 1 and 2.

produced large numbers of bastard offspring of mixed descent, thus swelling the ranks of the illegitimate population;

(*b*) a relatively high legitimate birth rate;

(*c*) a high death rate, though lower than in other sectors of the population thanks to the better conditions of life, housing, and regular diet;

(*d*) a relatively high natural growth rate, continually supplemented by new arrivals from Europe;

(*e*) a very high marriage rate.

The salient characteristics of slave demography, particularly in the areas of the great plantations geared to the export market and in the mining region, were:

(*a*) an abnormally low fertility rate due to the harsh conditions of life, segregation of the sexes, and above all the absence of any interest on the part of slaveowners in creating legal, stable families among slaves;

(*b*) an abnormally high death rate, not only due to the conditions of life, nutrition, housing, and hygiene, but equally to the high child and adult mortality from infections and parasitic diseases resulting from an insufficient as well as deficient diet, extremely bad sanitary conditions, and the abandonment of slaves when they ceased to be productive;

(*c*) a natural growth rate which was almost always nil and frequently negative, with the transatlantic slave trade as the only factor of growth;

(*d*) an almost nil marriage rate.

A third demographic pattern could be found among the poor free sector of the population, involved in productive activities which were marginal to the export economy. These inhabitants were distributed over wide areas on family-based plots producing varieties of food crops, the excess from which was sold for internal consumption (the captaincy of São Paulo, parts of southern Brazil, the valley of the river São Francisco), or else scattered over extensive cattle-raising areas which were dependent on and subsidiary to the plantations or mines (the north-eastern hinterland from Ceará and Piauí in the north to Bahia and Minas Gerais in the south and the far south of Brazil). In addition, there were settlers in the Amazon region involved in forest extraction who also fell into this demographic category. Predominant among these was the mestizo, often the hybrid product of white and Indian, but also the result of the crossing of this mixture with other groups such as the black and mulatto. As these were not economically attractive areas, their population reproduced mainly through natural internal growth. There was, it is true, occasional imbalance between the sexes, as adult men and youths tended to migrate to the more dynamic areas of the colonial economy. Nevertheless, the relative paucity of males was not such as to hinder the marriage rate, which likewise did not suffer interference from the dominant social stratum (as was the case in the slave sector). The family was therefore the basic unit of production and the effective workforce in the struggle for group survival. Consequently it was more stable, while not necessarily being legally constituted. The high rate of concubinage by no means diminished the degree of stability among free unions. In addition, the fact that farmsteads were isolated from one another, that regular dietary habits were guaranteed by the system of mixed agriculture and complemented by fishing, hunting, and gathering natural crops, means that the death rate, though high, was nevertheless among the least severe and was, of course, relatively unaffected by periodic food shortages and epidemics. The natural growth of the population was maintained consistently, due to a very high birth rate of over 1 per cent per year (over 150 births per year per 1,000 inhabitants). Evidence of this trend is provided by the study of the free population of the subsistence agricultural area of São Paulo between 1798 and 1828, referred to above (table 1). In addition a study of the captaincy of Minas Gerais in 1815 partly illustrates the variations in the growth rate according to social class (see table 4):

Table 4 *Birth, death, and growth rate trends in Minas Gerais, 1815*

	Birth rate per 1,000	Death rate per 1,000	% natural growth
Whites	36.6	27.4	0.92
Free coloureds	41.7	34.3	0.74
Slaves	33.4	32.9	0.05
Total	37.3	32.3	0.50

Source: H. Klein, in Merrick and Graham, p. 33.

In conclusion, table 5 provides a general estimate of the population of Brazil in 1819, by region and by captaincy, free and slave, on the eve of independence from Portugal.

Table 5 *The population of Brazil in 1819*

Regions and administrative areas	Population Free	Population Slave	Population Total
North	104,211	39,040	143,251
Amazonas	13,310	6,040	19,350
Pará	90,901	33,000	123,901
North-east	716,468	393,735	1,110,203
Maranhão	66,668	133,332	200,000
Piauí	48,821	12,405	61,226
Ceará	145,731	55,439	201,170
Rio Grande do Norte	61,812	9,109	70,921
Paraíba	79,725	16,723	96,448
Pernambuco	270,832	97,633	368,465
Alagoas	42,879	69,094	111,973
East	1,299,287	508,351	1,807,638
Sergipe	88,783	26,213	114,996
Bahia	330,649	147,263	477,912
Minas Gerais	463,342	168,543	631,885
Espírito Santo	52,573	20,272	72,845
Rio de Janeiro	363,940	146,060	510,000
South	309,193	125,283	434,476
São Paulo	160,656	77,667	238,323
Paraná	49,751	10,191	59,942
Santa Catarina	34,859	9,172	44,031
Rio Grande do Sul	63,927	28,253	92,180
Centre–west	59,584	40,980	100,564
Mato Grosso	23,216	14,180	37,396
Goiás	36,368	26,800	63,168
Brazil	2,488,743	1,107,389	3,596,132[a]

[a] Figure excludes *c.* 800,000 'tribal Indians'.

Source: Marcílio, 'Évolution historique', p. 14, based on Joaquim Norberto de Souza e Silva, 'População geral do Império', and Antonio Rodrigues Velloso de Oliveira, *Memória*, 159–99 and annexes.

Part Two

ECONOMIC AND SOCIAL
STRUCTURES: SPANISH AMERICA

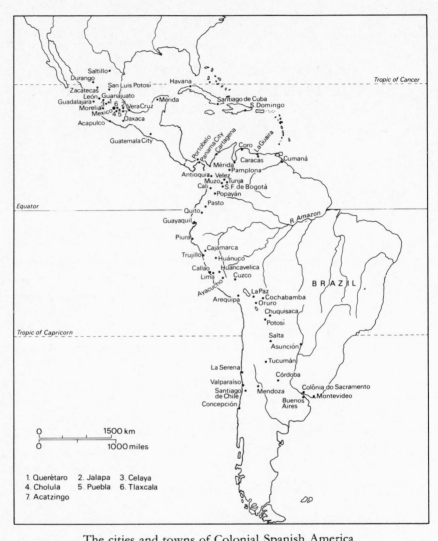

The cities and towns of Colonial Spanish America

3

THE URBAN DEVELOPMENT OF COLONIAL SPANISH AMERICA

THE URBAN IDEA

Like much of Spanish American colonial history, the region's urban development has two prehistories: one indigenous, the other peninsular Spanish. The *conquistadores* found many populous urban centres in Mesoamerica and, less markedly, in the central Andes. The Aztec capital of Tenochtitlán, with at least 150,000 and perhaps 300,000 inhabitants, became a Spanish viceregal capital. Eight more cities surrounded Lake Texcoco, while outlying centres of regional importance included Cholula, Tlaxcala, Tzin Tzun Tzan, Cempoala, and various sites in Yucatán and Guatemala. In the Inca realm the capital at Cuzco, while lacking the commercial importance of Tenochtitlán, had more than 100,000 inhabitants and exercised political sway over various centres along the Incaic *camino real*, some of pre-Incaic origin: Quito, Cajamarca, Jauja, Vilcas, Huánuco, and Bonbón. These urban hierarchies, in turn, were successors to earlier settlement complexes oriented towards centres at Teotihuacán, Monte Albán, Tajín, the Maya cities, Chan Chan, and Tiahuanaco.

Although the Spaniards converted some Indian cities like Tenochtitlán, Cholula, and Cuzco to their own uses, more pervasive influences on the European settlement scheme were the spatial distribution and village structure of the Indian populations. Indeed, if one were to carry the urban history of Spanish America only up to the late sixteenth century, the continuities with pre-conquest society would deserve a dominant emphasis. On a longer view, however, the political, social, and economic determinations of European rule, taken with the detribalization, relocation, and severe mortality of the Indian population, introduced many new vectors of change. The following treatment, then,

67

begins with European antecedents for urban development in the Indies. Pre-conquest patterns and their transformations are considered later.

Perhaps because Spanish America was for so long thought of as a predominantly agrarian realm, its urban history lay neglected until recently. Two noteworthy exceptions are books by an Argentine and a Peruvian, Juan A. García's sociological study of colonial Buenos Aires, *La ciudad indiana* (Buenos Aires, 1900) and Jorge Basadre's historical analysis of urban–rural relations in Peru, *La multitud, la ciudad y el campo en la historia del Perú* (Lima, 1929). It was not social and institutional aspects, however, but a controversy over physical form that finally brought Spanish American urban history to international scholarly attention. Since the 1940s the origins of the familiar chessboard layout with its spacious central plaza and monumental architecture have received detailed investigation. By now this research on the 'classic' Spanish American city plan has gone well beyond tracing formal precedents for design and has begun to reconstruct institutional and cultural process. Three groups of hypotheses that have emerged yield a convenient approach to our general topic.

First, some have emphasized that Spanish overseas colonization was part of a large imperial design made possible by the prior consolidation of the Spanish nation state. The gridiron plan for cities, while impractical for the irregular townscape of late medieval Spain, was invoked to rationalize the appropriation of vast overseas territories. Geometric layout was emblematic of the imperial will to domination and a bureaucratic need for order and symmetry. On this interpretation, the paradigm for Spanish overseas urbanism is taken to be the rectangular plan for Santa Fe de Granada, founded by the Catholic Monarchs in 1491 for the final siege of the Moors in southern Spain. The inspiration for this grid planning some have traced to ancient sources, notably Vitruvius, many of whose precepts for the ideal city reappear in the Spanish colonization ordinances of 1573.[1] Others hold that Santa Fe and the towns of the Indies found their pedigree in the regular layout of medieval bastide towns of southern France and north-eastern Spain. Still others point to the increasing influence of

---

[1] 'Ordenanzas de descubrimiento, nueva población y pacificación de la Indias, dadas por Felipe II en 1573', published in facsimile by Spain's Ministerio de la Vivienda (Madrid, 1973). For a partial English translation of the 1573 colonizing ordinances see Z. Nuttall, 'Royal ordinances concerning the laying out of New Towns', *Hispanic American Historical Review* [*HAHR*], 4/4 (1921), 743–53, and 5/2 (1922), 249–54.

Italian Renaissance or neoclassical planning on New World city building during the sixteenth century and later.

A second viewpoint reminds us that the Spanish conquerors and settlers were untutored in matters of urban design and could scarcely have been conversant with elegant styles of ancient, medieval, or neo-Roman origin. Their urban solutions were pragmatic, producing improvised and jumbled mining towns, cramped fortified seaports, and straggling rural hamlets as well as spacious and regular administrative centres. When geography and circumstances permitted, the grid was a natural, uncomplicated solution for practical leaders charged with making unequivocal land grants to contentious and ambitious settlers. The generous grid and plaza were congenial to the vastness of the territories newly annexed to Christendom. This solution, some conjecture, may even have echoed the grandeur of the Indian ceremonial sites, and E. W. Palm has suggested that the monumental form of the Aztecs' Tenochtitlán caught the attention of European planners through its influence on the 'ideal city' of Dürer.

Finally, some argue that while Spanish settlers made inevitable concessions to circumstance, and while Spanish legislators were aware of classical precedents, new town planning was ultimately a form of cultural expression ensconced in a matrix of traditions. Urban form in America was consonant with certain medieval Spanish treatises that in turn owed much to St Thomas Aquinas' *On the governance of rulers*. Gabriel Guarda in fact claims that the Spanish colonizing ordinances of neo-Vitruvian origin were less widely enforced than those of Thomist–Aristotelian inspiration. On this argument, urban form draws attention not on aesthetic or functional grounds but as a manifestation of social philosophy. We are reminded that whatever the constraints of place and circumstance, a town founding was a liturgical act sanctifying newly appropriated land. More than a mere exercise in cartography, urban design was the vehicle for a transplanted social, political, and economic order and exemplified the 'mystical body' that was central to Iberian political thought.

What began as a debate over the genealogy of urban design has evolved into a discussion of larger historical process, and our three sets of hypotheses turn out to be reconcilable. To be sure, certain propositions have been disproved, for instance that the Spanish grid plan was ubiquitous and unvarying or that neo-Vitruvian and Italian Renaissance theories were widely influential. But a large view shows that the rationalist, imperial, neo-Roman tradition was not incompatible with the Ibero-Catholic, Aristotelian one. Indeed, the two were intertwined from at least the era of the thirteenth-century legal code, *Las Siete Partidas*. It is moreover clear that this complex tradition made constant accommodation in the Indies to the predatory and populist spirit of the conquest; to economic and geographic imperatives; and to the presence of Indians and Africans, who together, despite their high mortality rates from disease and maltreatment, remained many times more numerous than the European population. One way to understand Spanish American cities, then, is to place the 'idea of a city' that came from Europe in dialectical relation with New World conditions of life.

At the close of the Middle Ages the Iberian city ideal drew from assorted classical and Christian sources that had been fused and reinterpreted since the thirteenth century. Prominent ingredients were: (1) the Greek notion of the polis, an agro-urban community based not on a 'covenant' among consenting individuals but on a 'political' entity of functionally integrated groups; (2) the imperial Roman notion that the municipality (*civitas*) was an instrument for 'civilizing' rural peoples and that *civitates* were the constituent parts of empire and, even more grandly, of a universal City of Mankind; (3) the Augustinian notion of a City of God or City of the Beyond that opposed a paradigm of Christian perfection to the sordid strivings and sins of the earthly city; (4) the chiliastic vision of an Edenic city of gold or terrestrial paradise that might be discovered in distant lands, or else a prospective city of poverty and piety that might arise under churchly guidance among overseas peoples newly consecrated to apostolic humility.

Save for the vision of a city of gold widely shared by the *conquistadores*, only jurists, theologians, and missionaries entertained these notions of urban community in explicit detail; yet the large premises on which they rested infused the mindset of settlers and city-builders. This cultural commitment stands in relief when compared to that of the New England Puritans. The Puritan congregation, or 'city upon a hill', did, to be sure, retain certain medieval principles of social subordination. All relations save those between parents and children, however, were voluntary and dependent on a covenant between contracting parties. The community had no 'corporate' identity in the sense that it was antecedent, or superior, to the contractual arrangements of its members. Each private conscience therefore bore extraordinary responsibility for preserving the purity of the 'bond of marriage' between God and the congregation.

While its members remained sinless, the community was an embodiment, not an imperfect replica, of the divine order. Moreover, those who emigrated from a parent community could found new congregations and initiate an independent relation to God. The Spanish American township, by contrast, had corporate identity in a system of empire that rested on hierarchies of urban and village units. Internally the town was composed of ethnic and occupational groups also knit by loosely hierarchical criteria. The urban unit was a microcosm of a larger imperial and ecclesiastical order, and responsibility for its proper functioning lay not with private consciences but with the discretion of bureaucratic, latifundiary, and ecclesiastical notables. The assumption of a 'sinless' community was relegated to chiliastic visions or to mission communities, like those of Jesuits and Franciscans, that served as exemplars or paradigms.

This complex vision of the urban community drew substance from Spanish institutional developments of the Middle Ages. Only in northern Spain along the pilgrimage route to Santiago de Compostela do we find the intrusion, starting in the eleventh century, of the 'communal' form of municipal organization that answered the mercantile preoccupations of travellers from across the Pyrenees. The municipal experience that was to shape Iberian overseas colonization was forged not here but in central Spain during the slow resettlement of lands taken from the Moors. On the meseta of León and Castile the term *burgués*, with its commercial implications, was rarely used and does not figure in the *Siete Partidas*. A propertied townsman was commonly a 'citizen' (*civis*), 'householder' (*vecino*), or 'decent man' (*omo bueno*). Monasteries and private persons accomplished the early resettlement, often under crown supervision. Later, control passed to municipal councils of the former Moorish realm, military orders, and nobles. Groups of free settlers received lands under stipulated conditions and privileges. A full-blown 'communal' municipal regime failed to develop, and the urban administration that managed rural activities was encompassed within the framework of the state. Towns were agro-urban units, and the commercial sector, so prominent in north-western Europe, vied here with military, ecclesiastical, agricultural, and pastoral interests.

In his *Tractado de República* (1521) the Spanish Trinitarian friar Alonso de Castrillo set forth symptomatic views on cities and citizenship. Addressing the crisis of the *comuneros* revolt of 1520–1, Castrillo criticized both the 'foreign' design for empire attributed to the entourage of Charles V and the excesses of the *comunidades* that opposed it – a tension between imperial strategy and local interest that had already appeared in Spain's new Caribbean settlements. Seeking a middle ground between absolutism and revolutionary constitutionalism, Castrillo reminded readers that the city was the noblest of human assemblages and that a kingdom was properly composed of cities, or 'republics', hierarchically arranged. Within cities, qualified citizens were to manage public affairs. Of the three classes of townsmen – nobles (*caballeros*), merchants (*mercaderes*), and artisans (*oficiales*) – only the first embodied civic virtues. Merchants were corrupted by private greed, while artisans were confined to horizons of private need. What Castrillo prophetically feared was a confluence of the cupidity of a few and the indigence of the many that would endanger the welfare of the republic.

THE URBAN STRATEGY

The 'Castilian' plan for urban development was not immediately asserted on Hispaniola, scene of the Spaniards' initial colonization effort in America. The early towns – including the ill-fated La Navidad of Columbus' first voyage, Isabela, founded on the second, and the subsequent mid-island chain of centres reaching the primitive south-coast city of Santo Domingo – had irregular plans and were akin to the fortified commercial 'factories' of the Italians in the Mediterranean and the Portuguese in Africa. Columbus himself frequently cited the Portuguese example. In a few years two things were clear: first, that the southern coast was more favourable than the northern for communication with Spain, control of the interior, and the staging of expeditions to Tierra Firme; second, that to use the inland chain of factories for tribute collection was not a viable social or economic strategy. Isabela, abandoned in about 1500, was by the 1520s a haunted ruin whose knightly inhabitants were said to salute the unwary visitor by doffing their heads along with their hats.

To remedy the bungled administration of the first decade, Nicolás de Ovando was dispatched to Santo Domingo as governor with instructions to found new settlements giving heed to natural features and population distribution. He was told that Christians should henceforth be clustered in municipal centres, thus setting the precedent for the segregation of Spanish *villas* from Indian *pueblos*. Ovando arrived in April 1502 with 2,500 settlers. When after two months a hurricane destroyed his capital, he resited it on the right bank of the Ozama to improve communications with the interior. The new city plan was the first instance of geometric layout in America. Soon Ovando devised a master scheme for a network of *villas* on Hispaniola, fifteen of which received the royal coat of arms in 1508. Some were sited in the west and south-east to control Indian labour; others were located near the gold deposits or in zones suited for agriculture and ranching. Santo Domingo city was the capital, main port, and terminus of roads to the north and west. For founding a town 50 vecinos seem to have been an average number. Certain towns received hospitals in a scheme of regionalized medical assistance. As co-ordinator of the plan, Ovando selected urban sites, controlled municipal appointments, and determined the disposition of lots (*solares*) around the plazas.

By the end of his term Ovando governed a European population of 8,000–10,000. He had created the underpinning for an integrated regional economy and promoted the island as a base for Caribbean exploration. Yet by the time he returned to Spain in 1509 his plans had gone awry. Proper roads were not built, and his decision to abolish the inept system of tribute collection, eliminate the caciques, and allocate the Indians to encomenderos, the mines, and the crown hastened the decline of the native population By the mid sixteenth century the settlements were desolate, and the north–south route established by the Columbus brothers had prevailed over Ovando's plan for east–west integration. This was to mean evacuation of the northern and western settlements in 1605–6 and eventual cession of western Hispaniola to the French.

In Cuba the governor, Diego Velázquez, chose seven urban sites that were plotted (1511–15), like those of Hispaniola, to profit from regional economic opportunities. Here, contrary to the case of Santo Domingo, Havana was relocated from the south to the north coast once the conquest of Mexico accentuated the importance of the northern shipping route. Eventually Havana overtook Santiago, the early capital, and was designated the rendezvous for Spain's Caribbean convoys.

The Caribbean phase of conquest saw the triumph of the municipal unit as an agro-urban instrument for colonization, and Ovando's experience informed the crown's elaborate instructions of 1513 to Pedrarias Dávila for colonization of Castilla del Oro.[2] By now the obstacles to the establishment of a prosperous network of centres were apparent: the lack of serviceable roads, the swift depletion of mineral

[2] Royal instruction of 1513 to Pedrarias Dávila, 'Ynstrucción para el governador de Tierra Firme, la qual se le entregó 4 de agosto DXIII', in M. Serrano y Sanz (ed.), *Orígenes de la dominación española en América* (Madrid, 1918), cclxx–xci.

resources, the decimation of the native population, and the lure of expeditions to the mainland. The drawbacks to regional planning under the close supervision of a crown-appointed bureaucrat were also evident. In both Hispaniola and Cuba assemblies of procurators soon appeared to assert municipal prerogatives. Although the crown would always oppose consolidation of a third estate, juntas of town procurators were convoked sporadically throughout Spanish America in the sixteenth century. In practice the procurator found his most effective role as a municipal representative at court who could bypass bureaucracy and petition the crown directly for redress of grievances.

The classic example of how municipal notables might choose their own caudillo and, through him, place themselves in vassalic relationship to the crown was the action of Hernán Cortés and his companions in repudiating the authority of their immediate superior, Diego Velázquez, at the start of the Mexican campaign. The so-called 'first letter' of Cortés, dispatched from the Rica-Villa of Veracruz on 10 July 1519, related to the crown that whereas Velázquez had wanted the expedition only to secure gold and return straightaway to Cuba, 'to all of us it seemed better that a town should be founded there in the name of your Majesties with a justiciary and council, so that in this land your Majesties might possess overlordship'. Cortés was 'well pleased and content' to designate *alcaldes* and *regidores* who in turn appointed him chief justice and *alcalde mayor*, completing the process of legitimation.[3]

These two branches of town government – *justicia* officered by *alcaldes* or magistrates and *regimiento* by *regidores* or councillors – had Castilian precedents. In the fourteenth century the crown curbed municipal liberty by converting these offices into prebends (*regalías*). In America the crown in principle controlled the *regimientos* but made concessions to the settlers with respect to *justicia*. Given the immense territory and diverse circumstances of the New World, the crown could not fully implant the Castilian system and was forced to accept various formulas to reconcile its interests with those of *conquistadores* and settlers. Although the municipality was conceived as embedded in the structure of the state, and the cabildo was in part bureaucratized, the regalist idea also permitted concession of *regimientos* in perpetuity. Cabildos enjoyed considerable autonomy during the early years, and those in outlying areas continued to do so after the higher structures of royal government were imposed.

[3] In J. B. Morris (ed.), *5 Letters of Cortés to the emperor* (New York, 1962), 1–29.

In the fourth book of his *Milicia y descripción de las Indias* (1599) an experienced New World caudillo, Bernardo de Vargas Machuca, offered a manual for town founders.[4] The settlers should reassure the Indians of their peaceful intentions, he advised, at the same time haggling over peace terms and exploiting tribal rivalries. The Indians should be encouraged to build houses sited conveniently for missionary purposes. The town itself should stand at the heart of its region to facilitate provisioning and military sorties. The site should be level and bare, not in a dangerous hollow, and close to water and firewood. To found the town Spaniards and Indian chieftains should erect a tree trunk, and the caudillo should sink his knife in it and proclaim his right to rule and punish, with the proviso that the town might later be rebuilt at a more suitable place. He would then declare:

I hereby found this community in the name of his Majesty, and in his royal name I shall protect it and keep peace and justice among all its inhabitants, Spaniards, conquerors, settlers, residents, and outsiders, and all its native population as well. I shall administer even-handed justice to the poor and the rich, to the humble and the exalted, and I shall protect their widows and orphans.

The caudillo would then brandish his sword, challenge any opponent to a duel, slash bushes at the site to establish possession, and place the community under royal jurisdiction. A cross should then be erected at the site of the future church, Mass said to impress the Indians, and the caudillo's cabildo appointments announced.

This done, the caudillo was to have the justices swear to keep order in the king's name, and soldiers desiring residence were to pledge to protect the townsmen. Citizens would then erect temporary tents and shacks on the plaza, which was to be rectangular but conform to the terrain. From it eight streets, each 25 feet wide, were to lead outward, creating blocks 200 by 250 feet divided into four lots. The church, cabildo, and gaol were to face the plaza, with remaining central lots assigned to the caudillo and chief officials. After earmarking space for *conventos*, hospitals, a slaughterhouse, and a butcher's shop, the caudillo was to allot land to householders. The Indian caciques should then provide workers to construct public buildings, level the open spaces, and plant crops under armed supervision of the Spaniards, who would need a stockade for emergency refuge. Adjoining residences of

[4] B. Vargas Machuca's instructions to town founders are in book 4 of his *Milicia y descripción de las Indias* [1599] (2 vols., Madrid, 1892).

Europeans should be connected by back doors or low walls in the event of a call to arms. With the town laid out, soldiers should reconnoitre the environs, bring Indian villages under Christian tutelage, assess economic possibilities, and compose reports for the cabildo with copies for higher officials. Further advice concerns colonization of new centres from the original nucleus; allotment of encomiendas according to the merits of the Spaniards and the suitability of the Indians; a warning to caudillos that, although entitled to a quarter of the land, they should not bite off more than they could chew; and the need to stimulate the Indians' self-interest by allowing them weekly markets, encouraging them to produce European commodities, and winking at their occasional pilferage. 'The Indian is thus made content, is better controlled, and gives twice as much service.'

Understandably, the historical experience that informed Vargas Machuca's instructions did not always exhibit so high a degree of formalism and calculation. A Jesuit's report of 1620 claimed that the founding of Asunción in the 1530s had been 'more by marriage than by conquest'. As the Spaniards were proceeding up the Paraguay river, he recounted, the local Indians

asked them who they were, whence they came, where they were going, and what they wanted. The Spaniards told them. The Indians replied that they should go no farther and that because they seemed like decent people they would give them their daughters to make them relatives. This pledge seemed fine to the Spaniards, and they stayed here.[5]

Yet for all their textbook character, Vargas Machuca's precepts contain three points that deserve emphasis: first, the wide discretionary powers enjoyed by caudillos and the hierarchical principle by which they rewarded followers; second, the umbrella of royal and ecclesiastical authority over any new municipal enterprise; third, the role of urban centres in appropriating territory and recruiting native peoples for the economic needs of the settlers and for the political and 'civilizing' purposes of empire. As time passed, personalist leadership gave way to control by municipal notables, often exercised outside the formal cabildo mechanism. Historians were once agreed that this regional oligarchical rule, supplemented by *cabildos abiertos* in occasional times of stress, made the municipality the only arena for effective self-government by creoles. This view draws attention to the considerable

---

[5] 'Informe de um Jesuíta anônimo' in J. Cortesão (ed.), *Jesuítas a bandeirantes no Guairá (1549–1640)* (Rio de Janeiro, 1951).

autonomy of local patriciates in outlying areas, but it exaggerates the discontinuity between the grass roots and superstructure of government. Creoles in fact attained positions of authority in the royal bureaucracy, while the towns themselves were not hermetic enclaves but a locus of tension between local ambition and imperial design. That is, the claims of a hinterland on those who would appropriate its produce and Indian labour competed with the claims of church and the state, sweetened by prebends and franchises, that aimed to win compliance from the notables and absorb the agro-urban unit within a scheme of empire.

Because the economy and society of colonial Spanish America are often described as archaic and resistant to change, one sometimes forgets that in the space of two generations after the Caribbean phase of conquest a few thousand Spaniards established an urban design for a continent and a half that has largely prevailed to this day. Indeed, by 1548 urban control centres, coastal and inland, had been created from the Mexican plateau south as far as Chile. Many of them are now familiar as modern national capitals: Mexico City, Panama City (resited in 1671), Bogotá, Quito, Lima, La Paz, Asunción, and Santiago. Caracas was founded in 1567 while Buenos Aires was founded permanently in 1580 after an ephemeral settlement in 1535–41. The broad reach of the settlement pattern reflected the colonizers' need for centres of control over prospective Indian workers and tributaries. Without Indians, the adage ran, there are no Indies. After the initial experiments, the commercial enclaves that characterized Portuguese, English, and Dutch overseas expansion were abandoned in the Spanish Indies in favour of direct appropriation of mineral and agricultural resources. In the words of Constantino Bayle:

The *conquistadores* were like the Roman legionaries who became colonists on leaving the wars, using lands distributed to reward their military efforts. The object of their campaigns to subdue native peoples was to establish themselves in the provinces, found cities, and work out ways to live comfortably as in Spain. Hence they did not stop at the coasts, and most of their foundings were mediterranean, where the fertility of the soil promised full compensation for their efforts. Division of land among the settlers was thus a necessary, indispensable complement to the municipality.[6]

As the chronicler López de Gómara put it, 'who fails to settle fails to conquer properly, and if the land is not conquered the inhabitants will not be converted'.

[6] Constantino Bayle, *Los cabildos seculares en la América Española* (Madrid, 1952), 85–6.

Colonization, then, was largely a labour of 'urbanization', that is, a strategy of settlement nucleation for appropriating resources and implanting jurisdiction. Urbanization taken in its simple demographic sense – designating population clusters that grow more swiftly than surrounding regions – is difficult to quantify for sixteenth- and seventeenth-century Spanish America even if one limits attention to towns of Europeans. To begin with, enumerations from the period are generally for vecinos, that is, householders controlling retinues or encomiendas rather than simple residents (*habitantes* or *moradores*) and transients (*estantes*), and the ratio of vecinos to *moradores* and to Indians varied greatly from place to place. Second, by the time the Spaniards' urban hierarchies were in place, the decline of the Indian population – rural, village, and urban – had become so precipitous as to render meaningless the usual measures, or significance, of urbanization and deurbanization. By using such tallies as are available, however, and by establishing weighted indices for urban functions, it is possible to draw certain conclusions about urban development for the period of roughly 1580 to 1630 (a time when the Indian population of central Mexico dropped from about two million to some 700,000). During this span it appears that larger administrative cities grew faster than smaller ones. Admittedly incomplete data indicate that in centres of over 500 vecinos at the terminal dates the number of vecinos had increased by 6.7 times, while in those of 100 to 500 vecinos it had risen by only one-third. The steadiest growth was in the larger bureaucratic centres provided with services, manufactures, and cultural resources. More dramatic growth occurred in favoured ports (Havana, Callao), mining towns (Potosí, Oruro, Mérida in New Granada, San Luis Potosí), and intermediate agricultural centres (Atlisco, Querétaro, Santiago de los Valles). Economic activities, however, tended to have only regional impact or else to be oriented to Spanish mercantilist design. The larger urban pattern was better defined at this time as a 'scheme' of cities than as a complex of interconnected urban 'systems'.[7]

The municipal strategy for appropriating resources derived from the Roman legal principle, revived in late medieval Spain, that separated the public and private domains, vesting in the crown rather than in the king as feudal lord the right to dispose of natural resources, including

---

[7] See J. E. Hardoy and C. Aranovich, 'Urbanización en América Hispana entre 1580 y 1630', *Boletin del Centro de Investigaciones Históricas y Estéticas* [*BCIHE*] (Universidad Central de Venezuela, Caracas), 11 (1969), 9–89.

land, by *merced real* or *gracia*. An early, idealistic policy statement appeared in a cedula of 1518 that allocated farmlands and urban lots to colonists and their heirs forever 'in ample quantity according to the willingness of each to cultivate them'. The cedula assumes a municipal unit as the distributive agent and accents the social or political concerns of the crown. These concerns were not to prevail against the predatory and personalistic character of colonization, and eventually they had to vie with the crown's own economic and fiscal interests in formulating land policy.

Spanish law gave grounds for three principal types of land grant. One was the *capitulación* that empowered an expedition leader to found towns and distribute lands, contingent on effective occupation for four to eight years. Second was a grant of vacant lands in accord with codified decrees stipulating, for example, that town founders could not be proprietors in existing towns, that prospective founders must guarantee the presence of at least thirty vecinos, and that new towns should be laid out on four leagues of land and be distant by five leagues from previous centres. Later, as the royal treasury became depleted and as better land near towns and along roads was appropriated, the crown increasingly favoured the exchange value of land against its use value. In a cedula of 1591, which Ots Capdequí calls an 'agrarian reform', lands not specifically conceded were to revert to the crown for a third type of disposal, sale by auction. Even then, a cabildo might arrange a collective land title for itself as a juridical person or, in the event of auction, appear as a single bidder and then redistribute the land under free title. The crown's early ideal of independent farm colonies was eclipsed by concentrated landholdings in privileged locations under competition that worked against latecomers and the impecunious. Crown income from land sales could not be fully realized given the difficulties of systematic surveying and title clearance and the fact that judges, trained in Justinian law, were reluctant to enforce policies that threatened outright ownership. In a second 'agrarian reform' the crown, by an *instrucción* of 1754, tried to reassert control over land sales and *composiciones*, prescribed leniency in handling Indian claims, and required legalization of land titles acquired after 1700. By then, however, the *de facto* territorial arrangements of the cabildos strongly resisted change.

What persisted, of course, was not a rigid design but a set of tendencies. Many of the original foundings proved ephemeral because of faulty site selection; disasters such as earthquakes, volcanic eruptions, or disease; Indian attacks; deficient natural resources and economic possibilities; or simply the lure of new prospects. The founders of Jauja, Peru, stipulated that their first site would be used only until a more suitable one was identified. Some towns were refounded six or more times. Nueva Burgos in New Granada has been called a 'portable' city, carried from place to place on its people's backs as they searched for a site where the Indians would leave them in peace to sow their fields. Some towns became apples of discord for competing caudillos, who might wrest control from one another and redistribute choice land to favourites. Other towns commandeered vast jurisdictions far beyond their capacity to settle them. Buenos Aires laid claim to much of modern Argentina, Quito to all of modern Ecuador and part of Colombia, Asunción to land in a hundred-league radius.

The study of seventeenth-century Tunja shows how a regional settlement plan might ramify and become consolidated.[8] Founded in 1559, Tunja was second in importance only to Bogotá in the New Granada highlands. The act of founding justified the site as offering 'caciques and Indians and available land to sustain the Spaniards'. By 1623 the city had 476 buildings, including twenty churches and convents but only seven 'public buildings or industries'. The population included 3,300 adult Spanish males and an indeterminate number of Indians, blacks, and mixed-bloods. City officials came from the 70 or more families of encomenderos occupying tile-roofed dwellings that might boast two storeys around interior patios and display stone trimming and coats of arms. Humbler Spaniards – merchants, master craftsmen, artisans – lived in cramped, thatch-roofed dwellings. Non-Europeans and half-castes were generally burden-bearers, living in *bohíos* outside the city plan.

Commerce took place on three levels. The fifteen leading merchants imported fine cloth and modest luxuries from Spain. Regionally, these and lesser merchants traded throughout New Granada, using the city's 30 horse and mule teams to export farm and ranch products, blankets, sandals, leather goods, and flour. Twice-weekly *tiangues* provided a local market for local produce and for the Indians' cotton blankets and pottery. Analogous three-tiered systems have been described for New Spain. The larger cities of Yucatán had long-distance merchants (*mercaderes*), usually immigrants well connected with the encomenderos; retail tradesmen (*comerciantes*), creoles or sometimes mestizos who

[8] V. Cortés Alonso, 'Tunja y sus vecinos', *Revista de Indias*, 25, 99–100 (1965), 155–207.

supplied local commerce and dealt with the countryside; and *tratantes*, often mestizos, Indians, or mulattos, who trafficked with the Indian communities. Similarly Querétaro's trade functioned at three levels: the first in the hands of factors from Mexico City, the second having a provincial radius and providing credit for industry and agriculture, and the third serving the city's retail outlets.

In the case of Tunja, the rudimentary state of manufacturing and finance and the agrarian orientation of the patriciate suggest that trade was secondary in the functional definition of the city. More decisive were the lines of political fealty and control. The social hierarchy represented in Tunja's concentric rings of architectural style symbolized other hierarchies, spatially extended but always centring on the plaza. Political functions loosely corresponded to the three levels of commercial activity. First, Tunja was a point of shifting equilibrium between the claims and favours of church and empire and the separatism of the encomenderos, many of them descended from the mutinous soldiers of Pizarro. If nine of the largest encomiendas belonged to the crown, it was also true that Tunja's encomenderos comprised the most powerful patriciate of New Granada and the only one to resist seriously the royal tax levies of the 1590s. Second, the city was the administrative base for surrounding towns colonized from Tunja, some of them 100 miles distant. Third, Tunja was the control centre for 161 encomiendas representing villages of 80 to 2,000 Indians.

Tunja usefully illustrates how superimposed schemes of dominion might intersect to produce a hierarchically ordered pattern of colonization. It also brings to the fore two aspects of Spanish American urban history – interethnic relations and commercial activity – that are a key not only to urban society but also to the formation of interurban settlement patterns.

TOWNS AND INDIANS

A central goal of Spanish settlement policy was the creation of two 'republics', one of Spaniards and one of Indians. The term 'republic' implied an agro-urban polis composed of functionally integrated social and occupational groups that was inserted into the structure of empire while enjoying a modicum of self-government, or at least self-administration. Although the notion of two republics suggests co-equality and, for the Indians, officially signified protective armature against exploitation, the republic of Indians became a euphemism for a regime of detribalization, regimentation, Christianization, tribute, and forced labour. What appeared in practice, moreover, was not implantation of the polis in the vision harboured by Las Casas but urban nucleation as designated by the terms *pueblos de españoles* and *pueblos de indios*. A cedula of 1551, later picked up in the *Recopilación*, ordered that 'the Indians be reduced to pueblos and not live divided and separated by mountains and hills, deprived of all spiritual and temporal benefits'. As the study of Central America makes clear, the towns of Spaniards and Indians were far from comparable. The arrangement of dwellings in the former reflected a social hierarchy, and the *plaza mayor* with its distinctive ecclesiastical, administrative, fiscal, and commercial structures identified the locus and functions of authority. In Indian towns, where social distinctions had been effaced or drastically simplified, residential location was not indicative of social or political ranking, while the plaza was but a 'vaguely defined vacant space dominated by a church, its sole architectural distinction'.[9]

The implications of Spanish colonization for the native peoples of New Spain are reasonably clear. On the eve of conquest large urban concentrations like Tenochtitlán were rare, and Indians generally lived in small, often contiguous settlements. Larger settlements had a market, temple, and residences for priests and nobles with outlying clusters for commoners. These were often fortified and located at elevations as wartime retreats for the adjacent population. Other centres were primarily ceremonial, inhabited only by priests. In many regions small dependent clusters of a few houses each were widely dispersed throughout the farmlands.

For a generation after conquest devastating epidemics, particularly of smallpox and mumps, had a far more punishing effect on the Indian population, especially those in populous centres and lowland areas, than did Spanish settlement schemes. A few strategic cities like Tenochtitlán were appropriated and rebuilt by the conquerors. The preferred sites for new towns, however, were precisely the valley regions that the Indians had regarded as less defensible or convenient. During these years the Spaniards imposed their urban vision less by relocation than by institutional redefinition. The pre-conquest Valley of Mexico was

---

[9] S. D. Markman, 'The gridiron town plan and the caste system in colonial Central America', in R. P. Schaedel, J. E. Hardoy, and N. S. Kinzer (eds.), *Urbanization in the Americas from its beginnings to the present* (The Hague, 1978), 481.

divided into numerous culturally and linguistically united 'city states'. These were formed of a central community of several thousand inhabitants organized by family groups (*calpullec*), where the local ruler (*tlatoani*; plural, *tlatoque*) resided, and its satellite communities composed of a single *calpulli* that controlled landholding. This city state, or *altepetl*, was larger than a hamlet and smaller than a river basin; it was, in Lockhart's words, 'less an urban complex than the association of a group of people with a given extended territory', and the word *altepetl* signified originally 'water and hill'. Upon this structure of lineage groups the Spaniards projected Iberian political nomenclature. That is, the central community became a *cabecera* subdivided into wards or *barrios*, while outlying clusters became *estancias* or *sujetos*. The whole settlement complex might become known as a pueblo, even though it quite lacked the close-knit structure and physical form associated with the Spanish prototype. The so-called pueblo in turn was wrenched from its position in Aztec imperial tribute organization and inserted into a European administrative hierarchy of *partidos* and, above them, *provincias*. Indian leaders soon learned the new rules and began vying to acquire privileges for their *cabeceras* or else to have their *sujetos* raised to *cabecera* status. By and large the dispersed pre-conquest settlement pattern endured to about 1550 and was even extended by the flight of Indian groups to remote places. What the Spaniards had managed was to accommodate a peninsular institution, encomienda, to an existing settlement pattern and an existing system for extracting tribute and labour. *Pueblos de españoles* were established incrementally as control centres, while the *tlatoque*, to whom Spaniards applied the Caribbean name *caciques*, served as intermediaries for new masters. A sizeable amount of the Indian labour made available was deployed to construct public works, churches, convents, and administrative headquarters for Mexico City and the *pueblos de españoles*.

This modified pre-conquest pattern inevitably yielded to the more sharply nucleated design that was the early preference of the Spanish crown. A demographic cause was the severe mortality of the Indian population, which made corporate life in dispersed centres unviable and called for the consolidation of survivors in accessible and manageable clusters. After the epidemic of 1545–8 royal orders explicitly commanded that natives be congregated in European-style pueblos near religious houses. Acceptance of this policy was assisted by the sometimes conflicting ambitions of ecclesiastics and encomenderos, both concerned to bring their wards under close supervision. The friars were the most successful agents of Hispanicization and Christianization, accomplished through large-scale creation of new towns, whether by merging existing centres or congregating scattered populations. Towns were named or renamed after Catholic saints; Indians were appointed to minor church offices; and municipal rituals, fiestas, and sodalities introduced Indians to the Christian calendar. Whether under the friars or under *corregidores*, Spanish municipal forms, the cabildo and its component offices, were widely introduced. By 1560 most of the original *cabeceras* had been moved to lower-lying, level sites and many Indians dispersed in remote areas were being relocated in new *cabeceras* and *sujetos*.

After another disastrous time of plague (probably typhus) and famine in 1576–81 the crown intensified the programme of forced congregation, urged on by clerics and encomenderos. As the new relocation strategy designed for most of New Spain took effect in 1593–1605, thousands of place-names vanished and the Spanish grid design with its broad plaza became a familiar sight. Enforced urbanization, however, met strong countercurrents. First, congregation made Indians more vulnerable to contagious disease. Second, Spanish appropriation of rural holdings abandoned by the Indians created a new productive institution, the hacienda, and these began to replace Indian towns as suppliers for the growing populations of the larger urban centres. Workers suffering from hunger and oppressive tribute schedules were drawn off to the greater security of hacienda labour, often in debt bondage. Thus the corporate structure of Indian municipalities atrophied as their economic life became precarious and control passed to hacendados and royal officials. The latifundium–large city binomial that was for centuries to govern settlement patterns and economic flows in large areas of Spanish America was swiftly taking shape. These new sources of organization for labour and the economy assisted the transition from a pre-conquest economic system to one that meshed more directly into the European mode of agro-pastoral, mining, and manufacturing production based on peonage and wage labour.

The great silver strike at Zacatecas in 1546 posed special problems of settlement, for this important site was at the centre of the north-central plateau that stretched north from a border along the Lerma river and was dominated by the bellicose, semi-nomadic Chichimeca tribes. Early efforts to protect traffic along the silver highways, to create defensive towns, and to tranquillize the Indians with guarantees for colonization all met with failure, although towns of future importance like Celaya, León, and Saltillo date from the 1570s. Not until after 1585 was a workable pacification policy devised, involving development of an effective mission system under the friars and relocation of sedentary Indians, notably the Tlaxcalans, to establish model agricultural communities. Zacatecas itself grew to a population of 1,500 Spaniards and 3,000 Indians, blacks, and mestizos by the early seventeenth century. Around the straggling layout of the core city, Indian townships grouped by 'nations' of origin soon took shape.

Although lacking monumental centres, the Chibcha settlements of the Bogotá *sabana* were similar to those of Mesoamerica.[10] Land occupation was dispersive and based on household groups (*utas*) organized into *sivin*, and these in turn into communities headed by a *sijipena* who became the Spaniards' cacique. The conquerors' policy of forced nucleation after 1549 met strong resistance, and by 1600 three-quarters of the 100 or so Indian settlements of the *sabana* were still intact. *Mestizaje* and Hispanicization of caciques were longer delayed than in Mexico. Spanish livestock were more effective than royal policy in forcing Indians to relocate and release land for use by the Europeans. Chessboard settlements became more common in the seventeenth century, although Indians preferred to remain on their scattered plots, leaving the towns as a scene for intermittent religious and fiscal functions and an eventual place of residence for whites and the racially mixed.

In its effects on Indian settlement patterns, the colonization of Peru was also analogous to the Mexican case, although differences in geography and resources, indigenous institutions, and pragmatic conquest solutions created significant variations. A central feature of the imposed urban system was that while the Spaniards occupied and rebuilt Cuzco, the Inca capital, their own capital was located at Lima on the coast. At the same time the mining boom of Potosí, far up in the highlands, brought that city a population vastly exceeding those of its Mexican counterparts. By 1557, twelve years after the discovery of silver, 12,000 Spaniards were counted; by 1572 the population had risen to 120,000 persons of all races, and by 1610, on the eve of decline, to 160,000, a figure which, if accurate, made Potosí the largest city in the hemisphere. Unlike Mexico–Tenochtitlán, Cuzco lost its function of political and cosmological integration as the 'umbilicus' of the Incaic

[10] J. A. and J. E. Villamarín, 'Chibcha settlement under Spanish rule, 1537–1810', in D. J. Robinson (ed.), *Social fabric and spatial structure in colonial Latin America* (Ann Arbor, 1979), 25–84.

world and became a point of linkage between two new poles of attraction. The Spaniards' predilection for the coastal zone and above all for Lima strongly conditioned what Wachtel calls the spatial 'destructuring' of the Andean realm.

At the regional level the Spaniards encountered again dispersed settlement with landholding managed by lineage groups (*ayllus*) under supervision of lords or *curacas* who became the caciques or go-betweens. The impact of the European market economy, however, may well have been more severe in Andean than in Mesoamerica. For here, pre-conquest exchange of products among regions of diverse climate depended not on market dealings but on the control of microhabitats at different altitudes by clusters of kin groups in a system of what have been called 'vertical archipelagos' – a solution also present in at least rudimentary form among the Chibcha. In opposition to these delicate networks of complementary production the Spaniards imposed their notions of land as a commodity, of tributary exaction, and of nucleated urbanization enhanced by all the accoutrements of European town life. Such policies received their prime impetus from the viceroy Francisco de Toledo (1569–81), nicknamed the Peruvian Solon, who ordered, for example, that 16,000 Indians of Condesuyo province be resettled from 445 villages into 48 *reducciones* and that 21,000 Indians of Cuzco be brought from 309 villages into 40 *reducciones*.

For Central America it is possible to trace the long-term erosion of the dichotomy between Spanish and Indian towns caused by race mixture and economic change. With miscegenation the original ethnic stocks produced intermediate groups of mestizos, mulattos, and zambos which by the late colonial period were collapsed into an indeterminate sector of *pardos* or *ladinos*. Towns, both Spanish or Indian, commanding productive hinterlands and favourably located for trade attracted all ethnic groups, becoming *pueblos de ladinos*. If isolated Indian towns, especially those of Dominican and Franciscan origin, stagnated and kept their early features, many others, for example in the indigo zones of the Pacific coast, drew mixed populations. Such centres became architecturally transformed with arcades around the plazas and monumental ecclesiastical and civic architecture. Similarly, a lively Spanish centre like Santiago de los Caballeros attracted an ethnically mixed population, accommodated in a progressively extended official *traza*. Some Spanish towns, on the other hand, never prospered and lost their regional dominance. On the Bogotá *sabana* the *pueblos de indios*, or *resguardos*, were increasingly infiltrated by whites, mestizos, and a few *pardos* and blacks, a change often signalized by the conversion of *resguardos* into *parroquias*. Breakdown of ethnic segregation has also been described by Marzahl for the Popayán region of modern Colombia, where latifundia and mining attracted many non-Indians to formerly Indian settlements. In the city itself the Spanish population mixed increasingly along the social scale with artisans and small farmers of Indian and half-caste extraction.

As this last example suggests, the 'two republics' principle was applied internally to biethnic cities as well as to systems of central places and satellites. Even a town like Querétaro, where Indians, blacks, mestizos, and Spaniards were mixed in the original residential pattern, eventually developed Indian barrios that preserved Indian languages, mores, and family habits. The classic case of segregation is Mexico City, where the central *traza* was laid out comprising some thirteen rectangular blocks in each direction and surrounded by four L-shaped, irregularly planned Indian barrios governed by Indian officials and providing a workforce for the central city. Inevitably, boundaries dissolved as miscegenation occurred and as the ratio of Indians to whites shifted from ten to one in the mid sixteenth century to one to two in the late eighteenth. On various occasions Indian–mestizo conflicts broke out, notably the riots of 1624 and 1692, and attempts were made to restore the original dichotomous arrangement. After the 1692 uprising a commission that included the eminent scholar Carlos Sigüenza y Góngora reported on 'inconveniences from Indians living in the centre of the city' and the need to congregate them in 'their barrios, curacies, and districts, where they should be organized for their better governance without being admitted to the central city'. The documents spoke of the 'insolent freedom' of Indians in the city, who abandoned their homes, impeding civil and churchly administration and tribute collection and filling 'this republic' with 'lazy, vagabond, useless, insolent, and villainous people', disposed to crime and 'confident in the impunity assured by their very anonymity and obscurity'. Blame was ascribed to both sides. First, the Indian barrios were infiltrated by blacks, mulattos, and mestizos, who were wayward, dishonest, thieving, gambling, and vicious and who either corrupted the Indians or forced them to find other sanctuary. Second, Spaniards living in the *traza* were willing to protect renegade Indians so as to rent them a room, or a shack, a relation cemented by *compadrazgo* ties sheltering 'the impudent behaviour that tries our patience'.[11] The trend towards ethnic mixture, both biological and spatial, was clearly beyond reversal. The city's new ecclesiastical and civil subdivisions of the late eighteenth century paid lip service to Indian segregation but did nothing to restore it.

Recent research on Antequera in the Oaxaca valley stresses the city's role in cultural integration throughout the colonial period.[12] A city census of 1565 identified ten ethnic categories of Indians, seven of them of the Nahua group, distributed within the *traza*, at its fringe, in the satellite community of Jalatlaco, or on near-by farms. Gradually these cultural identities dissolved as Indian barrios lost their ethnic character, native languages fell into disuse, the distinction between Indian nobles and commoners disappeared, and non-Indians took residence in Jalatlaco. Indians originally considered as *naborías*, or a source of labour 'in the city', became proletarianized urban Indians who were 'of the city'. The proliferation of mixed-race groups, the intermingling of white creoles and *castas* across the occupational hierarchy, and – after the region's economic upturn of the 1740s – the increased importance of economic as against ethnic status norms all went far towards effacing the distinction between colonized and colonizer.

On a broad view, it is clear that larger towns in the conquest period were a scene of extensive racial mixing among Europeans, Africans, and Indians, especially given the shortage of Spanish and African women. Subsequent stratification and conversion of racial groups into *castas*, it has been suggested by C. Esteva Fabregat, favoured 'both social separation and the relative sexual self-sufficiency of each ethnic group or *casta*'. A third stage saw the erosion of the system of *castas* at the very time that popular nomenclature for the increasing variety of racial combinations was undergoing baroque multiplication. In large cities particularly, this process was hastened by cityward migrations, political restlessness, and economic changes that undermined the corporate structures of society and nurtured a new psychology of malaise and aggressiveness. The suspension of ethnic categories in favour of a broad distinction between respectable folk and the populace, *gente decente* and *la plebe*, was an urban phenomenon reflecting a crisis of authority, a weakening of social controls, and increased assertiveness among the 'popular' sectors. In his study of 'crowds' in Peruvian history, written

[11] 'Sobre los inconvenientes de vivir los indios en el centro de la ciudad', *Boletín del Archivo General de la Nación* (Mexico), 9/1 (1938), 1–34.
[12] J. K. Chance, *Race and class in colonial Oaxaca* (Stanford, 1978).

Table 1 *Ibero-American population c. 1789 by ethnic group
and place of residence*

	Residents of 'urban' places			Residents of 'rural' places			Group totals	
	no. in ooos	% of urban pop.	% of total ethnic group	no. in ooos	% of rural pop.	% of total ethnic group	no. in ooos	% of total pop.
Indians*	1,728	36.8	22.0	6,132	65.3	78.0	7,860	55.8
Whites	1,670	35.6	51.8	1,553	16.5	48.2	3,223	22.9
Mestizos	666	14.1	64.4	368	3.9	35.6	1,034	7.3
Mulattos	419	8.9	39.1	653	7.0	60.9	1,072	7.6
Negroes	214	4.6	23.7	688	7.3	76.3	902	6.4
Totals	4,697	100.0	33.3	9,394	100.0	66.7	14,091	100.0

* Excludes *indios bárbaros*.
Source: Adapted from C. Esteva Fabregat, 'Población mestizaje en les ciudades de Iberoamérica: siglo XVIII', in F. de Solano (ed.), *Estudios sobre la ciudad iberoamericana* (Madrid, 1975), 599. Table contains rounding errors.

in 1929, Jorge Basadre posited an eighteenth-century transition from the religious and 'aulic' crowds who swarmed Lima's streets as spectators and celebrants to crowds that, although still 'prepolitical', were of a more frustrated and menacing disposition. The analogue in Mexico City was the urban culture of *leperismo*, publicized in foreigners' travel accounts and named for the racially indistinct *lépero*, who was pictured as insolent, vagrant, aggressive to women, and given to vice and assaults on property.

Using statistics from Alcedo's *Diccionario de América* of 1789, an attempt has been made to specify the racial composition of towns throughout Spanish America. Of the 8,478 settlements tabulated, 7,884 are considered as primarily rural pueblos, while 594 *ciudades, villas*, and mining centres, 7 per cent of the total, are claimed as having significant 'urban' functions based on commerce, services, and industry. This division does not yield a rural–urban split in the modern sense, for many so-called 'urban' centres were small and all of them included rural residents. Still the population distribution by this conjectural criterion reinforces the suggestion that the urban setting was the prime habitat for whites and racially mixed groups (see table 1). First, only 20–25 per cent of the Indians and blacks resided in urban places; second, whites and mestizos comprised 20 per cent of the rural population and 50 per cent of the urban; third, mulattos were about equal to blacks in rural places and almost double their number in urban ones.

Some have suggested that ethnic identification gave way to class identification in larger cities and even to an embryonic 'class consciousness' of the poor. This claim seems excessive when we recall that the class consciousness even of industrial workers in twentieth-century Latin American cities is problematical. It is more plausible to say that the mid eighteenth to mid nineteenth century was a time of absolute, if not necessarily relative, urban population growth and, especially during the independence movements, a relaxation of social controls that encouraged the urban poor to adopt contumelious attitudes towards constituted authority.

A generation after the conquest the native peoples of New Spain and Peru came to realize that they had lost primary identifications with their multifarious array of ethnic groups and were reduced to a common stratum of 'Indians'. Similarly, the variegated phenotypes of the late colonial urban *castas* lost social significance and were absorbed into an indistinct *plebe*. In both cases homogenization of the dispossessed marked the failure of the old ecclesiastical and juridical ideal of social 'incorporation'. The feeling this kindled was a common sense of disinheritance rather than a sense of common cause.

TOWNS AND COMMERCE

The contrast has more than once been made between the commercial impetus of the late medieval towns of north-west Europe and characteristic agro-administrative functions of colonial Spanish American towns. The first were points of crystallization for early forms of commercial capitalism; the second were centrifugal points of assault on the land and its resources. The first were seedbeds for a new economic and legal order; the second were vehicles for an established imperial order.

The contrast becomes less stark when one recognizes that, in time, commercial development gathered momentum in the Indies as local markets grew, marketable commodities were identified, and opportunities for overseas trade expanded. Even so, these trends did not undermine the old order and bring into being a new 'bourgeoisie' with a distinctive ideology. The merchant guilds (*consulados*) of large cities, even though they were closed groups with corporate *esprit*, were, in the words of Veitia Linaje's *Norte de la contratación de las Indias occidentales*, 'helped, protected, and favoured by the Kings and their Ministers'. In towns based on mixed economies like Arequipa and Popayán elites were resourceful at shifting the brunt of their economic involvements about among trade, mining, and agriculture as conditions changed. Colonial Havana, rendezvous port for homegoing fleets, was not a mercantile but a service city, with its port functions at the mercy of the erratic schedule of the fleet system. To compensate Havana for its utility to the mercantilist scheme the crown recognized the agrarian interests of its notables by granting their cabildo – one of only two so privileged in the Indies – the right to distribute land directly without royal approval.

In general, Spanish immigrants were favoured throughout the Indies over creoles in commercial careers, but their capital was often re-channelled into rural holdings and gifts to the church. Medellín, it appears, was an exception, given the narrow possibilities there for acquiring productive land; here sons tended to follow fathers into mining or trade, which offered high-status occupations.[13] But for Mexico City after the 1590s, although there are examples of two-generation merchant families, circulation of the merchant elite rather than consolidation was the norm.[14] Even in the outstanding 'commercial' city of late colonial Buenos Aires, where agricultural land beyond suburban *quintas* was not yet attractive to investors, merchants, it seems, did not create a stable class. Not only did their sons prefer ecclesiastical, military, and bureaucratic careers, but the institutions for business ventures were so rudimentary, and so vulnerable to inheritance laws, that commercial enterprises rarely survived beyond a generation.[15] Other cities in zones of quickening growth were still less progressive. Late colonial Caracas, the traveller Depons found, was more a workshop than a trade centre; the function of an exchange, of paper money, of discounting were all unknown. Havana, despite the economic impetus imparted by sugar exports after 1760, had no permanent banks until the 1850s. The Guayaquil of 1790, with cacao exports soaring, was a small city of 8,000 'with little in the way of financial institutions or, indeed,

[13] A. Twinam, 'Enterprise and elites: eighteenth-century Medellín', *HAHR*, 59/3 (1979), 444–75.
[14] L. S. Hoberman, 'Merchants in seventeenth century Mexico City: a preliminary portrait', *HAHR*, 57/3 (1977), 479–503.
[15] S. M. Socolow, *The merchants of Buenos Aires, 1778–1810* (Cambridge, 1978).

specialized commercial houses'.[16] A study of the credit market in eighteenth-century Guadalajara exemplifies what one means by the archaic financial capacity of Spanish American cities.[17] Here credit was largely controlled by the church, particularly in the early part of the century, with a lending potential derived from bequests left for masses, convent dowries, *cofradías*, tithe collection, and income from real estate. With such funds, the church could lend on a regular basis, while individuals – merchants, priests, widows – would lend but once or twice in a period of decades. Capital circulated within a small group of businessmen and clergy, reaching the hinterland through hacendados. That the money market achieved no great momentum in late colonial times is attested by the fact that the 892,000 pesos' worth of loans reported for Guadalajara in the 1760s had dropped to 773,000 by the decade 1801–10.

Yet if no Amsterdam or Philadelphia sprang up in the Indies, an important strand of the urban story features the varied commercial activity that gathered in volume to ratify, extend, or reorient the primitive design of empire and the contingent solutions of conquest. Because of the size of the stage on which it was played, the most dramatic episode was the rise to commercial hegemony of penurious Buenos Aires, favoured by strategic location but isolated by Spanish mercantilist policy, at the expense of Lima, the City of Kings and commercial capital of the southern viceroyalty.

Writing of the 'trade, splendour, and wealth' of Lima, the contemporary observer Bernabé Cobo, in his *Historia de la fundación de Lima*, gave little impression of a city where class structure, norms of behaviour, and economic decisions were powerfully shaped by commercial imperatives. He spoke, to be sure, of 'the tremendous volume' of its business and trade as 'the capital, emporium, and permanent fair and bazaar' of the viceroyalty and nearby regions. Most of the city's population made subsidiary incomes from commerce with Europe, China, and New Spain. Yet private wealth was attracted to extravagant consumption. Lima's four or five modest coaches at Cobo's arrival in 1599 had, 30 years later, become over 200, trimmed in silk and gold and worth 3,000 pesos or more apiece, a sum equal to half the annual income

---

[16] M. L. Conniff, 'Guayaquil through independence: urban development in a colonial system', *The Americas*, 33/3 (1977), 401.

[17] L. L. Greenow, 'Spatial dimensions of the credit market in eighteenth century Nueva Galicia', in Robinson, *Social fabric*, 227–79.

from an entailed estate (*mayorazgo*). Even the most affluent, with
fortunes of 300,000 or 400,000 ducats, suffered 'toil and anguish' to
maintain 'this empty pomp'. Persons worth as little as 20,000 were held
as poor. A large fraction of the city's wealth was displayed in furnishings
and jewellery; even the indigent possessed a gem or a gold or silver
plate. Lima's total stock of jewels and precious metals was calculated
at 20 million ducats, with the investment in slaves at 12 million – and
this exclusive of finery, tapestries, and articles of worship. So widespread
were luxurious habits of dress that one could scarcely distinguish social
groups. Merchants in Spain, where sumptuary laws applied, were
delighted at this distant outlet for silks, brocades, and fine linens. The
bulk of the city's fortunes were sunk in real estate (farms, vineyards,
sugar mills, ranches), *obrajes*, and encomiendas. Yet the total income
yielded by its fifteen or so *mayorazgos* was far exceeded by the million
ducats that flowed annually in salaries to ecclesiastics, bureaucrats, and
the military.

Buenos Aires, abandoned in 1541, was finally refounded in 1580 as
an Atlantic outlet for the inland settlements. Through their procurator
in Madrid the townsmen complained of the poverty of the region and
the lack of gunpowder, cloth, and wine for Mass. Trade with Upper
Peru was disallowed because Tucumán could supply it with agro-pastoral
products from a shorter distance. Accordingly, Spain authorized trade
between Buenos Aires and Brazil (then under the Spanish crown), first
(1595) for the import of slaves to expand agricultural production, then
(1602) to allow exports to Brazil of flour, dried beef, and tallow. Because
the Brazilian market was limited, merchants made their larger profits
on the re-export of slaves and tropical produce to Tucumán. Soon a
well-to-do class appeared, inflated by Portuguese immigrants. Bridling
at the threat to its fiscal interests, the crown abolished the Brazil trade
in 1622, limiting Buenos Aires to a yearly traffic with Spain of two 100-ton
ships. The possibilities for contraband, however, doomed to failure this
precarious design of maintaining a strategic outpost on the Plata estuary
while restraining its commercial development. Acarete du Biscay visited
the port in 1658, as he recalls in his *Account of a voyage up the Río de la
Plata, and thence over land to Peru* (London, 1698), to find a town of 400
earthen houses thatched with cane and straw and defended by only a
small earthen fort of ten guns, using twelve-pound ammunition or less,
and three 50-strong companies, captained by the vecinos and usually
undermanned because soldiers were 'drawn by the cheapness of Living

in those parts to desert frequently'. The houses, all of one storey, had spacious rooms, courtyards, and adjacent orchards and gardens. Beef, game, and fowl were cheap and plentiful, and while only 'the Savages' ate ostriches, their feathers made effective parasols for all. Better houses were 'adorn'd with Hangings, Pictures, and other Ornaments and decent Moveables' and served by many black, Indian, and mixed-blood servants. 'All the wealth of these Inhabitants consists in Cattle, which multiply so prodigiously in this Province, that the Plains are quite cover'd with 'em.' In the harbour Acarete found no less than 22 Dutch ships, each laden with some 14,000 hides bought for less than a crown apiece and saleable in Europe for five times as much. By now cattle were being sent to Peru as well; but although the cattle trade was profitable, the 'most considerable' merchants were 'they that Traffick in European Commodities'. The transfer of customs collection from Córdoba north to Salta and Jujuy in 1676 signalled Buenos Aires' domination of the whole Platine market.

Lima's merchants opposed a strong Buenos Aires–Tucumán regional economy that threatened their commercial sway over Upper Peru. They refused to buy cattle at the Salta fair and tried to corner the Charcas market through factors who intercepted produce from Buenos Aires and set their own price. Gradually, however, northern Argentina, Charcas, and even Chile fell from Lima's commercial control. The simple fact was that Buenos Aires was a more viable port than Lima-Callao. The expensive fleet system was not needed here; fewer pirates attacked ships, and less seaweed clogged their hulls at this latitude; shipments overland from Buenos Aires were cheaper and less troublesome than via Panama; contraband was less controlled at Buenos Aires, and *porteños* could pay with silver that had escaped the royal fifth; finally, after 1680 Sacramento was available as an immense warehouse. During the British *asiento* from 1713 to 1739, contraband opportunities increased, sales of hides and tallow jumped, and British commercial methods were learned. Population figures tell the story. While Lima's inhabitants remained steady at 55,000–60,000 for a century after 1740, those of Buenos Aires rose from 11,000 to 65,000. The elevation of the latter to a viceregal capital in 1776 authenticated commercial realities.

The Lima–Buenos Aires case exemplifies commercial forces that reshaped the settlement pattern of the whole southern continent and would eventually shift its economic axis from the Pacific to the Atlantic coast. Such forces, however, took hold also at the regional level, affecting the destinies of second-rank agro-administrative centres. Although the elite of Santiago de Chile drew its power and prestige primarily from landowning and political careers, the city's merchant interests managed to dominate producers in Chile's three main regional economies – those of Santiago, La Serena, and Concepción – to retard the growth of the last two and subordinate them to a commercial system that was centred on Santiago and oriented towards foreign suppliers and consumers.[18] In the Popayán region the early urban system underwent drastic redefinition, caused locally by changing mining locations and the shift from Indian to African slave labour, and externally by the rise of Cartagena as a port of entry (displacing Buenaventura) and the growth of textile manufactures in the Quito area. In the seventeenth century many centres became ghost towns, leaving Popayán, Pasto, and Cali as the urban mainstays. Popayán took the lead not by virtue of administrative rationalization from above – for its region was riven by cross-cutting civil, ecclesiastical, fiscal, and military jurisdictions – but by virtue of a privileged location for trade, mining and agro-pastoral pursuits, which in turn helped to consolidate its political role.[19]

In Mesoamerica Mexico City is the historic centre of bureaucratic, commercial, financial, and industrial dominance. Over the centuries it has internalized transformations that in South America are best exemplified successively in three cities: Lima (era of colonial mercantilism), Buenos Aires (era of commercial capitalism), and São Paulo (era of industrial, financial, and technological development). Yet the geography, resources, and settlement patterns of New Spain resisted such pervasive forms of spatial organization as Buenos Aires, São Paulo, and, most notably, Montevideo eventually imposed on their respective hinterlands. As James Lockhart has said, the Westernization of colonial Mexico did not occur in neatly concentric stages, 'since activity from the capital leapt great distances to areas of interest, leaving closer ones relatively isolated and unaffected'. It is possible to trace the growth of local resistance to the determination 'from without' of spatial organization and route patterns. It is true that economic and administrative requirements of the mother country reoriented the pre-Hispanic settle-

---

[18] M. Carmagnani, *Les mécanismes de la vie économique dans une société coloniale: le Chili (1680–1830)* (Paris, 1973).
[19] P. Marzahl, *Town in the empire: government, politics and society in seventeenth century Popayán* (Austin, 1978).

ment patterns of the central plateau or, in mineral and ranching zones, asserted themselves directly. Thus, wrote Moreno Toscano and Florescano:

> some Mexicans imagined the system as a huge mouth located in Spain and nourished by a wide conduit running from Mexico City to Cadiz via Jalapa and Veracruz which, in turn, was fed by lesser channels from the centres and cities of the interior. The route system linking centres and cities faithfully replicated that scheme.[20]

Yet this polarized pattern contained internal tensions and exceptions. Puebla, founded as a consolation prize for poorer Spaniards, soon attracted encomenderos, acquired an Indian workforce, and became a leading distribution centre for agricultural produce. The accretion of administrative, commercial, religious, and (as a textile producer) industrial functions allowed it to organize its own hinterland and on several counts resist domination by the capital. A similar case was Guadalajara, with its administrative, commercial, and educational functions. Another rivalry was that between the Veracruz merchants, who distributed imports via the Jalapa fair and were linked to Oaxaca and the Gulf coast's agricultural producers, and the Mexico City merchants, who sought control of the import trade and pressed for a route to the coast via Orizaba and bypassing Jalapa. Finally, there is the case of the Bajío, a prosperous agricultural and mining region supporting a network of specialized towns that resisted domination by either of the largest cities, Guanajuato or Querétaro. Here was an instance, unique for Mexico, of a complex, internally integrated regional economy. In its external relations it supplied agricultural products and raw materials to Mexico City while sending manufactures to northern Mexico in exchange for raw materials. Resulting profits were accumulated locally and not drained off to the capital.

In time, even modest agro-administrative centres became commercial catalysts for immediate hinterlands. For example, the original controls of taxation, forced labour, and administration emanating from Antequera over the Indian communities of Oaxaca were gradually complemented by trade involvements as market demands and cash reserves exerted their power. The city's growing need for pulque and other farm and ranch commodities not only increased rural production but

[20] A. Moreno Toscano and E. Florescano, 'El sector externo y la organización espacial y regional de México (1521–1910)', in J. W. Wilkie, M. C. Meyer and E. Monzón de Wilkie (eds.), *Contemporary Mexico* (Berkeley and Los Angeles, 1976), 67.

attracted village Indians to permanent or seasonal urban residence. Administration and regulation were no longer the rationale for Antequera's existence. According to William Taylor, 'trade, commerce, and manufacturing assumed new importance, and the city and countryside of the central valleys had begun to form a stronger regional system'.[21]

Urban places became important centres for the commercialization of Spanish American society and institutions, but ineffective vehicles for diffusing full-blown 'capitalism'. The spread of commercial impetus from cities and *pueblos de españoles*, for example, coexisted with 'commerce' for control and spoliation, as instanced by *corregidores* in their notorious practice of foisting useless merchandise at inflated prices on vulnerable Indian communities. Commercial activity was orchestrated within a framework of mercantilist design, patrician status objectives, and prebendary administration. Urban merchants failed to form a coherent and enduring 'class'. Lacking developed instruments and institutions for credit and financial accrual, they were adept at keeping open their options for social advancement and for orienting their progeny to alternative careers. Mario Góngora prefers to call the Chilean merchants a 'trading' (*negociante*) element, not a truly mercantile one, who pursued a *cursus honorum* that was 'part of an aristocratic, as opposed to mercantile or bourgeois, society'. Port cities, so often seedbeds for commercial innovation, were only intermittently active (Portobelo, the early Havana); or they served as stevedores to bureaucratic capitals (Veracruz, Callao, Valparaíso); or their commercial leadership was reinforced by core administrative, ecclesiastical, and service functions (Cartagena, Buenos Aires, Montevideo, the later Havana). In the 1690s the traveller Gamelli Carreri described Acapulco, with its makeshift houses of wood, mud, and straw, as a 'humble village of fishermen', not an emporium for trade with Guatemala, Peru, and the Orient and port of call for the Manila galleons. When ships from Peru arrived their merchants, carrying millions of pesos for Oriental finery, had to lodge in the miserable shacks of the town's mulattos.[22]

Cities were bastions of the Spanish political order and not conspicuous centres of innovative ideology and programmatic institutional change. This helps account for the diffuse quality of lower-class protest in the

---

[21] W. B. Taylor, 'Town and country in the valley of Oaxaca, 1750–1812', in I. Altman and J. Lockhart (eds.), *Provinces of early Mexico* (Berkeley and Los Angeles, 1976), 74.

[22] Gamelli Carreri's impressions of seventeenth-century Mexican cities are in *Las cosas más considerables vistas en la Nueva España* (Mexico, 1946).

late colonial years and for the decentralization of political structures
after independence and the flow of power to the rural domain. Even
so, it would be misleading to conceive of the colonial urban system
simply, in the imagery quoted above, as a huge mouth located in Spain
and fed by conduits running through the urban hierarchies of the Indies.
Semi-autonomous subsystems took shape, sometimes strong enough to
challenge the imperial prescription. Their vigour derived, however, not
from a 'capitalist' ethic but from their success at regional replication
of the Spanish metropolitan design, a process referred to by such
expressions as 'interiorization of the metropolis' or, more tendentiously,
'internal colonialism'. A classic example of how the city's 'develop-
mental' role was conceived is the proposal of a Mexico City magistrate
for the 'illness' of Hispaniola. In 1699 the *oidor* F. J. de Haro y
Monterroso advocated that the capital of Santo Domingo be transferred
to a central inland site, assembling the population of a score of scattered
villages and receiving the royal bureaucracies, the university, and the
colleges. 'The Court is the image of the heart', he wrote, 'and like it
should be located virtually in the centre so that justice and assistance
may be rendered with the greatest uniformity and dispatch.' Under such
conditions,

the Church, Tribunals, and Communities draw everything with them. Merchants, students, and claimants throng the highways: their trips increase the
welfare of many; neighbouring places benefit from consumption of their
produce, and the Royal Treasury profits from the numerous inns and
markets.[23]

The advice was never taken (although a similar proposal appeared as
late as 1858 in the Constitution of the Dominican Republic), but it
expresses a symptomatic view of the city as a patrimonial centre destined
simultaneously to stimulate, control, and hierarchize the forces making
for economic change.

LATE COLONIAL CHANGE

From the mid eighteenth century until the era of national independence
75 years later the urbanization of Spanish America can be related to three

[23] 'Medidas propuestas para poblar sin costo alguno (de) la Real Hacienda de la Isla de Santo
Domingo', in E. Rodríguez Demorizi (ed.), *Relaciones históricas de Santo Domingo* (Ciudad
Trujillo, 1942), 345–59.

Table 2 *Populations of larger Spanish American cities as a percentage of respective 'national' populations in selected years*

4 largest cities of Argentina	24 (1778)	14 (1817)
4 largest cities of Venezuela	15 (1772)	10 (1810)
3 largest cities of Chile	16 (1758)	9 (1813)
3 largest cities of Cuba	35 (1774)	22 (1817)
2 largest cities of Peru	8 (*c.* 1760)	7 (1820)
largest city of Mexico	2.9 (1742)	2.2 (1793)
largest city of Uruguay	30 (1769)	18 (1829)

general trends: faster population growth, Bourbon reform policies, and economic changes.

Having held somewhat steady at very roughly ten million inhabitants for a century or more, the population of the region rose to perhaps double that number by about 1825. Natural increase occurring with improved health conditions and the recuperation of Indian populations greatly assisted the upturn. So too did immigration. The eighteenth-century data so far collected, whether for European immigration or for European-born residents in America, are too deficient to allow a sequel to Mörner's perhaps conservative estimate of 440,000 Spanish transatlantic migrants for the period 1500–1650. Certainly a steady flow continued. For imports of African slaves Curtin's estimated yearly averages of 3,500 for the period 1601–1760 show a rise to 6,150 for 1761–1810.

General population growth contributed to urban growth, whether large cities, small towns, or fresh nuclei in frontier areas. When, however, we compare population increases in large cities with increases in what were to become the respective national territories, we find that the urban share declined during the decades before independence. The totals that supply the percentages in table 2 are sketchy, but the cumulative tendency is persuasive. Figures for several secondary centres corroborate this decline. From 1760 to 1784 the population of Trujillo, in coastal Peru, dropped from 56.5 per cent to 48.1 per cent of the provincial total,[24] while the three leading towns of central highland Ecuador – Latacunga, Ambato, and Riobamba – slipped from 9.6 per

[24] K. Coleman, 'Provincial urban problems: Trujillo, Peru, 1600–1784' in Robinson, *Social fabric*, 369–408.

cent (1778) to 4.6 per cent (1825) of the regional population, a trend associated here with natural disasters, economic depression, and the independence wars.[25]

The sources of population growth just reviewed explain in part the pattern of lagging urbanization. The decrease in Indian mortality rates was registered primarily in rural areas, where most of the Indians lived. Higher imports of African slaves went largely to rural areas; in fact, more than half the slaves introduced to Spanish America during 1774–1807 went to Cuba, with its burgeoning sugar economy. Spanish immigration, which may have fallen from earlier levels, presumably favoured urban centres, but here, as noted, data are weak. The uprooting of Indian communities, proletarianization of rural workers, and poverty in some of the mining areas swelled internal cityward migrations; but urban health conditions reduced their impact on urban growth. There were a minimum of 124,000 deaths from epidemics in Mexico City in the eighteenth century and 135,000 in Puebla. The 1764 smallpox epidemic in Caracas killed perhaps one-quarter of its population of 26,340.

If scattered statistics fail to show net urban growth, the Bourbon era did witness qualitative urbanization in the form of urban services, city planning, and elegant neoclassical public construction. The long-standing policy of urban nucleation was revived, particularly for colonization and frontier defence. Generally, in fact, Bourbon reform measures tended to favour decentralization of urban systems.

Mexico City received a new aqueduct, mint, custom house, and school of mines, and the Academy of San Carlos. The Alameda was doubled in length, shaded *paseos* were laid out, and the city's policing, paving, and street lighting were improved. Lima offered a cleaner slate for such modernization after its devastating earthquake of 1746. In towns throughout the Platine viceroyalty royal officials restored cathedrals, paved streets, improved drainage, and built schools, hospitals, aqueducts, bridges, granaries, and theatres. Santiago de Chile saw a wave of public construction and urban redesign after the 1760s, crowned by the work of the Italian architect, engineer, and urbanist Joaquín Toesca, who designed the cathedral, the Casa de Moneda, and the retaining walls of the Mapocho river. Dismayed by the rudimentary state of

---

[25] R. D. F. Bromley, 'The role of commerce in the growth of towns in central highland Ecuador 1750–1920', in W. Borah, J. Hardoy, and G. A. Stelter (eds.), *Urbanization in the Americas: the background in comparative perspective* (Ottawa, 1980), 25–34.

communications in their realm, viceroys assigned to New Granada after 1739 did what they could to improve the road system centring on the capital; in the 1790s Bogotá received its first police force, public cemetery, theatre, and newspaper.

The work of creating new towns was conspicuous in the increasingly productive regions of Chile and north-west Argentina, after 1735 under an expressly created Junta de Poblaciones and, from 1783 to 1797, under supervision of the intendant of Córdoba, the Marqués de Sobremonte. The new towns policy aimed to assemble dispersed rural populations in towns and villages and to bring Indians into *reducciones* or racially mixed centres. In addition to the foundings, some towns were reorganized or even rebuilt and resettled while others, like Concepción, were moved to new sites. The purposes envisioned were to bring schooling and administrative control to rural people, improve productivity, catechize Indians, and strengthen defences against hostile Indians. In all, some 80 new towns took root. Similar initiatives were taken in New Granada, two notable ones being a town founded in 1753 exclusively for convicts and named for Saint Anthony, patron saint of delinquents, and authorization for a community of runaway blacks to choose their own officers and to exclude white residents save for a priest. Distinctive among the frontier settlements in the Interior Provinces of northern Mexico were the 21 missions established in California between 1769 and 1823 and the new-style *presidios* which, as projected under a *reglamento* of 1772, anticipated the future boundary between Mexico and the United States. Although far from modern by European standards of the times, the *presidio* was greatly expanded over the primitive guard posts in the Chichimeca territory of two centuries before. It was now a spacious compound, hundreds of feet along a side, and enclosed by angular bastions and salient gun platforms. *Presidios* became internment centres for hostile Indians but also attracted, in addition to soldiers' families, those of whites, mestizos, and pacified Indians who sought protection and markets for their produce. By 1779 that at San Antonio, Texas with its surrounding *villa* contained 240 military, including families, and 1,117 civilians.

The creation of new towns, missions, and *presidios* had a combined effect of urban nucleation and systemic decentralization. Selectively it amounted to a new surge of conquest and settlement. This 'decentralization' of the late Bourbon period, however, was not the policy idealized by modern planners whereby local centres receive increased authority in day-to-day decision-making. Rather it was a policy aimed at dissolving emergent New World hierarchies and submitting the component parts to metropolitan control. Thus in New Spain after 1760 the intendant system was designed to increase royal power at the expense of corporations and privileged persons. Creation of twelve new administrative entities dependent on royal power rather than local elites interposed between Mexico City and local districts a series of subcapitals enjoying new administrative, judicial, and fiscal functions. In weakening viceregal power the crown achieved centralization by ostensible decentralization. Simultaneous commercial reforms broke the trade monopoly of Mexico City, favouring merchants in Veracruz and Guadalajara, who received their own *consulados* in 1795.

If the late Bourbon decades produced challenges to the older administrative capitals, they favoured accretion and consolidation of functions in hitherto peripheral centres. In the case of Buenos Aires, already discussed, the city's elevation to viceregal status recognized its prior control of a commercial hinterland. In its course towards primacy at the other end of the continent Caracas was more dependent on official reinforcement. On the eve of independence Humboldt observed that Venezuela's wealth was not 'directed at one point' and that it had several urban centres of 'commerce and civilization'. Over the centuries, however, Caracas, with certain marginal advantages of climate and location, had been favoured by successive increments of bureaucratic and cultural functions. The city's evolution can be seen as a complex interaction of economic advantage, political favour, and bureaucratic monopoly. After 1750, in John Lombardi's words, 'Caracas' centrality was created by the Spanish imperial government to serve the economic and military needs of that dying empire'. By a series of administrative decisions from 1777 to 1803 Caracas became seat of the new captaincy general, an *audiencia*, an intendancy, a *consulado*, and an archbishopric. Caracas' effective political control of Venzuela was still problematical; its communication with even nearby rural zones was precarious; other cities were more strategically placed for overseas trade. Yet the accrual of administrative functions gave the city a magnetic force that outlasted the turmoil of independence and the economic and political divisiveness of the early republican decades to ensure its pivotal role is national integration after 1870.

An important source of change for settlement patterns was the growing production for export made possible by expanding metropolitan markets and by the larger, faster ships employed in ocean trade. Port cities that were not merely 'stevedores' but themselves commanded productive hinterlands became particularly active: the sugar port of Havana, the cacao port of Guayaquil, the agro-pastoral port of Buenos Aires. Many inland towns also prospered, as did Antequera, which profited from the cochineal trade and a revived textile industry to evolve after 1740, in J. K. Chance's words, 'from a small, inward-looking agro-town into a highly commercial export centre of considerable size'. Though one might catalogue many more urban loci that responded to agricultural, mining, industrial, and commercial stimuli, we will here restrict ourselves to some broad generalizations about the pervasive effects of commercialization on patterns of settlement.

The eighteenth century witnessed an intensification and specialization of agro-pastoral production for foreign markets that has continued up to modern times. This trend signified many changes in the mode of production: a shift from labour-intensive to more technified, rationalized, and capital-intensive systems; a redirection of profits from consumption to productive infrastructure; new needs for intermediaries, credit facilities, and suppliers in urban centres; and, except for slave-based plantations, a shift from a workforce subject to paternalistic or coercive controls to a deracinated and underemployed 'rural proletariat'. These changes had various implications for urban development. Strategic maritime ports became more active. Larger cities prospered from financial and commercial activity. Patriciates were attracted to urban centres of power, providing a clientele for amenities and improved services. In rural areas, however, the export economies failed to strengthen settlement networks as they had the power and resources of privileged cities. New amenities and services went to latifundia, not to small towns. Commodity flows followed export channels, leaving regional urban networks weak. Traditional villages and *resguardos* were disrupted but not replaced by small commercial towns. Rural workers released from traditional settings who were not absorbed into peonage gained spatial mobility and entered the money economy, but as underemployed migrants, as members of the urban *lumpen*, or as residents of impoverished, makeshift villages. Woodrow Borah has described the impromptu late colonial rural clusters as being frequently 'a thickening of settlement at an existing crossroads, rancho, or hacienda', adapted to existing irregular roads and trails without resort to a formal grid.

The trends just indicated were not yet pre-emptive, and the patterning effects on urban systems of commodity exports, the rise to primacy of selected capitals, and proletarianization of rural workers were not to take more definitive hold until the era of national integration and accentuation of export dependency in the late nineteenth century. A modern planner transported to late Bourbon Spanish America might well have applauded the urban decentralization and colonization policies of the crown. He would have approved of the flourishing manufactures in regions outside the chief administrative centres, such as the Bajío, the Socorro region of New Granada, and the interior cities of the Platine viceroyalty. He would have noted that the rise in exports was accompanied in many places by higher levels and greater diversity of production for domestic consumption and thus by growing integration of economic regions. He would have been refreshed by the climate of intellectual inquiry and concern for applied science to be found in the urban environment. He might in fact have ventured to infer that large areas of Spanish America had embarked on modern economic 'development'. Whatever its basis for the Bourbon years, such a prognosis would not have held good for the early decades of independence. The independence wars themselves damaged productive facilities and many urban centres. As the new nations took form, the city-based bureaucracies of empire were dismantled, and political structures, particularly in the larger countries, were elaborated from provincial bases where wealth and power were more readily reconstituted. The achievements of domestic manufacturing were virtually cancelled by cheap foreign imports as the large cities became commercial headquarters for what have controversially been called new 'informal empires'. Statistically, the 'deurbanization' already discussed for the eighteenth century continued well into the nineteenth; but its causes and significance were in many ways altered by the independence wars and their aftermath.

4

MINING IN COLONIAL SPANISH AMERICA[1]

'Gold is the loftiest and most esteemed metal that the earth brings forth... Among other virtues which nature has bestowed on it, one is singular – that it comforts the weakness of the heart and engenders joy and magnanimity, takes away melancholy, and clears the eyes of cloudiness...'[2] So wrote a Spanish goldsmith half a century after the conquest of New Spain. Cortés perhaps spoke with less cynical intent than is often thought when he told Montezuma's messenger, 'I and my companions suffer from a disease of the heart which can be cured only with gold'.[3] But it was not so much gold as silver that awaited Spain in America. The accumulated gold of centuries was looted during the two decades, 1520–40, which saw the Spanish military conquest of Middle and South America. Thereafter, though gold was mined in varying and often substantial amounts, silver predominated in both volume and value produced.

[1] This chapter concerns the mining of precious metals: silver and, to a lesser extent, gold. Base metal ores, despite their common occurrence in Spanish America, were little exploited during the colonial period. The central Andes, particularly Charcas, was the region best endowed with such ores, and probably the most active in copper, tin and lead production. Copper was also produced in Chile and in Cuba, particularly in the sixteenth century, and in New Spain at various mines in Puebla, Jalisco and Michoacán. The iron supply was almost entirely imported from Spain. Indeed it generally seems to have been cheaper to import base metals than to produce them in America. An abundance of pearls was discovered around the island of Margarita, off the Venezuelan coast, during the early exploration of the Caribbean, but was depleted in the early decades of the sixteenth century. The emerald mines of eastern New Granada, however, which the Spanish learned of in the sixteenth century, continue to produce today.

In this chapter, colonial provincial names have been used. Thus New Spain corresponds to modern Mexico, New Granada to Colombia, Quito to Ecuador, Peru to Peru more or less as it presently exists, Charcas to highland Bolivia, Río de la Plata to central and northern Argentina.

[2] Juan de Arfe y Villafañe, *Quilatador de la plata, oro y piedras* (Valladolid, 1572; facsimile reproduction, Madrid, 1976), fo. 23v.

[3] Francisco López de Gómara, *Cortés. The life of the conqueror by his secretary* (Berkeley and Los Angeles, 1966), 58.

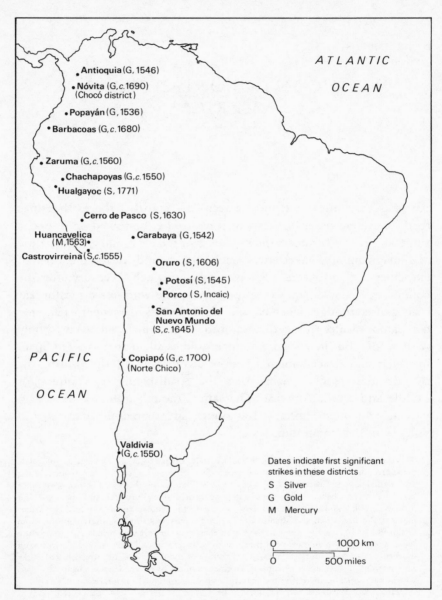

Centres of major mining districts in Spanish South America

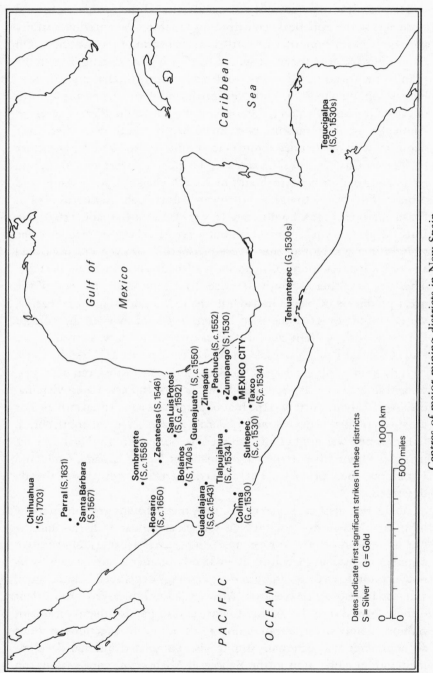

Centres of major mining districts in New Spain

Chihuahua
(S, 1703)

Parral (S, 1631)

Santa Bárbara
(S, 1567)

Sombrerete
(S, c.1558)

Rosario
(S, c.1650)

Zacatecas (S, 1546)

San Luis Potosí
(S, G, c.1592)

Bolaños
(S, 1740s)

Guanajuato (S, c.1550)

Zimapán

Pachuca (S, c.1552)

Zumpango (S, 1530)

Guadalajara
(S, G, c.1543)

Tlalpujahua
(S, c.1534)

MEXICO CITY

Taxco
(S, c.1534)

Colima
(G, c.1530)

Sultepec
(S, c.1530)

Tehuantepec (G, 1530s)

Tegucigalpa
(S, G, 1530s)

Caribbean   Sea

Gulf of
Mexico

PACIFIC

OCEAN

Dates indicate first significant strikes in these districts
S = Silver   G = Gold

1000 km

500 miles

The search for sources of both metals carried the Spaniards far and wide across the Americas, contributing much to the amazing rapidity with which they explored and settled their portion of the continent. On the promise of gold they first settled the Caribbean; finding little in the islands, they were lured on by golden visions to the Isthmus, then to New Spain, then to Peru. Both New Spain and Peru, as well as the north of New Granada, yielded gold booty. But even before Pizarro received Atahualpa's golden ransom, New Spain had begun to reveal her silver deposits, with discoveries about 1530 at Sultepec and Zumpango, close to Mexico City. In 1534, Taxco and Tlalpujahua were in action; and by 1543–4 the far western mines of New Galicia (Espíritu Santo and others). Then came the great northward silver rush: Zacatecas (1546), Guanajuato (*c.* 1550), Sombrerete (*c.* 1558), Santa Bárbara (1567), San Luis Potosí (*c.* 1592), to mention but a few. In the rear Pachuca came to light in 1552. Not all these were prosperous or even much worked at first; but the pattern of deposits was made clear in a few decades. The same was true in South America. In the late 1530s the first of the great goldfields of New Granada, in the Cauca and Magdalena basins, were located; by 1541 the gold of central Chile; in 1542 the gold of Carabaya in the eastern central Andes. By then silver was on the scene also: Gonzalo Pizarro worked the old Inca deposits at Porco by 1538. And the richest silver strike of them all, at nearby Potosí, came in 1545, to be followed by many lesser finds in Charcas. In Peru, Castrovirreina, discovered about 1555, was the first of numerous substantial strikes. For most of colonial times, however, Peru's greatest mineral contribution to the empire was not bullion, but mercury, discovered at Huancavelica in 1563. Other silver strikes were made in New Granada, Chile and Honduras, but proved trivial in comparison with those already described.

As the rich districts began to disgorge metal, towns grew up in many inhospitable regions – coastal New Granada, highland Charcas and the north Mexican plateau, for example – where only sparse and primitive populations had lived before. Roads and commerce spread rapidly as new economic circuits, energized by mining, developed. Cloth, wine, and iron from Spain, slaves from Africa, silks and spices from the Orient – these flowed into the mining towns; and to pay for them streams of bullion, mainly silver, began to flow in the opposite directions. But not all commerce was external. Mining also stimulated internal development: grain cultivation in the Bajío and Michoacán, wine making on the Peruvian coast and in Chile, cattle and mule raising in the Río de la Plata provinces, textiles in Peru and Quito; and everywhere freighting and craftwork. Very few large regions escaped the influence of the bullion flows.

Nature, in the guise of Tertiary orogenesis, had provided the wide dispersal of mineral wealth that gave rise to these currents. During the uplift of the Andean and Mexican ranges in the Tertiary age, rock fissures in many regions were filled with metallic minerals, among them those of silver. Far from all the resulting silver veins were rich, but enough were so to make the silver-mining centre a characteristic settlement over much of New Spain and the Andes. The veins were often formed at great heights – up to 15,700 feet at Potosí, for example – and mining settlements were therefore also high. Almost all were above 10,000 feet in Peru and Charcas, and between 6,000 and 8,000 in New Spain. Gold, conversely, was normally mined at lower levels, since most of it lay in alluvial deposits below the ranges from which it had been removed by hydraulic action. Many such deposits lay in rain forests, which presented their own difficulties of access and living conditions. Gold, by its chemical nature, appeared as native metal or as an alloy; not so silver, which was only occasionally found in a native state, but rather in compounds resulting from its reaction with other substances. Some of these compounds were useful ores. A brief account of the formation and nature of these will serve as a useful introduction to colonial mining and refining techniques.

The initial silver ores deposited in rock fissures from sources deep in the earth are known as hypogene or primary ores. These are normally sulphides. They may be rich – at Guanajuato they were – but frequently are not; and most of the great Spanish American silver centres drew their wealth from hypogene ores that had been enriched. This might happen in two ways. First, the action of descending water oxidized the hypogene sulphides, usually converting them into silver chloride (cerargyrite), which contains a higher proportion of silver. This enrichment by oxidation ceased, however, at the water table, since below it there was no free oxygen. But enrichment did continue below the water table through a second process – a rather complex one named secondary supergene enrichment, which produced sulphides of a higher silver content than that of the hypogene sulphides. Put simply, the effect of these processes was to create a zone of rich ores somewhat above and below the water table: silver chloride above, and sulphide below.

The difference between the two ore types was well known to colonial miners. The chloride ores were called *pacos* in the Andes and *colorados* in New Spain (the redness or brownness implicit in these names coming from the limonite, or blended soft iron oxides, generally found in the oxidized zone). *Pacos* were, for example, the common ores of the Potosí mountain, which was well oxidized 1,000 feet downwards from its summit. Chlorides were generally easy to refine by smelting or amalgamation. Sulphides were universally known as *negrillos*. Though they might be enriched through the supergene process, their sulphur content caused many problems of refining. In general, then, miners could expect increasing yields with depth, down to and beyond the water table, which generally lay at several hundred feet. But the chlorides, above the water table, were more profitable because easily refined. Once a mine dipped below the water table, not only intractability of ores but also flooding presented problems. There was then good reason to seek shallower chlorides elsewhere. The cyclical output of some districts was perhaps the result of a pattern of events deriving from the nature of the ore deposits, which may be summarized in this way: initial discovery of rich chlorides – output rises; deeper workings with some flooding and occurrence of sulphides – output levels off; further flooding and predominance of sulphides – output falls; new prospecting, revealing further shallow chlorides – output rises; and so on.

EXTRACTIVE TECHNIQUES

'Observing the working of mines in New Spain in general...one is surprised to find still in its infancy an art which has been practised in America for three centuries...'[4] So wrote the German traveller and mining engineer, Alexander von Humboldt, of the mining of silver ore in early nineteenth-century New Spain. He found powder wasted, workings made larger than necessary for adequate ventilation, and above all a lack of communication between different mine levels and shafts, which prevented the use of trolleys and animals to extract ore. Ore extraction was doubtless a less sophisticated and efficient process than the subsequent refining. But some qualification of Humboldt's judgement must be made.

The colonial silver miner normally attacked a vein with an open pit,

---

[4] Alexander von Humboldt, *Ensayo político sobre el reino de la Nueva España* (Mexico, 1966), 365 (book 4, ch. 11).

then burrowed deeper in search of particularly rich concentrations of ore. This procedure, which led to twisting, narrow tunnels, was sometimes called in New Spain the *sistema del rato* (meaning the 'opportunistic system', but later translated into English, wrongly but graphically, as the 'rat-hole system'). It persisted in small mines throughout, and indeed beyond, colonial times. The *sistema del rato* has been blamed for many colonial mining problems. But the method arose naturally and had certain advantages. It developed because the early miners were mostly amateurs. There were insufficient professionals initially in America to instil good underground practices into the thousands of individual prospectors who roamed the mining districts. And the crown did nothing to encourage rational exploitation of ores – rather, indeed, the opposite. It was anxious to maximize royalties on ·refined metals, and held that freedom of prospecting and extraction would lead to maximum production. Furthermore, laws limiting the size of claims to some 110 by 50 yards brought a proliferation of small mines, hardly worth exploiting carefully. Finally, the availability of Indian labour militated against good planning of workings: rather than cut special vertical shafts, for example, to extract ore with winches, it was cheaper to use the *sistema del rato* and employ labourers to carry out material through the resulting serpentine passages. This was particularly true in the early decades, when Indian labour was plentiful; by the later sixteenth century it was growing scarcer and dearer, and the signs of rationalization in workings that are visible by then probably resulted in part from this contraction of the labour supply.

The first notable improvement and rationalization of underground workings came with the cutting of adits (*socavones*): slightly rising tunnels driven from the surface to intersect the lower galleries of a mine. Adits provided ventilation, drainage and easy extraction of ore and waste. An adit was obviously most advantageous when driven into concentrated workings, cutting several mines at one blow. Such concentration existed at the peak of the Potosí mountain; so it is not surprising to find an adit begun there in 1556, nor that by the early 1580s there should have been nine in operation. In New Spain, even the great centres lacked such concentration of ores and mines. Nevertheless, Potosí's Mexican namesake, San Luis Potosí, used an adit to excellent effect in the early seventeenth century to exploit its main source of ores, the Cerro de San Pedro. Adits were by then a standard part of subterranean technique, and remained so. Adits also served to consolidate workings into larger systems. Miners began to pursue such consolidation by the mid-seventeenth century, buying adjacent claims and linking them with adits and galleries. The scale of these integrated workings grew with time, and was remarkable in some cases by the late eighteenth century, when large mining companies appeared. These might have numerous partners whose capital financed extensive underground workings. Here the Valenciana enterprise at Guanajuato stands as the supreme example – 'an underground city', according to one historian.[5] This was precisely the mine that Humboldt criticized. But, with its masonry-reinforced galleries, its many faces, its vertical shafts (especially the great octagonal San José shaft, 1,800 feet deep by 1810, and 33 feet across), the Valenciana was a far cry from the early 'rat-holes'. Large-scale integration occurred elsewhere in Mexico, but was rarer in South America, for reasons not yet elucidated.

Three other, more purely technological, developments in extraction may be mentioned. By the late sixteenth century pumps (*bombas*) were occasionally used for draining mines. These were probably lift, force or rag and chain pumps on the patterns shown in book VI of Agricola's *De re metallica*, a work consulted by Spanish American miners.[6] Some at least of the pumps built were human-powered. Water was also lifted in large hide bags, which could be dragged up sloping tunnels, whereas pumps required special vertical shafts. Animal-powered whims were possibly used for this task. Whims were the second notable technological development. By the eighteenth century in New Spain they had become a common means of extracting both water and ore, though they appear less frequent in the Andean mines. As mine workings grew, whims became more powerful. In the great Valenciana shaft no fewer than eight whims operated simultaneously. These were driven by mules or horses. Steam power did not reach Spanish America until the second decade of the nineteenth century. The third technological advance demanding comment is blasting. Its first European use was in Germany in 1627; but exactly when it was adopted in America is unclear. There is rather uncertain evidence for it at Huancavelica by 1635, and unequivocal evidence for it in the Potosí district in the 1670s. In the eighteenth century blasting was a standard technique and probably contributed

[5] D. A. Brading, *Miners and merchants in Bourbon Mexico, 1763–1810* (Cambridge, 1971), 287.

[6] Georgius Agricola, *De re metallica* (Basle, 1556), Eng. trans. Herbert Clark Hoover and Lou Henry Hoover (London, 1912).

much to the revival of Spanish American silver production in the first half of the century and to the extraordinary boom of the second.

The practices described so far were applicable to vein mining for gold, though such workings were far smaller than the typical silver mine. Gold vein mines were, moreover, unusual; the main examples occurred in the highlands of New Granada. Most gold came from alluvial deposits, from which it was extracted by placering techniques.

PROCESSING

Silver ore was broken up at the mine to eliminate useless material accompanying it. The resulting concentrate was then ready for processing, which was normally accomplished by amalgamation in a refinery known in New Spain as an *hacienda de minas* and in the Andes as an *ingenio*. The amalgamation refinery was a complex plant. Typically it consisted of a large walled square containing storerooms, stables, a chapel, accommodation for owner and workers, machinery to crush ores, tanks or paved courts to amalgamate them, and vats to wash them. Refineries were usually gathered in mining towns where they could take advantage of concentrated services and supplies, such as labour, crafts (especially carpentry and smithery), and food. Around 1600 Potosí, then at its zenith, had some 65 refineries; and New Spain a total of some 370. At any moment in colonial Spanish America there were probably 400–700 refineries operating, the number varying with prevailing conditions of boom or depression.

At the refinery the concentrated ore was milled to a fine, sand-like consistency, to ensure maximum contact between the silver minerals and mercury during amalgamation, and hence the maximum yield of silver. A stamp mill was the normal means of milling – a simple but massive machine consisting of a number of heavy iron-shod stamps (commonly six to eight of them) which were lifted in turn by cams fixed to a heavy rotating shaft, and allowed to fall on to a stone bed sometimes equipped with iron mortar blocks (see fig. 1). Each stamp shoe weighed up to 150 lb. Sometimes double mills were built, in which a single shaft extended on both sides of a central, vertical water-wheel. The total number of stamps in this case might reach sixteen.

Stamp mills were driven by water, or by horses or mules. (Human-powered mills existed at Potosí in the early 1570s, but quickly

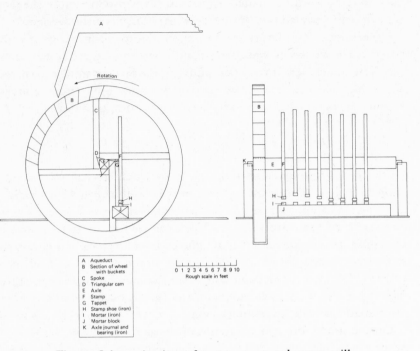

A   Aqueduct
B   Section of wheel
    with buckets
C   Spoke
D   Triangular cam
E   Axle
F   Stamp
G   Tappet
H   Stamp shoe (iron)
I   Mortar (iron)
J   Mortar block
K   Axle journal and
    bearing (iron)

0 1 2 3 4 5 6 7 8 9 10
Rough scale in feet

Fig. 1. Schematic view of a water-powered stamp mill

disappeared because of their inefficiency.) The choice of power source depended on local circumstances. Much of New Spain, for instance, lacked water enough to drive machinery, while many Andean districts were too barren to sustain the necessary animals. Thus, around 1600, only about a third of Mexican mills were water-powered, and these were mostly in central New Spain, a wetter region than the northern plateau; while in Potosí at the same time hardly any animal-driven mills remained, owing to lack of pasture and the consequent building of dams and aqueducts that provided water for year-round milling. Records from Potosí in the 1570s suggest, furthermore, that in general water-driven mills were more productive per unit of capital and labour employed in them than those driven by animals. For an equal capital investment in plant, a water-driven mill crushed over twice the quantity of ore in a day that an animal-powered mill would process, while the productivity of labour (the amount of ore milled per Indian worker per

day) was perhaps five times higher in the water-driven mill. Mining
districts well supplied with water were therefore at a distinct advantage.

Other types of milling devices existed – for example, the ancient
machine consisting of a large stone disc rolling on its edge over a
circular stone bed; but the stamp mill, with its large capacity, rapidly
prevailed in the major districts. Its design was already well established
in Europe when extensive ore processing began in America, and is
clearly illustrated in book VIII of Agricola's *De re metallica*. If further
pulverization of ore were required, another device might be used,
variously known as a *tahona, arrastre* or *arrastra*. This simple apparatus
consisted of a stone bed enclosed by a low circular wall, with one or
more hard, heavy stones suspended from a beam pivoted on a post at
the centre of the bed. Animals pulled the beam around, dragging the
stone over the bed. Ore placed on this was ground to a fineness which,
according to Humboldt, was unequalled in any European mining
centre. Nevertheless the *tahona*, though a design known from earliest
colonial times, seems to have been used mainly in eighteenth-century
New Spain – and not in all centres there. Its absence in other times and
places remains to be explained.

Once crushed, ore was ready for amalgamation. This slow but sure
process sustained the great edifice of silver production, because it
allowed cheap refining of the great masses of low-yielding ore available
in Spanish America. Debate continues over the identity of the originators
of the process in America, and indeed over whether it was an original
invention there at all. The general view is that the "inventor" was
Bartolomé de Medina, a Spaniard from Seville who, with some German
technical advice, pioneered the technique in New Spain in the early
1550s. It is generally accepted that though the principle of amalgamation
had been known since classical times, its first use on an industrial scale
came in the New World. It was so used in several Mexican centres in
the late 1550s, and in the central Andes from 1571 – the delay there
possibly resulting from the later discovery of the Andean mines and the
consequent later availability in them of good smelting ores, which made
amalgamation unnecessary for a time.

The classic amalgamation procedure in America took place on a *patio*
– a large, flat, stone-paved surface, sometimes roofed. On this, according
to one account, milled ore (*harina*) was piled in heaps (*montones*) of some
2,000–3,500 lb; then common salt was mixed in at the rate of $2\frac{1}{2}$–3 lb

per 100 lb (*quintal*) of ore. Other reagents might also be used. The commonest was roasted copper pyrites (*magistral*), added at the rate of 8–12 lb per *montón*. Then mercury was squeezed out over the ore through the weave of a sturdy cloth bag in the proportion of 10–12 lb per *montón*. Finally water was added, and the heap spread out to form a *torta* up to 90 feet across. Combination of silver and mercury now proceeded by chemical affinity, helped by much agitation. For most of colonial times Indians did this, paddling bare-legged through the muddy concoction; only in the 1780s were they replaced by horses or mules. After some time, normally six to eight weeks (though extremes of three weeks to five months occurred, depending on refining skill, ambient temperature and the nature of the ore) the refinery supervisor (*azoguero* or *beneficiador*) would determine by assay that the maximum possible fusion of silver and mercury had occurred, and the mixture was shovelled into a washing apparatus, commonly a large vat (*tina*) fitted with a paddle rotated by animal or water power. Water was then passed through the vat, carrying off waste while the heavy amalgam (*pella*) settled. The *pella* was then packed into a sock-like canvas bag, which was twisted to expel free mercury. Final separation of silver and mercury occurred by volatilization under a metal or clay hood, heat being applied to the *pella* from below, causing the mercury to vaporize. The hood itself was cooled so that the vapour condensed on the inner surface and metallic mercury was recovered.

The *patio* process was the standard technique in New Spain from the early seventeenth century on. Before then amalgamation was performed there in wooden troughs (*canoas*). In the Andean centres the *patio* was hardly, if ever, used. Generally in the Andes, refiners employed stone tanks (*cajones*) for amalgamation, each large enough to take 5,000 lb of ore and often, at least in the sixteenth century, built on vaulting so that a fire could be made beneath them. This moderated the low temperatures of the high Andes, accelerating amalgamation. After about 1600, however, and possibly because of the growing scarcity and cost of fuel, artificial heating died out, and refiners used only the sun's warmth.

The chemistry of amalgamation is complex. According to Modesto Bargalló, the modern authority on colonial refining, the basic equations are (in the case of silver sulphides):

$$CuSO_4 + 2NaCl \rightarrow CuCl_2 + Na_2SO_4$$
$$CuCl_2 + Ag_2S \rightarrow 2AgCl + CuS$$
$$2AgCl + nHg \rightarrow Hg_{n-2}Ag_2(\text{amalgam}) + Hg_2Cl_2$$

while other subsidiary silver-yielding reactions take place simultaneously.[7] Colonial refiners were, of course, ignorant of these chemical
processes. Their knowledge was purely empirical. Rapidly there
emerged from experience a series of accepted steps to be followed if
ore were of this or that appearance, or if mercury took on this or that
colour during amalgamation. These practices, often effective, were the
outcome of continual experimentation. Far from all of this was fruitful;
but a few important discoveries did emerge, the most profitable of them
being that of the utility of *magistral*, copper sulphate obtained by
roasting pyrites. This substance, as is clear from the equations just given,
was an integral part of amalgamation, especially in the processing of
sulphide ores. Its value may well have been discovered in Potosí in the
1580s. If so, the practice of adding *magistral* spread quickly, since it
clearly was present in northern New Spain before 1600, where it notably
improved yields. Before then Mexican refiners had probably relied,
unknowingly, on whatever natural copper sulphate their ores contained,
with erratic results.

No other single innovation in refining was as effective as *magistral*.
But small adjustments of amalgamation to local conditions took place
constantly throughout Spanish America, with positive results. And
when the crown in the late eighteenth century sent to America German
experts to teach the latest amalgamation method (that of the Baron von
Born, which was in fact an elaboration of the *cazo y cocimiento* (vat-boiling)
technique of the seventeenth-century Charcas refiner Alvaro Alonso
Barba), the Germans were finally obliged to concede that the traditional
American processes were best, in American circumstances. Indeed, one
of the Germans, Friedrich Sonneschmidt, after long experience in New
Spain, wrote in an excess of enthusiasm, 'It is not to be expected that
there will ever be found a method by which all varieties of ore can be
refined, having expenses lower than or even equal to those required by
the *patio* beneficiation'.[8] The method, he said, was slow. But it could
be set up almost anywhere; needed little water; used simple and
quickly-made apparatus and tools; had techniques rapidly taught even
to the ignorant. If Sonneschmidt had travelled to the Andes, he could
have said much the same of refining methods there.

---

[7] Modesto Bargalló, *La minería y la metalurgía en la América española durante la época colonial*
(Mexico, 1955), 194.
[8] Quoted in Modesto Bargalló, *La amalgamación de los minerales de plata en Hispanoamérica colonial*
(Mexico, 1969), 505.

The absolute efficiency of the colonial amalgamation processes – the proportion of the total silver content of the ore that they actually extracted – is unmeasurable, since the only estimate available of the ores' content is that made by the refiners themselves, and that they calculated according to the results amalgamation itself gave them. Nevertheless, an impression of amalgamation's essential ability – that of handling large amounts of poor ore – is conveyed in the fact that refiners could apparently break even with ores yielding only $1\frac{1}{2}$ oz of silver from each 100 lb of concentrate treated with mercury.

A secondary, but remarkably persistent and useful, refining technique was smelting. Here the Spanish borrowed initially from native technology, at least in the central Andes, where Indian miners had progressed beyond the primitive fire-setting techniques used by the native Mexicans and other Andean Indians to obtain certain metals, notably gold, silver, and copper. In Peru and Charcas true smelting had developed. First the ore was crushed under a *maray*, a boulder with a curved base, which was made to rock to and fro; then it was smelted in a small furnace, conical or pyramidal in shape, often only about three feet high. The sides were pierced with many air-holes through which the wind could blow when the furnace was placed in some exposed place. With llama dung or charcoal as fuel, the temperatures generated were sufficient to smelt ores. This was the famous *wayra* (Quechua: 'air') of the Andes; and in furnaces of this sort all silver was produced at Potosí until the arrival of amalgamation in 1571.

Europe, nevertheless, provided the dominant smelting technology, much of it introduced by German miners sent in 1528 by the Fugger banking company to the Caribbean islands and Venezuela. The crown had requested these experts for the improvement of mining and metallurgical skills in America, till then signally lacking among early settlers. Some of these Germans may have moved on to New Spain; others certainly arrived there in 1536, settling at Sultepec, where they built milling machines and furnaces. The basic smelting device was the Castilian furnace, an ancient design consisting of a hollow vertical column about three feet square and four to six feet high, built of stone or adobe. Its sides were pierced for bellows and the drawing of slag and molten metal. Ore, crushed by hand or in a mechanical mill, was packed into the furnace with charcoal. Bellows were essential; in any large establishment they were worked by water or animal power through gears and cranks. Smelted silver usually lacked purity, containing lead occurring in the ore, or that had been added as flux. So further refining was performed by cupellation, normally in a reverberatory furnace, though the Castilian type would serve.

Smelting persisted more strongly through colonial times than has been thought. It was the preferred technique of the poor individual miner or of the Indian labourer who received ore as part of his wage. A small furnace with hand bellows (a *parada de fuelles*) was cheap to make; hundreds of them sprang up in and around mining towns. But large-scale smelting also survived the coming of amalgamation, and particularly flourished when mercury was short, when new strikes of very rich ore were made, and where fuel was abundant. These conditions led, for example, to an important resurgence of smelting in parts of New Spain in the later seventeenth century.

Processing of gold consisted merely of separating the pure metal from whatever material it was found in – sand or gravel in streams and terraces, or some type of rock in veins. Panning or ground sluicing were the basic techniques in the first case. In the second, milling was necessary and could be done by hand or in a stamp mill. Amalgamation might then follow, to gather the gold from the crushed vein material. Gold often occurred in conjunction with silver ores, amalgamation of which then produced an alloy of the two metals. The preferred means of separating them, certainly until mid-colonial times, was the nitric acid method.

RAW MATERIALS

The processing of silver ores required a variety of raw materials, some of them in limited supply. Salt, essential for amalgamation, was easily obtained, either from salinas (in northern New Spain or in the central Andes) or, as in other parts of New Spain, from coastal deposits. Pyrites, from which *magistral* was prepared, occurred commonly enough in the silver districts. So did lead, which was needed as a flux for smelting (though much ore contained enough natural lead for the purpose). Iron, used in machinery and occasionally, in pulverized form, as a reagent in amalgamation, came wholly from Spain, but nevertheless was rarely scarce or excessively dear.

Rather less plentiful were wood and water. Wood was the basic construction material and fuel. Trees were consequently stripped quickly from areas around large mining centres, in some of which – the high Andes and the dry Mexican plateau – they can never have been plentiful. Timber then had to be brought in at high cost over great distances. In late sixteenth-century Potosí, the wooden axles for stamp mills, twenty feet long and twenty inches square, were brought from lower Andean valleys 100 miles or more off. Placed in Potosí they cost 1,300–1,650 pesos, as much as a medium-sized house. Wood or charcoal were also needed to fire furnaces; and charcoal makers ranged many miles from the mines, using scrub where no trees remained.

Water was essential for washing refined ores, and very desirable as a power source. With ingenuity – small dams and animal-driven washing vats – the supply could be stretched everywhere sufficiently to make washing possible. But only in some areas was water power possible – notably in central New Spain and in some parts of the Andes. By 1600 Potosí drew almost all its power from water, but only after some 30 dams with interconnecting canals had been built to store the summer rainfall.

A more crucial substance than any of these was mercury. Nearly all the mercury used in Spanish America came from three sources – in order of volume supplied, Almadén, in southern Spain; Huancavelica, in highland central Peru; and Idrija in the modern Yugoslavian province of Slovenia, then within the Austrian Habsburg domains. Trivial amounts also came now and then from China and various minor Spanish American deposits. In general, Almadén supplied New Spain, Huancavelica supplied South America, and Idrija was tapped when the first two proved inadequate.

Viewed broadly, the mercury supply met demand from silver mining (amalgamation of gold was inconsequential in comparison) in two of the three colonial centuries. In the sixteenth century Huancavelica, an all-but-virgin deposit, boomed; and Almadén's output grew quickly up to about 1620. And in the eighteenth century Almadén, as the result of the discovery of a massive ore body in 1698, so far surpassed its previous performance that it more than compensated for the weakness of Huancavelica. But in the intervening period, for much of the seventeenth century, there was a shortage of mercury, especially in New Spain. This resulted from low output at Almadén (caused by depletion of known ores and inefficient refining), and from a generally weaker showing at Huancavelica than that of the sixteenth century (caused by similar difficulties, compounded by problems of labour supply).

The resulting shortfall was in part met with mercury from Idrija, which was sent to America in substantial quantities from 1621 to 1645

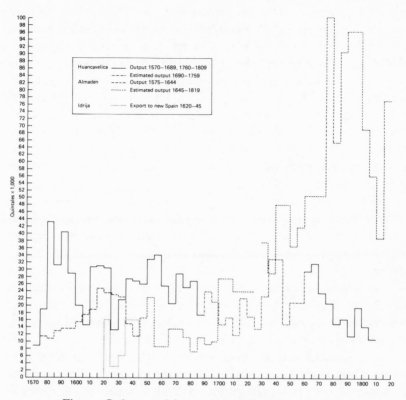

Fig. 2. Quinquennial mercury production, 1570–1820

Sources: **Huancavelica, 1570–1789:** Guillermo Lohmann Villena, *Las minas de Huancavelica en los siglos XVI y XVII* (Seville, 1949), 452–5; **1690–1759** (estimates): Manuel de Mendiburu, *Diccionario histórico-biográfico del Perú,* vol. 6 (Lima, 1933), 454–5; **1760–1809:** John R. Fisher, *Government and society in colonial Peru. The intendant system, 1784–1814* (London, 1970), 257. **Almadén, 1575–1644:** A. Matilla Tascón, *Historia de las minas de Almadén, 1: Desde la época romana hasta el año 1645* (Madrid, 1958), 107, 111, 121, 122, 137, 171, 182; **1645–1819** (estimates): M. H. Kuss, 'Mémoire sur les mines et usines d'Almadén', *Annales des Mines,* septième série, Mémoires, 13 (1878), 149–50. **Idrija, 1620–45:** exports to New Spain: P. J. Bakewell, *Silver mining and society in colonial Mexico, Zacatecas, 1546–1700* (Cambridge, 1971), 256. There were also substantial exports of Idrija mercury to Spanish America after 1786, in amounts still to be determined.

(see fig. 2). This mercury went mainly to New Spain, while Almadén's production was largely diverted from there to Peru, which was favoured in this way because up to then it had been the larger silver producer of the two viceroyalties. The crown found difficulty in paying for the Idrija mercury, and purchases ceased in 1645. 'German' mercury, presumably from Idrija, again appears in New Spain in the 1690s, as indeed does Peruvian mercury, which was imported until about 1730. But large shipments from Idrija did not resume until 1786, the result of a contract made in 1785 for the supply of 10,000–12,000 *quintales* annually to Spanish America. This mercury went to both New Spain and South America.

The crown not only exercised as close a control as possible over the production and distribution of mercury, but also determined the selling price. In principle, the price at a particular mining centre was equal to the sum of production costs and freight to that place; but the government tended to assess these to its own advantage. It is true that mercury prices show a downward trend throughout colonial times, as refiners petitioned constantly for reductions and the crown made concessions to the argument that low mercury prices would more than pay off in increased silver production. But the decline was slow. Between 1572 and 1617 the price was reduced in New Spain from 180 to 82.5 pesos. But no further reduction came until 1767, when the price was lowered to 62 pesos. In 1778 a final cut was made, to 41 pesos. In the Andes the price was consistently higher, perhaps because of large freight costs in the mountains, despite the relative closeness of Huancavelica to the silver centres. At Potosí the price fell from 104.25 pesos in the late sixteenth century to 97 in 1645, there to remain until dropping to 79 pesos in 1779 and 71 in 1787. Only in 1809 did mercury become almost as cheap in Peru, at 50 pesos, as it had normally been in New Spain in the late 1700s.

The general surge of silver output in the late eighteenth century, especially in New Spain, coincides closely with reductions in the price of mercury. This cannot be wholly fortuitous, and suggests that earlier reductions would have been profitable for the crown, especially once Almadén began to produce plentifully after 1700.

LABOUR SYSTEMS

Mining rested on Indian labour. Blacks, slave and free, had a part, but a small one except in gold mining, where they provided much of the workforce. The closest white men came to physical mining labour was prospecting; in general they were supervisors and owners. Mestizos could be found at physical mining tasks by the eighteenth century, but the more Spanish they appeared, the rarer they were in such jobs.

The standard labour systems of colonial times supplied mining with its Indian workers: in general chronological order of appearance, these were encomienda, slavery, draft, and hire for wages. The earliest colonial mining, placering and pit excavation for gold in the Greater Antilles before 1500, was performed by Indians whom Columbus distributed to settlers in an early and harsh form of encomienda. Enslaved natives of the Lesser Antilles and the Spanish Main were quickly added. And then, as the aboriginal population collapsed, not least under the demands of gold mining, black slaves were brought in. Meanwhile the use of Indians in encomienda and slavery for mining spread to Middle and South America as these were taken. The advancing conquest naturally yielded slaves, as everywhere there were some natives who resisted doggedly and so found themselves accounted justly enslaved when captured in war. So, for example, Cortés was able to employ some 400 Indian slaves in his Tehuantepec gold deposits in the 1540s.

Drafted Indian labour followed encomienda, but no clear line can be drawn between the two systems. In both viceroyalties draft labour for mining was extensively organized by the late 1570s, under the name *repartimiento* in New Spain and *mita* (Quechua: 'turn') in Peru. But the beginnings of these systems long antedate the 1570s. By 1530 in Guatemala, for instance, Spanish settlers and officials simply obliged gangs of nominally free Indians to wash gold for fixed periods. And by 1549, encomienda Indians being sent to Potosí by their masters from all parts of Peru and Charcas referred to their stay at the mines as mita – a set span of six or twelve months after which they were replaced by another group, and returned home. Their use of the Quechua term clearly indicates their association of this work for the Spanish with the mita imposed previously by the Incas, a draft for various sorts of public work, including mining. The Aztecs had operated a draft (*coatequitl*) also in their domain. The existence of these native antecedents doubtless facilitated the Spaniards' creation of drafts.

Gradually, over the mid sixteenth century, draft labour superseded encomienda and Indian slavery in mining. As the military phase of conquest passed, the supply of Indians taken in just war fell; and simultaneously laws limiting Indian slavery were more firmly enforced. Meanwhile draft labour began to present attractions to the crown and many settlers, since its fundamental effect was to remove Indians from the wide and largely arbitrary control of the encomenderos and make them available to the growing number of non-encomenderos among the Spanish. In this the crown perceived both a gratifying curtailment of the encomenderos' wealth and political power, and a more productive use of the shrinking Indian workforce. Officially organized drafts also gave the crown a chance to fulfil other purposes: first to create a salaried native workforce in America, for another distinction between official draft and encomienda was that drafted Indians should receive wages; second to limit the length of time that Indians worked, since drafts were assigned for specific though varied periods, according to local labour needs.

The largest, most highly organized, most famous, and – in common estimation – infamous, of all mining drafts was the mita of Potosí. Here it may stand as a model for other drafts in both New Spain and South America, though all varied in details. The Potosí mita and its harshness are usually made the personal responsibility of the Peruvian viceroy who created the system, Don Francisco de Toledo. But Toledo acted under general royal instructions to force Indians into mining – instructions that gave him such qualms of conscience that he hesitated for over two years before grasping the nettle. It was finally in late 1572, as he travelled from Cuzco to Potosí on his general inspection of Peru, that he began organizing the mita, instructing the leaders (*curacas*) of the high Andean towns to send able-bodied men to Potosí. The area finally designated for supplying workers was enormous, extending some 800 miles from Cuzco in the north to Tarija in the south, and a maximum of 250 miles across the width of the Andes; though only sixteen of the 30 provinces in this area were included, those excepted being mainly the lower and warmer ones whose inhabitants were feared too susceptible to disease if sent to the cold and height of Potosí. From the sixteen contributing provinces about 14 per cent (a seventh) of the tribute-paying population (males between eighteen and 50) were to go each year to Potosí for one year. According to the census Toledo made, this would provide enough labour for Potosí, about 13,500 men a year. This number was the *mita gruesa*, which, once in Potosí, was divided into three parts, each called the *mita ordinaria*, which worked by turn one week on and two off. So at any moment about 4,500 mita labourers (*mitayos*) were active in the draft.

Toledo then distributed the mitayos among mines and refineries according to their size and need, a process repeated thereafter by many incoming viceroys, and set daily wage rates: for interior mine work, 3.5 reales; for carrying ore to refineries, three reales; for refinery work, 2.75 reales.[9] The real worth of these wages is hard to estimate, as many prices, including those of the Indians' staples, maize and potatoes, are unknown. The week's wage of the mine mitayo would buy, however, about 30 lb of wheat flour. This may seem substantial; but a contemporary estimate put the cost of an Indian's journey to Potosí and one year's residence there at 100 pesos, while the total wage of a mine mitayo for seventeen weeks of six days was about 45 pesos. The normal work week soon fell, however, from six to five days. Sunday was a day of rest, or one, according to Spanish observers voicing the conventional criticism of Indians, of drunken idleness. On Monday, Indian officials from each province assembled the new week's *mita ordinaria* for distribution. Work began on Tuesday morning, continuing non-stop until Saturday night. Toledo's regulations specified a dawn-to-dusk workday; but mine owners soon began forcing mitayos to cut and haul ore by quota, set high so that rest and food had to be snatched when possible, above or below ground.

The mita clearly exposed the Indian to overwork, despite the legal safeguards created by crown and officials. Evidence suggests that wages were paid. But the labour burden grew, particularly as the Andean native population fell and a worker's turn came round more frequently than every seven years. In extreme cases by 1600, mitayos were having to spend every other year in Potosí. The mita itself clearly contributed to the depopulation, accelerating an existing decline by causing people to flee the provinces from which the draft was taken, by inclining some mitayos to stay in Potosí to seek anonymity amidst the town's large Indian population, and by disrupting the rhythms of agriculture and family life. Yet further abuses followed from the greater burden of

---

[9] There were eight reales to a peso. Here, and elsewhere in this chapter, the peso referred to is the *peso de a ocho* (known in New Spain as the *peso de oro común*) worth 272 maravedís.

labour. Those Indians able to do so bought themselves out of the mita by hiring replacements, or paying their own *curacas* or employers the cash necessary to do so. Many miners in the seventeenth century liked this practice of cash payments in lieu of labour, for if a mine were exhausted or a mill dilapidated, the sum the mitayos paid to avoid working might be greater than the value of the silver they would produce if they were working. To these cash payments the Spaniards gave the cynical title *indios de faltriquera* – 'Indians in the pocket'. This common practice was illegal, as was the equally common custom of including the mitayos assigned to a mine or mill in any sale made of these. The law strove to uphold the theoretical freedom of the Indian; but the mitayo was often treated – as when he was made part of a sale transaction – as a near-slave, while being deprived of the material benefits of slavery and of exemption from tribute.

Second to the Potosí mita in numbers of Indians drafted was the mita of Huancavelica, also created by Toledo. It drew, in the early 1620s, some 2,200 Indians a year, about a sixth of those sent to Potosí. But the Huancavelica mitayos may well have suffered more severely than those of Potosí, on account of the extreme hazards of those mercury mines: toxic vapours and soft, shifting rock. Elsewhere smaller drafts existed – for example, for gold production in Chile in the late sixteenth and early seventeenth centuries; for gold in Quito from, apparently, the sixteenth century; for silver in New Granada from the early 1600s; and for silver in New Spain from the mid 1500s.

The iniquities of the drafts were not ignored by the crown; and, indeed, despite the political and economic attractions that draft labour offered the crown, its imposition was much debated in Spain since it contradicted the fundamental principle that the Indians were free. Generally, however, the view that the public good required drafting Indians into mines prevailed. Abolition came only in 1812, though there were earlier attempts to bring it about, as for instance in a notable royal order of 1601 directed to New Spain, only withdrawn after remonstrations from the viceroy that such a step would mean disaster. But the crown did maintain its opposition – cancelling, for example, the assignment of 500 mitayos to Oruro by viceroy Esquilache in 1617. Other cases could be cited.

In the 1601 order the crown stated its desire for a voluntary workforce in mining. And indeed, voluntary labour by Indians in all types of production had from the beginning of colonial times been the ideal. But the natives' unfamiliarity with the work expected of them, with money wages, and their natural attempts to escape the heavy tasks placed on them (interpreted by the Spanish as inborn idleness) went against voluntary labour. There was always, however, some trace of it, originating in native society itself. In the Caribbean cultures the Spanish found the naboría, 'a commoner who was the direct dependent of a noble and who therefore did not participate fully in the general community obligations and privileges'.[10] To a similar social type in New Spain the Spaniards transferred the same name (later hispanized to *laborío*). In Inca lands the yanacona occupied much the same position. Indians of these sorts quickly shifted their allegiance to the new conquering Spanish lords, while growing numbers of other Indians who were in origin plain commoners imitated them, seeing advantages in being the direct personal dependants of Spaniards rather than their more remote servitors in encomienda. Naborías and yanaconas quickly turned to a wide range of tasks in early colonial society, for many of which they received wages, becoming the first wage labourers. Among their characteristic occupations was mining so that, for example, immediately after the discovery of the Zacatecas and Potosí ores in the mid 1540s there were naborías and yanaconas, respectively, working the mines, mixed with Indian slaves and encomienda labourers.

This early element of wage labour in mining grew quickly, for two reasons. First, mining demanded skills which, once acquired, were highly valued. An owner was willing to reward well an Indian who had learned ore-cutting or refining skills as a draft labourer, and would pay wages high enough to make permanent mining work attractive. Well before 1600 professional groups of Indian miners and refiners existed in the main centres. Second, many major mining districts existed in areas where the original native population was unsuitable for encomienda or draft, either because it was too sparse or too rebellious. Such was the case in northern New Spain, where mines were worked largely by wage labourers from the start. Figures for the composition of the Mexican mining labour force taken from a report of about 1597 show the importance of wage labour by then. The total force was 9,143 men, of whom 6,261 (68.5 per cent) were naborías, 1,619 (17.7 per cent) were draft (repartimiento) workers, and 1,263 (13.8 per cent) were black slaves. Also striking is that fact that all the repartimiento workers were

---

[10] Ida Altman and James Lockhart (eds.), *Provinces of early Mexico* (Berkeley and Los Angeles, 1976), 18.

in central Mexico, none in the west and north – the reason being that only in the centre had the native population been of sufficient density and sophistication to be organized into drafts. It was this population, moreover, that sent most of the naborías to the north and west.

A similar situation existed in Potosí. There, in 1603, some 11,000–12,000 workers were active at any one moment, of whom only about 4,500 were from the *mita ordinaria*. The rest were hired men (*mingas*). Undoubtedly many *mingas* were from the two-thirds of the *mita gruesa* that were 'off duty' (*de huelga*); but there is clear evidence that a permanent corps of *mingas* existed in Potosí by this time, consisting largely of mitayos who had stayed on after their year of draft. Their pay was up to five times that of the mitayo: for mine workers, 88 reales a week as opposed to seventeen. The cash wage of skilled ore cutters, who were normally salaried, was augmented in both Potosí and New Spain by ore which they took from the mines, legally or otherwise.

Wage labour was clearly the prevalent form of employment in the large mining districts from the late sixteenth century onwards. Earlier systems did not wholly disappear, especially in remote or unimportant districts: encomienda in seventeenth-century New Granada, even slavery on the northern frontiers of New Spain, where the fight against raiding Indians continued to yield legal slaves. But the waged worker became the norm, especially in New Spain, where growth of mining from the late seventeenth century generated such demand for skilled workers that by the late eighteenth labour costs comprised up to three-fourths of the total expenses in some enterprises. Draft survived in New Spain, but barely. In central Andean districts the mita remained more in evidence, supplying Potosí and Huancavelica with useful cheap labour until late colonial years; while informal (and strictly illegal) lesser drafts were probably organized by local government officials to aid other mines. But wage labour predominated here also. By 1789 only 3,000 came to Potosí in the *mita gruesa* – yielding a *mita ordinaria* of 1,000. But in 1794 the total Potosí workforce was 4,070 in mines and 1,504 in refining – figures suggesting that over three-fourths of workers were then salaried. Wage labour in the lower Peruvian districts in the late eighteenth century was also important.

Almost 14 per cent of Mexican mining labourers were blacks at the close of the sixteenth century – a by no means negligible proportion.

But, except in lowland gold-mining, this proportion can have been rarely exceeded. Many of the great silver districts were at considerable height, 8,000 feet or above; and it was a common opinion that blacks could not do heavy work and survive long in such cold, thin air. While the strict truth of this remains unclear, it certainly seems that at great heights black slaves could not perform heavy underground work efficiently enough to provide a return on their purchase price and maintenance. So at Potosí, for example, blacks were not put to underground tasks. They may have been employed in refining; but were normally found as craftsmen, typically carpenters and smiths, making and servicing tools and machinery, or as personal servants of miners and refiners – signals of success. At the lesser heights (6,000–8,000 feet) of the Mexican districts, some blacks did work below ground. At Zacatecas there are scattered references to black ore cutters (*barreteros*). But here again, surface tasks were far more common. An observer of Zacatecas in 1602 remarked: 'the blacks are mostly occupied in attending to milling and blending [with mercury] and washing the ores'.[11] Crafts also occupied many blacks in the Mexican mines.

The reportedly high mortality and low productivity of blacks in highland silver mining worked against the crown's frequent schemes to replace draft Indian labour with African slaves. But in tropical lowland gold mining, the opposite was true: blacks proved resistant to disease and capable of hard labour, while Indians perished (particularly highland Indians transplanted into the tropics, but also lowland Indians subjected to unaccustomed levels of work). A further difficulty with the lowland Indians was that they were generally lacking in economic and political integration, and so could not be easily organized into a labour force. Lowland gold mining was therefore the province of black workers. The greatest concentration of these undoubtedly occurred in eighteenth-century New Granada, where in 1787 the three main gold provinces (Antioquia, Popayán and the Chocó) held some 17,000 blacks, many of them in mining. Far from all were slaves by that time. In the Chocó in 1778, for instance, 35 per cent of a total of 8,916 blacks were free; by 1808, 75 per cent. The only major lowland gold region in which blacks did not predominate was Chile. There, in the sixteenth century, Indians, both slave and encomienda, worked the deposits; and in the eighteenth-century revival of gold, the labour force was heavily

[11] Alonso de la Mota y Escobar, *Descripción geográfica de los reynos de Nueva Galicia, Nueva Vizcaya y Nuevo León* (MS 1605?, Guadalajara, 1966), 68.

mestizo, there existing by that time a large mixed population willing
to work in mining for lack of other employment opportunities.

LABOUR CONDITIONS

As is clear enough from the foregoing account, working conditions
in mining and refining were always uncomfortable and often dangerous.
Below ground the least unpleasant job belonged to the most highly
skilled workers – the *barreteros*, who, with crowbars (*barras*), wedges
and picks, prized ore from the veins. This certainly demanded hard
physical effort in cramped, often hot, and always ill-ventilated and ill-lit
conditions. But far worse was the role of beasts of burden assigned to
the unskilled men who carried ores to the surface; and *barreteros* were
better rewarded, with both higher wages and the opportunity, sometimes
licit and sometimes not, to take pieces of rich ore for themselves. The
lot of the carriers (*tenateros* in New Spain, *apires* in the Quechua-speaking
Andean regions) was grim. Using a variety of receptacles for the ore
– rush baskets, hide buckets (*tenates*), sacks, or even, in early Charcas,
llama-wool blankets – they clambered through twisting passages often
no wider than a man's body. Ascents were negotiated with steps hacked
in the rock, or with steep ladders made from notched tree trunks or
strips of hides strung between poles. As the workings grew, large
cavities developed within them, with drops severe enough to kill a man
if he fell. Loads were heavy. Mine owners demanded a certain rate of
extraction even though ordinance forbade it. Difficult as it is to believe,
there is good evidence that *tenateros* in late colonial New Spain carried
300 lb on their backs. Working in darkness, often by the light of a single
candle tied to the front man's forehead or little finger, the carriers were
exposed to grave risks. Many fell to their deaths or to a severe maiming;
just how many cannot be known. Nor was physical injury the only risk.
In the high Andean mines, especially, changes of temperature between
the lower workings and the surface might cause illness. At Potosí, for
instance, even before 1600, some mines were 600 feet deep, and hot at
that level. After coming up with his load, the *apire* emerged at almost
16,000 feet into freezing temperatures. Respiratory disease was the
frequent outcome, often exacerbated by dust in the workings, especially
after blasting was introduced. Falls and disease were a greater risk than
collapses of workings, which, though they certainly happened, were
apparently not common.

Gold and mercury mining held their particular hazards. Since most gold workings were placers in low, wet areas, labourers in them were exposed to tropical diseases. They also often had the discomfort of working long spells in water. Far more unpleasant and dangerous, though, was mercury mining at Huancavelica – fortunately for workers the only permanent mercury mine in America. Clearly this was the most noisome and dangerous of all mines. The country rock surrounding the ores was soft and unstable, so that here collapses were common. But, worse, the workings were often filled with poisonous gases, which made labour in them particularly hazardous.

Refining also had its dangers, of which two were severe. Stamp mills produced much dust, which must inevitably have caused silicosis. And at various stages of amalgamation workers were exposed to mercury poisoning: in the blending of mercury with the ore, when the Indians were treading the mixture, bare-legged; in the distillation of mercury from the *pella*; and in the roasting of washings to recover mercury. In the latter two processes, attempts were made to trap and condense the mercury vapour, but some escaped.

SOCIAL REPERCUSSIONS

For both individuals and communities engaged in it, mining had profound social effects. To the immigrant from Spain or the poor colonist, mining offered a quick, if perilous, short cut to social distinction. The lucky few dozen, for example, who struck it rich in northern New Spain in the second half of the sixteenth century became figures of national prominence. In lordly style they put their fortunes and extensive entourages at the king's disposal, leading the fight against the nomadic northern tribes; assembled great estates from which they exported beef on a grand scale to central New Spain; married high – one of the founders and first miners of Zacatecas married a daughter of the viceroy Velasco I; another, a daughter of Cortés and doña Isabel Montezuma. Mining wealth brought not only social eminence, but political authority. For instance the greatest miner of late seventeenth-century Potosí, the Galician Antonio López de Quiroga, in his later years dominated the local governments of southern Charcas by placing his blood relations and sons-in-law as corregidores of various districts. Naturally, though, having elevated a man to high social and political places, mining might then cast him into the abyss. If the vein were lost, or workings suddenly flooded, then a mine would swallow silver as swiftly as it had previously disgorged it. Creditors closed in, seizing land, houses, belongings. Few families, indeed, remained prosperous in mining for more than three generations.

For the Indian, too, mining could bring profound social change. Most radical was the shift from rural to urban living that mining often imposed, a shift from traditional agricultural communities to sizeable Spanish-dominated towns. This translation was forced upon many Indians by a labour draft; but once having made the move, some decided to stay, so that from the late sixteenth century there was a corps of professional miners in the larger centres, working for wages and tending to adopt Spanish habits. They bought Spanish-style clothes and perhaps preferred wine to pulque or chicha. In doing so, they gradually lost their Indian identity and passed into the mestizo category, in culture if not in genetic type. This proletarianization and acculturation of Indians was not, of course, unusual in colonial towns, since these were the focus of Spanish presence while the countryside remained predominantly Indian. But the mining towns contributed especially strongly to the process because they drew such large numbers of Indians, because they offered relatively high buying power to the waged worker, and not least because they were almost the only Spanish settlements in several large regions – for example, northern New Spain, the Charcas altiplano, or northern Chile.

Whatever gain an individual Indian might have seen in settling in a mining town, the aggregate effect of mining on the native community was often grave. It is hard to gauge how much loss of Indian population mining caused, because other destructive forces were at work at the same time, and conditions varied from place to place. So, for example, the most severe fall in the Mexican Indian population appears to have happened before mining became widespread in New Spain. On the other hand, it is clear enough that the demands for gold production made of the natives of the Greater Antilles in the early colonial decades were a prime cause of their near annihilation by the mid-sixteenth century; and that two centuries later much the same happened in the central Chocó of New Granada, whose Indian population declined from over 60,000 in 1660 to 5,414 in 1778, as it was put first to washing gold, and then to providing food, housing and freighting for mines worked by blacks. The worst dislocation of Indian communities, although it cannot yet be described in numbers, probably occurred in the area serving the

Potosí mita, simply because this was the largest mining draft of all. The 13,500 mitayos assigned normally took their families with them when they left home for their year in Potosí. At a conservative estimate, therefore, some 50,000 people moved in and out of Potosí each year. Village agriculture was disrupted as people departed; reserves of food were depleted to sustain them on the journey, which from distant regions might last two months; many never returned home. Just how many died as a direct result of mining and refining will probably never be known. The proportion remaining in Potosí each year is also hard to judge; but an early seventeenth-century estimate that there were some 37,000 non-mita Indian males in the town suggests that it was large. Besides those who stayed, there were countless others who moved to isolated places in the mita area, or completely out of it, to escape the draft – with further ill effects for their original communities.

MINING AND THE STATE

Mining paid a substantial royalty directly to the crown; in stimulating trade it indirectly yielded sales taxes and customs dues; Indian tributes came quickly to be paid in kind; and it did certainly add dynamism to many parts of the colonial economy. So it is no surprise that kings displayed avid interest in the industry's fortunes. In principle the crown would have maximized its profit from mining by working the mines itself. Though this was too large an undertaking for general implementation, it was to a degree realized. By law in the sixteenth century a portion of any new vein was reserved for the crown. This requirement fell into neglect in New Spain, but was observed in Peru and Charcas, where such royal mines were leased out. On the refining side, there were in Potosí in the 1570s at least two royal refineries, run by salaried administrators. In mercury production the crown always preserved a direct interest. Ownership of both the Almadén and Huancavelica deposits remained totally in the king's hands, though until 1645 at Almadén and 1782 at Huancavelica the mines were actually worked by contractors from whom the crown bought the mercury at a negotiated price. After these dates the government did work the mines directly itself, with poor results at Huancavelica, though remarkably good ones at Almadén after 1700. In addition the crown monopolized the distribution of mercury and determined its selling price to refiners.

The vast gold and silver deposits of America, though, were beyond the scope of direct royal operation. Instead the crown, invoking its ancient right of universal ownership of precious metal deposits, demanded a royalty on production while conceding free prospecting and usufruct of ores to Spanish subjects. This procedure relieved the government of production costs while encouraging active prospecting. After being set initially at up to two-thirds of output, the royalty was fixed in 1504 at a fifth – the famous *quinto real*. To this was shortly added an assay charge of 1–1.5 per cent. Further royalty reductions were often made in later years, however, in attempts to stimulate mining, some of them going to as little as a twentieth. In time the basic rate became a tenth (*diezmo*). The first broad concession of this was made to Mexican miners in 1548 – temporarily at first but repeated until it became customary. Merchants and other non-miners or refiners bringing silver for royalty payment were still to pay a fifth. But this distinction proved impracticable, and by the mid seventeenth century little *quinto* was being collected on silver in New Spain.

In the Andean mines, however, the standard levy remained a fifth well into the eighteenth century. Some earlier concessions of *diezmo* were made to specific mines when a stimulus seemed necessary (for example, to Castrovirreina in 1621 and to Nuevo Potosí in 1640). But in the great mines of Charcas, Potosí and Oruro, despite their obvious decline, the full fifth was maintained until 1736. Then, finally, a standard *diezmo* was introduced in Peru and Charcas. Further cuts were made by Bourbon reformers after 1770 to encourage Mexican production. Several entrepreneurs attempting to revive old mines received total exemption from royalty until they recovered the cost of their efforts. Zacatecas, among others, benefited greatly from this policy. Research to date has not revealed any such concessions to Andean miners.

Royalties on gold long remained at a full fifth, being cut to a tenth in New Spain in 1723 and a twentieth in Guatemala in 1738. In the Andes, however, *quinto* was levied until 1778 – when a general reduction for all Spanish America was ordered: 3 per cent to be taken in the colonies and a further 2 per cent on arrival of gold in Spain. With its power to adjust royalties the Crown could and did exercise a powerful influence over mining. Royalty cuts were often followed by growth in production, and may sometimes have been foolishly delayed, as in the case of Potosí. Refusal to lower the rate probably cost the crown income that would have accrued from increased production. Similarly the Crown's attempt to profit from its control of mercury distribution by setting a price which, as has been seen, was often above cost, undoubtedly reduced silver output and hence many tax revenues.

Taken together, indeed, the crown's possession of three statutory powers over mining – control of royalty, control of mercury distribution and price, and power to assign or remove draft labour – does lend the industry something of the air of state enterprise. Administrators – viceroys, *audiencias* and treasury officials – clearly tended to see it in this light, regarding miners and refiners perhaps not as employees, but certainly as a special category of servants, of the crown. The miners themselves naturally resented governmental controls over their occupation, for example protesting at royalty rates or labour decrees; while trying, usually without success, to profit from their special standing, as when they played on their close connection with the crown to try to get subsidized supplies of black slaves.

In general, crown policy towards mining lacked co-ordination, creating uncertainty among miners. Some policies had distinctly adverse effects, as in the case of excessive royalty rates. The notable exception to this was the Bourbon mining policy implemented after 1770, which aimed to increase bullion production through a whole range of stimuli. Some were obvious: cheaper mercury; exemption from royalties for specially enterprising miners; creation of royal banks to buy silver from miners with coin, so saving them the heavy discounts charged by private buyers of raw silver; creation of banks to finance the industry; attempted improvement of mining and refining techniques through education, in the form of mining 'missions' of European experts – mostly not Spanish – trained in new techniques; and in New Spain a successful technical college specializing in mining, where teaching began in 1792. More subtle measures were also essayed in an attempt to raise the status and hence the attraction of mining. In both New Spain and Peru a mining guild on the pattern of the patrician merchant guilds was created. In particular miners were now to have a high privilege hitherto reserved for the great corporations of Spanish America, the church and the merchants: their own courts in Mexico City and Lima, which would remove mining litigation from the public forum of the Audiencias. Furthermore, mining law itself was modernized, with sixteenth-century ordinances finally being cast aside. In 1783 a new code appeared, drawn up by the Mexican mining court in consultation with the crown; and this code, modified to meet local conditions, became law in both Peru and the Río de la Plata viceroyalty in 1794.

This ensemble of reforms was certainly not responsible alone for the late eighteenth-century resurgence of mining. Indeed in Peru it seems to have been quite ineffective; and in New Spain several of its components (for instance the finance bank) failed. Nevertheless some part of the late colonial Mexican boom must be attributed to the Bourbon changes. And certainly these royal efforts to stimulate bullion production were the most comprehensive and cogent of any made in colonial times.

CAPITAL

No question is more important for an understanding of the functioning of mining than that of capital – its sources, cost and availability in different times and places. But for no question are manuscript sources scarcer and more enigmatic. Except for the case of late colonial New Spain, knowledge of mining capital is hardly more than generalized guesswork.

Early silver production by smelting required little capital investment: ores were generally near the surface, and the main piece of refining equipment, the furnace, could be built for almost nothing. Similarly, early gold mining in placers using Indian labour required a minimum of spending; though later gold production, in placers with black slaves, or by vein mining and the use of crushing mills, did demand investment in labour and plant. But this investment was not on the scale needed in amalgamation of silver. Here mines soon became deep, often demanding expensive adits; refining required a large set of buildings; powerful crushing mills were essential; and some power source had to be established, either a stock of animals or a water supply; a stock of mercury was needed. Prices of all these varied in place and time; but generally speaking a refining hacienda was among the most costly items exchanged in the colonies, on a par with estates, large town houses and ships. In early seventeenth-century Zacatecas and Potosí an *hacienda de minas* might cost, depending on size and condition, from 10,000 to 50,000 pesos.

To judge from the case of Potosí, the initial capital needed for amalgamation may not, contrary to expectation, have been difficult to assemble. In the previous smelting stage of refining, much ore had been mined that was then discarded as too poor for smelting, but which yielded great profits when amalgamated. Small, cheap machines sufficed initially to crush it, and profits were ploughed back in the form of larger mills able to handle growing amounts of less rich ores. At Potosí in the first six years of amalgamation (1571–6), 30–40 per cent of silver production after tax was probably used to build new refineries alone.

If no new finds of good ore were made, this stage of autonomous financing characteristically lasted two or three decades in any district. Then, as the better ores were depleted, the search began for external sources of credit to finance prospecting, adits, repair of machines, purchase of animals, and so on. The source commonly tapped was the merchant community in the mining centres. And so enters the scene that ubiquitous figure in Spanish American mining, the *aviador* (supplier of goods and credit). The appearance of aviadores was a wholly natural development. The first of them were general merchants who gave credit to the miners on supplies in the normal course of business. Soon they were also lending cash. In repayment they took refined but unminted silver, since most mining centres were too far from mints for refiners to take their silver in for coinage. The aviador therefore also became a buyer (*rescatador*) of raw silver. The aviador–rescatador naturally charged interest on his loans; but how much is so far impossible to tell. Receiving his payment in uncoined silver, he had to cover mintage charges on it as well as freight to the mint. In some cases he may also have paid the royalty. Silver producers constantly denounced the usury of aviadores, and indeed it often seems that aviadores prospered while miners went bankrupt. On the other hand, they doubtless had to absorb many bad debts, and they too suffered failures. The number of prosperous aviadores in any centre at any moment was probably no greater than the number of prosperous silver producers.

As the *avío* (supply and credit) system matured, a hierarchy of dealers developed. At its apex were the silver merchants (*mercaderes de plata*), who normally lived in the cities containing mints: in New Spain, Mexico City alone; in South America, principally Potosí but also Lima from 1683. Similar gold merchants existed in eighteenth-century New Granada, and probably earlier. There were perhaps no more than a dozen or two such merchants in each city. Their business was to buy up unminted silver at a discount with coin, have it minted, buy more silver, and so on, taking their profit from the discount. Their source of uncoined silver might be the refiners themselves, but more usually was the aviadores–rescatadores in mining towns. These in turn would buy from lesser district merchants as well as from refiners. Much of the credit loaned locally stemmed from the funds of the central *mercaderes de plata*.

The silver merchants are figures of the seventeenth century and later. By the eighteenth their businesses had in a few cases developed in New Spain into something resembling banking. The Fagoaga family in Mexico City traded at this level, giving extensive credit on account to important miners, and also taking in loans at 5 per cent interest from private institutions and persons. Even in prosperous eighteenth-century New Spain, however, there were never more than three such banks operating concurrently. As the eighteenth century progressed, miners and refiners tried setting up their own credit institutions to avoid the alleged rapacity of the merchants. This was done in 1747 in Potosí, for example, with some degree of success, especially when in 1752 the credit company expanded its activity beyond mere lending and began to buy silver for coinage from the producers. Later in the century, when the crown organized the mining guilds of New Spain and Peru, these were assigned funds to be lent to producers. Financial mismanagement combined with political opposition to limit severely the guilds' success as financiers. The crown did also, however, from about 1780 begin to establish its own funds for purchasing silver (*bancos de rescate*) in regional treasury offices, so freeing refiners to a degree from dependence on merchants for coin. Direct merchant financing of mining nevertheless continued to predominate until the end of colonial times. In the Andean districts local aviadores seem to have supplied most of it. In New Spain the large merchant houses of the capital were the source of much finance, especially after the implementation of the 1778 Free Trade law, which undermined their control of overseas commerce and caused them to seek other investments for their funds.

SILVER PRODUCTION

The most reliable source for gold and silver production is the record of royalty receipts kept by the treasury offices. The main town of a large mining district normally had its own office, and new ones were created when an important new district emerged or an old one grew notably. Another source, but one more distant from the actual production of metal, is the mintage record. Here the drawback is that not all bullion was minted, except perhaps after 1683, when coinage became obligatory. So in general royalties are preferable as indicators of output. How much bullion escaped paying them cannot be known; much clearly did. But the royalty accounts give at least a minimum estimate of production and

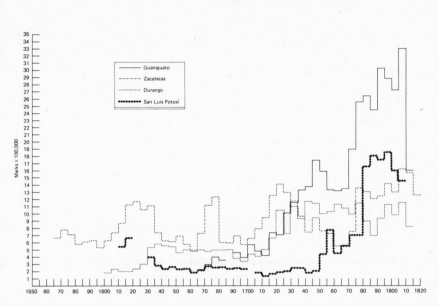

Fig. 3*a*. Quinquennial silver output, New Spain: the great northern mines, 1565–1820

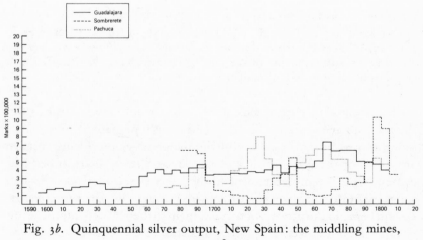

Fig. 3*b*. Quinquennial silver output, New Spain: the middling mines, 1595–1810

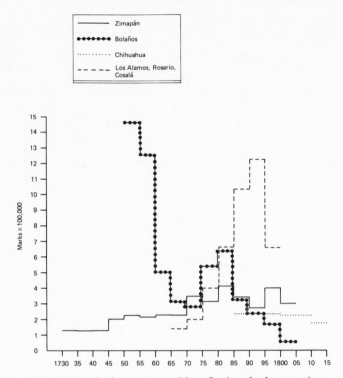

Fig. 3*c*. Quinquennial silver output, New Spain: the lesser mines, 1730–1815

Sources for Figs. 3*a*, 3*b* and 3*c*: **Zacatecas, 1565–1719,** and **Sombrerete, 1681–1719**: Bakewell, *Silver mining and society*, 246, 250. All other data here are from the treasury accounts of the mining centres shown in these figures – accounts being prepared for publication by Professor John J. TePaske.

do reflect its long-term trends. It is mainly from royalty records that the accompanying graphs (figs. 3–5) have been prepared.[12] They show quinquennial output for most of the major silver-producing districts and some of the gold districts. There are still many gaps to be filled, especially for the gold regions and the lesser silver districts. Adequate series of royalty receipts before the 1550s are rare, the American treasury system being in the process of formation up to then. Much interpolation, interpretation of data, and pure conjecture are necessary to estimate early production. A careful calculation from treasury ledgers in the Archive of the Indies was made by Haring, who modified and reduced

---

[12] The author is most grateful to Professor J. J. TePaske for supplying him, before their publication, with transcriptions of Mexican and Andean treasury accounts from regional treasury offices.

earlier estimates by Adolf Soetbeer and W. Lexis.[13] According to Haring, allowance being made for evasion of royalties, the quantities of gold and silver produced in Spanish America up to 1560 were:

Region	Pesos (1 peso = 272 maravedís)	Equivalent in marks of silver (1 mark = 2,380 maravedís)
New Spain:		
gold	5,692,570	650,579
silver*	26,597,280	3,011,429
Peru and Chile	28,350,000	3,240,000
Charcas	56,000,000	6,400,000
New Granada	6,081,000	694,971
West Indies and Tierra Firme	17,000,000	1,942,857
Totals	139,720,850	15,939,836

* The accounts did not permit separation of gold and silver output except in the case of New Spain.

In a later investigation, Jara managed to separate gold and silver output in Peru and Charcas from 1531 to 1600.[14] These figures contain no correction for royalty evasion.

Period	Gold (millions of maravedís)	Silver (millions of maravedís)	Total (millions of maravedís)	Equivalent of total in marks of silver (of 2,380 maravedís
1531–5	1,173	1,016	2,189	919,748
1536–40	325	371	696	292,437
1541–5	547	235	782	328,571
1546–50	406	4,371	4,777	2,007,143
1551–5	363	3,050	3,413	1,434,034
1556–7	52	1,439	1,491	626,471
1562–5	120	2,224	2,344	984,874
1567–70	65	2,106	2,171	912,185
1571–5	13	1,748	1,761	739,916
1576–80	181	7,930	8,111	3,407,983
1581–5	109	12,218	12,327	5,179,412
1586–90	56	14,463	14,519	6,100,420
1591–5	11	14,281	14,292	6,005,042
1596–1600	23	14,024	14,047	5,902,100

[13] C. H. Haring, 'American gold and silver production in the first half of the sixteenth century', *Quarterly Journal of Economics*, 29 (1915), 433–79.
[14] Alvaro Jara, 'La curva de producción de metales monetarios en el Perú en el siglo XVI', in *Tres ensayos sobre economía minera hispanoamericana* (Santiago de Chile, 1966), 93–118.

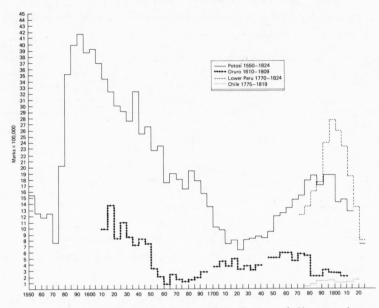

Fig. 4. Quinquennial silver output, Chile, Peru, and Charcas: the great
mines, 1550–1824

Sources: **Potosí, 1550–1735,** and **Oruro, 1610–1715:** P. J. Bakewell, 'Registered silver production in the Potosí district, 1550–1735', *JGSWGL*, 12 (1975), 67–103; **Potosí, 1736–89:** Potosí, Casa Nacional de Moneda, Cajas Reales MS 417. **Lower Peru, 1770–1824:** John R. Fisher, *Silver mines and silver miners in colonial Peru, 1776–1824* (Monograph Series no. 7, Centre for Latin American Studies, Liverpool, 1977), 124–5. **Chile, 1775–1819:** Marcello Carmagnani, *Les mécanismes de la vie économique dans une société coloniale: le Chili (1680–1830)* (Paris, 1973), 309.

Both Haring and Jara show clearly that in the first decade or so after conquest the bullion from a region was not so much mine output as booty. Large accumulations of gold, in particular, were seized in New Spain, New Granada, and Peru. Many gold deposits, especially in New Spain and Peru, had long been worked by the native peoples and were already partially depleted when the Spanish took them over. So gold production often trended downwards in the sixteenth century, except where the Spanish located new or little-tapped deposits, as in New Granada. Conversely, silver production tended to rise, since deposits

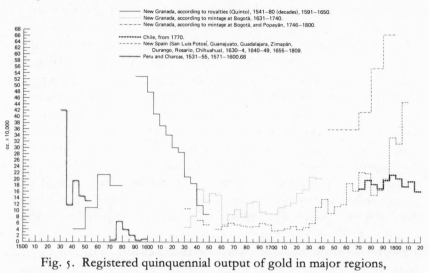

Fig. 5. Registered quinquennial output of gold in major regions, 1530–1820

Sources: **Peru** and **Charcas, 1531–55, 1571–1600:** Alvaro Jara, 'La curva de producción de metales monetarios en el Perú en el siglo XVI', *Tres ensayos sobre economía minera hispanoamericana* (Santiago de Chile, 1966), 93–118. **New Granada, 1541–80, 1591–1740:** Germán Colmenares, *Historia económica y social de Colombia, 1537–1719* (Medellín, 1973), ch. 5; **New Granada, 1746–1800:** Vicente Restrepo, *Estudio sobre las minas de oro y plata de Colombia* (4th edn, Bogotá, 1952), 197. **New Spain, 1630–4, 1640–9, 1655–1809:** treasury accounts of San Luis Potosí 1630–, Guanajuato 1665*–, Guadalajara 1670–, Zimapán 1735*–, Durango 1745–, Rosario 1770*–, and Chihuahua 1800–, being prepared for publication by Professor John J. TePaske. (Dates here, if asterisked, refer to the foundation of the town's treasury office; if not asterisked, to the first significant appearance of gold in the accounts of the office in question.) **Chile, 1770–1819:** Carmagnani, *Les mécanismes de la vie économique,* 367.

had previously been at most lightly exploited, and yielded well to new technology. It was probably in the late 1530s in New Spain and in the mid 1540s in the central Andes that the value of silver production first exceeded that of gold; and this continued for the rest of colonial times in those areas. In others, notably New Granada and Chile, gold always predominated. After the 1540s (at the latest) the total value of gold produced in Spanish America was always inferior to the value of silver.

Amalgamation ensured the ascendancy of silver. The effect of its introduction into New Spain cannot be appreciated because detailed accounts are lacking for the 1550s. But its influence in Peru and Charcas once it arrived in 1571 is evident from Jara's figures and from the enormous growth of Potosí's output (see fig. 4 above). After a period of decline resulting from depletion of smelting ores, Potosí's production grew almost sixfold in the period 1575–90, reaching, around 1592, not only its highest level ever, but a level exceeding that achieved by any other mining district in the whole colonial era. In the years 1575–1600 Potosí produced perhaps a half of all Spanish American silver. Such profusion of silver would not have been forthcoming without con-current abundance of mercury from Huancavelica, which in those same years was also yielding as never again (see fig. 2, p. 121). Another stimulant to Potosí was clearly the cheap and plentiful labour supplied through Toledo's mita. But without amalgamation little of the ore extracted by the mitayos could have been refined profitably. Potosí's main rival in this pre-1600 period was probably the Zacatecas district in New Spain (see fig. 3*a* above), though Pachuca and Taxco may have been very close also. Specific information on their production is not yet available. By 1600, however, Potosí had entered on a 130-year decline, interrupted occasionally, but not arrested, by new strikes in the district. The easily accessible ore concentration in the peak of the Potosí mountain became increasingly depleted in the seventeenth century, so that the Potosí industry developed into something far more diffuse than before, extending over much of southern Charcas. By 1660, 40 per cent of the silver paying royalties in Potosí originated in the district mines (though later this proportion did fall again somewhat). Oruro is not considered here as part of the Potosí district, as it had its own treasury office almost from the moment it became important (1606–7). It was possibly the second South American producer after the Potosí district in the seventeenth century, though it too suffered from ore depletion. Output series are not available for mines in Peru, nor elsewhere in South America, but indications are that they were comparatively poor.

Potosí and Oruro suffered no substantial mercury shortage in the seventeenth century, despite Huancavelica's erratic performance (see fig. 2). This, however, was at New Spain's expense. Huancavelica having faltered after 1595, the crown at length decided from 1630 to divert much of Almadén's output from New Spain to the Andean mines, which were by far the larger producers. Mercury for New Spain was bought from Idrija, but not in large enough amounts to keep the supply at previous levels. And New Spain was further deprived when the Idrija purchases were stopped in 1645. Mexican silver output thus fell from the 1630s, especially as the mercury shortage coincided with ore depletion in some districts. (The great exception was the Durango district, in which new strikes at Parral actually brought increased output in the early 1630s.) The downward trend in New Spain continued until the 1660s, when it was checked by an unexpected development: the revival of smelting. This is clear in the Zacatecas royalty records from 1670 and certainly had begun well before that. In the 1670s, 60 per cent of the Zacatecas district's output was smelted. The main centre for this was Sombrerete, which produced so prolifically that in 1681 it was allotted its own treasury office. By then the rest of the Zacatecas district had also widely converted to smelting, producing 48 per cent of its silver by that method between 1680 and 1699. After 1700 smelting continued to be commonplace in New Spain, as these figures show:

District	% output smelted in 1720s	% output smelted in 1760s
Guadalajara	26 (1730s)	8 (1770s)
Guanajuato	35 (1730s)	27 (1770s)
Pachuca	27	23
San Luis Potosí	86 (1730s)	54
Sombrerete	68	33
Zacatecas	c. 30	30
Zimapán	90+	94 (1795–9)

This notable return to smelting after a long predominance of amalgamation was evidently a response to the shortage of mercury from 1630 onwards. But explaining the success of this reversion will require more research. There is no apparent improvement in smelting technique; so high-grade ores must have been found in large quantities to allow profitable smelting on so large a scale. How was the necessary prospecting and expansion of existing mines financed after a long period of falling output? Possibly the answer lies in an acceleration of underground exploration through blasting.

Blasting must certainly be among the causes of the immense, ubiquitous and almost uninterrupted growth of silver output in eighteenth-century New Spain.[15] It is the one known radical innovation in the production process. Also conducive to greater output was the growing size and orderliness of workings, a trend glimpsed in the seventeenth century and now reinforced by the spread among at least some miners of a more rational and methodical approach to mining and its problems. While this cannot be quantified, the change may well have been fundamental to Mexican mining's success in the eighteenth century; it is only necessary to compare the cool, reasoned and precise accounts of their enterprises given by mid-eighteenth-century miners with the jumbled and often unintelligible ramblings of their counterparts a century earlier. Behind the great eighteenth-century Mexican boom lay also abundance of mercury and of labour. The table just given shows that smelting, though common after 1700, tended to decline with time. One reason for this was clearly the enormous growth of mercury production at Almadén, finally relieving the shortage that began in the 1630s. Even this abundance, however, failed to match demand in the late 1700s, so again Idrija mercury was bought, on a contract made in 1785 for the supply of 10,000–12,000 *quintales* annually to Spanish America. This mercury appeared in many Mexican centres in 1786. Plentiful mercury was matched with plentiful labour, as New Spain's population grew, doubling, in fact, over the second half of the eighteenth century (2.6 million in 1742 to 6.1 million in 1810). It is perhaps particularly significant that the population of the intendancy of Guanajuato, in which the most remarkable mines of the late eighteenth century lay, more than tripled in the 1742–1810 period. While no general study of mining wages exists in that century (or in any other for that matter), it is a reasonable supposition that this notable population growth tended to restrain wage increases, if nothing more – to the miners' advantage. This suggestion is supported by the overall stability of wages observed for Zacatecas after 1750 and by the apparent fall of workers' wages at Guanajuato in the final decades of the century. Mexican output was further augmented from about 1770 onwards by the governmental policies already described: reductions in mercury price, royalty concessions, improvements in the miner's status, and the introduction of education in mining, engineering, and geology. Some of these measures encouraged increased investment in mining, which resulted in larger and better-planned workings. And to these stimuli

[15] See Brading, *CHLA* I, ch. 11.

may possibly be added a growing demand for silver. This question needs closer examination; but it is arguable that the growth of population drove up demand for imported goods, which in turn increased demand for silver, the main export, to pay for them.

The great Valenciana mine at Guanajuato exemplifies many of the developments of late colonial Mexican mining. It was without a doubt the largest single mine ever worked in colonial Spanish America, employing at its peak over 3,300 underground workers and between 1780 and 1810 yielding 60–70 per cent of the total output of Guanajuato, itself the unchallenged silver capital of New Spain (see fig. 3*a*). The Valenciana owed its success to immense capital investment of the sort that the crown's fiscal encouragement of mining set out to evoke. Over a million pesos were spent on three great vertical shafts, which allowed cheap extraction of ore and acted as foci for numerous spacious galleries. Even these shafts ultimately proved inadequate, so that after 1800 another, the San José, was sunk. By 1810 this had reached a depth of nearly 1,800 feet. Its diameter of 33 feet permitted simultaneous operation of eight animal-driven hoists. The Valenciana was an enterprise of unprecedented horizontal integration. No single mine had previously possessed so many great shafts, nor such a multiplicity of galleries. There was also considerable vertical integration: the Valenciana partners ran refineries handling part of the ore coming from the mine. The rest they sold to independent refiners. Other enterprises in Guanajuato, however, carried vertical integration further still.

By the first quinquennium of the nineteenth century, according to Humboldt, New Spain was producing some 67.5 per cent of Spanish American silver – a proportion confirmed by the partial information shown in figs. 3*a*, 3*b* and 4, above.[16] This was the apogee of output. After 1805 disruption of the mercury supply by war, the crown's own increased fiscal pressure on New Spain, and finally damage by insurgents in 1810–11, brought production tumbling down.

The history of eighteenth-century Andean silver mining is less known, especially before 1770, than that of New Spain. For Potosí and Oruro in this period, there is hardly any more information available than the bare production figures. Neither has Peruvian mining in the first two-thirds of the century received attention. It seems, nevertheless, that the 1700s brought a larger recovery of Andean silver mining than has

[16] *Ensayo político*, 425 (book 4, ch. 11).

been thought. Potosí's output almost tripled from 1720 to 1780; the mines of Peru boomed remarkably after then (fig. 4). Potosí and Oruro may have benefited from blasting, and both certainly responded to the reduction in royalty from a fifth to a tenth in July 1736. Added to this was a clear though erratic growth in mercury supply from Huancavelica between 1700 and 1770 (fig. 2). After that Huancavelica slumped, but mercury was imported frrom Almadén and Idrija, so that the mines of Peru, and probably those of Charcas also, did not suffer shortage. The remarkable vigour of the Peruvian mines after 1770 may indeed owe much to abundance of mercury. Beyond this, as in New Spain, there was eighteenth-century population growth with its probably depressive influence on labour costs. And in Peru the late eighteenth century also witnessed an increased injection of capital into mining, resulting in improved workings. Although Peruvian enterprises remained far smaller than those of New Spain, investment did bring useful below-ground changes, most notably in the form of new drainage adits at Cerro de Pasco, which emerged as the most dynamic centre. This enlarged capital flow originated, it would seem, among the merchant community of Lima; though the funds were not invested directly, but reached miners through local aviadores. The new investments may reflect a growth in demand for silver caused by the separation of Peru from Charcas with the latter's incorporation into the new Río de la Plata viceroyalty in 1776. With their traditional source of silver cut off, since Charcas' output now had to be exported through Buenos Aires, the Peruvian merchants perhaps felt impelled to develop mines closer to home. The fall in Peruvian output after 1805 had general causes similar to those operating in New Spain, and a particular reason in the increasing depth and consequent flooding of the Cerro de Pasco workings after 1812.

In this discussion of production, one important but elusive influence has so far been omitted: the value of silver. This is elusive because price and wage series for colonial times are still rare, so that variations in the buying power of silver are scantily known. It is clear, though, that prices (as measured in silver) rose steeply in the late sixteenth and early seventeenth centuries in many places, in an inflation that owed much precisely to high silver production. This loss of value undoubtedly contributed to seventeenth-century declines in silver output. Later in the seventeenth century, prices may have been more stable, at least in New Spain; and may have continued so in the eighteenth. Such stability would have encouraged mining revival. The movement of the European bimetallic ratio tends to reinforce these suggestions: 1500–50 – *c.* 10.5:1; 1600 – *c.* 12:1; 1650 – *c.* 14:1; 1700 – *c.* 15:1; 1760 – *c.* 15:1. That is, until the mid seventeenth century, silver rapidly depreciated in terms of gold; after that the ratio remained steady.

GOLD PRODUCTION

Our knowledge of gold output is less extensive and secure than that of silver production, and is likely to remain so since gold, being much the more valuable, presented still greater temptations than silver to the royalty evader (and the smuggler). Royalties and mintage are therefore slighter indicators of real production of gold than they are for silver. For lack of others, though, these records have been used to prepare fig. 5, which shows output in four major gold regions for at least parts of the colonial era: New Spain, New Granada, Peru and Charcas, and Chile. These were certainly the areas that produced most gold. New Granada was first among them. For a few decades after settlement, several mainland areas – southern New Spain (Colima, Tehuantepec), Central America (Honduras), southern Quito (Zaruma), east central Peru (Carabaya), south central Chile (Valdivia), to mention only the most important – yielded plentiful gold. But only New Granada had deposits extensive enough to permit constantly growing output in the sixteenth century; and then, after a seventeenth-century slump, a still greater boom in the eighteenth. The leading sixteenth-century district in New Granada was Antioquia, between the Cauca and Magdalena rivers in the north. It was worked with encomienda and black slave labour, decline coming in the seventeenth century as the Indian population fell to disease and as the vein gold of Buriticá and placers in the rivers were worked out. The eighteenth-century boom owed much to the Chocó – the rain-forested Andean slopes facing the Pacific in central New Granada. Here river gravels rich in gold were extensively worked with black slaves and freedmen from the 1670s on. In several other areas of New Granada, notably Popayán in the south, there was also substantial gold mining.

In Chile, gold production seems to have become negligible by the mid seventeenth century, but revived again in the 1690s, climbing steadily in the eighteenth century. The reasons for this revival were the need for exports to balance Chile's trade, and the growth of a poor mestizo section of the population which, seeking some means of support, turned to small-scale gold mining in the centre north (Norte Chico).

Another major eighteenth-century gold region was northern New Spain, where gold often occurred in conjunction with silver ores. Recent investigation shows that San Luis Potosí was the first north Mexican district to yield much gold, beginning in the early decades of the seventeenth century. Between 1630 and 1635 it produced some 100,000 oz. Significant gold output began in the following districts, all northern except Guadalajara, at about the date indicated: Guanajuato (1665), Guadalajara (1670), Zimapán (1735), Durango (1745), Rosario (1770), and Chihuahua (1800). The growth of Mexican production, as shown in fig. 5 (which does not take account of any mines in the centre or south), was doubtless stimulated by royalty reductions, from a fifth to a tenth (*c.* 1720), and thence to 3 per cent (1778).

Few aspects of colonial life remained untouched by mining. Gold and silver gleamed in the eyes of conquerors and explorers. 'Great difficulty can be foreseen... in its satisfactory settlement and growth as long as there are no mines to stimulate the greed that will carry forward and facilitate the whole business', wrote the viceroy of New Spain in 1601 of the current Spanish advance into New Mexico, clearly having in mind the overall pattern of sixteenth-century Spanish settlement in America.[17] He predicted well. New Mexico remained a sparsely populated, poor and neglected section of the empire in large part because it revealed no significant bullion sources. Even New Mexico, though, counted heavily on mining for its existence, finding a market for animal and vegetable products in the silver towns of northern New Spain. Other regions of the empire poorly endowed with precious metals stood in similar relation to the mining zones (Quito to Peru, Tucumán and Buenos Aires to Charcas), with the exception of Paraguay, which suffered such extreme geographical isolation that even the immense market opportunities of Charcas failed to induce a flow of trade.

The conquest, exploration, settlement and exploitation of Spanish America were all spurred on by the prospect of mining; and mining determined to a remarkable degree the internal economic arrangement of the colonies. It had a scarcely less profound influence on internal political and administrative structure, since precious metal production led to the accumulation of wealth and population in regions that

[17] Archivo General de Indias, Mexico 24, Conde de Monterrey to king, México, 2 August 1601.

otherwise would have been of no weight. It is hardly necessary to stress further the social consequences of mining: the mobility, both upward and downward, to which mine owners were subject; the disruption of Indian communities and displacement of their people to distant regions; the frequent acculturation of these people in essentially Spanish mining towns to the ways of the colonizers. Nor should it be forgotten that many of these towns hold remarkable examples of colonial art and architecture. The great churches of the mining centres, particularly of those that flourished in eighteenth-century New Spain, are equally reminders of colonial mineral wealth and monuments to the successful miners whose patronage built them.

The external consequences of mining are, of course, almost beyond measure, since silver and gold were the foundation of the wealth that Spain drew from her American empire – wealth that excited the eager envy of other European states. The proportion of mining royalties in total royal income from America has not been calculated; nor would the figure have much interest, since bullion production also provided the cash in which all other taxes and duties were paid. Nor is the proportion by value of bullion in total exports from Spanish America known, though it must have been high – well over 75 per cent in most periods. Spain's rivals were naturally well aware of this gleaming current flowing across the Atlantic, and sought by various means to tap it in its course or at its source. Corsairs, particularly the English, had notable success in sixteenth-century raids in the Caribbean. In 1628 the Dutch West India Company dealt a spectacular blow to Spain by seizing the treasure fleet from New Spain off Cuba, though its reported plan (conceived in an excess of ambition and ignorance of geography) to seize Potosí from the Brazilian coast was beyond realization. More practical and successful was the strategy pursued strongly by the French and English in the eighteenth century of drawing off Spanish American wealth through commerce, some licit, but most not. Finally, independence opened the fabled mining regions themselves to direct foreign access. The flood of English capital into Mexican and Andean mines in the 1820s and '30s is a commonplace of nineteenth-century Spanish American history. But success was elusive. Steam power, Cornish miners, and English expertise were not readily transplanted. As the confident ventures collapsed, their disconsolate stockholders were made only too aware of America's recalcitrance in yielding up her precious metals, and of the magnitude of Spain's achievement in overcoming it.

5

THE FORMATION AND ECONOMIC STRUCTURE OF THE HACIENDA IN NEW SPAIN*

ECONOMIC TRANSFORMATION

The first revolution to transform the land in Mesoamerica was the invention in prehistoric times of agriculture itself. The second revolution took place some decades after the conquest, when the brutal decline in the native American population coincided with the Spaniards' penetration of the land and the propagation there of European plants and animals. The swiftness with which this process occurred may perhaps be explained by the previous acclimatization of European flora and fauna in the Canary Islands and the Caribbean. The mainland itself offered many different ecological zones for the reproduction of plants and animals. As early as the middle of the sixteenth century, the valleys of Puebla–Tlaxcala and the basin around Mexico City surprised the traveller with their diversified agricultural landscape, where maize, beans, squash, and peppers alternated with wheat, barley, and European vegetables and fruits.

European grain spread to the irrigated highlands south of Puebla (Atlixco, Tepeaca) and north of Mexico City (Tlalnepantla and Huehuetoca), and then on from there, pushing back the Chichimeca frontier (San Juan del Río, Querétaro). By the end of the sixteenth century, wheat and maize gilded the black soil of the Bajío and were harvested around Morelia and Guadalajara in the west and Oaxaca in the south. Within a relatively short period of time grain transformed the traditional landscape of the native countryside, opening up many hundreds of kilometres of fertile land to cultivation. Wheat farming introduced Spanish techniques of cultivation, such as the plough, the yoke, and

* Translated from the original Spanish by Dr Richard Boulind; translation revised by Clara García Ayluardo and the Editor.

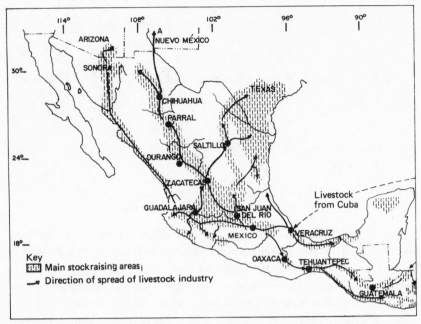

The spread of livestock economy in Mexico and Central America during the colonial era

Source: Robert C. West and John P. Augelli, *Middle America: its lands and people,* © 1966, p. 287. Reprinted by permission of Prentice-Hall, Inc., Englewood Cliffs, N.J.

irrigation, bringing them into permanent use in New Spain. By the mid-seventeenth century, the former wastelands of the Bajío had been converted into the most important, prosperous, and modern agricultural area of New Spain.

Another vehicle of great transformation in the physical as well as the social environment was sugar-cane. It was introduced into the *tierra templada* and *tierra caliente* south of the capital (valley of Cuernavaca and Atlixco) and into the lowlands of Veracruz from the 1530s, and a few years later it was also cultivated in the temperate valleys of Michoacán, New Galicia, and Colima. A crop demanding sun, water, and extensive flat land, sugar-cane also required heavy investment if the cane's juice was to be transformed into sugar crystals. Hence, from the first, the exploitation and processing of sugar-cane was associated with the powerful magnates. Hernán Cortés was one of the pioneers of sugar-cane in Cuernavaca and in the Veracruz lowlands. He set the example for other encomenderos and for rich officials who spent large sums buying land, constructing extensive irrigation systems, importing machinery for the rudimentary mills of the more complex refineries, building the *casas de prensas*, and *casas de purgar*, where the cane juice was extracted and refined, and providing housing for the managers and the numerous slaves. The estimated cost of a new sugar mill at the end of the sixteenth century was 50,000 pesos or more; it is therefore surprising that by then there were dozens of mills in operation. By the end of the sixteenth century, the first agro-industry that flourished in New Spain produced the highest volume of sugar in the Spanish dominions in America. Much of it remained in New Spain; as P. Acosta commented at the end of the century, 'the sugar that is retained and consumed in the Indies is almost beyond belief'. The rest of what was produced on the coast of Veracruz went to Spain.

European occupation of land was also stimulated by the demand for tropical products such as tobacco, cacao, indigo, dyewood and other plants, which from the second half of the sixteenth century onwards came to be grown on a commercial scale. However, it was the importation of livestock that had the most violent impact on the physical and cultural landscape of New Spain. Arriving from the Antilles, they followed in the tracks of other conquerors of the land. Among the many surprises which awaited the settlers, none had so great an impact as the way cows, horses, sheep, goats, pigs, mules, and donkeys multiplied in prodigious numbers, populating New Spain within a few years. In the two decades following the conquest, European livestock spread rapidly across the whole Valley of Mexico and across the valleys of Toluca, Puebla, Tlaxcala, Oaxaca and Michoacán. In these areas, densely populated by Indians using traditional farming methods, the European animals invaded and destroyed the open-field cultivation system, transformed arable land into pasture, dislocated the pattern of settlement, and reduced the Indians' sources of food. It is true that the Indians soon incorporated pigs, sheep, goats, and chickens into their nutritional system; but, on the whole, they lost rather than gained by the changes that transformed their relationship to the environment.

Cows, horses, and mules had a less adverse effect in the tropical lowlands, where epidemics had already decimated the Indian population, allowing the animals to find nourishing year-round pasture and grasses by the marshes and rivers. These conditions changed the coastal plains of Veracruz and the Pacific into areas of *ganado mayor*, as the Spaniards called estates where cattle, horses, and mules were bred. Even more

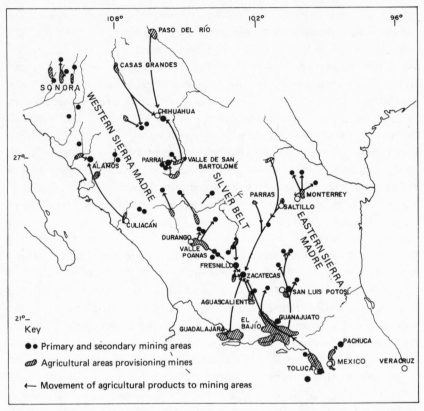

Mining and agriculture in northern New Spain: seventeenth and eighteenth centuries

Source: Robert C. West and John P. Augelli, *Middle America: its lands and people,* © 1966, p. 298. Reprinted by permission of Prentice-Hall, Inc., Englewood Cliffs, N.J.

attractive for both *ganado mayor* and *ganado menor* (lesser stock, i.e. sheep and goats) were the prairies of the north, opened up by settlements of miners. From 1540, the herds followed the northward route of the silver prospectors and, after 1550, overflowed into the semi-arid plains north of the Bajío. From the Valley of Mexico livestock migrated into the valley of Toluca, took possession of the Chichimeca country around San Juan del Río and Querétaro, reached into the north-east, where they populated the territories of San Miguel, Dolores, San Luis de la Paz, and Valles, and multiplied on the plains to the north of Zacatecas in Durango, Parral, and Chihuahua. In all these new territories at the end of the sixteenth century there were already hundreds of thousands of sheep, goats, cows, and horses. A vast new area of land was incorporated into the economy. Stock raising, agriculture and (most importantly) silver mining, attracted successive waves of white, Indian, and black settlement in these territories, and completed the process of colonization and the integration of the economy.

The spread of livestock led to the introduction of Spanish techniques of grazing – common use of lowland, hill, and wilderness pasture – and of the *mesta*, or guild of stock-breeders. This body prescribed rules for the pasturing, migration, and branding of livestock and for the resolution of disputes. A new technique for the breeding and selection of animals, the *rodeo*, was also developed in New Spain. This was a system for rounding up the yearlings annually to brand them and to choose which were to be sold or slaughtered.

These new activities created the man on horseback, the cowboy, who, together with the miner and the missionary, was one of the central figures in the colonization of the north. At the same time wagons and carts drawn by oxen, horses, or mules brought about a revolution in transportation, shortening distances and making the moving of merchandise and produce easier. These animals were the first non-human locomotive power used in New Spain, allowing transportation of equipment for milling and crushing minerals and for pressing and processing sugar. Cattle and goat hides engendered a healthy export trade and furnished articles needed for the extraction and transportation of mineral ores. Sheep's wool made possible the manufacture of textiles and clothing, which came into general use amongst whites, Indians, and mestizos. Since beef was cheap and abundant, the Spaniards and creoles of the north became consumers of it, while pig, chicken, lamb, and goat meat quickly transformed the eating habits of the native population. Some idea of the quantitative change in the physical landscape of New Spain after a century of Spanish colonization is given by Lesley B. Simpson, who estimated the head of cattle in 1620 at 1,288,000 (equalling the figure for the Indian population at that date), while sheep and goats taken together reached the incredible figure of eight million head.

The evangelizing friar was another agent of the great transformation of New Spain's ecology. Franciscan, Dominican and Augustinian missionaries, later joined by Jesuits and Carmelites, were active in introducing and adapting plants, animals, and agricultural and irrigation techniques. Every mission, convent, monastery, or Indian village that they founded saw the planting of European-type orchards with orange, lemon, and pear trees and grape-vines, vegetable gardens with new types of vegetables, and a system of dikes, aqueducts, ditches, and dams which extended the cultivated area and increased the seasonal supply of the fruits of the earth. In the centre and south of New Spain, the missionaries helped the speedy incorporation of these plants, animals, and techniques into the material culture of the settled Indians. In the north, these innovations were adopted by the mission towns, remote and isolated little settlements which were turned into self-sufficient units practising subsistence agriculture (wheat, maize, beans, garden, and orchard crops), stock raising, and cattle, sheep, and goat grazing as well as manufacturing their own textiles, clothing, soap, and artisan products. Between the middle and the end of the sixteenth century, the Dominicans, Augustinians, and Jesuits also built up their own sugar haciendas and cattle and sheep estates.

LAND DISTRIBUTION

Although in the days following the capture of the Aztec capital Cortés seized some of the best lands for himself and his soldiers, mainly those that had belonged to the state or to military or religious officials, the Spaniards were not interested in agriculture. At this stage, native food production was more than enough to satisfy demand. At first, only Cortés himself and a few others sowed European seeds on this fertile soil. They harvested the crops irregularly and with difficulty and frequently abandoned farming for other more profitable activities. Moreover, this type of cultivation lacked precise boundaries and had neither fixed equipment nor regular workers. Later, with the intention of interesting the *conquistadores* in agriculture and of limiting the size of estates, Cortés distributed plots of land called *peonías* to all foot soldiers participating in the conquest and *caballerías* (tracts five times larger than *peonías*) to all horsemen, but without significant success.

The first regular distributions of land were made by the *oidores* (judges) of the second *audiencia* (1530–5). Following the tradition of the *Reconquista* in Spain, and with the purpose of stimulating the 'safekeeping and preservation of the land', they empowered the *cabildos* (town councils) of the new towns and villages to give grants of land to anyone wishing to settle there permanently. Thus the *cabildos*, and

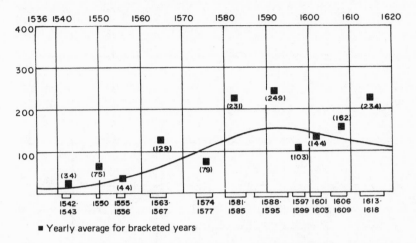

■ Yearly average for bracketed years

Fig. 1. *Caballerías* of agricultural land granted to Spaniards, 1536–1620

Source: L. B. Simpson, *Exploitation of land in central Mexico in the sixteenth century* (Berkeley and Los Angeles, 1952), 8.

later the viceroys, gave new settlers patents as *vecinos* (householders), with the right to a plot of land on which to build a house and plant a garden together with a grant of one or two *caballerías* to 'break and cultivate the soil'. Moreover, the new towns received an allowance for common lands and pastures. This was the model adopted for Puebla de los Ángeles, founded in April 1531, the first township of farmers who ploughed and cultivated the soil without encomienda Indians. It was later extended to the new towns founded in the north, and made general from 1573 by the New Laws of Settlement. For their part, the settlers undertook to live in the new town and promised not to sell their *caballerías* of land before ten years (later reduced to six) had elapsed, and not to transfer the land to any church or monastery or to the clergy.

From the mid sixteenth century the Spaniards' lack of interest in land and in agricultural activities suddenly changed; they now began to petition for extensive land grants. The distribution of *caballerías* of arable land became generalized, the area of a *caballería* being fixed at just under 43 hectares. To the end of the century there was a steady increase in grants of *caballerías* (see fig. 1). Two periods of extensive land distribution, 1553–63 and 1585–95, were linked to the great epidemics of 1545–7 and 1576–80 which decimated the Indian population. The

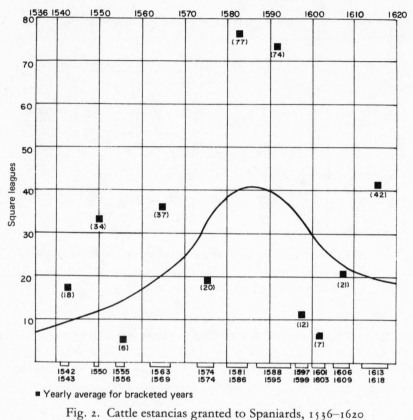

Fig. 2. Cattle estancias granted to Spaniards, 1536–1620

Source: Simpson, *Exploitation of land,* 9.

subsequent programmes for resettling the remaining Indians in *con-gregaciones* released thousands of hectares to be retained by the crown or distributed to Spanish settlers. According to the estimates of Lesley Simpson, between 1540 and 1620 redistribution was brought about by the granting of 12,742 *caballerías* of arable land to Spaniards, and of 1,000 to Indians; that is, some 600,000 hectares in all. (The *fundo legal* limited the size of each new Indian village to a maximum area of 101 hectares, as first specified in a viceregal order of 1567.) Village land was to be distributed as follows: one portion was reserved for the nucleus of the village, that is, the houses, gardens and personal plots of the inhabitants; another portion was reserved for the communal land and other areas where agricultural and stock-raising activities took place;

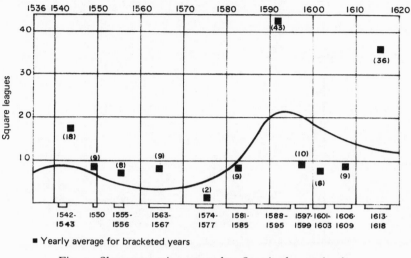

Fig. 3. Sheep estancias granted to Spaniards, 1536–1620
Source: Simpson, *Exploitation of land,* 10.

another consisted of untilled areas (hillside, woodland, grassland, and other areas for animal grazing and for the cultivation of wild fruits and plants); and the fourth and most important portion was divided into individual lots for each head of family to have as private property, but with so many limitations that, as in the pre-Hispanic age, it constituted only a right to the use of the land and in no way implied ownership in fee simple as conceived in Roman law.

The change in land use caused by stock raising, which from 1560 was encouraged by the crown, the viceroys, and the *cabildos* was no less massive or radical. Even though there is documentation of the granting of *asientos* or *sitios* (small farms) and later *estancias de ganado mayor* or *estancias de ganado menor* from 1530, it was not until 1567 that ordinances were enacted explicitly characterizing the area and the nature of such grants (see figs. 2, 3, and 4). François Chevalier, in his masterly analysis of the long process that began with the multiplication of herds and ended with the formation of the great ranching estate, observes that the latter was established in New Spain between 1560 and 1600, although it did not yet have the territorial characteristics of the later hacienda or latifundium. According to Simpson's calculations, by 1620 the grants of *estancia de ganado mayor* (each equal to one square league) had created

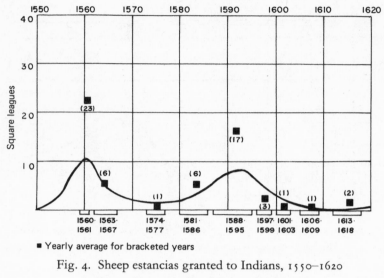

Fig. 4. Sheep estancias granted to Indians, 1550–1620
Source: Simpson, *Exploitation of land*, 11.

a newly cleared space of 2,576 square leagues. *Estancias de ganado menor* (each covering 0.44 of a square league) for the grazing of sheep and goats already came to 1,801 square leagues. A large part of this vast land area was not cultivated or devoted to stock raising at once, but its grant to private owners strengthened and greatly accelerated the massive agricultural transformation which was being brought about. Hundreds of new settlers benefited and a new group of landowners was created which was almost always antagonistic to the great encomenderos, who also benefited from land distribution and with whom they vied for land, workers, and markets.

The crown's decision to make a massive distribution of land and to divide it amongst many recipients institutionalized the original chaotic process of land settlement and gave the landowners stability precisely at the moment when the discovery of the mines, the expansion of settlement, and the decay of native agriculture made it necessary to create new sources of food production. This demand and the offering of grants of *caballerías* and estates attracted old and new settlers who lacked prior resources into the new agricultural towns which from 1560 onwards were established in the Bajío and further north, largely to supply the mining areas. Likewise, the rise in food prices and the abundant availability of land stimulated the formation of haciendas and mixed ranches (combining arable farming and stock-raising) which surrounded the cities and administrative capitals of the centre and south of the country. Under these stimuli, the livestock hacienda began to enclose within its boundaries wandering herds of cows, sheep, goats, and horses which, according to medieval Spanish tradition, were allowed to graze freely on wastelands and even to run on the farmlands after the harvest to feed on the stubble. In New Spain, this custom led to the recognition of pastureland, woodland, and land covered with stubble as land for common use. Out of this sprang a long series of complaints by Indian cultivators at the invasion of their open fields by herds of livestock. Such litigation was subsequently carried on by Spanish farmers themselves and was moderated only when territorial limits were set to livestock haciendas in 1567. Viceroys Luis de Velasco (1550–64) and Martín Enríquez (1568–80) also promulgated severe enactments to reduce the damage that livestock were causing, particularly in areas of native settlement. In Toluca and Tepeapulco, where Indians and livestock were concentrated in direct opposition to one another, fences were set up to stop animals trampling the seedbeds. Dates were also set to restrict the seasons of transhumance and of grazing on the stubble. Livestock owners were required to employ a set number of herdsmen on horseback to bar livestock from invading arable land. During these years, a policy was adopted which curtailed the grants for livestock estates in the basically Indian communities of the centre and south, but which gave them away freely in the newly colonized areas, both in the north and along the coast. In the north, these great unfenced spaces were covered with scrub, in the south they were savanna and woodlands. Stock-pens were situated far away from the pastures and the shack-like buildings where the estancieros (blacks, mulattos or mestizos), but not the owners, lived. In most cases, the herds grazed on wasteland and on the land left over between estates. Sometimes they took up an enormous space for the simple reason that nobody claimed it.

In the sixteenth century, occupying land without legal title was the most common way of extending one's property. This illegal occupation began to be regularized between 1591 and 1616, when the crown laid down new procedures for acquiring land. The most important measure was an ordinance of 1591 under which all irregular possessions of land purchases made illegally from the Indians, and land covered by a defective title could be regularized by means of a *composición* (a fee paid to the treasury). Between 1600 and 1700 most of the great haciendas of arable land, the livestock estates, and the large properties acquired by the church were regularized by this process. Thus in little less than a century the Spanish crown began and completed a vast programme of land redistribution which set the pattern for the later development of agriculture and landholding in the colony.

LABOUR

The hacienda attained stability when it succeeded in creating its own system for attracting, keeping, and replacing workers. It needed a little more than a century to achieve this, by means of constant struggle with the Indian community, the chief supplier of human energy at that time.

From 1521 to 1542, the encomenderos had free use of the labour power that the encomienda Indians gave them. The pre-existing native systems for the production of goods and the rendering of services were left unmodified. Under the encomienda, the Indian retained his bonds with the village and the people to which he belonged, setting up a temporary relationship with the encomendero, consisting in seasonal, unspecialized work. Because of its political character, this relationship was one of vassalage and did not involve any salary. Indians in encomienda were fed by what their community produced The communities also had to defray the costs of the worker's removal from his village of origin to the place where his services were rendered. In sum, encomienda Indians continued to be peasant producers, residing in their villages and performing a multiplicity of compulsory but temporary tasks for the encomendero. However, this system aggravated the exploitation of the Indians, since the rural villages and families had to produce what they needed for their own subsistence and reproduction, as well as a surplus to be transferred to the encomenderos, without receiving any benefit in exchange.

This situation began to change when the crown assessed the difference between the revenue the Indians paid in tribute and the revenue that agriculture, cattle-raising, and mining were beginning to furnish. However, as these activities needed a settled, permanent workforce that the encomienda could not provide, the Spaniards turned to slaves, both Indian and African. The initial exploitation of placer gold mining, silver mines and sugar mills thus encouraged the formation of a significant slave population in New Spain, which by 1550 had come to make up the permanent labour force of these activities. In 1548, Indian slavery was forbidden and many of the freed Indians became the first *naborías*, or wage-earners, who lived and worked permanently on the haciendas and the mines in exchange for pay. It was, however, African slaves who more often became the permanent workers, especially in the critical years from 1570 to 1630, when the native population plummeted. By 1570 there were already some 25,000 African slaves in New Spain, and it is estimated that between 1595 and 1640 over 100,000 more arrived.

African slaves formed an important part of the permanent labour force, but the development of agriculture, cattle raising and mining in New Spain would have been impossible without large numbers of seasonal workers, who could only be Indians. In order to break the encomenderos' monopoly of Indian labour the crown in 1549 ordered the abolition of personal services under the encomienda and in 1550 directed Viceroy Velasco to institute a system where Indians were to hire themselves out for a wage to Spanish enterprises. If they did not volunteer, the authorities should force them to do so. This draft labour system, known as *repartimiento* or *coatequitl*, became general from 1568 onwards and continued until about 1630.

During the greater part of the year, each Indian village was compelled to contribute between two and four per cent of its active work force, and ten per cent during the weeding and harvesting seasons. This percentage of workers was distributed in weekly shifts, so that each worker served an average of three to four weeks each year, in periods four months apart. The Indians were to be well treated, and they were only to do the work assigned to them at the time of hiring. In exchange, they were to be paid a daily wage, which, between 1575 and 1610, varied from half a real to a real and a half (1 peso = 8 reales). Between 1550 and 1560, it was also decreed that instead of paying tribute in many different products tribute should be paid only in two forms: in money or in kind, preferably in agricultural products, i.e. maize or wheat. Since the only way for the Indians to obtain money to pay the tribute was by working in the mines, on the haciendas, and in public services, this decree came to be another way of forcing them into employment in Spanish enterprises.

As all later history was to show, the Indians would not have consented to leave their communities and their traditional methods of production had they not been forced to do so, since neither the monetary wages nor other attractions in Spanish enterprises were any improvement over the way of life they enjoyed in their communities. The adoption of the new working system brought about radical changes in the Indian villages, principally because before the conquest and under the encomienda system the Indian used to produce his subsistence, as well as the surplus exacted by his overlords, in the same space and by the same methods of production. The new system of forced reparti-miento meant that the work to produce his means of subsistence was performed in his village and much of the surplus labour had to be done elsewhere under different conditions of production. Under the repartimiento, it was the Spanish authorities, not the native communi-ties, who determined the time of compulsory work and the wages, working conditions, and distribution of the workforce. These com-munities no longer had complete control over the organization of surplus labour. Moreover, when the repartimiento began, the natives were forced to work in specialized sectors of the Spanish economy (mining, agriculture, ranching) and with foreign means of production. Nonetheless, the peasant community did not remain apart from the new production process; on the contrary, it incorporated itself into it, with specific charges and functions.

Under the repartimiento system, the Indian village undertook the task of producing, with its own resources, the labour force required by the Spanish enterprises and of providing the seasonal workers required by the different haciendas, mines, public works, and the growing activities of the religious orders. This massive transfer of workers to the Spanish economy reduced the capacity for self-sufficiency that the native community had previously enjoyed. The constant flow of workers prevented the communities from producing for their own consumption, and this increased their dependence on goods produced by the Spanish economy. Thus, in order to replace the production of the Indians who went to work for the Spaniards, the Indian communities were forced to demand more work and increased production from their remaining members to compensate for the imbalance. However, a large part of that production had to be sent to the Spanish market, on the one hand, to obtain the income needed to make cash payments required from the communities as tribute, and, on the other, to buy goods they had ceased to produce or which political coercion on the part of their overlords forced them to purchase.

By the end of the sixteenth century and the early decades of the seventeenth, hacendados were beginning to oppose the forcible allocation of Indian workers by the *corregidores* (district magistrates) and to petition for the right to hire them in a 'free market' without interference from the authorities. They claimed that the Indians should be 'free to work for whomsoever they please and in any activity they choose, and to go to those employers who offer them the best conditions'. The owners needed more workers if they were going to cope with the demand of new and wider markets calling for a constant supply of agricultural and animal products that the Indian villages themselves could no longer satisfy, doubly weakened as they were by the demographic catastrophes and by the drain of workers. Hacendados began to keep Indian workers on their estates and pay them wages. In 1632, the crown ratified this new system of labour when it decided to suppress the compulsory repartimiento of agricultural workers and approved their hiring themselves out voluntarily in return for a day-wage. This decision benefited the great landowners, who had greater access to credit and more financial resources available and could make advances in clothing and money to workers to attract them and thus win the intense struggle for the scarcest of all resources. On the other hand, small and medium landowners saw themselves obliged to increase their own families' efforts, or to set up forms of joint production such as sharecropping or co-partnerships. By these means the owners of the great farming and stock-raising haciendas had, for the first time, a permanent non-slave workforce available throughout the year. The territorial expansion of the hacienda was consolidated by the acquisition of these workers, who from 1630 onwards settled down and multiplied within the boundaries of the hacienda, forming a resident peonage; that is, a body of workers who in practice had virtually no freedom of movement.

Under the new system, the crown not only lost the power by which it had hitherto been able to have its own official allocate and distribute the workforce, but it also, in effect, handed the workers over to the hacendados without any protection. From then on, the owners progressively became masters, legislators, judges, and magistrates over the hacienda residents. The hacienda ceased to be a simple 'arable farm' or 'stock-raising estate', as sixteenth- and early seventeenth-century documents term it, and became a self-contained unit of production. It was henceforth a permanently inhabited territorial area, with both fallow and cultivated lands, granaries in which the products of the harvest were kept, houses for the owners and their managers, shacks for the workers, small craft workshops, and toolsheds.

The conversion of the hacienda into a permanent economic and social unit engaged in the production of foodstuffs for the nearest urban and mining markets did not, nevertheless, assure it easily available permanent workers. The chief difficulty continued to be the absence of a labour market, since Indians who could have provided it had their own means of subsistence and shared in a peasant culture that was based on the corporate organization of the Indian village. Moreover, there were no sedentary Indian villages in the north whose inhabitants could be compelled to work on Spanish enterprises. Agricultural estates, stock-raising haciendas, and mines had to begin by having thousands of sedentary Indians sent to them from the south, by purchasing African slaves, and by enslaving hundreds of nomadic natives. Later on, the prosperity of the mines and the expansion of the haciendas that fed them attracted a continuous flow of rootless men, 'mestizos', a product of ethnic and cultural cross-breeding. Farming and livestock haciendas, as well as the mining and urban areas, were the crucibles in which New Spain's new population was forged. In the seventeenth century, the permanent workers on the livestock haciendas of the north and of the sugar haciendas in the coastal and tropical lowlands were African slaves, mulattos, creoles and mestizos, men without any secure position in either of the Indian or Spanish poles into which society was divided. However, they did have the necessary cultural adaptation to handle the new techniques and the new economic situation. Thus they became foremen and supervisors of work in the field, well qualified and trusted, and forefathers of a new generation of workers. However, studies now available show that even in the north, with its greater labour mobility, the most usual way to attract workers was to advance them money or clothing on future wages and that the most common way of retaining them was to go on lending them money, so as to keep them permanently indebted and legally tied to the hacienda. This was the system of debt peonage.

The Bajío was nearer to the nucleus of sedentary native peasants but, as a colonization zone, it bordered upon areas with unsubdued Indians.

Hacendados there also felt compelled to offer more attractions to permanent workers, giving them an additional weekly maize ration and putting into effect the system of cumulative debt. However, in contrast to the livestock haciendas, which mostly needed permanent workers, their biggest problem was that of having considerable numbers of seasonal workers available for the sowing, weeding, and harvesting seasons. In the seventeenth century, the hacendados of the Bajío solved this problem by renting out part of their lands to the peasants, under an agreement whereby the latter undertook to work for the hacienda on seasonal tasks. This solution was followed in many agricultural frontier zones, and also in the native centre and south. It gave rise to the existence of the so-called *arrimados* (squatters) and sharecroppers, and to forms of land tenure which in reality concealed labour relationships, as in the case of debt peonage and the *tienda de raya*, the hacienda store where wages were paid in kind. Thus the owner employed his most abundant and cheapest resource, land, to attract the scarcest and costliest resource, seasonal labour. In the majority of farming haciendas, the annual payroll constituted the biggest single running expense.

In the centre and the south, most of the haciendas drew their basic force of permanent workers from individuals of mixed Indian, African, and European blood. The worker received no wages but instead open credits allowing him to receive money loans and clothing, or alternatively compensation in kind, such as extra maize rations, housing, and the use of a small plot of land to cultivate within the boundaries of the hacienda. Besides these methods, hacendados had other ways of retaining workers compulsorily. One of the methods most generally employed was the obligation landowners undertook of paying the annual tribute of resident workers to the royal treasury officials, or of paying the fees that the workers owed the parish priest for marriages, funerals, and baptisms. These practices strengthened debt peonage; in Puebla and Tlaxcala the former practice was used as a pretext to keep workers permanently in the status of 'registered' bondsmen on the hacienda. Other forms of labour relations common in seventeenth- and eighteenth-century central Mexico were withholding all or part of the monetary wages (as in the case of several haciendas 'indebted' to their workers), refusing to accept the tender of payment of the worker's debt so that he could leave, manipulating the payroll in favour of the hacendado, and entering into collusive arrangements with royal officials and Indian caciques to retain workers without due cause. All in all, everything known to date about the means used to attract and retain permanent workers in the haciendas indicates the absence of a free labour market, and the prevalence not so much of a money wage as of means of subsistence (loans, food rations, housing, and the right to use hacienda land). It is also important to note that the permanent workforce of the haciendas did not draw as many members from Indian peasant villages, which maintained their own means of production and had a self-sufficient corporate economy, as from racially mixed groups which from their inception did not have the right to any land.

The pressure that the haciendas of the centre and south exerted on the Indian villages fell upon seasonal workers: it aggravated conflicts as markets expanded and as a bigger volume of production was needed, since this meant an increased demand for unskilled seasonal labour. The Indian villages eluded this pressure as long as they kept the balance between the area of their productive land and the size of their population. However, when land was no longer sufficient to support the population, individuals had to emigrate to the haciendas, the mines, or the cities. So one of the hacendados' principal strategies for acquiring workers was, precisely, to seize the lands of the Indian communities. Another, which the Spanish crown employed from the mid sixteenth century onwards, was to require the Indians to pay tribute in money: this necessarily compelled them to seek at least seasonal employment in Spanish enterprises. In the seventeenth and eighteenth centuries, this pressure increased, because religious fees also had to be paid in cash and, furthermore, because the Indians were coerced into buying merchandise from the *alcalde mayor* (district magistrate). This imposition, also known as *repartimiento*, was the cause of several native insurrections.

Even when continued emigration of workers progressively reduced the communities' capacity for self-sufficiency and compelled them to depend more on outside sources, most of the villages of the centre and south peacefully acquiesced in the relationship imposed on them by this system of domination. In areas where workers were scarcest, they even turned it to their own advantage, requiring landowners to grant them access to woods, quarries, and water supplies that the hacienda had appropriated for itself, in return for providing the hacienda with labour during the sowing, weeding, and harvesting seasons. In other cases, the landlord 'leased' a portion of his land to the Indian communities in return for seasonal workers. The landowners also set up a system of seasonal enlistment of workers, using a recruiter or contractor who visited the villages and, with the connivance of Indian caciques and governors, made up gangs of workers for the haciendas.

In this way, the system of domination gave the Indian villages the costly task of begetting and feeding the future labour force, as well as the obligation to train it in agrarian skills and make it available for the sowing and harvesting seasons. In return, the workers were offered a cash wage barely sufficient for them to meet the tribute, and to pay for the Spanish merchandise which the *alcalde mayor* made them buy. The means of subsistence which actually kept the seasonal workers alive came from their own work on plots of land within their native communities. Similarly the peons, or permanent hacienda workers, produced the major part of their own subsistence, since the maize rations or the plots of land that the landlord assigned to them within the hacienda, together with the labour of other members of their families, made up their true means of support. Thus a major part of the haciendas' economic success was a result of the surplus value extracted from peons' long workdays and from the exploitation of their families and of the peasant community. The remainder was achieved by the hacienda's adaptation to the market.

MARKETING

The hacienda emerged in order to satisfy the domestic demand created by the urban and mining-centre markets. Mexico City was the first market to give impetus to the formation of a belt of both agricultural and stock-raising haciendas around it. Later, its continuous population growth created a network of commercial channels supplying it with sugar, cotton, cacao, tropical fruits, and cattle from the north, the Pacific coast and Veracruz; wool, sheep, and lambs from the north-east; wheat and other grains from Puebla and the Bajío; and maize, the staple foodstuff, from the fertile lands of the areas surrounding the capital itself. The great mining centres of Zacatecas, Guanajuato, San Luis Potosí, Parral and Pachuca, along with other, smaller centres, were at first fed by the Indian agricultural areas of central Mexico, but in the late sixteenth century and during the two centuries that followed, they caused the development of agricultural and livestock haciendas in their own vicinities. In the Bajío and around Guadalajara, areas were settled with farmers and wide expanses were converted to growing crops and raising livestock intended primarily to supply the mining market.

Administrative capitals of provinces, such as Puebla, Guadalajara and

Valladolid (Morelia), were peopled by officials, members of the clergy and educational centres, and large groups of merchants, artisans and servants, and they, too, constituted important local and regional markets. But they never rivalled either in size or in importance the greatest market of all, the capital city itself. Mexico City was where the greatest number of people and the monetary profits of much of the economic activity of the viceroyalty were concentrated. Yet the capital city was no match for the dynamic mining markets, where the highest investments were made and the best salaries paid, and where the majority of the population used money or credit for trading. In other places where neither great investments nor important concentrations of wealth existed, where no great increase in population occurred, tiny markets barely provided sufficient outlets for small stock ranches requiring low investment and a minimal labour force. This was the case in Mérida, where the greater part of the foodstuffs that entered the city was provided by Indian farmers. The rest of the viceroyalty was a land of small farmers and of Indian villages where the population produced and consumed its own crops.

The commercial sector of agriculture in New Spain was thus concentrated around the two poles linking the colony to Spain: the mining complexes and the political and administrative centres. Agricultural production was conditioned not only by the area cultivated but also by frequent climatic variations. Droughts, frosts, hailstorms, and scarce or excessive rainfall substantially affected the volume of production and caused harvests to vary considerably in quality from year to year. As New Spain depended exclusively on domestic agricultural production to satisfy its needs, these tremendous cyclical fluctuations determined the volume of supply, the characteristics of demand, the level and variation of prices, and the market structure of basic staples such as maize, wheat, and meat. In years of abundant, regular rainfall the good yields brought a generous supply of grain and farm products into the markets. Although the owners of the large haciendas avoided selling in the months immediately following the harvest (November to April), the abundant supply provided by the Indians and the small and medium farmers pushed the price of maize down to its lowest level. It is important to note that maize was the basic foodstuff of the majority of the population as well as of draught and pack animals, livestock, pigs, and chickens. In these years of abundance, the grain trade in urban markets shrank considerably, because a large part of the native and mestizo population could rely on its own cereal production grown on tiny plots owned by families or individuals. A good harvest thus meant plentiful, cheap maize and the contraction of the market because of self-sufficiency, clear evidence that a considerable part of the urban population continued to possess small landholdings.

However, years of good harvests were interrupted by years of scanty rainfall, prolonged drought, early frosts, hailstorms, or a combination of those conditions. In the worst cases (1533, 1551–2, 1579–81, 1624, 1695, 1749–50, 1785–6 and 1809–10), the anticipated crop was reduced by half or more, sometimes throughout the whole agricultural zone, or in its main areas. Although bad weather afflicted all land equally, its effects were uneven. The great landowners' properties, rich lands, irrigated, well fertilized and sown with the best seed, were always the least affected. On the other hand, bad weather had fatal effects on the poor land, usually lacking in irrigation, animal manure, or selected seed, that belonged to Indians and smallholders. Because of this, and because the area of cultivation for commercial purposes was incomparably larger on the haciendas than on the lands owned by the native villages, the volume of grain that the hacienda had for sale in times of agricultural crisis would greatly exceed what the Indian communities or the small landholders could offer. Nonetheless, in years of agricultural crisis, the grain that arrived first in the urban and mining areas was that of native producers and creole and mestizo smallholders, bringing to the market what little they had salvaged from their crops to obtain cash with which to pay their tribute or their debts, or to repay loans incurred at the time of sowing. To do this they had to impose a strict diet on their own families for the rest of the year. The great landowners, on the other hand, hoarded their harvests in their granaries and sent grain to market only when prices were at their highest (May to October), when seasonal scarcity coincided with the crisis on the farms. Then, the opposite of what happened in the years of abundant harvest occurred; almost all the population became net consumers except the great landowners, whose volume of production and large storage capacity enabled them, as the only suppliers, to impose a 'seller's market'. In the severest agricultural crisis of the eighteenth century, prices of maize and wheat went up 100, 200, or at times even 300 per cent above the lowest price in the agricultural cycle. In other words, the great landowners obtained their highest profits in seasons when most of the population was suffering the onslaughts of soaring prices, hunger, and unemployment.

In every case of marked shrinkage in harvests, it was maize and wheat that led the rapid price rise, followed by meat, since both droughts and frosts destroyed the pasture and caused heavy mortality amongst cattle.

Years of bad harvests, then, meant a general scarcity of basic foodstuffs, a galloping rise in prices, and a swollen market of farm products. In such years, the volume of grain sales in city and mining markets would be two to three times what it was in years of good harvests. People who never purchased these products in times of plenty because they were self-sufficient producers consuming their own crops turned into full-scale consumers of the products of others in years of bad harvest. Moreover, in years of agricultural crisis, the whole supply system for foodstuffs operated to the advantage of urban and mining centres endowed with institutions whose function it was to buy up grain with municipal funds to maintain a constant cheap supply, and containing public granaries or municipal markets to which farmers were obliged to bring their grain for sale. These institutions' purchasing power, the authorities' pressure to make sure that crops were taken and sold there, the high prices, and the growing, urgent demand for food at these times combined to siphon the whole of the countryside's production into the chief cities and mining centres. In particular, high prices in the urban markets broke the barriers which normally made long-distance transportation of farm products unprofitable. This sequence of good and bad years, with its range of effects on the volume of production, supply, demand, and price levels, became a regular phenomenon, a recurring and immutable agricultural cycle with effects on the organization of the hacienda as a producing unit which was constructed precisely to counteract the most catastrophic effects of this cycle. In the short term, the hacienda's strategy was to extract the greatest possible profit from the seasonal changes in supply, demand, and agricultural prices by constructing enormous granaries which allowed hacendados to stockpile grain instead of having to sell it during the months of low prices. However, to combat the handicaps that arose from the variability of harvests, the restriction of markets, and the massive cheap supply from native producers and small landholders, the hacienda developed a more elaborate strategy which came to typify its characteristics as a producing unit.

Like every enterprise engaged in the sale of its products, the hacienda was organized so as to obtain a net surplus that its owner could treat as profit (that is, gross product minus the hacienda's own consumption requirements and minus the investment needed to renew its productive capabilities). To obtain this surplus, it was necessary to increase the volume of commercial production within the hacienda itself and extend the range of goods needed for home consumption and production, to avoid having to acquire these elsewhere. That is to say, the hacienda owners needed to increase their income from crop sales and to reduce their purchase of input goods to the minimum, so that they could devote themselves completely to maintaining their rank in society and to acquiring the European articles which they did not produce.

One way of attaining these objectives was to increase the size of the hacienda. As we have seen, the hacienda's losses or profits were unpredictable and depended on the vagaries of the climate and on the ups and downs of supply and demand. The owners therefore sought to equip their haciendas with the resources necessary to counteract the effects of these destabilizing factors. Within the boundaries of the hacienda, they sought to amass the greatest possible variety of land (irrigated or seasonal arable land and pastures) and of natural resources (rivers, springs, woodlands, and quarries) in an effort to create precisely the balanced economy which was lacking in the agricultural structure of New Spain. On the one hand this multiplicity of resources cut down the purchase of input goods from the outside, while on the other it protected the hacienda more adequately from the uncertainties of climate, with the availability of more extensive and diversified terrain. The most fertile and the best irrigated lands could be utilized for cash crops, and other areas planted with crops intended for home consumption, leaving the rest to lie fallow. All the haciendas of New Spain that have been studied show this characteristic of polyculture: alongside the cash crops (sugar-cane, maize, wheat, maguey, or live-stock) they produced an array of crops for their own consumption (maize, beans, peppers) and also exploited all other hacienda resources such as woodlands, lime-kilns, and quarries.

The acquisition of enormous expanses of land also helped the hacienda to fight off its competitors in the market. Every plot of land lost by the small farmer or the *ranchero*, and every piece of land wrested from an Indian village, reduced production for the hacendado's competitors and enlarged the market for his own production. The vast lands that the hacienda amassed and the many hectares that it kept lying fallow had, therefore, an economic logic. As we have already seen, robbing the Indians of their land came to be the best way of creating a labour force and also the best indirect way of multiplying consumers of the hacienda's products. For the dispossessed Indians there was no alternative but to hire themselves out to the hacienda as peons, to flock into the cities (and increase the number of urban consumers), or to flee to the most isolated areas of the country. However, in the jungle, the mountains, or the desert, Indian crops could not compete with those of the hacienda.

On the other hand, dividing the hacienda's extensive territory into areas for cash crops, areas producing for internal consumption, and areas lying fallow made a series of combinations possible whereby the owners could deal with the problems with which the agrarian and commercial structure of the colony presented them. Thus, in the sixteenth and seventeenth centuries, when markets were small, demand weak, and prices low, most of the growers concentrated on the fullest utilization of the areas reserved for internal consumption and on those left fallow, cutting back the area intended for cash crops. The area employed for home consumption exceeded that intended for cash crops so as to avoid low prices in the market and the purchase of commodities from outside. Also, the possibilities of polyculture were exploited to the maximum so that the fate of the hacienda did not depend on a single crop that could be ruined by bad weather. During these years of restricted demand and low prices, landowners often rented out a great part of the lands that the hacienda was not cultivating, with the dual purpose of securing another source of income and of having a reservoir of workers who tilled the hacienda land in return for the 'lease', without receiving any cash wages. Lastly, as the most important thing was to avoid money payment outside the hacienda, owners limited payment in money to expenditure that was really strictly necessary, that is, to advances in cash to attract workers.

In periods of demographic expansion, market growth, increasing demand, and rising prices, the mix and the use of the hacienda's resources were modified. As exemplified in the Bajío and the Guadalajara area in the later eighteenth century, the area intended for cultivation of cash crops and products for internal consumption was then enlarged at the expense of fallow lands, and it became necessary to lease or acquire new land. Land rose in value, and consequently, the most fertile was used for the more marketable products, while livestock and crops intended for internal consumption were moved to less fertile terrain. Use of marginal land increased, and the cultivated area generally was enlarged to meet the greater volume of products for the commercial market as well as for the growing number of hacienda workers. Owners then either raised rents or exacted more work from tenants, or simply evicted them so as to exploit the land directly and take advantage of the rise in prices in the urban market. It was at these times that pressure from the landowners on the territory of the Indian communities became stronger. When they failed to appropriate these lands, they were often leased, as happened in the Guadalajara area, where a great part of village land was leased to hacienda and ranch owners.

Consequently, in periods both of slackening and of appreciable rises in demand and prices, the hacendado always sought the maximum reduction in money outlay for incoming goods and an increase in his money income from direct sales in the market. Hence, the economic parameters of the hacienda were set by the monetary costs of inputs, on the one hand, and by the creation of monetary income through the sale of cash crops in the market, on the other. If the owner's lands were extensive and diversified, he could attract a labour force without having to spend great amounts of money, and through the proper blending of these resources he could produce at a cost low enough to be competitive in the market. However, if his land was scanty or infertile, or both, he was forced to seek labour and goods in exchange for money, and thereby raise his production costs, or else to increase the exploitation of family labour as the majority of ranchers and smallholders did. In the case of the owner of large expanses of diversified land, peons and seasonal day-labourers were made responsible for production for internal consumption as well as for sale in the market. A small farmer or rancher, however, would expect his own family to bear this burden.

Studies of colonial haciendas show that they all endeavoured to become self-sufficient in grain staples, especially maize, since corn rations were given in lieu of wages by all hacendados to both their permanent and their seasonal peons. A large number of the middle-sized haciendas and nearly all the large haciendas and latifundia were also self-sufficient in meat, dairy products, hides, and tallow, as well as in draught and pack animals. The great landed estates as well as the haciendas belonging to the religious orders, in addition to being self-sufficient in grain and animal products, were also self-sufficient in many basic consumer goods. There were carpenters and smiths right on the haciendas where agricultural implements and carts were made, and there were also small tanneries and soap and textile factories.

Haciendas also formed an interrelated and complementary production complex amongst themselves. In this way, anything that any of the haciendas did not produce in sufficient quantities was supplied by others without recourse to the open market. Likewise, in order to avoid the market, the miners of the north acquired extensive haciendas specializing in cereals and livestock, in order to provide food for their own workers, along with wood, charcoal, pack and draught animals, hides, tallow, and other materials required for the mining and refining of metals. Money was used as a measure of value, but it hardly ever actually changed hands. This practice became generalized in the seventeenth century. It regulated the relationships between the great hacendados and the powerful merchants of Mexico City, who cornered the greater part of the money supply, controlled the credit system, and had the monopoly of goods imported from Europe. Thus, for example, the owners of huge landed estates of the north, who had enormous herds of sheep and goats, sent livestock on the hoof, leather, and wool to the owners of the textile mills of Querétaro, San Miguel and Mexico City, receiving in exchange textiles, clothing, shoes, leather goods, and other merchandise. The balance in favour of one party or the other was accounted for by the Mexico City merchant, who acted for both sides as a credit institution and a clearing house. The procedure operated as follows: the textile mill owner opened an account for the livestock owner in a Mexico City mercantile house, where he credited him with the value of the livestock, leather or wool received from him. In turn, when the livestock owner received the textiles and other articles from the mill owner, he issued a receipt or *libranza* (letter of credit) in favour of the latter, likewise payable in the capital's commercial establishments or negotiable in exchange for other credits. This practice became common in transactions amongst hacendados and between hacendados and merchants. The latter, thanks to their experience and the power they had acquired over the money supply, credit, and imported goods, ultimately monopolized the dealings of the producers. Thus the lack of any effective monetary commercial exchange made producers dependent on merchants. Domestic producers of sugar, cotton, cacao, livestock, cereals, and other farm products sent their crops in great volume to the merchants in the capital, who sent them local and imported manufactures in exchange. The merchants, then, traded twice over, and hence their profits were substantial. On the one hand they resold the agricultural products at monopoly prices in the controlled markets of the capital and of the mining centres, and on the other they extracted great profits from trading foodstuffs and primary products for manufactures and imported goods. However, the large-scale producer of food, cereals, and basic agricultural products also stood to gain quite considerably. In the first place, although his trading with the merchant was not on an equal footing, the latter was a regular customer who was a sure outlet for his surplus production every year, and who could be relied on to pay immediately for it, or to give him merchandise or credit of an equal value. Secondly, the landowner resold the clothing, textiles, shoes and other manufactured goods that the merchant supplied him with to his own workers at a higher price, or frequently offered them as a part of their 'wages'. Sometimes, the hacendado himself opened a store in the area and dealt with other producers on the same terms as a Mexico City merchant did; that is, he took agricultural products in exchange for manufactured articles. Finally, the hacendado did not lose out because the cost of the inequality in trading was defrayed not by him but by his workers and by the Indian community. In the last analysis, since the profit resulting from these exchanges went to Spain, Spain stood to gain, together with the capital city and the middlemen. The losers were the small and medium-sized farmers and, above all, the Indian workers and the Indian villages.

Moreover, because they sold large amounts of their harvests to the merchants, the landowners used local markets to secure a year-round monetary income. Very soon, the great landowners' hoarding of the best lands nearest the urban markets, plus their access to credit and their family and economic ties with the officials responsible for supplying the cities with food, gave them monopoly control over the food supply. In the sixteenth century, native agriculture supplied the main cities of the central region, such as Mexico City and Puebla, but in the seventeenth and eighteenth centuries it was overtaken by the production of the haciendas that had grown up around them. The 200,000 *fanegas* of maize (one *fanega* equalled 1.55 English bushels or 55.5 litres) which Mexico City consumed each year came, at the end of the eighteenth century, for the most part from the haciendas of Chalco and of the valley of Toluca, owned by creoles, mestizos, and Spaniards. The same was the case in Guadalajara, where more than half the 80,000 *fanegas* of maize brought to market each year came from the haciendas of the great creole landowners. On the other hand, the share represented by native production, which between 1750 and 1770 already provided only about

25 per cent of the total of maize imported into the city, had fallen by
1810 to almost nothing. During the eighteenth century, every medium-
sized and large city showed this concentration of the maize supply in
the hands of the great hacendados. A further large share of Indians' and
smallholders' production of maize and cereals was also hoarded by
hacendados, merchants, and officials, who resold it in urban markets.
This process was consolidated by a continual fusion of hacendados with
city authorities, allowing the former to occupy the chief posts on the
cabildo, with the result that regulations on food supply were favourable
to the great landowners. Thus, although they were municipal institutions
intended, in theory, to maintain a constant cheap supply of maize for
the consumers, the granary and the corn exchange in fact came to work
in the interests of the big producers from whom they purchased the
greater part of their grain and who, as monopoly suppliers and sellers
of grain, were able to act as a pressure group on the price levels.

The case of wheat and flour is a good example. From the late sixteenth
century, hacendados (at first Spanish, but later creole) virtually
monopolized the production of wheat sold in the cities. In the
eighteenth century, the owners of large haciendas supplying the capital
usually had a harvest averaging over 1,000 *cargas* of wheat (one *carga*
equalled 149.5 kg), while the medium-sized haciendas could scarcely
supply more than 200 to 400 *cargas*. The large landowners' pre-eminence
in production induced them to build mills where wheat was ground,
and these turned into markets and storage centres for the flour the cities
consumed. Thus, in the eighteenth century, the chief mills around the
capital had a combined storage capacity of 50,000 *cargas* of flour, some
40 per cent of the city's annual consumption. Two mills in the
ownership of a single family controlled 30 per cent of the city's milling
and storage capacity. What happened in the capital of the viceroyalty
was repeated in Puebla, Valladolid, Oaxaca, Guanajuato, Zacatecas, and
Guadalajara. Early in the eighteenth century, most of the wheat and
flour entering the market in Guadalajara belonged to small and medium
farmers, but by the end of the century these producers had almost
disappeared, giving way to large hacendados who also owned the most
important mills. Hence, the capacity for growing wheat and for
producing and storing flour determined wheat prices in the urban
market.

The slaughter and sale of cattle was also controlled by municipal
authorities, whose chief officials included farmers and stock breeders.

The *abasto de carnes* (meat supply) was a municipal monopoly for the importation and sale of all the meat that was consumed in the city. The authorities leased it under contract to an individual, generally a stock breeder, who undertook to bring a given number of head of cattle during a given number of years. A few families were owners of the most extensive and numerous livestock haciendas around the viceregal capital, in the Bajío, and in the north, and therefore controlled the *abasto de carnes* and owned the three abattoirs that were licensed to operate. In Guadalajara in the late eighteenth century, one stock breeder alone, who was simultaneously *regidor y alférez real* (town councillor and royal standard-bearer) of the city, brought in 32 per cent of the livestock legally imported into the city for slaughter, and more than 70 per cent of the meat consumption was provided by five estates. The supply of sheep was even more concentrated, for just two haciendas sent Guadalajara more than 50 per cent of its total supply. In the second half of the eighteenth century, the hacendados of the Valley of Mexico also decided to exploit the enormous potential of the market that the capital, by then containing over 100,000 inhabitants, offered for the sale of pulque, the most popular beverage among the Indians and the castas (people of mixed race). In order to profit from this market, they converted into maguey fields the semi-arid lands north and north-east of the capital that were used for grazing and for the occasional growing of maize. Around 1760, the Jesuit estates concentrated in this area were producing 20 per cent of the pulque sold in the city; as much again came from the estates of the Conde de Jala, a powerful hacendado. At the end of the century the Jala family properties were incorporated with those of the Conde de Regla, and together they produced over half the pulque entering the viceregal capital. This monopoly of production was matched by control of the urban market: the same families that owned the haciendas had bought up the main shops in the city that were licensed to sell pulque.

Nevertheless, as the eighteenth century progressed, the monopoly of the large landowners disintegrated in Mexico City as well as in other principal cities of the colony. Almost every urban centre witnessed merchants taking over from producers the supply of meat, the marketing of maize, wheat, and flour, and the wholesale trading of sugar, cacao, hides, and wool. All the cases surveyed show that the great merchants displaced the large as well as the medium and small producers from marketing their products and from direct sale. This was done, on the one hand, through *habilitaciones* (loans) which the merchant advanced to the producer on the condition that most of the harvest be sold to him. On the other hand, with his command of cash resources, the merchant could exploit his position as the only potential purchaser; effectively, he was the only one able to make cash purchases of the bulk of the landowner's production. Whichever procedure was adopted, there can be no doubt that by the end of the eighteenth century the main commercial transactions in agricultural products were in the hands of merchants.

CREDIT

As we have seen, if a landowner did not combine in his own possession lands that were extensive, fertile, and diversified, or if he did not reduce to the minimum his cash expenditure, or if his cash reserves or his credit were not enough to permit him to ride out periods of falling demand and low prices, or to enable him to make rewarding investment in more land or equipment, his hacienda was simply not a good business. In other words, he was not producing any monetary surplus with which to obtain the goods and services which the colonial elite's urban lifestyle required. Conspicuous consumption was the essential manifestation of its power and status; however, it was very difficult for any one person to meet all the conditions necessary to ensure the stability of the hacienda. Recent studies have shown that very few families remained after two or three generations as owners of haciendas created by their ancestors.

The central problem in the formation of the hacienda certainly lay in the availability of ready cash to create, develop and maintain it. The history of the hacienda, therefore, is closely bound up with those individuals who possessed the scarcest resource of all, available capital and credit facilities. Everything we now know about the colonial economy of New Spain indicates that great estates did not arise from resources generated by agriculture alone, but from the investment in agriculture of income derived from encomienda, public office, mining, and commerce. The first Spaniards to accumulate land and cultivate it were the sixteenth-century *conquistadores–encomenderos* typified by Hernán Cortés; they were men who enjoyed a high annual income from public offices given to them as rewards for their exploits, who held hundreds of encomienda Indians yielding them free labour and tribute, and who, in addition to all this, had monetary incomes derived from commerce and mining. The founders of the enormous latifundia of the north were men of the same calibre: captains and governors of vast provinces which they had originally conquered and pacified, who became prosperous miners and finally owners of veritable territorial states where thousands of head of cattle grazed and where crops were grown to feed their mining and refining establishments. Later on, when the era of conquest and pacification was over, viceroys, judges, royal officials, magistrates, and officers of municipal councils acquired land. They used their official positions to obtain repartimiento Indians, credit, and special concessions enabling them to speculate in the market. The descendants of the original conquerors and encomenderos became united through marriage and economic and political ties to these powerful new men who handed out land and workers and who allowed access to the controlled urban markets. In this way, the luckiest retained and even extended their patrimonial estates. In the late sixteenth century and throughout the seventeenth, this generation of large landowners resisted the rise of a new generation of rich and powerful men: miners, merchants, and textile-mill owners. But they finally yielded and arranged new marriage, economic, and political alliances in order to survive.

The basis for the progressive symbiosis between landowners, officials, miners and the clergy was credit. The market characteristics already mentioned show that the chief difficulty faced by landowners was the availability of ready cash for seed, for purchasing and hiring implements, and for paying seasonal workers. Another problem was the need to borrow larger sums of money to build fences, granaries, and dams or to purchase more land. In these circumstances, the lack of liquid capital or the absence of cash transactions forced the landowner to seek loans. In the sixteenth and seventeenth centuries, in the absence of credit institutions, he obtained such loans from officials, mine owners, merchants, or the clergy. As security, he offered a socially prominent individual who was financially solvent or pledged rural or urban property. This meant that the landowners had to turn to individuals unrelated to agriculture in order to raise money or secure credit. This situation would give apparent support to the view that colonial agriculture was intrinsically incapable of yielding sufficient monetary profits to cover the running costs of the hacienda and to supply the owner with a surplus for savings, profitable investments, or for conspicuous consumption. Agricultural production did, in fact, produce a surplus, but it was diverted from the agricultural sector by the crown's economic policy and by the economic structure of New Spain.

The agricultural sector was affected by a political economy which impeded trade amongst the Spanish possessions in America. This worsened the effects of the cycles of good and bad harvests, of falling and soaring prices, and of the contraction and expansion of demand. That is to say, the impossibility of exporting grain when crops were abundant, or of importing it together with other foodstuffs in the years of agrarian crisis, made New Spain's agricultural cycle more extreme and the fluctuations in production and prices which so badly affected the economy more acute. Another economic policy decision which adversely affected the development of commercial agriculture in New Spain was the ban on the cultivation of certain plants, the processed products of which might compete with the manufactures exported by Spain. In reality, the enforced concentration on the growing of basic crops to feed the urban and mining areas meant that the agricultural sector was subsidizing silver production. However, most important of all was the crown's decision to appropriate almost all of New Spain's minted gold and silver. This action frustrated the development of a true mercantile economy, since it created a permanent outflow of the money supply. And the situation was further complicated by the fact that the monarch granted the merchant guild the monopoly of the now greatly reduced money supply.

Giving the merchants of the Mexico City *consulado* (merchant guild) the monopoly of trade with Spain, Asia, and – for a time – the Spanish possessions to the south and in the Caribbean enabled them to effect the greatest cash transactions, and reap the largest profits, in the unequal balance of trade between Spain and her colony. For example, manufactures were sold at monopoly prices in a captive market in exchange for precious metals and raw materials produced at low cost by exploiting the labour force, ensuring the predominance of the merchant over the producer. For the agricultural sector, this economic policy meant the transfer of its surplus production to the merchant, the permanent scarcity of money supply in the markets and the dependence on capital and credit monopolized by the merchant.

The relationship between the church and agriculture aggravated the distortions of agricultural development and made the situation of the hacienda more unstable. Unable to finance the immense effort of

indoctrination, pacification, social remodelling, and political legitimization undertaken by the church, the crown granted the latter the right
to collect and benefit from tithes. That is to say, the church extracted
10 per cent from agricultural and livestock production, the tithe being
a tax that had to be paid without any deduction allowed for 'seed, rent,
or any other expense'. No agricultural producer could evade the tithe,
not even the regular or secular clergy. Agricultural development was
further burdened by the innumerable and, at times, substantial monetary
donations made by the agricultural producers to churches, convents,
monasteries, confraternities, brotherhoods, hospitals, and other religious institutions. Since the landowners had no liquid capital, they
resorted to the procedure of taxing their estates with *censos* (mortgages),
which could be either redeemable or perpetually extended. In this way,
thousands of landowners burdened their holdings with *censos* payable
to the church. The mechanism consisted of burdening the hacienda with
a prescribed capital which was neither invested nor liable to total
repayment but on which the landowner undertook to pay an annual
interest of 5 per cent to the beneficiary of a pious donation. In other
words, without losing the ownership or use of his property, the
landowner diminished the annual income from the hacienda by payment
of 5 per cent interest on the amount donated to a religious institution.
This way of satisfying the pious feelings of the era was so massively
and so widely employed that at the end of the eighteenth century it was
said that there was no hacienda which was not burdened with one or
more *censos*.

The truth of the matter is that the unbridled multiplication of *censos*
on rural properties set up a process by which money was continually
drained from the producers' income. Ultimately, this situation helped
to destabilize the already precarious haciendas and ranches. As ecclesiastical and civil authorities alike recognized, hacendados and ranchers
were turned into mere administrators, leaving the religious institutions,
in effect, as the real landowners and beneficiaries of rural income.
Moreover, the accumulation of *censos* on haciendas brought about the
effective disappearance of the sale and purchase of rural property on the
basis of a cash transaction. Little money changed hands in the exchange,
since what actually occurred was the mere transfer of accumulated *censos*,
with the new owner incurring the obligation to pay the annual interest.
Through this process, rural land became 'property held in mortmain',
as Spanish liberals termed the accumulated ecclesiastical real estate

which never entered the market. In conclusion, even when agriculture did yield a surplus, this was channelled away by the continuous drain of capital which, added to the lack of cash-based commercial transactions, turned the hacienda, and especially the ranch, into a production unit highly vulnerable to the fluctuations of the agricultural and market cycles. The combination of these processes, in addition to the lack of access to credit, appears to provide the best explanation for the continual bankruptcies and divisions of ranches and haciendas.

Nevertheless, the great landowners did find effective ways to combat these ills and ensure the stability of the hacienda at the expense of the small and medium landowners. In the first place, they tried to secure the inheritance of the accumulated landed patrimony of the next generation. Every study of estates shows that after the death of most landowners their lands were divided among their children. The system of inheritance, then, became a further reason for the instability of the hacienda. Even when small or medium landowners did not inherit debts or mortgages with their properties, forcing their heirs to sell them, the division of land into small parcels determined the future loss of the patrimony since the *minifundio* and the tiny ranch were not suited to withstand violent climatic and price fluctuations. Faced with this threat, many hacendados in New Spain adopted the Spanish institution of the *mayorazgo* (entail) through which a family's rural and urban properties were made indivisible and had to be transmitted from one generation to the next through the succession of the eldest son. More than a thousand *mayorazgos* are known to have been created throughout the colonial period, many of them consisting of rural estates of modest proportions, instituted by farmers, the clergy, and members of provincial elites. Nevertheless, the most important *mayorazgos* formed vast estates in the ownership of a single family. These were originally founded by the descendants of the first *conquistadores* and encomenderos who had intermarried with rich miners and officials. Later on, in the eighteenth century, this group intermarried with the new rich families of merchants and miners, creating other important *mayorazgos*. The indivisibility and inalienability of the estates consolidated in a *mayorazgo* conferred economic stability on a landed patrimony that had been amassed over a generation and prevented its fragmentation or loss. On the other hand, it nullified individual aspirations nourished by the system of multiple inheritance, making the interests of every member coincide in the preservation of the wealth, power, prestige and distinction of the family as a unit through the perpetuation of a lineage. In the seventeenth and eighteenth centuries, titles of nobility were purchased by the richest hacendados, miners, merchants, and officials, who linked them to one or more territorial *mayorazgos*. Land, wealth, social prestige, and political power thus came together in a small nucleus of families who by the eighteenth century possessed the most extensive and fertile lands, monopolized the urban and mining markets, controlled the only sources of credit available, and derived the greater part of their money income by manipulating the network of external and internal trade.

The foundation of this oligarchy was the fusion of large landowner-ship with the monopoly of capital gained in the mining and commercial sectors. Credit was made available to the owners of large landholdings through the continuous marriage alliances that united their children with rich miners and merchants and through the accumulated land itself. Compared with the volatile fortunes made in mining and the hazardous adventures of commerce, the great landed estate came to be, in effect, the best way of preserving a patrimony and bequeathing it to succeeding generations, as well as constituting irrefutable proof of financial solvency. Furthermore, the new officials, miners, and merchants who had enriched themselves and who strengthened the landed patrimonies created by the early great landowners, were not alone. The church and the religious orders also turned rural (as well as urban) property into strong-boxes for the innumerable donations they received from private individuals. A portion of the money income received by way of *censos*, pious donations, bequests and chantries, was invested by the church and the religious orders in land and in urban properties. Another very substantial portion was given on loan to anyone who could pledge or mortgage rural or urban property, the best acceptable security of the period. In this way, the money that landowners, miners, merchants, manufacturers, and officials donated to the church in the form of pious donations returned to the richest families under the form of loans secured by their estates. These great landed families controlled the best and most valuable properties, its members also belonging to the religious orders that decided to whom the loans should be made. Recent studies of the amount of loans made by the religious orders and by the church to private individuals and the way in which these loans were made show that, without a doubt, the main beneficiaries of those funds were the principal families of landowners, miners, merchants, and officials. This small nucleus of interrelated families absorbed a large part of the available capital in New Spain as well as participating in the decision-making bodies of the various religious institutions.

The fact that merchants were inextricably bound up with an economic system which exported most of the surplus production to Spain prevented them from totally merging with the landowners, miners, and local manufacturers to form a colonial oligarchy with common interests. Moreover, the privileges that the Spanish crown granted to the merchants placed them at the apex of the dominant colonial economic system. Ultimately this new economic, political, and social status that the merchants gained during the eighteenth century was to put them at odds with the other members of the oligarchy. The concentration of credit and money supply in the hands of the merchants gave them greater political power than any other sector of the oligarchy. On the one hand, it made local, provincial, and viceregal officials dependent on them, because they needed cash securities to purchase public office. On the other hand, their enormous wealth allowed many merchants to buy public office for themselves and to preside over the main civil institutions. Furthermore, this same accumulated wealth began to finance the activities of municipal corporations, of the viceregal treasury, and even of the king of Spain.

Even though credit and the availability of liquid capital paved the way for the fusion of merchants with miners, the complete control that the former had over these resources made them the chief beneficiaries of mining. In exchange for the credit and commodities they provided the merchants appropriated the most substantial surpluses produced by the mining sector. The main measures by which agricultural producers were made subordinate to the merchants were the supply of credit and capital, and a greater monopoly over the external commercial sector. Merchants first deprived the agricultural producers of the marketing of export commodities and later displaced them from the domestic market. Throughout the eighteenth century and up to the time of New Spain's independence the great landowners depended on the capital and credit accumulated by the merchants.

6

THE RURAL ECONOMY AND SOCIETY
OF COLONIAL SPANISH SOUTH
AMERICA*

The Andean chain forms the warped backbone of South America. Its central ranges and plateaux constituted the heartland of the Inca empire. To a large extent, they maintained this role within the Spanish possessions throughout the colonial period, thanks to their enormous deposits of silver ore and their plentiful supply of hardy Indian workers. It is true that the northern and southern extensions of the Andes, with the adjacent basins of the Orinoco, the Magdalena and Río de la Plata, grew in economic importance. Yet colonial institutions and society bore above all the imprint of the Castilian conquest of the Inca realm.

Throughout the central Andean highlands (the sierra of present-day Peru, Bolivia, and Ecuador) vegetation, fauna and human conditions are determined primarily by the altitude. The percentage of cultivable land is exceedingly small. Also, the zone of pre-conquest agriculture was confined to between 2,800 and 3,600 metres above the sea. Here, after 1532, wheat and other Old World crops were added to the native maize and tubers. Above this zone, land can only be used for pasture. Here, European cattle and sheep gradually replaced the native llama as the chief resource. The eastern slopes (*ceja de montaña*) and also the deeper mountain valleys offer areas suitable for growing a wide variety of tropical products such as sugar, cacao, and coffee. The various vertical niches thus provide a surprisingly varied alimentary basis for human civilization, not only on a regional but often on a local level as well. Situated between the mountain barrier and cold water currents off-shore, the narrow Peruvian coastal strip (the *costa*) is a natural desert. However, in the course of the first millennium B.C., the construction of irrigation systems and the use of fertilizers allowed the development of agriculture

* Original text in English; revised and reduced in length by the Editor.

supporting a dense population and increasingly stratified societies. There was a continuous cultural interplay between costa and sierra until both merged under a common political structure, the Inca empire. Further north, the coast of Quito (Ecuador) comprises hot, humid lowlands suited primarily for plantation crops. The northern parts of the continent, New Granada (now Colombia) and Venezuela, defy simple characterization. The heartland of the former comprises the three north–south ranges of the Cordillera and between them the Magdalena and Cauca valleys. There is no easy access to either the Pacific or the Atlantic. In Venezuela, the highlands on the whole follow the northern coast. They are separated by vast grasslands (*llanos*) from the only major river, the Orinoco, which flows leisurely from west to east. Geographically and culturally, northern Colombia and all but the most western parts of Venezuela are very much a part of the Caribbean. South of the central Andes, Chile is a narrow strip along the ocean which stretches through three contrasting zones: desert in the north, a central 'Mediterranean' area with optimum conditions for agriculture and a forested, wet zone in the south. Across the Andes, the highlands of north-western Argentina form a continuation of the central Andean sierra, though the Tucumán and Mendoza areas form fertile and moist enclaves. Further south and east are the undulating grasslands of Paraguay, which were inhabited fairly densely by an Indian farming population. On the other hand, the grass-covered plains (the pampas) of Argentina were almost devoid of inhabitants at the time of conquest and would long remain so.

Even though each of these regions is immense and varied, we will use them to show some of the variations in colonial land tenure, labour systems, agricultural and pastoral production, and commercialization in Spanish South America.

LAND TENURE, CAPITAL, AND LABOUR

At the time of the conquest, the acquisition of land was not the main Spanish objective. Spaniards wanted primarily to re-establish in the New World the kind of urban-centred society they had left behind them in southern Spain. For provisions, these towns would rely on the surrounding native farming populations, subjected to a system of indirect colonial rule. The encomienda seemed to provide the ideal formula for this Spanish–Indian relationship. Entrusted to the protection and religious instruction of their encomenderos the Indians would deliver to them tribute in the form of commodities and/or labour service. As a legal institution, the encomienda did not imply rights to Indian lands. And in view of the density of Indian farmers in the nuclear areas as compared to the tiny clusters of European settlers, for a long time the demand for land was extremely limited.

Yet the legal instrument for land redistribution was an inherent feature of the very process of founding towns. Just as the householders (*vecinos*) received their ground plots by 'royal favour', they were entitled to receive larger or smaller tracts of land not cultivated already by the Indians for their own subsistence, as *mercedes de tierra* in the surrounding area. Depending on their prospective use, such land grants referred to farmlands (*mercedes de labor*) and grazing (*mercedes de estancias de ganados*) respectively. The type of grant used reflected the military reward character of the grants and the cautious approach of the crown: a *peonía* was originally a small piece of farmland granted to a foot-soldier; a *caballería*, the grant to a cavalryman, was about five times as much. A single *merced* often comprised more than one such unit, however. Grazing could also take place within the framework of town commons (*dehesas*) without giving rise to individual property rights.

Towards the middle of the sixteenth century Spanish immigration in the New World attained higher levels and some Spanish towns expanded quickly. Demand for food increased, particularly for products not yet readily supplied by Indian farmers, such as meat, wheat, sugar, and wine. Increasing numbers of Spaniards, encomenderos as well as others less privileged, took advantage of the land distribution machinery. Terminology for long remained vague but eventually land intended for grazing became known as *estancias*, while *chacras* were used for the cultivation of grains, vegetables or grapes. Various forms of labour were used for this expanding, but as yet small-scale, production. Some encomenderos used their Indians, although this was prohibited from 1549. Others secured part of the official allotment of paid Indian workers (*mitayos*), serving by turn to fill private as well as public labour needs. There was also a free, mainly Indian labour pool of day-workers (*jornaleros*). Another source of labour were Indian serfs (*yanaconas*) of a type existing under the Incas. African slaves, otherwise imported to be used as servants and urban artisans, also provided a growing share of rural labour in the neighbourhood of Spanish towns; but their high prices limited their use to clearly profitable agricultural enterprises.

Meanwhile, the encomienda, in the nuclear areas at least, steadily declined after the mid-century, not merely as a system of labour but also as an avenue to easy wealth and domination. This was, in part, a consequence of the drastic decline of the Indian population. Governmental rationing of labour (*repartimiento*) became increasingly necessary in view of the rapid expansion of the mining sector after the discovery of the rich silver mine of Potosí in Upper Peru in 1546. At the same time the concentration at Potosí in a most inhospitable environment, some 4,000 metres above sea level, of many tens of thousands of people, perhaps more than 100,000 at times, gave rise to a formidable demand for food, water, clothes (a very high priority in this chilly climate), stimulants (wine, liquors, coca leaves, yerba mate), fuel, construction materials, and beasts. Though declining in importance from the mid seventeenth century onwards, Potosí and other mines were to maintain their crucial role as centres of consumption until the very end of the colonial period.

The gradual growth of large-scale commercial agriculture and stock raising has to be seen in this context. There is little to sustain the view that the emergence of large-scale commercialized agricultural units and huge cattle ranches represents a seigniorial withdrawal from the larger economy to pursue the ideal of self-sufficiency on the early medieval model. As in New Spain, the great estates seem to have risen as integrated units within emerging regional markets surrounding mining and political–administrative centres. As the market for agricultural produce expanded the great landed estate expanded especially when land was readily available (as a result of Indian depopulation) and land prices were low. Thus, an element of speculation might creep into the building up of an estate. However, the prime incentive of landowners in acquiring more land was most probably to discourage competition from other landowners or to force the Indians, once deprived of their own lands, to provide them with cheap labour. For the large estates were formed through encroachments on the lands of neighbours, often Indians, as well as by means of *mercedes de tierra* and purchase. The legalization of this *de facto* situation took place as a consequence of the growing financial needs of the Spanish crown from the 1590s onwards. After due inspection, landowners were confirmed in hitherto questionable property rights after the payment of a fee (*composición de tierra*). This process obviously legalized many shocking abuses but it brought some order to a chaotic situation. The last *composiciones* took place in the course of the late eighteenth century.

Some landowners, especially larger ones, were absentees living in the towns who either let out their estates or had them run by *mayordomos*; but the large majority probably resided on their properties for at least a great part of the year. Some ensured that their estates passed from generation to generation without major divisions by taking advantage of the Spanish device of entailing their estates (*mayorazgo*). But recent research suggests that the opposite phenomenon of frequent changes in ownership by purchase was even more common. In the sugar-producing provinces of Lambayeque on the northern Peruvian coast between 1650 and 1719, only 22 per cent of estates changed hands by inheritance compared to 62 per cent by sale. *Composiciones*, donations, and dowries accounted for the remainder. Changes of ownership were facilitated by the often high level of indebtedness. In the case of Lambayeque we know that the debt burden of the haciendas totalled 36 per cent in 1681–1700, swelling to no less than 69 per cent a century later. By assuming the payment of various obligations – mortgage loans from the church (*censos*) or self-imposed obligations to the church to pay for masses or other religious services (*capellanías*) – the purchaser of an estate sometimes only had to pay a small sum in cash. At the same time, the large extent of these encumbrances made the division of properties more complicated and costly, and helped prevent excessive fragmentation. We do not know to what extent credits were also extended to landowners from non-ecclesiastical sources. But, in the eighteenth century at least, merchants sometimes ventured to give credit to landowners not solvent enough to receive church money but at higher rates of interest. One variety of credit was the *habilitación* (an institution combining the features of commission and loan), which was extended by merchants to, for example, owners of sugar plantations.

The size and relative importance of the great landed estates, usually called *haciendas* from the eighteenth century onwards, should by no means be exaggerated. First, most estates so called were probably quite modest and small with just a handful of workers. Secondly, Indian villages, reorganized as *reducciones* or *pueblos de indios* from around 1600 onwards, long controlled most of the land in the highland areas. They, too, became integrated to a degree within the emerging regional markets. With the decline of the Indian population discrepancies between the diminishing number of village Indians and their legally inalienable landholdings often arose. But non-Indian elements, notwithstanding legal prohibitions, quickly settled down among the Indians to cultivate part of their lands. Many former Indian *reducciones* were transformed into mestizo villages populated by small or medium-sized farmers. Others, albeit weakened, retained their corporative Indian character. They would become the communities (*comunidades*) of modern times.

During the colonial period the church, in particular religious orders such as the Jesuits, formed a more and more conspicuous element among landholders. The driving force behind Jesuit land acquisitions was the need to ensure a regular income for the upkeep of colleges and other urban activities. They were facilitated by gifts of land as well as cash from members of the elite. At times, land transfer to the church was also the consequence of individual landowners being unable to meet their financial obligations to some ecclesiastical body, these bodies being the main source of rural credit until at least the late eighteenth century. The land acquisition policy of the Jesuits was often strikingly systematic, so that properties specializing in different products complemented each other. They ran their holdings themselves, as a rule, while other ecclesiastics preferred to let them out. In Spanish South America, rural properties held by the church probably never constituted such a large share of total landholdings as in New Spain. Even so they often covered a great part of the very best lands, situated within a convenient distance of the main markets.

In 1767 the crown expelled the Jesuits from Spanish America and confiscated their extensive properties. Under state administration, these holdings became known as the *temporalidades*. Sooner or later, however, they were to pass into private hands, a process which remains to be systematically explored. It has been suggested that they were acquired by private owners 'almost always in the huge original units...at a fraction of their value'.[1] In the case of one district – Mendoza in Cuyo – we know, however, that the buyers were relatively modest people, not the existing local elite. In any event, the Jesuit loss meant a strengthening of the individual landowning sector, and the previous element of co-ordination, an important source of strength and profits, was mostly lost. In their pursuit of a regalist policy against the church,

---

[1] Arnold Bauer, 'The church and Spanish American agrarian structure, 1767–1865', *The Americas*, 28/1 (1971), 89.

the Bourbon governments also tried to reduce and regulate the ever increasing amount of landowner obligations to the church. In 1804 the redemption of self-imposed obligations (*obras pías, capellanías*) was decreed. Landowners would have to pay the capital value to the crown, which then would take over the financial responsibility towards the church. Although the effects of this revolutionary measure have been studied in the case of New Spain, where it cost many landowners their properties, almost nothing is known as yet as far as Spanish South America is concerned.

In the field of rural labour we also know much less about Spanish South America than New Spain. In the broadest terms African slave labour played an important role in the tropical lowlands, while Indians and mestizos provided the bulk of the labour force in the highlands. After the demise of the mita system rural labour there was legally free. The traditional idea of debt peonage as being the landowner's device for tying Indian labour to the estates has been increasingly undermined by recent research on New Spain. It is clear in the case of the viceroyalty of Peru that the opposite phenomenon, the withholding of wages, might have served exactly the same purpose. Probably, however, there were other reasons why landowners were able to compete successfully with miners and other employers for a supply of labour which, after shrinking steadily until the mid seventeenth century, slowly began to recover. The conditions of a hacienda worker, Indian or otherwise, given the usufruct of a parcel of land on which to grow food and some tiny wage in kind or cash, were simply less harsh than those of a mine worker. For that matter, they were also better than those of an inhabitant of an Indian village, continuously harassed by the authorities looking for mita labour, payment of tribute and fulfilment of other obligations.

On the Peruvian costa in the sixteenth century, while the Indian population declined and the income of the encomendero from tribute dwindled, the population of Lima, founded in 1535, grew quickly: in 1610 it numbered some 25,000 people, in the 1680s 80,000. Thus, a great many encomenderos and other Spaniards found it to their advantage to establish estancias and chacras on irrigated land in the valley of Rimac and neighbouring valleys with a view to supplying Lima's needs. The vanishing Indians were replaced as rural workers by imported African slaves. In the northern valleys, Spanish truck farms also appeared but, with less market stimulus, did not as a rule manage to thrive. Instead, they were absorbed or grew into larger units, some of which devoted themselves to ranching, others to the increasingly profitable cultivation of cotton or sugar. The territorial expansion of these haciendas was greatly facilitated by the steady decline of the Indian population which left community lands empty. For example, the community of Aucallama (Chancay), founded in 1551 with 2,000 people, had no Indians left in 1723 and its lands had little by little been auctioned off.

Side by side with the property of secular landlords, ecclesiastical holdings increased. In the valley of Jequetepeque, just north of Trujillo, the Augustinians maintained a virtual monopoly over the best lands for a couple of hundred years. Through contracts of perpetual lease (emphyteusis), however, their estates passed over to secular landlords from the 1780s onwards. In the valley of Chancay, on the other hand, several orders divided among them some of the best haciendas. The Jesuits possessed no less than eleven sugar haciendas in the northern and central valleys at the moment of expulsion in 1767. The growth of church properties, as well as the tapering off of the revenues of individual hacendados through *censos* and *capellanías*, was mainly a result of pious donations. But the Jesuits in particular also acquired many properties by purchase, financed either by profits or by loans obtained from inside or outside their order. The total value of 97 Jesuit haciendas in the whole of Peru in 1767 was 5.7 million pesos. On the southern coast properties tended to be smaller but more profitable than in the north. The great cash crop was wine. At first, Arequipa enjoyed an especially good location for diversified agriculture, being on the route from Lima to Potosí. In the surrounding valleys, encomenderos established prosperous estates. Later, however, from the 1570s onwards, the Upper Peruvian trade was channelled through the more southerly port of Arica and labour shortage also contributed to Arequipa's decline. This was not reversed until the mid eighteenth century, when Arequipa became a focal point on the trade circuit linking southern Peru, Upper Peru, and the Río de la Plata. African slaves formed an important part of the rural labour force on the Peruvian costa. The Jesuits in 1767 employed 5,224 slaves, 62 per cent on sugar plantations, 30 per cent in the vineyards. Slaves were often provided with plots on which to grow their own food. So were the permanent Indian workers (*agregados a las haciendas*). Gradually, the share of free black, mulatto, and mestizo labour also increased.

In the interior of northern Peru in the central Andean highlands, where sheep raising gave rise to numerous estancias as well as to textile workshops (*obrajes* and the smaller *chorrillos*), Spanish estates grew at the expense of Indian lands just as they did on the coast. Indians were the main labour force of sheep ranches as well as *obrajes*. At the same time, the non-Indian population steadily increased, so that at the end of the colonial period their numbers equalled those of the Indians, who had become peons on the great estates as their lands passed into the hands of the Spaniards.

Mines were often surrounded by haciendas which supplied them with their foodstuffs. To a degree Indian communities were also drawn into these local commercial networks. This was so in the case of Cerro de Pasco, north-east of Lima, where silver mining boomed towards the end of the eighteenth century. The mines of Huancavelica, the great deposit of mercury, were also surrounded by haciendas, which were character- ized by frequent changes of ownership by purchase. But in this case, they mostly served as reservoirs of labour for the mines. For consumption goods, Huancavelica had to rely on coastal producers.

Further south, the city of Cuzco constituted an important market and from early times was surrounded by *chacras*. By 1689, there were 705 haciendas in the region of Cuzco; in 1786, the number had decreased slightly to 647. Most were situated along the Camino Real, the road which, despite many difficult passages, connected Cuzco with Lima and Potosí. In 1689, a fifth of them were owned by gentlemen entitled to be addressed as 'don', 15 per cent by women (often widows) and no more than 7 per cent by the church and the religious orders. Ecclesiastical estates, though, included some of the largest and most profitable ones. The Jesuits owned the most important sugar estate, Pachachaca, located in a hot valley in Abancay, and the large *obraje*–hacienda of Pichuichuro in a higher, chillier part of the same province. Both were centres of networks of farming and ranching units, whose function was to supply the provisions needed by sugar and textile workers. Their ecological diversity clearly facilitated this type of economic integration. It also existed in the case of some huge *mayorazgos* such as that of the Marqués de Vallehumbroso. But most haciendas were probably quite modest and small. In 1689, a labour force of fifteen to twenty adult Indians seems to have been normal on Cuzco haciendas. Furthermore, most Indians were still living in their communities on the eve of independence. The non-Indian population of the Cuzco region increased slowly, from 5.7 per cent in 1689 to 17.4 in 1786.

In the cold region of Puno, Indian communities raising llamas and sheep were the main feature of rural society, though there were also scattered Spanish ranches. In Upper Peru, the valley of Cochabamba was one of the main granaries of Potosí. According to a seventeenth-century chronicler, the haciendas there were large and usually valued at 40,000–80,000 pesos. Only later did they begin to fragment as grain exports to Potosí ceased and landowners opted for letting out most of their lands to tenants.

The labour force of the haciendas in the central Andean highlands comprised three main categories. The mitayos (or *séptimas*) of the Indian villages served by turns in the same way as they did in the mines. The *yanaconas* constituted a permanent resident labour force, provided with the usufruct of small parcels of land for their subsistence but without pay and in fact tied to the estates. This category was of Inca origin but became more and more common in the course of the colonial period. Some free workers hired themselves out as *jornaleros*, paid mostly or wholly in kind and often indebted to the hacendado. Tenants or subtenants performed day work on the lands managed by the owner (*demesne*).

In the virtual absence of mining, the economic life of the Audiencia of Quito (present-day Ecuador) was geared to two major products: cacao in the wet tropical province of Guayas and woollen textiles in the highlands. On the coast, this gave rise to slave-based plantations; in the sierra both haciendas and, to a lesser extent, Indian communities tried to combine subsistence agriculture and sheep-raising with textile production. As in Peru, the haciendas of Quito were partly formed in extralegal ways, afterwards sanctioned by means of *composiciones*. In the case of the large hacienda of Gualachá, Cayambe, we know that it was transmitted by inheritance within the same family from the 1640s until 1819. But we do not know if this was typical or not. The ecclesiastical holdings were impressive. The Jesuits in 1767 possessed about a hundred haciendas, estancias and *obrajes*. They were valued at 0.9 million pesos, but were auctioned off at only 0.5 million. Some were taken over by creole aristocrats like the Marqués de Selva Alegre. Also in Peru, rural labour derived from the Inca institutions of *yanaconaje* and *mita*. But in Quito the *yanaconas* practically disappeared in the course of the seventeenth century. Instead, mitayos (here called *quintos*) came to form the bulk of the rural labour force. There was no competition in this case with the labour needs of mines. Through the concession of usufruct land parcels (here called *huasipungos*), however, and by making the mitayos incur debts, hacendados often succeeded in tying these temporary workers from the villages to their estates. Thus, their status became similar to that of the earlier *yanaconas*. Around 1740, two Spanish travellers gave a graphic account of this process on grain-producing haciendas and on cattle and sheep ranches. The shepherds are presented as possibly the least abused but much worse off than their counterparts in Spain. Worst of all were the conditions of those mitayos who were set to work in the prison-like *obrajes*. The Indians, of whatever origin, who were tied to the estates became known as *conciertos*, a somewhat ironic term because it means 'by contract'. Later, they would be called *huasipungueros*. By the end of the colonial period about half of the demographically stable Indian population of the highlands of Quito had become serfs of the haciendas.

In New Granada the encomenderos played a major role in the land appropriation process after the conquest (1537). In control of the town councils, they easily assigned themselves land within their encomiendas. The evolution of agrarian structures in New Granada offers considerable variety, however, because of the heterogeneous nature of the area.

Half of the high plateau called the *sabana* surrounding Santa Fe de Bogotá had passed into encomendero hands before the 1590s, when the Indians were gathered into *reducciones* (here called *resguardos*). The Spanish haciendas were consolidated through *composiciones*. One aristocrat got his 45,000-hectare property legalized for a mere 568 *pesos de oro*. *Mayorazgos* were few, however, and in the course of the seventeenth century some land was taken over by more modest landowners. The church was also able to acquire about half of the land. The Indian communities largely disappeared.

Until the 1590s encomienda Indians formed the chief source of labour in the *sabana*. After that the mita became the means of getting labour for agriculture as well as for mining and urban services. As in Quito, hacendados were often able to turn their six-month *concertados* into permanent, resident peons. A 'free' labour force also appeared in the eighteenth century, largely composed of mestizos, by now the majority of the population.

The *sabana* pattern was only different in degree from that of Tunja in the east. Here *resguardos* survived longer but were infiltrated by growing numbers of mestizo tenants. During the latter part of the eighteenth century the authorities allowed them to take over most of the land. The most humble, landless people in rural society, Indian as well as mestizo, became known as *agregados*.

Less populated regions presented a somewhat different pattern. In the Cauca valley, the control over the existing clusters of encomienda Indians was the point of departure for the formation of enormous latifundia soon to be filled with cattle. In the eighteenth century these holdings were divided up into more reasonable-sized hacienda units, largely devoted to the cultivation of sugar. They were worked by African slaves, in part transferred from the mining sector. Miners and merchants were conspicuous among landholders. The lands they acquired could be used as collateral for low-interest *censo* loans. Thus, the three economic sectors were variously intertwined and the decline of mining was to affect Cauca agriculture adversely towards the end of the eighteenth century.

The holdings of the Jesuits were scattered all over New Granada and comprised cattle ranches, grain-producing haciendas, as well as sugar, cacao, and banana plantations. They were valued at 0.6 million pesos in 1767. Plantations were worked by slaves, but they were fewer than on the more profitable plantations of the Peruvian Jesuits.

During the sixteenth century, the process of Spanish colonization in Venezuela was particularly disorderly and destructive. The Indian population, never dense, was severely reduced. In their unsuccessful quest for mines, or absorbed by the pearl industry, settlers were content to get their food supplies through encomienda tributes. But around 1600, with the cultivation of cacao, the structure of the Venezuelan economy was settled until the end of the eighteenth century. Cacao spread out from Caracas and the central coastal valleys. At the same time, cattle-raising was pushed southwards from the highlands into the northern parts of the llanos. *Mercedes de tierra* were, to begin with, given to very much the same individuals who received encomiendas.

We know how the increasing agricultural wealth was distributed among the citizens of Caracas in 1684. A quarter of these *vecinos*, 172 persons, held a total of 167 cacao plantations with 450,000 trees and 28 ranches with 38,000 head of cattle. By comparison, the wealth represented by wheat *labranzas* and sugar *trapiches* was insignificant. In the 1740s, when cacao production in the province of Caracas had multiplied by ten, the number of cacao proprietors had increased by only three. Some of them owned vast cattle ranches (*hatos*) as well. The process of concentration of land devoted to the overwhelmingly dominant commercial crop continued until the very end of the eighteenth century. More than 400 in the 1740s, by 1800 the owners of cacao plantations (*señores del gran cacao*) numbered no more than 160. They had benefited from *composiciones* and also deprived the small Indian pueblos of some of their land. The church controlled part of the landed wealth, about a fifth of the cacao area in the 1740s, but this was less than the properties of a single family, the Pontes. Absentee creole landlords concentrated in Caracas formed a homogeneous, ambitious elite which tenaciously fought royal functionaries and Spanish-born merchants, who from 1728 to 1784 monopolized external trade through the Caracas Company.

In Spanish American terms, landowners and their agricultural wealth in Venezuela toward the end of the colonial period had few counterparts. A French visitor was less impressed. In French Saint-Domingue, an infinitely smaller area, the value of rural production was ten times higher than that of the province of Caracas. What were the causes of this 'underdevelopment'? First, the well-known evils of *censos* and *capellanías*, in comparison with which tithes and sales-tax were less onerous because they adjusted to changes in production. There were also the price of absenteeism, greater costs to support often dishonest and inefficient administrators, as well as owners interested only in raising their socio-political status. Finally, the Frenchman also points at an external cause, the risky dependence on a continuous supply of African slaves, necessary because of their low fertility rate and the frequency of manumissions.[2]

Clearly, commercial agriculture in Venezuela had become increasingly dependent on slave labour. Apart from the extensive mission areas in the east and extreme south of the country, the remaining Indians had withdrawn into the age-old pattern of family units practising subsistence agriculture, based on manioc, maize, beans and plantains, and perpetuated through swidden. Also, many poor mestizos, free blacks and mulattos became *conuqueros* (smallholders) rather than hire themselves out for work. Slaves were therefore essential for cacao production and their productivity was relatively high. In stock-raising on the llanos, on the other hand, labour supply was never much of a problem. By the mid eighteenth century, there were a total of 3,500 peons, paid mostly

[2] Francisco Depons, *Viaje a la parte oriental de Tierra Firme en la América Meridional*, II (Caracas, 1960), 82–8.

in kind, and 400 slaves to take care of slightly more than 300,000 head of cattle in the areas of Guarico, Apure, and Cojedes.

In Chile, as the Indian population under Spanish control dwindled, a small number of encomenderos and other Spaniards were able to secure *mercedes de tierras* and divide most cultivable areas in central Chile among themselves. In 1614, Santiago was surrounded by about 100 chacras producing vegetables and grains and 350 estancias for cattle as well as grain production. Labour comprised a mixed lot of encomienda Indians, enslaved Mapuche prisoners from the south, Indian migrants from the other side of the Cordillera, blacks, and mestizos. But the small Spanish towns provided only a meagre market for agricultural produce. The main export was tallow, which could be sold at a profit in Peru, where it was used to make candles, a prerequisite for mining. The extensive cattle breeding with a view to providing tallow also had the advantage of requiring very little labour, a very scarce resource in seventeenth-century Chile.

After the earthquake of 1687 in hitherto wheat-growing districts on the Peruvian coast, a most promising market opened up for Chilean wheat. In response to external demand, wheat cultivation spread out from the ports, largely replacing stock raising. In the course of the eighteenth century, however, prices tended to slacken and, in some parts, yields also decreased. In this context, the subsequent concentration of landholdings, according to a recent study, should be interpreted as an effort to lower production costs.[3]

Also, a new way of securing labour was now tried. Within the framework of extensive cattle breeding, landowners often granted usufruct rights in marginal lots of land to Spaniards or mestizos of modest means in exchange for certain easily performed tasks, for instance in connection with rodeos. This was called a 'loan of land' (*préstamo de tierra*). With the increased value of land under the impact of wheat exports, coinciding with demographic growth, tenancy obligations (*arriendos*) were made more burdensome. Forced to pay heavy rents in kind or cash on their marginal terrains, tenants soon found themselves opting for rent in the form of day-work instead. By the end of the eighteenth century, in some parts such *inquilinos* already formed a more important source of labour than the ordinary farm-hands.

On the eve of independence, the landholding structure in the

---

[3] See Marcello Carmagnani, *Les mécanismes de la vie économique dans une société coloniale: le Chili (1680–1830)* (Paris, 1973).

Santiago region exhibited a high degree of concentration. There, 78 per cent of the number of units, worth less than 3,000 pesos, comprised less than 10 per cent of the total value. On the other hand, 11 per cent of the units, valued at more than 10,000 pesos, held more than 75 per cent of the total value. This structure also seemed quite stable. In the Valley of Putaendo in central Chile, the largest hacienda passed intact from one generation to another between 1670 and 1880. Sometimes, *mayorazgos* helped to keep the holdings within the family but usually they were not needed. Yet, in other cases, repeated divisions of properties initiated the process resulting in the minifundia of modern times. Finally, the composition of the landholding class was considerably modified in the eighteenth century when Spanish immigrants partly replaced old families of encomendero origin.

The immense region of the Río de la Plata proved disappointing because no mines at all were found there. In the north-west, colonization was merely an extension of that of Peru and Chile. Between 1553 and 1573 all the major towns had been founded and the sedentary Indian farmers distributed into encomiendas. Also, *mercedes de tierras* had been handed out in the areas around the towns. Meanwhile, direct expeditions from Spain only succeeded in establishing one permanent centre, Asunción, in 1541. Here in Paraguay, a rather dense Indian population was able to supply the Spaniards with farm produce – maize, manioc, and sweet potatoes. Paraguayan mestizos, a generation later, were the founders of Buenos Aires in 1580, but after the closing of its port fourteen years later, the city remained a sort of isolated island in the sea of pampa grasslands dependent on contraband for survival.

The north-western towns became linked, almost from the outset, to the Peruvian market, especially Potosí. First, they served as suppliers of textiles, based on wool in Córdoba and cotton in Tucumán and Santiago del Estero, later as suppliers of cattle and especially mules. In the seventeenth century, Paraguay also joined the Potosí network of trade as a supplier of yerba mate, the leaves of which were used to prepare a stimulating beverage. Yerba came from two sources, the citizens of Asunción and other towns using encomienda Indians for the harsh work of collecting it in faraway woods, and the Jesuit missions in the south and east of the area.

The other marketable products of the eastern Río de la Plata were pastoral. Towards the mid seventeenth century quickly formed herds of half-wild cattle (*ganado cimarrón*) appeared to constitute inexhaustible herds (*vaquerías*) to the south-west of Buenos Aires, in Entre Ríos and, on the northern shore of the Río de la Plata, Banda Oriental (now Uruguay). The way of exploiting the *vaquerías* was crude. *Vecinos* of Buenos Aires or of Santa Fe, up the river, asked the town council for a licence (*acción*) to round up and kill a certain number of beasts. Hides, tongue, and tallow only were of any commercial value. Indeed, external demand for them increased. It was only in the mid eighteenth century that a substantial number of estancias were set up by the Jesuit missions and around the Spanish towns, which now included Montevideo in the Banda Oriental. Often, previous *acciones* were taken as a basis for land property claims (*denuncias*). The minimum unit, a *suerte de estancia*, comprised about 1,875 hectares with a capacity of 900 head of cattle. Because land surveying was expensive, while land values remained exceedingly low, large areas were often held with doubtful titles. The owners as a rule lived in the nearest town. These estancieros were clearly subordinated to the rich merchant class. Around 1800, an estancia of 10,000 beasts was said to need no more than one overseer (*capataz*) and ten peons to run it. While urban labour was largely slave, cattle hands were usually free. Their wage level was high in Spanish American terms.

PRODUCTION

In the nuclear areas of advanced pre-Columbian agriculture, Indians used to produce not only for their own subsistence needs but also for those of non-productive upper strata with ceremonial and military roles. Conquest did not bring about any fundamentally new orientation of production. In peripheral areas, on the other hand, primitive farmers, hunters, and gatherers, if they survived conquest, had to be taught how to produce a surplus for their masters.

The basic pre-Columbian crops were tubers like manioc and potatoes, as well as maize, squash, and beans. Domesticated animals were scarce and supplied only a very small portion of dietary needs. Spaniards, however, refused to rely on native American crops. In 1532, every ship leaving for the New World was required to carry seeds, live plants, and domesticated animals to ensure the supply of all the food normally consumed by Spaniards. In the highlands, European crops were carefully fitted into the altitudinal scheme of pre-Columbian agriculture. Wheat could be grown up to 3,500 metres, barley to 4,000. In the case of a few commercial crops only, did the government at times discourage production in the New World because Spain's own exports of olives, silk, hemp, and wine were adversely affected. Spanish demands that Indian tributes in kind comprise wheat and other European crops made the natives learn how to produce them. The acculturation was obviously more rapid and thorough when the Spaniards were directing the production themselves, on chacras or haciendas. It was more difficult to change consumption habits, but just as in time non-Indians learned to appreciate native American produce, Indians began to grow some European plants for their own needs.

The spread of Old World domesticated animals was more revolutionary owing to the absence of New World counterparts, except for the llamas of the central highlands. Cattle multiplied with almost incredible speed in the South American grasslands. Sheep were accepted more easily by highland Indians due to their similarity with llamas. Horses were also accepted, even by the most bitter foes of the Spaniards, such as the Mapuches. Meat not only provided the main food of non-Indian populations but the free supply of meat also became a frequent condition set by Indian tribes for letting the missionaries gather them into *reducciones*.

The organization of production in highland Indian communities followed pre-Columbian patterns, in this respect only slightly modified by the introduction of Iberian municipal forms. On chacras, estancias, haciendas and plantations, naturally enough, European patterns prevailed. The plough was introduced but used almost exclusively on Spanish estates. On the steep slopes of the Andes the pre-Columbian foot plough (*chaquitaccla*) was clearly superior. The transfer of the European technology of the time was far from complete. While, for example, threshing with the use of beasts was introduced, irrigation with the help of a horse-drawn wheel (*noria*) was not. Due to the low level of technology, capitalization, and management, the sheer number of workers was the main determinant of agricultural production. There were also activities requiring special, usually more simple, varieties of productive organization, as in the case of the *vaquerías* of the Río de la Plata. Stimulants like coca and yerba were gathered in peripheral areas by Indians forced to do so by entrepreneurs and missionaries, often under very severe and dangerous conditions.

Little is known about the volumes of production, especially over time, even less about the rates of productivity. Furthermore, any data of this kind has to be related to similar information about other areas in or outside Latin America at the time, if they are to have any meaning. The fact that two-ninths of the tithes (*diezmos*) were entered in the records of the Royal Exchequer is one possible clue. It is very risky, however, to estimate volume of production on the basis of the monetary figures found in these accounts. The gathering of tithes was normally auctioned off to the highest bidder, which clearly implied a strong element of speculation in the transaction. The landed property of the bidder or of a guarantor (*fiador*) were used as security for these risky but sometimes very profitable ventures.[4]

In the Peruvian costa the process of change in agricultural production after the conquest was particularly profound. The major crops, like sugar and wine, domesticated animals, agricultural techniques, and the majority of the producers and consumers themselves came from abroad.

As early as *c.* 1550, Cieza de León commented upon the many sugar plantings of the district of Nazca. Towards the end of the eighteenth century, sugar production on the Peruvian coast totalled some 450,000 *arrobas* (1 arroba = 14.5 kg). However, the level of technology of the Peruvian sugar mills may have been lower than in other sugar-producing areas of the time. The cultivation of grapes and the resulting production of brandy and wines were concentrated in Ica and Moquegua on the southern coast. Ranching comprised the whole range of domesticated animals of the Mediterranean. Fodder crops like oats and alfalfa were also grown on a large scale. Although maize remained an important nutrient, white settlers preferred wheat. It was grown in great quantities despite a less than ideal climate. Towards the end of the colonial period, rice had also become an important food crop, grown especially in the Trujillo area. In Lambayeque, still further north, cotton was grown on a large scale from the seventeenth century onwards and used for the preparation of blankets.

The earthquakes of 1687 are said to have produced widespread sterility of the earth, thus bringing about a severe agricultural crisis. The destruction appears to have been limited to the environs of Lima, however, and the effects were probably only temporary. In the 1740s Lima was surrounded, two Spanish visitors wrote, by 'gardens, producing all the herbs and fruits known in Spain, and of the same

---

[4] By way of exception, the tithe collection was also entrusted to diocesan officials. Their estimates of actual harvest and livestock inventories (*tazmías de diezmos*) provide excellent sources on production, as is the case with the Cuzco diocese, 1781–6.

goodness and beauty, besides those common to America'. The extensive olive orchards, also, produced an 'oil...much preferable to that of Spain'.[5] Besides irrigation – by no means abandoned though probably less extensive than in pre-Columbian times – guano from the Chincha islands was still being used as a fertilizer, though this is often denied.

In the central Andean highlands considerably more pre-Columbian production patterns were retained than on the coast. A seventeenth-century chronicler stresses that in Upper Peru the Spanish scratch plough pulled by oxen and the native *chaquitaccla* were used side by side. The same blending of two different agricultural traditions was expressed by the dichotomies of maize and wheat, broad beans and potatoes, coca and sugar, llama and sheep. For each ecological niche, a choice could be made between Old or New World plants or animals. There was an element of disruption, however, when, for example, Spanish cattle invaded terrains hitherto reserved for farming. Also, the Indian networks of complementary, vertically integrated production units were often destroyed. On the other hand, the largest of the emerging Spanish estates often succeeded in incorporating different kinds of terrain in order to secure for themselves a wide range of products. Terracing and irrigation continued to be used, though to a lesser extent than in Inca times. Unirrigated tracts (*temporales*) gave inferior yields.

No overall picture of highland production can be obtained at the present time. For example, the parish of Ccapi (Paruro, Cuzco) produced, in 1689, an annual yield of 212 kg of grain per inhabitant. In another part of Cuzco, Calca y Lares, 148 kg of maize, 35 kg of wheat and 509 kg of potatoes were produced per inhabitant in 1786. These estimates compare favourably with present-day conditions, depressed due to overpopulation, erosion, and other factors. It is worth noticing that in Calca y Lares, in 1786, about a quarter of the wheat was grown by Indian communities, which also kept a third of the horses and half the cattle. On the other hand, Spanish haciendas produced 60 per cent of the maize and almost 30 per cent of the tubers. Apparently, the process of acculturation was advanced.

The oscillations of agricultural production were often violent owing to shifting weather conditions in a harsh environment where the extremes are very severe indeed. Droughts, early frosts, or floods would lead to famine and pave the way for epidemics which, in turn, might

[5] Jorge Juan and Antonio de Ulloa, *A voyage to South America*, ed. Irving A. Leonard (New York, 1964), 216–20.

cause crucial shortages of labour. It is interesting to note that harvest failure in 1782–3 caused a steeper rise in food prices in the City of Cuzco than the rebellion and siege by Tupac Amaru's Indians a couple of years earlier. Also, notwithstanding war destruction, the total tithe income of the diocese was higher in 1786 than in 1779.

A striking feature of highland rural society, in some of the northern as well as southern provinces, was the great extent of textile production based on wool from either llamas (vicuñas, alpacas) or sheep. Both the larger and smaller textile production units were, apart from a few towns, closely integrated with the rural economy, be it that of the haciendas or that of the communities. Where mining did not develop, textiles or perhaps the production of sugar, confined to deep hot valleys, or coca, carried out on the forested eastern slopes, provided the dynamics of rural society.

In the Audiencia of Quito the great variety and richness of tropical lowland production on the coast around Guayaquil, and in Esmeraldas, further north, never failed to impress visitors. First of all, there was the cacao tree producing 'its fruit twice a year, and in the same plenty and goodness'.[6] Also, the fertile but fever-ridden lands yielded cotton, tobacco, sugar cane, bananas, coconuts, manioc, peanuts, and many other fruits. In the highlands, production patterns hardly differed from those of the Peruvian sierra. In the case of the Guachalá hacienda, production stagnated during the late colonial period. This may have been a generalized phenomenon. There was, after all, very little stimulus for agricultural production in these isolated areas.

Bogotá, in the early seventeenth century, was considered a very cheap place to live, with an abundant supply of all kinds of provisions. This clearly reflected the great number of large and small producers in the *sabana* and also the proximity of higher as well as lower terrains, with their different crops. Looking at New Granada as a whole, the great variety of agricultural production is striking. There was no one dominant agricultural product. One would think that with the rapid decline of the Indian population throughout the region, the consumption pattern would be altered in favour of Old World crops. Yet a late eighteenth-century witness asserts that wheat consumption in Bogotá remained low because inhabitants preferred the indigenous maize. Wheat in the *sabana* was not merely produced for the people of Bogotá. It was also sent to distant markets along the Magdalena river and in

[6] *Ibid.*, 94.

the mining districts of Tolima and Antioquia. Thus, in the eighteenth century, agriculture in the *sabana* was adversely affected by the decline of mining and by competition, in Cartagena on the Caribbean coast, with imported North American grain. In fact agriculture in most of New Granada, beyond local subsistence, primarily functioned as an adjunct to mining. In the forested mining districts in the west, there were always plots where Indians or blacks cultivated maize, beans and manioc for the needs of some mining camp. Furthermore, the extensive cattle breeding in the Cauca and upper Magdalena valleys provided the mining and urban populations with abundant, protein-rich food. Tobacco was produced on a large scale and was subject to state monopoly from 1774 onwards. It was the single most important source of revenue in the viceroyalty of New Granada.

Venezuela's population remained relatively sparse throughout the colonial period. The urban centres were quite small and there was almost no mining sector. Thus, the question of subsistence was easily solved. The majority of the population derived their support from the swidden-based *conuco* agriculture of manioc, maize, and beans; and the abundant supply of meat from the cattle herds of the llanos made living fairly easy, even for the urban poor. In contrast to this extensively used rural landscape, the small areas devoted to cacao cultivation demanded a relatively big input of capital and know-how. The purchase of slaves alone represented a major investment. The question of labour subsistence was largely resolved by offering the workers space to grow their crops between the rows of trees entrusted to their care. Cacao requires an even water supply and towards the end of the colonial period elaborate irrigation and drainage works had been set up. To judge from export figures, production increased at an accelerated rate, from 1,000–2,000 *fanegas* (1 *fanega* = 110 *libras* = approx. 50 kg) in the 1630s to 125,000 *fanegas* in the 1790s.

In the shadow of cacao, other commercial cropps were late in developing. Only towards the very end of the colonial period did coffee, sugar, indigo, cotton, and tobacco expand in acreage and commercial importance. Tobacco was made a state monopoly in 1779. Unlike cacao, coffee, which would become Venezuela's next major crop, did not require irrigation and could thrive on slopes where drainage was not needed.

By the early seventeenth century in Chile, agricultural production in the area surrounding Santiago was already quite varied. Yet, for most items, such as grains, vegetables and wine, the city itself, still relatively small, and the troops on the Mapuche border were the only markets. In the Santiago area, some 40,000 head of cattle, and no less than 320,000 goats and 620,000 sheep, are reported. But on the whole, apart from tallow, which was exported, they served only local needs. The expansion of wheat cultivation for export towards the end of the seventeenth century naturally changed this pattern of production. To judge from tithe records, the value of production in agriculture and stock raising experienced a notable rise. In the area of Santiago, the yearly average has been estimated at 140,000 pesos in 1680–9, and at 341,000 in 1730–9, that is a yearly growth rate of 1 per cent, a considerable achievement in terms of a technically primitive economy. From the 1770s onwards, the rate of growth slowed down to 0.5 per cent. In the more southerly area around Concepción, the impact of external demand was felt with some delay and to a lesser degree. Further north, around La Serena, on the other hand, agriculture was mainly conditioned by mining, which experienced a recovery in the course of the eighteenth century. Thus here, the highest rate of growth in agriculture, 1.3 per cent, came as late as the 1790s. Still, Chile's productive capacity in agriculture was underutilized until the mid nineteenth century. Total demand was simply too limited.

Population in the Río de la Plata area remained exceedingly sparse throughout the colonial period. The major exception were the 30 Guaraní missions of the Jesuits, on and between the upper Paraná and Uruguay rivers. In the eighteenth century their population reached and occasionally exceeded 100,000. They were well organized economically and largely self-sufficient although they produced yerba mate largely for export. Overall the lack of domestic markets set very narrow limits on the production of most agricultural items. Those branches that did develop were geared to external demand. In the province of Tucumán, textiles were produced for Potosí until the Indian labour force declined in the early seventeenth century and better-situated producers took over that market. Then Tucumán became a mule-raising centre for Upper Peru.

The wasteful exploitation of the *vaquerías* of the pampas prior to the 1750s was geared to overseas demand. Production reached its peak during the period 1700–5, when 75,000 hides were exported each year. After 1750, when production was estancia-based, exports soon reached an even higher level, considerably more than 100,000 hides a year. Also, to some extent, not only fat and tallow, but also the meat was now exported. In the meat-salting plants (*saladeros*) of the Banda Oriental, jerked meat (*tasajo*) was prepared for overseas export too. In contrast, after the expulsion of the Jesuits in 1767, their vast estancias soon vanished. In the largest mission, Yapeyú, 57,000 head of cattle had been reduced to 13,000 and 46,000 sheep to 2,000 in 1798.

MARKETING

In view of poor overland communications and the great volume and bulkiness of most products of agriculture and stock-raising the distance to the centres of Spanish population was a crucial factor, largely responsible for the value of land and produce. When a mining boom subsided or a city lost population, the surrounding rural sector was inevitably affected adversely. On the other hand, specialized production of small-volume/high-value items like wine and sugar would lend themselves to long-distance trade and yet yield considerable profits. Also, the transportation of live animals, mules and cattle, though slow, could be a long-distance undertaking. Finally, water transport, if available, considerably reduced the problem of bringing agricultural produce to the market. Both the Pacific and the great rivers were used in this way. On the other hand, the existence of a great many excises and internal customs duties always hampered long-distance trade in comparison with the production costs of more local producers.

Price movements of agricultural products in colonial Spanish South America remain to be explored. Only a few series are known. One recent sample for late colonial Cochabamba suggests sharp seasonal and cyclical variations such as are known from New Spain. Prices probably also exhibited great local differences. Their impact was modified by the existence of a very large subsistence and barter sector. On the municipal level, efforts to regulate food prices in the interest of consumers as well as domestic producers were continually made.

Little is known about the ways in which marketing took place. Individual, very large-scale landowners, secular and ecclesiastical, sold the bulk of their products through their own agencies in Potosí and other towns (*remisiones*). Others preferred to sell their products on the spot or take them to the buyer's place (*ventas*). A system of regularly held fairs played a key role in some commercial activities such as the mule and cattle trade. Ecclesiastics, on the whole, seem to have preferred to sell their products direct to consumers rather than rely on merchants. Until legally suspended in the 1780s, the *reparto* or forced sale of merchandise to Indians and poor mestizos constituted a most important element of internal trade. In Peru, mules from the Río de la Plata and textiles from Quito and Cuzco constituted the main items of this trade. It has been estimated that *repartos* in Peru were more important as a means of transfer of Indian labour to the 'Spanish' sector of the economy than either the payment of tribute or mita obligations. *Reparto* implied a massive redistribution of Andean products like textiles and coca from producing to non-producing areas. The Indian administrators (*corregidores*) responsible for the *reparto*, were, however, probably to a great extent front men for professional merchants.

Inter-regional trade comprised a wide range of agricultural products as well as textiles. Perhaps a third of the sugar produced in the valleys of western Cuzco as late as 1800 found its way to the market of Potosí. The Peruvian sierra was supplied with continuous, large-scale imports of mules, bred on the plains and in the Andean foothills of the Río de la Plata area, and with yerba mate from Paraguay. Chile exported wheat to coastal Peru. On the other hand, agricultural products accounted for only a small, though increasing, share of Spanish South America's external trade. Exports of hides from the Río de la Plata region and cacao exports from Venezuela to Europe and New Spain, both expanded vigorously in the course of the eighteenth century. Otherwise, geographical isolation put South American producers at a disadvantage compared with those engaged in overseas trade in New Spain, so that imports into Spanish South America largely had to be paid for in specie.

The profitability of agriculture and stock raising can be measured only in relative terms against the backdrop of profitability in other branches of the economy. In eighteenth-century Spanish America a 'normal' yield in any activity would probably not exceed 5 per cent. We know that, for instance, Jesuit haciendas specializing in the growing of sugar and vines easily obtained much higher rates, but they were by no means typical. We do not yet have sufficient data to venture any generalization about the yield of privately owned haciendas. Available evidence suggests, however, that productive surplus was meagre. Furthermore, a great part of it was absorbed by obligations assumed to the church. For hacendados, the chance of making considerable profits depended on the exaction of exorbitant prices during harvest failures or on successful speculation through leases of tithe collection.

Around 1550, the chronicler Pedro de Cieza de León, deeply impressed by the fertility of the irrigated soils of the Peruvian costa and sierra, expressed the belief that the next generation would witness the export to other parts of Spanish America of 'wheat, wine, meats, wool, and even silks'.[7] This dream was not to be fulfilled, however, partly because these products were the same as those of New Spain. However, trade in agriculture soon developed on a considerable scale within the region. With a population of 25,000 in 1610 Lima, for example, consumed some 240,000 *fanegas* of wheat, 25,000 of maize, 3,500 head of cattle, 400 sheep, 6.9 tons of rice and 200,000 bottles of wine. These products came from areas as far away as Chile as well as from near-by. From the northern coast, sugar was exported to Guayaquil and Panama as well as to Chile. The ships bringing sugar to Chile returned with cargoes of wheat, thus reducing costs. In Lambayeque, where haciendas were few, even Indian communities learned to produce sugar for sale. Cotton was exported to the textile workshops of Quito. From the southern coast, Pisco brandy found markets in New Granada as well as Chile and wines even reached New Spain. Between the regions of Cuzco, Puno, and Arequipa another large channel of trade developed with Upper Peru and the Río de la Plata. In the 1770s the sugar producers of Cuzco and Arequipa are said to have competed on the Potosí market. The coca from Cuzco's *ceja de montaña* also met with increasing competition from Upper Peruvian producers. But the greatest threat to Peruvian commercial interests was the gradual saturation of the new viceroyalty of Río de la Plata towards the end of the eighteenth century with English textiles and Brazilian sugar. The opening up of the port of Buenos Aires to legal overseas trade with Spain in 1776 was, indeed, a crucial watershed, even though the decline of trade across the southern sierra was far from sudden.

Commercial exchange at local and provincial levels was less directly affected by such shifting trends at a regional level. The districts suffering from a chronic shortage of grains or meat had to get these products from better-situated neighbours in exchange for the products of artisans or other items. There were also the scattered clusters of miners, and textile and plantation workers who had to be fed and clothed. Not merely the haciendas, big and small, but also Indian communities took part in this kind of trade.

Special needs grew out of the commercial exchange itself. Some

[7] Pedro de Cieza de León, *La crónica del Perú* (Buenos Aires, 1945), 27 (ch. 113).

districts specialized in supplying the mules and mule-drivers (*arrieros*) instrumental in carrying out the trade. They served the land routes between the northern port of Paita and the city of Lima and between Cuzco, Arequipa, Arica, and Potosí. Mules from the Río de la Plata were bought at the fairs of Salta, Jujuy, and Coporaque. A traveller's report from 1773 gives a very vivid picture of this gigantic trade, which brought 50,000–60,000 mules annually to the highlands to be used in transportation as well as in the mines.[8]

The city of Quito was described in the early seventeenth century as a lively centre of commerce and an obligatory point of passage for those travelling between New Granada and Peru. But it was extremely difficult to move and carry merchandise between Quito and the principal port, Guayaquil. The stretch from the highland village of Chimbo to Guayaquil was called 'the worst road in the world, because it always rains on these mountain slopes so that the mules fall into the mire'.[9] Such was the bottleneck through which exports from Quito of textiles and imports of Peruvian wines and brandy, Mexican indigo needed to dye Quito textiles, and the rice, fish, and salt from Guayas had to pass. Freight costs became exceedingly high. Only in the neighbourhood of Chimbo was it worth while to grow wheat for sale to the coast. Otherwise, sierra agriculture merely served local subsistence needs. The extreme dependence on textile exports led to a depressed economic climate towards the end of the eighteenth century. The cacao of the coast, on the other hand, held its own in southern markets. If inferior in quality to the products of New Spain and Venezuela, Guayaquil cacao was nevertheless cheaper. Exports totalled 130,000 *cargas* (11,310 tons) in 1820.

Coming from Peru and Quito the Camino Real crossed New Granada passing through Pasto, Popayán, and Bogotá before entering the Venezuelan province of Mérida. It was supplemented by pack trails, but even the sure-footed mules often slipped in the incredibly rugged terrain. Human carriers of both men and cargo were a common sight in the highlands of New Granada. Thus river navigation, whenever feasible, proved more attractive than travelling overland, despite the

[8] 'Concolorcorvo', *El lazarrillo de ciegos caminantes desde Buenos Aires hasta Lima* [1773] (Buenos Aires, 1942), 112–61.
[9] Quote from Antonio Vázquez de Espinosa, *Compendio y descripción de las Indias Occidentales* (Washington, D.C., 1948), 339, 346.

sluggishness of the pole-boats (*champanes*) on the Magdalena and Cauca rivers. In the mining districts food prices were often high. Nevertheless, and despite the immense environmental variety of New Granada, internal trade did not develop very much, owing to the difficulties of communication. Also it was hampered by the fact that the urban centres were relatively small. In the 1690s, to take an example, even the diligent Jesuits decided that it was of no use to cultivate some large haciendas in Pamplona in the north-east because there were no markets for their produce. Also, the predominance of gold exports discouraged agricultural production for the external market. In 1788, agricultural produce accounted for only 15 per cent of the value of exports from New Granada.

In Venezuela, unlike New Granada, little use was made of waterways such as the Orinoco for the purpose of trade, and land communications were very poor. Thus, in the interior, agriculture remained mainly subsistence-orientated. The export sector was confined to the coast and the adjacent mountain range. In the early seventeenth century, before cacao dominated the export economy, there were some attempts at producing for distant markets. Hides were exported to Spain, mules bred for export to New Granada and even Peru, small quantities of wheat and maize were sent to Cartagena, Havana, Santo Domingo. From the beginning cacao was exported to Spain and Mexico but also, through contraband trade, to Curaçao, occupied by the Dutch in 1634. The belated answer to the predominance of contraband trade in Venezuela was the establishment of the Caracas Company, which was given a monopoly of the purchase and export of Venezuelan products in 1728. By gradually lowering purchase prices on cacao, the company forced an expansion of production on the part of plantation owners eager not to see their income reduced. In the 1780s this odious monopoly was finally dismantled and Venezuela began to enjoy the Bourbon version of 'free trade'; but wars increasingly disturbed shipping. Cacao deteriorates rapidly when stored in humid conditions, and it was gradually replaced by more easily stored export articles like coffee, cotton, and indigo. There was a sharply rising demand for cotton and indigo from an England now in the throes of the early stages of the Industrial Revolution.

In Chile in the early seventeenth century, a primitive pattern of distribution of rural produce characteristic of the post-conquest years still prevailed in marginal areas. Goods were actually distributed in the town houses of the landowning encomenderos, reducing the business space of ordinary grocers (*pulperos*). On the other hand, the tallow export trade to Peru was controlled, towards the mid-century, by merchants who bought the produce from the estancieros. The value of yearly exports of produce from the area of Santiago to Peru rose from 280,000 pesos in 1690–9 to 1,350,000 in 1800–9. At the end of the seventeenth century, these exports were about evenly divided between the products of stock-raising and those of farming. At the beginning of the nineteenth century, the proportions were 40 and 55 per cent, with minerals making up the rest. Yet, even though labour costs were low, freight costs were high and the profits of most haciendas must have been rather modest. In one case from central Chile (Maule) in the 1790s, the profits attained 6.6 per cent. Peru was Chile's only market and the trade was carried out by Peruvian vessels. Until the end of the colonial period, Lima merchants were basically in control of the setting of wheat prices.

Until the mid-eighteenth century at least in the Río de la Plata area an external monetary economy co-existed with a 'natural economy' in the domestic sphere characterized by barter trade and even the use of 'money in kind' (*moneda de la tierra*). The development of north-western trade was clearly dependent on Upper Peruvian mining. The yearly exports of mules increased from 12,000 beasts in 1630 to 20,000 in 1700. It then dropped during the nadir of mining until the mid eighteenth century. Towards the end of the eighteenth century, a level of 50,000–60,000 animals was reached.

Meanwhile, the exports of hides and other products of stock-raising through Buenos Aires, though only partly hampered by legal restrictions, reached higher levels after the commercial–administrative reforms of 1776–8. The gradual conquest of the Upper Peruvian market was now confirmed and the already sizeable drain of silver via Buenos Aires grew in size. The population of Buenos Aires reached 22,000 in 1770, some 50,000 in 1810 and the prosperity of the city also rose. But if the prospective market value of the city for, let us say, inland producers of wine and wheat increased, the exceedingly high freight costs across the pampas now made it more convenient for the people of Buenos Aires to import their supplies. Communications in the Río de la Plata were slow. Besides mule-trains, caravans of ox-carts, able to defend themselves against Indian attacks, were the normal means. The very first stretch, from Buenos Aires to Córdoba, easily covered by a horseman in five days, took about a month. Traffic via Mendoza to Chile had to cross the forbidding, 4,000-metre-high Uspallata pass.

In the course of the conquest, the timing and duration of which varied from area to area, Old World plants and animals thoroughly changed the resource basis of the South American continent. After an initial period of reliance on Indian food supplied in the form of encomienda tribute, Spaniards moved out from the towns and established networks of truck farms and livestock estancias. Thus a European-type market economy, based on exchange value, was superimposed on the traditional Indian economy based on use value and functioning through barter and collective work. The rise of the great landed estate was closely connected with the decline of the native American population and the growth of the Spanish and mixed population, and above all with the expansion of mining. Long-distance exports (for example, wheat from Chile and cacao from Venezuela) also promoted the emergence of large estates. Towards the end of the seventeenth century the basic rural institutions had attained stability and the pattern for the remainder of the colonial period had been set. On the whole, the eighteenth century witnessed agricultural expansion: upward demographical trends widened markets despite the ups and downs of mining and ensured a steady supply of labour. Agricultural and stock-raising enterprises in Spanish South America during the colonial period were, however, seldom able to produce at their full capacity: market size did not allow it.

The landowning elite was neither homogeneous nor stable in its composition. Landed properties varied widely with respect to size, production, indebtedness, market access, and labour supply. Succession through inheritance appears to have been less normal than acquisition through sale. The relative importance of the hacienda as compared to small and medium-sized landholdings and Indian communities also varied with respect to time and space. Large landowners were often simultaneously public officials, merchants and miners. They exerted a great amount of local power but were themselves dependent on non-agricultural sources of income or on credit from the church or urban merchants. They were profit-orientated and their haciendas were integrated into the market. Their labour systems were coercive although often paternalistic. Their enterprises did not normally reach high levels of profitability and their wealth was to a great extent put to non-economic use.

7

ASPECTS OF THE INTERNAL ECONOMY OF COLONIAL SPANISH AMERICA: LABOUR; TAXATION; DISTRIBUTION AND EXCHANGE

Colonies are structured by those who rule them to benefit the mother country and its ruling classes. To the extent that these rulers are successful in this aim colonies are, in Chaunu's word, extrovert. They are, at least in part, organized economically to send out to others significant portions of their most valuable or profitable raw materials and products. In colonial Spanish America much of the economic history which we know has emerged from studies of Spanish attempts to make the colonies serve metropolitan needs. One result has been an emphasis on the sea link, the *carrera de Indias*, and the fleet system. We know a fair amount about who went to the Indies and when, and what goods were carried in each direction across the Atlantic, more especially from Spanish America to Spain. Within Spanish America itself economic historians have allowed their interests to be shaped to some extent by what primarily interested the Spanish crown: above all, silver and gold mining and plantation agriculture, the bases of the great export trades, and the supply of labour to the mines and plantations. We know much less about the basic institutions, assumptions, systems and practices of the internal economy of colonial Spanish America. Drawing on the available secondary literature, which concentrates on a limited range of topics and regions, an attempt will be made in this chapter to examine three aspects of the internal economy: labour systems; taxation; and trade within the empire, both local and long-distance.

LABOUR

Colonial Spanish America began as a conquest society, and the first priority of the invaders was the extraction of wealth or capital from the conquered. During the conquest itself, and in the turbulent years which followed in each region, this extraction could be accomplished by direct seizure of previously accumulated surpluses of precious metals or stones. This took the form of looting or booty, an officially accepted way of paying soldiers or volunteer expeditionaries in the days before regularly paid standing armies. The best-known example is the ransom paid by Atahualpa to Pizarro's band of adventurers and the sharing out of this booty afterwards.

As the era of conquest came to an end and these surpluses were exhausted more systematic means of extraction were developed. One of the main methods became the direct exploitation of the native Americans themselves. Systems for utilizing local labour supplies varied quite widely over time and space in colonial Spanish America, but several underlying organizing forces and principles were at work. There was in the first place a close correlation between the socio-cultural organization of the Indian societies and the forms of labour organization that the Spanish settlers could impose on them. In complex stratified societies the invaders found existing conditions of slavery, servitude, and 'tied' labour. In many such cases they simply removed the apex of the social pyramid – the kings, royal houses, and rulers of large regions – and then governed using approximately the same labour systems, with lesser Indian rulers such as village chiefs as administrators. In areas where social organization was less advanced and stratified, where pre-Columbian labour had been less organized and disciplined, the conquering groups found labour much harder to employ systematically. This was especially true of nomads, unused to settled agriculture and occupying thinly settled areas. The regions where organized labour forces existed were also, of course, the areas of denser populations, such as central Mexico, highland Peru, and, to a somewhat lesser degree, the highland plateaux and valleys around Quito, Bogotá and Santiago de Guatemala (now Antigua). And along with dense, organized populations, themselves a form of accumulated capital, the first and succeeding generations of Spaniards found precious metals in Mexico and Peru, which were therefore heavily settled and became the core areas of the Spanish American empire. Regions of temperate climates and good soils like the pampas of the Río de la Plata and the ill-named Costa Rica were not settled heavily if they lacked aboriginal populations and precious metals or stones. Areas of relatively dense populations which held little other wealth sometimes attracted a modicum of Spanish settlement, but such areas could also be the most unfortunate of all after the conquest.

If they were fairly near to areas which had attracted Spaniards but which lacked a labour supply, then Indian slave exports became the main industry. In the second quarter of the sixteenth century many of the peoples of Nicaragua were sent as slaves to Peru, and above all to Panama. In a similar fashion the peoples of Trinidad, the Bahamas, Florida, Pánuco, and the Gulf of Honduras were used to restock the islands of the Caribbean. Perhaps the best known case was that of the pearl islands off the Venezuelan coast. Margarita and Cubagua attracted Spanish attention when beds of pearl-bearing oysters were discovered in their coastal waters. The pearlers imported Indians from Trinidad, the lesser Antilles, and points along the coast of Tierra Firme. This intensive exploitation soon depleted the oyster beds and the Indians of the pearl islands then became export material themselves. We find them in Panama and the islands of the greater Antilles. The European slave trade from Africa to the Americas is a larger version of this phenomenon, and it was also used at times as a way of installing replacement populations when aboriginal groups had disappeared.

Slavery was thus the first labour system almost everywhere. But it could not last and was soon for the most part brought to an end, although there were brief recrudescences of it, some legal, as after Indian rebellions, some illegal, as when labour-hungry settlers would advance into a nearby unconquered area to seize and bring out anyone they could catch. The crown, which opposed Indian slavery for humanitarian and political reasons, gradually asserted its authority. In regions such as Mexico and Peru, where sedentary village agriculture continued to be important, it was too disruptive. Spaniards who depended on village labour came to oppose the arbitrary removal of workers. Even in the rather anarchic Mexico of the 1520s and the turbulent Peru of the 1530s and 1540s the leaders of the invading Spanish groups recognized that they needed a rationing or distribution system which would provide labour for the powerful (and deny large quantities of it to the less powerful) in a way which would prevent too much strife – in this they failed notably in some cases – and which would be perceived as appropriate to the status of the individual. Castile of the *Reconquista* had known such a system. Kings had divided up conquered lands and peoples among those worthy of reward. Columbus brought this system of *repartimientos* or sharing out to the islands, although the rapid extinction of the local Indian populations prevented any great elaboration there. By the time Vicente Yáñez Pinzón negotiated a contract with the crown for the conquest of Puerto Rico (1502) the New World repartimiento was recognized by the crown. In that same year Ferdinand approved Governor Frey Nicolás de Ovando's grants of Indians to the settlers in Hispaniola. Later in Jamaica and Cuba similar grants were made as a matter of course. In Mexico and Peru, these labour repartimientos, later to be called *encomiendas,* became a way by which the most powerful and prestigious among the first settlers shared out the labour supply, more or less amicably, to the exclusion of those who did not have the power or position to do more than complain. Theoretically the crown was assigned the role of awarding encomiendas as a token of gratitude for the recipients' *hazañas* during the conquest or the subsequent early rebellions. In fact many *conquistadores* found themselves excluded from the early distributions whereas comparative latecomers who were better connected received handsome grants. In Peru and Nicaragua, for example, scenes of the exploits of the violent, rival gangs headed by the Pizarro, Almagro, Pedrarias and Contreras clans, grants of encomiendas were awarded, withdrawn, and reassigned as each new *adelantado* or governor was appointed, seized power, executed his predecessors, died, or fell from power. A man's military record during the conquest, or even his good behaviour in office or loyalty to the crown, were at best secondary considerations.

As time went on, nevertheless, it became apparent that in the core areas where the crown had vital interests most of the early settlers had made a tactical mistake in approving of the crown's assumption of primacy in the assigning of grants. The encomienda became, not a feudal fiefdom as Cortés had envisioned, but a contractual arrangement whereby a given number of Indian taxpayers was 'entrusted' to the material and spiritual care of a Spaniard and the cleric he was supposed to engage, in return for the right to extract certain roughly prescribed quantities of labour, goods or cash.

The crown was able to take gradual advantage of its regulatory position within the system and of its near monopoly of high patronage because the colonists, in addition to having an engrained loyalty reinforced by culture and status aspirations, needed the crown for prestige, titles, legitimacy, offices, and other emoluments. The royal government was under pressure too from humanitarians like Bartolomé de Las Casas. After one abortive and almost disastrous attempt to legislate the encomienda system out of existence, the so-called 'New Laws', which was a leading cause of the civil wars in Peru and of the

Contreras revolt in Nicaragua, the crown was able to restrict and manipulate the granting of encomiendas and of the rewards coming from them until encomiendas in the central densely populated areas were grudgingly recognized by all as belonging primordially to the crown, and as being temporary grants of income lasting for the recipient's lifetime and possibly, often in reduced form, throughout the lives of one or two of his successors.

Central government accomplished this by several avenues of attack. One was taxation and regulation. By a succession of laws the state seized more and more of the profits from encomiendas for itself and made the collection of these profits into a complicated series of stages. Some small encomiendas became more troublesome than they were worth and thus reverted to the crown. The state also made strenuous efforts to separate encomenderos from their charges. Encomiendas, it stressed, were grants of income, not of vassals. In the core areas encomenderos were prohibited from tarrying in or residing in their Indian encomiendas. *Calpisques, mayordomos*, village leaders, or other intermediaries collected the goods and money and delivered them to the absentee encomienda owners, thus increasing the legal and psychological distance between the two sides. The crown had swept away any vestiges of the lord and vassal relationship, and by the late sixteenth century the encomiendas in these central areas, heavily taxed and regulated, had become almost entirely part of the tributary tax, a pension system with many of the awards going to the widows and other dependants of poverty-stricken *beneméritos*, or to court retainers in Madrid who seldom if ever saw the Indies, far less the Indians 'entrusted' to them.

Other forces were at work to weaken the encomienda. One of the most important was population decline. Because of the lack of immunity to Old World diseases, and the economic and cultural disruptions caused by the conquest and the revolution which it brought, Indian populations disappeared by the million in the years after the conquest. The effect on the encomienda, composed entirely of Indian workers, was catastrophic. Encomiendas which had provided a Spanish family with an opulent living in the first generation could produce enough for a meagre existence two generations later, even if the nuclear Spanish family which lived off the early grant had not expanded into an extended family, as it usually had. Some encomiendas were vacated or abandoned in the late sixteenth century; the surviving Indians in them reverted to the crown.

For some early settlers the encomienda system became a trap. If a Spanish family had pretensions to nobility or a noble status the financial costs were heavy. A large seigniorial establishment was expected, including a large house, an army of retainers and hangers-on, a large family of spendthrift sons and dowry-consuming daughters, horses, arms, and expensive carriages and clothes. All this conspicuous consumption was carried out in a studied manner which placed high priority on an avoidance of the appearance of work and commerce. Such families, consuming all revenue, perhaps even destroying substantial amounts of capital, or at least converting it to poorly negotiable social prestige, were often destroyed by the shrinking, restricted encomienda if they waited too long. By the third generation they had fallen on relatively hard times, reduced to writing endless, bitter appeals to the crown containing inflated accounts of the merits and services of their conquest and first-settler ancestors, and wondering resentfully why so many rewards of the conquest had fallen to upstart latecomers.

In many of the central areas of the empire, however, the encomienda laid the base for many a fortune and thus contributed notably to economic development and the formation of elite wealth. It can be argued that the first encomiendas, at least in central Mexico, were so profitable and labour so plentiful as to distract attention away from land and land ownership. Some conquerors and first settlers, arriving in the New World with little of the world's goods, were astute enough to see this reward, this gift of more or less free labour and income, as a chance for a fresh start, an investment opportunity. Cortés and Alvarado, to name but two, used their encomiendas to pan gold, build ships, provision the shipyards, provision and crew the ships themselves, and provide porters and foot soldiers in the newly discovered lands. In the second and third generations, when the encomienda had become almost entirely a taxing system, astute encomenderos discerned that their grants were temporary and ultimately losing propositions. They extracted capital from them as fast as possible and diversified out of the dying institution, using it to invest in silver mines, commerce, herds of cattle, sheep, mules or horses, and above all land. Although there was no legal connection between the encomienda and land ownership, at least in the most important parts of the empire, the interrelationship is clear. In a number of cases the one financed the other.

Until recently, studies of the encomienda have concentrated on central Mexico, Peru, and the other important areas of the empire such as Quito and Bogotá. Later studies of more peripheral areas of the empire have had some surprising results. In areas such as Paraguay, Tucumán and perhaps even Chile – isolated, with little gold or silver and no dense agricultural populations, they were thinly settled by Spaniards and of slight economic interest to the crown – the encomienda survived in a fairly vigorous way until the end of the colonial period. Moreover, it either ignored or survived the impact of royal legislation and taxation, and retained some of its earliest attributes, including the right to commute tribute to labour and to use encomienda Indians as a labour force.

In central Mexico, Central America, Peru and Upper Peru, Quito, and New Granada the waning encomienda system was to some extent replaced as a major source of labour by various kinds of labour draft, although the two institutions coincided for many years. The emergence of a system of rotational labour drafts was closely tied to population decline. If the encomienda was, in part, a way for an emerging elite to control and share a major resource, labour, then repartimiento drafts were a way to ration an increasingly scarce supply. It is obvious from the names used for these drafts that in Mexico and Peru they were of pre-Columbian origin; the Mexican *coatequitl* and the Peruvian *mita* were further examples of the invaders' tendency to adopt existing functional institutions and to alter them slowly as circumstances demanded. In New Granada the labour draft for the mines also used the Quechua term but other drafts there were called *alquileres* or *concertajes*. In many parts of Central America people used the Castilian word *tanda*. In general the word *repartimiento* was used again, with its meaning of a sharing out or rationing of goods and services. Drafts were in use in Mexico by the 1550s, in Guatemala and the Andes by the 1570s, perhaps earlier, and in the highlands of New Granada by the 1590s.

In principle labour repartimiento was a paid labour draft in which a given percentage of the healthy, male, Indian population was obliged to travel away from home to work on assigned projects or at designated places. The time to be spent at this work was specified, as was the pay scale and, in general, the working conditions. In theory at least labour repartimientos were limited to public works projects or to industries or agricultures which were vital to public or state welfare. Certain tasks which the crown believed to be especially noxious to Indian health or well-being were specifically exempted from the repartimiento, at least in some places. Work on indoor sugar vats or on indigo plantations are two examples. Such legislation was often ignored or, as in so much else, its observance was brokered via a system of fines and bribes which, in effect, made the employment of Indians in some forbidden tasks subject to a royal fine or tax. Then, too, royal prohibiting legislation depended on the importance of the industry and on the availability of an alternative labour supply. Mercury mining at Huancavelica in Peru was almost certainly the most murderous repartimiento task of all, but it was essential after the use of the *patio* process for the refining of silver became important to the great mines at Potosí, and was granted large, organized repartimientos until late in the colonial period.

The labour repartimiento caused many complaints throughout its existence. Critics pointed out that proximity to a large city or to an intensive workplace, such as Mexico City and its *desagüe*, Potosí and its silver mines, the Huancavelica mercury mine, or even a new cathedral under construction, meant more frequent calls to the draft. The other side of the coin was that Indians called from a distance had to spend more time in travel to work and thus more time away from home. Both seasonal drafts, such as the ones for wheat farming around Mexico City and Puebla, and long-term ones for mining in Peru and New Granada, had important effects in Indian communities. Seasonal drafts for agriculture often coincided with the periods of intense agricultural activities in the villages – the harvest seasons for wheat and maize were almost exactly the same – so absent Indians found their crops maize were almost exactly the same – so absent Indians found their crops ruined, partly harvested, or expensive to harvest because they had to pay others. There are some cases where Spanish landowners took advantage of these circumstances, offering to allow their Indian repartimiento workers to return home earlier if they would forgo the pay to which they were legally entitled. Anxious to return to their sowing, weeding, transplanting, or harvesting, some Indians were eager to accept. Long-term absences had even greater impacts. Some villages in Upper Peru were reported to be sad places of elderly men, women, children, and invalids. Men often returned ill to these villages, especially those men involved in the mitas of Potosí and Huancavelica. Other *mitayos* never returned. Some died at the mines of overwork, lung diseases, or toxaemia. Many more stayed at the mines as free labourers, petty traders, or petty smelters, becoming more or less acculturated to the mining or city societies where they found themselves, and some passing into the amorphous class called variously *castas*, *cholos*, *ladinos*, or *mestizos*. This consequent distortion of the sex ratio in Indian society may not have had much effect on fertility – there were many other more important factors, such as diet, spacing of births, and epidemics – but it did seriously affect some forms of production, family patterns, Indian government hierarchies, and morale. Within some villages in southern New Spain the seasonal agricultural draft (*coatequitl*) may to some extent have worked against the general flattening of the Indian economic and social pyramid, the elimination of Indian class differentiation brought about by the conquest and its consequences. Relatively wealthy Indians were able to buy their way out of their turn in the draft, in spite of some protests from parish clergy and royal officials. Indian village officials were able to exempt themselves, their family males, their friends, and others who could pay them or exchange favours with them. In villages where repartimiento judges insisted on a given number of workers for each rotation the village poor had to serve additional turns. The gap between the relatively wealthy and the destitute in the village seems to have widened accordingly.

The repartimiento provided a limited range of economic opportunities to some sectors of the creole class. The office of repartimiento judge (*juez de repartimiento* or *juez repartidor*) did not carry much prestige, with its involvement with lower-class Indians, work assignments, and petty officialdom, but it did provide opportunities for accumulation of cash and goods. Indians and Indian villages bribed these judges to obtain exemptions, Spanish town councils and wheat farmers paid them or offered them favours in order to obtain more than their allotted number of workers or to ensure the official's silence in the face of illegalities in such matters as pay, working conditions, and length of work spell. Lesser creoles competed fiercely for such posts, especially in times of economic difficulties, and because the salary involved was minimal, the term of office usually short, and the prestige of the office small, it is clear that the potential for cash in the job was uppermost in their minds. Creole and mestizo farmers, especially those who required only seasonal labour, benefited too. The system provided them with a subsidized labour force which, in spite of legal restrictions or the bribes to be paid to avoid them, was probably less expensive than going into the free labour market to hire workers. Local Spanish government and the urban creole class in general benefited from this labour subsidy. Street cleaning (when it was performed), the construction and cleaning of aqueducts and irrigation canals, street and road repairs, construction and upkeep of public buildings such as churches, *cabildos*, and gaols, and city beautification programmes all depended heavily on labour drafts in many parts of the colonies. Near some cities local villages were obliged illegally to provide wood, stone, provisions, or hay to public or private institutions. This *corvée* labour did not disappear in some of the predominantly Indian parts of Latin America until the fourth or fifth decades of the twentieth century. Small vestiges of it still appear. Above all, the royal government depended heavily on the mita in the Peruvian silver industry, in the mines of New Granada, and to a much smaller extent in New Spain.

The longevity of the labour repartimiento varied widely and depended on local factors. Inheriting a previous pre-Columbian system gave it an important start. Other factors of importance were the size and organization of the labour force – large numbers of people were needed to make the system worthwhile; the speed of the demise of the encomienda system; and the conjunction of silver or gold mines, a shortage of nearby labour or alternative systems of labour, and the degree of competition for available labour between individuals, and between individuals and the crown. In central Mexico the system started early, and the crown's *desagüe* consumed large numbers. The crown had two main rivals. Spaniards in private agriculture, although individually powerful, could not compete with it, and in fact the crown had abolished agricultural repartimientos by 1632. Spanish landowners were forced to move towards various forms of peonage and free wage labour as alternatives. The crown's other rival, the silver-mining industry of Guanajuato and further north, was more powerful and resorted to free contractual labour as a way of enticing workers out of the central area. By the end of the eighteenth century there may have been half a million or more Indians between Guanajuato and San Luis Potosí, many in mining. In peripheral areas of Mexico, where the crown's need for labour was less strong, the agricultural repartimiento lasted longer. It was still to be found in Oaxaca in 1700 or even later. In Central America the crown attacked the encomienda system vigorously, and in Guatemala at least, most Indians seem to have been 'in the crown' by 1550. The crown had little use for Indian labour, although it collected the tribute enthusiastically and royal officials extracted large quantities of work and goods by extralegal means. On the other hand Spanish agriculturalists, especially around Santiago, had a need for labour on wheat farms. Spanish cities also petitioned the crown for drafts for public works.

Because of these local characteristics, repartimientos survived much longer than in most of Mexico, and some local roadwork *corvées* were abolished there within living memory. In the highlands around Tunja and Bogotá the presence of some gold mines meant a mita which endured into the eighteenth century, but there was heavy competition for a declining labour force. In Quito's jurisdiction, because of the *obrajes*, a similar history seems to have occurred. The great home of the labour draft was, however, highland Peru and Upper Peru. There the silver and mercury mines, especially Potosí and Huancavelica, were the main preoccupation of crown and colonists, and consumed such large numbers of workers that the demand could be handled only by massive, organized drafts. Because the mines were so important to the crown and because it faced weak opposition from alternative employers, it hesitated to disrupt a functioning system. The great mita of Potosí survived until the eve of independence in spite of extensive debates and recriminations over its harshness and destructive nature.

At the beginning of the sixteenth century the invading Spaniards found many systems of 'tied', semi-servile labour. One such institution which they inherited was *yanaconaje* in the Inca empire. In the Inca system *yanaconas* had sometimes constituted a special class of serfs, tied to lands and households rather than to individual villages or groups. Some of their social and economic functions still remain vague. The term may also have been applied to many client relationships, even among high nobility. In any event, the Spaniards augmented the system and incorporated vagabonds and others into it. *Yanaconas* were not slaves in that legally they could not be sold individually. They and their families could be sold with the land to which they belonged, however, and in many ways those who worked in agriculture closely resembled serfs *adscripti ad glebam*. As in Roman times the landowners paid the head tax assigned to each *yanacona* head of family. The number of *yanaconas* grew throughout the Peruvian colonial period as debt peons and other kinds of tied or coerced workers were added to their numbers. Indian villagers, burdened by tribute and mita obligations, often escaped into *yanaconaje* by choice, finding it the lesser of two evils. In Mexico the *mayeques* found by the Spaniards on their arrival may have been somewhat similar in function. Many *mayeques* melted into the villages where they were, often their home villages anyway. Some officials sent them back to their villages of origin, where they became *tributarios*. *Naboría*, a term originating in the islands, was another category of

Indians outside the encomienda and the village. *Naborías* were a class of personal employees at first, but as the sixteenth century advanced the term was used loosely, the word often became *laborío*, to describe various forms of Indian 'free' labour, a category which grew in Mexico throughout the colonial period. *Laborío* was a common term for workmen in the eighteenth century. *Yanaconas, laboríos, gañanes*, and other categories of waged or free workers became important as sources of labour for the mines. There is evidence that the mines pulled Indian village labour towards them, thus changing their category to one of these just mentioned. In general in nearly all parts of the colony there was a leakage from tribute paying, encomienda and repartimiento village Indians towards the free-labour categories. No doubt many of these escapees from the villages also acculturated and classified themselves as mestizos, castas, or cholos as time went on.

In Latin America historiography until quite recently, peonage was almost synonymous with entrapment by debt and with forced servitude. This simple picture has now dissolved and a new synthesis, if one is any longer possible, has not yet emerged. Some studies of peonage have become so revisionist that it is well to begin by reaffirming that debt peonage and severe repressive conditions did exist in many workplaces. In northern Mexico, and in other places in Spanish America where there were isolated desert mining camps, *obrajes* (textile workshops) or quarries, the *tienda de raya* or some other variation of the company store were common. In New Spain as far south as Nicaragua some peons were kept on haciendas by means of debt. Often this debt was not large, nor was it used overtly as a coercive device. In some places debt or advances were used by villagers as a means of tiding them over until the maize harvest, the debt to be repaid by seasonal work on the nearby hacienda, *labor* or workshop, at the next period of intensive labour requirements. Similar devices were used in the islands once sugar began to dominate in the eighteenth century. *Adelantos* carried the sugar workers through the dead season and were paid off at the *zafra*, or cane cutting. In other words, debt was sometimes and in some places used to recruit and discipline a permanent labour force, often in mines or on haciendas, but advances against future work were also used to recruit village labour for seasonal work, or to sustain an incipient 'free' rural proletariat during the times of the year when it was not needed on the plantation.

Perhaps the commonest form of peonage in colonial Spanish America was an arrangement whereby peasants rented small plots on large estates. The peasant family would build a hut, grow staples such as maize, beans, and potatoes, and keep a few chickens (guinea-pigs in the Andes), and a pig if they were lucky. The rent for both land and water use was sometimes paid in cash, or in a portion of the produce of the smallholding, a form of sharecropping, although this nowhere reached the importance it had later in the south of the United States. More often the rent was paid by an agreed-upon quantity of work on the hacienda. Where agricultural land was scarce and the labouring population was growing, landowners could exact more days of work. This situation seems to have obtained in many parts of Mexico, Central America, Quito and Peru in the middle and late eighteenth century. When land hunger was not severe and labour was scarce the situation was more favourable to the labouring classes. The population trough of the seventeenth century and the years immediately following major epidemics throughout the colonial period would give rural workers these small opportunities. These land-renting arrangements, although they were contracts between very unequal partners, satisfied many economic requirements for both sides. Landowners obtained a workforce without paying wages and by allowing the use of marginal lands which they seldom needed. Indians and other rural landless people rented subsistence plots without surrendering cash, and sometimes obtained the patronage and even the physical protection of the landlord and his *mayordomos* against intruders such as village and royal officials, labour press gangs, brigands, and vagabonds.

Many of the arrangements which brought resident workforces of peons into being on haciendas, *labores*, *obrajes* and other workplaces have not yet been uncovered. Some of these were informal and unwritten, and involved various local customs and understandings. Paternalism was pervasive and embraced numerous economic and social linkages between peons and employers. Godfatherhood or *padrinazgo* was used by both sides to create binding ties. *Compadrazgo* or ritual co-parenthood served the same purpose. Paternalistic owners bound the workers by psychological ties. The workers obtained a vague form of social security for themselves, and especially their children. Much of this cultural aspect of peon–landowner economic relationships awaits examination. What we do know is that many peons did not have to be coerced. By the late sixteenth century, and certainly when population growth among the lower classes began to increase, from the mid seventeenth century in New Spain and the early eighteenth century in Peru, the Indian village became an oppressive place in many parts of Spanish America. Tribute payments, tasks such as the labour repartimiento and work on village common lands, payments to village *cofradías* and community chests, the exactions of passers-by and of the Indian village leadership, land hunger in the eighteenth century, all made the Indian village less of a place providing community and protection and more of a place from which to escape. Often the Indian voted for the hacienda with his feet. On a few occasions, and increasingly in the late colonial period, Indian village authorities would sue in court for the return of villagers who had departed for other work and residences. In some of these suits, when villagers had a choice they chose for the hacienda and against the village.

The slightly rosier picture of peonage presented above certainly did not apply to all categories. The horrible conditions in some mines caused death, flight, and other manifestations of misery and desperation. Equally bad were some of the textile obrajes in central Mexico, and in the valleys around Quito, Ambato, Latacunga, and Riobamba. There peons were locked in at night, sometimes chained to their work-benches, abused physically, overworked, and detained for years. Legal officials helped obraje owners, and sometimes conspired with them, by sentencing lower-class offenders to terms in the factories. Richer obrajes could also afford African slaves, sometimes as guards or overseers, so that some of these sweatshops, worked by slaves and convicts, resembled Mediterranean galleys more than anything else in their work atmosphere. In all these categories – slavery, encomienda, repartimiento, and the various forms of peonage – regional variation and custom were so diverse that all generalizations, such as those above, fail to cover many situations.

Free labour is a puzzling category, partly because some of it was relatively unregulated and unobserved, partly because the category was so diverse. The free labouring force grew throughout the colonial period and by independence was the largest segment of the working class in many areas. For most of the period free labourers were almost entirely composed of castas, i.e. people of mixed race, acculturated Indians, free blacks, and a few déclassé whites. Royal government and local officialdom were ambivalent towards this population. After 1580 the crown tried to collect tribute from free blacks and mulattos, but not from mestizos. This never began in many areas, and collected little where it did, such as in parts of central and western Mexico. Ambivalence towards the free poor extended to their work. Technically free, they were an important part of the workforce and had to work. Laws arising from this paradoxical situation stated that castas who could prove that they held regular and wholesome employment should remain un-molested; those who could not so prove should be arrested and put to work. Freedom, in other words, did not extend to a permission to ape the leisure activities of the elites. Castas, moreover, bore a burden of suspicion. Most of them were not of Spanish racial origin, and their intermediate status, much less than full citizens of the elite, led Spaniards to worry that some of them might become disaffected, lead rebellions, stir up trouble among Indians, or collaborate with pirates and foreign intruders. These paradoxical views pushed free castas towards certain categories of work. The skilled became artisans, an intermediate grouping which possessed such essential accomplishments, for example carpentry, silversmithing, wheelwrighting, or coopering, that they could not be ignored or severely oppressed. Some of these skilled artisans belonged to craft guilds which in their written constitutions resembled medieval European models. Guilds in the sixteenth- and seventeenth-century Spanish colonies were nearly all urban and in their governance and functions represented a very typical 'trade-off' for such a hierarchically organized society. On the positive side membership in a guild assured a craftsman and his apprentices some minimal working conditions, some freedom of action in the market-place as to location and employer, restraint or prohibition of possible competition, and access to recognized due process for minor infractions of the law or civil suits involving jurisdictional, work-related, or market quarrels. Guild membership also provided some degree of job security and life insurance. Guild artisans were enthusiastic joiners of *cofradías* or religious fraternities which acted as funeral societies and minor savings and loan institutions. *Cofradías* and guilds, their festivals and other ceremonies, gave skilled artisans a place in the world, a recognized modicum of prestige and a kind of deference, but there was another side to the coin. Officials made sure that craft guilds were not challenged by too many rivals, that membership was exclusive rather than inclusive, but in return wages and other emoluments, especially high profits, were quite rigidly depressed. Many fees, hourly rates and perquisites were strictly defined by superior authorities, thus slowing any great social mobility on the part of most skilled free workers, and subsidizing the artisan needs of the upper classes and the church. Much of this rested on the concept of a fair wage, as understood at the time. Nevertheless, some artisans were able to advance to a kind of middle-class status.

Unskilled free castas occupied similar intermediate places. Many were *mayordomos*, managers, foremen, tax and rent collectors. Manual labour in the fields or workshops was avoided, and work was done which elites found unacceptable. Many free castas became petty merchants, *tratantes* (small local dealers), and horse-traders. Some of them were the agents of bigger merchants in the cities, and many of them owed varying sums of money or obligations – another form of debt bondage. Cattle haciendas provided the free poor with employment opportunities while at the same time affording them an opportunity to escape from the suspicion and daily harassment of the cities and more disciplined workplaces. The unsupervised style of life of these early cowboys, semi-nomadic, skilled horsemen, familiar with lances, lassos and skinning knives, further fed the fears of city-dwellers.

Many free poor and runaway Indian villagers – and, in monocultural areas, seasonal labourers, Indians commuting between villages and plantations, and escaped black slaves – reinforced this unfavourable attitude by turning to more socially unacceptable life-styles. By the late sixteenth century vagabondage was growing, and it worried the authorities and Indian villages. As labour shortages appeared authorities made strenuous efforts to tie down these wanderers, but every economic pause or dislocation increased their numbers, and the vestigial police forces of the colonial centuries could do little. Vagabondage, at least in the eyes of the authorities, was related to brigandage, the final and most desperate resolution of their paradoxical status for the free poor and the castas. Impressionistic evidence, and recurrent waves of mass executions of delinquents, would indicate that rural robbery, often by large organized gangs, was common, and greatly hindered officials, merchants, and travellers and their movements.

Slaves from Africa arrived in Spanish America with some of the earliest expeditions. In the first and second quarters of the sixteenth century we find them at work panning on the more profitable of the gold-bearing rivers, and in other workplaces where profits were high or an Indian workforce was absent, or both. In general, because of the distances and costs involved, African slaves were more expensive to acquire and maintain than Indian villagers, and there was no self-sufficient agricultural village to which they could return during the slow season. The growth of a large working population of African slaves had to await the disappearance or decline of the native American population. In many parts of Spanish America African slaves, like the early Indian slaves from places such as the Bahamas and the pearl islands, were a replacement population. This was especially true on the Caribbean islands and coasts, but slaves were sent inland to the mountains, too. One estimate finds that over 100,000 of them arrived in Mexico before the middle of the seventeenth century. In the large cities such as Mexico City and Lima household slaves and liverymen were a sign of status and the ability to consume conspicuously. Slaves also worked in the textile obrajes, sugar plantations and silver mines.

The best-known examples of blacks replacing Indian workers are in coastal Venezuela and the Chocó area of Colombia, tropical areas of sparse Spanish settlement. In Venezuela encomienda Indians were at first sufficient for the low level of economic activity there and for the poor market demand. Venezuela seemed destined to be another Paraguay. The growth of the cacao monoculture and of exports to Mexico in the second quarter of the seventeenth century changed all this. Some planters extracted labour from their encomienda Indians, and slave-raiding for new manpower continued, indeed persisted until the 1640s and possibly beyond. But it was obvious that a replacement population and a new organization of manpower was necessary. Cacao provided enough surplus capital to permit the purchase of African slaves in the late seventeenth and eighteenth centuries. In the Chocó, unlike Potosí with its huge, well-organized mita, the local Indians in the gold mines never constituted an adequate workforce. By 1700 most had fled or died and the gold-miners imported black slaves as replacements via the port of Cartagena. As the mining industry prospered in the early eighteenth century sufficient capital accumulated to bring in an ever larger number of slaves. By the 1750s gangs of hundreds were not uncommon. Both the region around Caracas and the Chocó were areas with profitable export industries. Agriculture for local markets seldom produced large enough profits to afford slaves. In the second half of the eighteenth century, as European sugar prices rose, areas of Cuba formerly devoted to cattle ranching and a little sugar and tobacco were given over to large-scale sugar plantations (*ingenios*) worked by large armies of slaves.

It would be simplistic to present black slavery in colonial Spanish

America, or anywhere else, as a uniform condition of manual labour servitude. Many slaves became house servants, artisans, foremen, guards, petty merchants, and shopkeepers. Much depended on their skills and cultural attributes before enslavement in Africa. Peasants may have remained peasants, but some townspeople and artisans from Africa were able to seize opportunities in the New World. Manumission was common. Some slaves developed remunerative skills and accumulated the price of their freedom. Masters freed slaves for a variety of reasons ranging from old age, guilt, and gratitude to hard times. In periods of economic stress some slave-owners freed slaves rather than feed and clothe them, literally tossing them out. Unscrupulous masters sometimes 'freed' the elderly or the sick. Freedmen in Spanish America joined the large amorphous groups of castas, neither slave nor exactly free. In the eighteenth-century Caribbean islands they were especially important, providing what might be described as the articulative strata of the local societies. They were the brokers, artisans, local merchants, carriers of goods, and suppliers of goods and services scorned by the white elites and not permitted to most of the slaves. Out of this group at the end of the eighteenth century came the leaders of the Haitian revolt: Toussaint L'Ouverture and Henri Cristophe, Alexander Pétion and Jean-Pierre Boyer.[1]

TAXATION

The various labour systems represent one of the most important means of extracting wealth in the Spanish American colonial economy. The other leading form of capital extraction and accumulation was taxation. For almost the entire colonial period, and indeed until the late nineteenth century in some parts of Spanish America, the main tax imposed on the lower classes was the tribute, a head tax collected almost entirely from Indians as a symbol of their subject status. This capitation tax, which took no account of property or income, had its origins in late medieval European poll taxes such as the *moneda forera* paid by the peasants of Castile. In the New World it appears at a very early date: for example, there is a royal command for its introduction included in the instructions given to Governor Ovando of Santo Domingo in 1501. Regular tribute assessment and collection was introduced to Mexico in

---

[1] Further discussion of Indian labour can be found in Bakewell, *CHLA* II, ch. 4, and Gibson, *CHLA* II, ch. 11. For a detailed treatment of slavery in colonial Spanish America, see Bowser, *CHLA* II, ch. 10.

the early 1530s, although it had existed well before then, based on the pre-Columbian Aztec head tax which the Spaniards had inherited. In Peru tribute became universal, regulated and standardized during the regime of Viceroy Francisco de Toledo (1569–81). Thereafter it was a major component of Spanish colonial government and administration almost everywhere within the American empire. It showed great adaptability and longevity, especially in the more isolated and economically backward parts of South America. It did not disappear from highland Bolivia and some areas of Peru until the 1880s.

The early tribute was paid mostly to encomenderos who had been granted the privilege of receiving it and of benefiting from it. As encomiendas reverted to the crown, and as the productive Indian population declined, it became a more important source of revenue to the crown, which began to collect it more carefully and rigorously. After some early hesitancy and a few errors the tribute was finely tuned – sometimes explicitly in legislation, more often not – to push Indians towards certain kinds of work and crops. Moctezuma's and Huascar's tributes had consisted almost entirely of local products, the specialties of each tributary region, although basic staples such as maize, beans, and cotton cloth provided the bulk of the payments. At first the Spanish conquerors made few changes except for the elimination of Indian products, such as feathers, which were of little use to them. By the 1550s in Mexico, and two decades later in Peru, tribute regulations were beginning to discourage the intricate polyculture of the native American Indian, the almost oriental pre-conquest 'gardening' of Mexico's lake country and the coastal oases of Peru. The general policy was designed to thrust the Indian agriculturalists towards the production of the staples needed in the large centres of consumption. Maize, beans, and cotton cloth persisted, but in addition new items from the Old World such as wheat, wool, and chickens were introduced. The Spanish goal was to simplify tributary items to one or two per village, with a marked preference for staples, although some local specialties, especially those of great value such as gold dust or cacao, persisted for the entire colonial period. Thus the tribute played a major economic role in the dissemination of new and originally unpopular crops and animals. Wheat and silk cultivation, cattle-, sheep-, and swine-herding became widespread partly because Indians were forced to pay tax in these commodities, or to look after wheat fields or cattle as part of their village obligations.

Another purpose of Spanish tributary policy was to bring the severely disrupted Indian economy more into the European market-place. To this end, Spanish officials and encomenderos began to demand part of the tribute payments in coinage, thus forcing the Indians to sell their goods for cash or their labour for wages. Some Indians travelled long distances to far-off zones of economic activity, in order to earn the cash to pay their tributes. Many preferred to pay in coinage, and found it less onerous. Viceroy Toledo in Peru quickly understood that tributes in cash were needed to recruit large numbers of Indians into the Potosí and Huancavelica labour drafts, but in areas where economic activity was not quite so intense, and where such large numbers of workers were not needed, Spaniards who moved too precipitously towards a tribute consisting entirely of cash found that they had made an error. By drifting too close to a completely monetary tribute in some parts of central Mexico, given the falling Indian population and the consequent shortage of local foodstuffs, the authorities and encomenderos forced some Indians too much into the market, where their expertise and diligence began to compete too well for the taste of some Spanish merchants. Exactions in cash forced the Indians to flee from their oppressive villages and to turn to vagabondage or to the paternalistic protection of the haciendas, where, in at least a few cases, the owner would pay the tribute for them. Cash payments led to an ever steeper decline in agricultural production in the villages, with a resulting increase in price inflation in the cities. In Mexico the cash tribute, where it was imposed, was soon corrected to a mixture of agricultural goods, usually maize, and cash.

The way in which tribute was imposed, assessed, and collected caused a general levelling in the Indian social structure, a levelling which transformed the pre-Columbian Indians into tributary peasants, but which also, like the mita recruitment system, brought some social differentiation. Spanish authorities or their agents usually counted the villagers but tended to report the results of their counts as totals. They assigned the task of collecting the tribute to intermediaries, usually the hereditary, appointed or elected leaders of the village. This delegation changed the tribute from a direct capitation tax to one of communal responsibility. The encomendero or corregidor, usually following the previous census, would assign a total tax quantity to a given village and its *anexos* or subsidiaries. Village *principales* collected the tax from those below them as they wished or as circumstances permitted. Some were egalitarian, believed in community cohesiveness, and spread the load more or less fairly. More often, as many noted, village quota systems led to an ever greater weight on the poor and to local tyrannies.

Indian tribute maintained its severity until near the end of the colonial period, as the Indian population at first decreased and then only slowly revived, as the Spanish population grew, and as the financial needs and indigency of the royal government increased. Many of those originally exempted from the tax were added to the rolls, and temporary increases, many of which became permanent, were imposed. In Mexico, for example, an additional tribute was levied in 1552 to help pay for the construction of the cathedral, and lasted for almost two centuries. The *servicio real* and the *servicio del tostón*, a tax of four reales, were added at the end of the sixteenth century to help with royal expenses and with the costs of the ineffectual *barlovento* fleet for the suppression of piracy in the Caribbean. The *tostón* lasted nearly until the end of the colonial period. Other local additions to the tribute, often to pay for local public works, were numerous in the seventeenth century. There is no question that the tribute was a detested burden.

The tribute also caused problems for Spanish society. Encomenderos, and especially the crown, frequently received tribute in goods which they did not need but which could be resold to other segments of society. The solution, a very imperfect one, was a system of royal and private auctions, which enabled the royal treasury and cash-hungry encomenderos to solve this problem of convertibility by selling the maize and other goods collected for cash. Such a system, besides the obvious inefficiencies arising from the double transportation of bulky perishable goods, drove prices up because of the multiple transactions, without benefiting the crown or the encomendero class as much as might be supposed. These auctions were controlled by a class of middlemen – inevitably restricted in number, because few could afford the large quantities of cash needed to participate. There is evidence, too, that these auction entrepreneurs did not bid against one another and sometimes conspired to keep bidding low. At least so the crown complained. After they bought the staples, the middlemen sold them to those who needed them. Maize, for example, went to weekly urban markets, mines, stores, and (less frequently) back out to the Indian villages. These middlemen were accused of monopolizing and hoarding. Some would wait, keeping items such as maize from the market until prices were high. This occurred at least once a year just before the main harvest came in. Thus the redistribution mechanisms for tribute goods were wasteful and expensive and caused hardship and discontent.

Payments in cash also brought difficulties. The Indians and the poor, as in all hierarchically structured preindustrial societies, were the traditional dumping ground for inferior, shaved, or falsified coins. Merchants and the wealthy kept their good currency for long-distance trade or for hoarding against the possibility of bad times. The inferior coinage used to pay Indians or to buy goods from them then became tribute and was unloaded onto the royal treasuries, much to the disgust of officialdom. Some of this inferior coinage then went to Spain, at first sight manifesting an aberrant working of the law often falsely attributed to Gresham.[2]

Besides the tributes, two other systems of taxation – or rather extortion – were widely imposed on the rural poor. The commonest system in some of the poorer areas of Spanish America was the *derrama*. Under this practice, Indian villagers, usually women, were forced to work materials, usually wool or cotton, to the next stage or stages of elaboration. Thus raw cotton was turned to thread, thread to plain cloth, plain cloth to dyed cloth, and so on. The women subjected to this primitive 'putting-out' industry were usually underpaid or unpaid, and thus subsidized the price of the product to the final buyer and the costs of manufacture to the trader involved. The trader was often the local corregidor or *alcalde mayor*, himself wretchedly paid but with social status to maintain and enough local power to compel the poor to work for him. Such an individual seldom had the investment capital to intensify this process. The quantities of cotton or wool involved were usually quite small. The system did perform a useful economic function in poorer areas, for it depressed the price of clothing, thus enabling local townspeople to buy below the costs and freight charges of the clothing coming either from the obrajes or from Europe or the Philippines. Other goods which needed only one or two simple processing stages entered this system at times. Thus the *derrama* both augmented the salaries of officials (a sort of indirect subsidy to the crown's payroll) and depressed the cost of basic goods such as clothing.

The other form of taxation or extortion was the forced sale, the *reparto* (*repartimiento*) of *mercancías* or *efectos*. *Alcaldes mayores*, corregidores, and other officials in Indian areas, often at the beginning of their terms of office, travelled through the villages selling goods which they

[2] For further discussion, see Gibson, *CHLA* II, ch 11.

had bought wholesale in the city markets. At times such sales performed a useful function. Staples came from one area to another where they were needed and Indians were pleased to buy them even at inflated prices. Often, however, these sales were exploitative, and unwanted goods – silk stockings, olives, and razors are among those mentioned – were foisted off on unwilling buyers, sometimes by force at exorbitant prices. Indians resold these goods, or those of them which had not rotted or spoiled, back into the Spanish market, often at lower prices than they had paid, in the hope of recouping some of their losses. The transaction involved here, besides the usual supplement to the salary and life-style of the corregidor, was a subsidy, paid by the Indian society, which lowered the cost of luxury goods to the Spanish society. Thus the people of Lima were able to purchase some silk from China without paying the full freight charge from Manila or all the profits of the middlemen between Manila, Acapulco and Lima.

The predominantly Indian, rural poor also had to suffer the graft of local officials. Salaries were little more than pittances, and by the time of Philip II's death almost all local positions had to be purchased either directly or indirectly by a gift to the royal coffers or to some royal nominee. It was fully expected by both sides that the office-holder would recover the cost of the office, augment his salary and probably increase his income, investments and status by extracting from his clientele and charges what the market would bear in the way of fees, bribes, gifts, and illegal assessments. Would-be office-buyers understood this system, and had a good sense of the price and value of individual positions. The price of any given office rose or fell depending on its potential as a source of income. Moreover, this understanding extended even to the lower classes. Graft is frowned upon in societies with an egalitarian ethos because it shifts capital upwards in the social structure in ways which are classified as immoral. In colonial societies, however, where the lower classes' access to power and decision-making was severely limited or almost absent, graft payments may have played a strangely 'democratic' role. They were one of the few ways in which the powerless, when they had a little surplus cash or goods, could lessen the pressure of the law, or even deflect its impact, not by participating in its enactment but by softening or stopping its implementation by *ex post facto* payments. Indians and castas recognized that graft payments to officials sometimes helped them, and gave corruption a grudging acceptance as a way of making colonial society, in at least a few instances, more humane. These payments, made essentially from the poor or lesser local elites, are another instance of the state delegating to others its governmental powers. Graft saved the state the trouble and some of the expense of governing. It should be noted that lower classes, including Indians, exacted payments from those above, too, in return for promptness, satisfactory work, and care of machinery, livestock and other property.

Perhaps the most common perquisite of office among lower officials was simply that of living off the land, or unpaid billeting. Officials, and for that matter parish priests, did not expect to pay for food, lodgings, or fodder for their horses and mules when travelling. These visits were burdensome in rural jurisdictions, especially if the corregidor, priest, prior or bishop was an enthusiastic, frequent *visitador*. Furthermore, clergy took advantage of a brief stay in a village to baptize, confirm, marry, or say requiem masses for those who had reached the life stages represented by these ceremonies since the last clerical visit. Each of these priestly duties carried a prescribed fee, but many other casual functions, such as catechizing children, visits to the sick, extra prayers or sermons in the village church, attendance at and blessing of village feasts, chapels, images or monuments, did not. Some clergy began to exact regular fees for each visit, presumably to cover these extra tasks. In poor areas these fees, called the *visitación*, the *salutación*, and a variety of other local names, did not amount to much, but an energetic priest with a good horse could cover many villages, and return to them too frequently for the villagers' economic well-being. In the same vein a corregidor passing through might take the opportunity to check the account books of the *caja de comunidad*, inspect the wheat or maize fields set aside for tribute payments, make sure that the village council house was swept out and in good repair, attest to the fairness and legality of the most recent municipal election, and so on, all in the expectation of a monetary payment above and beyond food and lodgings for himself, his retainers, and his horses and mules.

Indian villagers and other rural poor groups in the eighteenth century attempted to accommodate, avoid or resist these constant acquisitive intruders and tax collectors. If levies, legal and illegal, were pushed beyond understood limits some complained, rioted or revolted, tactics which were seldom more than temporarily successful and often prompted severe repression. Individuals, and occasionally whole villages, fled either to unconquered frontiers or into vagabondage or the anonymity of the cities. Most villages tried to create their own 'broker' or 'barrier' institutions to enable them to adjust to Spanish economic pressure. One of these institutions, the *caja de comunidad* or community chest, was borrowed from Spanish society; it became part of Indian society in the second half of the sixteenth century and spread to many parts of the empire. The purpose of the *cajas* was to place Indian community finances on an organized basis. They were supported by assessments on villagers and by assigned lands. Part of the tribute was diverted to them for local purposes such as payments to local officials, repairs to buildings, or loans to local people. Some *cajas*, in spite of legal prohibitions, were raided persistently by local officials and the clergy, and thereby became one more burden on heavily taxed villagers. Because of these depredations many ran permanent deficits which had to be made up by forced levies on the villagers. Yet some *cajas* appear to have run annual deficits by design. These porous community treasure chests were leaking to some purpose. They may have been a collective device whereby Indians banded together to spread the cost of buying off intrusive forces and over-zealous scrutiny from royal officials or the clergy. Having deflected the attentions and pressures from beyond the village boundaries these communities were then at greater liberty to pursue their own cultural and communal priorities.

Cajas de comunidad financed village projects, including church restorations and repairs to the council house of the village, thus, presumably, bolstering village solidarity and community pride. Some of the money collected was returned to villagers as pay for work performed. Many villages in Mesoamerica were required to put aside certain fields where the quantity of wheat or maize needed to pay the tribute was grown. The local Indians who planted, weeded, irrigated, harvested and gleaned these plots received pay from the *cajas* in many cases. Higher village officials too obtained cash payments from them, and these disbursements may have been of some importance to the perpetuation of hierarchies and traditions. Taking a senior position in village hierarchies could be a costly proposition and many Indians were understandably reluctant to assume the financial burdens associated with *cargos*. Financial rewards from the *cajas* in the form of salaries helped to solve this problem, although much of this money went to the more prosperous villagers, no doubt. Some cajas became wealthy and acted as banks and lenders to Indians and even to Spaniards, owned haciendas, estancias, sugar and flour mills and workshops, and invested in trade far beyond the boundaries of their villages of origin.

Another major Indian institution, also adopted from Spanish society, the *cofradía* or religious confraternity, built up funds not only to pay for communal religious ceremonies (some seen by the authorities as idolatrous) but also to pay fees to priests and bishops on *visitas*. Some *cofradías* foundered under economic and religious pressures from outside; some played partly successful brokerage roles; and a few prospered, and invested in land, herds, mortgages, and other goods. These wealthy *cofradías* were then targets for outside opportunists once again.

Tribute and other impositions upon Indian society, and responses to these pressures, were a large part of the story of taxation in Spanish America, but by no means all of it. The crown and its representatives tried to tax other groups and activities, with great imagination but with rather less success. Government did not have the bureaucrats, accounting systems or technology to tax systematically, so it tried to impose general and simple taxes, hoping to obtain what was possible rather than the optimum from any given tax. Taxes upon trade were one obvious possibility, but in a time of little supervision of land routes, of rudimentary police forces, and of no standardized weights, measures and coinage, such levies had to be haphazard and approximate. One method was to make use of natural and mercantilist trade bottlenecks. Trade to and from Spain was supposed to enter and exit through just a few ports, such as Callao, Panama, Portobelo, Cartagena, Veracruz and Havana. It was fairly easy to levy taxes in these ports with the help of the powerful local *consulados* or merchant guilds, who liked to impose exit and entry taxes of their own, to the disgust of secondary provinces which did not have a legal port. Evasion was common through bribery of officials, contraband carried on board legal ships, and outright smuggling, but except for some of the very bleakest middle decades of the seventeenth century the royal treasury could expect a considerable income from *almojarifazgo*, as these customs fees were called. The treasury tried to impose fees on internal trade by placing customs houses on the royal highways and by ordering that certain trades travel along one permitted route. Two examples of this were the route from the area of Tucumán to Potosí, which brought mules, sugar and other foodstuffs to the silver mines on the barren altiplano, and the road from Guatemala through Chiapas to Puebla and Mexico City which, in its heyday, carried large quantities of cacao and indigo. The tendency towards monopolistic control of bottlenecks was apparent at lower levels of society also.

Strategically placed towns on secondary trade routes tried to emulate the *consulados* of Veracruz and Seville and to tax passing traders for their use of local facilities. Cartago, the colonial capital of Costa Rica, sat astride the route between Nicaragua and Panama, a route which brought the mules raised on the pastures around the Nicaraguan lakes to the *trajín* or transisthmian haulage system of Panama. The Cartago town council levied a small tax per mule while local ostlers and feed-store owners were accused of manipulating prices for their services while the mule-trains were in the town. From time to time clans and other cliques in cities such as Guayaquil and Compostela controlled cabildos and through them whole regions and their products.

Customs dues, both external and internal, legal and illegal, were not the only taxes on trade. The *alcabala* or sales tax had been used in Castile before the conquest and reached America in the late sixteenth century. At first it was thought of as a Spanish or European tax, and the Indian population was theoretically exempt except when it traded in European goods, although some Indians paid heavily, even on maize sales. It was set at 2 per cent of the sale price of goods, but rose to double that amount in the seventeenth century. In times of war or other emergencies higher rates were used, and often lasted, as taxes will, long beyond the emergency. Late in the eighteenth century it was raised to 6 per cent, which caused some dissatisfaction and disturbances. Some smaller Spanish towns delayed the imposition of the alcabala, merchants and cabildos banding together to resist the surveys and listing of merchants necessary to start up the system. Other towns pleaded difficulties or disasters to obtain temporary exemptions. In Quito, when it was finally forced upon the locals in 1591, it caused threats of riots and sedition. In Guatemala, where it was ordered to begin in 1576, the first real surveys began in 1602. In many towns it was assessed on the town in general as a lump sum. The town then assigned the collection to a tax farmer, who had to rely to some extent on sworn statements from encomenderos, hacendados, merchants and shopkeepers as to the volume and worth of their exchanges in the recently-completed tax period. Self-assessment for tax is a poor way to collect money. Many basic items, such as bread, arms, religious ornaments, horses, and all gifts and inheritances, were exempt from alcabala. What with fraud, intermittent collection, illegal buying and selling from Indians, and quarrels over which goods qualified and which did not, most alcabalas from minor cities must have been a disappointment to the royal treasury. Probably it was collected more zealously in the larger cities. In central Mexico, with the increased activity and trade of the mid eighteenth century, it became, like the crown's tobacco monopoly, one of the most financially important branches of the royal treasury.

Most government offices were purchased both in America and in Spain – those in very wealthy communities bringing bids many times higher than the same posts in poorer communities – but this tax in advance was not sufficient for the crown in that it did not allow access to the official's income, frequently high, after he had taken office. To remedy this situation the government instituted two very crude income taxes. The *mesada* was a payment of a month's income by every new official, secular and ecclesiastic, upon entering his new post. In civil offices this was difficult to assess because office-holders seldom revealed the truth about the monthly yield of their positions. Benefices were public knowledge and so clerics holding them were taxed more accurately. In 1631 the crown increased the tax for secular officials to half of the first year's salary, or a *media anata*. (Thus, in the seventeenth century the remaining mesada became known as the *mesada eclesiástica*.) By 1754 the crown was demanding, and the papacy was consenting to, a *media anata* on the salaries of the high clergy, but it took several years to put this change into practice and for most clergy the mesada was the tax collected for much of the eighteenth century. Sometimes the *media anata* was also collected on the first year's profits from purchases of crown lands.

Since the days of the *Reconquista* the crown had claimed and received a share of booty and especially bullion. In the New World this share became the *quinto real*, or 'royal fifth', and once the conquests were over the *quinto* became a tax on the production of precious stones, pearls, gold, and above all silver. Sometimes, to stimulate production, it was lowered to one-tenth, and in some places of marginal importance the local guild of miners or the city cabildo was able to persuade the crown to be satisfied with one-twentieth. This was the case for most of the colonial period in the silver mines of Honduras and in the gold mines between Popayán and Cali. The *quinto* was easier to collect in the large mines or in any mines which used a mercury amalgam for smelting. Mercury mining was a royal monopoly and, although the quality of the silver ore was an important factor, there was a rough correspondence between the quantity of mercury used and the amount of silver refined. Silver, however, is a considerable spur to human ingenuity, and fraud was rife in the silver mines. Silver was adulterated, bars were shaved, miners and officials stole ore, government officials from time to time conspired in vast schemes of defalcation of the treasury. Nevertheless, fraud at the mercury-using mines never reached the proportions that it did in the mines which continued to use the old fire and oven smelting, the *huayras*, as they were called in Upper Peru. In these mines, which in many cases were worked only for a few months or a year or two, even the royal tenth or twentieth was very difficult to collect. Nevertheless, in spite of these difficulties the *quinto* was one of the most important taxes in the Spanish New World, extracting large amounts of money from labour and production, and remitting much, perhaps most, of it to Spain, other parts of western Europe, and eventually the Far East.

Government monopolies such as the mercury mining mentioned above, early seventeenth-century copper mining at Santiago del Prado in eastern Cuba, and above all the very remunerative *estanco* or monopoly on tobacco, came to be of great importance as sources of revenue. In the late colonial period monopolies on 'necessities' such as salt, paper, gunpowder, and tobacco became extremely unpopular among all classes and led to outbreaks such as the Tupac Amaru revolt and the early struggles which led to independence. Government also rented out its monopolistic rights, sometimes rights to whole regions, although these were usually areas that the government had been unable to develop. The Guipúzcoa company and the Campeche company of the eighteenth century were two examples.

The crown was obliged by its status as patron of the church to act as a redistributive agency for one tax. It collected the ecclesiastical tithe or *diezmo* on the 'fruits of the earth', roughly speaking all agricultural and domesticated animal products. Usually Indians did not pay the tithe except on products introduced to them by Europeans. The crown probably found the collection, administration and disbursement of the tithe to be a losing proposition. It kept one-ninth of the proceeds to cover its costs, almost certainly not enough, and spent the rest on bishoprics, cathedral chapters, construction and maintenance of churches, hospitals, poorhouses, asylums and schools, and on the parish clergy. The *diezmo* was a transfer of wealth out of the agricultural sector to the church, but part of it was returned, not only to the extent that the church satisfied some of the psychological and spiritual needs of its adherents, but also to the poor and the sick in the form of primitive medical attention, charity and hospitalization, and to the wealthier in the form of education, loans, and ritual opportunities for displays of social prestige. The other ecclesiastical tax, collected by clergy but administered by the government, was the *santa cruzada*, a system of sale of indulgences every other year which brought in considerable revenue, especially in the eighteenth century. To a very limited extent there was an attempt to turn the indulgences into an income or wealth tax, with assessments varying from two to ten pesos depending on wealth, class and caste. Collection was farmed out to the clergy, in the towns usually to members of the cathedral chapter, and its efficiency and fairness, even by its own terms, varied widely.

These taxes, which became more complicated and numerous as the colonial centuries advanced – head taxes on the peasantry, the control of trade bottlenecks and the assessment of towns by the approximate value of their business transactions, confiscations from captive groups such as government officials and dependent clerics, government monopolies and the sale of government monopolies, levies to support the state religion, and the appropriation of a share of the product of the most spectacular wealth-producing industry, in this case silver mining – were all very old devices, the most obvious sources of revenue for early empires and direct descendants of Roman imperial taxation. No great bureaucracy was needed, since almost all these taxes were farmed out, that is to say, the right to collect a specific tax was purchased by a private individual who recouped the costs of the office by holding back part of the taxes which he collected, or who agreed to deliver a specific amount to the authorities. Sometimes the tax farmer's share was expressed as a percentage of the total collected, an incentive to collect enthusiastically and thoroughly. And, of course, tax farmers, all the way from hacendados, wealthy merchants, and indigent creoles to *calpisques* and Indian village *principales* and *alcaldes*, trimmed, overcollected, underreported, and held back excessive amounts, as much as was possible, while keeping a close eye on the degree of amiability, indulgence, sloth, honesty, and indigence of the treasury officials to whom they had to account and deliver. It was not until the reign of Charles III, the first promoter of a modern state bureaucracy, that vigorous efforts were made to cut down tax farming and to increase collection by state functionaries, *intendentes* and *subdelegados*.

The Spanish state, a transitional system seeking desperately for funds and trying to be modern about it, devoted considerable thought to the problem of how to take a share of capital and income from the wealthy, a class which had to be pampered because it performed so many social control and other functions for the government. *Composiciones* or *indultos*, ex post facto payments to the crown for overlooking irregularities and criminal activities (often abuses of the labour force) and granting titles to dubiously acquired (usually Indian) land, was a poor income producer, although often expensive to the individual concerned, and was more of a series of rewards to supporters on whom government depended.

The best that the government could manage, given its relationship with the upper class, was the *donativo gracioso*, a 'voluntary donation', which was really a system of involuntary, negotiated assessments or confiscations resembling English royal benevolences. The crown began this practice of elaborate begging, sometimes for gifts, sometimes for loans, in the early sixteenth century, often invoking the costs of an emergency or a special celebration such as a war or the birth of a royal heir, as an excuse, but by the reign of Charles II it had become a system, recurring fairly regularly every few years, and with a recognized procedure for assessment and collection. Local officials, often the *audiencia*, which would then delegate the responsibility to local corregidores, were ordered to assess the wealthy of each jurisdiction for a donation. Lists of such people were drawn up with appropriate, suggested amounts. The corregidor or town official then collected these sums, or some approximation to them, at times after a prolonged period of bargaining. Royal officials were not exempt, and they too paid up short, sending long and elaborate letters of excuse to Spain explaining the underpayment. The crown had some latent means of threatening royal officials, but was in a difficult position vis-à-vis its wealthy private citizens. As its demands for gifts became more frequent, abject, and desperate, the importuned developed more and more sales resistance and the indigent crown was obliged to offer inducements such as pensions, titles of nobility, future exemptions, and freedom from government regulations in order to collect. The results of these donations were contradictory. Some of them in the late sixteenth and early seventeenth centuries produced large sums which helped the crown to surmount real emergencies, such as the million pesos sent by the viceroy of Mexico in 1629 to compensate for Piet Heyn's capture of the silver fleet. But the donations were also a form of disinvestment, a removal of capital from the colonies, and in the long run alienated a class on which the crown depended. The crown's financial and bargaining position was too weak to turn these practices into real taxes on wealth or incomes, or to make them of any long-term utility or advantage.

DISTRIBUTION AND EXCHANGE

Colonial Spanish America had several overlapping and intersecting systems of production, distribution and exchange, which went through many phases of prosperity and decline, expansion and contraction.

At the lowest level was peasant agriculture and village exchanges. Maize, beans, tubers, some pulque and chicha, salt, fowls and other small domesticates, and handwoven cloth were produced by Indian smallholdings, more or less communal villages and on the fringe areas of haciendas. To the extent that these basic goods were needed in larger markets such as Spanish cities the Indian community played the principal role in the early days of the encomienda, bringing large quantities of these staples for sale or, via the tribute, to auction in the cities. As the encomienda weakened and the Indian population declined, and as cities and mining centres became bigger and more attractive markets, local Indian producers and distributors were pushed aside to a considerable extent by Spanish farmers, owners of haciendas and obrajes, and Spanish or mestizo merchants. Indian production for the market was once more largely confined to the village level. The total quantity of goods involved certainly remained considerable, but individual quantities were small, moved about inefficiently, and lacked means of exchange. The system depended on the indefatigable industry and stamina of the Indian petty farmer and merchant, often the same person, and willingness to travel long distances with small quantities in search of meagre profits. Much of the exchange was by barter, or by substitute coinages such as cacao beans, cakes of brown sugar, or coca leaves. Money in its smallest denominations and falsified coinage were also common. The local *cabecera*, or sometimes a semi-vacant village which had been the pre-Columbian ceremonial centre, became the weekly market-place. People brought goods to these markets on their own backs or on the backs of mules or llamas. In the more 'Indian' areas such market days had cultural and religious functions which provided additional rewards to these merchants and made the profit margin slightly less important. In poor and marginal areas of Spanish America such as Paraguay, Tucumán, and rural Venezuela before cacao, areas with little Indian population and no important product to draw Spanish attention, the few Spanish settlers found that they had no alternative but to live off Indian production. It was in such areas that the encomienda lasted for most of the colonial period.

From time to time the emergence within the peasant economy of a desirable and profitable product (or, more frequently, the emergence within the European society of America, or in Europe itself, of a market for a previously ignored product) invited intrusion. Cacao, tobacco, cactus fibres, and in a slightly different way pulque and coca leaves are typical American crops which developed market values in the Europeanized economy because of changing patterns of distribution, changing tastes, or new ways of using products. Indian or peasant producers gradually lost control of the marketing system, and sometimes of the land and the productive process as well.

In some places and at some times Indian and other peasant groups were able to resist such intrusions and takeovers by displays of community solidarity. Usually peasant producers could limit, postpone, or prevent intrusion only by possession of a production or trade secret. A good example is cochineal, a dye which resulted from an intricate, skilled manufacturing process involving symbiotic relationships between humans, insects, and cactus. Spaniards, and even Indians from areas which did not produce cochineal, did not have the skills or patience to take over the production, and given its nature, the industry was difficult to rationalize or intensify. Economies of scale at the local level were counterproductive and led to declines in output. Production was in the hands of small producers – in this case Indian villagers in Oaxaca, the leading cochineal area – and so cochineal was delivered to many small village markets. Even at this stage it did not pay larger merchants or entrepreneurs to become involved. Petty merchants, Indians or castas, went around to these village markets buying up small quantities of the dye and delivering them to larger merchants. This is not to say that relationships in these local markets were fairer or more egalitarian. These petty traders, mule-skinners or more cosmopolitan Indian *principales*, often the main link between the peasant economy and the larger market economies, swindled, cajoled and coerced as much as they could. Both sides, Spanish above and Indian below, scorned them, as their common derisive names, such as *mercachifles* or *quebrantahuesos*, show. Thus Spaniards, through intermediaries, were able to profit from cochineal and to gather it together in sufficient bulk to make it a significant trade item as far away as Amsterdam and London, but they could not take over or fully control the production process, and the marketing system frustrated them until very late in the colonial period. Areas such as Oaxaca which had trade and marketing secrets which excluded non-Indians, were, of course, as a result able to remain more 'Indian'. Oaxaca, however, must be regarded as an exception. Most peasant areas which produced or marketed products which were of great value suffered massive intrusions, and major transformations in their production and marketing systems, and in their cultures, resulted.

By the early seventeenth century the expanding urban markets for meat, cereals (wheat as well as maize) and other basic foodstuffs in the more important parts of the empire were supplied for the most part not by Indian villages, except perhaps indirectly, but by large-scale, Spanish-owned estancias, sheep farms, pig farms, haciendas, wheat farms (*labores*) and market gardens. By the eighteenth century nine trade routes led to Mexico City, bringing into town hundreds of mule-trains and ox-carts laden with wheat, maize, cattle, pigs, hides, sugar, wines, and vegetables as well as textiles, dyes, and European goods. Several thousand mules entered the city each day, and Indian towns with grazing land near Mexico City became staging areas where cattle were rested and grazed until the city slaughterhouses were ready for them. Lima too was a big market, although the limited agricultural land near this desert oasis, and its coastal location, allowed Lima to draw some of its staples from a considerable distance, a luxury not logistically possible for inland, highland cities such as Mexico City, Bogotá or Quito. Lima's wheat came from the central valley of Chile and the northern oases of the Peruvian coast; its woods, cordage and pitch from Guayaquil or even from distant Nicaragua, and its maize and potatoes from the highlands of the hinterland. Lima was exceptional, however: most Spanish regional capitals of any size dominated interior highland valleys and created agricultural belts around them. The merchants who brought these staples to these cities were Spaniards or castas working for their own benefit, or as agents of Spanish farmers or larger city merchants. One exception was the Indian canoers in the canals approaching Mexico City from the south. The building, steering, and poling of canoes were skills or hard work which Spaniards scorned.

Distribution of staples within major cities was always a problem. Merchants, hacendados, wine growers and wheat farmers shared the basic colonial mentality which favoured monopoly and bottlenecks.

They tended to exclude competition and to withhold goods from the market to await shortages and higher prices. Groups of hacendados and wheat farmers quite obviously conspired towards these ends, and the result, if these monopolists were left unhindered, was shortages, even hardships, wild fluctuations in price, migrations among the poor, and chaotic market-places with outbreaks of looting and rioting. City authorities, *audiencias*, and even the viceregal governments intervened to make the system more just, to prevent shortages and exorbitant prices, and to preserve social tranquillity and the appearance of social control. The main devices used were the now familiar colonial ones which have already been discussed. Authorities ran monopolies themselves or auctioned off permission to monopolize and deliver a guaranteed quantity of goods. Government warehouses were called *pósitos* or *alhóndigas*. These institutions began in the New World in the late sixteenth and early seventeenth centuries and at first worked intermittently during times of shortages by confiscating and retaining Indian maize supplies brought into the city as tribute, and then redistributing the maize at set prices in the main city markets. In some cities the *alhóndigas* then became permanent features, buying up prescribed portions of the supplies of maize and other staples to depress the price and to control the profits of middlemen and monopolistic speculators. Cabildos themselves then became the monopolists to a certain extent, and some town councils, especially those controlled by tightly-knit cliques, played the market like true speculators. The town council, usually a far from affluent body in middle-sized and lesser Spanish towns, often borrowed heavily to buy staples for the alhóndiga, then found it tempting to recoup its outlays and perhaps even produce a small surplus for city reconstruction or beautification projects by holding up the redistribution from government warehouses until the price was just a little more favourable.

Some products such as meat, milk, and green vegetables could not be stored. In these cases the government could not monopolize purchase and redistribution and fell back on simply trying to ensure a dependable supply. This was done by auctioning the right to supply the city slaughterhouses or markets. A local hacendado would buy exclusive right to provision the city slaughterhouse, thus ensuring his monopoly and a right to charge high prices. The cabildo, abandoning fair prices to ensure a steady supply, was simply taking a percentage of his profits. The sufferers were those in the city who could not

Internal trade routes

afford to pay the monopoly prices. Most cities supplied their own basic manufactures. In 1781 Buenos Aires, for example, had 27 bakeries, 139 shoemakers, 59 tailors, and 76 carpenters, all producing for the local market.

The larger cities and the concentrations of rural populations near them also provided the markets for long-distance colonial Spanish American trade in non-perishable items or perishables with a longer life.

These longer-distance trades and trade routes, together with the bureaucratic networks which moved office-holders from place to place, were the only real ties which brought the American empire together as a unit, and, as the results of the wars of independence and subsequent attempts at common markets were to demonstrate, they were rather ephemeral links at best. If Spain was the metropolis for colonial Spanish America, then to a great extent central Mexico was the metropolis for large parts of the Caribbean, for Venezuela, the northern and southern extremes of continental New Spain, the Philippines, and even, for many purposes, the west coast of Spanish South America and its immediate hinterlands. More specifically, Mexico City, to a lesser extent Lima, and, for much of the colonial period, Potosí were dominant economic centres, magnets which drew and held large and sometimes distant catchment areas. In the middle to late eighteenth century, as the colonial economy went through a profound adjustment from its *ancien régime* of mercantilism towards a renovated mercantile era, and as new raw materials and products such as sugar, tobacco, and animal products became major exports to Europe, Buenos Aires, Caracas, and Havana joined the list of major urban markets.

At all times until the very late colonial period long-distance Spanish American trades were regulated or limited by the same logistical determinants of time, distance, cargo space and freight rates that dominated the trades between Spanish America and Seville or Cadiz. In general trade by sea was less expensive and more expeditious, so sea routes could deliver goods with higher perishability and lower profit margins from greater distances. In a similar fashion, although the differences were usually less, routes via coastal plains, at least during the dry season, could carry more perishable bulk goods than routes through the mountains. Where foodstuffs were involved, routes through relatively temperate climates entailed less spoilage than those which ran through hot, arid or humid tropics.

For much of the colonial period, beginning as early as the lifetimes of Hernando Cortés and the Pizarro brothers, the colonial axis of all these routes ran from Potosí through La Paz and Cuzco to Lima-Callao, and thence by sea up the coast to Panama and Acapulco, and ultimately Mexico City. Goods moved southwards more than northwards, and bullion moved more northwards than southwards, but at both ends of the colonial axis there was, significantly enough, a supply of silver to fuel exchanges and to provide incentives, although there were long periods when Potosí and the mines north of Mexico City did an inadequate job of providing either.

The distances involved in this colonial axis and the attractiveness of its main markets and main product, silver, encouraged the growth of regional specialization. Some of these were based on pre-conquest products and trade wares which continued on an increased scale into the colonial period because they fitted into Europeanized patterns of demand. The potteries of Puebla and Guadalajara, of the Ica and Nazca valleys, provided not only the kitchenware of the cities, towns and villages, but also the *botijas* or flagons which carried wine, oil, brandy, and pulque over long distances. Cacao in Colima and Soconusco fed the Mexican market until more European plantations, first around Caracas in the late seventeenth century, then later Guayaquil, took over the trade. Some of these regional specializations arose because of significant lacks near large markets. Lima could not grow its own wheat and had to look to small oases nearby. Even these were not sufficient and in the first half of the eighteenth century the central valley of Chile, relatively closer than Cuzco, Andahuaylas and Abancay because of the sea link, became Lima's main supplier. The barren altiplano around Potosí grew little and could provide grazing for only a few hardy sheep and American cameloids. So the valleys around Cochabamba and Sucre became its granaries, and mules were reared in large numbers as far away as Mendoza and driven to the mines through the mountains. Some specializations came into existence because of the availability of raw materials and skilled artisans. The bells and cannon of the foundries of Arequipa and Puebla supplied the churches, forts, and ships of the cities, ports, and routes along the axis. Other specializations arose because of European inability to supply many essentials at a great distance. The infamous textile obrajes or large workshops of central Mexico and Quito, the vineyards and olive groves of central Chile and of the Peruvian coastal oases, were local suppliers at first but expanded rapidly when Spain proved logistically and economically incapable of filling the colonial demand for cheap textiles, wine, brandy and oil. As regional specialities grew they challenged Spanish products even in Mexico and the Caribbean. Peruvian wine, for example, undercut the price of supplies from Andalusia in the Mexico City market, even after the government protected Sevillian monopolists by banning Mexican imports of Peruvian wine, thus driving it into contraband and raising its costs.

The obrajes represent the outstanding success story of colonial Spanish American industry and long-distance, inter-American trade. They grew up in two centres: the valleys of Quito, Otavalo, Riobamba, Ambato, Latacunga, and Alausí in the Ecuadorean sierra, and central Mexico from Puebla to Mexico City. The Quito complex supplied much of Pacific South America to regions as distant as Potosí and Cartagena. Mexico supplied New Spain and some of the islands of the Caribbean. Both industries rose to prominence in the late sixteenth century and lasted in various stages of prosperity until just before independence. The obrajes around Quito depended on vast herds of sheep – the valley of Ambato alone held about 600,000 in the late seventeenth century – and were challenged by few rivals for their Indian labour supply. Slaves, free castas, and a few convicts were all employed in the Quito sweatshops, but most of the workers were recruited quite simply by the old devices of encomienda and repartimiento. By 1680 there were some 30,000 people involved in the Quito obrajes, and the average mill employed some 160 people. Mexico's textile mills faced stiffer competition, not only from European and oriental textiles, but also from the labour requirements of silver mines and much larger cities. As a result its obrajes made heavier use of slave and convict labour and free wage labour. Wool was the principal cloth woven, but cotton was also widely used. Some mills were large and employed hundreds of workers. In the first half of the eighteenth century renewed competition both from Europe and other colonial centres – Cajamarca and Cuzco in Peru, Querétaro in New Spain – undermined the prosperity of Quito and Puebla somewhat. By the end of the century, however, they had successfully found alternative markets and started new lines of manufacture, although at the very end of the colonial period European competition was again a major problem.[3]

The main axis between Mexico, Acapulco and Callao, with its spur to Potosí, also stimulated shipbuilding. Guayaquil was a principal shipyard, thanks to its supplies of hardwoods and pitch, throughout the colonial period. Smaller ports such as Huatulco, San Blas and Realejo helped from time to time. All along the main inter-American trade route were important spurs. Mexico City, via its Caribbean port of Veracruz, traded with the islands and mainland ports. Routes between Veracruz and Havana – and, although later in starting, between Veracruz and La

[3] For further discussion of obrajes in eighteenth-century Spanish America, see Brading, *CHLA* I, ch. 11.

Guaira – became important carriers of silver, cacao, hides, dyes, and sugar. Mexico City was a distribution point not only for the vast sparsely populated expanses to its north, but also for areas as far south as Chiapas and Yucatán. Ports along the sea route between Acapulco and Callao traded with large hinterlands. Acajutla and Realejo were the ports for Central America, not only exchanging local goods for silver and wine from Mexico and Peru, but also bringing ashore illegal goods from Peru and sending them by land to Mexico to evade customs, and loading ships for Peru with silks and spices from the Philippines which had been brought illegally by land from Mexico City and Acapulco. The ports of northern Peru performed similar functions. Piura and Santa were not only the ports for Paita and the Callejón de Huaylas, but also the landing-stages for illegal goods from Mexico and the Philippines via Mexico which were trying to evade the vigilance of customs officers in Callao. In a similar fashion Guayaquil was the port for the highlands around Quito, and La Serena, Valparaíso, and Concepción were the ports for northern, central, and southern Chile and for the interior provinces on the other side of the Andes around Mendoza and San Juan.

An even more important southern spur was the one which ran from the southern silver terminus of the axis, Potosí, down through Salta, Tucumán, and Córdoba to Buenos Aires and the Portuguese smuggling depot at Colônia do Sacramento. Some of the goods travelling northwards along this route, for example the horses, mules and cattle of Tucumán which were sent to supply the silver mines, were legal and open. But Buenos Aires, for some two centuries after its definitive settlement, was also the illegal back door to Potosí, a surreptitious route and a shorter one from Europe than the legal one via Panama and Callao. European manufactures and some of the luxuries which mining boom towns demand moved slowly along this long land route. Of greater worldwide import was the silver which moved illegally in the other direction. From Buenos Aires the silver of Potosí passed on to merchants in Sacramento and Rio de Janeiro, and thence not only to Lisbon but directly to Portuguese India and China to finance the spread of Western intrusion there. From 1640, when Portugal broke with the Spanish crown, until about 1705 this large exchange system suffered many difficulties and some nearly complete interruptions, but in the late sixteenth and early seventeenth centuries, and again as the Spaniards were forced to give the Buenos Aires slave trade concessions to foreign companies, first French, then English, after 1702 and 1713, the Potosí–Buenos Aires silver trade was of great international importance. American silver reached the Orient by another route. The longest spur on the Mexico City–Lima–Potosí axis was the route between Acapulco and the Philippines. This route exchanged silk and oriental spices for Mexican and Peruvian silver, and in spite of mid-seventeenth-century difficulties, seems to have produced great profits. Thus the silver axes of the main colonial trade route financed European activities and imperialism in the Orient: the Potosí end via Buenos Aires, the Portuguese, and other foreigners; the Mexican end via the Philippines and Canton.

Internal colonial trade, both the system which supplied staples to city markets and the long-distance system carrying silver, textiles and regional specialities, required means of articulation. We have already mentioned such institutions as governmental and private auctions, *pósitos* and *alhóndigas*, guilds of merchants and artisans, and minor merchants and traders who collected small amounts of valuable items in village markets for delivery to larger houses in the cities. The dominant exchange mechanism, however, just as in the village economy and in Western Europe, was the trade fair. The largest fairs were in the big cities and the place and time of their occurrence and their internal governance were regulated by law and local inspectors. Other fairs took place at crossroads where the various systems intersected. The most unique and famous fairs were the ones which linked the three internal trade systems which we have described with the official transoceanic trades carried by the fleets and the various licensed ships. These fairs took place in the great official ports or nearby, especially Veracruz, Jalapa, and Portobelo. In a curious way these fairs, right at the top of the hierarchy of trade systems, closely resembled those at the very bottom. Indian fairs often took place in vacant ceremonial villages which would fill up for the two or three days of the fair, then fall back to their usual tranquillity. So too with Portobelo and many other unhealthy tropical ports. While the fleets unloaded and reloaded people would pack into the ports, renting rooms and buying food, drink, and transportation at enormously inflated prices. Tent cities and temporary canvas warehouses would spring up on nearby beaches, and roaring commercial and social interaction would give these places the appearance of frenzied, round-the-clock activity for a few days or weeks. When the fleets sailed and the mule-trains toiled away inland these cities would sink back to small collections of huts, many of them vacant, as the merchants and administrators headed with indecent haste for more salubrious spots.

Much less is known of the merchants in the two intermediate systems which supplied the large internal markets than of the great merchants of the *consulados* of Mexico City, Veracruz, Lima, Seville, and Cadiz. The small group of merchants in Quito in the closing years of the sixteenth century has, however, been studied. Its main preoccupation was not distance but time, more specifically *jornadas* or days of travel. Its other problem was delays in payment and thus in collecting profits. Borrowing was limited, so the typical merchant often waited for his profit from a venture before he could reinvest in a new one. Textiles to Potosí and Popayán, and leather, sugar, and hardtack to various destinations were his principal exports. European goods, wine from Peru, and silver from Potosí were his imports. A few traders worked as individuals but most had to band together because of the shortage of private capital and the relative lack of credit. Sometimes non-merchants were brought into the *compañía*, providing capital, mules, or labour in return for a share of the profits. Lack of a standard series of weights and measures, fluctuations in rates and values, the impossibility of knowing the demand for certain items in distant markets, and above all the lack of a good and stable currency caused disappointments, delays and losses. Some of these *compañías* of merchants spent months assembling the necessary capital and preparing for expeditions. Sometimes dozens of merchants became involved and the surrounding countryside had to be scoured for horses, mules, saddles, weatherproof containers, and fodder. Some of the caravans which left Quito were enormous, containing hundreds of mules. Failure rates among this generation of Quito merchants were low, and profits ranged between 10 and 30 per cent – good returns in a time of low inflation and fairly stable wages. The interest rates charged by lenders varied according to the destination, its distance in time, and its wealth as a market. Borrowing money for a trip to Guayaquil cost a merchant 10 per cent interest. The other extreme was Seville, for which lenders were unwilling to risk cash at less than 100 per cent. Potosí, with its high prices and wild spenders, cost less in interest than Panama. A loan towards sending goods to Cartagena by sea cost less in interest than a loan to send goods to Cartagena by land, in spite of the transhipments at Guayaquil and the isthmus. Merchants reinvested profits in the next venture, but even more in land, in consumption, and in the church. Businesses in this time and place seldom carried over to the next generation and ended with large distributions of assets when the merchant died. No doubt the Castilian laws of partible inheritance were much to blame in an era of large families. Merchants seem to have had no great feeling for their trade, did not found business 'houses', and did not hope that their heirs would follow in their footsteps. Their profits might be reinvested in another similar venture, or quite as easily in something entirely unrelated to trade. Merchants in very large commercial cities such as Mexico City and Lima were different. There some merchant families persisted over two or three generations and demonstrated a certain *esprit de corps* and status consciousness, partly because of the presence of the *consulados*. The merchants of Veracruz, Buenos Aires, Caracas, and Havana in the late eighteenth century were more professional and cosmopolitan than their earlier inland fellows. Nevertheless, there was always a marked inclination to get out of trade, to invest in land, and then to tie up fortunes in secure *mayorazgos* or entailed estates.

The history of prices and wages, another important aspect of production and exchange, has also perhaps not received the scholarly attention it deserves. Prices rose rapidly in the half-century or more after the conquest as the labouring population decreased, as silver mining monetized the economy quickly, and as the consuming population grew. This must have confused the calculations of producers and merchants considerably, but usually sixteenth-century inflation worked to their benefit, in the New World if not in the Old. Wages rose even more rapidly as labour not connected to slavery, encomienda and repartimiento/mita gained a comparative advantage because of its increasing scarcity. Producers, employers, and merchants had to balance off these increasing labour costs against the gains to be made from inflating prices. We do not know enough about this equation, but those who used large numbers of free labourers may have lost out slightly at the end of the day. Long-distance trades resulted in some wildly fluctuating prices because of the times and freights involved and because of the unevenness of supply. Famines, droughts, floods, volcanic eruptions, locusts, and epidemics brought temporary shortages and rapid price rises which were often worsened by eager monopolists. The price of Peruvian wine in Mexico, for example, varied greatly. We know little about wages, except for a general impression of stability in the seventeenth century which may have lessened in the eighteenth. Wages may have lagged behind prices, especially in late eighteenth-century Mexico, as the working population slowly increased, an additional long-term advantage to those who used wage labour.

Production and exchanges had to be financed. Credit sources included the church and its *capellanías*, or private endowments and benefices of the secular clergy, the royal exchequer, community chests, guilds and fraternities, and private individuals. Merchants themselves loaned money to other merchants and to miners and landowners. Speculators even played the market in the village economy by means of the *repartimientos de comercio*, advancing cash, equipment, horses, or mules in return for a share of the next harvest. Loans in general were fairly short-term and specific in purpose but land mortgages could last for years and the capital which such mortgages released was used for a wide variety of investments. Dowries were a very common means for transferring capital and financed many an enterprise or business expansion. In general credit instruments such as letters of credit and means of transferring capital and payments over distances and time were much poorer than in Western Europe. Because capital markets and the quantities of goods exchanged were relatively small, and because they were not backed by an extensive, widely understood and accepted system of credits and credit instruments, the system had to be backed by an agreed-upon valuable, which in this cultural context had to be bullion, especially silver. Not all of the marketing systems examined here needed the backing of a silver currency, at least not to the same extent. Village agricultural exchanges used barter or substitute coinages such as coca leaves or cacao beans. This is not to suggest that this economy was always a simple one. Studies of the various ecological niches and complementary zones of altitudes and specialization in the Andes and in Mesoamerica have demonstrated the existence of a 'vertical archipelago' of exchanges between different zones, governed by reciprocity and barter rather than calculated on strict and current market prices of the goods involved. Some of these barter exchanges could cover large distances, on rare occasions involving journeys taking weeks. Trade for the urban markets, however, especially long-distance trade and above all trade with Europe and the Orient, had to be backed by silver. There are several examples of ingenious traders relying upon alternative coinages. Cacao beans were used in Venezuela, Costa Rica, and in rural Mexico. Coca leaves were used in Upper Peru. There are even indications that the standard *botija* of wine or oil was understood as a measure of value, and thus became a sort of primitive money along the Pacific coast in the harder years of the mid seventeenth century. But in general, long-distance trades needed silver and when silver was scarce these trades languished.

Before 1535 the invading groups used barter or weighed pieces of gold and silver. The crown introduced a dangerous precedent by attempting to monetize the colonies and make some profit at the same time. It sent Castilian coins to the New World and declared them of higher value there than in Castile. Manipulation of the value of the coinage was a temptation to which the crown often yielded, with profitable, quick results and a disastrous impact on trading and on the confidence of the trading community in Spanish America.

Minting began in the New World in 1535 and for most of the colonial period the colonies produced their own coinage. From the beginning adulteration, falsification, and shaving of the coinage was rampant. Spaniards inherited an Aztec tradition of mixing gold with copper and this suspect *tipuzque* coinage circulated freely in Mexico past the mid sixteenth century. Thereafter Mexican coinage was considered more reliable. In Peru adulteration of silver with tin and lead pre-dated the conquest. Much early colonial Peruvian coinage was similarly mixed and Peruvian money remained an object of suspicion compared to that of Mexico for most of the colonial period. Potosí coins were a joke and were often rejected. At times falsified coinage was accepted in legal transactions, but at a discounted rate. Thus such coins were illegal technically but not in practice.

For much of the three centuries under discussion the standard coin was the *peso fuerte* or *peso de a ocho*, a silver coin divided into eight *reales*. In the lesser colonies this coin was often cut with a cold chisel, in two parts to make *tostones*, or in eight 'bits' or *reales*. *Moneda cortada* or *moneda recortada* did not inspire confidence. Cutting pesos often left *tostones* and *reales* of less than the correct size and weight. Clipping and shaving bits of coins reduced them to such shapelessness that coin weighing was a regular feature of small market-places. Good money was hoarded or exported and suspect *perulero* coins were the most common in America. To make matters worse the crown, Spanish merchants and foreigners drained the colonies of silver coinage with surprising efficiency, not only to Europe, but via Buenos Aires to Brazil and India, and via Acapulco to the Orient. Taxes were sent to Madrid, royal officers and merchants sent home substantial sums against the day of their retirement, and foreign smugglers preferred silver in exchange for the goods of north-western Europe or for African slaves. As silver mining declined in the mid seventeenth century, as the official Spanish fleet system deteriorated, and as smuggling and hoarding of good coinage increased, the colonies, especially the secondary ones of the circum-Caribbean area, suffered an intense currency shortage. And what remained was suspect trash. In the 1650s the state stepped in, tinkering with the debased coinage, devaluing the Peruvian *macacas*, and finally recalling them for restamping. None of these panic measures worked and the crown finally abandoned reform and left the situation to work itself out. Debased remnants were dumped on the Indian or free black communities and ended up in the treasury as payment of tribute and other taxes. Trade lost its main backing and stultified or became local. Barter grew but inhibited long-distance exchanges. Such monetary crises returned frequently after the mid seventeenth century. Southern Mexico was again troubled between 1700 and 1725. In 1728 the crown took over the mints, which had previously been leased to private companies, and tried to standardize coinage and stamping and to introduce the milled edge to discourage clipping – all seemingly to very little effect.

Coinage shortages and unreliability led to problems of convertibility, especially in rural or peripheral areas. Numerous complaints tell of powerful, wealthy regional figures who could not translate their capital to more desirable centres. A typical case would be that of a rancher in Mendoza or Sonora with thousands of head of cattle and countless hectares of land, trying to convert this obvious wealth into a move to Mexico City or even Madrid. How would such a man, or his widow, turn such holdings into a reliable coinage or its equivalent over long distances?

Currency and coinage, then, were a problem throughout the Spanish colonial period, an ironic situation given the wealth pouring out of the silver mines. In times of great shortages of coinage barter and substitute money returned, trade routes shortened because of lack of an agreed-upon means of exchange, and market confidence fell. When good coinage which enjoyed the confidence of traders was relatively abundant long-distance trade expanded and even local exchanges were quicker and easier. The state and quantity of silver coinage is one of the surest indicators of the general economic condition in such an early, unsophisticated money economy.

8

SOCIAL ORGANIZATION AND SOCIAL CHANGE IN COLONIAL SPANISH AMERICA

Less than two decades ago the topic that we now often call the 'social history' of early Spanish America, the study of its 'social structure' or 'social organization', was just beginning to be explored; a single thoughtful article was able to bring together nearly everything useful that was then known, most of it drawn from formal, self-conscious statements of contemporaries in laws, tracts, political manifestos, or official reports.[1] Since then a whole current of scholarship within the field of early Spanish American history has concentrated on precisely the opposite kind of social phenomena, informal patterns of thought and behaviour which were rarely given overt expression – some, indeed, may have been beneath the level of consciousness. Such work has been highly specific, tied to a certain time and place, giving detailed accounts of individual lives and individual families, businesses, or other local organizations in different periods and different regions.[2] The cases were sometimes chosen for their representation of general types and processes, but the typological aspect often remained implicit.

The time has now come for a provisional synthesis. The emphasis will be on processes and principles, although individual life stories and individual situations have ultimately provided the raw material. It may be felt by some that the colour – the humanity – is missing, that the regional variety has been attenuated, or that aspects of the chronology have been neglected. The first part of this chapter deliberately sets out to examine general patterns of social organization in a somewhat atemporal fashion. The second part discusses some of the dynamic principles of social evolution and change.

[1] Lyle N. McAlister, 'Social structure and social change in New Spain', *Hispanic American Historical Review* [*HAHR*], 43 (1963), 349–70.
[2] See *CHLA* II, Bibliographical Essay 8.

THE STRUCTURE OF SPANISH AMERICAN SOCIETY

Few would doubt the impossibility of finding an entirely static historical phenomenon. Nevertheless, some important features of the social organization of Spanish America did not change perceptibly during the 300 years of the colonial period. And there were many forms which, though not exactly universal, nor unchanging in actual fact, were immanent; under optimal conditions they regularly appeared and stabilized. Others indeed did change, but they are so characteristic of the period that their demise signals its end. The patterns and structures come in two very distinct sets, largely emanating from the Iberian and Indian backgrounds; they took shape in two almost equally distinct subsocieties within Spanish America. They will be treated separately before a number of overarching structures and interrelationships are considered.

The Spanish world

Conceived of in law as the *república de los españoles* or 'commonwealth of the Spaniards', the Spanish world was also a unit in social practice, held together by multiple mutually reinforcing ties despite its considerable diversity and spatial fragmentation. Even in the generation of the conquest this sector contained non-Spaniards, not only European foreigners, but Africans and Indian servants. In the mature colonial period some blurring occurred, but by practical consensus the Spanish world included all those who spoke fair Spanish, dressed and comported themselves in a more or less European manner, and normally circulated among Spaniards. In the latter part of the period this group ('Hispanics' in my terminology) tended to give itself the flattering designation *gente de razón*, 'people of reason', or those who lived a rational and orderly life as Europeans understood it.

Spanish society in America was essentially urban. The bulk of Hispanic and Hispanicized people, especially in the earlier half of the period, were urban dwellers. Widely scattered Spanish cities were separated by great stretches of Indian countryside, varying from thickly inhabited to almost empty. As the Hispanic sector grew, more centres arose and flourished, increasingly filling in the hinterland, but these replicated the older picture on a smaller scale, so that there was still a relative concentration of Hispanics. As we will see, only the very poorest and most marginal areas saw anything like true dispersal.

The city itself was always the primary locus of Hispanic society, reaching out beyond its streets and walls to take in the Hispanic inhabitants of the entire province as far as the beginning of the sphere of the next municipality. There was no scope for anything like a city–country or urban–rural rivalry; the only true counterweight to the city was the countryside inhabited by Indians. Not only did the city dominate in law, with its council representing the entire jurisdiction; in every branch of life the pattern was the same, the high and mighty in the city and the humble in the country, the successful converging on the centre and the marginal impelled from the city outward. All larger organizations, including agrarian estates, had city headquarters. Large-scale commerce and craft production, as well as the activity of higher professionals, tended to be located entirely in the cities.

The entire Hispanic sector of a given province made an indivisible, city-centred unit in every social, economic, and institutional dimension. Each economic or institutional network was also a stepped social hierarchy, and the city served the entire province as a social clearing-house. In any stable situation, there would tend to be a social convergence further unifying the province and its various province-wide organizations. Dominant families would form and, through inter-marriage, create a province-wide cluster, or sometimes rival clusters. Each of these families would attempt to place one or more of its members at high levels in each of the province's hierarchies; these and other members would also direct a set of interlocking economic enterprises; and in addition each family had poor relatives, dependants, and semi-dependants whom it deployed appropriately in its various affairs. The newly wealthy or powerful were attracted to the older dominant families and vice versa, with the new rich typically being absorbed into the ranks of the dominant through intermarriage. All this not only made the city–province unit a tightly knit one, it meant that in everyday life formal hierarchies meant rather less than they appeared to, and family matters, whether ties, lack of ties, or conflicts, meant a great deal.

Discussion of the largest social organism has thus led us quickly to the smallest. The nature of the family entities which allied, competed, or co-existed within the arena of the city–province profoundly affected the operation of all suprafamilial structures and distinctions. The patterns are best exemplified in the type of fully established, prominent family, wealthy in whatever the area offered, that one could find in any established province. As far as they could, smaller, poorer, or newer families operated in the same manner, and even a destitute orphan would act as representative of the family he might found. Family organization was inclusive, creating solidarity among sometimes quite disparate elements, and at the same time it gave each element its own weight, retaining distinctions.

Name and lineage were as important in the Iberian family as anywhere, but it was not just one line, or even the dual maternal–paternal aspect of the nuclear family, that was stressed. Names of several lines were embodied in succeeding generations and this attitude was also reflected in separate property holdings within families. A marriage was an alliance between two lines; that one side happened to be represented by a woman in no way affected the equality of the arrangement, and the bride's family continued to watch closely the holdings she took with her as dowry. Nor was strict primogeniture typical; despite a few entails, the norm even for the very wealthy was a relatively equal redistribution of the inheritance among all legitimate heirs, male and female. Each sought a slot for himself or herself within an overall family strategy that distributed the men in complementary walks of life and found the best alliances possible for the women. An excess of children could result in several of them going into the priesthood or a nunnery.

Another way to maintain coherence within diversity and flexibility was to keep everyone together; sometimes under the same roof and sometimes under the leadership of the eldest male (though not necessarily either), three or four generations, including cousins, aunts, uncles, and more distant relatives, would stay in very close touch, co-ordinating their activity the best they could and feeling responsible for each other – though fights over inheritance were endemic. The most characteristic feature of the system was a set of enterprises, of almost any nature, which were owned separately by individual family members but in fact operated as a unit.

The sense of family cohesiveness embraced different levels as well as different lines. Especially in the upper and middle walks of life, men married only when established, often living till then in informal unions with women of lower status, who bore them natural children. Married, established men often maintained a second household. As a result, there were numerous illegitimate relatives in almost any extended family. The family core neither rejected them nor treated them as equals, but took them in as servants or managers. Likewise, as a family spread its tentacles and time passed, it was inevitable that some would fare better than others, that certain members of the legitimate line and associated lines would fall on bad times; these poor relatives, too, met with a combination of assistance and subordination.

The role of women in the family was similar to that in southern Europe in the early modern period. Women immigrants did take part in the early occupation of Spanish America; in the central areas, Spanish women began to compare to men in numbers by the second generation. Indeed, in many places and times there were more women than there were good marriages for them, so there were a good many spinsters and non-remarrying widows. Somewhat misleadingly, they did not appear in the formal hierarchies, except as nuns, nor openly practise the professions and trades beyond some minor ones which convention assigned them – preparing and marketing certain kinds of food, inn-keeping, midwifery, and some others. Actually it was by no means uncommon for a woman, especially if she was the social or economic superior, to dominate her husband's estate or business informally, down to the details. Widows might quite openly direct enterprises and serve as heads of whole families. Spinsters made their own investments, in real estate and much else. As mentioned already, women could inherit and could hold property separately even within marriage (though under certain restrictions). To be sure, their commanding position was often largely derived from their family of origin, but the same was true of men.[3]

In other words, apart from questions of ethnicity and the kind of differentiation that one might call local colour (the effects of great distances, small numbers, fresh starts, exotic landscapes), the family in the Spanish world of the Indies operated along the same lines as its counterpart in Iberia.

The idea of gentility or nobility played a very large role in discussions of the social standing of individuals. Through the veiled, copious, constantly shifting terminology which was used, the concept itself is

[3] For a detailed treatment of the lives of women in colonial Spanish America, see Lavrin, *CHLA* II, ch. 9.

quite clear, as is the life-style it implied, but the exact range of its application was almost systematically ambiguous, so that a maximum of distinctions could be made. The highest circles were certainly exclusive enough, restricted to the top levels of the small number of prominent interlocking, long-established families; access to those circles was only through really major accretions of wealth or the holding of high official positions. Yet one can hardly speak of a tightly closed-off nobility with a strong *esprit de corps*, actively concerned to distinguish itself from all other sectors of life. At the top were a few, with the full set of external hallmarks, who represented the quintessence of nobility in the eyes of all. At the bottom of the Spanish world were obvious *gente baja* or 'low people' – taverners, muleteers, sailors. And there were modest people who were comfortable and respected enough but would never think of claiming the rank of gentry for themselves – artisans, estate foremen, shopkeepers, and the like. But anyone in the Hispanic sector who attained any sort of prominence or position at all became noble to some degree, in his own eyes and in those of others; he would use the current nobiliary terminology for himself, however timidly, and his pretensions would be reflected in his marriage, his retinue, and his residence. Nobility in a sense can simply be equated with prominence; just as one can be more prominent or less, so one could be more or less noble, and a large proportion of the Hispanic population placed itself somewhere in that continuum.

This did not, however, reduce the concept to meaninglessness. Rather, gentility was the mode in which prominence was perceived, giving the person so regarded an advantage in obtaining positions and access to connections. The fully established noble family had more connections, to equals as well as to inferiors, than did those lower on the scale. Attributes manifested by anyone aspiring to gentility differed little from those of nobles all over Europe. Of special social significance were the ideals of a magnificent urban residence, a numerous retinue, and permanent wealth from a broad-based estate rooted in all productive or profitable sectors of the local economy. Nobility was distinguishable from wealth, but the two drew each other irresistibly. Large and lasting wealth of any kind soon created nobility for its holders, and the already noble families would take any kind of locally viable base for their wealth, even plebeian-tainted industries such as textiles (in Quito) or pulque (in central Mexico), eventually changing the whole flavour of such endeavours in their respective regions. The wealth–nobility nexus does not seem peculiar to America, but a long-standing Iberian characteristic.

One of the idiosyncrasies of New World nobility was its close association with the first stages of the Spanish occupation of America. Not only did the first settlers or conquerors of any given region, including some patently humble persons, lay claim to nobility in their own lifetimes, obtaining coats of arms and other marks of distinction, but their successors continued to raise the claim throughout the colonial period. Repeated intermarriage with newcomers often made a near fiction of the vaunted descent, but a noble aura actually did adhere to these lines, as can be seen among other things in the fact that the new wealthy and occasional newly arrived nobles from the outside regularly sought to join them. The principle of noble status acquired through participation in great events and enhanced by antiquity was not new, but the result was to give each region and subregion of Spanish America something like a Hispanic nobility specific to itself.

Commonness is an even harder concept to pin down than nobleness. It did not, of course, embody a well-defined set of ideals; rather the noble's ideals were the general or Spanish ones, and the commoner attained them to the extent that he could. Certainly no one proudly laid claim to commonness. The important thing to note is that though there was not much overt legal distinction between nobles and commoners in the Indies, social practice, in most places and times, did treat a large body of Spaniards as commoners, less privileged than those above them. Although the higher levels are historiographically easier to handle, and patterns are more fully worked out there, we must remember that the great variety and number of Hispanic people in humble positions is perhaps as basic a characteristic of a province's full development as is a cluster of great established families. Moreover, the ordinary Hispanics were extremely important in the economy and in socio-cultural evolution; in every way they pulled their own weight, and were by no means simply the pawns of the great. The Hispanic world, and even the narrower segment of it consisting of those considered fully Spanish, thus contained a wide social spectrum and numerous internal distinctions.

One such set of distinctions, more tangible and often more informative about society or an individual than the noble–commoner dichotomy, consisted of the various functional or occupational categories, much the same ones which were prevalent in Iberia and other parts of Europe in early modern times. The highest such function was a rather amorphous one which we may call 'estate holder'. Although there were, of course, estates of many kinds, by no means all of them were large or prestigious. There was a strong presumption that any fully established person at the top of the Spanish world would be owner or co-owner of a fairly large estate. It is important on two counts, however, that we should not automatically associate this estate with land. First, the prestige and influence of the estate holder were associated perhaps more than anything else with his role as chief of the group of people involved, and after that with the object of his principal capital investment, be it machinery, livestock, or slaves. Second, the business of the estate was normally whatever branch of local enterprise produced the greatest steady revenue. Since the estate was invariably diversified, it always had some agrarian aspect, but the basis of it could be a silver-refining mill in Potosí, a textile workshop in Quito, or a gang of slaves to mine gold in Antioquia. Both revenue and prestige were associated with livestock long before they were with land; only as city markets grew did land become valuable, revenue-producing, and the quite direct basis for estates. Holders of the mainline enterprises of a region's economy would normally dominate its municipal councils – in Antioquia the *señores de cuadrilla* or gang owners, and so on – though at times they maintained only indirect control through lesser or newer members of their circle.

The literate professions of the law, the priesthood, and (less preferred) medicine, had a double aspect. First, the greatest and noblest families did not hesitate to send their sons into these fields, where they could expect quick advancement to high positions. Nor did professional practice at all preclude estate holding. Second, and more in line with the usual image of these professions, middle-level people used them as an upward avenue, and there were families largely devoted to the professions, secondary eminences hovering about the great. A similar flavour of high second rank was characteristic of the numerous notaries and secretaries of the Spanish world, though some of them too founded great families.

Of all the occupations, it is hardest to give any kind of relatively fixed social evaluation inside the Spanish world to that of merchant (*mercader*, later *comerciante* or *hombre del comercio* of a given centre). Even restricting the notion of merchant, as the Spaniards themselves did, to someone involved in large-scale, long-distance trade in goods of high market value (usually of European style or origin), one finds that the person so defined, though always literate and in some sense respected, varies over time and place from a near-outsider, distinctly a commoner, to the titled, propertied pillar of society. The long-distance aspect of commerce, particularly its close connection with Europe, tended to keep the merchant from identification with any one place and make him always a new arrival, more closely associated with Spain than the holder of any other kind of wealth. During parts of the colonial period great commercial enterprises tended actually to be based in Spain, and it was there that merchants aimed to establish families and lasting estates. But it also could and did happen that commerce became a province's steadiest source of large revenue, and that commercial firms, in view of the steady volume, took the province as their main headquarters. Then the conditions were set for the merchant to enter the highest ranks.

Always distinct from the true merchant was the petty local dealer known, among other terms, as the *tratante*. Humble, often at the very bottom of the Spanish hierarchy, and likely to be illiterate, the *tratante* dealt primarily in goods circulating in the regional economy, and lacked the capital and extensive network of the long-distance merchant. Nevertheless, when locally available products came into high demand, as sometimes happened, the *tratante* might advance to higher levels of commerce and society.

Artisans, of whom the wealthier areas had a full variety, using standard European techniques, were generally humble folk, though not necessarily so markedly so as the *tratantes*. Highly skilled and capitalized silversmiths might be almost bankers, and barber–surgeons were nearly professional men; the operator of a successful shop in almost any trade could be much respected, a man of substance. There were some trades, however, such as that of carter, where practically all the active practitioners were strongly plebeian. The shop system, with the owner as foreman, employing as many journeymen and apprentices as the size of his clientele would allow, made the successful artisan a person with a retinue. Like the *tratantes*, the artisans were petty retailers, and dealt in goods of local manufacture (though often made of imported materials). Artisans, too, sometimes advanced into larger commercial dealings, and they usually tried to gain some personal foothold in the region's estate economy; much more than the *tratantes*, some of whom were near-transients, they tended to be strongly rooted in local Hispanic society.

It would be going too far to describe colonial Spanish America as a society organized entirely on patron–client lines, but certainly the elements of such a mechanism are to be found everywhere. In many cases the substance of a person's activity was unimportant or changing, and the important thing was that one worked for someone else, perhaps supervising yet other people in the employer's name. Many people were most simply defined as the employees, at a certain level, of others; 'servants', they might be called at the time, but that meant not so much personal servants, most of whom were at the very bottom of the Spanish world, usually non-Spanish or at most ethnically mixed, as those who functioned as part of an estate structure. Working in such an organization could surely have had the flavour of personal service, since personalism and family relationships thoroughly penetrated the estate. But while any prominent family would have its estate and partly man it, the estate was a wider structure, the means through which an individual or family reached out into the environment, both social and physical, in the attempt to profit and dominate. Estate organization was the social vehicle of practically all Spanish economic activity. It appears, bent and adjusted to the respective purpose, in readily recognizable forms everywhere from cattle ranching to textile production and silver mining, and it can be seen in enterprises from small to large, truncated or greatly elaborated. Each function within it had a specific, relatively constant social profile.

Let us consider its full form. We have already spoken of the estate owner and the intrinsically high connotations of his position. Owners often took a very active part in their businesses, but whenever possible they were more concerned with overall, long-range matters than with everyday detail, and they defended the estate in the larger arena of other estates, families, and organizations. General consolidation, a high and permanent place in all basic aspects of the province's society, economy, and polity, was the owner's primary aim.

High-level supervision of operations was frequently delegated to younger relatives of the owner, or to collateral non-inheritors, or to truly poor or illegitimate relatives, who might appear fairly far down the structure. But there was also the specific type of the supervisor–manager or high-level steward, a person of consideration but without noble pretensions, strong in the skills of literacy and accounting. Truly extended, conglomerate estates might have an 'administrator' who was socially at the owner's level, but the ordinary major-domo or major-domos, responsible for production and sale in some detail, were distinctly a cut below the owners, although of course they always had their own ambitions.

Even the major-domos had general responsibilities and lived a correspondingly mobile existence. The secondary and tertiary supervisors, at the foreman level, were more tied to a certain process or subdivision and were in steady direct contact with workers. Their role was a humble one within the Spanish world, assigned to relatively marginal people of various kinds, with little formal education; it was as low a function as one would expect to find carried out by a fully Spanish person. Its general aura was comparable to that of the artisan, and indeed, when technicians and artisans were employed within an enterprise, this slot was usually theirs.

The next step down was the permanent worker, usually one with a good degree of skill specific to the enterprise. Wherever the Spanish world was immersed in an Indian one, this was its lowest position, and one rarely filled by people who were ethnically Spanish. It was, however, definitely located inside the Spanish world, whether the person in it was predominantly Hispanic in culture or not; in either case, the post presumed much Hispanicization of certain kinds.

At the bottom of the structure, in many kinds of estates, were more temporary, short-term, shifting workers doing less skilled tasks, especially during seasonal work peaks. In the classic rural estate of colonial Spanish America, such workers made up a majority of the staff. In many or most cases the temporary workers belonged to the Indian rather than the Spanish world, but since they are so important to estate organization, we cannot neglect to mention them here.

Whereas with the set of Spanish occupations we can speak only in the most general way of 'higher' and 'lower', and some are higher in one respect, lower in another, with the estate structure we are dealing with a true hierarchy, where each level gives orders to the one below: even the permanent workers often helped direct the temporary ones. Proceeding from bottom to top, each level is systematically higher on the Spanish social scale, and up to the manager level at least, each implies an increase in relevant skills (except that where the estate product was originally indigenous, as with pulque haciendas, the lowest-level workers may have had a high degree of product-specific skill). Where applicable, each higher level is more urban and ethnically more fully

Spanish. The type of organization described tends to extend beyond what one could by any stretch of the imagination call estates to larger organizations of all kinds, including governmental, even ecclesiastical and, by the late colonial period, military organizations.

Estate and family strongly conditioned the operation of other principles of social organization. One can see at times, especially in situations marked by great wealth and complexity, a tendency towards social corporatism, that is, for the practitioners of certain professions or trades to become a world in themselves, inside which their most important alliances and conflicts took place, with norms dictated internally. But this tendency could never go much further than a superficial, fleeting pressure-group solidarity, because the numerous strong family and estate complexes each contained within itself representatives of practically all the different occupations. Functional categories thus remained largely groupings rather than cohesive groups. Their unity was in the eye of the observer. In that sense they remained of great importance, assuring the exemplar of a given category the well-defined treatment accorded it by convention; hence the insistence on consistent use of epithets and titles of many kinds.

The principle of age progression also operated only within limits. Seniority counted greatly in all organizations, and in most walks of life one advanced over the years, reaching a peak at late maturity and staying there until senility. Yet one could rarely, within a single lifetime, entirely shake off one's original functional category, or advance very far up the estate hierarchy – at most by a single level, normally. On the other hand, while age meant authority and rank, if a person happened to inherit a great family's position early, he would appear while yet a mere youth as large estate owner and municipal council member.

A strong characteristic of the Spanish world was its lavish use of auxiliaries, people who entered into it and carried out many of the lower- and middle-level functions we have already discussed, but who were not entirely of it ethnically. Because this group was not entirely Spanish, and because of its importance to the relationship between the two socio-cultural worlds of Spanish America – Hispanic and Indian – it will be opportune to discuss its role at length in a later section. But one segment of the auxiliary population – the people of African descent – calls for treatment here, because not only was it without genetic relation to the Indian world, it was, even though internally distinct, wholly contained within the Hispanic sector.[4]

In most of Spanish America there was no African world in the sense that there were European and indigenous worlds, except perhaps in parts of the Caribbean. Rather than living in a separate sector, blacks were usually distributed among Hispanic families and their estates. While we can often detect African cultural content in their lives, they do not exhibit a distinct set of social patterns; instead, the latter are entirely those one would expect for marginal Spaniards. The sense in which blacks came closest to making up a subsector was that (with a thousand exceptions) they tended to marry among themselves and organize their own sodalities; but one could say the same of blacksmiths or Basques. They also had a fairly restricted range of roles, since their obvious physical difference from the Spaniards generally kept them out of the upper reaches, even when free and racially mixed, and the high original cost of importing African slaves meant that they would largely be put to remunerative, hence skilled and responsible, tasks. The archetypal positions for blacks were those of artisan and low-level supervisor (trusted personal servants constituting a subset of the latter). Petty commerce, at the *tratante* level, was another of their specialties, especially among women. They frequently descended as far as skilled permanent labour, but always at something intensive and well capitalized, and they occasionally rose as high as major-domo of a whole enterprise.

Slavery and manumission need not detain us here, although the overwhelming majority of blacks originally entering Spanish America did so as slaves, and manumission was a significant enough phenomenon to ensure that wherever there were black slaves there were also some black freedmen. We need make only two points. First, the socio-ethnic profile of the Spanish American slave: he is a person ethnically neither Spanish nor of the local aboriginal group, but originating (either himself or through recent ancestors) at a great geographical distance; he may change masters as frequently as the master's economic advantage dictates, and he functions fully inside Spanish structures. The African slave, and for that matter the minor but persistent phenomenon of the Indian slave, is at the opposite pole from the Indian of the rural corporate communities, who is within his own context, is less mobile, and is more likely to lack Hispanic language and skills.

[4] See also Bowser, *CHLA* II, ch. 10.

Second, the question of freedom or slavery made little difference to the social role of blacks. It is not only that free blacks and mulattos continued to be artisans, labour bosses, and trusted personal servants. The other side of the coin is that blacks sometimes rose as high as general supervisory functions while still slaves. Within Spanish American society overall, 'slave', aside from some obvious disadvantages, was a rather middling role.

Among Indians, the closest functional relatives of the blacks were those who, while not slaves, lived and worked full-time within the Spanish world. They too were quite mobile and removed from their original context, but far less so than the slaves or freedmen. One of the most significant and dynamic elements of the entire Spanish–Indian complex, they will receive attention after we have glanced at the context from which they came.

The Indian world

As a major division of mankind, comparable to the peoples of all Europe or all Africa, the aboriginal inhabitants of the western hemisphere were more a universe than a world. Only by reviewing the Indian sector of Spanish America exhaustively, taking one specific region at a time, would it be possible to achieve a unified and detailed description of its social phenomena. For the present purpose, let us merely sketch briefly three types of situation commonly seen, in each case looking first at the shape of pre-conquest society and then at colonial developments.[5]

In our first type, the fully sedentary society, modes of organization overlapped with those of Iberian society in many basic particulars, a fact not lost on the Spaniards. The sedentary areas boasted a well-defined provincial unit, typically even more autonomous and self-contained than the Spanish equivalent, with a dynastic head empowered to exact labour and tribute. (A central urban settlement might be either present and dominant, or nearly absent.) The nobleman–commoner distinction existed here, being if anything more deeply ingrained and insisted upon than among Spaniards. In many places there were certain commoners who differed from the others in making their living mainly from a particular craft or from commerce, rather than from the prevalent intensive agriculture.

Most sedentary societies in America, from the larger Caribbean

[5] See also Gibson, *CHLA* II, ch. 11.

islands to Peru and Mexico, also knew the social type of the person who, as the direct permanent dependant of the ruler or of some nobleman, was outside the general framework of public rights and duties. The Spanish system had no fully parallel phenomenon, though there were close approaches – one might mention the old arrangement, not brought to the New World, in which some Spaniards were vassals of a lord rather than directly of the king: and many people inside Spanish estate organizations in effect participated in broader society only as dependants of that estate and family. The position of the Indian permanent dependants was rather ambiguous; they may be thought of as usually lower than ordinary commoners, but in individual cases they could be powerful and well-rewarded henchmen of their noble lord. Since they sometimes belonged to a minority ethnic group or one recently conquered, or were refugees from overcrowding at home, the dependants seem to have originated primarily in marginal situations and to have been essentially a variety of commoner. Indeed, in central Mexico there was no universally accepted special term for this type, and they were often called by the word used for other commoners. On Hispaniola the term was *naboría*, and in the central Andes it was *yana*; these words, the latter in the plural-for-singular form *yanacona*, entered the general vocabulary of American Spanish.

But if society in the sedentary or central areas had much that Spaniards could find familiar, the relatively unfamiliar was equally important. A Spanish city–province, especially in the form existing in the Spanish world of the Indies, lacked firm subdivisions, but rather was characterized by a large number of strands and structures starting at the nucleus and spreading out and down to the very edges. The Indian province certainly had equivalent structures, up to a point, but it was organized in a more cellular fashion. A number of subdivisions, territorial as well as social, existed inside the province, each a reasonable microcosm of the whole (two well-known names for such units are *calpulli* in central Mexico and *ayllu* in the Quechua-speaking Andes). With each subunit firmly rooted in a territory and feeling strong micro-solidarity, the Indian world at the local level was very resilient and stable, even at times when pressures caused massive movement of individual people into and out of units, or reduction of overall numbers.

Further peculiarities of social organization stemmed from the basic principle of equal subdivision. Typically the provincial unit was structured by some symmetrical distribution of the subunits, which could then revolve and reciprocate in functions within the larger whole. Division into four parts was a classic device, but many other numerical schemes existed.[6] Quite frequently the province was divided into two moieties, not on a strict territorial basis, but with each moiety represented by subunits in all parts of the area, and each led by its distinct dynastic head. In many cases these divisions corresponded to historically separate ethnic subgroups, of which the local people were still touchily conscious. Another deviance from Spanish provincial organization was that one or more of the subunits might be non-contiguous with the rest; in the central Andes this was normal.

At the level of the individual there were yet more differences. In family organization, despite similarities as strong as the frequent presence of rival multilinear, multilevel family complexes, there were strong differences, such as generally less emphasis on parent-to-child inheritance and more on inheritance from older to younger sibling. Polygamy for prominent males was formal, rather than informal as among the Spaniards. Central Mexico, at least, had *teccalli* or noble houses which were almost complete subsocieties in themselves at times nearly overshadowing the *calpulli*, and organized more elaborately than any equivalent in early modern Spain, much less in the Spanish world of the Indies. The principle of age progression or grading was far more systematized in many Indian societies than among Spaniards, dictating personal functions and the shape of careers rather more rigidly and in greater detail. Nor was the sexual division of functions anywhere identical to the Spanish one, nor were blood relationships conceptualized in quite the same way, with consequent differences in the definition of kinship roles. Any given noble or priestly function would have specific prerogatives which were not quite those of the corresponding Spanish one, and it was the same with occupations; the central Mexicans, for example, were inclined to consider some of the crafts to be noble callings.

When the Spaniards came to occupy the sedentary areas, they took the continued functioning of Indian provincial society as the basis for the overall scheme. Recognizing a separate *república de los indios*, in each subregion they divided the Indian commonwealth into many distinct municipal polities, organized in quasi-Spanish style and together

---

[6] The same type of organization was characteristic of indigenous literary and artistic expression, at least in central Mexico. See Frances Karttunen and James Lockhart, 'La estructura de la poesía náhuatl vista por sus variantes', *Estudios de Cultura Náhuatl*, 14 (1980): 15–64, and John McAndrew, *The open-air churches of sixteenth-century Mexico* (Cambridge, Mass., 1965), 199.

constituting the hinterland of a single Spanish city. The Indians were presumed to be living in isolation from the Spaniards, and in the early period at least, Spanish social patterns of urban nucleation gave much reality to the presumption. The channelling role of the nobility, as well as the tax-paying, labour-supplying role of the commoners, found ample place in the new system. The Indian provincial unit was now the arena not only for its own traditional internal life, but for nearly all Spanish hinterland structures; its borders dictated those of encomienda, parish, Hispanic-style Indian town, and local administrative unit, and its mechanisms made those structures function. At first, then, the main pressure for social change was the introduction of new techniques and concepts, especially newly defined roles for Indians, such as that of alcalde, sacristan, and the like. But whenever the Indians took over one of these new roles, they practised it in the spirit of the most closely related role traditional in their own society. Thus, less in the way of direct internal social reorganization took place more than appeared on the surface. Those social patterns not in direct conflict with the operation of Spanish rural structures tended to persist, with Spaniards often ignoring or misunderstanding them. Full-fledged moiety organization, for example, lasted in places until the end of the colonial period.

The impact on corporate Indian society was only one side of the matter; the other, the absorption of individual Indians into the Spanish world as permanent servants, workers, and dependants of various kinds – a movement facilitated by the previous existence of the *naboría* or *yanacona* role – was in the long run equally significant.

A second major grouping includes what we may call the semi-sedentary societies, often located in forested areas; the Tupi of Paraguay and the Brazilian coast are perhaps the best known and studied, but the general type is widely distributed, around the edges of the fully sedentary peoples and elsewhere. As in the sedentary societies, villages existed and agriculture was practised, but the impressive array of coincidences with Spanish organization was largely lacking. Cultivation shifted sites quickly, and over time the villages did the same. There was no permanent, well-defined provincial unit to serve as arena and vehicle; even individual villages, though they might have war leaders and were sometimes organized in elaborate symmetrical subunits, had no dynastic ruler to demand tribute and give the entity a stable, unified direction. There was no distinction between nobleman and commoner, nor were there other specialized groups. The strongest unit of society was the extended lineage, sometimes living in one large house, usually under the leadership of the eldest male. This unit was so loosely integrated into the village that it might at times individually leave the settlement to join another group or to live in isolation. Age progression, kinship conventions, and sex divisions determined nearly all functions of individuals. A striking aspect of the sexual division of labour was that, whereas in the sedentary societies men bore the brunt of agricultural work, in the semi-sedentary ones women had this role, while men only helped with some tasks such as clearing, and were hunters, fishermen and warriors rather than farmers.

The social model for the Spanish occupation of the sedentary areas, that of a separate Spanish society, mainly urban, set down in a hinterland of separate semi-autonomously functioning Indian socio-political entities, was not viable in a situation such as that depicted above. Not only were mechanisms of tribute and command lacking; there were no large permanent indigenous structures of any description whatever. The deviance from Spanish society was too great for local Indian society to yield recognizable benefits to Spaniards without their own drastic direct intervention in some way.

One strategy was to attempt to remake the situation in the image of Mexico and Peru. The Spaniards in the areas we are speaking of established cities for themselves and tried to forge an Indian hinterland in the country surrounding (though in some regions these cities emptied or shifted location as frequently as Indian settlements had done, since no one place had any great advantage over another). They tried to create strong dynastic rulers for reorganized polities, which were to be encomiendas like the provincial units of the central areas and to deliver goods and labour from the surrounding countryside into the Spanish city. In Paraguay, the Spaniards attempted to propagate the specifically central Andean *mita*, or long-distance rotary draft labour, a device which implied an entirely different social organizational base from that of the local Guaraní.

Usually the local Spanish population did somehow manage to make the introduced structures work, but not at all in the fashion of the central-area originals. For example, in the encomienda variant of these areas, from Paraguay to Venezuela, women did tribute labour, following the aboriginal role definition, despite the fact that the standard encomienda, based on central-area social roles, had only men as tributaries.

Essentially, the two-society model collapsed. On the one hand, Spaniards entered deeply into Indian society; in the earliest stages, some went so far as to become in effect lineage heads, kinship being the only effective way to exercise authority. The Spaniards, including those of the highest rank, underwent racial mixture at a much earlier date than in the central areas, and they absorbed far more in the way of Indian language, food, and techniques. On the other hand, since local Indian organization, even with all the adjustments, did not serve Spanish interests very well, and the total aboriginal population was far smaller than in the central areas, the Indians tended to be drawn directly into the (now somewhat modified) local Spanish society, sometimes to the point that a separate Indian sector entirely ceased to exist. Inside Spanish structures Indians became dependent servants and permanent workers of other kinds, much like the *naboría-yanaconas* of the central areas, and the Spaniards were quick to make the connection; all over the Río de la Plata region and Chile such figures were, in fact, called *yanaconas*, and in this development too the Spaniards were re-creating a facet of the central areas which was without direct precedent in local aboriginal society. At any rate, the overall result of the movement in both directions was a single Spanish–Indian continuum in which one can pick out elements which are dominant or subordinated, intrusive or indigenous, but hardly distinguish two separate societies and economies.

Our third type of indigenous society was that of the non-sedentary peoples, who wandered over their territories in small bands, living by hunting or gathering. Their languages and many elements of their technology and culture were closely related to those of other American peoples, but because of their high mobility, their complete lack of stable settlements, their close adaptation to a specific natural environment (with corresponding ethos), and their warlike nature, they had few points of social contact with sedentary peoples, either indigenous or European. Hardly any social roles were shared between them and the sedentary societies, making the two types of society nearly impenetrable to each other. The result was mutual avoidance or conflict. Some non-sedentary groups remained entirely outside the Spanish sphere for centuries, or stayed independent by constant resistance, undergoing only a certain kind of self-generated social change, such as the evolution of larger confederations and stronger leaders for military purposes.

Not being willing or able to deliver sedentary labour or tribute as a corporate society, and also, owing to the nature of their accustomed roles, not easily able to enter sedentary society as individuals, these non-sedentary peoples could neither constitute a Spanish city's hinterland nor be taken there to work. When there was a Spanish presence among them, long-lasting mutual harassment and conflict would usually reign, while almost all social mechanisms through which the Spaniards tried to rule, absorb, or exploit them took the form of removing them abruptly and entirely from their own context. As to individuals, since the mechanism of the *naboría-yanacona* would not work, the Spaniards regularly resorted to slavery on the non-sedentary fringes, from southern Chile to northern Mexico. This was the only sort of situation in which enslavement of Indians persisted significantly after the conquest period. Though sometimes disguised as a term of servitude in punishment for resistance, it was nevertheless true slavery, with sale and resale provided for; the slave was almost always sent to a far-distant central area, where he had no recourse but to adopt the Spanish language and sedentary life. He was nearly as much an outsider there as the African slave; indeed, at a slightly lower social level and always in a minority, he appeared in the same functions as the African.

The other, more corporate institution for rendering the non-sedentary peoples sedentary was the entirely new settlement, carried out under official (most often ecclesiastical) auspices, in an arbitrarily chosen place with people collected from whatever subgroups they could be enticed to leave. This 'mission' settlement lacked complex internal subdivision, and in many other ways was the exact opposite of the Indian municipality of the central areas, which built on such a solid ethnic, territorial, and social base; yet the mission settlement was modelled on the central areas' Hispanic-style Indian polity and had, externally, the same kinds of Indian officers and governance. A leavening element was sometimes present in parties of sedentary Indians who had migrated or been brought from the older areas. What was being attempted was a total social revolution without a large occupying force, a movement destined from the start to failure or at most very limited success. Individual and mass flight from the new settlements was endemic, and the concentration of people, overall numbers being small, often brought about near-extinction by disease. In most of the cases in which the settlements flourished for long periods of time, the Indians were more semi-sedentary than non-sedentary. In any case, missions did generate certain numbers of Indians prepared to live a sedentary life and perform Hispanic-style tasks.[7]

An area with predominantly non-sedentary Indians was not likely to attract substantial Spanish immigration unless it was on a major trade route or had important mineral deposits. Even so, there was almost always some Spanish civil presence in such areas, and once missions were producing employable people, the Spaniards would, in the normal fashion, acquire some of them as servants and workers. There were severe limits on the magnitude of this type of interaction, however, and over time Spanish society in areas like this remained more simply Spanish in ethnicity, language, and other ways than in any other kind of American context, modified only by such Indian elements as were carried over from the sedentary and semi-sedentary areas. If a massive Spanish influx into such a region occurred, the non-sedentary Indian groups were apt soon to disappear, leaving little trace.

The interaction of the two worlds

The interrelationships between the Spanish and Indian worlds has already crept into the discussion; it has proved as impossible to discuss them separately as it was to keep the actual sectors apart during the colonial period. But the time has come to discuss directly the ways in which the two constituted a whole, operated within the same structures, or otherwise interacted.

The most nearly all-embracing social concept of the Spanish Indies was that of a schema or hierarchy in which each of the three major ethnic groupings – European, African, and Amerindian – had its fixed position. It was of course Hispanocentric; the general principle of its construction was that the more one was like a Spaniard in any way, the higher one ranked. The three categories were conceived of as 'Spanish' (*español*), 'black' (*negro*), and 'Indian' (*indio*). Note that the top rank is 'Spanish' rather than 'white'; the term *blanco* hardly appears in either

---

[7] The best study of the characteristic phenomena of areas of non-sedentary Indians remains Philip Wayne Powell, *Soldiers, Indians and silver: the northward advance of New Spain, 1550–1600* (Berkeley and Los Angeles, 1952).

popular or official usage until the late eighteenth century. The import of that fact is that the schema embraced both culture and phenotype, each to be weighed against the other, if necessary, in assessing a given category or individual. This is why it is not possible to give an entirely unequivocal answer to the question of which ranked higher, Indian or black. Indians looked more like Spaniards, blacks acted more like them. The use of the category 'black' rather than some term such as 'Moor' or 'Guinean' serves as a hint that in this case the physical distinction was felt to be the main one. The category 'Indian' is interesting in that it created a unity where none had existed and ignored vast societal distinctions, making possible a standard evaluation and treatment of all of the infinitely varied people who were so identified by virtue of inhabiting the western hemisphere.

The nature of the Indian category, indeed, raises the question to what extent people of non-Spanish origin accepted the Spanish ethnic schema. The 'Indians' were notably reluctant to accept that label either for themselves or for others so denominated (except for its occasional use when they spoke Spanish). In listings of the colonial period in Nahuatl, the language of central Mexico, aboriginal people are identified by provincial unit or subunit, and sometimes by trade, office or noble/commoner rank – but not as 'Indians'. All other Spanish ethnic designations, however, do appear in Nahuatl sources, used with the same meanings and connotations as among Spaniards. In the case of Nahuatl, by the middle colonial period the word *macehualli*, originally meaning 'commoner', 'vassal', was beginning to be used as a group designation with approximately the same field of reference as 'Indian', though without the same connotations. As to the blacks, they doubtless had their own interior evaluations, and those who were of the first generation from Africa possessed a quite different set of concepts and terminology, but to judge from external signs they appear to have grasped, utilized, and in that sense accepted the prevailing schema.

A crucial facet of the Hispanic American ethnic schema was that it recognized mixture. In actual social contacts, all discernible aspects of variation, both cultural and physical, were taken into consideration in an infinitely flexible way; in the schema, on the other hand, certain mixtures were conceived of as separate ethnic types, held fixed in standard terminology and attitudes. One should not expect too much stability of such concepts; in fact, the mere incorporation of mixture into the schema made of it a transitional device destined to phase itself out after a sufficient number of generations. The two most important intermediate categories were *mestizo*, for a mixture of Spanish and Indian, and *mulato*, for a mixture of Spanish and black (mixtures of Indian and black received only late and partial recognition as a separate category, being rather, in many cases, subsumed under *mulato*, whether from simple lack of interest in the distinction or because this mixture too brought the African nearer to the European physical type). Categories of mixture, though seeming to refer primarily to biological mixing, had important cultural connotations. In Guatemala there grew up the category *ladino*, 'Spanish-speaking', an adjective applied when appropriate to blacks and Indians in all parts of Spanish America, but here coming to be a substantive, meaning essentially the same people as those covered by *mestizo*, so that in this particular case the category for mixture is primarily a cultural rather than a biological one.

All in all, the place of the mixed categories is, as is to be expected, intermediate between the parent ethnicities. It is true that there were dissenting opinions; we can find many writings, by both Spaniards and Indians, which decry the mixed types as the scum of the earth, degenerated from the purer stocks. Very often, however, these complaints stem from highly placed people whose interests were served by the structure of two separate societies and who viewed the mestizos and mulattos as troublemakers; we cannot here go into what behaviour was viewed as trouble-making, but nothing could be clearer than that the mixtures, by their very existence, were the principal, ultimately unanswerable threat to the two-society structure. The derogatory opinion, then, is more a political position than part of a social concept; perhaps as a public stereotype it might have been an ordinary Spaniard or Indian's first word on the topic. But there also existed a more private, possibly less fully conscious evaluation of the mixed categories, which can be readily corroborated from their relative position in Spanish estate hierarchies and the like; people denominated by the terms indicating mixture are regularly higher than those labelled by the parent categories of black and Indian, while being lower than those called Spaniards.

One might then, in view of the ambiguities in the relative position of blacks and Indians, consider the schema as starting with Spaniard at the top and forking downward in two lines, one through mestizo to Indian and the other through mulatto to black. This is perhaps as far as one can go using a vertical schema. One can also, however, look at the schema as indicating, not level *per se*, but Spanishness, the degree to which a person is included in the Spanish world; this we can measure in the same way as before, by the position, relative to that sector, of the people bearing the respective labels. When such a standard is applied, a simple, unambiguous, linear arrangement results: the progression is Spaniard, mestizo, mulatto, black, Indian. Note that the two subordinated ethnic groupings reverse position after mixture. People in both the mixed categories had usually mastered Spanish culture quite thoroughly, so that at that level the closer phenotype could be decisive, whereas with the basic groupings it was not.

From the conquest period onward, Spanish society manipulated the ethnic categories whenever it felt the need, so that a person was not necessarily called by the label that a strict application of the criterion of biological descent would dictate; this allowed for flexibility at the edges of the categories, yet retained – indeed reinforced – their connotations and ranking. In the first great manipulation, a large portion of the earliest generations of mestizos were accepted (with some reservations) as Spaniards, there still being full awareness of blood relationships to Spanish individuals, and the latter still being very much in need of material for family-building. For most of the sixteenth century, the tendency was to call mestizo only those who were abandoned, destitute, or otherwise unfortunate. Throughout the colonial period, mestizos and mulattos who had influential Spanish relatives, or who acquired any sort of wealth or position, might escape the biological category and be considered Spaniards.

More common than the actual use of a new label, however, especially once a person was put in a certain category, was the dropping of the old label by the consensus of local usage. A person in any kind of contact with the Spanish world was ordinarily referred to by an ethnic epithet on every imaginable occasion, so much so that with blacks and Indians the label frequently displaced the surname. The one category for which usage was less consistent was that of Spaniard. Since 'Spaniard' was the point of reference, a name used without ethnic epithet was assumed to belong to a person of that category, who would employ as a status marker, instead of the ethnic designation, the name of an occupation or office, an academic or military title, 'don', or, with women, marital status. When a person in one of the lower ethnic categories achieved wealth, prominence or Hispanicization greater than was consonant with the stereotype of his category, community usage would drop the category and leave his name unmodified, with the result that it then sounded like that of a Spaniard (up to a point; we cannot here enter into the fine distinctions in naming patterns for the different ethnic groupings and even for prominent versus humble Spaniards). Non-labelling did not admit a person fully to any other category, but it did allow him to seek unopposed a marriage, a social circle, and honours corresponding to his cultural characteristics and economic position.

If we compare the ethnic ladder with the functional ladder, we find that each ethnic category combined in several functions. If persons called 'Spaniards' tended to monopolize the higher functions (joined on rare occasions by a Hispanicized Indian high nobleman), they also appear, and in greater number, far down the middle and lower rungs. And if 'Indians' tended to be the usual tillers of the soil, they exercised a hundred other functions in both worlds. (Only local units of Indians in the countryside, outside the Spanish world, represented fully functioning separate groups.) The people in mixed categories are more readily characterized as carrying out mainly middle-level functions, but here too the mestizos are constantly slipping through our fingers into close association or identity with the Spaniards. We are left with the combined mulatto–black grouping as one where ethnicity and function coincide tolerably well, since there was an overwhelming tendency (as we saw before) for those so designated to be involved in crafts or other intense, skilled work, or in low-level supervision, all of which were ranked the same in the Spanish world.

Apart from the more or less rural Indians, perhaps the way in which the ethnic groupings most closely approached group reality was as primary marriage pools. Other things being equal, most members of all ethnic groupings chose marriage partners from within the same grouping, and accordingly one's closest kin, friends, and peers were likely to bear the same ethnic label as oneself. However, an adequate match was not always available within the grouping, and as their wealth and position dictated, people married from within neighbouring groupings, 'higher' or 'lower' as the case might be. Studies of some specific situations in the middle and later colonial period indicate that among urban middle and lower groupings, a third to half of the marriages may normally have been outside the ethnic category.[8] Spaniards, rural Indians, and even large Indian concentrations on the

---

[8] See Edgar F. Love, 'Marriage patterns of persons of African descent in a colonial Mexico City parish', *HAHR*, 51 (1971), 79–91; D. A. Brading and Celia Wu, 'Population growth and crisis: León, 1720–1860', *Journal of Latin American Studies*, 5 (1973), 1–36; and John K. Chance, *Race and class in colonial Oaxaca* (Stanford, 1978), 136–8, 169.

edges of cities tended to marry inside their own groupings with greater frequency, but we cannot forget the prevalence of informal unions and illegitimate children; in these unions the woman was most often chosen from any category lower than that of the man. *Compadrazgo*, or ritual kinship through godparenthood, showed the same ambiguities. While perhaps the most frequent single use of this device was to reinforce existing ties among ethnic equals, it also often followed occupational lines regardless of ethnic origin, and served to create or strengthen patron–client ties between people who were widely separated on the ethnic scale.

Aspects of ethnic subcommunity formation are seen also in the history of *cofradías* or religious brotherhoods, which gave certain groups of people a meeting place, common festivities, group projects, mutual aid facilities, and *esprit de corps*. As with ritual kinship, this organizational element was by the mature colonial period spread through the entire society including the Indian sector, facilitating small sodalities; but ethnicity was only one of these. Here we cannot speak in atemporal terms. Originally *cofradías* were all-embracing. In the first years there would be only one or two such organizations for even the most important Spanish settlement; in the membership books of an early *cofradía* of Lima one can expect to see 'el gobernador don Francisco Pizarro' and 'Juan indio' on the same page. Very soon, new foundations would proliferate in the Spanish cities, specializing along the two lines of occupation (tailors, for example) and ethnic grouping (blacks, for example). Ultimately there came to be so many *cofradías* in the Spanish world that there was sometimes specialization by both criteria, ethnic within occupational, and by sex as well; among people labelled Spaniards there were also sodalities based on degrees of wealth and social prestige. In larger cities there would thus be *cofradías* specialized for each ethnic grouping, going as far as blacks from a specific part of Africa, with the exception, however, of mestizos, for whom specific *cofradías* were very rare, a fact which squares with their lack of corporate existence, noted above. In the Indian world, after a transitional period in which there would be one sodality per provincial unit, with prominent people from the whole area belonging to it, each subunit or hamlet would gradually develop its own, finding in it a good expression of its self-contained social organizational strength. Thus, while *cofradías* did sometimes give separate corporate expression to ethnic groups, at times ethnic categorization gave way to other criteria, and wherever there was insufficient scope for specialization, the organization actually worked in the diametrically opposed direction of uniting the different groupings in a single framework.

With residence patterns, the picture is again much the same. Only rural Indians lived in places where everyone was likely to be of the same ethnic label. From the time of their foundation, Spanish cities were divided into a central section, the *traza*, for Spaniards, and suburbs for Indians (varying from fully organized Indian municipalities to loose agglomerations of huts). In the dwellings and business complexes of the Spanish section there lived and worked people of all ethnic categories, grouped more vertically than horizontally. As the city grew it expanded into the Indian section, so that there were always people from the edges of the Spanish world, including Spaniards, people of mixed race, and blacks, who lived and owned property among the Indians. On the other hand, the Indians on the edge of town made their living mainly by working for or selling things to the people in the centre, so that though they may have had their houses in the Indian section, many spent more time in the *traza* than at home. A major city, long established and relatively flourishing, might develop a somewhat more specialized residential scheme, but as with *cofradías*, the specialization was as much by occupation and general status as by ethnic origin. Where blacks were especially numerous, there could come to be a black and mulatto section of town, as in Lima. However, like the Indian section, it did not contain all the blacks of the city. Many who lived there worked elsewhere, and there were also non-black residents.

In the central areas, by the middle colonial period, there were non-Indian people in most central settlements of Indian provincial units in the hinterland of any given Spanish city. These began to have somewhat the same structure as the city itself, with Spaniards congregating in the centre, even though they might not be officially represented in the local community, while prominent local Indians would hold their own rather than recede quickly to the edges. This left only the hamlets of the Indian provincial units untouched, and often enough even they were subjected to the same processes through their vicinity to a Spanish estate or other enterprise.

A major kind of interrelationship between the Spanish and Indian worlds, and one central to their gradual rapprochement, was contained in the group of people who functioned in the Spanish sector but came originally from the Indian sector. We have been calling them *naboría-yanaconas*, those being two words often applied to them by Spaniards in the first generations, taken from names in Indian languages for permanent dependants outside the ordinary framework of provincial unit and subunit. Often, however, the Indians-among-Spaniards were merely called servants, or referred to by some other occupational name, or given any of a plethora of partial synonyms (such as *gañán* in Mexico of the mature colonial period, for an Indian permanent hired man in a rural setting); or they might be left without any special denomination except Indian.

The existence of an analogous role in sedentary societies surely facilitated the rise of the *naboría-yanaconas*; apparently, when they first became a Hispanic American fixture on the island of Hispaniola, they were actual *naborías* of individual Indian noblemen, appropriated by individual Spaniards. Almost immediately the Spaniards in one way or another took to themselves many Indians who had never been *naborías*, but the familiarity of such a role in their own societies nonetheless made it possible for the new dependants to adapt to their situation readily, in some cases with a good deal of conviction. The aboriginal precedent must also have been important in the origin of the Spanish American practice whereby Indians who were attached to individual Spaniards or to Spanish enterprises were free of corporate Indian obligations, whether to provincial unit, encomendero, or crown, whether labour or tribute. (Despite a rather serious attempt in the mature and later periods to collect a universal monetary head-tax from persons labelled Indian, remission of all such duties was the norm for the group of which we are speaking.) The social type became so generalized and important within the overall scheme, even in areas which had never known the analogue in pre-conquest times, that we must consider it, the precedent notwithstanding, as something growing out of the needs of the Spanish world.

Wherever there was a dense sedentary Indian population, the Spaniards had an almost unlimited need for people with various Hispanic skills to fill intermediate positions in the vast structures they could build on the Indian base. Wherever the country was relatively empty, they needed the same kinds of people to hasten the building of anything at all. The ideal person for the role would be sufficiently non-Hispanic for subordination within a Hispanic structure to be natural for him, but divorced enough from the local scene to give his primary allegiance to the Spanish world, with which he would have to be in steady contact to learn the needed skills. The perfectly qualified type was the African, but since the expense of importing slaves set a sharp limit on African numbers, the Spaniards sought alternatives. Except for some Indians who were moved great distances during the conquests, and the continuing trickle of non-sedentary Indian slaves from the far fringes, the *naboría-yanaconas*, who were taken out of the Indian world but were still within their general culture area, were the primary answer, at least until the racially mixed increased in number. Perhaps it is necessary to add that these people were not slaves. Under certain conditions they were quasi-legally attached to an individual, especially in Peru, but they were not bought and sold like slaves, nor were they as totally out of contact with their own cultural ambience as were Spanish American slaves, both African and Indian. This group was everywhere the first category of Indian to work for Spaniards for a wage.

The *naboría-yanacona* was mobile and often somewhat out of his geographical context. He frequently followed his Spanish master in the latter's moves, and with the tie of his own provincial unit broken, might wander freely and far in search of opportunity in the Spanish world. His special skills could be required elsewhere; as the textile production of Puebla and Mexico City spread to other parts of Mexico, Indian weavers were attracted from the older centres to the new. Part of the Indian population of a large Spanish city would usually have originated in scattered regions all over the country. The archetypal move was the one to a Spanish city from an Indian provincial unit in that city's hinterland.

Physical movement was not, however, an absolute requirement. Much the same effect was achieved when a part of the Spanish world engulfed an Indian unit. A sheep estancia might take over a certain area containing two or three huts, whose inhabitants would before long be stock-watchers for the Spaniards rather than members of the local Indian community. Above all, this process affected the populations, often strongly organized, which lived on the sites where Spaniards founded their cities. In time, being located at the very centre of the Spanish world and surrounded by Indians in Spanish employ, the local inhabitants became much like the rest. In fact, in Peru some used the term *yanacona* to mean all town Indians, and it is true that even those who were not employed by Spaniards, but carried out crafts and operated branches of commerce on their own, generally did so using Spanish techniques or with the Spanish world as market.

This is not to deny that a functioning 'Indian world' could continue to exist inside a Spanish city for a long time, even in Mexico City, and more so still in the Andean highlands. In the Spanish Mexican city of Puebla, an Indian world actually took shape where none had been before; the elements migrating there coalesced, came to constitute a full municipality with subdivisions, and kept Nahuatl records, much affected by the style of pre-conquest annals, into the eighteenth century.[9] Also, the suburbs of a Spanish city, in areas with a surviving Indian hinterland, would at any given time contain some relatively unattached, unadjusted new arrivals from the country.

True to their original *raison d'être, naboría-yanaconas* characteristically did all the same things that blacks did, generally at a somewhat lower level. In the early years and on into the seventeenth century, a common picture was for an intermediate unit to consist of one black, the primary repository of skill and responsibility, and several Indians as his aides; this arrangement was seen in the resident staff of estancias, in artisans' workshops, in textile works, in Spanish urban households. In one respect the Indians predominated, since it was they who largely supplied the first generations of servant-mistresses for Spaniards. The role of permanent hacienda worker in temperate areas was also for a long time principally theirs, only sugar mills being able to afford larger numbers of blacks.

Over time, Indians-among-Spaniards, because of their maximum exposure to the Spanish world, were the fastest-changing group in colonial society. Their gain in Hispanic skills was cumulative across the generations, and they were the primary source of the growing numbers of mestizos, who represented new candidates for the same roles. Gradually they lost to people of the mixed categories their primacy as mistresses, while they and the mestizos gained on or overtook blacks and mulattos in qualifications for intermediary functions generally.

Belonging to Spanish organizations and learning Spanish skills or even language did not necessarily mean abandoning Indian modes. 'Cultures' are neither monolithic nor mutually exclusive, and one person may fully master two given cultures or any combination of discrete subsystems of each. Indian language was actually an advantage to the *naboría-yanacona* as a mediator in his contacts with the temporary

[9] Museo Nacional de Antropología (Mexico City), Colección Gómez de Orozco 184.

workers (in early times and in isolated regions, the language break was likely to be at the foreman level, and even the permanent workers would speak little or no Spanish). In both Mexico and Peru, labour arrangements at the level of permanent and temporary workers owe a good deal of both terminology and content to aboriginal modes of organization, proving that Indian culture was definitely still alive and capable of imposing its ways in this part of the Spanish world. It was able to do so even in the Mexican north, where the Indian employees were permanently out of contact with their central Mexican homeland. Here again, though, we cannot speak of the Spanish world's Indians without mentioning change over time: slowly where the Indian hinterland was strong, quickly where it was weak, the Indians in Spanish cities and other structures were gained for Spanish culture, lost to Indian.

'Race mixture' is not only ultimately inseparable from cultural mixture and fusion, but is also more a function of other processes than a well-defined and autonomous process in itself.[10] The Spaniards' nucleation where there was wealth, their use of numerous permanent auxiliaries from other ethnic groups, the relative distribution of the native American and African populations, the Iberian way of making many fine distinctions rather than drawing one single line between ethnic groupings – things such as these determined how many persons of mixed descent there would be in any given locality and what roles and ethnic labels would be assigned to them.

Iberian family organization, transposed to the New World, favoured the limited recognition and partial absorption among the Spaniards of the ethnically mixed persons who are inevitably produced when groups of different ethnic origin are in close long-term contact. As we have seen above, Spanish men at all the upper social levels had traditionally maintained secondary relationships with women of a somewhat lower position, especially before legitimate marriage, and they had recognized the products of such unions, allotting them a place somewhere between that of servants and that of relatives. In America these women of lower position were at first mainly permanent Indian servant women or black slaves, and their mestizo and mulatto children stepped naturally into the same roles that illegitimate offspring of secondary unions filled in

---

[10] Consider how Magnus Mörner's *Race mixture in the history of Latin America* (Boston, 1967) of necessity covers the entire range of topics central to social history.

Iberia, bearing the family name, acting as stewards for the family, or being put to a trade, or receiving some shred of the estate as their own, but distinctly subordinated, not competing with the legitimate and fully Spanish heirs. In line with the general use of marriage as part of family strategy, the Spanish fathers of mestizo daughters frequently arranged marriages for them with partners who were Spaniards but of lower rank than the father, very often persons actually working for the father. Yet ingrained Spanish familial practices could blur even this vital principle of recognition-plus-subordination as the standard fate of the ethnically mixed. In the Iberian system, when there were no legitimate heirs, the lot of the illegitimate ones improved drastically, and they might attain status nearly identical to that of the paternal family as to both wealth and social position. The same occurred with mixed offspring in the New World, especially during the time when a given local society was in its formative stage and in urgent need of persons who could pass for fully Spanish relatives, to be employed in cementing the local network of interfamily connections.

Here we already face the central fact concerning ethnic mixture in Spanish America, which is also the central historiographical dilemma for those attempting to study it. There was no permanent special role for the ethnically mixed. Rather, on the one hand, they had the same intermediary roles as the Indians-among-Spaniards or the blacks, the groups from whom they were descended and whom they partially replaced. On the other hand, many of them entered the Spanish grouping and became neither more nor less than Spaniards of varying degrees of marginality. As already seen, the mestizos in particular lacked every hallmark of corporate identity.[11] Wherever census records are surveyed, the result is that there are far fewer mestizos than we would expect (mulattos are counted nearer to their full strength because of their more marked phenotype). The mestizos who were openly so labelled were only the lower part of a population segment of unknown size which included a large number of persons labelled Spaniards – that is, if we are to define 'mestizo' biologically and not simply accept the contemporary judgement, for in the last analysis it was society's acceptance of a person as a Spaniard that made him one. No compilation of census figures, however careful, can get to the root of the matter,

---

[11] I subscribe fully to, and would generalize, the following statement by John Chance about Antequera de Oaxaca, which he studied meticulously in terms of census and parish materials: 'Mestizos did not constitute a group in the sociological sense, and their high intermarriage rate indicates that they did not share a common identity' (*Race and class in colonial Oaxaca*, 138).

because ultimately one is counting labels. Only extensive reconstitution of families in given localities, plus enough biographical research to elucidate those families' social and economic profiles, will allow us to see the subtle patterns of integration and discrimination which were doubtless at work within the group of ostensible Spaniards.

Meanwhile, there are certain general trends and sequences which are clear enough in rough outline. In peripheral places where there were very few Spaniards among larger numbers of Indians, Spaniards were at such a premium that any person with recognizably European-influenced features and culture was taken as Spanish, and the mestizo category hardly existed: Paraguay, as usually described to us, was a situation of this type. In an important sense, the treatment of mestizos on the periphery was a special case of the general tendency to minimize distinctions in the absence of wealth or numerous Spaniards; European foreigners and blacks also entered into the general Spanish population more easily and at higher levels on the fringe. In wealthy and well-developed local Hispanic societies, however, mestizos were more sharply subordinated and more likely to be labelled as such, again a part of the general elaboration and complexity of those situations.

There is also a sequence which can be observed in various local Hispanic societies starting from the time of their effective formation and extending into the time of their consolidation and maturity. When the various ethnic groupings come together in the first generations, the mestizos and mulattos are overwhelmingly illegitimate, children of Spanish fathers and non-Spanish mothers. Then as time passes, more of the people in the mixed categories are born of legitimate marriages in which both parents were themselves in mixed categories, or a parent from the *castas* had married a humble Spaniard or an Indian. Many parts of the Indies had passed into the second stage by the seventeenth century, but in some remote mining camps and other peripheral settlements the sequence was only starting then. The implications of all this for general social processes remain to be worked out in detail. By the time of the second stage, one would expect Spanish men to be drawing partners for informal unions more from the mixed groups or from among humble 'Spanish' women in families affected by mixture than from among blacks and Indians. It would also seem that the rate of absorption of persons of mixed ancestry, as a proportion of that group, would decrease, since proportionately fewer of them would have direct kinship ties to Spaniards.

At any rate, we can confidently surmise that by the later eighteenth century in many areas, the number of persons of mixed descent, above all biological mestizos, was growing explosively. Even the number so labelled expanded rapidly. The result was that mestizos were impelled or forced to go beyond the essentially intermediary positions they had, until then, normally occupied. Within the structure of estates and other enterprises, there were now too many of them to be supervisors and skilled operatives, though they did have the capacity to fill such roles; from Chile to Mexico they took to renting the edges of haciendas, sometimes attaining full independence thereby, but often instead falling into financial and labour obligations to the estates. Similarly the excess of mestizos ('excess', that is, from the point of view of the expectation that they would be restricted to certain positions half-way between Spaniards and Indians) led to their invasion and partial domination of the Indian world, a prime example being their wholesale entry into the *resguardos* or Indian reservations of New Granada, where they became a major factor in the demise of that entire system.

There is no denying the central role of ethnic mixture in the social constitution of Spanish America, but it remains something to be explained more than an explanation, a result of Spanish American social organization and of temporal and regional variations more than an independent causal agent. And the ethnically mixed person was only one of various types which in different situations filled marginal Hispanic positions and mediated between the Spanish and Indian sectors.

One final aspect of the relation between the two worlds should be emphasized. At the provincial or regional level the Spanish sector from the start was the heir of the large confederacies and empires which disappeared from the scene with the conquest. We must not ignore the constant movement of people directly out of one Indian provincial unit and into another; nor the long-continued conflicts between neighbouring units over possession of subunits; nor indigenous market networks of regional scope; nor the interdynastic marriages which prevailed for generations and in places for the whole colonial period, nor uniformities in language developments over large indigenous areas, implying continued interaction.[12] On the other hand, even where a

---

[12] For the latter aspect, see Frances Karttunen and James Lockhart, *Nahuatl in the middle years: language contact phenomena in texts of the colonial period*, University of California Publications in Linguistics 85 (Berkeley and Los Angeles, 1976), especially 49–51.

whole province had been in some way united before the coming of the Spanish, it was in most respects a functioning entity in post-conquest times only because of strands coming together in the Spanish city. The bulk of an Indian provincial unit's contacts with the outside normally consisted of confrontation with lower-level representatives of various Spanish hierarchies based in the city. In this one respect, the Indian social-political unit of the mature colonial period, even the rounded, stable entity of the central areas, was incomplete. Broader integration was through the Spanish world, and even high Indian nobles acknowledged it in due time by their tendency to establish themselves in the Spanish city. After about a century of the Spanish presence, it is a rarity to find the most generalized types of historical, political, or literary expression in Indian languages, even less written by persons identified as Indians, though the Indian world long retained the capacity. Following the *naboría-yanaconas*, the local Indian nobles adopted Spanish modes in addition to their own, and matters of more than local concern were increasingly expressed in these modes.

DYNAMICS OF SOCIAL CHANGE

We have already touched on some of the most basic dynamic factors in Spanish American social life: the tension set up by the close juxtaposition of two societies; the mixing of races and the recognition of different ethnic categories; the social continuum and urban–rural channelling inherent in the estate organizations and other hierarchies. Other essential elements which have not been discussed are demographic patterns and the constantly changing European markets for colonial exports. Then there is the steady overall growth of the Spanish world, fed from internal, European, and Indian sources – an aspect of the situation motivating many processes of social evolution and indispensable for understanding them, even though it in turn requires explanation.

Attraction

Let us start by considering some regular kinds of physical–social movement of individuals relative to the nuclei of the Spanish world. Perhaps the most fundamental way in which the two societies were connected was the movement of people out of the Indian world for short periods of work inside Spanish organizations, afterward returning to their homes. The distance involved might be half a mile to a nearby

Spanish holding, or many miles to a city or mining area. Originally, tribute obligation under the encomienda was the formal mechanism on the Spanish side, while on the side of the Indians it took the form of draft rotary labour of a kind well known to them, carried out by the provincial units through their own traditional devices and under their own supervision. But since many of the tasks were in European style, from building the encomendero's city house to planting wheat, there were also Spaniards, blacks, and *naboría-yanaconas* present to supervise and perform skilled tasks. Under later arrangements, governmental or informal, the role of Indian authorities stopped at recruitment, and the temporary workers were left entirely in the hands of the permanent staff of the Hispanic enterprise. Whether the locus was city, hacienda, or mine, there existed between these two groups, the temporary and the permanent, a relationship central to social change in Spanish America. The temporary labourers fed into the body of permanent labourers and hence into the Spanish world; at the mines of Potosí some of the *mita* workers stayed on to become *yanaconas*, and so it was in every area, with every group from household servants to stock watchers. Even where there were no sedentary Indians, and thus no obvious pool of temporary labour existed, a form of the standard mechanism would often appear. Thus the silver mines of the Mexican north were worked almost entirely by full-time labourers divorced from an Indian hinterland; yet the workforce divided into two parts, and the relatively quickly shifting shaft workers were a recruitment pool for the more skilled and permanent refinery workers.

Since markets and profitability were limited, Spanish enterprises kept the permanent staff as small as possible. Where the estates were close to the Indian units and the situation was sufficiently stable, there might be a long interim period when the short-term workers were employed so much of the time that they were nearly permanent; yet they retained their traditional residence and affiliations, coming each time out of their Indian world for a brief stint, and remaining subordinate to a better-remunerated, permanent staff.[13] Nevertheless, since the cities and the Hispanic world grew over time, even when total population was dropping, and consequently the market for Hispanic products expanded, there was an ever-increasing need for European-style skills, so

[13] For a situation of this kind see John M. Tutino, 'Provincial Spaniards, Indian towns, and haciendas: interrelated sectors of agrarian society in the valleys of Mexico and Toluca, 1750–1810', 190–1, in Ida Altman and James Lockhart (eds.), *Provinces of early Mexico: variants of Spanish American regional evolution* (Los Angeles, 1976).

that the proportion of permanent to temporary labourers increased decidedly, if slowly. Only in certain highly technical industries, or in areas without a large sedentary Indian population, had the permanent staff of Spanish enterprises reached a position of numerical majority by the end of the colonial period; but even so a major cultural and social population transformation had taken place (all without the slightest change in the principles of estate organization), and more was to come in future centuries.

The work movements also set up avenues of migration not connected with specific employment, as Indians in times of slack or difficulty moved to the edges of Spanish settlements in the mere hope of work, some of them becoming a permanent part of the urban Indian population. The topic is as yet little understood, but apparently such migration began to flow along regular channels from early on. Studies of the hinterlands of two Spanish cities, Lima and Mérida (Yucatán),[14] show the gradual formation of cityward migration routes for Indians. Starting some distance out from the city, each town (at least nominally Indian) served as a feeder for the next one in, until finally from the nearest town people moved into the city itself. Those arriving at the city might thus have spent years at several progressively more Hispanicized way-stations, and at times migration could proceed by one step per generation, a given town replacing the people it had lost cityward through marriages to newcomers from the next town back down the chain.

If the major effect of the temporary–permanent labour nexus was accretion to the Spanish world, it also had some corresponding impact on the Indian world. Constant movement in and out loosened self-contained local structures, and while the temporary workers took their own language and organizational customs with them to Spanish enterprises, they also brought something of Spanish organizational modes back with them, tying the two worlds into a more close-knit unit. Estates organized much like Spanish ones, recruiting from the same labour pool and serving the same markets, came to exist inside the Indian world, owned usually by noblemen. Indian commoners began to undertake petty regional commerce in the same style as the Spanish *tratantes* and muleteers.

[14] See Karen Spalding, 'Indian rural society in colonial Peru: the example of Huarochirí' (Ph.D. dissertation, University of California at Berkeley, 1967), and Marta Espejo-Ponce Hunt, 'Colonial Yucatán: town and region in the seventeenth century' (Ph.D. dissertation, University of California, Los Angeles, 1974).

Attraction worked at higher levels too. As we have seen, clerical personnel advanced from country to city in the course of their careers; people in various sorts of commerce and local administration did the same, and if a modest estate holder living in a nominally Indian town flourished beyond a certain point, he might relocate his residence in the city along with the really large estate owners. Urban-centred ideals and avenues of promotion were basic to such movements, but there was also a specific mechanism of physical movement in that the business of those mentioned, being connected with various urban-based hierarchies, took them to the city constantly. The process repeated itself on a larger, regional scale, drawing the successful along the various networks from provincial cities to the capital.

Marginalization

Processes of attraction helped the Spanish world to grow and nucleate in a very direct way. Marginalization, the expelling of marginal Hispanic people outward from the centre toward the edges, may at first glance appear to work in the opposite direction. But in fact it helped nucleation by reinforcing the principle of the assembly of upper elements in the city, and it spread lower elements into the Indian hinterland to thicken the Spanish net. One could view the process simply as the reverse side of attraction, disposing of the urban excess and replacing the rural vacuums which the latter movement produced, but the relationship was actually less clear cut. The despatch by organizations and families of their young and their poorly connected to perform subordinate tasks in the country may be viewed primarily as a cyclical mechanism of renewal, since, after all, most of those sent would come back in due course. But not all. Many people of quite impressive education and family, who were nevertheless somewhat removed from the family centre for reasons such as illegitimacy, belonging to a non-inheriting line, or coming late in too large a batch of children, were put out to pasture permanently, to return to the city at retirement or never. Not content with an interminable, spartan exile, they attempted to replicate city conditions more closely than the general structure would normally dictate. In one way or another they diverted their organizations' resources to provide themselves with quite fine housing and furnishings, and especially with urbanized servants. On the other hand, with their superiors' connivance or at their expense, they took independent steps to hasten their own return, the means often being the establishment of separate subsidiary enterprises, based at first entirely in the country and even serving country markets, wherever such had come to exist. The net effect was to create a back-current tending to increase the ethnic Spanishness and general urbanity of the country.

What we can call the educated marginal sector was not, however, the main part of the movement. The general process – assigning lower functions to those of momentarily lower social rank – was most visible in the outward motion from Spanish nuclei of those located toward the bottom of the Spanish world. The lower-ranking Hispanics, voluntarily or involuntarily, took up types of activity which were either inherently rural, involved much rural travel, or were easiest to break into in the country. Low-level supervision, petty commerce or transportation, and lower governmental functions at the level of constable or auctioneer cover most of the possibilities. The activity might be practised independently or as part of an organization; truck farmer was much the same thing as hacienda labour boss, and one might go back and forth between the two functions, or even carry them out simultaneously. Petty commerce was usually on an independent basis. With the independent activity, the decisiveness of the wealth factor is very clear; the humble entrepreneurs simply lacked the money to invest in more profitable enterprises. (Nevertheless, marginality cannot be equated with poverty; certain social attributes produced access to credit, while others did not.) Archetypally, the ambitious marginal person started with nothing, saved something through work in one of the urban–rural hierarchies, and then went independent in a modest way. Insofar as such people acquired any position, whether dependent or not, they tended to be irrevocably committed to country life by their lack of city connections, and thus they became the strongest force toward subnucleation, the creation of secondary Hispanic centres in the hinterland of an already existing Spanish city.

The core of the marginalization process is thus simple enough. What gives it an apparent complexity is that, owing to mechanisms of cultural and ethnic change mentioned previously, the definition of the marginal Hispanic person constantly and systematically shifts and tends especially to broaden as the Hispanic world grows. At all times, newness and ethnic differentiation were important defining characteristics. In 1550, the new or ethnically distinct in the Spanish sector were: Spaniards stepping off the boat as opposed to those who had been in the country longer; European foreigners; and blacks. As a general rule, *naboría-yanaconas* were not yet far enough into the Spanish world even to be marginal in it. A hundred years later, the same types as before are still important on the Hispanic margins, but mestizos and mulattos have joined them, and the new arrival is the immigrant direct from Spain now seen in contrast with the locally-born Spaniard, who hardly existed in 1550. Hispanicized Indians are also beginning to make themselves felt. By the mid eighteenth century the social margin of the Hispanic world still had much the same constitution, though now the types were so thoroughly intermixed as to be in places indistinguishable from each other; in general, the mixed categories and Indians were now more prominent than before, the others less. Again it should be emphasized that a person in a category tending to marginality was by no means destined to be marginalized if there were countervailing factors in his individual case.

Consonant with the nature of the Spanish city–province, the marginalization process worked with complete uniformity and in the same direction over the whole, starting at the centre and extending to the rim. The people on the edges of the city were the same kinds who filled Spanish rural structures, and were there for the same reasons; city growth and the Hispanicization of the countryside were one and the same movement. The process was repeated at the wider level, from a regional capital to its lesser cities and to its unsettled border areas (if any). In the conquest period, those whom later generations have sometimes called 'adventurers', because they left central Mexico and Peru for various deserts and jungles, were merely the new and the foreign, undergoing standard marginalization.

Within any given Hispanic unit, attraction and marginalization played back and forth in a roughly complementary way. Depending on economic and climatic conditions, one of the two might prevail over the other for a while; they also periodically produced overloading at one pole or the other, to be relieved by movement in the opposite direction. But both were always present, fomenting the indefinite growth of the Spanish world while always keeping predominance in the centre.

Immigration

Though it is related to both of the above processes, immigration differs from them in representing an absolute accretion to the local system, rather than a redistribution. Given the Spanish American exaltation of seniority in the Indies, one would expect to find a relatively low social evaluation of the first-generation immigrant from Spain. And so it is in many respects, as already hinted in the previous section. The new Spaniard was likely to be young, a beginner and outsider trying to find his way in. Compilations from the mature colonial period show far more of the Spanish-born in humble and middling positions than in high ones.[15] Indeed, for most of the colonial period, there was little awareness of the new Spaniard as someone radically distinct; he had no separate legal status, few functions peculiar to himself, and not even, until late in the game, a separate subethnic label. Even in the conquest generation, before any significant number of American-born Spaniards existed, the general mechanisms of attracting and absorbing the new immigrant were all fully developed, and his position relative to the resident Spanish population was definitively set. We would miss a vital line of social continuity if we failed to see that new to old in the first years is as Spanish-born to American-born in later generations. Where there was competition for certain positions between local Spaniards and outsiders (long confined to the mendicant orders), the line was normally drawn between natives of the immediate locality and people from all other places – be those the regional capital, other parts of the Indies, or Spain. Immigrants gravitated not to all other first-generation Spaniards, but specifically to people from their home region. It was as if the regionalism of Spain itself had simply been extended to the parts of the Indies, and all the various regions of both hemispheres made up a single system in which there was no sharp dichotomy.

Accordingly, the local assessment of the new Spaniard was not monolithic. Distinctions were made, on the same grounds which operated within the Spanish world of the Indies generally. The new arrival could be of high or low social rank, and trained in a high or low calling; he could belong to a local hierarchy (as with officials and merchants) or not, and he could even have local family connections or not.

Although entirely voluntary or gratuitous immigration certainly occurred frequently enough, family connections – and failing those, home-town connections – appear to have been the norm; in any case, there would be a specific invitation from an individual already in

[15] See, for example, J. Ignacio Rubio Mañé, 'Gente de España en la ciudad de México, año de 1689', *Boletín del Archivo General de la Nación*, 7 (1966), 5–406.

America to one in Spain. This seems to have been the mechanism for practically all female immigration, the newly arriving women stepping into the social circle of their relatives or friends and quickly marrying there, if not actually joining a husband or coming already married in a larger party. But despite the capital importance of women immigrants in helping create a subcommunity in the New World which was fully Spanish ethnically and culturally, the mainstream of immigrants over the centuries consisted of young single men.

Very often new Spaniards came in connection with a classic uncle–nephew sequence which was first fully recognized for the world of eighteenth-century import commerce, then seen to be characteristic of the entire period and of persons in all kinds of occupations. The successful immigrant would need trustworthy help in his business, but having married only when established, and lacking grown sons, he would write home requesting a nephew; over the years the nephew would become a partner, very likely marry his American-born cousin (his uncle's daughter), and on both scores end by heading the business in the next generation while the uncle's sons were aimed a step higher on the local social scale. The cycle could then repeat itself. It need not literally be a nephew; any young unattached man from home would do, since the regional tie was nearly as strong as the family one. Out of strands such as these grew up lasting traditions by which specific Spanish towns would send sons to specific parts of the Indies, the tie being strengthened further by a certain number of immigrants who returned home. Thus the apparently new Spaniard might have family and regional roots in his area of destination which were almost as strong as those of the locally born; while he had to go through a time of subordination and apprenticeship, he could hope eventually to come into a position already made for him.

Another type of immigrant received his entrée through being named from the outside to a position in one of the transimperial networks, whether governmental or ecclesiastical. He too might already have informal connections in the new area, but more probably the family and regional influences had been brought to bear at the other, appointing end. Unlike the immigrant of the 'nephew' type, he was not necessarily, or even usually, a youth. It is clear that high position in an important local hierarchy, plus many advantages of training and birth, immediately gave the new appointees social prestige and access to wealth and influence. On the other hand, they too were in some senses outsiders;

by no means can they simply be viewed as the apex of society. Almost all arrived deeply in debt. Many were at a given place only for a certain term and would later go elsewhere according to the practice of their hierarchy, as all were aware. Others, though likely to spend a lifetime in residence, still lacked the local familial and economic connections which they needed, not only to attain their private goals, but even to be able to carry out their official functions properly. Often arriving inside the familial–regional cocoon of an entourage, they immediately set about making connections outside and, since they had much to offer in exchange, they were usually successful. Yet in a way they were no less supplicants hoping to join established circles than were immigrant merchants, artisans, and agriculturalists at their respective levels.

A minority of the immigrants returned to Spain; most prone to do so were those of highest social rank, greatest liquid wealth, and closest connection with transoceanic networks. The viceroy and the international merchant were archetypal returners, while humble and unconnected new Spaniards were most often quickly marginalized into rural pursuits from which they rarely extricated themselves. As the Indies matured over the centuries, ever fewer returned, even in the official hierarchies. And whereas many of the largest merchants of the Indies were at first representatives of combines in Seville and had careers of a corresponding shape, in time the transatlantic firms fragmented, leaving the great import merchants with headquarters in the Spanish American capitals, and thenceforth they began to settle in the New World much more firmly, although till the end of the colonial period the nephew mechanism and the direct mercantile tie to Europe kept them predominantly first-generation Spaniards. (In some areas less developed than Peru and Mexico, the earlier pattern of firms based in Spain may have persisted well into the eighteenth century.)

Apart from representing a major and long-lasting population movement, Spanish immigration was a standard part of the process of family renewal in America. (This is the role of the newcomer in almost any society, and due to the strength of immigration, it was above all the immigrant from Spain who was the newcomer in the various provinces of the Spanish world of the Indies.) On the lower levels, new agriculturalists, artisans, or modest merchants, after gaining an economic foothold, married their partners' (sometimes mestizo) daughters or other women like them, or gained entry to the far edges of the locally prominent group. At a higher level, those who had position or wealth which was more closely related to the outside world – the officials, larger importers and sometimes miners – often married directly into the top rank of the area's Spanish society. Between the two types of absorption, it would be hard to find a Spanish family in the Indies of the later eighteenth century which had not been penetrated in this fashion more than once. The entry and renewal process, perhaps most acute in centres of great wealth, was nevertheless fully operative also in secondary and remote areas such as Chile, New Granada's Popayán, and Yucatán. A prominent family of any given area in late colonial Spanish America was apt to be a mixture of old and new, the maternal lines going back to the region's first settlers and the paternal ones to newcomers of various vintages. Like the kinds of more local centripetal and centrifugal motion discussed above, and even more directly than they, immigration was a steady force for the maintenance and growth of the Spanish sector. And again, like the other movements, it allowed for change and adjustment while retaining the essential character of the local scene.

These three processes – attraction, marginalization, and immigration – together made the Spanish Indies a world in which a great deal of physical mobility was normal, and in which people at all social levels often lived and worked at locations which by standard expectations would not be their final destination. Whenever a new region or a new economic opportunity opened up, such mobility was greatly accelerated. At these times and others, the attracting process had a great tendency to overfill the need, leaving people momentarily at a loose end at the point of attraction. These phenomena are at the root of the vagabondage so frequently mentioned in officials' reports and older histories. Recent investigators of primary sources generally find the stories vastly exaggerated, as to both the extent of wandering and its nature; apparently officials and economic pressure groups decried as vagabondage all movement of individuals which seemed to work against their own short-term interests. To the Peruvian encomendero, the *tratante* who bought llama wool from his Indians and made his tribute harder to collect was a vagabond.

Unstudied and nearly unstudiable as vagabondage is, some of the limits on it are already clear. Many of the 'vagabonds' were in fact carrying out specific economic activities – especially seasonal labour and peddling – in absolutely normal ways; others, and surely most others, moved along set channels in the reasonable hope of opportunities, rather than wandering aimlessly. Since a large number of transients was normal, there were large capacities for absorbing them. The magnate prided himself on the number of his guests, servants, and followers (all much the same thing, from his point of view). Family and regional connections assured help and hospitality at all levels. A state of emergency was not endemic, but confined to times of famine, gold rushes, and the like, as in other societies.

These limitations once acknowledged, two further aspects of the situation are worthy of note. First, the various social mechanisms already discussed had a long-range tendency to produce larger numbers of people of fully Hispanic culture than the economy was able to employ in functions befitting the ethnic stereotypes of the mature colonial period, so that persons located all along the middle and lower part of the scale were likely to view their positions as too low and be looking impatiently for something better. Second, the constant movement of people and valuables across undeveloped spaces was essential to the overall system, and this fact, plus the extreme social marginality of those employed in the transport business, was propitious for banditry – though again this phenomenon must not be exaggerated; its weight in shaping structures or trends is negligible. (One persistent feature of the countryside was the robbery of humble folk going to and from temporary work or local markets by alienated permanent estate workers, especially runaway slaves or *naboría-yanaconas*.)

Consolidation and dispersal

We have been discussing patterns and trends in the movement of individuals. There are also certain overall configurations of the Spanish world which appear regularly under the proper conditions. Given the organizational framework and processes already described, Spanish society will tend to nucleate, elaborate, and stabilize wherever and to the extent that there is a steady source of negotiable wealth. This process may be called consolidation. Wherever and to the extent that negotiable wealth is lacking, society will be diffuse. Since Hispanic people would not stay where there was no wealth at all, there was bound to be some degree of consolidation in any area occupied by Spaniards for very long. The decisive variables, as just asserted, seem to be economic ones; factors of distance often translate back into economics, in that certain activities are profitable in an isolated area that could not stand the competition of a nearby metropolis, while on the other hand products that could be sold profitably near a large centre lose value with distance. One could also think of the number of people of Hispanic culture as crucial. Certainly there is a general correspondence between larger numbers and higher degrees of consolidation. However, high degrees of consolidation occurred with relatively small numbers in the early post-conquest years.

Perhaps it can be useful to give labels to certain degrees of consolidation. What we can call 'minor consolidation' occurs when an area within the sphere of an already existing Spanish city proves distinct and tenable enough for people at the lower and middle levels to identify with it permanently, although overall dependence on the larger city remains, with everyone above a certain socio-economic level automatically belonging to the city proper, which is still the base of major hierarchies of all kinds. Until this point in time, middle-level estate personnel and small traders view all activity in the area as temporary; they mean to return after some years to the city, with which they maintain ceremonial and social ties. If they fail to return, they try similar activities in altogether different areas. For both reasons, turnover is extremely high. Then at the time of what I am calling minor consolidation, these people begin to develop some local ceremonial organizations, request burial in a favoured local church rather than in the city, marry mainly among themselves, convert one of the area's settlements into their principal seat, and in general replicate many of the social phenomena of the mother city, though always in a secondary way, closely adjusted to the influences and structures emanating from the larger centre. In central Mexico, the important subregions of Toluca and Tlaxcala attained minor consolidation in the later sixteenth century and then remained very stable at that level for the rest of the colonial period, without advancing to another stage.[16]

For a given settlement to become a Spanish city with its own autonomous municipal council was often the symbol of a higher degree of consolidation, but at times ephemeral or minor foundations bore these hallmarks, so we must look further for the symptoms of 'normal consolidation', which occurs when a city becomes the permanent primary social-economic centre for a large surrounding area. The

---

[16] Examples of the stages of consolidation in this section are taken mainly from Mexico; several of the regions mentioned have chapters devoted to them in Altman and Lockhart (eds.), *Provinces of early Mexico.*

prominent families intermarry tightly, develop local aristocratic pride even if in some sense they might bow to a distant great capital, establish some chaplaincies and entails, acquire some noble titles and honorific offices, build palaces, and make sure of staffing local governmental and ecclesiastical organizations from their own circles. An independence appears or is sought in many branches of activity: good-sized mercantile combines take the city as their main base; relative self-sufficiency in the crafts and professions is attained; the city may acquire a bishop, or if not, its main religious establishment may become cathedral-like. The outward-extending hierarchies of all kinds will stiffen and overlap with each other in personnel. In Mexico, Guadalajara and Mérida of Yucatán attained normal consolidation at an early date, while Querétaro, nearer to Mexico City, reached that stage only in the eighteenth century, having persisted until then in the kind of minor consolidation characteristic of Toluca.

'Major consolidation' is the same phenomenon as normal consolidation, but at the macroregional level, occurring under the stimulus of great and lasting assets of interest to the international economy. One predominant city takes all the others into its orbit, and while allowing them internal autonomy, tends to draw off their wealthiest inhabitants or integrate them into capital-based families, businesses, and other hierarchies. Magnificent social and physical establishments arise as the regional headquarters of each hierarchy. Through strands reaching outward in all directions from the capital, the entire area becomes much more tightly interwoven, and familial–personal convergence in the upper levels of the hierarchies reaches a maximum. In the capital itself extreme occupational specialization at all levels occurs. The power of suction exerted by the major centre is such that normal consolidation is impeded in a wide area all around. The two examples of major consolidation in colonial Spanish America are, of course, Mexico City for the Mexican orbit and Lima for a broad South American one, both cities being halfway between great silver-mining areas and major Atlantic ports.[17] Both attained the status well before the end of the sixteenth century. No single economic complex could contain more than

---

[17] For aspects of consolidation in the capitals, see Fred Bronner, 'Peruvian encomenderos in 1630: elite circulation and consolidation', *HAHR*, 57 (1977), 633–58; Paul B. Ganster, 'A social history of the secular clergy of Lima during the middle decades of the eighteenth century' (Ph.D. dissertation, University of California, Los Angeles, 1974); Dominic A. Nwasike, 'Mexico City town government, 1590–1650: a study in aldermanic background and performance' (Ph.D. dissertation, University of Wisconsin, 1972).

one such centre; hence major mining towns such as Zacatecas and Guanajuato went no further than normal consolidation after the extent of their deposits was clear. Other regions would have to wait centuries before corresponding assets brought corresponding developments. Buenos Aires and the Río de la Plata region began in the mid eighteenth century, completing the movement far into the nineteenth; major consolidation for Santiago and Chile was approximately contemporaneous.[18]

Wherever there were sedentary Indians, some form of normal consolidation would occur, and even among the semi-sedentary societies there would be cities as Spanish nuclei (although weak, unelaborated, and unstable); in both these cases it was always possible for Spaniards to gain some economic leverage. But where Indians were absent or non-sedentary and other economic assets were extremely weak, a quite radical dispersal could occur. Such areas might totally lack the two most essential nucleating elements, the city–province and the urban–rural estate. Hispanic migration to these areas would be minimal, mainly motivated and subsidized by more central areas in the general interests of their self-protection and expansion. Ecclesiastical and military establishments would loom large, constituting separate nuclei and containing persons of the highest social rank, who remained outsiders committed to their own hierarchies rather than becoming local inhabitants. Urban settlements for the Hispanic population would contain very humble persons in the main, and far from dominating a region, would hardly exhibit the signs of minor consolidation. There being no appreciable local market, estates were neither profitable nor prestigious; a certain number of persons of the type which elsewhere provided lower supervisors would maintain rural holdings where, with few or no employees, they would live as well as work, related as much to the official establishments as to the Spanish towns. In the Mexican far north, the Upper California of the late colonial period was of this type, while Santa Fe of New Mexico, surrounded originally by the more sedentary Pueblo Indians, approached a minimal normal consolidation.

[18] See Diana Balmori and Robert Oppenheimer, 'Family clusters: generational nucleation in nineteenth-century Argentina and Chile', *Comparative Studies in Society and History*, 21 (1979), 231–61, for discussion of both the specific developments and aspects of the general processes.

Regional variation

Regional variation being basic to the overall picture of Spanish American social phenomena, the preceding sections have touched upon it repeatedly. In discussing the Indian world we have already seen the reason for and even the nature of much of the variation. Indian society in sedentary areas could persist *in situ* and support the early erection upon it of an elaborate Hispanic-style urban-centred society, with crucial roles for the intermediate type of the *naboría-yanacona* and for persons coming temporarily from the Indian world to work within Spanish structures. Semi-sedentary Indian societies could support neither such elaboration nor such separateness; Spanish society had to be much simpler and smaller here, and the two societies had to interpenetrate more, affecting each other's modes of organization in a more direct way, while characteristic forms took shape slowly, over generations. Among non-sedentary Indians there might be no Spanish presence at all; where there was, it was likely to have a rudimentary organization unless there were other factors which attracted migrants. In the latter case, Hispanic society would be more purely Spanish than elsewhere, without any real connection to an Indian hinterland. With blacks and expatriate *naboría-yanaconas* as the lowest-ranking types, and the corporate Indians altogether absent, society overall was more mobile, both physically and organizationally, than in other kinds of areas.

Nearly all the social differences between regions which are not directly attributable to the Indian base are produced by the mechanisms which we have already examined: attraction/marginalization, immigration, and consolidation in response to wealth. The entire Spanish Indies were a single field of social action in which the high went to the centre and the lowly to the edge, in which immigration was attracted to wealthy regions and not to poor ones. Areas of greatest wealth quickly started on the path to maximum elaboration and nucleation, stabilizing at what has been called the stage of major consolidation, while in other areas, corresponding to the degree of relative poverty, society was truncated, less differentiated, and more diffuse or fragmented.

There is no need to remain entirely on the plane of abstraction. For Spanish America until at least the middle of the eighteenth century, there were two overwhelmingly important sources of wealth: silver, and the structures of the sedentary Indian societies. The combination of these gave Peru and Mexico such advantages over all other regions that it is not an exaggeration to call them simply the central areas, with regions such as the Mexican far north, the Río de la Plata area, and Venezuela as the peripheries, while other regions such as Chile and New Granada were intermediary. The peripheries were first penetrated and occupied by marginal people from the centre, often new immigrants, European foreigners, mestizos, and *naboría-yanaconas*. Because of this direct historical connection, the peripheries, as we have seen, frequently took the centre as the model for social organization, although with small success. On the periphery, whole specialized branches of central-area life were weak or absent: the professions, the crafts, long-distance (especially transatlantic) commerce. One observes what appears to be the 'democratization' of the periphery. In Chile of the conquest period, for example, foreigners, mestizos, and even a black or two held encomiendas and other honours which would have been denied them in Peru. But this appearance is merely the result of the fact that the greater central-area pool allowed for the more consistent drawing of distinctions. In peripheral areas too, the usual distinctions would re-emerge at the first sign of economic–demographic growth.

As time went on, the difference between the centre and the periphery tended to grow, as change at the centre was much more rapid. It was there that the increase in Hispanic numbers primarily took place, and immigration was overwhelmingly towards the centre as the locus of wealth. One might call what went on growth rather than change, since it was all in all simply the realization of the potential for consolidation inherent in any Hispanic society, coloured by the absorption of constituents of different ethnicity. But even if basic structures were constant, forms evolved toward complexity and flexible adjustment to more varied interests. In the centre the first dominant estate form, the encomienda, receded quickly under the pressure of new claimants, some from outside and some from within. Encomenderos' labour rights were lost almost immediately, tribute income followed, and before many generations even inheritability was lost. On the periphery, on the other hand, the encomienda (though greatly modified to adapt to local indigenous populations, as seen earlier) tended to remain significant, retaining both labour power and inheritability, until the last years of the colonial period. And so it is in other aspects: in the middle and later periods one expects to find on the periphery many archaic social features not characteristic of the centre since the sixteenth century. Indeed, except for features taken directly from the local indigenous base, much regional differentiation can be reduced to chronology, similar forms and processes appearing everywhere and in the same sequence, but at a different rate.

The centre is perhaps more a line than an area – a trunk-line leading from silver mine to great capital to major port. Elaboration and Hispanicization will concentrate all along this line and be less intense in areas to the side of it, even though they be located in Mexico or Peru. Parts of southern Mexico and the central Peruvian highlands which had dense sedentary Indian populations but were off the silver line still had a sixteenth-century aspect at the end of the colonial period, their Indian world intact and not inundated with Hispanics.

In accordance with the patterns which have been discussed, any given ethnic grouping, occupation or organizational form will have a differential distribution pattern. With the African element, if we take the mainland as our field (acknowledging the partial distinctness of the Caribbean islands), we find that because of the money required for slave importation, blacks concentrate in central areas or elsewhere on the trunk-lines along which they passed. The heaviest concentration of all is to be found in coastal portions of the centre, which lost their Indian population to disease; here blacks may become the majority of the total population, taking over entirely those functions ordinarily shared with mestizos and Hispanicized Indians. (In a present-day Nahuatl dialect of the Mexican Gulf coast, the word for 'mestizo' is *tiltic*, 'black'.)[19] Identical coastal strips not related to the central areas will have fewer or no blacks, as is true of the periphery in general.

One must not, of course, freeze the concepts 'centre' and 'periphery' entirely. New opportunities for wealth tend to produce new central areas. The growing viability of bulk exports and the different transport conditions of the eighteenth century were producing, by the latter part of the colonial period, possibilities of wealth in the former periphery which were comparable to those of Mexico and Peru much earlier. All the phenomena of centrality and consolidation, except those tied to sedentary Indians, promptly appeared in the areas affected, although the processes were far from their culmination at the time of independence, and many traces of peripherality remained.

[19] Antonio García de León, *Pajapan: un dialecto mexicano del Golfo* (Mexico, 1976), 105.

Chronological patterns

In view of the systematically varying pace of developments, one does not expect absolutely uniform chronology in the evolution of Spanish American social forms, whether cities, estates, or mercantile combines. There was, however, one vital process of social change, the biological and cultural intermixing of the various ethnic groups, which went inexorably forward almost as a simple function of the passage of time. Men in all ethnic categories from Spanish down continued to produce children from informal matches with women in lower categories than theirs, while for the middle categories and Indians-among-Spaniards, ethnic intermarriage was so prevalent as to become the norm. (That women were numerous in the Spanish category and that most marriages there were inside the ethnic grouping has no direct bearing on the progress of mixture; perhaps we still need to emphasize that miscegenation did not occur because of any lack of Spanish women. The great multiplication of people in mixed categories comes in the later period, long after the short-lived under-representation of Spanish women in the conquest generation.)

While exceptions must be made for any number of isolated areas, one can say that all over Spanish America, by the time of independence, the mature colonial period's system of ethnic categorization had, through its own normal operation, come into crisis. Being based on the recognition of mixture, the system would naturally respond to further mixture by further recognition, that is, by creating finer distinctions. Beyond a certain point, however, ethnic categories on the basis of fine genealogical distinctions among humble people with short genealogies, or none, would prove unrealistic, and the system would revert to simplicity or be abandoned. With ongoing ethnic and cultural fusion as the constant underlying reality, society's reaction in fact was not to sharpen distinctions to the utmost and then abandon them, but to do both almost simultaneously.

Over time, categories for subtle degrees of mixture and cross-mixture proliferated, the heyday being the later eighteenth century. An ethnic subgroup had to reach a certain numerical significance before receiving a label and a stereotype. The splinter groupings did take on a certain reality in the public mind. Sometimes they are even found embodied in separate *cofradías* or taken into account in sober parish records. Yet the long lists of types, some whimsically named, which were assembled for curious foreigners in the late colonial period never constituted a serious description of society. At the same time as distinctions were multiplying, all the lower groupings inside the Hispanic world were becoming more assimilated to each other than ever, in function as well as in subculture. And, in fact, society increasingly recognized them as one group under the concept *castas*, a term which as most used it included all mixtures plus blacks, or everyone except Spaniards and Indians.

The thrust of some of the new distinctions was to cut off avenues of advancement. From quite early in the mature colonial period artisans began to form guilds and prohibit the ethnically mixed from full membership or master status. By the end of the period there existed a considerable body of ordinances barring the lower ethnic groups from higher functions, for example denying anyone with any African ancestry access to a university. On paper the late period thus looks more restrictive than the earlier. No actual new tightening is involved, however. In the earlier time, there was no occasion to spell out restrictions which enforced themselves by the lower groups' simple and obvious lack of qualifications. The late legislation represents a somewhat alarmed and ineffectual attempt to maintain the literal status quo in the face of challenge by people whom centuries of cultural change had fully qualified to do what local Spaniards did; their increasing entry is the very reason for the restrictions. Further evidence of the growing strength and acculturation of the castas (along with the Hispanicized Indians) was the gradual displacing of blacks, alluded to above in another connection. By the end of the colonial period kinds of intensive skilled work which had once been virtually a black monopoly were being carried out by persons of mixed ancestry or by Indians. The rate of importation of slaves diminished, and except on the coasts and in former peripheral areas which were now expanding, persons of discernible African descent began to recede, through intermixture, as an element of the population.

For Indians within still functioning provincial units, their ethnic category was no more problematic at the end of the colonial period than it had been in previous centuries – perhaps less so, since local city-state self-consciousness had been worn down somewhat by cross-provincial Spanish structures, and increased contact with Hispanics of various types brought greater awareness of a general Indian ethnicity. But in areas formerly held by non-sedentary peoples, such as the Mexican north, there were many people called Indians whose ancestors had migrated from other regions generations before, who spoke principally or exclusively Spanish, and who carried out the same functions as the castas. In and around the large cities of the central areas there were

Indians functioning as equals among the castas and even among humble Spaniards. The Indian-among-Spaniards had outgrown the connotations of the stereotype; insofar as they clung to him and subordinated him beneath the level of other castas, he was with good reason one of the most volatile, discontented elements in late colonial society.

With Spaniards as well as other categories, the late period brought a tendency to make the most of distinctions. In all that has been said here, 'Spaniard' means the *español* of the time, a person presumed to be a Spaniard, regardless of whether he was born to the east or to the west of the Atlantic Ocean. Until the day of independence, there was no radical distinction, no sharp division of roles. 'Creole', such a standard part of the present-day scholarly vocabulary, remained a derogatory nickname, taken originally from the term for Africans born outside of Africa; by the end of the colonial period the locally born sometimes appropriated the term to themselves in public political statements, but even at that time 'creole' had no legal status and was not used by individuals for self-description in the ordinary affairs of life.[20] Over the centuries, American-born Spaniards took over more and more functions, not in the spirit of pushing out rivals, but as part of a natural maturation and growth, the same process which caused ever fewer immigrants to go back to the homeland. By the last third of the eighteenth century 'creoles' manned and dominated all posts and activities, including those in government and church, except for ones which had a foot on either side of the Atlantic. Only the viceroy, the archbishop, and the great import merchants were left as predominantly peninsular-born. Such an extreme state of affairs produced, it is true, a reaction in which the mother country repopulated many high posts with people born in Spain. This perhaps hastened polarization. In the late colonial period a separate census category of 'peninsulars' or 'Europeans' distinct from local 'Spaniards' began to be recognized. At independence some of the peninsulars were expelled. However, the distinction was never so sharp, nor the enmity so great, as might be imagined from the political sloganeering of the independence period.

At the end of the colonial epoch the social structure consisting of two separate worlds articulated by a well-defined ethnic hierarchy was

---

[20] The term is most frequently seen in the phrase *criollo de*, followed by a place-name, meaning in effect 'born in' that place, and in Mexico at least, in the eighteenth century it was standard practice for Indians (among others, mainly in the lower ranges of society) to be so described in legal documents. Thus used, the term referred only to place of origin, without connotation of ethnicity.

generally in ruins, in the sense that its parts had grown into each other irretrievably, as was predictable from the beginning. But all the processes that had brought about this state of things continued in full operation, as well as the basic organizational structures and even the multitude of distinctions, made thenceforth in a more flexible manner. Meanwhile, the more isolated areas of Spanish America continued to manifest features of the classic system far into the future.

9

WOMEN IN SPANISH AMERICAN COLONIAL SOCIETY

The history of women in colonial Spanish America is still in the process of being written, and thus contains many lacunae and raises many questions which have not yet been answered. Much of what we know so far about colonial women reflects the life of the upper echelons of society. However, enough research has been carried out to point to significant similarities and differences in life-styles, attitudes, motivations and aims among colonial women of all walks of life. Women's history in the colonial period cannot be measured by events or developments of a political character – the marks of distinction of a man-orientated world. Women were not personally or institutionally encouraged to assert themselves through actions that were in any way political; yet it cannot be said that their role was totally passive or marginal. They must be approached through the specific institutions of which they formed an intrinsic part, forms of collective behaviour, the manners and mores of classes or groups. Change was slow and not deliberate. Certain traditions were preserved at the personal level by unfailing observance; others by legal means. Thus, continuities are more apparent than changes.

Among the most significant topics to be examined in this chapter are: (1) the first movement of Spanish women to the newly discovered lands, which, although not long-lasting, helped to shape the cultural transfer and to form the biological nucleus of a social elite; (2) marriage, as the basis for the formation of families and kinship; (3) the legal status of women and the ways it helped to define their behaviour and opportunities within society; (4) the social mores surrounding male–female relationships; (5) forms of social deviance and their punishment; (6) education as it applied to different groups; and (7) conventual life, of special significance during the colonial period. All these are topics which in one way or another, and in varying degrees, touched the lives of the majority of colonial women, and thus they help delineate a broad picture of half of the population. Indian and black women have received special consideration under separate headings, although they are represented in the rest of the chapter. In accordance with the slow tempo of change in women's lives and in the institutions through which they expressed themselves, the chronology has been divided into very general periods: early colonial (1500–1620); middle colonial (1620–1760) and late colonial (1760–1810).

SETTLEMENT AND MIGRATION OF PENINSULAR WOMEN

The first large contingent of peninsular women reaching the Caribbean islands came as settlers and wives. Even though legislation issued in 1502 and 1503 encouraged families to emigrate, during the first decades of Spanish conquest and settlement single women were in the highest demand as prospective wives for the large number of single *conquistadores*.

The number of Spanish women emigrating to the New World after the conquest was never very large. Different estimates establish that women constituted between 5 and 17 per cent of the total number of migrants arriving during the first two decades of the sixteenth century. After the mid sixteenth century the number of women arriving increased considerably, reaching 28.5 per cent of all migrants between 1560 and 1579. Most of them came from Andalusia and had Mexico and Peru as their destinations. Since the crown was officially unwilling to tolerate the abandonment of wives in Spain while the settlers engaged in multiple illicit relationships in the Indies, it established that married men travelling to the colonies had to prove their wives' consent, and that married men already overseas had to seek reunion with their wives. There is evidence that many men were obliged to comply with the law but historians suspect that a much larger number did not.[1]

The women who emigrated to the New World had obvious expectations of a fast upward social shift, but not all of them fitted easily into the new environment. One-sixth of the women migrating between 1560 and 1579 were registered as servants. For those who actually intended to serve the likelihood of remaining for long in such occupations was

[1] Peter Boyd-Bowman, 'Patterns of Spanish emigration to the Indies until 1600', *Hispanic American Historical Review* [HAHR], 56/4 (1976), 580–604.

small, owing to the availability of a large body of cheap female Indian labour. It has been suggested that many of those registering as servants were prostitutes in disguise. Although this is conjectural, there were many complaints about the behaviour of some peninsular women, especially in areas such as Peru with a large body of unruly men. A royal administrator in the 1560s requested the crown to stop sending peninsular women to Peru, despite the lack of white women, because their conduct was scandalous and set a bad example to the younger ones.[2]

However, these, and other unusual women whose lives form the core of the anecdotal and exceptional history of women in the early and mid colonial periods, were atypical. Most women came to settle, to be protected, to carve out a better future for themselves. Some succeeded, but others failed to attain those goals in the difficult conditions of settlement in such areas as Chile, Central America or Paraguay. Other women married men whose skills or merits were insufficient for success. Towards the end of the sixteenth century there was a significant number of peninsular women for whom the promise of a better life had not materialized, and who found themselves as destitute widows or penniless daughters of *conquistadores* and first settlers. They wrote numerous letters to royal authorities requesting pensions or financial aid. Some received such compensation, and the less lucky could still hope for a different form of help. Wealthy and pious patrons, encouraged by the church, founded shelter homes (*recogimientos*) to which poor women of Spanish descent could retreat with the dignity expected of representatives of the ruling social elite.

Studies of migration patterns after 1600 are scarce, but indicators such as parochial and municipal censuses, marriage and death records, suggest a sharp decline in the number of peninsular women migrating to Spanish America in the seventeenth century. Once the first generation of American-born creole or mestiza women matured, the market for pensinular women started to narrow. Men continued to travel to Spanish America alone, eventually marrying women born in the colonies. But, during the sixteenth century, migrant women fulfilled an important task. They acted as the transmitters of Hispanic domestic and material culture, and of religious and social values. The usual women migrants were not cultivated or lettered, yet they set up models for all

---

[2] Roberto Levillier (ed.), *Gobernantes del Perú. Cartas y papeles. Siglo XVI* (Madrid, 1921), III, 40.

the detail of daily life such as dress and fashions, cooking, the material needs of the home, entertainment, courtship, and childcare. The replication of many important aspects of the Hispanic way of life was largely made possible by the stream of women who brought it from the motherland.

MARRIAGE AND KINSHIP

Marriage was one of the pillars of Spanish American society, as the foundation of the family, and as the basis for the legitimization of the progeny. Both Spanish and indigenous cultures ascribed strong social value to marriage and in the sixteenth century both cultural streams merged to consolidate matrimony as the essential foundation for a good and ordered society. Marriage ensured settlement and stability, which the Spanish crown sought to establish and maintain in the new colonial environment after the turbulent years of the conquest. For its part, the church regarded marriage as a holy sacrament, essential to good Christian living, and sought to make Indians and Spaniards (and later other ethnic groups) see the need to observe its fulfilment. The eradication of polygamy among the Indians who practised it was part of a policy of encouraging marriage pursued vigorously by crown and church, especially during the first half of the sixteenth century.

The age of marriage among women, the incidence of marriage in different areas, at different periods and among different groups, and the patterns of marriage in a multiracial society, have only recently begun to be investigated by historians and historical demographers. Available studies focus on certain areas and periods, making generalizations risky. However, some general trends can be observed. The incidence of endogamous marriages among Indian females, and those of Spanish descent, during the middle and late colonial periods was higher than that of other groups of women. *Casta* or mixed-race women were more likely to intermarry with men of a more diverse ethnic background, perhaps because their own background stressed much less need for racial homogeneity. The incidence of marriage was lowest among blacks. Certain specific preferences of mestiza women for Hispanic men and of Indian females for *pardo* (free black) males have been observed in several studies of Mexican society. Another noticeable trend was the higher incidence of marriage in rural than in urban areas, probably as a result of greater supervision or social pressure. On the whole, since so few studies of marriage for most of Spanish America are available, any attempt at defining specific trends, or preferences of some groups for others, must remain tentative and applicable only to the areas for which they have been carried out.

Despite the high social and moral value placed on it, marriage was not universally practised. Consensual unions – the source of *mestizaje* to a very large extent – were numerous, but its very nature makes the exact magnitude of this social phenomenon difficult to gauge. Generalized poverty, a less devoted and numerically insufficient clergy, and the acceptance of specific social mores which encouraged extra-marital relations (see below) are all possible explanations for the incidence of such unions. The crown and the church seemed to have lost their taste for the role of marriage broker. Towards the end of the eighteenth century, however, the issue of marriage again became a concern for the crown, but then the circumstances and the policy adopted were very different from those of the early sixteenth century. In 1776 Charles III issued a royal *pragmática* regulating the marriage practices of the upper social classes. The law prescribed that until children reached the age of 25 for males and 23 for females, they had to seek and obtain parental consent in order to marry. The thirteenth-century *Siete Partidas* had already granted that right to parents, and the revival of such legislation at the end of the colonial period has been interpreted as a belated effort to curtail exogamous marriages among the leading socio-economic groups. (Indians were only advised to obey the *pragmática*, and castas were exempted from its observance.) This legislation had the potential for creating havoc between parents and children in cases of disagreement over the choice of partners. There is no conclusive evidence about the effectiveness of the *pragmática*. Archival records show letters from sons and daughters seeking parental or familial approval, and cases of suits either seeking to prevent some marriages or protesting parental opposition. Whether or not this piece of legislation contradicted or reinforced well-established marriage practices remains to be elucidated. What is relevant is the stress on the assumption that the state had regulatory powers over the individual for the purpose of creating or maintaining a desired social structure. The most successful form of marriage control was that exerted over the military. Officers needed the approval of their superiors and royal permission to contract marriage. This represented an effort to preserve the elite character of the corps, since the rules forbade marriage with castas. Because of the cohesiveness of the army, few individuals succeeded in challenging such a form of social control.

Marriage was the basis for establishing social networks through kinship, which consolidated an individual's or a family's social position. This was particularly important to the Hispanic sector of society. Young peninsular immigrants, after several years of service and training, joined the established mercantile, landed, or mining families through marriage. Marriage was also the means of joining the ranks of those in control of the municipal governments and the royal judicial and administrative bureaucracy, and was thus the gateway to political power. Building up kinship ties through marriage was a process that took time and planning. Networks of families started to develop from the late sixteenth century. Wealthy entrepreneurs – whether from trading or mining – and successful bureaucrats formed new elite groups which managed to interrelate to the older families built on encomiendas and land. This process became more complex in the eighteenth century, but basically those power groups remained unchanged and by the end of the colonial period they were related to each other through marriages which followed a general endogamic pattern. Women's role in the building of these family networks was obvious. Several daughters could mean several marriages to bureaucrats, landowners or wealthy merchants, which would strengthen the position of their families as a whole. These marriages maintained the avenues of mobility open to male heirs, whose task was to preserve or improve the status of the family. As producers of heirs women were indispensable in a physical sense, but only instrumental in the larger politico-economic framework of a male-controlled society. What marriage meant for women themselves can only be guessed, since few personal records of their feelings exist. One may only infer that they were conditioned by education and religion to see their roles as natural and appropriate. Women benefited from their own or their family's socio-economic ascent, which guaranteed them access to a comfortable life and a secure future for their progeny. Only by keeping to traditional marriage formulas could they ensure such benefits.

STATUS AND OCCUPATIONS

Spanish American colonial societies shared with Spain the idea of the intrinsic weakness of the female sex, and inherited a legal system which was aimed at protecting women from their own frailty or potential abuse by men. This legal system contained both restrictive and protective concepts emanating from medieval and early Renaissance codes such as the *Ordenamiento de Alcalá* (1386), the *Ordenanzas de Castilla* (1484), the *Siete Partidas* (1265), and the Laws of Toro (1505). This combination of restriction and protection gave women considerable advantages, although the concept of the primacy of male over female remained paramount.

Women were under their father's control before marriage and their husband's after it. This situation, however, did not mean total subjection to men. The wife, as a mother, could and did exercise parental control over the children as their guardian, after the father's death, although sometimes she had to share this authority with a co-guardian. After marriage a woman needed her husband's legal consent to engage in any activity by herself (sales, purchases, partnerships, etc.). Once this permission was granted, the woman had complete freedom to act. In Spanish American colonial usage some of the protective legal restraints emanating from medieval codes were deliberately renounced by the women as a common legal practice to ease some kinds of transactions, and give the woman more freedom to act as a juridical person.

Women could maintain control over property owned prior to marriage (*bienes parafernales*). This meant that they could bequeath it according to their own will. The inheritance system was bilateral, and children could inherit both from the mother and the father. Thus, the legal and economic personality of the woman was not absorbed by the marriage. The property acquired throughout the years of marriage (*bienes gananciales*) was divided equally between wife and children after the father's death. In order to avoid potential fragmentation of a family's estate the parents could either entail part of the total property or allocate a third or a fifth of their part of the estate to a particular child. Other legal protecting devices were the dowry and the *arras*. Although usually interpreted as a bait for marriage, the dowry had a more significant purpose: that of providing extra financial security for the woman at the death of her husband. The husband had to notarize the dowry at the time of receipt, and promise to repay its value from his estate prior to any division it might undergo after his death. Many grooms added the *arras*, a gift of no more than 10 per cent of his present or future assets. This capital also went to the wife along with the dowry, since it was considered part of it. The man administered the dowry during his lifetime, and although cases of mismanagement and squandering are recorded they were the exception, not the rule. The legal obligations were observed. Dowries were most useful to a man when they consisted of cash, property, or even a bureaucratic position. If the dowry consisted mostly of goods which depreciated with time, in the long run it could be a liability for the man, since he was committed to returning its full original value. On the other hand, dowries were always an asset for women.

Dowries were mostly used by the Hispanic sector of society. Indian women rarely brought dowries similar to those of the elites, and castas had none as a rule. Dowries were a clue to the status of the bride and her family, and a form of investment for the benefit of the couple, not just the man. They were more popular in the seventeenth and early eighteenth century than in the late colonial period. As an institution dowry does not seem to have much survived the impact of the wars of independence.

Another institution which, although not designed to benefit women directly, contributed to enhance their status in early colonial society was encomienda. Encomiendas were specifically designed to reward men for services to the crown during the reconquest of Spain, and were grudgingly accepted as a form of compensation for the *conquistadores* in the New World. Encomiendas were tied to marriage and could only be bequeathed to legitimate heirs. The New Laws (1542) forbade women from holding encomiendas, but this was disregarded in practice and in the absence of male children they could be inherited – and sometimes administered – by wives or daughters. The crown also tried to establish that women marry or remarry within a year after inheriting an encomienda, but this was never fully enforced. Thus, some encomiendas were preserved in a family for two or even three generations. In the seventeenth century some women were awarded pensions or income derived from encomiendas. Encomiendas were also used as dowries, and thus enhanced the social position of a certain number of women.

A balance in the negative and positive implications of the legal concept of protection – what it took away and what it furnished – gave colonial women a considerable measure of freedom and authority, which compared favourably with women of other cultures in the same period. The system did not give women the ultimate freedom, that of being able to divorce their husbands; but this was consonant with Western Christian tradition. The Catholic Church allowed physical separation only under extreme circumstances, such as scandalous adultery on the part of the husband, long-term physical abuse, or abandonment of the home. Owing to the length of the procedure, the financial hardship it implied, and the social embarrassment it produced, not too many women were willing to engage in divorce proceedings, and many of those who did simply wished to obtain a reform in their husbands' behaviour. The overwhelming majority of women remained married for life, fulfilling their functions as mothers and wives.

Mothering was such an important occupation because the family's hope for the future rested on successful reproduction and child-rearing. Yet although it absorbed most of women's energies during their prime, little is known about it. A recent study of fertility among the wives of merchants in late eighteenth-century Buenos Aires provides data which, although based on a specific group, suggests that the pattern was similar to other groups elsewhere in Spanish America. Women were married in their late teens, to older and already established men. After they reached majority at 25 years of age, they were regarded as becoming too old for marriage. The average number of children for women who lived to be 45 was 9.7. Large families and relatively high fertility were the rule, even though the merchants' inclination to join Third Orders, which required vows of celibacy, seem to have lessened the number of children after women were 31.[3] This is a situation not applicable to other social groups. Studies in human fertility are rare for colonial Spanish America, but genealogical data, censuses, and other sources of vital statistics suggest that long years of childbearing were the rule for most women, both upper- and lower-class. An apparently high infant mortality rate, however, undermined the long years of fertility among all women. Women of the lower classes had the added burden of work. Slave women and indigenous groups seem to have had much lower fertility rates due to a variety of reasons such as breakdown of the family owing to complsory work, long periods of separation or irregular partnerships, disease, a n [poor diet. No concious attempt at

[3] Susan Socolow, 'Marriage, birth, and inheritance: the merchants of eighteenth-century Buenos Aires', *HAHR*, 60/3 (1980), 387–406.

contraception was made by the majority of the population, although folk medications for abortion were known.

Important as it was, motherhood did not totally absorb the lives of all women, especially women from the lower classes. After the late sixteenth century some women seem to have gauged the parameters of their legal and social territory and successfully engaged themselves in activities to which their sex was no impediment. Women's activities varied according to social and ethnic group, some being considered more appropriate for the urban non-affluent white woman, and others most commonly carried out by Indians, castas or blacks. Both creole women and mestizas have been found engaged in the administration of small shops, either as proprietors or as partners of men who tended the stores for them. The administration of small ranches or haciendas was less common, but from the sixteenth century onwards it was carried out by women of all ethnic groups who lacked male relatives. Money lending on a small scale, sewing, pottery making, weaving, the preparation of beverages such as pulque and chicha or food for sale in the streets or markets, and the sale of a variety of products in the local markets, are all occupations which women, mostly of the lower classes, carried out in colonial society. In some urban centres women administered bakeries and worked in wax and tobacco factories. Self-employment carried a higher status than domestic service or work in a sweatshop. Seamstresses and self-appointed teachers considered themselves superior to market vendors. Single, married, and widowed women alike engaged in these occupations. Marriage did not always provide competent or sufficient economic support. Among the poor, men often earned hardly enough to maintain a family and women were obliged to make extra income as the family grew.

Attempts were made during the reign of Charles III (1759–88) to incorporate women into several industrial schemes in Spain and Spanish America. Textile and tobacco factories controlled by the state opened their doors to women, and in 1779 Charles abolished the guild rules barring women from certain crafts. The wars of independence, however, put a halt to the development of a greater variety of women's occupations. In retrospect, the general picture of women's work at the end of the colonial period was only slightly better than at the beginning. Nevertheless, women engaged in a surprising number of occupations, considering the prejudices and inhibitions surrounding their sex. Only a few of those occupations, however, enhanced their status, while others, important and necessary as they were for the economy and the comfort of the upper classes, elicited neither recognition nor social mobility for the women who were obliged to engage in them.

SOCIAL MORES

Male–female relationships in colonial Spanish America were as complex as all other social relations. Ideal models of behaviour were harsh and very demanding on women. Spanish didactic and religious literature assumed that women were fragile beings and thus needed special protection in the form of seclusion, special parental and familial overseeing, and the refuge of religion. The assumption that women were weaker than men transcended the physical, involving their character as well. Women were assumed to have less resistance to temptation, to be less rational, more emotional and more violent than men. At the same time, however, they were burdened with more moral responsibilities than men. Of these, the preservation of their own and their family's honour was paramount. This consisted in the protection of their purity and virginity until marriage and the maintenance of absolute fidelity to their husbands after it. A woman's reputation depended heavily on the social assessment of her chastity, virtue, and fidelity, whatever her station in life. Men were not exempt from moral responsibilities, however. Among the most important for them was to protect the honour of the female in their households, since their own honour was at stake if hers failed. Thus, men and women were interlocked in the all-important task of preserving each other's honour. However, in this relationship one element, the female, was considered weak, and the other, the male, had special prerogatives that allowed him to break the rules outside his own home. Double moral standards made it easier for men to indulge in practices which were totally condemned for women. It was possible for a man to keep a concubine and preserve his social standing, while adultery was the worst personal and social offence a woman could commit. In Spanish America, the advantages men enjoyed were enhanced for the ruling class by the availability of countless Indian, casta or slave women, who were seen as less respectable or easier targets for male sexual aggressiveness or exploitation than the more closely guarded women of the upper classes.

Strained relations between the sexes were generated by the combination of social mores deeply concerned with the concept of honour and a religion which regarded worldly love as a lesser kind of emotion, emanating from irrational needs and causing more sadness than joy in the long run. Little communication between men and women took place after childhood. Rules of behaviour kept them apart, physically and intellectually, giving them a limited understanding of each other and resulting in a predominance of stereotyped notions about the opposite sex. Concepts of sexuality evolving from this complex situation assumed that male lust was natural and irrepressible. Women, on the other hand, were continually tested for their uprightness and virtue on the grounds that their sexuality, if released, would be dangerous to themselves and their families.

In this constant challenge many men and women 'failed' to live up to the high standards expected of them. Ecclesiastical records such as matrimonial investigations and inquisitorial records show that pre-marital sexual relations were frequent.[4] Women of the social elite figure less commonly in these records than those of the lower classes, but their absence is perhaps more a sign of greater discretion than of perfect behaviour. Women of the lower classes were under less social pressure than elite women. For them, consensual unions were not necessarily a bad thing. While many of them worked at an unskilled level, few were economically independent. A relationship with a man could mean extra economic, social, and emotional protection, and a measure of social mobility for their offspring if the father belonged to the upper classes.

Women who could not afford, or did not wish, to face the social embarrassment of concubinage or illegitimate offspring, or who wished to obtain some form of economic redress, could try to force the man to marry them, or at least to endow them with a sum of money. Long

---

[4] Matrimonial records found in the archives of bishoprics and archbishoprics involve cases of pre- or extramarital sexual relations among persons related by some degree of consanguinity, or who felt that they were so related. These records also contain cases of adultery, divorce and rape. Such cases could also be aired at the *audiencias*, as criminal cases. The Inquisition dealt with bigamy or polygamy, relationships between the clergy and lay women, and cases of sorcery for obtaining sexual favours. Little material from matrimonial records is in print. The historical surveys of the several offices of the Inquisition in Spanish America by José Toribio Medina furnish a partial view of the many cases of bigamy and clerical incontinence. See, for example, his *Historia del Tribunal del Santo Oficio de la Inquisición en México*, expanded by Julio Jiménez Rueda (Mexico, 1952); *Historia del Tribunal del Santo Oficio de la Inquisición en Chile* (Santiago de Chile, 1952); *Historia del Tribunal de la Inquisición en Lima* (2 vols., Santiago de Chile, 1956). For my own research I have used material from the Archivo del Antiguo Obispado de Michoacán (Mexico) available in microfilm at the Utah Genealogical Society, and from the Bienes Nacionales section in the Archivo General de la Nación, Mexico City. I have also consulted, to a lesser extent, material in the Biblioteca Nacional, Lima, and the Archivo Histórico de la Nación, Santiago de Chile.

and involved lawsuits related to these claims reveal that a factor contributing to the high incidence of consensual unions or premarital relations was the promise of marriage or *palabra de casamiento*. This mutual promise carried legal and religious weight even if it was not witnessed by anybody. A man who promised to marry a woman and subsequently deflowered her was accountable for her honour before civil and ecclesiastical authorities. Women thus engaged in illicit relationships in hope of an eventual marriage. Many accepted living with a man and bearing his children for many years without any complaint unless he decided to marry someone else. Jealousy and abandonment moved women to bring men to court on grounds of broken promise of marriage and loss of virginity. Most men denied having promised marriage or taken the woman's virginity – both very personal questions which not even the presence of many witnesses on both sides could establish firmly. If the man was willing to marry the woman and erase the 'sin' in which both had engaged, the church most often blessed the union, except in cases of close consanguinity or patent moral turpitude. The frequency of cases involving the loss of virginity under the promise of marriage, and the high illegitimacy rate in some urban centres, suggest a tension between accepted models of feminine propriety and a reality which belied such models. Such tension, in turn, points to strong underlying currents of repressed sexuality in male–female relations.

The problem of illegitimacy was acute in certain areas. Baptism records, especially in the cities, show scores of children registered as of 'unknown parents' (either mother, father, or both). In Lima, one of the few cities studied in detail for this phenomenon, the rate of illegitimate children among whites and mestizos between 1562 and 1689 was never below 40 per cent.[5] From 1610 onwards children start being registered as of unknown mother, and in 1619 10 per cent of all illegitimate children were so listed. It has been suggested that two types of women could use that device: a white woman seeking to protect her identity, or a slave woman seeking to ensure freedom to her offspring. The rate of illegitimacy among Indians, blacks and mulattos was extremely high in the same period: 50 per cent from 1594 to 1604, 74 per cent from 1618 to 1629, and 69 per cent from 1640 to 1649. Such figures suggest the magnitude of the problem in some areas. The several

[5] Claude Mazet, 'Population et société à Lima aux xvie et xviie siècles: la paroisse de San Sebastián (1562–1689)', *Cahiers des Amériques Latines*, 13/14 (1976), 53–100.

angles of this social problem – economic, ethnic, moral and sexual – remain in need of further investigation.

SOCIAL DEVIANCE

Female involvement in crimes, either as perpetrators or as victims, is another aspect of women's history which is barely known. Studies of criminality in colonial Mexico and Argentina suggest that women were more frequently the victims than the perpetrators of crime, even though an exceptional case of sadistic behaviour, that of Catalina de los Ríos, has received undue attention.[6] As victims both urban and rural women were the objects of homicide, rape, and physical violence. Women of the lower classes, who lived unsheltered lives, were most commonly reported as injured parties, with men of similar backgrounds as the offenders. What took place among members of the upper classes is much less known because it was not often reported. Personal violence of men towards women was common throughout the colonial period. The most common form of personal abuse was wife-beating, accepted as a man's prerogative, and not punishable unless it became injurious to the woman's health. Many women seeking divorce alleged physical abuse as one of the main causes for separation. They were obliged to present witnesses and prove continuous mistreatment. Light mistreatment was seldom considered cause for divorce. However, constant beating could bring the man a light gaol sentence.

Sexual abuse of women in the form of rape was most frequently reported among Indians and castas. During the early stages of the conquest rape of Indian women was frequent, but it was rarely punished. With the gradual enforcement of moral canons, it became abhorrent and punishable by forced work or physical exile. Rape was not as severely punished as sodomy, which brought death by burning to a few of its practitioners in the seventeenth century.[7] Rape could be due to personal lust, or animosity against the woman or her family,

[6] Susan Socolow, 'Women and crime: Buenos Aires, 1757–1797', *Journal of Latin American Studies*, 12/1 (1980), 39–54; William B. Taylor, *Drinking, homicide and rebellion in colonial Mexican villages* (Stanford, 1979), 44, 84–5, 88, 104–7. I have also used material from the archives of the Real Audiencia of Nueva Galicia, available at the Biblioteca Pública del Estado de Jalisco, Guadalajara. On Catalina de los Ríos, see Benjamín Vicuña Mackenna, *Los Lisperguer y la Quintrala* (Valparaíso, 1908).

[7] Antonio de Robles, *Diario de sucesos notables* (3 vols., Mexico, 1946), I, 137; for similar punishment in Spain, see José Deleito y Piñuela, *La mala vida en la España de Felipe IV* (Madrid, 1948), 63–6.

where the perpetrator wished to stain the family's honour through the woman. Rape could also be part of courtship, especially as a means to overcome parental opposition to a marriage – in which case it can hardly classify as a crime. Since premarital sexual relations were common among the lower classes, violence had to be involved in order to prove rape. Seduction also classified as a crime, although of a lesser degree than forced rape. To prove seduction, the woman's unwillingness had to be established, since many women routinely accused their lovers of seducing them to force a marriage. Among the most common cases of seduction were those of friars and priests accused of soliciting and of actual sexual intercourse with women under their spiritual care. These cases were dealt with by the Inquisition, and the customary punishment for a proven culprit was exile and perpetual prohibition from confessing women. Rarely was a member of the church defrocked for seduction.[8]

Some ambiguous forms of criminal activity, such as quackery and sorcery, warranted investigation by the Inquisition, which, since its establishment in Spanish America in the 1570s, dealt with the women accused of such activities. Most commonly, although not exclusively, these women were either Indians or castas. Their behaviour could be interpreted as a show of defiance against civil and religious authorities, a sign of incomplete assimilation of Christianity, and a bid for power and authority in a society in which they were marginalized. There were white women involved in these enquiries, many of them Spanish immigrants in the late sixteenth century. Obviously, superstition had not been uprooted from the peninsula itself. Europe was experiencing a wave of witchcraft and witch-hunting in the sixteenth and seventeenth centuries, but the most immediate roots of the practice of magical arts in Spanish America were indigenous. Most of the cases of sorcery investigated dealt with the concoction of spells or potions to attract the opposite sex. The punishment for proven engagement in such practices could be flogging, participation as a penitent in an auto-da-fé, or exile.[9] Sorcerers were never burnt in Spanish America. However, Judaizers were. The Inquisition considered religious dissent a crime which was harshly repressed, especially in the period from 1580 through 1650. In fact, hardly any other crime committed by women brought such

---

[8] See works by José Toribio Medina cited in n. 4, above.
[9] Noemí Quezada, *Amor y magia amorosa entre los aztecas* (Mexico, 1975); Solange Alberro, 'Noirs et mulâtres dans la société coloniale mexicaine', *Cahiers des Amériques Latines*, 17 (1978), 57–88.

intensive scrutiny and such dire results for them. Although the number of women burnt on the charge of being Judaizers is not large, the fact that women were punished as criminals under such charges warrants their inclusion in the larger spectrum of criminal activities touching women's lives.

The study of criminal activities among women in colonial Spanish America is still in its infancy. Murder seems to have been infrequently committed by women. The most common crimes among them were petty theft, illegal sale of liquor, sorcery, blasphemy, bigamy, and sexual incontinence. Whether sexual incontinence simply meant prostitution by another name, and whether it was widespread among women, remains obscure. The records on prostitution are uneven and it is doubtful whether organized prostitution flourished in Spanish America as it did in Spain or Europe, despite the licensing of a whorehouse in Hispaniola in 1526. Only in a few large towns could open prostitution prosper; anywhere else the church proved strong enough to stop it from being anything but a profession carried out by largely unorganized individuals.

The correction of crime was undertaken in *casas de recogidas*, gaols or *obrajes* (textile workshops). In all of them women worked for a number of years to atone for their alleged crimes. Conditions in municipal gaols and *obrajes* were notoriously bad, but there are insufficient data on how women were treated there to allow us to venture any conclusions. *Casas de recogidas* started to develop in the late sixteenth century as an answer for two social problems: virtuous but unsheltered women, and women who had 'fallen' and needed correction to prevent them from further sinning or contaminating other women. Some houses of shelter were strictly for the first category of women; others housed both, physically separating the 'good' from the 'bad'. *Nazarenas* or *Magdalenas* were the names given to institutions acting as gaols for women condemned to prison. During the mid-colonial years all of these types of institution were founded by lay individuals or ecclesiastical authorities, and were orientated towards the regeneration of women. There were also privately operated houses of shelter, where ecclesiastical authorities or private parties sent some women either for punishment or for protection. Women sent by their families received no benefit of trial or judgement; they were simply interned as their families willed. This situation suggests the extent to which women of the lower classes could be manipulated by the very mechanisms designed to protect them. In the late colonial period, the state started to take over some *recogimientos*, using them to accommodate inmates it did not want to send to the (usually inadequate) municipal facilities. This signalled a change in the punishment of female crime. Increasingly this became the responsibility of the state: *recogimientos* began to be regulated and taken over by municipalities, and their inmates came to be regarded as delinquents, not as souls in need of repentance.[10] This secularization in the process of the administration of justice was strengthened by the movement for independence, when conspiracy and insurgency were added to the list of crimes for which women could be answerable.

EDUCATION

Sixteenth-century Spanish literature on the education of women was heavily biased towards training them to be wives and mothers, and clearly defined two different spheres of activity for men and women. The activities of the woman were centred in the home, those of men outside it. Within the home, the duties of the man as husband–father were not so well delineated as those of the woman as wife–mother. The works of Fr Hernando de Talavera, Fr Martín de Córdoba, Fr Luis de León, Bishop Antonio de Guevara, Fr Luis de Granada, and Luis Vives, sought to instruct women in how best to perform their social and family functions. On the whole, their advice to women was to live a chaste life before marriage while learning the skills they would later need as wives, such as spinning, embroidery, cooking and so forth. Parties, dances, too many friendships, excessive spending on clothes for outings, and frivolous behaviour with young men were to be avoided at all times. Honest recreation at home, such as reading good literature or religious tracts, music and prayer, were allowed. Talavera, de León, and de Guevara specifically advised women on how to be good wives, stressing careful home administration, marital fidelity, and good care of the children.[11]

The cultural implications of sixteenth-century prescriptive literature

[10] Samuel Kagan, 'Penal servitude in New Spain: the colonial textile industry' (Ph.D. dissertation, City University of New York, 1977), 73–84; Josefina Muriel, *Los recogimientos de mujeres: respuesta a una problemática novohispana* (Mexico, 1974), *passim*.

[11] Fr Hernando de Talavera, 'De como se ha de ordenar el tiempo para que sea bien expendido. Avisación a la...muy noble señora Doña María de Pacheco, Condesa de Benavente', *Escritores místicos españoles* I (Madrid, 1911), 93–103; Fr Martín de Córdoba, *Jardín de nobles doncellas* (Madrid, 1953); Fr Luis de León, *La perfecta casada* (Mexico, 1970); Fr Antonio de Guevara, *Libro primero de las epístolas familiares* (Madrid, 1950), 262–5, 286, 291, 363–400; *Reloj de príncipes y Libro de Marco Aurelio* (Madrid, 1936); Julia Fitzmaurice-Kelly, 'Women in sixteenth century Spain', *Revue Hispanique*, 70 (1927), 557–632.

were deep. 'The opinion in which woman was held by theologians and moralists became a determinant in her status', it has been well said.[12] Even though these norms were addressed to the elite, they affected all social classes insofar as they became the ideal against which all women were tested. Not everybody complied with the norms, but they were transmitted through formal and informal education or through the confessional for several centuries. In the late eighteenth century doña Josefa Amar y Borbón wrote a book on the education of women which did not depart much from the basic canons established by the earlier male writers. Her most important contribution was to grant women more credit for their intellectual abilities than they had so far been given. She pleaded for a broader education which would allow women to use those abilities and thus add more meaning to their lives.[13] Her book, however, had a section on childcare, since she still saw woman's main role as that of a loving mother and wife. All this educational literature dictated a limited territory of action for women, and a pattern of behaviour which would support and nurture, not challenge, the heads of the Spanish and Spanish American patriarchal societies.

Female education in colonial Spanish America was based on the norms described above, but it may be better understood if a distinction is made between formal and informal education – the former being the methodical training of women in schools by a teacher, and the latter the general preparation for adult life imparted at home. All women received some kind of informal education during their childhood and puberty which was consonant with their prospective roles as wives and mothers, and also with their station in life, since class determined significant differences in expectations and behaviour.

The education of indigenous women prior to European colonization consisted of practical training in the occupations of their sex, which in their case included weaving, pottery making, and animal husbandry.[14] Such learning by experience remained unchanged throughout the colonial period. In fact, so important were these tasks for the Indian community that after the conquest of Mexico, when missionaries attempted to enclose Indian women in convent-like schools, their

[12] *Ibid.*, 557.
[13] Josefa Amar y Borbón, *Discurso sobre la educación física y moral de las mujeres* (Madrid, 1790).
[14] See the description and illustration of the duties of women from childhood onward, in Felipe Guamán Poma de Ayala, *Nueva corónica y buen gobierno* (Paris, 1936); Fr Bernardino de Sahagún, *Historia general de las cosas de Nueva España* (Mexico, 1975), 345, 400, 559–63.

parents objected, since such enclosure would deprive their daughters of the learning they needed to enhance their economic value in the eyes of their future husbands.[15] The majority of colonial women, whether slave or free, white, casta or mestiza, aspired to little else beyond that kind of informal education and some rudimentary understanding of the principles of Catholicism, with stress on the preservation of honour and feminine patterns of behaviour. However, a small number received training in elementary reading and writing, Latin for those who professed as nuns, and music and vocal training. The girls who received that education, whether at home or in convents and schools, belonged to the socio-economic elite. This is truer for the early and middle colonial periods than for the late years of the eighteenth century, when public and private schools started to spread, opening their doors to girls of all social classes. In fact, the acceptance, towards the end of the colonial period, of the idea that it was desirable to educate all women was one of the most significant changes in social attitudes about women.

The bases of formal education, narrow as they were in their character and the number of women they affected, were laid out in the sixteenth century, as part of the general transfer of culture from Spain to the colonies. In Spain education for upper-class women was not frowned upon as long as it remained a discreet virtue not to be flaunted in the face of society, and it trained women for their biological destiny. Education at home or within the walls of a cloister was acceptable. Nuns in nunneries, *beatas* in *recogimientos*, or *amigas* in their own homes, imparted education in Spanish America. A minority of women throughout the colonies wrote well, read books and even engaged in creative writing. Their literary efforts have not received adequate publicity because they were written for small audiences and did not rival the more skilled and polished works of men. Although a few lay women acquired reputations as writers, the majority of the women writers of the colonial period were nuns.[16] Convents offered the double incentive of instruction and a measure of freedom for self-expression. In Peru and Chile several nuns wrote mystical poetry and prose, but the best examples of religious writing are found in New Granada and in New Spain. In the Franciscan convent of Santa Clara in Tunja, Sor Francisca

---

[15] José María Kobayashi, *La educación como conquista* (Mexico, 1974), 289–90.
[16] The best source for a panoramic view of women's education and literary achievements in colonial Spanish America is Guillermo Fúrlong Cárdiff, S.J., *La cultura femenina en la época colonial* (Buenos Aires, 1951).

Josefa de la Concepción del Castillo (1671–1742) wrote several works which still stand as models of religious literature for their sensitivity and delicacy. In New Spain, María Ana de San Ignacio, a nun from Puebla, had her works printed by her bishop in 1758.[17] However, all other female writers are overshadowed by Sor Juana Inés de la Cruz (1648–95), who during her lifetime was known as 'the Tenth Muse', and who remains the most exceptional woman intellectual produced in all of colonial Spanish America. Her numerous secular and religious writings are kaleidoscopic in character, ranging from plays and love poems written before her profession to religious songs and meditations for nuns.[18] Sor Juana was an early proponent of education for women, which she defended passionately in a letter to a bishop of Puebla. Yet, like many other women in the seventeenth century, she had very narrow options for action and had to follow many of the conventions of her times. She retreated to a convent at the age of 21. In her own words, she took orders for lack of interest in matrimony and the world, but she certainly did not give up communicating with the world, and during the most productive years of her life she received constant attention and even adulation from a devoted public. The life of the convent offered her the right environment to reach an intellectual peak few other women could dream of.

Most colonial women, however, were illiterate. But illiteracy was no obstacle to the performance of activities which took them beyond the confines of the home. Legal transactions requiring notarization were signed for women by available witnesses. The administration of small shops, bakeries or property was carried out without a formal education. Thus, since literacy was not essential for anybody, female education remained in a state of benign neglect, as a curiosity to be admired but not necessarily emulated. After the third decade of the eighteenth century, attitudes began to change. Women's intellectual capacity came to be accepted and the promotion of formal education for them followed as a natural consequence. The first innovation in educational practices in the eighteenth century came wrapped in a religious cloak. The convents of the Order of Mary (*Enseñanzas*), institutions founded in

[17] Sor María Ana Agueda de San Ignacio, *Devociones* (Puebla, 1758); Sor Francisca Josefa de la Concepción del Castillo y Guevara, *Afectos espirituales* (2 vols, Bogotá, 1962); *Mi vida* (Bogotá, 1942); *Obras completas* (2 vols., Bogotá, 1962).

[18] Sor Juana Inés de la Cruz, *Obras completas* (Mexico, 1969); Anita Arroyo, *Razón y pasión de Sor Juana* (Mexico, 1971).

seventeenth-century France, began a consistent effort to educate upper-class colonial women. Convents of La Enseñanza were founded in Mexico City (1753), Bogotá (1770), and Mendoza (1760). Nuns expressly trained as teachers began to improve upon the haphazard educational efforts of other nuns in previous centuries. Lay schools patronized by confraternities or lay persons were the next step. In Mexico City the Basque Confraternity of Nuestra Señora de Aranzazú maintained a school founded in 1767. The Hermandad de la Caridad, in Buenos Aires, also maintained a school. Although they fostered women's education, their goals remained conservative, as they still educated women mostly for their roles in the home. One positive innovation, however, was the acceptance of poor girls at either morning or afternoon classes.

The final stage in the process of development of feminine education was the appearance in the late eighteenth century of public schools supported by municipal sources or by patriotic societies, encouraged by the educational concepts emanating from Spain and the European Enlightenment. In Spain men such as the Conde de Campomanes were proposing that women be trained in arts and crafts to enable them to earn a living in the absence of a husband, and to contribute to the general effort of industrializing Spain and the empire.[19] Notwithstanding these lofty ideals, the range of arts and crafts taught in most of Spanish America was limited to the classic feminine occupations. Also, since schools were founded exclusively in the cities, the benefits of education were limited to city-dwellers. However, the popularization of the idea of education for women was a real accomplishment which was gaining impetus when the movement for independence started. The disruptions caused by the wars set back this trend, and feminine education only started picking up its threads again in the 1830s.

CONVENT LIFE

Whereas the majority of women in Spanish America married – or lived in consensual unions – and raised children, a small number chose to take the veil as nuns, dedicating their lives to the service of God. This choice was not open to all women, though, making convent life a way of life for the chosen few. The first nuns sent to the New World were destined

---

[19] Pedro Rodríguez, Conde de Campomanes, *Discurso sobre la educación popular de los artesanos y su fomento* (Madrid, 1775), 301–15, 357–63.

to serve as teachers and models of the virtuous life to indigenous women. The latter, as pupils and neophytes, were consistently denied the right to take orders on grounds of spiritual unpreparedness. With few exceptions, this policy was in effect throughout the sixteenth and seventeenth centuries until a nunnery for noble Indians was founded in Mexico City in 1724. Thus, Spanish American nuns were consistently white creoles, with a few peninsulars who came as founders of several orders.

From the foundation of the convent of Nuestra Señora de la Concepción in Mexico in the decade 1540–50, nunneries spread relatively fast throughout Spanish America. Every major city wanted to boast a nunnery as a sign of both urban rank and religiosity. Deeply involved in the Counter-Reformation in Europe, and stirred by figures such as Teresa of Ávila, Spain could not adopt a policy other than the support of convents where women could fulfil a religious vocation and find a place of refuge in times of adversity. Late sixteenth-century and early seventeenth-century petitions for the royal approval of convents often stress the latter need. Many female descendants of *conquistadores* or marginalized settlers needed temporary or permanent retreat for economic reasons, and nunneries provided both. Other para-religious institutions such as *beaterios* and *recogimientos* served the same purposes without requiring the commitment of full religious vows.

Urban communities requesting royal permission for the foundation of nunneries, and the crown itself, consistently regarded nunneries as centres of moral and religious edification for the population at large, and the women who professed as selfless and pious beings dedicated to the highest form of life. Nuns elicited the reverence and praise of their contemporaries. Despite its limited accessibility and the small number of women involved, convent life left deep social, economic, and cultural marks on colonial Spanish America. The seventeenth century witnessed a rapid expansion of conventual institutions as the Conceptionist, Franciscan, Augustinian, Dominican, and Carmelite orders spread out from Spain to America. Feminine convents were strictly urban-based, contemplative institutions. Hospital work was not carried out by nuns until the nineteenth century. As mentioned before, no teaching order was established until 1753. This physical growth was sustained by the patronage of both the rich and the poor, lay and religious, who consistently donated cash or properties to help the institutions survive bad times and eventually expand. Helping to found or sustain a convent was considered a most commendable form of piety and charity.[20]

Within the walls of the cloisters women obtained not only protection and religious fulfilment, but a reasonable education for the period. While few historians argue about these points, the motivation for religious professions and the quality of vocation of many nuns has been the object of some debate. Often nunneries are mentioned as places where parents dumped their unmarriageable daughters, as if that had been the convents' sole purpose or as if all the postulants had been personal failures or economic burdens to their families. Examples of dissolute behaviour among nuns, frivolity within the cloisters, and forced professions may be found in colonial Spanish America;[21] but at the same time Spanish America produced two female saints – St Rose of Lima (1586–1617) and St Mariana de Jesús (1618–45) – and many *beatas*. As for getting rid of a daughter cheaply, it must be remembered that most convents required postulants to bring dowries comparable with those that most parents provided for their daughters' marriages. Nuns also bought cells within the cloisters and brought slaves or servants into them. All these expenses could only be afforded by families of some economic means. Nuns with a firm vocation but little money usually managed to amass their dowries by collecting donations from pious patrons. The barefoot orders, observing austere poverty, admitted nuns without dowry or with small endowments. These were the institutions which only the most resolute would enter. Underestimating or misjudging the depth and extent of religious influence over individual women, or women in general, may be as naïve as assuming that all nuns were utterly perfect. Religious life was an alternative choice for those women who did not wish to marry, who had strong religious vocations, or who appreciated the relative independence that the cloisters gave them.

Convents were not merely centres of spirituality, however. They were socially and economically tied to the colonial social elite from which many of the nuns came and which supported them morally and

[20] Asunción Lavrin, 'Religious life of Mexican women in the 18th century' (Ph.D. dissertation, Harvard University, 1963); Sister Ann Miriam Gallagher, R.S.M., 'The family background of the nuns of two *monasterios* in colonial Mexico: Santa Clara, Querétaro, and Corpus Christi, Mexico City (1724–1822)' (Ph.D. dissertation, Catholic University of America, 1972); Josefina Muriel, *Conventos de monjas en Nueva España* (Mexico, 1946).

[21] Antonio de Egaña, S.J., *Historia de la iglesia en la América española. Desde el descubrimiento hasta comienzos del S. XIX* (Madrid, 1966), 299–451; Peter Marzahl, *Town in the Empire. Government, politics and society in seventeenth-century Popayán* (Austin, 1978), 143.

financially. As recipients of capital from these patrons in the form of cash, mortgages or properties, many nunneries wielded significant economic power. During the late sixteenth century and part of the seventeenth many of the recently founded convents were far from being affluent and depended heavily on personal and community charity, having spent much of their original capital on the construction of their buildings or in necessary repairs and expansion. However, by the eighteenth century some of these institutions had consolidated their economic position and had reached economic stability, and even considerable wealth in some instances. They became important property owners and sources of credit. The most powerful institutions, such as the convents of La Concepción or La Encarnación in Mexico City, could lend large sums of money to chosen individuals and controlled a significant amount of urban property. The impact of the nunneries on the local economy and the credit market of a number of cities is only incompletely known for some areas of Spanish America and needs further attention from researchers.[22]

INDIAN WOMEN

The status and historical role of Indian women in colonial society was a result of the gradual accommodation between the values and customs of their societies prior to the discovery of America and those brought by the Spaniards from the peninsula. Because of the great variety of indigenous cultures in the vast territories of Spanish America, the following brief discussion of Indian women's social roles will focus only on Mesoamerica and the Andes.

Both Aztec and Inca societies were hierarchical, and in both women were subordinate to men in the state and in the family. Their general social status depended on the class to which they belonged, which was determined by the male head of the household. Wives of the nobility or highly-placed warriors shared their husbands' status and were well above the humble female peasant. Polygamy was widely practised among the upper classes, and this opened an avenue of social mobility for certain women, as, for example, the beautiful young girls who were chosen to be the concubines of nobles and warriors among the Incas. In both societies a special status was conferred on priestesses, such as

[22] Asunción Lavrin, 'Women in convents: their economic and social role in colonial Mexico', in Berenice Carroll (ed.), *Liberating women's history. Theoretical and critical essays* (Urbana, 1976), 250–77; 'El convento de Santa Clara de Querétaro. La administración de sus propiedades en el siglo XVII', *Historia Mexicana*, 25/1 (1975), 76–117.

the Inca Virgins of the Sun, who dedicated themselves for life to the cult of the sun. In Aztec societies girls could serve in two different kinds of temple (*telpochcalli* and *calmecac*). Unlike the Virgins of the Sun, these girls married when they came of age. Service in the temple was less a matter of status among the Aztecs, and more concerned with a desire on the part of parents to protect their daughters. In neither case was this service comparable to that of male priests; women were mostly aides to the males.

Although the Inca and Aztec societies were patriarchal, women had a definite and recognized role in society. It has been proposed that among the cultures preceding the Aztecs women had greater political power than at the time of the conquest. One author suggests that the glorification of warfare among the Aztecs changed the character of their society, replacing a more egalitarian society, in which women had a higher status, with one based on the philosophy of male domination.[23] Whether or not women could achieve political power as 'lords' in Inca society is still a subject of debate, but their system of inheritance at the time of the conquest was based on the marriage of the Inca to his sister in order to preserve the purity of the lineage. Among northern Andean indigenous cultures and in pre-Inca societies as well, lordship passed to the son of the sister of the chief if the latter had no heirs. It has been asserted that in those societies matriarchal lines of descent were common.[24]

Sex determined occupational roles for women in most indigenous cultures. Apart from the usual household occupations, women engaged in agricultural tasks, in the preparation of beverages and medicines, and in market activities in those cultures where they were well developed. Women also helped to raise tribute with their work, especially weaving, whether tribute exactions came from their own rulers, as with the Incas, or from conquering groups. The economic value of female work was acknowledged as essential for the household and the community, and this raised the status of the women who engaged in it, as essential elements in the production cycle.

The education of indigenous women for their social and family roles

---

[23] June Nash, 'The Aztecs and the ideology of male dominance', *Signs. Journal of Women in Culture and Society*, 4/2 (1978), 349–62.

[24] Judith Prieto de Zegarra, *Mujer, poder y desarrollo en el Perú* (2 vols., Lima, 1980), II, 65–164, 209–50; Juan A. Villamarín, 'Kinship and inheritance among the Sabana de Bogotá Chibcha at the time of the Spanish conquest', *Ethnologie*, 14/2 (1975), 173–9; Pedro Cieza de León, *La crónica del Perú* (Madrid, 1962), 85, 135, 140, 161, 173, 175.

was administered informally at home or through community tasks. Among the Aztecs, mothers and fathers had carefully worded advice for their daughters emphasizing fidelity, submission, endurance, and abstinence. Premarital virginity was highly recommended, although exceptions were made to allow for the existence of women of pleasure for the solace of warriors. However, moral codes were strict, and in both Aztec and Inca societies adultery was punishable with death for both the guilty man and the woman. The normative moral canons were rigid and demanding, and resembled those of Roman Catholicism. In many ways, this similarity of attitudes about women's social roles and mores facilitated the merging of the two societies during the colonial period.

Indian women were a crucial factor in the conquest of America. Liaisons with Indian women provided the first generation of *conquistadores* with allies, interpreters, personal care and sexual satisfaction. Throughout the conquest period, and even for several decades after it, Spanish and Indian societies experienced a period of relaxation of sexual and social mores. Behaviour previously unacceptable for both became daily routine, and it mostly affected women. Spaniards kept several Indian mistresses and sired numerous children. Concubinage became an entrenched social practice which was to prove very difficult to eradicate from colonial society.

The institution of the family among indigenous societies suffered severe dislocations during much of the early colonial period, as a result of the forced separation of husbands and wives and the intrusion of a new male element competing for Indian females. Throughout and after the conquest Indian women travelled long distances with marching troops, and were abducted from their homes or enslaved in certain areas if their communities resisted the conquest. The institutions of repartimiento, mita and encomienda aggravated the situation of women; despite the regulations of the Spanish crown against the abuse of women, they in fact rendered service under all three in different areas. The imposition of tribute on the household indirectly placed a heavier burden of work on Indian women. More directly, women paid tribute from the time they married, and widows paid half the taxes. Encomenderos demanded work from women as cooks, maids or wetnurses. With the gradual decline of the encomienda economic necessity forced many women to continue to serve for wages or for food and shelter.[25]

[25] Elinor Burkett, 'Indian women and white society: the case of sixteenth-century Peru', in Asunción Lavrin (ed.), *Latin American women: historical perspectives* (Westport, Conn., 1978),

For some time during and after the conquest women were pawned by their families in an effort to win the friendship and protection of the Spaniards. The choicest women were thus either given to or taken by the Spaniards, and even though some of these liaisons were temporary they saved the women involved from the harsher treatment received by humbler females. Many of these unions had a political purpose for the conquerors, who sought access to power in the Indian communities and to obtain their eventual allegiance. For the indigenous women involved they had deeper significance. Indian women's continuous interaction with Spanish society, especially in urban areas, meant that many of them eventually understood and adopted Spanish institutions and culture. Women in Spanish households became socio-cultural mediators between both societies. The degree to which rural women were removed from this process, and the role they played in helping indigenous communities succeed in maintaining their own identity, remains to be explored. As Spaniards recognized social hierarchies, many women of high status were able to retain rights and privileges for themselves and their families and thus for the ethnic group as a whole. This process was also fostered by the access of Indian women to the legal rights held by all women under Spanish legislation. Indians quickly adopted the Spanish bilateral inheritance concept as well as those of *bienes gananciales* (property acquired during marriage) and tutorship. In areas where originally lordship was inherited through the mother's side, pre-Columbian and Hispanic traditions converged to strengthen the position of the indigenous elite woman. However, all Indian women had similar legal rights, and archival sources indicate the concern for ownership and inheritance rights even among the humblest women.[26]

The degree to which Indian women intermarried with Spaniards or other ethnic groups throughout the colonial period remains to be assessed. The few studies available indicate that after the conquest and the early colonial period, Indian women interacted much less with men

---

101–28; William L. Sherman, *Forced native labor in sixteenth-century Central America* (Lincoln, 1979), 304–21; Julián B. Ruiz Rivera, *Encomienda y mita en Nueva Granada* (Seville, 1975), 244, 302, 336–7. Ruiz discusses the variations in the enforcement of tribute on women. See also M. Cristina García Bernal, 'Los servicios personales de Yucatán durante el siglo XVI', *Revista de la Universidad de Yucatán*, 19/110 (1977), 73–87.

[26] Delfina E. López Sarrelangue, *La nobleza indígena de Pátzcuaro en la época virreinal* (Mexico, 1965); J. O. Anderson, Frances Berdan and James Lockhart (eds.), *Beyond the codices. The Nahua view of colonial Mexico* (Berkeley, 1976); Pedro Carrasco P. and Jesús Monjarás-Ruiz, *Colección de documentos sobre Coyoacán* (2 vols., Mexico, 1978), documents in vol. II. See also Prieto de Zegarra, *Mujer, poder y desarrollo*.

of the ruling elite. The availability of other women led the Spaniards into other types of alliance. Also, the crown's initial policy of encouraging marriages with indigenous women was abandoned by the mid sixteenth century, and replaced increasingly by an official policy of separation and protection of the Indians. Intermarriage was never barred; it apparently lost personal appeal and social prestige.

Throughout the colonial period the most powerful cultural influence on Indian women was exerted by the Catholic Church, which significantly changed several aspects of women's lives and reinforced others. The eventual eradication of polygamy among the upper classes had important consequences for the Indian hierarchy, since it helped deplete their numbers, and closed an avenue of personal mobility for many non-elite women. The adoption of Christianity, on the other hand, reinforced many of the attitudes about women's functions in society. It also gave all Indian women a new source of authority and influence to look up to, the parish priest or the regular clergy in missionary centres. Their general message about women's social and family roles was basically Hispanic, but it dovetailed with concepts traditionally observed in the indigenous cultures. Thus, socio-economic divisions of male and female spheres were reiterated and reinforced.

How and to what degree life changed for Indian women during the colonial period as a result of the superimposition of Spanish over indigenous values is not easy to determine, but for those in the cities it may be partially illustrated by a brief description of the Indian women of Lima as they appear in a census carried out in 1613.[27] The majority of the population, male and female, was young, between the ages of twenty and 29 (50 per cent of women and 65 per cent of men). Whereas in the agricultural areas of Peru women predominated because the men had been drawn to the cities or the mines, in Lima there were twice as many Indian men as women. Lima's Indian female population was predominantly migrant, having come from all over Peru and as far away as Chile and New Granada. It was an uprooted population with only the vaguest notion of its past. Many of the women could not tell much about their families or their towns of origin. Among the younger ones most did not know who their parents were, having been brought into Lima to serve in Spanish homes. The majority (61.5 per cent) of the women were married, mostly to Indian men. Only 32 women out of a total of 630 were married to non-Indians, and of these, only three to

[27] Miguel de Contreras, *Padrón de los indios de Lima en 1613* (Lima, 1968).

Spaniards. In contrast to the majority of men, who had a variety of occupations and trades, most women knew no craft or art, and were mostly servants and housewives. The typical servant was young and single or, less frequently, a widow. A few coming from Chile were slaves. Among the housewives less than twenty worked outside the home, either as maids or as vendors in the market, selling corn, chicha and 'other things'. The other occupation mentioned in the census was that of seamstress. Only a handful of Spanish homes (mostly those of *oidores* and bureaucrats) had several Indian servants and among these only three had a work contract.

No doubt this picture must have varied in time and according to region. Even for Peru it only describes the capital. Life for women in other areas must have been different. For example, it is probable that more women engaged in market activities in small towns than in Lima. It has also been established that in the second half of the eighteenth century, in urban centres such as Caracas and Mexico City, women outnumbered men. It is probable that, as time passed, Indian and casta women migrated into the cities in search of work opportunities. However, it is important to stress that, as in early seventeenth-century Lima, Indian and casta females continued to be engaged in low-status occupations. The problem of illegitimate children persisted as another characteristic feature for urban women of low status.[28] The complexities of urban and rural life of the female Indian population – as well as of mestizas – have only recently begun to be appreciated.

BLACK WOMEN

Another group of women which is still hard to document and delineate is that formed by black and mulatto women, whether free or slaves, about whom some of the most basic questions have not been adequately answered as yet. For example, the ratio of male to female slaves arriving in Spanish America throughout the colonial period is still a topic of debate among historical demographers. Most of them suggest that female slaves arrived in numbers roughly one-third of that of the male slaves. Whether or not this imbalance continued to be a feature of the colonial black slave population has not been established. Some authors

[28] C. Mazet, 'Population et société à Lima aux xvie et xviie siècles'; John V. Lombardi, *People and places in colonial Venezuela* (Bloomington, 1976), 75–80; Silvia M. Arrom, 'Marriage patterns in Mexico City, 1811', *Journal of Family History*, 3/4 (1978), 376–91.

report an imbalance in favour of the male, as for example in late sixteenth-century Peru, while in other areas the reverse was true, especially in the seventeenth century. A greater mortality rate among male slaves possibly explains the fact that during the middle and late years of the colonial period in areas such as the Chocó and some Jesuit plantations in Peru, the slave population was roughly equal with regard to male and female, or exhibited a larger number of women.[29]

Since until recently the study of slavery focused largely on the trade, the historical personality of the female slave remained submerged in that of the group as a whole. The use of notarial records, various ecclesiastical sources, legal suits, and censuses permits recent historiography considerably more insight into the lives of black women, but the picture is still far from being satisfactory and must remain more impressionistic than exact.

The overriding theme emerging from the sources is the struggle to reconcile the legal human rights of the slaves with their actual situation in society. Slaves were guaranteed several basic rights by medieval Spanish law, especially the *Siete Partidas*, such as the freedom to marry and not to be separated from their families (a matter of great concern for women), and the right to seek their freedom through purchase, testamentary award or appeal to the legal system. They had also acquired the right to own property and the right to demand to be sold if their masters did not treat them humanely. These rights often went unheeded, and while the majority of slaves did not know how to take recourse to legal means to obtain redress, some of them did, appealing to civil and ecclesiastical authorities, and, in the process, leaving important witness to their existence, goals in life, problems, and personal feelings.[30] Most of the complaints of slave women were about mistreatment by their masters, opposition to their free choice in

---

[29] Nicholas P. Cushner, S.J., 'Slave mortality and reproduction in Jesuit haciendas in colonial Peru', *HAHR*, 55/2 (1975), 175–99; William F. Sharp, *Slavery on the Spanish Frontier. The Colombian Chocó, 1680–1810* (Norman, Okla., 1976), 154, 203; Fernando Montesinos, *Anales del Perú* (2 vols., Madrid, 1906), II, 197–8. A census of nine cities in Peru in 1614 showed 9,111 black or mulatto women (51.2 per cent) against 8,661 men.

[30] Frederick P. Bowser, *The African slave in colonial Peru, 1524–1650* (Stanford, 1974), 256–71; Colin Palmer, *Slaves of the White God: blacks in Mexico, 1570–1650* (Cambridge, Mass., 1976), 84–118; Eugenio Petit Muñoz, Edmundo M. Narancio and José M. Traibel Nelcis, *La condición jurídica, social, económica y política, de los negros durante el coloniaje en la Banda Oriental* (Montevideo, 1947), 228–36. The archives of the Real Audiencia of Nueva Galicia and Santiago de Chile contain a number of legal suits started by slaves. Like the free poor, slaves had access to the services of an advocate appointed by the *audiencia* when they started a suit. There is no study of the incidence of cases won or lost by slaves.

marriage, separation from their families, and obstacles to their manumission. Sexual abuse, which was frequent, because many male owners
regarded their female slaves as pieces of property they could use, did
not elicit as many complaints as might have been expected. Illegitimate
children among the female slave population were the rule, not the
exception. In most bills of sale throughout Spanish America, the
affiliation of children was made through the mothers, not the fathers.
Of course, the children of slave mothers remained slaves. Legitimate
marriages did take place, and were encouraged by the church and by
faithful and law-abiding masters. Studies of marriage records in several
colonial Mexican parishes indicate that female slaves married mostly
black slave males, although marriages with free men were surprisingly
frequent at times.[31] Family life was always precarious: separation from
the children could take place at any age and was expected as part of
life. The rural slave might perhaps have a more stable life if she belonged
to a large religious-owned plantation. Regulations for the management
of Jesuit haciendas stipulate with considerable detail the care to be taken
with the slaves. Since cohabitation was regarded as sinful, the Jesuits
established strict separation of the sexes. Young women were supervised
by older women until they were married, so as to avoid opportunities
for promiscuity. Marriage was encouraged and special bonuses were
issued at the time of marriage and the birth of children. Midwives were
provided, and infant care was available during the day when the slaves
were engaged in their appointed occupations. This minimum number
of humane rules seems to have been followed, as administrative
hacienda books corroborate their enforcement.[32]

The occupations of female slaves were varied, ranging from household work and street vending to heavier agricultural and mining work.
In sugar plantations they weeded the fields, cut cane, cooked, and
performed minor tasks in the sugar mill. In mines they sorted stones
and panned. The Jesuits, despite their humane regulations, put female
slaves to work in *obrajes*, a dreary and demanding task. The treatment
female slaves received was, perhaps, slightly better than that meted out

[31] See, for example, Edgar F. Love, 'Marriage patterns of persons of African descent in a colonial
Mexico City parish', *HAHR*, 51/1 (1971), 79–91; Patrick J. Carroll, 'Estudio sociodemográfico
de personas de sangre negra en Jalapa, 1791', *Historia Mexicana*, 23/1 (1973), 111–25; Gonzalo
Aguirre Beltrán, *La población negra de México* (Mexico, 1972), 242–64.

[32] James Denson Riley, *Hacendados jesuítas en México. El Colegio Máximo de San Pedro y San Pablo,
1688–1767* (Mexico, 1976), 161–83; François Chevalier (ed.), *Instrucciones a los hermanos jesuítas
administradores de haciendas* (Mexico, 1950), 61–84.

to male slaves, but patterns of good or bad treatment cannot be established with confidence.

The possibility of manumission lightened some of the dark aspects of slavery. In all regions where manumission records have been studied, female urban slaves were more frequently manumitted than rural women, or men in general. In this respect, women's sex was thus an asset. Personal endearment to a mistress or a master, or sexual services to a male owner resulting in offspring, could and did open the road to freedom to many female slaves. This manumission could be obtained by self-purchase or by the will of the master. The women manumitted ranged in age from infancy to old age, but most frequently they were in the prime of life, which was not the case with male slaves. Research for some areas and periods indicates that more manumissions were purchased than granted and that women slaveowners freed fewer slave women than men. The latter may be explained by the greater economic dependence of some female slaveowners, such as single and widowed women, on the income produced by their slaves. Also, since many female slaves were part of dowries, their owners were reluctant to sell them. Conditional manumissions, in which the owner attached some strings to freedom, seem to have been fairly common in Peru, but much less frequent in Guadalajara, for example, pointing to diversity rather than uniformity in the practice.[33] Prices of purchase or manumission for female slaves varied according to area, age of the slave, and period, being higher in the early colonial period and in some regions distant from the ports of entry. The prime of female slaves, in terms of price, was from the ages of twenty to 40. In general, prices declined in the eighteenth century, especially after the declaration of free trade, starting in 1789. Women always carried a lower price tag than men, despite their potential for producing children and thus multiplying the master's investment. A man's potential for work apparently had more economic appeal than the reproductive potential of a woman.

Still to be explored are the lives of free mulatto and casta women, whose freedom gave them a greater degree of mobility, a broader spectrum of activities and a different social rank. Casta and mulatto women were an important element of the labour pool in colonial cities

---

[33] Lyman L. Johnson, 'Manumission in colonial Buenos Aires, 1776–1810', *HAHR*, 59/2 (1979), 258–79; Bowser, *The African Slave*, 272–301. In my own research in the notarial archives of Guadalajara in the sixteenth and seventeenth century I have found very few conditional manumissions.

and rural areas. They ran and owned small shops, plots of land, and small houses, worked in factories when the latter were established in the late colonial period, and lent money to other women and men of their social stratum. Their wills show that they had the same interest in material possessions as members of the Hispanic group, whose behaviour probably served as models for theirs. In terms of marriage, these women seem to have interacted with men of most ethnic groups, but married mostly within their own group. Their social mobility was limited by their lack of *limpieza de sangre* (purity of blood), but in this they shared the same obstacles as other women of the non-white majority.

This survey of the various aspects of women's lives in the colonial period strongly suggests that their historical experience was tightly defined by their sex. Their social functions, their duties, and their rights were sharply different from those of men, and shaped to complement them, although from a subordinate level. Women accepted men's views of themselves as persons in need of special treatment and protection. They respected the clear distinctions between what was feminine and what was masculine. This does not deny the existence of strong female characters, or of active and energetic women, but it means that, on the whole, women rarely challenged their assigned roles in society as wives and mothers.

As a result, women displayed strong family ties. A strong or open involvement with the community in civic or political terms was precluded by legislation and attitudes which barred them from what was perceived as a strictly masculine preserve. One community outlet offering the possibility of action to women was the church. Through it, women exercised to a limited extent some of the activities associated with social welfare. However, when women – like men – acted as patrons of hospitals, endowments, religious institutions or chaplaincies, they were strongly motivated by personal religious, or even family interests. They regarded their actions as contributing as much towards the salvation of their souls as to the benefit of society at large. In this connection, it is important to stress the influence of the church over women's lives. It dictated the norms of their behaviour and had the institutional power to punish deviance, both physically and spiritually. It was also the vehicle for communal activities such as processions, religious feasts and confraternity membership, and gave women an alternative in terms of life-style, with profession as a nun or commitment as a *beata* to substitute for marriage.

Despite their subordinate position and their general want of formal education, women did not lack the initiative or capacity to direct their own lives without help from men when the circumstances called for it. Such circumstances, though, were restricted by law and by custom, and were mostly experienced by single adult women after their parents' death or when the latter were destitute and dependent, or by widows and women abandoned by husbands or lovers. Newly discovered or reinterpreted archival material points to a greater participation by women than has been assumed in socio-economic activities such as the foundation of schools and convents, the administration of family estates, the sharing of labour in local markets, the management of small shops, and so forth. We are thus forced to re-evaluate our notion of what was considered acceptable feminine behaviour for women of the several socio-ethnic groups, at different periods in time and at different stages in women's own lives. Previous characterizations of women as a homogeneous group have been rendered inadequate.

If we were to venture some general characterizations of women's historical roles throughout the subdivisions suggested for the colonial period, it could be said that in the early colonial period women's roles were more fluid than later, owing to the as yet undefined character of the colonial society. Several ethnic groups faced each other and tried to accommodate, assimilate or superimpose their own cultural, social, and economic concepts on each other. Social climbing and social demotion took place with considerable speed; there were opportunities for geographical mobility and for activities beyond the confines of the home. This situation ended around the late sixteenth century – depending on geographical area – with the rooting of the personal and social interests of those who succeeded in consolidating themselves as a socio-economic elite and in strengthening their position through endogamic unions. Throughout the mid-colonial period the hardening of class lines was encouraged by the increasing ethnic complexity of society and the availability of black and indigenous female labour, which placed the woman of Spanish descent in a paramount position. Divisions of class and wealth were difficult to bridge and created significant differences in the life-styles of women. Class consciousness, strong kinship ties, and the acceptance of traditional roles for women were strong in the seventeenth century and the first part of the eighteenth. The late colonial period, however, witnessed a number of changes in regard to women that suggest changing patterns of behaviour and attitudes. The Enlightenment favoured broader educational opportunities, and gave rise to an official willingness to allow women a place outside the home in occupations suitable to themselves and, above all, acceptable to the larger interests of the state. This implied a softening of the prejudice against women of the better classes involving themselves more openly in intellectual life and in work. These changes were not radical, however, and they must be regarded as evolutionary, co-existing alongside well-established social patterns. They came too close to the end of the colonial period to alter the character of women's lives significantly, but they prepared many men and women to accept a more active and independent stand in society after the wars of independence.

10

AFRICANS IN SPANISH AMERICAN COLONIAL SOCIETY

Africans accompanied, as slaves, the earliest voyages and expeditions to the New World. Until the last quarter of the sixteenth century, however, with a numerous if already declining native American population to exploit, the demand for African slave labour in Spanish America was modest, except to some extent in the Caribbean islands and the tropical coasts of the mainland, from which Indians virtually vanished in the early stages of colonization. For the period from 1521 to 1550 the most reliable estimate, that of Philip D. Curtin, puts the total number of blacks shipped to Spanish America at 15,000 (an annual average of 500), and for the years 1551–95, the figure rose only to 36,300 (an annual average of 810).[1] It would be an overstatement to term the African slave a luxury item during this period – slaves can be found in gold panning and in plantation agriculture (mainly sugar) as well as in domestic service – but the distribution of blacks was relatively generalized, and no particular region was as yet dependent on slavery as a labour institution. However, as the Indian population in the main centres of the Spanish empire, Mexico and Peru, declined rapidly towards the end of the sixteenth century an increasing volume of petitions to the crown from colonists and government officials urged a supply of additional manpower, and the obvious source was Africa.[2]

The large-scale and systematic introduction of African slaves into Spanish America posed two problems, one moral and one economic. The moral problem had several aspects, the first of which concerned the probable impact of growing numbers of Africans on the

---

[1] Figures for African slave imports into colonial Spanish America are drawn from Philip D. Curtin, *The Atlantic slave trade: a census* (Madison, 1969).
[2] On the demographic catastrophe which followed the Spanish conquest and settlement of America, see Sánchez-Albornoz, *CHLA* 11, ch 1.

Christianization of the native Americans. Increasingly, Indians could not live year-long in isolated villages under the tutelage of a friar, since the forced labour systems dictated that they leave their homes to perform the services required. This process automatically brought them into contact with Spanish society, a connection which the church had in the first blush of missionary activity unrealistically hoped to avoid. How much worse it would be, many priests feared, if a large African population were to be transplanted to Spanish America, teeming hordes whose pagan beliefs, with a mere gloss of Christianity, could not fail to contaminate the souls of the newly converted natives.

There was also the troublesome question of the volume of the slave trade. Though African slavery had hardly been unknown in late medieval Iberian society, traffic in blacks was small-scale (perhaps no more than several hundred slaves per year) and supplemented by a flow of white slaves, some of them Christian, from the eastern Mediterranean and Black Sea areas. Smallness of scale and ethnic impartiality meant that the morality of these operations had rarely been called into question, beyond an occasional papal fulmination against the enslavement of Christians, and the unfortunate individuals involved were either assimilated into society at the lowest level or (in a cultural sense) ignored. But morality is often as much a question of degree as of principle, and the slave trade to America was a sharp break with comfortable tradition. To be effective, its magnitude had to be far greater than Spain's past dealings in the Mediterranean, and only one race would be involved, the African. Was such a vast increase in the scope of human bondage at the expense of a single ethnic group morally justifiable?

This question was in fact rarely posed until the momentum of the American slave trade seemed irreversible. And even as the horrors committed on the African coast and on the Atlantic crossing became better known, only a tiny, scarcely read body of literature critical of the traffic came into existence. Moreover, it is important to stress that even these critics did not doubt the legitimacy of slavery itself, and they agreed that the propagation of the true faith along the African coast, which was the moral prop that supported slavery, was a laudable goal. However, they argued, the incessant and increasing demands of the slave trade were making a barbarous people more barbarous still. In search of profit, Africans were coming to hunt each other like deer, bending the structure of law and custom to find ever more grounds for enslavement. Tribal warfare grew in the quest for captives, and even fathers were induced to sell their children into bondage. Surely, they argued, bringing to the African a knowledge of Christ and his teachings would be best accomplished not by enslavement, but by a more vigorous missionary movement in Africa itself, something that the Portuguese seemed unwilling or unable to inaugurate. As for conditions on the slave ships, these were detailed at length and found indefensible.

Yet more than one casuist (usually a cleric) found the means to dispel these moral doubts. The rulers of Africa were assigned all legal and moral responsibility for enslavement. Blacks, according to this rationale, were to be had for sale by their own people for just cause in the market-place. It was not the role of the European to quibble over the system of African justice or to meddle in African political affairs. It may well be, the argument ran, that blacks were sold into slavery without legal merit, but this was for the African seller to determine, not the European who bought in good faith. In any event, Africans purchased by slave traders were being liberated from a heathen existence and would receive instruction in the Christian faith. In tracts of this order, the conditions which prevailed on the Atlantic crossing were delicately skirted. Opponents of the trade were not slow to condemn the fallacies of this argument, but it maintained its hold, readily accepted by Spaniards whose overriding goal was self-enrichment.[3]

Both critics and defenders of the slave trade were in agreement on one point: the enslavement of the African could be justified only by the simultaneous propagation of the Catholic religion. The wise and the diligent, the priests in the field, soon learned that this was a goal easier to proclaim than to accomplish. To catechize perfunctorily among a small number of slaves was simple enough in Spain: the task became enormously more difficult among the thousands of Africans who came to be shipped to the Americas on an annual basis. In the first place, blacks from the west coast of Africa spoke a staggering multiplicity of languages and dialects. Not even the most dedicated of missionaries could have mastered them all, and merely to locate and train interpreters was a formidable burden. There was the larger, equally vexing problem of cultural variance. To become a Christian is to learn, at least in rudimentary form, a series of rather precisely defined abstractions, and many blacks found the tenets of the Christian faith incomprehensible.

---

[3] For an excellent discussion of the shaky moral underpinnings of the slave trade, see David Brion Davis, *The problem of slavery in Western culture* (Ithaca, 1966).

For example, an explication of the Holy Trinity to a novice is difficult in any language, and more difficult still when it has to be filtered through interpreters to frightened and demoralized captives. The missionary had to be content to make slow, painful progress with his numerous charges, a problem often compounded by a chronic shortage of personnel, and the time was short. An African brought from the interior of Angola to the slaving port of São Paulo de Luanda might remain there for only months or weeks before beginning the Atlantic crossing to (say) Cartagena, where perhaps a similar interval might be spent before transhipment to his final destination in accordance with the vagaries of the market.

Under these circumstances, even the most zealous missionaries soon resigned themselves to rudimentary instruction among the slaves, followed by baptism, and hoped that their colleagues elsewhere would have the time and patience to impart a broader and deeper knowledge of Christian doctrine. Still other friars quite simply gave up their duties in all but name and came to mirror the attitude of the population at large, treating newly arrived blacks with indifference. In fact, all too often the initial stages of conversion fell far short of the ideal. Of the religious orders of the colonial period, perhaps only the Society of Jesus fulfilled its responsibilities, and that most notably in the great slaving port of Cartagena on the coast of Colombia. Indeed, the most telling condemnation of the slave trade ever written by a Spaniard (*De instauranda Aethiopium salute*) came from the pen of the Jesuit Alonso de Sandoval (1576–1651), who was stationed there for 40 years.[4] The work of his colleague, Peter Claver, was so worthy of admiration as to earn him sainthood.

It was, however, the supply of slaves and the organization of the trade more than its morality which presented Spanish officials with problems throughout the colonial period. When by the treaty of Tordesillas in 1494 Spain and Portugal grandly divided the colonial world between them, the former nation had made one signal mistake. By this agreement, Spain had ceded to Portugal all rights to the exploitation of the West African coast, and with that concession, any direct participation in the slave trade. The error was not perceived for decades.

---

[4] Alonso de Sandoval, *Naturaleza, policia sagrada y profana, costumbres y ritos, disciplina y catechismo evangelico de todos Etiopes* (Seville, 1627; 2nd, revised edn, 1647). Republished under the title *De instauranda Aethiopium salute: El mundo de la esclavitud negra en America*, ed. Angel Valtierra (Bogotá, 1956).

At the time, Spain had little need for slaves, and in the early sixteenth century the eyes of officialdom turned west across the Atlantic, not south to Africa. The limited numbers of slaves imported into the Spanish American colonies during the sixteenth century were supplied, under royal authorization, by the Portuguese. As the demand for slaves intensified during the last quarter of the century the dynastic union which in 1580 forged Spain and Portugal into the first colonial empire on which the sun literally never set could not have been more fortuitous. Portuguese supply of blacks could be reconciled with colonial demand within the same imperial structure, permitting African slavery in Spanish America to become a much more important source of labour and government revenue than it had been in the past. During the fusion of the two crowns, which lasted until 1640, Spain manipulated by government contract the number of blacks shipped to the American colonies and assured profit for itself at the same time. Put simply, a Portuguese entrepreneur, in return for the payment of a lump sum to the crown, was awarded a monopoly contract to grant licences to his mercantile associates, usually based in Seville or Lisbon, which in turn empowered them to sell a specified number of Africans in Spanish America. The holder of this contract, which was known as the *asiento*, made his profit in two ways: he was allowed to charge his clients more than he paid to the government, and he had the right to trade directly in slaves if he so wished. During the period from 1595 (when the first such contract was let) to 1640, the average annual importation of blacks soared to 2,880 (a total of 132,600). Mexico and Peru, rich in silver but with various sectors of their economies now crying out for labour, absorbed the bulk of this increase; the remainder were scattered throughout Spanish America.

The Spanish government consistently underestimated colonial demand for slaves, precipitating an extensive contraband trade which in many years doubled or tripled the authorized import quotas. The crown did what it could to control these illegalities. Only two first ports of entry were allowed for the slave trade, Cartagena and Veracruz, where not only were the slaves counted but the ships were also searched for unauthorized merchandise from northern Europe. Regulation was piled on regulation, but the voracious demands of the market could not be denied. Slaves were landed at other ports, and not only in the Caribbean. Buenos Aires, in particular, officially closed to all but a limited amount of commerce, became an open wound in the Spanish commercial system.

Slaves – and manufactures – entered Buenos Aires and crossed the Andes despite every attempt at government control.

Worse still, the Thirty Years War (1618–1648) sounded the death knell of Luso-Hispanic domination over the colonial world. Though it was ostensibly a European conflict, it was during these war years that the Dutch subjects of Spain, locked in a bitter struggle against Habsburg rule for over half a century, at last found the strength and the will to establish a colonial empire of their own. Spanish power, stretched thin all over the world, could not summon the resources to resist. For example, the north-east of Brazil, rich in sugar but militarily weak, was just one area occupied by the Dutch in the middle decades of the seventeenth century, and its new conquerors discovered what the Portuguese had long known: there could be no sugar without slaves. The Dutch used their superior naval strength to break once and for all Portuguese domination over the African slave trade. Portugal regained independence from an increasingly impotent Spain in 1640, re-established its control of a substantial section of the West African coast (most notably Angola), had even expelled the Dutch from Brazil. But the slave trade was never to be the same. In Africa, where the Dutch had led the way, the English and the French were not far behind, and traffic in slaves became and remained an international affair. From this time forward, for Spain the slave trade resolved itself into the unenviable business of dealing with past and potential enemies. The Spanish reaction was predictably proud and unrealistic: for nearly a quarter of a century after 1640 the importation of Africans into Spanish America, where as it happened demand was temporarily low, was completely forbidden. Slaves, however, were illegally imported from the newly established Dutch, English, and French colonies in the Caribbean and in 1662 Spain reluctantly bowed to reality and revived the *asiento* system. Not only the Portuguese traders, to whom the Spanish had become accustomed, but also the Genoese, the Dutch, the French, and the English now tried their hands at selling blacks to Spanish America, legally and illegally. The most famous contract of the late colonial-period slaving enterprises was that of the South Sea Company, whose privileges were won by England in 1713 as a major concession at the Treaty of Utrecht, which marked the end of the War of the Spanish Succession.

It was in the middle of the eighteenth century that Spain first officially recognized the indispensability of a constant flow of African slaves to its American colonies. After prolonged negotiations extinguished the South Sea Company's right to trade in Spanish America, the Spanish crown tried several times, never successfully, to conclude another general *asiento*, and in the interim relied on individual Spanish merchants who bought their slaves primarily from French and English suppliers in the West Indies. Then, in 1789, at last convinced of the value of sugar on the European market, the government moved in a dramatic fashion, acknowledging in particular the agricultural potential of Cuba and its need for field hands. The futile centuries-old struggle to regulate scrupulously the volume of blacks imported into Spanish America was abandoned and the slave trade was opened to all comers. The import duties and arbitrary quotas of the *asiento* were no more, and Spaniards and Spanish Americans were free to trade with any foreign supplier of slaves who at the moment suited their mercantile convenience. The result was a spectacular upsurge in volume to certain regions. Even the bloody racial turmoil that erupted in Haiti two years later, though arousing deep apprehension among slaveholders and officials alike, did not alter the government's new policy. In fact, the elimination of Haiti as a supplier of sugar to Europe contributed to the prosperity of Cuba and to the growth of the Cuban slave trade.

To estimate the volume of the Spanish American slave trade from the dissolution of Portuguese monopoly in 1641 to independence in the early nineteenth century is a difficult and delicate undertaking. After 1739, the historian does not have even the falsely low official figures of the *asiento* as a point of departure, and there is the further problem of re-exportation (i.e., slaves ostensibly taken to the sugar islands of the English and the French but in fact intended for sale to the Spanish). Philip Curtin, the most careful student of the subject, chose to divide the period into two parts. The first stretches from 1641 to 1773, a time when little variation in the demand for slaves by region is to be discerned, and he posits a total importation of 516,000, or an annual average of 3,880. The second part of what Curtin terms the 'numbers game' spans the years from 1774 to 1807, and posits a total of 225,100 imported blacks, or an annual average of 6,600. Annual averages, however, can be deceptive. With the partial recovery of the Indian population and the rapid growth of the mestizo population during the second half of the colonial period,[5] the formerly important slave

---

[5] On the demographic recovery in Spanish America from the middle of the colonial period, see Sánchez-Albornoz, *CHLA* II, ch. 1.

markets of Peru and Mexico, and the latter in particular, lost much of their old importance. On the other hand, with growing European demand for their exports, Venezuela, Colombia (to a lesser degree), and most especially Cuba picked up the slack. During the 1774–1807 period, for example, Cuba accounted for more than half the African slaves introduced into Spanish America (119,000 out of 225,100). Given contraband and the patchy nature of the recorded evidence, the precise volume of the slave trade to Spanish America during the colonial period will never be known, but here we accept the estimate of Curtin that somewhat less than a million Africans were imported between the conquest and the early years of the nineteenth century. In large part because of the Cuban sugar boom, this figure soared to a total of some 1.5 million by 1870, when Great Britain was at last able to achieve its long-sought goal of abolishing the slave trade.

For reasons that have yet to be satisfactorily explored in detail, the slave populations of most (though not all) regions of Spanish America would have declined over time without constant infusions of new slaves from Africa. But even this attempt to compensate for a naturally decreasing slave population did not resolve the problem, and, ironically, even ensured that the trend would continue, since the African-born apparently suffered higher rates of morbidity and mortality than did the American-born, and the cargoes of imported slaves generally contained considerably more men than women, a sex ratio unfavourable to a high gross birth rate. Put another way, the importation of a thousand slaves into (say) Cuba in any given year did not increase the black population by an equivalent amount, since a fluctuating portion of the number merely cancelled out an excess of deaths over births among the blacks already in the area. Thus a high volume of importation does not imply a proportionate increase in the slave population. By contrast, the number of free persons of colour in Spanish America grew steadily decade by decade, a phenomenon not to be accounted for by manumission alone and perhaps the result of greater immunity to disease, better living conditions, and a greater willingness to bear children.

The size of the slave population of colonial Spanish America for any period is difficult to establish. In the first place, there was never a reason for Spain to determine the number of slaves in the American possessions; once import duties were paid, slaveholders were under no obligation except to pay the widely varying local rates of taxation on their blacks. Further, the bureaucrats and observers of the age were accustomed more to round numbers than to statistical exactitude, and, on the rare occasions when enumerations were made, slaves and free blacks were often lumped together. There is the further consideration that African slavery was not equally important in all places at all times. For example, in 1774 Cuba had by one estimate only 38,879 slaves, a figure that shot up to some 212,000 by 1811 and 286,000 by 1827 in response to the growing needs of the sugar plantations. By contrast, in a characteristically imprecise enumeration for Mexico in 1645, a contemporary observer hazarded a guess of 80,000, a total which dwindled to some 10,000 by 1793. If we wish to know the demographic results of over 300 years of slavery for the entire empire, only educated guesses are possible, but it seems reasonable to fix the slave population in the early nineteenth century at about 550,000, with the number of free blacks equalling and probably exceeding that figure.[6]

More significant to an understanding of the importance of the African slave in Spanish America than mere head counts is the part played by slaves in the economic activity of its various regions. In the underground mining of silver in Upper Peru (modern Bolivia) and Mexico, the African slave was of marginal importance. After the initial bonanza, profit margins were much lower than many had hoped, the rate of on-the-job accidents was high, and in the frigid altitudes of the silver-mining regions, a frightening death rate was commonly believed to result from the fact that slaves from tropical Africa could not adapt to the climate, though disease was probably as much or more to blame. In response, mine owners tended to rely on the free labour market in the case of Mexico and the *mita* in the case of Peru rather than buy expensive slaves of uncertain mortality.[7] In the gold-mining areas of New Granada – Antioquia, Popayán, and the Chocó – the situation was quite different. Slaves were needed in the eighteenth century to supplant a native population riddled with disease and hostile into the bargain, and blacks were a relatively safe investment since gold was found in placer deposits, which meant little risk during extraction. As these

[6] See the figures of Sánchez-Albornoz, *CHLA* II, ch. 1. The most recent estimate, 538,735 slaves, a composite for the years 1728–1812, can be found in Leslie Rout, Jr., *The African experience in Spanish America, 1502 to the present day* (Cambridge, 1976), 95–8. See also the dated but useful work of Wilbur Zelinsky, 'The historical geography of the Negro population of Latin America', *Journal of Negro History*, XXXIV (1949), 153–221.

[7] See Bakewell, *CHLA* II, ch. 4; also Colin A. Palmer, *Slaves of the white God: blacks in Mexico 1570–1650* (Cambridge, Mass., 1976).

strikes were quickly exhausted, the pattern is one of masters and their bands of slaves (both male and female) wandering from one claim to another with little permanent settlement. According to the census of 1778, 60 per cent of New Granada's slave population of around 70,000 were involved in the extraction of gold.[8]

In agriculture, black labour was of paramount importance. And the two richest colonies of Spanish America, Mexico and Peru, perhaps provide the most interesting examples of the variety of ways in which slaves were used. The labour force employed in the widely scattered Mexican sugar industry was predominantly black, at least partly because the government was unwilling to authorize the employment of Indians in so strenuous an occupation. In the agriculturally rich provinces of central Mexico, areas where crop production was less specialized, a different pattern obtained. Hacendados maintained a crew of black field hands to assist all year round, and then during the annual peak seasons hired temporary Indian and mestizo workers to help with the tilling, sowing, and harvesting. Coastal Peru provides yet another picture. There, with the decimation of the native population in the sixteenth century, slave labour figured in practically every agricultural endeavour, especially in the production of wine, sugar, and wheat, and in market gardening. As a Peruvian viceroy of the seventeenth century put it, there was 'no service but theirs [the slaves']', and so it remained until well toward the end of colonial rule; while the importance of slave labour in Mexico declined as the eighteenth century progressed. While Mexico was estimated to have only 10,000 slaves in 1793, Peru had 89,241 in 1812.

Black slaves played an important role in the seventeenth and eighteenth centuries in the production of cacao in Venezuela and Quito, and were prominent in the tending and cultivation of wheat, cattle, and wines in the Argentinian regions of Tucumán, Córdoba, and Mendoza. In the largely pastoral economies of Uruguay and Paraguay, and in wheat-oriented Chile, blacks were to be found in not insignificant numbers, though (with the exception of Panama) the same was not true of the still internalized economies of Central America. Most dramatically, as we have seen, African slavery was at the core of the Cuban sugar boom that began in the late eighteenth century to transform the island from a society with slaves into a slave society.

[8] On gold mining in the Chocó, see William F. Sharp, *Slavery on the Spanish frontier: the Colombian Chocó, 1680–1810* (Norman, Okla., 1976).

Slavery in Spanish America was also very much an urban institution. In families with any pretensions to respectability, a certain social cachet went with the possession of black servants: females to do the cleaning, cook the meals, and nurse and watch over the children; males to tend the garden, polish the brassware, curry-comb the horses, and drive the carriage. Indeed, on occasion government officials who feared slave unrest termed the number of black household servants excessive, maintained more for ostentation than for utility.

But urban slaves served for much more than prestige. Greatly to the profit of the master, slaves became pedlars of fruit and odds-and-ends; they were unskilled labourers, those who, for example, lifted bricks but did not know how to lay them; or they were workers in the notorious textile workshops (*obrajes*) that dotted the landscape wherever cotton and wool were available for cloth. If we are to believe the testimony of observers, females were often forced into prostitution, delivering a fixed quota of pesos to their masters. With luck and usually under Spanish guidance, slave (and free) blacks became skilled artisans, makers of clothes, shoes, tiles, ironware, and furniture. Whatever their occupations, it is clear that blacks in the cities were an integral part of the economy; perhaps adapting more easily to urban life than Indians, they were depended upon to do the jobs which needed doing but which white men disdained. Though the mention of Peru evokes the image of an Indian society, in fact the population of Lima in the middle of the seventeenth century was over half black, and (among other things) the beauty of its surviving churches is in no small measure a tribute to their industry and skill. Lima and Mexico City had in fact the largest concentrations of blacks in the western hemisphere. And figures for other cities and towns in colonial Spanish America, at times allegedly precise enumerations but more often the casual impressions of discerning observers, indicate substantial black populations.[9]

In short, the historian of Spanish American slavery confronts an institution introduced and maintained by shifting regional economic requirements for labour. Important to all manner of rural enterprise and to the functioning of the urban areas, slavery also became a custom, a tradition, almost a way of life for many masters. Doors were opened by blacks, meals were served by blacks, ladies were carried to morning Mass in sedan chairs by blacks. The habit of domination was easily

[9] On slavery in Lima, see Frederick P. Bowser, *The African slave in colonial Peru, 1524–1650* (Stanford, 1974). On Mexico City, see Palmer, *Slaves of the white God.*

acquired and soon came to seem the natural, the indispensable order of things.

We might now inquire what rewards, if any, slaves received for their industry. Or, put another way, were there at least possibilities in their lives to offset the certainties of unremitting labour and ultimate death? In 1947, the late Frank Tannenbaum argued in a highly influential book, *Slave and citizen: the Negro in the Americas*, that blacks in Latin America were more fortunate than their counterparts in the United States South. All too often, Professor Tannenbaum based his conclusions not on archival materials but on faulty printed sources, and his work was a shade too heavily influenced by the splendid researches of Gilberto Freyre for Brazil, but there is a certain validity to his assertions. The Spaniards (and the Portuguese), unlike the English, had grown accustomed to, almost at ease with, black slavery centuries before the colonization of the western hemisphere, and the status of those in bondage was more or less precisely defined. State and church alike recognized slavery as nothing more than an unfortunate secular condition. The slave was a human being possessed of a soul, equal to a free person before the eyes of God. The church applauded manumission as a noble act, and many masters, thinking of their own salvation, at some point in their lives obliged. This leniency, this tolerance, also facilitated the entrance of the ex-slave into the larger society, according to Tannenbaum. Oddly, he had very little to say about the growth, during the colonial period, of racial prejudice, so crucial to an understanding of the evolution of slavery. But he made his other points strikingly: Latin America, in his view, stood in sharp contrast to the Old South, where the institutions of church and state were immature and indifferent to the slave, and where Englishmen-turned-Americans were at a loss to know what to do about emancipation and the status of a free black in slave society.

The book made an enormous impact within a limited circle, and over the decades has influenced the publication of a large number of monographs on slavery in Spanish America and a few attempts at comparative history in more detail, many of which have taken issue with one or another aspect of Tannenbaum's general thesis. The problem throughout this debate over the relative liberality of Latin American slavery is that disciple and detractor alike have too often misread the meaning of what Tannenbaum had to say and have attempted either to bolster or destroy his argument with facts relating to the material condition of the slave. Quality of diet, incidence of marriage, mortality rates, severity of corporal punishment, and the like have been used, and not always consciously, to support, refute, or modify the thesis of *Slave and citizen*. The result, within a certain moral context, has been a rather sterile academic debate over the dubious merits of Spanish American slavery, an attempt to measure degrees of inhumanity. Tannenbaum, however, was ultimately concerned with higher, larger issues. Whether slaves ate more plantain than pork was incidental to the thrust of his work; he was concerned with problems of human acceptance and integration. One may argue that material and spiritual conditions cannot be separated, and it is true that his static, lofty approach to the essential question of equality, and the gradations thereof, mars his work. However, those who have followed in his footsteps have often fallen into the same trap, failing to grasp the impracticability of generalizations that encompass all of Spanish America at all times. An urban slave in Mexico City, for example, the product of generations of bondage, imbued with the language and at least part of the culture of whites, most certainly took a different view of his situation than a black fresh off the boat from Africa, panning for gold in the wilds of Colombia. The best histories of Spanish American slavery have been and will be those that combine the cultural and material approaches with a vivid sense of place and period.

On one point historians of all persuasions may agree. Legal codes devised in Spain could not and did not define Spanish American reality. One might assume, with Tannenbaum, that the same spirit under which laws were framed enjoining a master to Christianize his slaves, to treat them well, to encourage them to marry, also guided and motivated the slaveholder himself. But the fact is that while imperial law was clear enough, it was also relatively brief and undetailed with regard to the treatment of slaves in Spanish America, and except for denial of the right to exercise the death penalty, the colonial legal system supported the nearly absolute authority of the slaveholder. And masters intended that it remain so: in 1789, for example, when Charles IV proclaimed a new slave code which set limits on the corporal punishment that a master might inflict, the storm of colonial protest was so great that the decree was allowed to become a dead letter. Local slave codes were more detailed, but usually revolved around little more than the curfew, illegal peddling, and – of course – corporal punishment.

Thus the lot of a slave in Spanish America was determined not so much by law as by the personality of the master and by the social and economic environment, which varied enormously from region to region, decade to decade. For some slaves, the relationship with their masters was more like that of servant to employer, with all of its variations and nuances; that is to say, not greatly affected by the fact of bondage. A clever and faithful household slave, might, for example, enjoy all the subtle prerogatives of an English butler, and while cold legalities existed, they were mitigated by economic security, the prospect of manumission, mutual human respect, and (especially in the case of slave children) even love. On the other hand, a canecutter on a large plantation during the boom might not even know his master. It was the overseer who represented white society, and contempt and cruelty were far more likely than affection to dominate the relationship between white and black.

Despite the fact that some blacks may have fared better than others, it would be difficult to argue an easy existence for most African slaves. By and large, they slept with board-and-blanket for bed, either in hovels in the patio or in shacks behind the Big House. Urban blacks ate the cheapest food available in the market-place, while in rural areas slaves were often permitted, and sometimes forced, to grow their own, practices which implied an abundance of carbohydrates and a minimum of protein. Pathetically poor clothes were worn, replaced at most twice a year, and medical attention was received only when absolutely necessary, and often too late. Moreover, many Spanish American masters assumed that their proprietary rights over female slaves extended to carnal access, a notion which goes far to explain the growing mulatto population of the colonial period.

The historian must remember, however, that for the most part this was an existence shared with the free poor population of Spanish America of whatever colour. The fiat of the master defined the life of the slave; for persons liberated but disadvantaged, socio-economic realities worked to a similar end. Indeed, there is little reason to doubt that the equivalent of rape was as common among the free poor as it was between master and slave. It should also be observed that not all masters were wealthy owners of town houses, vast plantations, and large mines. Indeed, a sizeable number of blacks were owned by people of very modest means, whose living conditions were not much better than those of their slaves: a softer bed in a more spacious room; larger portions at meals with a bit more protein, wine, and the sugary confections so beloved of Spanish Americans; clothes that were perhaps respectable but scarcely luxurious; and greater access to medical care of doubtful efficacy. In other words, miserable living conditions were a fact of life for the vast majority of Spanish Americans, and the crucial distinction was not so much between slave and free as between rich and poor.

Confronted with the realities of slavery, the church was content to hold out the rewards of the hereafter for those who were patient on earth. Even Alonso de Sandoval, while lamenting the immorality of the slave trade as he witnessed its sordid practices in Cartagena, did not call the legitimacy of African slavery into question. Rather, the care and concern of the dedicated priest was to strive for the conversion and good treatment of a race assumed by all to be inferior.

When it came to the spiritual care of the African, the problem was one of mandate and concern. In theory, slaves who arrived from Africa were already knowledgeable, baptized Christians, and therefore under the ministrations of the secular clergy in Spanish America. But even the crown, with its penchant for legalistic falsehoods, was not prepared to accept this myth, and hence the activities of the Jesuits in the slaving ports, while not specifically authorized, were permitted and even welcomed. Although for long the largest slaveholder in the western hemisphere until its expulsion in 1767, the Society of Jesus took its missionary responsibilities seriously, and most notably among the newly arrived Africans (the so-called *bozales*), both in the slaving ports and at ultimate destination. In Lima, for example, one or more Jesuits on a daily basis went to the *obrajes* and the markets to preach the faith, and seem to have been regarded by the slaves with a mixture of gratitude, reverence, and fear. One Jesuit, a favourite of Viceroy Toledo, used to go into the central plaza of Lima on Sundays and holidays, sit down on a stone bench, and preach to the blacks who came and surrounded him. Another, Padre Portillo, was known as the Trumpet of God because, it was said, his stentorian tones were capable of inspiring fear in the heart of the most recalcitrant black when he described the punishments of hell; his colleague Padre González acquired such a reputation that, allegedly, masters had only to invoke his name in order to subdue restless slaves. Lacking authorization and (perhaps) determination, the other great religious orders – the Dominicans, the Franciscans, and the Augustinians – were less consistent in their work and seem to have preferred to address the spiritual needs of *ladino* blacks, those who had some knowledge of the Spanish language and culture. In any event, where a sufficient number of these orders existed, there was a semblance of Catholicity and concern.

With regard to the secular branch of the church, whose nominal responsibility it was to care for the spiritual welfare of the blacks, the verdict must be a mixed one. During the centuries of slavery, the crown was very critical of the efforts of the secular clergy among the slaves, and a stream of letters exhorting greater diligence and care flowed from Madrid. The reply of the bishops was invariably the same: the slave population was growing too fast to be ministered to with the funds and personnel at hand, and the government was urged to surrender a portion of its share of the tithes to correct the deficiency. This the crown refused to do, and not until the late eighteenth century, when the numbers of secular priests had grown and the slave population was more or less stabilized, did the observance of Christian ritual emerge in what the Spanish regarded as a normal fashion. For example, if we are to measure salvation in terms of the number of baptisms and marriages performed among blacks, the secular clergy of Cuba acquitted itself quite well during the early years of the sugar boom.

The results of the missionary efforts among Africans both slave and free, to whom European culture was in so many senses an abstraction, can never be known. However, abundant evidence for various areas indicates a measure of success, at least on the surface of things, and particularly among urban *ladino* blacks. Slave and free Africans alike were overwhelmingly illiterate, and therefore pens were not put to paper to affirm their beliefs, but it is certainly true that blacks often chose a Catholic framework for the very human need to associate with each other. The religious brotherhoods they established throughout Spanish America were as punctilious in their devotion to Catholicism as their Spanish counterparts; candles, incense, flowers, altars, muttered prayers, none were lacking. Upon inner conviction the historian can only speculate, though one might cite the exceptional but nevertheless remarkable example of Peru's famed black saint, Martín de Porres.

Any measurement of the work of the church among blacks in Spanish America is difficult to make, and the historian always comes back to an age-old question: is an institution which eases somewhat, but finally supports, an evil which would in any event exist to be praised or condemned? In this case, the church was the ultimate justification for what came to be regarded as unjustifiable servitude, but its attempts to ameliorate, however slightly, the fundamental humiliation of bondage cannot be lightly dismissed.

This is not to say, of course, that all blacks at all times accepted their condition. Apart from spontaneous reactions to cruel treatment or excessive work there were frequent rebellions. Indeed, organized black resistance to bondage has been the subject of considerable scholarly attention in recent years.[10] In Panama in the middle of the sixteenth century slave unrest became so serious and widespread that the crown temporarily banned the further importation of blacks. In the early seventeenth century a substantial area of eastern Mexico passed into the hands of black rebels, forcing the viceroy to negotiate when military efforts to remedy the situation failed. In Venezuela in 1749 a massive slave revolt was only narrowly averted when one of the conspirators revealed the details of the plot under torture. More serious was the slave revolt which began in Coro in 1795, since events in Haiti had by then frightened planters all round the Caribbean. However, when these disturbances are analysed by region and by decade, the inescapable conclusion is that the majority of African slaves resigned themselves to their fate. The manifest unease of Spanish American masters and authorities about slave unrest should not obscure the fact that slave revolts in most regions, while much feared, were rare. Further, though Spaniards were in general contemptuous of the ways of their slaves, they soon learned one essential fact about those beneath them. Africans of different tribal backgrounds were as much at odds with each other as they were resentful of white authority, and the Spanish were quite careful to cultivate this animosity. Religious brotherhoods, even the rarely permitted dances in the streets, were carefully segregated on tribal lines as dimly perceived by white masters. Africans from Guinea were not allowed to congregate formally with those from Angola. The strategy worked. Nothing resembling unity ever emerged among Africans in Spanish America, and therefore slave revolts were ultimately doomed to failure.

Two other manifestations of slave unrest were of greater concern to masters. The first might be termed passive resistance. Understanding the orders of the master perfectly well the first time, a slave would

---

[10] A list of the most important slave revolts and plots can be found in Rout, *The African experience*, ch. 4. For a perceptive comparative account, see Eugene Genovese, *From rebellion to revolution* (Baton Rouge, 1979).

require their repetition twice or three times and then perform the task improperly. Tools were broken or misplaced, livestock mysteriously killed or maimed, the canals of irrigation ditches diverted, and arson was not unknown. The list was lengthy, and only constant vigilance by the master or a reliable foreman could prevent recurrence. The same applied to household service. A cook, for example, might refuse to perform a certain chore not directly related to the kitchen and, if at last compelled, do it so badly that mistresses thought twice before issuing the command again. Thus slaves learned to give vent to their frustrations without quite crossing the thin line between perceived indolence and insolence. The former was grudgingly tolerated by the white master as a racial characteristic impossible, or difficult, to correct; but the latter received the tender mercies of the whip or worse.

Even more troubling to Spanish American slaveholders was the problem of slaves who, tired of the burdens and monotony that defined their lives, sought release through flight. These runaways were termed *cimarrones*, and some succeeded in making good their escape. Masters responded with watchful eyes and locks on doors, but obviously slaves had to be given some mobility if they were to be of any use. Agricultural workers had to go out into the fields, and the overseer could not be everywhere at once; the cook had to go to the market. The authorities did what they could to assist. Harsh legal penalties (including mutilation and death) were imposed for flight, and in many areas a constabulary known as the *Santa Hermandad* was established to capture and return runaways. These measures were partial successes at best, and the problem continued, never to be solved. In Spanish American cities, blacks who had escaped from bondage took refuge in urban anonymity and found work from cynical employers who asked no questions about background. In such rural areas as Panama, eastern Mexico, and Venezuela *cimarrones* tended to band together for mutual support and companionship in settlements known as *palenques* or *cumbes*. In 1720, for example, it was estimated that in Venezuela alone there were at least 20,000 runaways scattered in *cumbes* throughout the colony.

Though irritating, these congregations usually posed no serious threat to white authority. Obviously, slaveholders lost both money and pride when slaves escaped from bondage (whether temporarily or permanently), but runaway blacks were largely weaponless and wanted not so much to challenge white authority as to escape from it. The trouble was that the *cimarrón* communities were rarely self-sufficient, and their raids on nearby plantations time and again forced enraged agriculturalists to plead for action from the government. Those who governed Spanish America were obliging, but by the same token did not wish to spend the precious revenue of the crown in armed confrontations with well-established *palenques* in remote areas. In more than one instance, a compromise was reached whereby the runaway settlement acknowledged Spanish authority, admitted (and sometimes requested) a priest, and in fact became a self-governing community. But where there was no settlement to join, a penniless, unskilled runaway in constant fear of being discovered was often ready to exchange his terrifying freedom for the dreary security of slavery. At least in Cuba, we have the curious custom of *compadrazgo*, whereby a *cimarrón*, thinking twice about what he had done, secured the services of a third party to make amends to the master, thereby speeding his return to servitude without punishment.

As the colonial period advanced, slavery came less and less to be the predominant status of the African in continental Spanish America. During the eighteenth century a point was reached when the majority of black Spanish Americans were free. This was in the first place the result of manumission, although the numbers of free blacks were bolstered decade by decade by procreation. The steady growth of a free coloured population is not surprising. As perhaps most strikingly stated in the famous legal compilation of Alfonso the Wise (1221–84) known as *Las Siete Partidas* (1263–5), Spaniards and Spanish Americans assumed slavery to be nothing more than a cross to be borne, a secular blemish that was not indelible, having nothing to do with the soul. However, liberty was proclaimed as the ideal. Thus, after varying intervals and most often in their death-bed wills, when economic profit suddenly seemed less important than spiritual salvation, masters voluntarily freed their slaves with the observation that compassion and faithful service motivated the act. Data based on wills and letters of manumission in notarial records indicate that during the period from 1524 to 1650, 33.8 per cent of African slaves in Lima were freed unconditionally. Figures for Mexico City yield a percentage of 40.4 for the same period, and in the Mexican province of Michoacán the total for the years from 1649 to 1800 rose to 64.6 per cent. Smaller numbers of slaves were liberated on promise of future service until the death of the master, or were in other instances willed to destitute relatives until their deaths. These arrangements, in the case of elderly slaves, may have come to naught, but at least they ensured that surviving offspring would be free. The rest of the blacks (39.8 per cent in Lima, 31.3 per cent in Mexico City, and 34 per cent in Michoacán) either had their freedom purchased for them by third parties whose motives were rarely made clear, or bought their liberty for an agreed-upon price by being allowed to work in their own time to accumulate the capital towards this end.[11]

But Christian charity had its limits, and convincing evidence indicates that manumission was in the main an opportunity open to children and females. The labour of the adult male slave was too valuable to be surrendered lightly. Researches for Peru and Mexico provide ample proof of this phenomenon. For example, children under fifteen and women constituted 92.2 per cent of the slaves freed in Lima between 1524 and 1650, and the results for Mexico City, though fragmentary because many of the records were lost in the horrendous floods of the sixteenth and seventeenth centuries, yield similar evidence. In Michoacán for the years from 1649 to 1800, women and children still constituted a majority (about 70 per cent) of slaves freed, and the lower figure probably reflects the increasing irrelevance of black labour in the face of demographic recovery among the natives and the greater availability of mestizo labour, a hypothesis that is supported by the higher percentage of slaves who were freed unconditionally.

It should be emphasized that though in law liberation was an opportunity open in equal measure to both rural and urban slaves, close investigation reveals that practice was quite different. Rural slaves faced a bitter lot. Ignorant, isolated, usually with minimal linguistic skills and financial resources, they knew practically nothing of the law courts of Spanish America and the moral precepts for which they stood. In general, blacks on the plantations of Spanish America lived and died at the will of their masters and overseers, and there was little dialogue, merely an exchange of commands and acceptances, doubtless spiced by meaningless banter. In contrast, for the urban slave, far wiser in the ways of society and the operation of Spanish American justice, liberation was easier to secure. Blacks in the cities worked more closely with their masters, and their positions frequently inspired and demanded trust and mutual confidence. The ear of the humane master was usually available,

---

[11] Frederick P. Bowser, 'The free person of color in Mexico City and Lima: manumission and opportunity, 1580–1650', in Stanley L. Engerman and Eugene D. Genovese (eds.), *Race and slavery in the western hemisphere: quantitative studies* (Princeton, 1975), 350.

and he was relied upon for justice, for lenience, and quite often for a chance at freedom, though perhaps at a price. The greater sophistication of the urban slave is often illustrated by more lurid cases. For example, when masters carried the principle of carnal access to the point of procreation, slave mothers on occasion sued for the liberty of the child and often won.

The present state of research will not permit generalizations about the rate of manumission, i.e. the number of slaves freed in relation to the size of the black population in any given area. But the investigations of other scholars appear to confirm Tannenbaum's assertion that Latin Americans were willing to accept the presence of the free black, to assimilate him into the larger society (albeit at its lower levels), and even, were he an artisan or a militia officer, accord him a degree of respect. There were no lynchings in Spanish America, and the vociferous opposition to the free black that prevailed in the United States South did not obtain in the colonies of Spain to nearly the same degree, though this is not to deny a strong measure of subtle prejudice. However, even this was confused by the process of miscegenation between Spaniard, African, and Indian which continued through the centuries, oblivious to the strictures of crown and church. Despite comments such as that of one seventeenth-century observer in Peru, who noted that the shape of the ear invariably gave away those of African descent, with time it became quite difficult in most cases to distinguish the racial heritage of individuals. Suspicion and gossip, but not certainty, were prevalent. Instead of the strict definitions of black and white that evolved in the United States South, Spanish Americans developed what might be termed a 'sliding scale' of skin colour and features, and an individual rose or fell within a fairly wide range on that spectrum depending as much or more on economic status and social position as on physical aspect. Still, there is little doubt that even with freedom dark-skinned persons had a hard time fending for themselves.

In short, benevolence, self-purchase, and natural increase all contributed to the growth of the number of free Spanish Americans of African descent, a development both more visible and more significant in the urban areas than in the countryside. Faced with greater difficulties in obtaining his freedom, once liberated the rural black also laboured under disadvantages. Only infrequently could he possess agricultural property of his own. What Spanish American whites had not bought or stolen during the early centuries of the colonial period, the Indians were, with demographic recovery, quite reluctant to relinquish except in dire circumstances. With luck, a free black might purchase a miserable plot of land, he might become a sharecropper, he might return to waged labour for his former master or for another landholder, but little more. And there were more extreme cases. In the mining region of the Chocó, for example, free blacks in the eighteenth century, ambivalent towards the slaves beneath them and scorned by the whites above them, retreated to the most remote parts of the region and there scratched out a living as best they could.

In the urban areas, on the other hand, we find free persons of African descent possessed of some means. They made relatively good profits as pedlars (at least by their lights), they became artisans, and they were the owners of modest houses. In Morelia (Michoacán), for example, in 1759 one mulatto bought a lot for 290 pesos, built three houses on it (one for his residence and two for rental), and resold the property in 1781 for 1,200 pesos.[12] (Many whites did not do nearly as well in the urban property market.) Free urban blacks were faithful members of their carefully segregated religious brotherhoods, in the beginning divided on the basis of tribal origin in Africa and then more and more on the criteria of fairness of skin and economic status, as miscegenation and assimilation into higher levels of the white-dominated economy created classes within their ethnic grouping. They were people who made their wills, paid their sales taxes, and who were generally regarded as respectable members of the community.

Indeed, on rare occasions in the urban areas educational opportunities to the secondary level existed, though overwhelmingly white schools were quite ambivalent on this point. Certain positions were, of course, beyond the pale. Blacks might serve as officers in all-coloured militia units, but they did not command whites. Attendance at a university was beyond the reach of all but the fairest-skinned and most favoured, and thus the professions were denied them. Membership on a city council would have been unthinkable. But there was, short of the highest echelons, a measure of dignity and comfort available to the fortunate and the talented free person of colour.

The documentation for the period suggests that free blacks displayed little or no sympathy for their ethnic comrades in bondage. No sense of ethnic solidarity existed. Rather, the object of freedom, promoted with unconscious cleverness by the larger society, was to 'whiten'. To

[12] Unpublished research notes of the author from the Archivo de Notarías (Morelia, Michoacán).

be sure, on rare occasions a free black would marry a slave, or at least acknowledge parenthood, but in general those of African descent who obtained freedom strove to separate themselves from the slave population. Spanish culture was aped as faithfully as possible, the Spanish language was learned with care, separate religious confraternities were established, and marriages were arranged with those at least as white and economically advantaged as oneself. Until a certain level of gentility had been attained, for an individual black the struggles for emancipation, genuine independence, self-respect, and advantage in Spanish America were long and lonely.

In the struggles for Spanish American independence in the early nineteenth century slaves were, by and large, merely conscripts, fighting for royalists or so-called patriots with more or less equal lack of enthusiasm and probably moved by promises of freedom in return for loyalty. Bolívar, though himself disposed towards the emancipation of slaves, wrote gloomily towards the end of his life of the 'natural enmity of the colours', and feared the day 'when the people of colour will rise and put an end to everything'. As Spanish rule collapsed, black bondage was abolished in such areas as Argentina and Chile, where it had never been vitally important, and in Central America and Mexico, where growing Indian and mestizo populations had largely deprived it of economic point and function. In newly independent nations like Venezuela and Peru, where slavery remained strongly entrenched, the emancipation of blacks met with more resistance and was not accomplished until the 1850s, when African slavery on continental Spanish America ceased to exist.

In the islands of Cuba and Puerto Rico, the pathetic though profitable remnants of the Spanish empire in America, where the expanding sugar industry stimulated the slave trade and an enormous growth of the black population, African slavery was not finally abolished until 1886. Defended for centuries with sanctimonious sophistry on the rare occasions when it was challenged, slavery in Spanish America was everywhere abolished with great rhetorical flourishes laden with indifference for a black population no longer central to white concerns.

11

INDIAN SOCIETIES UNDER SPANISH RULE

In Spanish American studies Indian history of the colonial period is a relatively new topic. Throughout the nineteenth century and into the twentieth it was a widely held assumption that little or nothing of consequence in Indian life survived the conquests of the sixteenth century. The view was consistent with the classic writings on conquest, famous for their descriptions of massacres, tortures, and military victories unrelated to events before or after. The conquests appeared to be so concentrated, so cataclysmic, so dramatic in their confrontations of European soldiers with American natives, that no one questioned their power to annihilate. The classic writers knew that individual Indians survived to be utilized by the conquerors as slaves and labourers and tribute-payers. But the prevailing view was that none of the political, social, or cultural values of the American civilizations escaped destruction. The clear implication was that for Indians the aftermath of the conquests was deculturation and stagnation.

The view that no Indian culture persisted after the conquests was consistent with the Leyenda Negra (Black Legend), the tradition of anti-Hispanic criticism that developed in the sixteenth century, flourished in the seventeenth, eighteenth, and nineteenth centuries, and continued to exert an influence on interpretations of Spanish and Spanish American history in the twentieth century. The critics of Spanish colonialism argued that the *conquistadores* were inhumane and that an important consequence of their inhumanity was the unnecessary destruction of American Indian civilizations. Thus the Black Legend emphasized Spanish insensitivity, as if a less crude conqueror, or one with more appreciation for native American cultures, would have salvaged something for the post-conquest future. It is worth noting that the apologetic White Legend, in almost every other respect the reverse of the Black Legend, also emphasized the destructive character of the conquests. The defenders of Spanish colonialism took the position that the American civilizations, with their cannibalism, human sacrifice, and other barbarities, could deserve only to be destroyed.

In the nineteenth century, the same idea was reinforced by the literature of travel in Spanish America. The Indian described here was an impoverished and depressed person, essentially unchanged from the time of Cortés and Pizarro. Conquest had eliminated all that was good in Indian society and the remainder had been left to stultify. One of the earliest and most perceptive of the nineteenth-century travellers, Alexander von Humboldt, reported:

The better sort of Indians, among whom a certain degree of intellectual culture might be supposed, perished in great part at the commencement of the Spanish conquest... The remaining natives then consisted only of the most indigent race... and especially of those dregs of the people... who in the time of Cortés filled the streets of all the great cities of the Mexican empire.[1]

Later travellers used Humboldt's observations as their own. Their commentaries often took the form of rhetorical surprise that the Indians they encountered in Spanish America could be the descendants of the opulent, splendid Aztecs and Incas.

A hundred years after Humboldt, in the early twentieth century, much more was known about American Indians and about Spanish American history. But the knowledge was institutionalized and compartmentalized and in it the post-conquest centuries constituted a huge vacuum. One discipline, archaeology, concentrated entirely on the pre-conquest civilizations. In the archaeological view, Indian societies were 'pure' up to the time of white contact, after which they became contaminated and no longer fit for study. A second discipline, history, reported the details of conquest at length and proceeded to view the post-conquest period from an administrative and imperial perspective. Historians paid some attention to encomienda and the Christian mission, institutions in direct contact with the Indian population. But they had a very imperfect knowledge of post-conquest Indian societies themselves. Human history was understood to be a process involving change, and preferably progressive change, and although certain sectors of Latin America could be regarded as having undergone historic

---

[1] Alexander von Humboldt, *Political essay on the Kingdom of New Spain*, trans. John Black, ed. Mary Maples Dunn (New York, 1972), 53.

change these contrasted with the Indian sectors, which were seen as unchanged, unprogressive, and in some sense unhistorical. A third discipline, ethnology, picked up the Indian subject in contemporary times. Its preoccupation was with traits that might be identified as Indian or Spanish in origin, and the ratio between traits of supposedly Indian origin and traits of supposedly Spanish origin became a principal object of study. But this kind of taxonomic historicism was as far as ethnology was prepared to go in its recognition of the past. It paid minimal attention to real antecedents, and one of the discipline's conspicuous features was its contemporary orientation.

Thus, until very recently, knowledge of the American Indian remained fragmented and dispersed. The three disciplines continued to function separately, and none made intelligible the transition of Indian society from the conquest period to the present. The few individuals who were concerned with aspects of colonial Indian life were students of the codices, such as Eduard Seler, a leader in codical and epigraphical research in the late nineteenth and early twentieth centuries. Or they were students of native languages, such as Remi Siméon, who translated colonial Mexican annals from Nahuatl to French in the late nineteenth century. Or, in the aftermath of the Mexican revolution of 1910, they were *indigenistas*, such as Manuel Gamio, who advocated a comprehensive study of the Indian, combining archaeology, history, and ethnology, and whose great three-volume work, *La población del valle de Teotihuacán* (1922), was the first to examine a native community from its archaeological beginnings to modern times. In Peruvian studies a few dedicated persons – we think of Clements Markham, Hiram Bingham, and Philip Means – touched occasionally on colonial Indian subjects. But no one had as yet looked upon Indian post-conquest history as a topic worthy of separate treatment, with a character and identity of its own.

Serious research on colonial Indian history has been confined principally to the period since 1940. In Mexico it began as an extension of institutional studies concerned with labour and tribute, and demographic studies that used the statistics of tribute records. The demographic figures, or many of them, had been available for a long time, but it was only in the 1940s and 1950s that they were assembled and compared in a way that demonstrated a high population at the time of the conquest and a sharp decline thereafter. The studies focused new attention on local places and place-names, Indian family size, liability to tribute exaction, internal social structure, the decline of productivity, and the economy of the seventeenth century. In Peru, where colonial Indian studies for most topics began later and where they continue now in a less developed form, an important documentary stimulus has been the records of local tours of inspection (*visitas*). In both areas recent decades have witnessed the emergence of the intermediate discipline called ethnohistory. In Spanish American studies as elsewhere, social sciences have become more aware of a chronological dimension, and within all relevant disciplines the fashion for peasant studies, very evident in the 1960s and 1970s, has had a stimulating effect on research in colonial Indian history. The fact remains, nevertheless, that we are dealing with a new topic, still inadequately and unevenly known.

EARLY CONTACTS AND COLONIAL INSTITUTIONS

Indians first encountered Spaniards at the time of the discovery by Columbus in 1492. Thereafter for a period of 25 years Spanish expansion into new areas and additional Spanish contacts with Indians occurred only gradually, so that as late as 1517 the number of native peoples in direct or indirect association with Spaniards probably amounted to fewer than 10 per cent of the total aboriginal population of America. In the subsequent 25 years, between 1517 and 1542, with the rapid Spanish incursions into Central America, Mexico, Peru, northern South America, and northern Chile, and with the temporary Spanish penetrations into Amazonia and the region north of the Rio Grande, the percentage of Indians affected rose to 90 or more. After 1542 Spanish relations with Indians were modified in numerous ways, but few new contacts remained to be made, and those that were made occurred at a far slower pace.

In general, early Spanish–Indian encounters in the West Indies and mainland coastal areas resembled, and on the Spanish side were derived from, contacts with natives on the Atlantic coast of Africa and in the Canary Islands. The West Indian natives were sedentary agriculturists, distributed in small or medium-sized communities, with social classes, priests, a developed religion, warfare, a canoe-borne commerce, and local hereditary or elected rulers. The first island to become important in the West Indies was Hispaniola, where Indians of all classes were captured, enslaved, and put to work in farming, mining, carrying, construction, and related tasks. We lack reliable documentation on the coercion, the disruption of families, the illnesses, the mortality, and the economic dislocations of Indian society in the West Indies. But it is virtually certain that all these were present to an extreme degree, and we know that the population of the islands began at a very early date the precipitous decline that would end within a few generations in the total disappearance of Indians from this part of America. As the population dropped, Spanish slave raiding moved out into more distant islands, and an ever larger area fell under Spanish control. Miscellaneous military forays in other islands culminated in the organized military conquest of Cuba (1511), an event that served as precedent and model for the major conquests of the mainland. Conquest in its major phase terminated in 1542 with the Coronado expedition to the American West and the Orellana expedition down the Amazon. In general conquest proceeded most rapidly and proved to be most effective against the organized Indian states, for these fell to the Spaniards as unified entities. When an urban capital fell, the whole imperial area lost much of its power to resist. In the more loosely organized and weaker societies, on the other hand, Indians could fight on and each community could resist separately. Conquest was intense and disruptive, but its principal effect for the larger history is that it placed Indians under Spanish jurisdiction and rendered them liable to Spanish law and to the whole range of Spanish controls and influences, legal and illegal. Moreover, because Spanish imperialism was self-consciously monopolistic, conquest carried with it the implied or explicit rejection of other, non-Hispanic European influences upon Indians.

To these generalizations there were some significant exceptions. In parts of Spanish America (Hispaniola, fringe areas of the Aztec and Inca empires, California), where overt military conquest was absent or much reduced, its place was taken on the Spanish side by a force or threat of force sufficient to achieve an equivalent Indian subordination. Indians in some areas (northern Mexico, Florida, central Chile), resisted conquest for long periods, thereby postponing the imposition of Spanish rule. In a few places (parts of the Argentine pampas, southern Chile, remote and marginal regions everywhere) the native inhabitants were never conquered, and they remained effectively separate during the entire Spanish colonial period. Indian rebellions (Peru in the 1530s and the eighteenth century, New Mexico in the late seventeenth century, and many others) occasionally thwarted Spanish controls after they had been imposed, returning selected Indian societies, always temporarily, to an independent and hostile status. Individuals and groups, and in sixteenth-century Peru an entire Indian 'state', were sometimes able to flee from the areas of Spanish control and find refuge in remote regions.

Conquest was not a necessary preliminary to Christian conversion, but in practice in the Indian experience it was closely followed by conversion, and in both the Spanish and the Indian understanding there was a connection between the two. To Indians Christianity appeared to be what made the Spaniards strong. Christianity was especially impressive from the perspective of those whose own gods of war had failed them. On the Spanish side, Christian missionaries responded to the immense challenge of pagan America with a conversion effort unmatched in 1,500 years of Christianity. The principal campaign occurred in the early years, though subsequent efforts to extirpate remnant pagan idolatries were common in the seventeenth and eighteenth century. Conversion *per se* was restricted chiefly to the period of early contact in each area, for Spaniards were determined that Indians should be incorporated into colonial society as Christian vassals of the monarchy.

The most important early secular institution governing relations between Spaniards and Indians was *encomienda* or *repartimiento*. Its basic and universal feature was the assignment of groups of Indians to selected Spanish colonists (*encomenderos*) for tribute and labour. The terms *encomienda* and *repartimiento* referred essentially to the same institution, although the latter literally stressed the act of distribution and assignment while the emphasis of encomienda was on the responsibility of the encomendero towards his Indians. *Encomienda* was the preferred word in Spanish law and in ordinary metropolitan usage. The encomendero's responsibility included the Christian welfare of his Indians, and this meant that a resident or itinerant cleric was to be provided for. The basically secular character of encomienda was, however, never seriously questioned.

Encomienda developed in the West Indies during the second decade of the sixteenth century. It began as a substitute for slavery, or as an official compromise between the extreme enslavement practised by the first colonists and the free labour system theoretically approved by the crown. With respect to Arawaks, Caribs, and other Indians of the islands and mainland coast, from Venezuela north to Florida, early encomienda was a covering institution for the continuation of the armed raids, capture, removal, and enslavement practices of the first years. Encomienda in Mexico and Central America differed from the early insular prototype in its emphasis on the established Indian community as the assigned unit and in its dependence on community resources and social structures. Thus, on the mainland, sedentary Indian life was preserved in a more stable form than on the islands. In Peru encomienda followed the institutional model of New Spain, but it was delayed in its definitive establishment by the prolongation of conquest and civil war. Elsewhere in South America the institution might imply any of a number of degrees of assimilation. Where populations were sparse, where peoples were partly or wholly migratory, encomienda was inappropriate or appropriate only as a device for slave raiding. In Paraguay, where encomienda achieved its most stable lowland form, Indians served the encomenderos as labourers, servants, and polygamous wives. A mestizo society developed in Paraguay with kinship ties derived from Indian society. In extreme cases encomienda provided only a permit to trade with the designated Indian people. Thus the institution took a variety of forms, depending on the degree of Spanish pressure and the size and character of the Indian population. But the classic type, that which developed in the Aztec and Inca areas and their adjacent regions in western Mexico, Central America, Venezuela, Colombia, Ecuador, and northern Chile, was the large-scale exploitative institution involving an Indian society now fragmented into independent communities, each dominated by a Spanish encomendero and his staff.

The decline of encomienda in the second half of the sixteenth century was the consequence of a number of factors. Indian depopulation reduced the value of each holding. A progressively more effective royal legislation, motivated by Christian humanitarianism towards Indians and fear of a rising encomendero class in America, surrounded encomienda by ever more stringent regulations. Tribute and labour demands were progressively limited. Inheritance of encomienda from one generation to another was regulated or forbidden. Royal judicial authority established an effectual imperial law. By the late sixteenth century encomienda was well advanced in its long process of decline. In Yucatán, Paraguay, and a few other areas it persisted without major change, but elsewhere it gradually disappeared or was converted into a system of treasury grants to persons who were still called encomenderos but who exercised no control over Indian life.

As individual encomiendas reverted to the crown their Indians came officially under direct royal authority. This authority normally took the form of *corregimiento* (or *alcaldía mayor*), in which a royal official entitled *corregidor* (or *alcalde mayor*) was placed in charge of a local colonial jurisdiction. His duties included the exercise of local justice, exaction of Indian tribute, execution of royal law, and maintenance of order in the Indian community. Though sometimes aided by lieutenants (*tenientes*) and other staff members, the corregidor was regarded as the royal official in most direct control of local Indian areas. Corregidores represented royal rule in place of the personal, private rule of the encomenderos, and the intention was that they should treat Indians more humanely. In practice exploitation of Indians by corregidores in defiance of the law came to be accepted and institutionalized.

Beginning in the second half of the sixteenth century the private sector gained an immense new power, outside of encomienda, through land ownership, operation of mines, and commerce. This private sector was principally white, and it depended on Indian society for its raw materials and its labour. Royal officials, though forbidden to engage in the exploitative practices attendant on this development, did so with virtual impunity. Such practices were for the most part tolerated by the ineffective monarchy at least until the Bourbon reforms of the late eighteenth century, and they contributed to the classic types of Indian subordination, reorganization, and acculturation to which the main part of our discussion will now be devoted.

POLITICAL STRUCTURES

Spanish rule quickly fragmented all the larger political structures of native America. This was true of the Aztec and Inca empires as well as of the smaller and less developed Chibcha, Tarascan, northern Araucanian, and other political organizations. The largest Indian unit to survive the process of fragmentation was commonly the town, called *pueblo*, or the leading town, called *cabecera*. In theory at least, and to some extent in practice, the fragmentation re-established an Indian political society of discrete communities, the justification being that these units had existed prior to the creation of the Aztec, Inca, and other states and that they had been forced to join those states against their will. Thus the New Spanish state could be understood as a liberating agency rendering the rulers of local communities again 'independent'. Spanish theory postulated an alliance of king and local Indian ruler, each being understood to be a natural lord, a *señor natural*, in opposition to the illegitimate, and now rejected, imperial bureaucracies of Aztec and Inca and other Indian overlords.

The change from pre-colonial to colonial government involved a 'decapitation' of the native structure, with the cut coming just above the level of the native community. In place of Montezuma, Atahualpa, their councils, staffs, and aides, and the equivalents of these in other areas, the colonial organization introduced Spanish viceroys and the imperial apparatus down to the corregidor or his *teniente*. Only rarely did the colonial jurisdictions above the level of the town manifest a continuing Indianism. One might say, of course, that the two great colonial viceregal jurisdictions (*reinos*) themselves reflected the two great imperial areas of pre-conquest America. Other examples might be the early Spanish appointment of such 'puppet rulers' as Juan Velázquez Tlacotzin in Mexico and Manco Inca in Peru, or the area affected in a colonial labour summons, or a special political connection between one town and another. But all such survivals are interesting chiefly as isolated vestiges or as exceptions to the rule that Spaniards destroyed the larger native systems and concentrated on the unit town.

The term *cabecera*, principal town, is more specific here than the term *pueblo*, which may refer to any town, including a town subordinate to the cabecera. In the usual case, subsidiary political organizations below the level of the cabecera were permitted to remain. In Spanish terminology the smaller pueblos falling within a cabecera jurisdiction were its *sujetos*, and they were understood to owe allegiance to that cabecera and to be governed by it. *Sujetos* might be barrios, i.e., wards or quarters or subdivisions of the cabecera itself, or they might be estancias or ranches or *rancherías* situated at a distance. Other terms might be substituted for these, but the basic concept of the independent Indian town, subdivided into barrios and governing a local network of satellite villages or families, emerged as a fundamental and universal principle of colonial political structure. It was accepted by both Indians and Spaniards. In general it was this political unit, singly or in combinations of two, three, or more, that was granted in encomienda, that became a parish in the colonial ecclesiastical organization, and that became a corregimiento jurisdiction in the colonial political organization. It is true that the geographical jurisdictions of encomienda, parish, and corregimiento rarely coincided absolutely. But the differences among them were more the consequence of differing cabecera combinations and of minor deviations in boundary or structure than of any real change in the functioning of the cabecera–sujeto unit.

In theory the chieftains of these units – under the titles *tlatoani* in Mexico and *curaca* in Peru, and with other titles elsewhere – inherited their positions in accordance with Indian succession rules. But even in the early colonial period such chieftains were frequently interlopers. This was because succession rules were flexible and manipulable, because local dynasties came to an end in the conquest or the aftermath of the conquest, and because encomenderos and other Spaniards had an interest in inserting their own Indian protégés as local rulers. The term *cacique*, an Arawak word brought by Spaniards from the West Indies, increasingly displaced the various local mainland titles for such chieftains. The new usage may well have been fostered by the many usurpations of local dynastic offices, for a challenger could more easily assume the borrowed title 'cacique' than the local title to which he had no proper claim. Of course not all caciques were illegitimate rulers by native standards. Nevertheless there is a certain irony in the Spanish position that the regional caciques were to be identified as *señores naturales*.

Local Indian leaders in the towns, with whatever title, were instrumental in promoting the Spanish institutions of church, encomienda, and corregimiento. Clergy, encomenderos, and corregidores depended on the local Indian rulers to implement the colonial institutions. In cases of non-cooperation or outright resistance, clergy, encomenderos, and corregidores were in a position to use compulsion or in extreme cases to banish or kill local rulers and install more cooperative successors. Such practices, to be sure, contributed to the usurpations and the illegitimate *caciquismos* referred to above. But they also help to explain how Spaniards in the post-conquest world were able to establish Christianity, encomienda, and corregimiento with so little opposition from native peoples. Local caciques, even illegitimate ones, were persons of tremendous power in their communities, and Spaniards deliberately won them over by favours or by force.

Further political Hispanicization in the Indian towns occurred during the middle and late sixteenth century. This began in New Spain where the town were induced – by viceroys, clergy, encomenderos, and corregidores – to develop the governing institutions of peninsular Iberian municipalities. This meant *cabildos* (town councils), with *alcaldes* (judges), *regidores* (aldermen), and various lesser officials, all Indians. Indian towns responded positively to demands for such political Hispanicization, and this also may reflect pressure exerted by Spaniards upon key Indian leaders and a corresponding pressure exerted by these upon the communities. By the late sixteenth century large cabeceras in

New Spain commonly supported councils with two or four Indian judges, and eight, ten, or twelve Indian aldermen. Smaller cabeceras might have only a single judge, and two or four aldermen. All would be members of the upper class within Indian society. As in peninsular Spain the *regidores* might be representatives of particular barrios or *sujetos*. The Indian judges heard criminal cases involving Indians, thus maintaining a distinct court in the first instance. Some of the remarkable intricacy and complication of the Spanish municipal prototype was reflected in Indian political institutions of the mid sixteenth century and after, as in representative and rotational schemes for election and service. Ordinarily the judges and aldermen were elected by the incumbent town council itself or by a core of Indian voters, the *vecinos* or *vocales* of the Indian community.

In the sixteenth century the new native government by cabildo came to serve as the principal intermediary between the Spanish state and the Indian population. In some places a new Indian officer, generally called *gobernador* or *alcalde mayor*, was chosen by the *vecinos* or by the town council at intervals of one or two or more years, or in some cases was appointed by viceregal authority for longer periods. This new Indian officer presided over the cabildo and rivalled and eventually outdistanced the cacique in local power and influence. That caciques increasingly lost out to town councils in the struggle for political control meant a decline in the principle of hereditary *cacicazgo* in Indian life. In the seventeenth century a cacique might still be an influential local figure by virtue of his lands and wealth, but his grandson or great-grandson in the eighteenth century might be almost indistinguishable from the mass of the Indian population. Thus in the internal Indian government in the towns, the adopted Spanish principles of institutionalized, elective, or appointive conciliar government did prevail over the original Indian principle of dynastic, hereditary, personal government. It was a process that in some cases was accomplished within a few years in the sixteenth century, while in other cases it required a longer time. Like much else introduced by the Spaniards it appeared in a more pronounced and effective form in the main communities of the heavily populated zones. In less developed, less densely populated, and more remote zones the original rule by local cacique continued to the end of the colonial period.

In the larger Indian towns of New Spain sixteenth-century political Hispanicization proceeded still further. The town councils were housed in *casas de cabildo* built in Spanish municipal styles and situated on the main plazas. They contained courtrooms and residence quarters, various chambers, an assembly hall for the Indian cabildo, and frequently a gaol. Judges and aldermen entered their hall ceremoniously after the manner of Spanish council members in cities of Spaniards. The Spanish procedures of call to order, roll, discussion, and vote were imitated in these Indian town councils. Minutes were kept, sometimes in the Indian language now transliterated into a written language. The *alcaldes* as a whole legislated on local matters, assigned plots, regulated markets, arranged celebrations, organized tribute collection and provision of labour, and ruled on the multitude of matters that required attention in municipal government.

But it should be remembered that an Indian cabildo, however Hispanicized, was never a truly powerful institution. Its authority was confined to the narrow range of options permitted it by the local clergy, encomendero, and corregidor, and these persons, singly or in combination, made the chief local decisions. In addition, as with so many other aspects of Spanish American colonial history, the seventeenth and early eighteenth centuries witnessed a stagnation or retrogression with respect to political Hispanicization. It does not seem to be a question of reversion to original Indian practices of community government, for these were largely forgotten by the seventeenth century. Town councils throughout the Hispanic world, in white society as in Indian society, lost some of their meaning in the seventeenth century and became still more formalized, conservative, and limited. The huge demographic losses suffered by Indian America and the depressed condition of Indian society as a whole were clearly reflected in a loss of status by local Indian governments. An increasing miscegenation began to call into question the very concept of 'Indian' governments in the towns. Caciques and cabildo members were required by law to be Indians. But here as elsewhere the concept of 'Indian' permitted a degree of interpretation, and mestizos acting as Indians are known to have infiltrated the offices of Indian government occasionally in the sixteenth century and with increasing frequency thereafter.

The funding of the Indian town governments was always precarious, and local councils were constantly on the lookout for sufficient sources of income. Community treasuries were *cajas de comunidad*, as in towns of Spaniards. They received revenue from each Indian family head, who contributed a fixed amount to support the local government, often by the same process as that by which tribute payments to the Spanish government were made. Indian towns sometimes required their residents to supply maize or other commodities, which the cabildo could then sell for a money income. Plots of town land might be assigned for this purpose. The herding of sheep or other animals on town properties and the rental or sale of community lands to Spaniards or to other Indians were additional methods by which towns obtained funds. It was assumed by Spanish administrators that the communities would use such funds for both municipal expenses – such as salaries for council members, construction of town buildings, or payments on outstanding debts – and, in the colonial phrase, the *ornato del culto*, or the maintenance of the church and the performance of religious services. The treasuries might be wholly accessible to the local corregidor or the local cleric, or both, and these Spanish officials could in effect dictate the disposition of funds. Town financial records of the seventeenth and eighteenth centuries show large expenses for church and fiesta supplies – wine, flowers, food, gifts to clergy, fireworks, costumes – as well as the normal and expectable expenses for secular political operations.

Indian town governments provided additionally a structure for the maintenance of Indian class systems. In central New Spain the distinction was between upper-class Indians, generally called *principales*, and lower-class Indians, generally called *macehuales*. The *principales* were the descendants of a pre-conquest Aztec upper class whose members were called *pipiltin* (singular, *pilli*). The many special military and other titles of the *pipiltin* fell into abeyance or disappeared entirely during the sixteenth century. But in the Hispanicized municipal governments only the *principales* were eligible for positions in the cabildo. *Principales* did serve in council offices in the mid sixteenth century and after, and for the most part the holding of such an office was testimony to the upper-class rank of the individual concerned. But the restriction of office holding to *principales* was soon subjected to strain, for Spanish rules also required annual elections and forbade re-election of the same person to a council office. With population decline, particularly in the smaller towns, it became impossible to abide by these inconsistent regulations, and the usual solution was not the admission of *macehuales* to office-holding, as might be supposed, but rather a vigorous defiance of the rule against re-election. Thus a local Indian aristocracy successfully controlled the town governments for a time, and the same persons year after year occupied the new offices despite the law.

But the *principales* of central New Spain were unable to maintain their position in the deteriorating circumstances of later colonial times. Increasingly, in one cabildo after another, and in the society at large, the distinction between *principales* and *macehuales* faded away. Spaniards had at first emphasized the distinction between them, not only in council offices but with respect to other kinds of privilege, exemption, and status. The decline of the cabildos in the seventeenth century paralleled the decline of the *principales* and the elimination or neglect of their privileges. Some lost their lands and retainers and wealth and became indistinguishable from *macehuales*. Others left the Indian community, migrated to the city, and entered the company of mestizos, mulattos, Negroes, and the urban proletariat. Mestizos, mulattos, and Negroes meanwhile infiltrated the cabildos, contributing to the breakdown of the concept of 'Indian' town government, but particularly jeopardizing the traditional role of the *principales*, for they were the ones who had dominated the offices of that government.

In Peru the *curacas* emerged as powerful local authorities in the post-conquest world, and they filled the universal cacique role of puppet ruler in mediating Spanish and Indian society. In the sixteenth century their colonial territories commonly retained the pre-conquest sub-divisions and the subordinate officials in an unbroken continuity. Like their equivalents in Mexico, the Peruvian *curacas* were then threatened by the new Hispanicized, institutionalized Indian governments. Indian cabildos, first formulated for the principal towns in the mid sixteenth century, proliferated rapidly. By 1565 the city of Lima had three, one for the Indian residents, one for those who had migrated from elsewhere, and a third for the inhabitants of the immediately surrounding area. The cabildos' powers related to properties, markets, gaols, and other local affairs, of course under the superior jurisdiction of Spanish authorities. The Indian *alcaldes* exercised justice in the first instance and the Indian *alguaciles* constituted a local police force. Most communities had two *alcaldes*, but Cuzco had eight in the early seventeenth century, and Huancavelica had eighteen *alcaldes de minas* in the eighteenth century.

The *curacas* were able to take advantage of their situation in ways that were not available to their counterparts in Mexico. Beginning in the 1560s the Indian nobles in Peru petitioned for and received titles as *alguaciles* and *alcaldes mayores*. A typical petition described the aristocratic lineage and the services that the Indian author had contributed to

Pizarro or some other *conquistador*. A successful candidate for the position of *alcalde mayor* had the authority to appoint annual judges and aldermen and to administer local justice in the name of the king. Some were given charge of the maintenance of the roads, bridges, and way stations that had survived from Inca times. By 1600 Indian *alcaldes mayores* had been installed through the whole Incaic area from Quito to Potosí. The offices came in effect to be monopolized by *curacas*, who were able to prevent their falling into the hands of lesser Indians. The Peruvian institution thus served to support and prolong the class of *curacas* more than other classes. But by the end of the colonial period this also had deteriorated. Spaniards and mestizos pre-empted some of the offices of the council and even the office of *alcalde mayor*.

A subject that is still poorly understood and that requires intensive comparative research concerns the *calpulli* and the *ayllu*. These terms refer to the basic social units above the level of the family, in Mexico and Peru respectively. Students have debated the character of these units, whether or not they represented kin groups, whether or not they may be translated as 'barrio' or 'ward', the extent of the jurisdiction that they exercised. The terms need to be accurately differentiated from other terms, e.g. *tlaxilacalli*, which in Mexico appears to have had a meaning very similar to *calpulli*. The distribution and usage need to be studied (it appears that in the sixteenth century the term *calpulli* was more commonly used in Guatemala than in central Mexico). The point of special interest here, however, once we learn what the units really were, concerns their durability in the colonial period and thereafter. It has been argued that they were the essential Indian social elements, without which Indian life and culture could not have survived to modern times.

RELIGION

It was with respect to religion that the Spaniards made their most determined effort to modify Indian society. This was because many features of Indian religion were offensive from the point of view of Christianity and because Christianity was held by the Spaniards to be the only true religion. Spaniards were willing to use force on occasion to destroy temples and idols, extirpate human sacrifice and other practices, and punish recalcitrants. But in principle Spaniards believed in non-coercive Christianization, and the missionary effort, despite its intensity and its universality, was in most respects a peaceful operation.

In this it differed, and Indians could readily see that it differed, from the military conquests that immediately preceded it.

Native American religions were far from uniform, but they may be characterized as fundamentally polytheistic and animistic, with the worship of celestial bodies and natural phenomena, propitiation of deities, shamanism, and a participatory ceremonial. The most sophisticated American religions included cult objects, intricate calendars, temples and similar religious buildings, priestly classes, and rich astrological and narrative literatures. Some became celebrated among Spaniards for their inclusion of elements similar to those of Christianity, especially baptism, confession, marriage, and the symbol of the cross.

Serious, large-scale conversion efforts began in the 1520s in Mexico and spread rapidly through native America in the aftermath of the conquest armies. The missionaries' first task was to eliminate the outstanding evidences of paganism and to terminate or reduce the power of the native priests, and for the most part these steps were successfully accomplished during the first generation. Thereafter the missionaries placed a strong emphasis on the essential tenets, and the most visible features, of the Christian religion. Here the assumption was that the finer points of faith and doctrine could reasonably be postponed. Few active missionaries could devote time to the prolonged training necessary for full conversion. Especially at first the missionaries concentrated on mass baptism and rudimentary sacramental instruction. We have evidence from various parts of native America that Indians assembled willingly and enthusiastically for mass baptism. But other evidence suggests that the reports of enthusiastic early Indian attendance at mass baptism may have been exaggerated by the optimistic missionaries. The elements of native religion that resembled Christianity were sometimes utilized as aids or guides in Christian instruction, but it is also true that missionaries feared the similar pagan practices as the work of the devil, designed to trap the unwary and distort the Christian purpose. As time progressed, the need and occasion for mass baptism and initial learning of course diminished.

With respect to Indian religious belief the end result was syncretism, or the fusion of pagan and Christian faiths. The fusion appeared in a number of forms. Indians might retain a fundamentally polytheistic position by accepting the Christian deity as one additional member of a pantheon, or by giving first attention to the Trinity or the community of saints rather than to the Christian God. The crucifixion might appear as a form of human sacrifice. Indians who seemed to be worshipping in the Christian manner might place idols behind the altars, as if in the hope of a response if the Christian religion should fail. Particulars of the Christian faith might be incorporated into an essentially pagan world view. Clergy throughout the colonial period sought out and discovered evidence of surviving paganism in hidden cult objects or covert practices.

The first missionaries moved from town to town and area to area, but as their numbers increased an orderly episcopal and parochial system developed, with resident clergy in the larger Indian communities. Indians in outlying areas were then reached by regular or irregular visitation. Missionaries gave special attention to the sons of upper-class Indians, in the knowledge that these would become the leaders of the next generation and would be in a position to exert a Christian influence upon the community in the future. By the same principle, upper-class Indians who resisted Christianity or reverted, after conversion, to pagan forms of worship were liable to severe punishment. Numerous cases of whipping and imprisonment and occasional cases of execution for these causes are recorded. Clergy conducted Christian services in the towns, at first in temporary buildings or open chapels, subsequently in churches, often large and impressive churches, built by Indian labour. Local clergy in the sixteenth century frequently functioned within the institution of encomienda. This circumstance sometimes determined the location of churches or in other ways influenced the course of the Christianization programme.

In an Indian community of the seventeenth century anywhere in Spanish America, Christianity played a leading role. The church was the largest and most imposing structure in every town. It dominated a complex of subordinate buildings, sometimes including a monastery. All had been built by Indians, often in voluntary and unrecompensed labour, and maintenance and repair had likewise been Indian work. Unless it were a large community it would ordinarily have only one resident white priest. Indians were forbidden ordination as priests, but all minor church tasks were performed by Indians, and an Indian hierarchy of officials was basic to the maintenance of the religious community. The principal religious rites, including baptisms, marriages, and funerals, were conducted in the church and provided a predictable and orderly ritual for Indian lives. The day of the town's patron saint, often the saint after whom the town was named, was a great local festival day, distinguishing one Indian community from its neighbours, sometimes in an atmosphere of competition. Certain saints' images were locally celebrated for bleeding, sweating, talking, or healing. A few locations – Guadalupe in Mexico and Copacabana in Peru are outstanding examples – became Indian pilgrimage sites. In every community fiestas were semi-religious occasions, providing release from routine and promoting collective loyalty to church, state, and society.

A Christian institution to which the Indians of Spanish America came to give special attention was the *cofradía* (sodality). *Cofradías* appear not to have been established by the early missionaries, nor were they considered appropriate for Indians during the first 50 years or so of Christianity in the colony. They grew up in Indian society in the late sixteenth and seventeenth centuries, and they then multiplied and spread. No student has yet catalogued the history and distribution of these sodalities in the Spanish colonies. But there can be no question that by the mid seventeenth century a large number had been established in the Indian towns. An individual parish, depending on circumstances, might have from one to six or more. Each had its functions in the maintenance of the church and in the fulfilment of the Christian life. *Cofradías* financed and managed chapels, Masses, ecclesiastical festivals, charities, and certain landed and other properties of the church. Indian members supported the *cofradía* treasury with initiation fees and regular dues, the funds then being allocated by the sodality's majordomo to meet the designated expenses. In some cases membership conferred plenary indulgence, and the funds were used to provide for shrouds, coffins, Masses, vigils, and burials when members died. Thus in addition to their other functions, *cofradías* might be institutions of individual insurance, guaranteeing favourable conditions for both body and soul after death. Their communal features reflect the developed, pervasive, institutionalized Christianity of the seventeenth and eighteenth centuries. They provided an organized mode of life, and Indians were perhaps the more attracted to them as the secular institutions of Indian society increasingly failed to provide equivalent satisfactions. The sodality records sometimes reveal a deliberate Indianism, a sense of the Indians' separation from and distrust of white society.

That Indians should pay tribute was one of the earliest and most fundamental of Spanish convictions in the colonial world. The tradition derived from Spain, where peasants were *pecheros*, payers of *pecho* or tribute. In America, where colonists paid no *pecho*, the tribute obligation fell on the new, non-Spanish lower class. In theory Indians paid tribute as the obligation of 'vassals' (this term was used in the colonial period) to the crown, and in return for the benefits or supposed benefits of Spanish civilization. Many Indians had paid tribute in their pre-conquest state, a fact that facilitated both the theory and the practice of Spanish tribute exaction.

Spanish seizures of goods, especially gold, in the early, Caribbean phase of conquest and settlement came gradually to be regulated in encomienda, by which the king granted to an intermediary, the encomendero, the privilege of receiving the tribute that Indians otherwise owed to the crown. Tribute became one of the principal devices of control exercised by encomenderos over Indians, and their tribute collectors, themselves commonly Indians, were among the most feared of the encomenderos' agents. A large part of the contemporary commentary on encomienda to the mid sixteenth century concerns excesses in tribute collection.

As in other aspects of encomienda, excesses in tribute collection were made possible by the encomenderos' reliance on local Indian leaders. Tribute was delivered first to the cacique in the early period, and a portion was then extracted under the cacique's direction to be turned over to the encomendero. In the absence of such co-operation from caciques or their equivalents, Spaniards had no reliable means of requiring tribute payments from Indians. But this co-operation also permitted caciques to drain off large parts of the Indians' tribute for their own enrichment. Early criticisms of the encomenderos, to the effect that they were extortionate in their demands, often failed to allow for the Indian caciques, who might be even more extortionate. The situation provides one of our most telling examples of colonial oppression within Indian society itself.

Royal efforts to curb the encomenderos meant that fixed amounts of tribute, ordinarily based on counts or estimates of the Indian population of the encomiendas, were now legislated. Given the methods of collection, which were well known, the crown was obliged to set limits both on the encomenderos' and on the caciques' incomes from tribute, and this was done. As local Indian governments increasingly drained power from caciques, tribute payments became more regularized and confined within an approximation of the legal limits. Caciques' incomes, like other evidence of caciques' authority, declined in the late sixteenth and the seventeenth centuries. The substitution of cabildo government for cacique government was a significant step in the process of establishing royal control over tribute exaction. In places where the town councils did not come into being Spaniards used other methods, including coercion, reward, and substitution, to ensure that caciques could both receive and pass on tribute without excessively exploiting the system to their own advantage.

Family heads were full tributaries in colonial Indian society. Widows, widowers, bachelors, and spinsters were half-tributaries. Encomiendas in the second half of the sixteenth century were legally limited to a tribute computed by multiplying the number of tributaries by the unit amount that each was to pay. The figure constantly changed, for the Indian tributary population declined, a fact that explains why we have so many recorded population counts in the second half of the sixteenth century. But the familiar irregularities and complications persisted. Because Indians were still the collectors, i.e. the persons who visited the individual tributaries and received their payments, a basically Indian system of assessment could frequently be retained under the guise of a uniform capitation tax. This meant the covert perpetuation of group exemptions, computations based on land or wealth, embezzlement of funds, and additional practices that Spaniards were in no position to control. On the Spanish side also many obstacles stood in the way of an equitable system of payments by Indian tributaries. The unit tributary amount was still ordinarily made up of a money payment and a payment in kind, and the values of these varied markedly from place to place. In addition, the Spanish government, ever more in need of funds in the later sixteenth and the seventeenth centuries, imposed a number of new taxes on Indians, under such special titles as *servicio*, for naval defence, and *ministros*, for the costs of Indian litigation. Like the original 'tribute' these were also subject to local variation. Indian liability to the taxes designed for Spaniards, such as the *alcabala* (sales tax), likewise differed in time and place, and many local exactions, originally imposed temporarily and arbitrarily by agents of the state or the church, came to be permanently established by custom. It is not simply that Indians in Chile paid different amounts from those paid by Indians in Mexico. The inhabitants of two neighbouring towns in either colony might also pay quite different amounts. The Spanish effort to arrive at uniformity in assessment was never successful.

The tribute practices described above relate to encomienda, but it should be noted that the escheatment of encomiendas to the crown did nothing to halt irregularities in tribute exaction. Contemporary observers often found corregidores to be more demanding than encomenderos. Corregidores, like encomenderos, relied on the caciques or cabildos and conspired with them to reward the Indian tribute takers with a portion of the excess taken. They enforced illegal exactions in money, food, or other goods, and arranged tribute sales at illegal prices, with secret payments. They demanded *derechos* (fees or bribes) for population counts, investments in office, approval of council legislation, and other functions that by law should have been performed gratis. Corregidores found willing accomplices in malfeasance in Indian council members, who charged illegally for fiestas, voted additions to their own salaries, and in various ways used their offices to increase and divert tribute funds for their own profit.

Within the Indian community the exactions of tribute had some important influences upon local productivity. Many Indian goods – maize, cacao, native textiles, and numerous others – continued to be paid in tribute. Sometimes the tribute requirements were for payment in European goods, such as wheat, woollen textiles, money, chickens, or eggs. Indians raised or made European goods in order to sell them for the money that would be paid in tribute. Undoubtedly the cultivation or manufacture of European products constituted a step in the direction of Hispanicization. Yet it is clear that goods were frequently raised or made by Indians exclusively as tribute goods, without any intent or desire to adapt them into Indian life.

LABOUR

Legal and illegal enslavement of Indians for purposes of labour occurred principally in the West Indies and in the adjacent mainland from Central America to Venezuela. In Mexico and Peru the *conquistadores* were more concerned with encomienda than with outright slavery, but they did make slaves of Indians captured in the wars, justifying the action by the *Requerimiento* (which threatened slavery for Indians who refused to surrender and receive the Christian gospel) or by the principle that captives taken in a just and Christian war could be legitimately enslaved. *Conquistadores* also argued that Indians who were slaves in their own native society should continue to be slaves after the conquests, since this involved merely perpetuation of a pre-existing status and not a new act of enslavement. For a time the crown permitted Indian enslavement in cases of rebellion and as punishment for particular crimes. Throughout the sixteenth century and on into the seventeenth we find instances of Indian slavery among captives taken in frontier wars and among individuals sentenced for crime. But in general, after the Laws of Burgos (1512), the prevailing principle was that Indians were free persons and not slaves.

Information on the Spaniards' use of Indian labour in the West Indies after the establishment of encomienda leaves much to be desired. Critics charged, probably accurately, that encomienda labour hardly differed from slavery, and that Indians continued to be overworked and mistreated as they had been during the first years. Encomienda Indians were sometimes sold or rented out by their encomenderos in defiance of the law; little was done to ensure the labourers' Christianization or to provide for their welfare in the way required by law. Mining, transportation, agriculture, building, and military service were the main categories of work. In the West Indies the encomiendas came to an end within two generations through the extinction of the native population. But it should not be assumed that the severe conditions of labour either in slavery or in encomienda constituted a direct cause of this extinction. As elsewhere, diseases introduced by Spaniards may be supposed to have been the chief cause. It is true, of course, that the diseases may have had more lethal consequences because of the fatigue, malnutrition, and other conditions attending Spanish labour practices.

Encomienda on the mainland was an onerous institution for Indians, but in the principal areas its labour component was limited to the first colonial generations. For central Mexico we have an abundant documentation on the subject, including some critical views by Indians themselves. It is quite clear the encomenderos exploited their Indians with respect to labour as they did with respect to tribute. As in tribute they depended on caciques or other Indians as intermediaries and local bosses. From the start the crown regarded the labour portion of encomienda as a temporary and unsatisfactory expedient pending the establishment of free wage labour, and it was this royal position that resulted in the removal of Indian labour from the encomenderos' control. The removal took place in the mid sixteenth century in central New Spain and a generation later in the central Andes. Thus by the late sixteenth century in the densely populated areas encomienda had become an institution for the exaction of tribute and could no longer be regarded as a source of private labour. Encomenderos desiring Indians as workers in these areas were now obligated to rely upon the new institution of labour *repartimiento* or *mita*.

Again we have a difference between the central and the outlying zones. Outside the central areas, in regions where the encomenderos were less numerous, encomienda continued to be an institution for regulating labour as well as an institution for collecting tribute. Even in the very late colonial period, surviving encomenderos still exercised this labour power in Chile, Paraguay, Yucatán, and elsewhere where the encomienda itself survived. The marginal survivals may perhaps be explained as instances of default. They were not important enough, from the metropolitan perspective, to constitute a threat to the crown or to provoke repressive legislation. In addition these were regions where the native social structures did not lend themselves to large-scale, organized labour drafts for agriculture or mining. The small-scale labour encomienda was the more appropriate institution in these areas because the local societies were fragmented or because they lacked the markets and mines and resources to sustain a comprehensive tribute or labour organization.

Labour *repartimiento*, as it was called in New Spain, or *mita*, the term used in Peru, was the new institution designed to regulate the work of Indians in the public sector following the separation of this work from the private or encomienda sector. Repartimiento was a response both to the increased number of Spaniards and to the reduced number of Indian labourers. It was a more economical system for the distribution of Indian labourers following the excesses and waste of manpower of encomienda. In repartimiento, each Indian community at periodic intervals became responsible for releasing a fraction of its able-bodied male population for labour. Each labouring group worked for its employer for a given period, ranging from a week to four months or more. The Indian workers then received a modest wage and returned to their communities while a new contingent, recruited and assigned in the same manner, took their places. As we have seen, encomenderos in the principal areas were now obliged to request repartimiento workers in the same way as other Spaniards.

The mita labour for the Peruvian mines at Potosí represents repartimiento in its most impressive form. Here in the late sixteenth and seventeenth centuries the flow of workers to and from the mine assumed the proportions of mass migrations. Local Indian officials directed the selection and organization. When the appointed day came the labourers formed a huge procession, with their families, llamas, food, and other supplies. From a distant province the journey required several months. In the seventeenth century many thousands of persons and animals were constantly wending their way to and from Potosí. Workers and their families might be away from their communities for a year or more. No other labour draft of the colony compared with this one for numbers of persons, duration, and intensity. The closest rivals in Mexico were for the rebuilding of Tenochtitlán in the sixteenth century and for the drainage of the Valley of Mexico in the early seventeenth century.

Repartimiento served the labour needs of the colony more effectively than encomienda had done, but it was increasingly subject to strain as the Indian population continued to decline. An Indian community of 400 tributaries, one that might originally have been required to supply eight or twelve or sixteen workers for each repartimiento draft, inevitably found itself less and less able to meet the quota as its population fell to 200 or 100 or even less. Spanish officials made some effort to adjust the quotas downward, but adjustments were commonly in arrears of the population loss, and in any case a lowering of the quota necessarily reduced the effectiveness of repartimiento as a means of labour recruitment. Indian communities now sought to hire outside workers or to send youths, the aged, or women to the repartimiento in order to fulfil their obligations. The strain on the communities and their Indian governments became severe, especially in those agricultural and mining areas where population loss was greatest.

In central New Spain the agricultural employers, no longer able to secure the workers they needed through repartimiento, made private labour contracts with individual workers, loaned money to Indians for repayment in labour, and in other ways defied or circumvented the system. The agricultural repartimiento deteriorated further and was finally abolished in 1633. The mining industry in New Spain had already ceased to depend on it, and this meant that only a few state-controlled operations, notably the drainage of the Valley of Mexico lakes, continued to receive such workers in substantial numbers.

Thus in the later seventeenth and eighteenth centuries, in central New Spain, most Indian labour was 'free'. As the native population again increased, conditions in the rural labour market became the reverse of what they had been. There were now too many workers for the number of jobs. Unemployed workers overflowed their pueblos and roamed the countryside. Because of the competition for employment the rural labourer's wage, having risen steadily from the early sixteenth century to the mid seventeenth century, remained almost constant for the next 150 years. The situation was advantageous for the hacendados, who kept a core of workers on their premises for year-round labour and could hire any number of additional labourers for seasonal needs.

In the central Andes a different situation prevailed. Here the mita remained the principal instrument for assembling the labour at Potosí and at other Peruvian mines throughout the colonial period. The mining technology was far behind the Mexican. In the eighteenth century great hoists were lifting the ore to the surface in Mexico, while in Peru Indian labourers were still climbing tiers of ladders carrying ore on their backs. In agriculture the Peruvian employers found many of the same deficiencies in the labour system that Mexican employers found. But the agricultural estates of Peru accommodated a special class of workers, the *yana* or *yanaconas*, formerly servants and workers for the Inca upper class. The *yanaconas* grew in number, relatively if not absolutely, in the sixteenth century as other Indians escaped the pressures of community life to join them. They were protected by law, favoured by the Spaniards, exempted at least in theory from tribute and mita, and bound to the land. The detailed history and further implications of the differences in labour conditions between the Andean highlands and central Mexico, both densely settled areas attractive to Spanish estate holders and employers, require further study and explanation.

Students have frequently identified peonage as the classic labour form of rural Spanish America. The supposition has been that hacienda owners and other landed employers characteristically compelled Indians to work by advancing them money and requiring repayment in labour. 'Classic' peonage assumes (1) an authoritarian hacendado unable or unwilling to maintain a labour force of hired workers, and (2) a group of impoverished Indian labourers desirous of escaping from their predicament but held through the circumstance of their debt. Through a series of subsequent loans, the hacendado then ensured that the debt would never be repaid in full. In extreme cases, after the original peon died, the still unredeemed debt was inherited by his son, and thus generation after generation whole Indian families were obligated to remain on the hacienda and commit themselves to lifetimes of labour. Peonage has been understood as an institution through which unscrupulous employers extracted the maximum of service from a controlled labour force at minimal expense. But recent studies suggest that peonage in these terms was less extensive in the colonial period than has been believed. The colonial record provides many instances of peonage in agriculture, mining, and other labour. But in particular areas the complex of pressures on Indian livelihood was such that Indian labourers did not need to be held by debt. An Indian of the seventeenth century, landless, unable to pay his tribute, without the resources to feed his family, willingly moved from his village to the hacienda. He might count himself fortunate to arrive and remain there, to work a plot of land, to receive a wage or a payment in advance of a wage, and to have the protective patronage of the owner. The hacienda sometimes assumed responsibility for his tribute payment, and it functioned further as an institution of credit, allowing him to fall into arrears in his obligations without incurring punishment or losing his job.

In the Spanish American cities, as in rural areas, Indians performed most of the labour. But the urban conditions were quite different from those of the countryside. Repartimiento labour for urban tasks was common in the sixteenth century, and it persisted intermittently, sometimes with long interruptions, throughout the colonial period. Food, fuel, fodder, and other goods for the city's officials and other residents were often supplied in a repartimiento institution that combined tribute in kind with the tasks of transporting and storing it. Some labour was for the construction or expansion of the urban zone. A class of Indians skilled at masonry, carpentry, and related occupations came quickly into being to serve as the teachers and bosses of the unskilled mass. The cities constantly needed workers. Houses had to be constructed and kept in repair. Churches and cathedrals were under construction for decades. Shops and public edifices, streets and bridges, water supplies and sewage systems all required labour, first for construction, then for repair, and finally for rebuilding. Indian residents of the towns and of the cities' environs were always regarded as the appropriate labourers for these tasks. They were summoned by repartimiento, and even after the formal repartimientos for these tasks were abolished, as they were for some cities, new ones kept the Indian labourers at special work.

An important difference between Indian labour in the cities and in the towns and countryside relates to crafts and craft guilds. Crafts in rural areas focused upon the utilitarian arts of native domestic and agricultural life: weaving of textiles, manufacture of pottery and baskets, fashioning of simple tools. Crafts in the city were far more complex. Spaniards expressed amazement at the rapidity with which Indians acquired the skills of Spanish manufacturing. In Mexico City Indians quickly learned to make gloves, shoes, saddles, glassware, and ironware. Within a generation following the fall of the Aztec capital, Indians were turning out doublets, waistcoats, breeches, and all the Spanish garments for sale in the Spanish markets of the city. The competition was acutely felt by Spanish tailors, shoemakers, silversmiths, and other craftsmen, who organized themselves in guilds and sought to resist or control the new Indian production. But by degrees Indians were admitted into the guilds as apprentices and journeymen and even as masters of some of the trades, and they progressively fused at these and all other social levels with Negroes, mestizos, and mulattos in the dense, mixed, crowded conditions of the city.

One more urban labouring institution is relevant to Indian life. This is the *obraje*, a workshop designed particularly for the production of woollen cloth. Obrajes began in the sixteenth century, with Indian labour. The chief tasks were washing, carding, spinning, and weaving. By the seventeenth century the obrajes had developed into exploitative sweatshops, and they became famous for their low wages and disreputable conditions. Indians and others found guilty of crimes were sentenced to obraje labour for periods of months or years, and Indians in this condition were known as slave labourers throughout colonial times.

LAND

In theory the Spanish imperial government respected Indian landholding and sought to confine Spanish lands to vacant areas or tracts whose transfer to Spanish ownership would not prejudice Indian interests. But in practice this principle was not adhered to. Spaniards naturally assumed possession of the valuable urban zones conquered in Tenochtitlán and Cuzco, and Indians were quite unable to resist the property pre-emptions in these and other cities by Cortés, Pizarro, and their *conquistador* followers. The land-granting authorities of the Spanish colonial government – cabildos, viceroys, and their agents – characteristically gave higher priority to Spanish interests than to Indian interests. Spanish colonists argued that they required more land for large-scale agriculture and cattle grazing than Indians did for their intensive, small-scale crop cultivation. To Spaniards the lands that Indians used for hunting or other community purposes seemed 'vacant' and hence available to them. There is a sense in which all the lands in America that ultimately came into Spanish possession were usurped from Indians. But the 'usurpations' were of many kinds, including purchase, trade, and voluntary bestowal by individual Indians, and the question of conflicting Spanish and Indian 'claims' is one of great complexity.

Historical attention has been directed in large part to the alienated 'village lands', lands that formerly fell under the jurisdiction of Indian communities and were then lost, usually to white hacendados or other property owners. In extreme cases all of a community's lands might be lost, for a hacienda could completely surround a town-site, causing the community in effect to be incorporated within the hacienda's jurisdiction. But the more common outcome in the colonial period was the loss of a portion of the community lands. This permitted the survival of the community in a politically independent status, but it increased the likelihood of its economic subordination to the hacienda. The relationship of political separation and economic domination served the interests of the hacienda, for the hacendado was relieved of the obligation of providing for the town and the continued availability of a nearby labour supply was assured.

Spanish colonists were originally attracted to the densely settled zones of central Mexico and the central Andes less for land than for booty, labour, and tribute. These zones were accordingly the areas of the major conquests and of the earliest and largest mainland encomiendas. Encomienda was the appropriate early institution here, and significantly it involved not a grant of land but a grant of Indians for tribute and work. In the Spanish peninsular heritage land ownership had traditionally provided economic profit and social status. But the transplanting of this tradition to the New World was delayed in the central zones of the colony precisely by the large, dense, landholding Indian population. Only with the decline of this population in the sixteenth century would quantities of land become available. One of the first and most consistent consequences of Indian demographic decline was the taking over of abandoned lands by Spanish colonists.

The process was not a simple one. In the Indian tradition a parcel of land vacated by the death of its occupant normally reverted to the community for reassignment to a new occupant. It was not understood to be available for occupation from outside. If there were no candidate within the community to whom the parcel might be assigned, the elders, the cacique, or the Indian cabildo might hold it unassigned as community property, pending the appearance of an appropriate holder. The holder in any case would have only the usufruct of the property. He could occupy it so long as he raised crops on it and used it to support his family. This characteristic communal Indian understanding of land use conflicted with the Spaniards' sense of absolute property and complicated any simple substitution of Spanish for Indian ownership when land became 'unoccupied' through death.

The community's capacity to retain its land, on the other hand, was severely strained under colonial conditions. Indian communities were weakened, not just reduced in size, by depopulation. When the difficulties became severe enough, Indian communities were forced to yield. If the Indian cabildo needed money to pay the town's tribute, it seemed preferable to rent out or sell property to Spaniards than to go to gaol for arrears in payment. The council members might further withhold properties from persons in their own community in order to have properties to rent or sell. The problems usually grew more pressing over time. Though they might be relieved to some extent by a year of abundance, they became progressively more critical in years of shortage. It was especially in periods of stress that Indian communities lost land and Spaniards gained it. In such periods, Indian communities were the more willing to sell land to Spanish colonists, and the colonists were the more anxious to buy, especially at reduced prices. Spanish colonial law, derivative as always from European precedents, tended to regard sale as a legitimate contractual arrangement between two willing persons irrespective of the surrounding circumstances.

Spanish law, at first supportive and protective of Indian landholding, subsequently provided new means for the transfer of Indian land to Spanish hands. In both Mexico and Peru the state policy of *congregación* (*reducción*) in the late sixteenth and seventeenth centuries meant that whole Indian town sites were destroyed, their occupants moved ('congregated' or 'reduced') to other places, and their lands sequestered. The justification was that Indians should live in compact units for the sake of social and political order, religious instruction, municipal control, and an acceleration of the civilizing process. In principle all Indian landholders resettled in *congregación* were to retain their landed possessions, or, if the resettlement were at too great a distance, to be compensated with equivalent lands near the new location. Spaniards always denied that *congregación* was designed as a means of land transfer. But this was its universal consequence.

When *congregación* was further implemented by the legal devices of *denuncia* and *composición*, the result was still more damaging for Indian land. *Denuncia* permitted any Spanish colonist to claim vacant land and, after some formalities and the payment of a fee, to hold it as legal owner. *Composición* permitted him to gain full legal possession of ('compose') any portion of his property that suffered from defective titles. *Denuncia* and composition were particularly appropriate to the seventeenth century, the period of reduced Indian population, for this was a time of vacated land and weakened Indian resistance. Land rendered unoccupied by depopulation could be denounced or simply seized and held, and later composed. It is true that Indians, and not simply whites, were authorized to employ both these means for securing property. But in fact very few Indians did so, for Indians in general remained ignorant of the law, lacked the requisite funds, and had relatively few opportunities for turning the situation to their advantage. Even the increase in Indian numbers in the eighteenth century failed to stimulate any appreciable native recourse to *denuncia* or composition, both for the reasons stated and because by this time so much of the land, and especially the productive and usable land, had passed to other owners.

Apart from legal transfers the records of colonial land transactions are filled with evidence of falsification, threats, and other illegal practices. Individual Indians were persuaded to 'sell' portions of the community's common land to Spaniards. Spaniards negotiated for the sale of one property and received, or took, a more desirable one. Spaniards bribed or forced Indians to donate land. Indians rented out land to Spaniards and after receiving rent for a period of years were given to understand they had been receiving instalments on a sale and that a full transfer of ownership was now required. Against such practices the Indian community was sometimes able to offer short-term resistance or to blunt or delay the effect. Indians are known to have surreptitiously moved boundary markers, presented forged documents of title, and sought to deceive Spaniards in other ways. Indian communities able to afford the expense could bring legal action, and we know of many cases in which Indian communities won lawsuits in colonial courts against Spanish colonists who seized their land. But the long-term advantage lay on the Spanish side, for the Spaniards were wealthier and stronger, could offer higher prices and bribes, could employ more skilful lawyers, and could afford to await the next favourable opportunity. For the most part it was a process that proceeded in one direction. Lands that came under Spanish control rarely reverted to Indian possession.

ACCULTURATION

Most educational institutions established by Spaniards for Indians were associated with the campaigns for religious conversion. This was the case in the areas of dense Indian population during the early period, and it was the case afterwards on the frontiers, where missionaries continued to come into contact with unconverted Indians. In addition to the religious training, mission schools made some effort to provide the rudiments of a secular education. Selected members of the Indian upper class, especially sons of caciques, did emerge from such schools with a knowledge of the Spanish language and the ability to read and write. At the one outstanding and exemplary school of this type, the Colegio de Santa Cruz de Tlatelolco (part of Mexico City), upper-class Indian students learned Latin and were offered a humanistic education roughly comparable to that provided by aristocratic *colegios* in Spain. But the effective period of Santa Cruz de Tlatelolco was confined to the mid sixteenth century, and although the seventeenth-century Colegio del Príncipe in Lima had some of the same objectives, nothing quite like Santa Cruz is known elsewhere or at any other time.

One of the leaders of the sixteenth-century missionary work, Vasco de Quiroga, sought to establish utopian Indian societies in two small communities, both called Santa Fe, in New Spain. His regulations called for a literate Indian population, common property, rotational office holding, and an economy based on agriculture and craft skills. His purpose was to realize in practice the idealistic society conceived by Thomas More and to demonstrate the doctrine of Indian perfectibility.

Quiroga's work is of importance for what it reveals of the missionary mentality and the philosophy of Christian humanism in a New World form. But in practical terms its implications for change in Indian society were very slight.

The histories of Santa Cruz de Tlatelolco and of the two communities of Santa Fe suggest that large-scale Indian acculturation, where it occurred, was not the result of Spanish efforts at formal education. Rather it was the result of other kinds of interaction between Spaniards and Indians. Native adaptations in speech, dress, social activities, economic productivity, and daily life depended on Indian class and status, Indian proximity to centres of Spanish population, and the character of the relevant relations between Indians and Spaniards. Only with respect to religion do we find widespread teaching on the Spanish side and an acceptance, or partial acceptance, of that teaching on the Indian side.

In the sixteenth century, members of the Indian upper class, particularly the caciques, had the foremost opportunities for Hispanicization. Caciques knew that the role of local puppet ruler would win them privileges, and they were quick to exploit the possibilities. Caciques and other members of the Indian upper class were permitted to carry firearms, wear swords, dress in Spanish clothing, ride horses, and fraternize with white colonists. In the sixteenth century a surprising number of upper-class Indians travelled to Spain to present themselves at the royal court, where they requested additional privileges, titles of nobility, and coats of arms in official recognition of their rank and of the supportive role, real or assumed, that they or their fathers had played in the Spanish conquests. Caciques lived in houses constructed in Spanish styles and furnished with Spanish beds, tables, chairs, tapestries, and similar accoutrements otherwise unknown in native life. They were landholders, sometimes on a large scale, with servants, labourers, flocks of sheep, and agricultural enterprises. A few even became encomenderos. They owned Negro slaves, made large charitable donations to Spanish institutions, bought and sold expensive things, and notarized their contracts. They married within the Indian upper class and willed their estates to their successors.

The decline of the cacique class in the seventeenth and eighteenth centuries was the result of the many new circumstances in the later history of the colony. Caciques lost their native retainers to disease, to the repartimiento, or to the estates of Spaniards. Their political power suffered under the competition of the Hispanicized cabildos in the towns. Their communities no longer supported them, and they lost out to white or mestizo entrepreneurs. A limited number of cacique families, especially in Peru, survived with their wealth, power, prestige, and economic enterprises intact at the end of the eighteenth century. But many others failed, preserving only a memory of the family's past and an ineffective claim to status. A crucial factor seems to have been that Spanish society now had no further use for the caciques and no longer needed them to perform a puppet role.

For the mass of the Indian population the adoption of Spanish traits and products was a much slower and more selective process than it was for the caciques or other Indians of the upper class. Most Indians did not learn the Spanish language. The native languages came to include a number of Spanish terms, but these were chiefly loan-words for which the languages had no equivalents. Most Indian houses and methods of house construction in the eighteenth century differed little from those of the fifteenth. In dress some Indians adopted trousers, shirts, hats, and woollen cloth, while others preserved the original Indian clothing in whole or in part. European chickens were widely accepted through Indian America, and chickens and eggs were frequently included among the tribute goods that Indians paid to Spaniards. Wheat, often required in tribute also, played a lesser role in native life than did chickens. Some products that had been confined mainly to the Indian ruling classes in pre-conquest times came to be much more generally consumed in the colony, the outstanding examples being pulque in Mexico and coca and chicha in Peru. Indians raised pigs and sheep on a limited scale. The raising of horses and cattle seems to have become more an Indian practice in Peru than in central Mexico, perhaps because the native llama served as a psychological preparation. In the settled agricultural zones of Mexico, where Spaniards established haciendas and ranches, cows and steers were feared and hated by Indians, at least partly because of their destructive intrusions into agricultural lands. But, as is well known, horses became an important adjunct to the migratory Indian life beyond the Mexican frontier, among the Navajos and Apaches, where they facilitated raiding, theft, and contraband. A similar Indian adoption of horses, for similar reasons, occurred in Venezuela, Chile, the eastern Chaco, and other locations where Indians could retain attitudes of hostility around the edges of the settled zones and live a migratory, marauding life.

The reasons for the various acts of acceptance and rejection are quite complex, and they remain inadequately studied. In the case of the caciques, we have perhaps a sufficient explanation in their strong motivation for Hispanicization and in the absence of any material obstacle or preventative. In the case of the large, sedentary populations of Mexico and Peru we may postulate both a less powerful motivation and a much larger number of obstacles. The Indian masses, unlike the caciques, did not need motivation to preserve power and status, for they had no power or status to preserve. They were prevented from taking steps towards Hispanicization by Spanish prohibitions, by their own poverty and low estate, and by their often fierce loyalties to traditional Indian society. Mass Indian society continued to function by its own rules, and the pressures of these rules inhibited a single individual from moving in the direction of Hispanicization. Spaniards forbade ordinary Indians to carry swords or firearms. But for most of those who lived in Indian society carrying swords or firearms would have been an antisocial act. Moreover, most could not have afforded swords or firearms if they had wanted them. On the other hand Spaniards did not forbid Indians to use ploughs, and Indians could have constructed the simple Spanish ploughs readily, using only a few pieces of wood. But the obstacles were many. Ploughs would have meant draft animals, together with the problems of feeding, storage, and maintenance, with which Indians were for the most part unfamiliar. A plough agriculture would have meant changing the assignment of properties in the areas of small agricultural plots. It would have meant abandoning the existing intensive agricultural methods and adjusting further to this change. The plough would have modified the rhythm of the agricultural calendar, on which individual and collective life depended. Agricultural practices for Indians were closely bound up with traditional ceremonies and group behaviour. Given the total situation it is not surprising that Indians in the sixteenth century preferred the familiar native digging-stick.

The Indian community itself was a conservative institution, impeding acculturation. Nostalgia for the vanished splendours of the native past was more characteristic of the towns of Peru than of those of Mexico, for the Inca rulers continued to be remembered in drama, pageantry, portraiture, and impersonation in the life of the former Inca empire. Incaic ideology was present to some extent in the foremost of the eighteenth-century Indian rebellions, that of Tupac Amaru. But even in the absence of this kind of reminiscence the Indian community characteristically and positively asserted Indian values. It could absorb a Hispanicized Indian government and the Christian religion and some other powerful influences from the Spanish world and still retain its integral, pervasive, controlling Indian character. Indian godparenthood (*compadrazgo*) and the Indian *cofradías* may perhaps both be understood as defensive institutions. They promoted solidarity and a closing of Indian ranks against outside pressures of all kinds. Against both Spaniards and other Indians an Indian community could proclaim its identity and assert its superiority by the character of its patron saint, the size of its church, or the brilliance of its fireworks at fiesta time. Saints, churches, and fireworks, like godparenthood and the *cofradía*, were Spanish introductions, and they therefore represent a degree of acculturation. But they reinforced the sense of Indian communality in the same way as did the dances and costumes and masks and the other genuinely Indian means of accomplishing the same thing.

An important late colonial instrument of forced acculturation was the *repartimiento* (or *reparto*) *de efectos*. In this the corregidores, though forbidden to engage in commercial activities, were the promoters and main agents of economic distribution among Indians. In some cases they took over this function from Indian merchants, or from white middlemen or itinerant sellers, whose practice in the sixteenth and seventeenth centuries was to visit Indian communities and distribute goods in native markets. In the seventeenth and eighteenth centuries corregidores were able to dispose of surplus goods and goods in general by requiring Indians to purchase them. In some districts corregidores were the covert partners of private merchants in these operations; in others they held an effectual and illegal monopoly on the Indian trade, controlling supplies, sales, and prices. The forced-sale repartimiento was designed to liquidate any produce in the Spanish exchange economy at the expense of the Indian and to extract from Indian hands any money remaining after tribute, ecclesiastical fees, sodality dues, and other expenses had been paid. The Indians were compelled to accept, and pay exorbitant prices for, animals, household goods, clothing, and luxuries such as silk stockings and jewellery that were totally superfluous in Indian life. In the late colonial period some legalization of the *repartimiento de efectos* occurred, but the practice itself continued and the legal limits placed on the amounts and prices of the distributed goods were never restrictive.

It should be observed that changes over time had an important bearing on Indian acculturation. The obstacles, whether physical or psychological, that prevented the adoption of particular Spanish products in the sixteenth century might disappear or change appreciably during the ensuing 200 years. Indians did gradually gain familiarity with Spanish agricultural methods in the labour repartimiento of the sixteenth century and the haciendas and plantations of the seventeenth century. Each type of Spanish enterprise induced a new or incremental acculturation. The two classic types were the wheat farm and the sugar plantation, but there were many others. Apart from agriculture, the accelerated migration to the cities, the further penetration of Spaniards into the hinterland, the unrelieved extension of _mestizaje_, the many Spanish goods that found their way into Indian markets, were all factors inducing a progressive Indian acculturation. The process was slow but it was a cumulative and an accelerating one. Backward steps in the direction of a return to pure Indianism were extremely rare. Acculturation proceeded most rapidly where Indians were few and where whites, Negroes, mestizos, and mulattos were numerous, and the tendency was always for Indian populations to shrink in relation to the other populations. Acculturated Indians ceased to _be_ Indians culturally or in the understanding of the time, and eventually much of the Indian population loss could be attributed to the acculturation itself, the siphoning off of individuals into other groups, the departure of Indians from their towns, and the 'passing' of persons who ceased to behave like Indians and began to behave like mestizos. In time those who left the village and spoke Spanish were understood to be mestizos, and those who stayed and spoke Indian languages were understood to be Indians. Thus the cultural criteria superseded the biological criteria, and the society that was called 'Indian' remained as a residue in constant process of diminution. Again and again the traits of this residue, even those of European origin, were identified as Indian traits.

During the centuries following the conquests Indian community life tended to be overtly peaceful. But local rebellions sometimes erupted, directed against specific controls, such as new taxes, labour demands, _repartimientos de efectos_, and land usurpations. Women and children as well as men characteristically participated. Like so much else in Indian life the rebellions were community enterprises, expressing a corporate Indian protest. They were emotional, intense, and short-lived, often lasting only a few hours. The typical uprising did no serious injury to

Spanish government and was quickly suppressed. The most celebrated uprising, that of Tupac Amaru in Peru in the 1780s, had numerous community implications but differed from others in affecting a larger area, the central and northern Andes, and extending over a longer period, from 1780 to 1782.

Generalizations about Indians under Spanish rule frequently do violence to the variety of conditions in colonial Spanish America. Important differences distinguished one area from another, and in each the situation changed over time. Students of this subject have identified as especially relevant determining factors: the density and social organization of the original Indian population; the proximity of that population to mines and Spanish cities; and the suitability of the area under consideration for Spanish haciendas and plantations. Even in regions at great distances from each other, if conditions such as these were similar, the historian may expect to find approximately similar relations between Spaniards and Indians. Thus the densely populated areas of Mexico and South America reveal a number of points in common, and the same may be said of the lowlands of both coasts. The Chichimeca on the northern frontier were more like the Araucanians on the southern frontier than either people was like any of the intermediate peoples in the 5,000 miles that separated them.

The populous and organized societies of the Mexican and Andean highlands strenuously resisted Spanish conquest, but they succumbed relatively intact. They came into Spanish hands with their internal structures and institutions still in working order, at least at local levels. This meant that families and individual Indians rarely came into direct contact with Spaniards. Indian families and towns survived and individuals retained their relations with their families and their towns. The society's capacity to deliver tribute and labour was not basically modified by conquest. Indians had delivered tribute and labour to their own rulers, and they continued to do so after suffering drastic depopulation and the pressures of the late sixteenth and the seventeenth centuries. Both the depopulation and the pressure were roughly parallel in the central areas of the two viceroyalties, and the Indian responses remained basically similar. From conquest times on we can identify a chronological lag between Mexico and Peru, and we have spoken above of some particular points of difference, but even in the seventeenth and eighteenth centuries central Mexico and central Peru may be classified together and contrasted with other areas.

In the coastal zones the original populations were less dense and the demographic losses more severe than in the highlands. Indian agriculture tended to be 'slash-and-burn' and Indian towns to be less structured and less able to protect their lands. This meant an earlier and larger opportunity for Spaniards to pre-empt fertile valleys and establish haciendas and plantations. Indian agriculture and Indian technology were insufficient to provide the surpluses that were necessary if tribute collection were to be successful. Labour shortages also were more acute. Spaniards dealt directly with Indians as individuals and imported Negro slaves to supplement the declining labour force. Other Indian workers migrated from the highlands and formed new communities or lived on the Spanish estates. Epidemics, forced labour, peonage, racial mixing, and eventually the virtual obliteration of the Indian population characterized Central American and South American coastal areas. The lowlands ceased to be Indian and became mestizo. Similar processes affected large parts of northern Mexico, where the original Indian population was sparse and where Spaniards were attracted by the silver mines. In northern Mexico Indian workers, imported from the south, became labourers in haciendas or mines and eventually disappeared in the mestizo–mulatto mixtures.

Highland and lowland areas, because of their differing climatic and ecological conditions and because of the different types of native society they supported, may thus be broadly distinguished with respect to Indian history under Spanish domination. But a number of other solutions should also be noted. The Jesuit congregations in the Guaraní region of South America provide one of history's foremost examples of benevolent tutelage under ecclesiastical auspices. The Jesuits imposed a strict supervisory control and a communal regimen for which Indians had no alternative after the Jesuits were expelled in 1767. Likewise, in the Yaqui region of northern Mexico a mission society was maintained by communal agricultural labour. The proceeds supported both Indians and Jesuits in the seventeenth and eighteenth centuries. In these marginal mission areas acculturation proceeded in the absence or virtual absence of encomienda, corregimiento, tribute, hacienda, mining, and a lay Spanish population, all of which were so instrumental in the processes of acculturation in other places. The cases are not important in terms of numbers of Indians, for only minuscule populations, in contrast to the large and thickly settled population of the Aztec and Inca empires, were involved. But they indicate something of the typological variety among Spanish influences and Indian responses.

What survived of Indian culture in Spanish America may be identified mainly at the level of individual, family, and community life. The tendency was for communities to become independent of one another, to resist Spanish pressures in community forms, and to survive as depositaries of a remnant Indianism. Upper-class native culture disappeared, not, as Humboldt thought, through death in the conquests, but more gradually over time, and through historical processes of extirpation or adaptation. With some exceptions the caciques, the original leaders in Hispanicization, abandoned Indian society in their own private interests. Others who were not caciques, and not even *principales*, left the villages to join haciendas, plantations, mines, or cities, or to hide in the forests, or to wander the country roads. But the village survivors supported one another in resisting change. They retained, so far as they could, their own forms of activity in agriculture, dress, daily life, food, and local customs. It is a mistake of course to conceive of what happened in Indian America exclusively in terms of what survived and what did not. We are dealing with a complex of relationships, within which mere survival is only one of the significant features of any trait. Others are the place of that trait in the total configuration, its origin and meaning, the emphasis or de-emphasis accorded it, and its convergence or interaction or deviation with respect to other traits. These subjects, and the modifications of all of them over time, we are still in the early stages of understanding.

Part Three

ECONOMIC AND SOCIAL
STRUCTURES: BRAZIL

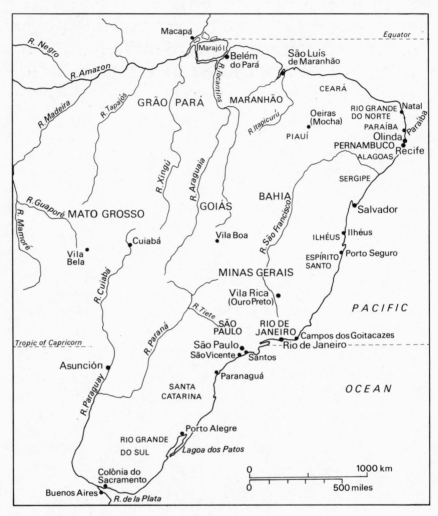

R. Negro
R. Amazon
R. Madeira
R. Tapajós
R. Guaporé
R. Mamoré
R. Cuiabá
R. Paraná
R. Paraguay
R. Xingú
R. Araguaia
R. Tocantins
R. Itapicurú
R. São Francisco
R. Tiete

Macapá
Marajó I.
Belém
do Pará
São Luís
de Maranhão

Equator

GRÃO PARÁ
MARANHÃO
CEARÁ
Oeiras
(Mocha)
RIO GRANDE
DO NORTE
Natal
PARAÍBA
PARAÍBA
Olinda
PIAUÍ
PERNAMBUCO
Recife
ALAGOAS
SERGIPE
BAHIA
MATO GROSSO
GOIÁS
Salvador
Vila Boa
ILHÉUS
Ilhéus
Cuiabá
ESPÍRITO
SANTO
Porto Seguro
Vila
Bela
MINAS GERAIS
PACIFIC
Vila Rica
(Ouro Preto)
SÃO
PAULO
RIO DE
JANEIRO
Campos dos Goitacazes
Rio de Janeiro
Tropic of Capricorn
São Paulo
São Vicente
Santos
Asunción
Paranaguá
OCEAN
SANTA
CATARINA
Porto Alegre
RIO GRANDE
DO SUL
Lagoa dos Patos
Colônia do
Sacramento
Buenos Aires
R. de la Plata

0   1000 km
0   500 miles

Colonial Brazil

12

COLONIAL BRAZIL, *c.* 1580–*c.* 1750: PLANTATIONS AND PERIPHERIES

SUGAR AND SLAVES

'A sugar mill is hell and all the masters of them are damned', wrote Father Andrés de Gouvea from Bahia in 1627.[1] Time and time again observers who witnessed the roaring furnaces, the boiling cauldrons, the glistening black bodies and the infernal whirling of the mill during the 24-hour day of the sugar *safra*, or harvest, used the same image of hell. Along with mining, the production of sugar was the most complex and mechanized activity that Europeans carried out in the sixteenth and seventeenth centuries, and its 'modern' and industrial nature shocked its pre-industrial observers. Yet it was from this nightmarish scene that the society and economy of Brazil grew. During the century from 1580 to 1680 Brazil was the world's largest producer and exporter of sugar. It was in the context of plantation agriculture and sugar that colonial society was formed. Like the sugar-loaf itself, society crystallized with white Europeans at the top, tan-coloured people of mixed race receiving lesser esteem, and black slaves considered, like the dark *panela* sugar, to be of the lowest quality.

By the final decades of the sixteenth century Brazil no longer resembled the trading-fort establishments of the Portuguese West African and Asian colonies. The shift from private to royal initiative in the exploitation and settlement of the vast Brazilian coastline, the creation of the captaincy system in the 1530s, the subsequent establishment of royal control in 1549, the elimination and enslavement of Indian peoples and the transformation of the principal economy from dyewood cutting to sugar-cane agriculture were all central elements in the

[1] Arquivo Nacional de Torre do Tombo (Lisbon) [ANTT], Cartório dos Jesuitas, maço 68, n. 334.

colony's formation. Although missionaries and prospectors or slavers occasionally penetrated the interior, for the most part settlement remained concentrated along the narrow coastal strip, where good soils, adequate climatic conditions, labour supply, and cheap transport to ports favoured the sugar industry during a period of increasing demand in European markets. Effective governmental control was restricted to the coast and above all to the archipelago of ports and small agricultural towns along the eastern littoral from Pernambuco to São Vicente. By 1580 Brazil, with a population of some 60,000 of whom 30,000 were Europeans, had become a colony of settlement, but of a peculiar kind; a tropical plantation colony capitalized from Europe, supplying European demand for a tropical crop and characterized by a labour system based on the enslavement first of American Indians and then of imported African workers.

Climatic, geographic, political, and economic factors made the captaincies of Pernambuco and Bahia the centres of the colonial sugar economy. Successful cane cultivation depended on the right combination of soil and rainfall. Brazilian planters favoured the thick black and dark red *massapé* soils whose fertility obviated the need for fertilizer. Colonial authors spoke of lands planted in cane continuously for 60 or more years. It was said that a common planter's test was to stamp his boot into the ground: if his foot sank up to the ankle in the *massapé*, then the land was good for sugar. Over time much cane was also planted in sandier soils, the *salões* of the uplands, which while less suitable were adequate for sugar-cane. A reliable rainfall of 1,000–2,000 mm, needed for cane cultivation, was found along the coast.

As the sugar industry of the north-east was above all an export activity, the siting of the plantations in relation to the ports was the key factor in their precise location. Land transport depended on large ox-carts and their use was hindered by the lack of roads and bridges. The fact that the *massapé* turned into a quagmire after heavy rains made land transportation even more difficult. Water transport was therefore crucial. Mills (often driven by water power) on the *beira mar* (sea coast) or on rivers were always more valuable because of their location. In Pernambuco the industry developed particularly in the *massapé* of the flood plain (*várzea*) of the Capibaribe, Ipojuca and Jaboatão rivers. Here the soils were good and transport down river to the port facilities of Recife was relatively easy and inexpensive. In Bahia,

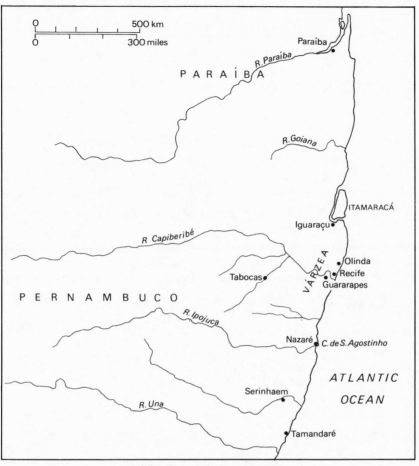

The Pernambuco coast

Source: C. R. Boxer, *Salvador de Sá and the struggle for Brazil and Angola 1602–1686* (London, 1952),

the Bay of All Saints was an excellent inland sea and even contemporaries noted the particular Bahian dependence on boats for moving goods to the *engenhos*[2] and sugar to the wharves of Salvador. The biggest and most

---

[2] The term 'plantation' was never used by the Portuguese or Spaniards of this period but while, strictly speaking, *engenho* referred only to the mill for grinding the sugar cane, the term came to be applied to the whole unit: the mill itself, the associated buildings for boiling and purging the cane syrup, the canefields (*fazendas de canas*), pastures, slave quarters, estate house (*casa grande*), slaves, cattle, and other equipment. In this chapter it is used to describe both the sugar mill itself and the entire economic complex.

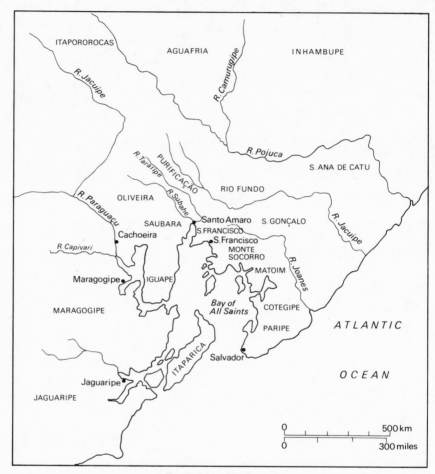

The Bahian Recôncavo

productive mills in the Bahian Recôncavo were at the water's edge.
Some regions had adequate soil and rainfall but nevertheless failed to
develop into major centres of production. Ilhéus provides a good
example. Besides constant Indian attacks, the distance from a major port
retarded the sugar industry throughout the colonial period. Some Ilhéus
sugar was shipped to Europe from Salvador, but the area did not
prosper.

Because the documentary record of Brazil's economic history in the
sixteenth century is thin and because newly established engenhos were

Table 1 *Growth of the Brazilian sugar industry, 1570–1629*
(number of engenhos)

Captaincy	1 Gandavo 1570	2 Cardim 1583	% growth p.a. (1 to 2)	3 Campos Moreno 1612	% growth p.a. (2 to 3)	4 Cadena 1629	% growth p.a. (3 to 4)
Pará, Ceara, Maranhão							
Rio Grande				1			
Paraíba				12		24	(4.3)
Itamaraca	1			10		18	(3.5)
Pernambuco	23	66	(8.4)	90	(1.0)	150	(3.1)
Sergipe				1			
Bahia	18	36	(5.4)	50	(1.1)	80	(2.8)
Ilhéus	8	3		5		4	
Porto Seguro	5	1		1			
Espírito Santo	1	6		8*		8	
Rio de Janeiro		3		14*	(5.8)	60	(7.9)
São Vicente, Santo Amaro	4					2	
Totals	60	115	(5.1)	192	(1.8)	350	(3.6)

Sources: Frédéric Mauro, *Portugal et l'Atlantique* (Paris, 1960), 102–211. Column 1 based on Pero de Magalhães [de Gandavo], *The Histories of Brazil* (2 vols., New York, 1922). Column 2, Fernão Cardim, *Tratados da terra e gente do Brasil* (3rd edn, São Paulo, 1978). For a slightly higher figure (120) based on a synthesis of a number of sources (1583–5) see Johnson, *CHLA* 1, ch. 8, table 1. Column 3, Diogo de Campos Moreno, *Livro que dá razão do Estado do Brasil* [1612] (Rio de Janeiro, 1968). Additional figures (starred) from report of Jácome Monteiro [1610] printed in Serafim Leite, *História da Companhia de Jesus no Brasil* [*HCJB*] (10 vols., Lisbon, 1938–50), VIII, 393–425. Column 4, (Pedro Cadena de Vilhasanti), 'Descripción de la provincia del Brasil', in Frédéric Mauro (ed.), *Le Brésil au XVIIe siècle* (Coimbra, 1963). See n. 4 below.

granted a ten-year exemption from the tithe by an *alvará* (royal decree) of 20 July 1551, thereby making tithe records unreliable for calculating the sugar economy's growth, it is difficult to trace the progress of the sugar industry. Between 1570 and 1630 various observers in Brazil did, however, leave descriptions of the colony which included estimates of the number of sugar mills in each captaincy. While these figures vary and are sometimes inconsistent, it is possible to establish from them a secular trend in engenho construction as an indication of the industry's growth (see table 1).

In 1570 Pedro Magalhães de Gandavo reported that there were 60 engenhos in Brazil, of which two-thirds were located in the captaincies of Pernambuco (23) and Bahia (18) (table 1, column 1). During the next fifteen years the number of mills appears to have almost doubled, according to reports written between 1583 and 1585 (table 1, column 2). The rate of growth in Pernambuco, 8.4 per cent per annum, was considerably more than in Bahia, but the industry's growth in both captaincies was striking. The rapid growth seems to have resulted from continually rising prices for sugar in the European market and the availability of capital for investment in Brazil. Negative factors were overcome. For instance, the first legislation against Indian slavery appeared in 1570 but seems to have been successfully circumvented by the planters so that large numbers of Indians were still available as 'cheap' labour. It was also during this period that a regular slave trade from Angola and Guinea to Brazil was established.

The next period, between the mid-1580s and 1612 (table 1, columns 2 and 3), was one of much less rapid growth in the major sugar-producing captaincies, although the formerly undeveloped Rio de Janeiro area experienced considerable expansion. The whole colony's annual rate of new engenho construction dropped from 5.1 per cent to only 1.8 per cent. A report by Diogo de Campos Moreno of 1612 placed the number of mills in Pernambuco at 90, with another 23 in the neighbouring captaincies of Paraíba, Itamaracá, and Rio Grande. While this was a significant increase over the 66 mills reported for Pernambuco in 1583, the rate of growth was considerably less than in the previous period. The pace of increase in Bahia was even slower, going from 36 mills in 1583 to 50 in 1612, an annual growth rate of only 1 per cent. Brazil had by now almost 200 engenhos producing about 5,000–9,000 metric tons of sugar each year.

In the period following Campos Moreno's report engenho construction began to speed up again. Expansion in the post-1612 period seems to have been stimulated more by a new technical innovation than by favourable prices. European prices, in fact, were unstable in the 1620s and planters could not depend on a steadily rising curve as they had done previously. Sometime between 1608 and 1612 a new method of mill construction based on an arrangement of three vertical rollers was either introduced into Brazil or developed there. While it is not yet clear what effect this new system had on productivity, it does appear that the new mills were much less expensive to build and operate. The three-roller mill, the *engenho de tres paus*, eliminated some of the processes previously needed and reduced the complexity of making sugar. This innovation seems to explain the somewhat surprising expansion of the industry in the face of unstable market conditions.[3] Older mills were converted to the new system and many new ones were built.

Pedro Cadena de Vilhasanti's report of 1629 (table 1, column 4)[4] listed 150 mills in Pernambuco and 80 in Bahia, indicating a growth rate of 3.1 and 2.8 per cent per annum respectively between 1612 and 1629. Also striking was the effect of the invention on other captaincies, such as Paraíba, where the number of mills doubled to 24 (4.3 per cent per annum). The lands of Guanabara bay around Rio de Janeiro, which had previously been devoted mostly to manioc agriculture, were now also turned over increasingly to sugar. In 1629 there were 60 engenhos operating there, although most of these appear to have been small in scale. By the time of the Dutch invasion of Pernambuco in 1630 there were approximately 350 sugar mills operating in Brazil (table 1, column 4). The year 1630, in fact, probably marked the apogee of the engenho regime, for, while the number of mills was to expand and prices were occasionally to recover in the future, never again would Brazilian planters be as free from foreign competition, nor would Brazilian sugars dominate the Atlantic markets in the same way. Neither was the Brazilian sugar economy to be free of internal structural problems. Brazil's first historian, Fr. Vicente do Salvador, had complained in 1627 that the three-roller mill and the expansion it had engendered were a mixed blessing. 'What advantage is there', he asked, 'to making so much sugar if the quantity decreases the value and yields such a low price that it is below cost?'[5] It was a prophetic question.

How much sugar was produced? Just as it is difficult to establish with any certainty the number of engenhos, it is no easier to ascertain their size or productive capacity. It was said that a small mill could produce

---

[3] Antônio Barros de Castro, 'Brasil, 1610: mudanças técnicas e conflitos sociais', *Pesquiza e Planejamento Econômico*, 10/3 (Dec. 1980), 679–712.

[4] The anonymous report of 1629, 'Descripción de la provincia del Brasil', published by Frédéric Mauro in *Le Brésil au XVIIᵉ siècle*, 167–91, is the same as that of Pedro Cudena [*sic*] offered by him in 1634 to the count-duke of Olivares. Cudena is surely Pedro Cadena de Vilhasanti, Provedor mór do Brasil. His report is found in Martin Franzbach's bibliography published in *Jahrbuch für Geschichte von Staat, Wirtschaft und Gesellschaft Lateinamerikas [JGSWGL]* (1970), VII, 164–200.

[5] Fr. Vicente do Salvador, *História do Brasil* (4th edn, São Paulo, 1965), cap. 47, 366.

3,000–4,000 arrobas (43–58 metric tons) per annum and a large unit
10,000–12,000 arrobas (145–175 tons.)[6] Productivity in a given year
depended on climate, rainfall, management, and exogenous factors such
as the interruption of maritime trade. Thus estimates made by colonial
observers vary widely from averages per mill of 160 tons in Bahia to
15 tons in Pernambuco. It appears that the average Brazilian production
per engenho decreased in the later seventeenth century owing to the proliferation of smaller units in Rio de Janeiro and Pernambuco. Moreover,
individual mill productivity also seems to have declined in the eighteenth
century, although the reasons for this are not clear. Table 2, below,
presents various estimates of productivity, among which those of Israel
da Costa in 1623, the Junta do Tabaco in 1702, and Caldas in 1754 are
noteworthy because they are based on actual counts, not estimates. Total
Brazilian production rose from 6,000 tons in 1580 to 10,000 in 1610.
By the 1620s a productive capacity of 1–1.5 million arrobas
(14,545–21,818 tons) had been reached, although it was not always
fulfilled. These levels do not appear to have been altered until the period
after 1750. Even so there were changes within the structure of the
industry that complicate calculations of production. It is difficult to
estimate sugar production in Dutch Brazil (1630–54). Pernambuco and
its neighbouring captaincies had 166 engenhos in 1630 but warfare and
disruption had reduced that number to about 120 mills in operation by
the end of the decade. The total productive capacity of Dutch Brazil
probably never exceeded 600,000 arrobas despite the efforts of Governor
John Maurits of Nassau to stimulate the industry. Dutch operations
against Bahia destroyed engenhos there as well and the military
campaigns and guerrilla operations in Dutch Brazil after 1645 devastated
that sugar economy. Pernambuco took over a century to recover from
the destruction of mills, cattle, and capital resources. In the later
seventeenth century Pernambucan mills were smaller on the average
than those of Bahia, which was by that time the leading Brazilian sugar
producer. By the 1670s all Brazilian regions faced new competition from
Caribbean production. When in 1710 André João Antonil published his
account of Brazilian sugar production he estimated a total of under
18,500 tons, a figure falling within the range already reached in the
1620s.

[6] The Portuguese *arroba* = 14.5 kg. All weights here are given in metric units unless otherwise
stated.

Table 2 *Estimates of sugar production, 1591–1758*

	Date	Region	Number of engenhos	Total production (arrobas)	Production per engenho (arrobas)	(tons)
A	1591	Pernambuco	63	378,000	6,000	87
B	1610	Bahia	63	300,000	4,762	69
C	1614	Brazil	(192)[a]	700,000	3,646	53
D	1623	Pernambuco	119	544,072	4,824	70
E	1637	Brazil	(350)[b]	937,500	2,678	39
F	1637	Brazil	350	900,000	2,571	37
G	1675	Bahia	69[c]	517,500	7,500	109
H	1702	Bahia/Sergipe	(249)[d]	507,697	2,039	30
I	1710	Brazil	528	1,295,700	2,454	36
		Bahia	146	507,500	3,476	51
		Pernambuco	246	403,500	1,750	26
		Rio de Janeiro	136	357,700	2,630	38
J	1751	Pernambuco	276	240,000	870	13
K	1755	Bahia	172	357,115	2,076	30
L	1758	Bahia	180	400,000	2,222	32

[a] Number of engenhos from Campos Moreno's account of 1612.
[b] Number of engenhos from Pedro Cadena; see source **G**.
[c] Number of engenhos is obviously too low.
[d] Number of engenhos is probably too high, since the production of all growers including those without mills was listed.

Sources: **A.** Domingos de Abreu e Brito, *Um inquérito à vida administrativa e económica de Angola e do Brasil* (Coimbra, 1931), 59; **B.** Father Jácome Monteiro in Leite, *HCJB*, VIII, 404; **C.** Report of André Farto da Costa, Arquivo Histórico Ultramarino (Lisbon) [AHU], Bahia, papéis avulsos, caixa 1a; **D.** Joseph Israel da Costa, in *Revista do Museu do Açúcar*, 1 (1968), 25–36; **E.** Geraldo de Onizio in Serafim Leite (ed.), *Relação diária do cerco da Bahia* (Lisbon, 1941), 110; **F.** Pedro Cadena in Mauro, *Le Brésil au XVII* *siècle*, 170; **G.** Francisco de Brito Freyre, *História da guerra brasílica* (Lisbon, 1675), 75; **H.** ANTT, Junta do Tabaco, various maços; **I.** André João Antonil, *Cultura e opulência do Brasil por suas drogas e minas* [1711] (ed. Andrée Mansuy; Paris, 1968), 274–5; **J.** José Ribeiro Jr., *Colonização e monópolio no nordeste brasileiro* (São Paulo, 1976), 67, 136–7; **K.** José Antônio Caldas, *Noticia geral desta capitania da Bahia* (Salvador, 1951), 420–38; **L.** Coelho de Mello in *Anais da Biblioteca Nacional do Rio de Janeiro* [*ABNRJ*], 31 (1908), 321.

The engenho, the central feature of Brazilian life, was a complex combination of land, technical skills, coerced labour, management, and capital. Sugar production was a peculiar activity because it combined an intensive agriculture with a highly technical, semi-industrial mechanical process. The need to process sugar-cane in the field meant that each engenho was both a factory and a farm demanding not only a large agricultural labour force for the planting and harvesting of the cane but also an army of skilled blacksmiths, carpenters, masons, and technicians who understood the intricacies and mysteries of the sugar-making process. In order to understand the social organization of the Brazilian colony it is essential to know how sugar was transformed from the cane into its refined state.

Although there were regional variations in the seasons and intensity of the sugar-making cycle, the general process and technology was the same throughout Brazil. We shall use the cycle of Bahia as an example. Sugar-cane is a perennial plant and will yield crops for a number of years, although the yield of juice will gradually diminish. After planting, the cane needs fifteen to eighteen months to mature before being cut for the first time, but it can be harvested again after nine months. In Bahia there were two planting seasons. New fields planted in July and August could be cut between October and November the following year. The second planting cycle, in late February and March, was designed to provide cane in August and September of the next harvest. Once planted the cane needed to be weeded three times, an onerous task usually performed by gangs of 30 to 40 slaves. Timing the planting of fields to ensure a constant supply of cane during the *safra*, or harvest, required particular skill and foresight.

The sugar cycle in Brazil was determined by the *safra*. In Bahia it began in late July and continued until late May. This was a time of intense activity, for to obtain the highest yields of juice the cane had to be cut at exactly the right moment, and once cut it had to be processed quickly, otherwise the cane would dry out and the juice go sour. During the safra the engenho was alive with activity. Groups of two or three dozen slaves were placed in the cane fields in pairs, often consisting of a man and a woman. Each pair, called a *fouce* (literally, a scythe), was given a quota of canes to cut and bind which was expressed in 'hands and fingers'; ten canes to each bundle, ten bundles to each finger, and seven hands or 4,200 canes a day to be cut by the man and bound by the woman.[7] The canes were then placed in ox-carts, often driven by children or older slaves, or were loaded in boats to be brought to the mill.

The mills were of two types: those driven by water-wheels (*engenho*

---

[7] This is the quota reported in Antonil, *Cultura e opulência*. These quotas were subject to change according to time and place.

real) and those powered by oxen or, more rarely, horses. The original method of milling made use of large millstones or presses using a screw arrangement. A major technological advance was the introduction in the first decade of the seventeenth century of a mill press composed of three vertical rollers, covered with metal and cogged in such a way that it could be moved by one large drive-wheel powered by water or animals. The new mill arrangement was apparently cheaper to build and operate, especially for animal-powered mills. This innovation led to a proliferation of engenhos and, since water-power was no longer so essential, an expansion of sugar mills into areas farther from water courses. Aside from this innovation, the technology of the sugar mills changed very little until the late eighteenth century.

During the safra the pace of work was exhausting. The engenhos began operations at four o'clock in the afternoon and continued until ten o'clock the following morning, at which time the equipment was cleaned and repaired. After a rest of four hours, the mill began again. Slave women passed the canes through the rollers of the press and the juice was squeezed from the cane. The juice was then moved through a battery of copper kettles in which it was progressively boiled, skimmed, and purified. This was one of the most delicate stages of the process and it depended on the skill and experience of the sugar master and the men who tended each cauldron. The task of stoking the furnaces under the six cauldrons was particularly laborious and was sometimes assigned as a punishment to the most recalcitrant and rebellious slaves.

After cooling, the cane syrup was poured into conical pottery moulds and set into racks in the purging house. There, under the direction of the *purgador*, slave women prepared the sugar pots for draining the molasses, which could be either reprocessed to produce lower-grade sugar or distilled into rum. The sugar remaining in the mould crystallized and after two months was taken from the mould and placed for drying on a large raised platform. Under the direction of two slave women, the *mães do balcão* (the mothers of the platform), the sugar-loaves were separated. The higher-quality white sugar was separated from the darker, lower-quality *muscavado*. In Brazil the larger mills usually produced a ratio of two to three times the amount of white to *muscavado*. The sugar was then crated under the watchful eye of the *caixeiro* (crater), who also extracted the tithe and, when necessary, divided the sugar between the mill and the cane farmers. The crates were then stamped

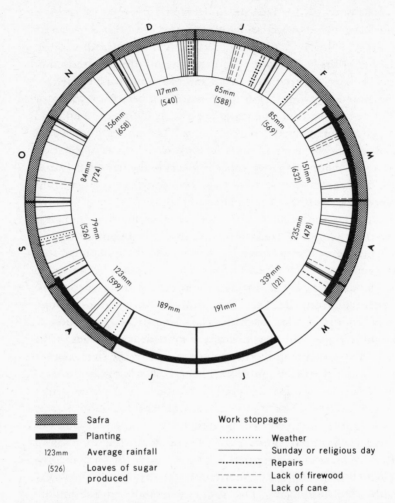

Safra

Planting

123mm   Average rainfall

(526)   Loaves of sugar
         produced

Work stoppages

············   Weather
—————   Sunday or religious day
–··—··—··–   Repairs
– – – – –   Lack of firewood
––––––––   Lack of cane

Fig. 1. Sugar plantation in Bahia: the agricultural cycle (based on the
Engenho Sergipe safra of 1650–1)

with marks indicating weight, quality, and ownership before being
transported by boat or ox-cart to the nearest seaport.[8]

The eight- to ten-months-long safra was a distinguishing feature of
the Brazilian sugar industry and its distinctive advantage. Records from

[8] The weight of the sugar crates varied over time. In the early seventeenth century, 15–20 arrobas
(480–640 lb) was common. By the eighteenth century, the average weight was calculated at
35–40 arrobas (1,120–1,280 lb).

the Jesuit-owned Engenho Sergipe do Conde in Bahia reveal an average safra lasting some 300 days. This figure compares favourably with the 120-day average of Jamaican sugar mills in the eighteenth century. There were, however, constant stoppages for Sundays, saints' days, poor weather, breakdowns, and shortages of cane and firewood. In Engenho Sergipe's 310-day safra of 1651, no cane was milled on 86 days: 56 for religious reasons, twelve for repairs, and eighteen for shortages.[9] Figure 1 represents the Bahian sugar year using the work stoppages of Engenho Sergipe in 1650–1 as an example of the interruptions experienced. Lay planters, it should be noted, were far less careful about observing Sundays and holy days, despite the denunciations and warnings of various churchmen. Thus, the Engenho Sergipe cycle represents a minimum number of working days. Finally, it should be noted that, despite costly interruptions, the Brazilian engenho enjoyed a favourable environment for sugar-cane cultivation and a comparative advantage in the length of its productive year. These were conditions especially conducive to slavery as a form of labour. The Brazilian sugar year had virtually no 'dead period', no time when slaves were unprofitably left without any useful occupation. Slaves could be used almost throughout the year, and they were. Given the length of the safra, the nature of the labour, and the rhythm of the working day, it is little wonder that high slave mortality was a constant feature of the Brazilian sugar industry.

Even this brief sketch of the sugar-making process makes clear its intensity and complexity. Given the existing technology, the peculiarities of sugar production imposed a certain rhythm and pace on the operations that made the period of the safra one of both exhausting labour and delicate precision. Integrating the sequence of planting, harvesting, milling, boiling, and purging demanded skilled management in order to avoid shortages or surpluses and to ensure a constant level of production. Technicians were needed to build and maintain the mill machinery, and at each stage of the sugar-making process skilled and experienced personnel were needed. The construction and supply of an engenho demanded a large capital outlay and access to credit in the face of the harvest's uncertainties. Engenhos often employed ten or twenty free men as artisans, managers, or skilled labourers. Salaries for such personnel could equal a quarter of the mill's yearly operating costs. Large quantities of firewood for the furnaces and great numbers of oxen

[9] *Documentos para a história do açúcar* (3 vols., Rio de Janeiro, 1954–63), II, 495–532.

for motive power were also constant items of expenditure. But, when planters discussed the operating cost of an engenho, it was the slaves who demanded their attention above all else. An average engenho needed 60–100 slaves, but a large estate producing over 100 metric tons a year could have 200 or more. Above all, the nature and organization of the labour force of the engenho determined the pattern of Brazilian society.

'The most solid properties in Brazil are slaves', wrote Governor Luís Vahia Monteiro in 1729, 'and a man's wealth is measured by having more or fewer... for there are lands enough, but only he who has slaves can be master of them.'[10] By 1580 slavery was already firmly established as the principal form of labour in the colony. The early expansion of the sugar industry took place with Indians working both as slaves and as contract workers drawn from Jesuit-controlled villages. In the 1560s the Indian population was devastated by a series of epidemics. Thereafter demographic collapse combined with physical resistance and aversion to plantation labour to make the use of Indian slaves less desirable for the Portuguese planters. In addition, under pressure from the Jesuits, the crown began to turn against the enslavement of Indians. The first prohibition was issued in 1570 and after the Iberian union further laws were promulgated in 1595 and 1609. Although this legislation did not eliminate Indian slavery entirely, in conjunction with high mortality, low productivity, and the general resistance of the Indian peoples, it made the seemingly stronger and more easily controlled African labour more attractive even though more expensive. The Portuguese had already made use of African bondsmen at home and in the Atlantic sugar colonies of Madeira and São Tomé. There is some evidence to show that the first Africans introduced as plantation labour had already been trained in the complexities of sugar-making and were placed in the more skilled positions where the planters' investment in training was less likely to be lost through disease. Europeans generally considered the value of Indian labour to be less than that of African, a situation which was reflected in the pricing of Indian slaves at one-third to one-quarter of the value of Africans. Even as free workers, Indians were paid less than free blacks and mulattos performing similar tasks.

The transition from Indian to African labour, although under way from the 1570s on, was slow and not fully achieved in the plantation

---

[10] *Publicações do Arquivo Nacional* (1915), xv, 364–5.

areas until the third decade of the seventeenth century. In Pernambuco, where there were 66 engenhos in 1585, Father Cardim reported 2,000 African slaves. Assuming an average of 100 slaves on each engenho, it would appear that two-thirds of the slaves were still Indians. Cardim also reported that Bahia had some 3,000 Africans and 8,000 slave and free Indians on its engenhos. At the Engenho Sergipe the transition can be plainly seen. Its slave force in 1574 was only 7 per cent African, but by 1591 it was 37 per cent African, and by 1638 totally African or Afro-Brazilian.

Statistics on the slave trade and general population figures are lacking for the period under discussion, so it is difficult to ascertain the size of the slave population. The best estimates at present are that about 4,000 slaves a year were imported between 1570 and 1630 and that there was a total African slave population of 13,000–15,000 in the colony by 1600. The level of imports rose to 7,000–8,000 a year until 1680, when the total slave population was about 150,000. Imports probably declined over the next two decades until the need for slaves in the gold-mining areas created a vast new demand. In the first half of the eighteenth century Bahia took some 5,000–8,000 slaves a year. Rio de Janeiro received 156,638 from Luanda alone between 1734 and 1769. By the eighteenth century slaves composed about half of the population in the north-eastern captaincies, but in sugar-growing regions they often constituted between 65 and 70 per cent of the inhabitants.

Slave trade figures were particularly important in the Brazilian case because it appears that natural increase in the slave population was negligible, if it existed at all. High levels of infant and adolescent mortality and a marked sexual imbalance were the major factors responsible for this situation. A survey of agricultural slaves in the Bahian Recôncavo reveals a sex ratio of two men to every woman.[11] This imbalance was continually exacerbated by the tendency within the slave trade to favour men over women and adults over children. Brazilian planters became particularly tied to the Atlantic trade and tended to reject natural growth as a viable alternative because child mortality rates were high and raising a slave child for twelve or fourteen years until maturity was a risky investment. Less than 20 per cent of the slave force was under the age of fourteen. The low fertility and high

---

[11] These figures and those that follow in this section are based on preliminary analysis of 1,740 slaves listed in Bahian inventories of agricultural properties between 1689 and 1826 drawn from Arquivo Público do Estado da Bahia (Salvador) [APB], secção judiciária.

Table 3 *Slave productivity in relation to original purchase price* (réis)

Date	1 Price per arroba of white sugar	2 Price per male slave	3 Annual value of slave output (col. 1 × 40)[a]	4 Monthly value of slave output (col. 3 ÷ 12)	5 'Replacement life' in months (col.
1608	1$080	30$000	43$200	3$600	8.3
1622	556	29$000	22$290	1$860	15.6
1635	812	39$000	32$749	2$730	14.3
1650	1$125	49$000	45$151	3$760	13.0
1670	1$177	45$000	47$080	3$923	11.5
1680	1$109	43$000	44$360	3$696	11.6
1700[b]	1$600	80$000	64$800	5$400	14.8
1710[c]	1$200	120$000	48$000	4$000	30.0
1751[d]	1$400	140$000	56$000	4$666	30.0

[a] Estimate of one crate of 40 arrobas per slave from José da Silva Lisboa (1780).
[b] Values represent averages from 1698 to 1704.
[c] Figures based on Antonil, *Cultura e opulência.*
[d] AHU, Bahia, caixa 61 (paper submitted to Mesa da Inspeção). All other figures based on accounts of Engenho Sergipe, Bahia.

mortality rates, estimated by planters at 5–10 per cent a year, could be offset by the high sugar prices and the readily available replacements through the slave trade. Throughout the first half of the seventeenth century a slave could produce enough sugar to recover his original cost in between thirteen and sixteen months, and, even after the steep rise of slave prices after 1700, replacement value could be earned in 30 months (see table 3).[12] Thus there was little incentive to ameliorate the conditions of labour or to change the existing manner of slave management. The engenhos consumed slaves and the slave trade replaced them.

Finally, the pattern of the slave trade had two other effects: one demographic and the other cultural. Because mortality seems to have been particularly high among the newly-arrived (*boçal*) slaves, high levels of importation, together with the sexual imbalance, tended to

[12] Table 3 presents a calculation of slave productivity in sugar in relation to the original purchase price of a male field hand. The calculations are based exclusively on the higher-priced white sugar, which was produced in ratios of 2 : 1 or 3 : 1 over *muscavado* on most Brazilian engenhos. This method of calculation probably lowers the estimate of months for replacement by one-third. At present it is not possible to calculate slave maintenance costs, although a report of 1635 set these at about 2 milréis per slave a year. Since slaves also produced food crops which also cannot be measured, I have left both the maintenance costs and non-sugar production out of the table.

create a self-perpetuating cycle of importation and mortality throughout most of the period under discussion. Moreover, the constant arrival of newly enslaved blacks tended to reinforce African culture in Brazil. There were regional variations. Rio de Janeiro, for example, was closely tied to Angola and Benguela, while Bahia traded intensely with the Mina coast. While a great deal is known about the Yoruba traditions introduced in the late eighteenth century, it is more difficult to say much about the African cultural elements brought by the earlier slaves. Planters and administrators complained about 'witchcraft' in a general fashion. *Calundus*, or ceremonies of divination accompanied by music, were reported in the early eighteenth century by one observer, who complained that planters ignored these rites in order to get along with their slaves, and that the latter then passed them on to freedmen and even to whites.[13]

While slaves were used for all kinds of labour, most could be found working on the engenhos and cane farms. The majority of these were field hands, 'slaves of sickle and hoe' (*escravos de fouce e enxada*), but those who had artisan skills and those who worked inside the mill house as kettlemen were more highly valued by the masters. House slaves, often mulattos, were favoured but relatively few in numbers. Occasionally an engenho would employ slaves in managerial roles, as drivers, for instance, or (more rarely) as the sugar master. In the Bahian survey mentioned above, 54 per cent were listed as field slaves, 13 per cent worked in the mill; 13 per cent were house slaves, 7 per cent were artisans; 10 per cent were boatmen and carters; while slaves in managerial roles constituted only 1 per cent of those listed with occupations. Brazilian-born blacks (*crioulos*) and mulattos were preferred as house slaves and mulattos were often chosen for artisan training.

The occupational distribution of the slave force reflects the hierarchies of the slave society. Distinctions were made between the *boçal*, newly arrived from Africa, and the *ladino*, or acculturated slave. In addition, a hierarchy of colour was also recognized in which mulattos received preferential treatment. The two gradations of colour and culture intersected in a predictable fashion, with Africans tending towards one end of both scales, mulattos at the other and *crioulos* between. The preference shown towards mulattos, and their advantages, were accompanied by prejudice against them as inconstant, sly, and 'uppity'. These hierarchies of colour and culture were, of course, created by the

---

[13] Nuno Marques Pereira, *Compendio narrativo do peregrino da America* (Lisbon, 1728), 115–130.

slaveowners, and it is difficult to know how far they were accepted by the slaves themselves; but the rivalry between Africans and *crioulos* in militia units and the existence of religious brotherhoods based on colour or African 'nationhood' indicate that these distinctions were maintained by the coloured population.

The once popular myth of the benign nature of Brazilian slavery has to a large extent been laid to rest by scholarship in the last two decades. Most contemporary observers commented that food, clothing, and punishment were the essentials of slave management. There seem to have been generous portions of the last, but provisions for slaves in the plantation zones were minimal. While there were considerable efforts to convert slaves to Catholicism and to have them participate in the sacraments of the church, the reality seems to have been quite different. High rates of illegitimacy among the slave population and low birth rates indicate that legal marriage was infrequent. Rather than viewing slaves as members of an extended family, it would seem that a natural hostility born of the master–slave relationship was paramount. The administrator of Engenho Santana in Ilhéus complained that the 178 slaves under his care were 'so many devils, thieves, and enemies'.[14] The counterpoint of plantation life was formed by the master's demands and the slave's recalcitrance – expressed by flight, malingering, complaint, and sometimes violence. Planters cajoled and threatened, using both punishments and rewards to stimulate effort. Slaves in the mill were given sugar juice or rum, slaves might receive extra provisions, 'gifts', or even the promise of eventual freedom, in order to coax them into co-operating. The following statement made by an engenho administrator in the 1720s describes vividly the texture of Brazilian plantation slavery and the slaves' ability to manoeuvre within their subordinate position:

the time of their service is no more than five hours a day and much less when the work is far off. It is the multitude that gets anything done just as in an anthill. And when I reprimand them with the example of whites and their slaves who work well, they answer that the whites work and earn money while they get nothing and the slaves of those whites work because they are given enough clothes and food...It is sometimes necessary to visit the quarters two or three times a day to throw them out,...those that are only feigning illness. God knows what I suffer by not resorting to punishment in order to avoid runaways. And when I complain, they point to their stomach and say, 'The belly makes

14 ANTT, Cartório dos Jesuitas, maço 15, n. 23.

the ox go', giving me to understand that I do not feed them. It is my sins that have sent me to such an *engenho*.[15]

There were a limited number of responses to the conditions of slavery, ranging from acquiescence to rebellion. The most common form of resistance was flight, which was endemic in the plantation areas. Inventories of properties almost always list one or two slaves who had escaped. Planters hired slave-hunting 'bush captains' (*capitães do mato*), themselves often free blacks, to hunt down the fugitives. In 1612 'bush captains' were created in the eight parishes of Pernambuco for slave control and by 1625 the town council of Salvador was setting fixed prices for the capture of fugitive slaves. When they could the escapees formed themselves into exile communities (*mocambos* or *quilombos*), in inaccessible areas. Usually small in size (under 100 people), they survived by a combination of subsistence agriculture and raiding. Expeditions were organized to destroy them, led by 'bush captains' in command of Indian auxiliaries. While most of the *mocambos* were short-lived, usually a few fugitives would escape recapture, and a new community would spring up.

In the period under discussion the most important escapee community was the great group of villages located in present-day Alagoas and known collectively as Palmares. The first *mocambos* in this region were probably formed around 1605 and the number of inhabitants swelled during the period of the Dutch invasion of Pernambuco. Expeditions were sent out periodically by both Portuguese and Dutch authorities to destroy Palmares, but all of them were unsuccessful. By the 1670s, the number of escaped slaves in Palmares was reported at over 20,000, probably an exaggeration since such numbers would have equalled all the slaves on Pernambuco's engenhos. Nevertheless, Palmares was by all accounts a very large community, containing thousands of escaped slaves and encompassing several villages and at least two main towns, called by this time by the Kimbundu term *quilombo* (*ki-lombo*). Major Portuguese punitive expeditions were carried out in 1676–7 under Fernão Carilho, followed in 1678 by fruitless treaty negotiations. After a heroic defence in 1695 the *quilombo* of Palmares was finally destroyed and its leaders executed. But *quilombos* died hard and as late as 1746 slaves and Indians were still gathering at the site of Palmares.[16]

The other major outlet from slavery was provided by manumission.

---

[15] Jerónimo da Gama (Ilhéus, 1753), ANTT, Cartório dos Jesuitas, maço 54, n. 55.
[16] AHU, papéis avulsos [PA], Alagoas, caixa 2 (2 August 1746).

Iberian traditions of slavery provided some basis for the phenomenon of voluntary manumission. Slaves who had performed long and faithful service or children raised in the plantation house were singled out for awards of liberty, but just as important was the process of self-purchase, in which slaves raised funds to buy their own freedom. A study of Bahian manumission charters from 1684 to 1745 reveals that women were freed twice as often as men.[17] Males had their best opportunities for freedom as children. *Crioulo* and mulatto slaves were freed far more frequently than Africans relative to their numbers in the population. The proportion of purchased to free manumissions rose during the eighteenth century to a point in the 1740s when the two forms of grant were made in almost equal numbers. The large numbers of purchased manumissions must discount to some extent the arguments sometimes made about the humanitarian aspects of manumission in Brazil, as does the fact that about 20 per cent of the charters were granted conditionally dependent on further service by the slave.

The patterns of manumission once again reveal the hierarchies of colour and acculturation that characterize other aspects of Brazilian slavery. As a group mulattos were the smallest sector of the slave population, but in manumission they were particularly favoured. Brazilian-born blacks followed and Africans, in this period, came last, receiving the fewest number of charters while composing the largest segment of the slave population. The manumission process was itself a complex mixture of Iberian religious and cultural imperatives and economic considerations, but it is clear that the more acculturated the slave and the lighter his or her colour, the better the chances for obtaining freedom. During the course of the seventeenth century manumission slowly began to produce a class of freedmen, former slaves who filled a series of low and intermediate roles in Brazilian economic life. The pattern of freeing women and children also tended to increase the reproductive capacity of the free coloured population while depleting that capacity among the slave population, thereby adding another reason for the negative natural growth rate of the Brazilian slave population.

Since the engenhos formed the core of the colony's economy, it is not surprising that the planters (*senhores de engenho*) exercised considerable social, economic, and political power. While some titled nobility in

[17] Stuart B. Schwartz, 'The manumission of slaves in colonial Brazil: Bahia, 1684–1745', *Hispanic American Historical Review* [*HAHR*], 54/4 (Nov. 1974), 603–35.

Portugal, like the duke of Monsanto, owned mills in Brazil, they did not come in person to administer them and were content to depend on agents and overseers in the colony. Most of the early *sesmarias* (land grants) went to commoners who had participated in the conquest and settlement of the coast. In general, then, the planter class was not of noble origin but was composed of commoners who saw in sugar the means to wealth and upward mobility. The title of *senhor de engenho* in Brazil was said to be like that of *conde* (count) in Portugal, and Brazilian planters tried to live the part. Their wealth and luxury drew the notice of visitors. And while they also made a great display of piety and some maintained full-time chaplains at their engenhos, ecclesiastical observers were often not impressed. Father Manuel da Nóbrega wrote, 'this people of Brazil pays attention to nothing but their engenhos and wealth even though it be with the perdition of all their souls'.[18]

The striving for social status and its recognition through the traditional symbols of nobility – titles, membership in military orders and entails – must be seen as a predominant mark of the planter class. A government report of 1591 suggested that the planters' aspirations could be manipulated for royal ends since the *senhores de engenho* were 'so well endowed with riches and so lacking in the privileges and honours of knighthoods, noble ranks, and pensions'. Eighteenth-century genealogists constantly strove to blur the distinction between families of noble origin and lineage and those whose claim to high status rested simply on longevity or success. In works like that of the Pernambucan Borges da Fonseca, planter families become 'noble' by 'antiquity' and even Indian origins are explained away.[19] A family like the Monteiros could be described as 'having maintained itself pure and finding itself today with sufficient nobility'. In fact, although the Brazilian planter class exercised considerable influence in the colony, it did not become a hereditary nobility; titles were not given, entails of property (*morgados*) were awarded only in a few cases, and even membership in the military orders was not granted often. The *senhores de engenho* were a colonial aristocracy, invariably white or accepted as such, locally favoured and powerful, but not a hereditary nobility. Lacking the traditional privileges and exemptions of a hereditary estate, the planters were relatively weak in their access to royal power.

The traditional historiography of colonial Brazil has tended to

[18] Serafim Leite (ed.), *Cartas do Brasil e mais escritos do Padre Manuel da Nóbrega* (Coimbra, 1955), 346.
[19] António José Victoriano Borges da Fonseca, 'Nobiliarchia pernambucana', *Anais da Biblioteca Nacional de Rio de Janeiro [ABNRJ]*, 47 (1925) and 48 (1926) (Rio de Janeiro, 1935), 1: 462.

encrust the planter class with a romantic patina that makes it difficult to perceive their social characteristics. Genealogists emphasizing the antiquity of important planter families projected a false impression of stability among the planter class. The sugar industry, in fact, created a highly volatile planter class, with engenhos changing hands constantly and many more failures than successes. Stability was, in fact, provided by the engenhos themselves, for the same mill names and properties appear continuously for hundreds of years. The owners and their families seemed to be far less stable. Undue emphasis on the few dominant families that survived the vicissitudes of the colonial economy has clouded this point.

There has in fact been little serious research on sugar planters as a social group. The main exception is a detailed study of 80 Bahian *senhores de engenho* in the period 1680–1725.[20] A century or more after the establishment of the industry almost 60 per cent of these planters were immigrants or the sons of immigrants, a pattern that indicates considerable mobility and flux within the planters' ranks. While the great families like the Aragão, Monis Barreto, or Argolos were third- or fifth-generation Brazilians, there were patterns of behaviour that allowed entrance to immigrants. The Portuguese-born merchant who acquired a mill and who himself (or whose son) married the daughter of a Brazilian planter family was a common phenomenon. While the old planter families tended to intermarry, room was always found for sons-in-law who were merchants with access to capital or high-court judges and lawyers bringing prestige, family name, and political leverage. Obviously, the arranged marriage was a key element in the strategy of family success.

The common pattern seems to have been for planters to live on their estates. In fact, the lack of absenteeism has been suggested by some as a major feature in the development of a patriarchal relationship between masters and slaves. While it is true that Brazilian planters resided in the *casa grande*, most of the engenhos of Bahia and many of those in Pernambuco were quite close to the port cities, so that constant interchange and movement between the engenho and the city was possible. Many planters kept urban residences and transacted their business in the city in person. Ownership of more than one mill was

---

[20] Rae Flory, 'Bahian society in the mid-colonial period: the sugar planters, tobacco growers, merchants, and artisans of Salvador and the Reconcavo, 1680–1725' (Ph.D. thesis, University of Texas, 1978). The period covered by this study was a time of crisis and thus the findings must be used with care, but it remains the only study to date.

also not uncommon and some engenhos were owned by religious establishments and administered for them by majordomos. The picture of the resident planter family must thus be modified somewhat. Neither were the sugar planters akin to feudal barons living in isolation, surrounded by their slaves and retainers and little interested in the outside world. Planter investment in cattle ranches, shipping, and urban properties was common, and often a merchant who had acquired a sugar mill continued his mercantile activities. The latest quotation on the Lisbon or Amsterdam sugar market was of constant interest. One viceroy in the eighteenth century, homesick for the salons of Europe, complained that the only conversation he heard in Brazil was on the prospects for next year's harvest.

From its origins the sugar industry of Brazil depended on a second group of cultivators who did not own their own mills but who supplied cane to the engenhos of others. These cane farmers were a distinctive stratum in colonial society, part of the sugar sector and proud of their title *lavrador de cana* yet also often at odds with the *senhores de engenho*. In the seventeenth century there were perhaps, on average, four to seven cane farmers for each engenho, supplying cane under a variety of arrangements. The most privileged *lavradores de cana* were those who held clear and unencumbered titles to their own land and were thus able to bargain for the best milling contract. When cane was scarce these growers were much pampered by the *senhores de engenho*, who were willing to lend slaves or oxen or provide firewood in order to secure the cane. Many growers, however, worked *partidos da cana*, that is land that was 'obligated' to a particular mill. These *lavradores* of 'captive' cane might be sharecroppers working an engenho's lands on a shares basis, or tenants, or those who owned their own land under conditions such as a lien on their crop in return for money or credit. Contractual arrangements varied from place to place and at different times, but the standard division was one-half of the white and *muscavado* sugar to the mill and one-half to the grower, with all lower grades the property of the mill. In addition, those with 'captive cane' then paid a rent in the form of a percentage of their half of the sugar. This, too, varied from one-third to one-twentieth depending on time and place, but the *senhores de engenho* preferred to lease their best lands to growers of considerable resources who could accept the one-third obligation. Contracts were commonly for nine or eighteen years, but a parcel was sometimes sold with an obligation for 'as long as the world shall last'.

In theory, the relationship between the *lavrador de cana* and the *senhor de engenho* was reciprocal, but most colonial observers recognized that ultimate power usually lay in the hands of the *senhor*. The *lavrador de cana* accepted the obligation to provide cane to a particular mill, paying damages if the cane went elsewhere. The *senhor de engenho* promised to grind the cane at the appropriate time, so many *tarefas* per week. While these arrangements sometimes took the form of written contracts (especially when part of sales or loans) they were often oral. Ultimate power usually rested with the mill owner, who could displace a grower, refuse to pay for improvements of the land, give false measure of the sugar produced or, even worse, refuse to grind the cane at the appropriate time and ruin a whole year's work. This unequal relationship caused tension between the millowners and cane farmers.

Socially, the *lavradores de cana* came from a spectrum that was economically broad but racially narrow. Humble men with two or three slaves and wealthy growers with twenty or 30 slaves could be found as cane farmers. Merchants, urban professionals, men of high military rank or with claims to noble status, could all be found among the *lavradores de cana* – people in every respect similar to the planter class in origin and background; but alongside them were those for whom the growing of a few hectares of cane exhausted all their resources. Thus, once again, as with the *senhores de engenho*, there was a certain instability in the agrarian population, people taking a chance, planting a few *tarefas* and then failing. In eighteen safras at Engenho Sergipe between 1622 and 1652 almost 60 per cent of the 128 *lavradores* appeared in less than three harvests. In this period, however, *lavradores de cana* were, almost without exception, European or Brazilian-born whites. Few people of colour could overcome the disadvantages of birth or the prejudice of creditors against *pardos* and enter the ranks of the sugar growers. In short, the *lavradores de cana* were 'proto-planters', often of the same social background as planters but lacking the capital or credit needed to establish a mill. The value of the average cane farm was perhaps one-fifth of that of the average engenho, surely a reflection of the relative wealth of the two groups.

The existence of a large class of cane farmers differentiated the colonial Brazilian sugar economy from that of the Spanish Indies or the English and French Caribbean islands. In the early stages of the industry it meant that the burdens and risks of growing sugar were widely distributed. It also meant that the structure of slave-owning was complex since large numbers of slaves lived in units of six to ten rather than the hundreds of the great plantations. Evidence from the late colonial period suggests that perhaps one-third of the slaves who worked the sugar were owned by *lavradores de cana*. Finally, the existence of *lavradores de cana* added to the problems of colonial Brazil when the sugar economy entered hard times in the late seventeenth century. Various attempts were made to limit the construction of new mills, but limiting the opportunity for *lavradores* to become *senhores de engenho* was perceived as even more injurious to the health of the industry than the proliferation of mills. It was felt that the industry had to hold out at least the hope of social mobility to attract cane growers, even though increasing output had an adverse effect on the price of sugar, already falling through foreign competition.

Despite the natural antagonisms between the *senhores de engenho* and the *lavradores de cana*, these two groups are best viewed as substrata of the same class, mainly differentiated by wealth but sharing a common background, aspirations, and attitudes. Conflicts between them might be bitter, but together the two groups constituted a sugar sector with similar interests in matters of taxation, commercial policy, and relations with other groups and both enjoying the highest political and social positions in the colony, dominating the town councils, prestigious lay brotherhoods, and militia offices.

Of considerably lower social status were the whites and free people of colour who performed a variety of tasks as wage labourers on the plantation. Records from the seventeenth century rarely speak of the attached agricultors, the *agregados* or *moradores*, who are common in the eighteenth century, but engenhos regularly employed woodmen, boatmen, carpenters, masons, and other craftsmen. There were, in fact, two kinds of employees on the plantations: those who received an annual salary (*soldada*), and those who were paid a daily wage or for each task carried out. The former generally included the sugar master, crater, overseers, boatmen, and sometimes kettlemen. Carpenters, masons, and woodcutters were employed as needed. Once again, hierarchies of colour and race emerge from the records. In this case Indians, no matter what their occupation, were invariably paid less than whites or free blacks performing similar tasks. Moreover, Indians were usually hired by the job or by the month and paid in goods rather than cash, indications that they were not wholly integrated into a European wage-labour market. Artisan occupations were one area where free people of colour could hope to find some opportunity for advancement. But, as in other productive activites, artisans on the engenhos often owned their own slaves.

Despite a historiography that has emphasized the seigniorial aspects of the planter class, sugar-growing was a business greatly concerned with profit and loss. By contemporary standards the establishment of an engenho was an expensive operation. An average engenho in the mid seventeenth century required about 15,000 milréis of capital investment. Lands were acquired by grants of *sesmaria* or by purchase, but in this period land does not seem to have been the most important factor of production, since transactions and wills rarely specified its extent or value. Much more care was devoted to the identification and evaluation of the labour force. It was estimated in 1751 that slaves were the most expensive factor of production, constituting 36 per cent of a plantation's total value. Land was valued at 19 per cent, livestock at 4 per cent, buildings at 18 per cent, and machinery equipment at 23 per cent. Yearly operating costs were high and once again labour topped the list. Salaries for free labourers were calculated at 23 per cent of the total annual costs, slave maintenance at 16 per cent, and the replacement of slaves at 19 per cent for an estimated loss of 10 per cent of the slave force each year.[21] Labour-related costs, then, were almost 60 per cent of annual expenditure. Firewood was the other major item of expense, 12–21 per cent of costs, depending on its availability and the plantation's location. With so few plantation records available, the profitability of the industry is difficult to establish in any but the most general terms. Early observers of Brazil always commented on the opulence and luxury of the planter class, while the planters themselves were continually seeking exemption from taxes or a moratorium on debt payments on grounds of poverty.

Credit and capital for the establishment and operation of *engenhos* came from a variety of sources. In the sixteenth century some direct investment from Europe seems to have been made in the Brazilian sugar industry, but there is little evidence of this in the seventeenth century. One method of raising funds for investment in a sugar mill might be called the 'Robinson Crusoe' pattern, since Defoe's hero practised it

[21] Câmara of Salvador to crown, AHU/PA/Bahia, caixa 61 (1751). Cf. Frédéric Mauro, 'Contabilidade teórica e contabilidade prática no século XVII', *Nova história e novo mundo* (São Paulo, 1969), 135–48.

during his stay in Bahia (1655–9?) and it was reported by other sources as well. This was the growing of manioc, tobacco, or some other crop with the hope of accumulating enough capital or credit with a local merchant to permit the building of a sugar mill. Probably the best opportunities for this approach were to be found in raising sugar-cane for processing at someone else's engenho. Loans came from various religious institutions such as the charitable brotherhood of the Misericórdia and the Third Orders of St Francis and St Anthony. The interest rate charged by these institutions was fixed by canon and civil law at 6.25 per cent and thus their loans tended to be low-yield, low-risk contracts made with members of the colonial elite, many of whom were members of these bodies. These institutional lenders favoured the sugar industry. The 90 loans of the Misericórdia of Salvador secured by mortgages on agricultural properties in 1694 included 24 on engenhos and 47 on cane farms. One suspects that institutional lenders preferred to make loans for the original capital expense in setting up a mill or cane farm, but that loans for operating expenses were much more difficult to obtain.

For the operating costs, and for those who could not gain access to the sources of institutional credit, the next alternative was private lenders, principally merchants. While also constrained by laws against usury, merchants found ways of extracting much higher interest rates, often by lending funds against a future crop at a pre-determined price. Further sources of credit were urban professionals or other *senhores de engenho*, but the study of Bahia's engenhos between 1680 and 1725 indicates that almost half the money lent came from religious institutions and another quarter from merchants.[22] Despite social fusion between planters and merchants, the debtor–creditor relationship created antagonism and tension between them and at many junctures caused them to take hostile – one might say class – positions towards each other.

In the long run, questions of finance and profitability cannot be viewed in static terms. International political events, the price of sugar, and local conditions in the colony all produced changing patterns of profit and loss. In general, it can be said that during most of the period under discussion Brazil was faced with rising costs and falling prices for its sugar. The rising cost of slaves, who as we have seen were a major item of expenditure, signalled to the planters the problem that they

[22] Flory, 'Bahian society', 71–5.

faced. We can make the same calculation that the planters made: how much sugar did it take to replace a slave? The answer provided in table 3 above is that it was about four times as much in 1710 as it had been in 1608.

It was on the wharves of Amsterdam, London, Hamburg, and Genoa that the ultimate success of the Brazilian sugar economy was determined. The European price for sugar rose sharply throughout the last half of the sixteenth century. After a slight drop in the 1610s price levels rose again in the 1620s, owing in part to the disruption of the sugar supply to Europe caused by Dutch attacks on Brazil and the losses suffered by Portuguese shipping. With the end of the Twelve-Year Truce between Spain and the United Provinces in 1621, Brazil became a major target for attack, and from 1630 to 1654 the Dutch held most of north-east Brazil, half of the colony, including Pernambuco, the major sugar-producing captaincy. Sugar continued to be produced in this area by Luso-Brazilian planters, but the Dutch West India Company began to call in the loans it had made to those persons who had acquired engenhos during the period of Dutch rule. The Luso-Brazilian rebellion, which erupted in 1645, was in part a response to the falling price of sugar and the straits in which the planters found themselves. During the war, between 1645 and 1654, production in Brazil was disrupted; while the price of sugar rose on the Amsterdam exchange it fell in Brazil.

The Dutch period was, in terms of the social and political development of the north-east, a historical hiatus. After the 30 years of Dutch rule few tangible vestiges of their presence remained. In broader economic terms, however, Brazil's place within the Atlantic system was never the same again, nor was the regional concentration of economic resources within the colony ever to be as it had been before 1630.

First, the destruction and disruption caused by the fighting seriously impaired the production and export of sugar. The seizure of Salvador in 1624 resulted in the loss of much of two safras and the capture of many ships. Similar losses resulted from the expeditions against Bahia in 1627 and 1638. The Dutch attack on the Recôncavo in 1648 brought the destruction of 23 engenhos and the loss of 1,500 crates of sugar. During the war, Portuguese shipping was decimated: between 1630 and 1636 199 ships were lost, a staggering figure except when compared with the 220 vessels lost in 1647-8. After the beginning of the Luso-Brazilian revolt of 1645 both sides burned engenhos and canefields as a matter of course.

Within the captaincies under Dutch control the confiscation of property and the flight of owners meant that 65 out of 149 engenhos were inactive (*fogo morto*) in 1637. During the revolt of 1645–54, one-third of the engenhos were out of action. While, around 1650, estimates of Pernambuco's capacity were set at about 25,000 crates, the captaincy actually produced only 6,000. Planters from Pernambuco fled southward to Bahia or even Rio de Janeiro, bringing slaves and capital with them. After 1630 Bahia replaced Pernambuco as the captaincy with the most slaves and as the centre of the Portuguese-controlled sugar economy. Rio de Janeiro's sugar economy was characterized by smaller units often producing rum for export. By the 1670s it was expanding northward into the area of Campos de Goitacazes.

While the sugar economy of Pernambuco suffered badly in the 1640s, Bahia and its surrounding captaincies did not enjoy the new leadership without problems. Brazilian sugar production had begun to level off in the 1620s and the fighting of the following decade simply intensified a process already begun. During the Dutch occupation of the northeast, the Portuguese crown sought to generate funds in order to carry out the war and meet its defence needs, but found that the slackening in Brazilian sugar production made doing so ever more difficult. Its response was to tax sugar production and trade ever more heavily. In 1631 a tax of one cruzado (= 400 réis) per crate was imposed followed by another of ten cruzados per crate in 1647. It was only natural that the crown should hope to finance its defence of the colony by taxing sugar. In Pernambuco about 80 per cent of government receipts resulted from various sugar taxes. Planters, of course, complained loudly about these imposts and other wartime measures such as requisitioning boats and quartering troops.

The damage to the sugar economy, the lower world price for sugar as a result of competition from the Caribbean, and the War of Restoration in Portugal all prevented the crown from abolishing the imposts on the sugar industry. But continuing taxes impeded rebuilding and expansion of the industry. In turn, the fall in output meant lower revenues from the tithe and other normal imposts, thus making the extraordinary taxes still necessary. Attempts to break this vicious circle were unsuccessful. For example, a proposal to declare a moratorium on all debts contracted before 1645 and thereby enable the planters to accumulate capital met with stiff resistance from Portuguese merchant-creditors.

By the end of the war in 1654, when Brazil was once again fully under Portuguese control and a return to its former prosperity might have been expected, the Atlantic community's sources of sugar and Brazil's share of them had changed considerably. The English, Dutch, and French colonies in the Caribbean which had begun to grow sugar during the favourable price conditions of the 1630s now began to compete heavily with Brazil. Increased production from these new suppliers tended to keep prices low, especially during the 1670s and 1680s, when a period of general European peace after 1675 permitted a regularization of the slave trade and an unrestrained growth of tropical agriculture. On the Lisbon market the price of an arroba of sugar fell from 3$800 réis in 1654 to 1$300 in 1688.

The 1680s, in fact, marked a low point in the fortunes of the Brazilian sugar economy. The colony was hit by a severe drought lasting from 1681 to 1684, there were smallpox outbreaks from 1682 to 1684, and a yellow fever epidemic that first struck Recife in 1685–6. Added to these problems was a general economic crisis in the Atlantic world after 1680. In 1687 João Peixoto Viegas penned his famous *memorial* identifying the problems of Brazilian agriculture and forecasting the ruin of the colony, but events in 1689 quickly turned the situation around. The outbreak of war between France and England disrupted the supplies of those nations and offered Brazil higher prices and increased opportunities for its sugar. Planters who, like Peixoto Viegas, had prophesied doom in 1687 could by 1691 think of regaining their former prosperity, despite the rising cost of slaves and other imported commodities. However, the recovery of the 1690s was short-lived. The uncertainties of war made sugar prices fluctuate wildly until 1713, when the earlier decline was resumed. Despite occasional recoveries the secular trend was downward into the middle of the eighteenth century.

Meanwhile, the discovery of gold in Minas Gerais after 1695 created a vast new demand for labour in Brazil and drove slave prices up to unprecedented peaks, reaching a rate of increase of over 5 per cent per annum in the decade between 1710 and 1720. The discovery of gold was itself certainly not the cause of export agriculture's problem. As we have seen, the sugar industry had suffered bad times intermittently since 1640, especially in the 1670s and 1680s, but the gold rush created new pressures on coastal agriculture. As early as 1701 attempts were made to limit the slave trade to the mines and after 1703 planters' complaints about labour shortages and the high cost of slaves were continuous. By 1723 the municipal council of Salvador complained that 24 engenhos had ceased to function and that sugar production had fallen because of the high price of slaves and the planters' inability to compete with the miners for the purchase of new labourers. After 1730 the north-eastern sugar economy entered a period of depression reflected in a declining annual production.

The unhappy history of sugar just outlined made difficulties for planters, merchants, and Portuguese crown alike. Planters complained of excessive taxes, high prices for slaves, droughts, and extortion by merchants; royal officials laid the blame on the planters' profligacy and lack of foresight; and merchants claimed that planters overspent and that their fraudulent weighing and quality-marking on Brazilian sugar crates had lowered the value of sugar in European markets. More perceptive observers realized that foreign competition and English and French protectionism had also cut deeply into the available market for Brazilian sugar. Such steps as were taken by the crown and by the planters themselves to meet the crisis had only limited effect. The Brazilian sugar industry in the eighteenth century steadily lost ground to its Caribbean rivals.

SUBSIDIARY ECONOMIC ACTIVITIES

The cutting and export of wood, so important in the early years of the colony's development, continued throughout the colonial period, although the emphasis shifted from dyewood to varieties used for furniture or shipbuilding. A new royal monopoly on brazilwood was established in 1605 in which contracts for cutting and shipping the wood were granted to private individuals. Contraband was always a special problem because some of the best wood was to be found in Porto Seguro, Ilhéus, and Espírito Santo, captaincies far from the centres of government control. Similar royal monopolies were established over whaling and salt, in which contractors would lease the rights to exploit those resources. While these activities undoubtedly generated funds for the crown, agriculture remained the basis of the colony's economy.

An agricultural hierarchy ranged according to the export possibilities of the crops prevailed in the colony. The best and most valuable lands were always given over to export crops, preferably sugar-cane but also tobacco. Subsistence farming, especially growing manioc, was considered to be the 'least noble' occupation, and was usually relegated

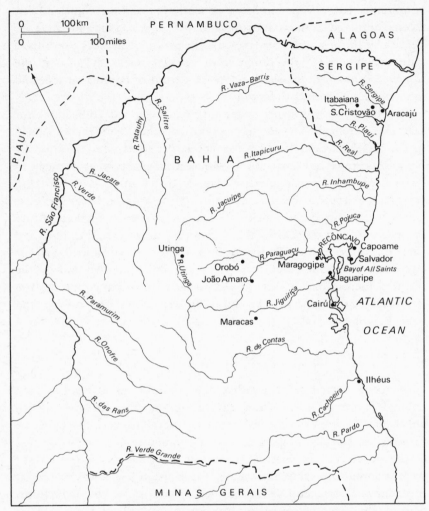

The Bahian *sertão* in the seventeenth century

Source: Stuart B. Schwartz (ed.), *A governor and his image in Baroque Brazil* (Minneapolis, 1979).

to marginal lands and often left to the humblest cultivators. Cattle-raising, at first for internal consumption and later for export, differed somewhat from the general pattern not only because it could be carried out effectively on land unsuited for export crops but also because the mobility of cattle on the hoof made it unnecessary for the ranches to be near the coast.

The agricultural hierarchy was closely paralleled by a hierarchy of colour amongst agriculturalists, and this in turn was matched by differences in the numbers of slaves they employed. Sugar planters and cane farmers were almost invariably white, tobacco farmers nearly always white, whereas manioc farmers included *pardos, mestiços* and free blacks. The number of slaves in each branch of agriculture, as well as the average number per holding, decreased according to the type of farming. A *senhor de engenho* might own a hundred slaves, a tobacco farmer fifteen or twenty on average, and a manioc grower only two or three, or even none at all. Clearly the highest return on investment in slave labour was in the export sector.

Tobacco

After sugar the most important export crop grown in Brazil up to the mid eighteenth century was tobacco or, as the Portuguese so poetically and accurately called it, *fumo* (smoke). Some tobacco was grown in Pará, Maranhão, and the captaincy of Pernambuco, but by far the most important centre of this husbandry was Bahia south and west of Salvador, especially the area around the port of Cachoeira at the mouth of the Paraguaçú river. It is not clear when tobacco cultivation in this zone began. Gabriel Soares de Sousa's description of the Recôncavo in 1587 does not mention the crop, but by the 1620s some tobacco was clearly being grown and exported from the Brazilian north-east. While the sandy and clay soils of the fields (*campos*) of Cachoeira were the focal point of production in Bahia, smaller zones could be found around Maragogipe and Jaguaripe in the Recôncavo, Inhambupe towards the *sertão*, the arid backlands, and to the north-east of Salvador on the Rio Real and in Sergipe de El-Rei. It is estimated that these Bahian regions produced nine-tenths of the tobacco exported by Brazil in this period.

Tobacco growing had some special features that influenced its social organization and its position in the Brazilian economy. Its six-month growing season was shorter than that of sugar and under proper conditions offered the possibility of double cropping. Its cultivation demanded intensive care: the seedlings had to be transplanted and then kept constantly weeded and protected from pests until the harvest, when the leaves had to be picked by hand. The gang labour of the canefields was not well suited to this activity. In fact, tobacco could be grown as efficiently on small family farms of a few acres as on larger units with twenty to 40 slaves. The scale of operations varied widely. Mixed cattle and tobacco farms were common, because the best-grade tobacco was produced using manure as fertilizer. But lower grades could be produced without the benefit of fertilizer. After the harvest the most difficult task was the preparation of the crop for sale. Brazilian tobacco was usually twisted into ropes, treated with a molasses-based liquid, wound into rolls (of eight arrobas for the Portuguese trade and three arrobas for the African coast) and then placed in leather casings. The onerous yet precise process of twisting and rolling had usually to be given to skilled slaves and was thus an item of some expense, but the poorer growers did not need to maintain their own processing unit; they simply paid *enroladores* to do this task.

Opportunities for profit, then, existed at various levels of production. Small family farms of four to seven acres existed alongside much larger slave-based units, although a survey of land sales at the turn of the eighteenth century placed the average unit at around 100 acres.[23] While cattle and a processing unit were essential for large producers, tobacco generally needed a smaller capital outlay and labour force than sugar and its preparation was a less complicated and costly process. The Bahian Superintendent of Tobacco wrote in 1714: 'There is much land that does not produce any other fruit, inhabited by many people who have no other means of support, since this agriculture is among the least costly and thus the easiest for the poor who practise it.'[24] In fact, in 1706, it was reported in Pernambuco that slaves themselves were producing low-grade tobacco in their free time.[25]

As in sugar agriculture, a variety of social types and classes were associated with tobacco, but in comparison with sugar they tended to be concentrated at a somewhat lower social level. While it might be profitable, the title of tobacco grower did not bring great social prestige or political power. Evidence drawn from notary records indicates that the average tobacco–cattle *sítio* was worth only about one-third of the value of the average cane farm and less than 1 per cent of that of an engenho. Thus, former manioc farmers and poor immigrants from Portugal were attracted to this crop, although there were also wealthy producers who combined tobacco cultivation with other activities. In the Cachoeira region families like the Adornos and Dias Laços had received enormous *sesmarias* when the area was first opened to European settlement. Some dozen families who raised sugar in Iguape (a zone of

23 *Ibid.*, 172.
24 ANTT, Junta do Tabaco, maço 97A.   25 *Ibid.*, maço 97 (21 Jan. 1706).

transition), ran cattle in the sertão, and also grew tobacco were the political and social elite of the area. Large growers like these might produce 4,000 arrobas a year, while there were others who grew less than 100 arrobas. Types of tenure varied and renting of tobacco lands was common. During the eighteenth century the number of small growers rose. Moreover, as a group their complexion darkened. Whereas a sample of 450 *lavradores de tabaco* between 1684 and 1725 revealed that only 3 per cent were *pardos*, a similar study for the late eighteenth century raised that figure to 27 per cent.[26] Tobacco, then, was a less prestigious, less expensive, and less exclusively white branch of export agriculture than sugar. However, tobacco agriculture was firmly based on slave labour and the census returns of tobacco-growing parishes at various points of time always show at least half the population to be slave – a lower proportion than in the sugar zones, to be sure, but one large enough to dispel any illusions that tobacco growing was based on yeoman husbandry.

The fortunes of tobacco as an export commodity were closely tied to those of Atlantic commerce and to the rhythm of Brazil's own economic development. The Dutch seizure of the Portuguese slaving station at São Jorge de Mina in 1637 disrupted the normal pattern of slave supply to Brazil. This, plus the loss of Angola in 1641, led to royal legislation in 1644 allowing direct trade between Brazil and Africa without any benefit to the metropolis. The Dutch limited Portuguese trade to four ports on the Mina coast and prohibited the introduction of any goods except Brazilian tobacco. This stimulated the expansion of tobacco cultivation in Brazil. The creation of a royal monopoly administration, the Junta da Administração do Tabaco, in 1674 was an attempt to control this product, but its major efforts were aimed at limiting production and contraband in Portugal itself.[27] While Brazilian planters complained about the monopoly, they continued to derive regular profit from the sale of tobacco to both Africa and Europe. Their position was considerably strengthened by the discovery of gold in Minas Gerais in 1695 and the resultant soaring demand for slave labour in the colony. Brazilian tobacco and gold became the items necessary for the slave trade in the eighteenth century.

[26] Cf. Flory, 'Bahian society', 158–217; Catherine Lugar, 'The Portuguese tobacco trade and the tobacco growers of Bahia in the late colonial period', in Dauril Alden and Warren Dean (eds.), *Essays concerning the socioeconomic history of Brazil and Portuguese India* (Gainesville, 1977), 26–70.

[27] Carl Hanson, 'Monopoly and contraband in the Portuguese tobacco trade', *Luso-Brazilian Review*,19/2 (winter, 1968), 149–68.

Two curious paradoxes marked the Brazilian tobacco trade. First, in order to make sure that it had a supply of the best-quality tobacco, Portugal had prohibited the export of either of the first two grades to Africa. The third grade, *refugado*, had to be liberally treated with molasses syrup, a sugar by-product, so that it could be wound into cords, but it was exactly this treatment that gave it the sweet taste and aroma that made it so popular on the African coast and as a major trade item with the Indians in the Canadian fur trade. The Portuguese monopoly also attempted to fix the price of high-quality tobacco to ensure a profit to metropolitan merchants. This situation led planters to concentrate on growing lower grades for sale in Africa or to enter the thriving contraband trade in tobacco. By the 1730s the crown was trying various measures to control the trade to Mina and to sustain the amounts going to Portugal, but, as figure 2 demonstrates, they had little effect. Finally, in 1743, the Mina trade was reorganized in favour of the Brazilian merchants. Only 30 ships a year – 24 from Bahia and six from Pernambuco – were allowed to trade on the Mina coast, thereby guaranteeing limits on supply and high prices for Brazilian goods. In 1752 it was estimated that a Mina slave could be bought at Whydah for eight rolls of tobacco or 28$800 réis, transported for another 26$420 réis, and sold in Bahia for 100$000 réis, yielding a profit of almost 45 per cent.

It is difficult to establish the levels of tobacco production and export and almost impossible to do so for the period prior to the creation of the Junta da Administração do Tabaco in 1674. Not only are statistical series lacking, but contraband was always rife, especially after the creation of an *estanque*, or monopoly, on tobacco sales in Portugal in the 1630s. Despite prohibitions and stiff penalties, the crop was grown in Portugal and, even more important, sailors and masters in the Brazil fleets seemed to be involved in smuggling on a grand scale. Occasionally contemporary estimates can be found. Antonil placed Bahian annual exports at 25,000 rolls in the first years of the eighteenth century. An estimate of 1726 placed levels of exports from Cachoeira alone at 20,000 rolls to Portugal and another 20,000 to Mina in the slave trade.

The best figures for the period under consideration here can be obtained from the lists kept by the Junta do Tabaco. This board, which controlled the importation and sale of tobacco, rented the regional monopoly contracts, licensed sale in Portugal and set prices recorded each year, the size of the annual cargo of tobacco and sugar in the Bahia

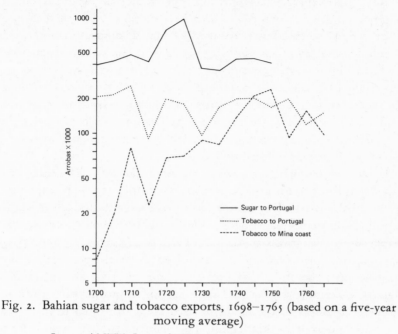

Fig. 2. Bahian sugar and tobacco exports, 1698–1765 (based on a five-year moving average)

Source: ANTT, Junta do Tabaco, maços 96A–106 *passim.*

fleet and the amount that was shipped to Africa. Records for the period before 1700 are incomplete, but for the seven years between 1680 and 1686 total annual imports averaged around 20,500 rolls. After 1700, a rather full record of the Bahian trade to both Portugal and Africa can be compiled until the end of the fleet system in 1765. If we assume that Bahian production was 90 per cent of the total output, then these figures provide the best available estimates. Figure 2 demonstrates that the highest levels of Bahian production, about 400,000 arrobas a year, were reached in the 1740s and that the percentage of production destined to the Mina coast as part of the slave trade rose sharply over the first half of the century.

Livestock

Various types of European domestic animals had been introduced into Brazil in the sixteenth century. Horses thrived in Bahia and by the 1580s there was a trade in horses from Bahia to Pernambuco and even to Angola, where mounted troops were used with success against the

Africans. However, cattle were more important. The engenhos required large numbers of oxen for carts and, in the smaller mills, as the motive force. It was estimated that an engenho needed between 30 and 60 oxen at any one time and their mortality rate during the safra was apparently high. In addition, engenhos needed tallow, hides, and beef in quantity. Most engenhos maintained some pasture for their resident herds, but the presence of grazing cattle near agricultural land always caused trouble. Cattle-raising was restricted by custom to the margins of the settled coastal areas. Eventually in 1701 cattle grazing within 50 miles of the coast was prohibited by law.

Forced out of the better agricultural zones, cattle herds began to grow rapidly in the interior sertão, north of Pernambuco, in the captaincies of Paraíba and Rio Grande do Norte (conquered in the 1580s), and especially in the region of Sergipe de El-Rei between Pernambuco and Bahia along the banks of the São Francisco river. This region was opened up in the 1590s with the aid of government-sponsored expeditions against the Indians. Ranchers, some of them also planters or related to planter families, and their herdsmen pushed their cattle out along both banks of the São Francisco river and by 1640 there were over 2,000 corrals in this region. The history of much of the interior of the north-east can be summarized as exploration, extermination of the Indians, large land grants, and the establishment of cattle ranches. By the first decade of the eighteenth century, there were over 1,300,000 head of cattle in the north-east, supplying the needs of the sugar and tobacco industries and the coastal cities.

Landholding in the sertão was truly extensive. Although there was legislation limiting the size of *sesmarias* to three square leagues, this restriction was simply disregarded. The *sesmarias* on which cattle ranches (*fazendas de gado*) were established sometimes exceeded hundreds of thousands of acres. At the close of the seventeenth century there were landholdings in the Bahian sertão larger than whole provinces in Portugal. Domingos Afonso Sertão, one of the great lords of the interior, owned 30 cattle ranches and another 30 farms totalling over 1,206,000 hectares. A great ranching family like Garcia d'Avila of Bahia, or a merchant turned rancher like João Peixoto Viegas, whose herds were on the upper Paraguaçú, might run over 20,000 head on their scattered ranches, but such 'potentates of the sertão' were the exception and ranches of 1,000 to 3,000 head were more common. As a rule, the interior cattle-ranching zones tended to be divided into large estates, sparsely populated by cowboys and subsistence farmers and dominated by great rancher families who were often linked to the planter elite of the coast. Farther from the centres of royal government, less constrained by municipal institutions, and controlling vast tracts of land, the cattle ranchers wielded more unrestrained power than did the sugar planters.

The great age of cattle expansion into the sertão in conjunction with the sugar industry dates between the opening of Sergipe de El-Rei in the 1590s and the creation of Piauí in the first decade of the eighteenth century. During this period a distinctive social organization and life-style developed. The missionary orders, especially the Jesuits, often played a crucial role in the opening up of new areas and the pacification of the Indians. Eventually, conflicts between ranchers and Jesuits developed because the Jesuits controlled Indian labour and owned extensive herds. The contact between cattlemen and Indians eventually produced a mixed-race population, regionally called *cabras* or *caboclos*. Miscegenation was common and the population of the sertão was composed principally of people of colour, Indians, *caboclos*, and blacks. Despite claims sometimes made that the cattle frontier was too free and uncontrolled to make much use of slaves, more recent studies have revealed that slavery was also a characteristic labour form in the sertão. The common pattern was to use both slaves and free workers as *vaqueiros* (cowboys), placing them on a distant ranch with their families and leaving them to guard the stock fairly independently. Periodically accounts were made and workers were sometimes allowed to keep a portion of the yearly increase in calves as an incentive to good service. There was nothing incompatible between cattle ranching and slavery.

Loosely structured and free of much direct interference from the crown, the society of the sertão developed its own peculiar character-istics. The *fazendeiros* exercised broad social and political power over their slaves and *agregados* (retainers). Control of river banks and waterholes was essential for success. The great ranchers apparently left broad expanses of their territory unused and refused to sell or rent any of it, in order to ensure that they themselves had adequate pasture and to deny the peasants and *agregados* alternative opportunities. In the scrub brush of the arid sertão the horse became a way of life and milk and beef the daily fare. Materially poor, the people literally lived on hides. Everything was made of leather – clothing, household utensils, saddles, window coverings, and tools. This was a society poorer than that of the coast, but more mobile and less constrained by metropolitan law;

but it was also totally dependent on the dominant economy, ranching, which was in its turn linked to the sugar industry.

From the sertão, herds of cattle (*boiadas*) covering up to 40 miles a day were brought down to fairs on the edges of the sugar districts and coastal centres of population. The system seemed to work well from the planters' viewpoint. The price of a team of oxen in the 1690s was about half what it had been in the 1590s, despite a general inflationary trend in the colony. Only after 1700, when the herds were diverted towards Minas Gerais, did the coastal population complain of shortages. Two other movements could also be noted in the eighteenth century: the expansion of the cattle frontier northward into the Maranhão and westward into Goiás, and the development of cattle products for export. By 1749 Pernambuco alone had 27 tanneries employing over 300 slaves and both Pernambuco and Bahia were exporting large quantities of hides and leather.

Manioc

Manioc, the Indian staple, had been quickly adopted by the Portuguese, who found that their familiar wheat and other grains did not flourish in the tropics. Manioc was relatively easy to grow and it could be prepared in a number of ways. Ground into flour it was easy to transport and store and it became the bread of everyday life. In the sugar-growing regions manioc and subsistence farming in general were pushed onto the most marginal lands. Peasant cultivators were allowed to grow foodstuffs on their *roças* on lands that could not be planted to cane. Along the roadways or on hilly uplands in the plantation zones the *lavradores de roça* eked out their humble lives, growing food for themselves and selling a very small surplus in local markets. But, in general, sugar planters disliked the presence of subsistence farming in the same region both because of their desire to use all good land for sugar cane, and because the manioc *roça* tended to destroy the forest which supplied the firewood so essential to sugar production. The result of this hostility was the development of a regional specialization with some areas devoted to sugar and others to manioc.

There were, in fact, two kinds of food-crop agriculture in colonial Brazil. One was the subsistence farming of peasant cultivators producing mainly for themselves and their families and selling a very small surplus in local market fairs, and the other was the production of large quantities of manioc flour destined to be sold to the engenhos and cities of the coast. In Pernambuco, the parishes of Una, Porto Calvo and Alagoas were important provisioning grounds for the captaincy. In Bahia, Maragogipe and Jaguaripe in the southern Recôncavo and towns southward along the coast, like Cairú and Camamú, were the major producers. While little is known about the internal organization of manioc agriculture for market, it is clear that foodstuff production was not necessarily a peasant family husbandry. Cairú and Camamú, for example, were manioc-producing regions of great fame, yet an ecclesiastical census of 1724 revealed that about half the population of these parishes were enslaved. This situation seems to indicate a slave-based economy of production for the supply of internal markets. A somewhat later account, of 1786, listed 188 manioc farmers in Cairú, of whom 169 owned a total of 635 slaves.[28]

Planter hostility towards subsistence agriculture and regional specialization in foodstuffs meant that the populations of cities and the inhabitants of sugar estates were dependent for their daily bread on sources of supply often beyond their control. Shortages, high prices, and near-famines were endemic in the plantation regions. One problem was the attraction which export agriculture held for manioc farmers. As early as 1639 attempts were made to force colonists in Cairú and Camamú to plant manioc instead of tobacco, and in 1706 residents of Maragogipe and Cachoeira sought to be released from prohibitions against growing tobacco or sugar-cane. A similar situation developed somewhat later in Pernambuco as farmers sought to plant cane, a more 'noble occupation', rather than grow manioc. Again, with the expansion of the slave trade, Brazilian manioc producers found that even their crop could be exported. By the 1720s, over 6,000 *alqueires* a year were being shipped in the Mina trade alone, to say nothing of what was shipped to Angola. Then, too, producers of foodstuffs could hold back supplies in order to maintain high price levels, a ploy made possible by the ease with which manioc flour could be preserved. Complaints against the cupidity of the manioc farmers and their regulation of supply were continually voiced in the coastal cities.

Colonial government took various measures to ensure adequate food supplies, but with very limited success. The first measure, already discussed above, was the requirement that certain regions be excluded from practising any agriculture except the growing of foodstuffs. This

---

[28] Lista das mil covas de mandioca, Biblioteca Nacional de Rio de Janeiro [BNRJ], 1–31, 30, 51 (Cairú, 25 Oct. 1786).

approach was unsuccessful because the growers were reluctant to comply and because they could control supply and thus raise prices. A second approach was to require sugar planters and cane farmers to plant enough manioc to support their own slave force. In Dutch Brazil, Count Maurits of Nassau had imposed this law in 1640. In 1688, at the urging of the *câmara* (city council) of Salvador, a similar law was issued in Bahia, requiring each *senhor de engenho* and *lavrador de cana* to plant 500 *covas* of manioc per slave. In 1701 further steps were taken. Cattle (except those needed by the growers) were prohibited from grazing within 50 miles of the coast and any cultivator with fewer than six slaves was prohibited from growing sugar-cane, a provision that brought heated complaints from the small-scale cane farmers of Rio de Janeiro. The idea behind these measures was that one-third of the manioc produced would feed the grower and his slaves while the rest would reach the market. Finally, merchants in the Mina trade were also required to maintain manioc farms to supply their needs. This last provision caused considerable tension between the merchants of Salvador, who argued that the roles of merchant and manioc farmer were incompatible, and a city council tired of the constant shortages and high prices.

One final response to the problem of food supply deserves to be mentioned. Caribbean sugar planters spoke of the 'Brazil system', by which planters allowed slaves to maintain their own plots, growing their own food supply and sometimes marketing the surplus in local fairs. While this system was reported in various places and usually evoked comment by travellers to Brazil, it is not clear how widely it was practised. It was reported in Bahia in 1687 that 'there are many engenhos that do not have their own lands to plant manioc and ... the owners who do have them usually rent them out'.[29] It has been suggested that the system of slave plots was a 'peasant breach' in Brazilian slavery. There is evidence that the privilege of maintaining a *roça* was desired by the slaves. From the planters' viewpoint the system shifted the burden of sustenance to the slaves themselves. Moreover, it could have direct benefits to estate management. The overseers of Fazenda Saubara were instructed to allow slaves and poor people in the area to plant their *roças* in scrublands, but never in the same place for more than a year so that new lands for pasture would be continually cleared.[30] At Engenho Santana in Ilhéus, manioc was bought from

---

[29] AHU/PA/Bahia, caixa 15 (9 Aug. 1687).

[30] Regimento que ha de seguir o feitor de Fazenda Saubara, Arquivo da Santa Casa de Misericórdia da Bahia (Salvador) [ASCMB], B/3a/213. Saubara was a manioc-producing parish in the

slaves at 20 per cent below the rate paid to freemen. However, the complaints of shortage and famine indicate overall that slave plots were inadequate as a major source of food. As Antonil noted, for the slaves of the many engenhos near the sea and rivers, 'shellfish was their salvation'.

PERIPHERIES OF NORTH AND SOUTH

At the northern and southern extremes of Portuguese colonization along the Brazilian littoral, settlements took shape that differed considerably from the plantation zones on the humid north-eastern coast. São Vicente in the south and Maranhão-Pará in the north were peripheral areas throughout the seventeenth century, lacking a European population of any size and only marginally integrated into the export economy of the rest of the colony. Geography, climate, difficulties of communication, and the nature and distribution of the local Indian populations propelled these regions along distinctive economic and social trajectories. While the far north and the far south were dissimilar in many ways, both were poor frontiers with few white men, fewer white women, little wealth, and hardly any black slaves. The institutions of Portugal were reproduced in these areas, but existed in an attenuated form. Culturally and ethnically both regions were markedly Indian in character. A relatively large mestizo population developed and in both São Vicente and in Maranhão-Pará exploitation of the resources of the sertão and of the Indian population became a way of life.[31]

The southern extremes

The origins of São Vicente and its neighbouring areas to the south were much like those of the other captaincies. Portuguese and Spanish voyages had passed along the southern coast in the early sixteenth century; a few castaways had settled there among the Indian population and a few small landing points had been established. Granted to Martim Afonso de Sousa in 1533, the captaincy of São Vicente at first centred on the port from which it took its name, but during the next two decades other settlements were established. São Vicente proved to

Recôncavo. This *fazenda* worked by slaves produced manioc for the hospital of the Misericórdia of Salvador.

[31] For further discussion of the northern and southern peripheries, see Hemming, *CHLA* II, ch. 13.

be unsuitable as a port and it was replaced in importance by Santos, a town founded in 1545 by Bras Cubas, a wealthy and energetic royal official. Along the humid coast behind these small coastal settlements sugar mills were established; the most famous of them was originally built by Martim Afonso but eventually came into the hands of the Schetz family of Antwerp. Sugar was produced for export, but the added distance from Europe and the lack of suitable land put São Vicente at a disadvantage in competition with Pernambuco and Bahia. Nevertheless, these coastal settlements looked much like poorer reproductions of those further to the north.

The future of the southern captaincies did not, however, rest with the ports. Behind the coastal strip, the Serra do Mar range rises steeply to a height of 800 metres. Beyond lies a plateau formed by the Tietê and others rivers, whose rolling hills dotted with trees, temperate climate, and relatively dense Indian population attracted the Europeans. A small settlement developed at Santo André da Borda do Campo, but it was soon surpassed in importance by São Paulo de Piritininga, originally a Jesuit village established in the midst of the Indians of the plateau. The two settlements were merged in 1560 and in the following year São Paulo was raised to the status of a township (*vila*). The Jesuits continued to play an important role in the pacification of the local Indian groups in the next two decades, and by the 1570s São Paulo's existence was secure. Separated from the coast as São Paulo was by the Serra do Mar, the 50 miles between it and Santos could be travelled only by footpath and goods had to be transported on the backs of human porters. São Paulo became the point of control and contact with the Indian population of the interior, serving both as a forward base against the hostile Tamoio to the north and the Carijó to the south and as a supplier of Indian captives to the engenhos of the coast.

By the end of the sixteenth century, the coastal settlements of São Vicente were in decline but on the plateau the basic social and economic features of São Paulo for the next century or so were already well established. Despite the remarks of Jesuit observers who felt that the town and its regions greatly resembled Portugal, São Paulo did not become an Iberian peasant community. From the beginning the Portuguese lived in a sea of Indians as Jesuit missionaries and military expeditions subdued the tribes of the immediate vicinity.

The community was poor and modest. The town had less than 2,000 inhabitants in 1600. Few Portuguese women were attracted to the area and the Portuguese households and farms were filled with captive and semi-captive Indians. Illicit unions between Portuguese men and Indian women were common and a large number of *mamelucos* (the local term for *mestiços*) resulted. Well into the seventeenth century the wills of *Paulistas* (residents of São Paulo) listed Indian slaves, and despite the anti-slavery legislation beginning in 1570, loopholes were always found. Many Indians who were legally free but held in a form of temporary 'tutelage' as *forros* or *administrados* also appear in the wills, passed along like any other property. Indians were used as servants and labourers but also as allies and retainers, linked to the Portuguese by the informal unions and the ties of kinship that resulted from them.

Indians also served as the principal resource in the captaincy. The Portuguese of São Paulo measured their wealth by the number of slaves and supporters they could call upon. 'Rich in archers' was a common description of the most prominent citizens of the plateau. The frontiersman Manoel Preto, for example, was reported to have almost 1,000 bowmen on his estate and, while such numbers were surely an exception, units in the hundreds were not uncommon. While the hierarchical distinctions of noble and commoner were transposed from Portugal, the general poverty of the region, its small European population, and the need for military co-operation against hostile tribes tended to level social differences among the Europeans, who included a relatively large number of Spaniards, Italians, and Germans. In the early period of São Vicente's history, little distinction was made between *mamelucos* and Portuguese so long as the former were willing to live according to what passed in the region for European norms.

The extent of cultural fusion, in fact, was notable. Indian material culture – tools, weapons, handicrafts, foods, and agricultural practices – were widely adopted and used by the Portuguese. The Paulistas were often as skilled with the bow as they were with firearms. The principal Indian language, Tupí, was spoken at all levels of society until well into the eighteenth century. The Portuguese, surrounded by Indian servants, slaves, allies, and concubines, spoke it as a matter of convenience and necessity, and at least some Paulistas were more fluent in it than in their native Portuguese. European forms and institutions were always present, especially in matters of government and religion, but they were limited by the poverty, the sparse European population, and the relative isolation of the region, far from the centres of colonial and metropolitan control.

Throughout the sixteenth and much of the seventeenth centuries the town of São Paulo itself remained small and poor. The most important families lived on their *fazendas* and either maintained a second residence in the town or simply came in periodically to serve on the municipal council or to participate in religious processions. Material possessions were few: a shirt or a musket were highly valued, a pair of boots or a European-style bed a real luxury. The local economy often suffered from a lack of coinage and much trade was done by barter. But by the mid-century some of the rusticity had gone from São Paulo. The Carmelites, Benedictines, and Capuchins of Saint Anthony had built churches, joining the Jesuits, whose college was one of the town's major buildings. Wills and testaments from the mid-century also seem to reflect less poverty than earlier ones. European crops grew well on the plateau. Grapes and wheat were cultivated alongside cotton, small amounts of sugar, and vegetables. Cattle were also raised. By 1614, a flour mill was operating in São Paulo and eventually flour, wine, and marmalade were exported to other captaincies. In 1629 the town's external commerce was estimated to be one-third that of Rio de Janeiro, although only one-fortieth that of Bahia.[32] By the mid seventeenth century the captaincy of São Vicente was no longer isolated from the rest of the colony, although its role was primarily that of a supplier to other captaincies more closely linked to the export sector.

The decline of the local Indian population and rumours of gold, silver, and emeralds in the interior led the Paulistas to turn their ambitions towards the sertão. The Tietê, Paranaíba, and other rivers that flowed westward towards the Paraná system were natural routes to the interior. By the 1580s mobile columns led by the Portuguese and *mamelucos*, but composed mainly of Indian allies, struck westward or southward in search of Indian captives and mineral wealth. These expeditions were organized into quasi-military companies called *bandeiras* (banners), and their participants often spent months or even years in the sertão, preferring to do that, said one governor, rather than serve someone else for a single day. At times the town of São Paulo was half deserted because so many men were absent. Those who stayed behind often acted as outfitters, providing supplies and arms in return for a share of the Indians captured. The sertão and the bandeiras became a way of life. In the forest, the Indian background of the Paulistas was

---

[32] 'Descripción de la provincia del Brasil' [1629], in Mauro, *Le Brésil au XVIIe siècle*, 167–91.

invaluable: they dressed, spoke, ate, and lived more or less like the Indians they led and hunted.

While there is an extensive and often laudatory literature on the Paulistas and their bandeiras, the economic aspects of their operations are both poorly documented and often confusing. Earlier writers such as Alfredo Ellis and Afonso de Escragnolle Taunay continually emphasized the poverty and isolation of São Paulo and ascribed to these causes the thrust into the sertão. However, even if we accept these authors' descriptions of the scope and success of the bandeiras, we are then presented with some puzzling questions about the Paulista economy. Jesuit observers estimated that over 300,000 Indians were taken from the Paraguay missions alone, to say nothing of those captured in the sertão. While such estimates may have been an exaggeration, other observers also provide high figures. Lourenço de Mendonça, prelate of Rio de Janeiro, claimed that in the decade prior to 1638 between 70,000 and 80,000 Indians had been captured.[33] According to Taunay there was a great migratory wave of Indian captives from São Paulo[34] to the engenhos of Bahia and Pernambuco, but there is little documentary evidence to support this view.

Rather than the north-east, it was probably Rio de Janeiro and São Vicente that absorbed the majority of the Indian captives. As we have seen in table 1, the sugar industry in Rio was expanding in this period, reaching an annual growth rate of about 8 per cent between 1612 and 1629. The demand for labour was met to some extent by Indian slaves. Slaves were brought to Rio from São Paulo by sea and also marched overland. As late as 1652 one-third to one-quarter of the labour force on the Benedictine engenhos in Rio de Janeiro was Indian.[35]

It well may be that the *fazendas* of São Paulo itself were the major consumers of Indian labour. Wheat, flour, cotton, grapes, wine, maize, and cattle were all produced on the plateau and some of these products

---

[33] *Memorial*, Biblioteca Nacional de Madrid, Códice 2369, fos. 296–301. Mendonça reported that of 7,000 Indians taken near Lagoa dos Patos in 1625, only 1,000 arrived in São Paulo. High mortality rates then may provide an explanation of what was happening to the captured Indians, but at the same time they provoke questions about why the Paulistas continued to engage in such a risky and uncertain enterprise.

[34] For the arguments against the traditional view, see Jaime Cortesão, *Introdução à história das bandeiras* (2 vols., Lisbon, 1964), II, 302–11, and C. R. Boxer, *Salvador de Sá and the struggle for Brazil and Angola, 1602–1686* (London, 1952), 20–9; see also the curious appendix in Roberto Simonsen, *História económica do Brasil (1500–1820)* (4th edn, São Paulo, 1962), 245–6.

[35] Arquivo Distrital da Braga, Congregação de São Bento 134 (1648–52).

were sent to other captaincies or to the Río de la Plata. A Spaniard long resident in São Paulo estimated wheat production at 120,000 *alqueires* in 1636 and also placed the number of Indian slaves on Paulista estates at 40,000.[36] This estimate seems to be supported by the many references by the eighteenth-century genealogist Paes Leme, who often spoke of large *fazendas* with hundreds of Indians in the seventeenth century. Given the small population of the captaincies, units of this size make sense only if they are producing for more than the local market. Thus, by the export either of Indians or of foodstuffs, São Vicente was drawn into increasing contact with the rest of the colony. Indian labour and the enslavement of Indians remained central aspects of the Paulista economy throughout much of the seventeenth century and a matter of vital concern in the captaincy.

The isolation that had characterized São Paulo in the sixteenth century and contributed to its social and cultural formation began to change after 1600. While São Paulo remained a relatively small town and never achieved the wealth of Salvador or Olinda, it was by the end of the seventeenth century a reasonable facsimile of those centres. It dominated the plateau and was increasingly surrounded by smaller settlements like Mogi das Cruzes (1611), Taubaté (1645), and Itu (1657), the results of bandeira activity and agricultural expansion. In 1681 São Paulo was made the capital of the captaincy and in 1711, two years after the creation of the enlarged captaincy of São Paulo e Minas de Ouro, its status was raised from town to city.

A few great families dominated São Paulo's social life and municipal institutions. For much of the seventeenth century the Pires and Camargo clans carried on an intermittent feud which had originated in a point of family honour but later took on political overtones. Royal control in the region was minimal. In 1691 the governor-general of Brazil wrote that the Paulistas 'know neither God, nor Law, nor Justice'. A few years later they were described by another crown officer as 'deeply devoted to the freedom in which they have always lived since the creation of their town'.[37] São Paulo was called a veritable La Rochelle in 1662, but in fact its loyalty to the crown of Portugal was constant. When in 1640 a small pro-Spanish faction tried to separate the captaincy from the rest of Brazil, it was frustrated by the majority of the population and by the loyalty of Amador Bueno, who refused its offer of leadership.

[36] Cortesão, *Introdução*, II, 305.
[37] Charles R. Boxer, *The Golden Age of Brazil, 1695–1750* (Berkeley and Los Angeles, 1964), 34.

At the same time, any interference in matters directly affecting Paulista interests was strongly opposed. Royal magistrates who meddled in 'matters of the sertão' (i.e. Indians) were often subjected to threats or violence. In 1639 the Spanish Jesuits, objecting to the raids against Guairá and Tape, obtained the bull *Commissum nobis* from Pope Urban VIII, which reiterated the prohibitions against Indian slavery and specifically mentioned Brazil, Paraguay, and the Río de la Plata. This document and the accompanying royal law of March 1640 caused a furore among the principal consumers and suppliers of Indian labour. There was rioting in Rio de Janeiro and the Jesuits were physically expelled from Santos and São Paulo in 1640. Although the Jesuits were allowed to return in 1653, the truculent independence of the Paulistas caused the crown to move cautiously in the captaincy. It was not really until their defeat in the War of the Emboabas in Minas Gerais (1708–9) that the Paulistas' 'pretensions' were brought under control.

While the crown often found the peculiar qualities and attitudes of the Paulistas a nuisance or a problem, it began to call increasingly on their skills and abilities to further royal aims. Expeditions were still often privately organized, but the Portuguese crown and its representatives in the colony began to find definite uses for the bandeiras. The great bandeira of Antônio Rapôso Tavares (1648–52) which crossed the Chaco, skirted the Andes northwards, and followed the river system of the continent's interior to emerge at the mouth of the Amazon was apparently commissioned by the crown and had a geopolitical purpose. Other uses were found for the Paulistas in the arid sertão of the north-east, especially in southern Bahia. From the 1670s onwards, groups of Paulistas could be found in the sertão, ranching on their own lands, Indian-slaving when they could and willing to be employed by the state. Paulistas and Bahians were principally responsible for opening up the area of Piauí to settlement in the 1680s. The Paulista Domingos Jorge Velho helped to open up Piauí and then joined another Paulista, Matias Cardoso de Almeida, in resisting a major Indian rebellion, the *Guerra dos Bárbaros*, which erupted in Rio Grande do Norte and Ceará (1683–1713). Participation in these government-backed actions was particularly attractive because they were considered to be 'just wars' and therefore the Indian captives taken could legally be sold as slaves. Indians captured during the *Guerra dos Bárbaros*, for example, were sold in the city of Natal.

The crown derived increasing benefit everywhere from using the skills and bellicosity of the Paulistas for state purposes. Fighting the

Indians was a primary employment, but other threats to internal security could also be met by the Paulistas. After years of intermittent warfare, it was the same Domingos Jorge Velho who between 1690 and 1695 led the final campaign against the escaped slave community of Palmares. In the far south also, traditional Paulista interests and activities naturally led to state sponsorship in the Portuguese push into the debated frontier with Spanish America.

Both the Paulistas and their traditional rivals, the Spanish Jesuits of Paraguay, had been involved in the opening up and settlement of the lands that lay to the south of São Vicente. Gold had been reported near Paranaguá in the 1570s, and although a town was not established there until 1649, the region was already well known by that time. Further to the south the Jesuits had apparently hoped to extend their Tape missions all the way to the sea at Lagoa dos Patos, but the bandeiras of the 1630s had forced their retreat. The Jesuits returned after 1682 and between that date and 1706 they established seven missions east of the Uruguay river in what was to become Rio Grande do Sul. The cattle introduced into the region from São Paulo and those left to roam by the Jesuits multiplied on the temperate plains into great feral herds. The upland pastures of Santa Catarina were known as the *vaqueria dos pinhais* and those of Rio Grande do Sul and the Banda Oriental as the *vaqueria do mar*. By the 1730s there were Portuguese cattle hunters who exploited these herds for the hides.

The creation in 1680 of a Portuguese outpost at Colônia do Sacramento on the banks of the Río de la Plata was a move with geopolitical and economic motives, designed to stake Portugal's claim to the region and to serve as a base for trade with Upper Peru (and the flow of silver). The subsequent history of the far south was a filling-in of the territory that lay between the small settlements of Paraná and the outpost at Colônia. It was also a story of the interplay between the actions of government and private enterprise. Settlements were made in Santa Catarina in the 1680s, the most important being Laguna (1684), which was settled by Paulistas and Azorean couples sent by the crown. By 1730 the discovery of gold in Minas Gerais had created a strong demand for the livestock of the south and a road had been opened from Laguna to São Paulo by way of Curitiba and Sorocaba, over which mules and horses destined for the mining region were driven.

Early penetration of the lands further to the south had been made by various bandeiras, but by the 1730s there was royal interest in occupying these lands. In 1737 Rio Grande do São Pedro was founded, and in the following year, it and Santa Catarina were made sub-captaincies of Rio de Janeiro. By 1740 more Azorean couples were arriving to serve as frontier settlers. Between 1747 and 1753 about 4,000 couples arrived, joining the Paulistas who also began to move into the region.

Society in the regions lying to the south of São Paulo varied to some extent according to the major economic activities in each. The region of modern Paraná, with its settlements of Paranaguá and Curitiba, was an extension of São Paulo. Early mining activity was characterized by the use of Indian slaves, and by the middle of the eighteenth century blacks were being used in increasing numbers. Eventually, the cattle *fazendas* that developed in the region were also based on slave labour, as the early *sesmarias* make clear. Further to the south life was organized around the scattered military posts and the exploitation of the cattle herds. The horse was an essential element of life, as was maté tea and barbecued beef. Small settlements developed around military posts or at river crossings. In general, it was a simple pastoral society in which cattle-rustling, smuggling, and hunting were the major activities.

The equatorial north

The northern periphery, although separated from São Paulo and the plains of the southern frontier by thousands of kilometres, and despite a strikingly different climate and geography, exhibited many parallels in the development of its society and economy with the extreme south. In the north the failure to create a suitable export economy, the sparse European population (especially the lack of women), the few black slaves, the independent attitude of local government, the cultural and biological fusion of Europeans and Indians, and, most of all, the central role of the Indian in the region's life all duplicated the patterns of the far south.

Although hereditary captaincies had been created for the northern coast of Brazil in the 1530s, these had not been occupied by the Portuguese. Instead, the French were the first to take an active interest in the 'east–west coast' of the north. Only after a group of French nobles led by the Sieur de la Ravardière established a settlement around a fort on Maranhão island in 1612 did the Portuguese show any interest in the area. And only after the surrender of St Louis (São Luís) in 1615 did they expand their control to the Amazon, establishing the town of Belém in 1616. Belém then served as a base of operations against small Dutch and Irish trade forts on the lower Amazon, which the Portuguese destroyed. In 1621 the vast region of northern Brazil was created as a separate state of Maranhão, with its own governor and administration and São Luís as its first capital, although after the 1670s governors began to spend much of their time at Belém, which became the capital in 1737.

Given the meagre population and resources of the state of Maranhão, the crown once again created hereditary captaincies as a means of shifting the burden of colonization into private hands. Cumá, Caete, and Cametá were created in the 1630s, as was Cabo do Norte (present-day Amapá), which in 1637 was given to Bento Maciel Parente, a courageous but rapacious Indian-fighter and backwoodsman (*sertanista*). Eventually, in 1665, Marajó island (Ilha Grande de Joanes) was also made a hereditary captaincy.[38] None of these grants proved particularly successful and they were eventually abolished in the mid eighteenth century. Until the 1680s, effective Portuguese control was limited to the areas around the two cities São Luís and Belém and a few river outposts designed to control canoe traffic and Indian slaving. Of these, Gurupá, which served as a toll station and control point some ten or twelve days' journey up the Amazon from Belém, was probably the most important.

As in São Vicente, the colony in the north was oriented towards the interior. Belem and São Paulo stood symbolically at the extremes of effective settlement. Both lay at the entrance to major river systems that facilitated movement into the interior, and both were bases for continual expeditions.

In the north, the Portuguese and their *caboclo* sons, accompanied by Indian slaves or workers, organized *entradas*, or expeditions, up the rivers in search of forest products like cacao and vanilla or Indians who might be 'rescued' from their enemies and made to serve the Portuguese. The life of these *sertanistas* was difficult and dangerous. Their river expeditions often lasted for months at a time. In the interior, the Europeans adopted many aspects of Indian life. The hammock, the canoe, manioc flour, and forest lore were all copied from the Indians among whom the Portuguese lived. A form of Tupí was spoken as a *lingua franca* throughout the state of Maranhão and remained the

[38] A sixth captaincy, Xingu, was created in 1685 but was never occupied.

dominant language of the area until well into the eighteenth century. The steel axe and the Catholic Church symbolized the cultural influences moving in the other direction, but in the far north, as in the south, the Indian impact was much greater and lasted longer than in the plantation zones of the coast.

The frontier nature of the state of Maranhão was underlined by its tiny European population. In 1637 the Jesuit Luíz Figueira complained of the lack of European women and decried the sins that resulted from illicit unions with Indians in terms exactly like those used almost a century earlier by Jesuits in Bahia and São Paulo. Efforts to rectify this situation had been made as early as 1619, when Azorean immigrants were sent to São Luís. We have already seen how this technique of sponsored immigration from the Atlantic islands to the frontiers was used in the far south, and it was to be employed again at later times in the Amazon region. But despite such measures, the European population remained small. In 1637 São Luís had only 230 citizens and Belém only 200. By 1672 the whole state of Maranhão was thought to contain no more than 800 European inhabitants. However, Belém began to grow in the eighteenth century. From about 500 in 1700, its population reached 2,500 by 1750. By that time the total population of Pará and Rio Negro was estimated at 40,000, including the Indians under Portuguese control.

As in the south, the small number of Europeans, the physical isolation from the centres of colonial government, the high percentage of Indians in the population, and the economic opportunities presented by the exploitation of the sertão and the Indians combined to create conditions in which Portuguese institutions were attenuated and European culture was deeply penetrated by indigenous elements. The two cities housed the senior government officers, a few merchants, and, eventually, the main establishments of the missionary orders. The wealthier colonists lived there, often combining interests in agriculture with the financing of slaving expeditions to the interior. The *entradas* were usually led by Europeans, but the canoes were paddled by Indians. In the scattered forts and outposts that were eventually established up the rivers, small garrisons of poor conscripts lived in isolation. Soldiers, frontiersmen, and deserters became *cunhamenas* ('squawmen'), fathering *mestiço* children and often living as agents for missionaries or government-sponsored *entradas*.

Royal control over the region was tenuous. The colonists of Pará and

Maranhão proved to be as truculent and as independent as the Paulistas had been. The municipal councils of Belém and São Luís forced governors to appear before them to explain policy until the crown put an end to the practice. Royal officers who favoured the settlers' interests in matters of taxation or the use of Indian labour were supported; those who favoured the missionaries' efforts to limit the use of Indians were opposed. Curiously enough, António Vieira, the great Jesuit missionary, called Maranhão 'Brazil's La Rochelle', the same term used to describe São Paulo's resistance to royal authority. As in São Paulo, it was usually 'matters of the sertão' (i.e. Indians) that provoked the strongest reactions on the part of colonists. The Jesuits were expelled from the main cities on two occasions and in the 1720s a campaign of vilification and complaint against them was mounted that eventually contributed to their ultimate expulsion from Brazil. The colonists sometimes found considerable support from those governors who were themselves violators of the laws against Indian slavery. This could be said of Cristóvão da Costa Freire (1707–18), or Bernardo Perreira de Berredo (1718–22), whose *Anais históricos* is still a major source for the region's history. The virulence of the struggle between the colonists and the missionary orders sprang ultimately from the economy and the central role of Indian labour within it.

From the beginning, the Portuguese had attempted to create an export-oriented economy in the north. In the immediate vicinity of Belém and São Luís both crown and colonists tried to develop sugar plantations like those of Pernambuco or Bahia. As early as 1620 privileges were given to those who promised to build engenhos in Maranhão.[39] Some sugar was eventually produced, especially near São Luís, but there were serious problems impeding the industry's growth, such as a persistent shortage of artisans and technicians, despite efforts to attract and maintain them. In 1723 the town council of Belém complained that there was only one blacksmith to serve the twenty mills of the area. Even more serious was a chronic shortage of labour. The importation of Africans prior to 1682 was sporadic. In that year the Companhia de Commercio de Maranhão was formed to supply slaves to the region. Its failure to do so, along with mismanagement and price-fixing, contributed to a settler revolt in 1684 that was also directed against the Jesuits. The crown suppressed the revolt, but it loosened the restrictions on using Indian slaves. The colonists continued to

[39] AHU, cod. 32, fos. 58–60.

agitate for the importation of Africans and, with local private capital in short supply, the crown itself sponsored a new company, the Companhia de Cacheu e Cabo Verde, to supply at least 145 slaves a year to the state of Maranhão. This trickle of slaves did little to stimulate production and caused much grumbling. Colonists complained of the high prices charged and the settlers of Pará claimed that the ships unloaded the best slaves at São Luís. Prior to 1750 probably only a few thousand Africans reached the north of Brazil.

Sugar production suffered from other problems as well. Shipping to the north was often irregular. In 1694 only one ship called at Belém. The sugar, already inferior in quality to that of Bahia, often lay for long periods on the docks, where its value fell even lower. Increasingly, the colonists and the missionary orders who owned engenhos turned to the production of rum for local consumption rather than sugar for export. Despite royal attempts in 1706 to stop distilling, production continued. By 1750 there were 31 engenhos and 120 small-scale *engenhocas* in the state of Maranhão.[40] While a few of these estates were large operations like those of the Carmelites and Jesuits, the majority were small units producing rum for local use.

Other cash crops were also produced. Cotton was grown, especially in Maranhão. It was used to make homespun cloth throughout the north and it also circulated widely as a form of currency, but did not figure as an important export until the late eighteenth century. Attempts were made to develop other crops. Indigo and coffee were introduced or sponsored by the crown, but with little success. Faced with the general failure to develop any export crop, the colonists depended increasingly on the products of the forest: vanilla, sarsparilla, anatto dye all found markets in Europe, but of all these so-called *drogas do sertão* none was so important as cacao.

The crown tried with little success to stimulate cacao production between 1678 and 1681 by offering tax exemptions and other advantages to producers. The colonists preferred to send their Indians after the wild cacao of the Amazonian forest rather than cultivate the sweeter domesticated variety. Cacao grew wild throughout the region and little capital was needed to gather it. *Tropas* of canoes paddled by Indians would move upriver, set up temporary bases while they gathered the fruit, and then return down river to Belém after about six months. Desertion,

---

[40] *Relatório* of Ouvidor João Antônio da Cruz Denis Pinheiro (1751), printed in J. Lucio de Azevedo, *Os Jesuitas no Grão-Pará* (2nd edn, Coimbra, 1930), 410–16.

Indian attacks, and the lack of commercial opportunities all presented difficulties to the cacao trade. Slowly, however, as markets for Amazonian cacao developed in Italy and Spain, the trade increased. In the mid-1720s about 100 licences a year were granted to canoes going to gather cacao. By the 1730s this figure had risen to 250 and by 1736 it stood at 320. During this era of open but licensed exploitation, before 1755, cacao was Pará's major export. Between 1730 and 1744 it constituted over 90 per cent of the captaincy's exports. Between 1730 and 1755 over 16,000 metric tons of cacao were exported from the Amazon region, and it was the major attraction for ships calling at Belém. At times Amazonian cacao fetched higher prices on the Lisbon market than Bahian sugar, but after 1745 exports became more irregular because of scarce labour, shortage of shipping, and a drop in cacao prices.

The failure to develop a dependable export crop during most of the seventeenth century underlined the essential poverty of the north. The settlements ran at a deficit. The tithe collected in Maranhão usually failed to cover the costs of government and it was the same in Pará until 1712. Government licences and the tithe on forest products were the principal sources of government revenue. Belém and São Luís were poor towns. As in São Paulo, imported goods were a rarity and the population depended on rough, locally-made products. There was little capital available for investment and a chronic shortage of coinage. Until 1748, when Lisbon minted coins specifically for Maranhão-Pará, almost all transactions were carried out by barter or by using cotton cloth or cacao as a means of exchange. What currency did exist circulated at twice its face value and the commodities used for exchange were often given an official rate of exchange different from their market value, thus making business difficult.

Ultimately, it was the Indian who became the key to the development of the north. The crown, the colonists, and the missionary orders all sought, for various reasons and under various pretexts, to bring Indians under European control. Almost from the beginning of the northern settlement this issue brought the colonists into direct conflict with the missionary orders, especially the Jesuits, and often with the crown and its representatives as well.

Northern Brazil became a great mission field. The Franciscans were established in Pará as early as 1617, but by the 1640s the Jesuits had replaced the Franciscans as the major missionary order in the north. With the arrival in 1653 of the remarkable and energetic Father António

Vieira as Provincial, the Jesuits' attempts to protect the Indians and to bring them under their control intensified. Vieira used the power of pulpit and pen to condemn the many abuses committed against the Indians in Maranhão and Pará, and his advocacy eventually resulted in a new law of 1655 against Indian enslavement. This legislation followed the lines of the early laws of 1570, 1595, and 1609 mentioned above, but it did leave loopholes that permitted defensive expeditions against hostile Indians and allowed those who 'rescued' Indians to exact five years of personal service, after which those Indians would become part of the general free labour pool. The law was, in reality, a compromise: the crown wanted to respond to the arguments of the Jesuits, but was unwilling to eliminate completely colonists' access to Indians because of the unrest it would create and because it had itself begun in 1649 to tax all slaves brought in from the interior. The Jesuits were given free rein to bring Indians from the interior by peaceful means and to establish them in mission villages where they would provide a pool of labour the colonists could draw upon.

The law of 1655 did little to eliminate the Indian slave trade and the Jesuits soon discovered that bringing in Indians by peaceful persuasion was also very difficult. Moreover, such limitations as the law imposed were the cause of continual complaints by settlers against the Jesuits, who were even expelled from São Luís and Belém in 1661–2 as a result of their Indian policy. A further law of 1680 which prohibited all Indian slavery and increased Jesuit control over Indian souls and Indian labour provoked even more virulent reactions from the colonists and contributed to the expulsion of the Jesuits from Maranhão in 1684. The Jesuits were reinstated with royal support and a new ordinance, the *Regimento das Missões* of 1686, was issued to regulate Indian affairs and to grant the missionary orders even greater powers. But two years later a further law also provided for government-sponsored *tropas de resgate* ('rescue troops') to bring in Indian slaves and distribute them among the colonists. In this arrangement, the Jesuits were to accompany each troop to ensure its compliance with the rules for slaving. To decide whether Indians captured by the state-sponsored *tropas* were taken under the limitations of the law, a Junta das Missões (Board of Missions) composed of representatives of the missionary orders and a royal judge met periodically in Belém. While the Jesuits were reluctant to co-operate with this legalized slaving, they were astute enough to realize that some compromise was necessary. The legislation of 1686–8 remained the basic law governing Portuguese–Indian relations until the middle of the following century.

The state of Maranhão, then, depended on a variety of forms of Indian labour, all based more or less on coercion. Indian slaves acquired legally or illegally were used everywhere and could be found in the governor's household, on the plantations of the Jesuits, and on the estates of the settlers. In addition, 'rescued' Indians and those who had come in of their own free will were placed in *aldeias* (villages) under missionary control. By 1730 the Jesuits alone had over 21,000 Indians in 28 mission villages and the Franciscans controlled another 26 aldeias. It is estimated that by the 1740s about 50,000 Indians lived under the missionaries. The aldeias were of various types. Those near the centres of Portuguese population provided labour under contract to the colonists. A few were royal villages used exclusively by the government to provide canoemen or workers in the salt-pans. The missionary orders were also entitled to the exclusive use of some villages for the upkeep of their establishments. Deep in the interior were frontier aldeias whose labour was only occasionally called on when a *tropa de resgate* passed by.

It was the success of the aldeias and the missionaries' interference in the colonists' access to Indian labour, together with the economic activities of the religious orders, that brought ever more vehement complaints from the settlers. The Jesuits were as always the prime target. They had acquired and developed extensive holdings in the north: cattle ranches on Marajó island, engenhos, cotton and cacao plantations. They had introduced new crops into the region and were also very active in gathering the *drogas do sertão*. In 1734 over one-third of the wild cacao registered at the Gurupá customs station belonged to the Jesuits. While the Mercedarians and Carmelites also had extensive properties, it was always the Jesuits who drew the sharpest criticism, probably because of their unaccommodating attitude on the issue of Indian slavery. Their greatest critic was Paulo de Silva Nunes, a retainer of Governor Costa Freire, who held some minor posts in the colony and later became the settlers' official representative in Lisbon. His angry petitions eventually led to a royal investigation in 1734 which exonerated the Jesuits, but the inquest itself indicated a stiffening of royal policy towards the religious orders which eventually resulted in the expulsion of the Jesuits and the secularization of the missions.

We should keep in mind that, from the Indian perspective, the problem was not one of labour but of survival. The demands made by the Portuguese and the mistreatment they meted out took their toll. In addition, epidemic diseases periodically decimated the Indian population. There were smallpox epidemics in 1621 and 1644 and then a region-wide outbreak in 1662. The following century brought no relief, with smallpox again in 1724 and a devastating measles epidemic in the 1740s. Each outbreak was followed by a shortage of labour that led to renewed slaving. Regions were depopulated by disease or were 'slaved out'. As the Portuguese penetrated the region of the Negro, Japura, and Solimões rivers, they found it increasingly difficult to trade for captives with the river tribes who already had access to steel tools and weapons acquired by trade with peoples in contact with the Dutch on the lower Essequibo. Faced with this situation the *tropas* depended increasingly on direct force.

North-western Amazonia was opened up in the late seventeenth century. By the 1690s a small outpost had been established near Manaus at the mouth of the Rio Negro and after 1700 Portuguese slaving on the Solimões river and the Rio Negro was common. These activities eventually led the populous Manao people to resist. They were defeated in a series of punitive campaigns in the 1720s, the survivors being sold as slaves in Belém. The region was given to the Carmelites as a mission field. They established some missions, but their efforts were often directed more towards economic gain than spiritual care of the Indians. Finally, it was also on this far frontier that, as in the south, the interests of Portugal came into direct conflict with those of Spain. Beginning in 1682, the Bohemian-born Jesuit Samuel Fritz, working out of the Spanish province of Quito, had established missions among the Omagua people along the Solimões river. Eventually, after diplomatic manoeuvring and some fighting, the Spanish Jesuits were forced to withdraw from the region. In 1755 north-western Amazonia became a separate captaincy, Rio Negro, establishing Portuguese authority well beyond the line of Tordesillas.

To summarize: the northern and southern extremes of Portuguese America seemed in many ways to lag behind the centres of settlement. The life and concerns of Belém and São Paulo in 1680 were much like those of Salvador or Olinda in 1600: the role of the missionaries, access to Indian workers, tapping the Atlantic slave trade. The relative racial proportions of the population – small numbers of whites, few Africans, many *mestiços* and a high percentage of Indians – in both peripheries also recalled earlier periods in the plantation zones of the coast. The differences, however, were not chronological but structural. They were related to the way these peripheries were integrated into the export economy of the colony. São Paulo first began to grow as a supplier of labour and foodstuffs to other captaincies. Then, with the development of mining in the captaincy, especially after 1700, the early pattern began to change; and, as it was drawn into the supply and exploitation of the mines, São Paulo came increasingly to resemble the captaincies of the north-east. In Amazonia change came more slowly. The failure to develop an export crop was the main reason. Although by the 1730s cacao and other forest products found some outlet, it was only after 1755 with state intervention in economy and society that the northern periphery was also drawn into the Atlantic commercial system.

THE URBAN FABRIC

The cities of Brazil, whether in the zones devoted to plantation agriculture or at the extremities of Portuguese settlement, were essentially a creation of the export economy. All the major centres were ports, points of exchange between the products of Brazil and the incoming flow of manufactures, immigrants, and slaves from Europe and Africa. The few secondary towns that existed were usually small riverine agricultural settlements or minor ports, tied by coastal trade to the maritime centres. In the north-east, secondary towns were few and slow to develop because of the attraction of the engenhos. Populations and economic resources tended to concentrate on the sugar plantations, so that during the safra the engenho, with its hundreds of labourers, its artisans, its chapel, and sometimes even its resident priest, provided many of the functions and services of a town. Noticeably absent were the small peasant villages on the Portuguese model; but in the context of slave-based plantations they would have made little sense. Only São Paulo and the towns of the plateau developed as inland settlements relatively free of the export orientation of the rest of the colony; they were of course small and unimportant throughout much of this period and were greatly overshadowed by Olinda and Recife, Salvador, and Rio de Janeiro.

Between 1532 and 1650 six cities and 31 towns or *vilas* were established in Brazil. The first foundations were concentrated along the coastal strip between Olinda and Santos, but after 1580, with the northward expansion of the colony, there was a new wave of foundations as Natal (1599), São Luís (1615), and Belém (1616) were established. Once again all these cities were ports and it was not until the second quarter of the eighteenth century and the opening of Minas Gerais that the urban network began to spread inland. In fact, it can be argued that Brazil had no network of cities, but only an archipelago of ports, each surrounded by its own agricultural hinterland and in closer contact with Lisbon than with each other. This was the result of the export orientation of the economy and of the Portuguese imperial structure, which sought to keep each captaincy directly dependent on the metropolis. The coastal location of Brazilian cities made fortification and defence matters of constant concern and expense. Dutch and English interlopers regularly attacked Brazilian ports in the period 1580–1620 and after 1620 these cities became vulnerable to attack as part of wider conflicts, as in the Dutch seizure of Salvador in 1624 or the French attack on Rio de Janeiro in 1710.

By contemporary European standards Brazilian cities were small and unimposing. The population of Salvador, the largest, grew from about 14,000 in 1585 to 25,000 in 1724, and reached nearly 40,000 by 1750. About half its residents were slaves. Olinda, the capital of Pernambuco, had a population of perhaps 4,000 in 1630 and only 8,000 in 1654. (Its port facility, Recife, did not really take form as a separate municipality until the Dutch made it their capital.) The cities of the north were even smaller. In the 1660s São Luís contained only 600 *moradores* (white inhabitants) and Belém only 400. Rio de Janeiro remained small throughout the seventeenth century, growing to 40,000 by the middle of the eighteenth after the opening up of Minas Gerais. These cities served as civil and ecclesiastical centres. The governor-general and the High Court sat in Salvador and after 1676 that city was also the archepiscopal see. In the capital city of each captaincy resided the governor and chief magistrate as well as the principal fiscal officers. Export cities, cities of ships, docks, and warehouses, cities of stevedores, sailors, and slave markets, the Brazilian ports acquired a certain similarity of plan born of necessity and function. Business concentrated near the wharves and warehouses where the sugar, tobacco, and hides were gathered, weighed, and taxed. The wealthy residents, planters or merchants often sought to remove themselves from the world of the wharves – hence the separation of the docks from the residential areas. In Salvador there was an upper city of government buildings and homes and a lower city of commerce. In Pernambuco, the port facility developed at Recife a few kilometres away from Olinda. High ground was preferred for public buildings and churches, usually the best constructions in a city. Cut stone and tile had been shipped from Europe in the 1570s and 1580s as ballast, and by 1600 impressive civil and religious buildings were being raised in the major cities. Many of these were then replaced, rebuilt, or improved in the mid seventeenth century. The Jesuit colleges built in the main cities at the close of the sixteenth century were among the most important buildings, as were the Franciscan churches and monasteries. The churches defined the quarters of the cities, for the parish was also the neighbourhood and reference point for civil and religious purposes.

One distinguishing characteristic of the Brazilian city of this period was the absence of its wealthiest and most prominent citizens for much of the year. The sugar planters and ranchers maintained urban residences but spent much of their time on their estates. Much has sometimes been made of the 'rural dominance' of Brazil's social and economic life. While this is true, it is misleading. City and plantation, or port and hinterland, were not polar opposites but part of an integrated continuum. Interaction between city and countryside was continuous and was faciliated by the fact that the vast majority of the rural population lived within a few days' journey of the coastal cities.

The cities had come to life under a variety of political conditions. Where the original donataries were weak, private power did not greatly constrain municipal authority. In Pernambuco, however, the Albuquerque Coelho family exercised its authority well into the seventeenth century, while in Rio de Janeiro the Correa de Sá clan remained predominant until the 1660s. In Salvador the presence of the chief royal officials of the colony also hampered the local exercise of political authority by the municipality. Smaller, more remote towns were less inhibited and tended to advocate without restraint the interests of the locally dominant economic groups expressed through municipal institutions.

Political life centred on the *senado da câmara*, the senate or town council, usually composed of three or four councillors, one or two municipal judges, and a city attorney. The voting members of the council were chosen by a complicated system of indirect elections from lists of men with the proper social qualifications. These *homens bons* were expected to be men of property, residents of the city, untainted by artisan origins or religious or ethnic impurity. While there were exceptions to these requirements, especially in frontier communities, they were generally honoured. Not so, however, the prohibitions against consecutive terms and relatives serving together, which were usually ignored, with the excuse that there were not enough men qualified to hold public office.

All aspects of municipal life and often those of the surrounding countryside fell under the control of the câmaras. The minutes of a typical month's activities in the mid seventeenth century might include regulating sanitation, fixing the price of sugar, municipal taxes, awarding the slaughterhouse contract, and organizing an expedition to hunt down runaway slaves. In time, and to the displeasure of royal governors, magistrates, and prelates, the town councils sought to extend their authority. Câmaras often wrote directly to Lisbon and some maintained attorneys in Portugal to look after their interests. When legislation or royal policy seemed to threaten the interests of the local elite, opposition coalesced around the câmara. Prohibitions against Indian enslavement provide a case in point in the seventeenth century. In Salvador (1610), Rio de Janeiro (1640), São Paulo (1640), and Belém (1662), the câmaras spearheaded resistance to royal policy and led movements that resulted in the arrest or expulsion of governors or Jesuits who were held responsible for anti-enslavement legislation.

It is clear that, while the câmara sought to promote the welfare of the municipality in general, these bodies represented most actively the interests of the locally dominant groups. In Salvador, the one city where the lists of councillors are almost complete, it can be seen that the câmara members were most often drawn from the *senhores de engenho* and *lavradores de cana* of the region. Of 260 men elected to voting office on the câmara of Salvador between 1680 and 1729, over half were mill owners, cane farmers, or large landowners; if the merchants and professionals who had acquired lands by the time of their election are added, the proportion rises to over 80 per cent.[41] Membership in the municipal council, then, was not the exclusive domain of one group, but the sugar sector clearly dominated and the same family names appear year after year. If this was the case in a large city with a high degree of social differentiation, then we can assume that the pattern of limited representation was even more intense in smaller places where the

---

[41] Cf. Charles R. Boxer, *Portuguese society in the tropics* (Madison, 1965), 72–110; Flory, 'Bahian society', 139–44.

number of potential councilmen was reduced. The câmaras tended to define the common interest in terms of the interests of the economic groups from which they were drawn. Thus, the councils of Belem and São Paulo ardently sought to ensure the right to send out Indian slaving expeditions, while those of Rio de Janeiro and Bahia were often concerned with establishing a moratorium on debts incurred by sugar planters or combating a royal trade monopoly.

Within the context of urban political life it is appropriate to discuss two social classes, the artisans and the merchants, whose political fortunes varied greatly in the cities of colonial Brazil. In contrast to Portugal, where artisan representation in town councils was a permanent characteristic of urban life and where artisan corporations (*bandeiras*) and the artisan council (*casa do vinte-quatro*) had exercised considerable influence, the Brazilian senates were usually without such representation. When artisans did participate in the town councils it was usually only in matters of direct interest to the crafts and trades, such as licences or price-fixing. The artisan crafts had not been well represented in Brazil in the early years of settlement, and even in the mid seventeenth century their numbers were small. Salvador, the largest city, had only 70 registered artisans in 1648. Artisan organizations became more active in the years after 1640, electing judges for each trade in Salvador and advising the senate of Rio de Janeiro on certain issues. In Salvador artisan representatives led by a *juiz do povo* (people's tribune) had formal representation in the town council from 1641 to 1711, but their position was so secondary that they were forced to sit out of earshot of the main table to prevent their participation in matters that did not concern them. Artisan complicity in the project to limit the number of new engenhos and in a tax riot in 1710 won them the enmity of the planters and brought their representation to an end.

The small number of urban artisans and their relatively weak political position was due to a number of related phenomena. First, the demand for many artisan skills on sugar plantations drew men in these occupations to the countryside, lessening their numbers and power in the cities. 'Mechanical office' was an 'ignoble' profession according to traditional concepts of society and artisans suffered discrimination on that ground. Royal office, membership in knightly orders, and other such honours were beyond their reach. In the Misericórdia of Salvador artisans were relegated to secondary status as brothers of lower condition and in the militia regiments artisans rarely received commissions. Contributing to their lowly status was the influence of slavery. Many slaves learnt to perform the 'mechanical offices' with skill. In addition, free people of colour looked upon the skilled trades as a step upward and set up shop whenever they could. Slave labour tended to depress wages and weaken the traditional qualitative distinctions of master (*mestre*) and apprentice of the Portuguese guild system. The existence of a small but growing percentage of *pardo* artisans lessened the prestige of the craftsmen as a group. In short, artisan status, never high in Portugal, was further lowered in Brazil within the context of a slave society. But this is not to say that artisans were unimportant in Brazilian cities. In the building and clothing trades, goldsmithing, tanning, and many other occupations, artisan brotherhoods, organized under the protection of a patron saint, assumed their obligations in municipal processions and festivals. Still, their power as trade guilds was weak and they remained for the most part under the thumb of the town councils or governors.

As for the political and social position of the merchants, it can be said that the Portuguese maintained a Ciceronian attitude towards business. Cicero had written: 'Commerce, if it is on a small scale, is to be considered mean; but if it is large-scale and extensive, importing much from many places and distributing to many without misrepresentation, it is not to be greatly censured.'[42] This was exactly the sentiment in colonial Brazil, where real distinctions existed between the export–import merchants, the *homens de negócio*, and the retail traders or shopkeepers, the *mercadores de loja*. In theory, any commerce in one's own name was considered a non-noble occupation, and mercantile origins were, like artisan background, cause for exclusion from honour and civil distinction. To this disability was added the fact that merchants were considered to be mostly of New Christian (i.e. Jewish) stock and thus suffered discrimination on that ground as well. While this New Christian connection has sometimes been overstated, a study of Salvador reveals that in the seventeenth century about half the resident merchants were New Christians.[43] But in the context of an export-oriented economy in which commerce was an essential element of life, such disabilities did not remain unchallenged or, at least, immutable. The

---

[42] Cicero, *De officiis*, I, 150–1. This work was known in Brazil. A copy appears in the inventory of *senhor de engenho* João Lopes Fiuza, APB, secção judiciária, maço 623, 4.

[43] Much of this section is drawn from Rae Flory and David G. Smith, 'Bahian merchants and planters in the seventeenth and early eighteenth centuries', *HAHR*, 58/4 (Nov. 1978), 571–94.

shopkeepers found their upward mobility continually blocked but the export merchants, who were involved in trade with Africa and Europe and, during the Iberian union, in a brisk contraband with Spanish America, could not be excluded from social and political advancement.

Though never great in absolute numbers, the merchants had some attributes that facilitated social advancement. The overwhelming majority of them were Europeans, many often coming to Brazil as agents for merchants at home or brought over by some uncle or cousin already doing business in Brazil. It is not surprising that many married Brazilian women, often daughters of the landed elite, who were willing, in some cases, to overlook the New Christian 'taint'. Success also cleared its own trail, as wealthy merchants were able to buy engenhos or ranches and gain membership in the prestigious Misericórdia or Franciscan tertiary brotherhoods. In many ways, the merchant class was absorbed into the landed elite in a gradual process that by the late seventeenth century blurred the social distinctions between the two groups.

Such fusion, however, did not eliminate the inevitable antagonism between merchants and producers born of their economic relationship. Planters' complaints against the merchants' 'extortion' persisted throughout the period in all the captaincies. The planters' habit of buying necessary equipment on credit for 20–30 per cent above the Lisbon price by mortgaging the next harvest at a set price below its market value was the cause of endless acrimony and remonstrance to the crown. In 1663, and periodically thereafter, planters managed to stop engenhos and canefields from being sold piecemeal to satisfy debts, but the mercantile interest was always strong enough to prevent the realization of the planters' dream – a complete moratorium on debts. The merchants' dictum, as expressed by Francisco Pinheiro – 'Do everything possible to obtain the highest price' – did nothing to mitigate the economic antagonism between them and the agrarian groups in the colony.[44]

The social and political rise of the merchants signalled by their increasing participation in town councils, commissions in militia regiments, membership in prestigious lay brotherhoods, and absorption into the planter aristocracy seems to have begun in the mid seventeenth century and intensified in the first decades of the eighteenth century. This was an epoch of severe strain in the Portuguese Atlantic empire,

[44] The most complete set of merchant records are those of Francisco Pinheiro (1707–52) contained in Luís Lisanti (ed.), *Negócios coloniais* (5 vols., Brasilia, 1973).

to which the crown responded with a series of mercantilist measures designed to shore up the flagging economy. The creation of the Brazil Company in 1649 (transformed into a government agency in 1663) with monopoly rights over the trade in certain commodities and the responsibility to provide a well-protected fleet was a wartime measure. It was followed in 1678 by the creation of a similar Maranhão Company designed to provide slaves to the north and granted control of commerce in that region. Such measures, while they sometimes struck at the interests of Brazilian merchants, were viewed with particular dislike by the planters and other colonists and tended to intensify the traditional planter–merchant conflict. Thus, during a period in which merchants were becoming increasingly important and prominent as a class, resistance towards them and towards royal mercantilist measures became intense.

In two places this conflict erupted into a violent confrontation. In 1684, the colonists of São Luís, led by a sugar planter named Manuel Beckman, rose against the company, declared its monopoly void, and took control of the city. The revolt petered out and Beckman was captured and executed. More serious was the civil conflict that broke out in Pernambuco, where the planter aristocrats of Olinda resisted the rise of neighbouring Recife as an independent city and suppressed the Portuguese-born merchants who resided there and to whom they were often indebted. The merchants, for their part, objected to their lack of representation in the câmara of Olinda, which levied the taxes on Recife. Matters came to a head in 1710–11 in a bitter but not particularly bloody civil war between the two factions of Olinda planters and Recife-based *mascates*, or merchants. This War of the Mascates revealed the natural tensions between merchants and planters and also the fact that within the colony's increasingly mercantilist orientation the merchant class would play an important role.

The turn of the century had brought not only more active merchant participation in Brazilian social and political life, but an intensification of the crown's role in municipal government as part of a new state activism. A major alteration in local government occurred between 1696 and 1700, with the creation of *juizes de fora* in the major Brazilian cities. These royally appointed professional magistrates presided over the câmaras and exercised authority in the preparation of electoral lists. The crown's justification for their use in Brazil was the elimination of favouritism and nepotism in the town councils, but their ultimate effect was to diminish the local autonomy of the câmaras. In addition, the expansion of settlement into the interior and the growth of secondary towns near the coast led in the first decades of the eighteenth century to the establishment of new municipal senates, a development which diminished the former authority of the coastal centres. For example, planters elected to the town council of Salvador increasingly declined to serve, preferring to attend to their engenhos or to take office on the senate of the new rural câmaras like those of Cachoeira or Santo Amaro, founded in 1698 and 1724 respectively. While planters continued to dominate Salvador's senate throughout the colonial period, there were increasing opportunities in other port cities for the merchants. The positions that they acquired by the middle of the eighteenth century, however, were in less powerful institutions.

SOCIAL STRUCTURE

Brazil was from its early period of settlement too large an area with too complex and diversified an economy for its social and political forms to become simply the sugar plantation writ large, but as we have seen, the demands of sugar agriculture and the peculiarities of its organization contributed in no small way to the ordering of society. The Portuguese had brought with them an idealized concept of social hierarchy buttressed by theology and a practical understanding of social positions and relationships as these functioned in Portugal. These concepts and experiences defined the terminology of social organization and set the parameters within which society evolved. But export agriculture and the plantation created their own hierarchies and realities.

As early as 1549 Duarte Coelho, donatary of Pernambuco, described his colonists in a way which unconsciously outlined the social hierarchy of his captaincy:

some build engenhos because they are powerful enough to do so, others plant cane, others cotton, and others food crops, which are the principal and most important things in the land; others fish, which is also very necessary; others have boats to seek provisions...Others are master engenho builders, sugar masters, carpenters, blacksmiths, masons, potters, makers of sugar forms, and other trades.[45]

Here was a natural social order in an economy based on commercial agriculture. Mill owners came first, followed by cane farmers. Next,

---

[45] Letter of 15 Apr. 1549, *Cartas de Duarte Coelho a El Rei* (Recife, 1967), 71.

those engaged in other export activities were mentioned. Men in subsistence farming or other such activities received special mention just as peasants in Europe were usually singled out for praise as the foundation of all else, but they were mentioned last among the agricultors. With a bare mention of commerce and merchants, Duarte Coelho then turned to the artisans, listing them roughly in the order of their importance in the sugar-making process, or, put another way, according to the annual salary that each would expect to earn on an engenho.

Duarte Coelho's description is revealing both in what it includes and what it omits. The hierarchy described is a functional–occupational order directly linked to export agriculture, primarily sugar. While reflecting an essential reality, it is incomplete in that it describes only the free population. The vast majority of the colonial population – the Indians and, later, the African slaves – do not figure here. In reality, in addition to this agrarian occupational hierarchy, Brazilian society was ordered by two other principles: a juridical division based primarily on distinctions between slave and free, and a racial gradation from white to black.

In the sixteenth century some attempt had been made to maintain the traditional legal distinctions between noble and commoner and the divisions of a European society of estates or orders. But the planter class failed to evolve into a hereditary nobility and all whites tended to aspire to high rank. *Fidalgos* (nobles) and churchmen continued to enjoy certain juridical rights and exemptions. On solemn or important occasions representatives of the traditional estates were convoked. Such was the case, for example, when, in reaction to a property tax in 1660, the câmara of Rio de Janeiro was joined by representatives of the nobility, clergy, and people, or when, at the founding of the town of Cachoeira, 'men of the people' and 'serious men of government' met to establish the town ordinances.[46] In Brazil, however, other forms of social organization made these traditional principles of stratification less important.

Juridically, Brazilian society was divided between slave and free status. Because of the large numbers of unfree labourers, Indian and African, the distinction between slave and free was crucial. But even

[46] Cf. Vivaldo Coaracy, *O Rio de Janeiro no século XVII* (Rio de Janeiro, 1965), 161; Arquivo Municipal de Cachoeira, Livro 1 de Vereação (1968). See also José Honório Rodrigues, *Vida e história* (Rio de Janeiro, 1966), 132.

within the clear legal separation of slave and free status there were intermediate categories. Indians who had been captured and placed under the tutelage of colonists, the so-called *forros* or *administrados*, were legally free but treated little differently from slaves. Moreover, those slaves who had arranged to make payments for their freedom or who had received their liberty on condition of future services or payments apparently enjoyed as *coartados* a legal position that distinguished them from slaves. Thus, while the juridical divisions of a European society of estates existed in Brazil they were of less importance in a colony where the distinctions of a slave society exercised great influence on social stratification.

Moreover, the existence of three major racial groups – Europeans, American Indians, and Africans – in a colony created by Europeans resulted in a colour-based hierarchy with whites at the top and blacks at the bottom. The place of people of mixed background – the mulattos, *mamelucos*, and other such mixtures – depended on how light or dark in colour they were and on the extent of their acculturation to European norms. To the free people of colour fell the less prestigious occupations of small trade, artisan craft, manual labour, and subsistence agriculture. Despite their legally free status they suffered from certain disadvantages. They were excluded from municipal office or membership in the more prestigious lay brotherhoods such as the Third Order of St Francis. Occasionally municipal councils passed sumptuary legislation. Slaves were prohibited from wearing silk and gold in Salvador in 1696 and by 1709 the restrictions were expanded to include free blacks and mulattos, as was done, it was argued, in Rio de Janeiro. There were other restrictions, too. According to a law of 1621 no black, Indian, or mulatto could be a goldsmith in Bahia, and in 1743 blacks were prohibited from selling goods on the streets of Recife.[47] The fact that such discriminatory laws were sometimes circumvented does not negate the limitations under which the free coloured population lived. That they realized their disadvantage and tried to do something about it is made clear by incidents such as that of 1689, when mulattos had sought to be admitted to the Jesuit College in Bahia where they wished to 'improve the fortune of their colour' by education and had been denied admission.[48]

[47] BNRJ, II–33, 23, 15, n. 4 (20 Feb. 1696); *Documentos históricos da Bibliotica Nacional de Rio de Janeiro* [*DHBNRJ*] 95 (1952): 248; Biblioteca Geral da Universidade de Coimbra [BGUC], Códice 707.

[48] AHU/PA/Bahia, caixa 16 (30 Jan. 1689). The crown ordered that the Jesuits admit them.

The antipathy towards people of colour was profound and penetrated all aspects of life. In Ceará in 1724 and in Rio Grande do Norte in 1732 it was suggested that, although mulattos and *mamelucos* had held public office when there had been a shortage of whites, there should now be restrictions on their service, 'since experience has demonstrated that they are less able because of their inferiority and because unrest and trouble is more natural to them'.[49] They were, as the câmara of Salvador put it, 'low people who have no honour nor reasons for the conservation and growth of the kingdom and seek only their own convenience'.[50] The ultimate comment on their disability is the fact that the freedom of a former slave could be revoked for disrespect towards a former master.

Among the free people of colour institutions developed, paralleling those of white society, which provided a sense of community and pride. Black militia regiments, named the *Henriques* after Henrique Dias, a leader against the Dutch, existed throughout much of Brazil. Distinctions were maintained between black and mulatto regiments and there were even attempts in some black units to limit officer status to the Brazilian-born *crioulos*. Still, the militia units provided a point of cohesion and eventually a platform from which grievances could be expressed. Perhaps of even greater importance were the lay sodalities of blacks and mulattos that existed through the colony. Providing social services, alms, dowries, burials, and organized religious observance, the brotherhoods became a fixture in urban life and sometimes on the engenhos as well. Although some may have existed as early as the sixteenth century, it was not until the eighteenth century that they began to proliferate. Bahia, for example, had six black and five mulatto brotherhoods dedicated to the Virgin at the beginning of that century. Although some of the brotherhoods were open to men and women of all races, others were limited by colour or by African nation of origin. While such institutions did offer paths to participation in the dominant culture, separation by colour and nation also reflected the realities of a slave-based society and the disabilities suffered by people of colour, both slave and free. The blacks of the brotherhood of the Rosary, which had been housed in the see of Salvador, had left and built their own church because of the insults they had suffered from the white brotherhoods, which had treated them poorly 'because they were

---

[49] *Ibid.*, Ceará, caixa 1; Rio Grande do Norte, caixa 3.
[50] Arquivo da Câmara Municipal do Salvador [ACMS], 124.7 Provisões, fos. 171–3 (3 Dec. 1711).

blacks'.[51] For people of colour election to the board of a brotherhood or the winning of a militia commission was undoubtedly a matter of social achievement and success but within a limited and always restricted range of opportunities offered by colonial society.

In addition to the fundamental distinctions of civil status and race, there were others, particularly important among the white population. Married men with a fixed residence were the preferred colonists and were favoured for municipal office and rights. Ethnic or religious origins were also used as a social gradient. Those with 'New Christian' – that is, Jewish – ancestors or relatives were considered religiously and culturally suspect and suffered legal and financial disabilities. In Brazil, however, these were often overcome by economic achievements.

New Christians played a major role in the colony throughout the seventeenth century. The forced conversion of all Jews in Portugal in 1497 had produced a large group who were suddenly plunged into a new faith. In theory, religious distinctions had been eliminated at a stroke, but differences of custom, attitude, and thought could not be so easily obliterated. New Christians bore the stigma of their birth from generation to generation, and even those who were devout Catholics could suffer, under discriminatory legislation and practice, exclusion from office or honour because of a New Christian somewhere in the family tree. Both crypto-Jews and those who had not the slightest attachment to Judaism were lumped together by the society as a suspect group. However, New Christians had been involved in the Brazilian enterprise from its origins and the fact that the Portuguese Inquisition was not established until 1547 meant that the colony's early years were relatively free from the watchful eye of orthodoxy. In Brazil New Christians became not only merchants but artisans, sugar planters, and *lavradores de cana*, holding civil and ecclesiastical offices. In 1603 the Board of Conscience in Lisbon ordered the bishop of Brazil to appoint only Old Christians to religious offices in Pernambuco because the majority of the churches in that state were served by New Christians. A study of Bahia from 1620 to 1660 revealed that while 36 per cent of the New Christians were in commerce, 20 per cent were in agriculture, 12 per cent were in professions, and 10 per cent were artisans. Another 20 per cent held civil, military, or religious office.[52]

---

[51] 'Pellos desgostos que padecião com os Brancos...e por serem pretos os maltratavão'. AHU/PA/Bahia, caixa 48 (8 July 1733).

[52] Anita Novinsky, *Cristãos novos na Bahia* (São Paulo, 1972), 176; ANTT, Mesa da Consciência, Livro de registro 18, fos. 8v–9.

The period of the Iberian union (1580–1640) brought the New Christians to the centre of the stage in the colony. The Inquisitorial visits to Pernambuco and Bahia in 1591–5 and 1618 created great consternation in the New Christian community, but the inability of the Inquisition to establish itself permanently in Brazil may have been due to the influence of that group in the colony. Bishops had inquisitorial powers and used them on occasion, but persecution of New Christians was less efficient in Brazil than in Spanish America and the levels of New Christian immigration to Brazil rose during the early decades of the seventeenth century. Pressures on the New Christians in Brazil and opportunities for trade created by the union with Spain caused many to emigrate or establish trading ventures in Spanish America, especially in the viceroyalty of Peru. The *peruleiros* were thoroughly resented on national, economic, and religious grounds. The term 'Portuguese' became a synonym for Jew in Spanish America and with the separation of Spain and Portugal in 1640 a series of *autos-da-fé* were held in Lima, Mexico, and Cartagena, aimed primarily at Portuguese merchants.

Controversy rages among specialists over the extent to which the Brazilian and Portuguese New Christians were or were not Jews and whether the Inquisition's efforts were designed to promote religious orthodoxy or were simply a tool of the nobility to break, by persecution and confiscation, the back of a growing bourgeoisie. The Inquisitorial visits do certainly suggest that there were practising Jews among the sugar planters of Bahia and Pernambuco. Moreover, under the policy of religious toleration advocated by Count Maurits of Nassau in Dutch Brazil, those who were crypto-Jews were able to come into the open, and they were soon joined by Jews from Holland. Two synagogues were operating in Recife in the 1640s. Those who fought with the Dutch were allowed to leave Brazil as part of the surrender terms, emigrating to Surinam, Jamaica, or New Amsterdam or returning to Holland. New Christians in Portuguese Brazil were apparently divided in their loyalties, but all were considered potential traitors. The fall of Salvador in 1624 was attributed by the *vox populi* to a New Christian 'stab in the back', although subsequent historiography has proven this to be untrue.[53] Attempts made by the Jews of Dutch Brazil to contact the New Christians in Portuguese territory were generally unsuccessful, but

---

[53] Cf. Novinsky, *Cristãos novos*, 120; Eduardo d'Oliveira França, 'Um problema: A traição dos cristãos novos em 1624', *Revista de História* 41 (1970), 21–71. For an economic interpretation of the Inquisition, see Antônio José Saraiva, *Inquisição e cristãos-novos* (Oporto, 1969).

the cosmopolitan connections of New Christians with Italy, France, and Holland were considered cause for suspicion. Episcopal investigations were made in Bahia in 1635, 1640, 1641, and 1646, the last being particularly extensive.

After 1660 the concern with New Christians as a group seems to have diminished until the beginning of the following century. Arrests of judaizers were made throughout the century from Maranhão to São Paulo, but in small numbers. The traditional discrimination against New Christian membership in public office, the Misericórdias, or the more prestigious lay brotherhoods continued. With the discovery of gold the arrests and confiscations of the Inquisition intensified. Most of those arrested were from Rio de Janeiro and Minas Gerais. The Lisbon *auto-da-fé* of 1711 included 52 prisoners from Brazil. In all, about 400 Brazilian New Christians were tried by the Inquisition. By the eighteenth century, under the watchful eye of the Inquisition and their neighbours, the cultural and religious distinctiveness of the New Christians faded away, although they remained a disadvantaged segment of Brazilian society.

Finally, there was in Brazilian colonial society, in addition to the burdens of colour, creed, and origin, that of sex. Brazilians shared the typical European attitudes of the time towards women but with an intensity that made even their Spanish neighbours comment. In theory, women were to be protected and secluded from the affairs of the world and expected to be devoted to the life of an obedient daughter, submissive wife, and loving mother. A rigid double standard of female chastity and constancy and male promiscuity was condoned to the point of the law's permitting an offended husband to kill his wife caught in an act of adultery. Various institutions existed in colonial society to aid or to ensure compliance with expected norms of behaviour for women of 'good family'. Benefactors of the Misericórdias left funds for the dowries of orphan girls. Retirement houses were established for young women whose chastity was endangered by the loss of a parent. As early as 1602 residents of Salvador sought to have a convent established in their city. The request was finally successful in 1677, when the Convento do Destêrro was founded, and by 1750 most of the major cities had convents.[54] As in other areas of life, admission to these depended on 'purity of blood', and since the 'dowry' needed for admission was large,

---

[54] ANTT, Mesa da Consciência, Livro de registro 17, fos. 158–9; Susan Soeiro, 'A baroque nunnery: the economic and social role of a colonial convent: Santa Clara do Desterro, Salvador, Bahia, 1677–1800' (Ph.D. thesis, New York University, 1974).

the daughters of planters and merchants held most of the positions available. If we can believe the complaints made about the scandalous life in the convents and the boastful observations of French travellers like Foger and Dellon, the ideals of seclusion and chastity were in reality often circumvented.

In fact, the role of women in colonial society was more complex than is usually portrayed. While in a legal dispute a party might argue that his property had been endangered because it had been in the hands of his wife, and women were 'by nature ... timid and unable to care for such matters, surrounded by tender children and lacking protection ...', many women, in fact, assumed the role of household head in their widowhood or because of desertion.[55] Women were to be found as plantation owners, *lavradores de cana*, and owners of urban real estate. To some extent this situation resulted from the Portuguese laws of inheritance, which assured all heirs of an equal portion and provided that a surviving spouse should inherit a major portion of the estate. Moreover, as we descend through the layers of class and colour, women become increasingly obvious in active economic roles. For instance, the small-scale ambulating retail trade in the colonial cities was almost exclusively in the hands of women of colour, both slave and free.

Government and society in Brazil formed two interlocking systems. Government sought to bind individuals and corporate groups to the formal political institutions of the state and to create conditions that facilitated and maintained the productive capacity of the colony; while the principal factors which motivated society and held it together were personal relations based on the extended family and on kin groups, shared social status and goals, and common economic interests. Throughout the colonial period state and society were so linked as to ensure the survival of the colony and the social and economic dominance of those groups which controlled the production and distribution of Brazil's major exports.

There were at least three levels of government within the colony. Royally appointed officers – the viceroy, governors, *disembargadores* (high court judges), and other crown magistrates – were the direct representatives of Portuguese authority. They were, in theory at least, a bureaucracy of professionals. Those in the higher executive positions were usually drawn from the Portuguese nobility, who were supposed, by inclination and training, to be soldiers. Magistrates were *letrados*,

[55] APB, Ordens régias (royal dispatches), 86, fos. 234–6.

university-trained lawyers, who formed a growing class of professional royal administrators. Together, soldiers and lawyers filled the highest offices in the colony. Beneath them was the second level of government, a myriad of minor offices, treasury officials, customs collectors, market inspectors, probate judges, scribes, and watchmen. Originally, these positions had been filled by European-born Portuguese, but by the mid seventeenth century colonials held many of these offices, some of which were bought and others held by inheritance. Finally, there was, as we have seen, a third level, formed by the offices of municipal government, the elected judges and *vereadores* (councillors) of the câmaras and the many lesser positions appointed by these local colonial bodies. In the countryside government was often in the hands of the senior militia officers, who served paramilitary functions as policemen, tax collectors, and, eventually, census-takers.

From the time of the donatary captaincies private power had played an important role in the colony's organization and, while the crown continually asserted its authority, the dominant groups in the colony found ways to make government respond to their needs. Municipal offices were usually in the hands of the local economic elite, which also came to control many of the lesser offices of justice and the treasury. In rural areas it was rare to find a militia colonel who was not also a planter or rancher. Even the ranks of the most highly professionalized royal officials, the magistrates, were penetrated by and incorporated into the Brazilian elite. Despite a strict prohibition on Brazilians serving in high government positions in the colony, and against family ties that might influence a magistrate's impartiality, webs of kinship and association between crown officers and local society were formed. Between 1652 and 1752 ten Brazilian-born judges were appointed to the Relação of Bahia, and when a new high court was created in Rio de Janeiro in 1752, its first chancellor was a Bahian by birth. Twenty-five high court judges married Brazilian wives, usually the daughters of sugar planters, and others became linked to the colonial elite by godparenthood, business dealings, or common participation in lay confraternities. In short, the colonial elites sought and found ways to make royal and municipal government responsive to their interests and goals. Government was often ineffective, sometimes oppressive, and usually corrupt, but it was rarely viewed as an external and foreign force, even though Portugal tried to put its own interests first.

Quite clearly the family played a major political and social role in the colony. The predominance of the donatarial families in Rio de Janeiro and Pernambuco was paralleled by the more restricted but still extensive powers held by interconnected, but sometimes quite hostile, kin groups of sugar planters, cattle ranchers, and other rural magnates. The struggles between the Pires and the Camargos in São Paulo in the 1650s or the Vieira Ravascos and Teles Meneses in Bahia in the 1680s reflect the importance and power of the family as an institution in the colony. The extended patriarchal family, with its many members linked by blood, marriage, and godparenthood and including dependants and slaves, was an ideal concept cutting across the social hierarchies described above. The formation and maintenance of these elite families, their strategies of inheritance, linkage, and continuity are topics that greatly merit attention. Unfortunately, the study of the family in Brazil is still in its infancy and the lack of any census data earlier than 1750 makes the task a hard one.

The relationship of state and society must finally be looked at in the context of Brazil's economy and its dominant form of labour relations – slavery. The Portuguese state and law provided a framework for the control of property, commercial transactions, and the distribution and control of labour power. Once the colony was launched as a producer of export crops based on enslaved African or coerced Indian labour, the state intervened very little in the internal aspects of the economy, the ordering of the factors of production, or the relationship between master and slave. So long as the major economic inputs came from the planter class, they were given free rein and the crown was content to collect its tithe and the various taxes on imports and exports. After 1650, when prices for Brazil's agricultural exports fluctuated, the crown took a number of measures to stimulate and improve the position of the sugar planters, often to the detriment of the mercantile groups in Portugal and the colony. By the beginning of the eighteenth century, however, changing European conditions, a Colbertian approach to political economy, the growing importance of mercantile groups within Brazil and the metropolis, and the discovery of gold all combined to bring about a change in the relationship between the Portuguese state and its American colony. That the Brazilian agrarian elite was able to absorb the newly important mercantile and mining classes and to adjust itself to a more active and interventionist state was mainly because both it and the colonial state were so firmly based on the institution of slavery and its concomitant social distinctions.

13

INDIANS AND THE FRONTIER IN COLONIAL BRAZIL

The 'frontier' in this chapter is the European boundary, the limit of colonial expansion into Brazil. Each of the hundreds of native American tribes also had its own frontier, sometimes fluid and shifting but more often geographically defined and well known to every member of the tribe. Tribal frontiers were the boundaries between often hostile, warring groups, or were the limits of each people's hunting forays or annual collecting cycle. The European frontier was a sharper division: the limit of penetration or permanent occupation by an alien culture. It marked a divide between peoples of radically different racial, ethnic, religious, political and technological composition. To European colonists, the frontier was the edge of civilization. Beyond it lay the barbaric unknown of the *sertão* – the 'wilds', the bush or the wasteland of the interior – or the impenetrable *selva*, the Amazonian rain forests.

In practice, the frontier was less precise than it may have been in the colonists' perception. The men who explored, exploited or attacked the frontier were often *mamelucos* of mixed European and Indian blood. Many of them spoke Tupi-Guaraní or other Indian languages. They were almost invariably accompanied by Indian guides, auxiliaries or forced labourers, and they adopted efficient Indian methods of travel and survival. Even when European colonists were firmly established on conquered tribal lands, the frontier was not necessarily the boundary between civilization and barbarism. It was often the Indians beyond the frontier who were more civilized. In most forms of artistic expression and often in political organization and social harmony, the Indians had the advantage over the frontiersmen, who were usually tough, brutal, ignorant, greedy, and uncultured.

There was little to attract Europeans to the Brazilian frontier. There was a complete lack of precious metals among the tribes of the Atlantic seaboard, and there were few rumours or signs of any advanced civilizations in the interior. There seemed to be no chance of discovering any rich empires comparable to those of the Incas, Aztecs, or Muisca in the *campo* of the Brazilian plateau or the forests that lay beyond. Spanish adventurers, more determined or more self-deluding than their Portuguese counterparts, made the explorations that quickly established that there was no wealth to be looted in the heart of Brazil. Sebastiano Caboto, Juan de Ayolas, Domingo Martínez de Irala, and Alvar Núñez Cabeza de Vaca explored far up the Paraguay and Paraná rivers in the 1520s and 1530s, and Aleixo Garcia, a Portuguese working with the Spaniards, accompanied a group of Guaraní right across the continent to be the first European to see outposts of the Inca empire. During the 1530s, some of Pizarro's lieutenants led disastrous expeditions from the Andes to explore the western edges of the Amazon forests. During those same years, gold-hungry Spaniards and Germans were marching deep into northern South America, up the Orinoco and onto the headwaters of the north-western tributaries of the Amazon. As early as 1542, Francisco de Orellana made the first descent of the Amazon from Quito to the Atlantic Ocean; and it was another Spanish expedition, that of Pedro de Ursúa and the infamous rebel Lope de Aguirre, that in 1560 made the only other descent during the sixteenth century. The survivors of these expeditions emerged broken and impoverished; and Amazonia acquired a terrible reputation. Lope de Aguirre summed up contemporary thinking when he wrote to the king of Spain: 'God knows how we got through that great mass of water. I advise you, great King, never to send Spanish fleets to that cursed river!'[1]

There were desultory attempts to discover gold, silver, and precious stones in the endless expanses of central Brazil but until the last decade of the seventeenth century very little came of them. At the same time land was not an attraction sufficient to lure people to the frontier. There was no lack of land along the thousands of kilometres of the Brazilian coast. The idea of scientific discovery came only with the age of enlightenment at the end of the colonial period. Very few explorers achieved any fame or reward for their efforts: Pedro Teixeira was praised for his journey up and down the Amazon in 1638–9, but only because it was a geopolitical venture to push Portuguese frontiers far up the river.

---

[1] Lope de Aguirre to King Philip [V], in C. R. Markham (trans.), *Expeditions into the Valley of the Amazons* (Hakluyt Society, 24; London, 1859) xii.

The Brazilian interior had only one commodity of interest to Europeans: its native inhabitants. The rivers, plains, and forests of Brazil were full of tribes of robust men and relatively attractive women. This great human reservoir was an obvious target both for colonists desperate for labour and for missionaries eager to spread their gospel and swell their personal soul-counts.

The Indian population of the Brazilian coast and interior was, however, at the same time being annihilated during the sixteenth, seventeenth, and every subsequent century by imported diseases against which it had no genetic defence. Smallpox, measles, tuberculosis, typhoid, dysentery, and influenza rapidly killed tens of thousands of native Americans who were otherwise in perfect health and physically very fit. It is impossible to quantify the extent of this depopulation, but there are many clues in the chronicles. There are early references to dense populations and large villages close to one another in all parts of Brazil and Amazonia.[2] The chronicles are also full of references to depopulation and disease. The Jesuits are, as usual, our best informants: they wrote accurate descriptions of disease symptoms and provided numerical data on the decline in the numbers living in their missions. Whatever the actual figures, there can be no question that a demographic tragedy of great magnitude occurred.

THE SIXTEENTH AND SEVENTEENTH CENTURIES

There were four main theatres of expansion of the frontier during the period up to the discoveries of gold at the end of the seventeenth century: (1) the south – the area penetrated by Paulistas, embracing the modern states of Rio Grande do Sul, Santa Catarina, Paraná, São Paulo and southern Mato Grosso; (2) the centre, inland from Salvador da Bahia; (3) the interior of the north-east; (4) the Amazon, which was exploited from Maranhão and Pará.

The south

João Ramalho, a Portuguese who was shipwrecked on the coast of São Vicente in about 1510 and who managed to marry a daughter of the powerful chief Tibiriçá of the Goianá Tupinikin living on the

---

[2] For a discussion of the population of Brazil *c.* 1500, see John Hemming, *Red Gold. The Conquest of the Brazilian Indians* (London, 1978), appendix, 487–501.

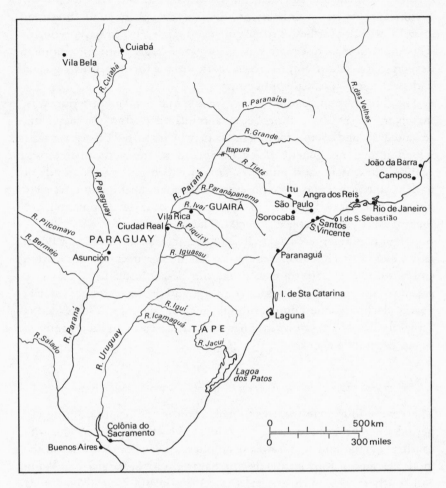

Southern Brazil

Piratininga plateau, fathered many sons and these in turn produced a sizeable *mameluco* offspring from many Indian women. By the time of the first Portuguese colony at São Vicente in 1532 and the founding of the Jesuit college and reduction at São Paulo de Piratininga in 1553, Ramalho's descendants were described by the Jesuit Manoel da Nóbrega as 'going to war with the Indians, their festivals are Indian ones, and they live like them, as naked as the Indians themselves'. Such racial intermingling was characteristic of São Paulo, where a century later children still spoke Tupi as their first language and went to school to learn Portuguese. By identifying themselves so closely with one Indian tribe, the Paulistas embroiled themselves in intertribal wars: the early history of their town was marked by bitter fighting against the Tamoio (allies of the French at Guanabara) and excursions down the Tietê against Gê-speaking tribes then known as Bilreiros ('wooden lip discs') or Coroados ('crowned', from their haircuts), who were presumably precursors of the modern Kaingáng and the now-extinct Southern Caiapó.

It was at the start of the seventeenth century that the tribes of southern Brazil began to feel the impact of two distinct European frontiers: Spanish Jesuits were pushing their missionary thrust east-wards across the Paraná and upper Uruguay from their bases near Asunción in Paraguay; and the Paulistas were beginning to make excursions into the forests in search of slaves. It was no accident that the Jesuits were more successful with the Guaraní of Paraguay and the closely related Carijó and Tape of southern Brazil than with any other South American tribes. These Guaraní-speaking peoples were deeply spiritual and were excellent farmers living in populous villages. They responded readily to the two benefits that the Jesuits had to offer: a well-disciplined existence regulated from cradle to grave by religious precepts, and plenty of food from efficient plantations and ranches. Alonso de Barzana, one of the first Jesuits in Paraguay, understood the potential of these Guaraní when he wrote in 1594:

All this nation is very inclined to religion, whether true or false... They know all about the immortality of the soul and greatly fear the *angüera* [devils] which are souls emerged from dead bodies that go about terrifying people and causing harm. They have the greatest love and obedience for the [Jesuit] Fathers if these give them a good example... These tribes are great farmers: they have vast quantities of food, especially maize, various kinds of manioc and other fine root crops, and a great amount of fish.[3]

In the last decade of the sixteenth century and the first decade of the seventeenth, Spanish Jesuit missionaries moved into an area they called Guairá – east of the Paraná and between its tributaries the Iguaçu and Paranapanema, roughly midway between Asunción and São Paulo and therefore, the Portuguese reckoned, on their side of the Line of Tordesillas. Their missionary activity was successful, and a series of *reducciones* (villages of Indians 'reduced' to Christianity and 'civilized' society) were soon full of Guaraní–Carijó converts. By 1594, the Spanish

---

[3] Alonso de Barzana to Juan Sebastián, Asunción, 8 Sept. 1594, in Marcos Jiménez de la Espada, *Relaciones geográficas de Indias* (Madrid, 1965), 85.

Jesuit Barzana was complaining that the greater part of his Society's original converts in Paraguay were dead from alien diseases or had fled to avoid persecution by settlers. Baffled by these epidemics and impotent to prevent the decline, the Jesuits did not desist from their proselytizing but merely looked hungrily at large native populations to the east and north-east.

The Paulistas were looking in the same direction, for less exalted motives. The town council of São Paulo explained the problem in 1585, in its first open reference to Indian slavery:

This land is in great danger of being depopulated because its inhabitants do not have [Indian] slaves as they used to, by whom they have always been served. This is the result of many illnesses...from which over two thousand head of slaves have died in this captaincy in the past six years. This land used to be ennobled by these slaves, and its settlers supported themselves honourably with them and made large incomes.[4]

São Paulo was a small hilltop town of only 2,000 white inhabitants in 1600. And yet the Paulistas, the citizens of this frontier town, embarked on a series of audacious expeditions that explored thousands of kilometres of south and central Brazil. These expeditions were called *bandeiras* (probably from the flag carried by a small company of troops), and the tough woodsmen who marched on them were *bandeirantes*. Although the bandeirantes hoped that they might possibly find precious metals or stones, their true purpose was to capture Indians. In the 1590s Jorge Correia, captain-major of São Paulo, and Jerónimo Leitão led slaving expeditions against the Carijó along the coast south to Paranaguá, and then for six years down the Tietê. Spanish Jesuits claimed that these Tietê campaigns destroyed 300 native villages and caused the death or enslavement of 30,000 people. Other expeditions 'raided and roamed the country' north to the Jeticaí (now called Grande) and Paranaíba rivers. In 1602 Nicolau Barreto led 300 whites and many Indians – a large proportion of the adult men of São Paulo – north for hundreds of kilometres to the Velhas and upper São Francisco rivers: they returned after two years of marching and many deaths, bringing 3,000 Temimino prisoners. Each year, bandeiras struck the Carijó and other tribes within easy reach of São Paulo.

It was inevitable that these expeditions would soon clash with the Spaniards pushing north-eastwards from Asunción. This was during the

[4] Acta da Câmara de São Paulo, 1585, in Afonso de Escragnolle Taunay, *História geral das bandeiras paulistas* (11 vols., São Paulo, 1924–50) I, 156.

60-year union of the crowns of Spain and Portugal (1580–1640), when many Portuguese felt their country to be occupied by Spain and there was no love lost between subjects of the Catholic dual monarchy of the Iberian peninsula. Paraguayan Spaniards tried to establish two towns in Guairá: Ciudad Real at the junction of the Piquiri and the Paraná, and Villa Rica on the lower Ivaí. Between 1607 and 1612, the Preto brothers led raids from São Paulo that captured hundreds of Indians working for the settlers in these towns. It was now that the Jesuits opened their missionary province of Guairá. For twenty years after 1610, Jesuit fathers under Antonio Ruiz de Montoya created fifteen villages or 'reductions' in the Paranapanema, Tibagi and Ivaí valleys. Indians flocked into these reductions to escape severe oppression from the Spanish settlers of Ciudad Real and Villa Rica.

The spectacle of large mission villages full of thousands of docile Guaraní was too tempting to Paulista bandeirantes. The bandeirantes and their bands of trained Indians and *mamelucos* had become expert woodsmen and trackers. They lived rough on their expeditions, eating a little roast manioc or any game or fish that their men could catch. If possible, they raided Indian villages and stole their stores of food. They were heavily bearded and wore high boots, skin or hide suits, padded cotton armour, and broad-brimmed hats as protection against strong sun or rains, or the insects and detritus that fall from tropical forests. Apart from food, swords, and firearms, their baggage included ropes and shackles to secure their victims, and some mining implements in case they might come across mineral deposits. One Jesuit marvelled at the effort that the bandeirantes expended on slaving expeditions that might last for several years. 'They go without God, without food, naked as the savages, and subject to all the persecutions and miseries in the world. Men venture for 200 or 300 leagues into the sertão, serving the devil with such amazing martyrdom, in order to trade or steal slaves.'[5] The Jesuit Diego Ferrer admitted that 'these Portuguese do and suffer incomparably more to win the bodies of the Indians for their service than I do to win their souls for heaven'.[6] To such desperadoes, it was infinitely easier to round up the inmates of a Jesuit reduction than to hunt hostile uncontacted or nomadic tribes in the depths of the forests.

[5] Anon. Jesuit, 'Sumário das armadas que se fizeram e guerras que se deram na conquista do rio Paraíba' [*c.* 1587] in *Revista do Instituto Histórico e Geográfico Brasileiro* [*RIHGB*], 36/1 (1873), 13–14.
[6] Diego Ferrer, Carta Anua of 21 Aug. 1633, in Jaime Cortesão, *Jesuítas e bandeirantes no Itatim (1596–1760)* (Rio de Janeiro, 1952), 45.

The first Paulista attack on outlying Indians of a Guairá reduction was by Manoel Preto, in 1616. He was back for another attack in 1619, and in 1623–4 his bandeira led over 1,000 Christian Indians from Guairá to slavery on plantations near São Paulo. Other attacks took place in ensuing years. The Jesuits sent furious complaints to King Philip of Spain and Portugal. They fulminated against 'Portuguese pirates... more like wild beasts than rational men... Men without souls, they kill Indians as if they were animals, sparing neither age nor sex.'[7] They reported that the bandeirantes killed babies or the elderly because they slowed down the marching column, and they killed chiefs to prevent them inspiring their people to rebel.

In 1628 an enormous bandeira of 69 whites, 900 *mamelucos*, and over 2,000 Indians left São Paulo under the command of the most famous of all bandeirantes, Antônio Rapôso Tavares. The Portuguese on this raid included two justices of São Paulo, two aldermen, the public prosecutor, and the son, son-in-law, and brother of the town's senior judge. The bandeira marched to the Ivaí valley and camped outside the reduction of San Antonio. Four months of uneasy calm ensued, with quarrels between bandeirantes and Jesuits over the ownership of various Indian groups. Finally, on 29 January 1629, the bandeirantes entered the mission to seize a particular chief. The spell was broken: this was the first time that Portuguese had penetrated within the walls of a reduction. They went on to round up 'all the others whom the Father was instructing. They themselves admit that they took 4,000 Indians from it...and they destroyed the entire village, burning many houses, plundering the church and the Father's house...'[8] The Portuguese regarded themselves as devout Christians, so they had to fabricate elaborate excuses for this violation of a Christian sanctuary – a negation of all the proselytizing claims advanced to condone Spanish and Portuguese colonizing of the Americas. Some claimed that the catechumens they led off to slavery were being taken into the bosom of the church; others pleaded that their country faced ruin without a supply of 'free' labour and that the Indians were technically free. Rapôso Tavares is said to have sounded a patriotic note, exclaiming: 'We have come to expel you from this entire region. For this land is

---

[7] Ruiz de Montoya to Nicolas Durán, Carta Anua of 1628, in Jaime Cortesão, *Jesuítas e bandeirantes no Guairá (1594–1640)* (Rio de Janeiro, 1951), 269.

[8] Justo Mancilla and Simón Masseta, 'Relación de los agravios que hicieron algunos vecinos y moradores de la Villa de S. Pablo de Piratininga...' in *ibid.*, 315.

[9] Antonio Ruiz de Montoya, *Conquista espiritual hecha por los religiosos de la Compañía de Jesús en las provincias de Paraguay, Uruguay y Tape* (Madrid, 1639), 35.

ours and not the king of Spain's!'[9] His bandeira went on to sack another empty village and to invade a flourishing mission on the Tibagi, shackling its entire population of 1,500 men, women and children. Two Jesuits accompanied the bandeira on the 40-day march back to São Paulo with thousands of captives herded along by the Paulistas' own Indians. The Jesuits were appalled to see the ease with which the slavers bribed the town's authorities with presents of captured Indians. 'Thereupon, after committing so many abominations, they were well received . . . No one who had not seen it with his own eyes could imagine such a thing! The entire life of these bandits is going to and from the sertão, bringing back captives with so much cruelty, death and pillage; and then selling them as if they were pigs.'[10]

Once Rapôso Tavares had destroyed and enslaved a Jesuit reduction with impunity, the Guairá missions were doomed. Two more villages were sacked by André Fernandes in 1630, and another by another bandeirante in 1631. The Jesuit fathers decided that their position was untenable. They assembled 10,000 Indians from their remaining Guairá reductions and sailed them down the Paraná in a convoy of hundreds of canoes. Spanish settlers tried in vain to prevent this exodus of what they regarded as their pool of labour. In 1632 the Paulistas turned against these settlers' towns, and Villa Rica and Ciudad Real were abandoned for ever. The refugees from Guairá were relocated in a region that the Jesuits were just beginning to penetrate. Four years earlier, two reductions had been established east of the upper Uruguay river, in what is now the Brazilian state of Rio Grande do Sul. After spiritual conflict with powerful shaman-chiefs – and some physical fighting by newly converted Indians against those who resisted the new faith – the Jesuits won over thousands of eager Guaraní. As always in Brazilian history, the missionaries used gifts of trade goods and the prestige of an advanced technology to buttress their proselytizing.

Having established reductions on the Ijuí and Ibicuí tributaries of the Uruguay, the Spanish Jesuits pushed on to the east. In 1633 they crossed the plain, in the territory of Tape Guaraní, to reach the Jacuí, a river that flowed directly into the Atlantic through the Lagoa dos Patos. They were coming close to achieving a stated geopolitical aim: the creation of a continuous belt of missions across the middle of South America, from the silver mining city of Potosí on the altiplano, across the Chaco and the Paraguay–Paraná basin to the Atlantic Ocean. This eastward push by Spanish Jesuits brought them into conflict with Portuguese

[10] Mancilla and Masseta, 'Relación de los agravios', 335–6.

interests in this section of the Atlantic seaboard. In the early sixteenth century, these southern coasts had been occupied only by occasional Spanish visitors. They lay on the Spanish side of the Line of Tordesillas. But with the failure of the Spaniards to make a permanent occupation, and with the growing Portuguese claim that Tordesillas ran from the mouth of the Río de la Plata to that of the Amazon, Portuguese from São Vicente and São Paulo were increasingly active in this southern region. By 1576 a chief of the Carijó of Santa Catarina complained that ships from São Vicente were coming twice a year to barter for slaves. With the dearth of slaves in and near São Paulo in the early seventeenth century, the traffic in slaves moved further south. Native middlemen called *mus* rounded up captives who were sold to Portuguese slavers and carried off in ships or overland. In 1635 the governor of São Vicente licensed a huge seaborne expedition to the Lagoa dos Patos. There was now no pretence to barter for slaves: the expedition was equipped for war, not trade. A Portuguese Jesuit saw the slavers' base in the lagoon, with fifteen seagoing ships and many large war canoes. He was shocked that the authorities had licensed 'ship after ship full of men with powder and shackles and chains, to make war on the heathen of the Patos, who had been at peace for so many years and some of whom were Christians'.[11]

In the year after this brazen raid on the lagoon, the bandeirante Antônio Rapôso Tavares marched south with a mighty expedition of 150 whites and 1,500 Tupi. He struck the northernmost of the Jesuits' new Tape reductions in December 1636. There was now no hesitation or delay. The Paulistas attacked at once, with drum and battle trumpet and banners unfurled. The Jesuits were also less timid. They had secretly started to arm and train their native converts, so the Portuguese were held off for a time by arquebus fire. That mission was destroyed. Another large bandeira spent the years 1637 and 1638 rounding up thousands of Christian Indians from the Jesuits' new villages on the Ibicuí. Finally, in 1639, the Spanish authorities in Asunción officially permitted the Jesuits to arm their converts to defend themselves against these outrages. Some Jesuit Fathers had had military experience before joining the Society, and these supervised the fortification of the remaining reductions and the training of their inmates. The result was the defeat of the next large bandeira, in March 1641. In a series of battles in canoes on the Mbororé tributary of the upper Uruguay, and in pitched

<hr>

[11] *Registro geral da Câmara Municipal de São Paulo* (Arquivo Público Municipal de São Paulo, 1917–), I, 500.

battles at palisaded missions, the Paulistas were routed. The pursuit lasted for days, through the rain-soaked pine forests of Santa Catarina and Paraná, and there was fierce hand-to-hand fighting. The victories of Mboreré put a stop to Paulista aggression against the Paraguayan missions, and affected the eventual boundary between Portuguese and Spanish possessions in southern Brazil.

At the time of the dispersal of the Guairá missions in 1631, one group of Jesuits moved westwards across the Paraná to establish a missionary province on the left bank of the Paraguay, north of Asunción. Although this new Jesuit province, called Itatín, lay far to the west of the Paraná and the Line of Tordesillas, and although it was protected by hundreds of kilometres of arid forests – the great dry forest or *mato grosso* that gave its name to the modern Brazilian state – it was soon attacked by bandeirantes. Spanish colonists conspired to help the Paulistas enter reductions of the hated Jesuits; until, having destroyed the missions, the Portuguese raiders attacked and demolished the Spanish settlers' own town, Jérez. There were bandeirante attacks on Itatín in 1632, 1638, and 1637; and the new missions were also harassed by fierce Guaicurú and Paiaguá warriors who controlled the banks and waters of the upper Paraguay. The final blow came in 1648 with a raid by Antônio Rapôso Tavares at the start of an epic 12,000-kilometre journey that the bandeirantes' apologist Jaime Cortesão has called 'the greatest bandeira of the greatest bandeirante'. Leading 60 whites and relatively few Indians, Rapôso Tavares marched along the watershed between the Paraguay and Amazon basins, across the Guaporé and northern Chaco to the eastern foothills of the Andes, then down the Mamoré and Madeira in the first descent of that great river, and on to Belém at the mouth of the Amazon. When he returned to São Paulo after many years' absence, his family scarcely recognized the ravaged old man. The Jesuit António Vieira deplored the bandeirantes' cruelty, but could not but admire this feat of exploration: 'It was truly one of the most notable [journeys] ever made in the world up to now!'[12] But at its outset, this bandeira had dealt the final blow to the Jesuit province of Itatín, destroying a mission on the Tare river that now forms the boundary between Brazil and Paraguay. A Jesuit father was shot and killed during this attack, and hundreds of Christian converts were again packed off to slavery.

The raids of the bandeirantes checked Spanish expansion from

---

[12] António Vieira to Provincial of Brazil, Parrá, Jan. 1654, Alfred do Vale Cabral (ed.), *Cartas Jesuíticas* (3 vols., Rio de Janeiro, 1931), I, 411.

Asunción and thus laid the foundations of Brazil's southern and western frontiers. But the great Brazilian historian Capistrano de Abreu asked: 'Are such horrors justified by the consideration that, thanks to the bandeirantes, the devastated lands now belong to Brazil?'[13]

The sugar engenhos of the captaincies of Rio de Janeiro and São Vicente and the *fazendas* around São Paulo were the major consumers of Indian labour. Many new towns, notably Parnaíba, Sorocaba, and Itú, were founded in the seventeenth century by bandeirantes and based on Indian labour. The leading citizens of São Paulo itself held 'administrations' over hundreds of Indians and boasted private armies of native bowmen. The captive Indians far preferred the manly pursuit of warfare – either on slaving expeditions or in the periodic feuds that occurred between Paulista families – to ignominious and abhorrent plantation labour. In Indian societies, men were traditionally responsible for clearing forest and for hunting and fishing; but agriculture was women's work. Members of a tribe helped one another and often shared the game they caught. The ideas of working for someone else, either for reward or from coercion, and the production of a surplus beyond the immediate needs of a man's family, were utterly repugnant to them.

Portuguese law required that Indians who had not been legally enslaved should live in mission villages or *aldeias*. The Jesuits in São Paulo attempted to administer a few such aldeias near the city, but these regimented missions, which functioned well enough when they were remote from frontier society, were unworkable when surrounded by colonists. The mission aldeias became lay parishes and their lands were constantly invaded by colonists and their cattle. The greatest problem was a legal requirement that mission Indians must work for part of the year – how many months varied with successive legislation – for adjacent colonists in return for 'wages' expressed in lengths of coarse cloth. The result was that the aldeias were often denuded of their menfolk. They were dismal places, constantly dwindling despite efforts to replenish them with a proportion of the Indians brought back by bandeirantes.

The mission aldeias were the subject of frequent dispute between Jesuits and citizens of São Paulo. The settlers' view of mission Indians was demonstrated in a declaration from a public meeting in 1611: 'There should be orders that the heathen work for the citizens for hire and payment, to tend their mines and do their labour. This would result

[13] João Capistrano de Abreu, *Capítulos de história colonial* (5th edn., Brasília, 1963), 115–16.

in tithes for God, fifths for the king, and profit for the citizens. It would give [the Indians] and their wives utility and the advantages of clothing themselves by their work. It would remove them from their continual idolatry and drunkenness...'[14] Although some Jesuits stoutly resisted such pressures, others wanted to abandon the thankless task of administering the aldeias because, in the words of Francisco de Morais, 'our presence in them serves only to affront and discredit the [Jesuit] Society... [and leads to] the ignominies and vituperation we suffer.'[15] During the 1630s a torrent of righteous protest by Spanish Jesuits led to Papal condemnation of Paulista slavers. The citizens of São Paulo were affronted. Matters came to a head with the expulsion of the Jesuits from Rio de Janeiro and then from São Paulo in July 1640. Mission villages were entrusted to the care of lay administrators, which ensured their rapid decline and exposed their remaining inhabitants to constant abuse. There were more strident protests from colonists and missionaries. But it was not until 1653 that the Jesuits returned to São Paulo, and then only on condition that they share the administration of the aldeias with laymen. During their absence, Governor Salvador de Sá testified that the populations of the four main villages of Marueri, São Miguel, Pinheiros, and Guarulhos had declined by almost 90 per cent, from a total of 2,800 families to 290.

The centre

Citizens of Rio de Janeiro and of the small towns of the long coastline between there and Salvador da Bahia were less concerned with the frontier than were the tough backwoodsmen of São Paulo. The reasons were both geographical and historical. Geographically, Rio de Janeiro was cut off from the interior by the granite pinnacles of the Serra dos Orgãos and the Serra da Mantiqueira. Similar coastal ranges and dense forests trapped the colonies of Espírito Santo, Pôrto Seguro and Ilhéus along a narrow belt of coastline. They were more concerned with maritime trade than exploration of the interior. Rio de Janeiro was a later foundation than São Vicente and São Paulo and its early years were spent in battles against the French and their Tamoio allies. It was not

[14] Declaration of 10 June 1612, São Paulo, in Pedro Tacques de Almeida Paes Leme, 'Notícia histórica da expulsão dos Jesuítas do Collegio de S. Paulo', *RIHGB*, 12 (1849), 9.
[15] Francisco de Morais to Simão de Vasconcelos, in Serafim Leite, S.J., *História da Companhia de Jesus no Brasil* (10 vols., Lisbon and Rio de Janeiro, 1938–50), VI, 97.

until 1567 that Estácio de Sá finally defeated the French in Guanabara; and 1575 before the Tamoio of Cabo Frio were subdued and forced to flee inland. There was a little slaving activity in the latter part of the century – the shipwrecked Englishman Anthony Knivet was employed by the governor of Rio de Janeiro on such ventures in the Paraíba valley in the 1590s – but nothing on the scale of the bandeiras. As late as the 1630s, the lethargic citizens of Rio de Janeiro were just moving into the fertile plains of the Waitacá, at the mouth of the Paraíba a mere 200 kilometres north-east of the city.

The stagnation of the colonies along the north–south coastline between the Paraíba and the Bahia de Todos os Santos was due to the success of the Aimoré tribes as much as to geographical constraints. The Aimoré were a Gê-speaking tribe with the usual Gê skills in archery, running, and forest tracking. According to Knivet – who may have been mistaken in this – they had adopted the Tupi practice of eating their enemies; but Knivet said that they did it for nourishment rather than for ritual vengeance in intertribal feuds. In battle, the Aimoré baffled the Portuguese by their use of camouflage, ambush, deadly accuracy with bows and arrows, and rapid dispersal after an attack. They did not mount the set-piece battles that made the Tupi vulnerable to European horses, swords, and firearms. Physically powerful, brave, and implacable, the Aimoré shrewdly resisted attempts to subdue or seduce them with trade goods. In 1587 Gabriel Soares de Sousa complained that 'There occurred in this land a plague of Aimoré, so that there are now only six [sugar] mills and these produce no sugar... The captaincies of Pôrto Seguro and Ilhéus are destroyed and almost depopulated from fear of these barbarians... In the past 25 years these brutes have killed over 300 Portuguese and 3,000 slaves.'[16] Pero de Magalhães Gandavo lamented that the Aimoré 'are so barbarous and intractable that we have never been able to tame them or force them into servitude like the other Indians of this land, who accept submission to captivity'.[17] A partial pacification of the Aimoré took place at the beginning of the seventeenth century. The governor of Brazil, Diogo Botelho, brought hundreds of newly pacified Tobajara and Potiguar warriors south from Ceará and Rio Grande do Norte, and was amazed when these achieved some military successes against the Aimoré. The ravages of disease and the

---

[16] Gabriel Soares de Sousa, *Tratado descriptivo do Brasil em 1587* (São Paulo, 1938), 57.
[17] Pero de Magalhães Gandavo, *Tratado da terra do Brasil*, trans. John B. Stetson (Cortes Society; 2 vols., New York, 1922), II, 110.

deceptive lure of 'civilized' society also helped persuade that fierce tribe to stop fighting. But despite this success there was no drive to push the frontiers of these captaincies inland throughout the colonial era.

The middle sector of the Brazilian frontier was inland from Bahia, up the Paraguaçu, Jacuípe, and Itapicurú rivers towards the great arc of the São Francisco river. Once Mem de Sá had defeated the tribes near the Recôncavo and their lands had been occupied by sugar plantations, excursions inland were in search of Indian labour. Movement into the interior of Bahia is relatively easy: the country is often open enough for movement by horse. The main impediment for expeditions into the sertão was lack of water or game.

In the 1550s the first wave of Jesuits settled thousands of Indians in missionary aldeias near Salvador da Bahia. Manoel da Nóbrega, Luís de Grã, José de Anchieta, and other Jesuit leaders were jubilant about the numbers of natives who accepted baptism. Two things destroyed these initial successes. One was the killing of the first bishop, Pero Fernandes Sardinha, who was shipwrecked north of Bahia in 1556 and eaten by pro-French Caeté. In an emotional reaction to this outrage, Mem de Sá permitted open war on the Caeté and enslavement of any captives. Settlers, desperate for labour, abused this edict to enslave any Indians they could catch. The other disaster was a wave of epidemics in the early 1560s that annihilated the missions. The most lethal disease appears to have been a form of haemorrhagic dysentery. One Jesuit said that 'the disease began with serious pains inside the intestines which made the liver and lungs rot. It then turned into pox that were so rotten and poisonous that the flesh fell off them in pieces full of evil-smelling grubs.'[18] Another described it as

a form of pox so loathsome and evil-smelling that none could stand the great stench that emerged from them. For this reason many died untended, consumed by the worms that grew in the wounds of the pox and were engendered in their bodies in such abundance and of such great size that they caused horror and shock to any who saw them.[19]

Whatever the diseases may have been, there is no question about the depopulation they caused. The Jesuits kept records of 30,000 dead in their missions near Bahia. Leonardo do Vale spoke of 'so much

---

[18] Simão de Vasconcelos, *Chronica da Companhia de Jesus*, bk 3 (Lisbon, 1663), 285.
[19] António Blásques to Diego Mirón, Bahia, 31 May 1564, in Serafim Leite, *Monumenta Brasiliae* (*Monumenta Historica Societatis Iesu*, 79–81, 87; Rome, 1956–60), IV, 55.

destruction along the coast that people could not bury one another. [In tribes] where previously there were 500 fighting men, there would not now be twenty.'[20] Such epidemics spread far beyond the frontier: this same Jesuit admitted that 'the Indians say this was nothing in comparison with the mortality raging through the forests'[21] beyond European control.

The immediate aftermath of this demographic disaster was a famine caused by the Indians' inability to grow their food. In desperation some Indians sold themselves or their families into slavery in return for emergency supplies of food; the Mesa da Consciência in Lisbon issued rulings on whether this was morally and legally acceptable. Other Indians followed tribal shamans on messianic quests for a 'land without ills': they developed curious mixtures of Christian and Tupi spiritual beliefs and fled inland beyond the frontier to illusory sanctuaries known as *santidades*. During the decades after the great epidemics, there were campaigns to conquer or win over these *santidades*, and this helped to push the frontier up the rivers that drained into the Bahia de Todos os Santos.

The other factor responsible for pushing the frontier inland from Bahia was the perennial shortage of labour. As in São Paulo, this shortage was heightened by the deaths of subject Indians, the influx of European colonists eager to enrich themselves and unwilling to perform manual labour, and the boom in sugar prices. The traffic in African slaves was in its infancy. African slaves were worth far more than Indian – when he wrote his will in 1569, Governor Mem de Sá valued his African slaves at from thirteen to 40 escudos each, whereas unskilled Indians were valued at only one escudo – but there was still intense demand for Indian labour, whether technically 'free' or slave. This inspired efforts to conquer uncontacted tribes of the interior or to lure them down to the coast by false promises. The governor who succeeded Mem de Sá in Bahia, Luís de Brito de Almeida, had no scruples about fighting Indians or taking slaves by any possible means. During his governorship, there were slaving expeditions such as that of António Dias Adorno, who was sent inland nominally to search for minerals but brought back 7,000 Tupiguen, or Luís Álvares Espinha,

[20] Leonardo do Vale, letter, in João Fernando de Almeida Prado, *Bahia e as capitanias do centro do Brasil (1530–1626)* (3 vols., São Paulo, 1945–50), I, 219.

[21] Leonardo do Vale to Gonçalo Vaz de Mello, Bahia, 12 May 1563, in Leite, *Monumenta Brasiliae*, IV, 12.

who marched inland from Ilhéus to punish some villages and 'not content with capturing those villages he went on inland and brought down infinite heathen'.[22] Other slavers used more cunning methods: they dazzled tribes with boasts of their military prowess, bribed them with trade goods and weapons, and deceived them with stories of the wonderful life that awaited them under Portuguese rule. The Franciscan historian Vicente do Salvador described how

with such deceptions and some gifts of clothing or tools to the chiefs,... they roused up entire villages. But once they arrived with them in sight of the sea they separated children from parents, brother from brother and sometimes even husband from wife... They used them on their estates and some sold them... Those who bought them would brand them on the face at their first [attempted] flight or fault: they claimed that they had cost money and were their slaves.[23]

When the Holy Inquisition visited Brazil in 1591, it investigated a number of professional slavers and its records contain interesting details of their activities. In order to gain the confidence of the tribes they planned to betray, these slavers would do things that disturbed the Inquisition – they ate meat during Lent, had numerous native women, traded weapons to the Indians, or smoked 'holy grass' with the shamans. The most famous of these professional slavers was Domingos Fernandes Nobre, whom the Indians called Tomacauna. The governor of Brazil employed Tomacauna as a slaver, and the Holy Office of the Inquisition was told how, in the course of his nefarious trade,

he sang and shook rattles and danced like [the Indians], and went naked like them, and wept and lamented just like them in their heathen manner... and he plumed his face with gum and dyed himself with the red dye *urucum*, and had seven Indian wives whom they gave him to keep in the Indian manner.[24]

Official wars against the Caeté and other tribes of the lower São Francisco, epidemics, and the activities of the slavers all combined to denude the sparsely populated sertão to the west of Bahia. One Jesuit was soon writing that 'the Portuguese go 250 or 300 leagues [1,500–2,000 kilometres] to seek these heathen since they are now so far away. And because the land is now deserted, most of them die of hunger on the

---

[22] Vicente do Salvador, *Historia do Brasil*, bk 3, ch. 20, in *Anais da Biblioteca Nacional do Rio de Janeiro* [*ABNRJ*], 13 (1885–6), 85.

[23] Salvador, *História do Brasil* (São Paulo/Rio de Janeiro, 1931), 92.

[24] Heitor Furtado de Mendonça, *Primeira visitação do Santo Officio às partes do Brasil: confisões de Bahia, 1591–92* (Rio de Janeiro, 1935), 172.

return journey.'[25] Another Jesuit marvelled at the 'boldness and impertinence with which [the slavers] allow themselves to enter the great wilderness, at great cost, for two, three, four, or more years'.[26] It was the same story as the bandeirantes, except that the men of Bahia were less determined woodsmen and they had fewer Indians to harass in their hinterland. They also lacked the lure of Jesuit reductions full of partly acculturated Christian converts.

The sertão that had been largely stripped of native inhabitants was found to be good cattle country. A map from the end of the sixteenth century showed a cattle corral at the mouth of the Paraguaçu, and during the ensuing decades cattle ranches spread up along this and the parallel rivers, across the Jacobina sertão towards the upper São Francisco, and along both banks of that great river. Some families became powerful cattle barons, *poderosos do sertão*, with lands stretching across many hundreds of kilometres of scrubby *campo* country. The descendants of Garcia Dias d'Ávila developed a ranch called the Casa da Torre, and they often quarrelled with another *poderoso*, António Guedes de Brito, and his heirs. Although a few acculturated Indians and half-castes made good cattle hands, most Indians were incompatible with cattle. They could not resist the temptation of hunting this large and easy game. The ranchers would not tolerate such killing, and were determined to clear all natives from lands they wanted for pasture. The result of this need for land for cattle was a series of campaigns against Indian tribes during the seventeenth century. This was warfare similar to the battles of the American West two centuries later. The opponents were plains Indians, generally Gê-speaking and as cunning as the dreaded Aimoré. In the 1620s Indians wiped out all settlers on the Apora plain; they moved on to evict those of the *chapada* of Itapororocas and to attack ranches on the lower Paraguaçu. It was not until after the Dutch wars that the authorities in Bahia resumed the offensive. In the 1650s there were military expeditions to destroy villages up the Maraú river and against the Guerens tribe of Aimoré. A lonely fort was established on the Orobo hills 250 kilometres west of Bahia, and there was an uneasy alliance with the Paiaiá of the Jacobina sertão to the north of these hills. The men of Bahia had little stomach for this tough, dangerous, and unrewarding

---

[25] Anon. Jesuit, 'Informação dos primeiros aldeiamentos da Bahia', in *José de Anchieta, Cartas, informações, fragmentos históricos e sermões*, ed. António de Alcântara Machado (Rio de Janeiro, 1933), 378.

[26] Anon. Jesuit, 'Sumário das armadas', 13–14.

fighting. Successive governors therefore turned to the Paulistas, whose bandeirantes had a reputation as Brazil's best Indian-fighters. Shiploads of Paulistas sailed north and were sent into the sertão with bloodthirsty orders to fight Indians, 'defeating and slaughtering them by every means and effort known to military skill...sparing only Tapuia [non-Tupi] women and children, to whom you will give life and captivity'.[27] Little was achieved during the 1660s, for the Paulistas were often outwitted by the 'Tapuia' tribes and they suffered in the dry interior of Bahia. Governor-General Afonso Furtado de Castro (1670–5), however, imported more Paulistas to lead bandeiras into Espírito Santo, present-day Minas Gerais, and especially the southern sertão of Bahia. He declared that hostile Indians must 'suffer stern discipline...Only after being completely destroyed do they become quiet...All experience has shown that this public nuisance can be checked only at its origin: by destroying and totally extinguishing the villages of the barbarians!'[28] The Indians fought hard. A campaign of 1672–3 brought back only 750 live captives (700 also died on the march to the coast), but its Paulista leader Estevão Ribeiro Baião Parente was authorized to found a town with the boastful name Santo António da Conquista, 260 kilometres from Bahia.

Some tribes avoided extinction by submitting to white conquest. They entered the service of the private armies of the cattle barons, or they accepted Christian missionaries and settled in mission aldeias. There was some activity by Franciscans, and the Jesuits had some missions on the middle São Francisco; but the most famous missionaries in the hinterland of Bahia and Pernambuco were French Capuchin (Hooded) Franciscans. One of these, Friar Martin de Nantes, wrote an account of his experiences among the Cariri between 1672 and 1683. He did his utmost to protect his native flock against oppression by the cattle barons.

At the beginning of the seventeenth century, settlers avoided the *cátinga* – dense, dry woods full of thorn bushes – that grew near the São Francisco river. But they later learned to clear and burn the *cátinga* and discovered that it contained stretches of good pasture. The result was the creation of immense cattle ranches along both banks of the river, and along the adjacent Vasa Barris, Real, Itapicurú and Jacuipe. By 1705

---

[27] Francisco Barreto, instructions to Bernardo Bartolomeu Aires, Bahia, 1 Feb. 1658, in *Documentos históricos da Biblioteca Nacional do Rio de Janeiro* [*DHBNRJ*] (1928–   ), IV, 71–2.
[28] Report by Alexandre de Sousa Freire, 4 Mar. 1669, in *DHBNRJ*, V, 213–14.

an author claimed that there were cattle ranches extending uninterrupted along 2,000 miles of the river. And a governor-general wrote in 1699 that the Paulistas had, 'in a few years, left this captaincy free of all the tribes of barbarians that oppressed it, extinguishing them so effectively that from then until the present you would not know that there were any heathen living in the wilds they conquered'.[29] All that was left of the original Gê and Tupi tribes were some groups in mission aldeias: Pancararú at Pambú island on the São Francisco (some of whose descendants survive at Brejo dos Padres, Tacaratú, Pernambuco); Ocren and Tupi-speaking Tupina and Amoipira upstream of them on the main river, and a mixture of tribes in the Jesuit aldeias of Pilar, Sorobabé, Aracapá, Pontal, and Pajehú towards its mouth; Cariri tribes at Caimbé and Massacará (where Garcia d'Ávila later kept part of his private native army), Jeremoabo on the Vasa Barris and Canabrava (now called Pombal) and Sahy (now Jacobina) on the Itapicurú.

Towards the end of the seventeenth century, saltpetre or nitrate was found on the river now called Salitre, and mission Indians such as the Paiaiá and Sacuriú – and soon the newly-pacified Araquens and Tamanquin – were forced to labour in the dangerous saltpetre quarries. At the beginning of the eighteenth century, the wild and nomadic Orí of the forested Cassuca hills near the headwaters of the Vasa Barris were pacified with the aid of Christianized Caimbé Indians. The civil authorities appointed a Cariri chief from Pontal aldeia to be governor of the Indians of the São Francisco, and he duly led his men into battle on behalf of the Portuguese against other Indians.

The north-east

The Indian frontier in the north-east – the interior of Pernambuco, Paraíba, Rio Grande do Norte, and Ceará – followed a similar pattern to that of Bahia and the São Francisco valley. In the sixteenth century the Tupi tribes of the Atlantic littoral were consumed and destroyed by warfare, imported disease, and forced labour in sugar plantations. The frontier then moved inland to the territories of more resilient Gê-speaking 'Tapuia' tribes, and sugar gave way to cattle in the dry sertão. There was the usual conflict between cattle barons and Indian tribes over land. But in one respect, Indians found it easier to come to

---

[29] João de Lancastro to Fernando Martins Mascarenhas de Lancastro, Bahia, 11 Nov. 1699, in _DHBNRJ_, xxxix (1938), 88–9.

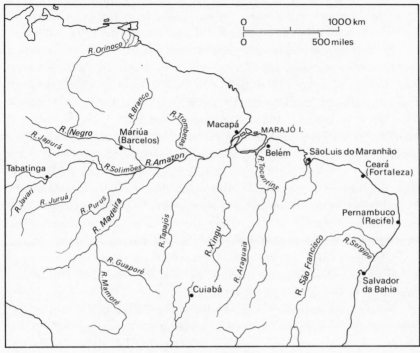

Northern Brazil

terms with a society based on cattle: they preferred the tough, lonely, mobile work of cattle hands to back-breaking, ignominious labour in sugar plantations.

Two factors made the north-east different from Bahia in its Indian affairs. One was the intrusion of other powers – the French and then the Dutch – and the attempts by rival European nations to manipulate Indian allies. The other was the existence there of large and cohesive native peoples: the Tobajara of Paraíba, the Potiguar of the long east–west coast from Rio Grande to Maranhão, and Chief Jandui's Tarairyu in the interior.

The fact that Pernambuco was the most successful of the captaincies that the Portuguese created in Brazil in the 1540s was due to the energy of the first donatory, Duarte Coelho, and to the suitability of the region for sugar planting. It was also due to an alliance with the Tupi-speaking Tobajara, which followed heavy fighting during the first years of the colony and which was sealed by the marriage of the donatory's brother-in-law Jerónimo de Albuquerque to a daughter of a Tobajara chief. Jerónimo de Albuquerque sired such a large family of *mamelucos* by his Indian wife that he became known as 'the Adam of Pernambuco'.

The Portuguese had more difficulty with the tribes to the south and north-west of Pernambuco. To the south, between the Cabo de Santo Agostinho and the mouth of the São Francisco, were the Caeté, the tribe that killed Bishop Sardinha and that welcomed French logwood traders. The Jesuit Jácome Monteiro complained that French Huguenots had made a 'La Rochelle' on the Sergipe river; but between 1575 and 1590 successive Portuguese campaigns ruthlessly destroyed the tribes of this stretch of coast. In the 1575–6 campaign, Governor Luís de Brito de Almeida himself led an attack from Bahia that 'gave such punishment as had never before been seen in those parts'.[30] The French, as usual, failed to reinforce or protect tribes that accepted their alliance. The Portuguese were thus able to crush the last native resistance in the Baepeba hills, when a force led by Cristóvão Cardoso de Barros in 1590 killed 1,500 Indians and captured 4,000, and founded the town of São Cristóvão at the mouth of the Sergipe river.

The large and bellicose Potiguar tribe successfully repelled Portuguese advances to the north of Pernambuco during the 1570s and early 1580s. Various Portuguese expeditions were defeated or left after only limited success. A Portuguese fort was established at São Felipe near the mouth of the Paraíba in 1584, but whenever its garrison ventured inland it was routed by Potiguar ambushes or attacks. A Jesuit complained of the Potiguar that 'none can resist the fury of this nation of victorious heathen. They are personally more spirited than any others, and so brave that they do not fear death.'[31] It was a judge from Recife called Martim Leitão who began to gain ascendancy over this formidable tribe. In expeditions in 1584 and 1585 he penetrated into the heart of Potiguar territory in Paraíba, and won some victories in heavy hand-to-hand fighting. By 1590 there was a Portuguese town on the Paraíba, with Jesuit and Franciscan missions among its Tobajara Indians. French ships were destroyed throughout these years and any Frenchmen caught on land were executed. By 1597 the Portuguese were ready to push northwards to Rio Grande, where the Potiguar had for many years been intermarrying with Frenchmen. Their expedition advanced by land and sea, and the land column contained a powerful force of Tobajara

---

[30] Soares de Sousa, *Tratado*, 43–4.
[31] Anon. Jesuit, 'Sumário das armadas', 25.

warriors. It also brought smallpox, which wrought havoc both on the Tobajara but even more on their Potiguar enemies. A fort called Reis Magos (Magi) was established on the Potengi and it resisted furious Potiguar attacks. In the end, a solemn peace treaty was concluded at Paraíba on 11 June 1599; a subsequent attack on the Reis Magos fort by 40,000 Potiguar was defeated, and by 1601 the Potiguar finally came under Portuguese control.

The next frontier was westwards along the coast of Ceará, towards Maranhão and the mouth of the Amazon. An Indian-fighter called Pedro Coelho de Sousa led an expedition of Tobajara and Potiguar across Ceará in 1604 and successfully attacked some French-influenced Tupinambá in the Ibiapaba hills near Maranhão; but he alienated his native allies by attempting to enslave both friendly and hostile Indians, and an attempt to colonize Ceará was ended by a disastrous drought. Jesuit missionaries were equally unsuccessful, when one of them was killed by 'Tapuia' tribes beyond Ibiapaba. It was a young Portuguese officer, Martim Soares Moreno, who succeeded in colonizing Ceará where warfare and religious proselytizing had failed. He succeeded by becoming a close friend of the Indians, adopting many of their customs and impressing them as a warrior. Martim Soares Moreno was in command of the fort of the Reis Magos at Natal, and he occupied Ceará 'with only five soldiers and a chaplain, trusting in the affection and friendship he had made with all the Indian chiefs on both banks [of the Jaguaribe]'.[32] The Portuguese frontier in Brazil was now close to Maranhão, approaching the Amazon and about to cross the Line of Tordesillas in northern Brazil just as it was in the south.

When the French made their last attempt to colonize Brazil, with the landing of three ships of colonists under the Sieur de la Ravardière on the island of Maranhão in 1612, the Portuguese, who had themselves failed to establish settlements there, dealt swiftly with the threat. The French tried to win over the Tupinambá of Maranhão by taking six chiefs to Paris, where they enjoyed lavish hospitality and a royal christening in Nôtre Dame. Such wooing was no match for Portuguese military skill and Indian alliances. The Portuguese mobilized the recently pacified Potiguar of Rio Grande under their chief Poti or Camarão ('Shrimp' in Tupi and in Portuguese), the 65-year-old *mameluco* Jerónimo de Albuquerque as commander with his Tobajara relatives, and the Ceará Indians of Martim Soares Moreno. The

[32] Diogo de Campos Moreno, *Livro que da razão do Estado do Brasil* [1612] (Recife, 1955), 211.

Portuguese sailed north-west with their Indians and established themselves in a fort at Guaxenduba, opposite Maranhão Island. Here, on 19 November 1614, they annihilated a larger and better-equipped force of French and Tupinambá; and within a year the French were gone for ever.

The frontier in the north-east would doubtless have advanced in a similar pattern to that of Bahia. The lands of the Rio Grande Potiguar who accepted the peace treaty of 1599 were rapidly parcelled out into cattle ranches. Cattle ranching would have spread into the dry interior – which was inhabited by Gê-speaking 'Tapuia' Indians, as was the interior of Bahia – during the first half of the seventeenth century. Such expansion was, however, delayed for a quarter-century by the advent of another European power: the Dutch. The Dutch wars (1624–54) halted expansion into the interior of the north-east and enhanced the standing of Indian tribes in the disputed areas. Both European powers enlisted native troops in their battles, and both regarded good relations with the Indians as important in ensuring control of the region. The struggle between Portuguese and Dutch was in part a war of religion, so that Catholic and Protestant missionaries redoubled their efforts to convert tribes and enlist them in the fighting. The Portuguese were lucky to have the young Potiguar chief Poti-Camarão, who turned into a formidable guerrilla leader, harassing the Dutch throughout the conquered provinces and deploying a force of Indians who had mastered all forms of European fighting. His men combined native skills in tracking and woodcraft with proficiency in handling European firearms. For their part, the Dutch had Indian warriors fighting under another Potiguar called Pieter Poti. The two native commanders were distant cousins and they corresponded in an unsuccessful attempt to persuade one another to change allegiance and religion.

Meanwhile, Calvinist pastors moved into the few remaining Indian villages and sought to convert the inhabitants to the Protestant faith. After initial superficial success they found, like the Jesuits before them, that the Indians had failed to grasp the finer points of Christianity. The Indians responded more enthusiastically to the great Dutch governor of Brazil, Count Johan Maurits of Nassau. Count Maurits had a genuine affection for the Indians. He wrote to his superiors that

the quiet and preservation of the colony of Brazil depends in part on the friendship of the Indians. With this in mind they should be permitted to enjoy their natural freedom...Orders should be issued that they are not to be outraged by their administrators, hired out for money, or forced to work in sugar mills against their will. Each should, on the contrary, be allowed to live in the way he understands and to work where he wishes like men of our nation.[33]

When Johan Maurits was recalled in 1644 a crowd of Indians insisted on accompanying him to his ship and demanded that he take them to Holland. A year later, in April 1645, the Dutch authorities organized an assembly of chiefs of the twenty Indian aldeias under their rule. The meeting was docile enough, but it made a powerful plea for Indian freedom to be observed in practice and not just in theory or in paper legislation. This meeting was unique in Brazilian history: not until the late twentieth century has there been a comparable gathering of tribal leaders in European-occupied Brazil.

For all their good intentions and their desire to win Indian allegiance, the Dutch proved little better than the Portuguese when it came to forcing Indians to labour for derisory pay expressed in lengths of cotton cloth. They sought to impose their Protestant religion and to eradicate 'heathen' practices with just as much vehemence as the Portuguese. They also unwittingly brought deadly diseases, such as smallpox or measles, which raged through the colony. As a result, when the Dutch began to be defeated most Indians turned against them. Many Dutch were massacred in a native rising in Maranhão and Ceará, and the survivors concluded that this was because 'instead of finding relief from us Dutch, the Indians are subjected to greater captivity'.[34]

One by-product of the Dutch invasion was increased knowledge of the Indians of the north-east. Contemporary accounts show terrible depopulation. Domingos da Veiga had reported that in 1627 there were 'little more than 300 bowmen divided among four villages [in Rio Grande]. There used to be such a quantity of them here that their numbers were not known.'[35] Twelve years later, Adriaen van der Drussen listed five villages in Rio Grande, five in Paraíba, five in Goiana, and four in Pernambuco, with a total of less than 2,000 men of all ages between them. Johannes de Laet gave a measure of the decline when he reported that in Ceará, where the Potiguar had once had 8,000 warriors, there were only 105 by 1635. In addition to the usual

[33] Johan Maurits van Nassau, report to States General, 27 Sept. 1644, in José António Gonçalves de Mello Neto, *Tempo dos Flamengos* (Rio de Janeiro, 1947), 234–5.
[34] Gedeon Morris de Jonge to Supreme Council, São Luís do Maranhão, 29 Jan. 1643, *RIHGB*, 58/1 (1895), 307.
[35] Domingos da Veiga, description of Rio Grande, 1627, in Barão de Studart (ed.), *Documentos para a história do Brasil e especialmente a do Ceará* (4 vols., Fortaleza, 1908–21), IV, 35.

epidemics and deaths in battle, there had also been widespread flight into the interior to avoid colonial oppression. According to Laet's figures, there was a total Indian population of only 9,000 in the 800 miles of coast between Ceará and the São Francisco river.

The Dutch also spread their influence inland, to try to bring the Gê-speaking tribes of the interior into the fighting on their side. Their emissary, Jacob Rabe, visited the Tarairyu of the hinterland of Rio Grande–Ceará and established excellent relations with the tribe's aged chief Nhandui or Jandui. Rabe and his successor Roulox Baro left careful descriptions of the society and religion of the Tarairyu, which reveal that they were very similar to modern Canela or Timbira of Maranhão or to the Krahô of northern Goiás. They were plains Indians, swift runners who maintained their agility through frequent log races between the two moieties of the tribe. Their marriage customs, religion, and even their physical appearance and bonnet-like haircuts were identical to those of their modern Gê-speaking counterparts. Thanks to Rabe's influence, the Tarairyu and other 'Tapuia' joined the Dutch and were particularly ferocious in the fighting against Portuguese settlers. In revenge, the settlers were merciless in slaughtering any Indians who fought with the Dutch, even when these surrendered under negotiated truce.

When the Dutch finally abandoned their Brazilian forts in 1654, 4,000 native people from the aldeias of Itamaracá, Paraíba and Rio Grande marched north-westwards to take refuge in Ceará. They were furious that the Dutch, whom they had served so faithfully for many years, had deserted them. They fortified themselves among the Tobajara in the Ibiapaba hills and sought to create an independent enclave which they called Cambressive. They even sent a Dutch-educated chief to Holland to beg for Dutch military assistance, as a reward for past services and to preserve the Protestant religion. This chief pleaded, in vain, that 'if help fails them, our people must inevitably finally fall into the clutches of the cruel and bloodthirsty Portuguese, who since the first occupation of Brazil have destroyed so many hundreds of thousands of people of that nation...'[36]

With the expulsion of the Dutch, Brazil was never again seriously threatened by a rival European invasion. The settlers of the north-east

[36] Appeal by Antony Paraupaba, The Hague, 6 Aug. 1654, in Pedro Souto Maior, *Fastos Pernambucanos* (Rio de Janeiro, 1913) and *RIHGB*, 76 (1913), 191.

were therefore able to push their frontier inland during the second half of the seventeenth century. Their frontier was similar to that of the Bahia hinterland: vast expanses of barren sertão good only for cattle ranching. After the Dutch wars the Tarairyu of Chief Jandui (whom the Portuguese continued to call 'Janduin' in his memory) were at peace for some years until their territories began to be invaded by cattle ranchers. Sporadic outbursts of fighting occurred during the ensuing decades. In the mid-1660s the Tarairyu and their allies the Paiacú attacked domesticated Tupi in the Jesuit missions of the Rio Grande and Paraíba coast. There were reprisal expeditions. But the explosion that had long been threatening finally occurred in 1687, when these Cariri tribes swept through Rio Grande slaughtering over 100 colonists and their retainers on isolated ranches and killing over 30,000 head of cattle. The governor reported that the settlers retreated into Natal and almost abandoned the captaincy.

At this time a few tough cattlemen had crossed the middle São Francisco and moved northwards into the valley of the Parnaíba, in what is now the state of Piauí. One of these pioneers was Domingos Afonso, nicknamed 'Mafrense' or 'Sertão', who pushed the frontier deep into this sparsely inhabited wilderness. The eighteenth-century historian Sebastião da Rocha Pitta told how he 'entered lands not previously penetrated by Portuguese and inhabited only by wild heathen, with whom he had many battles, emerging dangerously wounded from one but victorious in them all, killing many heathen and making the rest retreat to the interior of the sertão'.[37] Domingos Afonso died leaving the Jesuits 30 huge ranches stretching over almost 400 miles. Another pioneer of Piauí was Domingos Jorge Velho, who conquered territories to the west of Domingos Afonso; for a time the two cattlemen campaigned together. Each of these frontiersmen enlisted private armies of conquered Indians. Jorge Velho wrote to the king excusing his raids and conquests as being a way of 'domesticating' the tribes to a 'knowledge of civilized life' and introducing them to the mysteries of the Catholic church. He admitted that few missionaries were involved in this altruistic endeavour. Instead,

we enlarge our troops from those thus acquired and brought into settlements. With them we wage war on those who are obstinate and refractory to

[37] Sebastião da Rocha Pitta, *História da América Portugueza* (Lisbon, 1730), VI, 385.

settlement. If we later use them in our fields we do them no injustice, for this is to support them and their children as much as to support us and ours. Far from enslaving them, we render them a gratuitous service by teaching them to till, plant, harvest, and work for their livelihood.[38]

Despite this glowing account of his civilizing mission, the bishop of Pernambuco was appalled when he met Domingos Jorge Velho, describing him as

one of the worst savages I have ever met... He is no different from the most barbarous Tapuia, except in calling himself Christian. Although recently married, seven Indian concubines attend him – from which one can infer his other habits. Until now... he has roamed the forests hunting Indian men and women, the latter to exercise his lusts and the former to work on the fields he owns.[39]

As so often in Brazilian history, the Indians responded well to such a man and, once defeated by him, were willing to follow such a successful warrior. It was men like him, uncouth but brilliant woodsmen, who expanded Portugal's frontier in Brazil.

It was to Domingos Jorge Velho that the authorities turned when confronted by the Tarairyu war of 1687. He and his rugged army performed an extraordinary march across hundreds of miles of sertão. His 600 exhausted men engaged the Tarairyu or Janduin on the Apodi and many were killed on both sides in a fierce four-day battle. The Janduin had already shattered an expedition of 900 men sent against them from Pernambuco. There were the usual urgent appeals to the Paulistas, who were still rightly considered to be the only 'men accustomed to penetrate the sertão and endure hunger, thirst, and inclemencies of climate and weather. The regular infantry have no experience whatsoever of such conditions; nor do the local militia, who lack discipline and endurance.'[40] A Paulista commander, Matias Cardoso de Almeida, made an incredible 1,500-mile march north from the São Francisco and then led three years of campaigns against these Gê tribes. It was a ruthless war, in which the Portuguese commanders were ordered to slaughter all adult Indians they could catch, and in which

---

[38] Domingos Jorge Velho to king, Serra da Barriga, Palmares, 15 July 1694, in Ernesto Ennes, *As guerras nos Palmares* (São Paulo, 1938), 206; Eng. trans. in Richard M. Morse (ed.), *The Bandeirantes: the historical role of the Brazilian pathfinders* (New York, 1965), 118.

[39] Bishop of Pernambuco to Junta das Missões, 18 May 1697, in Edison Carneiro, *Guerras de los Palmares* (Mexico, 1946), 133–4.

[40] Archbishop-Governor Frei Manoel da Resureição to Câmara Coutinho, governor of Pernambuco, in Afonso de Escragnolle Taunay, *História das bandeiras paulistas* (2 vols., São Paulo, 1953), I, 175.

they launched murderous surprise attacks on native villages. The Janduin, in return, twice besieged Natal and mustered large armies of fearless warriors. As always, most of the fighting was done by rival Indians marching for or against the Portuguese. In the end, the Janduin achieved something that was common in North America in later centuries but rare in Brazil: a formal peace treaty with the king of Portugal that recognized their chief Canindé as an autonomous ruler and granted the tribe independence and large tracts of land within Portuguese sovereignty. The treaty was signed at Salvador da Bahia on 10 April 1692; but it was soon violated by ranchers' invasions of Indian territory and aggressions by Paulista commanders who remained in this part of the north-east.

The Amazon

It was very difficult to reach the mouth of the Amazon by ship from the north-east of Brazil: contrary winds, currents, and shoals meant that it was easier to sail from Maranhão and Pará to Lisbon than to Bahia. This isolation, together with the different vegetation and climate of the Amazon basin, meant that this frontier developed distinctly from the rest of Brazil. There was the added factor that even by the most pro-Portuguese interpretation of the Treaty of Tordesillas, the entire Amazon river lay within the Spanish rather than the Portuguese sphere.

With the failure of the Portuguese attempt to colonize Maranhão in 1535, and the failures of two Portuguese expeditions up the Amazon, that great river was visited only by Spaniards during the sixteenth century. Contact was made with hundreds of its tribes by the first discoverer, Vicente Yáñez Pinzón, in 1500; by Amerigo Vespucci, sailing under Gonçalo Coelho two years later; by Diego de Ordaz in an abortive attempt at settlement in 1531; and most notably during the first descent of Francisco de Orellana in 1542. The largest attempt to colonize the upper Amazon – in the mistaken belief that the lands of the Tupi-speaking Omagua of the Solimões-Amazon were the legendary kingdom of Eldorado – was the great expedition of Pedro de Ursúa of 1559–60, which ended in mutiny by the Basque traitor Lope de Aguirre. After this disaster the tribes of the Amazon were not molested by Europeans for a further half-century.

In January 1616, within two months of their eviction of the French from Maranhão, the Portuguese founded a fort 400 miles west on the

Pará river, which forms the southern mouth of the Amazon. This fort was to develop into the town of Belém do Pará. After initial calm, fighting soon erupted with the Tupinambá of the forested coast between Pará and Maranhão. During the ensuing decade there were savage wars of annihilation that left this region almost depopulated. Even the Tupinambá of Maranhão Island, whose populous villages had welcomed the French and who refused to join their compatriots in fighting the Portuguese, were not spared: for in 1621 they were struck 'by an epidemic of smallpox of such virulence that any who caught it – most of whom were Indians – did not survive for more than three days'.[41]

There is relatively little documentation of the first 35 years of Portuguese occupation of Pará and the lower Amazon: histories by the contemporary Vicente do Salvador and the later Bernardo Pereira de Berredo, a few official papers, and brief accounts by Capuchin missionaries or such explorers as Simão Estácio da Silveira. The picture that emerges from these sources is one of near-anarchy, a lawless time during which the Indians suffered. The settlers of the tiny town of Belém conquered the tribes on rivers flowing north to the Pará, on the lower Tocantins, and on other rivers between it and the Xingu. There was particularly heavy fighting against the Pacajá on the river of that name. Some tribes were lured down to Belém with promises of trade goods. Others were seized in surprise attacks by flotillas of canoes full of Portuguese and their Indian allies armed with firearms. Contemporary accounts speak of the destruction of hundreds of villages and heavy depopulation of all exposed coasts and rivers near Belém. The few missionaries in Pará at this time fulminated against the oppression of nominally free Indians who were 'forced to do very heavy labour such as making tobacco, in which they work for seven or eight months on end by day and night'.[42] Payment was in trivial lengths of coarse cloth, which the Indians themselves made; failure to work was punished by flogging in the stocks. The Indians had an obvious remedy in this forested land. As the Jesuit Luís Figueira wrote, 'Because of this oppression, they flee into the forests and depopulate their villages. Others die of despair in this labour without remedy.'[43] Any protest against violations of Pro-Indian legislation was greeted by howls of

[41] Bernardo Pereira de Berredo, *Annaes historicos do Estado do Maranhão* (Lisbon, 1749), bk 6, 211.
[42] Luís Figueira, 'Memorial sôbre as terras e gentes do Maranhão e Grão-Pará e rio das Amazonas', Lisbon, 10 Aug. 1637, in *RIHGB*, 94 (vol. 148) (1923), 431. [43] *Ibid.*

indignation from the colonists, and most of the early governors of Maranhão and Pará were themselves involved in raiding for slaves.

The most ferocious killer of Maranhão Tupinambá was a captain called Bento Maciel Parente. Yet this same Indian-fighter was appointed captain-general of Ceará in 1626 and a Franciscan complained that his treatment of its Indians was appalling even by contemporary standards: he kept the men constantly at work in his mills, without pay and with no breaks on Sundays or saints' days, and allowed no time for Indians dying of hunger to provide for their families. This Bento Maciel Parente was given royal authorization to make expeditions up the Amazon: and in 1637 he was given a hereditary captaincy of Cabo do Norte, which included the north shore of the Amazon as far upstream as the Paru river, a vast area corresponding to the modern territory of Amapá. This was the first time that a Spanish king of Portugal made an award to a Portuguese that was clearly west of the Line of Tordesillas; and the award was a licence to a notorious Indian-fighter and slaver to exploit at will its thousands of native inhabitants.

In that same year, the settlers of Pará were surprised by the arrival of a canoe containing two Spanish friars and some soldiers that had descended the Amazon from Quito. This inspired an expedition of great geopolitical importance in shaping the Brazilian frontier. The governor, Jacomé Raimundo de Noronha, determined to claim nothing less than the main Amazon river for Portugal. He sent Pedro Teixeira up-river with an important expedition of 70 Portuguese soldiers, with 1,100 mission Indians to paddle 47 canoes and to supply food by hunting and fishing. The governor gave Teixeira sealed orders to plant Portuguese boundary markers when he reached the lands of the Omagua, no less than 1,500 miles west of the Line of Tordesillas! The expedition was a triumphant success, thanks to the endurance of the Indians, who paddled upstream for months on end and eventually carried the flotilla up to Quito. The Spaniards sent observers to accompany the return journey and one of these, the Jesuit Cristóbal de Acuña, wrote a splendid account of his descent. He strongly urged the king of Spain to make an effective occupation of the Amazon: but his advice was ignored, and the boundary of modern Brazil is now far up the river, close to the place where Teixeira placed his marker.

Acuña observed the large and prosperous tribes that still existed on the Amazon. He was particularly impressed, as Orellana's men had been a century earlier, by the Omagua, who kept ponds stocked with thousands of turtles alongside their villages, and by the Curucirari, whose delicate polychrome pottery rivalled Chinese ceramics. But as the expedition descended the Amazon, Acuña witnessed increasing destruction by Portuguese slavers from Belém do Pará. He watched in horror while one of Bento Maciel's sons rounded up Tapajós men at gunpoint while permitting his own gang of Indians to rape their women and pillage their town. As he approached Pará, he saw increasing destitution and depopulation, with riverine settlements abandoned and no one left to cultivate the land. The small and primitive settlement of Belém was an incubus that steadily destroyed and denuded the Amazon and all its accessible tributaries. Pedro Teixeira's brother, the vicar-general of Maranhão, Manoel Teixeira, reckoned that in the first three decades after their arrival on the Amazon, the few hundred settlers of Maranhão and Pará were responsible for the deaths of almost two million Indians through their 'violent labour, exhausting discoveries, and unjust wars'.[44]

The Jesuits planned to operate in Pará, but their hopes were frustrated when a ship carrying their Provincial Luís Figueira and eleven Fathers foundered in full view of Belém in 1643 and the missionaries were captured and killed by hostile Aruan Indians of Marajó Island. It was ten years before the Jesuits returned; but they did so in 1653 in the towering person of António Vieira. Vieira was a Brazilian-born Jesuit who had risen to be the close confidant and confessor of Dom João IV of Portugal. He was famous for the brilliance of his sermons at a time when the pulpit was the most potent medium of communication. Vieira had been entrusted with secret diplomatic missions in Europe, and his was the most influential voice in shaping Portuguese foreign policy. It came as a surprise when this powerful man suddenly vowed to take up missionary field work, and actually sailed for the backwater of the Amazon.

António Vieira was appalled by the conditions he found in Maranhão and Pará. He preached fiery sermons against expeditions to 'rescue' or 'ransom' Indians which were really slaving expeditions and condemned any settlers who kept Indian slaves: 'All of you are in mortal sin; all of you live in a state of condemnation; and all of you are going directly

---

[44] António Vieira, 'Reposta aos capítulos que deu...Jorge de Sampaio' [1662, reply to ch. 24], *Obras escolhidas* (12 vols., Lisbon, 1951–4), v, 280.

to Hell!'[45] But his eloquence was wasted on colonists who had no intention of giving up any Indians and who were constantly clamouring for more native labour. After a journey up the Tocantins, Vieira returned to Portugal and persuaded the vacillating king to enact new legislation (1655) against Indian enslavement. The Jesuits were entrusted with the task of bringing the Indians from the interior by peaceful means and establishing them in mission villages under their control. Five years of euphoric activity ensued for the Jesuits. The Fathers accompanied expeditions up all the main tributaries of the lower Amazon and far up the Negro, and they had soon 'descended' some 200,000 Indians into 54 mission aldeias. The tribes came willingly, impressed by the reputation of the Jesuits and by their promises of material prosperity and religious enlightenment. The descents were, however, murderous deceptions. Many Indians died of alien diseases during the voyages down to Belém; but the missionaries consoled themselves that these victims of their misguided policy had at least received baptism before dying. Once settled in aldeias near Portuguese towns, the Indians were exposed to constant demands for their labour. Crowded into these settlements, they were particularly vulnerable to smallpox and measles, epidemics of which occurred with dismal regularity. The Jesuits could not reconcile the fundamental contradiction that stifled any royal wish for humane treatment of the Indians. The small European colonies in Brazil could not prosper without native labour and could not ward off attack by hostile tribes or rival colonial powers without docile native auxiliaries. The settlers knew that they could make the Indians work for them only by force; and in the impoverished Amazon they were too poor to afford African slaves. Life in this region depended on river transport and on fish and game, gums, fruits, and resins extracted from the forests. For such activities local Indians were far better than imported Africans. The Jesuits deluded themselves that the Indians in their missions would become loyal Christian subjects of Portugal. But they knew in practice that they were condemning them to forced labour and rapid destruction from disease, demoralization, malnutrition and social disruption.

Vieira himself performed two missions of which he was proud. In

---

[45] A sermon given by him at Maranhão, Lent 1653, can be found in Leite, *História da Companhia de Jesus*, IX, 211; Eng. trans. in E. Bradford Burns, *A documentary history of Brazil* (New York, 1966), 83.

1659 he undertook an embassy to the tribes of Marajó Island, who were known collectively as Nheengaíba (Tupi for 'incomprehensible languages'). These tribes had successfully resisted repeated Portuguese punitive expeditions, usually by disappearing into the labyrinth of channels on their island. Forty thousand of them now surrendered, accepting Vieira's assurances that Portuguese attitudes had changed with the new law of 1655. The Jesuits established themselves on Marajó, where their huge cattle ranches prospered, to the envy of the colonists and eventually of the government in Lisbon. In 1660 Vieira made a difficult journey to the remote Ibiapaba hills on the border between Maranhão and Ceará. He confronted the remnants of the north-eastern Indians who had fled there after the departure of the Dutch. All but the oldest accepted conversion to Catholicism and the presence of Jesuit missionaries.

The Jesuits' efforts to accommodate settlers' demands for Indian labour were in vain. Colonists who had hoped to make their fortunes in the Amazon were defeated by the difficult conditions and climate. As they saw their riverside clearings fail, they vented their frustration on the Jesuits, pious busybodies who seemed to be thwarting their supply of fresh Indian labour. Their fury erupted in May 1661 with a rising in São Luís do Maranhão against the Jesuit Fathers. Vieira and most of his men were arrested and shipped off to Portugal. A new law of 12 September 1663 installed lay *repartidores* in Indian villages to oversee the allocation of men to work on settlers' holdings. It was seventeen years before Vieira was able to influence a new king, Pedro II, to reinstate the Jesuits in full control of Indian aldeias and to forbid all forms of Indian slavery. During those years irreparable damage had been done to the Indians under Portuguese rule. The liberal law of 1 April 1680 awarded land to the Indians, since they were 'the original and natural lords of it'[46] – an important concept and a phrase still being quoted by pro-Indian activists in modern Brazil. But this law brought a reaction almost as swift as that to similar legislation in 1609 and 1655. In February 1684 the colonists of Maranhão rose in a revolt led by Manoel Beckman and Jorge Sampaio and again expelled the Jesuits. The revolt was soon crushed and the ringleaders hanged; but the Jesuits were alarmed and decided, albeit reluctantly, to compromise on two important issues. They were granted full temporal and spiritual control

---

[46] Law of 1 April 1680, in Agostinho Marques Perdigão Malheiro, *A escravidão no Brasil* (Rio de Janeiro, 1867), II, 70.

of the mission aldeias, although they agreed to increase the time that their charges must work for settlers to six months a year, and they undertook to administer these labour levies at wages to be agreed with the colonial governor. Not surprisingly, this wage was fixed at the derisory figure of two and a half yards of cloth for a month's work, and this wage remained in force for a century, even though it was only a fifth of the amount paid during the Dutch occupation. The cloth was almost valueless as an item of barter and could not purchase the tools or fish-hooks needed by the Indians; it was also produced from cotton worked by the Indians and was spun and woven by their women. The other terrible surrender was the reintroduction of legalized Indian slavery. As often throughout the colonial period, slavery was permitted for *índios de corda* – Indian prisoners of intertribal wars supposedly bound and ready for execution – and captives taken in 'just wars', which could now be waged on any tribe about which there was 'certain and infallible fear' that it might threaten Portuguese rule. Both these definitions were open to flagrant abuse. Official annual slaving (euphemistically called 'ransoming') expeditions were resumed, although they were accompanied by Jesuits to guarantee 'legality' and subject to a Junta das Missões composed of missionaries and a royal judge sitting in Belém. Contemporary documents are full of descriptions of slaving activities carried out against any tribes caught on the banks of the Amazon or its navigable tributaries. The traffic died down only when such areas were denuded, when tribes had retreated into the forests or up the tributaries beyond barriers of rapids, or when a few large tribes organized themselves for defence.

António Vieira himself drew up regulations for the daily conduct of life on Jesuit missions on the Amazon, the Regimento das Missões (1686) in what was now called Maranhão and Grão Pará. These regulations were later adopted for the rest of Brazil and with a few modifications remained in force until Pombal's secularization of Indian affairs in the 1750s. In 1693 the whole area was divided among the religious orders for missionary purposes. The Jesuits restricted their own activities to the south bank of the Amazon upstream to the mouth of the Madeira. The north shore of the Amazon to the Paru fell to Franciscan Capuchins of Santo António, as far as the Trombetas to Franciscans of Piedade and Conceição, to the mouth of the Rio Negro to the Mercedarians, and, later, the Negro itself and the Solimões to Carmelites. The missionary orders now adopted a policy of creating aldeias along the banks of the rivers, close to the original habitats of the tribes, rather than bringing Indians down-river in disastrous 'descents' for resettlement near Portuguese towns. This new policy provided a thin Portuguese presence along the Amazon, Solimões and Negro rivers. The existence of these aldeias (which were to become secular villages with Portuguese names under Pombal's legislation) was recognized in the Treaty of Madrid of 1750, which scrapped the Line of Tordesillas and awarded most of the Amazon basin to Portuguese Brazil.

THE EIGHTEENTH CENTURY

By the end of the seventeenth century the Brazilian frontier was static or in retreat except in Amazonia. Cattle ranching in the interior of Bahia and the north-east was reaching the limit beyond which animals could not be profitably driven to coastal markets. Bandeirante activity in the south was subsiding, with the disappearance of most Indians in the hinterland of Paraná and São Paulo and the realization that Indian captives were scarcely worth the effort now needed to capture them. Spanish Jesuits responded by pushing their Paraguayan missions back across the Uruguay river. Between 1687 and 1706 they established seven reductions on the east bank of the Uruguay and on its Icamaguá and Ijuí tributaries. These missions flourished, because of the industry of their Guaraní Indians and the immense herds of wild cattle that had bred during the half-century since the earlier missionary activity in the region. Such was their prosperity that Italian architects were imported to build great churches, and the Indians became highly proficient in performing sacred music or carving baroque sculpture.

New impetus to the expansion of the frontier, however, came from the discoveries of gold, in quick succession, in what are now Minas Gerais, west-central Mato Grosso, and Goiás. The upper Velhas river, which contained the largest gold deposits around Ouro Preto, had already been largely denuded of Indians by bandeirante raids. But the rush of miners seeking their fortunes in this area largely destroyed the remaining aldeias near São Paulo itself. Many Paulista families also used their private contingents of Indians to help on journeys to the mining area and to work in the mines themselves. Few of these ever returned.

The gold discoveries of Goiás involved the local Goiá and Araé tribes, for the bandeirante Bartolomeu Bueno da Silva, son of the original 'Anhangüera', recalled having seen gold ornaments on these

Indians. After repeated quests, he found the tribe again and persuaded its members to reveal where they had obtained their gold. Anhangüera the younger took a mass of his Carijó from São Paulo to work on the new deposits; but the brunt of the ensuing gold rush fell on the Goiá, who were forced to work with the miners and were soon extinguished. The long trail inland from São Paulo to the mining camp of Sant'Anna (Vila Boa de Goiás) was exposed to attack by groups of Gê-speaking Southern Caiapó, who mounted a determined and effective campaign to drive the Portuguese out of their forests and *campos*. After the failure of various punitive expeditions, the authorities called on António Pires de Campos, a Paulista who had gained the friendship of some of the Caiapós' traditional enemies, the Bororo of central Mato Grosso. Panic-stricken Goiás miners subscribed to bring this mercenary woodsman and his Bororo warriors to try to destroy the Caiapó. Between 1742 and 1751 Pires de Campos mounted a series of long raiding expeditions that, despite some Indian victories, eventually destroyed most Caiapó villages in a broad arc to the south and west of Goiás.

It was this same Pires de Campos who in 1719 had been one of the discoverers of gold in the depths of the South American continent, on the Coxipó river near Cuiabá. The long journey by flotillas (*monções*) of canoes from São Paulo to Cuiabá exposed adventurers on this gold rush to attack by three formidable Indian groups. After descending the Tietê and crossing the Paraná, the fleets portaged across onto the Paraguay watershed at a place called Camapuã. This place was exposed to ambushes by the same Southern Caiapó who harassed the Goiás miners. Further west, as the canoes descended the Aquidauana and paddled up the Paraguay, they were attacked by two of the most formidable nations of Indian warriors; the riverine Paiaguá and the Guaicurú of the Chaco and the Bodoquena hills. The Paiaguá were brilliant canoers and fearless fighters. They hid in the swamps and inlets of the Pantanal and sped out in light canoes to ambush passing Europeans. They had been opposing intruders ever since the first Spanish explorers of the sixteenth century, and it was they who killed many members of Rapôso Tavares' bandeira of 1648. They thus had no illusions about Portuguese intentions. António Pires de Campos described the Paiaguás' devastating fighting methods:

They were very highly skilled in handling their arrows and lances – they fired several shots during the time the bandeirantes took to fire one. Extraordinary swimmers, they advanced in their canoes and leaped into the water, tipping a side of their boat to act as a shield against musket balls. They would suddenly right the canoe again and fire another volley. If they felt they could not overcome the whites' resistance they submerged their boats; and before long dived and raised them again, and fled with such speed that they seemed to have wings.[47]

Paiaguá victories included the destruction of an entire flotilla of 200 people in twenty canoes in 1725; the destruction of most of the 1726 flotilla; and the capture of 900 kilos of gold and annihilation of most of its escort of 400 whites, blacks and Indians, in 1730. The Portuguese responded in 1734 with a formidable expedition of over 800 men in 100 canoes that ambushed and destroyed the main Paiaguá village; but fighting with this valiant tribe continued for some decades.

Part of the Paiaguá success was due to their alliance with the equally formidable Guaicurú. This tribe had also been fighting Europeans since the 1540s, and it gained a mastery over horses rivalling that of the North American plains Indians. A nomadic people, the Guaicurú lived only for their 7,000 or 8,000 horses, which they bred, trained, and tended with the utmost care. They considered themselves as an aristocratic people and dominated or terrorized neighbouring tribes. In order to remain mobile, Guaicurú women aborted most of their infants, so that the tribe had to raid to capture children from other tribes. Their superb horsemanship made the Guaicurú almost invincible in battle, and their lightning attacks could have destroyed all Spanish and Portuguese settlements in what are now northern Paraguay and southern Mato Grosso had they followed up their victories in sustained military campaigns; but they lacked the necessary will or leadership.

The Cuiabá goldfields lay in the territory of the Bororo; but although most of that nation were hostile to the Portuguese, they tended to avoid contact. Another large tribe affected by the discoveries of gold at Cuiabá and Vila Bela were the Arawak-speaking Parecis who lived north-west of Cuiabá near the upper Guaporé. This populous, docile, and civilized tribe was regarded as perfect potential labour by the miners. These unwarlike people were rounded up in hundreds to toil in the mines or to be shipped back to replenish the vanished stock of Indian labour at São Paulo itself.

[47] Antonio Pires de Campos, 'Breve noticia...do gentio bárbaro que ha na derrota...do Cuyabá', *RIHGB*, 25 (1862), 440.

The opening of the goldfields of Minas Gerais had an impact on the cattle areas of Bahia and the north-east. Hungry miners provided a splendid new market for cattle. With the peace treaty of 1692 that ended the Tarairyu (Janduin) wars there was a period of ugly violence as ranchers moved deeper into the interior of the north-eastern provinces. Official papers contain reports of atrocities against Indians on this nominally peaceful frontier. A Paulista commander, Manoel Álvares de Morais Navarro, slaughtered a village of peaceful Paiacú in 1699 during a parley; the primitive Tremembé, one of the few surviving tribes on the Atlantic coast, were annihilated by a punitive expedition from Maranhão; another Paulista, Francisco Dias de Siqueira, in 1692 ravaged the *corso* or roving tribes of the Maranhão interior but also attacked peaceful missions, and at the end of the century this old rascal was attacking uncontacted tribes in Piauí with a private army; in the final years of the seventeenth century there were slaving raids and Indian counterattacks on the Mearim and Itapicurú rivers of Maranhão; and between 1702 and 1705 the Vidal and Axemi of the Parnaíba valley were wiped out in a series of disgraceful violations of truces with them. One of the cruellest ruffians was António da Cunha Souto-Maior, who terrorized tribes from a camp on the Parnaíba. One 'barbarous entertainment'[48] devised by him and his brother was to release Anaperu prisoners one by one, ride them down on horses, and decapitate them with machetes. A rebellion by his own Indians in 1712 killed Cunha Souto-Maior and his Portuguese soldiers, and then spread rapidly into the most serious and widespread of all Indian rebellions. The insurrection was led by a mission-educated Indian called Mandu Ladino and it raged throughout southern Maranhão, Piauí and Ceará for seven years. It cost the Portuguese the loss of many lives and the destruction of hundreds of ranches. For a brief time Mandu's Gê tribes were allied to their traditional enemies, the Tupi tribes of Ceará. Had this alliance lasted, it could have expelled all Portuguese from Ceará; but the Tupi were placated by the authorities, and it was a force of Tobajara from Ibiapaba, fighting 'without any whites whatsoever, who were only an embarrassment to them in the forests',[49] who in 1719 caught and killed

---

[48] Antonio de Sousa Leal, report in Virginia Rau and Maria Fernanda Gomes da Silva (eds.), *Os manuscritos do arquivo da Casa de Cadaval respeitantes ao Brasil* (2 vols., Coimbra, 1956–60), II, 386.

[49] Father Domingos Ferreira Chaves to king, Ceará, 23 Nov. 1719, in Rau and Gomes da Silva (eds.), *Manuscritos*, II, 248–9.

Mandu and exterminated his 'Tapuia'. In 1720 the king called for a report on the situation of tribes in the north-east following the cattle boom. The resulting document was a litany of murders and outrages against its Indians during the preceding twenty years.

In north-western Amazonia the river Solimões ('poisons', because its tribes used curare), the main stream of the Amazon between the mouths of the Negro and the Javari at the modern boundary with Peru and Colombia, was scarcely claimed by either Spain or Portugal. In 1689 a Spanish Jesuit, Samuel Fritz, was active among the Yurimagua, who then lived near the mouth of the Purús. The Portuguese made occasional expeditions to this river in search of sarsaparilla, cacao or slaves. Fritz was taken to Belém and detained briefly in 1689 but was returned to his mission three years later. In 1697 Portuguese Carmelites appeared with a military escort to claim this stretch of river and expelled Fritz. During the ensuing decade the Iberian kingdoms disputed this long stretch of the Amazon, with Portuguese incursions upstream to the Napo and the arrest of a Spanish Jesuit near modern Iquitos in 1709. The result of all this was that the Portuguese eventually established a mission at Tabatinga, at what is now the frontier; but the Amazon was denuded by the squabbling. The Omagua and Yurimagua, once the most populous and advanced tribes on the Amazon, were dispersed and decimated. When the French scientist Charles de la Condamine descended the river in 1743 he reported that the Omagua lands were empty, with no Indians living on the 450 miles between Pebas and São Paulo de Olivença.

The early eighteenth century also saw the Portuguese pushing up the major tributaries of the middle Amazon. Jesuits found that their activities on the Madeira were impeded by the large and bellicose Tora tribe; but a powerful punitive expedition in 1719 'left them extinct'.[50] Other tribes of the lower Madeira agreed to descend to Jesuit missions near its mouth. The resulting vacuum was filled by the formidable Mura, a tribe that became implacable enemies of the whites after 400 of its people were enslaved while travelling peacefully towards a mission. The Mura learned to respect and avoid open combat against Portuguese firearms; but they were brilliant at ambushes and lightning attacks from

---

[50] José Gonçalves da Fonseca, 'Primeira exploração dos rios Madeira e Guaporé em 1749', in Cândido Mendes de Almeida, *Memórias para a história do extincto Estado do Maranhão* (Rio de Janeiro, 1860), II, 304.

the waterways of the lower Madeira. For many years during the mid eighteenth century the Mura prevented Portuguese settlement or movement on the rivers near their territory.

At this time, Carmelite missionaries were penetrating the Negro. Their advance was blocked by a 'rebellion' of the Manau under a paramount chief, Ajuricaba, in 1723. The Manau lived on the middle Negro, hundreds of miles upstream of the modern city that bears their name. During their war against the Portuguese they were in contact with the Dutch of Guiana, who supplied them with firearms, and for a time Ajuricaba flew a Dutch flag on his canoe. A large punitive expedition, based on the new mission of Mariuá (Barcelos), finally defeated the Manau and captured Ajuricaba in 1728. The great chief was brought in chains to slavery at Belém, but as he approached the city he and some fellow Manau tried to overpower their captors and then jumped into the river, still chained, preferring death to captivity.

In his monumental history of the Jesuits in Brazil, Serafim Leite lists no less than 160 expeditions made by the Fathers, most of them on the rivers of the Amazon basin during the century after 1650. There was also a steady succession of annual official and unofficial slaving expeditions. Through these activities the Portuguese penetrated far up all the Amazon's main tributaries, even if they tended to depopulate rather than to settle the areas they visited. There were also some longer explorations: in 1723 Francisco de Mello Palheta led a flotilla of canoes up the Madeira to Santa Cruz de la Sierra and back; in 1746 João de Sousa Azevedo made the first descent of the Arinos and Tapajós; others ascended the Negro to the Casiquaire canal, first discovered in 1744 by the Spanish Jesuit Manuel Román. These activities gave Portugal a physical presence in the Amazon basin, but at a terrible cost to the Indians. There were frequent epidemics of smallpox, influenza, and measles that destroyed the missions as fast as the missionaries could restock them with fresh converts. Father João Daniel reckoned that the Portuguese had descended or killed three million Indians from the Negro basin alone. He wrote that these rivers, once 'peopled with... Indians as numerous as swarms of mosquitoes, settlements without number, and a diversity of tribes and languages beyond count',[51] were reduced by 1750 to a thousandth part of their original population.

[51] João Daniel, 'Thesouro descoberto no maximo rio Amazonas', pt 2, ch. 15, *RIHGB*, 3 (1841), 50.

Travellers reported that hundreds of miles of the banks of the Amazon were 'destitute of inhabitants of either sex or any age'[52] and entire mission aldeias were abandoned.

It was Portuguese activity on the northern and southern extremities of Brazil – into the upper Paraná and Paraguay to the goldfields of Mato Grosso, and up the Amazon – that paved the way for the Treaty of Madrid, signed on 13 January 1750. This was a diplomatic triumph for the negotiators of Dom João V, for it recognized *de facto* occupation and thus awarded almost half South America to the Portuguese. The treaty sensibly sought to follow geographical features in fixing the boundary. It thus followed parts of the Uruguay, Iguaçu, Paraná, Paraguay, Guaporé, Madeira, and Javari rivers and, north of the Amazon, ran from the middle Negro to the watershed between the Amazon and Orinoco basins and along the Guiana watershed to the Atlantic.

The quarter-century after the Treaty of Madrid, the years of Dom José I and Pombal (1750–77), had a profound effect on the Indians of Brazil. Pombal's own half-brother, Francisco Xavier de Mendonça Furtado, was sent as governor of Maranhão-Pará and remained there from 1751 to 1759. He was shocked by the colonists' ignorance and abuse of Indians; but he was even more critical of the wealth, moral laxity, insubordination, and mistreatment of Indians by the missionary orders. In his letters to his brother he wrote that the various orders had some 12,000 Indians in 63 missions in Amazonia. On the island of Marajó, the Mercedarians had between 60,000 and 100,000 head of cattle on their ranches, the Jesuits 25,000–30,000, and the Carmelites 8,000–10,000. Although the Jesuits ran only nineteen missions, and although the governor approved of the fact that they alone kept Indian women decently clothed, it was the Fathers of the Society who most infuriated Mendonça Furtado. When he took a great fleet of canoes up the river in 1754 to supervise the frontier demarcations, he compared Jesuits' lack of co-operation unfavourably with the warm welcome he was given by the Carmelites on the Rio Negro.

The Jesuits appeared to be equally obstructive at the other extremity of Brazil. By following the Uruguay river, the new frontier established in 1750 isolated the seven prosperous and long-established Spanish Jesuit missions of Guaraní on what was to become Portuguese territory,

[52] Gonçalves de Fonseca, 'Primeira exploração...', 274.

and they were expected to move to new locations east of the Uruguay. But they refused, declaring that they had always occupied the lands of their villages and that these contained their consecrated churches and the burials of their ancestors. After the failure of various attempts at persuasion, a joint Portuguese–Spanish army determined to evict the Guaraní by force. On 10 February 1756 matters came to a head with the battle of Caibaté, in which in a few minutes European artillery and cavalry slaughtered 1,400 Christian Indians who were pathetically holding aloft their banners, crucifixes and holy images. This was the fate of the group of Brazilian Indians who had accepted Christianity most fervently during two centuries of conquest launched on the pretext of converting Brazil's heathen.

Those two centuries of missionary control of Brazilian Indians came to an end with two laws that Pombal persuaded the king to issue in 1755. An edict of 4 April 1755 theoretically ended all racial discrimination, declaring that half-castes 'will be fit and capable of any employment, honour or dignity'.[53] Then on 6 June came the Law of Liberties, which freed the 'persons, goods and commerce' of the Indians of Pará and Maranhão. Indians were declared to be free citizens, enjoying all the rights and privileges that went with citizenship. They were to be integrated into Portuguese society. Aldeias were to receive Portuguese names and would henceforth become ordinary towns. Anyone could trade with Indians and these could – in theory – work for whomever they chose, but at rates of pay to be fixed by the governor and officials. Indians themselves were to control their villages, and there were special punishments for any who invaded Indian land or tried to exploit Indian simplicity. In a ringing declaration of Indian freedom, the Law admitted that 'many thousands of Indians have been "descended", but they are being extinguished and the number of villages and their inhabitants is very small; and these few live in great misery'.[54] On the following day, Dom José issued an edict stripping missionaries of all temporal control of aldeias and limiting them to evangelical work among uncontacted tribes. To anticipate any outcry from the settlers, a decree on that same day created the Companhia Geral do Comércio do Grão-Pará e Maranhão, which would import black slaves to the region in order to develop its exports – tasks that it achieved with considerable success for a few decades.

53 Alvará of 4 Apr. 1735, *Ley sobre os casamentos com as índias.*
54 *Ley porque V. Magestade ha por bem restituir aos indios do Grão-Pará e Maranhão a liberdade das suas pessoas, e bens, e commercio,* 6 June 1755, in Perdigão Malheiro, *Escravidão,* II, 99.

The liberation of the Indians that was proclaimed so eloquently in the legislation of 1755 never took place. Pombal and his half-brother immediately began to worry in their correspondence that the Indians would revert to their primitive 'laziness' – they would concern themselves with feeding their own families instead of working for the Portuguese state or for the colonists. Governor Mendonça Furtado waited until 1757 before publishing the new law, and he then introduced on his own initiative a white 'director' into each native village. He pretended that these directors would be altruistic paragons concerned with teaching the Indians civilized ways and encouraging their commerce, so that they would become rich and civilized Christian citizens. This new system, known as the *Diretório de Indios*, was introduced to all former mission villages on 3 May 1757. In return for supposedly teaching the Indians the Portuguese language, European methods of farming and trade, and domestic skills, the directors were to handle all the commercial transactions of their charges and were to receive 17 per cent of any gross income from the sale of produce, to which the government added a further tax of 10 per cent. In addition to these heavy levies (which were on turnover rather than profit), all Indian males aged between thirteen and 60 were still required to work on 'public works' and to spend half of each year working for the colonists. Their chiefs and the new directors were to enforce this 'even to the detriment of the best interests of the Indians themselves'![55]

Observers in Brazil immediately warned that such appalling legislation would lead to disaster. There was ample precedent to show that laymen in control of Indians abused their charges atrociously. Bento da Fonseca warned that settlers would capture wild Indians 'without the slightest impediment, and [would rule] Indians of the aldeias, using them all as if they were their slaves, without paying them for their labour'. He also knew that the introduction of Portuguese soldiers to enforce the new Indian 'freedom' was no answer: 'If a religious order could scarcely maintain the defence of the Indians, it is certain that army captains could not – even if they had any inclination to do so.'[56] Despite these warnings, the directorate system was introduced throughout Brazil in August 1758. A year later the Jesuits were expelled from Brazil.[57] When in 1798, after almost universal condemnation by all

---

[55] *Diretório regimento*, 3 May 1757, in Perdigão Malheiro, *Escravidão*, 11, 110.
[56] Capistrano de Abreu, *Capítulos*, 185.
[57] For further treatment of the expulsion of the Jesuits, see Alden, *CHLA* 11, ch. 15.

experts on Indian affairs, the directorate system was finally abolished, the mission villages, particularly in the former Jesuit heartland in the south and also throughout the Amazon, were in complete disarray and abandon.

During the three centuries since the Portuguese first landed in Brazil the native American population of at least two and a half million had been reduced by probably three-quarters. At the end of the colonial period the few Indians living under Portuguese rule were pathetic creatures at the bottom of society, half acculturated, stripped of most of their tribal traditions and pride, but entirely failing to adapt to European ways or to grasp any of the finer points of European civilization. Those tribes which had managed to retreat deeper into the interior before the advancing Portuguese, to avoid destruction or absorption into Portuguese Brazil, were no more than a vague threat on a distant frontier. Poets such as José de Alvarenga Peixoto or José de Santa Rita Durão could afford to glorify and romanticize Indians, but in a style that bore no relation to reality. Apart from a handful of indifferent sixteenth-century chronicles, the Portuguese totally failed to record anything of anthropological interest about the tribes they destroyed. On the contrary, seventeenth- and eighteenth-century literature, whether by missionaries, officials or adventurers, is striking for its almost total lack of interest in or information about native societies.

14

COLONIAL BRAZIL: THE GOLD CYCLE, *c.* 1690–1750

For almost three centuries following the discovery of Brazil in 1500 the Portuguese court was flooded with reports of fabulous gold strikes in Brazil. These had often lacked foundation and had been a blend of misguided trust placed in native American legends, over-optimistic accounts by explorers, and the apparently undeniable logic that a continent which had rewarded the Spaniards with gold, emeralds, and silver must also possess precious metals in that part allocated to the Portuguese by the Treaty of Tordesillas (1494).

Not all these reports had been totally devoid of truth. Gold had indeed been found in São Vicente in the 1560s, and by the 1570s Paulistas had discovered alluvial gold in Paranaguá. There had been reports of gold strikes in the interior of the captaincy of Bahia by João Coelho de Sousa; his brother Gabriel Soares de Sousa had received official authorization (1584) to launch an expedition to confirm these findings. In the seventeenth century as the bandeirantes penetrated deep into the interior of Brazil in their search for Indian slaves and precious metals, reports from Paranaguá, Curitiba, São Vicente, Espírito Santo, and Pernambuco convinced the crown of the potential mineral wealth of Portuguese America. But only at the end of the seventeenth and during the first half of the eighteenth centuries did Brazil yield up her riches.

Around 1695 the governor of Rio de Janeiro received substantiated reports of major gold strikes within his jurisdiction, at Rio das Velhas in the region referred to in official correspondence initially as the 'mines of São Paulo'. There soon followed reports from the captaincy of Bahia of strikes in Jacobina, and in 1702 the governor-general notified the king of further strikes in Serro do Frio, Itocambiras, and in the sertão. Later strikes were confirmed in Rio das Contas. Concurrently, from the neighbouring captaincy of Espírito Santo there were reports of gold being found in 1701–2. In Bahia there was to be further successful exploration between 1726 and 1734 in Rio das Contas, Rio Pardo, and Rio Verde as well as in Araçuahi, Fanado, and Aguasuja in the sertão. In 1739 came reports of gold being found in the Serra da Baituração in Ilhéus, but this area was not exploited. These discoveries paled into insignificance beside events taking place within the area now known as 'general mines'. The discoveries in Rio das Velhas had triggered off widespread exploration and speculation. By 1720, when Minas Gerais was declared an independent captaincy, there was no part of it which was not being exploited profitably. Moreover, Minas Gerais was to serve as a base and stimulus for further exploration towards the west. The first result of such exploration was the discovery in 1718 or 1719 of gold on the river Coxipó and on the river Cuiabá, both in Mato Grosso. To the north further strikes were made about 1734 on the river Guaporé in the north-west of Mato Grosso. These were followed in about 1745 by a flurry of exploratory activity on the river Arinos, a tributary of the Tapajós, in the central northern area of Mato Grosso. In Goiás by 1725 discoveries in the area of Rio Vermelho in the central southern region augured well. By 1750 such major discoveries of gold as were to be made in Brazil had already been made, but this did not dampen further exploration. In the early 1750s mines in Trahiras and São Felix in Goiás were productive, as too were the mines of Kararis Novos in Pernambuco. Gold was discovered in the mid-century in the foothills of the Serra de Itabaiana in Sergipe, and in Espírito Santo in the Castelo mines. Bandeirante activity in the opening up of the sertão and exploration in a variety of regions continued throughout the century, but future developments merely served to confirm the royal designation (1754) of 'mining areas' as referring to São Paulo, Minas Gerais, Cuiabá, Mato Grosso, Goiás, and the judicial districts (*comarcas*) of Jacobina, Rio das Contas, and Minas Novas de Araçuahi in Bahia.

These discoveries of gold gave rise to two developments as unforeseen as they were confusing to the crown. The first was that during the first half of the century the crown received numerous requests for financial aid, concession of honorary titles, permission to use Amerindian labour as porters for expeditions, and the supply of mining equipment, powder, shot, and firearms. For the most part such claims were spurious or grossly inflated. Some were fraudulent. Petitioners had no intention of leaving coastal enclaves to undertake the promised expeditions, or else were trying to recoup financial losses incurred as the result of profitless speculation by claiming promising finds when the reality had been the reverse. Now that the potential of some regions had indeed been realized, the crown found it increasingly difficult to assess the validity of such requests. There are well-documented examples of the crown simply being duped. In contrast, deserving cases went unrecognized and unrewarded, and lack of royal support reduced the incentive for future exploration or exploitation of potentially productive areas which only later proved profitable. A second outcome was that the hope of royal favours led discoverers of anything remotely resembling precious or semi-precious stones or metals to submit their finds to the mints in Salvador, Rio de Janeiro, or Minas Gerais. The colonial mints often sent such samples to the Lisbon mint for expert evaluation. For the most part they proved to be valueless or low-value emerald, amethyst, garnet, and zircon.

More positively, the successful discovery of gold led to a careful scrutiny of old routes into the interior (*roteiros paulistas*), in some cases dating back to the sixteenth century, and intensified exploration which resulted in the discovery of mineral resources other than gold. During the viceroyalty of the Conde de Sabugosa (1720–35) numerous expeditions or *entradas* officially sponsored and led by Pedro Barbosa Leal, João Peixoto Viegas, António Velho Veloso, Pedro Leolino Mariz, and others, resulted in a gamut of mineral discoveries of varying significance, including lead, iron, copper, mercury, emery, and, above all, diamonds. The histories of saltpetre and silver offer two examples of mixed fortunes. As a prime ingredient in the manufacture of gunpowder, saltpetre was of critical interest to a crown in whose realms there were no natural deposits. In the 1690s deposits had been found near Jacobina but were exhausted within a decade. Experiments in Pernambuco proved unsuccessful. Finds in the Serra dos Montes Altos near the river São Francisco in the mid 1750s proved productive and were exploited in commercial quantities. In the governor-generalship of Dom João de Lancastre (1694–1702), and again during the viceroyalty of the Conde de Sabugosa, silver strikes were reported but the reality remained that as long as there was alluvial gold which afforded greater returns for less investment in time, effort, and cost, there was little incentive to engage in the more laborious and costly process of extracting silver ore.

COMARCA
DE
PARACATÚ

COMARCA
DO

SERRO FRIO

Tijuco
DIAMOND
DISTRICT

Vila do Príncipe

COMARCA DO

RIO DAS VELHAS

Pitangui

Vila Nova da Rainha

Sabará

Catas Altas

Vila Rica do
Ouro Preto

Mariana

Congonhas
do Campo

COMARCA DO

OURO PRETO

COMARCA DO

RIO DAS MORTES

S. José
del Rei

S. João
del Rei

Bom Sucesso

R. Jequitinhonha

R. Aracuahi

R. do Fanado

R. São Francisco

R. das Velhas

R. Paraopeba

R. São Francisco

SERRA DE S. ANTONIO

SERRA DA LAPA

Serra do Espinhaço

R. Doce

SERRA DO CARAÇO

SERRA DO ITACOLOMI

SERRA DA MANTIQUEIRA

R. Grandahi

R. Grande

0   km   100

0   50 miles

BRAZIL

Salvador

Rio de Janeiro

Minas Gerais in the early eighteenth century

The discovery and subsequent exploitation of gold were to have
immediate and far-reaching repercussions not only on the society and
economy of Brazil but also on the mother country and her political and
economic position within Europe. The crown did not wish to discourage
mining activities, but at the same time acted to protect those sectors
of colonial society and economy which might otherwise be adversely
affected by unrestrained gold fever. Despite initial optimism, it appears

that the crown could not believe its good fortune and, even in the case of the 'general mines', did not expect the results to be long-lasting. Optimism was also tempered by concern that once other European nations heard of the discoveries in Brazil they might invade Portuguese America. In 1703 the king ordered the governor-general to stop mining in Jacobina, Itocambiras, and Serro do Frio until their vulnerability to foreign invasion could be assessed. This prohibition also applied to new strikes in Espírito Santo. However, these orders either failed to arrive or were ignored. The governor-general lacked the military strength to enforce such orders in the hinterland, especially when confronted with the reality that in each area there was increasing gold production, a growing population, and, in the case of Jacobina, the important subsidiary economic development of cattle and horse raising. But for the next fifteen years the crown persisted in reiterating bans on mining in these areas. Only in 1720, the royal appetite whetted by gold returns and reassurances, did Dom João V authorize mining in Jacobina and shortly afterwards in Rio das Contas and other areas of the sertão. In 1729 the king was again to seek reassurance that Araçuahi and Fanado were not vulnerable to invasion from the sea, and in the 1750s development of mines at Itabaiana in Sergipe and at Castelo in Espírito Santo was refused because of their proximity to the coast.

The royal ban on development of mines in Bahia had been prompted by the strategic consideration that they would induce people to desert the city of Salvador and the Recôncavo. The king feared that there would then be an inadequate pool of manpower to defend the city against attack by foreigners or, once they saw the declining numbers of whites, by insurgent blacks or Indians. These fears were groundless, but the economic and demographic impact of the new discoveries did represent a serious threat to the coastal areas of the north-east and demanded strong measures. The city council of Salvador even petitioned the crown for a ban on all mining activities, a request which was ignored. Throughout the first half of the eighteenth century town and city councils in coastal areas attributed all their misfortunes to mining. A major complaint was that the lure of the mines siphoned off from the coastal areas whites and freedmen of colour who would otherwise have been involved in the cultivation of sugar, tobacco, or manioc. While some farmers may have deserted their fields for the mining areas, this was less prevalent than might be thought. Rather, the problem lay in the fact that farmers, no less than miners, needed slaves for working their fields. But miners had two advantages: first, they could afford higher prices for their slaves; second, instead of purchasing on credit and offering the yield of the next crop as security, they paid in cash. The result was that farmers in the coastal areas could not afford slaves of the best category (*primeiro lote*) and, even if they were interested, could not match prices offered by miners for slaves of the second category (*segundo lote*). The purchase of even inferior slaves stretched farmers' financial resources to the utmost. Many sold their holdings, or consolidated those few resources they had preserved intact, or were the victims of foreclosure for debt. Allied to increasing labour costs was the economic reality that export agricultural products were in any case (for more general, structural reasons) not as profitable to the producer in the first half of the eighteenth century as had been the case earlier.

Traditional lines of supply and demand for foodstuffs were also disrupted by the sudden increase in demand from the mining areas. When the town of São Cristóvão in Sergipe wanted to exploit the Itabaiana mines in 1750, one ground for the royal refusal to grant permission was that Sergipe was the cellar for Bahia: exploitation of the mines would disrupt and even paralyse the supply of foodstuffs to Salvador. Competition from mining areas severely disrupted the supply of meat to the coastal enclaves from the interior of Bahia, Pernambuco, Ceará, Piauí, and Maranhão. At the outset Minas Gerais was totally dependent on meat imports and, even with the development of its own industry, remained unable to support itself. Disruption of the supply and demand network was not limited to commodities produced in Brazil. Not only luxury items but such basic imports as salt underwent price increases and, in view of the inability of people in the coastal areas to meet these increased costs, were dispatched to the more profitable markets in the interior. In 1717 the viceroy reported that prices for basic commodities had skyrocketed. Breadwinners who had formerly supported a family could no longer do so and faced starvation or migration to the mining areas to try their luck. The result of these financial pressures was that many people from the coastal enclaves went into mining not so much because of the lure of ready wealth as because of impending starvation and poverty. Viceroy Sabugosa commented ironically in 1729 that the true golden age of Brazil had been before the discovery of gold; with the discovery of gold Brazil was experiencing an iron age.

The crown enacted a series of measures aimed at protecting agriculture while at the same time being careful not to discourage mining initiatives. In 1701 the king prohibited communication or transportation of cattle or foodstuffs from Bahia to the 'mines of São Paulo', or commerce in the opposite direction. Insufficient numbers of enforcement officers, coupled with the virtual impossibility of patrolling the vast areas of the hinterland, limited the effectiveness of such orders. In 1704 the crown forbade the re-export from Bahia to the mines of commodities imported from Portugal. Such restrictions were equally ineffectual; the lure of higher profits from sales in the mining areas was inducement enough to lead cattle drovers and merchants to evade controls and even to engage in hand-to-hand fighting with enforcement patrols rather than renounce their trading practices. The crown also forbade the opening of new roads to the mines. The king was moved in part by the desire to increase the effectiveness of patrols, but also by the more pressing need to exert some degree of control over the opening of new mining areas and the taxing of gold extracted from those already in operation. The vastness of the sertão, inadequately staffed patrols, and high returns on contra- band – be it in gold, cattle, slaves, or other commodities – made the clandestine opening of paths and roads inevitable.

More pressing was the need, first, to guarantee that Bahia and the north-east received their fair share of slaves from West Africa, and second, to ensure that once these had arrived in the ports of the north-east they were not immediately siphoned off to Rio de Janeiro or the mining areas. On the first issue, in order not to put the captaincies of the north-east at a disadvantage, in 1703 the king restricted ships trading directly from Rio de Janeiro or Santos to Angola and the Costa da Mina. But threats of exile and confiscation of ship and cargo failed to halt the trade. The king also prohibited slave exports to Minas Gerais from the ports of Brazil by land or by sea, i.e., by re-export from the north-east to Rio de Janeiro. A royal *alvará* forbade the sale to Paulistas of slaves arriving in Bahia. Such restrictions were to be modified. From an outright ban the king moved in 1701 to a quota of 200 slaves annually to be exported from Rio de Janeiro to Minas Gerais, and then went to the point of removing all restrictions on trade from Rio de Janeiro in favour of free trade to the mines. Challenged by other captaincies that this concession granted to Rio de Janeiro an unfair monopoly, the king resolved (10 November 1710) that there be no further restrictions on taking slaves to Minas Gerais from Rio de Janeiro or anywhere else. Free trade was conditional: evidence had to be furnished that slaves had not been taken from plantations, or, if they had, that they had been replaced by an equal number of slaves. Such crown measures were misdirected; rather than concentrating on exports or re-exports of slaves to the mining areas, the crown should have focused its attention on ensuring that slaves were available to farmers at prices they could afford. The result of this misplaced emphasis was a shortage of first-quality slaves for the plantations of Brazil in the first half of the eighteenth century.

The crown also acted to protect the society and economy of Portugal from the potentially disastrous results of an uncontrolled gold rush. Restrictions were placed on the numbers and types of people whom captains were permitted to transport to the New World. By 1709 the impact on Portugal's population, especially in the northern provinces, forced the king to reiterate earlier orders that potential travellers must have passports, obtainable from the secretary of state in Lisbon or, in the case of travellers from Oporto or Viana do Castelo, from the respective governors. Foreigners were only permitted to travel to Brazil if they could furnish evidence that their business was legitimate and posted bond before leaving Portugal to guarantee their return on the same fleet. Later this bond had to be increased because experience showed that windfall profits in the mining areas led many to forfeit their bond rather than return. Similarly, although clerics and friars were forbidden to travel to Brazil without the prior consent of their superiors or prelates, some signed on as ships' chaplains, while others obtained the requisite authorization for a temporary visit to Brazil for the collection of alms and simply failed to return. Despite severe penalties (1709) imposed on ships' captains found guilty of carrying prostitutes, many made their way to Brazil. There was always a way to gain passage, even if it were as a cabin boy or sailor, on payment of ten or fifteen gold coins. Measures were not strictly enforced at ports of departure. Oporto was notorious for the laxness of its authorities. In 1733 three ships from Oporto arrived in Bahia carrying over 700 passengers without permission. In 1742 the viceroy, the Conde das Galvêas, noted the large numbers of migrants to Brazil from Portugal and the Atlantic islands. Their destinations were Bahia, Pernambuco, Maranhão, and especially Rio de Janeiro as affording quickest access to the mining areas. He estimated that some 1,500 to 1,600 persons left Portugal annually for Brazil and that the majority went to the mines. Because so few returned to Portugal, he sounded a warning note on the prejudicial effects such migration could have on the mother country.

THE GOLD RUSHES

For prospective searchers after Brazilian gold there was no easy route to the interior of Brazil. High mountain ranges, densely wooded valleys, and swift-flowing rivers proved substantial barriers. The coastal plain, the sertão, and the central highland area afforded extremes of cold and heat, humidity and dryness, and alternate periods of drought and torrential rain. Wild animals, poisonous insects, snakes, and flora harmful to man (and, for the most part, unknown to Europeans) abounded. Hostile Indians were a constant threat and, although their presence may have decreased on some routes, they were nevertheless a force to be reckoned with throughout the hinterland of Brazil in the eighteenth century. Should the traveller survive these natural hazards, he still faced the dangers which arose from personal inadequacies. Many were totally unprepared either physically or psychologically for such journeys. Few appreciated the enormous distances they would have to cover even to reach the mines of Bahia, let alone those of Mato Grosso or Goiás. The logistics of ensuring adequate supplies of food and water, not to speak of protection against the elements, were complicated, and few of those arriving in Rio de Janeiro, Salvador, or Pernambuco had any previous experience to help them cope with these problems.

Two main networks of routes to Minas Gerais had been developed. The first served the needs of those seeking access to the 'general mines' from São Paulo and from the coastal areas of Rio de Janeiro and Santos and the intervening smaller ports such as Angra dos Reis and Paratí. From the coastal areas of the captaincy of Rio de Janeiro there were three principal routes. The Caminho Velho started at Paratí, climbed the Serra do Facão, and passed the town of Taubaté where the road divided to cross the Serra da Mantiqueira; from here one route ran to the mining townships of Rio das Mortes and Vila Rica and another to Rio das Velhas. Another route started at Santos, ascended to São Paulo and led thence to Taubaté, joining the first route at Guaratinguetá. The journey from the coast to the mining communities took about one month. The difficulties of this route led the governor of Rio de Janeiro Arthur de Sá e Meneses at the end of the seventeenth century to commission Garcia Rodrigues Paes to hack out a more direct route to Minas Gerais. This he did by going overland to Irajá, following the rivers Iguaçú, Paraíba, and Paraibuna, and thence to the mining areas. This route was known as the Caminho Novo. Writing in 1717, Dom Pedro de Almeida (later Conde de Assumar), who had himself travelled to his new appointment as governor from São Paulo, noted that all three routes were very rough going, full of outcrops, narrow ravines, high mountains, dense undergrowth, and heavily wooded terrain. During the rainy season there was loss of life and load by beasts and people alike. By 1725 a variant to the Caminho Novo started at Praia dos Mineiros, followed the river Inhomirim, and provided access via the river Piabanha to the river Paraíba. About the same time work was in progress on a road linking São Paulo directly to Rio de Janeiro.

A second network of routes was focused on the river São Francisco, which rises in Rio das Mortes in Minas Gerais and meanders north- and north-eastward before entering the Atlantic between Alagoas and Sergipe. Although it was navigable on its upper and lower reaches, the cataracts at Paulo Afonso were an obstacle to river transport over its whole length. Travellers from Salvador travelled by boat to the mouth of the river and thence from Penedo to Jacaré just below the cataracts, or by land or water through the Recôncavo to Cachoeira and thence started the long haul overland to the Arraial de Mathias Cardoso on the river. This was the converging point for travellers to Minas Gerais from Pernambuco, Ceará, Piauí, and Maranhão. Following the right bank of the São Francisco to the confluence with the Rio das Velhas, travellers could choose between a series of routes into central Minas Gerais or the isolated Serro do Frio. This route, known as the Caminho do Sertão or Caminho da Bahia, was over comparatively easy terrain, and had a ready supply of water, and the early establishment of cattle ranches guaranteed provisions. On the other hand the region of the São Francisco was unhealthy at certain times of the year and the greater distance meant a longer period of travel. Furthermore, even in the 1730s those Tupinambá who had been forced out of the Recôncavo during the governor-generalship of Afonso Furtado de Castro do Rio de Mendonça (1671–75) were still making lightning attacks on convoys en route to Minas Gerais, prompting the king to approve an outright war against these Indians in 1733. By the 1730s Jacobina was the centre for a series of routes from northern captaincies to the river São Francisco, as well as to Rio das Contas, and provided good access to

Salvador. From Salvador there was a route via São Pedro de Muritiba to Rio das Contas, crossing the treacherous river Una, and thence to Minas Novas de Araçuahi and finally to northern Minas Gerais.

Whereas travellers to the 'general mines' may have used river routes for part of their journeys, by and large overland travel predominated. Discoveries in Mato Grosso entailed a break with this tradition, at least in the early years. Furthermore, whereas the geographical position of Minas Gerais had made it equally accessible to Bahian and Paulista, circumstances favoured access to Mato Grosso by Paulistas and travellers from the coastal areas of Rio de Janeiro. These travellers exploited the network of rivers from Pôrto Feliz outside the town of São Paulo which all led to the river Cuiabá: those were the rivers Tieté, Paraná, Pardo, Anhandui, Aquidauna, and Paraguay. This route was to be modified and a portage developed from the river Pardo to the Coxim-Taquarí and thence by the river Taquarí to the river Paraguay.

Known as 'monsoons', voyages from São Paulo to Cuiabá took from five to seven months outwards and two returning because of lighter loads. Those leaving São Paulo between March and June caught the rivers in flood, which made shooting the more than 100 rapids between Pôrto Feliz and Cuiabá easier, although this was offset by exposure to malaria and other fevers at this season. Physical hardships were enormous and loss of life and stores from overturned canoes commonplace events. Perhaps the greatest danger was from hostile Indians on the upper Paraguay. The Paiaguá were river people and the Guaicurú were renowned horsemen. Together and separately, these two peoples killed many Portuguese. In two spectacular massacres the Paiaguá killed 600 in one single convoy in 1725, and 400 more in a fight lasting five hours in 1730. Before their virtual extinction in 1795, the Guaicurú were said to have accounted for 4,000 Portuguese. Physical hardship, distance, fear of Indians and the need for skilled canoe pilots forced prospective miners to travel in convoy as their best hope of survival. These convoys demanded organization, leadership, discipline and the subordination of the individual to the collective will. One of the largest, in 1726, was made up of some 3,000 passengers in 305 canoes and included the governor of São Paulo himself.

The route of Goiás, however, followed the more anarchic tradition characteristic of the rush to Minas Gerais. By the 1740s routes had been found from Rio das Velhas, from the north-east, and from Mato Grosso to Vila Boa de Goiás. The distance from Goiás to Salvador was estimated at 400 leagues (1,200 miles), but when Dom Marcos de Noronha was promoted from the governorship of Goiás to be viceroy in Salvador, he made the journey overland in eleven weeks to take up his new appointment in 1755.

Except in very general terms little is known of how many or what kind of people took part in the gold rushes which followed each new strike. The rush to Minas Gerais was by far the most important. It appears that migrants came from every walk of life, from the most diverse social backgrounds, and from all sorts of places: the coastal areas of Brazil, the Atlantic islands of Madeira and the Azores, and Portugal itself. There were a few English, Irish, Dutch, and French adventurers, especially in the early years before royal controls tightened; friars left monasteries in Salvador, Rio de Janeiro, and Maranhão, as well as Portugal; soldiers deserted from the garrisons of Brazilian port cities and Colônia do Sacramento; merchants, former planters, and people with claims to nobility were all infected with gold fever; freedmen of colour saw opportunity in the mining areas denied to them in the coastal enclaves; slaves abandoned their owners, or were dispatched under a factor to investigate the potential of mining; Paulistas, accompanied by their Indian slaves, were prominent both as discoverers and in subsequent gold rushes. Only one group appears to have been remarkable for its absence: women were, in the case of whites, virtually never present, and even among slaves were under-represented.

The rush to Mato Grosso was just as frenetic but the numbers were less. The reasons for this were various: the hardship of the journey was in itself a deterrent; second, even at this early date there were indications that disillusionment and failure in Minas Gerais had led some prospectors to have second thoughts; third, the dramatic rise in the price of slaves and the cost of provisions with no guarantee of return may have dissuaded potential prospectors. Finally, despite the discoveries at Cuiabá, there was not quite the same scattershot reporting of simultaneous discoveries which had characterized the early years in Minas Gerais. Many of these factors also held good for Goiás. The result was that participation by migrants from Portugal was smaller than had been the case in Minas Gerais.

The spectacular nature of the major rushes to Minas Gerais, Mato Grosso, and Goiás has diverted attention from the fact that gold fever did not die with the establishment of mining communities in the major regions of the interior. Throughout the first half of the eighteenth century there were lesser gold rushes in many parts of the interior. Secondary and even tertiary rushes from earlier strikes followed reports of newly productive areas. Discoveries in Rio das Contas in the early 1720s persuaded many miners to leave Minas Gerais in the hope of easier pickings. By the end of the decade new discoveries in Minas Novas de Araçuahi and Fanado and in the sertão of Bahia led the viceroy to report (1729) that Rio das Contas and Jacobina were virtually deserted. Much the same occurred in many areas of Minas Gerais. Discoveries in Goiás caused widespread desertion from Minas Novas and from Minas Gerais in 1736–7. Finally, there was the impact on gold miners of competing sources of wealth. The most famous were diamonds. Their discovery led gold miners from Bahia and Minas Gerais to desert their workings for Serro do Frio in the early 1730s. New strikes, and more especially rumours of potential riches, frequently disrupted the social and economic stability of the mining areas.

For a chosen few, there were indeed riches beyond their wildest dreams. But they were rare and hard-won. Although the Paulistas had the necessary skills for survival in the hinterland – as one enthusiastic governor said later, they could eke out an existence on bark and wild plants and by snaring animals and catching fish – they were in this regard unique among the first wave of miners. For most, already debilitated after long marches or perilous river journeys, arrival could only bring further physical deprivation. Especially in the early months of any mining encampment, before crops had been planted and harvested, food was in short supply and then only available at outrageous prices. Cats and dogs were as much sought after for food in Minas Gerais as they were in the early days in Cuiabá. Protection from rain and cold on the plateau was minimal – a wattle-and-daub hut with a straw roof, as likely to be destroyed by the elements as by fire. In the early years in Minas Gerais and, to a lesser degree elsewhere, the authorities imposed few restraints. Two visits to Minas Gerais by the governor of Rio de Janeiro in 1700–2 were little more than reconnaissance trips. Those few measures which were taken largely ignored the pressing social and economic needs peculiar to mining encampments and were directed instead at ensuring some return to the royal exchequer by setting up a system for allocating mining concessions and collecting the royal fifth, or *quinto*, on gold extracted. For many, poverty and an unmarked grave were the only rewards for their labours.

ADMINISTRATION

During the early eighteenth century the Portuguese crown introduced a series of administrative measures intended to curb the anarchy which characterized the mining areas and to establish a degree of stability. These measures had three main purposes: to provide effective government at the local and regional level; to administer justice and enforce the law; and to fulfil royal obligations as defender of the faith.

The prime instrument of this policy was the township or *vila*. In Portugal the *município* represented stability, the upholding of justice, a degree of self-determination at the local level, and – by virtue of its royal charter – a crown presence. All these aspects were also present in *vilas* overseas, where the last aspect took on especial importance. A royal order of 1693 had permitted the governor-general to establish *vilas* in the hinterland of Brazil, if these would assist in the introduction of law and order. In 1711 one of the first administrative acts of António de Albuquerque Coelho de Carvalho as governor of Minas Gerais and São Paulo was to raise three major mining encampments to the status of *vila*: Vila do Ribeirão do Carmo, Vila Rica do Ouro Prêto, and Vila da Nossa Senhora da Conceição do Sabará. São João del Rei (1713), Vila Nova da Rainha de Caeté (1714), Pitanguí (1715), São José del Rei (1718), and the more distant Vila do Príncipe (1714) completed the major administrative nuclei of Minas Gerais. In 1745 Vila do Carmo was the first *vila* of Minas Gerais to be accorded city status and was named Mariana. Perhaps the most spectacular example of the success of this policy came from Bahia. Between 1710 and 1721 532 firearm deaths occurred in Jacobina; once it was raised to a *vila* in 1721, in the succeeding four years there were only two violent deaths, one by a knife and one by a sword. The *vila* of Nossa Senhora do Livramento was raised in Rio das Contas in 1724, and in 1730 in Minas Novas de Araçuahi the town of Nossa Senhora do Bom Sucesso was established. In Mato Grosso and Goiás fewer towns were established. The most prominent were Vila Real do Senhor Bom Jesus de Cuiabá (1727) and Vila Bela da Santíssima Trindade (1752) in the former; in the latter Vila Boa de Goiás was officially installed in 1739. The order of priorities leading to the raising of these towns varied from region to region and from period to period. Before granting final approval for the establishment of a *vila* the king received reports on the following factors: the anticipated cost to the royal treasury and the extent to which it could be offset by increased revenues; current population and anticipated increase; the town's potential economic and military importance. In mining areas two questions were paramount. Would society be more stable and law and order more effective? Would revenues from the collection of the fifths (payment to the crown of a fifth part of any gold extracted) be enhanced? By offering various inducements such as land grants to new settlers and privileges and exemptions to members of town councils, and by providing new towns with sources of income in the form of lands to rent or fees on cattle, slaves, and other goods entering municipal territory, the crown not only encouraged the settlement of the interior but also provided a source of civic pride. Such towns served as points of departure for further exploration, and also became commercial and administrative centres for vast regions of their immediate hinterlands. The characteristic settlement pattern in the mining areas was of isolated nuclei at a considerable distance from each other; but, at least in Minas Gerais, the presence of concentric spheres of administrative influence helped to diminish such isolation and enhance administrative effectiveness. In the more sparsely populated regions of Mato Grosso and Goiás, the smaller number of towns sharply curtailed effective administrative control.

The move to the west and the rapidly growing importance of the Brazilian highlands and plateau also compelled the crown to create new captaincies, each with its own governor. These were carved out of the sprawling and undefined territories which fell under the jurisdiction of the governor of Rio de Janeiro. In 1709 the crown created a new captaincy, to be known as São Paulo e Minas do Ouro. By 1720 the importance of Minas Gerais and the impossibility of a single governor's effectively maintaining control over the territories of São Paulo and Minas Gerais led to the incorporation of Minas Gerais as a separate captaincy. The more westerly regions were slower in gaining administrative autonomy. Only in 1744 and 1748 respectively were the captaincies of Goiás and Mato Grosso carved out of the vast and largely undefined captaincy of São Paulo. The most dramatic indication of the transfer of strategic, demographic, economic, and political importance from the north-east littoral to the highlands of Brazil was the royal decision to move the viceregal capital from Salvador to Rio de Janeiro in 1763. This was the final step in a process which had started with the first gold strikes in Rio das Velhas some 70 years earlier and was to have profound effects on Brazil's future regional development.

In its attempt to bring justice to the backlands, the crown had to contend with the potent combination of distance from traditional seats of magisterial power coupled with the high inducements to corruption afforded to magistrates. The king attacked the first issue by creating judicial districts (*comarcas*) in new and existing captaincies where sudden shifts of population as the result of mining made a readily visible judicial presence desirable. In Minas Gerais, *comarcas* were initially created for Rio das Mortes, Rio das Velhas, and Vila Rica. Later, because of the territorial extent of Rio das Velhas and its prominence as a mining region as well as a pivotal route for commerce to and from the mining areas in legally sanctioned goods as well as contraband gold, a fourth *comarca* was established in Serro do Frio. Some *comarcas* were also established in Mato Grosso and Goiás. Perhaps the most telling example of the difficulties facing the crown and of the need to be responsive to a changing situation is provided by the saga of the *comarca* of Bahia do Sul. In 1714 the sertão of Bahia captaincy, which embraced the mining communities of Jacobina and Rio das Contas, as well as the much-travelled area of the river São Francisco, was described in an official document as a 'den of thieves'. After two decades of indecision coupled with long-winded discussion over the cost, a royal resolution of 10 December 1734 established a new judicial district to be known as the Comarca da Bahia da Parte do Sul.

The second manner in which the crown attempted to bring more effective justice to the mining areas was by authorizing judicial *juntas*. These had already functioned in the seventeenth century in more distant regions of Pernambuco and other captaincies, but it was in the eighteenth century in the predominantly mining areas where they were to be most common. Such *juntas* comprised the governor, the senior official of the royal treasury in the captaincy, and the senior crown judge of each *comarca*. The jurisdiction of the *junta* extended to passing sentence of death for crimes committed by blacks, mulattos, and Indians and there was no further recourse for appeal. In the case of whites the jurisdiction of such tribunals was prescribed by the social class of the accused. No records of the deliberations of these tribunals appear to have survived. Indeed, if the evidence from Minas Gerais is any indication, governors faced the continual problem of securing a quorum because crown judges were reluctant to travel considerable distances to a central meeting place for this purpose.

Within the institutional arena, the third recourse adopted by the crown to improve the effectiveness of the legal system in the mining areas was to create a second high court of appeals (*Relação*) in Rio de Janeiro. This started work on 15 July 1752 and represented the culmination of 30 years of lobbying by individuals and town councils in the mining areas. The grounds of their appeals were many: first, that judges handed down sentences arbitrarily, confident that the victim would lack legal expertise, money, and time to appeal to the only high court of appeals in the colony at Salvador; second, that even if such cases were appealed documents often were lost in the long overland journey by the Caminho dos Curraes, or ran the risk of the vessel carrying them being taken by pirates should they be sent by sea from Minas Gerais to Salvador, via Rio de Janeiro; third, that magistrates were so removed from traditional centres of justice that they were rarely held to account for their actions. First authorized by a royal resolution of 1734, the new tribunal found its final opening delayed by second thoughts over costs. When it did eventually become functional the new high court was composed of the same number of magistrates as its counterpart in Salvador and with the same authority. The new *Relação* became the appellate court for Rio de Janeiro and the captaincies to the south, but it was expected that its main area of effectiveness would lie in the mining captaincies of Minas Gerais, São Paulo, Mato Grosso, and Goiás.

Another problem concerned the quality and numbers of magistrates. There is no reason to believe that crown judges (*ouvidores*) of the mining areas were either more venal, or more virtuous than their counterparts elsewhere in Portugal or overseas. Indeed, before gaining such appointments they were expected to meet rigorous standards born of extensive training in the legal and administrative aspects of royal government and in many ways were viewed by the crown as a collective right arm. This royal trust resulted in the king imposing on his magistrates a range of responsibilities which were not primarily judicial. This was especially the case in the mining areas. In Minas Gerais crown judges took charge of the royal treasury in their respective regions until such time as the king saw fit to establish a royal exchequer headed by a *provedor mór*. Thus the crown judge became involved in the time-consuming task of supervising the fifths from the initial levying of the appropriate fees through to the final collection. Nor was it unusual for decisions over the granting of mining concessions, and the solving of unavoidable disputes, to be charged to the crown judge, although there were other officials with specific responsibilities for these areas. Many crown judges concurrently held the post of *provedor* of the dead and absent (*dos defuntos e ausentes*), which involved settlement of estates. Furthermore, it was to his crown judges that the king turned for additional information on the general state of their captaincies on the one hand or closer scrutiny of the conduct of an individual on the other. Inevitably the quality of justice deteriorated because of these many non-judicial demands.

But this was only part of the problem. Although crown judges were forbidden from engaging in commercial transactions or contracting marriages with local women without royal permission, neither constraint prevented them from making lucrative personal connections in their areas of jurisdiction. It was alleged that judges were more concerned about leaving at the end of their customary three years terms as wealthy men than in the administration of impartial justice. This may have been true in some cases, but ignores the many excellent magistrates of the highest integrity who served in the mining areas.

The crown also faced the difficulty of assessing what was a reasonable salary for magistrates in mining areas, and the extent to which they should be permitted *ajudas de custo* or expense allowances. This issue had a direct and negative impact on judges' effectiveness, especially when it came to administering justice away from their places of residence. In 1716 magistrates and other legal officials in Minas Gerais received authorization to set fees three times higher than their counterparts in Rio de Janeiro and the coastal captaincies, where the cost of living was lower. As the cost of living decreased with more extensive planting of crops in Minas Gerais, so accordingly were salaries reduced and in 1718 annual salaries of *ouvidores* were cut from 600$000 to 500$000 reis. Salaries regulated by Dom Lourenço de Almeida in 1721 were so clearly outmoded by 1754 that the king ordered a re-evaluation of salary scales for all judicial officers in the mining areas. The new rates of fees promulgated that year for the mining areas ranged between 50 and 300 per cent more than those for the coastal areas. Although on the whole such salaries remained higher than elsewhere in Brazil, so too were the costs of slaves, horses, living, and transportation. Moreover, in order to fulfil the obligation of making an annual 'visit of correction' (*correição*) to every part of a judicial district, *ouvidores* had to meet heavy expenses not only for transportation but also for replacing clothing and equipment spoilt during several weeks' travel on rough paths through the hinterland. Reluctance to meet such costs, coupled with the physical hardships of such judicial visits, resulted in crown judges' frequent failure to discharge this responsibility.

The crown was compelled to recognize that in the mining areas there was a chronic shortage of skilled lawyers, especially in the early years of settlement, and that governors had totally inadequate manpower at their disposal to enforce the law or bring criminals to justice. The appointment of additional judges known as *juízes de fora* was an administrative rather than a judicial expedient. In response to complaints about the absence of public notaries in rural areas which led to people dying intestate or without wills being witnessed, and to remedy the refusal of law enforcement officers to travel to outlying areas without substantial remuneration, the crown authorized town councils to appoint judges of the twentieth (*juízes da vintena*) in every parish more than one league distant from the nearest seat of municipal government. Such appointees were responsible for drawing up wills, deciding minor civil cases, levying fines, and arresting criminals. They lacked formal legal training and were unsalaried, their sole remuneration being fees derived from their services.

In enforcing laws and preserving the peace governors faced the problem of inadequate forces to patrol vast expanses of largely unmapped territory. There were no garrisons to which governors of Minas Gerais, Goiás, or Mato Grosso could turn in case of need. Unlike the coastal enclaves, such forces were rarely required for military duties. Rather their assignments reflected the social and economic priorities and pressures peculiar to mining areas: enforcing settlement of mining disputes; escorting bullion; curbing evasion of payment of the fifths; stopping illegal traffic in gold and other commodities; suppressing revolts and disturbances; enforcing curfews on slaves, shops, and taverns; arresting criminals; and holding in rein the 'powerful men of the backlands' (*poderosos do sertão*). Most effective were the two companies of professionally trained dragoons which arrived in Minas Gerais from Portugal in 1719. Under officers who had seen service in European and North African campaigns, they were immediately pressed into service to suppress a revolt in Pitanguí. They were to prove invaluable in maintaining law and order in Minas Gerais and were dispatched to Goiás when the need arose. Their example led Viceroy Sabugosa to establish a troop of dragoons in Minas Novas in 1729. Although lacking professional training, militia companies multiplied throughout the mining areas. Convoked in times of emergency and disbanded again, they proved to be valuable arms of the law. Militia companies were established on a regional or parochial basis, largely depending on the population density in a given area, but usually several companies were loosely regimented to form a *terço*. Such *terços* were composed mainly of companies of whites, but annexed to the regiments were companies of free blacks and free mulattos under their own commanders. Each numbering some 60 strong, these companies represented a cross-section of the free coloured population. Companies of free mulattos and half-castes (*pardos e bastardos fôrros*) were the most common in eighteenth-century Minas Gerais, followed by companies of free blacks and mulattos (*prêtos e pardos fôrros*), of free blacks and free mixed-bloods (*prêtos e mestiços fôrros*), and even of Indians and half-castes (*índios e bastardos*). Ethnic composition depended on the region. But official efforts were made, probably for reasons of security, to compose coloured companies of a mixture of blacks, Indians, and mulattos. Finally, reference should be made to the 'bush captain'(*capitão do mato*). Mining areas were characterized by a predominance of slaves and considerable laxity in supervising their activities as speculators. These factors, coupled with geographical isolation and inadequate policing, resulted in a high incidence of runaways. The responsibility for capturing such runaways and attacking smaller *quilombos* (groups of runaway slaves) lay with 'bush captains' – for the most part mulattos – who formed their own troops and worked on a commission basis.

Those factors – distance, accountability, corruption, and avarice – which hindered the effective enforcement of justice in the mining areas, contributed equally to difficulties confronting the Catholic Church in the hinterland, for which the crown had special responsibility because of the *Padroado Real*. As had been the case in conceding royal approval for new legal institutions, so too in the ecclesiastical area was the crown extraordinarily dilatory. The bishop of Rio de Janeiro was responsible for the newly populated areas of Minas Gerais, Mato Grosso, and Goiás as well as São Paulo during the period of their greatest economic and demographic expansion in the first half of the eighteenth century. Only in 1745 were bishoprics established at São Paulo and Mariana and prelacies in Cuiabá and Goiás. This dearth of ecclesiastical authority at the higher levels in the mining areas would in itself have been extremely prejudicial, but the degree of spiritual guidance available in these regions was further diminished by the royal ruling – inspired by fears that friars were traffickers in contraband gold – at the opening of the century forbidding the religious orders and the Society of Jesus from establishing themselves in Minas Gerais.

The religious and social repercussions were the subject of extensive correspondence between governors of Minas Gerais and the king. Governors complained that priests took concubines, worshipped the 'Mineral Church' (*Igreja Mineral*), raised families, engaged in mining, opposed efforts to collect the fifths, sowed dissent among the populace, and extorted outrageous fees for services performed at baptisms, marriages, and funerals as well as levying fees for communion. Little or no effort was made to catechize slaves arriving in Minas Gerais. In view of the great distances, there was little likelihood that wayward clerics would be reprimanded by their superiors. For his part, the bishop of Rio de Janeiro largely neglected complaints made by governors of Minas Gerais and either refused or was reluctant to collaborate with civil authorities in bringing the worst offenders to heel. The Conde de Assumar and his successors suggested numerous reforms including declaring Minas Gerais a mission area, making knowledge of an African language a prerequisite for appointment to a parish in Minas Gerais, and even using the tithes (*dízimos*) for their intended purpose rather than as yet another source of royal revenue. The crown issued decrees intended to curb some of the excesses, for example, that friars and priests without regular employment in the mining areas be expelled. Enactment of this single resolution ran into the practical problems of locating such churchmen, gaining the collaboration of vicars general, who were notoriously reluctant to co-operate with the civil authorities and not infrequently issued notices of excommunication against civil officers trying to perform their duties, as well as separating illegal clerics and friars from those to whom the crown had granted licences to come to the mining areas and collect alms for monasteries and churches in Portugal and the Atlantic islands.

As had been the case with the magistracy, the crown was in the final analysis reluctant to divest itself of any of its revenues, either by building new churches or by appointing more and better qualified priests. The former lack was partly offset by the initiative shown by the faithful who, both individually and corporatively, built and furnished churches in great profusion throughout the mining areas. As to the latter the king took two steps. The first was to terminate the situation whereby a parish priest was totally dependent on his flock for his income. In 1718 Dom João V ordered that parish priests in Minas Gerais be paid 200$000 reis annually from the royal exchequer. This measure, designed to improve the quality of clerics and reduce extortion, failed in practice. Nor did the introduction of permanent, salaried parochial appointments prove more effective. The second was to impose regulations concerning the fees priests could levy. As with judicial fees, these were modified in accordance with prevailing economic conditions. Although these regulations may have curbed some excesses, they were a palliative rather than a solution.

Administrative measures taken by the crown to cope with developments in the mining areas of Brazil in the first half of the eighteenth century also produced conflict and bitterness among the officials who had to implement them. In creating the new captaincies and making appointments, the crown failed to establish boundary lines for the new captaincies, *comarcas*, and different ecclesiastical jurisdictions. The peripheries of many of the newly designated captaincies were unexplored and at the time when the first migrations to Minas Gerais took place there was no qualified mapmaker in the colony. The crown failed to send any trained cartographers from Lisbon despite pleas from governors and viceroys, who were reduced to commissioning army engineers, marine pilots, and Jesuit mathematicians to determine the extent of their captaincies. Because his captaincy bordered on Bahia, Rio de Janeiro, Espírito Santo, Pernambuco, São Paulo, and Goiás the governor of Minas Gerais was constantly involved in disputes of this kind. In 1720, acting on royal orders, the Conde de Assumar had established boundary lines between Minas Gerais, Bahia, and Pernambuco. This resulted in a decade of challenges from the viceroy concerning the appropriateness of the bar of the Rio das Velhas as a point of division. The issue was critical because it would decide whether ecclesiastical appointments should be made by the archbishop of Bahia or the bishop of Rio de Janeiro, whether tithes and the fifths should be collected by appointees of the viceroy or the governor, and whether the crown judge of Rio das Velhas would have jurisdiction over that region. The dispute was finally resolved in favour of Minas Gerais. With the development of Minas Novas the question as to whether or not the area was in Bahia or Minas Gerais also produced conflict. According to the division made by Assumar, they were in Bahia, but his successor Dom Lourenço de Almeida challenged this. In 1729 the king ruled that Araçuahi and Fanado fell in Bahian territory, but that the crown judge of Serro do Frio (Minas Gerais) would have jurisdiction there. This did not end the matter. With the creation of the Comarca da Bahia da Parte do Sul, the king ruled that Araçuahi and Fanado would form part of the new judicial district, but in 1757 – faced with the fact that Fanado, although rich in diamonds, lay beyond the *Distrito Diamantino* – the king reversed his decision and ordered that Araçuahi and Fanado should henceforth be part of Minas Gerais. No aspect of colonial life in the new captaincies was untouched by the irritants of ill-defined boundaries and changes of the royal mind. The results were heated debates over a variety of issues such as the placing of registers, ecclesiastical appointments, collection of the tithes, contracts on road and river passages, creation of militia companies, the administration of justice, and the varying forms of imposing the royal fifth on the extraction of precious metals and stones.

Another problem the crown failed adequately to face up to was the impact on existing chains of command of newly created bureaucratic entities and the need for areas of jurisdiction to be clearly defined. Viceroy Sabugosa repeatedly complained that governors of Minas Gerais failed to keep him informed of events in the mining areas and did not accord him due respect. Dom João V ruled in favour of his viceroy, but this did not alter the fact that the transfer of the economic epicentre of the colony from the north-east to the highlands had been accompanied by a change in the traditional chain of command between king, the Overseas Council, viceroy, and governor. Greater distances and difficulties in communication between mining areas and even Brazilian coastal cities meant that by the time instructions were requested through normal channels, they might well no longer be applicable. Governors in the mining areas lived in highly volatile communities, where 'but a single spark could ignite a bonfire'. Such a spark could be an unpopular decision on the collection of the fifths, a slave uprising, a shortage of foodstuffs, or heavy-handed action by an over-zealous or arrogant crown judge. In the event of civil disorder, speedy decisions were essential. If time permitted or the matter was highly sensitive, governors bypassed the viceroy and the Overseas Council and wrote directly to the secretary of state in Lisbon, who had the royal ear. Should events break so fast that communication was impracticable, the governor, as the man on the spot, had to take a unilateral decision or attempt to reach a negotiated settlement in consultation with elected representatives of the people. Inevitably such decisions did not always meet with crown approval, and governors were accustomed to having their decisions overturned or being objects of royal anger. Nevertheless, there had been a fundamental change in the traditional method of decision-making in Portuguese America.

A governor's task was made more difficult in the mining areas because his areas of jurisdiction were ill defined. If the assertions of the Conde de Assumar were correct, he had apparently not been given any *regimento* establishing his own special responsibilities and setting guidelines for his relations with other organs of government. On at least one occasion his own views were overruled by crown judges whom he had convoked to implement crown policy. His relations with the mining bureaucracy were also ill defined. Although responsible for the stability of the mining areas, once Assumar started to appoint *guarda-móres* in isolated areas, he was immediately accused of abusing his powers. In dealing with renegade clerics and friars, governors were charged with usurping the jurisdiction of the ecclesiastical authorities. As if such conflicts of jurisdiction were not enough, the governor had to contend with a plethora of privileged groups, each jealously clinging to its own prerogatives. One such group were the minters; the *provedor* of the mint insisted that he was exempt from the governor's authority. Such conflicts of jurisdiction were not limited to the governor, but were shared by fiscal, judicial, and ecclesiastical officials especially in the early years of the establishment of royal government in Minas Gerais, Mato Grosso, and Goiás.

SOCIETY

The most evident characteristic of the emerging society of Minas Gerais, Mato Grosso, and Goiás was its 'instant' quality. In 1695 the population of the highland region of Brazil comprised assorted groups of bandeirantes, occasional cattle ranchers, a handful of missionaries, some speculators, and the Indians. Within less than two decades complete townships had been established and the bureaucratic machinery of government had begun to function. In human terms (and those figures which are available are as scarce as they are selective) in Minas Gerais the number of black slaves alone increased from zero to about 30,000 in the same period. The pattern was repeated elsewhere. By 1726 the population of Cuiabá was 7,000. Within three years of the first strikes in Minas Novas, the estimated population was 40,000, including whites and enormous numbers of black slaves. Within four years of being accorded municipal status, Bom Sucesso in Araçuahi had a permanent population of 1,000.

Inevitably, in the earlier years in Minas Gerais – and with each move to a major discovery or a minor strike in Mato Grosso or Goiás the process was to be repeated – there were popular 'revolts' against crown control. On the one side was the crown, following an essentially exploitative policy under the increasingly absolutist aspirations of João V, whose reign (1706–50) coincided with the development of the mining areas. On the other side were the settlers, notoriously independent, whose livelihood was at best unpredictable, and who felt bureaucratic and fiscal pressures increasing to the point of threatening their existence. The combination was explosive. Widespread evasion of authority took the forms of avoiding payment of the fifth, tithes, and other taxes, working new discoveries without reporting them, mining in forbidden areas, failing to license shops or taverns, and transporting slaves and other commodities through the mining areas without registration. Outright resistance was invariably due to changes in the method of collecting the fifth. By 1721 there had already been three revolts in Pitanguí. There were numerous reports of disturbances in the townships and outlying areas of the judicial district of Rio das Velhas, a region notorious for its population's resistance to any official measure. In the 1730s there were to be further disturbances in the sertão. All too frequently such revolts owed less to popular unrest than to the presence of *poderosos do sertão*, such as Manuel Nunes Viana or Manuel Rodrigues Soares, defending their authority and their profits.

By far the most serious popular uprising anywhere in Minas Gerais, Mato Grosso, and Goiás during the first half of the eighteenth century occurred in Vila Rica late on the night of 28 June 1720. It was directed against the local crown judge and new regulations (February 1719) for the collection of the fifths. Governor Assumar had little difficulty in restoring calm, with the help of the loyal populace of Vila do Carmo. He and his successors exploited the guilt of Vila Rica to induce the town council to contribute to the cost of building barracks, a mint, and a governor's residence by way of atonement. Furthermore, the lesson of evident differences between townships of Minas Gerais was not lost on governors, who adopted a policy of 'divide and rule' in their discussions with representatives of town councils and on the whole were successful in enacting royal policy.

The nature of settlement also made the mining region unusually susceptible to conflict between rival groups. The most famous is the so-called 'War of the Emboabas' in Minas Gerais in 1708–9. Briefly put, this was a series of clashes between Paulistas, who had made the discoveries, and Emboabas, or outsiders who flooded into the mining areas to profit from the strikes. A series of skirmishes in late 1708 in Rio das Velhas spread to the central mining area of Minas Gerais in the following year. The results were little, if any, loss of life, and a victory for the Emboabas. The Paulistas' hatred was not appeased by their (justified) impression that the authorities favoured the Emboaba cause. The *Guerra dos Emboabas* and later serious clashes between the two factions in Goiás in 1736 epitomized the divisions within the population of the mining areas. On the one hand were the Paulistas, of mixed blood with a strong Indian element, bilingual in Portuguese and Tupí-Guaraní, nomadic, consummate backwoodsmen, successful gold discoverers, with a well developed entrepreneurial streak, and distrustful of authority. On the other were the Emboabas – the term designated anybody not a Paulista – unversed in mining, with little interest in exploration, static, Portuguese-speaking, with no knowledge of the flora and fauna of Brazil, inexperienced once away from urban centres, and heavily dependent on others for their skills as well as for survival. Successive governors of Minas Gerais in the first half of the eighteenth century tried to integrate both factions by ensuring equal Paulista and Emboaba representation on town councils in newly developing areas such as Pitanguí.

The very nature of gold mining constituted a further threat to stability. Mining demanded speculation and speculation demanded mobility. The result was a constant ebb and flow of prospectors to new or highly touted discoveries. So sudden were these movements that there was no time to provide any infrastructure. Food shortages were a chronic problem. By 1726 the populace in Minas Gerais was so great that its fledgling cattle industry could not meet the demand. From the peripheral regions came a constant litany of complaint that people were kept away from promising discoveries by food shortages, droughts, floods, and sickness. Even where foodstuffs were available, miners' returns from panning the alluvial deposits were not always enough to permit them to buy much-needed supplies. This happened in Minas Novas in 1729: travellers bringing in food for sale did so at a financial loss because not enough gold was being extracted to permit the miners to pay for the goods. More frequently than has been appreciated, miners felt that the odds against success were too long. They sold their mining equipment and began to migrate back to the coastal regions.

Even for successful miners, the nature of gold mining exerted the kind of pressure unknown to the sugar planters of the north-east, for gold deposits were a wasting asset. Furthermore, higher immediate returns were more likely to be achieved with greater investment in machinery and labour. But higher fixed costs forced miners to keep producing if they wanted any profits. Even if these conditions were met, income was less certain for the miner than for the planter. Drought or flooding could halt mining operations. Collapse of a shaft or discovery of an unexpected rock face could mean loss of investment in time, labour, and machinery. Nor was there any guarantee that a given area actually held rich enough gold deposits to justify mining it. All these factors were characteristic of the mining areas of colonial Brazil. Risk notwithstanding, the lure of high profits resulted in a common tendency to over-invest and over-extend financial resources. The effective working of mines demanded a higher ratio of skilled to unskilled labour than was needed on a plantation. Slave carpenters, masons, or smiths were as expensive as they were essential to the miner seeking high yields from more sophisticated mining operations. The purchasing medium was the product – gold. Unlike the planter, who could in part offset higher costs by demanding more for his product, the miner was powerless to alter the price of gold: the selling price was set by the crown. The universal practice was to buy slaves and other commodities on credit. This could extend over three or four years at monthly interest rates of as much as 10 per cent. Collateral took the form of gold dust. Even successful miners lived in debt to Rio de Janeiro merchants for the purchase of slaves. In view of all these risks, failure was commonplace and could only contribute to the uncertainty and instability of mining communities.

The threat to stability did not reside solely in unrealized hopes of new finds, physical calamities, improvident provisioning, and acts of God. All too often the crown exacerbated an already insecure situation by policies whose intended objective was to increase royal revenues but whose unforeseen impact was the disruption of communities and individuals. One set of such measures placed restrictions on certain sections of the population that were held to constitute a potential threat to effective fiscal control or to security. Two examples will illustrate the impact of such measures on stable, settled families. Inevitably, because of their trade, goldsmiths fell under suspicion whenever there was discussion of contraband. In 1730 the king ordered the viceroy to forbid any goldsmith or foundryman to enter Minas Gerais, and announced that those already there should be expelled. This draconian order was enforced in Jacobina, Rio das Contas, Itocambiras, and Minas Novas; but when its enforcement was ordered in Minas Gerais the governor pointed out to the king that this would uproot not only goldsmiths who were currently plying their trade but also those who had ceased to practise and had families. A second ruling permitted those no longer practising to stay, provided that they signed an affidavit confirming renunciation of their trade. Others, regardless of family and home, had to sell up and leave the mining areas. The second example comes from Serro do Frio in northern Minas Gerais, which embraced the Diamond District. Suspicious of the presence there of free blacks and free mulattos, and in part to impress on the people that all mineral-bearing areas were crown property, in January 1732 the governor of Minas Gerais ordered the expulsion of all free blacks and mulattos from the *comarca* of Serro do Frio, famous not only for its diamond but also for its gold deposits. All pleas were rejected, as were testimonials by the town council as to the stability of the free blacks and mulattos and their valuable contributions to the tax base of the community. In September 1732 the Conde das Galvêas replaced Dom Lourenço de Almeida as governor and free blacks and free mulattos were permitted to stay.

Unrest and insecurity in the mining areas were increased by the crown's policy of revenue collecting. Virtually from the outset, the king realized that the thrust to the west, the dislocation of large numbers of people, their need for basic supplies, and their possession of gold, could be turned to the royal advantage in two ways. One was by restricting access to the mining areas and by controlling all entry points through which goods might be imported to the mining regions. No less than other colonists, inhabitants of the mining areas were affected by the crown monopoly of certain sectors of the import economy, such as salt, wine, and olive oil; but miners had to bear the additional burden of paying dues on imports into the mining areas. The crown followed a policy of tax-farming, and contracts usually for three years were auctioned off to the highest bidder. The contractor was at libery to establish registers on major routes to the mining areas. In addition to registers on land routes, similar contracts were auctioned off on river passages. To cover the costs of such contracts, fees were high and were sometimes collected ruthlessly. Tariffs were calculated on weight or volume rather than value, which bore particularly heavily on miners because, as a result of crown prohibition on manufacturing in the colony, tools, pickaxes, iron, and gunpowder all had to be imported. These fees had a dramatic inflationary impact on all sectors of the import economy, but nowhere more than on slaves – the *sine qua non* of mining. Taxes on slaves, gratuities to officials, fees – usually two *oitavas* of gold (1 *oitava* = 3.6 g) – payable at registers, and actual transportation costs, raised prices in the mining areas for slaves by as much as 200 per cent over the coastal costs. By 1735 the price of a male slave had soared to 400$000 reis in Minas Gerais and special skills could force the price even higher. Although in the long run such high prices reflected the miners' ability to pay, in the short term they spelt ruin for many.

Secondly, people in the mining areas had to pay all the usual taxes of tithes, etc., but were expected in addition to make extraordinary contributions to the building of barracks, a governor's residence, salaries for officials of the mint, wages for the dragoons, the rebuilding of Lisbon after the earthquake of 1755, the building of the royal palace at Mafra, dowries for royal marriages, and a so-called 'literary subsidy'. It was the responsibility of town councils to impose levies (*fintas*) fairly among the populace. In addition, town councils in mining areas faced higher costs than their coastal counterparts in building roads, bridges, gaols, municipal offices, water conduits, and fountains. The combination of higher costs for labour and materials, coupled with a higher incidence of need for replacements, imposed financial restraints on town councils which they tried to offset by heavy licensing fees for taverns, slaughter-houses, stores, and pedlars. Not only did such fees contribute to the inflationary spiral, but they encouraged active black-marketeering, hoarding of foodstuffs, and manipulation of the supply of foodstuffs to provide windfall profits for producers and middlemen.

The demographic pattern of the mining areas during the first half of the eighteenth century was fundamentally the same as that of the coastal enclaves of the north-east: a white minority in which males predominated; a black majority in which slaves predominated and males outnumbered females; a gradual growth in the number of manumitted slaves; a gradual increase in the number of mulattos. But there was a great difference in the relative numbers of each sector which dramatically affected their relationship and thus was sufficient to create an entirely distinctive society. Because the demographic data are culled primarily from capitation records, there is little information about the white population, but at least for the first half of the eighteenth century gubernatorial correspondence suggests that there was an overwhelming predominance of males, the majority of them unmarried. Few families migrated to the mining areas, especially in the formative period of each mining community when hardships were the greatest. Migration to the mining areas by whites was predominantly by bachelors, or bread-winners who had left wife and family in the security of Portugal or a Brazilian coastal city while they went in search of fortune. Some may have rejoined their families, but the records abound with pleas by daughters and wives for the authorities to trace missing fathers and spouses. Desertion or widowhood were often the lot of those left behind. The resulting dearth of white women of marriageable age was exacerbated by the practice of dispatching a daughter to Portugal rather than have her make a disadvantageous local marriage. In response to complaints by governors of Minas Gerais, the king finally (1732) laid down stringent conditions which had to be met before females could leave the colony. The results of this sexual imbalance among the white population were concubinage and a low marriage rate within the captaincy. Concubinage was a way of life in the mining regions and, although the sexual imbalance among whites was to be redressed somewhat in the course of the eighteenth century, many white males continued to prefer black or mulatto concubines even when white women were available. Recent research has suggested that the incidence of marriage overall in the mining areas was low, not only among white partners but also among blacks, and that 'marriage at the doors of the church' was related to the financial means of the prospective bride and groom.

The black and mulatto population in the mining areas also had distinctive characteristics. Based on evidence from Minas Gerais in the eighteenth century, certain generalizations are permissible. Most evident is the overwhelming black majority. This factor alone, coupled with the further characteristics, peculiar to mining regions, of excessively heavy concentrations of slaves in limited areas and considerable mobility permitted to slave speculators, was enough to keep the authorities in constant fear of a black revolt and constitute a threat to the preservation of law and order. Secondly, in the overall population of African descent males predominated, this again being largely attributable to the special labour needs of mining. This predominance was especially noticeable among slaves. In the course of the eighteenth century, two developments resulted in changing sexual ratios. The first was a dramatic increase in the numbers of manumissions. Whereas in the years 1735–49 *fôrros* accounted for less than 1.4 per cent of the population of African descent, by 1786 they accounted for 41.4 per cent of such persons and 34 per cent of the total population. More mulattos than blacks gained their freedom, and among mulattos females predominated. Secondly, there was an increase in the number of mulattos, both slave and free. These two factors had a startling impact on sexual ratios among people of African descent. By 1786, with the single exception of the category of black slaves (*prêtos*), there was a female majority among persons of African descent, be they slaves, free mulattos, or free blacks. In that year in Minas Gerais free female mulattos comprised the largest segment (22 per cent) of the free population of the captaincy.

ECONOMY

Despite physical hardships and royal fiscal and regulatory policies which placed a burden on every person in the mining communities, the increase of population alone is testimony enough to the very real opportunities which existed in Minas Gerais, Mato Grosso, Goiás, and the other mining regions of Brazil. In the course of half a century the economy of Minas Gerais developed from one based on a single commodity, gold, to one with a much broader base. From an initial function of directly servicing the miners, many commercial enterprises diversified markets and supply networks to embrace the community as a whole. In this way they became less dependent on the ebb and flow of mining fortunes and better able to survive the eventual collapse of the mining industry. The supply of foodstuffs to the mining regions and the growth of a construction industry afford two examples of this process.

The mining areas depended heavily on beef for food. Before the discovery of gold, cattle ranching had developed in the north-east with the cities of the coastal areas as the traditional markets not only for cattle on the hoof but also for jerked beef, the production of which was made possible by the presence of natural salt deposits. This industry received an enormous impetus from the development of Minas Gerais, Mato Grosso, and Goiás and expanded accordingly. In fact, such was the dependence of Minas Gerais on cattle imports that it offered an obvious point of exploitation for the *poderosos do sertão* such as Manuel Nunes Viana, who in the first two decades of the century threatened the stability of central Minas Gerais by his control of cattle moving from the upper São Francisco region around the bar of the Rio das Velhas into the towns of central Minas Gerais. Partly as a reaction to this dependence, cattle ranching developed within the mining regions themselves, although these could never be self-sufficient.

From the beginning of the eighteenth century *sesmarias* were granted by the crown within Minas Gerais, and especially along the routes to the mining areas, to people who wished to raise cattle. The same applied to the raising of pigs, the cultivation of manioc, and small poultry farms, which prospered alongside the mining industry. There were regional variations, and even within Minas Gerais Rio das Velhas was famed for its agriculture and smallholdings. The only restriction concerned the cultivation of sugar, in part because the crown feared that it would divert labour from mining.

The demands of an expanding industry and the needs of a growing population in the mining areas created a ready market for those with skills or trades. Mining areas attracted artisans in the building trades – stonemasons, carpenters, and blacksmiths – whose skills were needed to meet the surge in demand for civil and ecclesiastical building, as well as the requirements of mining enterprises. There were handsome profits for those willing to make modest investments in tile manufacture. Subsidiary industries developed: soap boiling, or the manufacture of pans essential to mining. In some instances these smaller industries conflicted with mining interests. Access to supplies of wood and water was hotly disputed by miners, soapmakers, and manufacturers of lime. Waxmakers, coppersmiths, cutlers, tinsmiths, saddlers, coopers, wood turners, and braziers, all found a ready demand for their skills, as did tailors, hatmakers, and hairdressers.

An interesting aspect of the relationship between economic growth and opportunities for artisans was the development of the decorative arts. Gold was not only a means of payment but also a medium of expression and there were many ways of working the precious metal for secular and religious decoration. Goldsmiths, gilders, and gold-beaters were much in demand. Brotherhoods of laymen and women commissioned painters, plasterers, cabinetmakers, woodcarvers, and sculptors to embellish the exteriors and interiors of the churches built in every parish. Even the fine arts benefited and musicians – instrumentalists, vocalists, and even composers – were sought after for religious services, municipal celebrations, or lavish welcomes for visiting functionaries. A musical tradition was born in Minas Gerais which was largely in the hands of mulatto performers.

Gold had been the reason for the migratory thrust towards the west. The obsessive and exclusive fascination it exerted in their early years brought individual mining settlements, and almost the entire region, to the verge of self-destruction. But the development of alternative outlets for entrepreneurial initiative and the possibility of social and geographical mobility provided the necessary safety valves. In the long run this permitted the waves of opportunist and speculative migrants differing in race, status, and origin to be moulded into a balanced and increasingly stable society. For a short span of time in the eighteenth century, Vila Rica do Ouro Prêto was to be the most dazzling town of the Portuguese overseas empire.

MINING

Gold was the basis of the economy and society of Minas Gerais, Mato Grosso, and Goiás during the first half of the eighteenth century. But there were in fact many types of gold, as surviving place-names – *ouro prêto, ouro podre, ouro branco* – reveal. The three essential criteria for assessing gold were form, colour, and touch. The most highly esteemed forms of gold were flakes and grains, which ideally would be smooth and devoid of roughness or splinters. As to colour, which ranged from bright yellow to black, a slight tendency towards darkness was preferable. The touch could only be determined by assaying and this was performed in mints or smelting houses. The best-quality gold needed little mercury to 'sweeten' it; consequently there was less wastage (*quebra*) in the foundry process. Gold of 23 carats was considered exceptionally good; 21 and 22 were the norm. It was important that there should be a uniform standard of gold from any region, even though it might have been extracted in different mines at different periods. Skilled assayers and technicians could establish the place of origin of gold samples, a skill which was especially valuable in determining whether the sample had originated in a particular area or had been brought there to avoid payment of the fifths. In the 1740s there were persistent reports that gold dust from Paracatú with a low touch was being imported into Minas Novas, renowned for the high touch of its gold. The unfortunate recipient of such gold was doubly defrauded because he himself would have to pay taxes in gold of the higher touch. In Minas Gerais there was a wide range of colour, form, and touch: the gold of Vila Rica, Vila do Carmo, and Sabará reached and could exceed 22 carats, whereas that of Rio das Mortes and Serro was lower and that of Borda do Campo never reached more than nineteen carats. In 1731 a report prepared in the mint of Salvador singled out the mines of Araçuahi and Fanado as giving gold which was superior in form, colour, and touch.

Gold deposits fell into two prime categories: gold found in veins, and gold found in rivers. The most widespread source of gold was placer mines. Prospectors (*faiscadores*) panned watercourses, using a wooden or metal pan (*bateia*). When the pan was oscillated gold particles sank because of their higher density and siliceous material was washed over the shallow sides. The same technique was used in more elaborate workings known as *taboleiros*, when a whole river bed was worked, or in *grupiaras*, which were workings in the banks of rivers or adjacent hillsides. Openings into hillsides were known as *catas*. Quartz and gravel were dug out and carried to the nearest water source to be worked by *bateias*, or else water was brought to the *cata* where the gravel beds could be worked by hydraulic pressure. The resulting sludge passed through a series of sluice boxes, each of which retained gold particles, to a trough where slaves panned the residue. Such enterprises were known as *lavras* and although they offered the highest yield they also demanded high initial investment. Lode or vein mining was rare in Minas Gerais but was the more common method in Jacobina. Regardless of the technique employed, the fact remained that water was critical to success. Too much could be as detrimental as too little.

Throughout the colonial period, mining technology remained rudimentary. Although the king had reportedly sent mining engineers to Brazil in the sixteenth century, requests in the eighteenth century for mining technologists from Hungary or Saxony went unanswered. As a result technical innovation was limited to the development of hydraulic machines to increase the availability of water for mining or to remove water from *catas*. Slaves of West African origin may have been more familiar with mining and metallurgy in general than their white owners and indeed were specifically selected for these skills. A writer at the beginning of the nineteenth century was to comment that the most ignorant miner of Minas Gerais was better informed than the best of Goiás, and the most ignorant miner of Goiás was infinitely more skilled than the best of Mato Grosso. Although in some regions Indian labour may have been used in mining, by and large the labour force was made up of African slaves. Among these, slaves from the Bight of Benin – the so-called 'Costa da Mina' – predominated. Miners' demands stimulated the slave trade to the Costa da Mina to the point that, during the first three decades of the eighteenth century, imports of Minas into Brazil exceeded those of Angolans. Minas were held to be better workers, more resistant to disease, and stronger than their Angolan counterparts. Gold mining made severe physical demands. Panning demanded immersion up to the waist in cold streams while the upper body was exposed to the heat of the sun. Sun poisoning, acute dysentery, pleurisy, pneumonia, intermittent fevers, and malaria were commonplace. Slaves in subterranean galleries were the victims of pulmonary infections resulting from inadequate ventilation, and death caused by fall-ins. Physical deterioration from overwork was rapid and slave mortality high. Estimates as to the useful working life of a slave in mining ranged from seven to twelve years.

Slavery in the mining areas provided points of contrast to plantation slavery. Prime among these was underproductivity. Estimates of the weekly takings (*jornaes*) of slaves varied from region to region. A report from Minas Gerais in 1721 recognized that a *jornal* of $\frac{1}{2}$ dram (*oitava*) was good. It was generally acknowledged that *jornaes* in Goiás were equal to or lower than Minas Gerais. In 1736 *jornaes* of half a *pataca* were reported from Goiás. *Jornaes* of half a *pataca*, twelve *vintéis*, a dram, and even $1\frac{1}{2}$ drams were reported from Rio das Contas in 1736 and there had been one fantastic *jornal* of 6 drams. Writing at a time of decline, in 1780 Teixeira Coelho suggested an average yield per slave of 20 drams in the course of a year. This productivity depended only in part on the slave's diligence and good health. Mining was often halted because of legal disputes, bureaucratic intervention, and seasonal changes. Owners prescient enough to engage in agriculture offset their losses by employing their labour force in the fields. For the owner engaged exclusively in mining the only way of cutting costs lay in a contractual arrangement with a slave which relieved the owner of the burden of providing sustenance by allowing the slave to prospect at will. The only condition was that at the end of the week he would return to his owner with the *jornaes*. Such an arrangement applied only to *faiscadores*; slaves on

lavras remained under close supervision. This licence had two immediate repercussions. The first was the presence in the mining areas
of both male and female slaves over whom there was no direct control
and who posed a constant challenge to law and order. The second was
that the potential for abuse was self-evident and the mining areas became
infested with *quilombos* of runaway slaves. However, for those who
remained within the law, there was a very real possibility of acquiring
enough gold dust to buy their freedom.

Technical limitations, exhaustion of the most readily available gold
deposits, and underproductivity were not the only factors contributing
to the failure to realize maximum extractive potential. All too often it
was the result of a combination of factors not directly related to the
availability of gold. For instance, it was alleged that declining
productivity was attributable to lack of incentives for discoverers.
Although a discoverer was accorded two mining concessions (*datas*),
many felt that the bureaucratic hassle was simply not worth the effort.
Repeatedly, governors recommended to the crown that greater incentives be instituted, with the direct object of enticing the Paulistas, who
virtually monopolized actual discoveries, to continue their endeavours.
Disease and Indian attacks also took their toll, but a powerful
disincentive was heavy taxation. The most oppressive tax was that on
the fifth part of all gold extracted. Of the variety of forms which were
experimented with (and which will be discussed later) most made little
or no allowance for the setbacks which beset the industry. The
combination of excessive taxation, maladministration, disillusionment,
lack of technical knowledge, and the gradual move to agriculture all
contributed to the decline in gold production. To these factors should
be added the failure of the crown to co-ordinate mining activities. The
result was uncontrolled exploitation in a series of regions isolated from
one another and for each of which a supporting economy was only built
up at the cost of financial and physical hardship. The chronic
individualism characteristic of mining meant that too little capital was
available in an industry where there was a well-established relationship
between capital investment and productivity. For instance, potentially
productive regions were not exploited because there was not enough
capital to build an aqueduct to bring water to the mining area. By failing
to stimulate collaborative efforts until late in the century, the crown
contributed to the decline in production.

This failure becomes understandable when seen against overall policy towards the mining area, which was characterized by an obsession with regulatory controls and taxation, especially the fifths. The first *Regimento das terras mineraes* dates from 1603, and this was amplified by a second set of regulations in 1618. Formulated before the major discoveries, these regulations proved inadequate to deal with the new American reality. A more detailed set of mining codes was issued by the governor of Rio de Janeiro in 1700 and approved by the crown in 1702. Taken in conjunction with royal orders of 1703 amplifying some areas and clarifying doubts, these regulations were to constitute the definitive mining code for the colony. A superintendent of mines, possessed of legal and administrative rather than mining skills, was to be appointed. To assist him in more technical matters he could appoint a *guarda-mór*, who could, if distance warranted it, appoint *guarda-menores*. The *guarda-mór* was responsible for the allocation of mining concessions. The discoverer received two *datas*, one as a reward for discovery and a second in his role as a miner. A third *data* was reserved for the crown, but was auctioned off to the highest bidder. All concessions were of 30 square *braças* (1 *braça* = 6 feet). Distribution of the remainder of the discovery was by lots and depended on the number of slaves a miner could put to work, i.e. a miner with twelve slaves received an entire *data* whereas a miner with fewer slaves received proportionately less. There was widespread abuse. One reason was that crown judges could also be superintendents. Thus, on being informed of a discovery, an *ouvidor* could intervene personally to make divisions, ignoring the rights of the discoverer to the first two *datas*, which he usurped for himself. But the major source of abuse was the 1703 ruling that superintendents and *guarda-mores* were themselves permitted to mine, thereby giving rise to conflict of interest. In the 1740s the crown judge of Cuiabá was also the superintendent of mining lands; in lieu of extra salary for the work involved in collecting the fifths, he received a preferential mining concession. In other cases, powerful local figures seized water supplies with impunity. Although all mining disputes should be referred to the *guarda-mór* in the first instance and, depending on the severity, to the *ouvidor* as superintendent, in 1733 the *juiz de fora* of Vila do Carmo tried to usurp this prerogative for himself. Further complaints were that *ouvidores* charged excessively for making visits to the mineral areas and that *guarda-mores* nominated totally unsuitable people as *guarda-menores* in return for financial favours. Although the *guarda-mór* could make recommendations it was the governor's duty to give the final stamp of approval and they were instructed to scrutinize more carefully all such nominations.

THE FIFTHS

If mining legislation remained comparatively unaltered in Portuguese America, the same cannot be said of the diversity of methods used by the crown in its attempts to collect, in the least inefficient manner, the *quintos*, or fifths, the tribute due to the crown of the fifth part of all gold extracted. During the colonial period at least a dozen different forms of collection were tried, only to be rejected or modified after costly experience. These fell into two general categories: collection by a form of capitation tax or collection in foundry houses. Capitation varied, ranging from a levy imposed on each *bateia* in operation to a more general tax imposed not only on slaves regardless of occupation but on shops, stores, taverns, slaughterhouses, and smallholdings for the cultivation of manioc, and even including taxes on those engaged in the mechanical trades and in business. A foundry house for the collection of the fifths had existed in São Paulo in the 1630s or 1640s, but it was in the eighteenth century that foundry houses were established throughout all major mining areas. Miners brought their gold to these buildings, where, after a fifth part had been removed for the crown, the remainder was cast into gold bars, stamped with the royal coat of arms, a sphere, and marked to identify the place of foundry. At various times mints played a similar function, returning a miner's share to him in coin.

Neither method of collecting the fifths met with the full favour of sovereign or subject. The crown claimed – wholly justifiably – that both methods afforded exceptional opportunities for evasion of payment and smuggling of untaxed gold. In the space of 30 years the search for the perfect method led the crown in Minas Gerais to go from a quota based on a form of capitation to a foundry house (1725), to capitation (1735) and back to foundry houses (1751). Evidence of royal frustration was the proposal floated in 1730 and again in 1752 to examine tax farming as an alternative to direct collection by the crown, but this was never adopted. The advantage of foundry houses (from the crown's perspective) was ease and speed of collection, whereas collection by capitation could result in delays of two or three years. As for the colonists, they were as adamant as they were inconsistent in their public opposition to one or the other method. Colonists in Minas Gerais who had openly challenged and physically resisted implementation of the royal law of 11 February 1719 concerning a foundry house, when confronted with a capitation tax, were to recall in the early 1740s the period of the foundry houses as being 'a time of joy'. When Viceroy Sabugosa established a foundry house in Minas Novas in 1730 he encountered no opposition; a decade earlier in Vila Rica this had defeated the best efforts of the Conde de Assumar. The major grievance against the capitation tax was that it failed to take into account the unpredictability of the industry's fortunes, not to mention death, sickness, or flight by slaves. It was also claimed that capitation imposed a heavy burden precisely on those whose potential productivity was highest – the owners of *lavras* who had invested heavily in the hope of higher returns. Miners argued with less justification that they should not have to shoulder the entire tax burden of their respective captaincies, especially when their expenses were the heaviest and the high prices they paid for slaves and essential tools were attributable to middlemen seeking to offset customs dues and other fees. Not surprisingly, this brought the rejoinder from other sectors of the community that legally the fifth was a tax imposed on the extractive industries, and that its imposition hit hard those not directly engaged in mining. Farmers were liable not only for the fifth but also for the tenth on their produce. A particularly sore point was that the clergy and public officials were exempt from the capitation tax on a stipulated number of slaves supposedly used in domestic service but in fact often used in placer mining. All agreed, however, that the method of collection resulted in extortion by over-zealous officials: collections were supposed to be twice a year, but officials advanced the collection date, thereby imposing an additional burden on miners and others. Furthermore, the heavy penalties for failure to pay did not discriminate between those who wilfully failed to register slaves and those who had complied with royal orders but had simply not been able to pay on time. As to the foundry houses, once the psychological hurdle had been overcome, it was generally agreed that this form of taxation at source was more equitable. But miners were wont to complain that in taking gold to the foundry houses they lost income while away from their workings, were exposed to robbery en route, and suffered delays through official harassment and dilatory processing of their gold.

The strength of popular sentiment on the issue of the fifths was shown on several occasions when the royal will was thwarted or implementation of an order delayed. Although in 1711 António de Albuquerque Coelho de Carvalho had with royal approval signed an agreement with the miners of São Paulo for collection on *bateias*, this was rejected two years later by miners of Minas Gerais. Despite royal anger and gubernatorial insistence, for over a decade the miners rejected all royal proposals and agreed only to a quota ranging from 25 to 37 *arrobas* annually. The royal law ordering the establishment of foundry houses was implemented only in 1725, following the revolt in Vila Rica in 1720 and scattered uprisings, especially in the district of Rio das Velhas, where discontent was fanned by powerful landowners. Such uprisings were as local in appeal as they were short-lived, but all opposed any change in the status quo, and claimed that the fiscal system did not allow for fewer discoveries or any decline in mining fortunes. So urgent was the need to return to full mining production that governors invariably pardoned the insurgents.

Indecision or inability to impose the royal will had adverse repercussions not only on the mining industry but on commerce in general. The crown's most serious failure was that it did not develop a single, uniform system. This was partly because the industry changed so rapidly: bureaucratic responses inevitably lagged behind new and unpredictable developments. Furthermore, the different types of mining could make one method of collection more advantageous to the crown than another and governors in different areas, sensitive to royal concern over revenue, authorized the locally more productive tax, unaware of the damage to the overall fiscal structure. In 1726, for example, the foundry house of Vila Rica was in full operation, but in Bahia the form of collection was by *bateias* and in São Paulo no systematic form of collection had been instituted. The result was a flourishing trade in gold exported illegally from Minas Gerais to Bahia, where it was claimed that it had been extracted locally and was thus not liable for taxation because the fifths had already been collected on the *bateias*, and to São Paulo, where it was alleged to have originated in the new discoveries in Cuiabá. The extent of this illicit trade was revealed by the diminished income in the foundry house of Minas Gerais. Similarly, the decision by Dom Lourenço de Almeida in 1730 to reduce the tax in Minas Gerais from 20 per cent to 12 per cent in the hope of stimulating internal productivity had the unforeseen effect of providing the incentive for illegal exporting of gold from Bahia to Minas Gerais, where it was used to buy coin, which was in turn clandestinely taken back to Bahia for the purchase of more gold. The result was a dramatic fall in gold entering foundry houses in Araçuahi and Jacobina because the Bahian miners hoped that the viceroy would issue a similar order. A royal order of 1732 ordered restoration of the 20 per cent tax in Minas Gerais. Bureaucratic inefficiency also played into the hands of smugglers: stoppages in gold smelting forced by exhaustion of supplies of mercury *ipso facto* encouraged people to seek alternative outlets for their gold dust rather than comply with royal orders for its dispatch to the mints of Salvador and Rio de Janeiro, where it would be smelted.

Inconsistency and frequent changes in policy could not fail to have an unsettling effect on commerce generally. Merchants struggled with greater controls on their movements, additional fees, and demands that they maintain strict records of imports, sales, and income. New methods of collecting the fifth were accompanied by additional regulations defining areas in which gold dust could circulate legally as the medium of trade, or where its circulation was forbidden and trade had to be conducted in bars or coin. Changes in the price of gold also had far-reaching repercussions on commerce to and from the mining regions. The periods immediately preceding the establishment of foundry houses were full of uncertainty: creditors harassed debtors to make their payments before the foundry houses came into operation, after which all gold would have to be smelted with the corresponding loss of a fifth. The result was insolvency and flight to the sertão by debtors unable to meet the sudden demands. Crown officials, priests, and merchants took advantage of this atmosphere of uncertainty to increase payments by a fifth, although the original services had been performed or contracts had been signed at a time when capitation was in effect.

The imposition of new systems proved extremely costly to the crown through bureaucratic confusion and because of loss of revenue through delays. Depending on the time and place, the actual task of collecting the fifths was divided between the public and private sectors. Town councils, *provedores* of the fifths, prominent citizens, and militia captains were all authorized to collect the fifths. The fiscal bureaucracy established by the crown to administer the industry participated to varying degrees. Most closely involved were the superintendents of foundry houses or intendants of the capitation; slightly removed were superintendents of royal mints, whose prime purpose was the minting of coin but who were called in to reduce dust to coin; further removed, but also with administrative oversight for some of the foundry houses, were the intendants of gold established in the port cities in 1751, whose direct responsibility was the reduction of contraband. Finally, there were treasury officials, crown judges, and governors and viceroy, who were held responsible in the final analysis not only for the collection of the fifths but for their safe passage to the coastal ports and thence to Lisbon. It was inevitable that conflicts of jurisdiction would reduce even further the effective collection of the fifths. There were two telling incidents in 1751: on one occasion the *provedor* of the royal treasury in Bahia refused to release funds for the purchase of materials for the smelting house at Jacobina; on the other the king had to intervene to decide a dispute as to whether the *provedor* of the mint or the intendant general in Salvador was the senior official (he ruled in favour of the latter).

Delay accompanied every change. Foundry houses had to be built, sometimes of stone (as in Vila Rica) and sometimes of wattle and daub (as in Minas Novas), but always there was a delay after the royal order was issued. Furthermore, all dies and equipment came from Portugal or, later, after the mints were established, from Rio de Janeiro and Salvador, and had to be carried over mountainous terrain often by Indian porters. Breakages, desertion by porters, or bad weather washing out roads and bridges, postponed the opening of foundry houses. All technical personnel – assayers and foundrymen – came from Portugal. When a smelting house was established at Vila Rica, the new *provedor* Eugenio Freire de Andrade, who had been *provedor* of the mint at Salvador, delayed his arrival; meanwhile, the technical staff had nothing to do but collect their salaries. Even when he did arrive, the equipment had not, and the governor employed the *provedor* in drawing up statutes for the royal treasury in the captaincy. Another source of delay was the grace periods during which people were permitted to make the adjustments necessary to comply with the new law, for instance by bringing gold dust to be smelted before the transition to foundry houses. In short, the administrative infrastructure was quite inadequate to cope with the logistic demands of changes in the method of collection. Even afterwards, foundry houses were sometimes brought to a standstill because promised shipments of mercury and other essential items such as printed tickets for the twice-yearly capitation *matrículas* either failed to arrive or arrived in over-generous quantities.

CONTRABAND

The very nature of gold, administrative inadequacies, the terrain, human greed, and the lure of high profits combined to make contraband rampant. Although generally short-lived, false mints and foundry houses existed in the colony. The former dedicated themselves to counterfeiting gold coins, especially the highly valued *dobrões* of 24$000 and 12$000 réis; the latter smelted bars from untaxed gold. These operations could usually count on the presence of a former employee of a royal mint or foundry house and the use of false dies, or dies which the authorities had failed to destroy. On a less organized level was the debasement of gold dust by the introduction of tin or other metals, a skill in which slaves were supposed to have reached a high level of sophistication. Gold dust was artificially coloured to raise its value from eight or ten *tostões* per *oitava* to twelve. Clipping and emptying of coins was common enough to force the crown to order a periodic recall to the mints when owners would be compensated on the basis of the intrinsic value of the coin. All these activities flourished, but the real profits to be made from contraband lay in smuggling gold on which the fifth had not been paid from the mining areas to the port cities. While the royal conviction that friars and lay priests were active in this trade was well grounded, the prime carriers of contraband gold were in fact cattle drovers and traders whose knowledge of back roads, sites of registers, and frequency of patrols made their services highly sought after. In order to evade the 1719 law that no gold should leave Minas Gerais unless it had first been smelted, subterfuges resorted to by individuals included fashioning gold dust, on which the fifths had not been paid, into rough and unpolished domestic utensils, chains and bracelets, or religious objects. It has already been noted that the vagaries in the collection of the fifth contributed to smuggling. In addition, official failure to close the loophole afforded by permitting the circulation of dust and coin concurrently in Minas Gerais meant that in the early 1730s merchants from Rio de Janeiro and Salvador could go to the mining areas, buy all available gold dust with coins minted in Rio de Janeiro and Salvador, and then clandestinely export the dust to the coast, where it could be worked into objects by goldsmiths or simply be sold. The authorities often claimed that miners had safe deposit boxes hidden in the convents of Bahia and Rio de Janeiro. Certainly there is evidence of the ease with which illegal gold could be transported. In his report of 1729 Dom Lourenço de Almeida estimated that over 200 arrobas of gold on which no taxes had been paid were being sold openly on the streets of Rio de Janeiro.

The crown did its best to curb this trade. Customs houses and registers were established on roads and rivers to the mining areas, especially in the Recôncavo of Bahia. Patrols were increased, especially on the Serra da Mantiqueira, and in the 1750s Indian soldiers were used to patrol Rio das Contas and the new road to Montes Altos. With the re-introduction of foundry houses, additional registers were created to cope with the growing population centres in outlying areas. On the judicial front special enquiries (*devassas*) were opened on counterfeiting and the debasement of gold. These measures produced few successes – the discovery of a false mint in Paraopeba in 1731 (after four years of successful clandestine operations) and the public burning in 1732 in Salvador of two counterfeiters. Investigations of this kind were made by local crown judges in the captaincies of the interior and, in the cities of Salvador and Rio de Janeiro, by the chief magistrate and crown judge for criminal affairs and the *juiz do crime*. In 1755 the king ruled that all such enquiries be carried out by the newly established intendant general of gold. Legislation was passed on 8 February 1730 reinforcing the law of 19 March 1720 forbidding the circulation of dust in Minas Gerais, as the presence of a mint there could no longer justify official toleration of those breaking the earlier law. Miners were permitted to have up to 500 *oitavas* in their possession but, with this exception, only coin and bar were to be the media for commerce. A law of 28 January 1735 made the crime of debasing gold punishable by death or exile and confiscation of property. The crown sought to meet the challenge of counterfeiting by a law of 29 November 1732 which ordered that the minting of coins exceeding 6$400 réis should cease; that a uniform die be introduced for all minters, the only variation being in the date and place; and that the collar (often illegally removed) be replaced by a milled edge, as this had proved successful in the minting of silver coins. The responsibilities of mints were extended to include verification of the origin of gold brought to them for making into coin, and in 1734 there was a ruling that mints should collect the fifth on all roughly fashioned gold utensils and chains submitted for coining. Goldsmiths had their purchases of gold placed under closer supervision. In 1752 the Conde de Atouguia received royal support for his proposal that the goldsmiths of the colony's capital be required to follow their profession in specially designated streets.

The second stage in the contraband cycle lay beyond the shores of Brazil, in Portugal, Africa, and northern Europe. Homeward-bound Indiamen put into Salvador or Rio de Janeiro, where officers and crew became carriers of contraband gold. This also applied to crews of vessels leaving Brazilian ports for Portugal, where the gold was distributed illegally. In 1729 it was alleged that officers carrying such gold illegally received a 3 per cent commission and that those of royal warships were preferred because they were less likely to fall prey to pirates. Passengers, soldiers, and sailors hid gold in firearms, barrels of molasses, hollowed-out wooden saints, and in concealed places in ships' hulls. The crown enacted legislation for the inspection of ships before leaving Brazil and on arrival in Lisbon. Laws of 1720 and 1734 required that all remittances of gold should be manifested before leaving Brazil and that payment of 1 per cent be made to the Junta da Companhia Geral do Comércio do Brasil. Captains were ordered to make manifests on board and submit these on arrival in Lisbon. Vessels from Brazil putting into the Tagus were visited by the crown magistrate for criminal affairs and gold and manifests were sent to the mint in Lisbon where the 1 per cent was collected and where the carrier or the consignee received his gold. But these laws were only partially effective, mainly because those on whom they depended – ships' captains and officers – themselves participated in the illegal trade. The crown's creation in 1751 of the intendancies general of gold was meant to control evasion, but the officials failed to live up to royal expectations.

Whereas Rio de Janeiro's contraband trade was directed primarily towards Portugal, that of Salvador was oriented towards West Africa. Despite royal orders that no gold should be exported to West Africa, the telling combination of demand for labour in the mines plus the ability to pay in gold rather than in officially sanctioned third-grade tobacco made this a profitable trade. In the 1720s ships from Bahia carried silver coins in addition to substantial amounts of gold, and it was opined that illegal exports of gold were increasing. In 1721 the viceroy estimated that 500,000 cruzados (1 cruzado = 480 réis) annually left Salvador illegally for the Costa da Mina; the following year unofficial estimates placed the figure at 90 arrobas. After the establishment of the factory at Whydah, intended originally to be a potential control on the trade in contraband gold, the factor regaled the viceroy with reports of Bahian ships arriving laden with gold. Sabugosa's draconian solution – the death penalty for anyone found taking gold from Salvador, Pernambuco, or Paraíba to West Africa – was overruled by the crown. In 1730 the viceroy claimed to have arrested the traffic by other means, but any success was short-lived. In the eyes of the crown the evil was twofold: first, loss of revenue; secondly, Brazilian gold falling into the hands of foreigners, notably the Dutch, who maintained a very lucrative trade with the Portuguese from their stronghold at El Mina. The result was that ships returned to Brazil from West Africa loaded with European merchandise simply because the purchase of the slave cargo alone could not provide an outlet for the large amounts of gold exported from Brazil. Five agencies were responsible for searching ships and it was only in 1756 that the king ordered this to be a major responsibility of the intendant general of gold.

Northern Europe also provided an attractive alternative for contraband. Between 1709 and 1761 the crown issued at least two dozen laws or decrees forbidding Portuguese subjects to trade with foreigners and ruling against the entry into Brazilian ports of foreign vessels except under extraordinary circumstances. Viceroys and governors were charged with implementing these decrees. One exception was for French and Spanish vessels homeward bound from the Río de la Plata, where a certain tolerance was exercised in the light of the viceroy's report of 1714 that their ability to pay in silver for provisions and services made such vessels welcome in Salvador. However, heavy penalties did not deter trade with foreigners, some of whom put into Brazilian ports alleging the need of emergency repairs or claiming to be engaged in whaling activities, while in fact carrying little or no whaling equipment but cotton, cloth, and powder instead. Others cruised off shore in order to make contact with agents who would arrange for light craft to bring out gold to the vessels. The problem facing the authorities was threefold. First, the extent of the Brazilian coastline made the task of patrolling it impossible. Secondly, the variety of ports included the smaller ports of Santa Catarina or Paratí as well as Rio de Janeiro, Salvador, and Pernambuco. In 1718 it was recommended that a fort be established at Paratí to curb the flood of foreign merchandise being unloaded there. Thirdly, such was the intensity of the foreign onslaught that any crown measures could only have been of limited effect. There were reports that companies had been established in London and Liverpool specifically to engage in this clandestine trade. Because foreign goods entering Brazil illegally paid no customs dues their vendors were able to undercut the sales price of identical merchandise from Lisbon. The result was very damaging to Portuguese merchants as well as those merchants who depended for their livelihood on the trade from Rio de Janeiro to Minas Gerais. The ineffectiveness of a century of royal measures was demonstrated in a report of 1799 giving the enormous amounts of gold in dust and bar as well as precious stones arriving in the ports of the United Kingdom.

A BALANCE SHEET

The vagaries and deficiencies in the collection of the fifths is doubly unfortunate. In the absence of production figures, fiscal records are our main source for assessments of gold production in the colony. Whereas the fifths collected in the foundry houses provide an indication as to levels below which production did not fall, during the periods when this tax was based on capitation our estimates have to be based on further calculations of the annual productivity of the slave population involved in mining. Both processes have obvious limitations. For a century and a half scholars from a variety of disciplines and nationalities have proposed wildly varying estimates. The results of the most recent research are contained in table 1, but further research in European and Brazilian archives and greater knowledge of production processes in Mato Grosso, Goiás, and Bahia (especially the latter) will doubtless result in further modifications. It appears that overall gold production in the colony increased almost fivefold within the first two decades of the eighteenth century, and progressively, but at a more leisurely pace, over the period 1720–35. The years 1735–50 witnessed another dramatic increase in productivity, reaching a climax in the mid-century. The second half of the century saw a steady decline. Overall figures conceal significant differences between rates of growth and decline in different mining regions, and even within different areas of the same captaincy. Minas Gerais remained pre-eminent throughout, but maximum levels of production were reached within three decades of the first significant discoveries. All major strikes had been made by 1720. In contrast, Bahia and Mato Grosso enjoyed two cycles of discovery: Jacobina and Cuiabá initially and, later, strikes in Minas Novas and the region around Vila Bela. Furthermore, less intensive exploitation coupled with smaller

Table 1 *Production of Brazilian gold in the eighteenth century (kg)*

	Minas Gerais	Goiás	Mato Grosso	Total
1700–1705	1,470			1,470
1706–1710	4,410			4,410
1711–1715	6,500			6,500
1716–1720	6,500			6,500
1721–1725	7,000		600	7,600
1726–1729	7,500		1,000	8,500
1730–1734	7,500	1,000	500	9,000
1735–1739	10,637	2,000	1,500	14,137
1740–1744	10,047	3,000	1,100	14,147
1745–1749	9,712	4,000	1,100	14,812
1750–1754	8,780	5,880	1,100	15,760
1755–1759	8,016	3,500	1,100	12,616
1760–1764	7,399	2,500	600	10,499
1765–1769	6,659	2,500	600	9,759
1770–1774	6,179	2,000	600	8,779
1775–1779	5,518	2,000	600	8,118
1780–1784	4,884	1,000	400	6,284
1785–1789	3,511	1,000	400	4,911
1790–1794	3,360	750	400	4,510
1795–1799	3,249	750	400	4,399

Source: Virgílio Noya Pinto, *O ouro brasileiro e o comércio anglo-portugûes* (São Paulo, 1979), 114.

populations resulted in a more protracted but less dramatic level of production than in Minas Gerais. In both cases the new discoveries offset the decline of gold production in the areas of initial discovery. In contrast, Goiás was characterized by transformation from rags to riches to rags again in the short span of four decades.

Overall production figures, based as they are on official fiscal records which indicate a decline in the amounts of gold reaching Lisbon only in the 1760s, tend to conceal the harsh reality that, although colonists may have contributed lavishly to the royal exchequer, even during their apparently most productive years mining communities were far from enjoying the benefits of a golden age. In 1730 the provedor of the royal treasury in Salvador lamented the decline of placer mining in the captaincy and two years later the mines of Cuiabá were described as 'offering no more than a shadow of former riches'. In Minas Gerais as early as 1732 ecclesiastical fees were modified in view of 'the wretched circumstances of these peoples because of the dearth of gold being extracted'. By 1741 the town council of Vila Rica referred to 'greatest poverty' occasioned by the absence of further discoveries and the alleged exhaustion of present deposits. Such was the plight of Brazil's richest captaincy that in the 1740s the governor reformed fee structures for a variety of services ranging from baptisms to medicines and even rewards for bush-whacking captains on the grounds that the original statutes had been made 'in another era when there was an abundance of gold'. This was no longer the case. Although miners, no less than sugar planters, were notorious Jeremiahs and such complaints should be taken with a grain of salt, everything indicates that the majority of the population in the mining regions enjoyed only fleetingly the benefits of their own production.

For over half a century the Portuguese crown derived enormous revenues not only from the fifths but from monopoly contracts, tithes, and a full range of duties on every aspect of colonial commerce. In addition, the crown turned to the mining areas in particular when seeking 'voluntary donations' for a variety of undertakings which included dowries for royal weddings, the building of Mafra, or the rebuilding of Lisbon after the earthquake of 1755. The fifths received by the crown represented not only revenues derived as the result of collection in the foundry houses or by capitation, but also included revenue from confiscations and proceeds from the sale of mining concessions. On the deficit side, deductions were made from the fifths for a variety of purposes. These included the twentieth due to the queen by virtue of a royal decree of 1720. The expenses of each intendancy were met from its own revenues; salaries of officials in the foundry houses were paid from revenue derived by these establishments. Gold derived from the first year of capitation in Minas Novas (1 September 1735–6) was directed to the building of an Indiaman for which the timber alone cost 60,000 cruzados. Against the fabulous revenues should be set the no less fantastic costs to the crown of the administration of the mining areas and the collection of the fifths: freight charges for materials for mints and foundry houses; salaries for officials and dragoons, which could exceed by four times those current in Portugal; costs of building mints in Rio de Janeiro (1702), Salvador (1714), and Vila Rica (1724), and foundry houses, of which eight had been authorized by 1755. Despite the contrary advice of governors and viceroys the crown persisted in the construction, maintenance, and overstaffing of these expensive undertakings. In 1721 and again in 1730 the governor of Minas Gerais tried in vain to curb royal enthusiasm for the building of foundry houses in the captaincy on the grounds that they could only be losing propositions and were thus against the royal interest. Both Dom Lourenço de Almeida and his successor as governor of Minas Gerais, the Conde das Galvêas, recommended that the mint of Vila Rica be abolished. In Bahia the building of foundry houses in Jacobina and Rio das Contas meant that the Salvador mint showed a deficit; in the 1730s and 1740s its staff was largely idle from lack of work. Revenue from seigniorage and brassage was inadequate to meet the expenditure on salaries. By 1789, the position of the mint in Salvador was so critical that a loan had to be sought from the royal treasury to meet payroll costs. The costs of collecting the fifths had led the crown to consider tax farming in 1752 but with this exception the Portuguese crown blithely ignored all advice to cut back on unnecessary expenditures. Even when the writing was on the wall the crown continued to follow a policy which oppressed the mining communities instead of stimulating growth and further discovery by the removal of all restrictions. By the time the crown had started slowly to move in this direction it was already too late.

The discovery and exploitation of gold had a major impact not only on the social and economic fortunes of the colony, but on the mother country, the south Atlantic economy, and the relationship of the Luso-Brazilian world with other European nations in the eighteenth century. In social and demographic terms a major impact was the sudden stimulus to migration – of freemen from Portugal and the Atlantic islands and of slaves from West Africa – to the New World, in a manner previously unparalleled in Brazilian history. The transatlantic phase was followed by a second phase which witnessed the dislocation of blacks and whites alike from coastal enclaves to the interior of Brazil. In contrast to the stability and permanence of settlements in agricultural areas on the coast, mining communities were characterized initially by their temporary nature and the fragility of their economic bases. Each area went through the experience of sudden population growth and intensive exploitation. Although the leading mining towns and cities could not rival their coastal counterparts in size, it was mining which stimulated urbanization in Brazil, something which agriculture had failed to do in the preceding two centuries.

The society of the mining areas shared many of the broad characteristics of the littoral regions, but the combination of special demands made on society by mining itself, the nature of settlement, and even the topography exaggerated and distorted them to such a degree as to result in a society which reflected only distantly that of the patriarchal plantation areas of the north-east or even of the port cities of Salvador or Rio de Janeiro. The sudden demographic growth made the mining areas true 'melting pots' for persons of widely divergent national, social, economic, racial, religious, and linguistic backgrounds. Never totally absent from the mining regions were tensions born of social differences, a highly competitive industry, both social and financial opportunism, and the distrust miners had of the crown and its representatives. The potential for social and financial self-advancement – be it represented by increased rates of manumission or the emergence of a comparatively prosperous middle class of miners, artisans, and smallholders in Minas Gerais particularly – was so unlimited and genuinely democratic in the focus of its aspirations as to constitute in itself a threat to stability.

From the crown's perspective the move to the west, the opening of new lands, and the development of extractive industries stretched Portuguese administrative resources to breaking point. Crown policy was characterized overall by restraint, caution, and restriction. The crown resorted to the narrowly legalistic expedient of issuing laws, edicts, and regulatory measures when the situation demanded imaginative policy dedicated to stimulating social and economic growth by fostering stability and a programme of incentives. Colonialist policies which had proved effective for the coastal areas and for agriculture were totally unsuited to the mining areas. The result was that large sectors of the population lived beyond the effective control of the crown. Popular challenges to royal authority were symptomatic of a society which was well aware of the fragility of crown authority and tested it to the full in a spirit of evasion, reticent co-operation, or outright revolt. The Portuguese crown may have secured new territories by the move to the west, but they proved an administrative liability.

The discovery of gold came at a time of recession in Brazilian agriculture attributable to the falling off in sugar and tobacco prices. Remittances to Portugal were therefore made in coin with a resulting severe shortage in the colony. Gold precipitated the dislocation of the economic epicentre of the colony from the north-east to the Brazilian highlands and plateau and from agriculture to mining. Thanks largely to the vociferous and repeated complaints by the city council of

Salvador in particular, alleging the disastrous impact on plantation economies of the north-east wrought by higher prices and the shortage of labour, the negative aspects of the impact of mining on agriculture have received undue attention. Certainly, the development of new markets represented a challenge which Salvador and Recife were initially unable to meet, resulting in shortages of foodstuffs and imports. But within a comparatively short space of time tobacco and sugar planters were taking advantage of the new markets for their products offered by the presence of mining communities, increased demand, and higher prices. In this respect the mining areas acted as stimuli not only for the agriculture of Bahia but also of Rio de Janeiro and São Paulo. The cattle industry of Bahia, Piauí, Ceará, Pernambuco, and Maranhão responded to increased demand in Minas Gerais, Goiás, and Mato Grosso by increasing production. Ranchers southwards from Curitiba to São Pedro do Rio Grande supplied cattle to the mining areas, using Paulista intermediaries. Gold therefore created new centres of production and consumption while stimulating the productivity of the more traditional regions of supply.

Higher prices in Minas Gerais had inflationary repercussions throughout the colonial economy, but the more prejudicial aspects were offset to some degree by greater flexibility in commercial transactions afforded by gold as a medium of exchange. Shortages of coin occurred frequently throughout the first half of the eighteenth century, but supplies from the colonial mints opened up new markets, increased competition, and moved certain parts of Brazil away from commodity exchanges and towards a monetary economy. The impact was readily apparent in the dramatic growth of commercial sectors in Salvador and Rio de Janeiro, which responded to increasing demands from Minas Gerais, Goiás, and Mato Grosso by acting as intermediaries for imports from Europe and Africa. The fortunes of merchants in these port cities were tied to the prosperity of gold. When production declined, so too did the demand and the acquisitive power, leading to retrenchment especially for Rio de Janeiro.

For Portugal, news of the discovery of gold came at a time of severe economic recession and balance of payments problems resulting from the Methuen Treaty (1703) with England. While in the short term Portugal was to be saved economically by imports of gold from Brazil, the long-term benefits to the nation's economy were limited because of the failure to develop any systematic agricultural or industrial policy.

The nature of the colonial pact was to be irremediably altered. That the colony had become wealthier than the mother country was self-evident. A universally recognized commodity of exchange – gold – placed Brazil vis à vis Portugal in a position of greater economic autonomy. Miners were in a better position than the Brazilian planters had been to dictate demands rather than being subservient to the Lisbon commercial establishment or to prices set in European markets. The demand came from the irresistible combination of growing population, urbanization, and the enhanced purchasing power of all sectors of the free community, which sought not only cloths and metal utensils, but luxuries such as spices, porcelain, silks, and velvets from Europe and Asia. Increased demand, which had proved so beneficial to the commercial growth of the port cities of Brazil, was no less so for Lisbon. But in the broader perspective the result was to reduce Portugal to the status of an entrepot, on the one hand for imports from England and northern Europe that Brazilians demanded but Portugal herself was unable to supply, and on the other for remittances of Brazilian gold which arrived in the Tagus only to be dispatched to London in payment for these imports. It was the presence of middlemen in this train of supply and demand which made contraband so attractive. As noted above, this could take the form of trade directly from Brazil to England or the illicit trade carried on by packet boats, vessels of the British navy, and merchantmen, whose ubiquitous presence in the Tagus at the time of the arrival of the Brazil fleets was a constant irritant to the Portuguese authorities. Brazilian gold, legal or contraband, stimulated English trade and exports to Portugal increased throughout the first half of the eighteenth century. (Brazilian gold may have laid the foundations for the future industrial revolution in England.) The decline in gold production, decreasing purchasing power, and reduced demand by the colonists were to be reflected in a decline in British exports to Portugal starting in the late 1750s. Truly prophetic had been the observation made in 1716 by the secretary of state in Lisbon to the Marquês de Angeja in Brazil: 'despite the floods of gold arriving from America, never was Portugal so poor because at the time of our greatest fortune the foreigners carry away everything from us'.

Brazilian gold had less measurable repercussions. In the political arena Dom João V was encouraged to emulate the despotism and the absolutist aspirations of Louis XIV. At no time did the king or his successors feel the need to convoke the Côrtes. Whether truly or falsely,

Dom João V enjoyed the enviable reputation of being the wealthiest sovereign of Europe. While much gold was squandered in both the mother country and the colony, enough remained to finance public works, royal academies and libraries, and social philanthropy. In the private sector remittances were made to Portugal for dependants, heirs, and charity. In Brazil, the increase in the mining areas in the number of brotherhoods of laymen and women devoted to the assistance of the less fortunate was a characteristic of eighteenth-century Minas Gerais. Such brotherhoods cut across differences of race, civil status, and ethnic heritage to include whites, free and slave mulattos, and blacks. Hospitals, foundling homes, and hostels for the destitute were the product of this charitable sentiment. Social philanthropy was paralleled by an increase in the building of convents and churches in the mining areas and in the coastal cities of Brazil. Although Brazil may have siphoned off skilled artisans from Portugal, there is every indication that it was in the mining areas that schools of native talent emerged whose best-known figure is the mulatto sculptor in wood and stone popularly known as Aleijadinho. Indeed, it is the interiors of the churches of Minas Gerais with their painted ceilings, carved pulpits, and altars and chapels laden with gold leaf which are the most enduring and the most visible legacy of the golden age of Brazil.

15

LATE COLONIAL BRAZIL, 1750–1808

If the years 1808–22, following the dramatic arrival of the Portuguese court at Rio de Janeiro, are considered for Brazil a period of transition from colony to independent empire, then the years 1750–1808 may be regarded as the last phase of Brazil's colonial experience. The era began as the mining boom was reaching its zenith; then, quite unexpectedly, the boom was over and an extended depression ensued. But Brazilians readjusted to the decline of the mineral sector by returning to agriculture, their traditional source of wealth. The result for coastal Brazil (but not the interior) was several decades of renewed prosperity based, in part, upon an expansion in the production of traditional staples, particularly sugar and tobacco, but also upon the development of new exports, especially cotton and rice, as well as cacao, coffee, and indigo. That recovery was accomplished without any fundamental improvements in technology or alterations in the patterns of land tenure, but through the growth of old and new markets and an intensified reliance upon slave labour. During this period Brazil accepted without protest the crown's decision to expel her most respected missionary order (the Jesuits) and to restrict the role of the remaining religious bodies. Portugal fought and lost two wars to secure Brazil's southern boundaries, but a third conflict (1801) gained Brazil rich agricultural and pastoral lands in the temperate south. Colonial Brazil had reached her territorial limits.[1] Though she virtually ignored the first American Revolution, Brazil became far more aware of the French Revolution. Not only did Europe's subsequent maritime wars open up new markets for Brazilian products but the Revolution's ideological underpinnings and its successes inspired the first serious

---

[1] See D. Alden, *Royal government in colonial Brazil* (Berkeley and Los Angeles, 1968), pt. 2; also Mansuy-Diniz Silva, *CHLA* I, ch. 13.

separatist conspiracies in several parts of the colony. Even though those movements were rigorously repressed, the call for reforms of the so-called colonial pact binding Brazil to Portugal became more insistent. The urgency for change became irresistible in 1807–8, when the Portuguese government found itself unable to withstand competing Anglo-French pressures and fled to the security offered by its richest and most populous colony.

DEMOGRAPHY

By the 1770s it becomes possible for the first time to obtain sufficient information to estimate the size and distribution of Brazil's population. In 1776 the colonial minister directed secular and ecclesiastical authorities throughout the colony to join together to provide complete counts of their inhabitants according to age and sex, but not, unfortunately, race. The crown's motives were obviously the traditional ones, those of determining the number of men capable of bearing arms and evaluating the number of potential taxpayers. In pursuance of that order, local officials (militia commanders and parish priests) compiled data from the *lista de desobrigas*, the parish register of persons receiving communion at Easter. Since that register excluded children under seven, their number was determined by actual count or (more likely) by estimate. The parish counts (*mapas particulares*) were forwarded to district officers; they sent condensed reports to their superiors, who remitted consolidated tabulations to the crown.

Such reports were supposed to be submitted to Lisbon annually, but with the exception of the captaincy of São Paulo they were seldom prepared so regularly. Many of the reports have been lost; others remain in the archives awaiting scholarly analysis. But a sufficient number have been gathered to permit estimates to be made of late colonial Brazil's population at two points in time. One clustering ranges from 1772 to 1782 and centres on 1776; the other spans the years 1797–1810, though most of the data reported for the latter year were compiled somewhat earlier, so that 1800 becomes a reasonable benchmark. The distribution of Brazil's enumerated inhabitants *c*. 1776 and *c*. 1800 is indicated in tables 1 and 2.

Several observations arise from these tables and the sources from which they are derived. First, it is evident that the census-takers substantially underestimated the number of children below the age of

Table 1 *Distribution of the population of Brazil, c. 1776*

Captaincy	Number of inhabitants	Percentage
Rio Negro	10,386	0.6
Pará	55,315	3.5
Maranhão	47,410	3.0
Piauí	26,410	1.7
Pernambuco	239,713	15.4
Paraíba	52,468	3.4
Rio Grande do Norte	23,812	1.5
Ceará	61,408	3.9
Bahia	288,848	18.5
Rio de Janeiro	215,678	13.8
Santa Catarina	10,000	0.6
Rio Grande do Sul	20,309	1.3
São Paulo	116,975	7.5
Minas Gerais	319,769	20.5
Goiás	55,514	3.5
Mato Grosso	20,966	1.3
Totals	1,555,200	100.0

Source: D. Alden, 'The population of Brazil in the late eighteenth century: a preliminary survey', *Hispanic American Historical Review* [*HAHR*], 43/2 (May 1963), 173–205.

fifteen. More will be said later about the consequences of such under-enumeration. Second, many Indians (estimated by one contemporary at 250,000) who were beyond the pale of Portuguese authority, especially within the Amazon basin, Goiás, Piauí, and Mato Grosso, were not counted; nor does it seem possible to provide any reliable approximation of their numbers. Third, in spite of repeated land 'rushes' to the mineral and pastoral lands of the interior west and south, during the eighteenth century, most of the enumerated population (78.8 per cent in 1776 and 73.4 per cent *c.* 1800) was still concentrated around the principal ports and hinterlands of the coastal captaincies, especially in the traditional staple export centres of Paraíba, Pernambuco, Bahia, and Rio de Janeiro, which contained more than half (51.1 per cent) of Brazil's recorded inhabitants in 1776 and 46.8 per cent *c.* 1800. Fourth, with minor exceptions, the general pattern of the distribution of Brazil's population did not change significantly during the last decades of the colonial period: the rank order of the captaincies was about the same in 1800 as it had been a quarter-century earlier. Fifth, while the urban

Table 2 *Distribution of the population of Brazil, c. 1800*

Captaincy	Date of report	Number of inhabitants	% of total population	Source
Rio Negro/Pará	1801	80,000	3.8	**A**
Maranhão	1798	78,860	3.8	**A**
Piauí	1799	51,721	2.5	**B**
Pernambuco	1810	391,986	19.0	**C**
Paraíba	1810	79,424	3.8	**C**
Rio Grande do Norte	1810	49,391	2.4	**C**
Ceará	1808	125,764	6.1	**D**
Bahia	1799	247,000	11.9	**E**
Rio de Janeiro	1803/1810	249,883	12.1	**F**
Santa Catarina	1797	23,865	1.2	**G**
Rio Grande do Sul	1802	38,418	1.8	**H**
São Paulo	1797	158,450	7.5	**I**
Minas Gerais	1805	407,004	19.7	**J**
Goiás	1804	52,076	2.5	**K**
Mato Grosso	1800	27,690	1.3	**L**
Totals		2,061,657	99.4	

Sources: **A**: Colin M. MacLachlan, 'African slave trade and economic development in Amazonia, 1700–1800', in R. B. Toplin (ed.), *Slavery and race relations in Latin America* (Westport, 1974), 136. **B**: F. A. Pereira da Costa, *Chronológia histórica do estado do Piauhy desde os seus primitívos tempos até...1889* ([Recife]), 1909), 109. **C**: Enclosure in Lord Strangford to Marquis of Wellesley, Rio de Janeiro, 20 May 1810, PRO, FO 63/84/ERD/2255 (copy courtesy of Dr F. W. O. Morton). **D**: Luiz Barba Alardo de Menezes, 'Memória sôbre a capitania do Ceará', [1808], *Revista do Instituto Histórico e Geográfico Brasileiro* [*RIHGB*], 34 (1871), 276, table 3. **E**: Luiz dos Santos Vilhena, *Recopilação de notícias soteropolitanas e brasílicas...em XX cartas*, ed. Braz do Amaral (3 vols., Bahia, 1921), II, 481. **F**: The data for the city of Rio de Janeiro is based on an 1803 census in Strangford to Wellesley, **C** above. Also included is the subordinate captaincy of Espiritu Santo, but I have deducted data for Santa Catarina. **G**: João Alberto de Miranda Ribeira, 'Dados estatísticos sôbre...Santa Catarina, 1797', Biblioteca Nacional do Rio de Janeiro [BNRJ], II–35, 30, 3. The census of 1810 (**C**) gives 31,911. **H**: 'Mappa de todos os habitantes da capitania do Rio Grande de São Pedro do Sul...1802', Arquivo Histórico Ultramarino (Lisbon), papéis avulsos (miscellaneous papers) [AHU/PA], Rio Grande do Sul, caixa 1. I have added to the existing total the uncounted 1,697 infants under one year. **I**: 'Mappa geral dos habitantes da capitania de S. Paulo no anno de 1797', Arquivo do Estado de São Paulo, *Publicação oficial de documentos interesantes para a história e costumes de São Paulo* [*DI*], 31 (1901), 151–5, 157. **J**: A. J. R. Russell-Wood, 'Colonial Brazil', in David W. Cohen and Jack P. Greene (eds.), *Neither Slave nor Free* (Baltimore, 1972), 97. **K**: Luis Antonio da Silva e Sousa, 'Memoria...de Goiás' [1812], *RIHGB*, 12 (2nd edn, 1874), 482–94. **L**: Caetano Pinto de Miranda Monte Negro to Visconde de Anadia, 17 April 1802, *RIHGB*, 28/1 (1865), 125–7.

Table 3 *Estimates and counts of principal Brazilian cities, 1749–1810*

City	Date	Number of inhabitants
Belém, Pará	1749	6,574
	1788	10,620
	1801	12,500
São Luís, Maranhão	1757	7,162
	1810	20,500
Recife, Pernambuco	1750	7,000
	1776	18,207
	1782	17,934
	1810	25,000
Salvador, Bahia	1757	35,922
	1775	36,393
	1780	39,209
	1807	51,000
Rio de Janeiro	1760	30,000
	1780	38,707
	1799	43,376
	1803	46,944
São Paulo	1765	20,873
	1798	21,304
	1803	24,311
Porte Alegre, Rio Grande do Sul	1808	6,035
Oeiras, Piauí	1762	1,120
	1810	2,000
Vila Boa, Goiás	1804	9,477
Vila Bela, Mato Grosso	1782	7,000
Ouro Preto, Minas Gerais	1740s	20,000
	1804	7,000

Sources: **Belém**: J. R. do Amaral Lapa, *Livro da visitação do santo ofício da inquisição ao estado do Grão Pará* (Petrópolis, 1978), 38. **São Luís**: AHU/PA/Maranhão, caixa 37; *RIHGB*, 17 (1854), 64. **Recife**: *Anais da Biblioteca Nacional do Rio de Janeiro* [*ABNRJ*], 28 (1908), 407; José Ribeiro Júnior, 'Subsídios para o estudo da geografia e demografia histórica do nordeste brasileiro', *Anais de História* (Marília, 1970), vol. II, 156–7; *ABNRJ*, 40 (1918), 102. **Salvador**: Thales de Azevedo, *Povoamento da cidade do Salvador* (2nd edn, São Paulo, 1955), 192; Vilhena, *Cartas*, II, map facing 480; Russell-Wood, 'Colonial Brazil', 97. **Rio de Janeiro**: Eulalia Maria Lahmeyer Lobo, *História do Rio de Janeiro*, I (Rio de Janeiro, 1978), 55; *RIHGB*, 47/1 (1884), 27; *ibid.*, 21 (1858), table facing 176; PRO, FO 63/84/ERD/2255, Strangford to Wellesley, 20 May 1810. **São Paulo**: Maria Luiza Marcílio, *La ville de São Paulo* (Paris, 1968), 119. **Porto Alegre**: *RIHGB*, 30/1 (1867), 69. **Oeiras**: Domingos Barreira de Macedo, 'Cenço das casas proprias e de aluguer q. occupa os moradores da cidade de Oeiras...', Sept. 1762, Arquivo Nacional da Torre do Tombo (Lisbon) [ANTT], Ministério do Reino, maço 601; *RIHGB*, 17 (1854), 56. **Vila Boa**: *RIHGB*, 12 (2nd edn, 1874), 482f. **Vila Bela**: José Roberto do Amaral Lapa, 'Ciclo vital de um polo urbano: Vila Bela (1751–1820)', *Anais do VII simpósio nacional dos professores universitários de história* (São Paulo, 1974), 315. **Ouro Preto**: Donald Ramos, 'Vila Rica: profile of a colonial Brazilian urban center', *The Americas*, 35 (April 1979), 495–526.

history of late colonial Brazil remains to be written, it is evident that the processes of urbanization were much more advanced in some parts of Brazil than in others. In the captaincy of Bahia, for example, 170,489 out of an estimated 193,598 persons in 1780 lived in the capital city, its immediate suburbs, and eight towns around the Bay of All Saints. By contrast, the average size of 36 municipalities in the captaincy of Rio de Janeiro (excluding the capital) was only 1,625 in the late 1770s. One further example: the 1782 census of Pernambuco reported that there were 169,043 persons living in 25 municipalities of the district (*comarca*) that included the captaincy's capital (Olinda) and its chief port (Recife), an average of 6,761 persons per community; but in the captaincy's other *comarca*, where there were twenty communities, the average fell by more than half, to 3,035.

Table 3 summarizes various contemporary counts and estimates of the size of Brazil's principal cities and towns during the last decades of colonial rule. All are low, in most instances excluding small children (0–7 years) and in some cases slaves as well. It is evident that throughout these years Salvador, the colonial capital until 1763, still retained a lead over its rival and successor, Rio de Janeiro, but that lead was to disappear during the years 1808–22, when Rio's population doubled. But whereas Salvador and its satellite communities claimed a large share of the captaincy of Bahia's inhabitants, that was untrue of other cities such as São Paulo. The city of São Paulo grew surprisingly little between 1765 and 1803. Moreover, while one in every four persons in the captaincy of São Paulo lived in its capital city in 1765, that proportion fell to one in eight by 1803, reflecting the growth of towns of intermediate size during the economic growth of the last colonial decades. While evidence is sparse, the seaports seem to have continued to increase more rapidly than did interior towns, the most notable of which, Ouro Preto, suffered a loss of more than half of its population after the mid-century because of the decline of the mining industry. Although colonial Brazil has generally been depicted as a distinctly rural colony, its leading cities were impressive for their size, if not for their beauty, cleanliness, or safety. By the mid 1770s Salvador was larger than every city in English colonial America save Philadelphia (pop. 40,000 in 1775) and possessed a larger population than did Bristol, Liverpool, Birmingham, or Manchester. Recife, only the fourth ranking city in Brazil, was then larger than Boston (25,000 in 1775), the third largest in English America, and very likely Rio de Janeiro was larger than

Table 4 *Racial composition of Brazil at the end of the colonial period*

		Percentage			
		Mulattos and blacks			
Place	Whites	Free	Slaves	Indians	Total
Pará[a]			23	20	80,000
Maranhão[b]	31	17.3	46	5	78,860
Piauí	21.8	18.4	36.2	23.6	58,962
Goiás	12.5	36.2	46.2	5.2	55,422
Mato Grosso[c]	15.8			3.8	26,836
Pernambuco	28.5	42	26.2	3.2	391,986
Bahia	19.8	31.6	47	1.5	359,437
Rio de Janeiro[d]	33.6	18.4	45.9	2	229,582
Minas Gerais	23.6	33.7	40.9	1.8	494,759
São Paulo	56	25	16	3	208,807
Rio Grande do Sul[e]	40.4	21	5.5	34	66,420
Average for eight jurisdiction[f]	28.0	27.8	38.1	5.7	

Source: PRO, FO 63/84/ERD/2255, Strangford to Wellesley, 20 May 1810.

[a] Not included in source. See MacLachlan, 'African slave trade', 136, where it is reported that 57% consisted of free persons. [b] Not included in source. I have substituted data derived from the census of 1801 cited in *ibid.* [c] Not included in source. I have used the census of 1800 (*RIHGB*, 28/1 (1865), 125–7), which gives 53.2% as *prêtos* and 27.2% as mulattos, but does not distinguish between slaves and free persons. [d] Based on the 1803 census for the city and later counts for the captaincy. Espíritu Santo and Santa Catarina excluded. [e] Data defective. See text. [f] Except Mato Grosso, Pará, Rio Grande do Sul.

pre-revolutionary New York (25,000 in 1775). At the turn of the century Rio was growing at the impressive rate of 9.2 per cent per year.[2]

When the crown began to require regular census counts in 1776, it did not stipulate that racial distinctions be included. However, some governors, especially those who administered captaincies where there were large numbers of slaves, did ask for such information themselves. Some of the resulting tabulations distinguished Brazil's four primary

[2] See Carl Bridenbaugh, *Cities in revolt. Urban life in America 1743–1776* (reprint., New York, 1964), 216 and 217 n. 4, and Jacob M. Price, 'Economic function and growth of American port towns in the eighteenth century', *Perspectives in American History*, 7 (Cambridge, Mass., 1974), 176–7. Cf. Gary B. Nash, *The urban crucible: social change, political consciousness, and the origins of the American revolution* (Cambridge, Mass., 1979), 407–9. Nash provides substantially lower estimates than Bridenbaugh or Price and makes the contrast between the largest English and Portuguese colonial cities appear even greater. For the 1799 census of the city of Rio de Janeiro, see *RIHGB*, 21 (1858), table facing 176; that of 1803 is cited in table 2, source C.

racial strains: whites, i.e., persons socially accepted as Caucasians; *pardos*, or mulattos; *prêtos*, or blacks; and Indians within effective Portuguese control. But other reports only differentiated between freemen and slaves. Since Indian slavery was officially (though not always in practice) abolished in the 1750s, it is evident that all slaves enumerated were persons of African origin, whether or not Brazilian-born, but what proportion of the slaves were black or brown is hard to say. Though we possess one or more censuses that do identify racial elements in one or another part of Brazil during the late eighteenth century, we do not have sufficient reports with comparable classifications for any decade to be able to generalize about the racial composition of Brazil as a whole.

Fortunately, soon after the arrival of the Portuguese court, the ministry of the interior did compile a census in which racial distinctions were included for major Brazilian captaincies. The results, as reported by Lord Strangford, the British minister at Rio de Janeiro, to his government in 1810, are summarized in table 4, which also includes somewhat earlier counts for captaincies missing in the Strangford dispatch. As table 4 demonstrates, nearly two-thirds of Brazil's population at that time was of African origin (blacks and mulattos), and there appear to have been more free persons of colour than whites in the colony. Regrettably, the ministerial census did not distinguish between mulatto and black freemen, but what we know from other studies suggests that six or seven out of every ten free persons of colour were mulattos, making them probably the most rapidly growing racial element in Brazil.

It is interesting to compare the racial data reported by Strangford with that derived from some of the censuses of the 1770s. In the far north the percentage of free persons (described as 'whites, mulattos, and other mixtures as well as... blacks') in Pará increased during the last three decades of the eighteenth century from 44.8 to 57, but in neighbouring Maranhão the percentage of free persons fell slightly (from 32.4 to 31). The racial composition of two of the most important sugar captaincies, Pernambuco and Bahia, is lacking in the earlier censuses, but the ministerial report shows a striking contrast: in Pernambuco there were substantially more free persons of colour than slaves; while the reverse was true in Bahia. As for the third-ranking sugar captaincy, Rio de Janeiro, in 1780 the percentage of free persons was almost equal to that of slaves (50.7 to 49.3), but the 1799 census reveals that the percentage of free persons had grown to 65.5. São Paulo was one of two captaincies where whites appear to have predominated numerically, though their percentage fell from 56.4 in the 1770s to 50.8 *c.* 1810. The racial data Strangford reported for Rio Grande do Sul does not accord with that contained in the censuses of 1798 and 1802, and the discrepancy must be due to clerical error. Those more detailed censuses indicate that whites comprised between 57.7 and 55 per cent of the population, compared with free persons of colour (5.5–6 per cent), slaves (34.5–35.5 per cent) and Indians (2.3–3.4 per cent). As might be expected, the interior captaincies were the least attractive to whites; coloured majorities predominated everywhere.

Since the censuses of the late colonial period are deficient by modern standards, it is not surprising that scholars differ as to the actual size of Brazil's population during these years. The evidence summarized here suggests that by about 1800 Brazil possessed more than two but less than three million inhabitants. Such a conclusion suggests several additional observations. First, by the turn of the nineteenth century Brazil held nearly as many people as did Portugal, whose population in 1798 stood at between three and three and a half million;[3] by contrast, Spanish America's population then outnumbered that of Spain by about 50 per cent. Second, it appears that during the course of the eighteenth century Brazil's population had grown between 2.5 and four times; however, what percentage of that growth was due to natural increase as opposed to immigration from Portugal or from Africa is impossible to say, though for the late colonial decades we do have far more abundant data concerning the volume of the slave trade than for earlier periods.

Brazil received its slaves from a number of African sources. Guiné, a major supplier during the sixteenth century, was only a minor source in the eighteenth, except for the Pará and Maranhão markets, which obtained nearly 70 per cent of their slaves from the ports of Bissau and Cacheu during the years 1757–77. Both the northerners and Mineiro gold miners preferred Guiné or Mina slaves over Angolan because they were considered more capable of withstanding hard labour. Bahians also favoured slaves from the Mina coast, i.e., four ports along the Dahomey littoral. They were able to exchange Bahian tobacco, sugar brandy (*cachaça*) and – illicitly – gold for slaves. After the Mina coast trade declined in the mid 1770s, the Bahian demand shifted mainly to the Bight of Benin. Rio de Janeiro drew the bulk of its slaves from the ports of

---

[3] *A população de Portugal em 1798. O censo de Pina Manique* (Paris, 1970), introd. Joaquim Veríssimo Serrão.

Luanda and Benguela in Angola, which is believed to have been the source of 70 per cent of the slaves sent to eighteenth-century Brazil.

Contemporary estimates of the number of slaves entering Brazil exceed those of modern scholars. Writing in 1781, the Bahian economic thinker, José da Silva Lisboa, advised his former mentor, Dr Domingos Vandelli, head of the royal botanical gardens in Lisbon, that Brazil imported more than 25,000 slaves a year. A decade later a Spanish agent of the British government stated that 19,800 slaves annually entered the three major Brazilian ports – Recife, Salvador, and Rio de Janeiro.[4] Neither informant provided sources to support his estimate and because of fraud, contraband, clerical errors, the frequent practice of counting several slaves as portions of a prime slave (a male in good health aged fifteen to 25), and scholarly differences over numerical proximates for slave tax records, as well as incomplete or missing documents, it is impossible to be certain how many slaves really did reach Brazilian ports during this period. Table 5 summarizes the best information that we possess concerning the volume and fluctuations in the slave trade.

Neither the figures offered here nor those of the well-known demographer of the slave trade, Philip D. Curtin, in his *The Atlantic slave trade: a census* (Madison, 1969), are complete. Curtin relies mainly on Mauricio Goulart, a Brazilian scholar who ignored northern Brazil and was sketchy on Pernambuco's imports. Both Curtin and Goulart ignore shipments from Guiné and Benin. But there are lacunae in our estimates as well. No reliable data have yet been found for Belém or São Luís at the beginning of the period, nor for Bahia or Rio de Janeiro in the late 1770s, nor for Pernambuco during the last fifteen years of the eighteenth century. Except for the years 1801–5, the estimates proposed here are lower than Curtin's, though they are based upon a wider array of sources. Still, the same general trends are observable: slave imports fell during the 1760s and continued to do so during the 1770s, reflecting the economic crisis of these decades; then came a revival in the 1780s, mirroring the growth of staple exports, which continued to expand, as did the slave trade, for the rest of this period.

If our knowledge of the number of slaves brought to late colonial Brazil remains incomplete, it is even more deficient with respect to the

[4] Lisboa to Vandelli, 18 October 1781, *ABNRJ*, 32 (1914), 505; 'Copia del papel que de a D^n Josef de Siqueira y Palma en respuesta de las preguntas que me hiso...', Madrid, 12 December 1791, British Library, Add. MS 13985, fo. 248r.

Table 5 *Estimates of annual slave imports into Brazil, by port of entry,*
1750–1805 ('000)

Inclusive dates	Belém do Pará	São Luís do Maranhão	Recife de Pernambuco	Bahia de Todos os Santos	Rio de Janeiro	Total	Curtin's estimates
1750–55	n.a.	n.a.	1.7	9.1	5.5	16.3 + }	16.0
1756–60	0.7	0.5	2.7	3.6	6.4	13.9 }	
1761–65	0.7	0.5	2.4	3.3	8.6	15.5 }	16.5
1766–70	0.7	0.5	2.4	2.6	7.8	14.0 }	
1771–75	0.7	0.5	2.4	2.3	6.7?	12.6 }	16.1
1776–79	0.6	0.5	2.4	4.0?	6.0?	13.5 }	
1780–85	0.6	1.2	1.0	2.4	9.2	14.4 }	17.8
1786–90	0.6	1.8	n.a.	2.4	8.9	13.7 + }	
1791–94	0.3	1.6	n.a.	3.4	8.9	14.2 + }	22.2
1795–1800	0.5	1.7	n.a.	4.4	10.0	16.6 + }	
1801–05	1.6	1.7	2.5	5.3	10.5	21.6	20.6

Sources: **Pará:** 'Recapitulação dos dois mapas dos escravos introduzidos pela companhia geral do Grão Pará e Maranhão... 1757 até 1777', AHU/PA/Pará, caixa 39; MacLachlan, 'African slave trade', 137; Joseph C. Miller, 'Legal Portuguese slaving from Angola. Some preliminary indications of volume and direction, 1760–1830', *Revue Française d'Histoire d'Outre-Mer*, 62 (1975), 171. **Maranhão:** 'Recapitulação dos dois mappas...'; MacLachlan, 139; Miller, 171. **Pernambuco:** 'Parallelo dos escravos que ficaram em Pernambuco de 10 annos antes do estabelecimento da companhia, com os 10 annos primeiros da mesma companhia...', Arquivo Histórico Ultramarino (Lisbon), codex series [AHU/CU/cod.] 1821, n. 13; António Carreira, *As companhias pombalinas de navegação, comercio e tráfico de escravos entre a costa africana e o nordeste brasileiro* (Bissau, 1969), 261; Miller, 171. **Bahia:** 'Relação dos escravos vindos da costa da Mina, desde o 1º de janeiro de 1750 thé o último de dezembro de 1755', Arquivo Público da Bahia, ordens régias (royal dispatches) [APB/OR], 54/83; P. Verger, *Flux et reflux de la traite des nègres entre le golfe de Bénin et Bahia do Todos os Santos du XVIIe au XIXe siècle* (Paris, 1968), 664; K. David Patterson, 'A note on slave exports from the costa da Mina, 1760–1770', *Bulletin de l'Institut Français d'Afrique Noire*, 33/2 (1971), 252; Carreira, 280–1; Biblioteca Nacional, Lisbon [BNL], cod. 6936; Miller, 170; Mauricio Goulart, *Escravidão africana no Brasil* (3rd edn, São Paulo, 1975), 212–15. **Rio de Janeiro:** Corcino Medieros dos Santos, 'Relações de Angola com o Rio de Janeiro (1736–1808)', *Estudos Históricos*, 12 (Marília, 1973), 19–20; Herbert S. Klein, *The Middle Passage: comparative studies in the Atlantic slave trade* (Princeton, 1978), 28 and 55; Miller, 169.

internal slave trade, i.e. the numbers of slaves admitted to one port and later transhipped to destinations elsewhere. During the first half of the eighteenth century the *câmaras* (municipal councils) of the north-eastern sugar captaincies constantly complained of shortages of slaves because of the re-export of new arrivals to the mining zones. Such complaints continued during the later decades. In 1754, for example, the câmara of Salvador protested that dealers in Rio de Janeiro and Salvador sold the best slaves to the premium markets of the interior, leaving only the refuse for local buyers. During the years 1750–9, 61.2 per cent (13,385) of the slaves brought to Pernambuco were subsequently forwarded to Rio de Janeiro for sale in the mines. But of the 21,299 slaves landed at Pernambuco between 1761 and 1770, only 1,653 (7.7 per cent) were reshipped to Rio, reflecting an upswing in the plantation economy of Pernambuco as well as a decline in the mining districts. Rio de Janeiro was the entrepot not only for slaves sold to buyers in that captaincy but also for those sent to São Paulo, Mato Grosso, and especially Minas Gerais. In 1756, for example, 3,456 slaves (37.5 per cent of those arriving at Rio that year) passed the Paraibuna checkpoint en route to Minas Gerais; in 1780 a well-informed magistrate reported that about 4,000 slaves a year, presumably including those smuggled, entered Minas from Rio. At the beginning of the nineteenth century Rio Grande do Sul, by then a prosperous agricultural and stock-raising captaincy, received 452 slaves from Rio de Janeiro and another 66 from Bahia; a few years later it took 515 from Rio de Janeiro, 28 from Bahia, and two from Pernambuco.[5] Though there is much more to be learned about slavery and the slave trade in colonial Brazil, it seems unlikely that the upswing in the trade at the end of our period significantly altered the magnitude of the population estimates offered here.

THE EXPULSION OF THE JESUITS

The expulsion of the Jesuits in 1759 constituted the first serious crisis to beset Brazil during the late colonial period. Since the first members of the Society of Jesus had entered Brazil with the founders of royal government in 1549, the Jesuits had become the premier missionary order in the colony. Their missions extended from Paraná in the south to the upper Amazon in the north, from the Atlantic coast to the Goiás plateau, though, along with other orders, they were excluded from Minas Gerais. Every major city and some interior towns like Belém de Cachoeira (Bahia) boasted Jesuit facilities: schools, seminaries, distinc-

[5] Câmara to viceroy, 6 February 1754, Arquivo Público do Estado da Bahia, ordens régias (royal dispatches) [APB/OR], 49/1051; 'Parallelo dos escravos que ficaram em Pernambuco...' (see table 5, Pernambuco); 'Lista dos escravos e cargoes que passarao neste registro da Parahibuna no anno de 1756 para o continente das minas', AHU/PA/Rio de Janeiro, 1º catalogo, caixa 40, no. 19,818; AHU/PA/Rio Grande do Sul, caixas 2–3.

tive, often sumptuous churches, religious retreats. In support of these facilities the Jesuits had become Brazil's largest landowner and greatest slave-master. Every sugar-producing captaincy possessed one or more Jesuit plantation; Bahia alone had five. From the Amazonian island of Marajó to the backlands of Piauí the Jesuits possessed extensive cattle and horse ranches. In the Amazon their annual canoe flotillas brought to Belém envied quantities of cacao, cloves, cinnamon, and sarsaparilla, harvested along the great river's major tributaries. Besides flotillas of small craft that linked producing centres with operational headquarters, the Society maintained its own frigate to facilitate communications within its far-flung network. The Jesuits were renowned as courageous pathfinders and evangelists, as pre-eminent scholars, sterling orators, as confessors of the high and mighty, and as tenacious defenders of their rights and privileges, which included licences from the crown to possess vast holdings of both urban and rural property and complete exemption of their goods from all customs duties in Portugal and in Brazil.

The Jesuits were also Brazil's most controversial religious body. From the outset they posed as champions of Indian freedom, untroubled by the fact that they themselves held thousands of blacks in slavery. They served as contentious intermediaries between Indian free workers and colonial planters and farmers. They were accused of providing asylum for legitimately ransomed Indians who had fled from merciless masters. Their economic competitors resented their special privileges and accused the Jesuits (and other religious orders) of monopolizing the spice trade of the Amazon, of engrossing lands belonging to their neighbours and tenants, and of engaging in forbidden commercial activities by means of retail sales conducted within their colleges. Such criticism was voiced by angry câmaras, which on several occasions expelled the Fathers from their captaincies during the seventeenth century, by court lobbyists, by rival churchmen, and by hostile royal officials. But the Jesuits always successfully defended themselves and, despite minor reverses, appeared to be as firmly rooted in mid-eighteenth-century Brazil as they had ever been.

The downfall of the Jesuits may be traced back to 1750, for that was the year of the ratification of the Treaty of Madrid, establishing a new boundary between Brazil and Spanish America, and of the appointment of Sebastião José de Carvalho e Melo (best known by his later title as the marquis of Pombal), a one-time Jesuit protégé, as one of the king's three ministers. He soon came to dominate the other ministers, as well as the sovereign himself (José I, 1750–77). Viewed by some writers as one of the most progressive, enlightened statesmen of the century and by others as a nepotistic, merciless, over-rated paranoiac, he was undoubtedly a proud, dynamic figure who found in the dogma of regalism the opportunities to modernize Portugal by means that had eluded his predecessors. Though Pombal became the arch-opponent of the Jesuits for two decades, the origins of his intense, uncompromising hatred for them remains unknown. The first indication that he was preparing for a fight came in 1751 in the instructions that he prepared in the king's name for his brother, Francisco Xavier de Mendonça Furtado, newly designated governor of the state of Grão-Pará and Maranhão and chief Portuguese boundary commissioner in the north. One of the instruction's secret articles warned that if the Jesuits offered opposition to the crown's policies in the Amazon, they should be informed that José I expected them to be the first to obey his orders, particularly 'because the estates which they possess are [held] entirely or for the most part contrary to the laws of the realm...'

Throughout the 1750s Mendonça Furtado, hard-driving, violent-tempered, gullible and suspicious, and the bishop of Pará, Dom Miguel de Bulhões e Sousa, a greedy, self-serving Dominican long known for his hostility towards the Jesuits and a zealous collaborator of Pombal and his brother, filled their dispatches to Lisbon with an endless stream of supposed Jesuit misdeeds. They repeated long-standing, unverified and, in fact, often discredited settlers' allegations concerning the Fathers' tyrannical mistreatment of the Indians, their monopoly of the spice trade, their reputedly enormous wealth, including that supposedly derived from hidden mines, and, on the basis of the discovery of a single cannon which the crown had authorized a generation earlier so that an exposed Jesuit mission could frighten off hostile Indian raiders, contended that the Jesuits had become an armed menace against the state and were even engaging in treasonable relations with Spaniards. (It was the Spanish Jesuits, of course, who were at the time organizing Guaraní resistance to the implementation of the Treaty of Madrid in southern Brazil.)

The voluminous dispatches that the governor and the bishop filed, those sent by Gomes Freire de Andrada, governor of Minas Gerais, Rio de Janeiro and southern Brazil, and a barrage of reports from remote Piauí concerning a bitter land dispute between the Jesuits and other landowners and a reforming royal magistrate, convinced Pombal that the Jesuits were the hidden hand behind every adversity that Portugal sustained. True, he did not blame them for the Lisbon earthquake of 1 November 1755, but he was incensed when a Jesuit orator dared to suggest that that calamity was a manifestation of God's judgement against the king's impious subjects. And he was even more indignant when another padre ill-advisedly warned that those who invested in one of Pombal's pet schemes – the Companhia do Grão-Pará e Maranhão – 'would not be members of the Company of Christ'.

Both Jesuit statements led to the arrest, imprisonment or exile of individual padres who joined others, notably foreign-born Jesuits, whom Mendonça Furtado had expelled for various alleged offences. In 1757, following a popular uprising in Oporto known as the Taverners Revolt, the Jesuits were accused of fomenting the tumult, though no proof of their involvement was ever found. Nevertheless, the charge served as the pretext for the banishment of the Jesuits from the royal palace and for the government's refusal to permit the Jesuits to continue preaching in Lisbon's cathedral. In his explanation of these measures to the papal nuncio, Pombal assured him that he possessed irrefutable proof that the Jesuits were guilty of the most heinous crimes and that if they were not immediately disciplined, within a decade they would become so powerful that all the armies of Europe would be unable to oust them from the heartland of South America, where they kept hundreds of thousands of Indians as slaves working on fortifications prepared by European engineers disguised as Jesuits. Such charges were further elaborated in a white paper prepared under Pombal's personal direction. Entitled 'Brief Account of the Republic founded by the Jesuits in the Overseas Territories of Spain and Portugal', it cited evidence purporting to demonstrate that the Jesuits constituted a state within a state, threatening Brazil's very security. Then, under Pombal's relentless prodding, the pope reluctantly designated a cardinal, a kinsman of Pombal and much beholden to him for past favours, to verify the government's charges, especially those concerning the Society's illicit commercial activities. Though he submitted no evidence and persistently refused to discuss the case with the papal nuncio, with whom he was obliged to consult, the cardinal quickly announced that all the charges were true, that every Jesuit facility was guilty of engaging in forbidden commercial and banking ventures. Two days after that report was issued, the patriarch of Lisbon, the highest ranking ecclesiastical dignitary of the realm, suspended all Jesuits within Portugal from preaching or hearing confessions.

Further humiliations followed. After an unsuccessful attack on José I in September 1758 (which may have been staged) several Jesuits were formally charged with being instigators of the regicide attempt, and in January 1759 the king ordered the arrest of all Jesuits in Portugal and the seizure of the Society's properties in the kingdom. On 3 September 1759, José I became the first Europen monarch to expel the Jesuits from all his domains and confiscate their properties.

When the top-secret instructions to arrest the Fathers and occupy their holdings were received in Brazil in late 1759, high magistrates accompanied by well-armed troops swiftly surrounded every Jesuit facility, arresting the occupants and ransacking their domiciles in the expectation of finding bullion and jewels – which, in fact, were not discovered. Closely guarded, the Fathers – approximately 670 of them – were returned to Portugal on the first available warships several months later. Although the crown had feared the possibility of popular uprisings in support of the Jesuits, none occurred, in part because of the military precision with which the detentions were accomplished and in part because the public response was conditioned by government-dictated anti-Jesuit pastoral letters distributed by co-operating bishops. As soon as former Jesuit properties were inventoried, those of a perishable nature, including crops, barnyard animals, and some (but not all) slaves, were auctioned off; in at least one captaincy, Rio Grande do Norte, they were actually distributed gratis to local inhabitants, particularly militia officers. Most of the urban properties, including blocks of rented shops, houses, and wharves, were quickly sold, but for a time the crown considered maintaining the large agricultural and stock-raising estates for their income; however, after it became obvious that such properties were constantly losing value because of mis-management and looting, they, too, were put on the auction block. Though the crown possessed a unique opportunity to diversify ownership of developed Jesuit lands by dividing them among small-holders, it refrained from doing so and sold the bulk of them to syndicates of wealthy landowners and merchants. Not all estates immediately found buyers. Some of the largest remained royal properties for as long as two decades; others, including more than 30 former Jesuit cattle ranches in Piauí and the great polycultural estate of Santa Cruz in Rio de Janeiro, remained state properties well into the twentieth century. The major Jesuit churches passed to the eager bishops and became their cathedrals, while most of the colleges were transformed into governors' palaces or military hospitals. The once impressive Jesuit libraries were pillaged and allowed to deteriorate until they became worthless.

It would, of course, be simplistic to conclude that the removal of the Jesuits and the dispersal of their assets were merely consequences of the paranoia of Pombal and his claque. The end of the Jesuits came about because of various other factors as well. Though not one of the criticisms uttered against them during the 1750s was fundamentally new, the uncompromising response of the Pombaline regime certainly did break with the tradition of church–state relationships in Portugal. The Pombaline regalists insisted that every element of society, particularly the religious, must be wholly subservient to the dictates of the king as interpreted by his ministers. The medieval concept of the two (and equal) swords was replaced by that of a single weapon ruthlessly and enthusiastically wielded by the king's ministers and their minions. Resistance, passive or active, could be interpreted only as a sign of disloyalty or treason. Certainly the reputedly enormous wealth of the Jesuits was tempting to a traditionally impecunious government, especially after it was beset by the hugely destructive Lisbon disaster. And for some years the windfall derived from the disposal of Jesuit properties lightened the crown's financial burdens, even if it failed to contribute to the development of the Brazilian infrastructure. Then, too, the physiocratic notion of the useful man was very much on the minds of the Portuguese elite, both at home and abroad. They were inclined to ridicule reclusive, contemplative monks or dedicated but impractical missionaries and to extol the virtues of the truly productive members of society, i.e., tax-paying heads of families who produced agricultural or industrial goods and who fathered sons. To men like the well-travelled diplomat Dom Luis da Cunha, Ribeiro Sanches, the peripatetic physician and self-proclaimed Jew, or the duke of Silva-Tarouca, long-time adviser to Maria Theresa of Austria, as well as Pombal himself and those who served under him, the day of the religious had passed. The modernizing state required other partners in its quest for advancement. Since the Jesuits were the largest, most influential, and most outspoken of the religious orders in the Portuguese dominions, they must be the first to be struck down.

The expulsion of the Jesuits had important but often overlooked consequences. One, especially noticeable in the 1760s, was a government campaign against former Jesuits, ex-Jesuit students and friends of Jesuits, many of whom were carefully watched and arrested on the slightest pretext and confined to gaols in Brazil or Portugal. That campaign was inspired by fears that ousted Jesuits were conspiring with the enemies of Portugal to infiltrate Brazil for seditious purposes, but it was also the product of a determined government policy to enforce religious orthodoxy in Brazil, and the episcopate of Brazil was expected to play a decisive role in the implementation of that policy through appropriate pastoral letters and close surveillance of the priesthood.

The most bizarre manifestation of that campaign was the dispatch of Giraldo José de Abranches, archdeacon of Mariana, Minas Gerais, to Belém do Pará in 1763. Abranches' mission was to conduct a special investigation for the Holy Office. Brazilians have taken pride in the fact that, unlike Spanish America or Portuguese India, colonial Brazil never had a branch of the Inquisition established there. While that is true, on several occasions during the late sixteenth and early seventeenth centuries special teams of inquisitors travelled from Portugal to Brazil to conduct lengthy inquiries. But the Abranches inquiry of 1763–9 was the first in a century and a half. Precisely why the commissioner was sent to Pará at that time remains obscure.[6]

Although the Visitor's authority extended throughout northern Brazil, he conducted hearings only in the ex-Jesuit college in Belém, and most of the 485 persons who appeared before him as confessants or denunciants seem to have come from that city and its environs. In spite of the tribunal's protracted duration, only 45 persons were identified as having committed serious offences, ranging from sorcery (21), blasphemy (6), and quackery (9) to sodomy (4), bigamy (5), heresy (2), and excessive corporal punishment of slaves (1). Nearly all were members of the lowest strata of society – Indians, black slaves, or free persons of colour – and only one was a (presumably white) sugar-mill proprietor.

The Abranches inquiry was an exceptional exercise of ecclesiastical authority in Brazil at this time, for it was more common for the bishops to be charged with responsibility for the suppression of deviance and

[6] The very existence of this mission remained unknown until 1963, when the manuscript of the tribunal was discovered in the National Library in Lisbon. See J. R. do Amaral Lapa, *Livro da visitação do santo ofício da inquisição do estado do Grão Pará* (Petropólis, 1978), which included the text of the official findings and a lengthy introduction.

the maintenance of ecclesiastical discipline. During the Pombaline era prelates were selected on the basis of evidence of severe piety, militant anti-Jesuitism, and abject subserviency to ranking secular authorities. Some of them conducted lengthy investigations during the early 1760s into alleged Jesuit misdeeds, enquiries which produced lurid if dubious testimony. After the expulsion, the episcopate was given complete authority over the religious orders and, once the Jesuits were no longer around to organize their defence, the others were powerless to resist. For a time the orders were prohibited from admitting any novices, and even after that right was restored special licences were required from the crown before new members could be admitted. Such consent was grudgingly given and by the end of the century many monasteries were half empty and most of their inmates advanced in years.[7]

Well might the heads of other orders shudder when the Jesuits were rounded up, for they knew that their turn would come. And it did. In the mid-1760s the most affluent of the remaining orders in the lower Amazon, the Mercedarians, were peremptorily recalled to the kingdom and their properties, consisting of vast cattle ranches on the island of Marajó, were seized by the crown. At the end of the same decade the crown imposed forced loans upon the wealthier religious orders which declined to surrender their properties voluntarily in exchange for government bonds. As a result of these and other measures, the religious orders in Brazil were weakened to such an extent that they never fully recovered. But the diocesan branch of the church was not much better off, and throughout the late colonial period its leaders were constantly appealing for funds to establish seminaries and augment the number of priests in non-urban areas. With rare exceptions, the crown turned a deaf ear to such requests. The enfeeblement of the Catholic church in Brazil in the nineteenth century can be traced back to the Pombaline era and to the generation that followed.[8]

[7] King to archbishop elect of Bahia, 30 June 1764, AHU/PA/Bahia, 1º catálogo, annex to no. 6554; *alvará* of 30 July 1792, Antonio Delgado da Silva (ed.), *Collecção da legislação portuguesa de 1750 a [1820]*, (9 vols., Lisbon, 1830–47), *1791–1801*, 152–3; colonial minister, circular to archbishop of Bahia, bishops of Rio de Janeiro, Funchal, and Angra, 30 January 1764, AHU/CU/cod. 603, no. 222; same to same and to bishop of Pernambuco, 19 August 1768, *ibid.*, cod. 604, no. 154; D. Antonio de Salles e Noronha, governor, to Martinho de Melo e Castro, 21 May 1781, AHU/PA/Maranhão, caixa 48; Fr Manoel de Santa Rosa Henriques to queen, *c.* 1793, AHU/PA/Pará, maço 3.

[8] George C. A. Boehrer, 'The Church in the second reign, 1840–1889', in Henry H. Keith and S. F. Edwards (eds.), *Conflict and continuity in Brazilian society* (Columbia, S.C., 1969), 114. The foregoing relies upon Manoel Barata, *Formação histórica do Pará* (Belém, 1973), 44, 78, 92–3; AHU/PA/Bahia, 1º catálogo, nos. 19,765–6, 19,687–9, and 22,826; for contemporary

ECONOMIC CRISIS AND REMEDIES

The prolonged economic malaise that afflicted Portugal and Brazil during the 1760s and 1770s constituted a deeper and more enduring crisis than that presented by the conflict between the state and the Jesuits, and remedies were less easily found. The economic crisis was preceded by the destruction of Lisbon, the imperial city and one of the leading cities of Europe, larger than Rome or Vienna, by earthquake and fire on Sunday morning, 1 November 1755 and the enormous cost of rebuilding it.[9] The crisis coincided with, and was partly caused by, two exceedingly expensive wars with Spain for control of the vast borderlands extending from São Paulo to the north bank of the Río de la Plata. The main cause of the crisis, however, was the precipitous fall in income, both public and private, from Brazil beginning in the early 1760s. There had, in fact, been warnings that the Brazilian milch cow was running dry even before the earthquake, particularly the repeated postponements in the departures of the great fleets from both peninsular and Brazilian ports during the early fifties, but such delays had occurred so often in the past that no one seemed unduly alarmed. The principal cause of the severe curtailment of the crown's income from Brazil was the declining yield of the gold and diamond mines of the interior. While the three leading bullion-producing captaincies reached peak levels of production at slightly different times, the maximum yield from the

comments on the decline of the Orders, see [Luiz Antonio Oliveira Mendes], 'Discurso preliminar...da Bahia' (c. 1789), *ABNRJ*, 27 (1905), 286, and Vilhena, *Cartas*, II, 464–5.

[9] The loss of life in the Lisbon earthquake of 1755 has been conservatively estimated at 10,000, but other guesses run much higher. The physical destruction, especially along the Tagus and in the eastern quarter of the city, was enormous. The great wooden royal palace that had graced the city's principal maritime square since the late sixteenth century, 33 noble palaces, 54 convents, all six of the city's hospitals, the newly finished patriarchal residence, the opera house, several foreign embassies, and most of the port's warehouses, filled with the cargoes of fleets recently arrived from Brazil, with shipments intended for the next outbound fleets, and with the year's wine harvest, all were gone. Out of 20,000 homes, 17,000 were in ruins. Additional damage occurred in other cities, especially Sintra, Santarém and even Coimbra. Estimates of total damage to property range up to 20,000 contos, three or four times more than the annual public revenues. The conto (1,000 milreis or 2,500 cruzados) was quoted on the London market at about £280 (1760–5 average); John J. McCusker, *Money and exchange in Europe and America, 1600–1775. A handbook* (Chapel Hill, 1978), 114. Inevitably Portugal's most important colony was expected to come to her rescue, and Brazilian cities responded generously. Salvador alone pledged to contribute 1,200 contos over the next three decades towards the rebuilding of Lisbon. Conde D. Marcos de Noronha, viceroy, to crown, 20 July 1759, C. R. Boxer manuscript collection; see also Ignácio Accioli de Cerqueira e Silva, *Memórias históricas e políticas da província da Bahia*, ed. Braz do Amaral [*MHB*] (6 vols., Bahia, 1919–40), II, 182–90. The most useful accounts of the earthquake are T. D. Kendrick, *The Lisbon earthquake* (London, 1956) and José-Augusto França, *Lisboa pombalina e o iluminismo* (Lisbon, 1976).

mining sector occurred during the latter half of the 1750s and between 1755–9 and 1775–9 there was a drop in output of 51.5 per cent. It was also during the late 1750s that the diamond mines of Minas Gerais began to give out, resulting in bankruptcy for several contractors and in an eventual royal takeover (1771), which, however, failed to reverse the steady fall in productivity of the mines. At the same time, the two major agricultural export crops of Brazil, cane sugar and tobacco, from Pernambuco, Bahia, and Rio de Janeiro, were in something of a slump, the former because of low European prices, the latter owing to difficulties with Mina coast slave suppliers. And exports of cacao from the Amazon had become irregular because of a scarcity of Indian collectors, a shortage of shipping, and a decline in prices.

One of the crown's leading sources of revenue had long been the fifths or *quintos* from Minas Gerais. During the years 1752–62 they generated an average of 108 arrobas (32 lb or 14.5 kg each) of gold a year, but that yield fell to 83.2 arrobas in the course of the next decade and to 70.8 between 1772 and 1777. Similarly, the fifths in Goiás declined by 33.6 per cent from 1752–62 to 1762–72, and by the years 1782–92 were only 29.5 per cent of the 1752–62 level.[10] One of the most lucrative customs houses in Brazil during the Age of Gold had been that of Rio de Janeiro, but between the mid-1760s and the mid-1770s its yield fell by 25 per cent. While the total value of public and private remittances sent from Rio de Janeiro to Lisbon dropped by 39 per cent between 1749 and the mid-1770s, the crown's share shrank even more alarmingly, diminishing by 73.8 per cent. Because the Rio de Janeiro branch of the royal exchequer was unable to pay its bills, its debt load increased to over 1,272 contos by 1780. But what concerned the colonial minister even more was that by that date the crown was owed over 4,000 contos from insolvent tax contractors and tax payers in ten Brazilian captaincies. Between 1752–6 and 1769 emissions by the royal mint in Lisbon declined by more than 38 per cent.[11]

Obviously this extended crisis affected many different interest groups – Brazilian planters, merchant factors, tax contractors, royal officials; Portuguese merchants, shippers, and government officials. For the

[10] 'Goiases, Rendim^{to} dos q^{tos}...', BNRJ, II–30, 34, 21, no. 1.

[11] Jorge Borges de Madeco, *A situação económica no tempo de Pombal*... (Lisbon, 1951), ch. 4; Antônio de Sousa Pedroso Carnaxide, *O Brasil na administração pombalina*... (Rio de Janeiro, 1940), 76–82; Alden, *Royal government*, 317–18, 328, 330 n. 68, 349–50, and 507–8; Corcino Medeiro dos Santos, *Relações comerciais do Rio de Janeiro com Lisboa (1763–1808)* (Rio de Janeiro, 1980), 60–2.

Portuguese government which had come to rely on the gold and diamonds of Brazil to finance the deficit in Portugal's balance of trade with the rest of the world, especially England, it was urgently necessary to find effective solutions to the problems besetting the Brazilian economy. Steps were taken to halt the decline in gold and diamond production – and to reduce smuggling – but without success. In order to improve the competitiveness of Brazilian sugars and tobaccos, the government, with rather more success, strengthened the powers of local boards of inspection (*mesas de inspecção*) previously established (1751) in major colonial ports. Presided over by high magistrates assisted by locally chosen deputies, the boards were responsible for setting quality standards for the export of both commodities, and later also of cotton; the determination of a just price between sellers and buyers; and the resolution of disputes between colonial shippers and European importers. More dramatic was the creation of two monopoly trading companies to promote the economic development of the backward north and the stagnant north-east.

The marquis of Pombal had become convinced that what Brazil and Portugal needed was a series of well-financed monopoly trading companies. Accordingly, in 1755 he persuaded a group of wealthy government officials and Lisbon merchants to invest in the Companhia do Grão-Pará e Maranhão. Its initial mission was to supply black slaves to the north, to offer attractive prices for colonial staples, existing (cinnamon, cloves, sarsaparilla, and especially cacao) and new (cotton and rice), and to transport these commodities to Portugal via its own armed convoys. By the early 1770s, however, the company began to perform other functions too. It served as a conduit through which the government conveyed large sums to maintain an expanded military presence and an augmented bureaucracy in the Amazon. It was also expected to cultivate a lucrative illicit trade with Spanish Quito via the Amazon and Mato Grosso,[12] and it was asked to develop a colonial market for the products of newly established factories in Portugal. Four years after the creation of the first company, its sister, the Companhia Geral de Pernambuco e Paraíba, was created to revive the faltering agrarian economy of the north-east. Each company was initially chartered for twenty years, the Maranhão company being nominally capitalized at 480 contos, that of Pernambuco at 1,360 contos. Shares were available to both domestic and foreign subscribers. Prominent

[12] 'Instrucção secretissima…para João Pereira Caldas', 2 September 1772, AHU/CU/cod. 599.

government officials, led by Pombal himself, were expected to invest heavily, and many did. Pressure was applied to other members of the nobility, lesser government functionaries, convents and other religious bodies, and affluent colonial merchants and planters to subscribe too. Those who purchased a minimum of ten shares were promised habits in the Order of Christ, a prestigious order of chivalry in Portugal, and exemption from certain taxes and from military call-ups. Much as they coveted those privileges and honours, colonial magnates did not rush to contribute: 90 per cent of the capital that financed the Maranhão company came from investors in the kingdom, as did 85 per cent of that behind the Pernambuco company. Of the two, the Maranhão company proved to be the better investment, yielding dividends averaging 8.4 per cent (1768–74) compared with under 6 per cent for the Pernambuco company (1760–79).

Neither company long survived the fall of the marquis of Pombal in March 1777, following the death of José I. Although Manuel Nunes Dias, the most indefatigable analyst of the Maranhão company (1755–78) confidently concludes that it was 'a great achievement (*êxito*) of enlightened Pombaline mercantilism', his own student and the author of a complementary study of the Pernambuco company (1759–79) regards that company mainly as a successful vehicle for exploitative European, especially British, capital. While both authors may be correct, it is not easy to determine how much the companies achieved for Brazil. Both obviously increased the levels of slave imports so essential for agricultural development (see table 5 above). Both provided a more dependable shipping service than had existed in the past; however, the Maranhão company did not lessen the Amazon's dependence upon cacao nor increase the volume of its exports, but it contributed to the beginnings of two new exports that would play important roles in the regional economy of the north in later decades – cotton and rice, discussed below. During the years 1760–80 the volume of both sugar and hide exports from the north-east increased significantly, though the Pernambuco company was unsuccessful in stimulating exports of new commodities in appreciable volumes. Both companies distributed to colonial markets impressive quantities of goods ranging from cotton and woollen cloth to hats, ribbons, china, silks, and hardwares manufactured in newly founded Portuguese factories, most of them opened since 1770. Lastly, both companies surrendered their monopolies but continued for many years to try to collect large sums owed them by colonial debtors, a source of continuing irritation to such planters and merchants.

Although there had been proposals to extend the system of monopoly companies to Bahia and Rio de Janeiro, they had proved stillborn, apparently because of a lack of available investment capital as well as strong British opposition. Instead, the government had moved in the opposite direction by terminating the convoyed fleet (*frota*) system that had been in effect since 1649. In spite of repeated efforts by the crown and the great Lisbon merchants to establish satisfactory shipping schedules at both ends of the vital Luso-Brazilian trade and to prohibit contraband, delays in Lisbon and in the colonial ports had become both costly and endemic and contraband rampant. After the Lisbon earthquake the number of sailings to Brazil had declined precipitously, from 262 departures in 1754–8 to only 191 in 1758–63. The Junta do Comércio (the board of trade) tried without success to reform the fleet system in order to safeguard the interests of Portuguese merchants and speed up payments to both the crown and merchants. In the end the crown decided in 1765 that the best way to accomplish that was to abolish the fleet system.[13]

The last fleets sailed together in 1766. Thereafter, with exception of wartime periods in the 1770s and in the late 1790s, properly licensed ships were free to sail whenever they pleased to Salvador and Rio de Janeiro and, after the termination of the monopoly companies, to other Brazilian ports as well. In addition, the crown also encouraged intra-Brazilian trade (*cabotagem*). Though some merchants attributed the declining volume of trade in the 1760s and 1770s to the cessation of the *frotas*, Jacome Ratton, a well-informed French businessman in Pombaline and post-Pombaline Portugal, was convinced that the establishment of free trade greatly accelerated Luso-Brazilian commerce, shortening the length of time peninsular merchants had to await their payments from the colony and making it possible for ships to make two voyages to Brazil in less than a year, whereas in the past they could expect to complete only two round trips in three years.[14]

Several other economic measures intended to stimulate trade may be briefly noted. The first was the creation of a centralized royal treasury in Portugal in 1761. One of the responsibilities of its colonial branches

[13] On the *frota* system and the monopoly trading companies, see also Mansuy-Diniz Silva, *CHLA* I, ch. 13.
[14] *Recordações sobre occurrencias do seu tempo em Portugal,...1747 a...1810* (London, 1813), 96–7.

was to offer subsidies and price guarantees to colonial producers of crops in which the crown was particularly interested (e.g., dyestuffs and fibres). Second, it was also in 1761 that the crown abolished the slave trade to Portugal, a measure undertaken not for humanitarian reasons, as some writers have contended, but to ensure an adequate supply of slaves for Brazil, where the Pombaline ministers believed they were most needed. Thirdly, in order to lessen Portugal's dependence upon foreign, especially English, manufactured goods, the government, for the first time since the reign of Pedro II (1683–1706), actively fostered the industrial sector of the kingdom. Brazil became a prime market for the output of the new factories, the source of 40 per cent or more of their earnings. It is not surprising, therefore, that in the mid-1780s, when the superintendent of contraband and thefts in Lisbon learned of the existence of small weaving shops capable of producing luxury cloths in Brazil, especially in Minas Gerais, he became seriously concerned. As a result, in 1785 the colonial minister ordered that all such shops be closed, their looms dismantled and shipped back to Portugal. Only coarse cottons intended for slaves were exempted from the well-known draconian decree of 1785, which symbolized Portugal's determination to keep Brazil exclusively an agricultural, ranching, extractive colony and to restrict most manufacturing activities to the mother country.[15]

But the crown did adopt other measures that were, in part, designed to benefit the Brazil trade. In 1797–8 it belatedly instituted a system of semi-monthly packets between the kingdom and major colonial ports to carry priority freight and mail, an innovation introduced long before in the British and Spanish empires. Then, in 1801, came a reform that had been under discussion for some years and one that must have been greeted in Brazil as a mixed blessing. The salt monopoly, in existence since 1631 and long viewed as oppressive to ranching, agricultural, and urban interests, was abolished. However, it was replaced by a system of taxes on salt extracted along the Brazilian littoral and at some points in the interior, by a new stamp tax, and by government monopolies on saltpetre and gunpowder.

Conspicuously missing from these efforts to stimulate trade was any step by the crown to facilitate transportation within Brazil, even though a programme of internal improvements might have paid large dividends in expediting the movement of goods from the interior to seaports. Not

---

[15] For further discussion of Portuguese economic policy in the late eighteenth century, see Mansuy-Diniz Silva, *CHLA* I, ch. 13.

untypical of the attitude of the government was the case of a proposed canal in Maranhão. In 1742 the câmara of São Luís called attention to the need for a canal between the Cachorro and Bocanga rivers to facilitate canoe traffic from the sertão. Submitting a plan drafted by a military engineer, it argued that such a project would also benefit the commerce on the larger Itapicurú and Mearim rivers, especially during winter months. In 1750 the crown directed the governor to contact important people in the captaincy to determine the proposal's fiscal feasibility, but they concluded that Maranhão was too poor to pay for such an undertaking. Again in 1756 the governor was directed to get the canal started and to find ways of raising local revenues to pay for it, but nothing came of that order either, because the level of exports, the only perceived taxable possibility, seemed too low. From time to time during the next two decades the câmara expressed the need for the canal, but nothing came of its appeals until 1776, when a special impost was levied upon cotton exports. Work then began on the canal but, for reasons not evident, was soon stopped. The cotton impost was still being collected in the early 1790s, even though no progress had been made on the canal for more than a decade.[16]

Land transportation remained extremely backward in late colonial Brazil. One must agree with Caio Prado Júnior that 'colonial roads were...almost without exception beneath criticism; they were no more passable even by travellers on foot and animals in the dry season, and in the wet season they became muddy quagmires, often defeating all hope of passage'.[17] What progress was made in this period came as a result of the efforts of energetic colonial governors and the co-operation, often coerced, of local communities. The most noteworthy example is the reconstruction of the *caminho do mar* between the plateau city of São Paulo and its chief port, Santos. Long in disuse because of the lack of maintenance, it was reconstructed between 1780 and 1792, thanks to the efforts of determined governors, the financial contributions of municipalities, merchants, mule-team owners, and exporters, and the labour of militia companies. The result was one of colonial Brazil's rare paved roads, one sufficiently wide so that 'two mule-teams meeting... could pass each other without stopping', and a vital avenue for opening up the agricultural possibilities of the rich plateau lands.[18] Another road

16 Martinho de Melo e Castro, 'Instrução para o governador...do Maranhão, D. Fernando Antonio de Noronha', 14 July 1792, AHU/CU/cod. 598, fols. 107r–110r.
17 *The colonial background of modern Brazil*, trans. Suzette Macedo (Berkeley, 1967), 298.
18 Elizabeth Anne Kuznesof, 'The role of merchants in the economic development of São Paulo 1765–c.1850', *HAHR*, 60 (November, 1980), 571–92.

that was improved in the late eighteenth century was the famed mule trail between Rio Grande do Sul and São Paulo. Further north, modest roads were built at the beginning of the nineteenth century in the manioc-producing regions of southern Bahia, and what was probably no more than a trail was opened up connecting the sertão with Parnaíba, Maranhão.[19] But there is not much progress to report elsewhere. It is significant that the first among the proposals suggested by a memorialist advocating the alleviation of the stagnant condition of Minas Gerais was the opening up of river routes from the coast to the interior and the construction of a series of internal highways.[20]

THE AGRICULTURAL RENAISSANCE

In the midst of the general Luso-Brazilian depression coastal Brazil began to make an economic recovery, but the depression lingered on in the interior. Given the imperfect quality of the statistics we possess, it is not possible to date the recovery precisely, but it could be said to have occurred by the early 1780s, when the agricultural renaissance of the coastal captaincies was already well established. Despite occasional downturns, that revival persisted for the remainder of the colonial period. In varying degrees the upsurge in the agrarian sector was a response to several factors: the measures adopted by the government of Pombal and his successors; the development of new industrial technology, principally in England and France (for example, in the cotton industry); the virtual disappearance of a major sugar supplier, the formerly flourishing French colony of Saint-Domingue, largely destroyed by a series of bloody upheavals beginning in 1791; and the deteriorating international situation, especially the resumption of Anglo-French hostilities beginning in 1793.

Sugar

Brazil's two leading agricultural exports, sugar and tobacco, both recovered and achieved new export levels during the late colonial

---

[19] For the Ilhéus road see Eulália Maria Lahmeyer Lobo, *História político-administrativa da agricultura brasileira 1808–1889* (Brazília, 1980), 26; the opening of the 'new road' beyond Parnaíba by João Paulo Diniz is mentioned by an anonymous writer in his 'Roteiro do Maranhão e Goiaz pela capitania do Piauí', *RIHGB*, 62/1 (1900), 64.

[20] Joze Eloi Ottoni, 'Memoria sobre o estado actual da capitn^a de Minas Gerais' (1798), *ABNRJ*, 30 (1912), 307.

period. The sugar industry, the mainstay of Brazil's exports during the seventeenth century but depressed for much of the eighteenth because of low market prices and high costs, especially of slaves, emerged from its slump. Spurred by more favourable prices, particularly at the end of the 1770s and in the 1790s, it significantly increased the volume and value of its exports. Although sugar was grown in many captaincies, the major export centres remained Pernambuco (plus Paraíba), Bahia (and the subordinate captaincy of Sergipe), and Rio de Janeiro; but at the end of the period sugar was also becoming a major crop in São Paulo. The industry had remained stagnant for decades prior to the establishment of the north-eastern monopoly company. In 1761 there were 268 engenhos in Pernambuco and Paraíba, not many more than had existed 40 years earlier. Furthermore, 40 of those mills were inoperative (*fogos mortos*) because of soil exhaustion, the disappearance of fuel supplies, the dispersal of slave gangs, and lack of maintenance. By the end of 1777, however, the number of mills in both captaincies had increased to 390 and exports had doubled.[21] We cannot trace the development of the industry in the north-east after 1777 until further research has been done.

From the data presented in table 6 below, it would appear that during the 1760s and 1770s Pernambuco regained the lead it had lost to Bahia in the middle of the seventeenth century as Brazil's principal producer, but that advantage may have been only temporary, for the industry also underwent expansion in Bahia. From 1759 until the late 1790s the number of mills in Bahia increased from just over 170 to 260, and by the latter date the sugar zone extended some 50 miles (sixteen leagues) north and north-west of the port of Salvador. By the end of the century there were also 140 engenhos in neighbouring Sergipe. Between the late 1750s and the late 1790s the level of exports, despite numerous fluctuations, increased from about 10,000 to about 11,500 crates (*caixas*); however, that figure is not as meaningful as it might seem, since the weight of the *caixa* tended to increase over time. In 1759 one contemporary wrote of crates varying from 26 to 45 arrobas while in 1781 another writer, also living in Bahia, spoke of crates of 40–60

---

[21] 'Relação do nᵒ de engenhos moentes e de fogo morto que ha nas capⁿⁱᵃˢ de Pernambuco e Parahyba...', 1 February 1761, AHU/PA/Pernambuco, caixa 50; 'Mapa dos engenhos que existem nas capitanias de Pernambuco e Paraiba...ate 31 de dezembro de 1777', AHU/CU/cod. 1821, no. 9.

arrobas. Still, the conversions generally employed in the tables of exports periodically reported to Lisbon are of crates of 40 arrobas, and that is the basis of the calculations summarized in this table. Between 1757 and 1798 the level of exports of Bahian sugars rose by 54.6 per cent and advanced another 9.3 per cent during the next decade. Since about 10 per cent of the sugar produced in Bahia was locally consumed, it appears that yearly production rose from nearly 360,000 arrobas in 1759 to about 880,000 *c.* 1807, or a gain of 69 per cent.

Dramatic changes in sugar production in this period also occurred in the captaincies of Rio de Janeiro and São Paulo. The most rapid growth in Rio de Janeiro was in the six northern parishes around the town of São Salvador dos Campos, the famous Campos de Goitacazes district, still an important source of cane sugar today. There, between 1769 and 1778, the number of engenhos nearly doubled (from 56 to 104) and production went up by 235 per cent. By 1798–9 there were 378 mills in the Goitacazes, more than half of the 616 engenhos in the captaincy.[22] Table 6 provides some idea of export levels in Rio de Janeiro from the 1770s until the end of the period. Most of the data is based on a carefully researched, recently published dissertation whose author probably understates the actual figures; at least his estimates are at considerable variance with those derived from other coeval sources.

Attractive prices and the construction of the *caminho do mar* stimulated the beginnings of an important sugar industry in São Paulo in the 1780s and 1790s. The two major areas of cultivation were along the coast north of Santos and the so-called quadrilateral defined by the townships of Sorocaba, Piracicaba, Mogi Guaçú, and Jundiaí, all situated within ten leagues of the city of São Paulo. By 1797 the plateau plantations were milling 83,435 arrobas for export. Sugar was destined to remain São Paulo's principal export crop until it was overtaken by coffee in 1850–1.

Considering the amount of scholarly attention devoted in recent decades to the Brazilian sugar industry, it seems surprising that the statistical base we possess for the late colonial period remains so incomplete. As is evident from table 6, we have estimates for the major growing areas – Pernambuco, Bahia, and Rio de Janeiro – for only two

[22] Santos, 49–51, 174; 'Mapa da população, fabricas e escravaturas do que se compoem as…freguezias da villa de…Campos…no anno de mil setecentos noventa e nove', *RIHGB*, 65/1 (1902), 295. Albergo Lamego, 'Os engenhos de açucar nos recôncavos do Rio de Janeiro, em fins do século xvii[i]', *Brasil Açucareiro* (March 1965), 18–25.

Table 6 *Estimated sugar exports from principal Brazilian regions, 1757–1807 (arrobas)*

Year	Pernambuco	Bahia	Rio de Janeiro	Totals
1757		407,824		
1758				
1759		321,584		
1760	8,000	200,000		
1761	69,720	226,000		
1762	359,080	226,000		
1763	165,320	226,000		
1764	495,640	200,000		
1765	178,400	160,000		
1766	282,160	160,000		
1767	263,120			
1768	284,160			
1769	332,160			
1770	278,160			
1771				
1772			131,515	
1773	377,760		80,184	
1774	405,480		156,515	
1775	404,640		23,779	
1776	313,200		106,773	
1777	271,000		103,926	
1778		480,000	634,349	
1779		480,000	127,741	
1780		480,000	154,944	
1781		480,000	146,082	
1782		480,000	144,200	
1783		480,000	91,750	
1784		480,000	180,141	
1785		480,000	101,141	
1786		480,000	84,053	
1787		480,000	117,140	
1788		480,000	104,646	
1789		480,000	110,027	
1790	275,000	400,000	115,615–200,000	790,643–875,000
1791			144,045–232,184	
1792			221,765	
1793			140,916–378,410	
1794			222,032	
1795			102,165	
1796			384,077	
1797		468,220	174,425	
1798		746,645	257,885–714,783	

Table 6 (*cont.*)

Year	Pernambuco	Bahia	Rio de Janeiro	Totals
1799			400,282	
1800			487,225	
1801			535,209	
1802			329,247	
1803			178,697	
1804			171,263	
1805			226,095	
1806			312,372	
1807	560,000	800,000	250,201–360,000	1,610,201–1,720,000

Sources: **Pernambuco**: 1760–77, Ribeiro Júnior, *Colonização*, 137; 1790, British Library, Add. MS 13,985, fol. 248v; 1807, Francisco Adolfo de Varnhagen, *História geral do Brasil*, v (5th edn, São Paulo, 1956), 61. **Bahia**: 1757 and 1759, João Antonio Caldas, 'Noticia geral de toda esta capitania de Bahia...desde o seu descobrimento até...1759' (fasc. ed., Salvador, 1951), fols. 438 and 442; 1760–6 and 1778–89, [Luiz Antonio Oliveira Mendes], 'Discurso preliminar...da Bahia' [*c.* 1789], *ABNRJ*, 27 (1905), 306, 315; 1790 and 1807, as for Pernambuco; 1797 and 1798, *MHB*, III, table facing 160 and 204–5. **Rio de Janeiro**: 1772–1807, Santos, *Relações comerciais*, 165; 1790 and 1807, as for Pernambuco; 1791 and 1793, 'Almanaque[s] da cidade do Rio de Janeiro... 1792...1794', *ABNRJ*, 59 (1937), 284 and 350 (from which 10% has been deducted for local consumption); 1798, Antonio Duarte Nunes, 'Almanac historico...do Rio de Janeiro' [1799], *RIHGB*, 21 (1858), 172.

years, 1790 and *c.* 1807. The former was provided by an apparently knowledgeable Spanish informant of the British government, the latter appears in the standard history of colonial Brazil and seems to be derived from contemporary sources. Those estimates suggest that Brazil's sugar exports in 1790 were about 11,500–12,700 metric tons and that by 1807 they had doubled to somewhere between 23,400 and 25,000 metric tons.

Tobacco

While several captaincies shared in the export of sugar, Bahia continued to be the dominant producer and supplier of tobacco in this period, as it had been since the inception of the industry. It was, of course, cultivated elsewhere – in Maranhão, Pernambuco, and Alagoas, for example. One of the tasks assigned to the boards of inspection in 1751 was the promotion of tobacco cultivation in areas where it did not exist or languished, but those efforts, for instance in Rio de Janeiro, were

Table 7 *Tobacco exports from Bahia to Portugal and the Mina coast,*
1750–1800, and re-exports from Portugal to foreign markets, 1764–1803
(arrobas)

Year	Shipments from Bahia			Re-exports by Portugal
	Portugal	Mina Coast	Total	
1750	161,423	150,094	311,517	
1751	(197,454)	179,367	(376,821)	
1752	254,089	(239,813)	(484,902)	
1753				
1754	201,148	(182,722)	(383,870)	
1755	199,339	97,674	297,073	
1756	186,866	75,922	262,788	
1757	247,832	124,377	372,209	
1758	80,765	139,165	219,930	
1759	173,237	146,094	319,331	
1760	125,341	118,884	244,225	
1761	151,638	127,208	278,846	
1762	56,547	179,364	235,911	
1763	292,560	(265,760)	(558,320)	
1764	33,460	(30,395)	(63,855)	102,267
1765	69,914	237,448	307,362	86,121
1766	184,942	(168,001)	(352,943)	54,452
1767				191,121
1768				100,873
1769				112,432
1770				123,850
1771				83,888
1772				97,711
1773				109,971
1774				97,161
1775				110,950
1776				175,641
1777				232,330
1778				266,410
1779				196,827
1780				122,944
1781				168,451
1782	272,296	(247,353)	(519,649)	195,406
1783	332,416	(401,976)	(634,382)	197,407
1784	374,676	(340,354)	(715,030)	286,205
1785	362,783	(329,551)	(692,334)	233,165?
1786	265,328	(241,023)	(506,351)	196,830
1787				180,175
1788				242,037
1789				224,048
1790				136,611

Table 7 (*cont.*)

Year	Shipments from Bahia			Re-exports by Portugal
	Portugal	Mina Coast	Total	
1791				174,799
1792				215,499
1793				187,996
1794				137,557
1795				171,947
1796				122,048?
1797	265,065	153,457	418,522	130,381
1798	371,607	(127,874)	499,481	130,168
1799	(253,155)	(229,965)	483,120	155,598
1800	209,734	190,403	405,859	176,178?
1801				177,535
1802				220,001
1803				233,539

Sources: **Shipments from Bahia:** 1750–66, Junta do Tabaco, Arquivo Nacional da Torre do Tombo (Lisbon) [ANTT], maços 96–106, courtesy of Prof. J. H. Galloway, Department of Geography, University of Toronto; 1782–6, 1799–1800, C. Lugar, 'The Portuguese tobacco trade and tobacco growers of Bahia in the late colonial period', in D. Alden and Warren Dean, *Essay concerning the socioeconomic history of Brazil and Portuguese India* (Gainesville, 1977), 48–9; 1797, annex to report of 1798, *MHB*, III, 204–5; 1798, 'Mapa da exportação dos produtos da capitania da Bahia para o reino e outros portos do Brazil e Africa...1798', APB, letters sent to the king, 139, no. 334. **Re-exports:** Lugar, 47.

Note: Blanks have been left when data for that year are missing. Data in parentheses have been reconstructed, based on assumption that on the average 52.4% of Bahian tobacco went to Portugal and that 47.6% went to Mina, the average for the complete years.

unsuccessful. Bahia remained the source of upwards of 90 per cent of the Brazilian tobacco that entered commerce. Though tobacco was grown in several parts of the periphery of the Bay of All Saints and in the Sergipe district, the prime centre of its cultivation, in terms of both the quantity and quality produced, was around the town of Cachoeira fourteen leagues north-west of Salvador, still a source of good cigars. Contemporaries reckoned that there were more than 1,500 tobacco farms in the Bahian region in this period and rated their annual production at about 35,000 rolls. During the eighteenth century the weight of rolls sent to Europe, as with that of cases of sugar, steadily increased from eight arrobas at the beginning of the century to between fifteen and twenty at its end, though tobacco rolls sent to Africa seem to have remained constant at about three arrobas. About a third of the annual Bahian crop was consumed within Brazil. Slightly more than half of the exports, the better qualities, were reserved for the European market (Portugal and her chief customers, the Italian ports, northern Germany, Spain, and sometimes France), while the rest, the so-called refuse, was dispatched along with sugar brandy and gold to Africa to purchase slaves.

Table 7 summarizes what is known about the volume of Bahian tobacco trade in this period and exposes several problems. First, there are the obvious lacunae which, where possible, I have tried to remedy (see note to table 7). Second, there was a market not included in the table, Angola. We know that Bahian tobacco was an important article of the slave trade there, as well as along the Mina coast. Between 1762 and 1775, for example, the Pernambucan company purchased 11,500 arrobas a year of Bahian tobacco to facilitate its Angolan slave purchases. Slaves sent to Rio de Janeiro from Angola were also procured by means of tobacco, but how much came from Bahia we do not know.

These lacunae make the generalizations that follow tentative at best. Yearly exports of Bahian tobacco appear to have averaged about 320,000 arrobas during 1750–66 and to have nearly doubled by the 1780s to almost 615,000. It has been suggested that the peak of eighteenth-century Bahian production came in the 1790s, but evidence is contradictory. Certainly prices were higher then than at any other time during the period, averaging nearly twice the level officially set in the early 1750s, and the number of ships that passed from Bahia to the Mina coast during the 1790s increased from about eleven a year (the average of the 1750s through the 1780s) to fifteen, though the number would nearly double during the first years of the nineteenth century.[23] But the known or estimated level of exports in the late 90s was markedly lower (averaging 452,000 arrobas) than during the 1780s. Furthermore, re-exports of Brazilian (mainly Bahian) tobacco by Portugal, which had increased from 108,000 arrobas a year during the 1760s to nearly 150,000 in the 70s, seem to have peaked at just under 205,000 in the 1780s, and then to have fallen to about 177,000 in the 1790s, before reaching a new plateau of close to 200,000 in the early 1800s. There is much that we still need to learn about the tobacco industry, but three conclusions seem

[23] Verger, *Flux et reflux*, 654.

firm. First, the industry was vitally important to Bahia not only because of its European earnings but especially because of the slave trade. Secondly, the industry was still expanding at the end of the colonial era, but that phase would abruptly stop in 1815, when Great Britain moved to restrict the slave trade. Thirdly, by the late eighteenth century tobacco was vastly overshadowed as a Brazilian export not only by sugar but also by an entirely new commodity, cotton.

Cotton

Though native to Brazil, cotton was not grown for commercial purposes until 1760, when the Maranhão company began making modest purchases. Its cultivation, initially confined to the delta formed by the Mearim and Itapicurú rivers, spread rapidly throughout the length of the Itapicurú until, by the 1790s, production came to centre around the town of Caxias, 184 miles south-east of São Luis.[24] Long before, cotton raising had leapt beyond the confines of Maranhão, to Pará by the early 1770s and to the littoral extending from Ceará to Pernambuco by the latter part of that decade. By the 1780s the cotton frontier was moving from the coastlands to the drier interior, where rains were less severe and the soils were sandy (e.g., the intermediate *agreste* zone of Pernambuco) and advancing into the hinterlands of Bahia, Piauí, Goiás, and Minas Gerais. Effectively those were the limits of successful cotton cultivation in this period, for efforts to spur production in Rio de Janeiro and São Paulo were unfruitful.

As table 8 indicates, Maranhão remained the leading cotton-producing captaincy for four decades. Cotton was then to Maranhão what cacao was to Pará and sugar to Bahia, Rio de Janeiro, and São Paulo, a dominant staple that justified dispatching considerable numbers of ships on a regular basis to colonial ports to load such staples and less important commodities. As Ralph Davis has reminded us, 'what really mattered to the shipowner [in the seventeenth and eighteenth centuries] was weight and volume, not value. What created demand for shipping was mass, not price.'[25] But by the early 1800s mass was shifting to the north-east – to Ceará, Rio Grande do Norte, Paraíba, and especially

---

[24] A sense of how rapidly cotton developed in Maranhão is given by Joaquim de Melo e Povoas, governor, to Mendonça Furtado, colonial secretary, 17 June 1767, ANTT, Ministerio do Reino, maço 601 (orig.).

[25] Ralph Davis, *The rise of the English shipping industry in the seventeenth and eighteenth centuries* (London, 1962), 176.

Table 8 *Brazilian cotton exports to Portugal, 1760–1807 (arrobas)*

Year	Pará	Maranhão	Ceará	Pernambuco	Paraíba	Bahia	Rio de Janeiro	São Paulo
1760		6,510						
1761		5,197						
1762		3,396						
1763		3,659						
1764		6,476						
1765		7,521						
1766		11,217						
1767		12,705						
1768		23,810						
1769		25,470						
1770		15,542						
1771		12,015						
1773		37,236					115	
1774	60	40,813					176	
1775	12	25,886						
1776	879	25,521				89	245	
1777	2,053	40,553	80			54		
1778	3,386	38,051	241					
1779	5,155	40,386					635	
1780	4,912	42,159					2,975	
1781	8,572	54,421					1,780	
1782	7,315	57,697					255	
1783	7,188	49,756					1,515	
1784	6,608	54,090					2,330	
1785	4,908	46,724					1,380	
1786	3,795	66,750					330	
1787	4,212	73,496			451		620	
1788	5,718	63,510		37,000	5,529		70	
1789	4,743	68,016			7,292		155	
1790		62,756			3,163		895	
1791		63,675			8,883		1,110	
1792		74,365	30,937	100,905	15,879		2,795	
1793		67,565		100,905			800	
1794	7,832	99,600		100,905	7,397		5,583	
1795		105,935		100,905	6,440		1,050	
1796	12,666	123,400		100,905	15,320		590	
1797	7,974	94,410		100,905		13,831	72	
1798	8,341	91,215		83,311		31,223	10,013	4,686
1799	11,569	152,485					880	
1800	15,930	203,256					1,630	
1801	10,931	145,410		107,905			2,000	160
1802	14,040	216,595		235,000			2,000	
1803		226,560		183,114			5,552	13

Table 8 (*cont.*)

Year	Pará	Maran-hão	Ceará	Pernam-buco	Paraíba	Bahia	Rio de Janeiro	São Paulo
1804	15,236	228,412	3,047	164,934		55,533	4,529	10
1805	14,710	168,693	6,248	278,329		73,955	2,608	44
1806	11,098	177,009		245,254			3,449	20
1807		206,449		334,914			1,792	

Sources: **Pará**: Except for 1804–6, Manoel Barata, *A antiga producção e exportação do Pará...* (Belém, 1915), 3–7; the remaining years from 'Balanças gerais do comércio' series, cited in Alden, 'The significance of cacao production in the Amazon in the late colonial period', American Philosophical Society, *Proceedings* (April 1976), 120/2, 134–5. **Maranhão**: 1760–78, Dias, *Companhia geral*, 353; 1783, 1788 and 1805–7, Gaioso, *Compêndio*, tables 2–3, facing 210; 1782–90 from AHU/CU/cod. 598, fols. 127 and 119; 1791–7, 1799, and 1801–3, Luiz Amaral, *História geral da agricultura brasileira* (1940 edn), II, 210–11, as quoted in Santos, *Relações comerciais*, 172–3. Amaral's figures are substantially lower than other sources used here. **Ceará**: Amaral (1956 edn), II, 30 and 'Balanças gerais' series. **Paraíba**: von Spix and von Martius, *Viagem*, II, 439. **Pernambuco**: 1788 and 1802, Frédéric Mauro, *Le Brésil du xvᵉ à la fin du xviiᵉ siècle* (Paris, 1977), 171; 1792–99, derived from data in source in n. 27; the remainder from the 'Balanças gerais' series. **Bahia**: *MHB*, III, 204–5, and 'Balanças gerais' series. **Rio de Janeiro**: Except for 1798, 1802, 1804–6, which are taken from the 'Balanças gerais' series, based on Santos, 172–3. **São Paulo**: von Spix and von Martius, I, 226–7, and 'Balanças gerais' series.

Pernambuco – whose product was esteemed as finer and cleaner than that of Maranhão.[26] The importance of cotton to Pernambuco amazed the bishop of Olinda, who wrote that its rapid progress had been so 'extraordinary' that by the turn of the century it 'almost equals [in value] sugar and all other products combined'.[27]

Several factors account for the rapid growth of Brazilian cotton. One was the ease of its cultivation and processing and another was the prospect of handsome earnings. Cotton was a far less complicated crop

[26] For near-contemporary assessments, see Henry Koster, *Travels in Brazil*, ed. C. Harvey Gardiner (Carbondale, Ill., 1966), 80, 170; L. F. de Tollenare, *Notas dominicais tomadas durante uma viagem em Portugal e no Brasil em 1816, 1817 e 1818* (Bahia, 1956), 113f; and J. B. von Spix and C. F. P. von Martius, *Viagem pelo Brasil*, translated from the German by Lucia Furquim Lahmeyer (3 vols., Rio de Janeiro, 1938), II, 455–7. The classic description and defence of the superiority of Maranhense cotton is Raimundo José de Sousa Gaioso, *Compêndio histórico-político dos princípios da lavoura do Maranhão* (1818; reprinted Rio de Janeiro, *c.* 1970); see especially pp. 178–81, 263–5.

[27] D. Jose Joaquim Nabuco de Araujo to D. Rodrigo de Souza Coutinho, colonial secretary, Recife, 16 November 1799, AHU/PA/Pernambuco, maço 21.

to produce than sugar and required no expensive equipment. The ground was prepared by the immemorial practice of slash-and-burn, which in Maranhão began after the first rains in January. A dozen seeds were then dropped into small holes three to four inches deep and spaced at intervals of five to six feet. In the north-east a variable number of seeds, depending on whether the land was situated in a humid or a dry zone, were carefully placed in furrows and covered over. Corn, beans, or manioc were sometimes interplanted with cotton, although one contemporary complained that, as with sugar cultivation, planters too often neglected to grow food crops. In Maranhão harvests began in October and November, while they started in May in Pernambuco. The processing consisted of picking the balls from the bushes and, as Whitney's gin was unknown, separating out the lint by primitive techniques. This was then baled and sacked. The sacks (weighing up to 200 lb in Maranhão and about 140 in Pernambuco) were transported to seaport warehouses by mules or river boats.

It was reckoned that a single slave could produce only 20 arrobas of cotton lint a year, half the amount expected of a slave in the sugar industry,[28] but the cotton-grower's potential profits were higher. Apart from the purchase of slaves, the owner's major expenses included their maintenance and clothing, the cost of sacking, freight, and the tithe. Even when warehouse charges, commissions, and insurance fees were added, one informant, Raimundo Gaioso, calculated that a planter's profits might come close to 50 per cent of his costs. Significantly, he had in mind a typical Maranhão planter who possessed about 50 slaves, a large and expensive gang, larger, in fact, than the slave force of many sugar planters elsewhere in Brazil. It should not be forgotten that there were risks, some peculiar to cotton-growing. Epidemics might wipe out the workforce, who were becoming increasingly expensive to replace throughout this period. And the crop might be ravaged by a plague of caterpillars, grubs, or other vermin, or rotted by excessive rains.

What made the risk worth taking was favourable prices and a constantly rising demand. In 1772 the Maranhão company was offering twice as much for an arroba of cotton as the Pernambuco company was paying for sugar. And prices continued to soar – from 3,200 réis an arroba in the 1770s to 4,500 réis in the early 1790s and to 5,900 réis by the late 1790s and early 1800s.[29] The principal reasons why prices

[28] See Schwartz, *CHLA* II, ch. 12, table 3.
[29] Melo e Castro, 'Instrução para...Noronha', fol. 96r; von Spix and von Martius, II, 502 n. 1.

continued to rise were the rapid expansion of the cotton textile industry, especially in England and France, made possible by a technological revolution, and the demand for high quality fibres for the manufacture of fine fabrics. Though much Brazilian cotton ran to coarser grades, some of that produced in Pernambuco and Paraíba was considered by Portugal's major customers as among the best available from any world source.[30]

For twelve of the years between 1776 and 1807 – 1776, 1777, 1789, 1796, and 1800–7 – we have adequate data to measure Brazilian cotton exports to Portugal and re-exports from it. During those years 5,433,087 arrobas were shipped to the kingdom, of which more than three-quarters (76.1 per cent) was sent to foreign markets, chiefly England (55.4 per cent) and France (31.2 per cent). Between 1781 and 1792 Brazil's share of the English market for raw cotton increased from 5.8 to over 30 per cent. By 1800 cotton represented 28 per cent by value of Portugal's re-exports from Brazil, compared with 57 per cent for sugar and only 4 per cent for tobacco.[31]

For another two decades cotton was to flourish in Brazil, then wither away in the face of competition from the more technologically advanced United States. Why Brazilian cotton could not successfully match that competition, who its leading producers and brokers had been, and whether, as seems likely, life on a Brazilian cotton plantation was even less bearable for slaves than it was on a sugar plantation, are among the important questions that scholars need to explore.

Rice

During the late colonial period Brazil also became a source of two important cereals, rice and wheat. Rice had long been an article of general consumption in Portugal, but it was dependent upon foreign sources of supply, especially northern Italy down to the beginning of the 1730s and from that decade onwards the new English colony of South Carolina. Carolina rice was also exported to Brazil, though a less attractive type, called *arroz da terra* or *arroz vermelha*, was apparently indigenous to Brazil. The processing of this rice was handicapped by

---

[30] Edward Baines, *History of cotton manufacture in Great Britain* (2nd edn, New York, 1966), 304–6; Michael M. Edwards, *The growth of the British cotton trade, 1780–1815* (New York, 1967), 83–4, 103.

[31] Jorge Borges de Macedo, *O bloqueio continental. Economia e guerra peninsular* (Lisbon, 1962), 44, table 5; Lugar, 'Portuguese tobacco trade', 46.

Table 9 *Brazilian rice exports to Portugal, 1767–1807 (arrobas)*

Year	Pará	Maranhão	Rio de Janeiro	São Paulo
1767		225		
1768		273		
1769		555		
1770		627		
1771		8,133		
1772		30,217	1,782	
1773	935	57,465	68	
1774	7,163	50,920	3,550	
1775	19,480	109,599	1,418	
1776	27,872	75,154	725	
1777	40,346	144,845	5,161	
1778	29,473	129,032	4,130	
1779	89,236	96,748	79,000	
1780	107,252	194,930	37,350	
1781	96,791	171,564	56,475	
1782	114,895		21,573	
1783	73,116	164,520	21,276	
1784	118,604		23,841	
1785	84,681		36,792	
1786	83,849		27,324	
1787	136,022		28,575	
1788	85,521	313,434	7,425	
1789	96,140		9,014	
1790		199,699	18,684	
1791			64,620	
1792			12,816	
1793			24,854	
1794	103,503		3,600	
1795			25,065	
1796	46,880		176,000	
1797	90,171		14,994	
1798	59,618		97,096	
1799	46,417			
1800	90,836	294,950	19,940	
1801	39,172		15,363	135
1802	65,467		9,310	891
1803			38,534	265
1804			11,088	
1805		235,243	33,961	21,472
1806		374,331	29,889	52,695
1807		321,595	135,078	62,525

Sources: **Pará**: Barata, *Antiga producção*, 3–7. **Maranhão**: 1767–78, Dias, *Companhia geral*, 353; 1779–81, 'Mapa dos effeitos exportados da cidade do Maranhão para Lisboa no anno de 1779...1780...1781', BNL, no. 7194; 1783, 1788, 1805–7, Gaioso, *Compêndio*,

the absence of husking and polishing mills. The first rice mill was built two leagues from the city of Rio de Janeiro in 1756, its owner being given the customary monopoly on the polishing of all rice produced in the captaincy. The initial rice shipments from Rio de Janeiro to the kingdom began about 1760, but the enterprise did not prosper.

That venture, however, alerted Lisbon authorities to the possibility of stimulating rice culture elsewhere. In 1766 the local administrator of the Maranhão company was directed to distribute Carolina rice seed to farmers in Maranhão. Though exports from that captaincy began by the latter part of the decade (see table 9), their level was disappointingly low, partly because growers preferred to cultivate local rice, which was heavier and larger grained, and also because of a shortage of processing mills. The governor and company officials exerted pressure upon growers to switch to Carolina rice, and new mills, modelled in part after one built by a wealthy local planter and slaver, an Irishman known as Lourenço Belfort, were constructed. Rice culture became firmly established in Maranhão by the early 1770s. Its success there prompted the crown to instruct the governor of neighbouring Pará to introduce Carolina rice there too, and with the aid of a French-born engineer, Theodosio Constantino Chermont, rice cultivation began in Pará in 1772. By 1781 Portugal was receiving sufficient rice from Brazil to be able to bar further entry of all foreign rice.

The sketchy statistics available concerning the levels of Brazilian rice exports in this period are summarized in table 9. It is evident that Maranhão, where rice was cultivated primarily in the lower Itapicurú river and where it became the second most important crop after cotton, continued to be the major source of supply. In Pará, where the rice bowl was around the town of Macapá, north-west of Belém, rice followed cacao as the captaincy's leading export, but after the 1780s exports became increasingly irregular, for reasons that remain to be determined. In Rio de Janeiro rice continued to be grown in low-lying areas north of the capital, but much of that captaincy's harvest was locally

tables 2–3, facing 210. 'Resumo da exportação...1805 a 1812', 220. **Rio de Janeiro**: Except for 1779, 1796, and 1807, based on Santos, *Relações comerciais*, 165 (where the data is expressed in sacks, which I have assumed corresponded to the legal definition of 2.25 arrobas, though I suspect that they may have weighed more); for the sources for 1779 and 1796, see Alden, 'Manoel Luis Vieira: an entrepreneur in Rio de Janeiro during Brazil's...agricultural renaissance', *HAHR*, 39 (Nov. 1959), 536–7; 1807, 'Balança geral...1807', BNL, no. 9198. **São Paulo**: von Spix and von Martius, I, 224.

consumed. There were occasional shipments from Bahia and shortly after 1800 São Paulo, a dominant supplier in modern times, began to export rice, apparently from plantations north of the port of Santos.[32]

Wheat

The south, specifically Rio Grande do Sul, also became a wheat exporter of consequence in this period – an especially welcome development from the crown's point of view, since Portugal had long suffered from chronic wheat deficits, the yields of peninsular crops being supplemented in the eighteenth century by imports from northern Italy, the Low Countries, England, and the Azores. During the Pombaline years 15–18 per cent of the grains consumed in the kingdom came from abroad. Wheat, together with codfish, olive oil, and wine, was one of the principal cargoes brought to Brazilian ports by the annual fleets, and when supplies were short governors and câmaras strove frantically to control supplies of the major alternative, manioc flour, which, though widely produced throughout tropical Brazil, was commonly disdained by the elites as fit only for slaves and other common folk.

Wheat growing in Rio Grande do Sul began about 1770 but, as with the cultivation of rice, its production was initially restricted by the absence of grist mills or of a knowledge of how to make them. In 1773 the crown dispatched a master carpenter and a master miller from Lisbon to remedy that problem, and three years later they returned from Rio Grande do Sul having apparently accomplished their mission. By 1780 wheat was being sown at the northern and southern extremities of the Lagoa dos Patos, around the towns of Porto Alegre and Rio Grande, the first centres of wheat farming in the captaincy, and in exceptional years yields as high as 70:1 were attained. Grain shipments to other parts of Brazil began in the early 1790s, averaging nearly 94,000 *alqueires* (75,200 bushels)[33] a year, and by the turn of the century the annual harvest reached nearly 160,000 bushels. Half of the crop was sent to Rio de Janeiro, Bahia, and Pernambuco, and wheat joined processed beef and hides as one of Rio Grande do Sul's most conspicuous exports. The availability of a local grain source within Brazil meant that Portugal was able to reduce wheat shipments to Brazil and apparently to lessen her dependence on foreign sources.

[32] D. Alden, 'Manoel Luis Vieira', 521–37.
[33] The local *alqueire* was approximately twice the volume of that of the kingdom.

Cacao

One Brazilian export for which Portugal had only limited use was cacao. The Maranhão company had been set up in part to stimulate and stabilize cacao exports from the Amazon, which had been irregular since the 1740s. By the time the company's charter lapsed, cacao was also being produced in two other captaincies, Maranhão and Bahia; by 1800 Rio de Janeiro would also become an exporter. But Pará remained the dominant supplier. Between 1777 and 1807 its share of Brazilian cacao exports never fell below 87 per cent and was usually much higher. Pará's export levels (ranging from 1.6 to 1.9 million lb a year) remained about the same throughout the late 1770s and 1780s, at a time when European prices were generally low. Although prices rose rapidly during the 1790s, when the long cycle of maritime wars began, Pará did not immediately respond by increasing its exports, perhaps because insufficient shipping was available. However, the continued shortage of cacao derived from other New World sources, especially from Venezuela, during the first years of the nineteenth century did stimulate a spectacular increase in shipments from the Amazon which averaged 5.5 million lb (171,875 arrobas) a year (1800–7), much the highest level attained in colonial times. By then Brazil had become the second- or third-ranking New World supplier. One-half to two-thirds of Brazilian cacao was re-exported by Portugal to seven European lands, led by France and the north Italian ports.[34]

Coffee

Cacao was to remain the dominant export of the Amazon for another half-century. Long before then, however, it was to be superseded as Brazil's most important beverage source by its rival, coffee. The origins and early development of Brazilian coffee are still curiously murky. It seems surprising that coffee aroused so little interest in either Brazil or Portugal during the eighteenth century. It was the subject of few *memórias* or royal directives, and contemporaries who wrote about the state of the economy of Brazil rarely mentioned coffee, nor was it commented on by foreign visitors to Brazil. And while the archives are full of petitions framed by other interest groups, especially sugar

---

[34] Alden, 'Cacao production', 103–35.

Table 10 *Coffee exports from Brazil, 1750–1807 (arrobas)*

Year	Pará	Maranhão	Pernam-buco	Bahia	Rio de Janeiro	São Paulo
1750	4,944					
1751	5,483					
1752	1,429					
1753	9,944					
1754	256					
1755	7,214					
1756	3,590					
1757	3,641					
1758	852	740				
1759	4,344	4,035				
1760	8,470	2,295				
1761	5,919	7,440				
1762	3,833	6,775				
1763	2,639	1,695				
1764	4,292	2,390				
1765	6,270	4,735				
1766	5,104	5,300				
1767	6,422	5,418				
1768	4,052	6,017				
1769	189	4,639				
1770	3,088	2,021				
1771	7,393	4,284				
1772	4,815	5,202				
1773	4,273	2,646				
1774	141	2,547				
1775	4,468	4,005				
1776	5,792	7,000		33	3	
1777	3,542	3,600				
1778	6,579					
1779	4,513	101			10	
1780	3,122	68			60	
1781	2,838	81			10	
1782		14			810	
1783					120	
1784	1,796				70	
1785	1,683				25	
1786	1,282				445	
1787					345	
1788		30			560	
1789					625	
1790					470	
1791					609	
1792					2,752	
1793					180	

Table 10 (*cont.*)

Year	Pará	Maranhão	Pernam-buco	Bahia	Rio de Janeiro	São Paulo
1794	2,811				3,171	
1795	5,150				235	
1796	4,042	165		1,983	8,454	13
1797	3,576	23		758	5,231	107
1798	5,019	155		2,020	14,642	528
1799	3,224	97	20	4,917	17,147	
1800	4,903	304	137	5,193	41,582	
1801	2,562	208		4,872	20,678	132
1802	4,793			6,433	31,836	116
1803	6,255		584	6,927	53,191	675
1803						243
1805	2,623			4,267	61,868	954
1806	2,656	132	303	553	70,574	1,060
1807		257		4,979	103,102	2,184

Sources: **Pará**: 1750–5, 'Mappa dos differentes generos que…da cidade do Pará consta se exportarao do seu porto…1730…1755…', AHU/PA/Pará, caixa 38; 1755–72, Dias, *Companhia geral*, 291–2; 1773–1802, Barata, *Antiga producção*, 3–7; 1803, 1805–6, 'Balanças gerais do comércio' series, in Alden, 'Cacao production'. **Maranhão**: 1758–77, Dias, 293; 1779–81, BNL, no. 7194; 1782 and 1788, Gaioso, *Compêndio*, tables 2–3; 1796–9 and 1806–7, 'Balanças gerais' series. **Pernambuco and Bahia**: 'Balanças gerais' series. **Rio de Janeiro**: 1776–95, Santos, *Relações comerciais*, 165; remaining years from 'Balanças gerais' series. **São Paulo**: 1796–8, 'Balanças gerais' series; 1801–7, Afonso de Escragnolle Taunay, *Historia do café no Brasil*, II (Rio de Janeiro, 1939), 281.

planters and tobacco growers, coffee planters were as strangely silent as manioc farmers were.

Coffee has been so long identified with São Paulo that it may seem surprising to recall that its first Brazilian home was the Amazon. Seed, brought apparently from Cayenne, was planted in farms around Belém in the 1720s, and the first trial shipments to Lisbon were made in the early 1730s. In 1731 the crown, primarily interested in the development of Amazonian stocks of cinnamon, offered producers of cinnamon or coffee exemption from all customs duties for a dozen years. Thirteen years later, in response to a plea from the câmara of Belém, the crown prohibited foreign imports of coffee, even though between 1736 and 1741 only 1,354 arrobas had reached Lisbon from Pará, compared with 564 from India and 1,494 from other foreign sources.[35] By 1749, according to a regional historian, there were 17,000 coffee trees in Pará,

[35] Overseas council to king, 26 June 1742, AHU/PA/Pará, caixa 10.

yet exports remained below 2,500 arrobas, compared with nearly 58,000 for cacao. In fact, coffee never really flourished in Pará. At no time in the late colonial period did exports of it exceed 8,500 arrobas and the same was true of Maranhão, where coffee was first grown in the 1750s (see table 10).

Between the 1760s and 1790s coffee-growing spread from the north of Brazil to Pernambuco, Bahia, Rio de Janeiro, Minas Gerais, and São Paulo. In Rio de Janeiro, where the crop first attained significance, it was cultivated near the capital in such now fashionable sections as Lagoa de Rodrigo de Freitas, Gávea, and Tijuca. By the nineties, if not earlier, coffee-houses – prototypes of the ubiquitous *cafezinho* bars so characteristic of modern Brazilian cities – made their appearance in Rio de Janeiro, increasing from 26 to 40 during the last lustrum of the century.

By the 1790s, 70 years after its introduction, coffee was finally becoming a significant Brazilian export, at least from Rio de Janeiro. Between 1798 and 1807 its coffee exports grew sevenfold, attaining nearly 1.5 million kg by the latter year. By the early 1800s, in spite of its reputation for tasting bitter because of improper drying procedures, Brazilian coffee was to be found in markets all the way from Moscow to Venice, in Hamburg, Copenhagen, Amsterdam, Paris, Lisbon, and the ports of the Barbary coast.

Both traditional and new commodities thus contributed to the economic revival of late colonial Brazil. The dramatic increase in the volume of Brazilian exports in just over a decade at the very end of the period is depicted in table 11.[36] The table clearly indicates the declining importance of gold, now less than half the value of hides, for example, and the rise of Rio de Janeiro and its chief dependency, Rio Grande do Sul. Because of sugar, coffee, indigo, hides, and gold, Rio de Janeiro had become the economic centre of Brazil in this period and, like Pernambuco, had surpassed Bahia, long the economic mainstay of the colony. In spite of persistent high expectations and very considerable crown investment, Maranhão and, more particularly, Pará lagged far behind the rest of coastal Brazil.

It should be remembered that the economic gains registered during this period were achieved using backward forms and techniques. Despite the elimination of the Jesuits and the harassment of other

[36] See also Mansuy-Diniz Silva, *CHLA* I, ch. 13, table 7.

Table 11 *Principal Brazilian exports to Portugal, 1796 and 1806 (contos de réis)*

Place	Foodstuffs[a]		Chiefly tobacco[b]		Drugs[c]		Cotton		Hides		Gold		Totals	
	1796	1808	1796	1806	1796	1806	1796	1806	1796	1806	1796	1806	1796	1806
Rio de Janeiro[e]	1,457	2,109.6	53	97.7	139.4	189.7	28.5	26.9	233.5	1,393	1,790.5	853	3,702	4,670
Bahia	2,721	1,794.8	575.8	446.7	24.8	27.4	345.8	399.7	242.3	570	50	46	3,961	3,284.7
Pernambuco[d]	1,207	1,697	2.5	1.5	4.4	20.8	827	1,844.3	199.4	227	0.3	26	2,250	3,817.8
Paraíba	65				0.1		82.4		4.9		0.8		153	
Maranhão	171	316.6	7.3	19.4	1.1		845.9	1,148	28.6	32.5	8	8.8	1,055	1,527.7
Pará	186	614	0.8	0.6	8.8	78.1	71	71	22.6	16.4	5.9	5.6	297	785.9
São Paulo[e]	41.8	1.7			0.2		0.5		7.0		0.5		55	
Ceará						1.5		54		9.5				67.4
Totals	5,858.8	6,533.7	639.4	565.9	178.8	319.9	1,592.9	2,398.2	732	2,248.4	1,995.3	939.4	11,473	14,153.5

[a] Incl. rice, sugar, cacao, coffee. [b] Incl. wax (from Africa), snuff, etc. [c] Incl. indigo, quinine, sarsaparilla, brazilwood and hardwoods. [d] In 1796 included Ceará, Alagoas, and Rio Grande do Norte. In 1806 included Paraíba. [e] Incl. Santa Catarina, Rio Grande do Sul and (in 1806) São Paulo.

Source: Balbi, *Essai statistique sur le royaume de Portugal et d'Algarve...*, I (Paris, 1822), tables I and III, facing 430.

land-owning religious orders, no fundamental changes occurred in land tenure. The rise of cotton, the expansion of sugar, and the growth of livestock ranching, particularly in Rio Grande do Sul, merely accentuated existing patterns of latifundia. And the backbone of the plantation and ranch labour force remained, as it had been since the sixteenth century, black slaves. If the figures presented above in table 5 are reasonably accurate, it appears that slave imports increased by 66 per cent between 1780–5 and 1801–5, a direct consequence of the agrarian revival. But slave labour still meant hoe culture, for the plough was virtually unknown in Brazil at this time and, with the exception of tobacco growers, Brazilian planters still resisted the use of any form of fertilizer save wood ash.[37] Slash-and-burn practices, borrowed from the Indians, remained the customary method of land clearance and soil 'preparation'. Sugar planters continued with reckless abandon to destroy the forests to fuel their processing plants, further depleting an already scarce resource in many areas. Neither bagasse, the residue of crushed cane, nor the Jamaican train, both developed in the Caribbean sugar industry to economize on fuel, were extensively employed in Brazil. Though the need for agricultural innovations was certainly recognized, basic changes did not occur, and the agricultural improvement manuals that the government sent to Brazil, beginning in the 1790s, were expensive and, not surprisingly, often rotted in warehouses.[38]

Moreover, the benefits of the economic surge were largely confined to the littoral of Brazil, while the interior, which in minor ways contributed to the seaports' volume of exports, languished in decadence. Except for Minas Gerais, where gold mining continued on a reduced scale, and enlightened methods of stock raising accompanied subsistence agriculture, the interior became a largely barren land. Such was the case, for example, with Piauí, a region of extensive, mostly absentee-owned cattle ranches and little else. Once a major supplier of cattle to the gold

[37] The frustrating efforts of one enlightened governor to bring about agricultural improvements, including the use of fertilizer, may be seen in the correspondence of Dom Francisco Inocêncio de Sousa Coutinho, the governor of Pará, with his brother, Dom Rodrigo de Sousa Coutinho, the colonial minister, in Biblioteca e Arquivo Público do Pará. Belém [BAPP], cod. 683, nos. 5 and 99; cod. 685, no. 42 and annex; cod. 689, no. 200; and cod. 703, no. 34.

[38] For contemporary criticism of Brazilian agriculture, see Vilhena, *Cartas*, I, 174–5, and Diogo Pereira Ribeiro de Vasconcelos, 'Breve descripção geographica, physica e politica da capitania de Minas Gerais', (1806), *Revista do Arquivo Público Mineiro*, 6 (1901), especially 837–8. On the failure to protect forests, F. W. O. Morton, 'The royal timber in late colonial Bahia', *HAHR*, 58 (February 1978), 41–61.

camps of Minas and the urban market of Salvador, it saw the Mineiro market decline in the 1760s with the falling off in gold production and the development of a more efficient kind of pastoralism in Minas itself. By about 1770 the number of *boiadas* (drives) sent annually from Piauense ranches via the banks of the São Francisco river to Minas had declined to 50 per cent of their 1750s level, and soon they disappeared altogether. Twenty years later the most devastating of a series of eighteenth-century droughts (*secas*) destroyed half the Piauense herd, a blow from which the economy did not recover for decades. The inability of Piauí to supply its other major market, Salvador, after the onset of the 'Great Drought' enabled a distant economic rival, Rio Grande do Sul, to capture the Bahian market for processed (salted or sun-dried) beef.

The 'Great Drought' also devastated parts of the interior of Maranhão and Ceará, but it was probably most seriously felt in Goiás. There the rapid exhaustion of gold placers in the 1760s left no money-making alternative, such as cotton or rice, to stock raising, since agriculture had never developed at a more than rudimentary level and the difficulties of transport made it impossible to dispose of surpluses to the more populous littoral. The *seca* of the 1790s was thus a serious blow to the local economy. Little wonder that while royal expenses were kept at an average of 62 contos a year (1762–1802), income fell steadily from 87 contos in 1765 to less than 33 in 1802.[39]

But Portugal had long operated marginal parts of the empire at a deficit: for example, her remaining enclaves along the west coast of India, which were sustained throughout most of the eighteenth century by subsidies from Lisbon; Mozambique; and (in the late colonial period) Mato Grosso and the upper Amazon, the sub-captaincy of São José do Rio Negro. It had long been Portuguese practice to compensate for fiscal losses produced in some parts of its empire with surpluses gathered elsewhere. In the sixteenth century India produced a large share of imperial income, but it is doubtful in spite of the royal monopoly on brazilwood, whether the crown netted much income from Brazil at all.[40] One of the earliest estimates of imperial income for the seventeenth century is that of a career fiscal officer, Luiz de Figueiredo Falcão, who indicates that at the opening of the century the state (*estado*) of India provided 45 per cent of crown income (760 out of 1,672 contos),

---

[39] Santos, *Relações comerciais*, 72–5.
[40] On this point see Johnson, *CHLA* I, ch. 8.

compared with a mere 2.5 per cent (42 contos) from Brazil, scarcely more than the yield of the Azores.[41] If we may believe Fr Nicolao d'Oliveira, who published his *Livro das grandezas de Lisboa* in 1620, income from India fell precipitously during the intervening years (to 412.5 contos, or 23.6 per cent of total crown revenue), while that of Brazil increased to 54 contos (3 per cent of the total), but he notes that the entire yield from Brazil was spent within the colony.[42]

Without question Brazil's share of total royal income increased steadily during the seventeenth century and markedly during the eighteenth century, but by how much is hard to say. A calculation for 1716 indicates that out of a total royal income of 3,942 contos, 545 (13.8 per cent) came from Brazil. In 1777 the treasurer general reported to the queen that the crown's ordinary income amounted to 4,400 contos. But he showed only 636 contos as originating within the empire, of which 24.5 came from India and the rest from Brazil. However, 1777 was a singularly bad year for income from Portugal's leading colony because of the borderlands' conflict with Spain. Not recorded is a remittance of 297 contos from Rio de Janeiro and an additional 131.8 contos from various other captaincies, diverted to Rio de Janeiro to defray extraordinary expenditures of the viceregal exchequer. If we add both sums to the reported remittances, total royal income from Brazil would have been 1,195 contos, or 27.15 per cent of the crown's ordinary income that year.[43]

Unfortunately, from 1777 until 1805 we lack details concerning the levels of crown income. Balbi, the French geographer, reports that it peaked in 1805 at 11,200 contos, almost three times greater than receipts in 1777. Brazil's share of that total must have been very large, but it is not ascertainable since Balbi never received the promised income breakdown, nor has it subsequently come to light.[44]

There are, however, statistics that demonstrate the extent of Brazil's contribution to Portugal's foreign trade during the last years of this era. According to the Portuguese historian Jorge Borges de Macedo, between 1789 and 1807 the volume of that trade quadrupled. Table 12

---

[41] *Livro em que se contem toda a fazenda, & real patrimonio dos reynos de Portugal, India, ilhas adjacentes...& outras muitas particularidades* (1607) (Lisbon, 1859), 7f.

[42] Fr Nicolao d'Oliveira, *Livro das grandezas do Lisboa* (Lisbon, 1620), 173–185v.

[43] J[oão] Lúcio de Azevedo, *Épocas de Portugal económico...* (2nd edn., Lisbon, 1947), 463; 'Reflexões ao resumo da receita e despeza do erario regio do anno de 1777', Biblioteca da Ajuda, Lisbon, 51–x–11, no. 57; Alden, *Royal government*, 328, 339, and 344.

[44] *Essai statistique*, I, 304.

Table 12. *Origins of exports from Portugal to Europe, Barbary, and the United States of America, 1789, 1796, 1806 (contos de réis)*

	Place of origin						Percentage
Year	Portugal	Atlantic islands	Brazil	Asia	Other	Total	Brazilian
1789	3,251.1	0.6	3,965	702	20	7,534.5	52.6
1796	3,911.8	11.4	9,833	277	1,928	16,013	61.7
1806	6,080.2	34.0	14,506	624	2,010	23,255	62.4

Sources: 'Alfabeto das importaçoens e exportaçoens do reino de Portugal com as naçoens estrangeiras em...1789', Ministério das Obras Públicas, Arquivo Geral, fols. 31v–32r; Balbi, *Essai statistique*, I, 442.

demonstrates that during three of those years for which we have sufficient data Brazil supplied between one-half and two-thirds of the products that contributed to the expansion of the mother country's commerce. Thanks to Brazil's non-mineral exports, the balance of trade between Portugal and her principal trading partner, England, was completely altered at the end of the late colonial period. From the beginning of the century until 1791 that balance had always heavily favoured England, but from 1791 until 1810 it shifted substantially in Portugal's favour.[45] Of the products that Portugal sent to Britain during those two decades 35.7 per cent were of Brazilian origin. Similarly, the terms of trade between the kingdom and another important customer, France, also shifted in Portugal's favour in the early 1800s, mainly because of heavy purchases of Brazilian cacao, coffee, cotton, indigo, and sugar.[46]

Such statistics were naturally pleasing to Portuguese merchants and to high authorities, but there were others that caused concern. In spite of Portugal's favourable trade balances with her European markets, the value of Portuguese-made manufactured goods sent to the empire declined by 69 per cent between 1801 and 1807. Such a decline, which very likely began a decade earlier, was particularly alarming since nearly

[45] Excepting only 1797 and 1799. Balbi, I, 441. The Anglo-Portuguese trade balance from 1698 to 1775 is given in H. E. S. Fisher, *The Portugal trade 1700–1770* (London, 1971), 16; from 1776 to 1800 in Elizabeth Boody Schumpeter, *English overseas trade statistics 1697–1808* (Oxford, 1960), 17–18, tables 5–6; and from 1801 to 1810 in Macedo, *O bloqueio*, 41, where the data is expressed in contos, convertible at £ stg = 3,555.5 reis. See also Mansuy-Diniz Silva, *CHLA* I, ch. 13, tables 4, 6, and 7.

[46] Macedo, *O bloqueio*, 38, 42, 201–3.

Table 13 *Balance of trade between Portugal and leading Brazilian captaincies, 1796–1806 (contos de réis)*

Year	Rio de Janeiro[a]		Bahia		Pernambuco		Maranhão		Pará	
	Exp.	Imp.	Exp.	Imp.	Exp.	Imp.	Exp.	Imp.	Exp.	Imp.
1796	3,702	2,474	3,960	2,070	2,250	1,384	1,055	635	297	330
1797	916	3,721	1,661	2,734	850	1,270	352	462	256	226
1798										
1799	4,526	6,575	4,002	3,818	2,647	3,369	836	1,372	448	565
1800	4,840	4,080	2,640	2,306	2,270	1,733	1,956	1,819	628	418
1801	6,290	5,332	3,503	2,985	3,335	1,377	1,354	778	295	194
1802	3,643	3,579	2,620	2,506	2,295	2,362	1,378	1,143	417	538
1803	3,295	3,493	2,914	3,042	2,504	1,779	1,892	1,187	717	410
1804	3,245	3,959	2,700	2,858	2,914	2,880	1,807	978	512	645
1805	3,960	3,150	3,736	2,340	3,975	2,614	1,584	754	647	626
1806	4,670	3,056	3,385	2,110	3,818	1,789	1,528	832	786	653

[a] Includes São Paulo and Rio Grande do Sul.
Source: 'Balanças gerais', series, in Alden, 'Cacao production', 134–5.

four-fifths of such goods were supposed to find markets in Brazil, whose economy for the most part was flourishing.

The explanation for the lessening demand for Portuguese goods in Brazil is not hard to find. It lay in the growth of foreign, especially British, smuggling – 'a scandalous scourge', as the colonial minister bitterly declared, 'which extends to almost all the Brazilian captaincies'. If that minister's sources are to be trusted, by the mid-1780s a dozen English ships a year were boldly sailing direct from England to Brazilian ports in defiance of Portuguese laws to the contrary, and exchanging British manufactures for Brazilian raw materials.[47]

Smuggling had always been prevalent in Brazil, and to combat it the crown devised elaborate procedures to discourage unauthorized foreign ships from seeking admission to Brazilian ports under the pretext of being in distress but actually in order to engage in clandestine trade. Those procedures were often so rigorously enforced in the past that sea captains like James Cook charged zealous colonial officers with being despotic and inhumane. Nevertheless, they served to discourage all but three or four distressed vessels (*arribadas*) a year from entering, for

[47] Melo e Castro, 'Instrução', fols. 92v–98v.

example, Rio de Janeiro. But it is patent that by the 1780s and 1790s foreign ships were frequenting Brazilian ports in ever growing numbers, especially the premier port of Rio de Janeiro, where the number of British *arribadas* increased from eight to 30 a year between 1791 and 1800.[48]

As a consequence of the growth of the contraband trade in imported foreign manufactured goods and the increasing value of colonial exports because of an exceptionally strong European market, Portugal found herself in the undesirable – and from the perspective of crown officials absurd – position of having an adverse balance of payments with important parts of Brazil. The results are summarized in table 13.[49] Well might the colonial minister conclude that if the situation did not improve, 'within a few years this kingdom will be drained of money'. And, he might have added, the Brazilians might as well declare their independence.

SIGNS OF POLITICAL UNREST

The two decades before the transfer of the Portuguese court to Rio de Janeiro (1807–8) in fact witnessed several abortive conspiracies intended to free parts of Brazil from Portuguese rule. The first is the much-studied Mineiro conspiracy of 1788–9, organized in the city of Ouro Preto by a small group of Mineiro and Paulista intellectuals, some of whom were poets and admirers of the achievements of the first American revolution. Though Minas had obviously been in economic recession since the early 1760s, the immediate precipitant of the plot was the determination of the colonial secretary, Martinho de Melo e Castro, to collect large sums that he considered were due the crown. Melo e Castro (1716–95), an experienced diplomat and secretary of state for the navy and overseas territories since 1770, when he succeeded Pombal's late brother, Francisco Xavier de Mendonça Furtado, was the only person of his rank to survive in office after Pombal's dismissal. He shaped (or mis-shaped) Portugal's colonial policies for two and a half decades. Ignoring evidence to the contrary, he became convinced that the persistent shortfall in revenues from Minas was a consequence not of the exhaustion of the placers, but of the wilful negligence of public

---

[48] Santos, *Relações comerciais*, 119. Between 1791 and 1798, thirty-nine foreign ships were admitted to the port of Salvador under similar circumstances. Luis Henrique Dias Tavares, *História da sedição intentada na Bahia em 1798* ('*A conspiração dos alfaiates*') (São Paulo, 1975), 88.
[49] See also Mansuy-Diniz Silva, *CHLA* I, ch. 13, tables 5 and 8.

authorities in the captaincy and of the wholesale frauds perpetrated by mining entrepreneurs, tax contractors, and others. Brushing aside proposals to ameliorate the depression in Minas, he directed the newly designated governor, the Visconde de Barbacena, to undertake prompt efforts to collect the arrears, which in 1788 totalled 5,455 contos. Melo e Castro's 'root and branch' reform was bound to be painful to mine operators, tax contractors, ranchers, ecclesiastics, merchants, and even royal officials in the captaincy, yet, strangely, he saw no need to send troops from Rio de Janeiro to accompany the new (and untried) governor in enforcing such a draconian programme.

The conspirators, consisting of several ecclesiastics, a prominent landowner, two dragoon officers, one of whom was popularly called 'Tiradentes' (the tooth-puller), planned their uprising in December 1788. Associated with them was a larger, shadowy group including a local magistrate, several heavily indebted tax contractors, other land-owners, and troop commanders. Their intent was to establish a Mineiro republic, where existing restrictions on diamond extraction, coinage, and manufacturing would no longer exist, and all debts to the Portuguese crown would be excused. They planned to establish a university (none existed in colonial Brazil) and various social services. The republic was to be democratically governed by municipal assem-blies, a national parliament, and an annually elected head, whose title and functions remained undefined. Instead of a standing army, the republic would be defended by a citizen militia in which, presumably, Brazilian-born blacks and mulattos, to whom the revolutionaries promised freedom (without offering compensation to their former owners), would figure prominently. Precisely how such a republic might survive in the interior, surrounded by royalist-controlled captaincies, seems never to have been worked out, though it was apparently hoped that the Mineiro example would inspire similar uprisings in adjacent São Paulo and Rio de Janeiro.

There were about twenty conspirators. They intended to launch their revolt in mid-February 1789. That was when the governor was expected to announce his intention to collect an unpopular head-tax, the *derrama*, which was certain to provoke popular unrest. The rebels planned to fan that discontent until it became a full-fledged riot in the capital, Ouro Preto. During the tumult Tiradentes was to decapitate the governor and proclaim the establishment of the republic. However, the governor took the wind out of the conspirators' sails by suspending the *derrama*, and a few weeks later the plot was exposed. Following the arrest of the principal conspirators, three separate judicial inquiries were conducted, and in April 1792 sentences were handed down. Five of the conspirators were banished to Angola, but the sixth, Tiradentes, was sentenced to be hanged in a symbolic gesture of warning to others harbouring treasonable ideas. Shortly afterwards the sentences were carried out.

Rather more has been claimed for the significance of the Mineiro conspiracy than the evidence will support. According to its most recent interpreter, it represented a 'confrontation between a society growing in self-awareness and self-confidence within an economic environment that encouraged and stressed self-sufficiency, and a metropolis bent on the retention of dependent markets and the safeguarding of a vital producer of precious stones, gold, and revenue'.[50] Perhaps so, but it is not clear whether other towns and their elites in Minas, not to say the slaves, would have supported the revolutionaries, nor how many Mineiros were at the time really prepared to surrender their lives and their property – including their most important investment, their slaves – in an effort to secure their freedom by means of such an ill-conceived scheme.

Some of the participants in the Mineiro conspiracy possessed copies of books by some of the well-known French *philosophes*, but how much they were influenced by such works is hard to say. Familiarity with reformist French literature did inspire other plots or alleged plots in late colonial Brazil. One example of the latter is the so-called *conjuração* of Rio de Janeiro of 1794. There the viceroy, the Conde de Resende, prohibited all gatherings by intellectuals because of fear of revolutionary talk. When he was informed that nocturnal meetings were being held in the home of a regius professor of rhetoric, he immediately ordered the participants' arrest. Among those detailed were a woodcarver, a cabinetmaker, a shoemaker, a physician, a surgeon, a jeweller, and several businessmen. Though one of them possessed copies of works by Rousseau, Raynal, and the author of a religious treatise listed on the index of prohibited books, the 60 witnesses called before the enquiry panel had nothing more incriminating to report than the fact that the group discussed the current political situation in Europe, the incompetence of certain clerics, particularly Franciscans, and the probability that the Portuguese army could not stand up to French forces. No

---

[50] Kenneth R. Maxwell, *Conflicts and conspiracies: Brazil and Portugal 1750–1808* (Cambridge, 1973), 114.

conspiracy having been proven, the twelve were quietly released in 1797, after two and a half years' confinement in the dungeons of a local fortress.

A very different fate befell those who participated in the most fascinating conspiracy in Brazil during this period, the so-called 'Tailors' Conspiracy' of 1798 in Bahia. On 12 August of that year, handwritten manifestos were affixed to church walls and other prominent places throughout Salvador, addressed to the 'Republican Bahian people'. In the name of the 'supreme tribunal of Bahian democracy', the inhabitants were urged to support an armed movement claiming to include 676 persons – soldiers, ecclesiastics, merchants, even agents (*familiares*) of the Holy Office – whose purpose was to overthrow 'the detestable metropolitan yoke of Portugal' and to install a French-style republic. Although designating a shoeless Carmelite to head an independent church, the rebels issued dire warnings to clergymen who opposed the republic, in which 'all citizens, especially mulattos and blacks', would be equal, a regime based on 'freedom, equality and fraternity'. Slaves were promised freedom and soldiers pay rises; merchants, free trade with all nations, especially France; consumers, a rollback in prices, especially of manioc and beef, both of which had advanced 25 per cent in recent years.

The authorities, residing in a city where two out of three persons were black or brown and in a captaincy where whites were outnumbered five to one (see table 4 above), moved with alacrity to apprehend the culprits. Forty-nine suspects, including five women, were arrested. Most were free mulattos, including their leader, João de Deus do Nascimento, a penniless 27-year-old tailor, but eleven were slaves. In a society in which an estimated nine out of ten persons were illiterate, a surprisingly large number of the conspirators were able to read and, indeed, many possessed translations of incriminating French writings of the period. They ranged in age from sixteen to 38 but averaged just over 26. Although some historians insist in labelling the movement a mulatto plot to do away with whites, ten of the conspirators, including a schoolmaster whose greatest sin appears to have been his ability to read French, were white.

In spite of the apprehension of all but two of the suspects and the discovery of many suspicious documents, no revolutionary plan was ever discovered. Nor had any weapons been fired, although many of the conspirators were troops of the line or militiamen. Yet, upon the conclusion of a lengthy investigation, in November, 1799, João de Deus and three others were publicly hanged, their bodies being quartered and exhibited about the city; seven others were whipped and banished to other parts of the empire; others were confined for additional months in local dungeons; five were sent to Africa and abandoned in places not under Portuguese control.

This severe punishment of the Bahian 33 was carried out upon express orders from Lisbon. The clear objective was to convince persons of African origin of the futility of seeking to alter their status by radical means and to reassure the dominant white colonials that as long as they supported the existing regime, Brazil would not become another Saint-Domingue. Yet not all blacks were intimidated, nor were all whites reassured. In 1807 still another plot was uncovered in Bahia, this time involving plantation and urban slaves of Hausa origin. Though the plotters, armed with bows and arrows, pistols, and muskets, do not seem to have devised any political programme, their social goal was unmistakable: the massacre of all whites in the captaincy. Once again there were executions and whippings, but Bahian and other Brazilian whites must have wondered how long such measures would suffice.

Little wonder that few whites in Brazil favoured either an end to the slave trade or the elimination of slavery, both of which were so vital to their way of life and so intimately tied to the prosperity that coastal Brazil was then enjoying. It may be true that plots such as the Tailors' Conspiracy and the Hausa movement disposed the elites to accept compromises short of independence, but it is clear that while their spokesmen refrained from expressing the need for political reforms, they felt no reluctance about urging the crown to concede greater economic liberties that would benefit Brazil, or at least her dominant elites. One of the most influential of those spokesmen was José Joaquim da Cunha de Azeredo Coutinho (1742–1821). A member of the new rich sugar aristocracy of the Campos dos Goitacazes in Rio de Janeiro, Azeredo held many important ecclesiastical posts in Brazil and in Portugal and repeatedly prodded the government to undertake reforms that would benefit the economies of both the kingdom and her most vital colony. Thus, in 1791, he strongly opposed new price restrictions on sugar, arguing that higher prices would allow Brazilians to buy more goods from Portugal. Three years later he published a series of reform proposals in 'An economic essay on the commerce of Portugal and her colonies', in which he revived the century-old argument that the 'true mines' of Brazil were her agricultural resources, not the gold placers which had produced illusory gains. He urged the abolition of the salt monopoly (accomplished, as noted, in 1801), the elimination of restrictions upon the exploitation of Brazilian forests in order to promote the always disappointing shipbuilding industry, the development of a fishing industry based on Indian know-how; and the removal of restrictions on the manufacture of essentials. In a third essay on the state of the Brazilian mining sector (1804), the sometime bishop of Pernambuco reiterated a Mineiro appeal of a generation earlier, calling for a revival of gold mining through the introduction of the latest European knowledge and equipment.[51]

Although the bishop indicated general remedies that he believed would promote harmony between Portugal and Brazil, a group of Bahian critics were far more specific. In 1807 the governor of Bahia wrote to the câmara of Salvador to inquire whether it felt that there were particular circumstances that inhibited the development of agriculture and commerce in the captaincy. The câmara, in turn, consulted leading figures throughout Bahia, several of whom responded at length. Judge João Rodrigues de Brito, a member of the high court of Salvador, clearly spoke for many proprietors when he candidly wrote,

In order for the farmers to achieve full liberty which the wellbeing of agriculture demands, it is necessary for them to have (1) the liberty to grow whatever crops they deem best; (2) the liberty to construct whatever works and factories they judge necessary to utilize fully their resources; (3) the liberty to sell in any place, by any means and through whatever agent they wish to choose, free of special fees or formalities; and (5) the liberty to sell their products at any time when it best suits their convenience. Unfortunately, the farmers of this captaincy enjoy none of these liberties at present.

The judge and several other respondents particularized many specific grievances of the agricultural interests of Bahia, including many restrictions imposed by the very câmaras controlled by the proprietary interests. But they also criticized the shortcomings of the religious, especially those living in monasteries, and the board of inspection, which they felt inhibited rather than facilitated sales of sugar, tobacco, cotton, and other crops; and they stressed the need for educational reforms and for freedom of the press.[52]

---

[51] Sergio Buarque de Holanda (ed.), *Obras económicas de J. J. da Cunha de Azeredo Coutinho (1794–1804)* (São Paulo, 1966).

[52] João Rodrigues de Brito *et al.*, *Cartas económico-políticas sôbre a agricultura e commércio da Bahia* (Lisbon, 1821; reprinted Salvador, 1924 and 1940). The quotation appears on p. 28 of the 1821 edition.

The articulation of such complaints, so similar to those voiced in Spanish America at that time, as well as the appearance of the first revolutionary plots in Brazil, testify to the extent of dissatisfaction that existed in late colonial Brazil. Not only sansculottes but men of substance and eminence, Portuguese- as well as Brazilian-born men, focused the crown's attention upon the need for fundamental improvements, without which revolutionary sentiment was bound to grow. And Portugal depended on Brazil far more than the colony needed the mother country.

At the conclusion of his 'Economic essay', Bishop Azeredo Coutinho had predicted:

If Portugal...preserves an adequate navy and merchant marine; if, satisfied with her vast dominions in the four quarters of the globe, she renounces further conquests; if she promotes by every [possible] means the development of the riches which her possessions have the capacity to produce; if she maintains her vassals in peace and tranquillity and assures their right to enjoy the fruits of their estates; if she establishes manufactures only of the most indispensable necessities, and abandons those of luxury to foreigners, in order to allow them an opportunity to purchase her superfluities...no enemy will molest her, or disturb her quiet...[53]

Unfortunately for the bishop and for the kingdom, the enemies of Portugal did molest her and profoundly upset her tranquillity. Portugal, which for years had profited from the succession of European conflicts, was finally a victim of those conflicts herself. In August 1807 Napoleon had demanded that Portugal close her ports to British ships and seize British subjects and their property. For a time the government sought to comply with those demands, but on 16 November a British fleet appeared off the Tagus and threatened to destroy elements of the Portuguese merchant marine and navy and possibly to bombard Lisbon as well. In addition, the British foreign secretary spoke darkly about the necessity of taking Brazil if Portugal failed to accept the assistance the British had proffered to facilitate the government's escape. While the lion was waving its tail angrily, the French tricolour appeared on Portuguese soil at the head of Marshal Junot's army of occupation (19 November). Squeezed by the Anglo-French nutcracker, the government implemented an emergency plan whose origins went back to 1640, and sought safety in its most important colony. On 29 November 1807 the

---

[53] *Obras*, 172.

government of the regent prince Dom João, *de facto* ruler of Portugal and the empire since his mother, Maria I, had become mentally incompetent in 1792, fled from Lisbon and sailed for Brazil under British naval escort, accompanied by thousands of courtiers, bureaucrats, soldiers, servants, and others. He arrived in Salvador in January 1808 and two months later was safely installed in Rio de Janeiro.

For Portugal, the economic euphoria of the past two decades, stemming in large part from profits earned on the resale of Brazilian agricultural and pastoral products, was over. It remained to be seen whether the regime of the prince regent (the future João VI) could accommodate the Brazilians by means that would satisfy their demands for change without at the same time seriously alienating the people whom it had just abandoned.

Part Four

INTELLECTUAL AND CULTURAL LIFE

16

LITERATURE AND INTELLECTUAL LIFE IN COLONIAL SPANISH AMERICA*

THE DISCOVERY OF THE NEW WORLD

The writings of the first 'discoverers' of America at the end of the fifteenth and beginning of the sixteenth centuries convey the amazement, and frequently the awe, of Europeans confronted by a new world. The ship's log of Christopher Columbus, describing the landscape of the Lucayos Islands and of Santo Domingo, and also the Taíno Indians of the region, who gave the Europeans an idyllic welcome, was a splendid opening to a series of reports on a natural world and a race of men hitherto unknown. It was in Columbus' first letter (printed in Latin in Rome in 1493) that the European conception of the New World was born. Other navigators, such as Pigafetta, a companion of Magellan, and above all Amerigo Vespucci (whose publisher Waldseemüller disseminated the expression 'Terra America' to give a new name to 'Las Indias') in their turn described the coasts, the flora and the natives of these new lands, all presumed to be islands.

This first vision of the New World was soon succeeded by that of the victims of a long series of shipwrecks, who faced less welcoming Indians, like the Caribs or the people of the Gulf of Florida, armed with powerful bows and 'arrows capable of piercing even the oar of a whaleboat'. This was the new image of America presented in, for example, the *Naufragios* (Valladolid, 1542) of Alvar Núñez Cabeza de Vaca, an Andalusian gentleman who related his tribulations, lasting several years, among the Indians. Having run aground in Tampa Bay, Florida, he returned to Mexico via California. During his three-year odyssey he was successively a conquistador (but only briefly), a pedlar,

* Translated from the original French by Mr Julian Jackson.

a slave of Indian masters, and a shaman; finally he was rescued by a group of Spaniards in northern Mexico.

At the other extreme from Alvar Núñez, the 'conquered conqueror' (there were many others, but only he left a journal which constitutes a precious ethnographical source), are the accounts of the successful conquerors. Of these, the *Cartas de relación* of Hernán Cortés, conqueror of Mexico, the first important continental discovery, are undoubtedly the best example, in that they combine scientific curiosity with mineral prospecting, plans for agricultural development with accounts of battles, descriptions of buildings and people with descriptions of the company of *conquistadores*. The first of the four *Cartas* (1519–26) appeared in Leipzig in 1524, in Latin, 31 years after that of Columbus.[1] The leaders of many other expeditions published similar *cartas*, but without ever equalling those of Cortés, who was as much a writer as a warrior or statesman. Pizarro, who conquered the Inca empire some twenty years after Cortés had taken over the Aztec empire, did not himself have enough education to write a narrative of the conquest, and his secretary performed the task rather badly. One of his captains, Pedro de Valdivia, who later died in the conquest of Chile and the war against the Araucanians, also bequeathed interesting *cartas*. All these writings were in fact – if not always in form – service records (*relaciones de servicios*) intended for the Council of the Indies which dispensed royal favour to the valiant conquerors, the more or less loyal servants of the Spanish crown.

Simple soldiers like the German Ulrich Schmidel in Paraguay or his compatriot Nikolaus Federmann in Venezuela, described the New World and its inhabitants with genuine naiveté. But the masterpiece of this early American literature was undoubtedly the *Historia verdadera de la conquista de la Nueva España* (Madrid, 1632) written over 30 years after the conquest by a *conquistador* from Extremadura, Bernal Díaz del Castillo (1496?–1584).[2] A lieutenant of Cortés, he began to write at the end of his life to correct the *Historia de la conquista de Mejico* (1532) published by Francisco López de Gómara, who, as personal chaplain of Cortés, tended, according to the veteran Bernal Díaz, to overestimate

[1] Standard edition by Pascual de Gayangos (Paris, 1966). English trans., *Letters from Mexico*, ed. A. R. Pagden (New York, 1971). [References to modern editions of colonial texts and to English translations have been added throughout this chapter by the Editor.]

[2] 2 vols., Madrid, 1940, and many other editions. English trans., *The True History of the Conquest of New Spain* (2 vols., New York, 1927), and many other editions.

the role of his master.[3] This was also the view of the Council of the Indies, which had the work confiscated. Bernal Díaz, who had become a provincial figure of some eminence (he was *alcalde mayor* in Guatemala), was not a man of any culture, but he had a rare facility with words. Both his recollections of camp life and his descriptions of Mexico and of the peoples he encountered between the Gulf Coast and the Valley of Mexico are full of colour and teeming with life.

The missionaries came on the heels of the soldiers; and if the clergy who accompanied the military expeditions were hardly distinguishable from the laymen (they usually belonged to the Order of Mercy or to the secular clergy), the mendicant orders (Franciscans, Dominicans, Augustinians) who were entrusted with the task of systematic evangelization were men of faith who attempted to understand the Indians. Several of them produced works like that of the Franciscan Fr. Toribio de Benavente, better known under his Aztec pseudonym of 'Motolinía', who wrote a *Historia de los indios de la Nueva España* (1541) in which he described in detail and with insight the customs and beliefs of the Indians.[4] The nature of the relationship between Indians and missionaries – who were at the same time catechists and advisers on agricultural and craft techniques, students and teachers of native languages, and confessors – was much richer than the relationship of fear and domination which existed between the Indians and their military conquerors. Among numerous other accounts by missionaries, that of the Dominican Bartolomé de Las Casas, a settler in Santo Domingo, military chaplain in Cuba and then bishop of Chiapas, is one of the most significant, inasmuch as his *Apologética historia summaria* (1559), in contrast to many of the chronicles of the conquest, was an apologia for the Indians faced with the cruelty both of the conquerors and of their new masters, the encomenderos.[5] The image of the Indian presented by this first generation of writers on 'America' was full of contrasts and contradictions, depending on the intellectual background of the author, his status (lay or ecclesiastical), his role in the Indies, and finally his personality.

[3] 2 vols., Mexico, 1943. English trans., *Cortés*, by Lesley Byrd Simpson (Berkeley and Los Angeles, 1964).
[4] Barcelona, 1914; Edmundo O'Gorman (ed.) (Mexico, 1969); English trans., *Motolinía's History of the Indians of New Spain*, ed. Francis B. Steck (Washington, 1951).
[5] Edmundo O'Gorman (ed.), 2 vols., Mexico, 1967. English trans., *In Defense of the Indians*, ed. Stafford Poole (Dekalb, 1974).

It was the missionaries who were mainly responsible for the first serious studies of America and the Americans to go beyond initial impressionistic descriptions. The value of such studies was in no way affected by the fact that their explicit objective was a desire to know the Indians well in order to be in a better position to convert them to Catholicism and root out their ancestral beliefs. A whole literature, ethnographic before its time, had developed from the middle of the sixteenth century and continued until 1577, when Philip II, considering it to be suspect, had it banned and confiscated. Such was the fate of the *Historia eclesiástica indiana* (1596) by the Franciscan Fr. Jerónimo de Mendieta;[6] but this work was nevertheless brought to light in a history of ancient Mexico by another Franciscan of the next generation, Fr. Juan de Torquemada, in his *Monarquía indiana de los veinte y un libros rituales* (1615).[7] The *Historia del origen de los indios de esta Nueva España* (1587) by the Jesuit Juan de Tovar was less lucky: hidden from view until the nineteenth century it was only to be published in the twentieth.[8] One could cite numerous cases similar to that of the *Relación de las cosas de Yucatán*, written in the middle of the sixteenth century (*c.* 1560) by the bishop and inquisitor Diego de Landa, who, in his efforts to destroy Maya culture, preserved an essential part of it by presenting the first interpretative table of Maya hieroglyphics.[9] But the model of this literature of ethnographic investigation remains the *Historia general de las cosas de la Nueva España* (1565?), a work many years in the writing by the Franciscan missionary Fr. Bernardino de Sahagún.[10] The manuscripts (unpublished till the middle of the twentieth century) have the distinctive (but not exceptional) feature of being arranged in columns: one contains the transcription of the account given by Indian informants in the Nahuatl language, and the other contains a line-by-line translation in Spanish; the third column, left empty, was intended to receive a Latin translation. The last version of the *Historia* was confiscated in conformity with the decree of 1577, and Sahagún, who

[6] 4 vols., Madrid, 1945; Francisco Solano y Pérez-Lila (ed.), 2 vols., Madrid, 1973.

[7] Madrid, 1945; M. León-Portilla *et al.* (eds.), 7 vols., Mexico, 1975–80.

[8] English trans., *The Tovar Calendar*, ed. George Kubler and Charles Gibson (New Haven, 1951); French trans., *Manuscrit Tovar. Origines et croyance des Indiens du Mexique*, ed. Jacques Lafaye (UNESCO, Graz, Austria, 1972).

[9] Standard edition (in Spanish and French), ed. Abbé Brasseur de Bourbourg (Paris, 1864); English trans., ed. Alfred M. Tozzer (Cambridge, Mass., 1940; reprinted New York, 1968); modern Spanish edition by Angel María Garibay, Mexico, 1959.

[10] Angel María Garibay (ed.), 4 vols., Mexico, 1956; English trans., *General History of the Things of New Spain. The Florentine Codex*, ed. Arthur J. O. Anderson and Charles E. Dibble (12 vols., Salt Lake City, 1950–82).

had devoted more than twenty years to the preparation of this encyclopaedia of native Mexico, died a disappointed man.

In addition to the ethnography of the Indians – or rather as one of its essential aspects – the study of Indian languages attracted the full attention of the mendicant friars. Confronted with the difficulty of teaching the Indians Christian doctrine in Spanish or Latin, they decided to learn the Indian languages themselves so as to be able to preach the Word of Christ in the vernacular, as the Apostles had done before them. If one remembers that only a few hundred missionaries (a few thousands over the whole continent) evangelized hundreds of thousands of Indians, it is amazing quite how many linguistic works were published for the almost exclusive use of the missionaries in the Indies. One of the first of these bilingual dictionaries can also be considered among the most complete: this was the *Vocabulario en lengua castellana y mexicana* (i.e. Spanish–Nahuatl) by the Franciscan Fr. Alonso de Molina. Published in Mexico City in 1571, this book is still the obligatory reference work for historians trying to interpret manuscripts in classical Nahuatl. Also important were the *Arte y vocabulario de la lengua general del Perú* (by an anonymous author), published in Lima in 1586, the *Vocabulario quechua* of Fr. Domingo de Santo Tomás, the Latin–polyglot dictionary (comprising the most widely spoken languages of the former Inca empire) of Alonso de Bárcena, published in 1590, and the *Arte, gramática de la lengua aymara* published in Rome by Ludovico Bertonio. Most comprehensive of all – appearing a little later than the previous works, it is true – was the *Arte, vocabulario, tesoro, catecismo de la Lengua Guarani* (1640) by Antonio Ruiz de Montoya, a Jesuit from Paraguay. The most original venture in this field was that of another Franciscan, in this instance Flemish, Peter of Ghent, who composed a catechism in Mexican hieroglyphics intended for use by the Indians. This work, foreshadowing both the paperback and the strip-cartoon, shows the inventiveness of these pioneers of evangelization.

Although less directly related to the process of evangelization, the study of botany and zoology was carried on simultaneously with that of language. The Indians worshipped certain totemic animals and used numerous plants in their ceremonies: thus knowledge of American natural history was another way of uprooting ancient beliefs camouflaged by traditional ritual practices. Moreover, the use of plants, insects, and parts of the bodies of animals for therapeutic purposes or in magic was widespread among the Indians. And European surgery, pharmaceutics, and obstetrics, which had not progressed beyond the knowledge inherited from the ancient Greeks via the Arabs, profited greatly from this example. In these areas, it must be emphasized, laymen played a more important role than clerics. The best-known work is certainly the *Historia natural de las Indias* (Seville, 1535, although the *Sumario* of the history, dealing with the Antilles and Tierra Firme only, dates from 1526) by Gonzalo Fernández de Oviedo, a civil servant posted in Santo Domingo, who aspired to write a new natural history on the lines of that of Pliny for the ancient world.[11] The *Historia* was not, however, an exhaustive work, for its author was incapable of mastering the enormous bulk of available material. Far from fulfilling his encyclopedic ambition (embracing cosmography, geology, geography, climatology, botany, and zoology), he became distracted by the details of picturesque local sights. More original were the contributions of specialists with less grandiose initial objectives, such as Dr Juan de Cárdenas, author of the *Problemas y secretos maravillosos de las Indias* (1591), a remarkable inventory of the flora of Mexico. One should also remember that treasure house of Indian pharmaceutics and medicine, *Rerum medicarum Novae Hispaniae thesaurus* (1628), by Francisco Hernández, who was sent to Mexico by Philip II expressly to prepare such a work.[12]

Not unnaturally, the first subjects to engage the interest of the Europeans were cartography, geography, the art of navigation, and then, more broadly, cosmography. Columbus himself made the first drawing of the northern coast of Santo Domingo at the time of his first expedition in 1492. Other great navigators after him, including Sebastian Cabot, Amerigo Vespucci, and Magellan, were both pilots and cartographers. The classic treatise on navigation to the Indies to be published in the sixteenth century was the Andalusian Pedro de Medina's *Arte de navegar* (1545). The first overall view of the American continent and islands was that presented by Amerigo Vespucci in *De Ora Antartica* (published by Waldseemüller in 1505), his account of his large-scale reconnaissance of the whole length of the eastern coast of South America. But the credit for the first great critical synthesis of cosmography devoted to the New World must go to a Jesuit and

---

[11] *Historia*, ed. Juan Pérez de Tudela (5 vols., Madrid, 1959); *Sumario*, ed. José Miranda (Mexico, 1950); English trans., *Natural History of the West Indies* by Sterling A. Stoudemire (Chapel Hill, 1959).
[12] Spanish trans., *Antigüedades de la Nueva España* (Mexico, 1945).

confidant of the viceroy of Peru, Father José de Acosta, for his *Historia natural y moral de las Indias* (1590).[13] The achievement of Acosta was to update the vision of the world inherited from Ptolemy and corrected only in certain details by Arab geographers and their French successor Pierre D'Ailly (whose *Imago mundi* had undoubtedly inspired Columbus' attempt to reach the East Indies via the west). It was Acosta who realized the ambitious project of Gonzalo Fernández de Oviedo. On the other hand it is to an author who had above all set out to write a work of history, Francisco López de Gómara, that we owe an overall geographical picture of the American continent, especially South America, with its main geomorphological features; in comparison with such contemporary works as the *Historia del descubrimiento y conquista del Perú* published in Antwerp in 1555 by Agustín de Zárate, a former royal civil servant in Peru,[14] Gómara's *Historia general de las Indias* (published in Saragossa in 1552) is a remarkable work of synthesis which has provided a valuable source for numerous later works right up to the present.

At the same time as this attempt to carry out geographical reconnaissance and to reach a rational understanding of peoples and their customs – an attempt we have here surveyed only very briefly – there developed an epic literature. *La Araucana* (1569–92) by Alonso de Ercilla, the poetical narrative of the defeat of the Araucanians, is a perfect example of a Renaissance epic, which, however, goes beyond its Ariostan models by having as its protagonist a collective hero, the Araucanian people, incarnated in leaders like Lautaro, Caupolican, and Colocolo.[15] But one also finds among the prose writers and among the first chroniclers of Chile, such as González de Nájera and Góngora Marmolejo, that events are constantly being compared with the history of the people of Israel and the wars of the Old Testament, in order to give the American conquests an epic dimension, even to give them the eschatological significance of a repetition of biblical history. This supernatural aspect, inspired by biblical exegesis, was later to develop in quite different directions. But present even in the first chronicles of

[13] Mexico, 1940; Madrid, 1954; Edmundo O'Gorman (ed.), Mexico, 1962. English trans., *The Natural and Moral History of the Indies* (1604), ed. Sir Clements R. Markham (2 vols., Hakluyt Society, 1st series, nos. 60 and 61, London, 1880; reprinted New York, 1969).

[14] Dorothy MacMahon (ed.), Buenos Aires, 1965. English trans., *A History of the Discovery and Conquest of Peru*, ed. D. B. Thomas (London, 1933).

[15] José Toribio Medina (ed.), 5 vols., Santiago de Chile, 1910–18; modern edition, Santiago de Chile, 1956.

the conquerors was a medieval, fantastical element, such as one finds particularly in the books of Amadis, which swarm with the most unlikely exploits. Bernal Díaz confessed naïvely that on entering the Aztec city of Tenochtitlán (Mexico City) the conquerors had believed themselves to be discovering the 'enchanted palaces mentioned in Amadis'. Beside these chivalric traditions there were the myths and legends inherited from classical antiquity: the Amazons, the Cyclops, the Fountain of Youth, Atlantis. Between Cuba and Florida the navigators searched for the Island of Bimini, site of the Fountain of Youth (where women possessed supreme beauty), with the same fervour as they hunted for gold. The search for the Amazons gave rise to the expedition of Francisco de Orellana, who travelled through tropical forest down the longest river in the world and gave it the name Amazon.

Moreover, a whole host of myths was born out of the conquest of America itself. The most well known is probably that of Eldorado. The origin of this legend was the story of an Indian chief of Peru, a Chibcha, who dived into a lake, having been first ritually smeared with gold dust. Fascinated by this tale, Sebastián de Benalcázar decided to set out in search of the gilded Indian ('el Dorado'). This myth became a perfect expression of the European frenzy for gold, and 'Eldorado' came to designate a fabulous empire, an imaginary (or, after the conquest of the Aztec and Inca empires, only half-imaginary) goal for the *conquistadores* greedily in quest of gold. Other beliefs, such as the 'Seven Cities' or the identification of the Cannibals with the Carib Indians of the Guianas and the West Indies, were a combination of the legends of the European middle ages and the imagery of the New World. The myth of the 'Seven Cities' derived from seven legendary bishops of Portugal who, fleeing the Moorish invasion, were supposed to have embarked on a ship in the direction of the Indies. But Cabeza de Vaca was not dreaming when on the horizon (in the North American desert which has since become the classic landscape of the 'Western') he caught sight of natural reliefs which he took to be the walls of towns (perhaps they were natural hills adapted for their own use by the Pueblo Indians); he believed that he was seeing the 'Seven Cities'. And on this testimony alone the viceroy of Mexico, Antonio de Mendoza, organized an important expedition to conquer the 'Seven Cities' of the Cíbola. In South America, too, expeditions were organized by the conquerors to discover a legendary city (probably an imaginary reflection of the Inca capital, Cuzco), the 'City of the Caesars' – perhaps Machu Picchu. Similar to the legend of Eldorado was the belief in a mountain of silver, the 'Sierra de la Plata', which was originally nothing more than the vivid description of Upper Peru given by the Guaraní Indians of Paraguay. And if the discovery by Juan Díaz de Solís of the river of silver, the 'Río de la Plata', turned out to be an illusion, the mountain of silver did indeed exist: it was the mountain of Potosí in Upper Peru with its fabulously rich silver mines. In this way the persistence of the myths and mirages was sustained in people's minds by a few providential cases where they coincided with reality.

There were certain beliefs of another kind which it was more dangerous to spread, given the atmosphere of the age: these were the myths derived from biblical prophecies or from later texts with only questionable right to be incorporated into the Scriptures, such as the Acts of St Thomas. A whole set of problems which would today fall under different scientific disciplines were in this period considered to be related: for instance, the origin of the native peoples of America and the question of their probable evangelization by an Apostle. Were the Indians human, and descendants of Adam? Pope Paul III's bull of 1537, *Sublimis Deus*, soon put an end to this controversy. But once this doubt had been settled a host of new ones arose: where did they come from? Were they descendants of the Iberians, of the Carthaginians, of the Andalusians, or of the Jews of the diaspora of the period of Salmanazar? All these hypotheses had numerous legal, historical, eschatological and, therefore, political implications. If the Indians were indeed descended from the Iberians, the Castilian monarchy had no need of the papal donation contained in the Alexandrine bulls to strengthen its right to the Indies (which suited the kings of Spain very well). If on the other hand the Indians were Jews, the numerous 'Portuguese' (the word was synonymous with Jewish) refugees in Mexico and Peru had found their forgotten brothers and could dream of revenge against a monarchy which had set up against them the tribunals of the Inquisition. Finally, the biblical prophecies announced that the rediscovery and conversion of the 'hidden Jews' would be the prelude to the end of the 'intermediary age' in the Christian view of history, and Christianity would at last become 'catholic', that is to say 'universal'. Such revelations could not but increase the ardour of the missionaries, but also the mood of subversion (or, as it was described, *la preocupación* and *las novedades*) which was already being stimulated from other sources – political ones – as shown in the rebellion of the Pizarros in Peru.

The question of a possible evangelization of the Indians by one of Christ's Apostles was no less charged than the question of their origins. What is more, they were linked, as we can see from the project of a Dominican creole, Fr. Gregorio García, who published a critical work of synthesis devoted to the *Origen de los Indios del Nuevo Mundo e Indias Occidentales* (Valencia, 1607) and another to the *Predicación del Evangelio en el Nuevo Mundo viviendo los Apóstoles* (Baeza, 1626), drawing attention to the essential unity of his work. If the Indians did indeed belong to the lineage of Adam (and to deny it was to contradict the official monogenism of the church, deriving from Genesis), how could the Lord have 'forgotten' them when he sent his Apostles to evangelize the whole world? There were two opposing views on this question. One was that the Indians were so corrupt that God had intended to let them stagnate in spiritual darkness for sixteen centuries longer than other people; the Spanish mendicant orders had been elected by Providence to extract them belatedly from 'captivity'; and the military conquest and its atrocities were the scourge of God. The other view, which was that of Las Casas among others, rejected discrimination of this kind as incompatible with the mercy of God: in this optimistic hypothesis the initial metaphysical problem was transformed into an exciting detective game. The objective was to identify the Apostle of the Indies, and to track down material traces left by him on the highways of the continent and spiritual traces in the beliefs of the Indians. Among the numerous authors with an amazing ingenuity and consistency Fr. Antonio de la Calancha, an Augustinian creole from Peru, argued in his *Crónica moralizada de la Orden de San Agustín en el Perú* (Barcelona, 1638) that St Thomas was the Apostle of the Indies, and identified him with certain divinities of the different populations of the Andes. The truth is that the hero bringing civilization held an important place in the pantheon of most polytheist religions, as much in Mesoamerica as in South America: he was Viracocha among the Incas, Quetzalcoatl among the Aztecs, Kukulkan among the Mayas, and so on, comparable to Pay Zume among the Tupi and Guaraní of Paraguay and Brazil. It was the Jesuits of Brazil, notably Manoel da Nóbrega, who seem to have started this tradition. Also preceding Calancha in the field was a Dominican from Mexico, Fr Diego Durán, whose *Historia de las Indias de Nueva España e islas de Tierra Firme*, written about 1585, was kept hidden because the author identified the original migrations of the Aztecs towards the Valley of Mexico with that of the people of Israel towards the Promised Land.[16] This spiritual ferment, somewhere between archaeology and prophecy, was full of potential dangers – of Messianic revolts and political secessions – and it was for this reason that the Royal Council of the Indies attempted to stem it by a repressive policy of confiscation of manuscripts, seizure of books and inquisitorial trials, political rather than anti-heretical in intention.

SPANISH CULTURAL POLICY

Official action in the cultural domain was not entirely repressive; on the contrary it was predominantly creative and stimulating. And, although successive sovereigns of Castile sometimes took contradictory measures which reflected their uncertainties, the consistency of the objectives pursued gave the measures the overall appearance of a coherent cultural policy. The first objective of this policy (both chronologically and in order of importance) was the cultural assimilation of the Indians. To the extent that the Catholic religion was the spiritual and philosophical foundation of Spanish culture and that the members of the clergy had a monopoly in the care and education of the Indians, the Christianization and 'Latinization' (that is, the learning of Spanish as the starting point of cultural assimilation) of the Indians formed two aspects of a common cultural enterprise. The evangelizers were simultaneously teachers of languages (Spanish and Latin), of music and singing (liturgical) and of technical education (in agriculture and manufacture). The religious houses built by the Indians under the direction of the friars were also the colleges where young Indians learnt religious doctrine and Latin. The limited resources, given the size of the population and the small number of missionaries, made it possible only to instruct the sons of Indian chiefs – which also accorded with the aristocratic conception of society prevailing in Castile. The Franciscans of Mexico were, in 1536, the first to set up a real college for Indians, near to Mexico City. This model institution, the college of Santa Cruz de Tlatelolco, which remains associated with the names of Fr. Bernardino de Sahagún and Fr. Andrés de Olmos, received young Indians as boarders. They left it catechized and relatively Hispanicized; and as they were called upon to become chiefs of their ethnic groups of origin, their religious and cultural conversion was supposed to bring in its wake that of their 'vassals', as they were called in Spanish. The

[16] José F. Ramírez (ed.), 2 vols., Mexico, 1867–80; Angel María Garibay (ed.), Mexico, 1967.

college, which was the work of reformed Franciscans, did not, however, survive its founders, men of a visionary faith. When, several decades later, the Jesuits in their turn created colleges for the Indians, that of Tlatelolco was only a shadow of its former self. The Jesuits envisaged the creation of a native clergy, a subject which caused controversy within the only recently founded society. Jesuit missionaries like Juan de Tovar in central Mexico fought for the maintenance and development of these colleges, but partly for economic reasons, the Society did not continue the experiment. Colleges for the education of Indians had largely disappeared from the Indies by the last quarter of the sixteenth century. But the preoccupation with the need to teach the Indians Spanish continued, as is shown by a series of royal cedulas, dating from the earliest years of colonization, which made such teaching compulsory. The fact that these decrees, incorporated into the 'Laws of the Indies', were so often repeated suggests that they had never been put into effect. Until the end of the eighteenth century the bishops were creating schools where the Indians might learn Spanish, for, as the archbishop of Mexico City could still write in 1753, 'The Indians refrain from asking for the sacraments or attending sermons because they are completely ignorant of Spanish'.

The failure of the policy of cultural assimilation of the Indians which had been instigated by the pioneers of evangelization was not only due to the difficulties of its implementation. Some members of the religious orders applied a policy of cultural segregation of the Indians, in order to protect them from encountering creoles and mestizos whose dissolute moral behaviour provided a bad example. This was the aim of the *pueblos hospitales*, a Utopian enterprise (inspired by Thomas More's book, still new at the time) of the Franciscan bishop of Michoacán, Vasco de Quiroga, and, later, of the Jesuit *reducciones* of Paraguay and California. But the most immediate effect of giving up the cultural assimilation of the Indians was that the friars fell back on the towns of the *república de los españoles*, where the number of religious houses increased. The urban colleges created by the members of different religious orders at the beginning of the seventeenth century and well into the eighteenth accepted exclusively the children of the Spanish and creole minority. The Jesuit college of San Pedro y San Pablo in Mexico City was a model of its type, for it was where most of the intellectual majority of New Spain received its education. One could cite similar examples in Lima, Quito or other capitals of the viceroyalties or the captaincies general.

The creation of universities in the Indies, as also of colleges of higher education, was at first an initiative of the mendicant orders, sanctioned by royal decrees. From 1538 the Colegio Tomás de Aquino of the Dominicans in Santo Domingo took the name of university. In 1551 the University of San Marcos in Lima was established, and in 1553 the Royal and Pontifical University of Mexico City. Other universities were set up later, such as those of San Carlos Borromeo in Guatemala and San Francisco Javier in New Granada. In Córdoba, La Plata, Cuzco, and Santiago de Chile more universities were created in the seventeenth century. The case of the town of Quito, which had no less than three universities by this period, is a revealing sign of a certain saturation, a product of the rivalry between the religious orders: there was a Dominican, an Augustinian and a Jesuit university. But in the Indies as a whole the Jesuits had won supremacy in this area by the seventeenth century. The statutes of the universities of the Indies were modelled on those of the University of Salamanca, and among the reasons invoked by the Royal Council of the Indies for the creation of the University of San Marcos in Lima figured a desire 'to ennoble these kingdoms by providing access to learning'.[17]

The development of higher education was an essential aspect of a general policy of treating the vassals of the new kingdom on a strictly equal footing with those of the Iberian peninsula. This implied discrimination of a social rather than a racial kind: the noble Indians were allowed to enrol alongside the Spaniards and creoles, but members of the *castas* (mestizos of Indian, black and white origin) and Indian commoners were excluded. These universities were administered by a rector elected by the professors and 'the advanced and hard-working students' gathered in the same electoral college (*claustro*), on to which the professors were co-opted. The Royal Council of the Indies watched with great vigilance to ensure that the conferring of degrees, the election of professors and the functioning of lectures all took place according to regular procedures. From these decrees one learns, for example, that the professors of Lima took unlimited holidays, that others began their lectures so late they lasted only a quarter of an hour: abuses all stemming from the fact that chairs were given to cronies or to clients without any preliminary examination of their competence. This was especially true of the professorships in Indian languages (notably, for Quechua and

[17] Decree of 1551 in Diego de Encinas (ed.), *Cedulario indiano* [1596]. A. García Gallo (ed.), 4 vols., Madrid, 1945–6.

Aymara in Lima) intended for instructing aspiring missionaries in the languages of their future catechumens but held by people quite ignorant of them. The Council of the Indies instituted compulsory language exams – as much for the professors as the students – and those who failed to obtain the average mark by the end of the year were not permitted to be sent on missionary work. This situation had been reached by the very first year of existence of the University of Lima. But it was no better in Mexico City: candidates for the doctorate were forbidden to leave their homes during the month before the presentation of their theses, in order to prevent them bribing (usually by holding a banquet) the members of the examining jury.

In spite of such indisputable abuses – which also occurred in European universities during this period – the universities of the New World provided the creoles with the possibility of access to cultural advancement, and, to some extent, to promotion in public administration. The fully-fledged universities – San Marcos and Mexico City – consisted of the four traditional faculties: theology, the arts, law, and medicine. Except in the faculty of medicine, Latin was the sole language used in teaching, in examinations, and in the writing of theses. The other universities, responsible to a religious order, were mainly, if not exclusively, faculties of theology and canon law. The degrees were the *bachillerato*, the *licenciatura* and the *doctorado*; the curriculum was relatively standardized throughout the different universities of the Indies. The autonomy enjoyed by the universities was, in the case of the royal and pontifical universities, limited by their statutes, by the system of royal patronage (*patronato*), and by financial dependence. Universities belonging to a religious order had greater freedom, exercised especially in the recruitment of professors.

The colleges and universities were the primary instruments of public education and the advancement of learning, but they were not the only ones. That the monarchy, and particularly its representatives in the New World, the religious orders, were aware of this is clear from the fact that they encouraged the importation of books and the setting up of printing presses. There was certainly control over the circulation and sale of books, but nonetheless the facts are eloquent: inventories of private libraries show, for example, that the works of Erasmus, Petrarch, and Boccaccio had reached America before 1540. The catalogue, in this same year, of the stock of the first publisher–bookseller in Mexico City contained all the fiction 'best-sellers': *Amadis de Gaula,*

Espejo de caballería, Oliveros de Castilla, Roberto el Diablo. By combining in 1539 with Juan Pablos (Giovanni Paoli), a Lombard, Juan Cromberger, the first publisher of Mexico City and the New World, had obtained a profitable monopoly; he was the son of Jacob Cromberger, who had established the famous publishing house of Seville in 1500. In 1583 Riccardi (a native of Turin), newly arrived from Mexico City, set up Lima's first publishing house. It was only in the seventeenth century that other publishing houses appeared – at La Paz, Guatemala City, and Puebla. It should be noted that these first presses in the Indies printed almost exclusively preaching manuals and catechisms; thus they served above all the requirements (at this time considerable) of missionary policy. But they also on occasion published treatises on mining technology and on anatomy, and even works of poetry.

The fictional works that we have mentioned were for the most part imported from Europe. Indeed, as early as 1513 the Catholic queen, Isabella, had expressed concern over the harmful effects which *Amadis* and other novels of the fantastic might have on the Indians' imagination, and she gave instructions forbidding the export of such books to the Indies. In 1536 the Council of the Indies confirmed this decision in its instructions to the viceroy Mendoza 'in order that the Holy Scriptures do not lose the authority and confidence they inspired' among the Indians, who, being only recently Christianized, would not be capable of distinguishing between fiction and Revelation. The best solution was to forbid the Spanish themselves from having these books in their houses, in case they lent them to Indians! These instructions, like others, no doubt went unheeded, for a cedula of 1543 repeated the prohibition for Mexico and extended it to Peru and Santo Domingo. The campaign against profane literature went further still, and in 1569 Viceroy Toledo summoned to Lima all owners of bookshops and possessors of novels. The pressure increased considerably with the setting up of Inquisition tribunals in Lima (1570) and Mexico City (1571). But a combination of smuggling, corruption among government servants responsible for inspecting ships on their arrival in port, and the connivance of various other individuals, all caused the efforts of the Inquisition to be largely fruitless, as is demonstrated by the inventories of private libraries, or even of religious orders, drawn up at various times during the viceregal period. In the sixteenth century both publishing and the clandestine circulation of books expanded considerably, as we shall see later. Let it simply be noted here that if imaginative fiction popular in Spain was forbidden in the Indies, political literature (chronicles of the conquests) and ethnographic studies (the history and customs of the American Indians) were encouraged, controlled, and censored depending on the regimes and the circumstances of the time.

The Catholic monarchs, Ferdinand and Isabella, promoted within their entourage the development of a literature about the New World. It is certain, for example, that without royal encouragement the Italian humanist Pietro Martire d'Anghiera, who resided at the court, would not have written his Latin work *De Orbe Novo* (Alcalá, 1516), which followed closely the events of the conquest.[18] He was followed in this path by the official chronicler Gonzalo Fernández de Oviedo, who would not have been able to produce his *Historia natural de las Indias*, already mentioned, if royal instructions had not required government employees to provide him with the necessary documentation. The history of Peru by Agustín de Zárate, also published in Antwerp a year after that of Cieza de León, was stimulated by the entourage of Charles V. And besides acts of personal intervention accompanied by financial support (not always sufficient, as Francisco Hernández complained), the monarchy also took official measures: in the first place, the creation in 1526 of the office of 'royal cosmographer and chronicler of the Indies', analogous to those which already existed for the kingdoms of Aragon and Castile.[19] Although the first holders of the post were at times surpassed by more independent authors, the work of these early official chroniclers was far from negligible. One of their successors, Antonio de Herrera, published a *Historia general de los hechos de los castellanos en las islas y tierra firme del mar océano* (Madrid, 1601–15), inspired by the *chansons de geste* of the Christian kingdoms of medieval Spain, which was to remain a monument of the historiography of Spanish discoveries and conquests in the New World.[20] This book had already been preceded by the *Elegías de varones illustres de las Indias* of Joan de Castellanos, published in Madrid in 1589. Besides the official history of the conquests, the monarchy also encouraged by the writing of unofficial history of pre-Columbian America, such as Acosta's *Historia natural y moral de las Indias* (1590). In both cases the political intention was to undermine versions of the conquest which justified the dynastic

---

[18] English trans. by Francis Augustus Macnutt, *De Orbe Novo, the Eight Decades of Peter Martyr d'Anghera* (2 vols., New York, 1912).

[19] Decree of 1526 in *Cedulario indiano*.

[20] English trans., *The General History of the Vast Continent and Islands of America* (6 vols., London, 1725–6). Modern Spanish edition, 17 vols., Madrid, 1934–57.

pretensions of the descendants of the discoverers and *conquistadores*, and in particular to undermine the intrigues by the Columbus and Cortés families or the armed rebellion of the Pizarros. And we have already noted the spiritual and political risks of allowing the historical traditions of the Indians to be reinterpreted by friars imbued with biblical prophecy. There was an abundance of unpublished works claiming to reveal and interpret the history of the Indies and of the Indians of America; many of these, like the *De rebus indicis* (1583?) of Juan Calvete de Estrella[21] and the *Miscellanea antarctica* of Miguel Cabello Balboa (1586),[22] were only published for the first time in the middle of the twentieth century. In short, the crown's desire to encourage the writing of history was part of its policy of controlling its unruly subjects in the Indies.

It was during the long reign of Philip II (1556–98) that there developed a grand project for a general inventory of the kingdom of the Indies. A long and detailed questionnaire was put to the priests of urban and rural parishes, through the agency of their bishops. This survey was principally a demographic census and an economic report intended to revalue the tax assessments inherited from the pre-conquest administration of Peru and Mexico, and based on the *quipus* of the Incas and the *mapas de tributos* in Mexican hieroglyphics. Although considerable reservations can be expressed as to the accuracy of the information collected in these *Relaciones geográficas* during the last quarter of the sixteenth century, even as they stand they are a valuable source for the modern historian. It is well known that certain encomenderos concealed a number of their Indians, which means that the *Relaciones* in reality overestimated the demographic fall. And we know that various priests, either illiterate or reluctant to play the role of government servant which was hardly a part of their vocation, took no trouble over their work. But there remains that part of the investigation relating to social mores, family life, domestic technology, the artisan class, clothing, food and so on. And if the overall results of this enterprise of anthropological fieldwork at the level of a whole continent (using only the inadequate technical equipment and methods available at the end of the sixteenth century) did not provide the Council of the Indies with all that it had hoped for from an administrative point of view, they are far from insignificant for the cultural historian. Some of the famous *relaciones* were published in Mexico as a book: the

21 J. López de Toro (ed.), Madrid, 1950.   22 Luis E. Valcárcel (ed.), Lima, 1951.

Relación de Chalco Amaquemecam. Others were published at the end of the nineteenth century in Spain by the scholar Marcos Jiménez de la Espada.[23]

Laws and official regulations are important for the study of cultural life not only because they directly affected such areas as the universities and the trade in books, but also because the assimilation of the spirit of the law was an essential aspect of cultural policy. From 1512 the first *Leyes de Indias* were promulgated, then abrogated in 1542 and replaced by the *Leyes nuevas*. 1680 saw the publication of the first great *Recopilación de las leyes de las Indias*, which was the reference work not only of the members of the royal *audiencias*, but of all *letrados*, as lawyers and jurists were known. Besides these official collections, there also appeared, with royal approval or encouragement, such works as the *Gobierno del Perú* (1567) by Juan de Matienzo, which was a veritable manual of colonial administration as well as a programme of government.[24] In the same genre was the book by Antonio de León Pinelo, *El gran canciller de las Indias*, written in Lima around 1625; it acquired the status of a classic. A little later, at the beginning of the seventeenth century, Juan de Solórzano Pereira, a protégé of the Count of Lemos, settled in Lima. He had had a legal training at the University of Salamanca and produced the masterpiece of this kind of literature, the monumental *Política indiana* (1648).[25] This was a critical history of the administration of the empire of the Indies which did not spare the Council of the Indies itself any more than the local *audiencias*. Nor was it an isolated example. To cite only one other, the Latin treatise *De contractibus* by the Jesuit Oñate formed part of the same effort to codify and improve the law of the Indies.

COLONIAL CULTURAL REALITY

Behind the façade of a unified Christian culture one in fact finds a very heterogeneous cultural reality. There were various reasons for this, the main one being the cultural diversity of the European immigrants, even if a majority of them were natives of the Iberian peninsula. It is necessary to remember in this context that in principle only the subjects of the crown of Castile to which, however, belonged the north of Cantabria, Navarre, Extremadura, and Andalusia, were authorized to go to the

[23] Marcos Jiménez de la Espada (ed.), 4 vols., Madrid, 1881–97; 2nd edn, 3 vols., Madrid, 1965.
[24] Guillermo Lohmann Villena (ed.), Paris, 1967.
[25] José María Ots Capdequí (ed.), Madrid, 1930.

Indies and only if they could prove that they were long-standing Christians. Since expeditions to the Indies began with a long and dangerous Atlantic crossing, the first contingents to go were made up of sailors from the Atlantic ports: Laredo, Santander (birthplace of Juan de la Cosa) and Castro Urdiales, in the north; San Lucar de Barrameda, Palos (home of the Pinzón brothers), Cadiz, Puerto de Santa María, in the south. The major *conquistadores* originated from Trujillo and Medellín, small towns less than 100 kilometres apart, in Extremadura. Among the evangelizers, besides the Castilians, an important role was played by Basques like Fr. Juan de Zumárraga and Galicians like Fr. Juan de Betanzos. These facts are important since, at the end of the fifteenth century and during the sixteenth, Spain was not yet a unified political entity, far less a homogeneous cultural entity. To give their peninsular kingdom a religious unity, the Catholic Monarchs had expelled practising Jews (in 1492, the year that Columbus discovered the Indies) and created the tribunals of the Inquisition to persecute converted Jews (*conversos*) still secretly loyal to the faith of their forbears. Later, in 1609, Philip III decided to expel the *moriscos*, the Moors of Granada dispersed throughout the other kingdoms of the peninsula after the conquest of Granada (also in 1492) and suspected of having an attachment to Islam which threatened the security of the Mediterranean coasts of Spain. The Christians themselves (Galicians, Basques and Catalans, Aragonese) exhibited considerable linguistic and cultural diversity and enjoyed complete internal legislative and administrative autonomy. The *fueros* of Navarre are the best known because they resisted until the twentieth century, but they were only one example, typical of many others. The spirit of regional particularism represented by the first conquerors was transferred to American soil, considered by them as a *tabula rasa*. It is for this reason that in recent years it has been claimed that only a micro-history of colonial Spanish America is possible. Each village could be a cultural enclave; as well as the valleys of the Colombian Andes, where a whole Castilian village might be simply transplanted, one can also find a Mexican mining town inhabited by Italians from the sixteenth century onwards. This latter example draws attention to the existence of clandestine immigration, a very important phenomenon from the early stages of colonization. Many Jews from Portugal fleeing the rigours of the Inquisition took refuge in the Indies, where they attempted to preserve their traditions, though often in a very impoverished form.

Germans suspected of Lutheranism came in large numbers, especially
to Venezuela. Even English and French pirates, whether shipwrecked
or merely adventurous, succeeded in inserting themselves into this
'frontier' society. Without going as far as certain Huguenot historians
for whom the Indies were the refuge of the riff-raff of Europe, or for
that matter Cervantes, for whom 'America was a whorehouse', we
should stress the inevitable atomization of a society of this kind in this
period.

Besides the diversity which was of regional origin, there was an
enormous variety in the level of culture and in social origin. If one
excepts men such as Cortés, Cabeza de Vaca or Cieza de León, who were
capable of putting down their swords in camp at nightfall and taking
up their pens, the vast majority of the *conquistadores* were completely
illiterate. The 'books of the brave' (i.e. the romances of chivalry)
studied by Irving Leonard were read aloud only by those soldiers
capable of doing so, in the midst of a circle of listeners whose culture
was purely oral. (Note that 'oral' does not necessarily mean impoverished; the medieval tales, the *romancero*, were sometimes conserved
by oral traditions until the invention of the transistor radio.) Among
the literate, the cultural background of the mendicant friars was entirely
different from that of the *conquistadores* and the government's civil
employees (*contadores, letrados*, etc.). They were recruited from the
highest cultural and spiritual spheres of the peninsula, and from the
earliest missions they also included other Europeans; this phenomenon
of international recruitment increased in the last quarter of the sixteenth
century with the arrival of the Jesuits. Despite official discouragement,
French, Italians, Flemings, Germans, Czechs, and above all subjects of
the Kingdom of Naples (dependent on the crown of Aragon) came to
enrich the civilization of the Indies from the great storehouse of
different cultures whose achievements, especially in architecture and the
plastic arts, continue to excite admiration to this day.

The extent to which these different cultural contributions were fused
together depended on factors whose relative importance varied
according to time and place. Cultural dominance could depend on the
influence of a personality, often a religious missionary. (Owing to the
influence of the Franciscan Peter of Ghent, for example, Indian
neophytes flooded Mexico with holy pictures in the Flemish style.) But
one can find certain constants: the level of cultural Hispanicization was
a function of proximity to an administrative town or a religious house

(or a college). The Indian cultural substratum was most resistant among the sedentary and culturally advanced population of the former native empires. In these cases the missionaries even helped to extend the sphere of influence of certain common languages such as Quechua in Peru, Nahuatl in Mexico and Guaraní in Paraguay, at the expense of languages spoken by minorities. And Spanish borrowed many Indian words, especially for its botanical, zoological, and technological vocabulary; the influence of Indian syntax is also noticeable. As for the influence of shamanistic practices in popular medicine, of techniques employed in the manufacture of objects and the construction of buildings, in the growing of plants, in cooking, etc., the evidence is overwhelming. Dietary habits were radically modified: tomatoes, maize, sweet potatoes, tobacco, and chocolate all entered Spanish culture and, through it, the culture of Europe.

The physical and climatic conditions and, above all, the new structures of an emerging society (relatively stable from about 1570), significantly modified the main patterns of Spanish culture, markedly differentiating it from its European origins. The *conquistadores* had intended to re-create on the fresh soil of America a New Spain, a New Andalusia, a New Galicia, a New Castile, a New Granada; and they did indeed achieve this ambition. The monarchy helped them in this by sending missionaries to evangelize the Indies and jurists to establish a state of law. But this 'transculturation' was inevitably accompanied by a process of 'acculturation'. The American continent was far from being a human desert, a territory awaiting the arrival of those who could believe themselves chosen by God to inhabit it and exploit the rich store of precious metals which lay under its soils. Even after the great epidemics which decimated their numbers in the sixteenth century, native Americans continued to comprise a large majority of the population. Thus the pockets of Spanish culture – often sustained by a few families of encomenderos grouped together in a small town – were submerged in an Indian environment. The houses which surrounded the plaza belonged of course to the European *vecinos*, but on market days or during religious festivals the square itself swarmed with Indians. Just as the Virgin Mary and the Apostle St James became Indian deities which would one day serve to defy Spanish power, the creoles aspiring from the first generation to differentiate themselves from the Spaniards of the peninsula absorbed Indian ways of behaving, even Indian superstitions. Yet at the same time they directed their greatest efforts at differentiating themselves as much as possible from the *indios bárbaros* in the eyes of European Spaniards.

We are thus confronted with the culture of a colonial minority, historically the first of such importance to exist since the beginning of the modern era. According to the most authoritative estimates the total population of Spanish origin in the Indies at the end of the sixteenth century was in the order of 150,000 individuals, mostly young with a definite preponderance of men over women and children. Only a quarter of the population lived in the towns, most of which were small. It was here that Spanish culture was provincialized and soon became archaic for lack of contact with Spain. Only the viceregal capitals like Lima and Mexico City, and the large ports closest to Europe like Havana and Santo Domingo continued to undergo the direct influence of Spain. And only the viceregal courts, the *audiencias* and the religious houses were able to sustain a written culture and, at least episodically, stimulate a certain literary activity. Most encomenderos lived culturally isolated in an Indian environment; the same was true of the missionaries. The creoles and Spaniards taken as a whole represented something like a fifth of the total population.

The phenomenon known to demographers and anthropologists as 'miscegenation' (and perhaps more graphically described as uncontrolled interbreeding) resulted in a religious and cultural syncretism which is at the root of the popular culture of modern Latin America. In the period which concerns us here, the combined effects of segregation and miscegenation led to the growth of different cultures in different ethnic minorities. These marginal cultures can be quite simply considered as countercultures (in relation to official Spanish culture) to the extent that they were a form of group survival and a defence against the dominant Spanish culture. There is no more striking example than that of the Afro-American cultures which emerged from a turning in on themselves by the communities of African slaves uprooted from their native lands and subjected to the harsh life of the plantation worker. At the same time African cultural influence on creole culture was encouraged by the creole custom of giving black wetnurses to their children and by the fact that creole men frequented the company of black and mulatto women. Cookery and dance were only the most visible signs of this influence, which was very profound in the Caribbean and the hot coastal regions of the circum-Caribbean. The archives of the Inquisition show that from the middle of the sixteenth century most of the accused were blacks prosecuted as blasphemers, sorcerers, polygamists, and the like. The energy with which Spanish culture and ethics were defended is one sign among others of the true extent of their vulnerability in a lax society so distant from the influential centres of Spanish culture such as Toledo, Seville, Salamanca, and, in the seventeenth century, Madrid.

America was itself unable rapidly to produce centres with a comparable force of attraction. One should, however, note the precocious flowering, from the beginning of the sixteenth century, of the court of the viceroy Diego Columbus in Santo Domingo. For a few years there developed a court life on the European model in which the refinements of Italian Renaissance manners, music and poetry were maintained by the viceroy's thirst for prestige. After the decline of the Columbus family following its legal disputes with the monarchy, Santo Domingo lost its pre-eminent position, which unquestionably passed, from the last quarter of the sixteenth century onwards and above all during the seventeenth, to Mexico City. The country having been almost entirely conquered, the sons of the *conquistadores* could give themselves over to the pleasures of fashion and to showing off their finery on the Paseo de la Alameda. The harness of the horses (often in silver) matched the elegance of their riders; the dresses and the wit of the women were celebrated by the poet Bernardo de Balbuena in a poem revealingly entitled *Grandeza mexicana*, written in 1602. The splendour of the public and private palaces, the equestrian sports, the processions and the theatrical performances, the poetry contests on the occasion not only of fixed Christian festivals but the marriage of a prince, a military victory in Europe, the arrival of a viceroy – all this allows us to talk of cultural activity in the modern sense of the term. In the capital the density of the population of creoles and Spaniards was sufficient (besides the wealth produced by the Indian labour on the plantations and in the silver mines) to sustain an atmosphere conducive to artistic invention (especially painting) and poetic competition.

The university and, above all, the religious houses were the favoured places to pursue those activities which did not require the larger arena of the *plaza*. Several of the religious houses served both as colleges and as societies or clubs: at them, as Sor Juana Inés de la Cruz informs us, one could learn music and give concerts and recitals. The creole friars of the end of the sixteenth century were no longer soldiers of Christ like their predecessors, but rather city-dwelling clerics who often led a life highly secular in character. Laymen were welcome in the religious houses; they became like salons where the art of conversation flourished. In such places, among the books read by the creoles, it would not have been surprising to find, alongside the austere tradition of Boethius and Thomas à Kempis, either profane authors of antiquity like Horace and Ovid or those of *quattrocento* Italy. This brief account of aspects of the urban cultural life of Mexico City also applies to that of Lima, which quickly developed a markedly aristocratic character and where the magnificent quality of the theatre has remained famous. La Perichola, the famous favourite actress of the viceroy of Peru, was representative of the atmosphere of Lima from the end of the seventeenth century. Secondary capitals, such as Quito and Guatemala City, had a certain renown, though on a more modest scale (for the presence of a viceroy's court at Mexico City and Lima acted as cultural stimulants). But it needed all the patriotic fervour and sentimental attachment of the creoles to describe Guayaquil as 'the Athens of the New World'. More worthy of mention are Córdoba de Tucumán in the future viceroyalty of La Plata, or such secondary cities of New Spain as Puebla de los Ángeles, Guadalajara, and Querétaro. (Only much later, in the eighteenth century, did Havana, Caracas, and Buenos Aires come to life.) Considering the size of the continent and the extent to which the population of European origin was scattered, it is not surprising that one can observe the provincial ossification of a culture which reflected the mixture of aristocratic pretensions and archaic tastes and mentalities (the *rancio* spirit) characteristic of colonial environments. The history of the culture whose main features we will attempt to describe through the works it produced was of course only that of the small minority of an urban and educated class, in the midst of a creole minority itself very small in proportion to the overall population of the Indies. But these limitations only highlight how considerable was the extent of such writings and publications, and also, in some cases, their first-rate quality.

COLONIAL LITERATURE

In spite of those obstacles to the development of an original creole culture which we have already mentioned, the colonial societies of Hispanic America saw the emergence of writers and artists who created some great works. Although such a judgement might be disputed, the memoirs of the conquerors and most of those works of missionaries which were inspired by the Indian civilizations might be considered as already creole in spirit. We have cited several examples, such as the works of Alonso de Ercilla among epics of the conquest itself, and that of the Franciscan Bernardino de Sahagún in the field of ethnography. As early as the reign of Charles V New World literature was notable both for quantity and often for quality. If we describe works as creole even though their authors were not American creoles in the strict sense of the term (since they were born in Europe), it is because cultural phenomena cannot be considered simply according to biological or geographical criteria. A sense of their difference from the Spaniards of Europe, and above all from the Europeans newly arrived on American soil, quickly developed among the veterans of the conquest and evangelization of the New World. While the first generation of creoles and mestizos (those born in the first years of the sixteenth century in the West Indies, about twenty years later in Mexico, and 30 years later in Peru) were still children, new terms appeared which codified this sense of difference. At this time the word 'creole' did not apply exclusively to individuals of European origin but to all non-Indians who were acclimatized (physically and, above all, culturally) to America. Slaves who had been in the Indies for several years were referred to as *negros criollos* to differentiate them from newly arrived *negros bozales* who were still inefficient as workers. A Spaniard born in the Indies of parents born in Spain was described as an 'American creole' or an 'American Spaniard' (*español americano*); a newly arrived Spaniard was given the pejorative nickname of *gachupín* in Mexico and *chapetón* in Peru. The emergence of these qualifying adjectives – eventually to become nouns: in the eighteenth century *americano* replaced *español americano* – showed that what had taken place was the emergence of a society conscious of itself, that is, the birth of a new culture.

When, in about 1580, the Dominican Diego Durán, who was born in Spain but had come to Mexico as a small child, wrote the preface to his *Historia de las Indias*, he declared his intention to cleanse the name of 'his homeland' (that is, New Spain), which had been besmirched by the hasty and critical judgements of recently disembarked Spaniards. Spanish civil servants did indeed often lump together creoles, Indians, and mestizos as 'barbarians'. Durán was thus led to write an apologia of those Indian civilizations which constituted the past of his Mexican homeland. And from the moment that the bond of common soil had brought together all the inhabitants of America – whatever their race or ethnic origin – in a common relationship to the foreigners of the continent, a 'creole' culture, different from Spanish culture, had been born. The perception of this difference, or rather opposition, was so considerable that it extended to religious beliefs. In Mexico the Virgin de los Remedios, patron saint of the *conquistadores*, was described as *gachupina* to distinguish her from Our Lady of Guadalupe, the *virgen criolla* who had, according to tradition, appeared to an Indian shepherd in 1531, exactly ten years after the capture of Mexico City by Cortés and his companions. The first was led in procession for the *fiesta del pendón* (the anniversary of the conquest) and also invoked against drought; the second, invoked against floods, became the patron saint of Mexico City, then of numerous other towns in the country, and, finally, the national symbol in the war of independence. The Mexican example is only one among many. The Virgin of Copacabana, venerated near Lake Titicaca – previously a place of pilgrimage to one of the Incas' many gods – was, together with St Rose of Lima, an object of worship common to all the creoles of Peru. Our Lady of Guápulo in Ecuador played a similar role in this process of crystallization of an American creole consciousness. Negative proof of this is provided by the mistrust and incredulity shown by the Spaniards towards American sanctuaries and cults which had, however, not usually claimed to be more than the reproduction of the religious images and sacred places of the peninsula. Competition therefore developed and became more and more intense between the Spaniards and the creoles of the Indies in the search for, and possession of, signs of divine grace. It is thus not surprising that the first products of creole culture were holy pictures and devotional treatises, edifying lives of missionaries, and works (often published sermons) of religious apologetics. For the modern reader such writings are historical documents rather than literary works of any aesthetic interest.

Secular literature, of whatever variety, developed at the same time as religious literature, first as an imitation of the great contemporary Spanish works, but soon to become genuinely creative. It is undoubtedly the case that the great verse epics like the *Arauco domado* (1596) by Pedro de Oña, or *La Araucana* (1569) of Alonso de Ercilla, were written in imitation of the epics of antiquity or those of contemporary Spain or Italy. But the subject matter was quite new, and these 'epics from a barbarian world' cannot simply be dismissed as imitations of Ariosto or Herrera, even if they did have considerable stylistic perfection, in conformity with the taste of the period. In addition to the American verse epic, the Spanish tradition was continued by epics written first in prose, like that of Juan de Castellanos, and then transformed into verse. The historiography of the Indies was in large part the work of creoles and mestizos (i.e. creoles, culturally speaking), of whom the most famous was undoubtedly the Inca Garcilaso de la Vega. A descendant on his mother's side from the royal Inca line, Garcilaso was the son of one of the captains of the conquest, a companion of the Pizarro brothers and a relative of the great Spanish poet Garcilaso. Garcilaso's *Comentarios reales de los Incas* (Córdoba, 1609) are a perfect example of the assimilation of the style and methods of contemporary European humanism applied to a pre-Columbian subject.[26] The work, in its size, its balanced structure and its mastery of style, is a pure product of the high Spanish culture of the time; it was to Andalusia that this descendant of the Incas went to polish the learning he had acquired in Lima. Garcilaso had already written an *Historia de la Florida* (1605) inspired by Ariosto's *Orlando Furioso* and using chronicles written by participants in the conquest, the companions of Hernando de Soto; it is the clumsy form and lack of intellectual content of the raw material upon which he drew that shows up all the more the extent of Garcilaso's genius.[27] He also acquired a literary reputation as translator of one of the best-sellers of the century, the *Dialoghi d'amore* of Leon Hebreo. But if Garcilaso was the century's most outstanding example of acculturation he was by no means the only one. In Mexico, the chronicler Fernando de Alva Ixtlixochitl also deserves to be remembered; even if his mastery of style was far removed from the perfection achieved by Garcilaso, his vision of the Indian past seen through the eyes of the cultural half-caste was no less characteristic of the new American culture.

The last decades of the sixteenth century, a generation after the chronicles and epics of the conquest, saw the appearance of works exalting the new cities of the Indies with their aristocratic pretensions. The *Grandeza mexicana* (already mentioned) of the priest Bernardo de Balbuena, inspired by Ariosto's *Jerusalem Freed*, was the most accomplished of these frivolous poems devoted to the luxurious life of the creoles, but Mexico City was not in this regard unique among the

---

[26] *Obras completas*, 4 vols., Madrid, 1960. English trans., *Royal Commentaries of the Incas and general history of Peru*, ed. Harold V. Livermore (2 vols., Austin, 1965).

[27] English trans., *The Florida of the Inca. A History of the Adelantado, Hernando de Soto...*, ed. John G. Varner and Jeannette V. Varner (Austin, 1951).

capitals of the Indies. An anonymous chronicler, 'The Portuguese Jew', described Lima in the same period as 'an earthly paradise for the [creole] lords', parading through the streets on horseback dressed in silk and the finest cloths of Segovia while their wives were carried in sedan chairs to pay their social calls. The Alameda of Lima was quite as splendid as that of Mexico City. The inspiration of the poets, including now women like doña Leonor de Ovando of Santo Domingo, had entirely changed: the epic had been replaced by court poetry, especially the poetry of courtly love.

In Mexico City Petrarchanism flourished in such poets as González de Eslava. The name of Gutierre de Cetina, also in Mexico City, was praised by Cervantes himself; nor should we overlook the satirical poet Juan del Valle Caviedes, from Lima. The Mexicans Juan de Terrazas and Juan de la Cueva are today hardly more than names. But this is not the case of Sor Juana Inés de la Cruz (1648–95), the 'new American phoenix', as she was described by her contemporaries. Born in 1648 in the Valley of Mexico, Juana de Asbaje, who had lived in the entourage of the viceroy of New Spain, was the very incarnation of the 'Indian spring' (that is to say, 'of the Indies' or creole) celebrated by Balbuena; and yet she took her vows. The story of her renunciation of the world and even – on the urgent entreaties of a confessor more well-meaning than inspired – of her library, is well enough known. Sor Juana's philosophical and theological erudition was comparable to that of the greatest minds of her century, such as the Portuguese Jesuit António Vieira, with whom she conducted a controversy in her essay on 'the dream' and its interpretations. But she was above all a musician and a poet. However exceptional her case might have been owing to her unusual abilities, it nevertheless shows that the education of women in creole society (more specifically in the convents, where the novices gave private lessons to young girls) could be varied and sophisticated. The poetry of Sor Juana ranged from edifying drama like *El divino Narciso* to the traditional Spanish genre of the *villancico*, which she herself described as a 'salad' because it used the popular mixture of languages spoken by the Indians and the blacks. Thus her poetic achievement embraced the whole cultural spectrum of the multiracial society of Mexico.[28] But it would be wrong to consider Sor Juana as an isolated case. Her contemporary, Francisco Bramón, produced a work of religious inspiration and considerable literary elegance: *Los sirgueros de*

[28] Sor Juana Inés de la Cruz, *Obras completas*, ed. Méndez Plancarte (Mexico, 1969).

la Virgen sin original pecado (1620).[29] The subject of the cult of the Virgin and particularly the issue of the Immaculate Conception – by which the new doctors of the University of Mexico City had to swear an oath when receiving their degrees – was the centre of creole spirituality. The exaltation of the almost supernatural abundance of America and the way that its riches flowed forth for the creoles was a theme shared with Sor Juana and her Lima contemporary, Antonio de León Pinelo, author of *El Paraíso en el Nuevo Mondo* (written around 1640).[30] This exaltation, both sacred and profane, of America by creole authors had begun in the middle of the sixteenth century and became more pronounced during the next two centuries; it was an area in which the baroque style was to flourish at its most extravagant.

Theatre, which, we have already noted, had an early success in the Indies, held an important place in creole culture. First there was religious theatre, inspired by the *autos sacramentales*, mystery plays traditional in Spain. These were used by the first missionaries as a means of indoctrinating the Indians, who, however, spontaneously grafted them onto their dances (in Mexico, the *areitos*), inherited from their polytheistic rituals, in which mime played a large part. Later the secular Spanish *comedia*, imitated from Lope de Rueda and – in the seventeenth century – the plays of Lope de Vega were performed in the towns of America. It was possible to see plays not only in enclosed courtyards (*corrales*) as in Spain, but also in the palaces of the new creole lords, where private performances were given; and not only of works borrowed or imitated from Spain. One of the greatest writers of *comedias* of the Spanish Golden Age was a Mexican creole (often mocked because he was a hunchback), Juan Ruiz de Alarcón. He was the author of *La verdad sospechosa* and other theatrical successes. Alfonso Reyes believes that he senses in Alarcón the sort of twilight melancholy which he considers a constant feature of the literature of his country, distinguishing Alarcón from people like Lope de Vega or Calderón, whose rival he was.

Most magnificent of all was the spectacle presented by creole society on the *paseo*, or better still on those vast plazas, surrounded by arcades, where grand public occasions took place. The entry of a viceroy, the enthronement of an archbishop, the ceremony of an auto-da-fé, all gave rise to large popular gatherings and to sumptuous displays of civil and ecclesiastical power. It was no coincidence that this whole colonial

[29] Mexico, 1943.   [30] Raúl Porras Barrenechea (ed.), Lima, 1943.

period was punctuated by quarrels over precedence between various dignitaries – over their place in the processions or on the platform, over whether they should bow or kneel, over whether they should prostrate themselves before the banner, over where they should stand during funerals, and so on. We should remember that the obligatory festivals, especially that of Corpus Christi, were accompanied by dancing and theatrical performances paid for by the government, during which the different ethnic communities were given the opportunity to participate. A temporary decor for these occcasional festivals was provided by constructions in stucco which might depict both scenes of classical mythology, inspired by the Renaissance, and also the heroes and emperors of Indian history. Poetry was also written for the occasion, sometimes by distinguished authors. The Mexican creole, Carlos de Sigüenza y Góngora, nephew on his mother's side of the Andalusian poet, a former Jesuit and professor of mathematics in the university, was a master of the genre. In *Las glorias de Querétaro* and *Primavera indiana* (1668) he made a new contribution to the American sense of the marvellous in literature, a mixture of Christian devotion, pagan mythology and patriotic fervour. But the varied genius of don Carlos also introduced an entirely new form in his picaresque 'captivity story', *Los infortunios de Alonso Ramírez* (Mexico City, 1690), Spanish in technique but American in ethos, though set, in fact, in the East, especially the Philippines. In the same period Juan de Espinosa Medrano, a creole from Lima nicknamed 'El Lunarejo', was making himself a reputation as a writer. His poems and religious allegorical dramas could still excite the admiration of Menéndez y Pelayo at the end of the nineteenth century. Besides the courts of the more well-read viceroys, like the Prince of Esquilache, himself a poet, and the circles gathered with pretensions to nobility around the richest mine owners, acting as patrons of the arts, there were attempts to create academies; the first of these was the 'Academia Antartica' of Lima, a brilliant circle influenced by Italy and frequented by Italian humanists.

If the last embers of the Italian Renaissance were glowing in the Indies when the repression of the Counter-Reformation had already begun in Spain, this was due to the distance, the difficulty of control, and also the influence of personalities. Erasmus and Thomas More had profoundly marked the minds of the first evangelizers. And from the middle of the sixteenth century the same was true of the writers of Ancient Greece and Rome: *Tres diálogos latinos*, imitated from Plato, in which the *bachiller* Francisco Cervantes de Salazar described Mexico City, dates from 1554.[31] In these years one of the first Franciscans of New Spain, Fr. Alonso de la Veracruz, published an original philosophical work, the *Recognitio summularum*, while Tomás de Mercado translated Aristotle into Spanish. The main trends of the philosophical thought of the period – the criticism of Vivés as well as the ideas of Erasmus, Neoplatonism and the stoicism which a reading of Boethius helped to make fashionable – were present in the Spanish American universities in the sixteenth and seventeenth centuries. Certainly Thomist scholasticism dominated the teaching of theology, as it did in Catholic Europe at the time. But the distinctive spirituality of the creoles was rooted in the belief (supported, as we have seen, by somewhat dubious exegetic research) that the world that they were building by their own efforts was destined to become the *Paraíso occidental* (1683) of Sigüenza y Góngora, an author who tackled subjects as difficult as the study and interpretation of Indian traditions and the solution of mathematical problems; he was a fine example of a universal man, comparable to the scholars of the Italian *quattrocento*.

But the classic expression of creole culture in the area of religion was the sermon, together with the funeral oration directed towards morally edifying conclusions. In them one finds a hyperbole, half-religious and half-patriotic, which borders on heterodoxy; one preacher, carried away by his eloquence, talked of the 'Sun of Jesus eclipsed by the Moon of Mary', and another wanted to 'transport the throne of St Peter to Tepeyac' (that is, to the sanctuary of the Virgin of Guadalupe). The most amazing presumption was undoubtedly that of the Mexican *bachiller* Miguel Sánchez, who, in an apologetic essay in 1648, identified the image of the Virgin of Guadalupe of Tepeyac with the Woman of Revelation in the vision of the Apostle John. Religious creoles indeed remained fascinated by Christian eschatology, a fascination which had begun in the sixteenth century with the venerable Gregorio López's translation from Latin into Spanish of the *Treatise of the Apocalypse*, accompanied by an interlinear commentary. Besides spiritual anxiety there were also doctrinal quarrels, all the more intense because opposing views were defended by different religious orders, pitting the Jesuits, supporters of Suárez, against the Dominican Thomists and partisans of 'efficacious grace' against those of *scientia media*. An individual like the bishop of Puebla, Juan de Palafox y Mendoza,

[31] Mexico, 1939.

struggled a century before his time against the supremacy of the Jesuits, who had become the masters of the higher education system. This intellectual ferment, accompanied by various parochial quarrels, led fairly quickly to the publication of what was for the period an impressive amount of material. It was not only the number of published works (usually printed at the expense of a pious patron) which increased, but also the number of publishing houses. The menologies of the religious orders, the annual letters of the Jesuits, and the histories of the provinces (a Franciscan one for New Spain, an Augustinian one for Peru, a Dominican one for Chiapas, and so on) held an important place among these publications, and they provide the historian with general information (ethnographic, economic, social, cultural) which goes considerably beyond a chronicle of monastic life.

If we take a panoramic view of the rich abundance of literature produced between the mid sixteenth century and the mid eighteenth – a catalogue of which has been compiled by the Chilean scholar José Toribio Medina[32] – we can distinguish various stages. First, the foundation of colonial society, characterized by the chronicles and the epics, the inventories of the natural environment, and by a curiosity about the native American world and its past. Then, at the end of the sixteenth century, and especially during the seventeenth, the heroic age of military and spiritual conquest gave way to the period of exploitation of America's abundant resources, the accumulation of wealth, and the display of luxury. Obviously cultural life evolved in line with this profound mental transformation which separated the generation of pioneers from the generation enjoying its new riches. It is striking that the Indian, on whose labour the wealth of the Indies depended, does not appear in this literature (or at least not in any realistic form), with the exception of *Las virtudes del Indio* (1650?) by Palafox y Mendoza. The third stage, which began in the middle of the seventeenth century with individuals like Sigüenza y Góngora, is usually known as the 'age of the baroque', but this ambiguous expression is inadequate to define anything more than an aesthetic trend, apparent above all in religious architecture. Even more worthy of notice, however, in this third phase in the cultural life of the Indies was the dawning of an intellectual and spiritual anxiety expressed as much in Sor Juana's renunciation of the world as in the work of Sigüenza y Góngora, editor of the first Spanish

[32] See *CHLA* II, Bibliographical Essay 16.

American periodical, *Mercurio Volante* (1693). This publication was perhaps the first echo in the Indies of the development of rational knowledge in Europe, as was the same author's *Manifiesto filosófico contra los cometas* (1681), which attacked the superstitions about astrological interpretations of comets which were current in this period. In the other major centre of the Spanish American world, the rector of the University of San Marcos of Lima, Pedro de Peralta y Barnuevo, devoted himself with equal success to mathematics, cosmography, and several other branches of learning. In the same years a treatise on surgery was published in Lima; Descartes and Malebranche, banned from the universities, were read secretly; and the Jesuits Kino and Athanasius Kircher, the former in the field as a missionary, the latter a scholar in the library, enriched geographical and cosmographical knowledge by studying California. But to prevent people illegally practising medicine the Council of the Indies created Tribunales de Protomedicato (Medical Boards) in Lima, Mexico City, Bogotá, and other cities. There was, at the end of the seventeenth century, a flowering of intellectual enquiry full of promise for the future; this period, which Paul Hazard has called *The crisis of the European mind*, was an era of plenitude for 'the Hispano-American mind', which in its turn only entered into a critical phase three-quarters of a century later.

THE CENTURY OF ENLIGHTENMENT

The opening decades of the eighteenth century were hardly distinguishable from the closing decades of the seventeenth, except in developing and accentuating trends begun in the latter. The demographic recovery, especially important where Indians were most numerous, the revival of the mining economy, the increase in miscegenation – all these were factors which strengthened the American consciousness of the creoles. Indeed the characteristic phenomenon of this period, which I have examined elsewhere for the case of Mexico (at this time still called 'New Spain'), is what I have described as 'creole triumphalism'.[33] The spiritual roots of this climate of ideas went back a long way, since they originated in the belief that through the Virgin Mary, who had selected the soil of America as a dwelling place among men, God had set the creoles apart from the rest of humanity. This

---

[33] Jacques Lafaye, *Quetzalcoatl and Guadeloupe. The formation of the national consciousness in Mexico*, trans. from the original French by Benjamin Keen (Chicago, 1976).

divine choice was shown in many ways: by the abundance of edible fruits, and by the wealth of metals hidden in the entrails of the earth or even sometimes open to the sky. The boom in public and private building which accompanied urban development in Mexico, New Granada, and even Chile and the lands of La Plata only stimulated creole pride. The baroque eloquence of the preachers, an inheritance from the previous century, echoing the monumental splendour of the new neoclassical architecture, exalted 'imperial' Mexico City, 'the Rome of the New World'. There was a new development: despite the epidemics of 1725 and 1736, the population of Mexico City soon overtook that of Madrid. In other words, the 'imperial city' of the Spanish empire was, from the middle of the eighteenth century, no longer situated in the Old World but in the New. In this period, when the traditional system of values established after the conquests of the sixteenth century was still intact, any sort of superiority was interpreted as a sign from heaven, a sign inciting the creoles of America to free themselves from the bureaucratic control of, and religious dependence on, Spain. If all preachers did not go so far as to hope to 'transport the throne of St Peter to Tepeyac', many of them did dream of 'Guadalupanizing' Christianity. This was the significance of missionary expansion towards the north of Mexico, now stimulated more by creoles than by Spaniards. The Franciscans of the Seminario de Propaganda Fide de Querétaro, recruited from the families of the creole 'aristocracy', were, as the inspirers of this movement, comparable to the pioneers of evangelization in the sixteenth century. Alongside the Franciscans (who had been the most numerous since the beginning of colonization), the Jesuits undoubtedly played the leading role in what was an authentic spiritual revival. As teachers of young creole boys and confessors of the nuns who taught the young girls, the Jesuits in fact controlled the ideological and spiritual upbringing of the creoles. Thanks to its colleges, which produced the creole civil and ecclesiastical elite, the all-powerful Society (powerful also in the economic sphere owing to bequests of properties which it administered efficiently) contributed significantly to developing American patriotism. More open-minded than certain rival orders, such as the Dominicans (who held numerous chairs in theology), the Jesuits encouraged the introduction into the universities of the New World of the theories of people such as Suárez or Malebranche, which deviated considerably from the philosophical dogma of Thomist scholasticism. As the only religious order not under royal patronage and depending directly on Rome, the Jesuits could resist not only the bishops nominated by the king, but even the *audiencias* and viceroys; and discontented creoles could turn to them for moral support.

Against a background of continued demographic and economic growth, the social climate of the middle decades of the eighteenth century was marked by an increase in tension between creoles (*americanos*) and Spaniards (*gachupines* or *chapetones*). The colonial sense of inferiority which had since the sixteenth century led the creoles to protest against the disdain felt for them by the newly arrived Spaniards invested with administrative, judicial and military power had been replaced by a sense of the superiority of America. This new attitude among creoles aroused their sense of the injustice of their almost total exclusion from official civil offices (and their total exclusion from the high ranks of the army) and of the real inequality into which the system of 'alternation' between Spaniards and creoles in the religious orders had developed. This social climate is attested to by documents such as the *Representación vindicatoria que en el año 1771 hizo a su Magestad la Ciudad de Mexico, Cabeza de aquel Nuevo Mundo, en nombre de toda la nación española-americana*. Alongside a creole society of landed proprietors, aspiring to ennoblement or already ennobled by the purchase of a title, and found in the cities of the Andes or in central Mexico, there appeared a new creole society. This society was often descended from recent Spanish immigrants – the eighteenth century saw an important revival of immigration – who were often of Basque, Catalan or Valencian origin and no longer from Castile or Andalusia. A professional and commercial bourgeoisie developed, less in the seignioral towns of the interior than in the ports, which were more open to trade, legal and illegal, and therefore also to ideas. Books and prohibited engravings were at first smuggled in, especially from Holland. And it was in these 'bourgeois' towns that new universities were created, immediately becoming centres where creole self-consciousness was asserted. A good example of this was the University of San Jerónimo, created in 1728 in Havana, the gateway of America, *La Llave del Nuevo Mundo* (1761),[34] as it was described by Felix de Arrate, who was born there, in the title of a book which was not to appear until 1830. The universities of Santa Rosa, founded in 1725 in Caracas, and of Santiago de Chile (1738), are other signs of a new direction in cultural development which coincided with the apogee of the traditional creole spirit. Both, incidentally, like the universities of Mexico City and Lima,

[34] J. le Riverend (ed.), Mexico, 1949.

had medical schools. The economic expansion of the eighteenth century was accompanied by considerable creativity in the cultural field: the theatrical life of Lima went through a magnificent period; operas were composed, and in the middle of the century a symphony orchestra was founded in Caracas, which remained supreme in this field until the beginning of the twentieth century. This was also, of course, a brilliant period for neoclassical painting, as well as architecture, and the works (religious allegories and civil portraits) of several genuinely great painters have been preserved. But this is not the place to study further aspects of culture which developed alongside that of the written word.

Publishing, whether of books or periodicals, had remained rare on the continent, being confined essentially to Mexico City and Lima, owing to a protectionist policy which favoured the printers of Spain; but it now benefited from exemptions, especially in favour of the Jesuits. Many writers (largely of piety, it is true) were to be published by the presses of the College of San Ildefonso in Mexico City, which started to function in 1748. Much more significant was the setting up in 1753 of the publishing house for the *Bibliotheca mexicana* by Juan José de Eguiara y Eguren,[35] whose objective was to list the works of all Mexican (that is, creole) authors since the foundation of New Spain in order to show the *gachupines*, and indeed the whole world, that American Spaniards had been writing great works – and plenty of them – for the last two and a half centuries. A printer might print over 1,000 copies of a book, which, taking account of their high price and the illiteracy of all but a privileged minority of the population, implies that the potential market was much wider than simply the region of Mexico.

The first half of the eighteenth century was characterized, then, by the creoles' exaltation of their American homeland; by a recognition of the contribution of creole culture to that of Spain and the rest of the world; and by the setting up of universities and publishing houses which would become the centres of American dissent and eventually revolt. The decisive hour for Spanish America struck in 1759 with the accession of Charles III. The new king, who had spent some years in Naples as viceroy, was imbued with ideas of scientific and educational progress and administrative reform. Moreover, he surrounded himself with advisers like Jovellanos and Campomanes, who were determined to bring Spain into line with France and England. One of the most important of a series of 'reforming' decrees, important for its economic

[35] Only one volume (A to C) appeared, in 1755. Agustín Millares Carlo (ed.), Mexico, 1944.

and spiritual – and therefore political – consequences, was undoubtedly the expulsion of the Society of Jesus from all the territories of Europe and America belonging to the crown of Castile. In 1767 and the years which followed, more than 2,600 Jesuits from the Indies were put on boats for Corsica and Italy, carrying with them in their hearts the image of their American homeland, for many of them were by this time creoles. This measure not only caused violent upheavals as much in the Indian missions as in the religious communities linked to the Society, but also profoundly disrupted social, cultural, and intellectual life. At the same time the regular clergy as a whole came under pressure from Charles III to return to a strict observance of the rules of their orders and in particular to confine themselves to their cloisters. They found it increasingly difficult to fulfil their traditional role in creole education and culture.

The spirit of creole culture was changing. The first trial of Freemasons before a tribunal of the Inquisition had taken place in Lima in 1751, but fifteen years before this Mexico already had four lodges; and – the fact is worthy of note – in Cadiz, whose *consulado* still had control over maritime trade with the Indies, there was at this time a lodge of 800 Masons. It was in the middle of the century, then, before the accession of Charles III, that the creole bourgeoisie – in particular that of ports like Havana, Veracruz or Caracas – first discovered the forbidden fruit of secret societies, which to some extent satisfied their demands for new scientific and philosophical knowledge and liberty from the bureaucracy of Spain. This was all, however, still far removed from the spirit which was to inform the Independence movements at the beginning of the next century. The ambition of even the most daring creoles was still only for reforms which could give them what, as Americans, they considered their rightful and deserved place in the conduct of public affairs, what would today be called 'internal autonomy'. However, in the course of the second half of the eighteenth century the competition between the Spaniards and the creoles of America further intensified. Comparing the merits of Spain and New Spain became a standard exercise among the clergy, scholars and members of *cabildos* (municipal councils). What Antonello Gerbi has called *La disputa del Mondo Nuovo* (1955), which thrilled enlightened Europe on the eve of the French Revolution, was largely an anthropological and sociological argument which at the same time served as a screen for the political aspirations of the creoles. In his essay devoted to

America, *Recherches philosophiques sur les Américains* (Berlin, 1768), the Prussian priest Cornelius de Pauw claimed that although the awakening of the American creoles might have preceded that of the Europeans, they were nevertheless inferior to them owing to a lack of perseverance and a premature intellectual and physical decline. Even the fauna of America was compared unfavourably to that of the Old World. Such judgements naturally provoked the creoles to further counterattacks; and this time the affair assumed international proportions, owing to the presence in Italy of exiled creole Jesuits who took up the challenge. Francisco Javier Clavijero, an ex-Jesuit (the Society having been dissolved by the Pope), published at Cesena, in an Italian translation, a *Storia antica del Messico* (1780),[36] concluding with a series of 'dissertations' refuting Pauw's allegations point by point. The debate was taken up by one of the mouthpieces of the *Aufklärung*, the *Deutsche Merkur* of Weimar, which devoted three issues to it, including contributions in 1786 by both Clavijero and Cornelius de Pauw. The controversy about the supposed inferiority (whether biological or caused by the climate) of the Americans in relation to the Europeans, the creoles in relation to the Spaniards, in fact posed the question of the capacity of the creoles of America to govern themselves. As when, in the sixteenth century, Sepúlveda had invoked Aristotle against Las Casas to show that the native Americans were born to be slaves, so Pauw used the authority of Buffon to justify the colonial dependence of the American creoles.

The splendid flowering of the arts and sciences in Spanish America during the second half of the eighteenth century – and especially the last quarter – provided a striking rebuttal of the harsh (and pseudo-scientific) verdict of Pauw and his partisans. The famous Escuela de Minería of Mexico City, to which the name of León y Gama remains attached, was founded in 1772. Academies of fine arts were founded in both Mexico and Guatemala in the 1780s. A number of economic societies, notably those in Cuba and Guatemala, were established. In Bogotá in 1783 José Celestino Mutis (born in Cadiz) and the creole Francisco José de Caldas brought together a comprehensive collection of botanical plates of the flora of the New World. The town was already provided with a public library founded by Moreno y Escandón, very representative of the spirit of the Enlightenment; some years later an

[36] Spanish trans., *Historia antigua de México* (4 vols., Mexico, 1945; also 4 vols., Mexico, 1958).

astronomical observatory was also set up. Even a region like the Río de la Plata, which had only recently become a viceroyalty after two centuries of neglect, took part in this scientific and cultural awakening. Throughout the continent, both pure and applied sciences made progress. Four chairs of law were created in the University of Chile (in 1756), one in Córdoba, and one in Chuquisaca. A new generation of lawyers was trained who, less than 25 years later, were to become the theorists of the independence movements and the members of the constituent assemblies of the newly liberated states of Spanish America. This intellectual ferment was not confined to the universities and academies or the Masonic lodges as it had in the past been confined to the religious houses. New ideas and new knowledge were disseminated by the press. To the *Gaceta de Madrid*, reprinted in America since 1737, and the *Gacetas* of Mexico City and Lima were added new names like the *Diario Erudito, Económico y Comercial de Lima* – its title indicates how diverse were its interests – which became the future *Mercurio Peruano*. Others followed, like the *Mercurio Volante* of the Mexican Ignacio Bartolache and the *Primicias de la cultura*, published in Quito. Another indication of both the appetite of the reading public and the abundance of subject material – as well as of the existence of a certain press freedom – was the fact that the *Gaceta de Lima* started to come out fortnightly. At the same time as the appearance of this unprecedented number of periodical publications an attempt at synthesis was undertaken in a number of fields. In that of history we have already mentioned the name of Clavijero, but his was not an isolated case; a work like the huge five-volume *Diccionario geográfico histórico de las Indias* by the Ecuadorian Antonio de Alcedo, published in Madrid in 1786–9, is yet more evidence of the desire to bring together all that was known about the natural world as well as history.[37] Clavijero was a former Jesuit and Alcedo a soldier, captain of the Royal Guard: the spirit of the century had spread to the most important civil and religious institutions. Even more revealing of the growing confidence of the creoles was the *memorias* (at that time unpublished) of the Dominican creole Fr. Servando Teresa de Mier, descendant of a governor of Nuevo León and nephew of a Grand Inquisitor, who later gave up holy orders. Exiled to Spain after an imprudent sermon delivered in the presence of the authorities for the festival of the Virgin of Guadalupe in the

[37] English trans., 5 vols., London, 1812–15.

cathedral of Mexico City, Mier looked at Old Spain through the uncompromising eyes of a creole rejecting a dependence which he considered to be unjust. He wrote that in the whole of the diocese of Burgos he had been able to find only a single Bible – and that one was incomplete. He condemned the crudeness of the language of the Aragonese; with some forthrightness he denounced the delays and corruption of the royal bureaucracy of the Escorial and the crass ignorance of Spanish regular clergy, especially the Dominicans of the province of Santander (his first place of exile), who, knowing him to be Mexican, had been amazed that he was not a 'negro' – he, Servando Teresa de Mier Noriega y Guerra, scion of a celebrated creole family from New Spain! The indignation of clerics treated in this way burst out in all directions, as in the *Carta a los Españoles americanos* of the Peruvian priest, Vizcardo, or that of another ex-Jesuit from Tucumán, Diego León Villafañe, who would later participate in the *Revolución de Mayo* in the viceroyalty of La Plata.

All these individuals were clearly men of the eighteenth century. But it was among those more directly influenced by the spirit of the Enlightenment (which had spread widely owing to the importation and circulation of books and tracts which the Inquisition was no longer succeeding in confiscating and burning) that the participants of the independence movement are more often to be found. In these years, so decisive for the evolution of ideas in Spanish America, tens of thousands of books were imported and put on sale in Lima, as advertisements of the period make clear. Ideas were transferred through the works of Spanish authors like Feijóo, Jovellanos, and others, but especially important were books by English and French *philosophes*. The *Encyclopaedia* circulated widely, as did the works of Voltaire, Rousseau, and Bentham, and a book very critical of Spanish Colonization, the *Histoire philosophique et politique…des Européens dans les deux Indes*, by the enlightened priest, Guillaume Thomas Raynal, which went through numerous editions after that of 1770. Raynal had never, in fact, set foot in America. More fortunate – and also more credible, because more truly learned – was the Prussian Baron Alexander von Humboldt, who, accompanied by the Frenchman Aimé Bonpland, secured an authorization to travel through the Indies at the turn of the century. This mission resulted, over a period of several years, in several masterpieces, such as the *Essai politique sur le royaume de la Nouvelle Espagne*,[38] the *Voyage aux régions équinoxiales du Nouveau Continent*,[39] and the *Essai sur Cuba*.[40] Even though he was not able to complete his essay on Peru, he provided an irreplaceable account of creole society at the end of the eighteenth century and the beginning of the nineteenth. And his picture of the relations between creoles and Spaniards confirmed that presented by Jorge Juan y Santacilia and Antonio de Ulloa, two officers of the Spanish navy on an intelligence mission (1735–44) to the Pacific coast of South America, in their *Noticias secretas de Américas*,[41] who in turn reaffirmed what the Marqués de Barinas had predicted 50 years before them in his treatise *Vaticinios de la pérdida de las Indias* (1685).[42] But none of these authors was listened to, and through force of circumstance – or rather of ideas and the men who took up arms to defend them – the Spanish monarchy lost the Indies. Among those writers, orators and leaders of cultural and scientific activity who prepared mens' minds for independence, certain names stand out: Nariño in Colombia, Belgrano in Argentina, Lizardi in Mexico. The writings of José Joaquín Fernández de Lizardi (who had taken the pseudonym of *El Pensador Mexicano*, later (1817) to become the title of the newspaper he founded) criticizing the prevailing mores and social organization, led to his arrest by the viceregal authorities. In his most important novel, *El periquillo sarniento* (1816), he succeeded perfectly in adapting the spirit of the Enlightenment to the tradition of the Spanish picaresque novel. No less traditional, but equally modern in its critical inspiration, was *Lima por dentro y por fuera* (1792) by the Peruvian satiric poet Simón de Ayanque, which portrayed the realities of the society of the Peruvian capital, with its mixture of races and cultures, and played its part in undermining the established order.

Far from having been the last refuge of theocracy, obscurantism, and barbarism, as was long claimed by most European historians of the time

---

[38] Paris, 1811. English trans., *Political Essay on the Kingdom of New Spain* (4 vols., London, 1811); also trans. John Black, ed. Mary Maples Dunn (New York, 1972).

[39] Paris, 1808. English trans., *Personal Narrative of Travels to the Equinoctial Regions of the New Continent During the Years 1799–1804* (7 vols., London, 1814–29; 1852; reprint, 3 vols., 1971); modern Spanish edition, 5 vols., Caracas, 1941–2.

[40] First Spanish edition, 1827. English trans. (abridged), *The Island of Cuba* (New York, 1856); modern Spanish edition, *Ensayo político sobre la isla de Cuba* (Havana, 1960).

[41] Confidential report written in 1748, first published in London in 1826; 2 vols., Madrid, 1918. See also *Relación histórica del viaje a la América* (2 vols., Madrid, 1748); English trans., *A voyage to South America* (London, 1758); abridged version of 1802 translation, Irving A. Leonard (ed.) (New York, 1964).   [42] Caracas, 1949.

(and later by liberal historians of nineteenth-century Latin America), Spanish America had by the end of the eighteenth century reached a high level of cultural achievement. Humboldt's testimony about New Spain has remained justly famous: he enthused over the splendour of the monuments of Mexico City, comparable in his view only to St Petersburg and Paris, and claimed that no other town of the New World had universities and literary and scientific institutions of an equal standard. This judgement, formulated some 30 years before the political independence of Mexico, echoed those of the humanist scholar Cervantes de Salazar, written 30 years after the conquest of Mexico by Cortés, and the Neapolitan traveller Gemelli Carreri at the end of the seventeenth century. Honest foreign observers praised creole culture as much for its architectural achievements as for its institutions of higher education or its schools of technology. From the outset creole culture – far from remaining frozen in neoclassicism or trapped in an outmoded scholasticism – was open to outside influences. From the first decade of colonization the Indies were affected by the most representative spiritual and artistic traditions of the Renaissance (coming either directly from their origins in Italy or via Spain and Flanders). By the seventeenth century, the aesthetic ideas and achievements of the Golden Age of Spain – baroque and neoclassicism, *conceptismo* and *culteranismo* – were both imitated and rivalled in America. From the middle of the eighteenth century, as the ideas of the Enlightenment penetrated the Spanish possessions, American creoles had aspirations to the intellectual as well as the cultural leadership of the Spanish world. Finally, after the American War of Independence and the French Revolution many creoles took up revolutionary ideas which found expression in the speeches and proclamations of Hidalgo, Bolívar, and other leaders of the revolutions for Spanish American independence (1810–25).

A NOTE ON LITERATURE
AND INTELLECTUAL LIFE IN
COLONIAL BRAZIL

The first account of Brazil dates from Cabral's landfall on the coast of
South America in 1500: the letter of Pero Vaz de Caminha to Dom
Manuel I, 1 May 1500 (in William Brooks Greenlee (ed.), *The voyages
of Pedro Álvares Cabral to Brazil and India from contemporary documents and
narratives* (Hakluyt Society, London, 1937)). The three most important
sixteenth-century chronicles are, first, Pero de Magalhães de Gandavo,
Tratado da terra do Brasil and *Historia da Provincia da Santa Cruz* (Lisbon,
1576; Eng. trans., John B. Stetson, Junior, *The histories of Brazil* (2 vols.,
Cortes Society, New York, 1922)); secondly, Fernão Cardim S.J., *Do
clima e terra do Brasil* and *Do principio e origem dos indios do Brasil* [*c.* 1584],
published as 'A treatise of Brasil' in Samuel Purchas, *Hakluytus
Posthumus, or Purchas His Pilgrimes* (4 vols., London, 1625; 20 vols.,
Glasgow, 1905–7), and *Tratados da terra e gente do Brasil*, ed. Capistrano
de Abreu (Rio de Janeiro, 1925); thirdly, and most important of all,
Gabriel Soares de Sousa, *Tratado descritivo do Brasil em 1587* (first
published Rio de Janeiro, 1851; São Paulo, 1938). Especially interesting
and valuable are the letters and reports of the Jesuits who arrived with
the founders of royal government in 1549. Most notable are the writings
of Manoel de Nóbrega (during the period 1549–70) and José de
Anchieta (during the period 1554–94). There are a number of collections
of Jesuit letters. See, in particular, Serafim Leite, *Monumenta Brasiliae* (4
vols., Rome, 1956–60). The Jesuits set up ten colleges, four seminaries
and a novitiate, beginning with Santo Inácio (São Paulo) in 1554, Todos
os Santos (Bahia) in 1556, Rio de Janeiro in 1567, and Olinda in 1576.
The Jesuits dominated secondary education in colonial Brazil until their
expulsion in 1759. Unlike colonial Spanish America, no university was
ever established in colonial Brazil. There are numerous descriptions of
Brazil in the sixteenth century by non-Portuguese: André Thévet, Jean

de Léry, Ulrich Schmidel, Hans Staden, Anthony Knivet, Gaspar de Carvajal, and many others.

The foremost chronicle of the more complex society of seventeenth-century Brazil is Ambrosio Fernandes Brandão, *Os diálogos das grandezas do Brasil* (1618; ed. José António Gonsalves de Mello, Recife, 1962; 2nd edn, 1966). Also interesting is the satirical verse of the *bahiano* Grégorio de Matos (1633–90). The first history of Brazil, written by a Brazilian-born Franciscan (who drew heavily on Gabriel Soares de Sousa), is Vicente do Salvador's *Historia do Brasil* of 1627 (eds. Capistrano de Abreu and Rodolfo Garcia, 3rd edn, revised, São Paulo, 1931). The Dutch occupation of north-east Brazil (1630–54) produced important studies by Dutch scholars and scientists. The Jesuits continued to write about Brazil, especially about the interior: a notable contribution is Simão de Vasconcellos, *Chronica da Companhia de Jesus do Estado do Brasil* (Lisbon, 1663; 2nd edn, 2 vols., Lisbon, 1865), which deals largely with the second half of the sixteenth century. The exemplary literary figure of the seventeenth century is, however, the Jesuit António Vieira (1608–97); his sermons and writings, especially in defence of the Indians, represent one of the high points of Luso-Brazilian culture. See *Padre António Vieira: obras Escolhidas* (12 vols., Lisbon, 1951–4); *Padre António Vieira: Sermões* (14 vols., Lisbon, 1679–1710; 3 vols., Porto, 1908); *Cartas do António Vieira*, ed. J. L. de Azevedo (3 vols., Coimbra, 1925–8).

The most famous treatise on Brazil's natural resources and economy at the end of the seventeenth and beginning of the eighteenth centuries is *Cultura e opulência do Brasil por suas drogas e minas* by Giovanni Antonio Andreoni (João Antonio Andreoni) (1649–1716), an Italian Jesuit who wrote under the pseudonym Andre João Antonil. It was prepared over ten years beginning in 1693 and first published in Lisbon in 1711. There are various modern editions; by far the most scholarly is that edited by Andrée Mansuy (Paris, 1968). 1730 saw the publication in Lisbon of Sebastião da Rocha Pitta, *História da América Portuguesa* (3rd edn, Bahia, 1950), the first general history of Brazil by a Brazilian since that of Vicente do Salvador a century earlier.

Brazilians had to travel to Coimbra for a university education, but in the middle decades of the eighteenth century a number of attempts were made in both Bahia and Rio de Janeiro to set up scientific and literary academies and societies. The most notable were the Academia Cientifica (1771) and the Sociedade Literaria (1785) of Rio de Janeiro.

It was, however, in Vila Rica (Ouro Preto), Minas Gerais, in the 1780s that the literary and intellectual life of colonial Brazil reached its highest level. And outstanding were the *mineiro* poets: Claudio Manuel da Costa (*Vila Rica*), José Inácio de Alvarengo Peixoto, Manuel Inácio da Silva Alvarengo, José Basílio da Gama (*O Uraguay*), José de Santa Rita Durão (*Caramurú*) and Tomás Antonio Gonzaga (most famous for his satirical *Cartas chilenas*). Many of this brilliant generation of intellectuals and poets participated in the *Inconfidência mineira* (1788–9).

During the last decade of the eighteenth century and the first decade of the nineteenth, a number of important political and economic works were produced in Brazil, although, as always, published in Lisbon. (Until 1808 there was no printing press in Brazil.) Most worthy of note are José Joaquim da Cunha de Azeredo Coutinho, *Ensaio económico sobre o comércio de Portugal e suas colonias* (1794; in *Obras económicas*, ed. Sérgio Buarque de Holanda, São Paulo, 1966); Luis dos Santos Vilhena, *Recopilação de notícias soteropolitanas e brasílicas contidas em XX cartas* (1802; 3 vols., Bahia, 1921–2), the most important source on the economic, social, and political conditions of late colonial Brazil and especially Bahia, where the author lived from 1787 to *c.* 1804; and João Rodrigues de Brito, *Cartas econômico-políticas sobre a agricultura e o comércio da Bahia* (1807; Lisbon, 1821; Bahia, 1924).

For more detailed information on these and other colonial texts (and their various editions), see Samuel Putnam, *Marvellous Journey. A survey of four centuries of Brazilian writing* (New York, 1948); Rubens Borba de Moraes, *Bibliographia Brasiliana. A bibliographical essay on rare books about Brazil published from 1504 to 1900 and works of Brazilian authors published abroad before the Independence of Brazil in 1822* (2 vols., Amsterdam, 1958; rev. and enlarged, 2 vols., Rio de Janeiro and Los Angeles, 1983); Rubens Borba de Moraes, *Bibliografia brasileira do período colonial* (São Paulo, 1969); and José Honório Rodrigues, *História da história do Brasil*, 1: *Historiografia colonial* (São Paulo, 1979).

17

THE ARCHITECTURE AND ART OF
COLONIAL SPANISH AMERICA*

This chapter is divided geographically into two broad regions: first Mexico, Central America, and the Caribbean; then the rest of Spanish America, that is Spanish South America. Within each we shall look at architecture, sculpture, and painting. The emphasis will be on architecture, especially religious architecture, together with the quasi-architectural retables (a kind of 'fantasy architecture'). In the fields of sculpture and painting we shall encounter some distinguished artists and even some series of significant works which, with some difficulty, might be deemed to constitute a 'school', such as the Quito school in sculpture and the Cuzco school in painting. But only in the field of architecture do we find any coherence and continuity. It is therefore to architecture that we must look for the key to an understanding of the culture of colonial Spanish America.

Ninety per cent of what is interesting in Spanish colonial architecture falls into the category of religious architecture. Important cities possessed a cathedral plus a smaller or greater number of parish churches in the hands of the secular clergy. Belonging to the regular clergy of the religious orders, besides the convents themselves were the churches and chapels that depended upon them, known as *conventuales*. 'Religious' architecture, however, consisted not only of cathedrals, churches, and chapels but also hospitals, colleges, universities, and other institutions which in colonial society were the responsibility of the church, as well as estate and mission buildings. And as the financial resources of the church grew, its wealth was expressed in the increasing size and splendour of its buildings. The civil power was content to have typically Spanish public buildings with a positively spartan look about them in comparison with the relatively luxuriant structures, eclectic in

* Translated from the original Spanish by Dr Richard Boulind; translation revised by the Editor.

style, of the omnipresent religious establishment. Domestic architecture was still less pretentious and even more derived from purely Spanish influences, southern (Mediterranean) or northern.

The architecture and art of colonial Spanish America is certainly more than an imitation of Spanish or European models. On the other hand, compared with costume, cuisine, or music, for example, surprisingly few elements can be said to be of native origin. In general, Mexico, Central America, and the Caribbean were the areas most directly open to Spanish influence. Some areas of Spanish South America – Quito, for example – attracted many of the religious who came to the New World from European countries other than Spain and many non-Spanish architects and painters. Cultural developments were most original, 'mestizo' or 'American' in the more remote areas of Spanish South America like the highlands around Arequipa, the Collao, and the cities of the altiplano, even Cuzco and Potosí. In architecture the dominant style, particularly the basic structural technique of cross-vaulting, during the 'heroic age', the sixteenth century, when the religious orders – Franciscan, Dominican, Augustinian, and Mercedarian – competed with one another in the exploration of unknown territory, the conversion of Indians and the building of churches and convents, is reminiscent of European Gothic. We also find Mudéjar[1] ceilings, Plateresque[2] façades and cloisters, and Mannerist plans (most often imitations of Juan de Herrera (1530–97), the architect of the Escorial and the cathedral at Valladolid) in some large cathedrals, such as those of Mexico City and Puebla. The growing importance of the Jesuits was to coincide with the introduction of the baroque in architecture and the decorative arts and this was the dominant style from the middle of the seventeenth to the middle of the eighteenth centuries. Then, towards the end of the colonial period, the latter part of the Age of the Enlightenment, the baroque began to give place, first, to a more courtly style that was French in inspiration – the rococo – and then to a return to the Greco-Latin mode in the shape of neoclassicism. 'Style', however, is a fatally European concept in this context. Rather, we have to experiment with a new nomenclature and a thoroughly Spanish American classification of forms – one seen from within the continent itself and not, as has always been the case hitherto, from outside.

---

[1] A style in architecture and the decorative arts practised by the Arabs in Spain – both the converts (*moriscos*) and the subdued (*mudéjares*) working in the service of the Christians – between the twelfth and the sixteenth centuries.

[2] A typically Spanish style of the sixteenth century, more decorative than structural, in which Arab, late Gothic, and – predominantly – Italian Renaissance elements are combined.

MEXICO, CENTRAL AMERICA, AND THE CARIBBEAN

Architecture

Soon after the discovery of the Caribbean islands, the *conquistadores* in Hispaniola threw themselves into a vast programme of building with an intensity they could not hope to maintain when they began the conquest and settlement of the mainland. Early colonial buildings still standing in the city of Santo Domingo remind us how grandiose this programme was, even though it was completed neither there nor in Cuba and Puerto Rico. This first wave of construction relied on local materials combined with European techniques. When there was nothing to build with but adobe and straw, the settlers built themselves huts like those of the Taínos, but when they began to demand nobler edifices, they had to call in masons and sculptors who came directly from Spain. As might be supposed, these earliest constructions range in style from late Gothic to an Italian Renaissance, narrowly defined, in style. There was a time-lag of about a century, however, since we note here the direct imitation of *quattrocento* forms, or the copying of them at one remove, via the 'Spanish Renaissance' style known as *a lo romano*, which later was to be known as the Plateresque. Sometimes ceilings displayed the method of piecing woodblocks together that was a hallmark of the work of the Mudéjares. This method went under the name of *carpintería de lo blanco*. Those wooden ceilings that consisted of star-shaped polygons were especially prized, at least in the sixteenth and seventeenth centuries, although we sometimes encounter them in the eighteenth as well. They were not only a form of artistic expression; they actually constituted a structural procedure of high ingenuity, especially where there was a shortage of good straight building timber. Everything that was built in the early colonial period – from Santo Domingo to Mexico – was inevitably imbued with a certain rustic character. However, though it might be somewhat modest, architecture was expected to have some sort of impact, even nobility.

In Santo Domingo the best building of this period is without doubt the cathedral. It was planned by the first bishop, Alessandro Geraldini, who had been a friend of the 'Catholic Monarchs' Ferdinand and Isabella. Here was an Italian humanist at work, who could do no less than ensure that his own see – chronologically the first in America – should display some feature of his glorious native land. In fact, the cathedral's great façade consists of a double arch in Italian Renaissance style, incorporating a motif that embodies false perspective in the form of *trompe-l'œil*. Without much logic, this doorway is superimposed upon a Gothic structure that is quite modest in scale, with cross-vaulting and details finely sculpted by artists from Spain. Such luxury was, however, rare: in the so-called Alcázar, or House of Diego Columbus, we encounter a species of fortress – nowadays over-restored, unfortunately – which has two loggias of arcading, one on either side, just like the House of Cortés in Cuernavaca, Mexico, later. Also still standing are the convents of San Francisco (1544–55) and La Merced (1527–55), whose structures are basically Gothic: the first is an impressive ruin, but the second is still intact. The Hospital de San Nicolás (1533–52) is cruciform in plan, like the hospitals that the Spanish crown erected in Santiago de Compostela and Toledo. This, too, is nowadays in ruins, however. Finely sculpted Plateresque details are still to be seen in the Dominican convent and on certain façades in the city. The buildings of Cuba and of Puerto Rico date from a little later, and are more modest than this brilliant beginning in Santo Domingo. Except for a few churches, the centres of interest in ports of strategic importance like Santiago de Cuba, Havana, and San Juan de Puerto Rico will always be their fortifications, which were to attain their greatest splendour in the two centuries following.

When the Spaniards came to put down roots in Mexico, they knew what models to follow better than they had in Santo Domingo. At first, both the civil and the religious authorities occupied what were really only huts, of extreme simplicity and poverty. And when serious construction began, it was the religious orders – Franciscan, Dominican, and Augustinian – who led the way: they invented the kind of convent, entirely functional, that fitted their requirements and represented both the spiritual and the temporal powers that they intended to assert. The Spanish crown had assigned different regions of Mexico to each of the orders, which arrived there in the following sequence: first the Franciscans (1524), then the Dominicans (1526), third the Augustinians (1533), and finally the Jesuits (1572). The Franciscans secured a privileged position in Puebla and Tlaxcala. The Dominicans were further south, in the *tierra caliente*, where they were more exposed to earthquakes. Lastly, the Augustinians secured the grant of lands in the north of the Valley of Mexico and in Michoacán.

To appreciate the purpose and layout of these religious houses, we should not compare them with European buildings of the same period.

Rather we should refer back to Europe's eleventh century, to the era when people, although being Christianized, were still practising pagan religions and still perilously exposed to periodical invasion by the barbarians. In sixteenth-century Mexico and Guatemala the task was the same: the evangelization of a territory that was still not pacified. The best system for the friars was to root themselves in the land, working to make it productive at the same time as they undertook the 'spiritual conquest' of souls. The convent thus became a species of bridgehead – an operational base that was at once a fort, a church, and an agricultural estate. In any order, in any region, the typical convent consisted of a sizeable fortified church, together with subsidiary structures, a cloister, and an orchard. A great walled forecourt with several entrance gates extended across the entire front of the church. In the courtyard was a stone cross sited in front of the church, adjacent to an 'open chapel' – *capilla abierta* – or 'Indian chapel', from where the services could be followed without the congregation necessarily having to enter the church proper. Then, in the corners of the courtyard were 'chapels of rest' – *capillas posas* – little buildings where halts were made during liturgical processions. Clearly the 'programming', so to speak, of this architecture in New Spain is completely different from what we would find in any convent built in the same period in Europe. To be more specific, in the New World churches typically had a single nave with a polygonal apse; the walls were smooth and had buttresses and high windows to impede any intrusion from outside. The majestic nave was roofed with cross-vaulting, either real or imitation. Sometimes the façade and the sanctuary were richly adorned with a form of decoration that looked more like a theatre curtain superimposed on the building than a feature of the wall itself. The cloisters were simpler and sometimes had ogival arches, though they were more usually round or elliptical. The open chapels and the chapels of rest were another indication of the nature of the Spanish American convent. The former could be placed variously within the general plan; there was, moreover, a great deal of variety in their structure. Some (like Cuernavaca) have three bays, some (Teposcolula) five, some just one with a semicircular arch (Acolman, Actopan), while there are other designs too. When it came to the chapels of rest – little structures with pyramidal roofs – the master masons again had to use their imaginations, for there were no European models to give them inspiration. The most important of the Franciscan convents founded in the middle of the sixteenth century were Huejotzingo, Calpan, and Cuernavaca. Among the Dominican convents Yanhuitlán is outstanding; and of the Augustinian convents the most significant are Acolman and Actopan.

Traces of Romanesque practice, cross-vaulting that is Gothic in style, and Plateresque façades applied to a simpler structure behind them must not, however, be allowed to lead us astray. The master masons employed whatever structural methods, forms, and techniques were available and turned to whatever materials came to hand. Likewise, they depended upon craftsmen – architects, carvers, and painters – and labourers who could be found locally at the time. Until quite recently, art historians took the concept of deliberate design far too literally, whereas the truth was that executants of such work had, above all, to adapt themselves to a process of constant improvisation, with results that are often admirable. In addition to Spanish styles, we find in sixteenth-century Mexico occasional reminders of the Manueline style in Portugal, as in the doorway of the Porciúncula in the convent of Huejotzingo. To these unprejudiced constructors a use and value could be found for everything, for their aim was to build big, build solid, and build fast.

In the late sixteenth century, however, a different type of church made its appearance – one on a plan featuring a central nave, with side aisles. Such churches were mainly the work of the Franciscans at Tecali and at Zacatlán de las Manzanas (1562–7). They have tall columns supporting their wooden roofs. Around this time, however, the Dominicans built the great church of Cuilapán (now in ruins), in the area of Oaxaca; it was constructed between 1555 and 1568 and had a relatively low nave, with aisles on either side.

The seventeenth is the century of the cathedrals and great urban convents that are still standing in Mexico and Central America. Six or seven cathedrals were begun to replace primitive buildings that were falling down, or were destroyed by fire. The oldest of these is Mérida cathedral in Yucatán, where the west front adheres to Renaissance rules, and where the interior has high columns supporting vaults. These features are not in keeping with the old-fashioned, fortress-like effect that the building projects when viewed from outside. The cathedral of Puebla (1576–1626 and 1640–9) is the purest and the most classical of all the cathedrals. It was the work of an architect from Estremadura, Francisco Becerra (1545–1605), whom we shall meet again in Quito, Lima, and Cuzco. The vertical daringly predominates within the

building, and it has a magnificent façade in the style of Juan de Herrera
that consciously exploits the contrast between dark stone and marble.
In the interior the architect achieves an impression of great height by
artificially prolonging the proportions of the Tuscan columns. All in
all, Puebla is the most homogeneous of all that splendid flowering of
early cathedral building in Mexico. Yet Mexico Cathedral (built
between 1563 and 1700) has to be adjudged the greatest, both in size
and splendour. It was consecrated in 1667, even though it then still
lacked its dome and its towers. The work of the architect Claudio de
Arciniega (1528–93), it was, like Puebla cathedral, inspired by Jaén
Cathedral in Spain (begun in 1540). The Metropolitan Cathedral of
Mexico has three naves and two rows of side chapels closed off by grilles.
As in Puebla cathedral, its quality of verticality is achieved by Herreran
means. It is a chaste, majestic construction, with a covering of
saucer-domes also like Puebla cathedral. Neither the baroque retables,
nor the neoclassical parapets on the façade, nor the saucer-domes,
compromise the essential classicism of the interior.

As can be seen from the treatment so far, this is an attempt to study
Spanish colonial architecture by means of classification according to
period, region, and function rather than according to any insistence on
stylistic connections such as is so common even nowadays. However,
in this area of colonial cultural life history the term 'baroque' can be
properly employed only from the mid-seventeenth century onwards.
We find its first timid appearance in the shape of the 'Solomonic' – that
is, spiral, twisted, or convoluted – columns that were introduced into
the upper stage of the transept doorway of Mexico cathedral. There are
also in the capital of New Spain churches that reflect this style, such
as Santa Teresa la Antigua (1684), San Bernardo, San José de Gracia
(where rusticated[3] forms are employed), and, finally, the Sanctuary of
Guadalupe itself. The semi-hexagonal arches which then became so
popular elsewhere in Mexico are also a product of this period. So, too,
are the window-frames and the reliefs to be seen on the upper storeys
of church façades. Besides the examples in the capital already mentioned,
all sorts of architectural experiments can be seen in the provinces that
anticipate the great eighteenth-century developments known as the era
of the 'second baroque'. Thus, for example, Oaxaca witnessed the
building of the ponderous façades of the cathedral, of La Soledad (where

---

[3] From 'rustication': a mode of building in which the individual blocks or courses of stones
are emphasized by deeply recessed joints and often by a roughened surface.

they take the form of a screen), and of San Felipe Neri. In Morelia (formerly Valladolid) the city's austere cathedral was begun in 1640 by an Italian; its construction took more than a century to complete. In San Luis Potosí, too, there were efforts to get up to date.

Nevertheless, in general, it was a long time before the deeper message of the baroque was understood. Many years, in fact, were to pass before classical norms were at all seriously challenged, before there was any confident visible statement of the baroque in the shape of the three-dimensional forms that appear to 'lean out' towards the spectator, literally invading the space in which he is located. Only in the eighteenth century do we have an opportunity to witness the style's affirmation not only as a repertoire of forms, but also as to some extent a novel conception of the world. Above all, this transformation is to be seen in façades and altarpieces, since in general the plans of churches did not lend themselves wholeheartedly to the 'delirium' of the baroque. The transformation occurred, above all, in Mexico City, thanks to two great architects from Spain, Lorenzo Rodríguez (1704–74) and Jerónimo Balbás (active 1709–61). About this time also, or a little later, a number of Mexican architects began to reveal their abilities.

To summarize what was novel, first of all certain 'movements' were introduced into façades. One was the huge concavity, formed by a colossal niche, in the church of San Juan de Dios in Mexico City. Another innovation was the highlighting of contrasts in materials and textures, both for structural and for ornamental purposes. Thus *tezontle*, a deep red volcanic rock, would be set off by *chiluca*, a sand-coloured stone. Thirdly, the Solomonic column was gradually replaced by the *estípite*, a square-sectioned column of inverted pyramidal shape which seems, to some extent, to reproduce the proportions of the human body. The old-fashioned Spanish idea of concentrating decoration around door, windows, and on the upper portions of buildings remained influential, as is demonstrated by the church of Santa Prisca in Taxco, one of the few churches which we can identify as having been built all of a piece. Less authentic but nonetheless picturesque are the church of San Agustín (Querétaro) and the cathedrals of San Luis Potosí and Aguascalientes.

This 'second' or 'high' baroque, however, attained its greatest masterpieces not so much in façades as in some church interiors, such as Santa Rosa (Querétaro), La Valenciana (Guanajuato), La Enseñanza (Mexico City), and the church of the Tepotzotlán seminary. The style perhaps reached its climax in the Sagrario Metropolitano (1749–68), adjoining the cathedral of Mexico City, by Lorenzo Rodríguez, where the inverted pyramidal pillar is used profusely, in the Retable of the Kings in the apse of Mexico cathedral by Balbás, and in the work of this master generally. Later still, the very supports themselves – whether Solomonic columns or inverted pyramidal pillars – tended to disappear, while greater complexity of plan became common. In the Capilla del Pocito of 1777–91 in the Shrine of Guadalupe, the work of the architect Francisco Antonio Guerrero y Torres (*c.* 1720–92), curving walls of *tezontle* support three cupolas clad in glazed tiles, creating a dazzling and graceful ensemble.

The next stylistic episode was a brief rococo influence: more than any other style, it was exhibited by the interiors of certain convents for women. Later still, neoclassicism came upon the scene. By contrast with the baroque, this was, by definition, an academic style, whereas the baroque had been nothing if not popular.

The Academy of Fine Arts, founded in Mexico City by Charles III in 1785, was, from the beginning, supplied with good masters, the most eminent being the Valencian sculptor and architect Manuel Tolsá (1757–1816), active in Mexico from 1791. It was Tolsá who completed the towers, dome, and balustrade of Mexico cathedral. He also designed the magnificent School of Mining (1797–1813) in the heart of the city centre, which has come down to us in a fine state of preservation. In the provinces, Tolsá was succeeded by the Mexican Francisco Eduardo Tresguerras (1759–1833), who may be said to have designed virtually all of Celaya (Guanajuato) in the neoclassical style that he made his own.

By comparison with Mexico, Central America seems to have relatively little to offer in the field of architecture. But it is not entirely lacking in interest. Founded in 1532, Guatemala City enjoyed prosperity right up to the time of its almost total destruction in the great earthquake of 1773. Rebuilt on its new site, it is now called Guatemala la Nueva, while the other, earlier city, retains the designation simply of Antigua. Antigua's buildings, for the most part, are of brick and mortar, having a low and ponderous appearance, with decoration apparently poured over them. This architecture looks more naïve to us than that of Mexico, and the best façades and interiors have an unmistakably rustic feeling. Typically Guatemalan is the hospital and church of San Pedro (1645–65), which has a window-niche in its choir. The façade tries hard to appear correct, but it gets the proportions of its columns wrong, so they appear stunted. On the other hand, every possible expedient is resorted to in order to impart movement to inert surfaces. There is chiaroscuro, bathing some parts in light so that they contrast with those left shaded. Plaques are used to adorn the wall surfaces. Cheerful pastel colours are used to paint the buildings, all of which we now see in a semi-ruinous state. Other interesting buildings worth mentioning are the cathedral (1669–80), in which Enrique Marco Dorta identifies Italian Renaissance elements, and, particularly, La Merced (1650–90), the proportions of which are low-set, and which has niches set between chubby columns covered with white decoration that stands out in relief from a background of pale colour. Other important churches are San Francisco – which has undergone reconstruction – and El Carmen.

The best-known eighteenth-century builders were Diego de Porres, who was responsible for the Missionary College and for Santa Clara (1724–34), and Felipe de Porres, to whom the Shrine of Esquipulas must be attributed. The latter has four massive corner towers and an elevation in which distinct horizontal stratified layers of decoration repeat the same elements again and again – a design apparently contradicting the dynamic sense of movement which characterizes the baroque. Lastly, between 1751 and 1773 José Manuel Ramírez constructed the proud university building, with its cloister of mixed orders of arches. In contrast, the Colegio Tridentino exhibits a different original motif in its decoration – the rusticated pilaster. To some extent, this is to be seen all over Central America, for example in the churches of San José el Viejo and of Santa Rosa (both in Antigua), and in the cathedral of Tegucigalpa in Honduras. Amongst important civil buildings in Guatemala City are the Town Hall and the Palace of the Captains-General. These two buildings incorporate arcades with round arches springing from short columns, both in the lower and in the upper storeys.

In Cuba, too, it is the eighteenth that is the great century. Surprisingly, as if to contradict simplistic ideas about styles, its *tierra caliente* baroque cannot but strike us as being in fact both very controlled and deeply refined. The former Franciscan convent in Havana (1719–38), now the post office, is an extremely simple structure. After the short British occupation of Havana in 1762–3, the Spanish government granted the city privileges as a free port, and the whole region flourished. Angulo Iñíguez has noted the influence exerted by Cádiz on Cuba, and records for us the names of two important architects, Pedro de Medina and

Fernández Trevejos. Between them, they must have been responsible for Havana's three chief buildings of this period: the main post office (1770–92), the government house (1776–92), and the cathedral (1742–67 and later), which began life as the church of the Jesuits. Of these, the two former buildings are solid and well-proportioned. They have porticoes that are classical in type on their ground floors, and show little in the way of baroque detailing. The cathedral, on the other hand, has a façade that is virtually Borrominesque – it is full of movement, a movement created by curves that are both sober and highly effective.

Sculpture[4]

The sixteenth century begins brilliantly in Santo Domingo, as E. W. Palm, in particular, has shown. In the cathedral there is Gothic and Renaissance carving both in stone and mahogany, all of excellent quality. It must be the work of Spanish artists of high reputation, despite the fact that their names are unknown.

So far as Mexico in this period is concerned, research is difficult because of the enormous mass of artistic production it is necessary to analyse. The retable – which we shall examine first – may be said to have migrated to America fully equipped with Spanish Renaissance forms. This means that it was a sort of 'para-architecture'. Occasionally it was executed in mortar, but much more usually in wood and plaster; it combined panels of painting with three-dimensional images in niches, gilded, and painted in polychrome overall. This ensemble was halfway between theatre architecture – in that it was a sort of solider version of stage sets – and large-scale furniture. The genre progressed gradually from a Renaissance sensibility that was basically architectonic – the retable being conceived as a flat façade featuring superimposed orders[5] – to a more sculptural treatment. However, as we have already observed, art works in America tended to be an accumulation of Mannerist or baroque ingredients. The baroque style, at least in the way it had been created in Italy, had not yet been understood, so far as its deeper meaning was concerned; that is to say, it does not yet afford us any unified three-dimensional dramatic statement.

[4] Here the term 'sculpture' is used in its broadest sense – to include panelling, retables, stalls, pulpits, and confessionals as well as statues and images.

[5] The way of disposing on a façade columns or pilasters and their entablatures in a way such that each one corresponds to a single storey. As opposed to giant order: a column or pilaster extending over two or more storeys of a building. Sometimes called a colossal order.

In Mexico the retables of Huejotzingo and Xochimilco, for example, are still of the Renaissance type, with balustered or decorated columns in the lower third of the composition. Later – from the mid seventeenth century onwards – Solomonic or convoluted columns make their appearance in Mexico cathedral and in the church of Santo Domingo, Puebla, but without the retable yet achieving any sense of movement through the interplay of concave and convex shapes and the chiaroscuro that this produces. Only in the late seventeenth century, and above all in the eighteenth, does the Mexican baroque come to rely on the inverted pyramidal pillar or *estípite*, allowing it to push the style to its farthest extremes: *horror vacui*, scenery-like effects, emphasis on the sensation of depth. Clearly confirming this is the Retable of the Kings already mentioned, Jerónimo Balbás' work of 1718–32.

The great stall-carvers of seventeenth-century Mexico are the Spaniard Juan de Rojas and the Mexican Salvador de Ocampo. Rojas was the master of the sculpture in the cathedral choir (1695), and Ocampo created the stalls in the Augustinian church, also in the capital. The plasterwork of Puebla should not be overlooked, either. Originating there, the art spread to Oaxaca, where it manifested equal technical splendour. The best example in Puebla is without doubt the Chapel of the Rosary (dating perhaps from 1690), where work of great imagination transforms the chapel's dome into a 'golden grotto'. A similar effect was to be achieved a few miles away in the enchanting little church of Santa María Tonantzintla. This is an example of the same principles in décor, but here they are executed in a more popular vein. And although ceramics are scarcely sculpture, it seems appropriate here to mention the Puebla school of ceramics as an application of decorative style. Its ornamental tiles (*azulejos*) in general constitute one of the lasting glories of Mexican art, above all in the eighteenth century. This art, compounded of earth and fire, was a peculiarly Pueblan development: the province had little stone of its own. Thus, in the area around the city we find red tiles alternated with white plasterwork and with *azulejos*. This combination created an unmistakable local style, of which Puebla's Casa del Alfeñique is an example.

Let us now turn to three-dimensional sculpture proper. Beautiful pieces of sculpture possibly originating in the Iberian peninsula appear in Mexico from the sixteenth century onwards. The best are in the tradition of the Andalusian school, above all that of the great Juan Martínez Montañés (1568–1649). The seventeenth century saw the development of a Mexican school in its own right. The works in stone that it produced were placed in the porticoes of rural and urban convents – their gateways, open-air chapels, and chapels of rest – and are often splendidly wrought. The greatest period in the field of sculpture was, however, the eighteenth century. The 'second baroque' is *par excellence* a sculptural school of art. In wood, in stone, and in stucco-work, the level attained was tremendously high; more, however, on account of the decorative effect itself than of the quality of the sculpture proper. At the end of the century, however, when neo-classicism was already taking over as the dominant style, Manuel Tolsá was to show himself capable of producing an important non-religious sculpture in bronze. His equestrian statue of Charles IV in Mexico City (1803) is a genuine masterpiece in its genre.

In Guatemala, from the sixteenth century onwards, there was a school of sculpture which could boast at least two real masters – Juan de Aguirre and Quirio Cataño. The latter sculpted the so-called 'Black Christ' of 1595, which still exists in the shrine of Esquipulas. Most of the works Cataño produced were scattered across Central America or have since disappeared. Santo Domingo in the seventeenth century was poor in sculpture, in comparison with the heights attained there in the previous century. The only really interesting site (the interest derives from its iconographic value) is the Chapel of the Rosary in the Dominican church (1650–84), which has a representation of the signs of the zodiac in relief on the vault of the chapel. Nor is seventeenth-century sculpture better represented in Cuba, where only a bulky *St Christopher* by Martín de Andújar, a pupil of Martínez Montañés, deserves attention.

As for figure-carving, seventeenth- and eighteenth-century Central America imported a profusion of work from Spain, though some talented local artists also appeared. In the seventeenth century one of them was Alonso de la Paz, who sculpted the *St Joseph* in the Dominican church in Guatemala. In the eighteenth there was Juan de Chaves, the creator of a *St Sebastian* in Guatemala cathedral.

Painting

Each region and each period excels in one particular art form. Whichever one it may be, the speciality comes later to represent its period better than any other. We shall never know exactly why one art form captured the imagination and the expertise of a particular country or time more than any other. It is my belief, for example, that figure carving is relatively more important in South America – above all, in Quito – than it is in New Spain. On the other hand, in Mexico painting carries off the palm, so far as the arts of the colonial period are concerned, even though Mexican painting was heavily dependent on European models and was not as original as Mexican architecture.

In the sixteenth century there was an urgent need for figure painting to be produced rapidly, so that the Indians could be taught Christianity and European culture by seeing suitable images of them. For this purpose painting was no doubt a quicker and easier medium than sculpture. This eagerness to decorate the walls of churches and convents persisted right through the seventeenth century. Nonetheless, from the outset easel painting also enjoyed a privileged position. Religion was the inspiration of these two art forms, and the aims of both was spiritual edification. Non-religious painting was at first hardly cultivated at all in Spanish America: portraiture was not practised until the eighteenth century, when it became very popular.

Those friars who first wanted their walls decorated faced a severe shortage of capable artists, so they simply resorted to copying prints and to reproducing facsimiles from illustrated books, through the medium of the hand of some talented friar or more or less gifted Indian. Among Franciscan convents possessing wall paintings let us mention, in the first place, Huejotzingo and Cuernavaca. It is generally accepted that Augustinian convents were more luxurious than those of the other mendicant orders. And this luxury reveals itself, above all, in the abundance and quality of the wall paintings in their houses. Hence, for instance, we can admire those in the cloisters of the convent of Epazoyucán (Hidalgo), where the Flemish influence is most obvious. The convent that is richest in this sort of work is, however, Actopan, where frescoes still continue to be uncovered.

The earliest artist whose career can be documented is Juan Gerson, a precocious example of a native artist who produced work of the first importance. His paintings on *amate* paper – made from bark cut from trees – provided elegant medallions for the lower choir of the church of Tecamachalco (Puebla) in 1562. Also important is a Fleming, Simon Pereyns (or 'Perines', as he was called in Spanish), who was active, despite being tried and tortured by the Inquisition, from about 1558 to 1589. With him we move from wall painting to retable and easel painting. We are in a different world, one that is less naïve and more ambitious. We are no longer concerned with walls decorated to make the surroundings more luxurious; rather, we are now witnessing an eagerness to express religious scenes of greater spiritual meaning. To Pereyns we can attribute ten paintings inspired by Flemish compositions on the high altar at Huejotzingo (1586). He also produced the *Virgin of the Pardon*, once in the retro-choir of Mexico cathedral, but regrettably the victim of a fire in 1967. Andrés de la Concha (at one time known as 'the Master of St Cecilia') was a distinguished 'Romanist' active between 1575 and 1612. Several important works of his are preserved in the Museo Virreinal, amongst them the *St Cecilia* itself.

The turn of the seventeenth century saw the establishment in Mexico of an illustrious dynasty of painters, the Echaves. Its earliest representative came from Spain: Baltasar de Echave Orio (*c.* 1548–*c.* 1619). Amongst his better-known canvases are his *Prayer in the Garden of Olives* and his *Martyrdom of St Apronianus*, which display in various ways the influence of Italian Mannerism. Among artists of distinction in this period Luis Juárez (*c.* 1585–*c.* 1645) stands out. He was possibly of Mexican birth, and his training must be attributed to the Sevillian master Luis Alonso Vázquez and to Echave Orio. One of the latter's sons was Baltasar de Echave Ibía (1583–1660), painter of a famous *Immaculate Conception* (1622). More daring in his handling of perspective than Echave Ibía was the Dominican Fr. Alonso López de Herrera (1579–*c.* 1654). He, too, was probably of Mexican birth, and his best known works are a *Christ resurrected* and an *Assumption of the Virgin*.

One more step towards modernity was then taken by Sebastián de Arteaga (1610–56), a Baroque painter who was, in fact, a pupil of the Spanish painter Francisco Zurbarán (1598–1664) of Seville, and who, after a period of working in Cádiz, moved permanently to Mexico about 1643. His *Incredulity of St Thomas* is an important picture because of the new approach to painting it demonstrates. José Juárez (*c.* 1615–*c.* 1660) may have been trained with Arteaga, though beside the latter he at first sight appears somewhat archaic. His paintings include an *Adoration of the shepherds* and a *Martyrdom of St Justus and St Pastor*, both now in the Pinacoteca Virreinal.

We should also mention here Baltasar de Echave Rioja (1632–82). A son of Echave Ibía, who like both Arteaga and Juárez died at a relatively early age, Echave Rioja may be deemed the last of the *tenebrista* painters.[6] Pedro García Ferrer, on the other hand, is a painter who Marco Dorta believes was influenced by the Spanish painter Francisco Ribalta (1565–1628): some of his work, for example his *Immaculate Conception* in Puebla cathedral, is of great interest.

In Mexico City the seventeenth century came to a climax with a most accomplished artist: Cristóbal de Villalpando (1645–1714). For the influences on his work we have to look to Seville, more especially to Juan de Valdés Leal (1622–90). Although he may on occasion be open to reproach for careless draughtsmanship, there is no doubt that Villalpando evinces signs of eloquence in composition and brilliance in colouring. One of his works is *The Transfiguration and the brass serpent* (1683); other big canvases of his are to be seen in the sacristy of Mexico cathedral, in particular his *Church Militant* and *Church Triumphant*. The other famous painter represented in this sacristy is Juan Correa, who was active between 1674 and 1739. His works include two enormous paintings (1689–91) depicting *The Assumption of the Virgin* and *The entry of Jesus into Jerusalem*. Another work of his was the *Apocalypse*, once hanging behind the cathedral's Altar del Perdón, but unhappily lost by fire some years ago.

In the eighteenth century José Ibarra (1688–1756), a Mexican born in Guadalajara, is noteworthy. Although some claim the seventeenth was the great century for painting in Mexico, Ibarra has at least to be accepted as an outstanding draughtsman with an accomplished palette and a sense of decorative purpose. The Pinacoteca Virreinal has his *Woman taken in adultery* and an *Assumption*, the latter a more conventional treatment than the former. Miguel Cabrera (1695–1768) was a native of Oaxaca, and in his own time enjoyed a great reputation. He is best represented in the 1759 church of Santa Prisca in Taxco. In this church he painted a *Martyrdom of St Sebastian* and a *Martyrdom of St Prisca*, and also a great *Assumption* which still hangs in the sacristy. It is not so much the influence of Rubens that is observable in the latter as a certain superficial charm which stems from the French art of the period. Cabrera also painted a gigantic *Virgin of the Apocalypse*, now in the Pinacoteca Virreinal, and the celebrated portrait of Sor Juana Inés de la Cruz. Late eighteenth-century Mexican painting was poised between the baroque and the rococo. Neoclassical painting, it has to be

[6] *Tenebrismo* is a seventeenth-century Spanish style of painting derived from Caravaggio, where the contrast between light and shade is exaggerated so that a dark overall impression prevails.

admitted, did not have the time to attain the same stature. However, from that period there do remain to us a multitude of interesting portraits and self-portraits. Only the Valencian Rafael Jimeno y Planes (1759–1825) needs to be mentioned here, however: he came to Mexico as director of painting in the Academia de San Carlos, which Viceroy Revillagigedo founded in 1784.

In the case of Guatemala, the principal influence on painting was that of Zurbarán, exerted directly from Seville as much as from Mexico City, even though the latter was the viceregal capital. The Dominican church in Guatemala still houses a series of *Twelve Apostles* in the style of Zurbarán, among which the *St Matthias* and the *St John* may possibly be by the master himself. Guatemala still has some scattered works of Juan Correa, and some of the paintings that Villalpando did for the Franciscan church in Antigua. There were two relatively important painters who worked exclusively in Guatemala: Pedro de Liendo, a Basque who died in 1657 and who painted a *Life of St Dominic* which hangs in the Guatemala convent of that Order, and Captain Antonio de Montúfar (1627–65), an artist who unfortunately became blind, but who had painted scenes from the Passion in the church of the Calvary in Antigua.

In Puerto Rico we encounter the curious figure of José Campeche (1751–1809), who never left his native island, but who had the good fortune to be an intimate of the Spanish painter Luis Paret y Alcázar, whom Charles III had banished. Paret stayed only three years in Puerto Rico, but even during that short time Campeche learnt from him the arts of a miniaturist, which he backed up with clear and sophisticated colour values that were very much in the taste of the period. He has left us *An Amazon*, which is now in the Museo de Ponce, and the portraits (1792) of a high official and of his wife, which are now in private collections in Puerto Rico.

SPANISH SOUTH AMERICA

Architecture

The different regions of Spanish South America display even greater variety than those of Mexico, Central America, and the Caribbean. Almost every one of them can lay claim to an architecture with a character and a form of expression that are all its own. Thus in Panama, the only importance of which was to carry the route linking the two oceans, we find above all a proliferation of fortresses, or 'castles' (as they were then termed), for a defence against pirates. Panamá la Vieja was founded on the Pacific coast in 1519, but for many years it was only a collection of wooden shacks, plus a handful of convents that were scarcely more substantial. Later, in 1671, the city was destroyed by the English buccaneer Sir Henry Morgan, and afterwards it was moved to its present site. The best pieces of architecture in Panama, apart from the Customs House in Portobelo on the Caribbean, remained the forts. Most of them were built by military engineers, principally Giovanni Battista Antonelli, an Italian, and Cristóbal de Roda, a Spaniard.

In the northern part of continental South America – present-day Colombia and Venezuela – we observe a different type of colonization and hence of architecture. The undulating, fertile meseta offered sites for cities that were not just way-stations, like Panama. From the outset Tunja managed to build its town church in stone. It is a specially interesting church in that it consists of a nave and side-aisles of Gothic pillars (nowadays hidden in a casing of plaster), linked together by ogee arches carrying a wood-frame roof that is nowadays concealed by an ugly modern flat ceiling. The façade dates from only a little later, but it is classical in style, perfectly articulated on Herreran principles. The sixteenth and seventeenth were the centuries when the main religious orders built their churches, but many of the best retables in them date only from the eighteenth.

The chief building work in Bogotá was largely executed in the seventeenth century. Then, because of earthquakes, it was almost entirely rebuilt in the eighteenth century and even during the early years of the nineteenth. From the earlier period the best building still standing in Bogotá is the Franciscan church, belonging to a convent that is now otherwise demolished. It is a long narrow church with a simple roof in Mudéjar style, and a good retable from the sixteenth and seventeenth centuries. More classical in its proportions is the church of San Ignacio, from the hand of the Italian Jesuit Coluccini: it is admirable, above all, for the ingenuity shown in achieving correct style with brick and timber alone.

It is on the Caribbean coast that we find the third key city in the architectural history of northern South America: Cartagena de Indias. Cartagena was a bastion where the silver of Peru made a halt, having crossed the Isthmus, before it proceeded on its long transatlantic voyage to Spain. It was a fortified city, with a cathedral begun in 1575 which – at least as far as the interior is concerned – has recently been skilfully restored. In 1631 two 'castles' were built beside the harbour entrance known as the Boca Grande. The great San Felipe fortress which still dominates the city was completed, in its first version, between 1630 and 1657. The city wall was the work of the same Cristóbal de Roda whom we have already seen working in Panama.

In contrast, architecture in Venezuela was extremely modest during the first two centuries of Spanish hegemony. There are two distinguished churches from that era: the Assumption (1590–9) in Margarita, and the cathedral of Coro (1583). These two churches were to serve endlessly as prototypes, both as to plan and as to structure; they each had a nave with side-aisles on either side separated from one another by pillars or stanchions of timber, and a roof of simple beams covered with tiles. The scanty decoration is concentrated on the doorways, drawing on timid Renaissance motifs. Caracas was founded in 1567; its first cathedral fell down in 1641. In 1655 Juan de Medina began a great church with a nave and four side-aisles which is fundamentally the cathedral of today, even though the present façade dates from the eighteenth century. Venezuela, too, had important fortifications, the most significant being those on the peninsula of Araya, facing Cumaná, which were built in 1622–50.

In Ecuador, nearly everything is concentrated in Quito. Its cathedral – dating from 1562 – is the oldest in South America. As happened so often, it was partially destroyed in an earthquake, although the central nucleus remained standing. During the eighteenth century the cathedral suffered the addition of a dome quite unrelated to its original architecture, which featured square Gothic-style pillars and a Mudéjar roof. Quito is the most 'European' of colonial Latin American cities, doubtless because many of the Franciscans and Jesuits working there came from the Low Countries, Germany or Italy. From the early period we still have the enormous Franciscan convent, where there was – and in part still is – the best Mudéjar roof in the region, a roof which suffered a fire in the middle of the eighteenth century. The façade of its principal church is a Northern European interpretation of Italian Mannerist models, sometimes drawn directly from the famous architectural treatise of Sebastiano Serlio; the concave-cum-convex flight of steps ascending from the public square is a case in point.

The most distinctive architectural developments in Spanish South America occurred, however, at the heart of the Viceroyalty of Peru (present-day Peru and Bolivia), where at least two quite distinct structural procedures coexisted. In turn, these produced two equally distinct styles of architecture. There was the 'moulded' style of the littoral and the 'sculpted' style of the highlands. In the coastal area – which included Lima, Trujillo, Ica, Pisco, and Nazca – light materials were used, such as adobe, brick, and later *quincha* (a composition of reeds and dry clay which was then covered with plaster). In the highlands, on the other hand, architecture of any quality was always executed in hard stone – either granite or andesite.

In Lima the cathedral and the convents of the major orders were begun in the sixteenth century, and work on them continued throughout the seventeenth. Founded by Pizarro in 1535, Lima nonetheless had no permanent cathedral until 1569, when building began to the plans of the same Francisco Becerra whom we have already noted working in Puebla (New Spain). (When in Quito (*c.* 1580–2) on his way to Peru he may have drawn the plans for the Dominican and the Augustinian convents there, too.) The sanctuary end of Lima cathedral was at last begun in 1604, following a plan which appears also to have provided a prototype for Cuzco cathedral.

The great Viceroy Toledo had in fact already insisted, in 1583, that Cuzco, the ancient Inca capital, should have a great cathedral of its own, in place of the thatched cottage which had discharged this function since the earliest days of the Spanish occupation. It may well be that the plans for this colossal stone pile were Becerra's, but we know that from 1649 onwards Chávez y Arellano was architect in charge of the works. He was possibly also the designer of the 'retable-façade' which came to serve as a model throughout the region. The enormous edifice did not suffer too badly in the 1650 earthquake, so it was possible to consecrate the cathedral just four years later. Like Lima's, Cuzco's cathedral is wide, with a nave, two side-aisles and, beyond these again, two rows of deep side-chapels. Similarly, Cuzco cathedral is covered by cross-vaulting, a procedure which was understood from early days to be the most elastic, and the one best able to resist seismic movements. The difference between the two cathedrals lies in the fact that Cuzco's vaults are of brick whilst those of Lima were rebuilt in *quincha* after the great eighteenth-century earthquakes, particularly that of 1746.

The terrible Cuzco earthquake of 1650 was to be a turning point in the city's architecture. Almost the whole of the city was laid in ruins, the sole exceptions being the cathedral and part of the Franciscan church. Several of the religious orders – for example the Jesuits – decided to build their churches anew. The Society of Jesus possessed a plot next to the cathedral, right on the Plaza de Armas. It seems we owe the new Jesuit church to Father Gilles, a Fleming whose name when Hispanicized became Juan Bautista Egidiano. The church (1651–68) consists of a nave with a dome that displays great daring of conception. In contrast with the universal propensity for building low, and with horizontal emphasis, the Jesuit church in Cuzco is a high-spirited vertical composition with a magnificent retable type of façade and twin bell towers. Both of these were elements that were to be imitated as far away as Arequipa and Potosí.

Topographically the highland area nearest to Cuzco is what is known as El Collao, beside Lake Titicaca. The Dominicans were granted lands there in which to proselytize in the earliest period of settlement. Before Viceroy Toledo ordered them in 1569 to surrender their territory they had contrived to construct more than twenty churches, all of them long and narrow, with double-pitched roofs. Their only decoration was their simple but well-designed doorways, which included such early Renaissance elements as pilasters, decorative entrance frontispieces, and medallions in the spandrels. We shall meet these elements afresh when the Jesuits take them up.

In Upper Peru (present-day Bolivia) we find the Augustinians in possession of the area around Lake Titicaca from the sixteenth century onwards. In the place known as Copacabana they were later to build a famous shrine to the Virgin of that name. The plans for the convent were by the architect Francisco Jiménez de Sigüenza; construction took from 1610 to 1640. The convent has a great forecourt in the 'Mexican' style, so we find *capillas posas* in it, together with a central chapel called the Miserere, or Chapel of the Three Crosses, where divine service could be held in the open air.

A significant city in Bolivia that dates from the sixteenth century is the one now called Sucre – otherwise, in various times past, known as Charcas, Chuquisaca, or La Plata. Its cathedral is the work of Juan Miguel de Veramendi, and around 1600 its central nucleus was already finished, including the nave, to which side-aisles were added late in the seventeenth century (1686–97).

Though some other architectural works of consequence were built elsewhere in Spanish South America during the first century and a half of Spanish colonialism they were so impermanent it is not worth taking the time to review them. One exception perhaps is the Franciscan convent and its associated church (1572–1618) in Santiago de Chile, both of which survived the earthquakes, floods, and fires which periodically devastated the rest of the city.

We must now look at what happened during the last 120 years of Spanish hegemony – a period which certainly has left us a wealth of structures still standing, some in their original state, some subsequently rebuilt. Surveying the continent from north to south, we begin with Panamá la Nueva – the city as translated from its original site – where the only primary structure of real significance is the cathedral. This had been begun earlier, but serious work upon it dates only from 1726 and it was not completed till the end of the century.

In Bogotá most of the religious architecture dates from the seventeenth century, and the eighteenth is characterized mainly by remodellings, with substantial new work occurring only occasionally. The Italian military engineer Domingo Esquiaqui (1740–1820), for example, restored the tower of the Franciscan church, giving it a new façade into the bargain. Meanwhile, the Spanish architect Fr. Domingo de Petrés (1750–1811) busied himself with the interior, where he showed great historical sensitivity by restoring it without changing more than was necessary of what already existed. Petrés also worked on the churches of Santa Inés and Santo Domingo, both of which have since been demolished, and especially on that of San Ignacio, which was abandoned when the Jesuits were expelled in 1768. And he built the Astronomical Observatory, which still stands today. His masterpiece, however, was Bogotá's new cathedral, a splendid neoclassical building that consists of a nave with side-aisles and side-chapels, a dome, and a well-proportioned façade with two elegant towers. Among other eighteenth-century work in the viceregal capital of New Granada, we should also mention the church of the Third Order of Franciscans, begun in 1771, and the *espadaña*, or belfry, which was added to the old Las Aguas church and whose width exactly equals that of the façade. We meet Petrés again beyond the city limits of Bogotá, as it was he who planned the cathedral of Zipaquirá and the shrine of Chiquinquirá. One of the few important works in the Colombian countryside is the Franciscan convent at Mongui (begun in 1694 and not finally completed until 1858). It has a nave, side-aisles, a drumless dome, and a vaulted false ceiling that covers a simple roof structure. The most striking feature in this ensemble is the great staircase (1718), whose converging flights are placed alongside the cloister.

Important cities for eighteenth-century architecture are Cartagena and Popayán. In Cartagena, the most noteworthy building of the century is the Jesuit convent dedicated to St Peter Claver, which has an impressive church in coralline stone. This church presents an aristocratic façade to the world, a façade with a very smooth surface and made to a design after Herrera, incorporating two relatively low side-towers. Apart from churches, the so-called House of the Inquisition and the town-house of the Marqués de Valdehoyos should be mentioned. Both bear witness to how those who wielded power used to live in a fortified city in the tropics. All things considered, Popayán is the most 'baroque' city in a country which is, in fact, baroque not so much in its architecture as in its furnishings and its decorative detailing. Popayán's most distinguished churches are the Franciscan, the Dominican, and the Jesuit (nowadays known as San José). The Franciscan church is the work of the Spanish architect Antonio García. Its façade constitutes an example of authentic baroque style, and is crowned by an undulating profile which harmoniously plays down the contrast in height between the nave and the aisles. Popayán was largely destroyed by an earthquake in 1736. Among other buildings then ruined was the church of the Dominican convent. It was Gregorio Causí of Bogotá who set to work to rebuild it; its relatively small nave and side-aisles are visibly constructed of brick, the material that is characteristic of Popayán. The façade clearly retains something of the earlier church, giving an air of eccentricity to an ensemble which some art historians insist on terming 'baroque'. The Jesuit church is to the design of the German Simon Schenherr. He was summoned for the purpose from Quito, a city that influenced Popayán stylistically far more than did Bogotá. San José exhibits a great oblique arch in brick as the only decorative feature in its plain façade. Amongst provincial examples of virtually 'spontaneous' architecture there is, for example, the church of Santa Barbara in Mompox, on the Magdalena river. It is picturesque, but really it constitutes an exception to the rule, as it is chiefly noteworthy for its simple, white-washed octagonal bell-tower.

In Venezuela the eighteenth century is much more important than the seventeenth. In the first place, Caracas cathedral was completed in 1710–13: its façade is attributed to Andrés de Meneses. (The tower, on the other hand, dates from 1770.) Amongst many other interesting buildings we may cite the churches of Turmero (1781), El Tocuyo (*c.* 1776), Petare (*c.* 1772) and La Victoria (*c.* 1780). In what used to be Angostura and is now Ciudad Bolívar, the cathedral (1771–4) is by Bartolomé de Amphoux. Construction continued for a long time without the structure ever reaching completion.

In Quito the eighteenth century begins with the rebuilding of the Mercedarian church in 1737, influenced in style by the Jesuit church. This, in its turn, had been started in 1605, but the real inspiration of it derived from Marcos Guerra, an Italian religious, who corrected and completed the basic work. The façade, for instance, was begun by Fr Leonhard Deubler in 1722, but three years later Venancio Gandolfi, another Italian, replaced him. As for the church's interior, it too is the work of Deubler and of other Tyrolean religious such as Vinterer, and of Spaniards like Ferrer. The other important religious buildings from the eighteenth century in Quito are some convents for nuns like the Carmen Moderno (otherwise known as the Carmen Bajo), and the chapel of the Hospital. Above all, certain interiors deserve notice. These include the Rosary Chapel in the Dominican church, for instance, and the chapter-house (1741–61) in the Augustinian convent.

In Peru one must note the widespread use in this period of *quincha*, extensively employed in the reconstruction of Lima after the earthquake of 1746. Nearly all the important buildings were reconstructed by this method, thanks to the extreme lightness of the materials that it used. The same thing happened on the southern coast at Ica, Pisco and Nazca, where we find small churches that nowadays look more like the work of a stage designer than an architect. Despite their limitations of size, they at least possess a certain unity of conception that was lacking in earlier work. In Lima the chief eighteenth-century churches are generally those of the nunneries: Santa Teresa and the Nazarenes are leading examples. Some have fallen before the wrecker's ball whilst others, such as San Marcelo, have lost their façades. The typical church of this sort has only a nave, is painted in bright colours, and has a façade with a highly decorated doorway, two little low towers, and a wooden balustrade. The best example may be the Jesús María church (1722–36), which has undergone no alteration in two and a half centuries. Among the palaces of the period in Lima the Palace of Torre-Tagle, the most splendid family residence in the whole of South America, stands out. It has a gateway heavy with mouldings, two enormous Moorish-style fretted balconies – *mucharabíes* – in dark wood, and a courtyard with arcades of mixed design and *azulejos* on the lower walls. In Lima the new work shows the recrudescence of the baroque. Two façades that are covered in sculpted reliefs deserve mention: La Merced (1697–1704), and the Augustinian church (1720). Here we are dealing with true 'retable-façades'. The former is executed entirely in mouldings and the latter, still more extravagant, is wholly made up of a general profusion of three-dimensional curvilinear forms.

In several cities of Peru the eighteenth century was an especially active century. Trujillo, on the coast, was a city of *quincha* and timber, there used to simulate a regular form of construction in brick. Trujillo suffered greatly in the 1970 earthquake, and is at present undergoing careful restoration. Cajamarca, in the mountains, developed a structural technique of its own: everything is in stone, including the vaulting. A unique style characteristic of the town was thereby produced. In fact the decoration of the cathedral (1690–1737), San Antonio (1699–1704), and the Belén church consists of high relief applied in bands to emphasize the desired horizontality. Because of its ponderousness and naïveté, the baroque style in Cajamarca wears a provincial air which recalls Antigua Guatemala. Ayacucho is a smaller city high in the mountains, halfway between Lima and Cuzco. Its principal pride is its superb state of preservation. Most of its religious buildings were begun in the seventeenth century, but many of them underwent changes and additions of interesting detail in the course of the eighteenth. The Dominican church, however, is of the eighteenth century. It is on the plan of a Latin cross, with an exterior gallery transecting the façade. Ayacucho is remarkable for its cathedral, too: its interior is the more impressive aspect, as it contains some of the best retables of the period. Arequipa is another city of the highlands, facing us with a different stylistic problem, even though there too all building is of stone. The stone here is a volcanic tufa of a brilliant whiteness, and it is relatively soft and easy to cut, which gave rise to the so-called 'mestizo' style, that is to say, to a form of decoration in which traditional European motifs are intermingled with those taken from indigenous flora and fauna. The style can be found earliest in Arequipa, but it spread from there through the Collao to La Paz and Potosí. The Jesuit church in Arequipa was begun in 1590 and its side doorway dates from 1660, while its façade is eighteenth-century. It is the earliest affirmation of this mestizo style, which was later to spread to the other churches of the city and to ones around it, such as Paucarpata, Yanahuara, and Caima.

In Santiago de Chile there is only one church worth mentioning from the eighteenth century, the new Dominican church (1747–1771). It is basilica-like in plan and covered with a false vault of stucco. The present cathedral, now greatly altered, is the reconstruction of an earlier building which went up in flames in 1769. The late eighteenth-century neoclassical design was the work of Joaquín Toesca (1745–99), an Italian architect. Toesca's masterpiece is the Casa de Moneda (generally known as 'La Moneda'), the present-day seat of Chile's government. This is also a neoclassical design, but in complete contrast to what has happened to the cathedral, it has undergone very little modification although it was bombed during the coup of 1973. La Moneda has a great central doorway, windows with wrought-iron grilles, and a balustrade that is, if anything, too delicate – though it does provide the building with a finial and give it its unmistakable silhouette. Architecture in central Chile was influenced by that of Lima, via the maritime connections of the two countries. In the north of present-day Chile, however, originals on the Bolivian altiplano provided models for such churches as San Pedro de Atacama, Sotoca, Chiapa, and Huariña – which is not surprising since they were the outlets for the silver and mercury transported from Upper Peru. In the south of Chile, however, a certain ingenuity was needed to meet the challenge posed by having to build in timber alone, since that material was easily available locally. Typical is the church at Achao (1730–50): it has a nave and side-aisles separated by timber columns, supporting a multi-lobed vault also constructed of timber.

Present-day Argentina has little to show in the way of buildings from the seventeenth century. The most important is doubtless Córdoba cathedral, begun in 1677. The structure still needed a roof long after the walls were finished, so in 1729 a request was sent for the assistance of Father Bianchi (whose name when Hispanicized was Blanqui); this renowned Jesuit architect then closed the vaults and designed a façade which some people have described as Mannerist in inspiration. Another religious, the Franciscan Vicente Muñoz (1699–1784), executed the strange dome reminiscent of the Romanesque architecture of the region of León in Spain. Lastly, the towers with their relief work are by an anonymous master, probably of the later eighteenth century. The other Córdoba monument of interest is the Jesuit church (1645–71), the work of the Flemish Brother Philippe Lemaire, in Spanish Lemer (1608–71). By following the treatise of the French architect Philibert Delorme he managed in 1667–71 to cover the church with a timber roof constructed by shipbuilding techniques, as though it were a ship turned turtle. This roof was partially burnt some years ago, but more recently it has been faithfully restored. In Buenos Aires, too, the Jesuit church is the earliest one of importance. German and Italian masters were to work on San Ignacio there for many years. Juan Kraus began it in 1712; on his death two years later he was followed, successively, by Juan Wolff, Bianchi, Juan Bautista Primoli, and Pedro Weger. The façade is Germanic in character, with tall brackets set obliquely, and an undulating top flanked by two bell towers, though of the pair the one on the right dates only from the nineteenth century. The other well-preserved church in Buenos Aires is the Franciscan Recoleta church of the Pilar, Bianchi's work of 1716–32. It has a nave, vaulting, and side-chapels of shallow proportions. There is also a saucer-dome which is not visible from the exterior. Buenos Aires has had in all six successive cathedrals. The present one was constructed between 1754 and 1860, and is the work of the Savoyard Antonio Masella (*c.* 1770–74). He built it wide, providing it with a nave, side-aisles, spacious side-chapels, and a dome. Early in the nineteenth century it was given a classical portico designed by the French engineer Prosper Catelin.

In the province of Córdoba the Jesuits set up a number of estancias, notably Santa Catalina, Jesús María, and Alta Gracia. The churches on these estates all consist simply of a nave and a dome. Alta Gracia is remarkable for having its side walls convex, so that they appear to curve outwards to embrace the dome. There is a pronouncedly Germanic air about the façades: we know that Santa Catalina was the work of the Bavarian religious, Antonio Harls (born in 1725, he died in Italy after the 1767 expulsion of the Jesuits), while the churches at Jesús María and at Alta Gracia have been attributed to Bianchi. Much more important were the Jesuit missions of the province of Paraguay. They covered not only present-day Paraguay, but also some of the north-east of Argentina and the south-west of Brazil. Altogether 30 of these missions were established between 1609 and 1767, the year in which the Jesuits were expelled from America on the orders of Charles III. The missions were centres of agriculture and craft industries in which Indian converts freely contributed their labour for the benefit of the community. According to the Uruguayan historian Juan Giuria, the churches on these missions fall into three types. The earliest of them had a structure wholly of timber, with a nave separated from side-aisles by squared timbers that were sometimes covered with panelling. These pillars carry a simple superstructure consisting of a roof in two pents, covering a gallery that runs around the building, as well as the church itself. Only a very few examples of this form of construction remain, one being the San Ignacio Guazú mission in Paraguay. The second type of mission church was a mixed form structurally: the basic construction was of timber but, in contrast, the walls and the façade were constructed of stone according to a style peculiar to the missions called by some historians 'Guaraní baroque'. The outstanding example of this type may well be San Ignacio Miní in Argentina, whose architect was the Italian Jesuit Juan B. Brasanelli (1659–1728). The third and last type of mission church was still being developed when the Jesuits had to leave. More pretentious than the earlier types, it lacked much of the character that they had had. Some of these imposing edifices were the work of architects of renown, such as Father J. B. Primoli, mentioned above. Here we have buildings entirely constructed of carefully cut stone, adhering to canons of architecture that go back to the Italian *cinquecento*. The best-preserved of these churches are on the Jesús and Trinidad missions in Paraguay, and on the San Miguel mission in Brazil; the latter two are well-documented examples of Primoli's work.

An excellent example of a timber church of the first of these models is, in fact, the church of a Franciscan rather than a Jesuit mission – Yaguarón, on the outskirts of Asunción in Paraguay. The church of Yaguarón dates from 1761–85, is still standing, and is in excellent condition. It is 70 metres long and 30 wide. Its timber structure is manifest everywhere, except in the presbytery and the sacristy, where little vaults – also of painted and decorated timber – hide the true nature of the roof structure. The bell tower in fact consists of little more than a scaffolding built of square-sectioned tree-trunks: it is an early twentieth-century reconstruction, closely based on the original structure. The Jesuit missions of Moxos and Chiquitos in Bolivia should also be mentioned here. These were graphically described by the French naturalist Alcide d'Orbigny, who visited them in the nineteenth century. Architectually speaking they are perhaps of little importance, but from the cultural point of view they are supremely significant. The churches of these missions belong to what we have identified as the first model, differing from other examples only in that the columns of tree-trunks supporting them are carved *in situ* with a décor of convolutions, fluting, etc. Generally the churches were painted in bright colours, both inside and out. Still to be seen in Chiquitos is the well-restored church of San Francisco Xavier, the work of the Swiss Jesuit Father Schmid (1694–1772).

In the territory that is now Uruguay, for a long time the subject of bitter dispute between Spain and Portugal, the city of Montevideo at the mouth of the Río de la Plata (founded in 1726) is rather too recent in date to have much of importance from the colonial period. There is, however, the cathedral in Montevideo, known as La Matriz: it was built in 1784–99 to the plans of the Portuguese engineer José C. Sáa y Faría. It is an impressive building 83 metres long and 35 wide. The nave reaches a height of 18 metres and its towers ascend to a greater height – 35 metres. The other colonial building in Montevideo which deserves mention is the Cabildo. This was constructed in 1804–12, to the plans of the Spanish architect Tomás Toribio. It is an attractive neoclassical structure entirely of stone, with a great staircase, also of stone, rising proudly to the *piano nobile*.

Sculpture

Let us begin with ceilings, which in South America are often better preserved than they are elsewhere in the former Spanish Indies. These fall into two categories: the Mudéjar type composed of star-shaped polygons, and those ceilings that are based on Renaissance models. Surprisingly, the most beautiful examples of the Mudéjar type are nowadays to be found in Colombia, Ecuador, and Bolivia, as nearly all the Peruvian examples have been lost through earthquakes or on account of changes in fashion. There are Mudéjar ceilings in the cathedral of Tunja, in the church of the Conception and the Franciscan church in Bogotá, in Pasto cathedral, in the Franciscan and Dominican churches and the cathedral in Quito, and in the church of Santa Clara in Ayacucho, Peru. Lastly, Sucre has some more basic examples of Mudéjar style to offer, such as those in the Franciscan and the Mercedarian churches, and in the Jesuit church of San Miguel. Ceilings of Renaissance type are also abundant in Colombia. And there are two very famous ceilings in Lima which should not be overlooked: in the Sala de Visitas of the Dominican church, and in the ante-sacristy of the Augustinian church. There are more primitive, simpler examples to be seen in Cuzco as well.

Retables, on the other hand, exist everywhere, though they are not all of the same style, nor equal in quality. In Colombia and Venezuela, for example, they continue to be very 'architectural' in design right into the eighteenth century: that is to say, they have columns and entablatures, as though they were real buildings. Perhaps the most celebrated retable from this early period is one in the form of two facing walls in the Franciscan church in Bogotá. The composition, by an anonymous sculptor, consists of revetments in large square gilded panels in high relief. In Quito, however, we encounter important new departures, such as the grandiose semicircular altar in the presbytery of the Franciscan church. This is a great piece of northern Mannerist stage machinery, with its upper portion completed in the eighteenth century with elements derived from late baroque. Retables in seventeenth-century Peru, on the other hand, are more 'Hispanic', whilst those of New Granada are more 'Italian'. The Peruvian line of development of the retable cannot readily be traced in Lima, where too many examples of it have been lost; but in Cuzco it is clearly identifiable. We know the names of the sculptors of the period, for instance that of Martín de Torres, who carved the retable of the Trinity in the cathedral, and that of Pedro Galeano, who was responsible for the retable of the Solitude in the Mercedarian church. The most important artist is Diego Martínez de Oviedo, who made a timid beginning with the sort of baroque style that was later to be developed to unparalleled heights of extravagance at San Blas by the Indian artist Juan Tomás Tuyrú Túpac. The masterpiece of this era is, without doubt, the high altar of the Jesuit church by an anonymous artist.

Returning to Colombia, we must note the eighteenth-century artist Pedro Caballero, who created a highly original style, incorporating wildly proliferating vegetation, in the church of the Third Order of Franciscans in Bogotá. In Quito, however, the period's distinguished sculptors are the same practitioners as we already recorded as architects of the Jesuit church – Deubler, Vinterer, and Ferrer. Here it was the custom for those who carved the images also to carve the retables which were to house them: this was the case with Bernardo de Legarda, who worked on the high altar in the admirable Cantuña chapel. Quito's glorious sequence of retables culminates in the wide and relatively low one, a gilded pyramid, in the Rosary chapel of the Dominican church. The retable in the old Carmelite church already foreshadows the spirit of the rococo: it has smooth matched columns in pairs, and a pediment compounded of convex and concave curvatures.

The eighteenth-century history of the Peruvian retable can be followed better in Lima than in other cities. The earliest retable there to include columns was that of San Francisco Xavier, which dates perhaps from 1687. It is in the church of San Pedro, which, along with the Franciscan church and the church of Jesús María, houses the best-preserved retables to be found anywhere in Lima. Most of the designers are unknown to us, although we do have the name of José de Castilla (*c.* 1660–1739), the artist responsible for the high altar of the Jesús María church. Later, a sort of caryatid appears on the retables, for instance on the one executed by José Flores in 1764 for the church of San Francisco de Paula in Rimac, in the suburbs of Lima. For other examples one has to look outside Lima, at what is scattered about Trujillo, Ayacucho, and Cajamarca. These retables tend towards the rococo, although in the provinces this style never attained any unified expression. Towards the end of the colonial period there are some examples of neoclassicism in this area, notably the work of the Spanish architect Matías Maestro, who was both painter and sculptor.

As we have already noticed, each city seems to have had a speciality of its own: Lima and Cuzco, for example, were well known for choir-stalls. The stalls of Lima cathedral were the result of a 1623 competition won by the Catalan Pedro Noguera. He at once called upon the rivals he had just edged out – Luis Ortiz de Vargas and Martín Alonso de Mesa – to collaborate with him. The choir-stalls of Cuzco cathedral date from a little later, but are just as beautiful: according to a contract of 1631 they are the work of Sebastián Martínez. In Cuzco we are no longer in the late Renaissance period as we were in Lima, but seeing rather the baroque in full flower. Individual elements are observable in the stalls that we can also identify both in retables and in the stonework of church façades, since there were many opportunities for the transfer of motifs.

Pulpits are a world apart. In Colombia there are hardly any worth mentioning, save that in the Franciscan church in Popayán, which is possibly of 1756, and which Santiago Sebastián attributes to the sculptor Usiña. In Ecuador, however, there are excellent pulpits in the Franciscan church in Quito, in the Jesuit church there, and in the shrine at Guápulo (1716), the latter being the work of the sculptor Juan Bautista Menacho. The best pulpits are in Peru, beginning with those in the Herreran style in the Franciscan church in Cuzco (*c.* 1630), and in the Claretian church in Ayacucho (1637). The series of Mannerist–baroque pulpits in Cuzco can be established because we possess examples in Santa Teresa, then in the Jesuit church, then in the Dominican church, then in San Pedro, until we reach the culmination of the baroque in the church of San Blas (1696) attributed, as we saw, to Tuyrú Túpac.

Early images are relatively few and far between in Colombia and Venezuela, though some were brought in from Spain. By contrast, miniature or life-size images unquestionably constitute Ecuadorean art's chief glory throughout the seventeenth and eighteenth centuries. The series begins with Father Carlos, active between 1620 and 1680, and whose saints' images were examples of crude realism. Many of them are now in the Franciscan Museum. He was succeeded by his pupil José Olmos, known as 'Pampite', who was actively at work between 1650 and 1690. Pampite was, in fact, heavily influenced by Martínez Montañés: his specialities were figures of Christ and Calvary scenes, of which there are examples both in the Franciscan church and in Ecuador's National Museum. In Quito, image carving was exclusively carried out in wood: although the Quito school's use of line shows its affiliation to the school of Seville, its brilliant colouring is more reminiscent of the Castilian school. The line of succession continues in the early eighteenth century with the mestizo Bernardo de Legarda, creator of an unforgettable image known as the 'Dancing Virgin', which he executed many times over on different scales. Finally, the 'idealist' Legarda was succeeded by an out-and-out naturalist in the person of Manuel Chili, known as 'Caspicara': to him we owe, for instance, the moving *Descent from the Cross* which is the centrepiece of the high altar of Quito cathedral.

From eighteenth-century Peru it is the sculptor Baltasar Gavilán who stands out: his *Death* – a skeleton with bows and arrows – survives in the sacristy of the Augustinian church in Lima. Gavilán also executed an equestrian statue of Philip IV, but it was destroyed in the 1746 earthquake. Later, Matías Maestro seems to have been responsible for the destruction of several baroque retables in the course of introducing the neoclassical style.

In conclusion, although there is no space here to discuss adequately artists working in other regions of Spanish America, we should mention the sculptor Gaspar de la Cueva in Bolivia. Born in Spain in 1595, he was trained in the circle of Martínez Montañés. His best-known works are his *Ecce Homo* in the Franciscan church in Potosí and his *Christ tied to the column* in the church of San Lorenzo in the same city. The sculptors who worked in the Jesuit missions are well represented in the museums and private collections of Argentina.

Painting

For historical reasons that are not susceptible of easy explanation, there seems always to have been some non-Spanish influence in Hispanic painting in South America. Perhaps this is because the earliest important painters were Italian. Possibly it was because later Flemish engravings provided them with a significant source of inspiration. In later periods it may have been because, from the middle of the seventeenth century onwards, a number of Indian or mestizo artists succeeded in creating a variety of original means of expression.

Apart from some very early Spanish painters of relatively limited inspiration – Diego de Mora, the elder Illescas, and Reynalte Coello – the history of Hispanic painting in South America really begins with the Italian Jesuit Bernardo Bitti. Bitti (1548–1610) had studied in Rome in the circle of Giorgio Vasari (1511–74) and arrived in Lima in 1575. Some of his work is still to be found there, although it can also be seen in Arequipa, Cuzco, Ayacucho, Julí, La Paz, and Sucre. Bitti is a Raphaelesque painter and one strongly influenced by the Flemish school, as can be seen from works like the *Virgin and Child* (*c.* 1595) in the Jesuit church in Arequipa, and the *Immaculate Conception* in the Mercedarian convent in Cuzco. Of commanding importance was another Italian, Mateo Pérez de Alesio (?1547–?1628), although, unlike those of Bitti, few of his works have survived. Born in Rome, he learnt his craft there before moving first to Malta and then to Seville, where a colossal *St Christopher* from his hand is still preserved in the cathedral. He repeated it in Lima cathedral, but this later work was destroyed in an earthquake. Of the innumerable works that have been attributed to him, one of the few that remain is the *Virgin at Bethlehem*, or *Virgin suckling the Child*, an oil-painting on copper now in the Velarde Collection in Lima. The third influential Italian, and the one who travelled furthest – though he was not as accomplished as the other two – was Angelino Medoro (1565–1632). He was a Roman who was working in Tunja as early as 1586; some of his paintings are still to be seen there. Typical of his work are an enormous canvas for the Mercedarian convent in Bogotá, and an *Immaculate Conception* of 1618 for the Augustinian church in Lima. Medoro, more than the other two painters mentioned, is a Mannerist, presenting exaggeratedly fore-shortened figures and using chilly, iridescent colouring.

In Tunja, Colombia, we find two series of ceiling paintings from the middle of the sixteenth century. The less important is in the so-called 'Casa del Fundador'; the better is in the famous Casa del Escribano. What these two series show is noble heraldic achievements, mythological scenes, and even some emblems. Although the paintings are attributed to Medoro, the authoritative Martín Soria simply listed them as 'anonymous'. What is curious about them is above all that they exhibit a strange combination of elements deriving from Italian Mannerist, French, and Flemish models. One of the most surprising of the images is a clumsy reproduction of the well-known Dürer print depicting a rhinoceros.

Let us move on 100 years, but return to Peru. In the later seventeenth century two rival but complementary figures appear in Cuzco: Basilio de Santa Cruz, who was active from 1650 until his death in 1699, and the Indian Diego Quispe Tito, who lived from about 1611 to about 1681. Santa Cruz achieved enormous productivity, partly because he was the protégé of the powerful episcopal Maecenas Manuel de Mollinedo. He was a formally correct painter who adhered to European canons of art. There are several gigantic pictures of his dating from around 1690 and still to be seen in Cuzco cathedral, including a *St Barbara*, and a *St Isidore the husbandman*. Quispe Tito began by copying Flemish engravings, which he interpreted idiosyncratically: an example is his *Holy Family returning from Egypt* (1680) which is now in the collection of the Dirección de Monumentos Nacionales in Lima. Of his paintings, some of the most accomplished are preserved in the parish church of San Sebastián in the outskirts of Cuzco, for which he had originally painted them – his *Ascension* (1634), for example. He is the leader of the so-called 'Cuzco School', and was the preceptor of Melchor Pérez de Holguín, whom we shall examine later.

The Cuzco school of painting originated about 1680, in some of the work of Quispe Tito. The style is characterized, first, by an anti-realism expressed in the free adaptation of subjects from Flemish engravings. Second, it has a flatness of view, rejecting perspective. Third, there is a certain frontality, from the point of view of the observer. Fourth, the pictures incorporate arabesques made of gold leaf applied to the canvas. The Cuzco school's pictures which consist of single images thus turn out to be as hieratic as if they were actual icons. On the other hand, those of the school's compositions that include several figures appear rather naïve, partly owing to the extreme familiarity with which they treat sacred subjects.

Proceeding to Ecuador, we find in the seventeenth century a transitional figure in the person of Hernando de la Cruz (1591–1646). His most famous work, which still hangs in the sacristy of the Jesuit church in Quito, is a *St Ignatius*. His pupil Miguel de Santiago (1626–1706) was an altogether more all-embracing artist. His best-known works cover whole series of subjects, such as the scenes from the life of St Augustine painted for Quito's Augustinian convent and the *Miracles of Our Lady of Guadalupe* for the shrine at Guápulo on the outskirts of Quito. Nicolás Javier Goríbar (1665–1740), who studied with Miguel de Santiago, was more monumental but less cheerful and less refined than his master. He, too, is known principally for two series of paintings: *The prophets*, all of them compositions hanging in the Jesuit church, and *The kings of Judah*, for the Dominican church. He was active between 1688 and 1736. The only other Ecuadorean of the eighteenth century deserving some attention is Manuel Samaniego (1767–1824), a courtly painter with a highly individual personality. Among his works is an *Assumption of the Virgin*, a vast canvas in the choir of Quito cathedral. He also painted such profane themes as *The seasons* for a hacienda. He even wrote an interesting *Treatise on painting* (undated, and published for the first time by the Ecuadorean historian José María Vargas in 1975).

In New Granada a worthy school of painting can be identified early on. It started with Medoro and was subsequently embodied in his pupil Fr. Pedro Bedón of Quito. An artist with a very comprehensive range, Bedón produced delicate miniatures as well as extensive canvases. Further, the region around Bogotá gave rise to a dynasty of painters, that of the Figueroa family, which lasted for centuries. The founder of it was a Spaniard, known as 'Balthasar the Elder'. Among his children the most interesting was Gaspar de Figueroa, painter of the *Christ and the holy women* that is now in the Museo de Arte Colonial in Bogotá; he died in 1658. In his turn Gaspar had a son who was celebrated in his time, Baltasar de Vargas Figueroa (d. 1667), from among whose works we still possess a *Death of St Gertrude*, now in the Museo de Arte Colonial, and a *Virgin crowned by the Trinity*.

The most celebrated painter in New Granada was, with good reason, Vargas Figueroa's pupil Gregorio Vásquez de Arce y Ceballos

(1638–1711). He was a native of Bogotá, and worked there throughout his career. His production was enormous, showing both variety and versatility. A good draughtsman, he was also an excellent painter of all sorts of themes, including portraits. His great religious compositions include a *Purgatory*, painted in 1670 and preserved in the church of Funza, a *Last Judgement* (1673) in Santa Clara at Tunja, and an *Immaculate Conception* (1710).

Further to the south, in Bolivia, we find Melchor Pérez de Holguín (*c.* 1665–1724), who, according to Martín Soria, was possibly the best painter produced by colonial Spanish South America. There is no doubt that in his work this native of Cochabamba aspired to emulate the great Zurbarán. On occasion his designs are out of proportion and repetitious, but there is no doubt whatever that he displays a vitality of tone and a sense of the monumental form quite beyond those of his colleagues. One calls to mind his *St Peter of Alcántara*, now in the National Museum in La Paz, and his gigantic picture, painted in 1716, *The entry into Potosí of Archbishop Diego Morcillo Rubio de Auñón*, now in the Museo de América in Madrid. The only other artist from Upper Peru who requires discussion here is Gaspar Miguel de Berrío. Active between 1736 and 1761, he was a pupil of Holguín who practised two totally distinct genres of painting during his artistic career. One was totally academic; the other made generous use of the *brocateado* technique of applying gold leaf to canvas which was a characteristic of the popular Cuzco school of painting. Particularly noteworthy is his *Protection of St Joseph* (1737) in the Las Monicas church in Potosí.

Finally, still further south there are a few more artists, all of them eighteenth-century figures, who should be included in this survey. About Tomás Cabrera, born in Salta in 1740, we know very little, though many of his works still exist in some of the churches of Tucumán. In Buenos Aires his *St Joseph and Child* (1782) is to be seen in the Pilar church. His vast historical picture, *The peace treaty between Governor Matorras of Tucumán and the cacique Paykin*, painted in 1775, is now in the Museo Histórico Nacional. At this period Buenos Aires had two Spaniards actively at work – Ausell and Salas. Miguel Ausell, born about 1728 and active until 1787, was a Valencian who came to America in 1754. Only three of his pictures are known to present-day scholars: a *St Ignatius*, in the Buenos Aires church of that dedication, his *Resurrection of Our Lord* (1760), and a *St Louis* which was destroyed in the coup of 1955. José Salas was born in Madrid in 1735, and moved to Buenos Aires in 1772. Among the pictures he painted there was a *St Vincent Ferrer* for the Dominican convent. He is also known for some of his portraits, such as those of the Marqués de Loreto (now lost), and that of the foundress of the Casa de Ejercicios, Sor María Antonia de la Paz y Figueroa; this was painted in 1799 and is now in the Casa. Salas was still at work as late as 1816. Lastly, we have two Italians: Martín de Petris, who lived in Buenos Aires from 1792 to 1797, the year in which he must have painted his portrait of the *regidor* Mansilla Moreno, and Angel María Camponeschi, who was born in Rome in 1769, and was at work in Buenos Aires until 1810. Camponeschi was one of the most important artists active in the Río de la Plata area during this period. He excelled particularly as a portraitist and his work was in great demand. A picture he painted in 1804, *Fray José de Zemboráin*, is preserved in the Dominican convent in Buenos Aires.

18

THE ARCHITECTURE AND ART OF
COLONIAL BRAZIL

No firm or well-defined tradition of town planning was brought by the Portuguese settlers to Brazil. Unlike Italy, France and Spain, neither the regular gridiron nor the radial town plan had had any currency in Portugal. The suggestion has been made by Robert Smith that when Salvador da Bahia was built on two levels, the upper connected to the lower town by steep lanes, a traditional Portuguese layout – represented by Lisbon, Coimbra and Oporto, for example – was being followed. This suggestion remains conjectural. Certainly the fairly regular layout of upper Salvador, with four or five long, more or less parallel streets crossed at right angles by a dozen shorter ones, does have a few precedents in Portugal, especially in the north of the country, e.g. Bragança, Caminha, Viana do Castelo, Braga, Aveiro. Such orthogonal urban plans were part of the general western European cultural heritage derived from classical antiquity. Nevertheless they are not common in Portugal and comparatively rare in the early towns built by the Portuguese overseas. In Lusitanian India the fortress towns of Damaõ and Bassein were constructed on regular orthogonal plans, and the layouts of Cochim and São Tomé (Meliapor) were also basically orthogonal, though less regular.

The contrast between Portuguese colonial cities and those of Spanish America, particularly Mexico, has often been noticed. In Spanish America regular gridiron plans, confirmed from *c.* 1573 in the *Leyes de Indias*, are common. What has less often been observed is the contrast to be found in both empires between the capital city or administrative centre on the one hand and the mining town on the other. The organic, uninhibited growth of street systems in Guanajuato, Taxco and Zacatecas in Mexico, or Huancavelica and Potosí in Peru, precisely parallel those in Ouro Preto for example, or Sabará, where the town simply follows the auriferous stream, or São João d'El Rei in Minas Gerais. The elevation of Ouro Preto to the status of a town (*vila*) in 1711 integrated, without regularizing, half a dozen separate *arraiaes*, or encampments, established by the early leaders of the gold rush – the first two actually named after pioneer settlers, namely António Dias de Oliveira (1698) and Padre João de Faria Fialho (1699). In none of these inland mining towns was there any need for fortified enceintes, so there were no military considerations exerting pressure towards urban regularity.

Nevertheless, despite imperfect and tardy achievement of the aim, the basic intention in Brazil does seem to have been similar to that pursued in Spanish America, i.e. to give administrative centres orthogonal plans. As we have seen, the upper town of Salvador da Bahia (founded 1549) was given such a plan, in so far as the uneven site permitted. The focus was a typical rectangular central square or *praça*, the Terreiro de Jesus, approximately a double square aligned east and west. The whole town was enclosed within a roughly triangular enceinte fortified with bastions. Rio de Janeiro (founded 1567) was also given an orthogonal layout, and two centuries later the extension of the city was regulated by a more strictly uniform grid plan, influenced perhaps by the Pombaline *cidade baixa* of post-earthquake Lisbon. In 1816, when Niteroi was founded on the other side of Guanabara bay, it was given a completely regular chessboard plan. Other early examples of fairly regular orthogonal street plans are those of São Luis de Maranhão (founded 1615), Alcántara de Maranhão (created *vila* 1648) and Paratí (created *vila* 1667). Perhaps most interesting of all is the rebuilding of Mariana, early capital of Minas Gerais (founded *c.* 1710), on an orthogonal plan, which was undertaken directly after the establishment of a bishopric there in 1741.

Closely associated with the planning of towns was their fortification. Throughout the colonial period Brazil was subject to invasion, threat of invasion and piracy. Consequently much effort was spent on fortifying the principal coastal centres. At least fifteen forts were built to defend the city of Salvador and the Bahia de Todos os Santos between the sixteenth and eighteenth centuries, most of which survive; fourteen were constructed in Guanabara bay; and at least seven were built to defend Belém do Pará.

Of particular interest is the Forte dos Reis Magos defending Natal (Rio Grande do Norte). It was originally built of earth in 1598 to designs by Father Gaspar Samperes S.J. In need of repair by 1608, it was redesigned in 1614 – and then rebuilt in stone – by Francisco de Frias da Mesquita (b. *c.* 1578, d. after 1645) who had been nominated in 1603 *engenheiro-mór* of Brazil, where he subsequently served for over 30 years as architect, soldier and engineer. There is a general similarity in shape and outline between this fort and that of the Fortaleza de Jesus at Mombasa in East Africa, which was begun in 1593 to the design of the Milanese military architect G. B. Cairati, employed by the crown of Portugal as *engenheiro-mór das Indias* from 1583 to 1596. The Mombasa fortress has been the subject of a controversial suggestion (not yet, however, generally accepted) that the anthropomorphic plan was a conscious reference back to Renaissance notions of symbolic, and proportional, relationships between Vitruvian buildings and the human body, together with the allegorical concept that 'è la fortezza quasi un'altro corpo humano' (Pietro Sardi, *Il corno dogale della architettura militare* (Venice, 1639), p. 47). The outline of the Forte dos Reis Magos is much simplified compared with that of the Fortaleza de Jesus, so the anthropomorphic appearance of the former, though clear, is less strikingly apparent than in the African plan. This also applies to the somewhat similar seventeenth- and eighteenth-century forts of São Sebastião and Nª Sª da Conceição at Rio de Janeiro and the Castellinho de São Sebastião on the island of Terceira (Azores).

Francisco de Frias was also responsible for building in 1608–9 a polygonal (nine-sided) sea fort or *arx maritima*, known as the Fortaleza da Lage de São Francisco, defending Recife from the sea, and a similar fortress, this time square or triangular, known as the Forte do Mar de São Marcelo, defending the sea approach to Salvador da Bahia. The latter fort, still under construction in 1622, was converted to a round shape in 1654–66 and further strengthened 1714–28. Both forts, of which only the second survives, are said to have been designed by Tiburcio Spanochi, chief military engineer to Philip III of Spain (Philip II of Portugal), whose plans were sent out to Brazil in May 1606. Another Fortaleza da Lage was constructed in the bar of Guanabara bay in 1644–5. These forts are of interest not only from a specifically Portuguese point of view but also for the history of military architecture in general. *Fortezze in acqua* were discussed in theory by Girolamo Maggi and Jacomo Fusto Castriotto (*Della fortificatione* (Venice, 1564; 2nd edn, 1584), book III, chs. 1–8), who gave triangular, square and star-shaped designs for them, in each case sustaining a high circular cavalier; and a triangular sea fort was designed specifically for the defence of Lisbon by Francisco de Holanda in his memorandum *Da fabrica de Lisboa* of 1571. Nevertheless, very few such forts were ever actually built. The eventual completion in the second decade of the seventeenth century of the Tagus fort recommended by Holanda (built to the circular design of an Italian military engineer, G. V. Casale) was an exceptional achievement, and becomes still more impressive when we add to it the simultaneous realization of similar fortresses in the sea at both Recife and Salvador, soon followed by another defending Rio de Janeiro.

Germain Bazin, in his classic survey (1956–8) of colonial religious architecture in Brazil, catalogues 297 churches and chapels. To these may be added another 98 which, although less important, did nevertheless qualify for inclusion in the list of historic buildings maintained by the Património Nacional in 1955. Adding another ten recorded elsewhere, we arrive at an overall total of 405. This figure could obviously be increased or decreased according to the criteria adopted. Analysing the list geographically, three-quarters of these surviving colonial churches are scattered along the 4,000-km coastal strip between Belém do Pará just south of the Equator and Santos on the Tropic of Capricorn and are seldom found more than 50 km inland. The remaining quarter are situated in the mining provinces of Minas Gerais and Goiás, 200 to 400 km north and north-west of Rio de Janeiro.

Within the coastal belt one-third of the churches are concentrated in three major urban nuclei, those of Olinda–Recife, Salvador da Bahia and Rio de Janeiro. There is a similar concentration in the mining provinces – one-third being situated within the straggling, interconnecting urban complex of Ouro Preto and António Dias together with neighbouring Passagem and Mariana. The significance of these four major urban centres – three coastal and one inland – is still more sharply emphasized if we limit our view to the hundred most artistically and historically interesting colonial churches. Of these, between two-thirds and three-quarters are to be found within the four nuclei.

Turning now to the types of church built in colonial Brazil, the analysis of the 405 examples yields the following information: cathedrals and parish churches – 73; conventual churches (principally those of the Benedictine, Franciscan and Carmelite orders) together with those of Jesuit colleges – 61; chapels of Third Orders (mainly Franciscan and Carmelite) – 36; other churches and chapels in towns and villages, including the chapels of confraternities (for example, the seventeen belonging to that of Nossa Senhora do Rosario dos Homens Pretos) – 189; the most notable chapels, including those of missions, *fazendas*, sugar plantations (*engenhos*) and ranches – 46. The churches of the Benedictine, Franciscan and Carmelite convents, together with the Third Order chapels of the Franciscans and Carmelites, comprise about 18 per cent of the total, and no less than 36 per cent of the hundred churches thought to be the most important and remarkable.

From this large group of colonial churches ten representative examples have been chosen and are briefly described to illustrate the main aspects of art-historical interest – in particular stylistic development, regional variation and the decorative schemes employed.

By far the most important seventeenth-century structure surviving in Brazil is the former church of the Jesuit college, now the cathedral, at Salvador. It is a large building, measuring 58 by 27 metres. It still belongs to what William Beckford called 'the majestic style which prevailed during the Spanish domination of Portugal' (*Excursion to the monasteries* (London, 1835)). The name of the architect is unknown but he must certainly have been Portuguese. The precedents and parallels furnished by Jesuit churches in Portugal for the design of the façade and the interior arrangement have often been noticed. The visual impact of the façade is impoverished by the inadequacy of the towers, or rather belfries (*campanários*). In this respect the façades of the Jesuit churches at Belém do Pará and nearby Vigía (1718 and *c.* 1725 respectively, names of architects unknown) are more successful. The whole building is constructed of a fine Portuguese limestone known as *pedra lioz*, cut and shaped in quarries near Lisbon and shipped out as ballast in the Brazil fleets. The prime purpose was to accelerate construction, and completion was by this means achieved within the remarkably short span of fifteen years (1657–72). The volume of the interior is impressive, the cubic shape modified and offset by the huge vault (imitated in wood), painted and deeply coffered to a pattern which follows one given in Serlio's *Libro quarto di architettura* (Venice, 1537; 25 subsequent editions in seven languages, 1540–1619). The most eye-catching features of this splendid interior are, however, the reredoses (*retablos*) of the thirteen altars, dating from between the third quarter of the seventeenth century and the mid eighteenth, which admirably exemplify the stylistic development of reredos design in the Lusitanian world from the late Renaissance to full baroque.

The Franciscan convent at Salvador da Bahia offers another series of architectural and ornamental splendours – in particular the façade (1708–23) and interior decoration (second quarter of the eighteenth century) of the church, the cloister (1686–1750) and its *azulejaria* (1749–52). Virtually nothing is known of the architects or designers. The sober and dignified façade, built of a coarse, grey local sandstone (*pedra arenita*) plastered over, appears to great advantage at the end of a long narrow *praça*, furnished, like a forecourt (*adro*), with a central monumental cross. The composition is remarkable for the effective way in which, following the examples given by Serlio in his *Libro quinto* (Paris, 1547; thirteen subsequent editions in six languages, 1551–1619), a pair of tall, massive towers of uncompromisingly rectangular shape, crowned by pyramids, frame and offset a square three-bay façade (surmounted by a high gable) in which arched and scrolled forms somewhat abate the prevailing angularity. The lower section of the façade follows a triumphal arch pattern, adumbrating the framing of the chancel arch inside – both approximating to the arch of Septimius at Rome, recorded in Serlio's *Libro terzo* (Venice, 1540; twenty subsequent editions in seven languages, 1544–1619). The most interesting element of the design for the future was the series of loosely interwoven volutes which surround the rectangular centrepiece of the gable or *frontão*. These arrays of volutes represent the starting point of a baroque process of dissolution, or breaking of the bonds which the rigorous frameworks of late Renaissance architecture imposed. From this beginning, as the century advanced, a progressive emancipation from the constrictive rules of classical composition is visibly evident in the displacement of traditional orthogonality by new mobile curved forms and S-shaped profiles. (The development of subsequent Franciscan church façades in north-east Brazil well illustrates the progress of these innovations, culminating finally at Marechal Deodoro (Alagoas), where the façade, which dates from 1793, is almost completely liberated from constraint by the omission altogether of the lower entablature and the arching of the upper one in a series of dynamic curves. This creates such a light, volatile composition that the solid prismatic bulk of the *campanile*, here flush with the façade and tied to it by a row of identical apertures, is needed to stabilize the design as well as to complement it.)

Behind the sober façade of the Franciscan church at Salvador we find the whole interior glimmering with gold – an example of the so-called *igreja toda de ouro*, of which there are two other examples in Brazil: the

Third Order Franciscan church, or *capela dourada*, at Recife (1698–1724) and São Bento at Rio de Janeiro (begun 1717, completed after 1772). Far from being a bewildering riot of gilded foliage and *putti*, the organization of these dazzling interiors was carefully planned and controlled. The decoration is carved, usually from cedarwood, in high relief and, as Paulo Santos has pointed out, is inscribed within well-defined panels separated by broad mouldings. The shapes of the foliage, principally acanthus, are rhythmically interrelated and the influence of patterns given by Serlio at the end of his *Libro quarto* is manifest, as are other patterns of his in the panelling of the chancel vault and ceilings of the nave and sacristy. Contrasts of the kind we see in this church between a plain exterior and a lavishly decorated interior are not uncommon in Portuguese and Brazilian architecture (though seldom going to such lengths as here). And one has only to turn to such highly sophisticated examples as the Dominikus Zimmermann churches of the second quarter of the eighteenth century in Bavaria to recognize that these contrasts were in no sense accidental.

The sense of irreality, or mirage, induced by the mass of glittering ornament in the *igreja toda de ouro* confirms successful realization of the baroque aim, carried to its logical conclusion, of disintegrating structural outlines and dissolving frames of reference. The high degree of fragmentation achieved in the Spanish development of the *estípite* was not paralleled in Portugal or Brazil. Wendel Dietterlin's *estípite* models were either less well known in Portugal or, more likely, less congenial to Portuguese taste. The Corinthian column with a twisted shaft, or *salomónica*, which first reached Lisbon from Genoa in 1671, was soon being used in Brazil. Thereafter this column, covered with decoration of various kinds, remained the principal architectural element of Brazilian *retablos* until nearly the end of the eighteenth century, when neoclassical fashions supervened. Rules for shaping *salomónicas* had long been available in Vignola's treatise *Regola delli cinque ordini* (1st edn, Rome, 1562).

The cloister of the Franciscan convent at Salvador is another masterpiece of Brazilian colonial architecture. The lower walks are arcaded and vaulted whereas the upper storey is simply an open gallery or loggia with rafters left bare beneath a sloping roof. The design derives directly from a sixteenth-century Portuguese cloister type of which several examples survive – one of the finest being that of Viseu cathedral (*c.* 1550). The harmonious impression is enhanced by the magnificent pictorial *azulejo* decoration of the walls at both levels. Other splendid features of this Franciscan convent are the sacristy, the library, and the *capela do capítulo*.

The sculptured façade of the church of the Third Order of St Francis of Assisi at Salvador (dated 1702–3), which impresses by its exoticism and prolixity rather than by its originality, is doubtfully ascribed to Gabriel Ribeiro, about whom little is known. This façade represents the phenomenon of interior wood-carved decoration (in this case the closest parallel is in the superb jacaranda choir stalls of the convent church carved by Brother Luiz de Jesus, 'o Torneiro') translated to the exterior of a building and executed there in stone. It was not until a generation later in northern Portugal, thanks to the influence of the Italian architect Nicolò Nasoni (active in Portugal 1725–62), and a good deal later still in Minas Gerais, that façades enriched – if not (as here) laden – with sculptural decoration came into fashion. Appropriately, the interior of the Third Order Franciscan church at Salvador is quite simple, thus offering the reverse of the usual contrast between exterior and interior which is exemplified in the Friars' church next door. The small Ionic cloister with neo-Palladian pediments has exceptional charm.

The monumental church of São Pedro dos Clérigos at Recife (begun 1728; architect Manuel Ferreira Jácome) is distinguished by the vertical composition of its façade, which may have influenced subsequent Recife churches. However, it must also be recalled that due to the confined site, all building in Recife was taller than usual – colonial town houses here often having four or even five storeys when two were usual elsewhere. Inside the church a huge *trompe-l'œil* painting (1764–8, João Sepúlveda and Luíz Alves Pinto) on the nave ceiling has been preserved, but the most interesting feature is the shape of the nave, an elongated octagon. This shape was used in a more sophisticated quasi-oval design for the vaulted nave of the church of São Pedro dos Clérigos at Oporto (begun 1732, architect Nicolò Nasoni) and reappears in a provincial, decagonal, version in the *matriz* of Ouro Preto (1736). Some years later we find a similar shape used at Rio de Janeiro in the Mãe dos Homens church (1752–90) and, soon afterwards, in Goiás.

Given the problem of designing an interior comprising the two rectangular spaces of nave and chancel, the architect's attention would inevitably focus on the transition between the two. To smooth the sharp angles an obvious solution would be to carry the nave wall obliquely across the corners on either side of the chancel arch – a solution of which there are several examples in Brazil as well as Portugal. Next, for the sake of symmetry the other two corners of the nave would be similarly treated, thus producing a rectangle with canted angles which could be 'read' as a stretched octagon; and this is precisely what we see in a series of churches in Portugal and the Azores of the first half of the eighteenth century. From then onwards it would have been a natural, indeed logical, development to seek the greater elegance and spatial complexity of a more nearly equilateral elongated polygon, as was done at São Pedro Recife and in the churches at Oporto and Ouro Preto cited above. And after that it only required emancipation from deep-seated inhibitions against curved walls for elliptical and eventually double-elliptical plans to be accepted and tried out, and these new shapes allowed to appear externally. The canonical authority of Serlio's *Libro quinto* could be quoted (much more influential than buildings at Rome by Vignola, Bernini, etc., usually cited); and eventually indeed a church was built with a visibly oval nave. This was the pilgrimage church of Bom Jesus do Monte near Braga in Portugal (1722–5) described by M. A. Vieira in chapter XVI of his *Descripção do sanctuario* (Lisbon, 1793); but before long it threatened to collapse, had to be propped up and was eventually pulled down and replaced by the present neoclassical structure in 1803. The future for 'unstable' oval forms lay not in Portugal, where the 1755 earthquake would have reinforced conservative preference for 'stable' rectangular plans, but in Brazil, and precisely in earthquake-free Minas Gerais.

The splendidly situated hilltop church of Nª Sª da Glória do Outeiro at Rio de Janeiro, with its white walls articulated by stone structural members extended into the sky by tall pinnacles, is one of the most picturesque buildings in Brazil. It is also designed to be seen from all sides, unlike so many Bahian and Pernambucan churches. With its double-polygonal plan, the nave and chancel being respectively an elongated octagon and an elongated hexagon, it is also one of the most unusual buildings in the country. Unfortunately both its architect and date are uncertain. It may have been begun as early as 1714; but it was more probably built in the 1730s, which would be consistent with the *azulejaria*, mainly dating from 1735–40, and with the tradition that the designer was Lt.-Col. José Cardoso Ramalho, appointed *engenheiro-mór* of Rio de Janeiro in 1738 after ten years' service in the Brazil fleets.

Characteristically Portuguese are the whitewashed interior walls offsetting the wainscoting of blue and white *azulejos*, and the nave vault ribs of local pinkish granite. The siting of the bell tower over the entrance porch recalls the centralized church of N.S. da Cruz (1705) at Barcelos in Portugal, though the two buildings differ in other respects.

The monumental church of Nª Sª da Conceição da Praia at Salvador, designed by the military engineer Manuel Cardoso de Saldanha, was begun in the *cidade baixa* in 1739, dedicated in 1765, but not finally completed until the mid nineteenth century. As with the former Jesuit church in the same city, at which we have already glanced, the building stone employed was *pedra lioz* (or *pedra do reino* as it was called in Brazil), imported from Lisbon. Nª Sª da Conceição is also, like the Jesuit church, a large building, 57 by 44 metres, incorporating on either side of the church symmetrical wings which house administrative offices. It belongs stylistically to the *estilo joanino*, the Portuguese late baroque which was current during the reign of Dom João V (1706–50); and there is one unusual feature, namely the diagonal placing of the towers flanking the façade – a feature which we find subsequently repeated in Nª Sª da Piedade at Elvas (1756) in Portugal and at the *matriz* of Morro Grande (begun 1764, design attributed to António Francisco Lisboa, called 'o Aleijadinho' (the little cripple) (1738?–1814)) in Minas Gerais.

The beautiful colour and texture of the *pedra do reino* appear to particular advantage in the interior. The reredos of the high altar (1765–73, carved by João Moreira) is a late baroque masterpiece incorporating some rococo elements; but the most remarkable decorative feature is the magnificent architectural *trompe-l'œil* painting on the nave ceiling executed in 1773 by José Joaquim da Rocha.

The importation of this church from Lisbon bears witness to the easy accessibility of Salvador and other coastal cities (but not Minas Gerais) from Portugal, the high standards of the Bahian merchants who sponsored the construction and insisted upon the best metropolitan architecture and stone masonry, and also, conversely, the lack of sufficient craftsmen in Brazil.

The *matriz* of Nª Sª do Pilar of Ouro Preto (begun *c.* 1720, design attributed to the military engineer Major Pedro Gomes Chaves) belongs to a series of large parish churches mostly built in the 1720s and 1730s in the new towns of Minas Gerais. They all follow the traditional ground plan comprising two adjoining rectangular rooms, nave and chancel. At Ouro Preto, however, two years after the nave of Nª Sª do Pilar had been structurally completed (1734), an unusual modification was introduced, namely the insertion of an interior screen wall giving the nave an elongated decagonal shape inscribed within the external rectangle. The description of the impressive interior with its 'egg-shaped' nave given in June 1867 by Isabel Burton to her husband Richard is recorded in the latter's *Highlands of Brazil* in conscientious detail, down to the invocations of the six side altars.

Joaquim José da Silva, *vereador* (alderman) of Mariana, writing in 1790, assigns the construction of the decagonal nave of Nᵃ Sᵃ do Pilar to the stonemason–builder A. F. Pombal, uncle of o Aleijadinho, and says that the colossal Corinthian order applied by Pombal followed the rules given by Vincenzo Scamozzi's *L'idea della architettura universale* (Venice, 1615, and numerous subsequent editions in five languages). Later he records that o Aleijadinho's father, the carpenter–builder M. F. Lisboa, used the rules of Vignola's *Cinque ordini* for the interior of the *matriz* of António Dias. The reliability of J. J. da Silva's evidence (his memorandum has only survived thanks to a transcript made by R. J. F. Bretas in 1858) has been questioned, but there seems no reason to doubt that the architectural treatises he cites were available to builders in eighteenth-century Brazil, together with Serlio's *Libri d'architettura*, Padre Inácio da Piedade Vasconcellos' *Artefactos symmetriacos e geometricos* (Lisbon, 1733), and quite possibly other Italian, Spanish and French treatises such as those of Palladio, Lorenzo de San Nicolás and Fréart de Chambray.

The church of Nᵃ Sᵃ do Rosário at Ouro Preto represents the final, most advanced outcome of all the various experiments with polygonal and curved ground plans hitherto undertaken in Portugal and Brazil. It is an authentically baroque structure, not merely baroque in its decoration. It has a bow façade, round towers, and both nave and chancel are elliptical: only the sacristy remains rectangular. Also it is designed to be seen equally well from the sides as from the front. It was begun after 1753 and probably completed in 1785, the date inscribed above the pediment. At Mariana a 'sister' church, that of São Pedro dos Clérigos, begun at some time between 1748 and 1764, only differs substantially from the Rosário in having square towers (which were not completed until 1922). The *vereador* J. J. da Silva affirms that both these churches were constructed by the stonemason–builder José Pereira dos Santos to designs given by Dr António Pereira de Sousa Calheiros, about whom virtually nothing else is known: he was quite possibly a scholarly amateur who gave designs for buildings and *retablos* in the same way as did his contemporary André Soares at Braga. The name Calheiros is that of an armigerous Minhota family with its seat (*solar*) near Ponte de Lima.

For the curved plans of the Ouro Preto and Mariana churches, Sousa Calheiros is said to have been inspired by the Pantheon at Rome. That suggests acquaintance with Serlio's *Libro terzo*, and this particular book of Serlio's could also have been seen to authorize other prominent features of Nª Sª do Rosário. For example Serlio illustrates the ancient Roman gate of Spello near Assisi with a pedimented façade flanked by duodecagonal, i.e. quasi-cylindrical, cone-capped towers. He also illustrates the convex arcades of the Colosseum and other amphitheatres, and, most suggestive of all, a 'tempio fuori di Roma molto ruinata' with a double-circle plan. This last, as Angulo has shown, gave the plan – though not of course the elevation – for the Capilla del Pocito (1777, Guadalupe, Mexico City), a derivation which proves conclusively that the illustrations of treatises such as Serlio's really did exert influence on architectural design in colonial Latin America.

The immediate precedents for the double-ellipse ground plans of the two Mineiro churches were two small churches at Rio de Janeiro (a town closely linked to Minas because it was the principal seaport for the mines), namely Nª Sª da Glória do Outeiro, already mentioned, and São Pedro dos Clérigos (1733–8, architect unknown; destroyed 1943) which had a bow façade, an oval nave, rounded side chapels visible externally, and ambiguously shaped towers which could be equally well 'read' either as round or square. (Richard Burton ironically coined the term 'round-square tower style' to express this ambiguity.)

Robert Smith searched Portugal, and the Minho in particular, to find support for the notion that there might be a Portuguese origin for the bow façades and curved walls of naves, chancels and towers which distinguish the Carioca and Mineiro churches. However, the only fully elliptical design visible as such from outside and prominent and early enough to have exercised the alleged influence in Brazil was the nave, of 'forma quasi redonda', of the first church of N.S. Bom Jesus near Braga (consecrated 1725), which has been mentioned above. Otherwise there are only Nasoni's elongated polygonal nave for São Pedro dos Clérigos at Oporto (1732); two churches with flat façades which project forward between flanking towers with chamfered or rounded corners (Santa Marinha, Vila Nova de Gaia, 1745, architect Nicolò Nasoni; N.S.

dos Santos Passos, Guimarães, 1769, architect André Soares); and lastly a small church with an octagonal nave, dedicated to Nª Sª da Lapa, in the country town of Arcos de Val-de-Vez, 30 km north of Braga (built between 1758 and 1774, design attributed by Robert Smith to André Soares).

The possibility of course existed for the Portuguese at home as well as overseas to choose curvilinear, baroque architectonic forms. Illustrations and descriptions were certainly available in books and engravings, and information could also have been transmitted by Italian and Central European immigrants. The fact that only in Minas Gerais and Rio de Janeiro were those swelling baroque forms given a real welcome is no less puzzling than their virtually total rejection in the rest of the Lusitanian world. The experimentation in the mining province and its seaport took many different forms. At Rio there was Nª Sª da Lapa (1747–55) which has a round nave. At Ouro Preto there is the Third Order church of Nª Sª do Carmo (begun 1766 to a design by M. F. Lisboa, modified 1770 and subsequently) which has a serpentine façade and 'round-square' towers; also the undated chapels of São José (convex façade), São Miguel do Saramenha (semicircular apse) and São João Batista (bottle-shaped plan).

Parallels, if not precedents, for all the unusual features in these Mineiro churches are to be found in the eighteenth-century architecture of Piedmont and Central Europe; and the façade of the Kollegienkirche at Salzburg (1696, architect J. B. Fischer von Erlach) published in the architect's *Entwurff einer Historischen Architectur* (Vienna, 1721, book IV, plate 9; subsequent editions Leipzig, 1725, 1742, London, 1730, 1737) could among other exemplary designs perfectly well have been known to Dr António de Sousa Calheiros. But if there indeed were Central European or Polish influences in Minas Gerais that would paradoxically make Mineiro architecture in a sense all the more typically Portuguese, not less so, since foreign influences of various kinds in provincial Portugal, especially the Minho, are a recurrent theme in its architectural history.

The churches of the Third Order of St Francis of Assisi at Ouro Preto and at São João d'El Rei were seemingly begun in 1766 and 1774 respectively, to designs traditionally ascribed to o Aleijadinho. Representative of the fully developed Mineiro rococo (sometimes called the *estilo Aleijadinho*), they exemplify the zenith of sophisticated elegance achieved in the art and architecture of colonial Brazil. Richard Burton, who visited Minas in the winter (June–July) of 1867, devoted three pages of *The Highlands of Brazil* to describing what he called 'the show-church of São João d'El Rei if not of Minas Gerais'.

The decorated façades and rococo suavity of the forms of both these Franciscan churches contrast sharply with the robust baroque convexity and lack of ornament which distinguish N^a S^a do Rosário at Ouro Preto. Particularly remarkable in the São João d'El Rei church is the subtlety of the attenuated elliptical plan of the nave, virtually a tulip shape. On the other hand the Ouro Preto church also possesses great merits. The composition of the façade and integration of the towers is brilliantly successful, and the interior is unequalled with its pulpits, chancel ornaments and high altar (completed 1794) by o Aleijadinho. The *trompe-l'œil* ceiling painting (1801–12, Manuel da Costa Ataíde), as Robert Smith has said, 'evokes something of the spirit of the rococo of southern Germany'.

A notable feature of the *estilo Aleijadinho* churches is the extensive and elaborate rococo relief ornament applied to the façades, and to the portal in particular, carved in a greenish-blue local steatite (*pedra sabão*) with mixtilinear, wavy and crinkled architrave mouldings. Nasoni had been responsible, in the mid 1740s, for a series of architraves with undulant and mixtilinear profiles in buildings at and near Oporto; but the motif was not subsequently taken up in Portugal. André Soares made no use of it. Consequently it is all the more surprising that it should have been adopted, in a refined version, by o Aleijadinho for the surrounds of his church portals. Nevertheless, the rococo architecture of the Minho was occasionally more revolutionary than that of Minas Gerais. In the Malheiros-Reimões chapel at Viana do Castelo (which I have attributed on stylistic grounds to André Soares) the entablature has been eliminated – a radical liberty which was very seldom taken in Brazil.

The hilltop Sanctuary of N.S. Bom Jesus de Matosinhos at Congonhas do Campo is approached up the hillside by a zig-zag route past six chapels of the *Passos* (stations of the cross), beyond which a monumental double staircase gives access to the forecourt of the church. The remoteness of the site and the views bounded by far distant mountain ranges are extraordinarily impressive; and the elegant, curvilinear *adro* staircase with its twelve statues of prophets carved by o Aleijadinho on its parapets is an unforgettable sight. The simple *Passos* chapels and the conventionally designed church (1758–76) contribute compatibly to the ensemble without, however, having any intrinsic architectural merit themselves. Here again Portuguese parallels were unexpectedly more innovative. N.S. Bom Jesus do Monte near Braga (1722–5) and Nª Sª dos Remédios near Lamego (begun 1750) had an oval nave and an octagonal chancel respectively.

The Congonhas church is surrounded by a wide pavement enclosed by a parapet. This paved space is an integral part of the completed ensemble, comparable to the stylobate of a temple. In front of the church it expands to form the *adro*, which is conceived as an open-air narthex, or atrium, integrated with the church and functionally designed to accommodate an overflow of pilgrims still able to hear, through open doors, the service being said inside the building. Thus the *adro* provides a forward extension of the church, and the frontal walls of the *adro* staircase and its rounded flanks have the character of an advanced façade; and they do in fact follow a very similar alternating convex–concave rhythm to that of the façade of Nª Sª do Carmo at Ouro Preto.

Regarded in this way, the figures of the prophets are seen to possess an architectural as well as a sculptural value; and the overall effect achieved is authentically baroque in its concentrated theatrical intensity. One may usefully compare the Congonhas statues to the eleven surmounting the high mid-eighteenth-century façade of the church of St John Lateran at Rome. In both, the group of gesticulating figures fulfils a balancing function in the architectural composition. At Congonhas, however, the figures are brought forward and down to the level of the forecourt parapet, and thus are related to the portal in a horizontal plane instead of vertically as in the Roman church. From this point of view the Congonhas ensemble may also be recognized to represent the culmination of earlier *estilo Aleijadinho* experiments in the three-dimensional design and decoration of façades.

The modest showing of civil architecture in Brazil from the sixteenth to the eighteenth century is a reflection of Brazil's colonial status. There was no resident monarch before 1808, so there were no royal palaces. The position of the governor-general or viceroy contrasted markedly with that of even minor independent princes in Europe, who were free to imitate Versailles and did so. Little real power was delegated from Lisbon to Salvador or Rio de Janeiro, still less to the *capitanias*. Even inland Minas Gerais enjoyed an only slightly greater independence, conferred by its remote situation; but so jealous was the home government of its authority that a regulation was issued on 27 November 1730 prohibiting the governor of Minas from describing his residence as a palace. The status of the Brazilian cities can best be compared to that of provincial 'capitals' in the home country: one would no more expect to find a Mafra or a Queluz near Évora, Coimbra, or Oporto than near Salvador or Rio de Janeiro. Brazil was Portugal's 'milch cow' and ultimately of course expenditure on government buildings in Brazil could only reduce the revenue yielded. In marked contrast, the church and the religious orders were by their natures less centralized and enjoyed considerable independence from their parental institutions, as the urban physiognomy of colonial towns clearly demonstrates. Generally speaking, a certain parallelism is to be observed between civil and ecclesiastical architecture. Juan Giuria has pointed out that, in striking contrast to Spanish American practice, the formula generally adopted for church façades in the Brazilian coastal towns is virtually identical, below the main entablature, to that of a palace façade.

Although individually they may be of little architectural pretension, the impressive quality and aesthetic value of an environment of contemporary houses cannot be over-estimated. They furnish the background against which the great set pieces, represented by churches and convents, rise up and dominate the scene with their height and bulk. A prescient and laudable awareness of the irreplaceable value of the complete, integrated colonial townscape led the Brazilian government in 1933 to declare the whole of Ouro Preto a national monument, instead of just issuing a series of individual preservation orders for the principal buildings.

The most ambitious works of colonial civil architecture were the town halls, the residences of governors and bishops, the town houses or *solares* of patrician families, and the country houses on large sugar plantations (*engenhos*), ranches or farms (*fazendas*). A few eighteenth-century town halls survive – of which the magnificent structure, traditionally combining town hall with prison, at Ouro Preto is the most distinguished example. Begun in 1784 to a design given by the governor, Luiz da Cunha Menezes, who was an amateur architect, it faces the governor's residence (second quarter 18th century, design attributed to the military engineer José Fernandes Pinto Alpoim) across the *praça* on the central ridge, thus creating a scenic, monumental focus which pulls together and integrates an otherwise irregular, sprawling, centrifugal town. The single most impressive official residence in colonial Brazil was, however, the palace of the archbishop of Bahia (built

1707–15), a massive cubic structure of imposing gravity. Also striking, though in a quite different way, is the elegant Ionic Merchants' Exchange building, of English Regency style, in the lower town of Salvador (1815–17, architect Lt.-Col. C. D. da Cunha Fidié) which bears witness to the importance in colonial life of the business activities which its members pursued.

At the very end of the colonial period, the situation was transformed by the presence of the Portuguese court in Rio de Janeiro (1808–21). A group of French artists led by the painter Joachim Lebreton, invited to found an academy of fine arts, arrived at Rio in 1816. Among them was the architect A. H. V. Grandjean de Montigny (1776–1850), who gave designs for several large institutional buildings, and assured the predominance of French taste in Brazil for well over a century.

It must be recognized that if architecture is deemed a social art, then the design of private houses deserves particular attention. The category is a wide one extending from one- or two-room wattle and daub (*pau a pique*) cottages to stone-built town houses large even by European standards – such as the Casa dos Contos at Ouro Preto, completed in 1787 for João Rodrigues de Macedo with corner columns, central tower or belvedere (*mirante*), magnificent stone staircase, enclosed courtyard and even a garden – apparently the only colonial garden to have survived in Brazil.

Already at the turn of the seventeenth century fine town houses were being built in the middle of the city of Salvador, among which the Saldanha house (first decade 18th century) is particularly interesting because of its decoration. The front door and window above are surrounded by sculptured ornament of the same kind as that on the façade of the Third Order Franciscan church (1702–3); and if Gabriel Ribeiro was indeed responsible for the latter he was probably responsible for the Saldanha portal too. Entering through this imposing portal, we come into a vestibule with a fine stone staircase dividing above the landing into two flights giving access to the *piano nobile*, where the family lived. In the reception rooms in the front of the house there are panelled wooden ceilings, and on the walls a series of signed *azulejo* pictures, dating from *c.* 1703, representing hunting, pastoral and mythological scenes and surrounded with elaborate ornamental borders; and in the small chapel opening from the principal salon a magnificent framed *azulejo* panel. J. M. dos Santos Simões has rated the Casa Saldanha *azulejaria* among the most important in the Lusitanian world.

The internal arrangement of the Saldanha house and of other town houses at Salvador, and elsewhere in colonial Brazil, follows a traditional Portuguese distribution of rooms which is already apparent in a house at Olinda (Pátio de São Pedro, no. 7) probably dating from the early seventeenth century. In this layout there was on the ground floor a vestibule giving access to the stairs and to a corridor leading to the paved courtyard or *quintal* at the back of the house, where animals were also kept; also on the ground floor were a guest room, sometimes a shop, store-rooms, slaves' quarters, and separate rooms for the performance of various household tasks. On the first floor in front there was a large reception room with balconied windows, or a veranda, looking onto the street or the *praça* below. From this a central corridor led to the back of the house with small, often windowless, rooms or alcoves, some used as bedrooms, on each side; and at the back a large dining room and a kitchen, with an external staircase down into the *quintal*.

The *casa grande* of the *senhor de engenho* or *fazendeiro* also followed a more or less consistent pattern adapted from established practice in the home country, even to the extent of occasionally preserving the tower, symbol of aristocratic privilege in Portuguese manor houses. Other traditional features are the hipped roof, the external staircase and the loggia or veranda with a sloping raftered roof supported by a row of thick stone columns or pillars, usually of the Tuscan order. (A fine example is the mid-eighteenth-century *casa grande* of the *fazenda* of Colubandé, Rio de Janeiro.) These verandas are exactly similar in construction to the upper storeys of some Portuguese and Brazilian cloisters, including that of the Franciscan church at Salvador described above. A chapel was also provided, either incorporated in the house or built separately; and occasionally one of these chapels achieves distinction for its architecture or decoration – or for both in the extraordinary case of the chapel of Nª Sª da Pena (1660) of the *engenho velho* at the junction of the Iguape creek and Paraguaçú river in the Recôncavo da Bahia.

The most interesting of all surviving Brazilian colonial country houses – and the earliest (though in ruins) – is the Casa da Torre at Tatuapara on the coast north-east of Salvador, built by the *fazendeiro* Garcia d'Avila (d. 1607), who was a cattle farmer on a very large scale. This house, already recorded as existing in 1584, was enlarged by Garcia's grandson Francisco between 1607 and 1624. It is remarkable for its massive masonry construction, its tower, its hexagonal chapel and the open entrance courtyard, with symmetrical arcaded wings (i.e. the French Château de Bury (1511) plan – which was only gradually beginning to be adopted in Portugal during the first half of the seventeenth century).

Although there was little variation in the main characteristics of civil architecture throughout the colony, there were many small regional variations which have been lovingly recorded by José Wasth Rodrigues.

Finally it should be noticed that some valuable evidence on vanished early buildings has come down to us from Dutch sources, as a result of the Dutch invasion and settlement of north-east Brazil (1621–54). At Olinda the invaders are recorded to have admired the stone-built town houses they found there. The Olinda churches, which had some slight architectural pretensions, were recorded by Frans Post, who was in Brazil from 1637 to 1644 as painter to Count Maurice of Nassau. Post's charming landscapes of the Pernambucan countryside also show us the *engenhos* and the humble, barn-like, village churches with their characteristically Portuguese lean-to porches (*alpendres*). The most ambitious building enterprise of the Dutch themselves was in their capital, Recife, where a palace for the governor was erected in 1639–42 with flanking towers (fulfilling the functions of lighthouse and observatory) surrounded by a park. This palace, eventually destroyed *c.* 1782, exercised no influence on civil architecture in Brazil.

The stylistic development of the Portuguese and Brazilian *retablo* during the sixteenth and seventeenth centuries – from late Renaissance through baroque and rococo to neoclassical – has been exhaustively analysed and illustrated by Robert Smith and Germain Bazin; but the *raison d'être* of this elaborate decoration, upon which such large resources were spent, remains to be fully elucidated.

The psychological objective, or result, of the decoration may be one of dazzling and mesmerizing the beholder or of creating a visionary illusion. The artistic objective is more precise and specific, namely to overcome the impression upon the visitor, so graphically expressed by Richard Burton, 'that he stands in a large barn', which the architectonic naïveté of the parallelepipedic space conveys. The densely carved and richly gilded reredoses attract the eye magnetically – extending the space and dissolving its boundaries with suggestions of vibration and movement. Colour also enters into this process of visual disintegration

– the burnished, gilded, carved wooden ornament (*talha*) resonating with the red, green and violet of painted images, the light and dark blues of *azulejos* and the brown or black of polished jacaranda.

The impact of these chromatic and sculptural effects is to be seen enhanced in various ways in the truly marvellous baroque–rococo interiors of the chapel of Nª Sª do O at Sabará in Minas Gerais (second quarter 18th century), and the chapels of Nª Sª da Conceição dos Militares (*c.* 1740–80) and Nª Sª da Conceição das Jaqueiras (third quarter 18th century), both at Recife.

The comprehensive inventory of the surviving *azulejos* of colonial Brazil which has been compiled by J. M. dos Santos Simões may be regarded as definitive. There was no local manufacture: all were imported from Portugal. From the seventeenth century onwards, so firmly established was the taste for them that they were sometimes imitated by painted facsimiles. As a rule only *azulejos* of the very best quality were shipped to Brazil, so frequently the Brazilian examples are among the best in existence of their date and type, and a few are even unique. Already in Brazil in the eighteenth century, Portuguese monochrome *azulejos* started to be used extensively to enrich the exteriors of buildings and cupolas of towers as at the Franciscan convent at João Pessoa (Paraíba) – long before the custom was adopted in Portugal. *Azulejos* were not used for *ex votos*, but in Nª Sª da Boa Viagem at Salvador there are striking mid-eighteenth-century tile panels depicting miraculous escapes from death at sea.

The well-known device of opening up a ceiling or vault by *trompe-l'œil* painting was developed by seventeenth-century Italian artists to give worshippers in baroque churches visions of apotheoses and heavenly triumphs seen as if looking through architectural frames represented in sharply receding perspective. The techniques for achieving this highly effective means of disguising real architectural boundaries by eliminating them visually, and extending interior space without limit, were disseminated throughout Europe by the text-book treatise of Father Andrea Pozzo S.J., *Perspectiva pictorum et architectorum* (Rome, 1693–1700, and subsequent editions in Italian, Latin, German and English). The secrets were also transmitted by practitioners – in the case of Portugal by the Florentine Vincenzo Bacherelli, who arrived at Lisbon in about 1700 and trained Portuguese painters in the art, which became immensely popular. The earliest such ceiling in Brazil is that of São Francisco at Rio de Janeiro (begun 1737, Caetano da Costa Coelho). Thereafter many more were painted, notably in the churches of Salvador and Recife, and went on being painted, as we have seen, into the nineteenth century in Minas Gerais, though few of them contrived to achieve complete perspective consistency or technically correct foreshortening.

The new illusionist treatment displaced earlier systems of decorating ceilings and vaults with coffered or panelled compartments often following Serlian patterns. The opening up in a vertical direction of the enclosed space of the church which *trompe-l'œil* painting accomplished was paralleled by the advent of new open reredos designs superseding framed compositions firmly closed by concentric arches. These two parallel stylistic revolutions, similarly directed towards breaking spatial constraints, occurred during the first quarter of the eighteenth century in Portugal and the second quarter of the eighteenth century in Brazil.

The art of colonial Brazil reached a climax in the first decade of the nineteenth century with the rococo ceiling paintings of Manuel da Costa Ataíde and the statues of prophets carved by António Francisco Lisboa, o Aleijadinho, for the pilgrimage church at Congonhas do Campo. The latter have continuously attracted interest and admiration at least since Auguste de Saint-Hilaire visited Congonhas in 1818 (*Voyage dans...le Brésil* (Paris, 1833)) and have in our own time evoked several excellent studies and commentaries, though the choice of prophets, their placing, and the inscriptions they carry, raise questions not yet adequately answered.

O Aleijadinho was also responsible for some if not all of the 66 carved wooden figures housed in the six chapels of the *Passos* on the slope leading up to the church at Congonhas. No detailed comparison has yet been made between the individual figures and figural groups of these *Passos* and those at various pilgrimage centres in Portugal which could be considered precedents for Congonhas, although such a comparison might well give insight into the original composition of the Brazilian groups.

Among the principal precedents for the Congonhas ensemble are Santo António dos Olivais at Coimbra and N.S. Bom Jesus de Bouças at Matosinhos near Oporto, both dating from the second quarter of the eighteenth century and both with six chapels. Slightly later there are the much-elaborated versions, set in fountainous hillside gardens, of N.S. Bom Jesus do Monte near Braga and Nª Sª dos Remédios near Lamego.

It is easy to exaggerate the correspondence between the Congonhas and Braga shrines. Out of nineteen stone statues at Braga only Isaiah and Jeremiah figure among the twelve at Congonhas, and the resemblance stressed by Smith between the Pontius Pilate at Braga and o Aleijadinho's Nahum is insufficient to counteract their iconographical incongruity. As for the gardens with fountains, hardly a trace of them is left at Congonhas. There were apparently different intentions. Burton records that 'when [the *Passos* chapels at Congonhas] are finished, the place will be used as a burial ground for those who can afford it'. In many respects there is a much closer correspondence between the six simple square *Passos* chapels at Congonhas and the like number of equally small unassuming chapels at Coimbra and at Matosinhos – to the second of which the Brazilian shrine was of course in an important sense affiliated. Descriptions of the figural groups at Braga were available to the confraternity responsible for commissioning the *Passos* figures from o Aleijadinho in 1796. Full details had been published three years previously in M. A. Vieira's *Descripção*, referred to above.

Certain manifestations of popular art, including, as here, the popular super-realism of *tableaux vivants* largely made up of stereotypes or caricatures, pose aesthetic problems. Few critics have been inclined to accept them as fine art. Even Samuel Butler, who was exceptionally favourably disposed, only argued in favour of the very best work at Varallo (*Ex Voto* (London, 1888), ch. 6). At Congonhas, where o Aleijadinho, a sculptor of genius, was responsible for the *Passos* figures, they cannot of course be dismissed. There has therefore been a tendency to select a few which are thought to possess artistic merit, attributing those to o Aleijadinho himself and assigning the rest to assistants in the workshop.

The truth of the matter is that o Aleijadinho contracted for the *Passos* figures and was paid for them between 1796 and 1799. Thereafter he contracted for the twelve prophets and was paid for them over the years 1800–5. We have no reason to deny him and his workshop the credit for both; though how much he did himself and how much was done by helpers under his instructions can of course be debated. He must, however, have controlled the work and taken responsibility for fulfilling the contract in both cases. There can only be one conclusion: that he was an artist of unusually uneven accomplishment, the variations in the quality of his achievement perhaps partly reflecting the irregular progress of his crippling disease.

From the foregoing survey it will be evident that the study of Brazilian colonial architecture and art cannot be viewed meaningfully in isolation, apart from that of the parent country. So close was the relationship that, prior to independence (1822), Brazil must be regarded art-historically as being as much a part of Portugal as, say, the Minho; and just as we find significant idiosyncratic expressions in the art of the Minho, so also we find notable manifestations of artistic individuality in Brazil. There was no indigenous Indian, or African, artistic contribution to stimulate, or explain, the Brazilian individuality; and the Dutch occupation of Pernambuco (1630–54) left behind no artistic heritage. Original features in the architecture and art of the colony must therefore be attributed to other causes. Among these causes were: first, the influence of illustrated books (architectural treatises in particular) and engravings; secondly, personal contributions made by Italians and Central Europeans working in Brazil, though very few of these are documented, apart from the Italian architect A. J. Landi, who was active at Belém do Pará in the late eighteenth century; thirdly, the belated currency of artistic styles in Brazil making possible their further development after they had been superseded in Europe; and finally, in the special case of António Francisco Lisboa (o Aleijadinho), an extraordinary personal artistic talent.

A last word deserves to be said on a characteristic which generally distinguishes colonial Brazilian productions and which continually impresses the visitor who is familiar with the arts and architecture of Portugal and other parts of the Lusitanian world. That is the high standard of workmanship which the Portuguese colonists in America demanded and received and, in consequence, the fine quality of the greater part of it, whether imported from Portugal or executed in Brazil.

19

THE MUSIC OF COLONIAL SPANISH AMERICA

Colonial Spanish American music consists of several different strands: European music of the Renaissance and baroque periods; autochthonous music persisting from the pre-conquest period; African music transported chiefly from the sub-Saharan Atlantic coastal regions; and, of course, mixtures of all three – European, Indian and African.

As early as the 1550s, only half a century after the arrival of the Europeans, Latin America displayed the musical diversity which was to be characteristic of the entire colonial period. Juan Pérez Materano, the dean of Cartagena cathedral and resident in Cartagena since 1537, was putting the final touches to a treatise on music that discussed both polyphony and plain song. His royal printing licence, issued at Valladolid on 19 December 1559, permitted him to publish it anywhere in the Americas with copyright privilege lasting ten years.[1]

In Mexico City the 1550s witnessed a dramatic revival of Aztec cult songs (*xochicuicatl*). The 91 'flower songs' in a contemporary Nahuatl manuscript now known as *Cantares en idioma mexicano* (first published in facsimile by Antonio Peñafiel in 1904) contain evocations of slain warrior ancestors dated 1551, 1553 and later. Although lacking melodies in five-line European notation, the *cantares* nonetheless include musical rubrics ranging from the seventeen-syllable drum-beat pattern for strophes 49–54 to the 22-syllable pattern for strophes 55–60 of Song XLV. To show the variety of the drum-beat patterns required in these *cantares*, Karl A. Nowotny tabulated 758 different patterns, the most complex belonging to the latest songs.[2] The number of *huehuetls*

---

[1] Robert Stevenson, 'The first New World composers: fresh data from Peninsular archives', *Journal of the American Musicological Society*, 33/1 (Spring 1970), 98.

[2] 'Die Notation des *Tono* in den aztekischen Cantares', *Baessler-Archiv*, N.F. 4/2 [XXIX. Band] (December 1956), 186.

(upright membranophones, struck with bare hands) needed to accompany any given song in the collection ranges from one to ten. Since any single huehuetl produced two sounds a fifth apart, the ten huehuetls that accompanied Song XLV gave a rich accompaniment indeed. There are 60 strophes in this *tombeau* commemorating don Hernando de Guzmán, the renowned Indian manuscript illuminator who in 1569 inherited the lordship of Coyoacán.[3] The cacique don Francisco Plácido, who in 1563 governed the Otomí town of Xiquipilco, wrote three *cantares* dated 1551, 1553 and 1564. An alumnus of the Tlatelolco college for noble Indian youth, he gave the following musical instructions for the accompaniment of Song XIV: 'The huehuetl is played in the following fashion: first, a peal that dies away; then another peal doing the same; then three drum-strokes. Next comes a roll near the centre of the drumhead [sounding a fifth lower than the previous drum-strokes]. This breaks off, whereupon the pattern resumes – beginning with the single stroke at the rim of the huehuetl.'[4]

Augustinian missionaries sponsored the publication in Mexico City of the first music book printed in the New World. Their 80-page *Ordinarium* (1556), prefaced by a title-page compartment showing a nude Adam and Eve facing each other, contains chants for Kyries, Glorias, Sanctuses and Agnuses (but no Credos), together with formulae for intoning the gospels and for the *Ite missa est*. Prepared with extreme care by Diego de Vertauillo, Augustinian Provincial in Mexico from 1554 to 1557, and printed by Juan Pablos (= Giovanni Paoli), this *Ordinarium* was applauded not only in New Spain but also in the Iberian peninsula and in Peru. So great was its success that a reprint was issued in 1571 by the pioneer printer at Madrid, Pierres Cosin. Destined for use at Indian mission stations allotted to the Augustinians, the *Ordinarium* included none but ancient chants originating (according to Solesmes research) before 1200. Taking their cue from the 1556 *Ordinarium*, the Dominicans seven years later issued a *Psalterium Chorale*. Originally to have been printed by Juan Pablos but completed, after his death in August 1560, by his widow and Pedro de Ocharte of Rouen (1563), this *Psalterium* accords with a Dominican-sponsored book published at Venice in 1523 by Petrus Leichtenstein. Franciscan and Augustinian monasteries in Mexico City commissioned the *Missale Romanum*

---

[3] *Annales de Chimalpahin Quauhtlehuanitzin*, translated by Rémi Siméon (Paris, 1889), 210.
[4] See Robert Stevenson, *Music in Aztec and Inca territory* (Berkeley and Los Angeles, 1968), 47–8, for Nahuatl text.

Ordinarium (Antonio de Espinosa, 1560), called 'the most splendid product of the Mexican press'[5] during a century that saw publication of more than 220 books, fourteen of which (no mean percentage) were music books.

All these sixteenth-century Mexican music imprints, even the most luxurious – the 300-folio *Psalterium, An[t]iphonarium Sanctorale* sponsored by the Jesuits (Pedro de Ocharte, 1584) – were specifically intended for use at Indian missionary stations, where a profusion of native and European-style instruments accompanied the daily singing of hours and Mass. In a carry-over from Aztec custom, Indian church musicians enjoyed exemption from tribute payments.[6] The excess of both musicians and musical instruments of all types provoked the First Mexican Church Council of 1555 to pass an ordinance forbidding their further multiplication.[7] Printed in 1556, the statute of this council curbing musical excesses received royal reinforcement in a cedula of February 1561 ordering an abatement of 'trumpets, clarions, chirimías, sackbuts, flutes, cornetts, dulzainas, fifes, viols, rebecs and other kinds of instruments, an inordinate variety of which is now in use in the monasteries'.

As an instance of the more decorous music heard on such an occasion as Charles V's funeral commemoration held on 30 November and 1 December 1559 in the Mexico City church of San José, Francisco Cervantes de Salazar's *Túmulo imperial* (Mexico, Antonio de Espinosa, 1560) tells of a procession over two hours long attended by Indian governors of Mexico, Tacuba, Texcoco and Tlaxcala, accompanied by chieftains from 200 villages, and the Spanish archbishop, the bishops of Michoacán and Nueva Galicia, the heads of the three mendicant orders and 400 priests. Once inside the spacious church, they heard vigil music led by the youthful *maestro de capilla* of Mexico City cathedral, Lázaro del Álamo (b. El Espinar, near Segovia, *c.* 1530; d. Mexico City, 19 May 1570).[8] His choices included the invitatory *Circumdederunt me*,

[5] Samuel A. Green, *A second supplementary list of early American imprints* (Cambridge, Mass., 1899), 20.

[6] See, for example, Bishop Sebastián Ramírez de Fuenleal to Charles V, 3 November 1532, printed in Henri Ternaux-Compans, *Voyages, relations et mémoires originaux* (Paris, 1840), XVI, 218–19.

[7] Mexico City, archdiocese, *Constituciones del arçobispado...de Tenuxtitlan Mexico* (Mexico, Juan Pablos, 1556), fo. xxxiii (cap. 66).

[8] Each Spanish American cathedral employed a *maestro de capilla* (chapelmaster or music director), competitively chosen, whose duties included composing as well as conducting and daily teaching; an organist similarly chosen; a cadre of paid adult singers and instrumentalists; and a group of six to a dozen choirboys who received free instruction in music and grammar plus token salaries.

the psalm *Exultemus*, and the motet *Parce mihi* by the world-renowned Spanish composer Cristóbal de Morales (*c.* 1500–53), generally regarded as the best of the century. Álamo also directed his own compositions during the ceremony. His alternate-verse setting of *Domine ne in furore* enlisted the cathedral choirboys for the odd-verse polyphony.

In the viceroyalty of Peru, an inventory of Cuzco cathedral taken on 21 February 1553 itemized both stout volumes of *las misas de Xpoval* [*sic* for Cristóbal] *de Morales* published in Rome by the Dorico brothers in 1544, along with a half-dozen other polyphonic books.[9] One at least of the two organs stationed aloft on opposite sides of the choir enclosure was made at Seville in 1549. So far as locally composed music was concerned, the cathedral *maestro de capilla* Juan de Fuentes set a notable precedent at Corpus Christi in 1551. Dressing up eight mestizo boys in Inca costume (not six, as was the conventional number of choirboys in a Spanish cathedral, but eight in deference to Inca numerology), Fuentes had them sing an Inca *haylli*. At refrains, the Spanish-born adult choristers sang part-music, to Garcilaso de la Vega's delight (as he recalled in his *Commentarios reales* of 1609, fo. 101v, column 2). And not only to Garcilaso's delight, fortunately. So great was the success of Fuentes' mixing of Inca and Spanish music that the Cuzco cathedral chapter decided on 18 July 1552 to hire henceforth a full complement of choirboys, each earning an annual salary of 50 pesos.

Hernando Franco (1532–85), Mexico City cathedral *maestro* 1575–85, and Gutierre Fernández Hidalgo (*c.* 1553–*c.* 1620), Bogotá cathedral *maestro* 1584–6, were responsible for the earliest extant Latin polyphony composed in the New World. Antedating anything in a vernacular language, their Magnificats and Salves compare favourably with the finest settings of the Song of Mary and of the Marian antiphon composed around 1580 by leading peninsular composers such as Juan Navarro, Bernardino de Ribera and Rodrigo de Ceballos. Hernando or Fernando Franco, born in 1532 at Galizuela in Extremadura, began his musical career as a choirboy at the age of ten in Segovia cathedral. During his seven years there (1542–9), both he and his close companion Lázaro del Álamo studied with the Segovia cathedral *maestros* Gerónimo de Espinar (later the teacher of Tomás Luis de Victoria) and Bartolomé de Olaso. The Salamanca University doctor of canon law who at 28

[9] Cuzco cathedral, *Libro de auctos capitulares 1549–1556*, fo. 44, quoted in Robert Stevenson, 'Cuzco cathedral: 1546–1750', *Inter-American Music Review*, 2/2 (Spring–Summer 1980), 2.

became a professor at the University of Mexico, Mateo Arévalo Sedeño (1526–c. 1584), brought both Lázaro del Álamo and Hernando Franco to the New World. After a probationary year Álamo became Mexico City's *maestro* on 2 January 1556. Franco, after an unspecified period as Guatemala cathedral *maestro*, succeeded the prematurely deceased Álamo on 20 May 1575. The short interim between Álamo and Franco was filled by Juan de Vitoria, a native of Burgos, who composed music for the earliest extant New World theatre pieces, staged on 5 and 8 December 1584 – with choirboys.[10]

Archbishop Pedro Moya de Contreras, who much preferred Franco to the fidgety Vitoria, recommended him to the crown on 30 October 1580 as a *maestro* of exemplary character and high intellect, able to 'compete advantageously with any *maestro* in Spain. Moreover, he has placed the musical forces of the cathedral in excellent order.'[11] Although not pretending to the ability to assess Franco's contrapuntal technique, Moya de Contreras could well have added that Franco's compositions showed complete mastery of all the best polyphonic procedures of the period. With manuscript compositions nowadays scattered from Guatemala City to Chicago (Newberry Library), and from Puebla to Durango in Mexico, he enjoys greatest fame for his Magnificats in the eight church tones – a copy of which on parchment was presented to Mexico City cathedral on 5 July 1611 by his admiring successor, Juan Hernández.[12]

Just as Franco was the dominant Renaissance composer in North America, so Gutierre Fernández Hidalgo was the leading figure in South America. He spent 36 years in four Andean capitals. *Maestro* at Bogotá from May 1584 to January 1586, he served also as rector of the newly founded diocesan seminary during his last months there. So excessive did students find his musical demands, however, that they fled at the beginning of 1586. Disgusted by this 'student strike' he left Bogotá soon after, but memories of his musical genius persisted until the middle of the next century. From Bogotá he moved first to Quito (12 January

[10] Lota M. Spell, 'Music in the cathedral of Mexico in the sixteenth century', *Hispanic American Historical Review* [*HAHR*], 26/3 (August 1946), 310–11.

[11] Francisco del Paso y Troncoso, *Epistolario de Nueva España 1505–1818*, XII, 58–9, quoted in Robert Stevenson, 'Mexico City cathedral: the founding century', *Inter-American Music Review*, 1/2 (Spring–Summer 1979), 154.

[12] This 1611 manuscript, transferred from Mexico City cathedral to the viceregal museum at Tepotzotlán, served Steven Barwick for the transcription of fourteen Magnificats in all tones except tone III (the corresponding leaves are torn out of the manuscript), which he published in *The Franco Codex* (Carbondale, Ill., 1965).

1588 to 6 February 1590), then Cuzco (13 July 1591 to early 1597) and finally to La Plata (present-day Sucre) cathedral (6 May 1597 to 13 June 1620). In each cathedral he combined the roles of choral and instrumental director, choirboy and musical coach to the adult clergy with that of composer of Latin liturgical music and festive villancicos using vernacular texts. His instrumentalists were usually Indians or mestizos playing winds or brass. His singers ranged from costly, vain castrati to staid Spanish clergy. He composed his festival music setting vernacular texts for Christmas, Corpus Christi and Marian calendar events.

Hoping to have his collected works published in France or Spain, he signed a contract 22 January 1607 with Diego de Torres, the Jesuit Provincial of Paraguay, already famous for its music.[13] Under the terms of the contract he entrusted the Provincial with five volumes, one each of (1) Masses, (2) Magnificats, (3) Hymns (*en fabordón*), (4) Holy Week office-music and (5) motets. To pay for the printing, Fernández Hidalgo promised within a half-year to forward through Antonio de Vega, commissary of the Inquisition at nearby Potosí, the large sum of 1,500 pesos (equal to his salary as chapelmaster at La Plata cathedral for five years). For this amount he hoped to obtain 50 printed copies of each of the five volumes, or 250 printed books in all. To recompense him for his trouble, he offered Father Torres several gift-copies of each volume. He wished two of each to be given to his dearly beloved Cuzco cathedral, another two of each to the famous Encarnación convent at Lima; and one of each to Quito and Bogotá cathedrals. Only Bogotá among these various designated places now retains any of his compositions, and they are all in manuscript. The 204-page choirbook (hereafter referred to as GFHCB) contains his eight odd-verse Magnificats *a 4* in the eight tones plus an incomplete Magnificat *a 4* for tiples in tone III; nine Vespers psalms; and two Salve Reginas: one, *a 4* (GFHCB 118–21), for a long time was wrongly attributed to the Sevillian Francisco Guerrero (1528–98), the other was *a 5* (GFHCB 102–5). The first two verses of the Salve *a 5* (Vita dulcedo and Ad te suspiramus) join with two further verses (Et Jesum and O clemens) of a Salve *a 6* by a famous contemporary, Tomás Luis de Victoria (1548–1611), to make a complete work.[14]

[13] Archivo Nacional de Bolivia, Escrituras Públicas, tomo 12, Núñez 1607, fo. 756, quoted in Robert Stevenson, *The music of Peru. Aboriginal and viceroyal epochs* (Washington, 1960), 182–3.

[14] Fernández Hidalgo's *Magnificat quarti toni* (GFHCB 158–65). The Salve Regina, *a 5*, and tone III *Laetatus sum in his*, *a 4*, were recorded by the Roger Wagner Chorale on albums entitled *Salve Regina* (Angel S 36008, 1966), *Festival of early Latin American music* (Eldorado 1, 1975) and *Latin American musical treasures from the 16th, 17th and 18th centuries* (Eldorado 2, 1977). These same masterworks were published in *Latin American colonial music anthology* (Washington, D.C., 1975), 149–67.

Franco and Fernández Hidalgo were both born in the Iberian peninsula. Two other outstanding sixteenth-century *maestros* – Gonzalo García Zorro (1548–1617) and Diego Lobato de Sosa – were American-born mestizos born of Spanish fathers and noble Indian mothers. Son of a captain and a Chibcha princess, García Zorro preceded and followed Fernández Hidalgo as Bogotá cathedral's *maestro de capilla*. In an extensive report on García Zorro's musical ability[15] one witness, Juan Pacheco, a resident of Bogotá who had studied music with him for three years, described him as a bass singer, a harsh disciplinarian who taught nothing without blows, and an unskilful contrapuntist. Although not flattering to the musicianship of García Zorro (who later rose to cathedral canon), the statements that 'any worthy chapelmaster should know counterpoint and polyphonic composition, ought to conduct competently at the choirbook stand, and must be able to spot and correct any flaws in each singer's performance', give some idea of the technical competence expected of an Andean cathedral *maestro* in the 1580s – wherever born and trained. One critic complained that 'without inordinate practice, [García Zorro] cannot sing madrigals, villanescas, nor anything involving the major prolation'. Such an expectation itself gives some idea of the repertory and sight-singing skills deemed prerequisite for 'the post of chapelmaster in a metropolitan cathedral such as ours'.

Diego Lobato de Sosa, the son of a *ñusta* of Cuzco who had been one of Atahualpa's wives and a Spanish captain killed at the battle of Iñaquito on 18 January 1546, received his professional training at the Colegio de San Andrés in Quito. His music teachers included the two Flemish Franciscans, Josse (Jodoco) de Rycke of Malines and Pierre Gosseal of Louvain, both of whom arrived in 1534 and founded the Franciscan *convento* in Quito in 1535. After 22 years Fray Josse wrote a (frequently cited) letter dated 12 January 1556 commending his Indian pupils for 'easily learning to read, write, and play any instrument'. As his instrument, Diego Lobato chose the organ – which he mastered sufficiently well to be appointed organist of Quito cathedral in 1563. In 1564 Lorenzo de Cepeda, St Teresa of Ávila's brother, who had migrated to Quito, paid 234 pesos to help defray the cost of cathedral organs being installed by Pedro de Ruanes.[16] Cepeda also donated a

---

[15] Archivo General de Indias, Santafé 226, 2/8, fos. 65v–66 and 93v–94.

[16] Quito cathedral, *Libro del Cabildo desta Santa Iglesia...de 1562 a 1583*, fo. 46v (12 September 1564), quoted in Robert Stevenson, 'Music in Quito: four centuries', *HAHR*, 43/2 (May 1963), 249.

large cathedral bell, which was in use until it broke on 14 November 1676.

Between 22 March and 19 June 1566 the newly arrived Dominican bishop, Pedro de la Peña, ordained Lobato priest. In 1571 Bishop Peña named him *cura* of the new Indian parish of San Blas – a post for which his command of the Quechua spoken at Quito and the prestige of being closely related to the highest Quechua-speaking nobility fitted him admirably. In the meantime he continued as cathedral organist. Juan de Ovando praised him in a 42-folio report to the crown dated 1573, *La Cibdád de Sant Francisco del Quito*: 'He is virtuous and self-restrained, musically skilled, and he ministers to the Indians [200 pesos annually] while simultaneously serving as cathedral organist [250 pesos].'[17] The report continues by calling Quito cathedral music 'currently the best in the Peruvian viceroyalty'.

On 3 April 1574 Lobato was named *maestro* and commissioned by the cathedral chapter to compose the *motetes* (short Spanish liturgical compositions) and *chanzonetas* (festive pieces without estribillos) needed for Christmas and Corpus Christi. The lavishing of all these attentions on Lobato aroused envy. In the eight years between 1577 and 1585 Canon Ordóñez Villaquirán did Lobato great harm by threatening to appeal to the pope himself if monies spent on music in Quito cathedral were not reduced and by spurning him for being a mestizo. Another junior canon who interfered was Francisco Talavera. A native of Santo Domingo, Talavera had studied organ in the island with Manuel Rodríguez, a brilliant Spaniard who was Gregorio Silvestre's brother and who ended his career as Mexico City cathedral organist, 1567–94. However, Lobato survived these interferences to be again named titular *maestro de capilla* on 6 February 1590, following Gutierre Fernández Hidalgo's departure for Lima.

The earliest surviving music with Spanish text in Spanish-speaking America dates from the last decade of the sixteenth century. Tomás Pascual, village *maestro* at San Juan Ixcoi (Huehuetenango, Guatemala), completed a villancico collection on 20 January 1600 that contains coplas and villancicos dated 1595, 1597 and 1599. The earliest part-music with Nahuatl text dates from 1599, and consists of the two rhythmically enticing Marian chanzonetas that are copied at fos. 121v–123 of the Canon Octaviano Valdés Codex in Mexico City.[18]

---

[17] Eliecer Enríquez B., *Quito a través de los siglos* (Quito, 1938), 49–50.
[18] Facsimiles in Gabriel Saldívar y Silva, *Historia de la música en México (épocas precortesiana y colonial)* (Mexico, 1934), 102–5.

Throughout the seventeenth century the better Spanish American composers and conductors continued to cluster around the local cathedrals, notably, in New Spain, those of Mexico City itself, Puebla de los Ángeles and Oaxaca. The sumptuous cathedral of Puebla boasted a succession of six distinguished *maestros* – Pedro Bermudes (1603), Gaspar Fernandes (1606–29), Juan Gutiérrez de Padilla (1622–64), Juan García de Céspedes (1664–78), Antonio Salazar (1679–88) and Miguel Mateo de Dallo y Lana (1688–1705) – all of whom left testimonials to their talent in still extant compositions. Oaxaca cathedral had the distinction of hiring from 1655 to 1667 the first full-blooded *maestro de capilla* in colonial annals, the Zapotec Juan Mat[h]ías. One rare exception to the rule that the cathedrals attracted the most talented was 'don' Juan de Lienas in Mexico City during the years before 1650. Like Tomás Pascual in San Juan Ixcoi (Huehuetenango), Juan Matías at Oaxaca cathedral, and many others, Juan de Lienas was an Indian. He was also probably a cacique – and married. For some or all of these reasons he failed to gain a cathedral post, despite being the composer of superb single- and double-choir polyphony that excels in both expressiveness and carefully tooled craftsmanship. His Salve Regina *a 4*, transcribed from the so-called Convento del Carmen codex, is a tender, emotional work.[19] His works in the Newberry choirbooks brought to Chicago around 1899 by the collector Charles Lawrence Hutchinson (1854–1924) and catalogued as Case VM 2147 C 36, volumes 1–6 – the Magnificat (Newberry 1, at fos. 92v–97) and *Domine ad adiuvandum, a 8* (91v–92); the three vespers psalms *a 8* (Newberry 2, 5 and 6, *Dixit Dominus, Laudate pueri* and *Credidi*); a 12-verse double-choir *Magnificat primi toni* (2, 96v–100 and 6, 98v–102); a Salve, *a 8* (3 at fos. 1v–3 and 133v–134); a Nunc dimittis, *a 8* (3v–4 and 131v–132), and *Tu lumen tu splendor, a 6* (4v–5) – show the most signs of use among the various compositions in these manuscripts. Rather than holding a cathedral post, Lienas made his living as a *convento* chapelmaster. Wherever he conducted, he probably intended his double-choir works for tiples on higher parts, instruments on lower (lower voices typically lack texts in the Newberry choirbooks).

The three other Mexico City composers represented in the Newberry volumes were all cathedral *maestros de capilla*. Antonio Rodríguez Mata began with a half prebend 23 September 1614. From 1618 he composed

---

[19] Published as *Tesoro de la música polifónica en México* (Mexico, 1952); recorded on *Salve Regina*.

the villancicos and chanzonetas needed at Christmas and other high feasts, and from no later than 1632 until his death in 1643 was titular chapelmaster. His *Passio Domini nostri Jesu Christi secundum Lucam, a 4* (Newberry 2, fos. 115v–118) – like his Matthew and John Passions *a 4* (Mexico City Cathedral Choirbook (hereafter MCCB) II, fos. 1v–14, 72v–80), and like his two lamentations (MCCB II, 106v–114 and 114v–119) – eschews all artifice, and instead consists of dark-hued chords throughout. Like Victoria and Guerrero, Rodríguez Mata limited the polyphony in his Passions to crowd utterances and a few other sentences.

Fabián Pérez Ximeno (b. *c.* 1595; d. Mexico City *c.* 17 April 1654) earned a large salary for being cathedral assistant organist as early as 1 December 1623. Like Luis Coronado, who preceded him as cathedral chapelmaster (1643–8), and López Capillas, who followed him (1654–74), he functioned as both choir director and organist during his five years from 31 March 1648 to his death six years later. On 2 May 1651 he petitioned the cathedral chapter to 'dissolve certain competing choirs, and in particular one choir led by a Negro, because of the indecency of their singing and the nonsense which they utter when assisting at Masses and at other paid church functions'.[20] Long before 1651 blacks had been accused of disturbing the peace around Mexico City cathedral. Because they habitually gathered in the *zócalo* on Sunday afternoons to dance around the Aztec calendar stone, sometimes killing each other, Archbishop Alonso de Montúfar (1554–72) had ordered the stone buried. By 1598 African drums were so much better known in Mexico than the pre-conquest *tlalpanhuehuetl* that even an Indian historian, Hernando Alvarado Tezozomoc, in his *Crónica mexicana*, had felt obliged to explain the dread death drum of his ancestors by likening it to 'a drum of the Negroes who nowadays dance in the plazas'.

Ximeno's petition also articulated another long-standing grievance: payments to such unauthorized choirs took bread out of the mouths of duly appointed cathedral singers. Replying, the cathedral chapter reminded Ximeno that certain indigent singers would be left penniless if cathedral singers monopolized every paid engagement, and deputed the cathedral *provisor*, Doctor Pedro de Barrientos, a man 'well experienced in these wrangles between choirs', to resolve their

---

[20] Mexico City cathedral, Actas Capitulares, XI (1650–53), fo. 33v, quoted in R. Stevenson, *Christmas music from Baroque Mexico* (Berkeley and Los Angeles, 1974), 73–4.

differences with his usual prudence. In their discussion it becomes quite evident that the music of the *capilla del negro* pleased certain members of the chapter so well that they were ready to protect the black musician even at the risk of offending their most veteran musical staff. Sensing the need to brighten the sound of his own rather elderly choir, Ximeno next proposed the importation of a virtuoso harpist and some other instrumentalists from Puebla. During his last two years, trying to act as both chapelmaster and first organist proved too much for him. Discipline among his musicians deteriorated. To steer them back to a proper course, the chapter was forced to resort to the time-honoured system of fines.

As a composer Ximeno favoured great polychoral blocks of sound. His *Missa quarti toni*, *a 11* (Newberry 3, 49v–57, and 2, 42v–59 = 5, 62v–69) survives also in loose sheets at Puebla cathedral. As the model on which to base this Hypophrygian Mass abounding in fine antiphonal effects, he chose the tone IV psalm *a 11*, *Beatus vir*, by 'frai Jasinto'. Ximeno's *Missa de la Batalla*, *a 6* (*sexti toni*) belongs to the Spanish Battle Mass tradition inaugurated by Guerrero (*Della batalla escoutez*, *a 5* [1582]), continued by Victoria (*Pro victoria*, *a 9* [1600]), and exemplified in such other later works sent the New World as Vicente García's *Missa de Batalla*, *a 8* and Carlos Patiño's *Magnificat Batalla*, *â Ocho*. Still in the polychoral vein, Newberry 3, 59v–62 and 2, 52v–54 contain Ximeno's 'G minor' *Magnificat*, *a 11*. His bright-hued Newberry repertory *a 8* and *a 11* contrasts with the sombre colouring of his two funeral psalms *a 5* in MCCB III, fos. 73v–78 and 79v–84: *Qui inclinavit* and *Confitebor tibi Domine in toto corde*, each ending with a 'Requiem aeternam' verse. As a sample of his versatility, his march-rhythm F major *gallego a 5*, *Ay ay galeguiños ay que lo veyo* (for soprano solo, chorus of two sopranos, tenor and bass, plus unfigured continuo) proves him as much a master of the vernacular idiom as he was of learned Latin styles.[21] His recourse to jaunty repeated dactyls (crotchet followed by two quavers) gives this Galician-dialect villancico a flair that immediately captivates the most casual listener.

No villancicos survive by Ximeno's immediate successor in Mexico City cathedral, Francisco López Capillas (*c.* 1605 to 18 January 1674), who was appointed chapelmaster on 21 April 1654. Nonetheless, printed texts of villancicos sung in the cathedral on 12 December 1669

[21] Published in *ibid.* 181–7.

make López Capillas the first to have set to music poetry honouring the Virgin of Guadalupe.[22] What does survive from his pen are eight splendid Masses (including a *Batalla, a 6*), nine Magnificats, ten motets, two hymns and a Matthew Passion. In at least six of his eight extant Masses he displays extraordinary learning – *Missa super scalam Aretinam, a 5* (MCCB VII, fos. 2v–21), two Palestrina parody masses *a 4, Quam pulchri sunt gressus tui* and *Benedicta sit Sancta Trinitas* (MCCB VI, fos. [1v]–21 and 21v–43), a Juan de Riscos parody *Missa Re Sol, a 4* and two parody masses based on his own motets, *Aufer a nobis, a 4* and *Alleluia, a 5* (MCCB VIII, fos. 1v–17, 19v–35 and 74v–91). Whence came his erudition? Whatever he knew, he learned in Mexico – for it was there that he was both born and bred. His lengthy will, signed 13 January 1674 before a Mexico City notary, Francisco de Quiñones,[23] testifies to his having been born in the viceregal capital, to his having sisters living in Mexico City, and to his owning extensive real estate there. In a short musical treatise preceding his hexachord Mass (MCCB VI), he invokes the authority of 'Pedro de Guevara Loyola, Maestro desta Yglesia'. Justifying his elaborate notational conundrums, he appeals to precedents set by Morales, Richafort, Lupus Hellinck, Palestrina and Manchicourt. Among theory texts he cites Cerone's *El Melopeo y Maestro* (1613), book 8, chapter 9; and chapters 15, 17 and 21 of a now lost *Compendio de música* by the former cathedral *maestro* Guevara Loyola (or Loyola Guevara), who had published a 60-page *Arte para componer* (Seville, Andrea Pescioni, 1582) before emigrating to Mexico City. Such evidence proves López able to cite by chapter and verse European teachers, treatises and music[24] – all available during his youth in Mexico.

López's early professional years included a seven-year period at Puebla cathedral, 17 December 1641 to 15 May 1648. Until 13 September 1645 he played both bajón and organ, thereafter only organ. To avoid lowering his 400-peso annual salary, the chapter permitted him thenceforth to earn half for organ-playing, the other half for singing. A *bachiller* when hired in 1641, he became a *licenciado* before 15 January 1647. Concurrently with his studies, he imbibed no small part of his

[22] José Mariano Beristaín de Souza, *Suplemento especial III a la Biblioteca Hispano Americana Septentrional* (Mexico, 1951), 34–5; *Letras qve se cantaron...En los Maitines de la Apparicion de la Santissima Imagen de la Virgen Maria Madre de Dios de Gvadalvpe...Año 1669. En Mexico. Por la Uiuda de bernardo Calderon.*

[23] Archivo General de Notarías, 547 Q [*olim* 325], 1674, fos. 8–11v.

[24] Lester D. Brothers, 'A New-World hexachord Mass by Francisco López Capillas', *Yearbook for Inter-American Musical Research*, 9 (1973), 39–40, published the entire *declaración* prefacing MCCB VII.

musical learning from the incomparable Puebla cathedral *maestro* during his stay there, Juan Gutiérrez de Padilla. Ever eager to foster developing genius, Padilla recognized López's talents by recommending him for a 600-peso annual salary in 1647.

His musical earnings at Mexico City cathedral rank among the highest in colonial annals – rising from a yearly salary of 500 pesos in 1654 to 1,000 in 1674. Like Gaspar Fernandes at Puebla, 1606–29, and like his Mexico City predecessors Luis Coronado and Ximeno, he drew two salaries. Every other week he alternated on the organ bench with the deceased Ximeno's nephew, Francisco de Vidales, until the precocious Vidales departed for Puebla (d. Puebla, 2 June 1702). At double feasts when both were present, López Capillas directed and Vidales played. The *primera solemne dedicación* of the cathedral on 2 February 1656 inaugurated the most brilliant musical year of the century in the capital. The viceroy, the Duke of Albuquerque, had suggested on 28 January that López was genius enough to write a four-choir Mass in time for 25 July, when four bishops were to be consecrated – Mateo Sagada Bugeiro for the capital, Alonso de Cuevas Dávalos for Oaxaca, and two others. According to the viceroy's proposal, each of the four choirs would sing a Mass 'complete in itself' and different from all the rest. Choirs from the city under their own chapelmasters would make up the numbers needed for such a musical panoply. They would be 'so carefully divided into four equal choirs and well trained that the four different Masses sung simultaneously would blend into a perfectly harmonious whole'.[25] Easily the prince of Mexico City *maestros* since Franco, López acceded.

In 1661 López tried persuading the chapter that 'the offices of *maestro de capilla* and organist cannot properly be filled by the same person'. However, despite the archbishop's protection and his own acknowledged merits, the chapter adjured him to go on living with the 'bad custom' as best he could, because for 'justos motivos y causas superiores' no alleviation was in sight. Unable to persuade the chapter gently, López next tried the tactic of withholding a type of service always expected of *maestros de capilla* – namely, the annual composition of special new Christmas music. On 16 December 1664 the chapter summoned him to explain why no villancicos were being prepared and why so few singers were appearing for Saturday Salves. He replied that

---

[25] Actas Capitulares, XIII, fo. 16v: cited in Stevenson, 'Mexico City cathedral music: 1600–1750', *The Americas*, 21/2 (October 1964), 122.

composing special Christmas music was not a contracted part of his job, whereupon the chapter countered with the retort: 'For 80 years Mexico City chapelmasters have been annually composing the villancicos, and if López does not wish to continue doing so, a proper remedy will be found.'[26]

With the arrival in 1668 of the prelate Fray Payo Enríquez de Rivera, López's musical advice at last began being taken seriously enough for the chapter to engage Joseph Ydiáquez as principal organist. A graduate of the University of Mexico, Ydiáquez rivalled his sixteenth-century predecessor Manuel Rodríguez. No other Mexico City organists won such high praise for both their teaching and their virtuoso performances. Ydiáquez did so well that on 10 January 1673, within months of his being hired, the chapter voluntarily doubled his salary. A month later López began an intensive campaign to recruit fine singers from other parts of New Spain. At the same time, López was himself rewarded (cedula dated 23 March 1672 at Madrid, effective at Mexico City 7 May 1673) by promotion from half to full prebend. So large did his income now grow that two generations later his *renta* was a legend. In 1742 Juan Téllez Girón, who began as a cathedral choirboy in 1693 and became organist in 1697, cited him as the best-paid musician in Mexican memory.

Bachiller Joseph de Agurto y Loaysa, one of nineteen cathedral choristers hired in 1647 and López Capillas' successor as chapelmaster sometime before 1685, enjoys the distinction of having collaborated more frequently with the 'Tenth Muse', Sor Juana Inés de la Cruz (1651–95), than any other composer who set her poetry to music. Villancicos were so much his forte that he composed the music for five of her twelve canonical sets – those for Assumption in 1676, 1679, 1685, for Conception in 1676 and for St Peter in 1683. As if these were not enough, he composed the music also for the anonymous 1677 and 1686 Assumption-sets attributed to Sor Juana by Alfonso Méndez Plancarte.[27] Against this impressive record, Antonio de Salazar (b. Puebla, *c.* 1649; d. Mexico City, 25 March 1715) – appointed Mexico City cathedral chapelmaster on 3 September 1688 – composed only one canonical set and six 'attributed' sets; Miguel Mateo de Dallo y Lana of Puebla cathedral composed three canonical and one 'attributed'; and Mateo

---

[26] Actas Capitulares, XVI (1664–7), fo. 122v.
[27] Sor Juana Inés de la Cruz, *Obras completas*, II: *Villancicos y letras sacras*, ed. Alfonso Méndez Plancarte (Mexico City and Buenos Aires, 1952), 469, 499.

Vallados (appointed Oaxaca cathedral chapelmaster 23 March 1668; died there before 7 September 1708) one canonical.

The publication of baroque Mexican villancicos that began in 1934 when Gabriel Saldívar y Silva included two by Antonio de Salazar (1690, 1691) in his pathbreaking *Historia de la música en México* now colours the seventeenth century with a previously unsuspected iridescence. Padilla's *jácara, negrilla, calenda, juego de cañas*, and *gallego*[28] exemplify the extraordinary variety of his work. Not only Padilla but even more so his predecessor at Puebla, Gaspar Fernandes, imported from Guatemala in 1606, excelled in African-influenced *guineos, negros* and *negrillas*. Particularly captivating is Fernandes' *guineo a 5* beginning 'Eso rigor e repente' and rushing to the frenetic refrain, 'Sarabanda tenge que tenge'.[29] Eight of Sor Juana's villancico cycles include texts labelled *negro* or *negrilla* – those for 15 August and 6 December 1676; 31 January 1677; 15 August 1679, 1685 and 1686; Christmas 1680; and 19 March 1690. In her *negro* for 31 January 1677 a black sings to the accompaniment of his calabash a *puerto rico* beginning 'Tumba, la-lá-la; tumba, la-lé-le / wherever Peter enters, no one remains a slave.' In her other *negros*, tags such as 'gulungú, gulungú' and 'he, he, he, cambulé' add rhythmic zest.

Apart from rattles to accompany a 1677 *puerto rico* sung in St Peter's honour, the wide variety of instruments[30] used to accompany her 1691 villancico cycle honouring the 'keeper of the keys' comes to view in the following text set to music by Antonio de Salazar:

[Estribillo.] How well the cathedral honours her shepherd, [St Peter]! Hear the peal of the bells, tan tan talan, tan tan! Listen to the clarion, tin tin tilin, tin tin! Better still the sound of the trumpet, the sackbut, the cornett, the organ, and the bassoon. Jesus, what din they all make, so loud the violin can't even tune! Tan tan talan tan tan, tin tin tilin tin tin! [Coplas.] To lend added sparkle to Peter's sacred day, one instrument joins another in sweetest harmony: the

[28] Published from Puebla cathedral manuscripts in *Christmas music*, 113–45. *Las estreyas se rien* – Padilla's 'cane game' published in *Christmas music*, 129–40, and in *Seventeenth-century villancicos from a Puebla convent archive*, ed. R. Stevenson (Lima, 1974), 19–33 – was recorded on *Blanco y negro: Hispanic songs of the Renaissance from the Old and New Worlds* (Klavier KS 540, 1975), under John Alexander's direction.

[29] Recorded on *Festival of early Latin American music* and *Blanco y negro*. This *guineo* was included among exhaustive documentation of the black element in Spanish American colonial music in 'The Afro-American musical legacy to 1800', *Musical Quarterly*, 54/4 (October 1968), 475–502.

[30] Many instruments mentioned in Sor Juana's verse are shown in paintings by her Mexican contemporaries Cristóbal de Villalpando and Juan Correa. For colour reproductions of twelve paintings see *Ángeles músicos: homenaje a Sor Juana Inés de la Cruz*, ed. Salvador Moreno (Mexico, 1980). Villalpando's canvases show harps, lutes, portative organs, gambas, viol, krummhorn, transverse flute, guitar; Correa's show also a bajoncillo.

shawm accompanied by the violin. Tin tilin tin tin! Now the trumpet loudly blares, now the cornett trills, now the sackbut joins the fray of contending lines. Tan talan tan tan! Now the tromba marina squeaks above the double bass, their pitch stabilized by the bassoon. Now echo refines the zither's trill, alternating with the violin. Tin tilin tin tin! The tenor [shawm] gurgles, the vihuela runs in counterpoint, the small rebec lends its charm, the bandore takes a part, the harp quavers: and thus they all resound. Tan talan tan tan!

Not only does Sor Juana name Salazar's instruments in this 1691 villancico suite, but also she tells what specific consort accompanied each stanza of the coplas: trumpet, sackbut, and cornett, bassoon, and organ the first; shawm and violin the second; trumpet, cornett, and sackbut the third; tromba marina, double bass and bassoon, zither and violin the fourth; tenor shawm, vihuela, small rebec, bandore, and harp the fifth.

The black influences abundantly evident in New Spain also left their distinctive mark in South America. As early as 12 June 1568 a married mulatto named Hernán García signed a contract at La Plata (modern Sucre, Bolivia) with Juan de la Peña de Madrid to open a school ('para tener escuela') in which each taught his specialty: Madrid how to sing and dance, García how to play and dance. García's instrument was the vihuela; and to help him buy a large one for 60 pesos, Madrid advanced half its price ('treynta pesos de la mytad dela que costó vna viguela grande'). They contracted not only to share alike in the school's profits, but also to divide equally whatever payments they received for dancing and playing at Corpus Christi, Assumption and other festivals. Meanwhile García agreed to teach nowhere but in the school which they were to run, not to exercise his profession anywhere else, and above all to teach nobody except those who paid ('mostrar el dicho o fiar a nadie sino delo pagaren').[31]

Not surprisingly, both the San Antonio Abad seminary library in Cuzco and Sucre cathedral contain (or contained) numerous seventeenth-century *negros*, *negritos* and *negrillas*. Three revealing *negros* at Cuzco are catalogued as MSS 110, 115 and 344. *Bamo bamo en bona fe*, an alto–tenor ternary-metre duo in F major, has a refrain repeating the typical 'African' rhythmic tag words, 'gurugú' and 'gurumbé'. *Caia guinea bailamo lo congo* ('Stop talking, black man, let's dance the congo'), *1a 4*,

---

[31] Archivo Nacional de Bolivia, Escrituras Públicas, Águila 1568, fo. 226v and Bravo 1569, fo. 29v.

in C major, fast ternary metre, exploits ruthlessly repetitive rhythms and tonic–dominant major key harmony (as is everywhere the rule in the colonial *negro* repertory). The text continues: 'i mandinga con tumbaquetú, con tumbaquetú…asi mangulú, mangulú, mango' [repeat]; then, 'con tumbaquetú' [repeated several times]; next, 'vailamo lo congo'. *Pasqualiyo Antoniyo Flasiquiyo Manueliyo* for Christmas, begins as a solo answered by five-part ensemble (three tiples, alto, tenor). In F major, this *negro* sung in Cuzco cathedral on Christmas Eve 1753 exhibits all the traits typical of *negros* since Philippe Rogier (1560/1–1596) and Géry de Ghersem (1572/5–1630) started composing them in Spain and Gaspar Fernandes began in New Spain. The traditional traits include these: black-dialect text with refrain of 'African' words endlessly repeated, F or C major tonic–dominant harmonies, fast syncopated ternary-metre music with constant 'displaced' accents to suggest interacting African time lines.

The Sucre cathedral *negro* repertory includes a C major reel in $\frac{6}{8}$ accompanied by the paired violins and continuo that had become the Spanish American norm in even the remotest centres before the middle of the eighteenth century. Four tiples unite in summoning their fellow blacks to Bethlehem ('bamo a Beren') to see the Child ('beremo niño naciro') in this *negro* that begins: 'Antonuero bamo bamo a Beren'. Another more ambitious *negro a 8* sung at Sucre *c.* 1700 began 'Entle que entle / Venga que venga / Dansa que dansa / Buelta que buelta' ('Enter who will enter, come, dance, turn'). 'Cuçambú' is the refrain word tirelessly repeated in this C major, fast ternary-metre jamboree.

The supreme baroque genius of Spanish South America was Juan de Araujo (b. *c.* 1646, Villafranca, Spain, d. La Plata, 1712).[32] Araujo studied as a royal scholar at San Marcos University, Lima, whither his father, who was a *ministro*, had emigrated *c.* 1650. His independence of spirit offended Pedro Fernández de Castro y Andrade (1632–72), Count of Lemos and nineteenth viceroy of Peru, who had arrived in November, 1667. Banished from Lima, Araujo returned after Lemos' death to become *c.* 1672–6 *maestro de capilla* of Lima cathedral. In 1680 La Plata cathedral hired him as *maestro*. When he took over, the wealth of the cathedral had grown so enormous that three pages of fine handwriting could not list all the *perlas*, *esmeraldas*, *oro*, and other jewels and metals

---

[32] For catalogues of his works see Carmen García Muñoz and Waldemar Axel Roldán, *Un archivo musical americano* (Buenos Aires, 1972), 53–96, and R. Stevenson, *Renaissance and baroque musical sources in the Americas* (Washington, 1970), 40 and 231–5.

in the treasurer's safekeeping (27 October 1685). Amid such opulence, Araujo was able to call not only for the copying of some 200 of his now surviving compositions (among a total of 617 *tonos antiquísimos* thus far catalogued in the Sucre cathedral archive) but also to gather the forces necessary for their performance (many run to eight, nine and ten vocal parts with corresponding accompaniments). By 1693 he had so impressed the Audiencia of Charcas that this body recommended him to Charles II for a prebend or canonry. His punctilious teaching of choirboys, six of whom were still being boarded, lodged and taught in his house until the eve of his death, assured him of a continuous stream of tiples able to sing his high-pitched villancicos and *tonos*. After his death, a succession of his pupils and of their pupils kept La Plata music on as lofty a plane as any in South America to 1800.

The other centre that continued to be musically well served as late as 1700, despite drastic population decline, was Potosí. Antonio Durán de la Mota, *maestro de capilla* of the Potosí *iglesia matriz*, whom the La Plata cathedral chapter unsuccessfully tried to lure in 1712 after Araujo's death, ranks next to Araujo as the finest inland composer bridging the two centuries. His exquisite Vesper psalm *a 4*, *Laudate pueri Dominum* (1723), survives in parts at the San Antonio Abad seminary in Cuzco and received its highly praised modern premiere at the Carmel Bach Festival on 22 July 1970.[33] Another facet of his talents is shown in the fiery tribute to John of God, *Fuego fuego que Juan de Dios se abrasa*, *a 7* (1734).[34] One of twelve vernacular works to be found in the archives of Sucre cathedral, this vivid villancico demonstrates still further the amazingly high musical culture still prevalent at the Villa Imperial in a century of drastically reduced mining operations.

Lima's musical hegemony in the continent fluctuated with the *maestros* imported from Europe. For her *maestro de capilla* on 12 November 1612, when five adult singers, five instrumentalists (presumably all able to double as singers) and four boys constituted the paid musical corps, Lima employed the Sevillian Estacio de la Serna (*c.* 1565–1625), who before emigrating to Lima had from 5 December 1595 to *c.* 1604 been organist of the royal chapel at Lisbon. Serna composed two tientos.[35] His noble tone VI tiento[36] fully equals in quality and

---

[33] Recorded on *Festival of early Latin American music* and published in *Latin American colonial music anthology*, 102–12.

[34] *Latin American colonial music anthology*, 95–101.

[35] *Monumentos de la música española*, XII (1952), 246–55.

[36] Recorded on *Música de la Catedral de Lima* (Buenos Aires: FONEMA, Qualitón SQ1 4068, 1976) and *Latin American musical treasures*.

facture the best contemporary European product and amply justifies the financial rewards Lima rained on him. Martín de León's *Relacion delas exequias que el ex^mo Sr D. Iuan de Mendoça... Virrei del Piru hizo en la muerte dela Reina* (Lima, Pedro de Merchán y Calderón, 1613) lauds him as 'so famous for his art and for his other excellent qualities as to be known throughout all Spain', and claims for his 'newly composed music' (*musica nueuamente compuesta*) performed in the cathedral on 23 November 1612 to commemorate Queen Margaret (d. 3 October 1611) an 'incomparable sweetness'.

Financial superiority enabled Lima in 1622 to lure from Cuzco (where he had been hired on 18 June 1617 for a yearly 500 pesos) the choleric Cristóbal de Belsayaga. His seven-minute *Magnificat sexti toni, a 8*,[37] belies his reputation of being a strict disciplinarian and no-nonsense conductor by unfolding page after page of melting sweetness. Ever the taskmaster, Belsayaga obtained from the Lima chapter a ruling on 13 July 1623 that singers must henceforth habit themselves as early as 6 a.m. in summer and 6.30 in winter. After a further decade marred by many contretemps, he resigned on 11 April 1633, thereafter managing the business affairs of a rich Lima convent. Two years before his resignation there was published at Lima in Juan Pérez Bocanegra's *Ritual formulario* (Gerónymo de Contreras, 1631), the first part-music printed in the New World. The text of this fragrant processional is in purest Cuzco Quechua, *Hanacpachap cussicuinin*.[38]

The arrival at Lima in November 1667 of the count of Lemos as viceroy inaugurated a new era. In his train came Lucas Ruiz de Ribayaz. 'My grounding in music was acquired while serving the Condesa de Lemos y Andrade', wrote Ruiz de Ribayaz in *Lvz y Norte Mvsical* (Madrid, Melchor Álvarez, 1677), the compendium of dances for guitar and harp that he published on his return to Spain after the nineteenth viceroy's premature death on 6 December 1672. More important for Peru than Ruiz de Ribayaz was another retainer who sailed with the viceroy from Cadiz on 3 March 1667 – Tomás de Torrejón y Velasco (b. Villarrobledo, 23 December 1644; d. Lima, 23 April 1728). Up to his appointment on 1 January 1676 as Lima cathedral chapelmaster, colonial *maestros* had always been priests.

During his 52 years as Lima cathedral *maestro*, Torrejón's compositions spread from Cuzco to Guatemala. His fourteen vernacular works

[37] *Latin American colonial music anthology*, 59–66, and recorded in *Festival of early Latin American music*.

[38] Recorded on *Salve Regina*.

at Guatemala begin with a villancico of 1679 honouring the first American saint, Rose of Lima (1586–1617; canonized in 1671). This delightful tribute for tiple duet, tenor and harp enjoyed such popularity in Guatemala that it was reworked in 1748 with a new text lauding Our Lady. It was still sung in 1755. Another of his villancicos honouring Rose of Lima inspired a new arrangement in 1744 by Manuel de Quiroz, Guatemala cathedral *maestro* 1738–65. An even longer life can be documented for his frothy four-voice Christmas 'toy' (*juguete*), *Atención que para hacer en todo cabal la fiesta*. In this F major triple-metre dance (*vailete*) with harp accompaniment Torrejón y Velasco sets a text that alludes to authors as famous as Vergil and Lope de Vega. Four sacristans representing four churches distant from each other engage in a contest of wits. To vaunt their pseudo-learning, their macaronic coplas drip with oozings of Latin. When reviving it at Guatemala in 1772, Rafael Castellanos (cathedral *maestro* 1765–91) thickened the instrumentation but otherwise left the buoyant music intact. Torrejón y Velasco's Sacrament villancico in the archives of Guatemala, *Cantarico que bas a la fuente*, sets lines from Pedro Calderón de la Barca's *auto sacramental* entitled *Primero y segundo Isaac*, premiered at Madrid in 1678 with music by Juan Hidalgo. Since this *auto* was performed at Lima in 1681 and again in 1686, Torrejón's setting doubtless dates from one year or the other.

Certainly the most influential dramatist in colonial history, Calderón de la Barca supplied the libretto for the earliest extant opera produced in the New World, Torrejón's *La púrpura de la rosa*. It was staged in the Peruvian viceroy's palace in Lima on 19 October 1701 to celebrate Philip V's eighteenth birthday and first year on the throne.[39] This opera – or *representación música* as Torrejón called the work on the title page of the holograph score now at the Biblioteca Nacional in Lima (MS C1469) – belongs still to the baroque tradition of Juan Hidalgo (b. Madrid, *c.* 1614; d. Madrid, 30 March 1685). In place of Italian-style recitative, both Hidalgo and Torrejón preferred narrative coplas. In place of arias, they both stopped the action with choral ritornelli that correspond with the estribillos of villancicos. Torrejón was justified in casting treble choirboys in the roles of Adonis and Mars because Hidalgo had composed his adult male roles for women singers.

[39] *La púrpura de la rosa* has been published twice: In *Foundations of New World opera: with a transcription of the earliest extant opera, 1701* (Lima, 1973) and Tomás de Torrejón y Velasco, *La púrpura de la rosa* (Lima, 1976). Fragments were published in *The Music of Peru*, 250–86. The introductory choral loa plus a nymphs' chorus *a 7* from the opera are recorded on *Salve Regina*.

In eighteenth-century Spain the Bourbon dynasty favoured Italian performers and Italian composers. Farinelli, Corselli, Coradini, Falconi and others made Madrid an Italian fiefdom during Philip V's later years. Ferdinand VI and María Bárbara revelled solely in Italian opera, Italian keyboard literature and Italian chamber music. The shift in royal patronage, painfully apparent at Madrid, blew winds of change to even the most remote outposts of the Spanish empire. At Guatemala, Manuel de Quiroz rearranged opera excerpts by Francesco Ciampi, Nicola Conforto, Corselli, Giacomo Facco, Baldassare Galuppi, Leonardo Leo, Nicola Logroscino, Giambattista Pergolesi, Niccolo Porpora and Leonardo Vinci. At Cuzco the Augustinian friar Esteban Ponce de León, who began as cathedral *maestro de capilla* no later than 1738, composed Italian-style recitatives and arias for the revival of Agustín Moreto's *Antíoco y Seleuco* on 30 November 1743 to honour the newly installed bishop, Pedro Morcillo Rubio de Auñón. Although the play itself antedates 1654, Ponce de León's music belongs completely to 1743 and reflects not Torrejón y Velasco's influence, but rather the stylistic vogues introduced at Lima by Torrejón's successor, Roque Ceruti (*c.* 1686–1760), who was a native of Milan.

Ceruti reached Lima in 1708. Brought there by the twenty-fourth Peruvian viceroy, Manual de Oms y Santa Pau, who was himself a passable poet and guitar player, Ceruti composed and directed the music for the viceroy's *comedia harmónica* staged on 17 September 1708: *El mejor escudo de Perseo Fiesta real, que en el Patio de Palacio y en teatro hermosamente eregido* [se hizo]. This lavish spectacle, produced to celebrate the birth of the crown prince Luis, cost 30,000 pesos. As if the sumptuous costumes and changes of scenery in this 'musical play' were not enough, Oms y Santa Pau continued during the next two years patronizing other lesser works called *serenata* or *pastorale* with Ceruti's music to educate the Lima elite in the latest Italian vogues. From about 1721 to 1728 Ceruti directed music at Trujillo cathedral – returning to take the post of *maestro de capilla* at Lima on 1 August 1728. Ceruti's large extant repertory at the Archivo Arzobispal in Lima, La Plata cathedral, the Seminario de San Antonio Abad in Cuzco, and at La Paz (Julia Fortún collection) reveals him to have been the first Lima *maestro* who made a habit of writing da capo arias; he also wrote more brilliantly for paired violins than any of the Spanish-descended Lima chapelmasters. On the other hand, he was accused by Toribio del Campo of forgetting melody in the interest of figuration and harmonic sequences. Campo's article in *Mercurio Peruano* (16 February 1792) deplores Ceruti's 'strayings' (*descaminos*) from the right road of melodic beauty.

With admirable patriotic fervour, Campo preferred José de Orejón y Aparicio (b. Huacho, 1706; d. Lima, May 1765). The most gifted native-born Peruvian composer of the colonial period, Orejón became Lima cathedral's chief organist on 3 October 1742 and titular chapelmaster on 9 April 1764. The bitter-sweet melancholy of his Sacrament solo cantata, *Ya que el sol misterioso*, and the sensuous charm of his tiple duet honouring Our Lady of Copacabana, *A del día a de la fiesta*,[40] distinguish him from other more prosaic native-born South Americans of his century – the industrious Juan de Herrera (*c.* 1667–1738) of Bogotá, for example. To be sure, Herrera (appointed Bogotá cathedral *maestro* 16 January 1703) belonged aesthetically with the baroque, as his 26 Latin and nine vernacular works in the Bogotá archives amply reveal. Grandeur and power distinguish Herrera's polychoral Masses; a breezy raciness informs his festive villancicos.

Neither Paraguay, nor Chile, nor Argentina produced homegrown composers of the calibre of Orejón y Aparicio or Herrera during the colonial period. The Italian composer Domenico Zipoli (b. Prato, Italy, 16 October 1688; d. Córdoba, 2 January 1726) did, however, work for some years in Argentina. While Jesuit church organist at Rome, Zipoli had published a widely hailed keyboard collection, *Sonate d'intavolatura per organo e cimbalo* (1716). Sent to South America as a Jesuit missionary, he composed after 1717 an F major Mass for three voices, paired violins and continuo, that continued being sung at Potosí as late as 1784 and was successfully revived, recorded and published after discovery of the parts at Sucre cathedral in 1959.[41]

Mexico, on the other hand, which had already produced Juan Matías, Francisco López Capillas and Juan García de Céspedes, continued to foster native-born talents at least until the middle of the eighteenth century. Manuel de Zumaya (*c.* 1680–1755), an international celebrity, composed the first opera mounted in North America to Silvio Stampiglia's libretto, *La Partenope*. Produced 1 May 1711 in the viceregal palace in Mexico City, this opera paid tribute to Philip V's name-day. On 7 May 1715 Mexico City cathedral chapter appointed Zumaya to be the recently deceased Antonio de Salazar's successor as chapelmaster. In 1738 Tomás Montaño, Mexico City cathedral dean,

[40] *Latin American colonial music anthology*, 247–67.
[41] FONEMA, Qualitón SQ1 4059. The programme notes by Francisco Curt Lange are valuable.

took Zumaya with him when he was installed bishop of Oaxaca. After Montaño's death (24 October 1742) Zumaya elected to remain in Oaxaca, where on 11 January 1745 the cathedral chapter named him successor to Tomás Salgado (holder of the post of Oaxaca chapelmaster since 6 December 1726). Zumaya, whom many Mexican musicologists rate the finest composer in Mexican history, left a glittering array of Latin liturgical music in all genres. His 1714 *Missa te Joseph celebrent, a 6* (copy at Oaxaca), his Magnificats in tones I, II and III (Museo Virreinal, Tepotzotlán, choirbook dated 1717, fos. 4v–22), his psalms (1717 choirbook), hymn strophes (MCCB v*b*), and lamentations (MCCB IV, fos. 22v–33), count among the most profound and beautiful monuments of native-born colonial genius in any of the arts. His twelve villancicos at Guatemala and 25 at Oaxaca expose other brilliant facets of his kaleidoscopic genius.

Unable to find any other native-born *maestro* to rank with Zumaya, Mexico City cathedral fell back on European-born chapelmasters for the remainder of the eighteenth century. Ignacio Jerusalem y Stella, imported in 1742 to lead the Coliseo theatre orchestra, was a native of Lecce, Italy. In 1749 the cathedral authorities accepted him as interim chapelmaster. Within three years efforts were being made to replace him. He attended when he pleased, performed theatre music in sacred precincts, disdained Spanish liturgical traditions, and charged for instruction that his contract obliged him to give gratis. A decade rife with complaints against his negligence brought no relief. Only during the last eight years before his death in 1769 did he amend his freewheeling ways. What protected him against all charges was a pronounced creative talent that took flight in completely Italianate cantatas of rarest charm. His works, in demand from Guatemala to Alta California (at Santa Barbara a Jerusalem Mass is the oldest composition in the Mission archives), survive in enormous profusion in the Mexico City cathedral archives. Only Antonio Juanas, his Spanish-born successor in the post of Mexico City chapelmaster, exceeds him in the quantity of work extant.

In late eighteenth-century Venezuela mulatto composers grouped themselves around the wealthy Oratorian Padre Pedro Ramón Palacios y Sojo (1739–99), who was a brother of Simón Bolívar's maternal grandfather. The senior member of the so-called Chacao group was Juan Manuel Olivares (b. Caracas, 12 April 1760; d. El Valle [Caracas suburb], 1 March 1797). The eldest of nine children of a goldsmith, he and his father owned black slaves. His three largest cathedral-type compositions are: *Lamentación Primera a solo del Viernes S^{to}* (first Lamentation for Good Friday) for soloists, paired violins, flutes, French horns, viola and string bass; a Salve Regina for soprano–alto–tenor vocal trio supported by strings, oboes and horns; a Stabat Mater for vocal quartet and the same instruments specified for his Good Friday lamentation. Not only these three exquisite works but also a set of five Holy Week motets composed for Conceptionist nuns and a *Magnificat con fuga al final* (odd-verse, A major) survive at the Escuela de Música 'Jose Ángel Lamas' in Caracas, in copies dated 1810 and later. His eight mulatto pupils, who made such a mark in Venezuelan musical history, were (1) Juan Antonio Caro [de Boesi] (1758–1814), composer of an orchestrally accompanied D major Mass 'copied by a humble brother of St Philip Neri's Oratorio'; (2) Lino Gallardo (*c.* 1773–22 December 1837), putative composer of the Venezuelan national anthem, dubbed 'the Haydn of Caracas' in a *Gazeta* article (16 August 1820); (3) Juan José Landaeta (10 March 1780–17 October 1814), who disputes with Gallardo the title of having composed *Gloria al bravo pueblo*; (4) Juan Luis Landaeta (*c.* 1772–26 March 1812), a physician, slave-owner and double-bass player; (5) Pedro Pereira, the organist of San Felipe Neri whom Padre Sojo remembered with 50 pesos in his will; (6) Marcos Pompa, also bequeathed 50 pesos by Padre Sojo; (7) José Francisco Velásquez, Olivares' brother-in-law, an extremely prolific composer whose earliest extant orchestral Mass is dated 1787; father of a homonymous son also a composer; (8) Mateo Villalobos, flautist, bequeathed 100 pesos by Padre Sojo.

Not only do the works of these Venezuelan mulattos eschew anything 'African' but also their works remained sufficiently popular to be copied and recopied throughout the nineteenth century. Venezuela alone among Spanish American nations continued revering and reviving the works of her late colonial composers. To the mulatto group were joined two European-descended composers of prime consequence: Cayetano Carreño (b. Caracas, 7 August 1774–4 March 1836) and José Ángel Lamas (b. Caracas, 2 August 1775–9 December 1814). Carreño served as cathedral *maestro de capilla* from 3 June 1796 until his death 40 years later. Lamas, for whom the national school of music is named, was cathedral *bajonista* from 1796 to his death. His *Popule meus*, composed in 1801 when he was 26, has been continually sung throughout the intervening years and for decades was considered the supreme master-piece in the entire Venezuelan colonial repertory. Publication since 1942 of his orchestral Mass in D (composed in 1810), his *Gran Miserere*, and his Salve Regina in E flat prove him no less a master in the composition of larger works. The continued viability of the Venezuelan colonial repertory redounds all the more to the national credit because all composers thus far named were born and educated in Venezuela. They also adhered to the independence cause. The continued currency of music by Juan Antonio Caro [de Boesi], who was shot at Cumaná 16 October 1814, exemplifies what patriotic sacrifice can do to ensure a composer's lasting fame.

The foremost mulatto composer born in the Caribbean during the eighteenth century was Joseph Boulogne, Chevalier de Saint-Georges (b. Guadeloupe, 1739; d. Paris, 1799), who studied music in Saint-Domingue with the black violinist Joseph Platon before emigrating to Paris in 1752.[42] In Paris he built up a reputation comparable with that of Gossec (1734–1829). Beginning in 1775 he published eleven *symphonies concertantes*, three symphonies, ten violin concertos, fourteen string quartets, twelve sonatas for piano and violin and numerous smaller pieces. His operas included the three-act *Ernestine* (Paris, Comédie-Italienne, 19 July 1777), *La chasse* (12 October 1778) and a two-act 'comédie melée de ballets', *L'Amant anonyme* (8 March 1780). Joseph [Platon] played an unspecified Saint-Georges violin concerto at Port-au-Prince on 25 April 1780.

The brilliance of concert and operatic life at Cap-Français, Saint-Marc, Léogane, Cayes, Jérémie, Petit-Goave, Jacmel, and especially Port-au-Prince during the 27 years that can be documented from the *Gazette de St.-Domingue, Avis Divers et Petites Affiches Américaines*, and other later newspapers covering 1764 to 1791, rivalled or exceeded contemporary musical offerings in the Spanish viceroyalties. Apart from 23 operas by Grétry, six by Philidor, and lesser numbers of works for the lyric stage by Gluck, Dalayrac, Monsigny, Rousseau and Pergolesi, at least three operas by locally based composers were produced: Dufresne's *Laurette* (28 October 1775), Bissery's *Le sourd dupé* (21 June 1777) and *Bouquet*

---

[42] Barry S. Brook, *La symphonie française dans la seconde moitié du XVIIIe siècle* (Paris, 1962), II, 641–9 lists Saint-Georges' orchestral works; III, 143–70 publishes his Symphonie Concertante in G, Op. 13. The Black Composers Series, vol. 1 (Columbia M 32781, 1974) includes recordings of his Symphony No. 1 in G (Op. 11, No. 1), String Quartet No. 1 in C (Op. 1, No. 1), Symphonie Concertante in G (Op. 13), and a Scena from the opera *Ernestine*.

disputé (18 June 1783). Dufresne composed also a *grande symphonie concertante a deux orchestres et a echo* (25 August 1778) and Bissery a *concerto sur forte-piano* (22 February 1777). Petit at Port-au-Prince wrote two concertos (8 July 1783, 15 June 1785), Fontaine composed 'ariettes' and 'chœurs' for *L'Amant Loup-Garou ou Monsieur Rodomont* (16 November 1779). Rivière, a black composer, wrote symphonies concertantes performed at Cayes (12 October 1785), and also 'ariettes à grand orchestre', sérénades champêtres and pot-pourris for 'grand orchestre' (4 March, 23 November 1786; 18 January 1787). Maulan tried his hand at local colour compositions (24 January 1788; 11 March 1790).

The first black violinists in the Cap-Français theatre orchestra were three pupils of Tasset aged fifteen, sixteen and seventeen in 1764 and 1765. Rivière played a solo in the Port-au-Prince production of Grétry's *Le Tableau parlant* on 28 December 1779, and on 31 December 1781 the mandoline in a concerto for mandoline and guitar. Julien, another black violinist, played violin solos in a Davaux symphonie concertante (25 April 1780). Two mulatto sisters, Minette and Lise, sang in numerous concerts and operas of the 1780s, Grétry accounting for at least five of their operas: *Sylvain*, *Zémire et Azor*, *Aucassin et Nicolette*, *L'Amant jaloux* and *La caravane du Caire*.

Cuba's leading eighteenth-century composer was Esteban Salas y Castro (b. Havana, 25 December 1725; d. Santiago de Cuba, 14 July 1803), *maestro de capilla* of Santiago de Cuba cathedral from 1764. As catalogued in 1961 by Pedro Hernández y Balaguer,[43] his villancicos in that cathedral archive ran to 52. Eighteen masses, five psalms, twelve antiphons, 29 alleluia verses and other small liturgical works attest his sensitivity in Latin-text music. Although he wrote no virtuoso string or vocal parts, his command of figuration and his control of meshing lines ranks him as a studious and frequently inspired composer who does not need the false sobriquet of 'being the first native-born western hemisphere composer'[44] to justify his renown.

When the cry of Dolores (16 September 1810) heralded Mexican independence both the cathedrals of Mexico City and Puebla were employing foreign-born *maestros*. Lima – where Bartolomé Mazza (b. Novi Liguri, Italy, *c.* 1725; d. Lima, 1799) had been the dominant figure

[43] *Catálogo de música de los archivos de la Catedral de Santiago de Cuba y del Museo Bacardí* (Havana, 1961), 48–59.
[44] Edgardo Martín, *Panorama histórico de la música en Cuba* (Havana, 1971), 24.

as opera impresario and leader in all other phases of theatrical life during the late eighteenth century – continued to favour Italians. The cathedral employed as chapelmaster from 1807 to 1823 the Genoa-born cellist Andrés Bolognesi. At Buenos Aires, seat of a viceroyalty since 1776, the chief theatre composer from 1787 to 1792 was Antonio Aranaz, a native of Santander. The cathedral organist from 1785 to 1813 was the Basque Juan Bautista Gaiburú (b. Guipúzcoa, 1759; d. Buenos Aires, 1831). Blas Parera (b. Murcia, 1776 of Catalan parentage; d. Mataró near Barcelona, 7 January 1840) had arrived in Buenos Aires in 1797 and in 1812 composed the Argentine national anthem, before returning to Spain in 1818. The *maestro de capilla* of Santiago de Chile cathedral on the eve of independence was yet another Catalan, José de Campderrós, born at Barcelona. Chile's receptivity to Catalans even extended to the Chilean national anthem, composed (on commission from the Chilean envoy in London) by Ramón Carnicer (1789–1855).

Political independence merely strengthened the central role which European-born composers had come to play in the musical life of late colonial Spanish America. From Argentina to Mexico, throughout the nineteenth century, every nation that could afford imports fattened itself on a preponderantly foreign musical diet. Thus, the long struggle for political independence in Spanish America ironically produced regimes that all too frequently abdicated their responsibility to foster local composers, support local performers, and train local musicians.

DISCOGRAPHY

The three best-produced general anthologies of colonial Spanish American music are *Salve Regina* (Angel S 36008), sung by the Roger Wagner Chorale, directed by Roger Wagner, and recorded in 1966; *Festival of Early Latin American Music* (Eldorado 1, 1975), and *Latin American musical treasures from the sixteenth, seventeenth, and eighteenth centuries* (Eldorado 2, 1977), both also directed by Roger Wagner.

Blanco y Negro: Hispanic songs of the Renaissance from the Old and New World (Klavier Records KS 540), recorded in 1975 by the Ancient Consort Singers, directed by John Alexander, and the Ancient Instrumental Ensemble, directed by Ron Purcell, contains *negros* composed in viceregal Mexico. *Música virreinal* (Universidad Nacional Autónoma de México, Voz Viva de México), by the Orquesta de Cámara de la UNAM and the Conjunto Coral Universitario, directed by Luis Herrera de la

Fuente, contains Jesús Estrada's transcriptions of Hernando Franco, Manuel de Zumaya, and Ignacio Jerusalem selections. *Tablatura mexicana para guitarra barroca* (Angel SAM 35029), with Miguel Alcázar, guitar, contains items from the eighteenth-century MS 1560 in the Biblioteca Nacional de México.

Música de la Catedral de Lima (FONEMA, Qualitón SQ1 4068) recorded in Buenos Aires in 1976, joins two anthologies of Peruvian music recorded in Lima to illustrate the colonial Peruvian repertory: *Música peruana de los siglos XVII y XVIII* (Discos Sono Radio SE 9376) and *Música sacra de la época colonial en el Perú* (Virrey DVS 738-stereo), performed by the Coro de Cámara de la Asociación 'Jueves', directed by Arndt von Gavel.

For the Caribbean, *Chevalier de Saint-Georges* (Columbia M 32781, Black Composers Series, no. 1), recorded in 1974 by the London Symphony Orchestra conducted by Paul Freeman, the Juilliard Quartet, and other assisting artists, illustrates the works of Joseph Boulogne.

A NOTE ON THE MUSIC OF
COLONIAL BRAZIL

Brazil's known musical patrimony begins in the second half of the eighteenth century. The earliest music with a Portuguese text (found by Régis Duprat) is a cantata dated 1759 consisting of recitative and da capo aria for soprano, paired violins and continuo. Sung at Bahia during the 6 July 1759 session of the newly founded Academia dos Renascidos, this cantata celebrates the recovery from an illness of the academy's patron José Mascarenhas Pacheco Pereira de Mello, who had recently arrived from Lisbon.

The veteran *mestre de capela* of Bahia Cathedral who presumably wrote this delightful cantata, showing complete command of the Italian style in vogue at Lisbon in 1759, was Caetano de Mello Jesus – a native of the Bahia region and a protégé of a rich elected official of the Academia dos Renascidos. In 1759–60 he completed his *Escola de Canto de Orgão*, the lengthiest and most profound music treatise written in the Americas before 1850.[1] Mello Jesus argued for the use of all the key-signatures used in J. S. Bach's *Das Wohltemperiertes Clavier* (1722 and 1744). Unfortunately, however, none of Mello Jesus's music using seven-sharp or any other signatures survives at Bahia, where all colonial music seems to have perished.[2]

---

[1] The manuscript tomes, sent to Portugal for publication at the expense of a friend of Mello Jesus but never printed, can be found in the Biblioteca Pública et Évora, with call-numbers CXXVI/1–1 and/1–2. The second volume contains addenda by Brazilian-born *mestres de capela* in Recife (Ignácio Ribeiro Noya), Olinda (Ignácio Ribeiro Pimenta) and Rio de Janeiro (António Nunes de Siqueira).

[2] The copious information concerning colonial music in Bahia, Pernambuco, Rio de Janeiro and São Paulo that can be gathered from the Lisbon and Évora archives was conveniently assembled in Robert Stevenson, 'Some Portuguese Sources for Early Brazilian Music History', *Yearbook of the Inter-American Institute for Musical Research*, iv (1968), 1–43. Among European–descended *mestres de capela* André da Silva Gomes (1752–1844), for example, director of music at São Paulo Cathedral 1774–1822, left 87 works now in metropolitan curia archives.

Luis Álvares Pinto (1719–89), born in Recife of mulatto parents, displayed such musical talent that friends raised money for him to study in Lisbon with the cathedral organist Henrique da Silva Negrão. In 1761 Pinto wrote a 43-page manuscript treatise *Arte de solfejar*, now in the Biblioteca Nacional in Lisbon, that compares most advantageously with the earliest surviving Peruvian treatises – José Onofre Antonio de la Cadena's printed *Cartilla Musica y primera parte que contiene un methodo facil de aprehenderla à cantar* (Lima, Niños Espósitos, 1763) and manuscript *Dialogo Cathe-musico* (n.d., Seville, Archivo General de Indias, Indiferente General 1316). A devotee of eighteenth-century French treatises, Pinto nonetheless cites the chief theorists who had written in Spanish: Francisco de Montanos, Cerone and Andrés Lorente. Among writers in Portuguese, he is familiar with Pedro Thalesio (*Arte de Canto Chão*, 1618 and 1628), António Ferandes, João Álvares Frouvo, and Frouvo's pupil Manoel Nunes da Sylva (*Arte minima*, 1685, 1704, 1725). Cristóbal de Morales ranks as the earliest composer whom he considers a still valid model. On returning to Recife Pinto served São Pedro dos Clérigos as *mestre de capela*.[3] His lost works include three hymns to Nossa Senhora da Penha and Mãe do Povo with texts by the Olinda-born poet, Manuel de Souza Magalhães (1744–1800), *Maitinas* for São Pedro and for Santo António, numerous *ladainhas*, a Passion, and various sonatas. Jaime C. Diniz recovered and published at Recife in 1968 Pinto's *Te Deum*, *a 4* with continuo.

In the mid-1940s Francisco Curt Lange began recovering the music of a pleiad of eighteenth-century Minas Gerais mulatto composers headed by José Joaquim Emérico Lôbo de Mesquita (b. Vila do Príncipe (=Serro), 12 October 1746; d. Rio de Janeiro, April 1805). The natural son of the Portuguese adventurer José Lôbo de Mesquita and his slave Joaquina Emerenciana, the composer began the study of music with the *mestre de capela* of Nossa Senhora da Conceição church in the town of his birth. From about 1776 to 1798 he pursued a career combining church organ playing, office holding in various confraternities, and military service (*alferes do Terço de Infantaria dos Pardos*) at Arraial do Tijuco (=Diamantina), Minas Gerais. His many pupils at Arraial do Tijuco included his successor as organist of Santo Antônio church, José Lopes. Lôbo de Mesquita's extant œuvre includes at least

---

[3] In Brazil the *mestres de capela* were patronage appointments made at court. They had the right to license and collect fees from local musicians who made their livings playing for weddings, funerals and festivals.

five Masses (in F *c.* 1780, in E flat *c.* 1782, the rest undated), six Novenas, four *Ladainhas*, two Magnificats, three motets, four Marian antiphons, a Stabat Mater, a Te Deum, and various lesser Latin works.[4]

Until Pernambuco and Minas Gerais began yielding their colonial music treasures, Rio de Janeiro was always regarded as the principal centre of mulatto composition. José Maurício Nunes Garcia (b. 22 September 1767; d. 30 April 1830), born and educated at Rio de Janeiro, composed his first dated composition, *Tota pulchra es Maria*, in 1783. Ordained deacon on 17 December 1791 and priest on 3 March 1792, Nunes Garcia found no bar to his career through his colour. From 1791 to 1798 he was *mestre de capela* of the Igreja da Irmandade de S. Pedro dos Clérigos. On 2 July 1798 he succeeded João Lopes Ferreira as cathedral chapelmaster. For Christmas 1799 he composed *Maitinas* consisting of eight responsories, each an elaborate symphonic movement (instrumentation: violins 1 and 2, flute, 2 clarinets, 2 bassoons, 2 horns, 2 trumpets, figured organ part). Published in 1978, these *Maitinas* already demonstrate that he was a composer capable of competing successfully with the Eyblers and Süssmayrs of his epoch. When the royal court arrived in January 1808, Nunes Garcia was 41 and at the height of his creative powers. On 15 June the newly arrived bishop D. José Caetano transferred the cathedral from the Igreja da Irmandade de Nª Sª do Rosário e S. Benedito dos Homens de Côr to the Carmelite friars' church. On 26 November (1808) the Prince Regent Dom João assigned Nunes Garcia 600,000 réis yearly for being director and organist of the Real Capela and for giving music lessons to Rio de Janeiro youth at his house on the Rua das Marrecas.

Like all previously mentioned Brazilian mulattos, Nunes Garcia spent a long and fruitful career composing nothing reminiscent of Africa. Instead, all 237 works painstakingly catalogued in Cleofe Person de Mattos, *Catálogo temático das obras do padre José Maurício Nunes Garcia* (Rio de Janeiro; 1970), belong firmly to the European musical tradition. His favourite composers were Haydn, Mozart and Rossini. These are the three masters excerpted as examples for his sons Apolinário José (1807) and José Maurício (b. 1808) to imitate when in 1821 he wrote a

---

[4] Other members of the Minas Gerais mulatto group recovered by Lange include Inácio Parreiras Neves (*c.* 1730–*c.* 1793), Francisco Gomes da Rocha (*c.* 1746–1808), Marcos Coelho Neto (1746–1806) and his son Marcos Coelho Neto Filho (1763–1823) – all four of whom pursued their careers at Vila Rica de Albuquerque (= Ouro Preto). Lange began publishing what remains of their work in *Archivo de música religiosa de la Capitania Geral das Minas Gerais, Brasil, siglo XVIII* (Mendoza, 1951).

Compendio de música expressly for their instruction. As proof of his devotion to Mozart, in December 1819 at the Igreja do Parto in Rio de Janeiro he conducted the first New World performance of Mozart's Requiem. According to Sigismund Neukomm (1778–1858), a pupil of Michael and Joseph Haydn who spent 1816 to 1821 in Rio de Janeiro, Nunes Garcia on that occasion conducted a performance with full orchestra which, he wrote for the *Allgemeine Musikalische Zeitung* of Leipzig (19 July 1820), 'left nothing to be desired'.[5]

Even allowing for the loss of manuscripts after his death, his extant Masses number nineteen, his Requiems and funeral offices twelve, his Graduals 26. In comparison with his 225 extant sacred works with Latin texts, his secular works number only ten. They include an overture composed in 1803 to an opera *Zemira*, incidental music for a heroic drama *Ulissea* played on 24 June 1809, and incidental music for a drama by Gastão Fausto da Câmara Coutinho presented on 13 May 1810, *O Triunfo da América*. His first printed work was the modinha with piano accompaniment *Beijo a mão que me condena* (Rio de Janeiro, Pierre Laforge, 1837).

DISCOGRAPHY

Mestres do barroco mineiro (século XVIII) (Festa LDR 5005), performed by the Associação de Canto Coral do Rio de Janeiro, directed by Cleofe Person de Mattos, and the Orquestra Sinfónica Brasileira, conducted by Edoardo de Guarnieri, comprises music by José Joaquim Emérico Lôbo de Mesquita and other late eighteenth-century Mineiros (discovered by Francisco Curt Lange). The next six albums of music by José Maurício Nunes Garcia (1767–1830) make him the most recorded colonial composer: *Requiem Mass* (Columbia M 33431, Black Composers Series, no. 5), Helsinki Philharmonic Orchestra, directed by Paul Freeman, with chorus and soloists; *Missa pastoril para a noite de Natal* (Angel 3 CBX 262), Coro da Associação de Canto Coral do Rio de Janeiro, directed by Francisco Mignone with guest artists; *Missa de Requiem – 1816* (Festa LDR 5012), with the same choir and the Orquestra do Teatro Municipal, conducted by Edoardo de Guarnieri;

[5] On Neukomm, see Luiz Heitor Corrêa de Azevedo, 'Sigismund Neukomm, an Austrian composer in the New World', *Musical Quarterly*, 45/4 (October 1959). Neukomm so appreciated the art of the popular mulatto singer Joaquim Manuel da Câmara that he copied twenty of his modinhas into a manuscript that he bequeathed to the Paris Conservatoire (MS 7694). Sixteen of these he provided with piano accompaniment. Neukomm's fantasy for flute and piano *L'Amoureux*, op. 41 (Conservatoire MS 7703) quotes a sultry Joaquim Manuel melody. And he included a bold anonymous *lundú* in his piano caprice, *Amor Brasileiro*, op. 40.

and three anthologies of sacred works: CGC 57.576.159, Coral Ford-Willys e Orquestra, directed by Geraldo Menucci; Academia S. Cecília de Discos, Ltda., Coral e Orquestra de Câmara de Niterói, directed by Roberto Ricardo Duarte; and Abril Cultural, Grandes Compositores da Música Universal, no. 46, various artists. A five-volume anthology entitled *Música na Côrte Brasileira* (Angel 3 CBX 410–14), with various Brazilian groups and soloists, provides a survey of Brazilian music history up to 1900. Luis Álvares Pinto's *Te Deum* was recorded in 1968 by the Coro Polifónico do Paraná (Rozenblit, CLP 80032). Caetano de Mello Jesus's 1759 cantata has been recorded in its entirety by Olga Maria Schroeter and the Orquestra de Câmara de São Paulo, Olivier Toni conducting in an album entitled *Música Sul-Americana do Séc. XVIII.* (Chanticleer CMG, 1030), The aria from the cantata was recorded in 1977 by Mary Rawcliffe accompanied by an ensemble conducted by Roger Wagner in the album *Latin American musical treasures of the sixteenth, seventeenth, and eighteenth centuries* (Eldorado 2). José Maurício Nunes Garcia's sequence for four soloists, mixed chorus, and orchestra, *Lauda Sion Salvatorem*, composed in 1809, was included in the *Festival of Early Latin American Music* album recorded in 1975 (Eldorado 1).

BIBLIOGRAPHICAL ESSAYS

LIST OF ABBREVIATIONS

The following abbreviations have been used for works which occur repeatedly in the bibliographical essays:

ABNRJ	*Anais da Biblioteca Nacional do Rio de Janeiro*
CHLA	*Cambridge History of Latin America*
HAHR	*Hispanic American Historical Review*
HM	*Historia Mexicana*
JGSWGL	*Jahrbuch für Geschichte von Staat, Wirtschaft und Gesellschaft Lateinamerikas*
JLAS	*Journal of Latin American Studies*
LARR	*Latin American Research Review*
RHA	*Revista de Historia de América*
RIHGB	*Revista do Instituto Histórico e Geográfico Brasileiro*

I. THE POPULATION OF COLONIAL SPANISH AMERICA

Nicolás Sánchez-Albornoz, *The population of Latin America. A history* (Berkeley and Los Angeles, 1974), traces the general evolution of Latin America's population: chapters 3 and 4 deal with the changes that occurred during the period of Spanish rule. The work contains an extensive bibliography, and has undergone revision in its second Spanish edition, *La población de América latina. Desde los tiempos precolombinos al año 2000* (Madrid, 1977). The classic work of Ángel Rosenblat, *La población indígena y el mestizaje en América*, I: *La población indígena, 1492–1950*, and II: *El mestizaje y las castas coloniales* (Buenos Aires, 1954), while obviously now out of date, nevertheless contains information that is still useful relating to the native American population.

The sources for population history – tributary counts, parish registers, etc. – are abundant in Spanish America. The types of statistics, their quality, and the techniques their analysis requires have been examined, in general terms, in Woodrow Borah, 'The historical demography of Latin America: sources, techniques, controversies, yields', in P. Deprez (ed.), *Population and economics* (Winnipeg, 1970), 173–205; and in its Spanish edition (Bogotá, 1972). A preliminary checklisting of sources has been carried out in several countries, under the auspices of the Centro Latinoamericano de Demografía (CELADE), in collaboration with the Consejo Latinoamericano de Ciencias Sociales (CLACSO), and is entitled *Fuentes para la demografía histórica de América latina* (Mexico, 1975). Within the field of the joint Oxford–Syracuse project, Keith Peachy, 'The Revillagigedo census of México, 1790–1794: a background study', *Bulletin of the Society for Latin American Studies*, 25 (1976), 63–80, David J. Robinson and David G. Browning, in 'The origin and comparability of Peruvian population data, 1776–1815', *JGSWGL*, 14 (1977), 199–222, and others with work as yet unpublished, have begun to assess the demographic sources for the later colonial period. N. Sánchez-Albornoz, 'Les régistres paroissiaux en Amérique latine. Quelques considérations sur leur exploitation pour la démographie historique', *Revue Suisse d'Histoire*, 17 (1967), 60–71, discusses the historical value of parish registers, a question which has undergone reconsideration in Claude Morin, *Santa Inés Zacatelco (1646–1812). Contribución a la demografía del México colonial* (Mexico, 1973), and in Rosemary D. F. Bromley, 'Parish registers as a source in Latin American demographic and historical research', *Bulletin of the Society for Latin American Studies*, 19 (1974), 14–21.

The demographic research so far carried out for colonial Spanish America as a whole is assessed in Borah, 'Historical demography', focusing on the first century after the conquest. Woodrow Borah and Sherburne F. Cook, 'La demografía histórica de América latina: necesidades y perspectivas', in *La historia económica en América latina* (Mexico, 1972), II, 82–99, go on to suggest directions for further investigations. Mention should also be made of B. H. Slicher van Bath, 'De historische demografie van Latijns Amerika. Problemen en resultaten van onderzoek', *Tijdschrift voor Geschiedenis*, 92 (1979), 527–56. Ciro F. S. Cardoso, 'La historia demográfica; su penetración en

Latinoamérica y en América central', *Estudios Sociales Centroamericanos*, 9 (1973), 115–28, reviews modern developments in population history with special reference to Central America. H. Tovar Pinzón, 'Estado actual de los estudios de demografía histórica en Colombia', *Anuario Colombiano de Historia Social y de la Cultura*, 5 (1970), 65–140, carried out a comparable task for Colombia. As for bibliographies covering particular areas, there is for Mexico, Enrique Florescano, 'Bibliografía de la historia demográfica de Mexico (época prehispana–1910)', *HM*, 21 (1971–2), 525–37, and for the Andean region, Michael T. Hamerly, 'La demografía histórica de Ecuador, Perú y Bolivia: una bibliografía preliminar', *Revista del Archivo Histórico del Guayas*, 3 (1974), 24–63. On Spanish migration to America see Magnus Mörner, 'A bibliography on Spanish migration', in F. Chiapelli (ed.), *First images of America. The Impact of the New World on the Old* (2 vols., Berkeley and Los Angeles, 1976), II, 797–804. *Latin American Population History Newsletter* appears twice a year with information on work published, research in progress and professional meetings.

On the debate over the size of the native American population on the eve of the European invasion see note in *CHLA* I, 145–6. The debate on the ill effects that the conquest had on the native population focused initially on Mexico, because of the important contributions made by the Berkeley school (in particular, see S. F. Cook and W. Borah, 'The rate of population change in Central Mexico, 1550–1579', *HAHR*, 37 (1957), 463–70; *The Indian population of Central Mexico, 1531–1610* (Berkeley and Los Angeles, 1960); and W. Borah and S. F. Cook, *The aboriginal population of Central Mexico on the eve of the Spanish conquest* (Berkeley and Los Angeles, 1963), and 'Conquest and population: a demographic approach to Mexican history', *Proceedings of the American Philosophical Society*, 113 (1969), 177–83). It gave rise at once to a lively controversy (A. Rosenblat, *La población de América en 1492* (Mexico, 1967)), which has recently been revived (William T. Sanders, 'The population of the Central Mexican symbiotic region, the basin of Mexico, and the Teotihuacán valley in the sixteenth century', in William M. Denevan (ed.), *The native population of the Americas in 1492* (Madison, 1976), 85–150; B. H. Slicher van Bath, 'The calculation of the population of New Spain, especially for the period before 1570', *Boletín de estudios latinoamericanos y del Caribe*, 24 (1978), 67–95; Rudolph A. Zambardino, 'Mexico's population in the sixteenth century: demographic anomaly or mathematical illusion?', *Journal of*

Interdisciplinary History, 11 (1980), 1–27), and has been extended to other regions of Spanish America, once again partly through the initiative of S. F. Cook and W. Borah, in *Essays in population history: Mexico and the Caribbean* (2 vols., Berkeley and Los Angeles, 1971 and 1974). Denevan, *Native population*, recapitulates the debate and opens up fresh perspectives. On the population of the central Andes there has been some important recent work. See Daniel E. Shea, 'A defense of small population estimates for the Central Andes in 1520', in Denevan, *Native population*, 152–80, N. Sánchez-Albornoz, *Indios y tributos en el Alto Perú* (Lima, 1978), and, above all, N. David Cook, *Demographic collapse. Indian Peru, 1520–1620* (Cambridge, 1981). The role that epidemics played in bringing about demographic catastrophe has been highlighted in W. Borah, '¿América como modelo? El impacto demográfico de la expansión europea sobre el mundo no europeo', *Cuadernos Americanos*, 6 (1962), 176–85, Henry F. Dobyns, 'An outline of Andean epidemic history to 1720', *Bulletin of the History of Medicine*, 37 (1963), 493–515, and Alfred W. Crosby Jr., *The Columbian exchange: biological and cultural consequences of 1492* (Westport, 1972). As yet there are no specific evaluations of the impact of the other contributory factors.

For immigration into America from other continents there are several works of synthesis. Spanish migration has been minutely inventoried by Peter Boyd-Bowman, *Indice geobiográfico de cuarenta mil pobladores españoles de América en el siglo XVI*, I: *1493–1519* (Bogotá, 1964), II: *1520–1539* (Mexico, 1968); *Patterns of Spanish emigration to the New World (1493–1580)* (Buffalo, 1973); 'Patterns of Spanish emigration to the Indies until 1600', *HAHR*, 56 (1976), 580–604, and (assessed by M. Mörner), 'Spanish migration to the New World prior to 1810: a report on the state of research', in Chiapelli, *First images of America*, II, 737–82. Eighteenth-century immigration to Mexico has recently been analysed by Charles F. Nunn, *Foreign immigrants in Early Bourbon Mexico, 1700–1760* (Cambridge, 1979). David A. Brading, 'Grupos étnicos, clases y estructura ocupacional en Guanajuato (1792)', *HM*, 21 (1971–2), 460–80, calculates the proportion of Spaniards who were there around 1792. African migration is examined in Philip Curtin, *The Atlantic slave trade: a census* (Madison, 1969).

The widespread internal movements brought about by the policy of resettling the Indians has not so far been thought worthy of a new study to match the old one by H. F. Cline, 'Civil congregations of the Indians in New Spain, 1598–1606', *HAHR*, 29 (1949), 349–69. A renewal of interest in the subject is, however, displayed in A. Málaga Medina, 'Las reducciones en el virreinato del Perú (1532–1580)', *RHA*, 80 (1975), 9–45, Peter Gerhard, 'Congregaciones de indios en la Nueva España antes de 1570', *HM*, 26 (1976–7), 347–95, and Nancy M. Farriss, 'Nucleation versus dispersal: the dynamics of population movement in Colonial Yucatán', *HAHR*, 58 (1978), 187–216. For urbanization, see *CHLA* II, Bibliographical Essay 3.

Even though the first century after the conquest continues to attract most of the research in population history, a recent shift has begun to favour the late colonial period. This new trend is due, in part, to the higher quality of the sources for that period. Parish registers of baptisms, burials and marriages from the seventeenth and eighteenth centuries have begun to be investigated. Claude Morin, Thomas Calvo and Elsa Malvido published simultaneously three wide-ranging studies on the Puebla area: *Santa Inés Zacatelco*, mentioned above, *Acatzingo. Demografía de una parroquia mexicana* (Mexico, 1973), and 'Factores de despoblación y reposición de la población de Cholula (1641–1810)', *HM*, 23 (1973–4), 52–110. León in a later period is discussed in David A. Brading, *Haciendas and ranchos in the Mexican Bajío. León, 1700–1780* (Cambridge, 1978). Work based on the registers of urban parishes has so far achieved only a partial coverage: Lima has received attention from Claude Mazet, 'Population et société à Lime aux xvie et xviie siècles', *Cahiers des Amériques Latines*, 13–14 (1976), 53–100, and Valparaíso from R. Salinas Meza, 'Carácteres generales de la evolución demográfica de un centro urbano chileno: Valparaíso, 1685–1830', *Historia*, 10 (1971), 177–204. Lima's register begins as early as 1562. N. D. Cook is busy analysing a number of country parishes in the Collaguas region, where it was the custom to enter the various racial groups in different books. Even small subdivisions within the dual organization of this Andean community had separate registers. See N. D. Cook, *The people of the Colca valley. A population study* (Boulder, 1982). H. Aranguiz Donoso, 'Notas para el estudio de una parroquia rural del siglo xviii: Pelarco, 1786–1796', *Anales de la Facultad de Filosofía y Ciencias de la Educación*, 1969, 37–42, E. F. Love, 'Marriage patterns of persons of African descent in a colonial Mexico City parish', *HAHR*, 51 (1971), 79–91, and Marcello Carmagnani, 'Demografía y sociedad. La estructura social de los centros mineros del norte de México, 1600–1720', *HM*, 21 (1971–2), 419–59, compare differential behaviours by ethnic group.

From tax assessments and civil or ecclesiastical censuses the spatial

and social distribution of the population and its increase or decrease
have been studied. We cannot give details here of the many local
histories of varying importance, but only of those studies which cover
wide areas. Using late colonial censuses, G. Vollmer, *Bevölkerungspolitik
und Bevölkerungsstruktur im Vizekönigreich Peru zu Ende der Kolonialzeit
1741–1821* (Bad Homburg, 1967) analyses the ethnic composition of
Peru's population and its distribution; John V. Lombardi, *People and
places in colonial Venezuela* (Bloomington, 1976), does likewise for
Venezuela, using the ecclesiastical censuses of the diocese of Caracas.
S. F. Cook and W. Borah, *The population of the Mixteca Alta, 1520–1960*
(Berkeley and Los Angeles, 1968), M. Carmagnani, 'Colonial Latin
American demography: growth of Chilean population, 1700–1830',
Journal of Social History, 1 (1967), 179–91, M. T. Hamerly, *Historia social
y económica de la antigua provincia de Guayaquil, 1763–1842* (Guayaquil,
1973), and G. Vollmer, 'La evolución cuantitativa de la población
indígena en la región de Puebla (1570–1810)', *HM*, 23 (1973–4), 44–51,
trace the development of the population in the Mixteca Alta, Chile, the
coastland around Guayaquil, and the Puebla area respectively.

Census materials also make it possible to dissect the demographic
structure of groups (family, fertility, mortality and migratory movements). E. González and R. Mellafe, 'La función de la familia en la
historia social hispanoamericana colonial', *Anuario del Instituto de
Investigaciones Históricas*, 8 (Rosario, 1965), 57–71, started a general
debate on the family in Hispanic America, which has to be supplemented
by recent, more specific studies. Cook and Borah, *Essays in population
history*, vol. I, expound the transformation of the family in Mexico, from
the time of the conquest onwards. There are data on the evolution of
endogamy in Oaxaca in J. K. Chance, *Race and class in colonial Oaxaca*
(Stanford, 1978). Silvia Arrom, 'Marriage patterns in Mexico City,
1811', *Journal of Family History*, 3/4 (1979), 376–91, treats the urban
family in Mexico at the beginning of the nineteenth century. Late
colonial period variations in fecundity are discussed by S. F. Cook and
W. Borah, *Essays in population history*, vol. II. Nicholas P. Cushner,
'Slave mortality and reproduction on Jesuit haciendas in Colonial Peru',
HAHR, 55 (1975), 177–99, deals with one particular group, the slaves,
but has only a thin data base. Internal migrations in Peru have been
measured at their destinations by census data in N. D. Cook, 'Les
indiens immigrés à Lima au début du XVIIᵉ siècle', *Cahiers des Amériques*

Latines, 13–14 (1976), 33–50, and in more general terms, by Sánchez-Albornoz, *Indios y tributos*; J. Estrada Yzaca, 'Migraciones internas en el Ecuador', *Revista del Archivo Histórico del Guayas*, 11 (1977), 5–26, deals with this subject for Ecuador.

A sophisticated statistical elaboration of censuses and of vital records has been undertaken experimentally by the group of demographers in CELADE. Their works, narrow but suggestive for the methodology employed, concentrate on mortality: see Jorge L. Somoza *et al.*, *Estimates of mortality among members of religious orders in Chile in XVIII and XIX centuries* (Santiago de Chile, 1975), and C. Arretx *et al.*, *Adult mortality estimate based on information on age structure of death. The application to data for San Felipe around 1787* (Santiago de Chile, 1977).

Efforts to reduce mortality rates in the eighteenth century have been analysed by Donald B. Cooper, *Epidemic disease in Mexico City, 1761–1813. An administrative, social and medical study* (Austin, 1965), with reference to the epidemics Mexico underwent at that time. M. M. Smith, 'The "Real expedición marítima de la vacuna" in New Spain and Guatemala', *Transactions of the American Philosophical Society*, 64 (1974), 1–74, traces the spread of vaccination in New Spain and in Guatemala.

2. THE POPULATION OF COLONIAL BRAZIL

General studies on the structure and growth of the Brazilian population in the colonial period are rare. Attempts to calculate the size of the population and assess its growth at various dates have been carried out by Roberto Simonsen, *História econômica do Brasil (1500–1820)* (6th edn, São Paulo, 1969), and also by Celso Furtado, *Formação econômica do Brasil* (11th edn, São Paulo, 1971). Using information from the third quarter of the eighteenth century, when the first census surveys were carried out in each captaincy, various authors have assembled and organized statistics still preserved in archives, in an attempt to arrive at a demographic aggregate for the country during the period. The following studies, in particular, are worthy of note: Dauril Alden, 'The population of Brazil in the late 18th century: a preliminary survey', *HAHR*, 43/1 (May 1963), 173–205; Maria Luiza Marcílio, 'Accroissement de la population: évolution historique de la population brésilienne jusqu'en 1872', in CICRED, *La population du Brésil* (Paris, 1974); also M. L. Marcílio, 'Evolução da população brasileira através dos censos até

1872', *Anais de História* (Assis), 6 (1974), 115–37. Some scholars have based their figures on different sources. For example, using the more reliable nineteenth-century census figures, they have made retrospective estimates in order to arrive at a probable total for the population of Brazil in the eighteenth century. Such is the case of Giórgio Mortara, 'Estudos sobre a utilização do movimento da população do Brasil', *Revista Brasileira de Estatística* (Jan.–Mar. 1941), 38–46, who calculated the total population of Brazil by year, from 1772. As far as the post-1800 period is concerned, the most recent figures are those provided by Thomas W. Merrick and Douglas H. Graham, *Population and economic development in Brazil: 1800 to the present* (Baltimore, 1979).

Many items from colonial census surveys have also been published. A summary of the main items available in the archives of Rio de Janeiro is provided by Joaquim Norberto de Souza e Silva, 'Investigações sobre os recenseamentos da população geral do Império e de cada Província de per si, tentadas desde os tempos coloniaes até hoje', in *Relatório do Ministério dos Negócios do Império, 1870* (Rio de Janeiro, 1872), annex. This summary was utilized by F. J. de Oliveira Viana, 'Resumo histórico dos inquéritos censitários realizados no Brasil', in Brazil, *Recenseamento do Brasil, 1920* (Rio de Janeiro, 1922), vol. 1, Introduction. Colonial census surveys from several captaincies have been published in their entirety in many numbers of *RIHGB* and in the *Revistas* of the various state Historical Institutes, as well as in *ABNRJ*.

Catalogues of demographic sources are now beginning to be published. See, for example, M. L. Marcílio and L. Lisanti, 'Problèmes de l'histoire quantitative du Brésil: métrologie et démographie', in Centre National de la Recherche Scientifique, *L'histoire quantitative du Brésil de 1800 à 1930* (Paris, 1973); Marcílio, 'Catálogo de los datos bibliográficos documentales de naturaleza demográfico existentes en los archivos brasileños', in CLACSO–CELADE, *Fuentes para la demografía histórica de América Latina* (Mexico, 1975), 87–131; and finally, Marcílio, 'Levantamentos censitários da fase proto-estatística do Brasil', *Anais de História* (Assis), 9 (1977), 63–75.

The best study on the anthropological and racial formation of the Brazilian people is still Gilberto Freyre's classic work, *Casa grande e senzala* (10th edn, Rio de Janeiro, 1961), vol. 2. Equally important is Darcy Ribeiro, *As Américas e a civilização* (Petrópolis, 1977).

The indigenous population has been the subject of research by demographers and historians. Ethnographic and anthropological studies give account of the size and decline of the indigenous population during the colonial period. The classic study by Ángel Rosenblat, *La población indígena de América desde 1492 hasta la actualidad* (Buenos Aires, 1945), presents very low figures for the Brazilian Indian. At present, we have at our disposal far more reliable figures in William Denevan (ed.), *The native population of the Americas in 1492* (Madison, 1976), and particularly in John Hemming, *Red gold: the conquest of the Brazilian Indians, 1500–1760* (London, 1978).

The African slave trade to Brazil has always received attention from scholars. For Bahia, the pioneer study is that of Pierre Verger, *Flux et reflux de la traite des nègres entre le Golfe de Bénin et Bahia de Todos os Santos du XVIIe au XVIIIe siècles* (Paris, 1968). See also, by the same author, 'Mouvements de navires entre Bahia et le Golfe de Bénin (XVII–XIXe siècles)', *Revue Française d'Histoire d'Outre-mer*, 55 (1968), 5–36. The trade to the north-east has been studied by Antônio Carreira, *As companhias pombalinas de navegação, comércio e tráfico de escravos entre a costa africana e o Nordeste brasileiro* (Bissau, 1969). For Amazonia, see the work of Colin M. MacLachlan, 'African slave trade and economic development in Amazonia, 1700–1800', in Robert B. Toplin (ed.), *Slavery and race relations in Latin America* (London, 1974).

For the history of the slave trade to Brazil as a whole, the most complete study is that by Philip D. Curtin, *The Atlantic slave trade: a census* (Madison, 1969). See also, by H. S. Klein, 'The Portuguese slave trade from Angola in the 18th century', *Journal of Economic History*, 32/4 (Dec. 1972), 894–917, and *The Middle Passage: comparative studies in the Atlantic slave trade* (Princeton, 1978).

With regard to general studies on Brazilian slavery in the colonial period, one must begin by mentioning A. M. Perdigão Malheiro's classic work, *A escravidão no Brasil: ensaio histórico, jurídico e social* (3 vols., Rio de Janeiro, 1866/7 (new edn, 1944)). Of more recent studies, the most noteworthy are Maurício Goulart, *A escravidão africana no Brasil* (3rd edn, São Paulo, 1975); Kátia M. Queiros Mattoso, *Être esclave au Brésil, XVIe–XIXe siècles* (Paris, 1979); and Stuart B. Schwartz's important article, 'The manumission of slaves in colonial Brazil: Bahia, 1684–1745', *HAHR*, 54/4 (1974), 603–35.

One or two regional studies on the demography of the colonial period have begun to be published. The pioneer study is M. L. Marcílio, *La ville de São Paulo: peuplement et population, 1750–1850 (d'après les régistres paroissiaux et les recensements anciens)* (Rouen, 1968). See also Iraci del

Nero Costa, *Vila Rica: população (1719–1826)* (São Paulo, 1979), and M. L. Marcílio, 'Croissance de la population pauliste de 1798 à 1828', *Annales de Démographie Historique, 1977* (Paris, 1978), 249–69.

The structure, composition and organization of the family and households in late colonial Brazil has recently begun to attract attention: see Donald Ramos, 'City and country: the family in Minas Gerais, 1804–1838', *Journal of Family History* (Minneapolis), 3/4 (1978), 161–75, and M. L. Marcílio, 'Tendances et structures des ménages dans la Capitainerie de São Paulo (1765–1828) selon les listes nominatives d'habitants', in CNRS, *L'histoire quantitative*, 157–65. Also M. L. Marcílio, 'Mariage et remariage dans le Brésil traditionnel: lois, intensité, calendries', in J. Dupâquier *et al.* (eds.), *Marriage and re-marriage in past populations* (London, 1980).

3. THE URBAN DEVELOPMENT OF COLONIAL SPANISH AMERICA

Collections and guides

Proceedings of the eight Symposia on Latin American Urbanization from Its Origins to Our Time, held from 1966 to 1982 at meetings of the International Congress of Americanists, yield a broad view of contemporary research on Latin American urban history. They include more than 150 papers from many disciplines, ranging from pre-Columbian times to the present and from case studies to broad conceptual statements and bibliographic reviews. At least 50 deal with colonial Spanish America. The published proceedings are: J. E. Hardoy and R. P. Schaedel (eds.), *El proceso de urbanización en América desde sus orígenes hasta nuestros días* (Buenos Aires, 1969); J. E. Hardoy, E. W. Palm and R. P. Schaedel (eds.), 'The process of urbanization in America since its origins to the present time' in *Verhandlungen des XXXVIII. Internationalen Amerikanistenkongresses*, 4 (Stuttgart and Munich, 1972), 9–318; R. P. Schaedel *et al.*, *Urbanización y proceso social en América* (Lima, 1972); J. E. Hardoy and R. P. Schaedel (eds.), *Las ciudades de América Latina y sus áreas de influencia a través de la historia* (Buenos Aires, 1975); J. E. Hardoy and R. P. Schaedel (eds.), *Asentamientos urbanos y organización socioproductiva en la historia de América Latina* (Buenos Aires, 1977); J. E. Hardoy, R. M. Morse and R. P. Schaedel (eds.), *Ensayos histórico-sociales sobre la urbanización en América Latina* (Buenos Aires, 1978);

W. Borah, J. Hardoy and G. A. Stelter (eds.), *Urbanization in the Americas: the background in comparative perspective*, special issue, *Urban History Review* (Ottawa, 1980). Papers in the first three anthologies appear in the original languages; those in the next three are in Spanish; those in the last are in English. Publication of the eighth Symposium is planned. English versions of 21 papers selected from the first four Symposia were published in R. P. Schaedel, J. E. Hardoy and N. S. Kinzer (eds.), *Urbanization in the Americas from its beginnings to the present* (The Hague, 1978). Six papers from the Sixth Symposium appeared in English in *Comparative Urban Research*, 8/1 (1980).

Other collections: R. Altamira y Crevea *et al.*, *Contribuciones a la historia municipal de América* (Mexico, 1951); F. de Solano (ed.), *Estudios sobre la ciudad iberoamericana* (Madrid, 1975); and D. J. Robinson (ed.), *Social fabric and spatial structure in colonial Latin America* (Ann Arbor, 1979).

The basic bibliography for urbanization is F. de Solano *et al.*, *El proceso urbano iberoamericano desde sus orígenes hasta los principios del siglo XIX, estudio bibliográfico* (Madrid, 1973–4), listing over 1,800 items for the pre-Columbian and colonial periods (also in Solano, *Estudios*, 727–866). J. E. Hardoy *et al.*, *Urbanización en América Latina, una bibliografía sobre su historia* (Buenos Aires, 1975), the first of three projected volumes, covers pre-Columbian urbanization and the colonial period to 1540. For municipal sources see A. Millares Carlo, *Los archivos municipales de Latinoamérica: libros de actas y colecciones documentales, apuntes bibliográficos* (Maracaibo, 1961).

Backgrounds

The volumes by Solano *et al.* (*El proceso urbano*) and Hardoy *et al.* (*Urbanización*) cover pre-Columbian research. J. E. Hardoy, *Pre-Columbian cities* (New York, 1973) is a good conspectus with extensive references.

For the Spanish background: E. A. Gutkind, *International history of city development*, vol. III: *Urban development in Southern Europe: Spain and Portugal* (New York, 1967); A. García y Bellido *et al.*, *Resumen histórico del urbanismo en España* (2nd edn, Madrid, 1968); L. García de Valdeavellano, *Sobre los burgos y los burgueses de la España medieval* (Madrid, 1960); J.M.Font y Rius, 'Les villes dans l'Espagne du Moyen Age' in Société Jean Bodin, *La ville* I (Brussels, 1954), 263–95; J. Vicens Vives, *An*

Economic History of Spain (Princeton, 1969), section on 'Urban Economy'; J. A. Maravall, *Las comunidades de Castilla* (2nd edn, Madrid, 1970); A. Alvarez de Morales, *Las hermandades, expresión del movimiento comunero en España* (Valladolid, 1974); R. Ricard, 'La *Plaza Mayor* en Espagne et en Amérique Espagnole', *Annales, Économie–Sociétés– Civilisations*, 2/4 (1947), 433–8; R. Pike, *Aristocrats and traders, Sevillian society in the sixteenth century* (Ithaca, 1972). Some of the themes introduced in the first section of this chapter are expanded in R. M. Morse, 'A prolegomenon to Latin American urban history', *HAHR*, 52/3 (1972), 359–94.

Cartography

J. E. Hardoy surveys published and manuscript sources in 'La cartografía urbana en América Latina durante el período colonial. Un análisis de fuentes', in Hardoy, Morse and Schaedel, *Ensayos*, 19–58. Also: D. Angulo Iñiguez, *Planos de monumentos arquitectónicos de América y Filipinas existentes en el Archivo de Indias* (3 vols., Seville, 1933); F. Chueca Goitia and L. Torres Balbás, *Planos de ciudades iberoamericanas y filipinas existentes en el Archivo de Indias* (2 vols., Madrid, 1951).

General studies

If one construes urban history to include 'settlement patterns', if one accepts the central role of towns in Spanish colonization, and if one views urban centres as linked to regional and transatlantic economies, then the sources for urban history become almost coextensive with those for Spanish American history in general. The bibliographies cited above list some of this material.

Various general issues are mapped out in R. M. Morse, 'Some characteristics of Latin American urban history', *American Historical Review*, 67/2 (1962), 317–38; G. A. Kubler, 'Cities and culture in the colonial period in Latin America', *Diogenes*, 47 (1964), 53–62; C. Sempat Assadourian, *El sistema de la economía colonial* (Mexico, 1983); S. M. Socolow and L. L. Johnson, 'Urbanization in colonial Latin America', *Journal of Urban History*, 8/1 (1981): 27–59; and J. K. Chance, 'The colonial Latin American city: preindustrial or capitalist', *Urban Anthropology*, 4/3 (1975), 211–28. One can follow the urbanization process to 1630 in J. M. Houston, 'The foundation of colonial towns in Hispanic America', in R. P. Beckinsale and J. M. Houston (eds.), *Urbanization and its problems* (Oxford, 1968), 352–90; and J. E. Hardoy and

C. Aranovich, 'Urbanización en América Hispana entre 1580 y 1630', *Boletín del Centro de Investigaciones Históricas y Estéticas* (Universidad Central de Caracas) [*BCIHE*], 11 (1969), 9–89. G. Céspedes del Castillo traces the Lima– Buenos Aires rivalry in *Lima y Buenos Aires* (Seville, 1947). K. Davis takes a comparative hemispheric view in 'Colonial expansion and urban diffusion in the Americas', *International Journal of Comparative Sociology*, 1/1 (1960), 43–66, while R. R. Reed shows how Spain's New World experience influenced urbanization in the Philippines in *Colonial Manila, the context of Hispanic urbanism and process of morphogenesis* (Berkeley and Los Angeles, 1978).

C. Bayle gives an informed survey of municipal life and institutions in *Los cabildos seculares en la América Española* (Madrid, 1952). M. Góngora examines the legal context of municipal government in *El estado en el derecho indiano* (Santiago de Chile, 1951) and, more succinctly, in *Studies in the colonial history of Spanish America* (Cambridge, 1975), 98–119. J. M. Ots Capdequí, *España en América, el régimen de tierras en la época colonial* (Mexico, 1959) shows the importance of the municipality in controlling land distribution. For cabildos see also A. Muro Orejón, 'El ayuntamiento de Sevilla, modelo de los municipios americanos', *Anales de la Universidad Hispalense*, 21/1 (1960), 69–85, and F. X. Tapia, *El cabildo abierto colonial* (Madrid, 1966).

W. Borah reviews the voluminous literature bearing on the accommodation of Indians to urban life under Spain in 'Aspectos demográficos y físicos de la transición del mundo aborigen al mundo colonial', in Hardoy, Morse and Schaedel, *Ensayos*, 59–89. Also: C. Bayle, 'Cabildos de indios en América Española', *Missionalia Hispánica*, 8/22 (1951), 5–35; M. Mörner, *La corona española y los foráneos en los pueblos de indios de América* (Stockholm, 1970); F. de Solano, 'Urbanización y municipalización de la población indígena', in Solano, *Estudios*, 241–68.

W. Borah also assesses the often controversial literature on Spanish American urban design in 'European cultural influence in the formation of the first plan for urban centers that has lasted to our time', in Schaedel *et al.*, *Urbanización*, 157–90. See also G. M. Foster's chapter, 'Cities, towns, and villages: the grid-plan puzzle', in his *Culture and conquest* (Chicago, 1960), 34–49; G. Guarda, *Santo Tomás de Aquino y las fuentes del urbanismo indiano* (Santiago de Chile, 1965); E. W. Palm, 'La ville espagnole au nouveau monde dans la première moitié du XVIᵉ siècle', *La découverte de l'Amérique, 10ᵉ Stage International d'Études Humanistes* (Paris, 1968); L. Benevolo, 'Las nuevas ciudades fundadas en el siglo xvi en América Latina', *BCIHE*, 9 (1969), 117–36; L. M. Zawiska, 'Fundación de las ciudades hispanoamericanas', *BCIHE*, 13 (1972), 88–128; D. P. Crouch and A. I. Mundigo, 'The city planning ordinances of the laws of the Indies revisited', *Town Planning Review*, 48/3–4 (1977), 247–68, 397–418; G. Kubler, 'Open-grid town plans in Europe and America', in Schaedel, Hardoy and Kinzer, *Urbanization*, 327–42.

Other topics: F. Domínguez Compañy, 'Actas de fundación de ciudades hispanoamericanas', *RHA*, 83 (1977), 19–51; R. Archila, 'La medicina y la higiene en la ciudad' in Solano, *Estudios*, 655–85; F. de Solano, 'An introduction to the study of provisioning in the colonial city' and G. Gasparini, 'The colonial city as a center for the spread of architectural and pictorial schools', both in Schaedel, Hardoy and Kinzer, *Urbanization*, 99–129 and 269–81.

Regional studies

Antilles

C. O. Sauer presents a coherent account, with good maps, of Spanish town-founding in the Antilles and Tierra Firme to 1519 in *The early Spanish Main* (Berkeley and Los Angeles, 1966). J. M. F. de Arrate y Acosta, *Llave del Nuevo Mundo* (Mexico, 1949) is a descriptive and historical account of Havana by a town councillor, written in the 1750s and first published in 1830. E. W. Palm, *Los monumentos arquitectónicos de la Española, con una introducción a América* (2 vols., Ciudad Trujillo, 1955) is near-definitive for the topic and deals broadly with the origins of New World urbanization. Also: J. Pérez de Tudela, 'La quiebra de la factoría y el nuevo poblamiento de la Española', *Revista de Indias*, 60 (1955), 197–252; J. Artiles, *La Habana de Velázquez* (Havana, 1946); I. A. Wright, *Historia documentada de San Cristóbal de la Habana en el siglo XVI* (2 vols., Havana, 1927), *Historia documentada de San Cristóbal de la Habana en la primera mitad del siglo XVII* (Havana, 1930), and *Santiago de Cuba and its district (1607–1640)* (Madrid, 1918); Adolfo de Hostos, *Ciudad murada, ensayo acerca del proceso de la civilización en la ciudad española de San Juan Bautista de Puerto Rico* (Havana, 1948); M. A. Castro de Dávila, 'The place of San Juan de Puerto Rico among Hispanic American cities', *Revista Interamericana*, 6/2 (1976), 156–73.

Mesoamerica

C. Gibson treats the reorientation of pre-Columbian cities and settlement patterns under Spanish rule in Mexico in *Tlaxcala in the sixteenth century*

(New Haven, 1952), *The Aztecs under Spanish rule* (Stanford, 1964), especially the chapters 'Towns' and 'The City', and 'Spanish-Indian institutions and colonial urbanism in New Spain', in Hardoy and Schaedel, *El proceso*, 225–39. This theme also features in studies of Mexico's three main regions in I. Altman and J. Lockhart (eds.), *Provinces of early Mexico* (Berkeley and Los Angeles, 1976). A. Moreno Toscano and E. Florescano, 'El sector externo y la organización espacial y regional de Mexico (1521–1910)', in J. W. Wilkie, M. C. Meyer and E. Monzón de Wilkie (eds.), *Contemporary Mexico* (Berkeley and Los Angeles, 1976), 62–96, relates changing urban systems to economics, public policy and transportation. G. Kubler, *Mexican architecture of the sixteenth century* (2 vols., New Haven, 1948) has much to say on demography and urban form. M. Giménez Fernández, *Hernán Cortés y su revolución comunera* (Seville, 1948) shows Cortés' strategic use of municipal organization. P. W. Powell studies the special challenge of urban settlement on the Chichimeca frontier in *Soldiers, Indians, and silver, the northward advance of Spain, 1550–1600* (Berkeley and Los Angeles, 1952). Central American urbanization is treated in M. J. MacLeod, *Spanish Central America, a socioeconomic history 1520–1720* (Berkeley and Los Angeles, 1973) and, more explicitly, by S. D. Markman, *Colonial architecture of Antigua Guatemala* (Philadelphia, 1966), and several of his papers for the Symposia on Latin American urbanization, cited above.

On Mexico City: M. Toussaint, F. Gómez de Orozco and J. Fernández, *Planos de la ciudad de México, siglos XVI y XVII* (Mexico, 1938); E. W. Palm, 'Tenochtitlán y la ciudad ideal de Durero', *Journal de la Société des Américanistes*, N.S. 40 (1951), 59–66; S. B. Schwartz, 'Cities of empire: Mexico and Bahia in the sixteenth century', *Journal of Inter-American Studies*, 11/4 (1969), 616–37; E. Poulain, *Vie économique et sociale à Mexico d'après les 'Actas del cabildo de la ciudad de Mexico', 1594–1616* (Caen, 1966); R. E. Boyer, *La gran inundación, vida y sociedad en la ciudad de México (1629–1638)* (Mexico, 1975); L. S. Hoberman, 'Merchants in seventeenth-century Mexico City: a preliminary portrait', *HAHR*, 57/3 (1977), 479–503; R. Feijóo, 'El tumulto de 1624' and 'El tumulto de 1692', *HM*, 14/1 (1964), 42–70 and 14/4 (1965), 656–79; G. Poras Muñoz, *El gobierno de la ciudad de México en el siglo XVI* Mexico, 1982).

On other towns and cities: J. McAndrew, *The open-air churches of sixteenth century Mexico* (Cambridge, 1965); F. Chevalier, 'Signification sociale de la fondation de Puebla de los Ángeles', *RHA*, 23 (1947), 105–30; F. Marín-Tamayo, *La división racial en Puebla de los Ángeles bajo el régimen colonial* (Puebla, 1960); J. Bazant, 'Evolution of the textile industry of Puebla, 1544–1845', *Comparative Studies in Society and History*, 7/1 (1964), 56–69; M. Carmagnani, 'Demografía y sociedad: la estructura social de los centros mineros del norte de México', *HM*, 21 (1970–1), 419–59; P. J. Bakewell, *Silver Mining and Society in Colonial Mexico: Zacatecas 1546–1700* (Cambridge, 1971); J. K. Chance, *Race and Class in Colonial Oaxaca* (Stanford, 1978); E. Chinchilla Aguilar, *El ayuntamiento colonial de la ciudad de Guatemala* (Guatemala, 1961).

Northern South America

J. A. and J. E. Villamarín trace the reworking of native settlement patterns on the *sabana* of Bogotá in 'Chibcha settlement under Spanish rule: 1537–1810' in Robinson, *Social Fabric*, 25–84. Other regional studies: A. Castillero, *Políticas de poblamiento en Castilla del Oro y Veragua en los orígenes de la colonización* (Panama, 1972); C. Martínez, *Apuntes sobre el urbanismo en el Nuevo Reino de Granada* (Bogotá, 1967); G. Gasparini, 'Formación de ciudades coloniales en Venezuela, siglo XVI', *BCIHE*, 10 (1968), 9–43; A. Perera, *Historia de la organización de pueblos antiguos en Venezuela* (3 vols., Madrid, 1964).

On particular towns and cities: C. Verlinden, 'Santa María la Antigua del Darién, première "ville" coloniale de la Tierra Firme américaine', *RHA*, 45 (1958), 1–48; A. Rubio, *Esquema para un análisis de geografía urbana de la primitiva ciudad de Panamá, Panamá la Vieja, 1519–1671* (Panama, 1947); G. Gasparini, *Caracas colonial* (Buenos Aires, 1969); P. M. Arcaya, *El cabildo de Caracas* (Caracas, 1965); J. V. Lombardi, 'The rise of Caracas as a primate city' in Robinson, *Social Fabric*, 433–72; S. Blank, 'Patrons, clients, and kin in seventeenth-century Caracas', *HAHR*, 54/2 (1974), 260–83; E. Marco Dorta, *Cartagena de Indias, puerto y plaza fuerte* (Madrid, 1960); G. Arboleda, *Historia de Cali* (2nd edn, 3 vols., Cali, 1956); V. Cortés Alonso, 'Tunja y sus vecinos', *Revista de Indias*, 25/99–100 (1965), 155–207; P. Marzahl, *Town in the empire: government, politics, and society in seventeenth century Popayán* (Austin, 1978).

South America: West Coast and Andes

J. Basadre made a classic analysis of changing settlement patterns and their political implications from Incan to modern times in *La multitud, la ciudad y el campo en la historia del Perú* (Lima, 1929). G. Lohmann Villena studies the *corregidor*'s key role in *El corregidor de indios en el Perú bajo los Austrias* (Madrid, 1957). Newer scholarship offers further clues in: J. V. Murra, *Formaciones económicas y políticas del mundo andino* (Lima,

1975), especially the chapter entitled 'El control vertical de un máximo de pisos ecológicos en la economía de las sociedades andinas'; N. Wachtel, *Sociedad e ideología* (Lima, 1973); and K. Spalding, *De indio a campesino* (Lima, 1974). Administrative studies include J. P. Moore, *The Cabildo in Peru under the Hapsburgs* (Durham, 1954) and J. Alemparte, *El cabildo en Chile colonial* (2nd edn, Santiago de Chile, 1966). G. Guarda stresses military determinants for Chile in *Influencia militar en las ciudades del Reino de Chile* (Santiago de Chile, 1967); M. Carmagnani features economic factors in 'Formación de un mercado compulsivo y el papel de los mercaderes: la región de Santiago de Chile (1559–1600)', *JGSWGL*, 12 (1975), 104–33, and *Les mécanismes de la vie économique dans une société coloniale: le Chili, 1580–1830* (Paris, 1973); and M. Góngora treats social structure in 'Urban social stratification in colonial Chile', *HAHR*, 55/3 (1975), 421–48.

On particular cities: J. C. Super, 'Partnership and profit in the early Andean trade: the experiences of Quito merchants, 1580–1610', *JLAS*, 11/2 (1979), 265–81; M. L. Conniff, 'Guayaquil through independence: urban development in a colonial system', *The Americas*, 33/3 (1977), 385–410; J. Bromley and J. Barbagelata, *Evolución urbana de la ciudad de Lima* (Lima, 1945); M. Colin, *Le Cuzco à la fin du XVIIᵉ et au début du XVIIIᵉ siècle* (Paris, 1966); B. Arzáns de Orsúa y Vela, *Historia de la Villa Imperial de Potosí* (3 vols., Providence, 1965); L. Hanke, *The Imperial City of Potosí* (The Hague, 1956); A. Crespo R., *Historia de la ciudad de La Paz, siglo XVII* (Lima, 1961); M. Beltrán Ávila, *Capítulos de la historia colonial de Oruro* (La Paz, 1925); J. Urquidi Zambrano, *La urbanización de la ciudad de Cochabamba* (Cochabamba, 1967); R. Martínez Lemoine, 'Desarrollo urbano de Santiago (1541–1941)', *Revista Paraguaya de Sociología*, 15/42–3 (1978), 57–90; A. de Ramón, *La ciudad de Santiago entre 1650 y 1700* (Santiago de Chile, 1975).

The Río de la Plata Region

J. E. Hardoy and L. A. Romero provide a synthesis of Argentine urban history and a critique of sources in 'La ciudad argentina en el período precensal (1516–1869)', *Revista de la Sociedad Interamericana de Planificación*, 5/17 (1971), 16–39. J. Comadrán Ruiz supplies demographic context in *Evolución demográfica argentina en el período hispano (1535–1810)* (Buenos Aires, 1969). A classic study of colonial Buenos Aires, first published in 1900 and influenced by Le Play's sociology, is J. A. García, *La ciudad indiana*, in his *Obras completas* (2 vols., Buenos Aires, 1955), I, 283–475. See also A. Razori, *Historia de la ciudad argentina* (3 vols., Buenos Aires,

1945); R. Levillier, *Descubrimiento y población del norte de Argentina por españoles del Perú* (Buenos Aires, 1943); R. Zorraquín Becú, 'Los cabildos argentinos', *Revista de la Facultad de Derecho y Ciencias Sociales*, 11/47 (1956), 95–156; R. Zabala and E. de Gandía, *Historia de la ciudad de Buenos Aires* (2 vols., Buenos Aires, 1936–7); N. Besio Moreno, *Buenos Aires, puerto del Río de la Plata, estudio crítico de su población 1536–1936* (Buenos Aires, 1939); J. Comadrán Ruiz, 'Nacimiento y desarrollo de los núcleos urbanos y del poblamiento de la campaña del país de Cuyo durante la época hispana (1551–1810)', *Anuario de Estudios Americanos*, 19 (1952), 145–246; J. Álvarez, *Historia de Rosario (1689–1939)* (Buenos Aires, 1943); L. E. Azarola Gil, *Los orígenes de Montevideo, 1607–1749* (Buenos Aires, 1933); F. R. Moreno, *La ciudad de Asunción* (Buenos Aires, 1926); R. Gutiérrez, 'Estructura urbana de las misiones jesuíticas del Paraguay', in Hardoy and Schaedel, *Asentamientos*, 129–53.

Late colonial period

General: Two concise syntheses are W. Borah, 'Latin American cities in the eighteenth century: a sketch', in Borah, Hardoy and Stelter, *Urbanization*, 7–14, and D. A. Brading, 'The city in Bourbon Spanish America: elite and masses', *Comparative Urban Research*, 8/1 (1980): 71–85. Surveys and statistics for Latin America and for eight countries from 1750 to 1920 are found in R. M. Morse, *Las ciudades latino-americanas* (2 vols., Mexico, 1973), vol. II; urban statistics are also given in Borah's paper just cited and in R. E. Boyer and K. A. Davies, *Urbanization in 19th-Century Latin America: Statistics and Sources* (Los Angeles, 1973). E. M. Lahmeyer Lobo studies urban merchant guilds in *Aspectos da atuação dos consulados de Sevilha, Cádiz e da América Hispânica na evolução econômica do século* XVIII (Rio de Janeiro, 1965). C. Esteva Fabregat quantifies urban and rural racial composition in 'Población y mestizaje en las ciudades de Iberoamérica: siglo XVIII', in Solano, *Estudios*, 551–604.

Antilles and Mexico: M. Nunes Dias, *O comércio livre entre Havana e os pôrtos de Espanha (1778–1789)* (2 vols., São Paulo, 1965); A. R. Caro de Delgado, *El cabildo o régimen municipal puertorriqueño en el siglo* XVIII (San Juan, 1965); Jean Saint-Vil, 'Villes et bourgs de Saint Domingue au XVIIIeme siècle', *Conjonction*, 138 (1978), 5–32; A. Moreno Toscano, 'Regional economy and urbanization: three examples of the relationship between cities and regions in New Spain at the end of the eighteenth century', in Schaedel, Hardoy and Kinzer, *Urbanization*, 399–424; D. A. Brading, *Miners and merchants in Bourbon Mexico 1763–1810* (Cambridge, 1971); F. de la Maza, *La ciudad de México en el siglo XVIII* (Mexico, 1968); E. Báez Macías, 'Planos y censos de la ciudad de México 1753', *Boletín del Archivo General de la Nación*, 7/1–2 (1966), 407–84; A. Moreno Toscano and J. González Angulo, 'Cambios en la estructura interna de la ciudad de México (1753–1882)', in Hardoy and Schaedel, *Asentamientos*, 171–95; D. B. Cooper, *Epidemic disease in Mexico City 1761–1813* (Austin, 1965); R. Liehr, *Ayuntamiento y oligarquía en Puebla, 1787–1810* (2 vols., Mexico, 1971); L. L. Greenow, 'Spatial dimensions of the credit market in eighteenth-century Nueva Galicia', in Robinson (ed.), *Social fabric*, 227–79; E. Van Young, 'Urban market and hinterland: Guadalajara and its region in the eighteenth century', *HAHR*, 59/4 (1979), 593–635; D. E. López Sarrelangue, *Una villa mexicana en el siglo XVIII* (Mexico, 1966); M. L. Moorhead, *The Presidio* (Norman, 1975).

South America: A. Twinam, 'Enterprise and elites: eighteenth-century Medellín', *HAHR*, 59/3 (1979), 444–75; J. P. Moore, *The cabildo in Peru under the Bourbons* (Durham, 1966); V. A. Barriga (ed.), *Memorias para la historia de Arequipa, 1786–1796* (3 vols., Arequipa, 1941–8); G. Guarda, *La ciudad chilena del siglo XVIII* (Buenos Aires, 1968); G. O. Tjarks, *El consulado de Buenos Aires y sus proyecciones en la historia del Río de la Plata* (2 vols., Buenos Aires, 1962); J. L. Moreno, 'La estructura social y demográfica de la ciudad de Buenos Aires en el año de 1778', *Anuario del Instituto de Investigaciones Históricas* (Universidad Nacional del Litoral) [*AIIH*], 8 (1965), 151–70; S. M. Socolow, *The merchants of Buenos Aires 1778–1810* (Cambridge, 1978); L. L. Johnson and S. M. Socolow, 'Population and space in eighteenth century Buenos Aires', in Robinson, *Social fabric*, 339–68; F. J. Cervera and M. Gallardo, 'Santa Fe, 1765–1830: historia y demografía', *AIIH*, 9 (1966–7), 39–66; P. S. Martínez Constanzo, *Historia económica de Mendoza durante el virreinato, 1776–1810* (Madrid, 1961); D. J. Robinson and T. Thomas, 'New towns in eighteenth century Argentina', *JLAS*, 6/1 (1974), 1–33; R. Gutiérrez, *Estructura socio-política, sistema productivo y resultante espacial en las misiones jesuíticas del Paraguay durante el siglo XVIII* (Resistencia, 1974); three articles in *Revista Paraguaya de Sociología*, 15/42–3 (1978): R. E. Velázquez, 'Poblamiento del Paraguay en el siglo XVIII' (175–89), M. Lombardi, 'El proceso de urbanización en el Uruguay en los siglos XVIII y XIX' (9–45), and J. Rial Roade, A. M. Cocchi and J. Klaczko, 'Proceso de asentamientos urbanos en el Uruguay: siglos XVIII y XIX' (91–114).

Much information on late colonial urban conditions in northern South America and Mexico is found in: F. Depons, *Voyage à la partie orientale de la Terre-firme dans l'Amérique Méridionale (1801–1804)* (3 vols., Paris, 1806), A. von Humboldt and A. Bonpland, *Personal narrative of travels to the equinoctial regions of the New Continent during the years 1799–1804* (7 vols., London, 1814–29), and Humboldt's *Political essay on the kingdom of New Spain* (4 vols., London, 1811).

4. MINING IN COLONIAL SPANISH AMERICA

No adequate general book on colonial Spanish American mining yet exists. The only attempt at such a work, Carlos Prieto's *Mining in the New World* (New York, 1973) ignores important topics. The best introductory guide must therefore be the perceptive article by D. A. Brading and Harry E. Cross, 'Colonial silver mining: Mexico and Peru', *HAHR*, 52/4 (1972), 545–79. Modesto Bargalló, *La minería y la metalurgía en la América española durante la época colonial* (Mexico, 1955) concentrates on technical aspects of mining and refining, on which it is the best study available.

The fundamental bibliography is Eugenio Maffei and Ramón Rua Figueroa, *Apuntes para una biblioteca española de libros, folletos y artículos, impresos y manuscritos, relativos al conocimiento y explotación de las riquezas minerales y a las ciencias auxiliares* (2 vols., Madrid, 1871), reprinted VI Congreso Internacional de Minería, vols. 2 and 3 (León, 1970). This is updated by Justo García Morales, *Apuntes para una bibliografía minera española e iberoamericana (1870–1969)*, VI Congreso Internacional de Minería, vol. 4 (León, 1970).

Only one significant collection of colonial documents specifically on mining exists: Modesto Bargalló, *La amalgamación de los minerales de plata en Hispanoamérica colonial* (Mexico, 1969), indispensable on its topic. Various colonial treatises and histories on, or dealing with, mining are available. Among these are, for New Spain: Francisco Xavier de Gamboa, *Comentarios a las Ordenanzas de Minas* (Madrid, 1971), translated into English as *Commentaries on the Mining Ordinances of Spain* (2 vols., London, 1830), good on technical as well as legal questions; Fausto de Elhúyar, *Memoria sobre el influjo de la minería en...la Nueva España* (Madrid, 1825) and *Indagaciones sobre la amonedación en la Nueva España*

(Madrid, 1816); Jose Garcés y Eguía, *Nueva teórica y práctica del beneficio de los metales* (Mexico, 1802); Alexander von Humboldt, *Political essay on the Kingdom of New Spain* (4 vols., London, 1811–22), translated into Spanish as *Ensayo político sobre el Reino de la Nueva España* (Mexico, 1966). For South America, Luis Capoche, *Relación general de la Villa Imperial de Potosí* (Biblioteca de Autores Españoles, CXXII, Madrid, 1959), which is fundamental for Potosí up to *c.* 1585; Alvaro Alonso Barba, *Arte de metales* (Madrid, 1640; Eng. trans. London, 1923), a remarkable seventeenth-century refining treatise by a priest of Charcas; Bartolomé Arzáns de Orsúa y Vela (1676–1738), *Historia de la Villa Imperial de Potosí* (3 vols., Providence, Rhode Island, 1965); Pedro Vicente Cañete y Domínguez, *Guía histórica, geográfica, física, política, civil y legal del Gobierno e Intendencia de la Provincia de Potosí* [1787] (Potosí, 1952). Also important is Georgius Agricola, *De re metallica* (Basle, 1556; Eng. trans. London, 1912), a highly influential work in Spanish America.

Of all regions of Spanish America, it is New Spain that has most attracted the attention of modern mining historians. Henry R. Wagner, 'Early silver mining in New Spain', *RHA*, 14 (1942), 49–71, studies the early decades. P. J. Bakewell and Robert C. West examine important northern districts, particularly in the seventeenth century, in, respectively, *Silver mining and society in colonial Mexico, Zacatecas 1546–1700* (Cambridge, 1971) and *The mining community of northern New Spain: the Parral mining district* (Ibero-Americana 30, Berkeley and Los Angeles, 1949). Clement G. Motten, *Mexican silver and the Enlightenment* (Philadelphia, 1950) surveys the eighteenth century. D. A. Brading's fundamental *Miners and merchants in Bourbon Mexico, 1763–1810* (Cambridge, 1971) deals particularly with Guanajuato but also embraces other centres and multifarious topics related to mining. Walter Howe, *The mining guild of New Spain and its Tribunal General, 1770–1821* (Cambridge, Mass., 1949) is thorough. Humboldt's *Political essay* is indispensable for the late eighteenth century. See also, in general, Miguel León-Portilla *et al.*, *La minería en México* (Mexico, 1978).

Central American mining is treated by Murdo J. MacLeod in *Spanish Central America. A socioeconomic history, 1520–1720* (Berkeley and Los Angeles, 1973). For New Granada see especially Robert C. West, *Colonial placer mining in Colombia* (Baton Rouge, 1952) and Germán Colmenares, *Historia económica y social de Colombia, 1537–1719* (Medellín, 1976); also William F. Sharp, *Slavery on the Spanish frontier. The Colombian Chocó, 1680–1810* (Norman, Oklahoma, 1976). On Quito little is available, but Aquiles R. Pérez, *Las mitas en la Real Audiencia de Quito* (Quito, 1947) has information on mining as well as labour. The most thorough work for Peruvian mining is John R. Fisher's *Silver mines and silver miners in colonial Peru, 1776–1824* (Liverpool, 1977). Josep María Barnadas, *Charcas, 1535–1565: orígenes históricos de una sociedad colonial* (Centro de Investigación y Promoción del Campesinado, La Paz, 1973), is informative on early mining in that mineral-rich province. But Potosí still awaits a general study. Most comprehensive to date, among multitudinous shorter ones, are the introduction by Lewis Hanke to Capoche's *Relación general*, and that by Hanke and Gunnar Mendoza to Arzáns' *Historia*. For Chile, Ernesto Greve, 'Historia de la amalgamación de la plata', *Revista Chilena de Historia y Geografía*, 102 (1943), 158–259, is broader than it sounds. Marcello Carmagnani, in *El salariado minero en Chile colonial. Su desarrollo en una sociedad provincial: el Norte Chico, 1690–1800* (Santiago de Chile, 1963), describes mining and labour in an important gold district.

For mercury mining, see above all M. F. Lang, *El monopolio estatal del mercurio en el México colonial (1550–1710)* (Mexico, 1977) and Guillermo Lohmann Villena, *Las minas de Huancavelica en los siglos XVI y XVII* (Seville, 1949). For eighteenth-century Huancavelica, see Arthur P. Whitaker, *The Huancavelica mercury mine* (Cambridge, Mass., 1941); and for Almadén, A. Matilla Tascón, *Historia de las minas de Almadén*, vol. 1: *Desde la época romana hasta el año 1645* (Madrid, 1958).

Good brief studies on specific topics are Alberto Crespo Rodas, 'La "mita" de Potosí', *Revista Histórica*, 22 (Lima, 1955–6), 169–82; for legal and moral aspects of the mita, Jorge Basadre, 'El régimen de la mita', *Letras* (Universidad Mayor de San Carlos, Lima, 1937), 325–63; and Alan Probert, 'Bartolomé de Medina: the patio process and the sixteenth-century silver crisis', *Journal of the West*, 8 (1969), 90–124.

5. THE FORMATION AND ECONOMIC STRUCTURE OF THE HACIENDA IN NEW SPAIN

The study of the hacienda as a productive unit in the creation of new forms of exploitation of the soil and of labour is a relatively recent phenomenon in Mexico. Lesley B. Simpson, *Exploitation of land in central Mexico in the sixteenth century* (Berkeley and Los Angeles, 1952) illustrates with quantitative data the impressive, early conversion of Indian lands into agricultural and stock-raising enterprises owned and run by

Spaniards. François Chevalier, *La formation des grandes domaines au Mexique* (Paris, 1952; Sp. ed. 1956; Eng. ed. 1963) continued the traditional interest in forms of land tenure – for example Helen Phipps, *Some aspects of the agrarian question in Mexico* (Austin, 1925); George McCutchen McBride, *The land systems of Mexico* (New York, 1927); Silvio Zavala, *Las encomiendas y propiedad territorial en algunas regiones de la América Española* (Mexico, 1940); Jesús Amaya Tapete, *Ameca, protofundación mexicana* (Mexico, 1951) – and gave a new dimension to studies on land ownership and agriculture. Using a wide variety of private and official archives, Chevalier reconstructed the main processes which influenced the formation of the latifundia, traced their development over time, and related the expansion of the hacienda to the general development of the colony and in particular to the establishment of a new economic structure.

Although the dominant theme is still that of land ownership, most recent studies include an analysis of production and productivity, systems of labour, technology, administration, the market, and other micro- and macro-economic aspects. A detailed exposition of the themes and standpoints of such studies may be found in Magnus Mörner's review of recent literature ('The Spanish American hacienda: a survey of recent research and debate', *HAHR*, 53/1 (1973), 183–216), and in Reinhard Liehr, 'Orígenes, evolución y estructura socioeconómica de la hacienda hispanoamericana', *Anuario de Estudios Americanos*, 33 (1976), 527–77. Equally recent is the attempt to define more precisely the economic characteristics of the hacienda and to pinpoint the differences between it and the latifundium, the plantation and other institutions. This attempt to arrive at a more rigorous definition was begun by Eric R. Wolf and Sidney W. Mintz in 'Haciendas and plantations in Middle America and the Antilles', *Social and Economic Studies*, 6 (1957), 380–412. This has been followed up, albeit irregularly, in recent years. See, for example, James Lockhart, 'Encomienda and hacienda: the evolution of the great estate in the Spanish Indies', *HAHR*, 49/3 (1969), 411–29; Robert G. Keith, 'Encomienda, hacienda and corregimiento in Spanish America: a structural analysis', *HAHR*, 51/3 (1971), 431–46, and his introduction to the collective work he edited, *Haciendas and plantations in Latin American history* (New York, 1977), 1–35.

Since 1970, the analysis of agricultural problems during the colonial period has taken the form of regional studies, and in particular of monographs devoted to one or more haciendas. Over these years, a number of monographs have appeared which, apart from describing the formation of this type of landed estate, have tackled more deeply the growing problems of production, labour, the market and the influence of landowners on the social and political life of the region. Charles Gibson, *The Aztecs under Spanish Rule: a history of the Indians of the Valley of Mexico, 1519–1810* (Stanford, 1964) created a model for scholarly analysis at a regional level which has been adopted by many researchers interested in agricultural issues. The collective work, *Haciendas, lati- fundios y plantaciones en América Latina* (Mexico, 1975), edited by Enrique Florescano, brought together a series of essays which consider issues of property, production, labour and market outlets in various privately owned estates and in Jesuit haciendas, the latter being preferred for the richness and accessibility of their archives. In 1970, Ward Barrett published one of the best studies on the economy of the sugar hacienda, *The sugar hacienda of the Marqueses del Valle*, in which he paid special attention to the technical and administrative aspects of the hacienda, as well as to labour costs and productivity. However, the vast majority of studies have concentrated on the Jesuit-owned haciendas: Ursula Edwald, *Estudios sobre la hacienda colonial en México. Las propiedades rurales del Colegio Espíritu Santo en Puebla* (Wiesbaden, 1970); James D. Riley, *Hacendados jesuitas en México* (Mexico, 1976); Herman W. Konrad, *A Jesuit hacienda in colonial Mexico: Santa Lucía, 1576–1767* (Stanford, 1980).

Also numerous are studies which examine the formation and development of one or more haciendas over extended periods. See, for example, Jan Bazant, *Cinco haciendas mexicanas* (Mexico, 1974); Edith Boorstein Couturier, *La hacienda de Hueyapán, 1559–1936* (Mexico, 1976); Enrique Semo (ed.), *Siete ensayos sobre la hacienda mexicana, 1780–1880* (Mexico, 1977). These monographs and other economic studies have stimulated the analysis of agrarian problems region by region. William B. Taylor, *Landlord and peasant in colonial Oaxaca* (Stanford, 1972) is an important study which points to a sharp contrast between the development of Indian and Spanish properties in this region and the findings of Chevalier, Gibson and other authors with regard to the centre and north of Mexico. On the vast northern cattle-raising region, Charles H. Harris has written a fundamental work which traces the economic, social and political history of a large family-owned latifundium: *A Mexican family empire. The latifundio of the Sánchez Navarro family, 1765–1867* (Austin, 1975). The Puebla–Tlaxcala area has been the subject of continuing scrutiny by a group of German scholars, who have published such studies as that of Ursula Edwald, already cited, and Hans J. Prenn, *Milpa y hacienda. Tenencia de la tierra indígena y española en la cuenca del Alto Atoyac, Puebla, 1529–1650* (1978). Among these, particularly worthy of note is Herbert J. Nickel, *Soziale Morphologie der Mexikanischen Hacienda* (Wiesbaden, 1978), which gives us a general model of the Mexican hacienda and compares this with that of the Puebla–Tlaxcala area. One of the best analyses of the origin and development of the hacienda in a particular region is Robert Patch, 'La formación de estancias y haciendas en Yucatán durante la colonia', *Boletín de la Escuela de Ciencias Antropológicas de la Universidad de Yucatán* (July–August 1976).

On the Bajío, the main grain-producing region in the seventeenth and eighteenth centuries, David A. Brading's *Haciendas and ranchos in the Mexican Bajío. León 1700–1860* (Cambridge, 1978), is one of the first studies on the formation of the ranches. In his unpublished doctoral thesis, 'Creole Mexico: Spanish elites, haciendas and Indian towns, 1750–1810' (University of Texas, 1976), John Tutino examines the social stratification of landowners and the relationship between haciendas and villages in Central Mexico. Claude Morin examines these relationships, agricultural production and the situation of Indian workers in *Michoacán en la Nueva España del siglo XVIII* (Mexico, 1979). One of the best studies on the regional agricultural economy is Eric Van Young, *Hacienda and market in eighteenth-century Mexico: the rural economy of the Guadalajara region, 1675–1820* (Los Angeles, 1981), which considers production, labour, the market and the hacienda system in the region of Guadalajara. Ida Altman and James Lockhart (eds.), *Provinces of early Mexico* (Berkeley and Los Angeles, 1976), brings together a series of regional essays describing agrarian processes, the formation of haciendas and the relations between them and the Indian villages in Yucatán, Oaxaca, Toluca, Tlaxcala, the Valley of Mexico, Querétaro, Zacatecas and Coahuila.

The books by Chevalier and Simpson mentioned above provide the best information on the expansion of cattle raising and the formation of cattle estancias and haciendas in the sixteenth century. William H. Dusemberry, *The Mexican mesta. The administration of ranching in colonial Mexico* (Urbana, 1963), provides an overall analysis of the organization created by cattle breeders in order to regulate seasonal migration, grazing rights, legal matters and the slaughter of cattle.

Ramón Ma. Serrera, *Guadalajara, ciudad ganadera. Estudio regional novo-hispano, 1760–1805* (Seville, 1977), contains an analysis of the breeding of cattle, horses, mules and sheep, of the economic function of these activities in the region, and of the great ranching families.

Changes in the agrarian landscape brought about by the development of the haciendas and ranches and by the introduction of new crops and animals are treated in some of the works already mentioned. Alejandra Moreno Toscano offers us a general panorama of these changes in her *Geografía económica de México. Siglo XVI* (Mexico, 1968). Peter Gerhard has studied in some detail the effects of policies which obliged Indian villages to merge into larger units: see 'Congregaciones de indios en la Nueva España antes de 1570', *HM*, 26 (1976–7), 347–95, and 'La evolución del pueblo rural mexicano: 1519–1975', *HM*, 24 (1974–5), 566–78.

The transformation of large tracts of Indian land into private estates owned by Spaniards gave rise to new forms of soil exploitation based on new systems of labour, which in turn created a new pattern of relations between workers and landowners. Between 1929 and 1950, several studies presented an initial view of the chronological development of the systems of agricultural labour and some of their principal characteristics: Lesley B. Simpson, *The Encomienda. Forced native labor in the Spanish Colonia, 1492–1550* (Berkeley and Los Angeles, 1929), *Studies in the administration of the Indians in New Spain* (Berkeley and Los Angeles, 1938 and 1940), and *The encomienda of New Spain* (Berkeley and Los Angeles, 1950); Silvio Zavala, 'Los orígenes coloniales del peonaje en México', *El Trimestre Económico*, 10 (1943–4), 711–48; S. Zavala and María Castelo (eds.), *Fuentes para la historia del trabajo en Nueva España, 1552–1805* (8 vols., Mexico, 1939–46).

Based on these studies and on those of Gonzalo Aguirre Beltrán on the importation of black slaves (*La población negra de México, 1519–1810* (Mexico, 1940)), of George Kubler on the effects of the demographic crisis on the supply of Indian labour (*Mexican architecture in the sixteenth century* (2 vols., New Haven, 1948)), and on the research into the epidemics and demographic catastrophes of the sixteenth century he himself had carried out with S. F. Cook, W. Borah's important study *New Spain's century of depression* (Berkeley and Los Angeles, 1951) showed the devastating effects of the decline of the Indian population on agriculture, mining and the activities of Spanish settlers. According to Borah, the loss of the labour force which was one of the props of colonial society caused a general economic crisis, the organization of labour along different lines, namely the creation of a landless peasantry, and new forms of production and circulation of agricultural produce.

In *The Aztecs under Spanish rule*, Charles Gibson produced the most comprehensive study currently available on Indian labour in any one region. The analysis of systems of agricultural labour in the Valley of Mexico led him to suggest that debt peonage was no longer predominant in this region at the end of the eighteenth century, and that the methods of coercion used initially to retain workers had changed owing to the transformation of the hacienda into an institution which offered regular wages throughout the year and attractive living and social conditions for the Indians who had lost their lands or had cut their links with their community of origin. This hypothesis has been raised in almost all recent studies on the haciendas and agricultural labour, but none has proved convincingly that debt peonage and political coercion ceased to be important as methods of retaining labourers on the haciendas. The studies mentioned above on the haciendas rather confirm that the practice of retaining wages persisted, and prove that the worker did not usually receive payment in cash, but in credit facilities and goods, all of which demonstrates the presence of political and social pressures which curtailed the worker's freedom of movement and employment.

More recent studies (see, for example, John Tutino, 'Life and labor on north Mexican haciendas: the Querétaro–San Luis Potosí region: 1775–1810', and E. Florescano, 'Evaluación y síntesis de las ponencias sobre el trabajo colonial', in *El trabajo y los trabajadores en la historia de México* (Mexico, 1979), 339–77 and 756–97), show that the permanent labourers on the haciendas, the peons, constituted a new social grouping, a product of racial mixture, acculturation and the economic changes of the sixteenth and seventeenth centuries. On the other hand, the majority of seasonal labourers were from Indian villages (E. Florescano, Isabel González Sánchez *et al.*, *La clase obrera en la historia de México. De la colonia al imperio* (Mexico, 1980)).

Until the 1960s the predominant assumption in agrarian studies was that the hacienda was a self-sufficient unit of a feudal rather than commercial type. This thesis has been replaced by new interpretations which show that the hacienda originated in the introduction of the mercantile economy and that its development ran parallel to the growth of mercantile exchange and market outlets. In *Precios del maíz y crisis agrícolas en México, 1708–1810* (Mexico, 1969), E. Florescano examined the principal mechanisms which regulated the demand for and availability of grain on the urban market, and related fluctuations in the price of maize to agricultural crisis and seasonal shortages. Later studies have confirmed the presence of such mechanisms in various regions (see the works by D. A. Brading on León and Eric Van Young on Guadalajara cited above), and in the mining area (Richard L. Garner, 'Zacatecas, 1750–1821. The study of a late colonial Mexican city', unpublished doctoral thesis, University of Michigan, 1970).

The theoretical basis which permitted a deeper economic interpretation of the relationship between agriculture and the market and the dominant economic system was provided by recent Marxist studies, in particular the work of Witold Kula, *An economic theory of the feudal system* (original Polish edition, 1962; Buenos Aires, 1974; London, 1976). Inspired by this and other Marxist studies, Carlos Sempat Assadourian and Ángel Palerm, among others, have treated in a different way the problem of the articulation of the colonial economy with the world system, the characteristics which forged the development of the mercantile colonial economy and the subordinate role played in this by agriculture compared with mineral production. On this issue, see the studies by both authors in E. Florescano (ed.), *Ensayos sobre el desarrollo económico de México y América Latina, 1500–1975* (Mexico, 1979).

The dependence of primary producers in the face of the seasonal and cyclical fluctuations of the market (see Florescano, *Precios*; Brading, *Haciendas and ranchos*; Van Young, *Hacienda and market*; Garner, 'Zacatecas, 1750–1821') produced an even greater dependence among farmers and cattle raisers on commercial capital. During the eighteenth century this expressed itself, in the main urban and mining centres, through the domination of the mechanisms of circulation of agricultural produce and the control of market outlets by the merchant sector; for this, see the already mentioned study by Van Young and Harris, *A Mexican family empire*; Tutino, 'Creole Mexico', and Marco Bellingeri, *Las haciendas en México. El caso de San Antonio Teochatlaco, 1800–1920*, forthcoming. The studies by Asunción Lavrin on the credit extended by religious institutions to producers and merchants ('El capital eclesiástico y las élites sociales en Nueva España a fines del siglo XVIII', paper presented at the V Simposio de Historia Económica de América Latina, Lima, April 1978), R. B. Lindley on credit and family relations within the colonial elite ('Kinship and credit in the structure of the Guadalajara oligarchy, 1800–1830', unpublished Ph.D. thesis, Austin, 1976), Gisela von Wobeser on the contraction of debts among the owners of haciendas (*San Carlos Borromeo. Endeudamiento de una hacienda colonial, 1608–1729* (Mexico, 1980)), J. Tutino on the concentration of wealth and land within the commercial sector ('Creole Mexico') and Doris Ladd on the colonial aristocracy (*The Mexican nobility at Independence* (Austin, 1976)), all demonstrate the gradual erosion of the power of primary producers in the face of the credit and capital accumulated by merchants, and the formation of a small but powerful oligarchy of great families, predominant among which were merchants.

6. THE RURAL ECONOMY AND SOCIETY OF COLONIAL SPANISH SOUTH AMERICA

The rural history of Spanish South America finally began to receive some attention from scholars during the 1970s. Even now, far more research is devoted to the large estates than to smallholders and *comunidades*. See Magnus Mörner, 'The Spanish American hacienda. A survey of recent research and debate', *HAHR*, 53/2 (1973), 183–216; articles by Reinhard Liehr in H. J. Puhle (ed.), *Lateinamerika. Historische Realität und Dependencia-Theorien* (Hamburg, 1976), 105–46, and H. Pietschmann in G. Siebenmann (ed.), *Die lateinamerikanische Hacienda. Ihre Rolle in der Geschichte von Wirtschaft und Gesellschaft* (Diessenhofen, 1979), 37–48. Interesting perspectives are provided by Cristóbal Kay, 'Desarrollo comparativo del sistema señorial europeo y del sistema de hacienda latinoamericano', *Anuario de Estudios Americanos*, 31 (1976), 681–723. Agricultural productivity and technology during the colonial period have until now received very little attention. An older but still important study of the legal aspects is J. M. Ots Capdequí, *El régimen de la tierra en la América española durante el período colonial* (Ciudad Trujillo, 1946).

A general survey of Peruvian rural history is provided by V. Roel Pineda, *Historia social y económica de la Colonia* (Lima, 1970). Recent monographs include R. G. Keith, *Conquest and agrarian change: the emergence of the hacienda system on the Peruvian coast* (Cambridge, Mass., 1976); M. Burga, *De la encomienda a la hacienda capitalista. El Valle de Jequetepeque del siglo XVI al XX* (Lima, 1976); K. A. Davies, 'The rural domain of the city of Arequipa, 1540–1665' (Ph.D. dissertation, University of Connecticut, 1974); S. E. Ramírez-Horton, 'Land tenure and the economics of power in colonial Peru' (unpublished dissertation, University of Wisconsin, 1977); and M. Mörner, *Perfil de la sociedad rural del Cuzco a fines de la colonia* (Lima, 1978). The valley of Chancay has been studied in several contributions by J. Matos Mar and others. In vol. II of *Trabajos de historia* (4 vols., Lima, 1977) Pablo Macera studied Jesuit haciendas and the history of sugar production. See also Nicholas P. Cushner, *Lords of the land: sugar, wine and Jesuit estates of coastal Peru 1600–1767* (Albany, 1980). For labour see Frederick P. Bowser, *The African slave in colonial Peru, 1524–1650* (Stanford, 1974); for the role of the Indians as labour and in trade, K. Spalding, *De indio a campesino. Cambios en la estructura social del Perú colonial* (Lima, 1974). Food supply is discussed in O. Febres Villaroel, 'La crisis agrícola en el Perú en el último tercio del siglo XVIII', *Revista Histórica*, 27 (Lima, 1964), 102–99, and Demetrio Ramos, *Trigo chileno, navieros del Callao y hacendados limeños entre la crisis agrícola del siglo XVII y la comercial de la primera mitad del siglo XVIII* (Madrid, 1967). Irrigation is studied by H. Villanueva U. and J. Sherbondy (eds.), *Cuzco: agua y poder* (Cuzco, 1979).

The most serious work so far on the rural history of Upper Peru (Bolivia) is B. Larson, 'Economic decline and social change in an agrarian hinterland: Cochabamba (Bolivia) in the late colonial period' (unpublished dissertation, Columbia University, 1978). Labour aspects are dealt with by N. Sánchez-Albornoz, *Indios y tributos en el Alto Perú* (Lima, 1978). Articles by S. Rivera Cusicanqui and others have appeared in the journal *Avances* (La Paz, 1978–), and D. Santamaría has published two interesting articles on hacienda production and Indian land property rights from 1780 to 1810 in the journal *Desarrollo Económico*, 17 (Buenos Aires, 1977).

Mario Góngora has been the pioneer in the field of Chilean rural history. His works include: *Origen de los 'inquilinos' de Chile Central* (Santiago, 1960); (with J. Borde), *Evolución de la propiedad rural en el valle del Puangue*, I–II (Santiago, 1956); *Encomenderos y estancieros. Estudios acerca de la constitución social aristocrática de Chile después de la Conquista, 1580–1660* (Santiago, 1970); *Studies in the colonial history of Spanish America* (Cambridge, 1975). See also R. Baraona, X. Aranda and R. Santana, *Valle de Putaendo. Estudio de estructura agraria* (Santiago, 1969). An important and unique contribution is that of M. Carmagnani, *Les mécanismes de la vie économique dans une société coloniale: le Chili 1680–1830* (Paris, 1973).

For short surveys of the rural history of the Río de la Plata see C. S. Assadourian, G. Beato and J. C. Chiaramonte, *Argentina. De la conquista a la Independencia* (Buenos Aires, 1972); H. C. Giberti, *Historia económica de la ganadería argentina* (Buenos Aires, 1961); A. R. Castellanos, *Breve historia de la ganadería en el Uruguay* (Montevideo, 1971). Pedro Santos Martínez, *Historia económica de Mendoza durante el Virreinato, 1776–1810* (Madrid, 1961), is an important regional history. See also his *Las industrias durante el Virreinato (1776–1810)* (Buenos Aires, 1969). C. Garzón Maceda, *Economía del Tucumán. Economía natural y economía monetaria. Siglos XVI, XVII, XVIII* (Córdoba, 1968), is another penetrating study of general interest. Rural history is also dealt with in J. L. Mora Mérida, *Historia social de Paraguay, 1600–50* (Seville, 1973). On the Jesuit missions, see M. Mörner, *Actividades políticas y económicas de los jesuitas en el Río de la Plata. La era de los Habsburgos* (Buenos Aires, 1968), and his article on the rivalry of Uruguayan *ganado cimarrón* in *Revista Portuguesa de História*, 9 (Coimbra, 1961). See also E. A. Coni, *Historia de las vaquerías de Río de la Plata, 1555–1750* (Buenos Aires, 1956) and the articles by J. C. Garavaglia and T. Halperín Donghi in Enrique Florescano (ed.), *Haciendas, latifundios y plantaciones en América Latina* (Mexico, 1975). S. M. Socolow, 'Economic activities of the *porteño* merchants: the viceregal period', *HAHR*, 55/2 (1975), is also useful.

The Audiencia of Quito (Ecuador) is still little explored. More data on rural and social history than the title suggests can be found in C. Moreno Yáñez, *Sublevaciones indígenas en la Audiencia de Quito, comienzos del siglo XVIII hasta finales de la Colonia* (Bonn, 1976). See also E. Bonifaz, 'Origen y evolución de una hacienda histórica, Guachalá', *Boletín de la Academia Nacional de Historia*, 53 (Quito, 1970), and U. Oberem, 'Contribución a la historia del trabajador rural de América Latina: "conciertos" y "huasipungueros" en Ecuador' (Universitätsschwerpunkt Lateinamerikaforschung, Bielefeld, 1977, mimeo). On the coast, see M. T. Hamerly's excellent *Historia social y económica de la antigua provincia de Guayaquil, 1763–1842* (Guayaquil, 1973), and M. Chiriboga's article on the history of cacao plantations in *Estudios Rurales Latinoamericanos*, 1/1 (Bogotá, 1978).

In Colombia, the sociologist O. Fals Borda was the pioneer in rural history. See his work *El hombre y la tierra en Boyacá* (Bogotá, 1957), and his article on Indian 'congregations', 1595–1850, in *The Americas*, 13/4 (1957). On the Indian communities see also an article by T. Gómez in *Cahiers du Monde Hispanique et Luso-Brésilien*, 27 (Toulouse, 1977). The main contributions by G. Colmenares include *Haciendas de los jesuitas en el Nuevo Reino de Granada, siglo XVIII* (Bogotá, 1969); *Historia económica y social de Colombia, 1537–1719* (Bogotá, 1973); *Cali: terratenientes, mineros y comerciantes. Siglo XVIII* (Cali, 1975). See also J. A. Villamarín, 'Haciendas en la Sabana de Bogotá, Colombia, en la época colonial: 1539–1810', in Florescano, *Haciendas, latifundios y plantaciones*, and contributions by different authors in *Anuario Colombiano de Historia Social y de la Cultura* (Bogotá, 1963–).

In his pioneering work, *Economía colonial de Venezuela* (Mexico, 1946), E. Arcila Farías dealt mainly with commercialization. For a broader approach see, Federico Brito Figueroa, *Estructura económica de Venezuela colonial* (Caracas, 1963), an analysis in strictly Marxist terms. A fine study on the late colonial and early national periods is M. Izard, *La agricultura venezolana en una época de transición* (Caracas, 1972).

7. ASPECTS OF THE INTERNAL ECONOMY OF COLONIAL SPANISH AMERICA: LABOUR; TAXATION; DISTRIBUTION AND EXCHANGE

There are no satisfactory surveys of the Spanish American colonial economies. A provocative, thoughtful, but dated Marxist interpretation is Sergio Bagú, *Economía de la sociedad colonial: ensayo de historia comparada de América Latina* (Buenos Aires, 1949). Also somewhat dated is Emilio A. Coni, *Agricultura, comercio e industria coloniales (siglo XVI–XVIII)* (Buenos Aires, 1941). A more modern but less stimulating study is Demetrio Ramos, *Minería y comercio interprovincial en Hispanoamérica (siglos XVI, XVII y XVIII)* (Valladolid, 1970). Much useful material on economic institutions can still be found in C. H. Haring, *The Spanish empire in America* (New York, 1947). A study with a very different emphasis, as the title suggests, is the short book by Stanley J. and Barbara H. Stein, *The colonial heritage of Latin America: essays on economic dependence in perspective* (New York, 1970). For the Atlantic sea link, Atlantic trade and the Atlantic economy in general, see *CHLA* I, Bibliographical Essay 10.

Labour

A convenient summary of Indian colonial labour systems is by Juan A. and Judith E. Villamarín, *Indian labor in mainland colonial Spanish America* (Newark, Delaware, 1975). The evolution of such labour systems may be grasped by reading in sequence the introductions to the several volumes by Silvio Zavala and María Castelo (eds.), *Fuentes para la historia del trabajo en Nueva España, 1552–1805* (8 vols., Mexico, 1939–46). Readers should also consult Zavala's *El servicio personal de los indios en el Perú (extractos del siglo XVI, XVII, XVIII)* (3 vols., Mexico, 1978–80), which has extensive discussion of the Peruvian encomienda, mita and peonage. The encomienda, how it declined because of population loss and royal legislation, and how some entrepreneurs used it as a device for capital accumulation and diversification, are discussed in José Miranda, *La función económica del encomendero en los orígenes del régimen colonial (Nueva España, 1525–1531)* (Mexico, 1965). The link between the encomienda and land tenure in general is discussed in two very different essays: James Lockhart, 'Encomienda and hacienda; the evolution of the great estate in the Spanish Indies', *HAHR*, 49/3 (1969), 411–29; and Robert G. Keith, 'Encomienda, hacienda and corregimiento in Spanish America: a structural analysis', *HAHR*, 51/3 (1971), 431–46. The pioneer of studies on peonage is, once again, Silvio Zavala, in his 'Los orígenes coloniales del peonaje en México', *El Trimestre Económico*, 10 (1943–4), 711–48. See also Genaro V. Vázquez, *Legislación del trabajo en los siglos xvi, xvii y xviii* (Mexico, 1938); Samuel Kagan, *Los vagabundos en la Nueva España, siglo XVI* (Mexico, 1957); Richard Konetzke, 'Los mestizos en la legislación colonial', *Revista de Estudios Políticos*, 112–14 (1960), 113–30, 179–215; and Karen Spalding, *De indio a campesino. Cambios en la estructura social del Perú colonial* (Lima, 1974). For the literature on black slavery, see, *CHLA* II, Bibliographical Essay 10.

Taxation

Gabriel Ardant is the main authority on systems of taxation. See, for example, his massive *Théorie sociologique de l'impôt* (2 vols., Paris, 1965). José Miranda surveys the history and economies of Indian tribute in Mexico, in his *El tributo indígena en la Nueva España durante el siglo XVI* (Mexico, 1952). Nicolás Sánchez-Albornoz covers a later and longer period, including the post-independence tributes of the nineteenth century, in *Indios y tributos en el Alto Perú* (Lima, 1978). Ronald Escobedo Mansilla, *El tributo indígena en el Perú, siglos XVI y XVII* (Pamplona, 1979) is thorough but lacks interpretation and imagination.

Derramas and *repartimientos de mercancías* await detailed history and analysis. Meanwhile, a good study of the late colonial repartimientos in Peru is H. Moreno Cebrián, *El corregidor de indios y la economía peruana en el siglo XVIII. (Los repartos forzosos de mercancías)* (Madrid, 1977). We are equally lacking in definitive works on the specific institutions which Indians adopted so readily, the *caja de comunidad* and the *cofradía*. There are two unpublished dissertations containing extensive information: Francis Joseph Brooks, 'Parish and *cofradía* in eighteenth-century Mexico' (Ph.D. thesis, Princeton University, 1976); and Gary Wendell Graff, '*Cofradías* in the new kingdom of Granada: lay fraternities in a Spanish-American frontier society, 1600–1755' (Ph.D. thesis, University of Wisconsin, 1973). See also Gonzalo Aguirre Beltrán, *Formas de gobierno indígena* (Mexico, 1953); Pedro Carrasco, 'The civil religious hierarchy in Mesoamerican communities; pre-Spanish background and colonial development', *American Anthropologist*, 63 (1961), 483–97; appropriate parts of the impressive study by Pierre Duviols, *La lutte contre les religions autochtones dans le Pérou colonial* (Paris, 1971); and José Miranda and Silvio Zavala, 'Instituciones indígenas en la colonia', in A. Caso (ed.), *Métodos y resultados de la política indigenista en México* (Mexico, 1954), 29–167.

Distribution and exchange

On the *consulados* see, for example, Germán O. E. Tjarks, *El consulado de Buenos Aires, y sus proyecciones en la historia del Río de la Plata* (2 vols., Buenos Aires, 1962) and the older Robert S. Smith, *The Spanish guild merchant. A history of the consulado, 1250–1700* (Durham, N.C., 1940). Government *estancos* or monopolies are the subject of a series of works from the Escuela de Estudios Hispanoamericanos in Seville. The most recent is by José Jesús Hernández Palomo, *La renta del pulque en Nueva España, 1663–1810* (Seville, 1979). The crown's revenues are studied exhaustively in Francisco Gallardo y Fernández, *Orígen, progresos y estado de las rentas de la corona de España, su gobierno y administración* (8 vols., Madrid, 1805–8).

The Indian economy and market system are discussed in such well-known works as Charles Gibson, *The Aztecs under Spanish rule: a history of the Indians of the Valley of Mexico, 1519–1810* (Stanford, 1964); Josep M. Barnadas, *Charcas, 1535–1565: orígenes históricos de una sociedad colonial* (La Paz, 1973); and Magnus Mörner, *La corona española y los foráneos en los pueblos de indios de América* (Stockholm, 1970).

For long-distance commerce, routes and markets, the following should provide an introduction: Woodrow Borah, *Early colonial trade and navigation between Mexico and Peru* (Berkeley and Los Angeles, 1954); Marcello Carmagnani, *Les mécanismes de la vie économique dans une société coloniale: le Chili (1680–1830)* (Paris, 1973); Manuel Moreyra y Paz Soldán, *El comercio de exportación en el Pacífico a comienzos del siglo XVIII* (Lima, 1944); and María Encarnación Rodríguez Vicente, *El tribunal del consulado de Lima en la primera mitad del siglo XVII* (Madrid, 1960). Lawrence A. Clayton reviews some works on Pacific trade in 'Trade and navigation in the seventeenth-century viceroyalty of Peru', *JLAS*, 7 (1975), 1–21, and gives us a good picture of a colonial shipyard and port in *Caulkers and carpenters in a New World: the shipyards of colonial Guayaquil* (Athens, Ohio, 1980). The Potosí–Buenos Aires route has a large but scattered bibliography. Helpful are Mario Rodríguez, 'Dom Pedro of Braganza and Colônia do Sacramento, 1680–1705', *HAHR*, 38 (1958), 180–208; and Sergio Villalobos R., *Comercio y contrabando en el Río de la Plata y Chile, 1700–1811* (Buenos Aires, 1965). An amusing account of the journey between Buenos Aires and Lima is 'Concolorcorvo', *El Lazarillo, a guide for inexperienced travelers between Buenos Aires and Lima, 1773*, tr. Walter D. Kline (Bloomington, 1965). Fairs are discussed in Manuel Carrera Stampa's 'Las ferias novohispanas', *HM*, 2 (1952–3), 319–42, which also contains maps of trade routes, and in Allyn C. Loosley, 'The Puerto Bello fairs', *HAHR*, 13 (1933), 314–35. Carrera Stampa also wrote a pioneering work on craft guilds, *Los gremios mexicanos: la organización gremial en Nueva España, 1521–1810* (Mexico, 1954).

The literature on merchants is extensive, especially for the eighteenth century. Two articles on the less well-known early groups are John C. Super, 'Partnership and profit in the early Andean trades: the experiences of Quito merchants, 1580–1610', *JLAS*, 2 (1979), 265–81, and Louisa Schell Hoberman, 'Merchants in seventeenth-century Mexico City: a preliminary portrait', *HAHR*, 57 (1977), 479–503. Work on colonial industries has also been voluminous. For recent studies of the textile *obrajes*, see John C. Super, 'Querétaro *obrajes*: industry and society in provincial Mexico 1600–1810', *HAHR*, 56 (1976), 197–216; Robson Tyrer, 'The demographic and economic history of the Audiencia of Quito: Indian population and the textile industry, 1600–1810' (Ph.D. thesis, University of California at Berkeley, 1976); Javier Ortiz de la Tabla Ducasse, 'El obraje colonial ecuatoriano. Aproximación a su estudio', *Revista de Indias*, 27 (1977), 471–541;

G. P. C. Thomson, 'Economy and society in Puebla de los Ángeles 1800–1850' (D.Phil. thesis, Oxford, 1978); Richard J. Salvucci, 'Enterprise and economic development in eighteenth-century Mexico: the case of the obrajes' (Ph.D. thesis, Princeton University, 1982).

Other colonial industries have interested scholars such as Eduardo Arcila Farias, who described Venezuela's cacao in *Economía colonial de Venezuela* (Mexico, 1946), and the trade in it to Veracruz in *Comercio entre Venezuela y México en los siglos XVI y XVII* (Mexico, 1959); Manuel Rubio Sánchez, *Historia del añil o xiquilite en Centroamérica* (2 vols., San Salvador, 1976–7); and John E. Kicza, 'The pulque trade of late colonial Mexico City', *The Americas*, 27 (1980), 193–221. There is a census of the small manufacturers of Buenos Aires in Lyman L. Johnson, 'The entrepreneurial reorganization of an artisan trade. The bakers of Buenos Aires, 1770–1820', *The Americas*, 27 (1980), 139–60.

Sixteenth-century price inflation was the object of a study by Woodrow Borah and Sherburne Cook, *Price trends of some basic commodities in central Mexico, 1531–1570* (Berkeley and Los Angeles, 1958). Enrique Florescano covered the same problems for the last century of the colonial period in his *Precios de maíz y crisis agrícolas en México, 1708–1810* (Mexico, 1969).

For opposing views on the seventeenth-century crisis, see Woodrow Borah, *New Spain's century of depression* (Berkeley and Los Angeles, 1951), and volume II of John Lynch's *Spain under the Hapsburgs* (2 vols., Oxford, 1965, 1969). The colonial boom of the eighteenth century and the partial setbacks which took place in the years before independence have been studied in many of the works already cited. The other side of the eighteenth-century economic boom is nowhere better summed up than in D. A. Brading's *Haciendas and ranchos in the Mexican Bajío: León, 1700–1860* (Cambridge, 1978). See also Eric Van Young, *Hacienda and market in eighteenth-century Mexico: the rural economy of the Guadalajara region, 1675–1820* (Berkeley and Los Angeles, 1981).

8. SOCIAL ORGANIZATION AND SOCIAL CHANGE IN COLONIAL SPANISH AMERICA

Sophisticated discussion of Spanish American social organization is extremely rare. This chapter draws to some extent upon the following pieces by James Lockhart: 'Encomienda and hacienda: the evolution of the great estate in the Spanish Indies', *HAHR*, 49/3 (1969), 411–29; introduction to Ida Altman and James Lockhart (eds.), *Provinces of early Mexico: variants of Spanish American regional evolution* (Los Angeles, 1976); 'Capital and province, Spaniard and Indian: the example of late sixteenth-century Toluca', in Altman and Lockhart, *Provinces of early Mexico*, 99–123. See also Woodrow Borah, 'Race and class in Mexico', *Pacific Historical Review*, 23 (1954), 331–42; Enrique Otte, 'Träger und Formen der wirtschaftlichen Erschliessung Lateinamerikas im 16. Jahrhundert', *JGSWGL*, 4 (1967), 226–66; and Richard Boyer, 'Mexico in the seventeenth century: transition of a colonial society', *HAHR*, 57 (1977), 454–78. The latter two articles are perhaps more economic than social in orientation. Two broad thematic works by Magnus Mörner cover all Spanish America for the entire colonial period and are in a part social, part legal vein: *Race mixture in the history of Latin America* (Boston, 1967), and *La corona española y los foráneos en los pueblos de indios de América* (Stockholm, 1970). See also Guillermo Céspedes' synthesis, *Latin America: the early years* (New York, 1974), summarizing much recent basic research. James Lockhart and Enrique Otte, *Letters and people of the Spanish Indies, sixteenth century* (Cambridge, 1976) contains analysis of general social types and processes together with specific examples; Otte's 'Die europäischen Siedler und die Probleme der Neuen Welt', *JGSWGL*, 6 (1969), 1–40 contains additional similar material. The principles of the present chapters are illustrated on a wider canvas in James Lockhart and Stuart B. Schwartz, *Early Latin America: a history of colonial Spanish America and Brazil* (Cambridge, 1983).

The remarkable recent florescence of writing on the social history of early Latin America has mainly taken the form of works at once specific and theoretical, specific in that they closely reconstruct the progress of individual persons or organizations in a specific time and place, and theoretical in that thereby they reveal previously unknown categories and patterns basic to the general social process. James Lockhart, 'The social history of colonial Latin America: evolution and potential', *LARR*, 7 (1972), 6–45, surveys this literature up to *c.* 1970, including such notable contributions as Mario Góngora, *Grupos de conquistadores en Tierra Firme (1509–1530)* (Santiago de Chile, 1962) and James Lockhart, *Spanish Peru, 1532–1560. A colonial society* (Madison, 1968). The following are some of the more important monographs published since then: Pedro Carrasco *et al.*, *Estratificación social en la Mesoamérica prehispánica* (Mexico, 1976); Enrique Otte, *Las perlas del Caribe: Nueva*

Cádiz de Cubagua (Caracas, 1977); J. Lockhart, *The men of Cajamarca: a social and biographical study of the first conquerors of Peru* (Austin, 1972); Frederick P. Bowser, *The African slave in colonial Peru 1524–1650* (Stanford, 1974); Mario Góngora, *Encomenderos y estancieros: estudios V acerca de la constitución social aristocrática de Chile después de la conquista, 1580–1660* (Santiago de Chile, 1970); Góngora, 'Urban social stratification in colonial Chile', *HAHR*, 55 (1975), 421–48; Peter Marzahl, *Town in the empire: government, politics, and society in seventeenth century Popayán* (Austin, 1978); P. J. Bakewell, *Silver mining and society in colonial Mexico: Zacatecas 1546–1700* (Cambridge, 1971); D. A. Brading, *Miners and merchants in Bourbon Mexico 1763–1810* (Cambridge, 1971); Brading, *Haciendas and ranchos in the Mexican Bajío: León 1700–1860* (Cambridge, 1978); Leon G. Campbell, 'A creole establishment: the Audiencia of Lima in the later eighteenth century', *HAHR*, 52 (1972), 1–25; Philip L. Hadley, *Minería y sociedad en el centro minero de Santa Eulalia, Chihuahua (1709–1750)* (Mexico, 1979). Two more general works are Arthur J. O. Anderson, Frances Berdan and James Lockhart (eds.), *Beyond the Codices* (Berkeley and Los Angeles, 1976), being a collection of Nahuatl documents from inside the Indian world of colonial Mexico, with extensive introductory materials, and Altman and Lockhart, *Provinces.*

Another kind of work exists, which is more aggregate or statistical without prior close attention to functioning entities; naturally it throws far less direct light on social categories or processes, yet seen in conjunction with the type of research just cited, it can yield valuable insights. See, for example, Peter Boyd-Bowman, 'Patterns of Spanish emigration to the Indies until 1600', *HAHR*, 56 (1976), 580–604; Julia Hirschberg, 'Social experiment in New Spain: a prosopographical study of the early settlement at Puebla de los Angeles, 1531–1534', *HAHR*, 59 (1979), 1–33; Robert G. Keith, *Conquest and agrarian change: the emergence of the hacienda system on the Peruvian coast* (Cambridge, Mass., 1976); Stephanie Blank, 'Patrons, clients, and kin in seventeenth-century Caracas', *HAHR*, 54 (1974), 260–83; Asunción Lavrin and Edith Couturier, 'Dowries and wills; a view of women's socioeconomic role in colonial Guadalajara and Puebla, 1640–1790', *HAHR*, 59 (1979), 280–304; Germán Colmenares, *Historia económica y social de Colombia, 1537–1719* (Bogotá, 1973); John K. Chance, *Race and class in colonial Oaxaca* (Stanford, 1978); Leon G. Campbell, *The military and society in colonial Peru 1750–1810* (Philadelphia, 1978); Christon I. Archer, *The army in Bourbon Mexico, 1760–1810* (Albuquerque, 1977); Mark A. Burkholder and D. S. Chandler, *From impotence to authority: the Spanish crown and the American Audiencias, 1687–1808* (Columbia, Missouri, 1977); John V. Lombardi, *People and places in colonial Venezuela* (Bloomington, 1976); Lyman L. Johnson, 'Manumission in colonial Buenos Aires', *HAHR*, 59 (1979), 258–79; Herbert S. Klein, 'The structure of the hacendado class in late eighteenth-century Alto Perú: the Intendencia de la Paz', *HAHR*, 60 (1980), 191–212; Susan Migden Socolow, *The merchants of Buenos Aires 1778–1810* (Cambridge, 1978); Ann Twinam, 'Enterprise and elites in eighteenth-century Medellín', *HAHR*, 59 (1979), 444–75; Doris M. Ladd, *The Mexican nobility at independence 1780–1826* (Austin, 1976); William B. Taylor, *Landlord and peasant in colonial Oaxaca* (Stanford, 1972); and Taylor, *Drinking, homicide and rebellion in colonial Mexican villages* (Stanford, 1979).

9. WOMEN IN SPANISH AMERICAN COLONIAL SOCIETY

The development of social history in the last decade has awakened interest in the role of women in history, but the growth of a bibliography on the topic for the colonial period in Spanish America has been slow. There are still relatively few recent works to consult and for many subjects the reader must refer to old standard works. Furthermore, much information needs to be retrieved in small amounts from a variety of studies dealing with other subjects of a social, economic or intellectual character.

The migration of Spanish women to the New World seems to have been significant only in the sixteenth century, and few studies focus on that topic. Among them are Peter Boyd-Bowman, 'Patterns of Spanish emigration to the Indies until 1600', *HAHR*, 56/4 (1976), 580–604, Nancy O'Sullivan Beare, *Las mujeres de los conquistadores. La mujer española en los comienzos de la colonización americana. Aportaciones para el estudio de la transculturación* (Madrid, 1956), and Analola Borges, 'La mujer pobladora en los orígenes americanos', *Anuario de Estudios Americanos*, 29 (1972), 389–444. The values on and attitudes to women and the family prevalent in Spain and carried by both women and men to the Indies is a lateral theme in the history of Spanish America which, nonetheless, helps in understanding the formation of a new society. For such a purpose the following should be helpful: Ángel Valbuena Prat,

La vida española en la edad de oro (Barcelona, 1943); Antonio Domínguez Ortiz, *La sociedad española en el siglo XVII* (2 vols., Madrid, 1963); José Deleito Piñuela, *La mujer, la casa y la moda en la España del rey poeta* (Madrid, 1946). James Lockhart has explored the topic of the transfer of culture and the role of the first generation of Spanish women in the Indies in his *Spanish Peru, 1532–1560. A colonial society* (Madison, 1968).

The legal rights of all women in Spanish America were defined by Spanish legislation, which may be studied in Marcelo Martínez Alcubilla, *Códigos antiguos de España* (2 vols., Madrid, 1885) and José María Ots Capdequí, 'Bosquejo histórico de los derechos de la mujer en la legislación de Indias', *Revista General de Legislación y Jurisprudencia*, 132 (1918), 161–82; and in *El estado español en la Indias* (Mexico, 1946), 83–156. The general premises set up by Spanish legislation must be implemented by the *ad hoc* legislation issued by the crown throughout the colonial period to redress the human and economic problems created by the development of the overseas possessions. For that purpose, see Richard Konetzke (ed.), *Colección de documentos para la historia de la formación social de Hispanoamérica, 1493–1810* (3 vols., Madrid, 1953–62); Silvio Zavala, *El servicio personal de los indios en Perú* (2 vols., Mexico, 1978).

The deeds of several exceptional women form a body of anecdotal popular history which, although mostly descriptive, is useful to introduce the subject of women to beginners. In this category are Stella B. May, *The Conqueror's Lady* (New York, 1930) for Inés de Suárez, and Alejandro Vicuña, *Inés de Suárez* (Santiago, 1941); Nicolás León, *Adventuras de la monja alférez* (Mexico, 1973); Ventura García, *La Pericholi* (Paris, 1940); Mirta Aguirre, *Influencia de la mujer en Iberoamérica* (Havana, 1947). Although difficult to read, Benjamín Vicuña Mackenna, *Los Lispersguer y la Quintrala (Doña Catalina de los Ríos)* (Valparaíso, 1908) provides information on a truculent female figure and the complicated genealogical history of a Chilean family. The fascinating figure of Micaela Bastidas, wife of Tupac Amaru II, is well treated by Lillian E. Fisher, *The last Inca revolt, 1780–1783* (Norman, Okla., 1966) and Francisco A. Loayza (ed.), *Mártires y Heroínas* (Lima, 1945). The lion's share in bibliography and historical attention belongs to the outstanding poet, Sor Juana Inés de la Cruz, one of whose biographers offers an eleven-page bibliography on her. Among the better studies of Sor Juana are Anita Arroyo, *Razón y pasión de Sor Juana* (Mexico, 1971); Fanchon Royer, *The Tenth Muse: Sor Juana Inés de la Cruz* (Paterson, N.J.,

1952); Julio Jiménez Rueda, *Sor Juana Inés de la Cruz en su época* (Mexico, 1951).

A work by Judith Prieto de Zegarra, *Mujer, poder y desarrollo en el Perú* (2 vols., Lima, 1980) is a full-length study of women in Peru from Inca times to the end of the nineteenth century. Most new work is in the form of articles or chapters in books. A general treatment of some of the features of the history of women in New Spain is found in Asunción Lavrin, 'In search of the colonial woman in Mexico: the seventeenth and eighteenth centuries', in A. Lavrin (ed.), *Latin American women: historical perspectives* (Westport, 1978), 23–59. In the same volume Johanna S. R. Mendelson surveys the image of women and women's world as reflected in late colonial newspapers, in 'The feminine press: the view of women in the colonial journals of Spanish America, 1790–1810', 198–218.

Marriage and the family are topics critical to the study of women which have only been approached by a handful of researchers. The importance of marriage, family ties and kinship among the social elite is stressed by Doris Ladd in *The Mexican nobility at independence, 1780–1826* (Austin, 1976); Susan M. Socolow, *The merchants of Buenos Aires, 1778–1810* (Cambridge, 1978); and Stephanie Blank, 'Patrons, clients and kin in seventeenth-century Caracas: a methodological essay in colonial Spanish American social history', *HAHR*, 54/2 (1974), 260–83. Historical demographers are starting to make inroads into topics such as marriage patterns and fertility. Illustrative works are Susan M. Socolow, 'Marriage, birth, and inheritance: the merchants of eighteenth-century Buenos Aires', *HAHR*, 60/3 (1980), 387–406; Michael M. Swann, 'The spatial dimensions of a social process: marriage and mobility in late colonial northern Mexico', in David J. Robinson (ed.), *Social fabric and spatial structure in colonial Latin America* (Syracuse, N.Y., 1979); Silvia M. Arrom, 'Marriage patterns in Mexico City, 1811', *Journal of Family History*, 3/4 (1978), 376–91. John K. Chance, *Race and class in colonial Oaxaca* (Stanford, 1978) has useful information on marriage patterns and their influence on race relations. A general but brief overview of the meaning of the family in colonial Spanish America is provided by Elda R. González and Rolando Mellafe, 'La función de la familia en la historia social hispanoamericana colonial', *Anuario, Instituto de Investigaciones Históricas* (Universidad Nacional del Litoral, Santa Fe, Argentina), 8 (1965), 55–71. Studies of women within the family are rare. Edith Couturier's 'Women in a noble family: the Mexican Counts of Regla, 1750–1830', in Lavrin, *Latin American women*, 129–49 is one of the few attempts at this genre. Other studies explore the evolution of a family as a whole, highlighting but not focusing on its women. See, for example, Ida Altman, 'A family and region in the northern fringe lands: the Marqueses de Aguayo of Nuevo León and Coahuila', in Ida Altman and James Lockhart (eds.), *Provinces of early Mexico* (Berkeley and Los Angeles, 1976); Patricia Seed, 'A Mexican noble family; the Counts of the Orizaba Valley, 1560–1867', M.A. thesis, University of Texas, Austin, 1975; José Toribio Medina, *Los Errázuris. Notas biográficas y documentos para la historia de esta familia en Chile* (Santiago de Chile, 1964). Intimately related to the family, dowries and wills have been used as sources by Asunción Lavrin and Edith Couturier to delve into women's socio-economic power in colonial Mexico in 'Dowries and wills: a view of women's socio-economic role in colonial Guadalajara and Puebla, 1640–1790', *HAHR*, 59/2 (1979), 280–304.

The status and role of women in pre-Columbian societies, essential for understanding continuities and transformations during the colonial period, may be elicited from several of the available surveys of the major cultures. On the societies of the Aztecs and Incas, see *CHLA* 1, Bibliographical Essays 1 and 3. More specifically, Pedro Carrasco has written 'The joint family in ancient Mexico: the case of Molotla', in Hugo Mutini *et al.* (eds.), *Essays on Mexican kinship* (Pittsburgh, 1976). The predicament of indigenous women immediately after the conquest has been well documented and discussed by Elinor C. Burkett, 'Indian women and white society: the case of sixteenth-century Peru', in Lavrin, *Latin American Women*, 101–28, and William L. Sherman, *Forced labor in sixteenth-century Central America* (Lincoln, 1979). A comparison between the pre-Columbian and the twentieth-century Indian woman in Mexico is available in Anna-Brita Hellbom, *La participación cultural de las mujeres: Indias y mestizas en el México precortesiano y postrevolucionario* (Stockholm, 1967). For information on female slaves, see the works cited in *CHLA* 11, Bibliographical Essay 10, especially Miguel Acosta Saignes, *Vida de los esclavos negros en Venezuela* (Caracas, 1967). Also, Elinor Burkett, 'Early colonial Peru: the urban female experience', Ph.D. dissertation, University of Pittsburgh, 1975, chapter v, 'Black women and white society', 252–95.

Although the concept of formal education for women did not start to develop until the late colonial period, the concept of informal education and, later, the institutional approach to the formal education bear enquiry. The works of Spanish educators and philosophers have been mentioned in the notes. To those references may be added a Mexican educational novel, published in the early nineteenth century but representing the ideas of the last decades of the empire: José Joaquín Fernández de Lizardi, *La Quijotita y su prima* (Mexico, 1967), and a recent study of Luis Vives by G. Kaufman, 'Juan Luis Vives in the Education of Women', *Signs. Journal of Women in Culture and Society*, 3/4 (1978), 891–6. For the development of educational institutions, see Elisa Luque Alcaide, *La educación en Nueva España* (Sevilla, 1970), 163–204; Pablo Cabrera, *Cultura y beneficencia durante la colonia* (2nd edn, Córdoba, 1928); Gloria Carreño Alvarado, *El colegio de Santa Rosa de Santa María de Valladolid, 1743–1810* (Morelia, Michoacán, 1979).

With few exceptions female conventual life and related activities have been neglected by historians of the church. Thus, for information on that subject one must turn to older general histories of the church or monographs on the foundation and development of convents. A comprehensive work such as Antonio de Egaña, S.J., *Historia de la iglesia en la América española. Desde el descubrimiento hasta el S. XIX* (Madrid, 1966) offers a good start. Local histories are best reflected in less broad works. Fr Mariano Cuevas, S.J., *Historia de la iglesia en México* (5 vols., Mexico, 1921–8) is informative and biased, but has an overview of the female convents. Others are less complete, but still useful. See, for example, José Manuel Groot, *Historia eclesiástica y civil de Nueva Granada* (2 vols., Bogotá, 1869). Histories of the regular orders written during the colonial period also give information on the female convents. See, for example, Antonio de la Calancha and Bernardo Torres, O.S.A., *Crónicas Agustinianas del Perú* (2 vols., Madrid, 1972); Fr. Diego de Córdova Salinas, O.F.M., *Crónicas franciscanas de las provincias del Perú* (Washington, D.C., 1957); Fr. Alonso de Zamora, R.P., *Historia de la provincia de San Antonio del Nuevo Reino de Granada* (Caracas, 1930); Agustín Dávila Padilla, *Historia de la fundacion y discurso de la provincia de Santiago de México de la orden de predicadores* (3rd edn, Mexico, 1955). Colonial histories of nunneries are less numerous than the histories of religious orders. Two good examples are Ventura Travada, *El suelo de Arequipa convertido en cielo en el estreno del religioso monasterio de Santa Rosa de Santa María*, in Manuel Odriozola (ed.), *Documentos literarios del Perú*, x (Lima, 1877), 5–326; and Carlos Sigüenza y Góngora, *Paraíso occidental*

(Mexico, 1648), which deals with the convent of Jesús María in Mexico City. Despite the fact that all these sources have an overtly pious character, they are rich in detail and well reflect the spirit of the period in which they were written.

Most of the modern works on nunneries focus on New Spain. Josefina Muriel has written extensively on colonial women. Her better-known works are, *Conventos de monjas en la Nueva España* (Mexico, 1946) and *Los recogimientos de mujeres: Respuesta a una problemática novohispana* (Mexico, 1974), both of which are very informative. Indian nuns flourished in eighteenth-century New Spain and two works deal specifically with them: Josefina Muriel, *Las indias caciques de Mexico* (Mexico, 1963) and Sister Ann Mirian Gallagher, R.S.M., 'The Indian nuns of Mexico City's *monasterio* of Corpus Christi, 1724–1821', in Lavrin (ed.), *Latin American women*, 150–72. Sister Gallagher's doctoral dissertation 'The family background of the nuns of two *monasterios* in colonial Mexico: Santa Clara, Querétaro, and Corpus Christi, Mexico City (1724–1822)' (Catholic University of America, 1972) has valuable material originating in the archives of the nunneries themselves. As well as a doctoral dissertation focusing on eighteenth-century nunneries in general, 'Religious life of Mexican women in the 18th Century' (Harvard University, 1963), Asunción Lavrin has written several shorter works mostly on the socio-economic aspects of nunneries. Among them are 'The role of the nunneries in the economy of New Spain in the eighteenth century', *HAHR*, 46/3 (1966), 371–93; 'El convento de Santa Clara de Querétaro. La administración de sus propiedades en el siglo XVII', *HM*, 25/1 (1975), 76–117, and 'Women in convents: their economic and social role in colonial Mexico', in Bernice Carroll (ed.), *Liberating Women's History* (Urbana, 1976), 250–77.

A dissertation recently finished is the latest addition to the historical literature on colonial women. It is Patricia Seed, 'Parents vs. children. Marriage opposition in colonial Mexico, 1610–1779' (University of Wisconsin, 1980), and examines the historical record of conflicts between parents and children over the choice of marriage partners.

10. AFRICANS IN SPANISH AMERICAN COLONIAL SOCIETY

The past 30 or so years have witnessed a remarkable flowering in the study of slavery in colonial Spanish America. A survey of the literature, which was published scarcely a decade ago (Frederick P. Bowser,

'The African in colonial Spanish America: reflections on research achievements and priorities', *LARR*, 7 (1972), 77–94), though still useful, is already dated in many important particulars.

A clear picture of the trade in Africans to Spanish America, along with the most detailed and reliable estimate of the volume of the slave trade to appear in print, can be found in Philip D. Curtin, *The Atlantic slave trade: a census* (Madison, 1969). This work is not likely to be superseded for many years. The interested reader will also wish to consult Jorge Palacios, *La trata de negros por Cartagena de Indias* (Tunja, 1973); Enriqueta Vila Vilar, *Hispanoamérica en el comercio de esclavos* (Seville, 1977); Herbert S. Klein, *The Middle Passage: comparative studies in the Atlantic slave trade* (Princeton, 1977), and Colin A. Palmer, *Human cargoes: The British slave trade to Spanish America 1700–1739* (Urbana, 1981).

Two other works are indispensable: the monumental study of trade between Spain and America by Pierre and Huguette Chaunu, *Séville et l'Atlantique (1504–1650)* (8 vols. in 11, Paris, 1955–60), and the classic account by Georges Scelle, *La traite négrière aux Indes de Castille* (2 vols., Paris, 1906). But the reader should be warned. The Chaunus were more interested in Spanish commerce through Seville in general than in the intricacies of the slave trade, and their approach to the latter at times borders on the casual. For all its merits, the work of Scelle belongs to a different historiographical age; legalisms, useful though they are to know, dominate a consideration of economic realities.

As far as slavery in colonial Spanish America is concerned, Frank Tannenbaum's *Slave and citizen: the Negro in the Americas* (New York, 1947), discussed in the text, effected a scholarly revolution. Slavery, and the related subjects of manumission, abolition and race relations, became worthy of serious investigation and thought. Tannenbaum's thesis was further refined, though perhaps with an overemphasis on the United States, by Stanley Elkins in his *Slavery: a problem in American institutional and intellectual life* (Chicago, 1959), and in many respects received additional, and perhaps unexpected, support in the brilliant work of Eugene D. Genovese, *The world the slaveholders made* (New York, 1969), a Marxian analysis of slavery in the western hemisphere tinged with a delightful bent towards the aristocratic. (An admirable corrective to the work of Elkins is to be found in the review by Sidney Mintz, *American Anthropologist*, 63 (1961), 579–87.) See also the thoughtful work of David Brion Davis, with its analysis of the moral justifications of slavery, in *The problem of slavery in Western culture* (Ithaca, 1966); reprinted in E. Genovese and Laura Foner, *Slavery in the New World: a reader in comparative history* (Englewood Cliffs, 1969).

Despite growing interest in the history of slavery in colonial Spanish America, general surveys remain few. The classic study is José Antonio Saco, *Historia de la esclavitud de la raza africana en el Nuevo Mundo y en especial en los países américo-hispanos* (4 vols., Havana, 1938), but the work reveals more about the prejudices of a Cuban seeking independence from Spain than it does about slavery during the *colonia*. At present, the most useful account is by Leslie B. Rout, Jr., *The African experience in Spanish America, 1502 to the present day* (Cambridge, 1976). See also Rolando Mellafe, *La esclavitud en Hispanoamérica* (Buenos Aires, 1972); Eng. trans. *Negro slavery in Latin America* (Berkeley and Los Angeles, 1975). On slave revolts, Richard Price, *Maroon societies. Rebel slave communities in the Americas* (New York, 1973), and Vera Rubin and A. Tuden (eds.), *Comparative perspectives on slavery in New World plantation societies* (New York, 1977), section VI.

Over the past 30 years the most spectacular advances in our knowledge of colonial Spanish American slavery have been made in regional studies. For Mexico, the work of Colin A. Palmer, *Slaves of the white God: blacks in Mexico, 1570–1650* (Cambridge, Mass., 1976) evokes in fine fashion the realities of slavery in that colony during its zenith, and largely replaces in utility the pioneering work of Gonzalo Aguirre Beltrán, *La población negra de México, 1519–1810* (2nd edn, Mexico, 1972) though the latter can still be read with profit for the late colonial period. Also worthy of mention is the work of Ward Barrett, *The sugar hacienda of the Marqueses del Valle* (Minneapolis, 1970), a thoughtful and beautifully detailed study of the operations of the Cortés estate and the role of slavery as a labour source. Reference should also be made to David M. Davidson, 'Negro slave control and resistance in colonial Mexico, 1519–1650', *HAHR*, 46 (1966), 235–53, perhaps the best account in print of the phenomenon of *cimarronaje* and Spanish attempts to deal with it.

For Peru, the splendid researches of James Lockhart, *Spanish Peru, 1532–1560: a colonial society* (Madison, 1968), have been supplemented and expanded by Frederick P. Bowser, *The African slave in colonial Peru, 1524–1650* (Stanford, 1974). Both accounts rely heavily and profitably on notarial records. See also Nicholas P. Cushner, 'Slave mortality and reproduction in Jesuit haciendas in colonial Peru', *HAHR*, 55 (1975), 175–99.

Cuba has also received an impressive amount of scholarly attention. The seminal works of Fernando Ortiz Fernández, especially *Hampa afro-cubana: los negros esclavos* (Havana, 1916), may now be read in conjunction with studies of more detailed scholarship written from a different perspective. Foremost among these is Franklin W. Knight, *Slave society in Cuba during the nineteenth century* (Madison, 1970), which provides profound insights into the role of sugar and slavery in the transformation of the socio-economic structure of the island. (By the same author, see also 'Origins of wealth and the sugar revolution in Cuba, 1750–1850', *HAHR*, 57 (1977), 231–53.) An interesting contrast is the work of Herbert S. Klein, *Slavery in the Americas: a comparative study of Virginia and Cuba* (Chicago, 1967), which attempts to put the Tannenbaum thesis into practice at the level of detailed research. See also Gwendolyn M. Hall, *Social control in slave plantation societies. A comparison of St. Domingue and Cuba* (Baltimore, 1971). The nineteenth-century Cuban slave trade and the political agonies of its abolition have been detailed by Arthur F. Corwin, *Spain and the abolition of slavery in Cuba, 1817–1886* (Austin, 1967) and David Murray, *Odious commerce. Britain, Spain and the abolition of the Cuban slave trade* (Cambridge, 1980).

Though slavery was less important as a source of labour on the sister island of Puerto Rico, an account of its significance is still curiously lacking. In the interim, the reader is referred to Luis M. Díaz Soler, *Historia de la esclavitud en Puerto Rico, 1493–1890* (2nd edn, Río Piedras, 1965), and Sidney Mintz, 'Labour and sugar in Puerto Rico and in Jamaica, 1800–1850', *Comparative Studies in Society and History*, 1 (1959), 273–80.

For Colombia, a welcome and significant book has recently appeared by William Frederick Sharp, *Slavery on the Spanish frontier: the Colombian Chocó, 1680–1810* (Norman, 1976) which details the all-important role of blacks in the gold-mining operations of that colony in an area which to this date retains a striking degree of underdevelopment. In his preface (p. ix) Sharp lists other useful works on slavery in Colombia, but two should be accorded mention here: the overview by James F. King, 'Negro slavery in New Granada', in *Greater America: essays in honor of Herbert Eugene Bolton* (Berkeley, 1945), and Jaime Jaramillo Uribe, 'Esclavos y señores en la sociedad colombiana del siglo XVIII', *Anuario*

Colombiano de Historia Social y de la Cultura, 1 (1963), 3–55. See also David Chandler, 'Family bonds and the bondsman. The slave family in colonial Colombia', *LARR*, 16 (1981).

Two works are of paramount importance for the student of Venezuelan slavery: Miguel Acosta Saignes, *Vida de los esclavos en Venezuela* (Caracas, 1967), and John V. Lombardi, *The decline and abolition of Negro slavery in Venezuela* (Westport, 1971), perhaps the finest account in print of the emancipation process in Spanish America. See also Lombardi's *People and places in colonial Venezuela* (Bloomington, 1976), and Robert Ferry, 'Encomienda, African slavery and agriculture in seventeenth-century Caracas', *HAHR*, 61/4 (1981), 609–35.

A general account of black slavery in Argentina is still lacking, but several notable monographs should be mentioned: Emiliano Endrek, *El mestizaje en Córdoba: siglo XVIII y principios del XIX* (Córdoba, 1966); Ceferino Garzón Maceda and José Walter Dorflinger, 'Esclavos y mulatos en un dominio rural del siglo XVIII en Córdoba', *Revista de la Universidad Nacional de Córdoba*, II, 2nd series (1961), 627–40; Lyman L. Johnson, 'Manumission in colonial Buenos Aires 1776–1810', *HAHR*, 59/2 (1979), 258–79; Jose Luis Masini, *La esclavitud negra en Mendoza* (Mendoza, 1962); and Elena F. Scheüss de Studer, *La trata de negros en el Río de la Plata durante el siglo XVIII* (Buenos Aires, 1958).

African slavery in Chile likewise awaits its historian, but note should be made of two works: Rolando Mellafe, *La introducción de la esclavitud negra en Chile: tráfico y rutas* (Santiago de Chile, 1959); and Gonzalo Vial Correa, *El africano en el reino de Chile: ensayo histórico-jurídico* (Santiago de Chile, 1957).

Slavery in the other regions of Spanish America has yet to receive deserved attention, but the most important titles are listed below. Beyond categorization but well worth reading is Paulo de Carvalho Neto, *Estudios afros: Brasil–Paraguay–Uruguay–Ecuador* (Caracas, 1971). Taken by area, the following titles are of significance:

Bolivia: Inge Wolff, 'Negersklaverei und Negerhandel in Hochperu 1545–1640', *JGSWGL*, 1 (1964), 157–86.

Panama and Central America: Alfredo Castillero Calvo, *La sociedad panameña: historia de su formación e integración* (Panama, 1970); Quince Duncan and Carlos Meléndez, *El negro en Costa Rica* (San José, 1972); Oscar R. Aguilar, 'La esclavitud en Costa Rica durante el período colonial (hipótesis del trabajo)', *Estudios Sociales Centroamericanos*, 5 (1973), 187–99.

Ecuador: Julio Estupiñan Tello, *El negro en Esmeraldas: apuntes para su estudio* (Quito, 1967).

Dominican Republic: Franklyn J. Franco Pichardo, *Los negros, los mulatos y la nación dominicana* (2nd edn, Santo Domingo, 1970); and Carlos Larrazábal Blanco, *Los negros y la esclavitud en Santo Domingo* (Santo Domingo, 1967).

Paraguay: Josefina Plá, *Hermano negro: la esclavitud en el Paraguay* (Madrid, 1972).

Uruguay: Ildefonso Pereda Valdés, 'El negro en el Uruguay', *Revista del Instituto Histórico y Geográfico del Uruguay*, 25 (1965).

In general, information concerning slavery in colonial Spanish America has been drawn from the titles cited above, but works on two specialized topics deserve citation. The first of these is manumission and the role of free blacks in Spanish America, and the reader may wish to consult the following titles: Frederick P. Bowser, 'Colonial Spanish America', in David W. Cohen and Jack P. Greene (eds.), *Neither slave nor free: the freedman of African descent in the slave societies of the New World* (Baltimore, 1972); Bowser, 'The free person of color in Mexico City and Lima: manumission and opportunity, 1580–1650', in Stanley L. Engerman and Eugene D. Genovese (eds.), *Race and slavery in the western hemisphere: quantitative studies* (Princeton, 1975), 331–68; Alan Kuethe, 'The status of the free pardo in the disciplined militia of New Granada', *The Journal of Negro History*, 56 (1971), 105–18; and Magnus Mörner, *Race mixture in the history of Latin America* (Boston, 1968).

Second, the problem of slave discontent and rebellion requires mention of two impressive works that transcend area: Eugene D. Genovese, *From rebellion to revolution* (Baton Rouge, 1979), a series of lectures that explores the topic in hemispheric perspective; and Carlos Federico Guillot, *Negros rebeldes y negros cimarrones: perfil afroamericano en la historia del Nuevo Mundo durante el siglo XVI* (Buenos Aires, 1961).

II. INDIAN SOCIETIES UNDER SPANISH RULE

A bibliography of Spanish American ethnohistory up to 1967, by Howard F. Cline, is contained in section B, pp. 117–48, of Charles C. Griffin (ed.), *Latin America. A guide to the historical literature* (Austin, 1971). The section provides references to some 300 basic works relating to both pre- and post-Columbian ethnohistory, with evaluative commentary. Many of the entries are original in the *Guide*. Others are taken from the *Handbook of Latin American Studies*, which initiated a section on the ethnohistory of Mesoamerica by Henry B. Nicholson in no. 22 (1960), and a section on the ethnohistory of South America by John V. Murra in no. 29 (1967). The *Handbook of Latin American Studies* is the foremost bibliographical work for continuing reference. The sections on ethnohistory are now published as part of the Humanities volumes, issued every other year. The student should note that works bearing on Indian history in the colonial period may sometimes be found in sections other than Ethnohistory, especially in History and Ethnology.

A major work of reference for the ethnohistory and particularly the ethnohistorical bibliography of Mesoamerica is the *Guide to ethnohistorical sources*, which comprises the four final volumes (12–15) of Robert Wauchope (ed.), *Handbook of Middle American Indians* (Austin, 1964–75). The four volumes were edited by Howard Cline and they contain articles on the relevant bibliographical materials, the *Relaciones geográficas*, the chronicles and their authors, the pictorial manuscripts (codices), materials in the native and in the European traditions, and much else. There is no comparable guide to the ethnohistorical source material of South America, but two summary articles survey the bibliography and the current state of research: John V. Murra, 'Current research and prospects in Andean ethnohistory', *LARR*, 5 (1970), 3–36, and Karen Spalding, 'The colonial Indian: past and future research perspectives', *LARR*, 7 (1972), 47–76.

Basic works on Spanish institutional controls over Indians include Clarence Haring, *The Spanish empire in America* (revised edn, New York, 1963), which is still the most satisfactory one-volume general summary, and a series of writings on special topics: Alberto Mario Salas, *Las armas de la conquista* (Buenos Aires, 1950) on conquest, warfare, and weapons; Silvio Zavala, *La encomienda indiana* (Madrid, 1935) and *Las instituciones jurídicas en la conquista de América* (Madrid, 1935; revised edn, 1971); L. B. Simpson, *The encomienda in New Spain* (revised edn, 1950); Guillermo Lohmann Villena, *El corregidor de indios en el Peru bajo los Austrias* (Madrid, 1957); Constantino Bayle, *Los cabildos seculares en la América española* (Madrid, 1952); and many others. Peter Gerhard, *A guide to the historical geography of New Spain* (Cambridge, 1972) is fundamental for the history of encomiendas, corregimientos, town foundations, and local institutions and events. Special note should be taken of Lewis Hanke, *The Spanish struggle for justice in the conquest of*

America (Philadelphia, 1949), on the campaign for fair treatment of Indians, and of Edward H. Spicer, *Cycles of conquest. The impact of Spain, Mexico and the United States on the Indians of the South-West 1533–1960* (Tucson, 1962), an examination of white–Indian contacts in northern Mexico and the south-west of the United States.

The classic treatment of Indian conversion in Mexico to the 1570s is Robert Ricard, *La 'conquête spirituelle' du Mexique* (Paris, 1933; also in Spanish and English translation). The historical literature on northern Mexican and borderlands missions is too extensive to summarize here. For South America see especially Fernando de Armas Medina, *Cristianización del Perú* (1952); Antonine Tibesar, *Franciscan beginnings in colonial Peru (1532–1600)* (Seville, 1953); and Pierre Duviols, *La lutte contre les religions autochtones dans le Pérou coloniale. 'L'extirpation de l'idolâtrie' entre 1532 et 1660* (Lima, 1971).

Important writings on tribute, land and labour, largely from the Spanish administrative point of view, are José Miranda, *El tributo indígena en la Nueva España durante el siglo XVI* (Mexico, 1952); L. B. Simpson, *Exploitation of land in central Mexico in the sixteenth century* (Berkeley and Los Angeles, 1952); François Chevalier, *La formation des grands domaines au Mexique. Terre et société aux XVIe–XVIIe siècles* (Paris, 1952; also in Spanish and English translations); and the series of introductions to the volumes of Silvio A. Zavala and María Costelo (eds.), *Fuentes para la historia del trabajo en Nueva España* (8 vols., Mexico, 1939– 46). All relate to Mexico, and again there are no comparable studies for South America. An important recent work on the hacienda in Peru is Robert G. Keith, *Conquest and agrarian change. The emergence of the hacienda system on the Peruvian coast* (Cambridge, Mass., 1976). A general survey of labour is Juan A. and Judith E. Villamarín, *Indian labor in mainland colonial Spanish America* (Newark, Delaware, 1975). On relations between Spaniards and Indians the article by Elman R. Service, 'Indian–European relations in colonial Latin America', *American Anthropologist*, 57 (1955), 411–25, and the general treatment by Magnus Mörner, *Race mixture in the history of Latin America* (Boston, 1967), are worthy of attention.

The study of Indian society under colonial conditions owes much to the seminal work of the California demographers L. B. Simpson, Sherburne F. Cook and Woodrow Borah, beginning in the 1940s and continuing to the present, and published principally in the Ibero-Americana series. See Bibliographical Essay 1, above. Borah especially has developed the original demographic materials in studies of Indian social organization, tribute payment, labour and prices. Pioneering work in the analysis of Nahuatl texts and codices for what they yield on Indian social structure and social history has been accomplished by Pedro Carrasco, Joaquín Galarza, Hanns J. Prem and others. Frances Karttunen and James Lockhart have also examined the colonial history of the Nahuatl language in *Nahuatl in the middle years. Language contact phenomena in texts of the colonial period* (Berkeley and Los Angeles, 1976). Treatments of colonial Indian society in particular areas of Mexico include Delfina López Sarrelangue, *La nobleza indígena de Patzcuaro en la época virreinal* (Mexico, 1965); Charles Gibson, *Tlaxcala in the sixteenth century* (New Haven, 1952) and *The Aztecs under Spanish rule* (Stanford, 1964); William B. Taylor, *Landlord and peasant in colonial Oaxaca* (Stanford, 1972) and *Drinking, homicide and rebellion in colonial Mexican villages* (Stanford, 1979); Ronald Spores, *The Mixtec kings and their people* (Norman, Oklahoma, 1967); and the collection of studies edited by Ida Altman and James Lockhart, *Provinces of early Mexico* (Berkeley and Los Angeles, 1976).

In South America comparable work began later and the studies are not so far advanced as in Mexico, but current research is making rapid headway. A pioneering survey was George Kubler, 'The Quechua in the colonial world' in vol. II (1946) of the *Handbook of South American Indians*, ed. Julian H. Steward. Most of the recent contributions are in the form of specialized articles. But see Nathan Wachtel, *La vision des vaincus* (Paris, 1971; also in English translation), a wide-ranging, imaginative, structuralist analysis of Indian life and thought in Peru. Articles and special studies by Waldemar Espinosa Soriano, Alvaro Jara, Udo Oberen, María Rostworowski de Diez Canseco and Karen Spalding examine Indian social organization, labour, *curacas*, *visitas*, *señoríos* and related topics, especially for the sixteenth century.

12. COLONIAL BRAZIL, *c.* 1580–*c.* 1750: PLANTATIONS AND PERIPHERIES

Guides, general histories, collections

The works of José Honório Rodrigues are fundamental tools. *Historiografía del Brasil, siglo XVI* (Mexico, 1957) and *Historiografía del Brasil, siglo XVII* (Mexico, 1963) discuss the major sources. *História da história do Brasil*, 1: *Historiografia colonial* (São Paulo, 1979) covers the eighteenth century as well. The sources and scholarship in English are contained with annotations in Francis A. Dutra, *A guide to the history of Brazil, 1500–1822* (Santa Barbara, 1980). Rubens Borba de Moraes, *Bibliografia brasileira do período colonial* (São Paulo, 1969) is a catalogue of works by Brazilians published before 1808. A good specialized bibliography is Robert Conrad, *Brazilian slavery: an annotated research bibliography* (Boston, 1977).

Sérgio Buarque de Holanda (ed.), *História geral da civilização brasileira, I A época colonial* (2 vols., São Paulo, 1960) provides a succinct survey of major themes. Pedro Calmon, *História do Brasil* (7 vols., Rio de Janeiro, 1959) has the most detailed colonial sections of the many modern histories. The classic *História geral do Brasil* (6 vols.; 7th edn, São Paulo, 1962) by Francisco Adolfo de Varnhagen, originally published in 1857, is still valuable. Together, C. R. Boxer's *Salvador de Sá and the struggle for Brazil and Angola, 1602–1686* (London, 1952), and his *The Golden Age of Brazil, 1695–1750* (Berkeley and Los Angeles, 1964) provide the best available overview in English of Brazilian history for the period. Frédéric Mauro, *Le Brésil du XVᵉ à la fin du XVIIIᵉ siècle* (Paris, 1977) is a brief survey based on recent scholarship. Dauril Alden (ed.), *Colonial roots of modern Brazil* (Berkeley and Los Angeles, 1973) presents an important collection of papers on colonial themes. A. J. R. Russell-Wood (ed.), *From colony to nation* (Baltimore, 1975), is primarily concerned with the post-1750 period but does have a number of articles pertinent to the earlier era. The *Anais do Congresso Comemorativo do Bicentenário da Transferência da Sede do Governo do Brasil* (4 vols., Rio de Janeiro, 1966), contains many items of interest, as do the various publications of the Luso-Brazilian Colloquium (1st Proceedings or *Actas* published in Nashville, 1953).

Government and economy

The structure of Portuguese government in Brazil is summarized in Eulália Maria Lahmeyer Lobo, *Processo administrativo Ibero-Americano* (Rio de Janeiro, 1962). Dauril Alden, *Royal government in colonial Brazil* (Berkeley and Los Angeles, 1968), contains much useful material. Stuart B. Schwartz, *Sovereignty and society in colonial Brazil* (Berkeley and Los Angeles, 1973), discusses the judicial structure of the colony. A useful collection of royal instructions is Marcos Carneiro de Mendonça, *Raízes da formação administrativa do Brasil* (2 vols., Rio de Janeiro, 1972). A provocative interpretative essay that touches on the early colonial era is Raymundo Faoro, *Os donos do poder* (1st edn, Rio de Janeiro, 1958). Other works on the organs of colonial government in Portugal itself are cited in *CHLA* 1, Bibliographical Essay 12.

General studies of the colonial economy are few. Frédéric Mauro's invaluable *Portugal et l'Atlantique* (Paris, 1960) is an essential quantitative study of Brazil within the Atlantic system. For other works on the Atlantic economy, again see *CHLA* 1, Bibliographical Essay 12. Mauro has also published important collections of essays such as *Nova história e nôvo mundo* (São Paulo, 1969). Roberto Simonsen, *História económica do Brasil* (São Paulo, 1937) is still valuable although many of the figures presented need revision. A number of volumes by Mircea Buescu, such as his *300 anos da inflação* (Rio de Janeiro, 1973), make good use of colonial economic data. The synthesis of Caio Prado Júnior, *Colonial background* (see *CHLA* II, Bibliographical Essay 15) and Celso Furtado, *The economic growth of Brazil* (Berkeley and Los Angeles, 1963) provide excellent overviews. Especially provocative is Fernando Novais, *Estrutura e dinâmica do sistema colonial* (Lisbon, 1975) which has also appeared in a Brazilian edition.

Various economic activities have received monographic attention, although the record here is spotty. A major difficulty that the chapter reflects is a lack of serial economic data for the period prior to 1750. There are no adequate studies of manioc- or tobacco-farming for this period. A good study of the ranching society in the north-east is provided by Luiz Mott, 'Fazendas de gado do Piauí (1697–1762)', *Anais do VII Simpósio Nacional de Professores Universitários de História* (São Paulo, 1976), 343–69. On this topic Lycurgo Santos Filho, *Uma comunidade rural no Brasil antigo* (São Paulo, 1956), is also useful. The best single monograph on sugar is Wanderley Pinho, *História de um engenho no Recôncavo* (Rio de Janeiro, 1946). Unfortunately, similar studies do not exist for the engenhos of Rio de Janeiro and Pernambuco. António Barros de Castro, 'Escravos e senhores nos engenhos do Brasil' (Ph.D. thesis, University of Campinas, 1976), is an excellent overview based on printed primary sources. Still indispensable for any study of the colonial economy is André João Antonil (pseudonym of Antonio Giovanni Andreoni, S.J.), *Cultura e opulência do Brasil por suas drogas e minas* (Lisbon, 1711), a work whose value has been greatly increased by the notes and introduction provided by Andrée Mansuy in the Paris edition of 1968. Myriam Ellis has contributed solid studies such as *Aspectos da pesca da baleia no Brasil colonial* (São Paulo, 1958), and Alice P. Canabrava's analysis of Brazilian trade in the Río de la Plata, *O comércio português no Rio da Prata, 1580–1640* (São Paulo, 1944) remains essential reading.

Slavery

A lively debate is being conducted in Brazil over the nature of the colonial economy and the role of slavery within it. Jacob Gorender, *O escravismo colonial* (São Paulo, 1978) is a major statement based on a wide reading of printed sources. It has produced considerable reaction as is demonstrated in the group of essays in José Roberto do Amaral Lapa (ed.), *Modos do produção e realidade brasileira* (Petrópolis, 1980). An earlier essay by Ciro Flamarion S. Cardoso, 'El modo de producción esclavista colonial en América', in *Modos de producción en América Latina* (Buenos Aires, 1973), is still an important theoretical formulation of the problem.

The form of labour and its relation to the social and economic structures of the colony has been a major theme in Brazilian history. The most complete study of Portuguese Indian policy is Georg Thomas, *Die portugiesische Indianerpolitik in Brasilien, 1500–1640* (Berlin, 1968), but it should be used in conjunction with Kieman's book on Indian policy in the Amazon (cited below) and with the works of Father Serafim Leite on the Jesuits. John Hemming, *Red gold. The conquest of the Brazilian Indians 1500–1760* (London, 1978) is a well-written narrative account. Stuart B. Schwartz, 'Indian labor and New World plantations: European demands and Indian responses in northeastern Brazil', *American Historical Review*, 83/1 (February 1978), 43–79, deals with Bahia, but studies of other regions are sorely needed.

Despite the centrality of African slavery to colonial Brazil, the coverage of the topic is very uneven. To some extent this is a problem of sources available for the pre-1750 period. Some of the best books about slavery in Brazil often have little information on the early colonial period and are forced to infer the previous history. Such is the case with Gilberto Freyre's classic, *The masters and the slaves* (New York, 1946), originally published in 1933 in Brazil. Present concerns have also oriented research. Thus, we have a large and growing literature on slave resistance and especially Palmares as is represented by Edison Carneiro, *O quilombo dos Palmares* (3rd edn, Rio de Janeiro, 1966), but little on the early slave trade. On that topic Maurício Goulart, *A escravidão africana no Brasil* (São Paulo, 1949) is still a good starting point.

Portuguese attitudes towards slavery have been studied by A. J. R. Russell-Wood, 'Iberian expansion and the issue of black slavery', *American Historical Review*, 83/1 (February 1978), 16–42, and David Sweet, 'Black robes and black destiny: Jesuit views of African slavery in 17th-century Latin America', *RHA*, 86 (July–December 1978), 87–133; but many other issues need investigation. Questions concerning the profitability, demography, family structure and internal organization of Brazilian slavery in this period all remain to be studied. An example of what can be done is provided by Francisco Vidal Luna, *Minas Gerais: Escravos e senhores* (São Paulo, 1981), an essentially quantitative study of slave ownership. On slave culture, Roger Bastide, *The African religions of Brazil* (Baltimore, 1978) remains the essential introduction. A useful popular survey that incorporates the best recent scholarship is Katia M. de Queiros Mattoso, *Être esclave au Brésil XVIe–XIXe siècle* (Paris, 1979).

Social aspects

In some ways the literature on free people of colour and race relations is better developed than that on slavery itself. A. J. R. Russell-Wood, 'Colonial Brazil', in David W. Cohen and Jack P. Greene (eds.), *Neither slave nor free: the freedman of African descent in the slave societies of the New World* (Baltimore, 1972), incorporates much of the author's own work and follows the approach of Charles R. Boxer, *Race relations in the Portuguese colonial empire* (Oxford, 1963). Stuart Schwartz, 'The manumission of slaves in colonial Brazil: Bahia 1684–1745' (*HAHR*, 54/4 (1974), 603–65) is a quantitative study. A. J. R. Russell-Wood, 'Black and mulatto brotherhoods in colonial Brazil', *HAHR*, 54/4 (1974), 567–602, is a good general discussion, but it should be used together with Patricia Mulvey, 'The black lay brotherhoods of colonial Brazil: a history' (Ph.D. thesis, City University of New York, 1976), and Manoel S. Cardozo, 'The lay brotherhoods of colonial Bahia', *The Catholic Historical Review*, 33/1 (April 1947), 12–30.

Social change and social groups before 1750 have received little attention. Francis Dutra has produced a number of studies of institutional response to social change of which 'Membership in the Order of Christ in the seventeenth century', *The Americas*, 27/1 (July 1970), 3–25, is a good example. The role of women remains mostly unstudied except for chapters by Susan Soeiro and A. J. R. Russell-Wood in Asunción Lavrin (ed.), *Latin American women: historical perspectives* (Westport, 1978), 60–100, 173–97. Various social groups have been best studied in Bahia (see below), but many important topics need to be examined. We have, for example, no studies of wage labourers or artisan organizations in the early period.

One social group, the New Christians, has received extensive treatment. Arnold Wiznitzer, *The Jews in colonial Brazil* (New York, 1960), is a general study. Anita Novinsky, *Cristãos novos na Bahia* (São Paulo, 1972) brings a great deal of new material into the debate about the Judaism of the New Christians. Regional studies like José Gonçalves Salvador, *Os cristãos-novos. Povoamento e conquista do solo brasileiro* (São Paulo, 1976), on the southern captaincies, and the excellent piece by Gonsalves de Mello, 'A nação judaica do Brasil holandês', *Revista do Instituto Arqueológico, Histórico e Geográfico de Pernambuco* [*RIAHGP*], 49 (1977), 229–393, on Pernambuco, have deepened our understanding of their story. The history of the New Christians was intimately, if unfortunately, tied to that of the Inquisition. A good recent study of that institution and especially of its structure and operation is Sónia A. Siqueira, *A inquisição portuguesa e a sociedade colonial* (São Paulo, 1978).

On the Brazilian cities and towns, the fundamental work is Nestor Goulart Reis Filho, *Evolução urbana do Brasil (1500–1720)* (São Paulo, 1968). Also useful are Edmundo Zenha, *O município no Brasil* (São Paulo, 1948), and Nelson Omegna, *A cidade colonial* (Rio de Janeiro, 1961). A recent thesis with emphasis on the late colonial era is Roberta Marx Delson, 'Town planning in colonial Brazil' (Ph.D. thesis, Columbia University, 1975). An excellent interpretative essay is Richard M. Morse, 'Brazil's urban development: colony and empire', in Russell-Wood, *From colony to nation*, 155–81.

Regional studies

The historiography of the period before 1750 is regionally unbalanced. Bahia has received far more attention than other areas. Thus, many generalizations contained in the chapter are based on findings for Bahia which remain to be demonstrated for other areas.

For Bahia there are excellent social and institutional studies. A. J. R. Russell-Wood, *Fidalgos and philanthropists* (Berkeley and Los Angeles, 1968), studies the Misericórdia. Susan Soeiro, 'A baroque nunnery: the economic and social role of a colonial convent: Santa Clara de Desterro, Salvador, Bahia, 1677–1800' (Ph.D. thesis, New York University, 1974), is good on women in society and the financial role of that institution. C. R. Boxer's chapter on the câmara of Salvador in *Portuguese society in the tropics* (Madison, 1965) is particularly valuable. David G. Smith, 'The mercantile class of Portugal and Brazil in the seventeenth century: a socio-economic study of the merchants of Lisbon and Bahia, 1620–1690' (Ph.D. thesis, University of Texas, 1975), is the most thorough study of merchants. Rae Flory, 'Bahian society in the mid-colonial period: the sugar planters, tobacco growers, merchants, and artisans of Salvador and the Recôncavo, 1680–1725' (Ph.D. thesis, University of Texas, 1978), is based on notarial records. Stuart B. Schwartz, 'Free farmers in a slave economy: the *lavradores de cana* of colonial Bahia', in Alden (ed.), *Colonial roots*, 147–97, looks at that group based on plantation records. José Roberto do Amaral Lapa, *A Bahia e a carreira da Índia* (São Paulo, 1968), deals with Salvador as a port and shipyard. Thales de Azevedo, *Povoamento da Cidade do Salvador* (3rd edn, Bahia, 1968), and Afonso Ruy, *História política e administrativa da cidade do Salvador* (Bahia, 1949), are still invaluable.

For Pernambuco and its adjacent areas the situation is in general much worse. José Antônio Gonsalves de Mello has done much in *RIAHGP* to rectify this situation. Also valuable is Francis A. Dutra, *Matias de Albuquerque* (Recife, 1976). On the war of the Mascates, see Norma Marinovic Doro, 'Guerra dos Mascates – 1710' (Master's thesis, University of São Paulo, 1979), and J. A. Gonsalves de Mello's excellent 'Nobres e mascates na câmara de Recife', *RIAHGP* (forthcoming).

The best recent scholarship on the Dutch occupation of the north-east is represented by C. R. Boxer's *The Dutch in Brazil, 1624–54* (Oxford, 1957) on military and political affairs; José Antônio Gonsalves de Mello, *Tempo dos Flamengos* (2nd edn, Recife, 1978), on social matters; and Evaldo Cabral de Mello, *Olinda Restaurada* (São Paulo, 1975), on the economy. These works incorporate the earlier classic studies. In addition, the above authors have all edited important documents of the period. Representative of them and extremely valuable is J. A. Gonsalves de Mello (ed.), *Relatório sôbre as capitanias conquistadas* by Adriaen van der Dussen (Rio de Janeiro, 1947). E. van den Boogaart (ed.), *Johan Maurits van Nassau-Siegen, 1604–1679* (The Hague, 1979), presents recent Dutch and Brazilian scholarship on the period.

Modern social and economic history on Rio de Janeiro before 1750 is virtually nonexistent. Joaquim Veríssimo Serrão, *O Rio de Janeiro no século XVI* (2 vols., Lisbon, 1965), is valuable for the documents it reproduces. Vivaldo Coaracy, *O Rio de Janeiro no século XVII* (2nd edn, Rio de Janeiro, 1965), contains useful information. The many works of Alberto Lamego on the sugar economy of Rio de Janeiro were extensively used by William Harrison, in 'A struggle for land in colonial Brazil: the private captaincy of Paraiba do Sul, 1533–1753' (Ph.D. thesis, University of New Mexico, 1970), but much remains to be done.

There is an extensive historiography on São Paulo, although much of it concentrates on the exploits of the bandeiras and was written prior to 1950, thus reflecting older historical concerns. A provocative essay on the early history of São Paulo is Florestan Fernandes, *Mudanças sociais no Brasil* (São Paulo, 1960), 179–233. There are a number of histories of the region of which Afonso d'Escragnolle Taunay, *História seiscentista da Vila de São Paulo* (4 vols., São Paulo, 1926–9) is the most thorough. Taunay is also the dean of bandeira studies, and his *História geral das bandeiras paulistas* (11 vols., São Paulo, 1924–50), is the basic study. Alfredo Ellis Júnior, *Meio século de bandeirismo* (São Paulo, 1948) and Jaime Cortesão, *Rapôso Tavares e a formação territorial do Brasil* (Rio de Janeiro, 1958) are standard works by other specialists. There has been in recent years considerable interest in the society of São Paulo in the period after 1750, but for the early times the literature is limited. Alcântara Machado, *Vida e morte do bandeirante* (São Paulo, 1930), uses the series *Inventários e testamentos* (São Paulo, 1920–) to evoke everyday life. The works of Sérgio Buarque de Holanda, such as *Caminhos e fronteiras* (Rio de Janeiro, 1957) and *Visão do paraíso* (Rio de Janeiro, 1959), are indispensable. Richard M. Morse (ed.), *The Bandeirantes: the historical role of the Brazilian pathfinders* (New York, 1965) presents excerpts from many important works. Suggestive essays are contained in Jaime Cortesão's *Introdução à história das bandeiras* (2 vols., Lisbon, 1964).

On the extreme south, José Honório Rodrigues, *O continente do Rio Grande* (Rio de Janeiro, 1954) provides a succinct essay. Guillermino César, *História do Rio Grande so Sul* (Pôrto Alegre, 1970) has interesting social information. Dauril Alden, *Royal government*, provides the best summary in English.

For the Brazilian north prior to 1750 the bibliography is not large. J. Lúcio de Azevedo, *Os Jesuitas no Grão-Pará: suas missões e a colonização* (Coimbra, 1930) is still valuable. Mathias Kieman, *The Indian policy of Portugal in the Amazon region, 1614–1693* (Washington, D.C., 1954) remains indispensable. Artur Cezar Ferreira Reis, *História do Amazonas* (Manaus, 1935) is representative of his many works on the region. João Francisco Lisboa's *Crônica do Brasil Colonial: Apontamentos para a história do Maranhão* (Petropolis, 1976), is a republication of an earlier and still useful work. Two articles by Colin MacLachlan, 'The Indian labor structure in the Portuguese Amazon', in Alden, *Colonial Roots*, 199–230, and 'African slave trade and economic development in Amazonia, 1700–1800', in Robert Toplin (ed.), *Slavery and Race Relations in Latin America* (Westport, Conn., 1974), 112–45, are useful. On the economy, Sue Ellen Anderson Gross, 'The economic life of the Estado do Maranhão e Grão-Pará, 1686–1751' (Ph.D. thesis, Tulane University, 1969) provides a survey. Dauril Alden, 'The significance of cacao production in the Amazon region during the late colonial period: an essay in comparative economic history', *Proceedings of the American Philosophical Society*, 120/2 (April 1976), 103–35, is the best study of that topic. On the society of the Amazon region, the most thorough study to date is David Sweet, 'A rich realm of nature destroyed: the middle Amazon valley, 1640–1750' (Ph.D. thesis, University of Wisconsin, 1974).

13. INDIANS AND THE FRONTIER IN COLONIAL BRAZIL

Literature on Brazilian Indians is far richer for the sixteenth than for subsequent centuries. On contemporary authors and secondary literature, see Hemming *CHLA* I, chapter 5, and *CHLA* I Bibliographical Essay 5.

On the west and the south in the seventeenth century, the fundamental study, although sometimes confusing, is Afonso de Escragnolle Taunay, *História geral das bandeiras paulistas* (11 vols., São Paulo, 1924–50). The majority of documents about bandeirante–Jesuit conflict are in the seven volumes edited by Jaime Cortesão and Hélio Vianna, *Manuscritos da Coleção De Angelis* (Rio de Janeiro, 1951–70), and in Jaime Cortesão, *Rapôso Tavares e a formação territorial do Brasil* (Rio de Janeiro, 1958) and *Introdução à história das bandeiras* (2 vols., Lisbon, 1964). See also Alfredo Ellis Júnior, *Meio século de bandeirismo* (São Paulo, 1948), José de Alcântara Machado, *Vida e morte do bandeirante* (São Paulo, 1943), and the works of Sérgio Buarque de Holanda. Many key sources have been translated in Richard M. Morse (ed.), *The Bandeirantes: the historical role of the Brazilian pathfinders* (New York, 1965). There is contemporary information on the bandeirantes in Pedro Tacques de Almeida Paes Leme, *Nobiliarchia Paulistana* and *Historia da Capitania de S. Vicente* (1772) and in collections of documents such as: *Actas da Câmara Municipal de S. Paulo* (São Paulo, 1914–), *Inventários e testamentos* (São Paulo, 1920–) and the large but disorganized *Documentos interessantes para a história e costumes de São Paulo* (86 vols., São Paulo, 1894–1961). Aurélio Porto, *História das missões orientais do Uruguai* (Rio de Janeiro, 1943) is important, and the history of the Jesuits' Paraguayan missions is documented in Nicolau del Techo, S.J., *Historia de la Provincia del Paraguay* (Liège, 1673), José Sánchez Labrador, S.J., *El Paraguay católico* [1770] (3 vols., Buenos Aires, 1910–17), and Antonio Ruiz de Montoya, S.J., *Conquista espiritual...en las provincias del Paraguay, Paraná, Uruguay y Tapi* (Madrid, 1639), and, among modern accounts, Pablo Pastells, S.J., *Historia de la Compañía de Jesús en la Provincia del Paraguay* (8 vols., Madrid, 1912–59), Magnus Mörner, *The political and economic activities of the Jesuits in the La Plata region* (Stockholm, 1953), and Guillermo Fúrlong, *Misiones y sus pueblos de guaraníes* (Buenos Aires, 1962).

For Bahia and the north-east in the seventeenth century, Diogo de Campos Moreno, *Livro que da razão do Estado do Brasil* [1612] (Recife, 1955) is useful, as are André João Antonil, *Cultura e opulência do Brasil...* (Lisbon, 1711; modern edns, São Paulo, 1923 and Paris, 1968), and Ambrosio Fernandes Brandão, *Os diálogos das grandezas do Brasil* [c. 1618] (Recife, 1962). The Franciscan Martin of Nantes wrote an interesting chronicle of his mission with the Bahia Cariri: *Relation succinte et sincère...* (Quimper, c. 1707; Salvador, 1952). There is some good material in Barão de Studart (ed.), *Documentos para a história do Brasil e especialmente a do Ceará* (4 vols., Fortaleza, 1908–21), but by far the most material is in the vast and disorganized *Documentos históricos da Biblioteca Nacional do Rio de Janeiro* (Rio de Janeiro, 1928–). In English, see Charles Boxer, *Salvador de Sá and the struggle for Brazil and Angola, 1602–1686* (London, 1952); and Stuart B. Schwartz, 'Indian labor and New World plantations: European demands and Indian responses in northeastern Brazil', *American Historical Review*, 83/1, February 1978, 43–79.

The impact of the Dutch wars on the Indians of the north-east is reported in the contemporary works of Caspar Barlaeus, *Rerum in Brasilia gestarum historia* (Cleef, 1660; Rio de Janeiro, 1940), Roulox

Baro, *Relation du voyage...au pays des Tapuies* [1647], Adriaen van der Drussen, *Report on the conquered captaincies in Brazil* [1639] (Rio de Janeiro, 1947); various letters and reports by Gedeon Morris de Jonge in *RIHGB* 58/1 (1895), and Joannes de Laet, *Novus Orbis* (Leyden, 1633; French trans. *Histoire du Nouveau Monde*, Leyden, 1640) and *Historie ofte Iaerlick Verhael van de Verrichtinghen der Geotroyeerde West-Indische Compagnie* (Leyden, 1644; trans. *ABNRJ*, 30–42 (1908–20)). From the Portuguese side: Diogo Lopes de Santiago, 'Historia da guerra de Pernambuco...' [1655], *RIHGB*, 38–9 (1875–6), Raphael de Jesus, *Castrioto Lusitano* (Lisbon, 1679), and papers in *Documentos holandeses* (Rio de Janeiro, 1945). For modern works on the Dutch in north-east Brazil, see *CHLA* II, Bibliographical Essay 12.

For Maranhõ and the Amazon, the basic contemporary history is Bernardo Pereira de Berredo, *Annaes historicos do Estado do Maranhão* (Lisbon, 1749). The 'Livro grosso do Maranhão', *ABNRJ*, 66–7 (1948) is full of good information. The *Anais* of the Biblioteca Nacional also published early reports by Jacomé Raimundo de Noronha, Simão Estácio da Sylveira and others. For the later seventeenth century, there are João de Sousa Ferreira, 'America abreviada, suas noticias e de seus naturaes, e em particular do Maranhão' [1686], *RIHGB*, 57/1 (1894), and Francisco Teixeira de Moraes, 'Relação histórica e política dos tumultos que sucederam na cidade de S. Luiz do Maranhão' [1692], *RIHGB*, 40/1 (1877).

As usual, missionaries produced the bulk of written material on the Amazon region. Venâncio Willeke has recorded the activities of the early Franciscans, *Missões Franciscanos no Brasil, 1500–1975* (Petrópolis, 1974). But the Jesuits were the most active, and their mission was inspired by António Vieira, for whom the basic sources are: *Obras escolhidas* (12 vols., Lisbon 1951–4, of which vol. 5 deals with Indians); *Cartas* (3 vols., Coimbra, 1925–8); and *Sermões* (14 vols., Lisbon, 1679–1710, or 3 vols., Pôrto, 1908); André de Barros, *Vida do apostólico Padre António Vieyra* (Lisbon, 1745). Two vivid and important memoirs by missionaries are: João Felipe Bettendorf, 'Chronica da missão dos Padres da Companhia de Jesus no Estado do Maranhão' [1699], *RIHGB*, 72/1 (1901), and João Daniel, 'Thesouro descoberto no maximo rio Amazonas', *RIHGB*, 2–3, 41 (1840–1, 1878). There is also a history of the Jesuits and a *Memorial sobre o Maranhão* by the eighteenth-century Jesuit José de Moraes, in Cândido Mendes de Almeida, *Memórias para a história do extincto Estado do Maranhão* (2 vols.,

Rio de Janeiro, 1860) and in A. J. de Mello Moraes, *Corografia histórica...do Império do Brasil* (Rio de Janeiro, 1860), both of which contain other useful works on Maranhão despite rather jumbled presentation. The basic history on the Jesuits, apart from Serafim Leite's monumental work, is João Lúcio d'Azevedo, *Os Jesuítas no Grão-Pará: suas missões e a colonização* (Coimbra, 1930). See also his life of Vieira (2 vols., Lisbon, 1920), and, in English, C. R. Boxer, *A great Luso-Brazilian figure, Padre António Vieira, S.J., 1608–1697* (London, 1957), and Mathias C. Kieman, *The Indian policy of Portugal in the Amazon region, 1614–1693* (Washington, D.C., 1954). For the quarrels with Spanish Jesuits, Samuel Fritz, *Misión de los Omaguas...*(Eng. trans., Hakluyt Society, 2nd series, 51; London, 1922) and José Chantre y Herrera, *Historia de las misiones de la Compañía de Jesús en el Marañón español* (Madrid, 1901).

For eighteenth-century Amazonas, there are useful reports by Governor João da Maia da Gama and by the Jesuit Bartholomeu Rodrigues, all published in Mello Moraes, *Corografia histórica*. The papers of Pombal's half-brother Mendonça Furtado are in Marcos Carneiro Mendonça (ed.), *Amazônia na era Pombalina* (3 vols., São Paulo, 1963), and reports on travels related to the frontiers of the Treaty of Madrid are in José Gonçalves da Fonseca, *Primeira exploração dos rios Madeira e Guaporé em 1749* (in Mendes de Almeida, *Memorias*, II), José Monteiro de Noronha, *Roteiro da viagem...até as últimas colonias do sertão...*(Barcelos, 1768 and Belém, 1862), and Francisco Xavier Ribeiro de Sampaio's *Diario* of his voyage of 1774–5 (Lisbon, 1825) and report on Rio Branco (*RIHGB*, 13 (1850)). Finally, scientific travellers start to appear on the Amazon: Charles Marie de La Condamine, *Relation abrégée d'un voyage fait dans l'intérieur de l'Amérique Méridionale* (Paris, 1745) and Alexandre Rodrigues Ferreira, 'Diario da viagem philosophica pela capitania de São José do Rio Negro' [1786] (parts in *RIHGB*, 48–50 (1885–8); also São Paulo, 1970). David Sweet's excellent thesis, 'A rich realm of nature destroyed: the middle Amazon Valley, 1640–1750' (University of Wisconsin, 1974) is essential.

There is little about Indians in literature on central and north-east Brazil during the eighteenth century. Apart from works already cited, there are reports on abuse of Indians in the north-east, in Virginia Rau and Maria Fernanda Gomes da Silva (eds.), *Os manuscritos do arquivo da Casa de Cadaval respeitantes ao Brasil* (2 vols., Coimbra, 1956–8) and in Sebastião da Rocha Pitta, *Historia da America Portugueza* (Lisbon, 1730).

An interesting report on Indian policy at the end of the century is José Arouche de Toledo Rendon, 'Memoria sôbre as aldeas de índios da Provincia de São Paulo' [1798], *RIHGB*, 4 (1842).

Most interest in Indians was in southern Brazil. For the Guaicurú and Paiaguá, who harassed convoys to Cuiabá, see José Sánchez Labrador, *El Paraguay católico*, Manuel Felix de Azara, *Viajes por la America Meridional* [1809] (Madrid, 1923), Francisco Rodrigues do Prado, 'História dos índios Cavalleiros ou da nação Guaycurú' [1795], *RIHGB*, 1 (1839), Martin Dobrizhoffer, *Geschichte der Abiponer*...(3 vols., Vienna, 1783–4; Eng. trans., London, 1822), Ricardo Franco de Almeida Serra, 'Parecer sôbre o aldêamento dos índios uaicurús e guanás...' [1803], *RIHGB*, 7 and 13 (1845 and 50) and 'Discripção geographica da Provincia de Matto Grosso' [1797], *RIHGB*, 6 (1844). For Bororo and other tribes near Cuiabá, Antonio Pires de Campos, 'Breve noticia...do gentio barbaro que ha na derrota...do Cuyabá' [1727], *RIHGB*, 25 (1862). A general history of that region is Joseph Barbosa de Sá, 'Relação das povoaçõens do Cuyabá e Matto Grosso...' [1775], *ABNRJ*, 23 (1904).

For the War of the Sete Povos, the Treaty of Madrid and the expulsion of the Jesuits, Jacintho Rodrigues da Cunha, 'Diario da expedição de Gomes Freire de Andrade às missões do Uruguai' [1756], *RIHGB*, 16 (1853), Thomaz da Costa Corrêa Rebello e Silva, 'Memoria sobre a Provincia de Missões', *RIHGB*, 2 (1840), Jaime Cortesão, *Do Tratado de Madri à conquista dos Sete Povos (1750–1802)* (Rio de Janeiro, 1969) and *Alexandre de Gusmão e o Tratado de Madri* (8 vols., Rio de Janeiro, 1950–9), and works on the Jesuits already cited. Among modern works, Guillermo Kratz, *El tratado hispano-portugués de Límites de 1750 y sus consecuencias* (Rome, 1954), deserves mention. A comprehensive treatment of the Indians and the expansion of the frontiers up to the expulsion of the Jesuits is John Hemming, *Red gold. The conquest of the Brazilian Indians* (London, 1978).

14. COLONIAL BRAZIL: THE GOLD CYCLE, *c.* 1690–1750

Studies on the 'golden age' of Brazil have focused on only one area – Minas Gerais, which was the major gold-producing region of the colonial period. There has been an erroneous assumption that what was true for Minas Gerais was equally applicable to auriferous zones of Bahia, São Paulo, Goiás, Mato Grosso, Pernambuco and Espírito Santo. Readers should be cautious of generalizations based on the Mineiro experience and recognize that differences in topography, chronology, demography, racial composition, political importance, degree of effective crown administration and relative importance within the overall economic context resulted in wide variations between the gold-bearing regions of Brazil. The diamond industry lies beyond the scope of this chapter, but an excellent introduction is provided by Augusto de Lima Júnior, *História dos diamantes nas Minas Gerais* (Lisbon and Rio de Janeiro, 1945) and Joaquim Felício dos Santos, *Memórias do Distrito Diamantino da Comarca do Serro do Frio* (3rd edn, Rio de Janeiro, 1956).

Many contemporary or near-contemporary accounts of gold strikes, exploitation, consolidation and decline are available. André João Antonil (pseudonym of Antonio Giovanni Andreoni, S.J.) is valuable for the early years in Minas Gerais, although it is doubtful if he ever visited the region. Available in a modern edition (edited by Andrée Mansuy, Paris, 1968), his *Cultura e opulência do Brasil por suas drogas e minas* (Lisbon, 1711), especially part 3, contains information not available elsewhere. It remains unsurpassed for bringing to the reader the intensity and raw emotions of the initial gold rush. Dr Caetano Costa Matoso's notes form the basis for the *Relatos sertanistas. Colectânea*, with introduction and notes by Afonso de Escragnolle Taunay (São Paulo, 1953). A commentary on the medical state of the captaincy is Luís Gomes Ferreira's *Erário mineral dividido em doze tratados* (Lisbon, 1735), based on his residence for two decades in Minas Gerais. Charles Boxer has made some of the few studies of the author and his medical treatise: see *The Indiana University Bookman*, 10 (November 1969), 49–70; 11 (November 1973), 89–92. The moral tract *Compendio narrativo do peregrino da America* (Lisbon, 1728) of Nuno Marques Pereira, whose literary Maecenas was none other than the *sertanista* Manuel Nunes Viana, contains many insights. See also *Notícias das minas de São Paulo e dos sertões da mesma capitania, 1597–1772* (3rd edn, São Paulo, 1954) by the Paulista Pedro Taques de Almeida Paes Leme (1714–77). The intensely spiritual life of the captaincy is revealed in the *Triunfo Eucharistico exemplar da Christandade Lusitana*...by Simão Ferreira Machado (Lisbon, 1734). There are numerous memoranda, of which the most penetrating was penned by José João Teixeira Coelho, an eleven-year resident as crown judge: 'Instrucção para o governo da Capitania de Minas Gerais (1780)', first published in *RIHGB*, 15/3 (1852), 257–463, reprinted in *Revista do Arquivo Público Mineiro* [*RAPM*], 8/1–2 (January–June 1903), 399–581, and translated in part by E. Bradford Burns (ed.), *A documentary history of Brazil* (New York, 1966), 155–63. Other commentaries, many of them published in *RAPM* (Ouro Prêto, 1896– ; Belo Horizonte, 1903–), focus on the decline of the economy of Minas Gerais. The best overview is undoubtedly the *Pluto Brasiliensis* of the German mining engineer Baron Wilhelm Ludwig von Eschwege (Berlin, 1833), portions of which have been published in *RAPM* and in the *História e Memória da Academia Real das Ciencias de Lisboa*, 4/1 (1815), 219–29, as 'De uma memória sobre a decadencia das minas de ouro de Capitania de Minas Gerais e sobre outros objetos montanísticos'. Technical aspects of processing gold and silver were the subject of a monograph by António da Silva, *Directorio practico da prata e ouro, em que se mostram as condiçõens, com que se devem lavrar estes dous nobilissimos metaes; para que se evitem nas obras os enganos, e nos artifices os erros* (Lisbon, 1720). For Minas Gerais such accounts may be complemented by those of nineteenth-century travellers; e.g. John Mawe, *Travels in the interior of Brazil, particularly in the gold and diamond districts* (London, 1812), Johann Baptist von Spix and Carl Friedrich von Martius, *Reise in Brasilien in den Jahren 1817 bis 1820* (3 vols., Munich, 1823–31), of which a partial English translation by H. E. Lloyd is available (2 vols., London, 1824).

Other mining captaincies have been less favoured than was Minas Gerais by contemporary chroniclers and commentators, although a great deal can be found, for example, in the pages of *RIHGB* and *Revista do Instituto Histórico e Geográfico de São Paulo* [*RIHGSP*] in the nineteenth and early twentieth centuries.

Contemporary scholarship has been fascinated by the Brazilian pathfinders, the *bandeirantes*, and the frontier. Myriam Ellis, 'As bandeiras na expansão geográfica do Brasil', in *História geral da civilisação brasileira, I A época colonial* (2 vols., São Paulo, 1960), and her essay in *Revista de História de São Paulo* [*RHSP*], 36 (1958), 429–67, survey the field. For fuller discussion of the literature, see *CHLA* II, Bibliographical Essay 13. On the search for gold, more particularly in the period before the so-called 'golden age', see: Myriam Ellis Austregésilo, 'Pesquisas sobre a existência do ouro e da prata no planalto paulista nos séculos XVI e XVII', *RHSP*, 1 (1950), 51–72; Lucy de Abreu Maffei and Arlinda Rocha Nogueira, 'O ouro na capitania de São Vicente nos séculos XVI e XVII', *Anais do Museu Paulista* (1966); Joaquim José Gomes da Silva, 'História das mais importantes minas de ouro do Estado do Espírito Santo', *RIHGB*, 55/2 (1893), 35–58; Madalena da Câmara Fialho, 'Muragem do oiro nas capitanias do norte do Brasil', *Congresso do mundo português*, 10/2, 2a secção, 1a pte (Lisbon, 1940), 85–94.

Manoel da Silveira Cardozo describes the roller-coaster nature of the crown's hopes in 'Dom Rodrigo de Castel-Blanco and the Brazilian El Dorado, 1673–1682', *The Americas*, 7/2 (October 1944), 131–59. Well-publicized but abortive attempts to discover significant mineral deposits brought acute embarrassment to both the king and to Afonso Furtado de Castro do Rio de Mendonça during his governorship of Brazil (1671–5); a manuscript by a mysterious Spaniard Juan Lopes Sierra, acquired by the Bell Library of the University of Minnesota, has been translated into English by Ruth E. Jones and edited with notes by Stuart B. Schwartz under the title *A governor and his image in baroque Brazil* (Minneapolis, 1979). Cardozo has surveyed the Minas Gerais phase of the initial gold rush in his classic article 'The Brazilian gold rush', *The Americas*, 3/2 (October 1946), 137–60. Routes from São Vicente and Rio de Janeiro are described by Richard P. Momsen, Jr., *Routes Over the Serra do Mar* (Rio de Janeiro, 1964). Several authors have discussed the relationship between Brazilian gold strikes and moves to the west in the first half of the eighteenth century. The most succinct account in English is David M. Davidson, 'How the Brazilian West was won: freelance and state on the Mato Grosso frontier, 1737–1752', in D. Alden (ed.), *Colonial roots of modern Brazil* (Berkeley and Los Angeles, 1973), 61–106. In Portuguese there is Capistrano de Abreu, *Caminhos antigos e povoamento do Brasil* (4th edn, Rio de Janeiro, 1975); Sérgio Buarque de Holanda, *Monções* (Rio de Janeiro, 1945) and *Caminhos e fronteiras* (Rio de Janeiro, 1957); Taunay, *Relatos monçoeiros* (São Paulo, 1953), and his 'Demonstração dos diversos caminhos de que os moradores de S. Paulo se servem para os rios de Cuiabá e Província de Cochiponé', *Anais do Museu Paulista*, 1 (1922), 459–79. Francisco Tavares de Brito's account of travel from Rio de Janeiro to Minas Gerais (Seville, 1732) was republished in *RIHGB*, 230 (January–March 1956), 428–41. Exploration, settlement and consolidation in Goiás occupied Taunay in *Os primeiros anos de Goyaz, 1722–1748* (São Paulo, 1950), *separata* from vol. 11 of his *História geral* (*q.v.*).

Crown government and the fiscal administration of the mining areas has received remarkably little attention from scholars, and what few studies there are have focused on Minas Gerais. The first governor of Minas Gerais and São Paulo was chronicled by Aureliano Leite in his *António de Albuquerque Coelho de Carvalho, capitão-general de São Paulo e Minas do Ouro no Brasil* (Lisbon, 1944). Francisco de Assis Carvalho Franco's *História das minas de São Paulo. Administradores gerais e provedores, séculos XVI e XVII* (São Paulo, 1964) holds useful information: the most penetrating study of a local crown administrator is Marcos Carneiro de Mendonça, *O Intendente Câmara. Manuel Ferreira da Câmara Bethancourt e Sá, Intendente geral das minas e diamantes, 1764–1835* (São Paulo, 1958). Early minutes of the town council of Vila Rica have been published in the *Annaes da Biblioteca Nacional*, 49 (1927; published in 1936), 199–391, and in *RAPM*, 25/2 (1937), 3–166. The struggle between officialdom and *poderosos do sertão* is described by A. J. R. Russell-Wood, 'Manuel Nunes Viana: paragon or parasite of empire?', *The Americas*, 37/4 (April 1981), 479–98. Augusto de Lima Júnior focused on the establishment of municipalities in Minas Gerais in several of his many works: *A Capitania das Minas Gerais (Origens e formação)* (3rd edn, Belo Horizonte, 1965); *As primeiras vilas do Ouro* (Belo Horizonte, 1962), *Vila Rica do Ouro Prêto. Síntese histórica e descritiva* (Belo Horizonte, 1957). See also Yves Leloup, *Les villes de Minas Gerais* (Paris, 1970) and A. J. R. Russell-Wood, 'Local government in Portuguese America: a study in cultural divergence', *Comparative Studies in Society and History*, 16/2 (March 1974), 187–231. Francisco Iglesias has placed the events in Minas Gerais in broader context in 'Minas e a imposição do estado no Brasil', *RHSP*, 50/100 (October–December 1974), 257–73. If the administration of mining areas has not received the attention it deserves, the same cannot be said of the legal aspects of mining, especially the collection of the royal fifths: as to the former, indispensable are Francisco Ignácio Ferreira, *Repertorio juridico do Mineiro. Consolidação alphabetica e chronologica de todas as disposições sobre Minas comprehendendo a legislação antiga e moderna de Portugal e do Brasil* (Rio de Janeiro, 1884) and João Pandiá Calógeras, *As Minas do Brasil e sua legislação* (3 vols., Rio de Janeiro, 1904–5). Information on the fifths is contained in C. R. Boxer, *The Golden Age of Brazil, 1695–1750* (Berkeley and Los Angeles, 1969); Kenneth Maxwell, *Conflicts and conspiracies: Brazil and Portugal, 1750–1808* (Cambridge, 1973); and Virgílio Noya Pinto, *O ouro brasileiro e o comércio anglo-português* (São Paulo, 1979). Manoel de Silveira Cardozo's early studies are still the best available: 'Alguns subsídios para a história da cobrança do quinto na capitania de Minas Gerais até 1735' (Lisbon, 1938; reprint from *1 Congresso da história da expansão portuguesa no mundo*, 3a secção (Lisbon, 1937)); 'The collection of the fifths in Brazil, 1695–1709', *HAHR*, 20/3 (August 1940), 359–79; 'Os quintos do ouro em Minas Gerais (1721–1732)', *1 Congresso do mundo português*, 10/2, 2a secção, 1a pte (Lisbon, 1940), 117–28. Robert White focused on the capitation tax of 1735 in 'Fiscal policy and royal sovereignty in

Minas Gerais', *The Americas*, 34/2 (October 1977), 207–29. Cardozo returned to fiscal aspects in his later article 'Tithes in colonial Minas Gerais', *Catholic Historical Review*, 38/2 (July 1952), 175–82.

For the social history of the mining areas the articles of Donald Ramos are of great interest: 'Marriage and the family in colonial Vila Rica', *HAHR*, 55/2 (May 1975), 200–25; 'Vila Rica: profile of a colonial Brazilian urban centre', *The Americas* 35/4 (April 1979), 495–526; 'City and country: the family in Minas Gerais, 1804–1838', *Journal of Family History*, 3/4 (winter 1975), 361–75. On the slave trade, see *CHLA* 1, Bibliographical Essay 12. A. J. R. Russell-Wood, *The black man in slavery and freedom in colonial Brazil* (London, 1982), 104–27, examines the impact of gold mining on the slave trade, and the institution of slavery in the mining regions. Studies of persons of African descent have focused on two very different areas, namely religious brotherhoods and runaways. The former have been studied by Fritz Teixeira de Salles, *Associações religiosas no ciclo do ouro* (Belo Horizonte, 1963), Julita Scarano, *Devoção e escravidão: A irmandade de Nossa Senhora do Rosário dos prêtos no Distrito Diamantino no século XVIII* (São Paulo, 1976), and A. J. R. Russell-Wood, 'Black and mulatto brotherhoods in colonial Brazil: a study in collective behavior', *HAHR*, 54/4 (November 1974), 567–602. Runaways are discussed in Waldemar de Almeida Barbosa, *Negros e quilombos em Minas Gerais* (Belo Horizonte, 1972). An interesting dialogue between a sometime miner and a lawyer on the evils of slavery has been translated by C. R. Boxer under the title 'Negro slavery in Brazil. A Portuguese pamphlet (1764)', *Race*, 5/3 (January 1964), 38–47. A general survey is Aires da Mata Machado Filho, *O Negro e o garimpo em Minas Gerais* (2nd edn, Rio de Janeiro, 1964).

There are no satisfactory general surveys in English of life in mining communities. Chapters in Boxer's *The Golden Age* on the gold rush to Minas Gerais, the struggle between Paulistas and Emboabas and life in eighteenth-century Vila Rica have yet to be bettered. General surveys include: João Camillo de Oliveira Tôrres, *História de Minas Gerais* (5 vols., Belo Horizonte, 1962); Francisco Adolpho de Varnhagen, *História geral do Brasil* (5 vols., 9th edn, São Paulo, 1975), especially vol. 4; Miran de Barros Latif, *As Minas Gerais* (2nd edn, Rio de Janeiro, 1960). Afonso de Escragnole Taunay's monograph *Sôb el Rey Nosso Senhor. Aspectos da vida setecentista brasileira, sobretudo em São Paulo* (São Paulo, 1923; an earlier version appeared in the *Anais do Museu Paulista*, 1 (1922)) can still be read with profit. Mário Leite, *Paulistas e mineiros. Plantados de cidades* (São Paulo, 1961) is useful. Much can be gleaned on events in central Minas Gerais from an excellent account of the Diamond District: Aires da Mata Machado Filho, *Arraial do Tijuco. Cidade Diamantina* (2nd edn, São Paulo, 1957).

Much ink has been expended on two incidents in the history of Minas Gerais in the first half of the eighteenth century: one so-called 'war' and one revolt. The first was the War of the Emboabas, for which there is adequate material for thought in Manoel da Silveira Cardozo's 'The *Guerra dos Emboabas*: civil war in Minas Gerais, 1708–1709', *HAHR*, 22/3 (August 1942), 470–92, and the scholarly chapter in Boxer's *The Golden Age* together with the references there cited. The second was the 1720 revolt in Vila Rica, also treated by Boxer, and in more detail by P. Xavier da Veiga, *A revolta de 1720 em Vila Rica, discurso histórico-político* (Ouro Prêto, 1898).

If the social history of the mining areas has yet to receive its due from historians, no such neglect has been present in treating the spiritual, intellectual, musical, architectural and artistic vitality of Minas Gerais in the eighteenth century. The *Triunfo Eucharístico* (Lisbon, 1734) and the *Aúreo Trono Episcopal* (Lisbon, 1749) have been reproduced, with introduction and notes by Affonso Avila, under the title *Resíduos seiscentistas em Minas. Textos do século do ouro e as projeções do mundo barroco* (2 vols., 2nd edn, Belo Horizonte, 1967). Diogo de Vasconcelos, *História do bispado de Mariana* (Belo Horizonte, 1935) and Cônego Raimundo Trindade's *Arquidiocese de Marianna. Subsídios para a sua história* (2 vols., 2nd edn, Belo Horizonte, 1953 and 1955) provide an introduction. Intellectual life is addressed in José Ferreira Carrato, *Igreja, iluminismo, e escolas mineiras coloniais (Notas sobre a cultura da decadência mineira setecentista)* (São Paulo, 1968) and his earlier *As Minas Gerais e os primórdios do Caraça* (São Paulo, 1963); Eduardo Frieiro, *O diabo na livraria do cônego* (Belo Horizonte, 1957), and E. Bradford Burns, 'The Enlightenment in two colonial Brazilian libraries', *The Journal of the History of Ideas*, 25/3 (July–September 1964), 430–8. Resurrection of a long-forgotten musical tradition in eighteenth-century Minas Gerais is attributable to the unflagging efforts of Francisco Curt Lange: see *CHLA* II, Bibliographical Essay 19. The greatest scholarly interest has focused on baroque art and architecture in Minas Gerais: see *CHLA* II, Bibliographical Essay 18.

Turning from the social and cultural history of the mining areas to the economic aspect, the reader is better supplied. The mining process is well described by Antonil (*Cultura e opulência*, pt 3, ch. 14 and elsewhere); Calógeras, *As minas*, 1, 111–32; and Eschwege. To these contemporary accounts can be added Mawe, *Travels*, and Paul Ferrand, *L'or à Minas Gerais* (*Brésil*) (2 vols., Belo Horizonte, 1913), especially 1, 21–67. Labour arrangements occupied Lucinda Coutinho de Mello Coelho, 'Mão-de-obra escrava na mineração e tráfico negreiro no Rio de Janeiro', *Anais do VI simpósio nacional dos professores de história*, 1 (São Paulo, 1973), 449–89. Productivity of slaves in Goiás was studied by Luís Palacin, 'Trabalho escravo: produção e produtividade nas minas de Goiás', *Anais do VI simpósio*, 1, 433–48. Estimates as to actual production vary enormously: see Eschwege; Calógeras; Roberto C. Simonsen, *História económica do Brasil, 1500–1820* (4th edn, São Paulo, 1962); Visconde de Carnaxide, *Brasil na administração pombalina* (São Paulo, 1940); Adolph G. Soetbeer, *Edelmetall-Produktion and Werthverhältnis zwischen Gold und Silber seit der Entdeckung Amerikas bis zur Gegenwart* (Gotha, 1819). Revenue yields for Minas Gerais are contained in appendices to Boxer, *The Golden Age* and Maxwell, *Conflicts and conspiracies*. The most recent study of the subject is Noya Pinto, *O ouro brasileiro*, 39–117. Numismatists may wish to consult A. C. Teixeira de Aragão, *Descripção geral e histórica das moedas cunhadas em nome dos reis, regentes e governadores de Portugal* (3 vols., Lisbon, 1874–80); K. Prober, *Catálogo das moedas brasileiras* (São Paulo, 1966); Vitorino de Magalhães Godinho, *Prix et monnaies au Portugal, 1750–1850* (Paris, 1955); Alvaro de Salles Oliveira, *Moedas do Brasil. I. Moedas e barras de ouro. Elementos para o seu estudo* (São Paulo, 1944); Severino Sombra, *História monetária do Brasil colonial. Repertório com introdução, notas e carta monetária* (enlarged edn, Rio de Janeiro, 1938); Alvaro da Veiga Coimbra. *Noções de numismática brasileira – Brasil colônia* and *Noções de numismática – Brasil independente*, reprints 18 and 21 in the series Coleção da Revista de História (São Paulo).

The economies and commerce of the mining areas have been the subjects of fewer studies. Problems of supply lines and the domestic economy were well described by Antonil and, more recently, by the well-documented studies of Myriam Ellis, *Contribuição ao estudo do abastecimento das áreas mineradoras do Brasil no século XVIII* (Rio de Janeiro, 1961) and Mafalda P. Zemella, *O abastecimento da capitania das*

Minas Gerais no século XVIII (São Paulo, 1951). The cattle industry is mentioned by Rollie E. Poppino, 'Cattle industry in colonial Brazil', *Mid-America*, 31/4 (October 1949), 219–47. The importance of mule-teers is described by Basílio de Magalhães, 'The pack trains of Minas-Gerais', *Travel in Brazil*, 2/4 (1942), 1–7, 33. The most detailed study of any single commercial activity is by Miguel Costa Filho, *A cana-de-açúcar em Minas Gerais* (Rio de Janeiro, 1963).

General studies of the Brazilian economy include sections on mining: the reader is referred to the still useful *Obras económicas* of J. J. da Cunha de Azeredo Coutinho, available in a modern edition (São Paulo, 1966) edited by Sérgio Buarque de Holanda; Roberto Simonsen, *História económica*; Caio Prado Jr., *História económica do Brasil* (8th edn, São Paulo, 1963); P. Pereira dos Reis, *O colonialismo português e a conjuração mineira* (São Paulo, 1964). There is extensive literature on the Atlantic trade in gold and its impact on Portugal and on Anglo-Portuguese relations; see *CHLA* I, Bibliographical Essays 12 and 13.

15. LATE COLONIAL BRAZIL, 1750–1808

For reference material on the colonial period as a whole, see Biblio-graphical Essay 12. To the bibliographies cited there, that compiled by Abeillard Barreto, *Bibliografia sul-riograndense* (2 vols., Rio de Janeiro, 1976), easily the best regional survey, might be added.

The forthcoming volume of Joaquim Veríssimo Serrão, *Historia de Portugal*, 5 vols. to date (Lisbon, 1972–80) will include the late colonial period and may be expected to be as comprehensive as are the preceding volumes. Other general histories of the period, such as Fortunato de Almeida, *História de Portugal*, IV (*1580–1816*) (Coimbra, 1926), and Damião Peres (ed.), *História de Portugal* (8 vols., Barcelos, 1928–66), are badly dated but may still be profitably consulted. Although uneven in quality, there are many informative essays in Joel Serrão (ed.), *Dicionário de história de Portugal* (4 vols., Lisbon, 1962–7, and a later, expanded printing). For more specialized studies of Portugal under Pombal and his successors, see *CHLA* I, Bibliographical Essay 13.

For a century and a quarter the classic history of colonial Brazil has been Francisco Adolfo de Varnhagen, *História geral do Brasil* (7th edn, 6 vols., São Paulo, 1962). While it continues to be worth consulting because of the sources utilized by the author and added to by subsequent editors, it is unsatisfactory as a synthesis for this period because of its defective organization. More readable is the fourth volume of Pedro Calmon, *História do Brasil* (7 vols., Rio de Janeiro, 1959), but the treatment of the post-1750 years in Sérgio Buarque de Holanda (ed.), *História geral da civilização brasileira*, I *A época colonial* (2 vols., São Paulo, 1960) is woefully incomplete and generally disappointing. No modern study supersedes the seminal analysis and range of insights supplied by Caio Prado Júnior, *The colonial background of modern Brazil*, translated by Suzette Macedo (Berkeley and Los Angeles, 1967), first published in Portuguese more than three decades ago.

On peninsular aspects of the Luso-Brazilian economic relationship during this period, the fleet system, and the Pombaline monopoly companies, see *CHLA* i, Bibliographical Essay 13.

Two recent Ph.D. dissertations, one already published, examine the emergence of Rio de Janeiro as Brazil's chief entrepot in this period: Corcino Madeiros dos Santos' conscientiously researched *Relações comerciais do Rio de Janeiro com Lisboa (1763–1808)* (Rio de Janeiro, 1980), and Rudolph William Bauss' industriously prepared 'Rio de Janeiro: the rise of late-colonial Brazil's dominant emporium, 1777–1808' (Tulane University, 1977). Additional details may be found in the opening chapter of Eulália Maria Lahmeyer Lobo's encyclopaedic *História do Rio de Janeiro* (*Do capital comercial ao capital industrial e financeiro*) (2 vols., Rio de Janeiro, 1978), but we await comparable studies of other Brazilian seaports.

On the slave trade, see *CHLA* i, Bibliographical Essay 12 and, for the late eighteenth century, Jean Mettas, 'La traite portugaise en haute Guinée, 1758–1797: problèmes et méthodes', *Journal of African History*, 16/3 (1975), 343–63, and J. C. Miller, 'Mortality in the Atlantic slave trade: statistical evidence on causality', *Journal of Interdisciplinary History*, 11/3 (Winter, 1981), 385–423, which demonstrate what the archives and modern methodologies are able to tell us. Joseph C. Miller (compiler), *Slavery: a comparative teaching bibliography* (Waltham, Mass., 1977) and supplements, reports on most of the known literature concerning this vast topic.

On the treatment of slaves in colonial Brazil and the socio-economic status of emancipated slaves, especially mulattos, which warrants further investigation, see *CHLA* ii, Bibliographical Essay 12.

Apart from Caio Prado Júnior's incisive essays in *Colonial background*, no reliable history of Brazil's agricultural development during these years exists. Luiz Amaral, *História geral da agricultura brasileira* (2nd edn, 2 vols., São Paulo, 1958), remains standard but is badly digested and does not reflect newer, archive-based findings. Though primarily concerned with the nineteenth century, Eulália Maria Lahmeyer Lobo, *História político-administrativa da agricultura brasileira 1808–1889* (Brasília, 1980) is useful for its bibliography and for some of its details.

In spite of their vital importance to the Brazilian diet, no modern study of the beginnings of wheat or manioc cultivation and trade exists. We are better served with respect to the tobacco industry. Its origins have been deftly traced by Rae Jean Flory, 'Bahian society in the mid-colonial period: the sugar planters, tobacco growers, merchants, and artisans of Salvador and the Recôncavo, 1680–1725' (Ph.D. dissertation, University of Texas, 1978), ch. 5, and its further development analysed by Catherine Lugar, 'The Portuguese tobacco trade and tobacco growers of Bahia in the late colonial period', in D. Alden and Warren Dean (eds.), *Essays concerning the socioeconomic history of Brazil and Portuguese India* (Gainesville, 1977), 26–70; see also José Roberto do Amaral Lapa (ed.), 'O tabaco brasileiro no século xviii (Anotações aos estudos sobre o tabaco de Joaquim de Amorim Castro)', *Studia*, 29 (April 1970), 57–144, reprinted in *Economia colonial* (São Paulo, 1973), 141–230. Geancarlo Belotte, 'Le tabac brésilien aux xviiie siècle' (Thèse pour le doctorat de 3me cycle, Université de Paris-Nanterre, 1973), organizes most of the known statistics but is otherwise unimpressive.

The socio-economic background for the revival of the sugar industry in Bahia is closely examined by Flory (see above), but its development there, in Pernambuco, and in Rio de Janeiro during the years after 1750 requires further study. See, however, Alberto Lamego, 'Os engenhos de açúcar nos recôncavos do Rio de Janeiro, em fins do século xvii[i]', *Brasil Açucareiro* (March 1965), 18–25; José Honório Rodrigues, 'Agricultura e economia açucareiras no século xviii', *Brasil Açucareiro*, 26 (July 1945), and portions of Alberto Lamego's chaotically organized *A terra Goitacá a luz de documentos inéditos* (8 vols., Rio de Janeiro, 1913–47), for the spectacular rise of sugar in the Campos district of Rio de Janeiro. Maria Thereza Schorer Petrone, *A lavoura canavieira em São Paulo* (São Paulo, 1968), is a model study.

The literature on other aspects of the agricultural renaissance is fragmentary. José Ribeiro Júnior has promised a study of the cotton industry of Pernambuco. We badly need it and a comparable monograph on the cotton industry of Maranhão. Some features of the cattle industry in the interior of the north-east have been explored by Luiz R. B. Mott in several essays, including 'Fazendas de gado do Piauí (1697–1762) [*sic* for 1772]', *Anais do VIII Simpósio Nacional dos Professores Universitários de História* (São Paulo, 1976), but no comparable account of stock raising in other key areas, especially Minas Gerais and Rio Grande do Sul, has been published. The beginnings of rice cultivation have been examined by D. Alden, 'Manoel Luis Vieira: an entrepreneur in Rio de Janeiro during Brazil's...agricultural renaissance', *HAHR*, 34/4 (November 1959), 521–37. The only study of the production of dyestuffs in this period is D. Alden, 'The growth and decline of indigo production in colonial Brazil: a study in comparative economic history', *Journal of Economic History*, 25 (March 1965), 35–60. Surprisingly, no adequate history of the beginnings of Brazilian coffee has appeared, but see Afonso de Escragnolle Taunay, *História do café no Brasil*, ii (Rio de Janeiro, 1939). For the development of cacao, see D. Alden, 'The significance of cacao production in the Amazon in the late colonial period', American Philosophical Society, *Proceedings* (April 1976), 120/2. Myriam Ellis, *O monopólio do sal no estado do Brasil (1631–1801)* (São Paulo, 1955) remains unsurpassed.

The economic decline of the interior during this period has never been adequately assessed. A masterful account of efforts by royal and private enterprise to link the back-country with the seacoast is David M. Davidson's 'Rivers and empire: the Madeira route and the incorporation of the Brazilian far west, 1737–1808' (Ph.D. dissertation, Yale University, 1970), of which the only published excerpt is 'How the Brazilian west was won: freelance and state on the Mato Grosso frontier, 1737–1752', in D. Alden (ed.), *Colonial roots of modern Brazil* (Berkeley and Los Angeles, 1973), 61–106. The transportation and marketing problems of the backlands at this time warrant systematic explication.

Another vital economic activity that scholars have ignored is colonial Brazil's coastal fishing industry. Only whaling has received attention: see Myriam Ellis, *Aspectos da pesca da baleia no Brasil colonial* (São Paulo, 1958), and D. Alden, 'Yankee sperm whalers in Brazilian waters, and the decline of the Portuguese whale fishery (1773–1801)', *The Americas*, 20 (January 1964), 267–88.

We will obtain a far better understanding of how particular branches of the Brazilian economy fared during this period when we possess adequate price histories for major markets. Two pioneering studies are Harold B. Johnson, Jr. 'A preliminary inquiry into money, prices, and wages in Rio de Janeiro, 1763–1823', in Alden, *Colonial roots*, 231–83, and Kátia M. de Queirós Mattoso, 'Conjuncture et société au Brésil à la fin du xviiie siècle: prix et salaires à la veille de la révolution des alfaiates – Bahia 1798', *Cahiers des Amériques Latines*, no. 5 (Paris, 1970), 33–53.

Colonial administration during this period is discussed in detail in D. Alden, *Royal government in colonial Brazil* (Berkeley and Los Angeles, 1968), and more briefly by Caio Prado Júnior in the final chapter of *Colonial background*. A more favourable appraisal of the religious policy of the Pombaline regime than that offered here is Henrique Schaefer, *Historia de Portugal*, 5 (Porto, 1899), 208–13; see also Fortunato de Almeida, *História da igreja em Portugal*, new edn by Damião Peres, vol. 3 (Porto, 1970), which is a mine of useful data. See also Thales de Azevedo, *Igreja e estado em tensão e crise* (São Paulo, 1978). No one is likely to improve significantly upon the meticulously researched, carefully organized, forcefully presented works by Serafim Leite, S. J. His *História da companhia de Jesús no Brasil* (10 vols., Rio de Janeiro, 1938–50) is one of the major works ever produced on Brazil's colonial experience and appears in a condensed version as *Suma histórica da companhia de Jesús no Brasil...1549–1760* (Lisbon, 1965). See also D. Alden, 'Economic aspects of the expulsion of the Jesuits from Brazil: a preliminary report', in Henry H. Keith and S. F. Edwards (eds.), *Conflict and continuity in Brazilian society* (Columbia, S.C., 1969), 25–65. A recent study of the role of parish priests is Eugenio de Andrade Veiga, *Os parocos no Brasil no período colonial 1500–1822* (Salvador, 1977). The cultural role of the church in the interior is analysed by José Ferreira Carrato, *Igreja, iluminismo e escolas mineiras coloniais* (São Paulo, 1968), while the ubiquitous black brotherhoods have been restudied by Patricia A. Mulvey, 'Black brothers and sisters: membership in the black lay brotherhoods of colonial Brazil', *Luso-Brazilian Review*, 17/2 (1980), 253–79. For additional bibliography, see *CHLA* II, Bibliographical Essay 12, and *CHLA* I, Bibliographical Essay 15.

Without question the best serial runs of demographic evidence for this period pertain to São Paulo. They have been analysed closely in two recent dissertations: Maria Luiza Marcílio, *La ville de São Paulo 1750–1850: peuplement et population* (Rouen, 1968), and Elizabeth Anne Kuznesof, 'Household economy and composition in an urbanizing community: São Paulo 1765 to 1836' (University of California at Berkeley, 1976). The latter of these particularly demonstrates what can be done with adequate resources, sound methodolgy and access to computer time. See also Kuznesof, 'The role of the female-headed household in Brazilian modernization: São Paulo 1765 to 1836', *Journal of Social History*, 13 (Summer 1980), 589–613, and 'The role of merchants in the economic development of São Paulo 1765–c. 1850', *HAHR*, 60/4 (November 1980), 571–92. While demographic materials are less extensive for other parts of Brazil, much remains in Brazilian and Portuguese archives to challenge future scholars. See also *CHLA* II, Bibliographical Essay 2.

The opening chapter of Lobo's *História do Rio de Janeiro* helps to fill the gap that exists concerning the urban history of that city during this period. We have better coverage for Bahian society and the city of Salvador than we do for any other part of Brazil during the eighteenth and early nineteenth centuries. In addition to the outstanding dissertation by Flory, there is David Grant Smith and Rae Jean Flory, 'Bahian merchants and planters in the seventeenth and early eighteenth centuries', *HAHR*, 58/4 (November 1978), 571–94; John Norman Kennedy's 'Bahian elites, 1750–1822', *HAHR*, 53/3 (August 1973), 415–39; and two well-researched dissertations that span the late eighteenth and early nineteenth centuries: F. W. O. Morton, 'The conservative revolution of independence, Bahia 1790–1840' (Oxford, 1974), the first half of which concerns the years before 1808, and Catherine Lugar, 'The merchant community of Salvador, Bahia 1780–1830' (SUNY at Stony Brook, 1980). Still valuable is Thales de Azevedo, *Povoamento da cidade de Salvador* (3rd edn, Bahia, 1968). Would that we possessed studies for other major cities comparable to Kátia M. de Queirós Mattoso's sophisticated, carefully researched and lucidly presented *Bahia: a cidade do Salvador e seu mercado no século XIX* (Salvador, 1978), portions of which concern the late colonial period. The curious emergence of Brazilian Levittowns, i.e., planned, model communities, in the Amazon, the far west and the south-east, mostly established between 1716 and 1775, is examined by Roberta Marx Delson, *New towns*

for colonial Brazil (Ann Arbor, 1979). Still useful is Paulo F. Santos,
'Formação de cidades no Brasil colonial', v Colóquio Internacional de
Estudos Luso-brasileiros, *Actas*, 5 (Coimbra, 1968), 7–116.

For a detailed analysis that places the conspiracies of this period
within a broad context, see Kenneth R. Maxwell, *Conflicts and conspiracies:
Brazil and Portugal 1750–1808* (Cambridge, 1973), which is mainly
concerned with the Mineiro plot. The Tailors' insurrection has inspired
several fascinating studies: Afonso Ruy, *A primeira revolução social
brasileira* (2nd edn, Bahia, 1951); Kátia M. de Queirós Mattoso, *Presença
francesca no movimento democrático Baiano de 1798* (Salvador, 1969); and
Luis Henrique Dias Tavares, *História da sedição intentada na Bahia em 1798*
('*A conspiração dos alfaiates*') (São Paulo, 1975) are the major Brazilian
studies, but the outstanding chapter in Morton's thesis should not be
missed. In addition to Buarque de Holanda's fine introduction to
Azeredo Coutinho's works, see E. Bradford Burns, 'The role of
Azeredo Coutinho in the enlightenment of Brazil', *HAHR*, 44 (May
1964), 145–60, and Manoel Cardozo, 'Azeredo Coutinho and the
intellectual ferment of his times', in Keith and Edwards, *Conflicts and
continuity*, 72–112.

16. LITERATURE AND INTELLECTUAL LIFE IN COLONIAL
SPANISH AMERICA

There is no recent general work on the cultural history of Spanish
America in the colonial period. But there are two older works which
remain useful: *De la Conquista a la Independencia* (Mexico, 1954) by the
Venezuelan Mariano Picón Salas, translated into English as *A cultural
history of Spanish America* (Berkeley, 1962), is a work about culture in
the traditional sense of 'high culture', that is, books and fine arts;
George Foster's *Culture and conquest* (Chicago, 1960) concerns culture
in the anthropological sense of the word and stresses the cultural
contribution of Spain to the daily life of Spanish America in the colonial
era. The chapters devoted to America, by Guillermo Céspedes del
Castillo (for the sixteenth and seventeenth centuries) and Mario
Hernández Sánchez-Barba (for the eighteenth) in the monumental
Historia de España y América, ed. Vicens Vives (Barcelona, 1957; 2nd
edn, 1977) supplement the information contained in this chapter. A
recent general survey is Mario Hernández Sánchez-Barba, *Historia y
literatura en Hispano-América 1492–1820: la versión intelectual de una*

experiencia (Valencia, 1978). Mario Góngora, *Studies in the colonial history of Spanish America* (Cambridge, 1975) discusses many aspects of intellectual and cultural life. On Hispano-creole urban civilization, see José Luis Romero, *Latinoamérica: las ciudades y las ideas* (Buenos Aires, 1976).

A number of bibliographical reference works are indispensable, especially the researches of the Chilean scholar José Toribio Medina, which appeared at the beginning of this century and are therefore somewhat inaccessible, except in specialized libraries: his *Historia de la Imprenta en América y Oceanía*, followed by *Imprenta en Mexico*, *Imprenta in Puebla*, *Imprenta en Guadalajara* and others, all of which appeared in the first fifteen years of the century, give an impression of the quantity of books – and authors – from the different towns of colonial Spanish America. Medina's works on the Inquisition in Chile, Mexico and Peru are no less important. Two in particular may be mentioned: the *Historia del Tribunal de la Inquisición de México* (Santiago de Chile, 1905) which has been expanded by Julio Jiménez Rueda (Mexico, 1952); and the *Historia del Tribunal de la Inquisición de Lima*, republished in 1954 in Santiago de Chile with a preface by Marcel Bataillon.

The bibliographical and biographical work of the Mexican Joaquín García Icazbalceta, a contemporary of Medina, has needed little updating; it was published in ten volumes of *Obras* (Mexico, 1896–9). See also Francisco Esteve Barba, *Historiografía indiana* (Madrid, 1964), a guide to the major writings of the colonial period. The best guide to works translated into English remains R. A. Humphreys, *Latin American history. A guide to the literature in English* (London, 1958).

Among recent monographs the following deserve mention: John H. Elliott, *The Old World and the New 1492–1650* (Cambridge, 1970); F. Chiapelli (ed.), *First images of America. The impact of the New World on the Old* (2 vols., Berkeley and Los Angeles, 1976); Antonello Gerbi, *The dispute of the New World*, translated from the original Italian edition of 1955 (Pittsburgh, 1973), and by the same author *La naturaleza de las Indias nuevas: De Cristóbal Colón a Gonzalo Fernández de Oviedo*, translated from the 1975 Italian edition (Mexico, 1978); Alain Milhou, *Colón y su mentalidad mesianica en el ambiente franciscanista español* (Valladolid, 1983); Lee E. Huddleston, *Origins of the American Indians, European concepts, 1492–1929* (Austin, 1967); Anthony Pagden, *The fall of natural man. The American Indian and the origins of comparative ethnology* (Cambridge, 1982); Lewis Hanke, *All Mankind is One: a study of the disputation between*

Bartolomé de las Casas and Juan Ginés de Sepúlveda in 1550 on the intellectual and religious capacity of the American Indians (Dekalb, 1974); Juan Friede and Benjamin Keen (eds.), *Bartolomé de las Casas in history: towards an understanding of the man and his work* (Dekalb, 1971); J. Lockhart and E. Otte, *Letters and people of the Spanish Indies* (Cambridge, 1976); John Leddy Phelan, *The Millennial Kingdom of the Franciscans in the New World: A study of the writings of Gerónimo de Mendieta, 1525–1604* (Los Angeles, 1956; revised edn, 1970); Shirley B. Heath, *Telling tongues. Language policy in Mexico, colony to nation* (New York, 1972); Demetrio Ramos Pérez, *El mito del Dorado: su génesis y proceso* (Caracas, 1973); Benjamin Keen, *The Aztec image in Western thought* (Rutgers University Press, 1971); Jacques Lafaye, *Quetzalcoatl and Guadalupe. The formation of the national consciousness in Mexico* (Chicago, 1976), translated from the original French edition by B. Keen. Older but still useful are Irving Leonard, *Books of the brave: being an account of books and of men in the Spanish conquest and settlement of the sixteenth-century New World* (Cambridge, Mass., 1949) and *Baroque times in Old Mexico. Seventeenth-century persons, places and practices* (2nd edn, Ann Arbor, 1959); Lewis Hanke, *The struggle for justice in the conquest of America* (Philadelphia, 1949); Arthur P. Whittaker, (ed.), *Latin America and the Enlightenment* (Ithaca, 1942). On the universities: John Tate Lanning, *Academic culture in the Spanish colonies* (New York, 1940), *The university of the kingdom of Guatemala* (1955), and *The eighteenth century Enlightenment in the University of San Carlos de Guatemala* (1957). On the development of a creole consciousness in the eighteenth century: Miguel Batllori, *La cultura hispano-italiana de los jesuitas expulsos* (Madrid, 1966); Gloria Grajales, *Nacionalismo incipiente en los historiadores coloniales* (UNAM, Mexico, 1961); André Saint-Lu, *Condition coloniale et conscience créole au Guatémala* (Paris, 1970); Ruth Wold, *El Diario de México* (Madrid, 1970).

Since the cultural colonization of the Philippines was in many ways comparable to that of the Indies and the Philippines (administratively and religiously dependent on New Spain) were linked to Spain through the Indies, John Leddy Phelan, *The Hispanicization of the Philippines* (Madison, 1967) is important.

17. THE ARCHITECTURE AND ART OF COLONIAL SPANISH AMERICA

Among the pioneers in writing the history of the art and architecture of colonial Spanish America, the prominent figures in Mexico were

Manuel Romero de Terreros, with his *Historia sintética del arte colonial* (Mexico, 1922), and Manuel Toussaint, author of the classic *Arte colonial en México* (2nd edn, Mexico, 1962; Eng. trans. *Colonial art in Mexico*, Austin, 1967). A comparable role was played in Peru by the architect Emilio Harth-terré, who never actually wrote a book, but whose numerous articles have now been collected into one volume: *Perú: monumentos históricos y arqueológicos* (Mexico, Pan-American Institute of Geography and History, 1975). See also Héctor Velarde, *Arquitectura peruana* (Mexico, 1946) for a number of interesting points of view. In Argentina there were three specialists who were active and who differed greatly from one another – Ángel Guido, Martín S. Noel and Miguel Solá. On the whole Guido was a theorist who made his name with *Eurindia en el arte hispanoamericano* (Santa Fe, 1930). Martín Noel, architect, theorist (see his *Teoría histórica de la arquitectura virreinal* (Buenos Aires, 1932)), and connoisseur, was most importantly the editor of a series of studies entitled *Documentos de arte colonial sudamericano*, published in Buenos Aires between 1943 and 1957 by the Academia Nacional de Bellas Artes. However, even today the most comprehensive and coherent book is still that of Miguel Solá, *Historia del arte hispanoamericano* (Barcelona, 1935). Some of these works were indeed to attain the status of authorities, but they were, in point of fact, either incomplete or over-concise. The major work was to be that undertaken by a Spanish historian, Diego Angulo Iñíguez, the chief author of a monumental *Historia del arte hispanoamericano* (3 vols., Barcelona, 1945–56), in which he was assisted by another Spaniard, Enrique Marco Dorta, and by the Argentine architect Mario José Buschiazzo.

Little by little, a new generation of art historians began to emerge in each of the major countries, especially in Mexico, where Francisco de la Maza, a brilliant essayist, left several fundamental studies, such as *El Churrigueresco en la Ciudad de México* (Mexico, 1969), and *La ciudad de Cholula y sus iglesias* (Mexico, 1959) and the historian Justino Fernández produced a most useful little book, *Arte mexicano* (Mexico, 1958), plus (among others) *Arte mexicano del siglo XIX* (Mexico, 1967). Víctor Manuel Villegas, *El gran signo formal del barroco* (Mexico, 1956) remains the classic study of the *estípite* or square inverted pyramidal pillar. Later the same author collaborated with a Spaniard, A. Bonet Correa, in *El barroco en España y en México* (Mexico, 1969), a curious and controversial work.

Pre-eminent amongst the foreigners who have interested themselves in this field are North Americans, especially George Kubler, with his

Mexican architecture of the sixteenth century (2 vols., New Haven, 1948). Later, he was the author, jointly with Martín Soria, of a major volume, *Art and architecture in Spain and Portugal and their American dominions* (1959, Penguin History of Art series). If this work is open to criticism it is for being too compressed by comparison with the learning of the authors. New directions, also, were marked out by the work of Harold E. Wethey, particularly in his *Colonial architecture and sculpture in Peru* (Cambridge, Mass., 1949) and his later 'Hispanic American colonial architecture in Bolivia', published in the *Gazette des Beaux-Arts* (New York), 39 (1952); a version in Spanish exists as *Arquitectura virreinal en Bolivia* (La Paz, 1961). About the same time Alfred Neumeyer's article 'The Indian contribution to architectural decoration in Spanish colonial America', *The Art Bulletin*, 30 (1948), attracted a great deal of attention. Robert C. Smith and Elizabeth Wilder, *A guide to the art of Latin America* (Washington, D.C., 1948) constituted a major step forward. And since then the *Handbook of Latin American Studies* (Library of Congress, Washington, D.C.) has included a section on colonial art in its Humanities volume. Also in English was the important but hotly debated Pál Kelemen, *Baroque and Rococo in Latin America* (New York, 1951). Later, Kelemen brought out a brief textbook, *Art of the Americas, ancient and Hispanic* (New York, 1969). Both books are exceptionally well illustrated. Other monographs began to appear: for example, Joseph Armstrong Baird, *The churches of Mexico, 1530–1810* (Berkeley and Los Angeles, 1962), and John MacAndrew, *The open-air churches of sixteenth-century Mexico* (Cambridge, Mass., 1965), both books already classics in the field. More recently, the study of colonial art has been revived in the United States by such important new contributions as Robert James Mullen, *Dominican architecture in sixteenth-century Oaxaca* (Tempe, Arizona, 1975). Another influential thinker in this field equal in influence to George Kubler has been the German scholar Erwin Walter Palm. Among his many works, 'The Treasure of the Cathedral of Santo Domingo', *Art Quarterly* (Detroit), 1950, and his major work, *Los monumentos arquitectónicos de la Española* (2 vols., Ciudad Trujillo, 1955) might be singled out.

Turning to the present generation of Latin American art historians, in Mexico, the most important is Elisa Vargas Lugo: *Las portadas religiosas de México* (Mexico, 1969) and *La iglesia de Santa Prisca en Taxco* (Mexico, 1974). She is a member of the Instituto de Investigaciones Estéticas at the Universidad Nacional Autónoma de Mexico, founded in 1939. Also there are Xavier Moyssén Echeverría (*La escultura de la Nueva España en el siglo XVI*; Mexico, 1965), Manuel González Galván (*De Guatemala a Nicaragua: diario del viaje de un estudiante de arte*; Mexico, 1968), Jorge Alberto Manrique (*Los dominicos y Azcapotzalco*; Xalapa, 1963) and Marco Díaz (*Arquitectura religiosa en Atlixco*; Mexico, 1974). The Institute publishes an important journal, *Anales*. There are also interesting researchers working outside the Institute, for example Carlos Flores Marini, author of *Casas virreinales en la Ciudad de México* (Mexico, 1970). Of all the Latin American countries, Mexico publishes the largest number of books and journals in this field.

The countries of Central America and the Caribbean are rather poorly served, although the publications of the Pan-American Institute of Geography and History are useful: there are, for instance, volumes on Guatemala (1953), Panama (1950) and Haiti (1952). Guatemala alone has been studied to any significant degree, and there are several important works such as Sydney D. Markman, *Architecture of Antigua Guatemala* (Philadelphia, 1966). See also Verle Lincoln Annis, *La arquitectura de la Antigua Guatemala, 1543–1773* (bilingual edn, Guatemala, 1968) and, in recent years, the publications of the two Guatemalans Luis and Jorge Luján Muñoz. Heinrich Berlin, *Historia de la imaginería colonial en Guatemala* (Guatemala, 1952) is indispensable. For Cuba, it has become traditional to resort to Joaquín E. Weiss y Sánchez, *Arquitectura cubana colonial* (Havana, 1936). To bring the student up to date, there are the works that have recently been published by Cuba's Dirección del Patrimonio Colonial and, particularly, those by the Argentine architect Roberto Segre.

In the case of Colombia, on the other hand, both surveys and detailed studies abound. Still useful, if uneven, is the work of the late Carlos Arbeláez Camacho, in collaboration with the Spaniard Francisco Gil Tovar – *El arte colonial en Colombia* (Bogotá, 1968); with another Spanish scholar, Santiago Sebastián, Arbeláez Camacho contributed *La arquitectura colonial* (Bogotá, 1967) as volume IV of the *Historia extensa de Colombia*. Santiago Sebastián's shorter publications may also be read with profit: for example, his *Arquitectura colonial en Popayán y Valle del Cauca* (Cali, 1965) and his *La ornamentación arquitectónica en Nueva Granada* (Tunja, 1966). An author interesting for his qualities as a polemicist is Germán Téllez, a noted architect and photographer: see his contribution (as well as those of Gil Tovar, Sebastián and others) to the most recent collective work on the subject, the well-illustrated *El arte colonial en*

Colombia (Barcelona, 1977–). For colonial sculpture in Colombia, apart from the works already cited, one may consult Luis Alberto Acuña, *Ensayo sobre el florecimiento de la escultura en Santa Fé de Bogotá* (Bogotá, 1932). For painting there is Gabriel Giraldo Jaramillo, *La pintura en Colombia* (Mexico, 1948). In their general conclusions these studies were, however, supplanted by the outstanding work of the late Martín Soria, *La pintura del siglo XVI en Sudamérica* (Buenos Aires, 1952).

In Venezuela Carlos Manuel Möller has been writing articles on aspects of the history of colonial art since 1951. However, the whole subject was transformed by an Italian architect, Graziano Gasparini. His many publications include *Templos coloniales de Venezuela* (Caracas, 1959) and more general polemical, *América, barroco y arquitectura* (Caracas, 1972). He also founded the *Boletín del Centro de Investigaciones Históricas y Estéticas de la Universidad Central*, which has been published in Caracas without interruption since 1964. On the other arts, one may consult Alfredo Boulton, *Historia de la pintura en Venezuela* (2 vols., Caracas, 1964–8), and Carlos F. Duarte, *Historia de la orfebrería en Venezuela* (Caracas, 1970). See also Duarte and Gasparini, *Los retablos del período colonial en Venezuela* (Caracas, 1971).

In Ecuador, the earliest scholar to win a reputation for the study of its art was José Gabriel Navarro, above all for *El arte en la provincia de Quito* (Mexico, 1960). Following in his footsteps, and drawing on an abundance of archival material, has been the Ecuadorean Dominican Father José María Vargas. His *Historia del arte ecuatoriano* (Quito, 1964) and his *Patrimonio artístico ecuatoriano* (Quito, 1967) are both somewhat ill arranged, but are books to which it is essential to refer. The architect H. Crespo Toral is the author of a number of monographs. Both Father Vargas and Crespo Toral have contributed (anonymously) to *Arte colonial en Ecuador* (multi-volume, Barcelona, 1977–), which is profusely illustrated in full colour. For Ecuadorean painting and sculpture one has to turn to authors already named – Navarro, Vargas and Crespo Toral – to certain other Ecuadorean writers such as F. Samaniego, and to foreigners such as the Bolivian couple José de Mesa and Teresa Gisbert and the Spanish Santiago Sebastián, who have all contributed important essays in this field.

The bibliography available for Peru is not as prolific as might be imagined. Apart from the works by Wethey and Harth-terré already cited, the many articles, and several books of the late Rubén Vargas Ugarte, S.J., especially his *Diccionario de artistas coloniales de la América*

Meridional (Buenos Aires, 1947), are essential. Currently the leading figures in the field are Francisco Stastny, Humberto L. Rodríguez Camilloni, J. García Bryce and Jorges Bernales Ballesteros. Stastny is the author of *Pérez de Alesio y la pintura del siglo XVI* (Buenos Aires, 1947), while Rodríguez Camilloni has produced several valuable monographs, and García Bryce has brought out an interesting study of Matías Maestro. Bernales Ballesteros – a Peruvian who lives in Seville – has produced the best documented of all studies of Lima, *Lima: la ciudad y sus monumentos* (Seville, 1972). Peru, as the richest area of South America – historically speaking – has naturally received attention from foreign scholars as well as Peruvians: for example, Mesa and Gisbert, the Argentine Héctor Schenone, and the Chilean Alfredo Benavides Rodríguez, author of *La arquitectura en el Virreinato del Perú y en la Capitanía-General de Chile* (Santiago, 1941).

For Bolivia, it is essential to consult the work of José de Mesa and Teresa Gisbert. They not only translated Wethey on Bolivia but also have to their credit a myriad of articles and monographs, notably *Historia de la pintura cuzqueña* (Buenos Aires, 1962), *Bolivia: monumentos históricos y arqueológicos* (La Paz, 1970), and *La escultura virreinal en Bolivia* (La Paz, 1972). Furthermore, since 1972 they have been publishing the journal *Arte y Arquitectura* under the auspices of San Andrés University. Not to be overlooked is the work of Mario Chacón Torres, *Documentos sobre arte colonial en Potosí* (Potosí, 1959).

In Chile, besides Benavides Rodríguez, already cited, there is the historian Eugenio Pereira Salas, author of the monumental *Historia del arte en el Reino de Chile* (Santiago, 1965). Amongst younger historians, the Benedictine Father Gabriel Guarda stands out, and, likewise, M. Rojas-Mix, author of a somewhat tendentious book, *La Plaza Mayor* (Barcelona, 1978), on town planning. Nowadays there are other scholars active in the field, such as Myriam Weissberg, an architect of Valparaíso.

Argentina is better served. This is, in the first place, due to Mario José Buschiazzo's founding of the Instituto de Arte Americano y de Investigaciones Estéticas: between 1948 and 1971 it published 24 issues of its journal *Anales*, as well as several important books, not all of them by Argentines. From among the multiplicity of Buschiazzo's own works one may, perhaps, single out his *Bibliografía de arte colonial argentino* (Buenos Aires, 1947) and a brief but excellent handbook, *Historia de la arquitectura colonial en Iberoamérica* (Buenos Aires, 1961). Other researchers are at work in Argentina, including Héctor Schenone, author of a

number of valuable articles and a book written in collaboration with
Adolfo Luis Ribera, *El arte de la imaginería en el Río de la Plata* (Buenos
Aires, 1948). Several architects stand out from among the younger
generation: A. Nicolini, Robert J. Alexander and Ramón Gutiérrez.
Either on their own, or as a team, they have published books both on
Argentinian and on continent-wide themes; a good example is their
Evolución urbanística y arquitectónica del Paraguay (Resistencia, n.d.).
Paraguay was the object of the attention, also, of the late Uruguayan
historian Juan G. Giuria: *La arquitectura en el Paraguay* (Buenos Aires,
1950). He has, however, also written about his native country: *La
arquitectura en el Uruguay* (2 vols., Montevideo, 1955–). For painting one
has to turn to the three-volume work of José León Pagano, *El arte de
los argentinos* (Buenos Aires, 1937–40), or else to separate monographs.
Highly useful in this category are the works of the late Argentine Jesuit
Father Guillermo Furlong Cardiff, particularly his *Arquitectos argentinos
durante la dominación hispánica* (Buenos Aires, 1946), and its companion
Artesanos argentinos durante la dominación hispánica (Buenos Aires, 1946).

Lastly, there is a recent polemical work on the art and architecture
of colonial Spanish America as a whole: Damián Bayón, *Sociedad y
arquitectura colonial sudamericana* (Barcelona, 1974).

18. THE ARCHITECTURE AND ART OF COLONIAL BRAZIL

The extensive critical literature now available to scholars covering most
aspects of Brazilian colonial architecture and art dates back to 1937,
when the first numbers appeared of the *Revista* and *Publicações* of the
Serviço do Património Histórico e Artístico Nacional, Ministério da
Educação e Cultura [SPHAN]. These two series have provided the solid
basis of documentation and critical analysis which has opened up the
subject for serious study.

In the same year, 1937, there was published the first important general
survey of Brazilian colonial architecture: Juan Giuria, 'La riqueza
arquitectónica de algunas ciudades del Brasil', *Revista de la Sociedad
Amigos de la Arqueología* (Montevideo), 8 (1937). Three further general
studies of outstanding merit have since appeared: Robert C. Smith,
'The arts in Brazil', in H. V. Livermore (ed.), *Portugal and Brazil*
(Oxford, 1953), Germain Bazin, *L'architecture religieuse baroque au Brésil*
(2 vols., Paris, 1956–8) and A. C. da Silva Telles, *Atlas dos monumentos
históricos e artísticos do Brasil* (Rio de Janeiro, 1975). Among surveys

limited to particular areas the following are especially valuable: for Bahia, Edgard de Cerqueira Falcão, *Relíquias da Bahia* (São Paulo, 1940), with very good illustrations, and R. C. Smith, *Arquitectura colonial bahiana* (Bahia, 1951) containing some useful special studies; for Bahia, Pernambuco and Paraíba, Clarival do Prado Valladares, *Aspectos da arte religiosa no Brasil: Bahia, Pernambuco, Paraíba* (Rio de Janeiro, 1981), with very good illustrations; for Minas Gerais, R. C. Smith, 'The colonial architecture of Minas Gerais in Brazil', *Art Bulletin*, 21 (1939), E. de C. Falcão, *Relíquias da Terra do Ouro* (São Paulo, 1946; 2nd edn, 1958), with very good illustrations, and Sylvio de Vasconcellos and Renée Lefevre, *Minas, cidades barrocas* (São Paulo, 1968; 2nd edn, 1977); for Ouro Preto, Paulo F. Santos, *Subsídios para o estudo da arquitetura religiosa em Ouro Preto* (Rio de Janeiro, 1951) with measured ground plans, elevations and sections.

In addition to the well-documented monographs on particular churches published in the two SPHAN series, other important studies are: Pedro Sinzig, 'Maravilhas da religião e da arte na igreja e no convento de São Francisco da Bahia', *RIHGB*, 165 (1932; pub. separately 1933), R. C. Smith, 'Nossa Senhora da Conceição da Praia and the Joanine style in Brazil', *Journal of the Society of Architectural Historians*, 14 (1956), R. C. Smith, 'Santo António do Recife', *Anuário do museu imperial*, 7 (1946), Augusto Carlos da Silva Telles, *Nossa Senhora da Glória do Outeiro* (Rio de Janeiro, 1969), Mario Barata, *Igreja da Ordem Terceira da Penitência do Rio de Janeiro* (Rio de Janeiro, 1975) and R. C. Smith, *Congonhas do Campo* (Rio de Janeiro, 1973).

The art and architecture associated with particular religious orders has attracted some specialized studies. Among those on the Jesuits the following deserve notice: P. F. Santos, *O barroco e o jesuítico na arquitetura do Brasil* (Rio de Janeiro, 1951), and Serafim Leite, *Artes e ofícios dos Jesuítas no Brasil* (Lisbon, 1953). For the Benedictines there are the works of Clemente Maria da Silva Nigra, in particular *Frei Bernardo de São Bento* (Salvador, 1950) and *Os dois escultores Frei Agostino da Piedade, Frei Agostino de Jesus e o arquiteto Frei Macário de São João* (Salvador, 1971).

Among individual artists most attention has naturally been paid to o Aleijadinho. The first biography by Rodrigo José Ferreira Brêtas, 'Traços biográficos relativos ao finado Antonio Francisco Lisboa, o Aleijadinho' (1858) was republished by SPHAN in 1951. Germain Bazin's monograph *Aleijadinho et la sculpture baroque au Brésil* (Paris, 1963) has not been superseded, but Sylvio de Vasconcellos, *Vida e obra de*

Antonio Francisco Lisboa, o Aleijadinho (São Paulo, 1979) is also valuable.

On civil architecture the outstanding work remains José Wasth Rodrigues, *Documentário arquitectónico relativo à antiga construção civil no Brasil* (São Paulo, 2nd edn, 1975). There are a few studies of individual buildings in the SPHAN publications; and to these should be added R. C. Smith, 'A Brazilian merchants' exchange', *Gazette des Beaux-Arts* (1951). On military architecture the most detailed examination of a representative group of fortresses is Gilberto Ferrez, *Rio de Janeiro e a defesa do seu porto, 1550–1800* (2 vols., Rio de Janeiro, 1972). Luís Silveira, *Ensaio de iconografia das cidades portuguesas do ultramar*, iv (Lisbon, 1957) provides basic documentation on Portuguese colonial cities, while Sylvio de Vasconcellos, *Vila Rica. Formação e desenvolvimento* (Rio de Janeiro, 1951; 3rd edn, São Paulo, 1977) examines one important colonial town in some depth.

The definitive work on *azulejos* is J. M. dos Santos Simões, *Azulejaria Portuguesa no Brasil (1500–1822)* (Lisbon, 1965). The famous *azulejos* in the Franciscan convent at Salvador are well illustrated in Silvanisio Pinheiro, *Azulejos do convento de São Francisco da Bahia* (Salvador, 1951).

Knowledge of developments in the mother country is indispensable as background for the appreciation of the art and architecture of colonial Brazil. Particularly useful for this purpose are the Portuguese studies of R. C. Smith, notably: 'João Federico Ludovice', *The Art Bulletin*, 18 (1936), *A talha em Portugal* (Lisbon, 1962), *Nicolau Nasoni* (Lisbon, 1967), *The art of Portugal 1500–1800* (London, 1968), *Frei José de Santo António Vilaça* (2 vols., Lisbon, 1972) and *André Soares* (Lisbon, 1973).

Finally, some valuable evidence on colonial art and architecture is contained in records, graphic and literary, made by early visitors to Brazil. In the seventeenth century there are the paintings of Frans Post (standard monograph: Erik Larsen, *Frans Post: interprète du Brésil* (Amsterdam and Rio de Janeiro, 1962)). In the nineteenth century the most important evidence is that of Richard F. Burton (*Explorations of the highlands of the Brazil* (2 vols., London, 1869)), who took a lively interest in colonial churches, some of which were still being completed when he visited them.

In conclusion mention should be made of Clarival do Prado Valladares, *Nordeste histórico e monumental* (4 vols., Bahia, 1982–4), a magnificently illustrated record of colonial architecture and art in the north-east of Brazil, from Maranhão to Bahia.

19. THE MUSIC OF COLONIAL SPANISH AMERICA

The first histories of music written by Spanish Americans which include sections on the colonial period are José Sáenz Poggio, *Historia de la música guatemalteca* (Guatemala, 1878; republished in *Anales de la Sociedad de Geografía e Historia de Guatemala*, 22/1–2 (March–June 1947), 6–54) and Ramón de la Plaza, *Ensayos sobre el arte en Venezuela* (Caracas, 1883; facsimile reprint, 1977). Serafín Ramírez, *La Habana artística* (Havana, 1891) and Laureano Fuentes Matons, *Las artes en Santiago de Cuba* (Santiago de Cuba, 1893), although riddled with errors, contain some still useful information on the early nineteenth century. The historian Gabriel Saldívar y Silva (1909–80) published at 25 his authoritative *Historia de la música en México (épocas precortesiana y colonial)* (Mexico, 1934); it still remains uniquely valuable. In contrast with earlier Latin American music researchers, Saldívar was a palaeographer who exploited numerous documents in the ecclesiastical and secular archives of Mexico City. To him and his collaborator, his wife Elisa Osorio de Saldívar, belongs the honour of having preceded all other Latin Americans in treating their continent's musical past dispassionately, and of having placed its study on a sound footing. The next scholar to write a history of his nation's music was Eugenio Pereira Salas (1904–79). His *Los orígenes del arte musical en Chile* (Santiago de Chile, 1941) still remains a model of method even though superseded in some factual aspects by Samuel Claro Valdés, *Oyendo a Chile* (Santiago de Chile, 1979). Alejo Carpentier, *La música en Cuba* (Mexico, 1946) is still quoted, partly because of the author's fame in other fields. To him belongs the credit of having been the first to unveil Cuba's leading colonial composer, Esteban Salas y Castro (1725–1803). Lauro Ayestarán (1913–66) provided an exhaustive account of his nation's past in *La música en el Uruguay*, 1 (Montevideo, 1953). José Antonio Calcaño (1900–78) corrected many mistakes in Ramón de la Plaza when he published his masterful *La ciudad y su música, crónica musical de Caracas* (Caracas, 1958; facsimile reprint 1980). Vicente Gesualdo, *Historia de la música en la Argentina, 1536–1851* (Buenos Aires, 1961; 2nd edn, 1977) covers colonial music in the Río de la Plata region. José Ignacio Perdomo Escobar (1917–80) included important colonial data in his *Historia de la música en Colombia* (3rd and 4th edns, Bogotá, 1963 and 1975). Andrés Pardo Tovar's lengthy *La cultura musical en Colombia* (Bogotá, 1966) was sponsored by the Academia Colombiana de Historia (*Historia extensa de Colombia*, 20; *Las artes en Colombia*, 6).

Among lexicons, Rodolfo Barbacci, 'Apuntes para un diccionario biográfico musical peruano', *Fénix* (Lima, Biblioteca Nacional), 6 (1949), 414–510 and Carlos Raygada, 'Guía musical del Perú', *Fénix*, 12–14 (1956–7) itemize useful colonial data. Otto Mayer-Serra's two-volume *Música y músicos de Latinoamérica* (Mexico, 1947), brings together in a systematic way material extracted from previous publications. Much more up-to-date are the colonial articles in *Riemann Musiklexicon Ergänzungsband Personenteil: A–K* (Mainz, 1972) and *L–Z* (1975); in *Die Musik in Geschichte und Gegenwart*, xv and xvi (Bogotá, Cuzco, Guatemala, Lima and Mexico City in the supplements for 1973 and 1979); and in *The New Grove Dictionary of Music and Musicians* (London, 1980). Nicolas Slonimsky's classic *Music of Latin America* (New York, 1945; reprinted 1972) focuses on twentieth-century developments to the detriment of earlier music history, but Gerard Béhague's *Music in Latin America, an introduction* (Englewood Cliffs, 1979) is valuable for the colonial period. Léonie Rosentiel's chapter on 'The New World' in the *Schirmer History of Music* (New York, 1982), 837–946, is especially useful for its colonial summary.

Among researchers whose monographs are basic for colonial music, Francisco Curt Lange stands pre-eminent, with 49 substantial publications in Spanish, Portuguese, German and English, itemized in *The New Grove*, x, 447. Robert Stevenson published numerous articles on colonial topics in *Die Musik in Geschichte und Gegenwart* (beginning with volume IX (1961)), in Italian-, French- and Spanish-language lexicons, in *Grove's Dictionary of Music and Musicians*, 5th edn (1954) and in *The New Grove*. His books with colonial sections include *Music in Mexico: a historical survey* (New York, 1952, 1971), *The music of Peru. Aboriginal and viceroyal epochs* (Washington, 1960), *La música colonial en Colombia* (Cali, 1964), *Music in Aztec and Inca territory* (Berkeley and Los Angeles, 1968, 1976), *Renaissance and Baroque musical sources in the Americas* (Washington, 1970), *Foundations of New World opera* (Lima, 1973), *Christmas music from Baroque Mexico* (Berkeley and Los Angeles, 1974), *A guide to Caribbean music history* (Lima, 1975), *Latin American colonial music anthology* (Washington, 1975) and *Tomás de Torrejón y Velasco: La púrpura de la rosa* (Lima, 1976). In *Inter-American Music Review* he has since 1978 published fully documented essays on colonial music in Caracas, Cuzco, Guatemala, Mexico City, Puebla, Quito, and San Juan, Puerto Rico.

INDEX

895